RESTRICTING LIBERTY TO PREVENT TERRORISM

RESTRICTING LIBERTY TO PREVENT TERRORISM

The Belgian and UK Approaches to Direct Restrictions to the Right to Liberty to Prevent Terrorism

Ward Yperman

INTERSENTIA

Cambridge – Antwerp – Chicago

Intersentia
Lefebvre Sarrut Belgium SA
Rue Haute, 139/6
1000 Bruxelles
Belgium
contact@larcier-intersentia.com

Distribution for the UK and
Rest of the World (incl. Eastern Europe)
Ingram Publisher Services UK
1 Deltic Avenue, Rooksley
Milton Keynes MK13 8LD
United Kingdom
Tel: +44 1752 202 301 | Fax: +44 1752 202 331
Email: orders@nbninternational.com

Distribution for France and other countries
Interforum Editis
92 avenue de France
75013 Paris
France

Distribution for the USA and Canada
Independent Publishers Group
Order Department
814 North Franklin Street
Chicago, IL 60610
USA
Tel: +1 800 888 4741 (toll free) | Fax: +1 312 337 5985
Email: orders@ipgbook.com

Restricting Liberty to Prevent Terrorism. The Belgian and UK Approaches to Direct Restrictions to the Right to Liberty to Prevent Terrorism

Cover design by Danny Juchtmans / www.dsigngraphics.be
Cover image: Danny Juchtmans

ISBN 978-1-83970-438-3
D/2025/06040/0020
NUR 828

British Library Cataloguing in Publication Data. A catalogue record for this book is available from the British Library.

CONTENTS

List of abbreviations xv

INTRODUCTION 1

Chapter I.
Issue and context 3

Chapter II.
Prevention 7

METHODOLOGY 17

Chapter I.
Scope of the topic 19

Chapter II.
Research objectives and questions 23

Chapter III.
Countries for comparison 27

Chapter IV.
Relevance 29

PART I.
NORMATIVE FRAMEWORK 33

Introduction 35

Chapter I.
General principles 39

Section I. Scope of application 39
    Subsection I. Deprivation vs. restriction 39
    Subsection II. Practical application 44
Section II. Right to liberty 50
    Subsection I. Protecting against arbitrariness 50
    Subsection II. Subparagraph (a) 61

Subsection III. Subparagraph (b) 64
Subsection IV. Subparagraph (c) 67
Subsection V. Subparagraph (e) 79
Subsection VI. Other safeguards 81
Subsection VII. Practical application 98
Section III. Freedom of movement 105
Subsection I. Restrictions 105
Subsection II. Practical application 110

Chapter II.
Application in the context of terrorism prevention 117

Section I. Criminal law 117
Section II. Administrative law 119

Chapter III.
Main principles used throughout this book 121

Section I. Operationalising main principles 121
Section II. Legal certainty 124
Section III. Proportionality 127

PART II.
BELGIUM 131

Introduction 133

Chapter I.
Restrictions to the right to liberty 143

Introduction 143
Section I. Principal sentences 143
Subsection I. Alternative sentences 143
Subsection II. Suspension of sentencing and postponement of enforcement 148
Section II. Additional limitation of liberty 151
Subsection I. Supervision by the Sentence Enforcement Court 151
Subsection II. Security measure for the protection of society 155

Chapter II.
Article 137 CC 159

Section I. *Actus Reus* 159
Section II. *Mens Rea* 163

Section III. Sentences 167
Section IV. Political offence? 177
Section V. Constitutional Court 181
Section VI. Practical application 184

Chapter III.
Article 140 CC 189

Section I. Terrorist groups 189
Section II. Participating in the activities of a terrorist group (§1) 192
Subsection 1. *Actus Reus* 192
Subsection 2. *Mens Rea* 198
Subsection 3. Sentences 205
Section III. Participating in the taking of any decision regarding the activities of a terrorist group (§1/1) 209
Subsection I. *Actus Reus* 209
Subsection II. *Mens Rea* 210
Subsection III. Sentences 210
Section IV. Leadership of a terrorist group 212
Subsection I. *Actus Reus* 212
Subsection II. *Mens Rea* 213
Subsection III. Sentences 214
Section V. Practical application 215

Chapter IV.
Article 140*bis* CC 221

Section I. *Actus Reus* 221
Section II. *Mens Rea* 226
Section III. Sentences 227
Section IV. Constitutional Court 230
Section V. Practical application 231

Chapter V.
Article 140*ter* CC 235

Section I. *Actus Reus* 235
Section II. *Mens rea* 237
Section III. Sentences 237
Section IV. Constitutional Court 238
Section V. Practical application 239

Chapter VI.
Article 140*quater* CC 241

Section I. *Actus Reus* 241
Section II. *Mens rea* 242
Section III. Sentences 242
Section IV. Constitutional Court 243
Section V. Practical application 244

Chapter VII.
Article 140*quinquies* CC 247

Section I. *Actus Reus* 247
Section II. *Mens rea* 250
Section III. Sentences 250
Section IV. Constitutional Court 251
Section V. Practical application 252

Chapter VIII.
Article 140*sexies* CC 253

Section I. *Actus Reus* 253
Section II. *Mens rea* 254
Section III. Sentences 256
Section IV. Constitutional Court 257
Section V. Practical application 260

Chapter IX.
Article 140*septies* CC 263

Section I. *Actus Reus* 263
Section II. *Mens rea* 267
Section III. Sentences 269
Section IV. Practical application 271

Chapter X.
Article 141 CC 273

Section I. *Actus reus* 273
Section II. *Mens Rea* 275
Section III. Sentences 277
Section IV. Practical application 279

Chapter XI.
Proposed new offences 281

Chapter XII.
Pre-trial detention 283

Section I. Numbers 283
Section II. Initial deprivation of liberty 283
Section III. Arrest warrant 288
Section IV. Further pre-trial detention 291
Section V. Detention during and after trial 295
Section VI. Article 5 safeguards 298

Chapter XIII.
Analysis 301

Section I. Offences 301
Subsection I. The goal of this Chapter 301
Subsection II Legal certainty 301
a) Constitutional Court 19 March 2019 301
b) Analysis 303
Subsection III. Proportionality 309
Section II. Supervision by the Sentence Enforcement Court 310

PART III.
THE UK 313

Introduction 315

Chapter I.
Criminal law 327

Section I. Restrictions to the right to liberty 327
Section II. Defining terrorism 334
Section III. Terrorism *sensu stricto* 338
Subsection I. Various pieces of legislation 338
Subsection II. Sentences 342
Subsection III. Practical application 346
Section IV. Offences related to proscribed organisations 347
Subsection I. Proscribed organisations 347
Subsection II. Membership and support 349
a) S. 11 TA 2000: Membership 349
b) S. 12 TA 2000: Offences related to support 350
c) Sentences 352
d) Practical application 353
Subsection III. Uniform and publication of images 354
a) S. 13 TA 2000: Wearing uniforms or insignia 354

b) S. 13 (1A): Publication of images 355
c) Sentences 355
Subsection IV. Criticism 356
Section V. Offences related to terrorist property 358
Subsection I. Terrorist property 358
Subsection II. Offences 358
a) S. 15 TA 2000: Fund-raising 358
b) S. 16 TA 2000: Use and possession 359
c) S. 17 TA 2000: Funding arrangements 359
d) S. 18 TA 2000: Money laundering 360
e) Sentences 361
f) Practical application 362
g) Criticism 362
Section VI. Training 363
Subsection I. S. 54 TA 2000: Providing or receiving weapons training 363
Subsection II. S. 6 TA 2006: Providing or receiving training for terrorism 364
Subsection III. S. 8 TA 2006: Attendance at a place used for terrorist training 365
Subsection IV. Sentences 366
Subsection V. Criticism 367
Section VII. Directing a terrorist organisation 368
Section VIII. Possession for terrorist purposes and collection of information ... 369
Subsection I. S. 57 TA 2000: Possession 369
Subsection II. S. 58 TA 2000: Collection of information 371
Subsection III. Sentences 375
Subsection IV. Practical application 376
Subsection V. Criticism 379
Section IX. Information about acts of terrorism 381
Subsection I. Offence S.38B TA 2000 381
Subsection II. Sentence 383
Subsection III. Practical application 384
Subsection IV. Criticism 385
Section X. Eliciting, publishing or communicating information about members of armed forces 385
Subsection I. Offence S. 58A TA 2000 385
Subsection II. Sentence 386
Section XI. Designated area offence 386
Subsection I. Offence S. 58B TA 2000 386
Subsection II. Sentence 388
Subsection III. Criticism 388
Section XII. Encouraging terrorism and dissemination of terrorist publications 388

Subsection I. S. 1 TA 2006: Encouragement of terrorism 388
Subsection II. S. 2 TA 2006: dissemination of terrorist publications . . . 394
Subsection III. Sentences 396
Subsection IV. Practical application 398
Subsection V. Criticism 399
Section XIII. Preparation of terrorist acts 401
Subsection I. S. 5 TA 2006: Preparation 401
Subsection II. Sentence 403
Subsection III. Practical application 405
Subsection IV. Criticism 406
Section XIV. Offences involving radioactive devices and materials and nuclear facilities and sites 409
Subsection I. Mixture of terrorism *sensu stricto* and *sensu lato* 409
Subsection II. S. 9 TA 2006: making or possessing radioactive devices or materials 410
Subsection III. S. 10 TA 2006: misuse and damage 410
Subsection IV. S. 11 TA 2006: Threats 410
Subsection V. Sentences 411
Subsection VI. Criticism 411
Section XV. Extraterritorial offences 412
Subsection I. Inciting terrorism overseas 412
Subsection II. Other extraterritorial jurisdiction 413
Section XVI. Investigative and pre-trial detention 416
Subsection I. General rules on arrest and detention 416
Subsection II. Terrorism specific rules on arrest and detention 421

Chapter II.
Administrative law 427

Introduction 427
Section I. Anti-Terrorism, Crime and Security Act 2001 427
Section II. Control Orders 432
Section III. Terrorism Prevention and Investigation Measures (TPIMs) 446

Chapter III.
Analysis 461

Section I. The goal of this Chapter 461
Section II. The right to liberty in the UK 461
Section III. Offences 463
Subsection I. Legality 463
Subsection II. Proportionality 466
Section IV. Administrative law 469

PART IV.
COMPARATIVE ANALYSIS AND RECOMMENDATIONS............. 473

Introduction.. 475

Chapter I.
Comparative analysis... 477

Section I. General comparison 477
Section II. Administrative law.. 478
Section III. Criminal law 480
Subsection I. Restrictions of liberty 480
a) Principal sentences.. 480
b) Additional restrictions of liberty 482
c) Pre-trial detention... 484
Subsection II. Terrorism *sensu stricto*............................... 486
Subsection III. Terrorism sensu lato.................................... 490
a) Offences relating to terrorist groups 490
b) Financing 495
c) Recruitment and inciting... 497
d) Training 499
e) Preparation... 502
f) Traveling.. 504
g) Possession and information offences............................... 506
Subsection IV. Conclusions 508

Chapter II.
General observations 511

Chapter III.
Recommendations 521

Section I. Introduction 521
Section II. Minimal changes 523
Subsection I. Article 137 CC 523
Subsection II. Article 138 CC.. 524
Subsection III. Article 139 CC... 525
Subsection IV. Article 140 CC 526
Subsection V. Article 140*bis* CC 526
Subsection VI. Article 140*ter* CC 527
Subsection VII. Article 140*quater* CC 527
Subsection VIII. Article 140*quinquies* CC........................... 528
Subsection IX. Article 140*sexies* CC.................................. 528

Subsection X. Article 140*septies* CC 528
Subsection XI. Article 141 CC 529
Subsection XII. Article 141*ter* CC 529
Subsection XIII. Pre-trial detention 529
Subsection XIV. Being at the disposal of the Sentence Enforcement Court 530
Section III. Thorough reform 530

General Conclusion 535
Bibliography 539

LIST OF ABBREVIATIONS

AMSA 1990
Aircraft and Maritime Security Act 1990 (UK)

ASA 1982
Aviation Security Act 1982 (UK)

ASD
Autism spectrum disorder

ATCSA 2001
Anti-Terrorism, Crime and Security Act 2001 (UK)

BA 1976
Bail Act 1976 (UK)

CAA 1982
Civil Aviation Act 1982 (UK)

CC
Criminal Code (Belgium): Strafwetboek 8 juni 1867, *BS* 9 juni 1867, 3133

CCC
Cellules Communistes Combattantes

CCP
Code of Criminal Procedure (Belgium): Wetboek van Strafvordering 17 november 1808, *BS* 27 november 1808

CJCA 2015
Criminal Justice and Courts Act 2015 (UK)

CPS
Crown Prosecution Service (UK)

CTA 2008
Counter-Terrorism Act 2008 (UK)

CTBSA 2019
Counter-Terrorism and Border Security Act 2019 (UK)

CTSA 2015
Counter-Terrorism and Security Act 2015 (UK)

CTSA 2021
Counter-Terrorism and Sentencing Act 2021 (UK)

DHKP-C
Devrimci Halk Kurtuluş Partisi-Cephesi

ECHR
European Convention of Human Rights 1950

ECtHR
European Court of Human Rights

ETPIM
Enhanced Terrorism Prevention and Investigation Measure (UK)

EU
European Union

FATF
Financial Action Task Force

FRA
European Union Agency for Fundamental Rights

FTF
Foreign terrorist fighter

GICM
Groupe Islamique Combattant Marocain

HRA 1998
Human Rights Act 1998 (UK)

IED
Improvised explosive device

IRA
Irish Republican Army

IS
Islamic State

ISIS
Islamic State of Iraq and Syria

JCHR
Joint Committee on Human Rights (UK)

MICAS
Mesure individuelle de contrôle administratif et de surveillance (France)

MOIS
Ministry of Intelligence and Security (Iran)

OAPA 1861
Offences against the Person Act 1861 (UK)

OCMW/CPAS
Openbaar centrum voor maatschappelijk welzijn/Centre public d'action sociale (Belgium)

PACE 1984
Police and Criminal Evidence Act 1984 (UK)

PT CCP
Preceding Title to the Code of Criminal Procedure (Belgium): Wet 17 april 1887 houdende de voorafgaande titel van het wetboek van strafvordering, *BS* 25 april 1887, 1265

PTA 2005
Prevention of Terrorism Act 2005 (UK)

SA 2020
Sentencing Act 2020 (UK)

SIAC
Special Immigration Appeals Commission (UK)

TA 2000
Terrorism Act 2000 (UK)

TA 2006
Terrorism Act 2006 (UK)

TFEU
Treaty on the Functioning of the European Union 2007

TPIM
Terrorism Prevention and Investigation Measure (UK)

TPIMA 2011
Terrorism Prevention and Investigation Measures Act 2011 (UK)

UK
United Kingdom

UN
United Nations

US
United States

WERP
Statute on the External Legal Position (Belgium): Wet 17 mei 2006 betreffende de externe rechtspositie van de veroordeelden tot een vrijheidsstraf en de aan het slachtoffer toegekende rechten in het raam van de strafuitvoeringsmodaliteiten, *BS* 15 juni 2006, 30455

WPA
Statute on the Police (Belgium): Wet 5 augustus 1992 op het politieambt, *BS* 22 december 1992, 2712

INTRODUCTION

CHAPTER I
ISSUE AND CONTEXT

1. The risk society, prevention of harm and terrorism – The accomplished social scientist Ulrich Beck famously wrote that human society had become a risk society.[1] He theorised that modern society had become a risk society in the sense that it is increasingly occupied with debating, preventing and managing risks that it itself has produced.[2] More recently Garland spoke of a culture of control, in which '*protecting the public has become the dominant theme of penal policy.*'[3] Other criminologists and legal experts have since then elaborated and built upon these theories.[4] 9/11 is often seen as a pivotal moment in world history and in the history of (counter-)terrorism, as terrorist networks

---

1 See also: Claudia Aradau and Rens Van Munster, 'Governing Terrorism Through Risk: Taking Precautions, (Un)Knowing the Future' (2007) 13 European Journal of International Relations 89, 90; Stéphanie De Coensel, *Counter-Terrorism & Criminal Law: A Normative Legitimacy Test of Terrorism-Related Offences on Expression, Information and Movement* (Maklu 2020) 41–42; Simon Hale-Ross, *Digital Privacy, Terrorism and Law Enforcement: The UK's Response to Terrorist Communication* (1st edn, Routledge 2018) 105–106; Maartje Amalia Hermina van der Woude, *Wetgeving in een veiligheidscultuur: totstandkoming van antiterrorismewetgeving in Nederland bezien vanuit maatschappelijke en (rechts)politieke context* (Boom Juridische uitgevers 2010) 5.

2 Ulrich Beck, *Risk Society: Towards a New Modernity* (SAGE Publications 1992).

3 David Garland, *The Culture of Control: Crime and Social Order in Contemporary Society* (Oxford University Press 2001) 12. See also: De Coensel, *Counter-Terrorism & Criminal Law: A Normative Legitimacy Test of Terrorism-Related Offences on Expression, Information and Movement* (n 1) 42; Andrew Lynch, Nicola McGarrity and George Williams, 'The Emergence of a "Culture of Control"' in Nicola McGarrity, Andrew Lynch and George Williams (eds), *Counter-terrorism and beyond: the culture of law and justice after 9/11* (Routledge 2010); van der Woude (n 1) 5–6.

4 De Coensel, *Counter-Terrorism & Criminal Law: A Normative Legitimacy Test of Terrorism-Related Offences on Expression, Information and Movement* (n 1) 41–43. See e.g.: Petter Asp, 'Preventionism and Criminalization of Nonconsummate Offences' in Andrew Ashworth, Lucia Zedner and Patrick Tomlin (eds), *Prevention and the Limits of the Criminal Law* (Oxford University Press 2013); Aradau and Van Munster (n 1); BA de Graaf and Q Eijkman, 'Terrorismebestrijding en securitisering: een rechtssociologische verkenning van de neveneffecten' [2011] Justitiële Verkenningen 33; Klaus Günther, 'Responsibility to Protect and Preventive Justice' in Andrew Ashworth, Lucia Zedner and Patrick Tomlin (eds), *Prevention and the Limits of the Criminal Law* (Oxford University Press 2013); R Pieterman, *De voorzorgcultuur: streven naar veiligheid in een wereld vol risico en onzekerheid* (Boom Juridisch 2008); van der Woude (n 1); Leanne Weber and Murray Lee, 'Preventing Indeterminate Threats: Fear, Terror and the Politics of Preemption' in Stephen Farrall and Murray Lee (eds), *Fear of crime: critical voices in an age of anxiety* (Routledge-Cavendish 2009).

went global. Shortly after 9/11, Beck wrote an article in which he identified terrorism as one of three different global axes of conflict in world risk society.[5] Over 20 years later, terrorism is still considered to be a considerable problem that must be tackled.[6] Fortunately, most governments seem to be succeeding fairly well in developing a counter-terrorism approach which has probably reduced the number of victims.[7]

2. International and European context – As terrorism networks became more and more international, so did the fight against terrorism.[8] Chiefly under the auspices of the United Nations (UN),[9] several terrorism-related conventions were negotiated in the second half of the 21st century.[10] More recently, the UN Security Council issued several resolutions on combatting terrorism.[11]

5 The other two being ecological conflicts and global financial crises. See: Ulrich Beck, 'The Terrorist Threat: World Risk Society Revisited' (2002) 19 Theory, Culture & Society 39. See also: De Coensel, *Counter-Terrorism & Criminal Law: A Normative Legitimacy Test of Terrorism-Related Offences on Expression, Information and Movement* (n 1) 41.

6 Johan Delmulle and Stefaan Guenter, 'Gerechtelijke aanpak inzake terrorisme', *Strafrecht en Strafprocesrecht* (Wolters Kluwer 2006) 3.

7 Christian De Valkeneer, 'Les Réponses Face Au Terrorisme : Les Glissements Du Judiciaire Vers l'administratif' [2017] Journal Tribunaux 707, 707. For data, see: Datagraver.com.

8 Elise Delhaise, *Infractions terroristes* (Larcier 2019) 13–19; I De La Serna, 'Des infractions terroristes', *Les Infractions* (Larcier 2013) 169–174; Véronique Hameeuw, 'Strafbaarstelling van terroristische misdrijven: van Europees Kaderbesluit tot het Belgische Strafwetboek' [2005] Tijdschrift voor Strafrecht 2; Alain Winants, 'De invloed van terrorisme op de strafwetgeving: actualia materieel strafrecht' (2019) 14 Nullum Crimen 343, 344; Lucia Zedner, *Security* (2009) 118–120.

9 There was the European Convention on the Suppression of Terrorism of 27 January 1977, *ETS* 90, Strasbourg. This was a Council of Europe Convention. However, belying its much more encompassing name, this convention only covers extradition.

10 Petter Asp and Iain Cameron, 'Terrorism and Legal Security – a Swedish and European Perspective' in Mattias Dahlberg (ed), *Uppsala-Minnesota Colloquium: Law, Culture and Values* (Iustus förlag 2009) 267; Alex Conte, *Human Rights in the Prevention and Punishment of Terrorism* (Springer Berlin Heidelberg 2010) 39–47; De La Serna (n 8) 169–170; Julien Féret and Ana Peyro Llopis, 'La lutte contre le terrorisme: instruments et institutions' in Ludovic Hennebel and Damien Vandermeersch (eds), *Juger le terrorisme dans l'État de droit* (Bruylant 2009) 265–271; Daniel Flore, 'La Loi du 19 Décembre 2003 relative aux infractions terroristes: Genèse, principes et conséquences', *Questions d'actualité de droit pénal et de procédure pénale* (Bruylant 2005) 209–210; An Fransen and Jan Kerkhofs, 'Het materieel terrorismestrafrecht' in Jan Kerkhofs, Antoon Schotsaert and Philippe Van Linthout (eds), *Contra-terrorisme: De gerechtelijke aanpak van terrorisme in België* (Larcier 2018) 4–5; Andrea Gioia, 'The UN Conventions on the Prevention and Suppression of International Terrorism' in Giuseppe Nesi (ed), *International cooperation in counter-terrorism: the United Nations and regional organizations in the fight against terrorism* (Ashgate 2006); Jean-Christophe Martin, *Les règles internationales relatives à la lutte contre le terrorisme* (Bruylant 2006); Winants (n 8) 345. See e.g.: Convention on Offences and Certain Other Acts Committed On Board Aircraft of 14 September 1963, Tokyo, *United Nations Treaty Series* 1969, 220; International Convention for the Suppression of Terrorist Bombings of 15 December 1997, New York, *United Nations Treaty Series* 2001, 256.

11 E.g. the UN Security Council Resolution S/RES/2178 (24 September 2014). See also: Conte (n 10) 47–60; Féret and Peyro Llopis (n 10) 289–306; Fransen and Kerkhofs (n 10) 10–12.

Specifically in Europe, there is the Council of Europe Treaty on the Prevention of Terrorism.[12] Last but definitely not least, the European Union has been active in the fight against terrorism.[13] In 2002 the European Union (EU) issued a Framework Decision on Combatting terrorism.[14] The creation of a counter-terrorism framework was an issue that had surfaced before, but 9/11 provided enormous political momentum and sped up the process.[15] This Framework Decision was amended by another one in 2008 because of the introduction of

12 Warsaw, 16 May 2005 [2018] *Pb. EU* 159/3. See also: Delhaise (n 8) 17; Féret and Peyro Llopis (n 10) 272–273; Fransen and Kerkhofs (n 10) 8–10; J Petersen, 'Naar nieuwe verbale uitingsmisdrijven in de strijd tegen terreur?' (2019) 14 Nullum Crimen (NC) 50, 53–54.

13 For an overview and analysis of EU measures see: Sophie Perez and Thierry Thibaud, 'Les instruments de lutte contre le terrorisme au sein de l'Union Européenne', *L'Union Européenne et la lutte contre le terrorisme: état des lieux et perspective* (Larcier 2010). See also: European Parliament Research Service, 'The fight against terrorism' PE 621.817 May 2018; Féret and Peyro Llopis (n 10) 273–277; Francesca Galli and Anne Weyembergh, 'Introduction' in Francesca Galli and Anne Weyembergh (eds), *EU counter-terrorism offences: What impact on national legislation and case-law?* (Editions de l'Université de Bruxelles 2012) 13–20; Sabine Gless, 'The Two Framework Decisions: A Critical Approach' in Francesca Galli and Anne Weyembergh (eds), *EU counter-terrorism offences: What impact on national legislation and case-law?* (Editions de l'Université de Bruxelles 2012); Ben Hayes and Chris Jones, 'Taking Stock: The Evolution, Adoption, Implementation and Evaluation of EU Counter-Terrorism Policy' in Fiona de Londras and Josephine Doody (eds), *The Impact, Legitimacy and Effectiveness of EU Counter-Terrorism* (1st edn, Routledge 2015); Cian C Murphy, *EU Counter-Terrorism Law: Pre-Emption and the Rule of Law* (1st edn, Hart Publishing 2012); Oschinsky Suzanne and Oschinsky Yves, 'Le point sur la legislation antiterroriste' (2005) 501 Journal des Procès 14; Petersen (n 12) 54.

14 Council Framework Decision 2002/475/JHA of 13 June 2002 on combating terrorism [2002] *OJ* L164/3. For analysis, see: Ali Bounjoua, 'L'harmonisation des infractions de " l'entraînement au terrorisme " et du " voyage à des fins de terrorisme " en droit pénal Européen à l'aune des départs et des retours de zones de conflits au sein d'états tiers à l'Union Européenne' [2022] Revue de droit international et de droit comparé 645, 664–665; Marieke De Goede, 'The Politics of Preemption and the War on Terror in Europe' (2008) 14 European Journal of International Relations 161, 169–170; De La Serna (n 8) 170–174; Delhaise (n 8) 15–17; Flore (n 10) 209; Fransen and Kerkhofs (n 10) 6–8; Sabine Gless, 'Fighting Terrorism in a "Rechtsstaat"' in Toine Sapens, Marc Groenhuijsen and Tijs Kooijmans (eds), *Universalis: Liber amicorum Cyrille Fijnaut* (Intersentia 2011) 931–939; Jean-Claude Paye, 'De la définition légale de l'organisation criminelle à l'incrimination du terrorisme' (2002) 435 Journal des Procès 9; Anne Weyembergh and Laurent Kennes, 'Le Titre Iter du Livre II du Code Pénal: Des infractions terroristes', *Droit pénal spécial: tome 1* (Anthémis 2011) 105–107; Anne Weyembergh, 'L'impact du 11 septembre sur l'équilibre sécurité/liberté dans l'espace pénal européen' in Emmanuelle Bribosia and Anne Weyembergh (eds), *La convention Européenne des droits de l'homme à l'épreuve de la lutte contre le terrorisme* (Bruylant-Nemesis 2002) 161–173. See also: Martin (n 10) 109–110. For an analysis of the Framework Decision and its implementation in several countries not discussed in this book, see: Erling Johannes Husabø and Ingvild Bruce, *Fighting Terrorism through Multilevel Criminal Legislation: Security Council Resolution 1373, the EU Framework Decision on Combating Terrorism and Their Implementation in Nordic, Dutch and German Criminal Law* (Brill | Nijhoff 2009).

15 Maria Luisa Cesoni, 'Les "infractions terroristes": de la répression des actes à la police de la pensée' in Christian De Valkeneer and Henri D Bosly (eds), *Actualités en droit pénal 2019* (Larcier 2019) 230; De La Serna (n 8) 170–171; Hameeuw (n 8) 2; Raf Jespers, 'La nécessité d'une vision critique sur la lutte contre le terrorisme' (2004) 393 Journal des Procès 12, 14; Murphy (n 13) 17–27; Winants (n 8) 346.

the Council of Europe Treaty and the fact that the terrorist threat had grown and evolved.[16] Finally, it was replaced by the Directive on Combatting Terrorism in 2017.[17] For many states these international and European instruments, and for EU countries especially the EU instruments, were strong drivers in the development of their counter-terrorism offences.[18] For example, the Belgian law of 19 December 2003,[19] which introduced the first terrorist offences in Belgian criminal law, was enacted mainly to comply with the obligations of the EU Framework Decision on Combatting Terrorism.[20]

16 Council Framework Decision 2008/919/JHA of 28 November 2008 amending Framework Decision 2002/475/JHA on combating terrorism [2008] *OJ* L330/21–23; Bounjoua (n 14) 665; De La Serna (n 8) 174; Delhaise (n 8) 18; Fransen and Kerkhofs (n 10) 9–10; Gless (n 14) 934. For an analysis of this Framework Decision, see: Sophie Lavaux, 'Terrorisme: la stratégie de l'Union Européenne en matière de radicalisation et de recrutment (suite)' [2011] Vigiles 68, 68–71.

17 Directive (EU) 2017/541 of the European Parliament and of the Council of 15 March 2017 on combating terrorism and replacing Council Framework Decision 2002/475/JHA and amending Council Decision 2005/671/JHA [2017] *OJ* L88/6. See also: Bounjoua (n 14) 666; Delhaise (n 8) 19; Fransen and Kerkhofs (n 10) 12–15.

18 Andrew Ashworth and Lucia Zedner, *Preventive Justice* (Oxford University Press 2014) 171; De La Serna (n 8) 170.

19 Wet 19 december 2003 betreffende terroristische misdrijven, *BS* 29 december 2003, 61689.

20 Council Framework Decision 2002/475/JHA of 13 June 2002 on combating terrorism [2002] *OJ* L164/3, now replaced by Directive (EU) 2017/541 of the European Parliament and of the Council of 15 March 2017 on combating terrorism and replacing Council Framework Decision 2002/475/JHA and amending Council Decision 2005/671/JHA [2017] *OJ* L88/6; Marie-Aude Beernaert, 'La Loi du 19 Décembre 2003 relative aux infractions terroristes : Quand le droit pénal Belge évolue sous la dictée de l'Union Européenne' (2004) 24 Journal des tribunaux 585, 585–586; Delmulle and Guenter (n 6) 3; De La Serna (n 8) 168 en 174; Hameeuw (n 8) 2; Adrien Masset, 'Terrorisme' [2013] Postal Memorialis – Lexicon strafrecht, strafvordering en bijzondere wetten 411, T60/1 and T60/3; Winants (n 8) 345.

CHAPTER II
PREVENTION

3. THE NEED TO PREVENT – The wave of terrorist attacks that were carried out in Europe during the first two decades of the century, has abruptly brought the issue of terrorism to our doorstep. Terrorism has induced fear in the population[21] and governments are trying to control the risk posed by terrorists,[22] who are seen as 'dangerous people'.[23] The idea of risk management has shifted the focus from repression to prevention.[24, 25] Avoiding a large number of people suffering

---

21 Shamila Ahmed, 'The "emotionalization of the 'War on Terror'": Counter-Terrorism, Fear, Risk, Insecurity and Helplessness' (2015) 15 Criminology & Criminal Justice 545, 546–548; Pedro Caeiro, 'Concluding Remarks' in Francesca Galli and Anne Weyembergh (eds), *EU counter-terrorism offences: What impact on national legislation and case-law?* (Editions de l'Université de Bruxelles 2012) 309; Marie-Helen Maras, *Counterterrorism* (Jones and Bartlett 2013) 92–93; Anthony Richards, 'Conceptualizing Terrorism' (2014) 37 Studies in Conflict & Terrorism 213, 221.

22 De Coensel, *Counter-Terrorism & Criminal Law: A Normative Legitimacy Test of Terrorism-Related Offences on Expression, Information and Movement* (n 1) 46–47. More generally, see: Garland (n 3).

23 Heidi Mork Lomell, 'Punishing the Uncommitted Crime: Prevention, Pre-Emption, Precaution and the Transformation of Criminal Law' in Barbara Hudson and Synnove Ugelvik (eds), *Justice in the Risk Society: Challenging and Re-affirming Justice in Late Modernity* (SAGE Publications Ltd 2012) 83; Maras (n 21) 217; John Vervaele, 'Terorrism and Security' in Steven Dewulf (ed), *la [CVDW] Liber Amicorum Chris Van den Wyngaert* (Maklu 2017) 603; Lucia Zedner, 'Fixing the Future? The Pre-Emptive Turn in Criminal Justice' in B McSherry, A Norrie and S Bronitt (eds), *Regulating Deviance: The Redirection of Criminalisation and the Futures of Criminal Law* (Hart Publishing 2009) 37–39.

24 In scholarship the term 'pre-emption' is also extensively used. See e.g.: Jude McCulloch and Sharon Pickering, 'Pre-Crime and Counter-Terrorism: Imagining Future Crime in the "War on Terror"' (2009) 49 The British Journal of Criminology 628; Jude McCulloch and Dean Wilson, *Pre-Crime: Pre-Emption, Precaution and the Future* (Routledge 2016); Lucia Zedner, 'Seeking Security by Eroding Rights: The Side-Stepping of Due Process' in Benjamin Goold and Liora Lazarus (eds), *Security and Human Rights* (Hart Publishing 2007) 259. The term pre-emption implies that the offence is not only prevented but even the unspecified threat of harm is prevented (or rather pre-empted). It emphasises the remoteness of the harm. However, for simplicity's sake, we will use the term 'prevention' in this book.

25 MvT wetsontwerp 5 juli 2016 houdende diverse bepalingen ter bestrijding van terrorisme (III), *Parl.St.* Kamer 2015–16, no. 54 1951/001, (4) 12; Ahmed (n 21) 551–552; David Anderson, 'Shielding the Compass: How to Fight Terrorism without Defeating the Law' (2013) Independent Reviewer of Terrorism Legislation 6; Andrew Ashworth, 'The Unfairness of Risk-Based Possession Offences' (2011) 5 Criminal Law and Philosophy 237, 237; Ashworth and Zedner (n 18) 180; David Cole, 'The Difference Prevention Makes: Regulating Preventive Justice' (2015) 9 Crim Law and Philos 501, 501–502; Conte (n 10) 451; De Coensel, *Counter-Terrorism & Criminal Law: A Normative Legitimacy Test of Terrorism-Related Offences on*

harm is the main reason why terrorist attacks should be prevented, which gives governments an imperative and even an obligation to prevent them.[26] Under the European Convention of Human Rights (ECHR) states have a positive obligation to protect the right to life, to family life, and to a home to the people under their jurisdiction and to protect them against inhuman or degrading treatment and torture.[27] Doing nothing to prevent terror attacks could therefore be a

Expression, Information and Movement (n 1) 43–44; De Goede (n 14); De Valkeneer (n 7) 709; Helen Fenwick, 'Preventive Anti-Terrorist Strategies in the UK and ECHR: Control Orders, TPIMs and the Role of Technology' (2011) 25 International Review of Law, Computers & Technology 129, 129–130; Helen Fenwick and Gavin Phillipson, 'Covert Derogations and Judicial Deference: Redefining Liberty and Due Process Rights in Counterterrorism Law and Beyond' (2011) 56 McGill Law Journal 863, 865–866; Cyriel Fijnaut, 'De belangrijke rol van het strafrecht bij de bestrijding van (islamitisch) terrorisme' (2005) 2005 Rechtsgeleerd Magazijn THEMIS 210, 212; Francesca Galli, 'The War on Terror and Crusading Judges: Re-Establishing the Primacy of the Criminal Justice System' in A Masferrer (ed), *Post 9/11 and the State of Permanent Legal Emergency* (Springer 2012) 159–160; Barbara Hudson, 'Justice in a Time of Terror' (2009) 49 The British Journal of Criminology 702, 712; Lomell (n 23) 83; Lynch, McGarrity and Williams (n 3) 5; Maras (n 21) 94 and 124; Manuel Cancio Meliá, 'Terrorism and Criminal Law: The Dream of Prevention, the Nightmare of the Rule of Law' [2011] New Criminal Law Review 108, 113–114; McCulloch and Pickering (n 24) 629–630; McCulloch and Wilson (n 24) 4–5; John P McLoughlin, Gregory P Noone and Diana C Noone, 'Security Detention, Terrorism And The Prevention Imperative' (2009) 40 CASE W. RES. J. INT'L L. 463, 464; Valsamis Mitsilegas, 'The Criminalisation of Travel as a Global Paradigm of Preventive (in)Justice: Lessons from the EU Response to "Foreign Terrorist Fighters"' (2023) 14 New J Eur Crim L 183, 183; Phil Palmer, 'Dealing with the Exceptional: Pre-Crime Anti-Terrorism Policy and Practice' (2012) 22 Policing and Society 519; Dan Squires, 'Terrorism and Pre-Emptive Civil Processes' (2016) 20 The International Journal of Human Rights 684, 685; Katja Sugman Stubbs and Francesca Galli, 'Inchoate Offences: The Sanctioning of an Act Prior to and Irrespective of the Commission of Any Harm' in Francesca Galli and Anne Weyembergh (eds), *EU counter-terrorism offences: What impact on national legislation and case-law?* (Editions de l'Université de Bruxelles 2012) 291; van der Woude (n 1) 8–9; Frank Verbruggen, Ettina Prakken and David Roef, *Voorbereidingshandelingen in het strafrecht* (Wolf legal publishers 2004) 98–99; Vervaele (n 23) 603; Nigel White, 'Preventive Counter-Terrorism and International Law' [2013] Journal of Conflict & Security Law 181, 181; Christopher Alister Wood, 'Risk Assessment, Counter-Terrorism Law & Policy; A Human Rights-Based Analysis: Assessing the UK's Pre-Emptive and Preventative Measures of Countering Terrorism, Interaction with Article 5 and 6 of the European Convention on Human Rights, and the Potential Role of Risk Assessment,' (Durham University 2017) 11; Zedner, 'Fixing the Future? The Pre-Emptive Turn in Criminal Justice' (n 23) 39–44; Zedner, *Security* (n 8) 73–74.

26 H Fenwick, 'Recalibrating ECHR Rights, and the Role of the Human Rights Act Post 9/11: Reasserting International Human Rights Norms in the "War on Terror"?' (2010) 63 Current Legal Problems 153, 154; McCulloch and Pickering (n 24) 632; McCulloch and Wilson (n 24) 58–73; Palmer (n 25); Don E Scheid, 'Indefinite Detention of Mega-Terrorists in the War on Terror' (2010) 29 Criminal Justice Ethics 1, 2; Sugman Stubbs and Galli (n 25) 295–296; Clive Walker, 'Keeping Control of Terrorists without Losing Control of Constitutionalism' (2007) 59 Stanford Law Review 1395, 1395–1396; George Williams, 'Anti-Terrorism Laws and Human Rights' (2015) 19 Review of Constitutional Studies 127, 130.

27 Sébastien Van Drooghenbroeck, 'Note relative à l'application des principes de proportionnalité et subsidiarité en matière pénale dans de droit de la Convention européenne des droits de l'Homme', Annex 2.7 to the Report on behalf of the Committee on Justice on the Bill on the Code of Criminal Procedure, *Parl.St.* Senaat 2005–06, no. 3–450/20, (1398) 1400–1401; *L.C.B. v. United Kingdom* App no 14/1997/798/1001 (ECtHR 9 June 1998); *Osman v. United Kingdom* App no 87/1997/871/1083 (ECtHR 28 October 1998); *Z. and others v. United Kingdom* App no

violation of human rights.[28] However, states cannot blindly intervene and the European Court of Human Rights (ECtHR) has emphasised the need to *'strike a fair balance between the defence of the institutions of democracy in the common interest and the protection of individual rights.'*[29]

4. Criminal law and administrative law – If there is a form of consensus on the fact that terrorism should be prevented, the answer to the question of how to effectively do so, is less straightforward. Even just defining terrorism has proven to be a difficult task for states and academics.[30] What exactly is understood as 'terrorism' differs from state to state and will be discussed in the Parts covering national legislation. From a legal perspective, countries mainly

---

29392/95 (ECtHR Grand Chamber 10 May 2001) 73; *Opuz v. Turkey* App no 33401/02 (ECtHR 9 June 2009); *Soare and others v. Romania* App no 24329/02 (ECtHR 22 February 2011) 127; *Oshurko v. Ukraine* App no 33108/05 (ECtHR 8 September 2011) 67–68; *Austin and others v. United Kingdom* App nos 39692/09, 40713/09 and 41008/09 (ECtHR Grand Chamber 15 March 2012) 55; *Tagayeva and others v. Russia* App no 26562/07 and 6 others (ECtHR 13 April 2017) 482; Amnesty International, 'Veiligheid & Mensenrechten: Maatregelen tegen terrorisme en radicalisering', Letter to the Belgian Chamber of Representatives following a hearing on 12 May 2015 (2015) 5; Andrew Ashworth, 'Criminal Law, Human Rights and Preventative Justice' in B McSherry, A Norrie and S Bronitt (eds), *Regulating deviance: The redirection of criminalisation and the futures of criminal law* (Hart Publishing 2009) 101; Andrew Ashworth, Lucia Zedner and Patrick Tomlin, 'Introduction' in Andrew Ashworth, Lucia Zedner and Patrick Tomlin (eds), *Prevention and the Limits of the Criminal Law* (Oxford University Press 2013) 7; Olivier De Schutter, 'La Convention Européenne Des Droits de l'Homme à l'épreuve de la lutte contre le terrorisme' in Emmanuelle Bribosia and Anne Weyembergh (eds), *La convention Européenne des droits de l'homme à l'épreuve de la lutte contre le terrorisme* (Bruylant-Nemesis 2002) 86–89; Günther (n 4) 86–87; Jos Silvis, 'Terrorism and Human Rights' in Koen Lemmens, Stephan Parmentier and Louise Reyntjens (eds), *Human Rights with a human touch: Liber amicorum Paul Lemmens* (Intersentia 2019) 656–657; Stefan Sottiaux, *Terrorism and the Limitation of Rights* (Hart Publishing 2008) 3–4; Jan Velaers, 'La lutte contre le terrorisme et les Droits de l'homme: Dévelopements récents en Belgique' in P D'Argent, D Renders and M Verdussen (eds), *Les Visages de L'Etat: Liber Amicorum Yves Lejeune* (Bruylant 2017) 775; Frédéric Vanneste, 'Het Europese Hof Voor de Rechten van de Mens en de overheden die terrorisme bestrijden: brothers in arms?' (2003–2004) 41 Rechtskundig Weekblad 1665, 1667; White (n 25) 186–187.

28 Tagayeva and others v. Russia App no 26562/07 and 6 others (ECtHR 13 April 2017); Guide the case-law of the European Court of Human Rights on terrorism (2020) 10–11.

29 *Klass and others v. Germany* App no 5029/71 (ECtHR 6 September 1978) 48–49 and 59; *Brogan and others v. United Kingdom* App nos 11209/84, 11234/84, 11266/84 and 11386/85 (ECtHR Plenary 29 November 1988) 48; *Fox, Campbell and Hartley v. United Kingdom* App nos 12244/86, 12245/86 and 12383/86 (ECtHR 30 August 1990) 28.

30 Ashworth and Zedner (n 18) 172–174; Asp and Cameron (n 10) 256–265; Gerhard Hafner, 'The Definition of the Crime of Terrorism' in Giuseppe Nesi (ed), *International cooperation in counter-terrorism: the United Nations and regional organizations in the fight against terrorism* (Ashgate 2006); Liora Lazarus, Benjamin Goold and Caitlin Goss, 'Control without Punishment: Understanding Coercion' in Jonathan Simon and Richard Sparks, *The SAGE Handbook of Punishment and Society* (SAGE Publications Ltd 2013) 461; Maras (n 21) 4–12; Richards (n 21) 213–219; NJ Schrijver and LJ Van Den Herik, 'Counter-Terrorism Strategies, Human Rights and International Law: Meeting the Challenges' in ER Muller, U Rosenthal and R De Wijk (eds), *Terrorisme: studies over terrorisme en terrorismebestrijding* (Kluwer 2008) 885–886; Vervaele (n 23) 593–594.

use two different tools to prevent terrorist attacks: the criminal justice system and administrative measures.[31]

5. 'Traditional' criminal law – Normally, criminal law is repressive, it addresses acts that are 'public wrongs' and punishes people for them.[32] Society (ultimately represented by the judge or jury) punishes someone who has committed criminally reprehensible behaviour and has thereby damaged a protected legal interest ('*rechtsgoed*') and caused a public harm.[33, 34] For example, larceny violates the right to property, manslaughter violates the right to life, and so on.[35] Traditional criminal law sometimes goes further and punishes people even before they have caused the public harm. This is the case for inchoate offences, which '*criminalize acts that are intrinsically dangerous because they require proof of some conduct in which the actor loses control of the effects of his criminal intentions because their actions pose a direct threat to the asset.*'[36] An example of this is the doctrine of the criminal attempt (see nos 266 and 465).[37] Both traditional offences and inchoate offences criminalise acts

---

31 White (n 25) 189–191.

32 Ashworth and Zedner (n 18) 95–96; Ashworth, Zedner and Tomlin (n 27) 1; Emma Dekrem, 'Naar een veralgemeende strafbaarheid van voorbereidende handelingen?' [2020] Nullum Crimen 133, 134; Lomell (n 23) 84–85; Tim Nikolas Mueller, 'Preventive Detention as a Counter-Terrorism Instrument in Germany' (2014) 62 Crime, Law and Social Change 323, 323; Verbruggen, Prakken and Roef (n 25) 23–25; Zedner, 'Seeking Security by Eroding Rights: The Side-Stepping of Due Process' (n 24) 259.

33 The so-called harm principle is the most widely recognised ground for criminalisation. See: De Coensel, *Counter-Terrorism & Criminal Law: A Normative Legitimacy Test of Terrorism-Related Offences on Expression, Information and Movement* (n 1) 101.

34 Ashworth and Zedner (n 18) 95–96; Dekrem (n 32) 134; Chris Van den Wyngaert, Steven Vandromme and Philip Traest, *Strafrecht en strafprocesrecht in hoofdlijnen* (11th edn, Gompel&Svacina 2019) 239; Steven Vandromme and Chris De Roy, 'De strafbaarheid van voorbereidingshandelingen en uitvoeringshandelingen: de nieuwste ontwikkelingen in het leerstuk van de strafbare poging en de gevolgen ervan voor het strafprocesrecht', *Strafrecht en Strafprocesrecht* (Wolters Kluwer 2006) 509–510; Frank Verbruggen, 'Schaduwboksen in het donker: de dogmatische onderbouw van het strafrechtelijk overheidsoptreden tegen georganiseerde criminaliteit' (Faculty of Law of KU Leuven 2001) 163–174; Verbruggen, Prakken and Roef (n 25) 23–25.

35 Vandromme and De Roy (n 34) 509; Winants (n 8) 359.

36 Peter Ramsay, 'Democratic Limits to Preventive Criminal Law' in Andrew Ashworth, Lucia Zedner and Patrick Tomlin (eds), *Prevention and the Limits of the Criminal Law* (Oxford University Press 2013) 215. See also: Peter Ramsay, *The Insecurity State: Vulnerable Autonomy and the Right to Security in the Criminal Law* (Oxford University Press 2012) 142. For an analysis, see also: Douglas Husak, *Overcriminalization: The Limits of the Criminal Law* (Oxford University Press 2008) 160; Sugman Stubbs and Galli (n 25) 291–294.

37 Ashworth and Zedner (n 18) 96–97; Conte (n 10) 437–438; Dekrem (n 32) 134; Lomell (n 23) 85; McCulloch and Wilson (n 24) 18; Ramsay, *The Insecurity State: Vulnerable Autonomy and the Right to Security in the Criminal Law* (n 36) 142; Ramsay, 'Democratic Limits to Preventive Criminal Law' (n 36) 215–216; Sugman Stubbs and Galli (n 25) 294; Vandromme and De Roy (n 34) 510; Zedner, 'Seeking Security by Eroding Rights: The Side-Stepping of Due Process' (n 24) 259. Note that Alexander and Ferzan argue that a completed attempt is in fact not an inchoate offence and only an incomplete attempt is. See: Larry Alexander

which are in themselves dangerous for the legal asset that we as a society deem worthy of protection.[38] A traditional concept within criminal law is that of the *iter criminis*, the criminal path or 'road to the offence'. It is the symbolic road the perpetrator takes, which starts at the idea of committing an offence and culminates in the actual perpetration of the offence.[39] Along this road, several phases can be distinguished: the idea, the preparation, the start of the execution and the completion of the offence.[40] It is up to the legislature to decide at which point on this path to intervene.[41] The traditional doctrine briefly set out above means that criminal law intervenes when the perpetrator has reached the 'start of the execution' phase on the *iter criminis*.[42] Mere ideas are not punishable, and often very hard or even impossible to prove.[43]

6. Preventive criminal law – When using criminal law to tackle terrorism,[44] governments have to use it in a way it is not traditionally used. In order to prevent terrorist attacks, a repressive point of view is insufficient since it intervenes after the fact. To be able to use criminal law in a preventive manner, states have started to criminalise 'precursor crimes' or 'pre-inchoate offences', i.e. the criminalisation of preparatory acts and facilitative acts (e.g. financing, providing training, etc.).[45] These acts in themselves do not cause

---

and Kimberly Kessler Ferzan, 'Risk and Inchoate Crimes: Retribution or Prevention?' in GR Sullivan and Ian Dennis (eds), *Seeking Security: Pre-Empting the Commission of Criminal Harms* (Bloomsbury Publishing 2012) 105–106. They state that '*Only if the actor retains control over whether those future crimes occur do we have a true inchoate crime.*'

38 Ramsay, *The Insecurity State: Vulnerable Autonomy and the Right to Security in the Criminal Law* (n 36) 142–143.

39 H Berkmoes, 'Algemeen' in M De Busscher and others (eds), *Strafrecht: duiding* (Larcier 2018) 83–84; De Coensel, *Counter-Terrorism & Criminal Law: A Normative Legitimacy Test of Terrorism-Related Offences on Expression, Information and Movement* (n 1) 38; Dekrem (n 32) 137; A De Nauw and F Deruyck, *Overzicht van het Belgisch algemeen strafrecht* (Die Keure 2017) 66; Françoise Tulkens and others, *Introduction Au Droit Pénal* (10th edn, Wolters Kluwer 2014) 417; Vandromme and De Roy (n 34) 509.

40 Corr. Luik (vakantiekamer) 19 juli 2017, *JLMB* 2017, 1391; Berkmoes, 'Algemeen' (n 39) 84; De Coensel, *Counter-Terrorism & Criminal Law: A Normative Legitimacy Test of Terrorism-Related Offences on Expression, Information and Movement* (n 1) 38; Dekrem (n 32) 137; De Nauw and Deruyck (n 39) 65; Sugman Stubbs and Galli (n 25) 292; Van den Wyngaert, Vandromme and Traest (n 34) 357.

41 Daniel Ohana, 'Responding to Acts Preparatory to the Commission of a Crime: Criminalization of Prevention?' (2006) 25 Crim. Just. Ethics 23, 23.

42 Berkmoes, 'Algemeen' (n 39) 84; De Coensel, *Counter-Terrorism & Criminal Law: A Normative Legitimacy Test of Terrorism-Related Offences on Expression, Information and Movement* (n 1) 38; De Nauw and Deruyck (n 39) 67; Lomell (n 23) 85; Sugman Stubbs and Galli (n 25) 292–293; Van den Wyngaert, Vandromme and Traest (n 34) 357.

43 Sugman Stubbs and Galli (n 25) 292; Vandromme and De Roy (n 34) 513.

44 Note that this does not only apply to terrorism, but also to other parts of criminal law, e.g.: many traffic violations, some drug offences, etc.

45 Ashworth, 'Criminal Law, Human Rights and Preventative Justice' (n 27) 90; Asp (n 4) 27–28; Conte (n 10) 438; Elise Delhaise and Coline Fievet, 'Frontières intelligentes et nouvelles incriminations pénales : L'Union Européenne face à la problématique des " foreign terrorist

public harm[46] and are not intrinsically dangerous to a legal asset, but are steps taken in preparation of a terror attack (i.e. the public harm). They are preventive offences aimed at finding and convicting people before they can commit an attack or assist others in doing so,[47] and are in themselves far from causing harm and sometimes even far from creating a danger (or risk) of harm.[48] Since the authorities cannot however afford to wait until the actual attack is

---

fighters"' [2017] Journal des tribunaux 113, 119–120; RA Duff, *Answering for Crime: Responsibility and Liability in the Criminal Law* (Hart Publishing 2007) 159–166; Galli (n 25) 160–162; Lazarus, Goold and Goss (n 30) 464; Lomell (n 23); McCulloch and Pickering (n 24) 633–634; Mitsilegas (n 25) 183; Mueller (n 32) 329; Ramsay, *The Insecurity State: Vulnerable Autonomy and the Right to Security in the Criminal Law* (n 36) 142–143; Ramsay, 'Democratic Limits to Preventive Criminal Law' (n 36) 215–216; Vervaele (n 23) 598–602; Clive Walker, 'The Impact of Contemporary Security Agendas Against Terrorism on the Substantive Criminal Law' in Aniceto Masferrer (ed), *Post 9/11 and the State of Permanent Legal Emergency: Security and Human Rights in Countering Terrorism*, vol 14 (Springer Netherlands 2012) 129; Lucia Zedner, 'Terrorizing Criminal Law' (2014) 8 Criminal Law and Philosophy 99, 100. For Belgium see: Art. 140–141 CC; Luik 18 oktober 2017, *JLMB* 2017, 1878; Corr. Oost-Vlaanderen (afd. Gent) 16 oktober 2017, *NjW* 2017, 805, noot W. Yperman en S. Royer; Delhaise (n 8) 44–45; De Valkeneer (n 7) 709; An Fransen, Jan Kerkhofs and Pieter Verrest, *Terrorisme: Een analyse van het Belgische en Nederlandse Materieel Strafrecht* (Wolf Legal Publishers 2017) 42–103; Masset (n 20) 427–434. For different conceptual analyses, see also: CM Billiet, P De Smedt and H Van Landeghem, 'Vlaamse milieuhandhaving nieuwe stijl' [2009] Tijdschrift voor Milieurecht 326, 362; De Coensel, *Counter-Terrorism & Criminal Law: A Normative Legitimacy Test of Terrorism-Related Offences on Expression, Information and Movement* (n 1) 104; Petersen (n 12) 53; Jeroen Ten Voorde, 'Prohibiting Remote Harms: On Endangerment, Citizenship and Control' (2014) 10 Utrecht Law Review 163, 166; Vandromme and De Roy (n 34) 542–544; Van den Wyngaert, Vandromme and Traest (n 34) 239–240. For the UK see: s. 11–19, s. 38B and s. 54–59 TA 2000; s. 1 – 11 TA 2006; Anderson, 'Shielding the Compass: How to Fight Terrorism without Defeating the Law' (n 25) 7; Ashworth and Zedner (n 18) 98 and 179–181; Conte (n 10) 438; Helen Fenwick, 'Terrorism and the Control Orders/ TPIMs Saga: A Vindication of the Human Rights Act or a Manifestation of "Defensive Democracy"?' [2017] Public law. 609, 621–622; Zedner, 'Terrorizing Criminal Law' 112–115. For an analysis of the concept of precursor crimes, see: Manuel Cancio Meliá and Anneke Petzsche, 'Precursor Crimes of Terrorism' in Genevieve Lennon and Clive Walker (eds), *Routledge Handbook of Law and Terrorism* (Routledge 2015).

46 See e.g. on some of the UK offences: Victor Tadros, 'Justice and Terrorism' [2007] New Criminal Law Review 658, 675–676.

47 MvT wetsontwerp 22 juni 2015 tot versterking van de strijd tegen terrorisme, *Parl.St.* Kamer 2014–15, no. 54-1198/001, 6; Luik 18 oktober 2017, *JLMB* 2017, 1878; Corr. Oost-Vlaanderen (afd. Gent) 16 oktober 2017, *NjW* 2017, 805, noot W. Yperman en S. Royer; Conte (n 10) 438; Delhaise (n 8) 44–45; De Valkeneer (n 7) 709; Fransen, Kerkhofs and Verrest (n 45) 42–103; Galli (n 25) 160–162; Hale-Ross (n 1) 106; Masset (n 20) 427–434; Coline Moreau, 'Droit pénal de l'ennemi versus droit pénal du citoyen: réflexions sur la fonction sécuritaire du système de droit criminel mise en avant par les infractions terroristes incriminées par les articles 140*sexies* et 140*septies* du Code Pénal' [2021] Revue de Droit Pénal et de Criminologie (Rev. dr. pén.) 101, 101; Vervaele (n 23) 598–602; Zedner, 'Terrorizing Criminal Law' (n 45) 100.

48 Ashworth, 'The Unfairness of Risk-Based Possession Offences' (n 25) 238; Asp and Cameron (n 10) 267–272; Moreau (n 47) 101–103; Ramsay, 'Democratic Limits to Preventive Criminal Law' (n 36) 216–217; Ten Voorde (n 45) 167; Zedner, 'Fixing the Future? The Pre-Emptive Turn in Criminal Justice' (n 23) 50; Zedner, *Security* (n 8) 131. European Union Agency for Fundamental Rights, *Directive (EU) 2017/541 on combatting terrorism: Impact on fundamental rights and freedoms* (2021) 7.

committed, they 'punish' people for these preparatory acts in order to prevent any attacks.[49] This aim is achieved by intervening at an increasingly early stage on the *iter criminis* and punishing people who are ever further removed from the perpetration of the actual attack.[50] The earlier on the *iter criminis* the legislature intervenes, the more vague the offences will be, since they are further removed from the perpetration of the actual harm, the acts will be harder to interpret and the core of the offence will shift to the *mens rea*.[51] Intervening earlier also greatly reduces the possibility of the perpetrator to desist from their plans without intervention (thus removing part of the agency of the offender).[52]

7. Terrorism offences *sensu stricto* and *sensu lato* – Terrorist offences can be divided into two categories. Firstly, there is terrorism *sensu stricto*: terrorist murder, manslaughter, the hijacking of aircraft, and so on. In short, the commission of a terrorist attack, or at least threatening to commit such an attack. These are forms of traditional, repressive criminal law. Secondly, there are offences that target terrorism *sensu lato*. These are acts which prepare or facilitate a terrorist offence *sensu stricto*, for example, travelling with terrorist intent, receiving training with terrorist intent or financing terrorism. They are so-called pre-inchoate, pre-emptive or preventive offences.[53]

---

49 MvT wetsontwerp 22 juni 2015 tot versterking van de strijd tegen terrorisme, *Parl.St.* Kamer 2014–15, no. 54-1198/001, 6; Noémie Blaise and Elise Delhaise, 'La répression des voyages à visée terroriste à l'aune des droits fondamentaux' [2019] Journal Tribunaux 173, 174; Delhaise (n 8) 44; Meliá and Petzsche (n 45) 203; Moreau (n 47) 101; Petersen (n 12) 67; Sugman Stubbs and Galli (n 25) 294; Van den Wyngaert, Vandromme and Traest (n 34) 359; Winants (n 8) 359. In Belgium, the moment of intervention is potentially moved even more forward through proactive investigating. See: Art. 28*bis*, §2 CC. See also: Lionel Delval, 'Société du risque et gestion des crises: les pouvoirs publics Belges sont-ils organisés pour faire face à un risuqe majeur? type de risque: menace terroriste' in Marc Cools and others (eds), *1915–2015 Het verhaal van de Belgische militaire inlichtingen- en veiligheidsdienst* (Maklu 2015) 433–434.

50 Marie-Aude Beernaert, 'Renforcement de l'arsenal législatif anti-terroriste: entre symboles et prévention' [2015] Journal des tribunaux 833, 833; Dekrem (n 32) 134–135; Ignacio De La Serna, 'Des infractions terroristes' in Christian De Valkeneer and Ignacio De La Serna, *À la découverte de la justice pénale : Paroles de juriste* (Larcier 2015) 213; Flore (n 10) 221–222; Moreau (n 47) 123; Isabelle Thomas, 'La mise en oevre en Droit Européen des dispositions internationals de lutte contre le terrorisme' [2004] Revue générale de droit international public 463, 473; Philip Traest, 'Ontwikkeling van nieuwe deelnemingsvormen' [2007] Nullum Crimen 241, 261; Winants (n 8) 358–359; Zedner, 'Fixing the Future? The Pre-Emptive Turn in Criminal Justice' (n 23) 50.

51 Inneke Onsea, *De bestrijding van georganiseerde misdaad: de grens tussen waarheidsvinding en grondrechten* (Intersentia 2003) 44. See also: Amnesty International, 'Veiligheid & Mensenrechten: Maatregelen tegen terrorisme en radicalisering', Letter to the Belgian Chamber of Representatives following a hearing on 12 May 2015 (2015) 9.

52 Moreau (n 47) 116–117; Ohana (n 41) 24.

53 See e.g.: Ashworth and Zedner (n 18); McCulloch and Wilson (n 24); Zedner, 'Fixing the Future? The Pre-Emptive Turn in Criminal Justice' (n 23).

8. Preventive administrative measures – Administrative measures, which operate outside (and potentially alongside) of the criminal justice system, are also frequently used to prevent terrorism. They do not have to abide by the same procedural standards as the criminal justice system, but the consequences of an administrative measure are in principle less severe.[54] Administrative measures are for example: asset freezing, the confiscation of passports, relocation orders, etc.

9. Criticism – Scholars and organisations such as Amnesty International have warned against the dangers of extensive counter-terrorism legislation.[55] The criminal justice system has been shaped to avoid abuse by the state when exercising the extensive powers it awards to the state (e.g. *habeas corpus*, right to appeal, sentence ranges proportionate to the offence, etc.). When preventive administrative counter-terrorism measures started being used more and more, scholars warned that the safeguards built into the criminal justice system do not fully apply.[56] Because of these issues, some scholars have welcomed the employment of the criminal justice response instead of the administrative response.[57] However, other scholars have also warned that this path is not without danger either.[58] Specifically because when criminal law is used in a

---

54 De Valkeneer (n 7) 709–710.

55 Amnesty International, 'Veiligheid & Mensenrechten: Maatregelen tegen terrorisme en radicalisering', Letter to the Belgian Chamber of Representatives following a hearing on 12 May 2015 (2015); Amnesty International report, 'Dangerously disproportionate, the ever-expanding national security state in Europe' (2017); Ashworth and Zedner (n 18) 171–172; Hudson (n 25) 710–712; McCulloch and Pickering (n 24) 632–633; Vervaele (n 23) 603–604; Zedner, 'Terrorizing Criminal Law' (n 45) 102–105.

56 Ashworth and Zedner (n 18) 186–189; Ipek Demirsu, *Counter-Terrorism and the Prospects of Human Rights* (Springer International Publishing 2017) 90–91; De Valkeneer (n 7) 709–710; Susan Donkin, *Preventing Terrorism and Controlling Risk: A Comparative Analysis of Control Orders in the UK and Australia*, vol 1 (Springer New York 2014) 2; Fenwick, 'Recalibrating ECHR Rights, and the Role of the Human Rights Act Post 9/11' (n 26) 153; H Fenwick and D Fenwick, 'The Role of Derogations from the ECHR in the Current "War on Terror"' in Eran Shor and Stephen Hoadley (eds), *International Human Rights and Counter-Terrorism* (Springer 2019) 18; Galli (n 25) 172–173; Mordechai Kremnitzer and Lina Saba-Habesch, 'Executive Measures against the Liberties of Terrorism Suspects' in Genevieve Lennon and Clive Walker (eds), *Routledge Handbook of Law and Terrorism* (Routledge 2015) 224–225; Lazarus, Goold and Goss (n 30) 467; Moreau (n 47) 111–112; Weyembergh and Kennes (n 14) 129–130; White (n 25) 189–191; Wood (n 25) 27; Zedner, 'Seeking Security by Eroding Rights: The Side-Stepping of Due Process' (n 24) 264–271; Zedner, 'Terrorizing Criminal Law' (n 45) 105–107. See also: Ashworth, Zedner and Tomlin (n 27) 7. European Union Agency for Fundamental Rights, *Directive (EU) 2017/541 on combatting terrorism: Impact on fundamental rights and freedoms* (2021) 11.

57 Ashworth and Zedner (n 18) 180–181; Fenwick, 'Preventive Anti-Terrorist Strategies in the UK and ECHR: Control Orders, TPIMs and the Role of Technology' (n 25) 139; Galli (n 25) 173–175; Velaers (n 27) 791–792; Walker, 'Keeping Control of Terrorists without Losing Control of Constitutionalism' (n 26) 1463; Zedner, 'Terrorizing Criminal Law' (n 45) 107–111.

58 McLoughlin, Noone and Noone (n 25) 472–476; Meliá (n 25); Mueller (n 32) 331–332; Ohana (n 41); Sugman Stubbs and Galli (n 25) 298–300; Vervaele (n 23) 598–604; Anne Weyembergh

preventive way, it could lose some of its traditional safeguards as well (e.g. a sentence proportionate to the offence, a sufficiently clear definition of the offence, etc.).[59] Because of this, both ways to tackle the problem of terrorism prevention are open to misuse. An extreme but definitely not the only example is Guantanamo Bay.[60] The main danger in restricting liberty when preventing terrorism is an arbitrary application of those intrusive powers because of the lack of certainty and transparency. This is the same for both preventive use of criminal law[61] (e.g. the case of the 'Nottingham Two',[62] who were wrongfully taken into pre-trial detention under suspicion of having committed a very broadly formulated precursor offence before the police realised their mistake) and administrative law (e.g. the use of secret evidence when imposing control orders[63] so the person subject to the order does not even know exactly why it is being imposed on them).

10. Summary – Governments have an obligation to intervene preventively and avoid terror attacks. They have done so by either employing criminal law in a preventive way or by using preventive administrative measures. Both of these tools, however, have been criticised as endangering human rights and

---

and Laurent Kennes, 'Domestic Provisions and Case Law: The Belgian Case' in Francesca Galli and Anne Weyembergh (eds), *EU counter-terrorism offences: What impact on national legislation and case-law?* (Editions de l'Université de Bruxelles 2012) 158. See also: Amnesty International, 'Veiligheid & Mensenrechten: Maatregelen tegen terrorisme en radicalisering', Letter to the Belgian Chamber of Representatives following a hearing on 12 May 2015 (2015).

59 De Coensel, *Counter-Terrorism & Criminal Law: A Normative Legitimacy Test of Terrorism-Related Offences on Expression, Information and Movement* (n 1) 46; De Valkeneer (n 7) 709; Lazarus, Goold and Goss (n 30) 464; Murphy (n 13) 47; Sugman Stubbs and Galli (n 25) 298–300; van der Woude (n 1) 10; Vervaele (n 23) 603–604; Walker, 'The Impact of Contemporary Security Agendas Against Terrorism on the Substantive Criminal Law' (n 45) 133; Comité T, 'Rapport 2020: Evaluation des mesures visant à lutter contre le terrorisme à la lumière des droits humains', 15. See also: Stefan Braum, 'Are We Heading towards a European Form of "Enemy Criminal Law"? On the Compatibility of Jakob's Conception of "an Enemy Criminal Law" and European Criminal Law' in Francesca Galli and Anne Weyembergh (eds), *EU counter-terrorism offences: What impact on national legislation and case-law?* (Editions de l'Université de Bruxelles 2012) 241. Tadros actually compares the use of criminal law and the use of control orders in the UK and concludes that the use of some form of control orders is preferable. See: Tadros, 'Justice and Terrorism' (n 46) 687–689.

60 Human Rights Watch, 'Guantanamo: Facts and Figures' (2017), www.hrw.org/video-photos/interactive/2017/03/30/guantanamo-facts-and-figures; Zedner, *Security* (n 8) 122.

61 This is one of the things Amnesty International Belgium explicitly warned against in 2015. See: Amnesty International, 'Veiligheid & Mensenrechten: Maatregelen tegen terrorisme en radicalisering', Letter to the Belgian Chamber of Representatives following a hearing on 12 May 2015 (2015) 11.

62 H. Yezza, 'Britain's terror laws have left me and my family shattered' (*The Guardian 2008)* www.theguardian.com/commentisfree/2008/aug/18/terrorism.civilliberties.

63 A Lynch, T Tulich and R Welsh, 'Secrecy and Control Orders: The Role and Vulnerability of Constitutional Values in Australia and the United Kingdom' in D Cole, F Fabrini and A Vedaschi (eds), *Secrecy, national security, and the vindication of constitutional law* (Edward Elgar 2013).

specifically for their potential of arbitrary application. The question therefore arises whether the criticism is justified and whether these systems do leave room for arbitrary application. If so, we will ask ourselves which type of intervention is least conducive to arbitrary application and how these systems can be improved to minimise this danger of arbitrariness.

METHODOLOGY

CHAPTER I
SCOPE OF THE TOPIC

11. NEED FOR LIMITATION – Before going into detail on the relevance, research questions and choice of countries for comparison, we have to delineate the scope of the topic. As explained, there are two main types of counter-terrorism measures. We will first look at which administrative measures fall within the scope and then at which criminal law measures do so. Since there is a myriad of measures on both sides of the equation, certain choices have been made in order to make an in-depth analysis feasible.

12. ONLY ADMINISTRATIVE MEASURES WHICH LIMIT LIBERTY AND FREEDOM OF MOVEMENT – 'Administrative measures' is a very broad concept, and we thus need to limit it in order to clearly define the scope of the research. These measures can affect many human rights, such as the right to privacy, the right to a fair trial[64] or the freedom of expression.[65] The potential sentences for terrorist precursor offences are however severe. We therefore need to compare them to the most invasive administrative measures: measures that impact the right to liberty of the people subject to them. The discussion on measures like these focusses on two fundamental rights: the right to liberty (Art. 5 ECHR) and the free movement of persons (Art. 2 of the 4th protocol to the ECHR).[66]

13. ONLY MEASURES WITH DIRECT EFFECT ON THOSE RIGHTS – This demarcation of the scope about measures that impact the right to liberty or free movement of the person subject to them still casts a wide net. E.g. the freezing of assets[67] restricts a person's free movement too since they cannot travel anywhere if they do not have access to the funds to do so. To further narrow it down, the focus will be on measures that have a direct impact on freedom of movement or liberty. This excludes the freezing of assets and other measures that

---

64 Maria Luisa Cesoni, 'Terrorisme et involutions démocratiques' [2002] Rev Dr Pén Crim 141, 150–151.

65 Petersen (n 12) 59–67.

66 See e.g.: *De Tommaso v. Italy* App no 43395/09 (ECtHR Grand Chamber 23 February 2017).

67 Council Common Position 2001/931/CFSP of 27 December 2001 on the application of specific measures to combat terrorism [2001] *OJ* L344/93; KB 28 december 2006 inzake specifieke beperkende maatregelen tegen bepaalde personen en entiteiten met het oog op de strijd tegen de financiering van het terrorisme, *BS* 17 januari 2007, 1898.

restrict proprietary rights whilst only having an indirect impact on a person's freedom of movement or liberty. Furthermore, we will exclude measures related to migration law and laws on citizenship (migration detention, revocation of citizenship, passports[68] or ID-cards, etc.) because they were the topic extensive PhD research conducted by Louise Reyntjens.[69]

14. Criminal law – On the criminal law side of the equation, the focus will be on offences explicitly introduced to combat terrorism. Other offences potentially committed by terrorists (e.g. petty theft in order to finance a terrorist organisation) are excluded. While the focus of the research will be on material criminal law offences, we cannot completely ignore criminal procedure. First of all, this would be very artificial as some material criminal law cannot be fully understood without the procedural context. Second, the criminal justice system does not always require a conviction for a criminal offence before limiting a person's right to liberty. The rules on pre-trial detention will therefore be relevant as well.[70] We will, however, exclude rules applicable to the execution of the sentence (e.g. special prison regimes, special probation rules, etc.). This is because they require a very different focus and at that point the main preventive decisions (taking somebody into pre-trial detention, convicting them, etc.) have been made.

15. Normative framework: ECHR – As this research aims to answer a normative research question (see no. 16), a normative framework is needed. As explained in this Chapter, the focus of the book is on measures with a direct effect on the right to liberty or the free movement of people so these two human rights make for a good starting point in order to analyse what the appropriate normative framework would be. In terms of human rights, by far the most relevant jurisdiction is that of the ECtHR, which is also the overarching jurisdiction for the two states used for comparison: Belgium and the UK (see nos 21–22). Therefore, Article 5 ECHR (right to liberty) and Article 2 of the Fourth Protocol to the ECHR (free movement of people) will be the starting point for this analysis. The EU free movement rules and jurisprudence of the European Court of Justice will not be analysed in detail for several reasons.[71]

68 The confiscation of which is a restriction to the right to free movement. See: *Baumann v. France* App no 33592/96 (ECtHR 22 May 2001) 62–63; *Kerimli v. Azerbaijan* App no 3967/09 (ECtHR 16 July 2015) 47; *Rotaru v. Republic of Moldova* App no 26764/12 (ECtHR 8 December 2020) 22.

69 Louise Reyntjens, Ex-citizens and the European convention on human rights: citizenship deprivation examined under the ECHR (PhD Thesis KU Leuven 2022) 327 p.

70 Art. 16 §1 Statute on pre-trial detention; S. 41 and schedule 8 TA 2000; Ashworth and Zedner (n 18) 189–190.

71 For a detailed analysis of deprivations of liberty and EU rights, see: Leandro Mancano, *The European Union and Deprivation of Liberty: A Legislative and Judicial Analysis from the Perspective of the Individual* (Hart Publishing 2019).

First, as the UK is no longer an EU Member State (and was never a member of the Schengen area), the EU rules no longer apply to it. This does not make the EU rules irrelevant as they still fully apply to Belgium; but does make them less interesting to use as a normative framework as they only apply to one of the two jurisdictions discussed. Second, when it comes to human rights, the European Court of Justice gives the ECHR special significance as a guide principle, in its case law, and the meaning and scope of rights in the EU Charter is the same as those laid down by the ECHR.[72] Therefore, the ECtHR makes most sense as a benchmark. Third, while the EU free movement rights have evolved since their inception, they find their origins in economic considerations (free movement of workers).[73] Nowadays they are applied more broadly to all EU citizens, but as their origins lie in economic considerations, they allow for relatively broad limitations for reasons of public policy and public security.[74]

72 Art. 52 Charter of Fundamental Rights of the European Union (2000/C 364/01) [2000] *OJ* C364/1; Allan Rosas, 'The Court of Justice of the European Union: A Human Rights Institution?' (2022) 14 Journal of Human Rights Practice 204.

73 Art. 45 TFEU; Mancano (n 71) 21.

74 Art. 27 Directive 2004/38/EC of the European Parliament and of the Council of 29 April 2004 on the right of citizens of the Union and their family members to move and reside freely within the territory of the Member States amending Regulation (EEC) No 1612/68 and repealing Directives 64/221/EEC, 68/360/EEC, 72/194/EEC, 73/148/EEC, 75/34/EEC, 75/35/EEC, 90/364/EEC, 90/365/EEC and 93/96/EEC (Text with EEA relevance) [2004] *OJ* L158/77.

CHAPTER II
RESEARCH OBJECTIVES AND QUESTIONS

16. Main research question – The objective of our research is to compare the ways in which Belgium and the UK have used very intrusive measures in order to prevent terrorism and ascertain how best to do so. The most intrusive measures a state can employ are those which have a direct impact on the right to liberty of people, so that is where the focus of this book lies. Therefore, the starting point of the analysis is the right to liberty (Part I). Next, the Belgian legal framework is examined, as Belgium is the main jurisdiction in question (Part II). Then, the same is done for the UK (Part III). The UK has been faced with a similar problem as Belgium but chose to react to it differently. Therefore, the UK approach might provide valuable insights in how the Belgian system could be improved. In order to achieve these insights, a detailed comparison between the two jurisdictions is undertaken in Part IV, after which general conclusions on the prevention of terrorism through direct restrictions to the right to liberty are drawn and recommendations are made on how to improve the Belgian legislation. In short, our research sought an answer to the following question:

Is the Belgian or the UK approach to prevention of terrorism through direct restrictions to the right to liberty preferable in light of this right; and how could the Belgian approach be improved?

17. First part – In the first Part we establish our evaluative and normative framework. The starting point are the two human rights introduced above: the right to liberty and free movement of persons. The overarching jurisdiction shared between Belgium and the UK is that of the European Court of Human Rights (see no. 15). Therefore, Part I opens with an elaborate analysis of the ECtHR case law on these two rights. As is made clear, avoiding arbitrariness is the central thread running through this case law. The second Chapter of Part I recapitulates the important principles from Chapter I and applies them to terrorism prevention. In the third and final Chapter of this same Part, we distil and operationalise two main principles from the ECtHR case law which will serve as the evaluative and normative framework for this book: legal certainty and proportionality. However, when applying these principles throughout the book, we should never lose track of the goal of preventing terrorism, as terrorism

prevention remains a necessity. The research questions in the first Part are descriptive, using as the starting point for their answer the ECHR and applying a grammatical and systematic interpretation mainly based on the jurisprudence of the ECtHR. The sub-questions covered in Part I reflect the short overview above. They are:

1.1. Descriptive question: What is the scope of application of Article 5 ECHR (right to liberty) and Article 2 Protocol 4 ECHR (free movement of persons)?
1.2. Descriptive question: How does the ECtHR interpret Article 5 ECHR in its case law?
1.3. Descriptive question: How does the ECtHR interpret Article 2 Protocol 4 ECHR in its case law?
1.4. Descriptive question: How are these two rights applied in the context of terrorism prevention?
1.5. Descriptive question: Which main principles can be derived from the case law and how will they be operationalised in the context of this book?

18. Second part – The second and third Parts focus on Belgium and the UK. The second Part studies the choices made in Belgian legislation and case law and the motives behind them. These choices are subsequently evaluated in light of the normative framework established in Part I. Question 2.1, being a descriptive question, is answered based on the Belgian Criminal Code and other relevant legislation. A mixture of a grammatical, systematic and legal-historic interpretation is used, based on jurisprudence, legal doctrine and explanatory memorandums. In addition, a quantitative case law analysis made in the context of the Reguide project is used to study the practical application of the Belgian terrorist offences.[75] Research question 2.2 is evaluative based on internal criteria and using the framework established and operationalised in Part I. The following sub-questions are answered:

2.1. Descriptive question: How has Belgium used direct restrictions to the right to liberty to attempt to prevent terrorism?
2.2. Evaluative question: In which ways is the Belgian approach in line with our framework?

19. Third part – The third Part will do the same as Part II, using the same methodology, but for the UK. This Part analyses the following sub-questions:

3.1. Descriptive question: How has the UK used direct restrictions to the right to liberty to attempt to prevent terrorism?

75 For more information, see: https://reguide.be/.

3.2. Evaluative question: In which ways is the UK approach in line with our framework?

20. Fourth part – In the fourth Part, the systems of both countries, which have been analysed independently from each other in Parts II and III, are compared. This comparison includes their strengths and weaknesses in light of our framework. Then, general conclusions regarding the prevention of terrorism through direct restrictions of liberty are drawn on the basis of the preceding analysis. Finally, the framework created in the first Part is used to make recommendations to improve the Belgian legislation. This framework thus serves as both the evaluative framework in Parts II and III and the normative framework in Part IV. The recommendations in Part IV are specific and hierarchical in the sense that they consist of two sets. First, proposals for minimal and therefore more moderate changes and second proposals for more extensive changes. The right to liberty aims to '*ensure that no one should be deprived of that liberty in an arbitrary fashion.*'[76] Therefore, our goal is to create a system where the risk of arbitrariness is as small as possible. The final sub-questions are:

4.1. Comparative question: How do the Belgian and UK legal systems compare in the ways they directly restrict the right to liberty to prevent terrorism?
4.2. Comparative question: Which of these attempts is most in line with our framework?
4.3. Normative question: Which changes can be made to the Belgian legislation to create a system where the risk of arbitrariness is as small as possible without unduly hindering the government's ability to prevent terrorism?

[76] Guide on Art. 5 of the convention: Right to liberty and security (2014) 5.

CHAPTER III
COUNTRIES FOR COMPARISON

21. Belgium – The issues explained above (see nos 1–10) arose in many states across the globe. The extent to which countries use criminal law and administrative law in the aforementioned ways varies. This PhD compares the legal systems of Belgium and the UK, using Belgium as the starting point for comparison. The UK was part of the EU until 2020, Belgium still is, and both are part of the Council of Europe. The same legal instruments thus bound them in their recent struggle against terrorism. Within the group of EU countries, Belgium is interesting because of its strong tradition of using criminal law and avoiding the use of administrative measures where possible. Belgium has implemented some administrative measures to prevent terrorism (e.g. asset freezing or the confiscation of passports) but has mainly used traditional criminal justice tools.[77] It does not (yet) have any administrative counter-terrorism measures that have a direct impact on the right to liberty or freedom of movement. A proposal to introduce electronic monitoring for suspected terrorists in Belgium was put forward in 2015 but appears to have been shelved.[78]

22. The UK – The UK has a large amount of experience with terrorism and is considered somewhat of an example in terms of counter-terrorism measures.[79] The relevant EU instruments (see no. 2) have also been influenced by the UK legislation and its point of view on counter-terrorism. In addition, the UK has made extensive use of intrusive administrative measures to prevent terrorism,[80] having created a system of 'Terrorism Prevention and Investigation Measures' (TPIMs): administrative measures that can have far-reaching consequences for a person's liberty.[81] These TPIMs can include overnight house arrest, forced

---

77 Art. 137–141*ter* CC; Fabienne Brion and others, 'Impact Assessment of Belgian De-"Radicalisation" Policies Upon Social Cohesion and Liberties' (2022) AFFECT 25; Fransen, Kerkhofs and Verrest (n 45) 42–103; Masset (n 20) 427–434.

78 Lijst van contra-terrorismemaatregelen, plenaire sessie Kamer van Volksvertegenwoordigers, 19 november 2015.

79 See e.g.: Jean-Claude Paye, 'Lois Anti-Terroristes. L'exemple Anglais' [2004] Journal des Procès 14; Kent Roach, *The 9/11 Effect: Comparative Counter-Terrorism* (Cambridge University Press 2011) 257.

80 Ashworth and Zedner (n 18) 182.

81 Terrorism Prevention and Investigation Measures Act 2011; s. 16 – 20 Counter-Terrorism and Security Act 2015; Fenwick, 'Preventive Anti-Terrorist Strategies in the UK and ECHR: Control Orders, TPIMs and the Role of Technology' (n 25) 135–138; Fenwick, 'Terrorism and

relocation, restrictions on the use of electronic communication, etc. The UK has a long history of confronting terrorism and has been using this tactic for decades now.[82] The UK also derogated from Article 5 ECHR shortly after 9/11, making it the only European state to do so until France issued a derogation in 2015 (see no. 28). This should not come as a complete surprise as the relationship between the UK and the ECtHR has been tense at times and the UK has pushed the boundaries of what is accepted by the European Court. There are several reasons why the UK uses administrative measures and Belgium does not. An important reason is that the prohibition on the use of intercept evidence in court in the UK has steered cases away from court proceedings and forced them to make more use of administrative measures.[83] The method used, is a functional micro-comparison, comparing the administrative and criminal justice regimes which have a direct effect on the right to liberty in both jurisdictions.[84]

the Control Orders/TPIMs Saga: A Vindication of the Human Rights Act or a Manifestation of "Defensive Democracy"?' (n 45) 615–621; Zedner, 'Terrorizing Criminal Law' (n 45) 106.

82 Anderson, 'Shielding the Compass: How to Fight Terrorism without Defeating the Law' (n 25) 8–9; Ashworth and Zedner (n 18) 182–187; David Feldman, 'Deprivation of Liberty in Anti-Terrorism Law' [2008] The Cambridge Law Journal 4, 4–8; Fenwick, 'Preventive Anti-Terrorist Strategies in the UK and ECHR: Control Orders, TPIMs and the Role of Technology' (n 25) 123–136; Fenwick, 'Terrorism and the Control Orders/TPIMs Saga: A Vindication of the Human Rights Act or a Manifestation of "Defensive Democracy"?' (n 45) 612–619; Maras (n 21) 217–221; Zedner, 'Terrorizing Criminal Law' (n 45) 105–106.

83 S. 17 Regulation of Investigatory Powers Act 2000.

84 Lina Kestemont and Paul Schoukens, *Rechtswetenschappelijk Schrijven* (Acco 2012) 57–62.

CHAPTER IV
RELEVANCE

23. Academic – Terrorism itself is a problem of great relevance. People are afraid and there is no easy solution. The need to minimise the threat of future attacks is a strong incentive to intervene harshly. Governments have proven to be willing to do away with certain human rights protections in order to achieve increased security (or at least the feeling of increased security). Scholars have warned against this both when it comes to administrative measures and when it comes to the preventive use of criminal law. Therefore, we will take into account both systems, compare them in a systematic manner and provide concrete recommendations on which steps to take to minimise the potential for arbitrariness. In doing just this, our research is able to add valuable information to the debate on how best to tackle terrorism in a democratic society based on the rule of law.

24. Societal and practical – The societal and practical relevance are high as well. In preventing terrorism, governments have sometimes intervened harshly and arbitrarily (e.g. extraordinary renditions,[85] indefinite detention in Guantanamo or Belmarsh).[86] Getting a clear view of which measures are least conducive to arbitrariness and which safeguards can be put in place is essential in order to react appropriately to the threat that terrorism poses. Sometimes human rights protection and security are seen as antithetical, but this is not our view at all.[87] We believe it essential to combat terrorism within a human rights framework since human rights violations are likely to produce the terrorists of

---

85 Amnesty International, 'Veiligheid & Mensenrechten: Maatregelen tegen terrorisme en radicalisering', Letter to the Belgian Chamber of Representatives following a hearing on 12 May 2015 (2015) 5.

86 Benjamin Freeman, 'Preventive Detention, Extraordinary Rendition and Torture: Counter-Terrorism Initiatives and the Unjustifiable Curtailing of Individual Rights and Liberties' (*Ethics, Terrorism, United States, War & Conflict*, 22 March 2016); Claire Hamilton, 'The European Union: Sword or Shield? Comparing Counterterrorism Law in the EU and the USA after 9/11' (2018) 22 Theoretical Criminology 206, 214–216; Zedner, *Security* (n 8) 122.

87 See also: White (n 25) 191. See also: Tiberiu Dragu, 'Is There a Trade-off between Security and Liberty? Executive Bias, Privacy Protections, and Terrorism Prevention' (2011) 105 American Political Science Review 64. Dragu's analysis focusses on the right to privacy. One of the conclusions is that there could be situations in which decreasing privacy reduces security from terrorism.

tomorrow.[88] People who feel oppressed are more likely to resort to terrorism against the government which is responsible and against the society that allows it.[89] Moreover, many terrorist groups want to create a society with fewer freedoms (one can think of IS and its interpretation of the Sharia[90]).[91] Counter-terrorism legislation that does away with human rights and restricts hard-won freedoms actually does the job for them.[92] In Belgium, preventive administrative counter-terrorism measures that have a direct impact on the right to liberty do not exist yet. However, the idea has already been put forward and it does not seem unlikely that similar proposals will be advanced in the future.[93] Our research is therefore especially valuable in guiding the decision of whether or not to implement such measures in Belgium; and whether they provide advantages compared to the preventive use of criminal law.

---

88 See also: Ashworth and Zedner (n 18) 190; Conte (n 10) 688–689; De Valkeneer (n 7) 708; Fenwick, 'Recalibrating ECHR Rights, and the Role of the Human Rights Act Post 9/11' (n 26) 155; Victor Tadros, 'Controlling Risk' in Andrew Ashworth, Lucia Zedner and Patrick Tomlin (eds), *Prevention and the Limits of the Criminal Law* (Oxford University Press 2013) 140; Wood (n 25) 256–257.

89 M. Scheinn, 'Ten areas of best practices in countering terrorism', report by the Special Rapporteur on the protection of human rights and fundamental freedoms in the fight against terrorism, A/HRC/16/51, 2010, 6–7; Secretary General of the UN, 'Uniting against terrorism: recommendations for a global counter-terrorism strategy', A/60/825, 2006, 114 and 118; De Valkeneer (n 7) 708; Fenwick and Fenwick (n 56) 20; Wayne McCormack, 'Detention of Mega-Terrorists: It's About Crime' (2011) 30 Criminal Justice Ethics 82, 83–84; Meliá and Petzsche (n 45) 204; E Newman, 'Exploring the "Root Causes" of Terrorism' [2006] Studies in conflict and terrorism 765, 765–766; Eran Shor and others, 'Terrorism and State Repression of Human Rights: A Cross-National Time-Series Analysis' (2014) 55 International Journal of Comparative Sociology 294, 295; Wood (n 25) 43; Zedner, 'Terrorizing Criminal Law' (n 45) 104–105.

90 G. Wood, 'What ISIS really wants' (*the atlantic* 2015) www.theatlantic.com/magazine/archive/2015/03/what-isis-really-wants/384980/.

91 Jan-Werner Müller, 'Militant Democracy' in Michel Rosenfeld and András Sajó (eds), *The Oxford handbook of comparative constitutional law* (1st ed, Oxford University Press 2012) 1255–1256.

92 Peter Chalk, 'The Response to Terrorism as a Threat to Liberal Democracy' in Alan O'Day (ed), *War on terrorism* (Ashgate 2004); Helen Fenwick, 'The Anti-Terrorism, Crime and Security Act 2001: A Proportionate Response to 11 September?' (2002) 65 The Modern Law Review 724, 724; Fenwick, 'Terrorism and the Control Orders/TPIMs Saga: A Vindication of the Human Rights Act or a Manifestation of "Defensive Democracy"?' (n 45) 609; Hale-Ross (n 1) 18–19; Hudson (n 25) 710; Moreau (n 47) 123; Müller (n 91) 1254–1255; Petersen (n 12) 73; Sottiaux (n 27) 5; Philip A Thomas, 'Emergency and Anti-Terrorist Powers' [2002–2003] Fordham Int'l L.J. 1193, 1218; K Van Cauwenberghe, 'Kan terrorisme de rechtstaat onderuit halen?' (2015) 318 Juristenkrant 13; Walker, 'Keeping Control of Terrorists without Losing Control of Constitutionalism' (n 26) 1403; Wood (n 25) 41; Lucia Zedner, 'Securing Liberty in the Face of Terror: Reflections from Criminal Justice' (2005) 32 Journal of Law and Society 27, 510.

93 Lijst van contra-terrorismemaatregelen, plenaire sessie Kamer van Volksvertegenwoordigers, 19 november 2015.

Disclaimer: quotes which were not originally in English are translated to the best of our abilities. References to the original source material, which is usually in Dutch or French, are always provided. It cannot be ruled out that small nuances were accidentally lost or added in translation.

PART I

NORMATIVE FRAMEWORK

INTRODUCTION

25. Goal of Part I – This Part of the book aims to establish the evaluative and normative framework. As was explained in the introduction (see nos 12–13), the focus of this book is on measures that directly impact the physical liberty of people. Within the framework of the ECHR, this means that Article 5 ECHR, which protects the right to liberty and security, is of paramount importance. However, this is not the only relevant Article. Article 2 of the Fourth Protocol to the ECHR protects the freedom of movement and also directly relates to people's physical liberty.

26. Article 5 ECHR – Article 5 of the ECHR reads:

1. Everyone has the right to liberty and security of person. No one shall be deprived of his liberty save in the following cases and in accordance with a procedure prescribed by law:
   (a) the lawful detention of a person after conviction by a competent court;
   (b) the lawful arrest or detention of a person for non-compliance with the lawful order of a court or in order to secure the fulfilment of any obligation prescribed by law;
   (c) the lawful arrest or detention of a person effected for the purpose of bringing him before the competent legal authority on reasonable suspicion of having committed an offence or when it is reasonably considered necessary to prevent his committing an offence or fleeing after having done so;
   (d) the detention of a minor by lawful order for the purpose of educational supervision or his lawful detention for the purpose of bringing him before the competent legal authority;
   (e) the lawful detention of persons for the prevention of the spreading of infectious diseases, of persons of unsound mind, alcoholics or drug addicts or vagrants;
   (f) the lawful arrest or detention of a person to prevent his effecting an unauthorised entry into the country or of a person against whom action is being taken with a view to deportation or extradition.
2. Everyone who is arrested shall be informed promptly, in a language which he understands, of the reasons for his arrest and of any charge against him.
3. Everyone arrested or detained in accordance with the provisions of paragraph 1 (c) of this Article shall be brought promptly before a judge or other officer authorised by law to exercise judicial power and shall be entitled to trial within a reasonable time or to release pending trial. Release may be conditioned by guarantees to appear for trial.

4. Everyone who is deprived of his liberty by arrest or detention shall be entitled to take proceedings by which the lawfulness of his detention shall be decided speedily by a court and his release ordered if the detention is not lawful.
5. Everyone who has been the victim of arrest or detention in contravention of the provisions of this Article shall have an enforceable right to compensation.

27. Article 2 Protocol no. 4 – Article 2 of Protocol no. 4 to the ECHR reads:

1. Everyone lawfully within the territory of a State shall, within that territory, have the right to liberty of movement and freedom to choose his residence.
2. Everyone shall be free to leave any country, including his own.
3. No restrictions shall be placed on the exercise of these rights other than such as are in accordance with law and are necessary in a democratic society in the interests of national security or public safety, for the maintenance of *ordre public*, for the prevention of crime, for the protection of health or morals, or for the protection of the rights and freedoms of others.
4. The rights set forth in paragraph 1 may also be subject, in particular areas, to restrictions imposed in accordance with law and justified by the public interest in a democratic society.

28. Derogations under Article 15 ECHR – Before discussing the abovementioned ECHR rights in detail, it is important to note that the ECHR allows for Member States to derogate from its rights. This is not the case for all of them, however. The prohibition of torture and the prohibition of slavery, for example, are absolute.[94] Non-absolute rights, such as the right to liberty and free movement can be derogated from, but only in the event of war or other public emergency threatening the life of the nation.[95] Moreover, this is only possible to the extent that the seriousness of the situation strictly requires such measures and provided that they are not in conflict with other obligations under international law. Terrorism has already been accepted as a ground for application of Article 15 ECHR and can thus threaten the life of a nation.[96]

94 Art. 3 and 4, section 1 ECHR. See also: Conte (n 10) 284–287.

95 Daniel Alati, *Domestic Counter-Terrorism in a Global World: Post-9/11 Institutional Structures and Cultures in Canada and the United Kingdom* (1st edn, Routledge 2017) 92–93; Conte (n 10) 309–312 and 528–534; Claire Macken, *Counter-Terrorism and the Detention of Suspected Terrorists* (Routledge 2011) 80–88; Sottiaux (n 27) 50–51; Jean Spreutels and Sylviane Velu, 'La lutte contre le terrorisme dans la jurisprudence de la Cour Consitutionnelle de Belgique' in Koen Lemmens, Stephan Parmentier and Louise Reyntjens (eds), *Human rights with a human touch: Liber amicorum Paul Lemmens* (Intersentia 2019) 130–131; Vanneste (n 27) 1674–1675; Diane Webber, *Preventive Detention of Terror Suspects: A New Legal Framework* (Routledge 2016) 69–70.

96 Art. 15 ECHR; *Lawless v. Ireland (no. 3)* App no 332/57 (ECtHR 1 July 1961) 28–30; *Ireland v. United Kingdom* App no 5310/71 (ECtHR 18 January 1978) 205 and 212; *Brannigan and McBride v. United Kingdom* App nos 14553/89 and 14554/89 (ECtHR 25 May 1993) 44–47; *Aksoy v. Turkey* App no 21987/93 (ECtHR 18 December 1996) 70; *A and others v. United Kingdom* App no 3455/05 (ECtHR Grand Chamber 19 February 2009) 175–181; *Guide to*

Belgium has not derogated from the ECHR rights in the fight against terrorism, but the UK has (see also no. 22). This UK derogation is discussed in detail below (see nos 497–500).

29. Overview Part I – The rest of this Part of the book is structured as follows. Chapter I outlines the general principles set out in the case law of the ECtHR concerning the two aforementioned rights. This Chapter contains three Sections, the first covering research question 1.1[97] on the scope of application of the two rights, with a focus on the boundary between the right to liberty and the freedom of movement. Section II then covers research question 1.2[98] and zooms in on the right to liberty and the cases in which a deprivation of liberty can be justified. The third and last Section answers research question 1.3[99] and does the same as Section II but now for the freedom of movement. In Chapter II, as per research question 1.4,[100] the general principles from Chapter I are applied to our specific case: restricting liberty to prevent terrorism. Chapter III concludes this Part by answering research question 1.5[101] and distilling from the case law the main elements that will serve to operationalise the normative framework throughout the rest of this book, being the principles of legal certainty and proportionality.

the case-law of the European Court of Human Rights on Terrorism (2020) 39. France also claimed that terrorism threatened the life of the nation when it in 2015 declared the state of emergency and deviated from its obligations under the ECHR. (Declaration contained in a letter from the Permanent Representative of France to the Council of Europe, dated 24 November 2015, registered at the Secretariat General on 24 November 2015, www.coe.int/en/web/conventions/full-list/-/conventions/treaty/005/declarations?p_auth=0e9U611h&_coeconventions_WAR_coeconventionsportlet_enVigueur=false&_coeconventions_WAR_coeconventionsportlet_searchBy=state&_coeconventions_WAR_coeconventionsportlet_codePays=FRA&_coeconventions_WAR_coeconventionsportlet_codeNature=10). See also: Anderson, 'Shielding the Compass: How to Fight Terrorism without Defeating the Law' (n 25) 4; Ashworth and Zedner (n 18) 178; Conte (n 10) 543–547; De Schutter (n 27) 129; RA Duff, 'Pre-Trial Detention and the Presumption of Innocence' in Andrew Ashworth, Lucia Zedner and Patrick Tomlin (eds), *Prevention and the Limits of the Criminal Law* (Oxford University Press 2013) 121; Fenwick, 'Terrorism and the Control Orders/TPIMs Saga: A Vindication of the Human Rights Act or a Manifestation of "Defensive Democracy"?' (n 45) 624; Fenwick and Fenwick (n 56) 8–11 en 18–19; Silvis (n 27) 657–658; Sottiaux (n 27) 49–50; Vanneste (n 27) 1674–1675; Velaers (n 27) 791.

97 What is the scope of application of Art. 5 ECHR (right to liberty) and Art. 2 Protocol 4 ECHR (free movement of persons)?

98 How does the ECtHR interpret Art. 5 ECHR in its case law?

99 How does the ECtHR interpret Art. 2 Protocol 4 ECHR in its case law?

100 How are these two rights applied in the context of terrorism prevention?

101 Which main principles can be derived from the case law and how will they be operationalised in the context of this book?

CHAPTER I
GENERAL PRINCIPLES

SECTION I. SCOPE OF APPLICATION

SUBSECTION I. DEPRIVATION VS. RESTRICTION

30. Deprivation vs. restriction – The ECHR establishes certain human rights and explains under which circumstances these rights can be limited. This way the ECHR aims to protect people from arbitrary interferences with any of the protected rights. In its case law on Article 5, the ECtHR often repeats that the aim of that Article is to ensure that no one is deprived of their liberty in an arbitrary fashion.[102] Mere restrictions to the liberty of movement are not covered

---

102 *Engel and others v. Netherlands* App nos 5100/71, 5101/71, 5102/71, 5354/72 and 5370/72 (ECtHR 8 June 1976) 58; *Winterwerp v. Netherlands* App no 6301/73 (ECtHR 24 October 1979) 37; *Schiesser v. Switzerland* App no 7710/76 (ECtHR 4 December 1979) 30; *Guzzardi v. Italy* App no 7367/76 (ECtHR Plenary 6 November 1980), 92; *X. v. United Kingdom* App no 7215/75 (ECtHR 5 November 1981) 43; *Ashingdane v. United Kingdom* App no 8225/78 (ECtHR 28 May 1985) 41; *Quinn v. France* App no 18580/91 (ECtHR 22 March 1995) 42; *Amuur v. France* App no 19776/92 (ECtHR 25 June 1996) 42; *Giulia Manzoni v. Italy* App no 19218/91 (ECtHR 1 July 1997) 25; *Riera Blume and others v. Spain* App no 37680/97 (ECtHR 14 October 1999) 28; *Labita v. Italy* App no 26772/95 (ECtHR Grand Chamber 6 April 2000) 170; *Mancini v. Italy* App no 44955/98 (ECtHR 2 August 2001) 16; *Lavents v. Latvia* App no 58442/00 (ECtHR 28 November 2002) 62; *Vasileva v. Denmark* App no 52792/99 (ECtHR 25 September 2003) 33; *McKay v. United Kingdom* App no 543/03 (ECtHR Grand Chamber 3 October 2006) 30; *Sissanis v. Romania* App no 23468/02 (ECtHR 25 January 2007) 91; *Saadi v. United Kingdom* App no 13229/03 (ECtHR Grand Chamber 29 January 2008) 63; *Ladent v. Poland* App no 11036/03 (ECtHR 18 March 2008) 45; *A. and others v. United Kingdom* App no 3455/05 (ECtHR Grand Chamber 19 February 2009) 162; *Abdolkhani and Karimnia v. Turkey* App no 30471/08 (ECtHR 22 September 2009) 125; *Rantsev v. Cyprus and Russia* App no 25965/04 (ECtHR 7 January 2010) 314; *Medvedyev and others v. France* App no 3394/03 (ECtHR Grand Chamber 29 March 2010) 73; *Louled Massoud v. Malta* App no 24340/08 (ECtHR 27 July 2010) 58; *Iskandarov v. Russia* App no 17185/05 (ECtHR 23 September 2010) 139; *Khayredinov v. Ukraine* App no 38717/04 (ECtHR 14 October 2010) 26; *Osypenko v. Ukraine* App no 4634/04 (ECtHR 9 November 2010) 50; *Kharin v. Russia* App no 37345/03 (ECtHR 3 February 2011) 31; *Soare and others v. Romania* App no 24329/02 (ECtHR 22 February 2011) 232; *Sarigiannis v. Italy* App no 14569/05 (ECtHR 5 April 2011) 39; *Creangă v. Romania* App no 29226/03 (ECtHR Grand Chamber 23 February 2012) 84; *Austin and others v. United Kingdom* App nos 39692/09, 40713/09 and 41008/09 (ECtHR Grand Chamber 15 March 2012) 56; *James, Wells and Lee v. United Kingdom* App nos 25119/09, 57715/09 and 57877/09 (ECtHR 18 September 2012) 187; *Ostendorf v. Germany* App no 15598/08 (ECtHR 7 March 2013) 65; *M.A. v. Cyprus* App no 41872/10 (ECtHR 23 July

by Article 5 ECHR, which explicitly uses the terms '*deprived of his liberty*.'[103] This does not mean states can restrict people's physical liberty without restraint. Restrictions have to meet the criteria of the freedom of movement in Article 2 of the Fourth Protocol to the ECHR.[104] An important question which thus arises is where to draw the line between a deprivation and a restriction of liberty.

31. WHERE TO DRAW THE LINE? – In assessing whether there has been a deprivation of liberty the ECtHR does not consider itself bound by any legal conclusions of the domestic authorities. Its assessment is autonomous.[105] With

---

2013) 186; *Bergmann v. Germany* App no 23279/14 (ECtHR 7 January 2016) 95; *Buzadji v. Republic of Moldova* App no 23755/07 (ECtHR Grand Chamber 5 July 2016) 84; *Khlaifia and others v. Italy* App no 16483/12 (ECtHR Grand Chamber 15 December 2016) 64; *J.N. v. United Kingdom* App no 37289/12 (ECtHR 19 May 2016) 74; *Mehmet Hasan Altan v. Turkey* App no 13237/17 (ECtHR 20 March 2018) 123; *Şahin Alpay v. Turkey* App no 16538/17 (ECtHR 20 March 2018) 102; *S., V. and A. v. Denmark* App nos 35553/23, 36678/23 and 36711/12 (ECtHR Grand Chamber 22 October 2018), 73; *I.S. v. Switzerland* App no 60202/15 (ECtHR 6 October 2020) 41; *Selahattin Demirtaş v. Turkey (no. 2)* App no 14305/17 (ECtHR Grand Chamber 22 December 2020) 311; *Denis and Irvine v. Belgium* App nos 62819/17 and 63921/17 (ECtHR Grand Chamber 1 June 2021) 123–124; *Kerem Çiftçi v. Turkey* App no 35205/09 (ECtHR 21 September 2021) 27. See also: *Guide on Article 5 of the European Convention on Human Rights: Right to Liberty and Security* (2020) 8; Macken (n 95) 52; Webber (n 95) 52.

103 *Engel and others v. Netherlands* App nos 5100/71, 5101/71, 5102/71, 5354/72 and 5370/72 (ECtHR 8 June 1976) 58; *Guzzardi v. Italy* App no 7367/76 (ECtHR Plenary 6 November 1980) 92; *Foka v. Turkey* App no 28940/95 (ECtHR 24 June 2008) 73; *Gillan and Quinton v. United Kingdom* App no 4158/05 (ECtHR 12 January 2010) 56; *Villa v. Italy* App no 19675/06 (ECtHR 20 April 2010) 41; *Creangă v. Romania* App no 29226/03 (ECtHR Grand Chamber 23 February 2012) 84; *S.M. v. Italy* App no 18675/09 (ECtHR Decision on admissibility 8 October 2013) 21; *De Tommaso v. Italy* App no 43395/09 (ECtHR Grand Chamber 23 February 2017), 80; *Zelčs v. Latvia* App no 65367/16 (ECtHR 20 February 2020), 34.

104 *Guzzardi v. Italy* App no 7367/76 (ECtHR Plenary 6 November 1980), 92; *Ashingdane v. United Kingdom* App no 8225/78 (ECtHR 28 May 1985) 41; *Raimondo v. Italy* App no 12954/87 (ECtHR 22 February 1994), 39; *Amuur v. France* App no 19776/92 (ECtHR 25 June 1996) 42; *Denizci and others v. Cyprus* App nos 25316–25321/94 and 27207/95 (ECtHR 23 May 2001) 404; *H.M. v. Switzerland* App no 39187/98 (ECtHR 26 February 2002) 40; *Lavents v. Latvia* App no 58442/00 (ECtHR 28 November 2002) 62; *Sissanis v. Romania* App no 23468/02 (ECtHR 25 January 2007) 91; *Foka v. Turkey* App no 28940/95 (ECtHR 24 June 2008) 73; *Rantsev v. Cyprus and Russia* App no 25965/04 (ECtHR 7 January 2010), 314; *Gillan and Quinton v. United Kingdom* App no 4158/05 (ECtHR 12 January 2010) 56; *Villa v. Italy* App no 19675/06 (ECtHR 20 April 2010) 41; *Stanev v. Bulgaria* App no 36760/06 (ECtHR Grand Chamber 17 January 2012), 115; *Creangă v. Romania* App no 29226/03 (ECtHR Grand Chamber 23 February 2012), 84; *Austin and others v. United Kingdom* App nos 39692/09, 40713/09 and 41008/09 (ECtHR Grand Chamber 15 March 2012) 57; *Nada v. Switzerland* App no 10593/08 (ECtHR Grand Chamber 12 September 2012) 225; *Ostendorf v. Germany* App no 15598/08 (ECtHR 7 March 2013) 63; *S.M. v. Italy* App no 18675/09 (ECtHR Decision on admissibility 8 October 2013) 21; *Buzadji v. Republic of Moldova* App no 23755/07 (ECtHR Grand Chamber 5 July 2016) 103; *De Tommaso v. Italy* App no 43395/09 (ECtHR Grand Chamber 23 February 2017) 80; *Aftanache v. Romania* App no 999/19 (ECtHR 26 May 2020) 78. See also: L Todts, *Bestuurlijke en strafrechtelijke vrijheidsbeperkingen ter handhaving van de openbare orde* (die Keure 2021) 91.

105 *H.L. v. United Kingdom* App no 45508/99 (ECtHR 5 October 2004) 90; *Creangă v. Romania* App no 29226/03 (ECtHR Grand Chamber 23 February 2012) 92; *Austin and others v. United Kingdom* App nos 39692/09, 40713/09 and 41008/09 (ECtHR Grand Chamber 15 March 2012)

regard to this assessment, the Court has repeatedly stated that '*the difference between deprivation and restriction of liberty is one of degree or intensity, and not one of nature or substance*.'[106] According to the Court's case law, the notion of deprivation of liberty contains an objective element, being a person's confinement in a particular restricted space for a not negligible length of time, and an additional subjective element, meaning that the person has not validly consented to the confinement in question.[107] The starting point of this analysis should be the concrete situation of the person.[108] A whole range of factors must be taken

61; *Popoviciu v. Romania* App no 52942/09 (ECtHR 1 March 2016) 57; *Buzadji v. Republic of Moldova* App no 23755/07 (ECtHR Grand Chamber 5 July 2016) 103; *Khlaifia and others v. Italy* App no 16483/12 (ECtHR Grand Chamber 15 December 2016) 71; *Zelčs v. Latvia* App no 65367/16 (ECtHR 20 February 2020) 35; *Aftanache v. Romania* App no 999/19 (ECtHR 26 May 2020) 79.

106 *Guzzardi v. Italy* App no 7367/76 (ECtHR Plenary 6 November 1980) 93; *Ashingdane v. United Kingdom* App no 8225/78 (ECtHR 28 May 1985) 41; *Amuur v. France* App no 19776/92 (ECtHR 25 June 1996) 42; *H.M. v. Switzerland* App no 39187/98 (ECtHR 26 February 2002) 42; *Lavents v. Latvia* App no 58442/00 (ECtHR 28 November 2002) 62; *H.L. v. United Kingdom* App no 45508/99 (ECtHR 5 October 2004) 89; *Sissanis v. Romania* App no 23468/02 (ECtHR 25 January 2007) 91; *Foka v. Turkey* App no 28940/95 (ECtHR 24 June 2008) 74; *Rantsev v. Cyprus and Russia* App no 25965/04 (ECtHR 7 January 2010) 314; *Gillan and Quinton v. United Kingdom* App no 4158/05 (ECtHR 12 January 2010) 56; *Medvedyev and others v. France* App no 3394/03 (ECtHR Grand Chamber 29 March 2010) 73; *Villa v. Italy* App no 19675/06 (ECtHR 20 April 2010) 41; *Iskandarov v. Russia* App no 17185/05 (ECtHR 23 September 2010) 139; *Shimovolos v. Russia* App no 30194/09 (ECtHR 21 June 2011) 49; *Stanev v. Bulgaria* App no 36760/06 (ECtHR Grand Chamber 17 January 2012) 115; *Austin and others v. United Kingdom* App nos 39692/09, 40713/09 and 41008/09 (ECtHR Grand Chamber 15 March 2012) 57; *Nada v. Switzerland* App no 10593/08 (ECtHR Grand Chamber 12 September 2012) 225; *M.A. v. Cyprus* App no 41872/10 (ECtHR 23 July 2013) 186; *S.M. v. Italy* App no 18675/09 (ECtHR Decision on admissibility 8 October 2013) 21; *Bergmann v. Germany* App no 23279/14 (ECtHR 7 January 2016) 95; *Popoviciu v. Romania* App no 52942/09 (ECtHR 1 March 2016) 56; *Buzadji v. Republic of Moldova* App no 23755/07 (ECtHR Grand Chamber 5 July 2016) 103; *Khlaifia and others v. Italy* App no 16483/12 (ECtHR Grand Chamber 15 December 2016) 64; *De Tommaso v. Italy* App no 43395/09 (ECtHR Grand Chamber 23 February 2017) 80; *Zelčs v. Latvia* App no 65367/16 (ECtHR 20 February 2020) 34; *Aftanache v. Romania* App no 999/19 (ECtHR 26 May 2020) 78. See also: Richard A Edwards, 'Police Powers and Article 5 ECHR: Time for a New Approach to the Interpretation of the Right to Liberty' (2020) 41 Liverpool Law Review 331, 335; Feldman (n 82) 5; Fenwick, 'Recalibrating ECHR Rights, and the Role of the Human Rights Act Post 9/11' (n 26) 166; Sottiaux (n 27) 199; Todts (n 104) 95–96; Wood (n 25) 240.

107 *Storck v. Germany* App no 61603/00 (ECtHR 16 June 2005) 74; *Stanev v. Bulgaria* App no 36760/06 (ECtHR Grand Chamber 17 January 2012) 117. See also: Guide on Article 5 of the European Convention on Human Rights: Right to Liberty and Security (2020) 10; Fenwick, 'Recalibrating ECHR Rights, and the Role of the Human Rights Act Post 9/11' (n 26) 167; Sottiaux (n 27) 199; P Van Dijk and others, 'Chapter 9. Right to Liberty and Security', *Theory and Practice of the European Convention on Human Rights, 5th edition (hardcover)* (Intersentia 2018) 444.

108 *Engel and others v. Netherlands* App nos 5100/71, 5101/71, 5102/71, 5354/72 and 5370/72 (ECtHR 8 June 1976) 58; *Guzzardi v. Italy* App no 7367/76 (ECtHR Plenary 6 November 1980) 92; *Ashingdane v. United Kingdom* App no 8225/78 (ECtHR 28 May 1985) 41; *Amuur v. France* App no 19776/92 (ECtHR 25 June 1996) 42; *Riera Blume and others v. Spain* App no 37680/97 (ECtHR 14 October 1999) 28; *H.M. v. Switzerland* App no 39187/98 (ECtHR 26 February 2002) 42; *H.L. v. United Kingdom* App no 45508/99 (ECtHR 5 October 2004) 89; *I.I. v. Bulgaria* App no 44082/98 (ECtHR 9 June 2005) 86; *Storck v. Germany* App no 61603/00 (ECtHR 16 June

into account such as the type, duration, effects and manner of implementation of the measure.[109] Relevant in this assessment are for example the possibility to leave the restricted area, the degree of supervision and control over the person's

2005) 71; *Sissanis v. Romania* App no 23468/02 (ECtHR 25 January 2007) 91; *Iliya Stefanov v. Bulgaria* App no 65755/01 (ECtHR 22 May 2008) 71; *Foka v. Turkey* App no 28940/95 (ECtHR 24 June 2008) 74; *Abdolkhani and Karimnia v. Turkey* App no 30471/08 (ECtHR 22 September 2009) 125; *Rantsev v. Cyprus and Russia* App no 25965/04 (ECtHR 7 January 2010) 314; *Gillan and Quinton v. United Kingdom* App no 4158/05 (ECtHR 12 January 2010) 56; *Medvedyev and others v. France* App no 3394/03 (ECtHR Grand Chamber 29 March 2010) 73; *Villa v. Italy* App no 19675/06 (ECtHR 20 April 2010) 41; *Iskandarov v. Russia* App no 17185/05 (ECtHR 23 September 2010) 139; *Osypenko v. Ukraine* App no 4634/04 (ECtHR 9 November 2010) 46; *Shimovolos v. Russia* App no 30194/09 (ECtHR 21 June 2011) 49; *Stanev v. Bulgaria* App no 36760/06 (ECtHR Grand Chamber 17 January 2012) 115; *Creangă v. Romania* App no 29226/03 (ECtHR Grand Chamber 23 February 2012) 91; *Austin and others v. United Kingdom* App nos 39692/09, 40713/09 and 41008/09 (ECtHR Grand Chamber 15 March 2012) 57; *Nada v. Switzerland* App no 10593/08 (ECtHR Grand Chamber 12 September 2012) 225; *M.A. v. Cyprus* App no 41872/10 (ECtHR 23 July 2013) 186; *S.M. v. Italy* App no 18675/09 (ECtHR Decision on admissibility 8 October 2013) 21; *Popoviciu v. Romania* App no 52942/09 (ECtHR 1 March 2016) 56; *Buzadji v. Republic of Moldova* App no 23755/07 (ECtHR Grand Chamber 5 July 2016) 103; *Khlaifia and others v. Italy* App no 16483/12 (ECtHR Grand Chamber 15 December 2016) 64; *Rozhkov v. Russia (No. 2)* App no 38898/04 (ECtHR 31 January 2017) 74; *De Tommaso v. Italy* App no 43395/09 (ECtHR Grand Chamber 23 February 2017) 80; *Zelčs v. Latvia* App no 65367/16 (ECtHR 20 February 2020) 34; *Aftanache v. Romania* App no 999/19 (ECtHR 26 May 2020) 78. See also: Edwards (n 106) 335; Todts (n 104) 96.

109 *Guzzardi v. Italy* App no 7367/76 (ECtHR Plenary 6 November 1980) 92; *Ashingdane v. United Kingdom* App no 8225/78 (ECtHR 28 May 1985) 41; *Amuur v. France* App no 19776/92 (ECtHR 25 June 1996) 42; *Riera Blume and others v. Spain* App no 37680/97 (ECtHR 14 October 1999) 28; *H.M. v. Switzerland* App no 39187/98 (ECtHR 26 February 2002) 42; *Lavents v. Latvia* App no 58442/00 (ECtHR 28 November 2002) 62; *H.L. v. United Kingdom* App no 45508/99 (ECtHR 5 October 2004) 89; *I.I. v. Bulgaria* App no 44082/98 (ECtHR 9 June 2005) 86; *Storck v. Germany* App no 61603/00 (ECtHR 16 June 2005) 71; *Sissanis v. Romania* App no 23468/02 (ECtHR 25 January 2007) 91; *Iliya Stefanov v. Bulgaria* App no 65755/01 (ECtHR 22 May 2008) 71; *Foka v. Turkey* App no 28940/95 (ECtHR 24 June 2008) 74; *Abdolkhani and Karimnia v. Turkey* App no 30471/08 (ECtHR 22 September 2009) 125; *Rantsev v. Cyprus and Russia* App no 25965/04 (ECtHR 7 January 2010) 314; *Gillan and Quinton v. United Kingdom* App no 4158/05 (ECtHR 12 January 2010) 56; *Medvedyev and others v. France* App no 3394/03 (ECtHR Grand Chamber 29 March 2010) 73; *Villa v. Italy* App no 19675/06 (ECtHR 20 April 2010) 41; *Iskandarov v. Russia* App no 17185/05 (ECtHR 23 September 2010) 139; *Osypenko v. Ukraine* App no 4634/04 (ECtHR 9 November 2010) 46; *Shimovolos v. Russia* App no 30194/09 (ECtHR 21 June 2011) 49; *Stanev v. Bulgaria* App no 36760/06 (ECtHR Grand Chamber 17 January 2012) 115; *Creangă v. Romania* App no 29226/03 (ECtHR Grand Chamber 23 February 2012) 91; *Austin and others v. United Kingdom* App nos 39692/09, 40713/09 and 41008/09 (ECtHR Grand Chamber 15 March 2012) 57; *Nada v. Switzerland* App no 10593/08 (ECtHR Grand Chamber 12 September 2012) 225; *M.A. v. Cyprus* App no 41872/10 (ECtHR 23 July 2013) 186; *S.M. v. Italy* App no 18675/09 (ECtHR Decision on admissibility 8 October 2013) 21; *Popoviciu v. Romania* App no 52942/09 (ECtHR 1 March 2016) 56; *Buzadji v. Republic of Moldova* App no 23755/07 (ECtHR Grand Chamber 5 July 2016) 103; *Khlaifia and others v. Italy* App no 16483/12 (ECtHR Grand Chamber 15 December 2016) 64; *Rozhkov v. Russia (No. 2)* App no 38898/04 (ECtHR 31 January 2017) 74; *De Tommaso v. Italy* App no 43395/09 (ECtHR Grand Chamber 23 February 2017) 80; *Zelčs v. Latvia* App no 65367/16 (ECtHR 20 February 2020) 34; *Aftanache v. Romania* App no 999/19 (ECtHR 26 May 2020) 78. For an analysis of possible factors, see also: Edwards (n 106) 335; Todts (n 104) 96–119. Note that the Court of Justice of the European Union also follows this line of reasoning. See: *JZ v. Prokuratura Rejonowa Lodz* C-294/16 (CJEU 28 July 2016) 44–57.

movements, the extent of isolation and the availability of social contacts.[110] That a person is not physically restrained, e.g. by being handcuffed[111] or put in a cell,[112] is not a decisive factor in establishing the existence of a deprivation of liberty.[113] House arrest, for example, can be a form of detention as well and thus a deprivation of liberty.[114] Finally, even relatively short detentions (as short as 30[115] or 45 minutes[116]) can amount to a deprivation of liberty, depending on the circumstances.[117] This means not all short detentions are deprivations of liberty. For example, a stay at the police station of a few hours which does not go beyond the necessary time for certain formalities does not amount to a deprivation of liberty.[118] The purpose of the measure taken by the authorities is not decisive for the assessment.[119] This is only relevant at a further stage of the analysis, when

110 See e.g. *Guzzardi v. Italy* App no 7367/76 (ECtHR Plenary 6 November 1980) 95; *H.M. v. Switzerland* App no 39187/98 (ECtHR 26 February 2002) 45; *H.L. v. United Kingdom* App no 45508/99 (ECtHR 5 October 2004) 91; *Storck v. Germany* App no 61603/00 (ECtHR 16 June 2005) 73. See also: *Guide on Article 5 of the European Convention on Human Rights: Right to Liberty and Security* (2020) 11.

111 *Riera Blume and others v. Spain* App no 37680/97 (ECtHR 14 October 1999) 33.

112 *Austin and others v. United Kingdom* App nos 39692/09, 40713/09 and 41008/09 (ECtHR Grand Chamber 15 March 2012) 59; *Nada v. Switzerland* App no 10593/08 (ECtHR Grand Chamber 12 September 2012) 226. See also: Fenwick and Phillipson (n 25) 883.

113 *I.I. v. Bulgaria* App no 44082/98 (ECtHR 9 June 2005) 87; *M.A. v. Cyprus* App no 41872/10 (ECtHR 23 July 2013) 193; *Popoviciu v. Romania* App no 52942/09 (ECtHR 1 March 2016) 59. See also: Todts (n 104) 94.

114 *N.C. v. Italy* App no 24952/94 (ECtHR 11 January 2001) 33; *Mancini v. Italy* App no 44955/98 (ECtHR 2 August 2001) 17; *Lavents v. Latvia* App no 58442/00 (ECtHR 28 November 2002) 63; *Nikolova v. Bulgaria (no. 2)* App no 40896/98 (ECtHR 30 September 2004) 60; *Danov v. Bulgaria* App no 56796/00 (ECtHR 26 October 2006) 80; *Dacosta Silva v. Spain* App no 69966/01 (ECtHR 2 November 2006) 44; *Ninescu v. Republic of Moldova* App no 47306/07 (ECtHR 15 July 2014) 53; *Buzadji v. Republic of Moldova* App no 23755/07 (ECtHR Grand Chamber 5 July 2016) 104–105. See also: Todts (n 104) 94. *Contra*: Fenwick, 'Recalibrating ECHR Rights, and the Role of the Human Rights Act Post 9/11' (n 26) 166; Janneke Gerards, 'Freedom of Movement' in P Van Dijk and others, *Theory and Practice of the European Convention on Human Rights* (Intersentia 2018) 937.

115 *Gillan and Quinton v. United Kingdom* App no 4158/05 (ECtHR 12 January 2010) 57.

116 *Shimovolos v. Russia* App no 30194/09 (ECtHR 21 June 2011) 50.

117 *Novotka v. Slovakia* App no 47244/99 (ECtHR Decision on admissibility 4 November 2003) 2; *Iliya Stefanov v. Bulgaria* App no 65755/01 (ECtHR 22 May 2008) 71; *Rantsev v. Cyprus and Russia* App no 25965/04 (ECtHR 7 January 2010) 317; *Iskandarov v. Russia* App no 17185/05 (ECtHR 23 September 2010) 140; *Osypenko v. Ukraine* App no 4634/04 (ECtHR 9 November 2010) 47; *Shimovolos v. Russia* App no 30194/09 (ECtHR 21 June 2011) 49; *Creangă v. Romania* App no 29226/03 (ECtHR Grand Chamber 23 February 2012) 93; *Ostendorf v. Germany* App no 15598/08 (ECtHR 7 March 2013) 64; *M.A. v. Cyprus* App no 41872/10 (ECtHR 23 July 2013) 190; *Zelčs v. Latvia* App no 65367/16 (ECtHR 20 February 2020) 36 and 40; *Aftanache v. Romania* App no 999/19 (ECtHR 26 May 2020) 80; *Kerem Çiftçi v. Turkey* App no 35205/09 (ECtHR 21 September 2021) 28; *Järvinen v. Finland* App no 30408/96 (European Commission of Human Rights 15 January 1998) 2.

118 *Foka v. Turkey* App no 28940/95 (ECtHR 24 June 2008) 75; *Osypenko v. Ukraine* App no 4634/04 (ECtHR 9 November 2010) 47.

119 *Austin and others v. United Kingdom* App nos 39692/09, 40713/09 and 41008/09 (ECtHR Grand Chamber 15 March 2012) 58; *M.A. v. Cyprus* App no 41872/10 (ECtHR 23 July 2013) 189; *Rozhkov v. Russia (No. 2)* App no 38898/04 (ECtHR 31 January 2017) 74.

examining the compatibility of the measures with one of the exceptions listed in Article 5(1) ECHR (see nos 45–61).[120] Drawing the line between a restriction and a deprivation of liberty based on these rules can be difficult. In the *Guzzardi* case, the Court itself admits that '*the process of classification into one or other of these categories sometimes proves to be no easy task in that some borderline cases are a matter of pure opinion.*'[121] The uncertainty which arises has been the subject of criticism in legal scholarship.[122]

SUBSECTION II. PRACTICAL APPLICATION

32. Goal of this Subsection – In this Subsection, we look at some concrete examples from the case law to get an idea of the practical application of the abovementioned rules and to be able to see where exactly the ECtHR draws the line between a deprivation and a restriction of the right to liberty. For similar reasons, the other two Sections of this Chapter also have a Subsection containing case law. The discussion of the cases is focussed on the parts of each case which are relevant for the analyses of Articles 5 ECHR and 2 Fourth Protocol ECHR. Some of the cases included analyses of other Articles or paragraphs of Articles of the ECHR, which was omitted.

33. Guzzardi (1980) – Mr. Guzzardi was an Italian national who was tried for conspiracy and for being an accomplice to an abduction. He was remanded in custody during the investigation but was acquitted over three and a half years later. Another three years later, however, the acquittal was overturned by the Court of Appeal, and he was eventually convicted.[123] The Italian legislation only allowed his pre-trial detention to continue for a maximum of two years.[124] Therefore, it had to end well before the judgment in first instance. On the day this two years ran out, Mr. Guzzardi was released from prison, but immediately subjected to a measure of special supervision for a term of three years.[125] These special supervision measures could be imposed by the Regional Court on several categories of people, including people '*who may be regarded as having committed*

120 *Austin and others v. United Kingdom* App nos 39692/09, 40713/09 and 41008/09 (ECtHR Grand Chamber 15 March 2012) 58; *M.A. v. Cyprus* App no 41872/10 (ECtHR 23 July 2013) 189; *Rozhkov v. Russia (No. 2)* App no 38898/04 (ECtHR 31 January 2017) 74.

121 *Guzzardi v. Italy* App no 7367/76 (ECtHR Plenary 6 November 1980) 93. See also: Fleur Dhont, 'Art. 5 EVRM' in J Vande Lanotte and Y Haeck, *Handboek EVRM, Deel 2* (Intersentia 2004) 279; Edwards (n 106) 335.

122 Edwards (n 106) 335–336; Feldman (n 82) 8; Fenwick, 'Preventive Anti-Terrorist Strategies in the UK and ECHR: Control Orders, TPIMs and the Role of Technology' (n 25) 879; Jim Murdoch, 'Safeguarding the Liberty of the Person: Recent Strasbourg Jurisprudence' [1993] International and Comparative Law Quarterly 494, 495–499; Todts (n 104) 23.

123 *Guzzardi v. Italy* App no 7367/76 (ECtHR Plenary 6 November 1980) 9.

124 *Guzzardi v. Italy* App no 7367/76 (ECtHR Plenary 6 November 1980) 10.

125 *Guzzardi v. Italy* App no 7367/76 (ECtHR Plenary 6 November 1980) 11–12.

offences endangering the physical or mental integrity of minors or posing a threat to health, security or public order' and people '*who must be considered as habitually living, even in part, on the proceeds of crime or on the rewards of complicity therein*.'[126] The measure was imposed upon application by the chief of police, who first had to send a warning to the person to mend their ways. In execution of this special supervision, the police took him to an island where he had to reside, and only a small section of which he had access to. In addition, he had to:

- start looking for work within a month, establish his residence in the prescribed locality (i.e. the island), inform the supervisory authorities immediately of his address and not leave the fixed place without first notifying them;
- report to the supervisory authorities twice a day and whenever called upon to do so;
- lead an honest and law-abiding life and not give cause for suspicion;
- not associate with persons convicted of criminal offences and subjected to preventive or security measures;
- not return to his residence later than ten pm and not go out before seven am, except in case of necessity and after having given notice in due time to supervisory authorities;
- not keep or carry any arms;
- not frequent bars or night-clubs and not take part in public meetings;
- inform the supervisory authorities in advance of the telephone number and name of the person telephoned or telephoning each time he wished to make or receive a long-distance call.

The court which imposed this measure, based it on a report by the Milan Chief of Police which stated that although Mr. Guzzardi claimed to be working in the building trade, he was actually engaged in illegal activities and belonged to a mafia group. The report furthermore listed four prior convictions and described him as '*one of the most dangerous*' of individuals.[127] The goal of these measures was to remove Mr. Guzzardi from his (criminal) surroundings and isolate him from possible other criminal elements. Mr. Guzzardi appealed the imposition of the measures, as it turned out that there was no adequate accommodation for his family on the island, nor opportunities for permanent employment. However, this appeal was rejected,[128] as was a further appeal to the Italian Court of Cassation.[129] After serving almost half of his three-year special supervision

---

126 *Guzzardi v. Italy* App no 7367/76 (ECtHR Plenary 6 November 1980) 46. See also: *De Tommaso v. Italy* App no 43395/09 (ECtHR Grand Chamber 23 February 2017) 34.
127 *Guzzardi v. Italy* App no 7367/76 (ECtHR Plenary 6 November 1980) 12.
128 *Guzzardi v. Italy* App no 7367/76 (ECtHR Plenary 6 November 1980) 17.
129 *Guzzardi v. Italy* App no 7367/76 (ECtHR Plenary 6 November 1980) 19.

on the island, Mr. Guzzardi was moved to the mainland, where he served the remainder of his supervision living in a specified area. This was done to separate him from one of his co-accused, who was also subject to a special supervision measure on the island.[130] Regarding his stay on the island, the ECtHR stated that special supervision and compulsory residence do not always come within the scope of Article 5, this depends on the manner of implementation of the measure.[131] In this case the Court noted that Mr. Guzzardi could only access a tiny fraction of the island, the buildings in which he was housed were in a state of disrepair and he lived principally in the company of other people subject to special supervision and policemen (the permanent residents of the island were allowed to visit, but very rarely did and he was not allowed to visit the town itself). Therefore, there were few opportunities for social contacts, other than with his own family, the other people under special supervision and the supervisory staff. Furthermore, the court took note of the fact that he needed to stay indoors between ten pm and seven am, had to report twice a day, had to inform the authorities about who he corresponded with over the telephone and needed permission for trips off the island, which were rare and under supervision. Failure to comply with any of these measures could have led to being arrested. The Court stated that any of these individual factors were not strong enough to amount to a deprivation of liberty, but in combination they did.[132] Note that the Court was far from unanimous on this point. Seven judges dissented on the point that this was a deprivation of liberty and not a mere restriction.[133] Of these dissenters, judges Teitgen and Garcia De Enterria did note that they found the question of whether there was deprivation of liberty a borderline case. Judge Bindschedler-Robert on the other hand had a much more fundamental issue with it and doubted that the difference between deprivation and restriction is one of nature or substance. He argued for an interpretation of the right to liberty limited to paradigm cases of deprivations of liberty. In his dissenting opinion, judge Sir Gerald Fitzmaurice argued that the majority did not take into account the terrorist context, by which he meant that public order in Italy was seriously menaced by threats coming essentially from political terrorism and the mafia, and argued that the measure in question did not amount to a deprivation of liberty but a mere restriction of the freedom of movement.

---

130 *Guzzardi v. Italy* App no 7367/76 (ECtHR Plenary 6 November 1980) 21–22.

131 *Guzzardi v. Italy* App no 7367/76 (ECtHR Plenary 6 November 1980) 94.

132 *Guzzardi v. Italy* App no 7367/76 (ECtHR Plenary 6 November 1980) 95. See also: Feldman (n 82) 5; Fenwick and Phillipson (n 25) 884; Todts (n 104) 95. One question we could ask ourselves is how the evolution of technology might have influenced this. Current technology would make it much easier to communicate, even over longer distances, with family and friends and would therefore ease the social isolation.

133 Being judges Zekia, Sir Gerald Fitzmaurice, Bindschedler-Robert, Teitgen, Garcia De Enterria, Matscher and Pinheiro Farinha.

34. Cianciminio (1991) – Mr. Cianciminio was an Italian politician who was prosecuted for involvement with the mafia and subjected to a compulsory residence order and special supervision (see no. 33). He had to reside in a specific district and could not leave it without permission, had a curfew from 8 pm to 7 am and had to report to the police once a day.[134] After about three years, the compulsory residence order was substituted by a ban to reside in certain districts. The European Commission on Human Rights noted that Mr. Cianciminio could move freely within the district during the day and his living conditions were not dissimilar to those of the rest of the population.[135] Therefore, the measure did not constitute a deprivation of liberty.[136]

35. Trijonis (2006) – In the *Trijonis* case, a man was subject to house arrest as a bail condition while awaiting trial. Originally the house arrest was 24 hours per day, every day of the week. After about a month, it was amended to house arrest during weekends and from 7 pm until 7 am on weekdays, so Mr. Trijonis could go to work during the day.[137] The ECtHR held that the complaint on the 24-hour house arrest was admissible, but the amended house arrest was not a deprivation of liberty.[138]

36. Villa (2010) – Mr. Villa, having been found partially irresponsible for his actions, was convicted by the Italian courts to a prison sentence of three months and 15 days, which was automatically replaced by seven months 'controlled freedom' (the prohibition of leaving town, the obligation to report to the police station daily, etc.)[139] for threatening to kill and injuring his father.[140] In addition to this sentence, because Mr. Villa was considered socially dangerous, a security measure was imposed on him, consisting of one year probation.[141] This probation included the following obligations[142]:

- to report to the police once a month;
- to maintain contact with a psychiatric centre;
- to live at his specified address;

---

134 *Vito Ciancimino v. Italy* App no 12541/86 (European Commission of Human Rights Decision on admissibility 27 May 1991) 119.

135 *Vito Ciancimino v. Italy* App no 12541/86 (European Commission of Human Rights Decision on admissibility 27 May 1991) 122.

136 *Vito Ciancimino v. Italy* App no 12541/86 (European Commission of Human Rights Decision on admissibility 27 May 1991) 123.

137 *Trijonis v. Lithuania* App no 2333/02 (ECtHR Decision on admissibility 17 March 2005) 2–3.

138 *Trijonis v. Lithuania* App no 2333/02 (ECtHR Decision on admissibility 17 March 2005) 7. Note that there was no decision on the merits of this case. The case was struck out of the list because of the inactivity of the applicant. See: *Trijonis v. Lithuania* App no 2333/02 (ECtHR 15 December 2005).

139 *Villa v. Italy* App no 19675/06 (ECtHR 20 April 2010) 14.

140 *Villa v. Italy* App no 19675/06 (ECtHR 20 April 2010) 6–8.

141 *Villa v. Italy* App no 19675/06 (ECtHR 20 April 2010) 8.

142 *Villa v. Italy* App no 19675/06 (ECtHR 20 April 2010) 15.

- not to move away from the commune where he resided;
- to stay at home between 10 pm and 7 am;
- to have with him at all times the document setting out his obligations and to present it to the police authority on request.

After about two months, Mr. Villa was placed in a psychiatric hospital, where he stayed for about 11 months, after which he was released on probation for another two years and seven months.[143] The ECtHR, without much extra explanation held that this probation did not amount to a deprivation of liberty and thus was only a restriction of the freedom of movement.[144]

37. S.M. (2013) – Mr. S.M. had been convicted of two counts of theft and was suspected of two robberies. An Italian District Court considered him socially dangerous and therefore placed him under special police supervision (see no. 33) for two years.[145] This measure entailed the prohibition of leaving his city of residence without prior permission, the prohibition to move to a different city, the obligation to stay at home between 10 pm and 6 am (unless in situations of real necessity which had to be communicated to the police) and to present himself at the police station every Sunday.[146] Mr. S.M. appealed and on appeal, more than two years after the imposition of the measure, the Court of Appeal held that a procedural error had been made. It sent the case back to the District Court in order for that court to make a new decision, but in the meantime terminated the supervision measure.[147] During this new procedure before the District Court, the public prosecutor dropped the application for special supervision as the circumstances had changed and Mr. S.M. was no longer dangerous.[148] The ECtHR found that this measure did not amount to a deprivation of liberty and thus did not come within the scope of Article 5 ECHR.[149]

38. De Tommaso (2017) – The case of *De Tommaso v. Italy* concerned Mr. De Tommaso, who was subject to special police supervision (see no. 33) and a compulsory residence order because he was believed to be involved in criminal activities and to be a dangerous individual.[150] The measures entailed the following obligations:

- to report once a week to the police authority responsible for his supervision;
- to start looking for work within a month;

143 *Villa v. Italy* App no 19675/06 (ECtHR 20 April 2010) 17–19.
144 *Villa v. Italy* App no 19675/06 (ECtHR 20 April 2010) 42–43. Note that Art. 7 ECHR was not raised.
145 *S.M. v. Italy* App no 18675/09 (ECtHR Decision on admissibility 8 October 2013) 3 and 9.
146 *S.M. v. Italy* App no 18675/09 (ECtHR Decision on admissibility 8 October 2013) 9.
147 *S.M. v. Italy* App no 18675/09 (ECtHR Decision on admissibility 8 October 2013) 11–14.
148 *S.M. v. Italy* App no 18675/09 (ECtHR Decision on admissibility 8 October 2013) 15.
149 *S.M. v. Italy* App no 18675/09 (ECtHR Decision on admissibility 8 October 2013) 22.
150 *De Tommaso v. Italy* App no 43395/09 (ECtHR Grand Chamber 23 February 2017) 11–16.

- to live in Casamassima and not to change his place of residence;
- to lead an honest and law-abiding life and not give cause for suspicion;
- not to associate with persons who had a criminal record and who were subject to preventive or security measures;
- not to return home later than 10 pm or to leave home before 6 am, except in case of necessity and only after giving notice to the authorities in good time;
- not to keep or carry weapons;
- not to go to bars, nightclubs, amusement arcades or brothels and not to attend public meetings;
- not to use mobile phones or radio communication devices; and
- to have with him at all times the document setting out his obligations and to present it to the police authority on request.[151]

The ECtHR considered that, unlike Mr. Guzzardi, Mr. De Tommaso was not forced to live within a restricted area and was not unable to make social contacts.[152] Furthermore, the inability to leave the house between 10 pm and 6 am did not amount to house arrest.[153] Therefore, referring back to its previous case law, the Court ruled that Mr. De Tommaso was not deprived of his liberty and Article 5 did not apply.[154] In their partly dissenting opinions, judges Pinto De Albuquerque, Sajó and Kūris argued that the measures in question did amount to a deprivation of liberty. According to them, the measures imposed on Mr. De Tommaso were similar to those in *Guzzardi* and thus did deprive him of his liberty.

39. Timofeyev and Postupkin (2021) – Mr. Postupkin was sentenced to seven years and six months' imprisonment for drug trafficking.[155] After serving his prison time in full, the District Court placed him under administrative surveillance. The reasons for this were the fact that he had been convicted of an offence qualifying as dangerous recidivism, that he had not complied with the prison rules and that 23 disciplinary penalties had been imposed on him. The administrative surveillance measure entailed an obligation for Mr. Postupkin to present himself to the authorities once a month, not to leave his residence between 10 pm and 6 am and to report any change of residence within three working days.[156] The ECtHR, referring to the *De Tommaso* case, reiterated that overnight house arrest and the obligation to report to the police at regular intervals are limitations of the right to free movement. The same goes for the

151 *De Tommaso v. Italy* App no 43395/09 (ECtHR Grand Chamber 23 February 2017) 17.

152 *De Tommaso v. Italy* App no 43395/09 (ECtHR Grand Chamber 23 February 2017) 85.

153 *De Tommaso v. Italy* App no 43395/09 (ECtHR Grand Chamber 23 February 2017) 86.

154 *De Tommaso v. Italy* App no 43395/09 (ECtHR Grand Chamber 23 February 2017) 89.

155 The other applicant, Mr. Timofeyev did not allege a violation of his right to freedom of movement and his case will thus not be discussed.

156 *Timofeyev and Postupkin v. Russia* App nos 45431/14 and 22769/15 (ECtHR 19 January 2021) 124.

obligation to report any change of residence.[157] So the measures imposed on Mr. Postupkin, cumulatively as well as separately, limited his right to free movement but did not deprive him of his right to liberty.

SECTION II. RIGHT TO LIBERTY

SUBSECTION I. PROTECTING AGAINST ARBITRARINESS

40. Exhaustively listed exceptions – On several occasions the Court has underscored the importance of the right to liberty and security in a democratic society within the meaning of the Convention.[158] As explained above, the main goal of Article 5 ECHR is to protect against arbitrary interferences with the right to liberty. In order to achieve this goal, the Article contains a list of situations in which a person can be deprived of their liberty. These exceptions to the right to liberty are listed exhaustively[159] and need to be interpreted

157 *Denizci and others v. Cyprus* App nos 25316–25321/94 and 27207/95 (ECtHR 23 May 2001) 403–404; *Bolat v. Russia* App no 14139/03 (ECtHR 5 October 2006) 65–66; *Tatishvili v. Russia* App no. 1509/02 (ECtHR 22 February 2007) 45; *Timofeyev and Postupkin v. Russia* App nos 45431/14 and 22769/15 (ECtHR 19 January 2021) 125.

158 *De Wilde, Ooms and Versyp v. Belgium* App nos 2832/66, 2835/66 and 2899/66 (ECtHR 18 June 1971) 65; *Winterwerp v. the Netherlands* App no 6301/73 (ECtHR 24 October 1979) 37; *Zervudacki v. France* App no 73947/01 (ECtHR 27 July 2006) 40; *Ladent v. Poland* App no 11036/03 (ECtHR 18 March 2008) 45; *Medvedyev and others v. France* App no 3394/03 (ECtHR Grand Chamber 29 March 2010) 76; *Iskandarov v. Russia* App no 17185/05 (ECtHR 23 September 2010) 143; *Khayredinov v. Ukraine* App no 38717/04 (ECtHR 14 October 2010) 26; *Kharin v. Russia* App no 37345/03 (ECtHR 3 February 2011) 43; *Oshurko v. Ukraine* App no 33108/05 (ECtHR 8 September 2011) 96; *James, Wells and Lee v. United Kingdom* App nos 25119/09, 57715/09 and 57877/09 (ECtHR 18 September 2012) 187; *Buzadji v. Republic of Moldova* App no 23755/07 (ECtHR Grand Chamber 5 July 2016) 84; *Ali Osman Özmen v. Turkey* App no 42969/04 (ECtHR 5 October 2016) 68; *Oravec v. Croatia* App no 51249/11 (ECtHR 11 July 2017) 44; *Mehmet Hasan Altan v. Turkey* App no 13237/17 (ECtHR 20 March 2018) 122; *Şahin Alpay v. Turkey* App no 16538/17 (ECtHR 20 March 2018) 101; *Zelčs v. Latvia* App no 65367/16 (ECtHR 20 February 2020) 44; *I.S. v. Switzerland* App no 60202/15 (ECtHR 6 October 2020) 41; *Selahattin Demirtaş v. Turkey (no. 2)* App no 14305/17 (ECtHR Grand Chamber 22 December 2020) 311. See also: Dhont (n 121) 275; Sottiaux (n 27) 197.

159 *Eriksen v. Norway* App no 17391/90 (ECtHR 27 May 1997) 76; *Witold Litwa v. Poland* App no 26629/95 (ECtHR 4 April 2000) 49; *Enhorn v. Sweden* App no 56529/00 (ECtHR 25 January 2005) 34; *Saadi v. United Kingdom* App no 13229/03 (ECtHR Grand Chamber 29 January 2008) 43; *A. and others v. United Kingdom* App no 3455/05 (ECtHR Grand Chamber 19 February 2009) 163; *Abdolkhani and Karimnia v. Turkey* App no 30471/08 (ECtHR 22 September 2009) 128; *M. v. Germany* App no 19359/04 (ECtHR 17 December 2009) 86; *Rantsev v. Cyprus and Russia* App no 25965/04 (ECtHR 7 January 2010) 322; *Garayev v. Azerbaijan* App no 53688/08 (ECtHR 10 June 2010) 93; *Gatt v. Malta* App no 28221/08 (ECtHR 27 July 2010) 35; *Louled Massoud v. Malta* App no 24340/08 (ECtHR 27 July 2010) 59; *Grosskopf v. Germany* App no 24478/03 (ECtHR 21 October 2010) 42; *Schwabe and M.G. v. Germany* App nos 8080/08 and 8577/08 (ECtHR 1 December 2011) 69; *Stanev v. Bulgaria* App no 36760/06 (ECtHR Grand Chamber 17 January 2012) 144; *Creangă v. Romania* App no 29226/03 (ECtHR Grand Chamber 23 February 2012) 84; *Austin and others v. United Kingdom* App nos 39692/09, 40713/09 and 41008/09 (ECtHR Grand Chamber 15 March 2012) 60; *Nada v. Switzerland*

narrowly.[160] Article 5 therefore does not allow for a broad range of justifications as is the case for Articles 8 to 11 ECHR.[161] Nor is there a possibility to allow for detention which does not fall within the scope of any of the subparagraphs of

---

App no 10593/08 (ECtHR Grand Chamber 12 September 2012) 224; *Suso Musa v. Malta* App no 42337/12 (ECtHR 23 July 2013) 89; *Del Rio Prada v. Spain* App no 42750/09 (ECtHR Grand Chamber 21 October 2013) 123; *Petkov and Profirov v. Bulgaria* App nos 50027/08 and 50781/09 (ECtHR 24 June 2014) 41; *Ruslan Yakovenko v. Ukraine* App no 5425/11 (ECtHR 4 June 2015) 45; *Klinkenbuß v. Germany* App no 53157/11 (ECtHR 25 February 2016) 45; *J.N. v. United Kingdom* App no 37289/12 (ECtHR 19 May 2016) 74; *Aboya Boa Jean v. Malta* App no 62676/16 (ECtHR 2 April 2019) 52; *Al Husin v. Bosnia and Herzegovina (no. 2)* App no 10112/16 (ECtHR 25 June 2019) 96. See also: Conte (n 10) 300; Mueller (n 32) 325.

160 *Winterwerp v. Netherlands* App no 6301/73 (ECtHR 24 October 1979) 37; *Guzzardi v. Italy* App no 7367/76 (ECtHR Plenary 6 November 1980) 100; *Bouamar v. Belgium* App no 9106/80 (ECtHR 29 February 1988) 43; *Ciulla v. Italy* App no 11152/84 (ECtHR Plenary 22 February 1989) 41; *Quinn v. France* App no 18580/91 (ECtHR 22 March 1995) 42; *Giulia Manzoni v. Italy* App no 19218/91 (ECtHR 1 July 1997) 25; *K.-F. v. Germany* App no 144/1996/765/962 (ECtHR 27 November 1997) 70; *Labita v. Italy* App no 26772/95 (ECtHR Grand Chamber 6 April 2000) 170; *Mancini v. Italy* App no 44955/98 (ECtHR 2 August 2001) 23; *Čonka v. Belgium* App no 51564/99 (ECtHR 5 February 2002) 42; *Vasileva v. Denmark* App no 52792/99 (ECtHR 25 September 2003) 33; *Epple v. Germany* App no 77909/01 (ECtHR 24 March 2005) 33; *Zervudacki v. France* App no 73947/01 (ECtHR 27 July 2006) 41; *Ladent v. Poland* App no 11036/03 (ECtHR 18 March 2008) 46; *Kandzhov v. Bulgaria* App no 68294/01 (ECtHR 6 November 2008) 55; *A. and others v. United Kingdom* App no 3455/05 (ECtHR Grand Chamber 19 February 2009) 171; *Medvedyev and others v. France* App no 3394/03 (ECtHR Grand Chamber 29 March 2010) 78; *Khayredinov v. Ukraine* App no 38717/04 (ECtHR 14 October 2010) 26; *Osypenko v. Ukraine* App no 4634/04 (ECtHR 9 November 2010) 50; *Kharin v. Russia* App no 37345/03 (ECtHR 3 February 2011) 31; *Soare and others v. Romania* App no 24329/02 (ECtHR 22 February 2011) 232; *Sarigiannis v. Italy* App no 14569/05 (ECtHR 5 April 2011) 39; *Shimovolos v. Russia* App no 30194/09 (ECtHR 21 June 2011) 51; *Oshurko v. Ukraine* App no 33108/05 (ECtHR 8 September 2011) 96; *Ostendorf v. Germany* App no 15598/08 (ECtHR 7 March 2013) 65; *Magee and others v. United Kingdom*, App nos 26289/12 and 2 others (ECtHR 12 May 2015) 73; *Buzadji v. Republic of Moldova* App no 23755/07 (ECtHR Grand Chamber 5 July 2016) 84; *Ali Osman Özmen v. Turkey* App no 42969/04 (ECtHR 5 October 2016) 68; *Khlaifia and others v. Italy* App no 16483/12 (ECtHR Grand Chamber 15 December 2016) 88; *Mehmet Hasan Altan v. Turkey* App no 13237/17 (ECtHR 20 March 2018) 123; *Şahin Alpay v. Turkey* App no 16538/17 (ECtHR 20 March 2018) 102; *S., V. and A. v. Denmark* App nos 35553/23, 36678/23 and 36711/12 (ECtHR Grand Chamber 22 October 2018) 73; *Ilnseher v. Germany* App nos 10211/12 and 27505/14 (ECtHR Grand Chamber 4 December 2018) 126; *Moustahi v. France* App no 9347/14 (ECtHR 25 June 2020) 88; *I.S. v. Switzerland* App no 60202/15 (ECtHR 6 October 2020) 45; *Selahattin Demirtaş v. Turkey (no. 2)* App no 14305/17 (ECtHR Grand Chamber 22 December 2020) 312; *Denis and Irvine v. Belgium* App nos 62819/17 and 63921/17 (ECtHR Grand Chamber 1 June 2021) 124; *Kerem Çiftçi v. Turkey* App no 35205/09 (ECtHR 21 September 2021) 27; *McVeigh and others v. United Kingdom* App nos 8022/77, 8025/77 and 8027/77 (European Commission of Human Rights 18 March 1981) 162. See also: Macken (n 95) 52–53; Sottiaux (n 27) 200; Todts (n 104) 91.

161 *McKay v. United Kingdom* App no 543/03 (ECtHR Grand Chamber 3 October 2006) 30; *Magee and others v. United Kingdom*, App nos 26289/12 and 2 others (ECtHR 12 May 2015) 73; *Buzadji v. Republic of Moldova* App no 23755/07 (ECtHR Grand Chamber 5 July 2016) 84; *Ali Osman Özmen v. Turkey* App no 42969/04 (ECtHR 5 October 2016) 68; *S., V. and A. v. Denmark* App nos 35553/23, 36678/23 and 36711/12 (ECtHR Grand Chamber 22 October 2018) 73; *Selahattin Demirtaş v. Turkey (no. 2)* App no 14305/17 (ECtHR Grand Chamber 22 December 2020) 312.

Article 5(1) based on a balancing of the interests of the state with those of the detainee.[162]

41. LAWFULNESS – Even if a measure falls within one of the subparagraphs of Article 5(1), it is not automatically justified. In addition to falling under one of the subparagraphs of Article 5(1), any deprivation of liberty must be lawful.[163] This means that '*a procedure prescribed by law*' must be followed and the deprivation thus has to comply with national law,[164] but this alone is not

---

162 *A. and others v. United Kingdom* App no 3455/05 (ECtHR Grand Chamber 19 February 2009) 171. See also: Dhont (n 121) 276.

163 *Winterwerp v. Netherlands* App no 6301/73 (ECtHR 24 October 1979) 39; *Kemmache v. France (no 3)* App no 17621/91 (ECtHR 24 November 1994) 42; *K.-F. v. Germany* App no 144/1996/765/962 (ECtHR 27 November 1997) 63; *Saadi v. United Kingdom* App no 13229/03 (ECtHR Grand Chamber 29 January 2008) 67. See also: *Epple v. Germany* App no 77909/01 (ECtHR 24 March 2005) 33; *McKay v. United Kingdom* App no 543/03 (ECtHR Grand Chamber 3 October 2006) 30; *Kafkaris v. Cyprus* App no 21906/04 (ECtHR Grand Chamber 12 February 2008) 116; *Abdolkhani and Karimnia v. Turkey* App no 30471/08 (ECtHR 22 September 2009) 130; *M. v. Germany* App no 19359/04 (ECtHR 17 December 2009) 90; *Rantsev v. Cyprus and Russia* App no 25965/04 (ECtHR 7 January 2010) 322–323; *Gatt v. Malta* App no 28221/08 (ECtHR 27 July 2010) 40; *Kharin v. Russia* App no 37345/03 (ECtHR 3 February 2011) 35; *Kováčik v. Slovakia* App no 50903/06 (ECtHR 29 November 2011) 49; *Stanev v. Bulgaria* App no 36760/06 (ECtHR Grand Chamber 17 January 2012) 143; *Reiner v. Germany* App no 28527/08 (ECtHR 19 January 2012) 82; *Creangă v. Romania* App no 29226/03 (ECtHR Grand Chamber 23 February 2012) 84; *Lolova-Karadzhova v. Bulgaria* App no 17835/07 (ECtHR 27 March 2012) 28; *James, Wells and Lee v. United Kingdom* App nos 25119/09, 57715/09 and 57877/09 (ECtHR 18 September 2012) 188; *Kakabadze and others v. Georgia* App no 1484/07 (ECtHR 2 October 2012) 62; *Ostendorf v. Germany* App no 15598/08 (ECtHR 7 March 2013) 74; *M.A. v. Cyprus* App no 41872/10 (ECtHR 23 July 2013) 197; *Suso Musa v. Malta* App no 42337/12 (ECtHR 23 July 2013) 92; *H.W. v. Germany* App no 17167/11 (ECtHR 19 September 2013) 64; *Del Rio Prada v. Spain* App no 42750/09 (ECtHR Grand Chamber 21 October 2013) 125; *Ruslan Yakovenko v. Ukraine* App no 5425/11 (ECtHR 4 June 2015) 57; *Bergmann v. Germany* App no 23279/14 (ECtHR 7 January 2016) 101; *J.N. v. United Kingdom* App no 37289/12 (ECtHR 19 May 2016) 75; *Khlaifia and others v. Italy* App no 16483/12 (ECtHR Grand Chamber 15 December 2016) 91; *Ivan Todorov v. Bulgaria* App no 71545/11 (ECtHR 19 January 2017) 33; *Merabishvili v. Georgia* App no 72508/13 (ECtHR Grand Chamber 28 November 2017), 186; *Paci v. Belgium* App no 45597/09 (ECtHR 17 April 2018) 64; *Ilnseher v. Germany* App nos 10211/12 and 27505/14 (ECtHR Grand Chamber 4 December 2018) 135; *Rooman v. Belgium* App no 18052/11 (ECtHR Grand Chamber 31 January 2019) 190; *Aboya Boa Jean v. Malta* App no 62676/16 (ECtHR 2 April 2019) 54; *Zelčs v. Latvia* App no 65367/16 (ECtHR 20 February 2020) 51; *Aftanache v. Romania* App no 999/19 (ECtHR 26 May 2020) 89; *Denis and Irvine v. Belgium* App nos 62819/17 and 63921/17 (ECtHR Grand Chamber 1 June 2021) 126; *Kerem Çiftçi v. Turkey* App no 35205/09 (ECtHR 21 September 2021) 27. See also: Elizabeth Gibson-Morgan, 'Police Custody in England and France: A Lawful Deprivation of Liberty?' in Marion Charret-Del Bove and Fabrice Mourlon (eds), *Pre-trial detention in 20th and 21st Century Common Law and Civil Law Systems* (Cambridge Scholars Publishing 2014) 120; Sottiaux (n 27) 200.

164 *Pantea v. Romania* App no 33343/96 (ECtHR 3 June 2003) 220; *I.I. v. Bulgaria* App no 44082/98 (ECtHR 9 June 2005) 88; *Creangă v. Romania* App no 29226/03 (ECtHR Grand Chamber 23 February 2012) 101; *H.W. v. Germany* App no 17167/11 (ECtHR 19 September 2013) 64; *Popoviciu v. Romania* App no 52942/09 (ECtHR 1 March 2016) 62; *Selahattin Demirtaş v. Turkey (no. 2)* App no 14305/17 (ECtHR Grand Chamber 22 December 2020) 313; *Denis and Irvine v. Belgium* App nos 62819/17 and 63921/17 (ECtHR Grand Chamber 1 June 2021). This means that in cases where Art. 5(1) of the Convention is at stake, the Court must exercise a certain power to review whether national law has been observed.

sufficient.[165] In turn, national law must be in conformity with the Convention,

165 *Winterwerp v. Netherlands* App no 6301/73 (ECtHR 24 October 1979) 39; *X. v. United Kingdom* App no 7215/75 (ECtHR 5 November 1981) 43; *Ashingdane v. United Kingdom* App no 8225/78 (ECtHR 28 May 1985) 44; *Bozano v. France* App no 9990/82 (ECtHR 18 December 1986) 54; *Weeks v. United Kingdom* App no 9787/82 (ECtHR 2 March 1987) 42; *Bouamar v. Belgium* App no 9106/80 (ECtHR 29 February 1988) 47; *Van der Leer v. Netherlands* App no 12/1988/156/210 (ECtHR 21 February 1990) 22; *Wassink v. Netherlands* App no 12535/86 (ECtHR 27 September 1990) 24; *Kemmache v. France (no 3)* App no 17621/91 (ECtHR 24 November 1994) 37 and 42; *Benham v. United Kingdom* App no 19380/92 (ECtHR 10 June 1996) 40; *Amuur v. France* App no 19776/92 (ECtHR 25 June 1996) 50; *Chahal v. United Kingdom* App no 22414/93 (ECtHR Grand Chamber 15 November 1996) 118; *K.-F. v. Germany* App no 144/1996/765/962 (ECtHR 27 November 1997) 63; *Aerts v. Belgium* App no 61/1997/845/1051 (ECtHR 30 July 1998) 46; *Steel and others v. United Kingdom* App no 67/1997/851/1058) (ECtHR 23 September 1998) 54; *Assenov and others v. Bulgaria* App no 90/1997/874/1086 (ECtHR 28 October 1998) 139; *Riera Blume and others v. Spain* App no 37680/97 (ECtHR 14 October 1999) 31; *Baranowski v. Poland* App no 28358/95 (ECtHR 28 March 2000) 50–51; *Witold Litwa v. Poland* App no 26629/95 (ECtHR 4 April 2000) 72–73; *Ječius v. Lithuania* App no 34578/97 (ECtHR 31 July 2000) 56; *Čonka v. Belgium* App no 51564/99 (ECtHR 5 February 2002) 39; *Stafford v. United Kingdom* App no 46295/99 (ECtHR Grand Chamber 28 May 2002) 63; *Vasileva v. Denmark* App no 52792/99 (ECtHR 25 September 2003) 32; *Novotka v. Slovakia* App no 47244/99 (ECtHR Decision on admissibility 4 November 2003) 2; *H.L. v. United Kingdom* App no 45508/99 (ECtHR 5 October 2004) 114; *Enhorn v. Sweden* App no 56529/00 (ECtHR 25 January 2005) 36; *Epple v. Germany* App no 77909/01 (ECtHR 24 March 2005) 33; *Öcalan v. Turkey* app no 46221/99 (ECtHR Grand Chamber 12 May 2005) 83; *Ambruszkiewicz v. Poland* App no 38797/03 (ECtHR 4 May 2006) 27; *Zervudacki v. France* App no 73947/01 (ECtHR 27 July 2006) 42–43; *Nasrulloyev v. Russia* App no 656/06 (ECtHR 11 October 2007) 70; *Ladent v. Poland* App no 11036/03 (ECtHR 18 March 2008) 47–48; *Varga v. Romania* App no 73957/01 (ECtHR 1 April 2008) 45; *Foka v. Turkey* App no 28940/95 (ECtHR 24 June 2008) 80; *Kandzhov v. Bulgaria* App no 68294/01 (ECtHR 6 November 2008) 55; *A. and others v. United Kingdom* App no 3455/05 (ECtHR Grand Chamber 19 February 2009) 164; *Krejčíř v. Czech Republic* App no 39298/04 and 8723/05 (ECtHR 26 March 2009) 76; *Stephens v. Malta (no. 1)* App no 11956/07 (ECtHR 21 April 2009) 61; *Oral and Atabay v. Turkey* App no 39686/02 (ECtHR 23 June 2009) 26; *Mooren v. Germany* App no 11364/03 (ECtHR Grand Chamber 9 July 2009) 72; *Abdolkhani and Karimnia v. Turkey* App no 30471/08 (ECtHR 22 September 2009) 130; *Medvedyev and others v. France* App no 3394/03 (ECtHR Grand Chamber 29 March 2010) 79; *Garayev v. Azerbaijan* App no 53688/08 (ECtHR 10 June 2010) 95; *Gatt v. Malta* App no 28221/08 (ECtHR 27 July 2010) 40; *Louled Massoud v. Malta* App no 24340/08 (ECtHR 27 July 2010) 61; *Iskandarov v. Russia* App no 17185/05 (ECtHR 23 September 2010) 144–145; *Khayredinov v. Ukraine* App no 38717/04 (ECtHR 14 October 2010) 27; *Osypenko v. Ukraine* App no 4634/04 (ECtHR 9 November 2010) 50; *Kharin v. Russia* App no 37345/03 (ECtHR 3 February 2011) 35; *Soare and others v. Romania* App no 24329/02 (ECtHR 22 February 2011) 232; *Sarigiannis v. Italy* App no 14569/05 (ECtHR 5 April 2011) 39; *Oshurko v. Ukraine* App no 33108/05 (ECtHR 8 September 2011) 97; *Kováčik v. Slovakia* App no 50903/06 (ECtHR 29 November 2011) 49; *Korneykova v. Ukraine* App no 39884/05 (ECtHR 19 January 2012) 33; *Reiner v. Germany* App no 28527/08 (ECtHR 19 January 2012) 82–83; *Creangă v. Romania* App no 29226/03 (ECtHR Grand Chamber 23 February 2012) 84; *Lolova-Karadzhova v. Bulgaria* App no 17835/07 (ECtHR 27 March 2012) 28; *Simons v. Belgium* App no 71407/10 (ECtHR 28 August 2012) 28; *James, Wells and Lee v. United Kingdom* App nos 25119/09, 57715/09 and 57877/09 (ECtHR 18 September 2012) 190–191; *Kakabadze and others v. Georgia* App no 1484/07 (ECtHR 2 October 2012) 62–63; *Plesó v. Hungary* App no 41242/08 (ECtHR 2 October 2012) 59; *Yefimenko v. Russia* App no 152/04 (ECtHR 12 February 2013) 101; *Ostendorf v. Germany* App no 15598/08 (ECtHR 7 March 2013) 74; *M.A. v. Cyprus* App no 41872/10 (ECtHR 23 July 2013) 197; *Suso Musa v. Malta* App no 42337/12 (ECtHR 23 July 2013) 92; *Petkov and Profirov v. Bulgaria* App nos 50027/08 and 50781/09 (ECtHR 24 June

including the general principles expressed or implied in it.[166] These implied general principles are: '*the principle of the rule of law and, connected to the latter, that of legal certainty, the principle of proportionality and the principle of protection against arbitrariness which is, moreover, the very aim of Article 5.*'[167]

42. Rule of law – The preambule of the ECHR explicitly refers to the rule of law, which is part of the core principles of the ECHR.[168] In its case law on

2014) 41; *Ruslan Yakovenko v. Ukraine* App no 5425/11 (ECtHR 4 June 2015) 57–58; *J.N. v. United Kingdom* App no 37289/12 (ECtHR 19 May 2016) 76; *Strogan v. Ukraine* App no 30198/11 (ECtHR 6 October 2016) 86; *Khlaifia and others v. Italy* App no 16483/12 (ECtHR Grand Chamber 15 December 2016) 91; *Ivan Todorov v. Bulgaria* App no 71545/11 (ECtHR 19 January 2017) 33; *Rozhkov v. Russia (No. 2)* App no 38898/04 (ECtHR 31 January 2017) 78; *Oravec v. Croatia* App no 51249/11 (ECtHR 11 July 2017) 45–47; *Mehmet Hasan Altan v. Turkey* App no 13237/17 (ECtHR 20 March 2018) 137; *Şahin Alpay v. Turkey* App no 16538/17 (ECtHR 20 March 2018) 116; *Paci v. Belgium* App no 45597/09 (ECtHR 17 April 2018) 64; *Ilnseher v. Germany* App nos 10211/12 and 27505/14 (ECtHR Grand Chamber 4 December 2018) 135–136; *Rooman v. Belgium* App no 18052/11 (ECtHR Grand Chamber 31 January 2019) 190; *Al Husin v. Bosnia and Herzegovina (no. 2)* App no 10112/16 (ECtHR 25 June 2019) 97; *Zelčs v. Latvia* App no 65367/16 (ECtHR 20 February 2020) 51–52; *Aftanache v. Romania* App no 999/19 (ECtHR 26 May 2020) 89–90; *Denis and Irvine v. Belgium* App nos 62819/17 and 63921/17 (ECtHR Grand Chamber 1 June 2021) 126–127; *Kerem Çiftçi v. Turkey* App no 35205/09 (ECtHR 21 September 2021) 27.

166 *Winterwerp v. Netherlands* App no 6301/73 (ECtHR 24 October 1979) 45; *Brogan and others v. United Kingdom* App nos 11209/84, 11234/84, 11266/84 and 11386/85 (ECtHR Plenary 29 November 1988) 65; *Kemmache v. France (no 3)* App no 17621/91 (ECtHR 24 November 1994) 37; *Chahal v. United Kingdom* App no 22414/93 (ECtHR Grand Chamber 15 November 1996) 127; *Baranowski v. Poland* App no 28358/95 (ECtHR 28 March 2000) 51; *Ječius v. Lithuania* App no 34578/97 (ECtHR 31 July 2000) 56; *Novotka v. Slovakia* App no 47244/99 (ECtHR Decision on admissibility 4 November 2003) 2; *Ambruszkiewicz v. Poland* App no 38797/03 (ECtHR 4 May 2006) 27; *Nasrulloyev v. Russia* App no 656/06 (ECtHR 11 October 2007) 71; *Varga v. Romania* App no 73957/01 (ECtHR 1 April 2008) 46; *A. and others v. United Kingdom* App no 3455/05 (ECtHR Grand Chamber 19 February 2009) 202; *Mooren v. Germany* App no 11364/03 (ECtHR Grand Chamber 9 July 2009) 72; *Garayev v. Azerbaijan* App no 53688/08 (ECtHR 10 June 2010) 96; *Louled Massoud v. Malta* App no 24340/08 (ECtHR 27 July 2010) 39; *Kováčik v. Slovakia* App no 50903/06 (ECtHR 29 November 2011) 49; *Simons v. Belgium* App no 71407/10 (ECtHR 28 August 2012) 28; *Plesó v. Hungary* App no 41242/08 (ECtHR 2 October 2012) 59; *M.A. v. Cyprus* App no 41872/10 (ECtHR 23 July 2013) 198; *Ruslan Yakovenko v. Ukraine* App no 5425/11 (ECtHR 4 June 2015) 58; *J.N. v. United Kingdom* App no 37289/12 (ECtHR 19 May 2016) 76; *Khlaifia and others v. Italy* App no 16483/12 (ECtHR Grand Chamber 15 December 2016) 128; *Ivan Todorov v. Bulgaria* App no 71545/11 (ECtHR 19 January 2017) 33; *Oravec v. Croatia* App no 51249/11 (ECtHR 11 July 2017) 47; *Etute v. Luxembourg* App no 18233/16 (ECtHR 30 January 2018) 24; *Mehmet Hasan Altan v. Turkey* App no 13237/17 (ECtHR 20 March 2018) 137; *Şahin Alpay v. Turkey* App no 16538/17 (ECtHR 20 March 2018) 116; *Paci v. Belgium* App no 45597/09 (ECtHR 17 April 2018) 65; *Moustahi v. France* App no 9347/14 (ECtHR 25 June 2020) 100. See also: Dhont (n 121) 289; Macken (n 95) 52.

167 Guide on Article 5 of the European Convention on Human Rights: Right to Liberty and Security (2020) 32. See also: Simons v. Belgium App no 71407/10 (ECtHR 28 August 2012) 32; Denis and Irvine v. Belgium App nos 62819/17 and 63921/17 (ECtHR Grand Chamber 1 June 2021) 127.

168 Preambule to the ECHR. See also: *Rotaru v. Republic of Moldova* App no 26764/12 (ECtHR 8 December 2020) 23; Gibson-Morgan (n 163) 120; Philip Traest, 'Rechts(on)zekerheid

Article 5 ECHR, the ECtHR consistently refers to the rule of law[169] as well as the principle of legal certainty,[170] which is a central element of the rule of law.[171] However, its analysis seems to focus exclusively on legal certainty. The Court often states that is essential for domestic law to clearly define the conditions for detention and that domestic law should be sufficiently accessible, precise and foreseeable in its application.[172] It is therefore required that the person, if need

in materieel en formeel strafrecht en strafrechtelijk legaliteitsbeginsel' [1993–1994] Rechtskundig Weekblad 1190, 1204.

169 *Winterwerp v. Netherlands* App no 6301/73 (ECtHR 24 October 1979) 39; *Amuur v. France* App no 19776/92 (ECtHR 25 June 1996) 50; *Stafford v. United Kingdom* App no 46295/99 (ECtHR Grand Chamber 28 May 2002) 63; *McKay v. United Kingdom* App no 543/03 (ECtHR Grand Chamber 3 October 2006) 30; *Nasrulloyev v. Russia* App no 656/06 (ECtHR 11 October 2007) 71; *Kafkaris v. Cyprus* App no 21906/04 (ECtHR Grand Chamber 12 February 2008) 116; *Mooren v. Germany* App no 11364/03 (ECtHR Grand Chamber 9 July 2009) 76; *Abdolkhani and Karimnia v. Turkey* App no 30471/08 (ECtHR 22 September 2009) 130; *M. v. Germany* App no 19359/04 (ECtHR 17 December 2009) 90; *Medvedyev and others v. France* App no 3394/03 (ECtHR Grand Chamber 29 March 2010) 117; *Louled Massoud v. Malta* App no 24340/08 (ECtHR 27 July 2010) 61; *Kakabadze and others v. Georgia* App no 1484/07 (ECtHR 2 October 2012) 62; *Plesó v. Hungary* App no 41242/08 (ECtHR 2 October 2012) 59; *H.W. v. Germany* App no 17167/11 (ECtHR 19 September 2013) 66; *Del Rio Prada v. Spain* App no 42750/09 (ECtHR Grand Chamber 21 October 2013) 125; *Magee and others v. United Kingdom* App nos 26289/12 and 2 others (ECtHR 12 May 2015) 73; *Buzadji v. Republic of Moldova* App no 23755/07 (ECtHR Grand Chamber 5 July 2016) 84; *Khlaifia and others v. Italy* App no 16483/12 (ECtHR Grand Chamber 15 December 2016) 91; *Oravec v. Croatia* App no 51249/11 (ECtHR 11 July 2017) 47; *Merabishvili v. Georgia* App no 72508/13 (ECtHR Grand Chamber 28 November 2017) 186; *Mehmet Hasan Altan v. Turkey* App no 13237/17 (ECtHR 20 March 2018) 137; *Şahin Alpay v. Turkey* App no 16538/17 (ECtHR 20 March 2018) 116; *Paci v. Belgium* App no 45597/09 (ECtHR 17 April 2018) 65; *Zelčs v. Latvia* App no 65367/16 (ECtHR 20 February 2020) 51; *Selahattin Demirtaş v. Turkey (no. 2)* App no 14305/17 (ECtHR Grand Chamber 22 December 2020) 312; *Aftanache v. Romania* App no 999/19 (ECtHR 26 May 2020) 90.

170 *Baranowski v. Poland* App no 28358/95 (ECtHR 28 March 2000) 52; *Ječius v. Lithuania* App no 34578/97 (ECtHR 31 July 2000) 56; *Enhorn v. Sweden* App no 56529/00 (ECtHR 25 January 2005) 36; *Zervudacki v. France* App no 73947/01 (ECtHR 27 July 2006) 43; *Nasrulloyev v. Russia* App no 656/06 (ECtHR 11 October 2007) 71; *Varga v. Romania* App no 73957/01 (ECtHR 1 April 2008) 46; *Paladi v. Moldova* App no 39806/05 (ECtHR Grand Chamber 10 March 2009) 74; *Mooren v. Germany* App no 11364/03 (ECtHR Grand Chamber 9 July 2009) 72; *Garayev v. Azerbaijan* App no 53688/08 (ECtHR 10 June 2010) 96; *Oshurko v. Ukraine* App no 33108/05 (ECtHR 8 September 2011) 98; *Kováčik v. Slovakia* App no 50903/06 (ECtHR 29 November 2011) 49; *Korneykova v. Ukraine* App no 39884/05 (ECtHR 19 January 2012) 33; *J.N. v. United Kingdom* App no 37289/12 (ECtHR 19 May 2016) 76; *Ivan Todorov v. Bulgaria* App no 71545/11 (ECtHR 19 January 2017) 33; *Oravec v. Croatia* App no 51249/11 (ECtHR 11 July 2017) 47; *Mehmet Hasan Altan v. Turkey* App no 13237/17 (ECtHR 20 March 2018) 137; *Şahin Alpay v. Turkey* App no 16538/17 (ECtHR 20 March 2018) 116.

171 Christina Peristeridou, *The Principle of Legality in European Criminal Law* (Intersentia 2015) 55; Clive Walker, 'Counterterrorism within the Rule of Law? Rhetoric and Reality with Special Reference to the United Kingdom' (2021) 33 Terrorism and Political Violence 338, 339–341.

172 *Amuur v. France* App no 19776/92 (ECtHR 25 June 1996) 50; *Baranowski v. Poland* App no 28358/95 (ECtHR 28 March 2000) 52; *Ječius v. Lithuania* App no 34578/97 (ECtHR 31 July 2000) 56; *Hilda Hafsteinsdóttir v. Iceland* App no 40905/98, (ECtHR 8 June 2004) 51; *Enhorn v. Sweden* App no 56529/00 (ECtHR 25 January 2005) 36; *Zervudacki v. France* App no

be with appropriate advice, can foresee the consequences of their actions to a degree that is reasonable in the circumstances.[173] This is also referred to as the 'quality of law' or in some cases as 'safeguards against arbitrariness'. Examples of relevant factors in this assessment are the existence of clear legal provisions for ordering detention, for extending detention, and for setting time-limits for detention[174] and the existence of an effective remedy by which the applicant can contest the lawfulness and length of his continuing detention.[175, 176]

73947/01 (ECtHR 27 July 2006) 43; *Nasrulloyev v. Russia* App no 656/06 (ECtHR 11 October 2007) 71; *Varga v. Romania* App no 73957/01 (ECtHR 1 April 2008) 46; *Paladi v. Moldova* App no 39806/05 (ECtHR Grand Chamber 10 March 2009) 74; *Mooren v. Germany* App no 11364/03 (ECtHR Grand Chamber 9 July 2009) 76; *M. v. Germany* App no 19359/04 (ECtHR 17 December 2009) 90; *Medvedyev and others v. France* App no 3394/03 (ECtHR Grand Chamber 29 March 2010) 80; *Garayev v. Azerbaijan* App no 53688/08 (ECtHR 10 June 2010) 96; *Louled Massoud v. Malta* App no 24340/08 (ECtHR 27 July 2010) 61; *Sarigiannis v. Italy* App no 14569/05 (ECtHR 5 April 2011) 39; *Oshurko v. Ukraine* App no 33108/05 (ECtHR 8 September 2011) 98; *Korneykova v. Ukraine* App no 39884/05 (ECtHR 19 January 2012) 33; *Creangă v. Romania* App no 29226/03 (ECtHR Grand Chamber 23 February 2012) 101 and 120; *Kakabadze and others v. Georgia* App no 1484/07 (ECtHR 2 October 2012) 62 and 68; *M.A. v. Cyprus* App no 41872/10 (ECtHR 23 July 2013) 198; *H.W. v. Germany* App no 17167/11 (ECtHR 19 September 2013) 66; *Del Rio Prada v. Spain* App no 42750/09 (ECtHR Grand Chamber 21 October 2013) 125; *Ruslan Yakovenko v. Ukraine* App no 5425/11 (ECtHR 4 June 2015) 58; *J.N. v. United Kingdom* App no 37289/12 (ECtHR 19 May 2016) 77; *Ivan Todorov v. Bulgaria* App no 71545/11 (ECtHR 19 January 2017) 33; *Oravec v. Croatia* App no 51249/11 (ECtHR 11 July 2017) 47; *Merabishvili v. Georgia* App no 72508/13 (ECtHR Grand Chamber 28 November 2017) 186; *Paci v. Belgium* App no 45597/09 (ECtHR 17 April 2018) 65; *Zelčs v. Latvia* App no 65367/16 (ECtHR 20 February 2020) 51; *Aftanache v. Romania* App no 999/19 (ECtHR 26 May 2020) 90; *Moustahi v. France* App no 9347/14 (ECtHR 25 June 2020) 90; *Denis and Irvine v. Belgium* App nos 62819/17 and 63921/17 (ECtHR Grand Chamber 1 June 2021) 128. See also: Sottiaux (n 27) 201.

173 *Steel and others v. United Kingdom* App no 67/1997/851/1058 (ECtHR 23 September 1998) 54; *Baranowski v. Poland* App no 28358/95 (ECtHR 28 March 2000) 52; *Ječius v. Lithuania* App no 34578/97 (ECtHR 31 July 2000) 56; *Hilda Hafsteinsdóttir v. Iceland* App no 40905/98, (ECtHR 8 June 2004) 51; *H.L. v. United Kingdom* App no 45508/99 (ECtHR 5 October 2004) 114; *Enhorn v. Sweden* App no 56529/00 (ECtHR 25 January 2005) 36; *Varga v. Romania* App no 73957/01 (ECtHR 1 April 2008) 46; *Paladi v. Moldova* App no 39806/05 (ECtHR Grand Chamber 10 March 2009) 74; *Stephens v. Malta (no. 1)* App no 11956/07 (ECtHR 21 April 2009) 61; *M. v. Germany* App no 19359/04 (ECtHR 17 December 2009) 90; *Medvedyev and others v. France* App no 3394/03 (ECtHR Grand Chamber 29 March 2010) 80; *Garayev v. Azerbaijan* App no 53688/08 (ECtHR 10 June 2010) 96; *Oshurko v. Ukraine* App no 33108/05 (ECtHR 8 September 2011) 98; *Korneykova v. Ukraine* App no 39884/05 (ECtHR 19 January 2012) 33; *Creangă v. Romania* App no 29226/03 (ECtHR Grand Chamber 23 February 2012) 120; *Kakabadze and others v. Georgia* App no 1484/07 (ECtHR 2 October 2012) 62; *Del Rio Prada v. Spain* App no 42750/09 (ECtHR Grand Chamber 21 October 2013) 125; *Ruslan Yakovenko v. Ukraine* App no 5425/11 (ECtHR 4 June 2015) 58; *Khlaifia and others v. Italy* App no 16483/12 (ECtHR Grand Chamber 15 December 2016) 92; *Ivan Todorov v. Bulgaria* App no 71545/11 (ECtHR 19 January 2017) 33; *Oravec v. Croatia* App no 51249/11 (ECtHR 11 July 2017) 53; *Zelčs v. Latvia* App no 65367/16 (ECtHR 20 February 2020) 51; *Aftanache v. Romania* App no 999/19 (ECtHR 26 May 2020) 90.

174 *Abdolkhani and Karimnia v. Turkey* App no 30471/08 (ECtHR 22 September 2009) 135; *Garayev v. Azerbaijan* App no 53688/08 (ECtHR 10 June 2010) 99.

175 *Louled Massoud v. Malta* App no 24340/08 (ECtHR 27 July 2010) 71.

176 *J.N. v. United Kingdom* App no 37289/12 (ECtHR 19 May 2016) 77.

Finally, promptness or speediness of the judicial supervision is of the essence as well.[177]

43. PROPORTIONALITY – The proportionality principle is a little less straightforward. In its case law, the Court states that there needs to be a relationship of proportionality between the ground of detention relied on and the detention in question.[178] However, it adds that the scope of the proportionality test varies depending on the type of detention.[179] Therefore, the rules on proportionality will be included in the discussion under the different relevant subparagraphs.[180] In certain cases the Court also states that a measure is only justified where other less severe measures have been found to be insufficient.[181] This is what is traditionally called subsidiarity, but it can also be seen as part of a suitability and necessity test and thus proportionality (see no. 98).[182] Here as well though, the test varies depending on the type of detention. The case law concerning Article 5(1)(f) for example, explicitly states that detention with view to deportation or extradition does not need to be reasonably considered necessary to avoid the perpetration of offences or absconding.[183]

---

177 *McKay v. United Kingdom* App no 543/03 (ECtHR Grand Chamber 3 October 2006) 30; *Selahattin Demirtaş v. Turkey (no. 2)* App no 14305/17 (ECtHR Grand Chamber 22 December 2020) 312.

178 *James, Wells and Lee v. United Kingdom* App nos 25119/09, 57715/09 and 57877/09 (ECtHR 18 September 2012) 195; *Ruslan Yakovenko v. Ukraine* App no 5425/11 (ECtHR 4 June 2015) 61. See also: *A. and others v. United Kingdom* App no 3455/05 (ECtHR Grand Chamber 19 February 2009) 164.

179 *James, Wells and Lee v. United Kingdom* App nos 25119/09, 57715/09 and 57877/09 (ECtHR 18 September 2012) 195; *Ruslan Yakovenko v. Ukraine* App no 5425/11 (ECtHR 4 June 2015) 61.

180 In the case law on subparagraph (e), which will not be discussed in detail, the necessity in the circumstances is an often-recurring issue. See e.g.: *Witold Litwa v. Poland* App no 26629/95 (ECtHR 4 April 2000) 78; *Enhorn v. Sweden* App no 56529/00 (ECtHR 25 January 2005) 36; *Kharin v. Russia* App no 37345/03 (ECtHR 3 February 2011) 35; *Plesó v. Hungary* App no 41242/08 (ECtHR 2 October 2012) 62.

181 *Stanev v. Bulgaria* App no 36760/06 (ECtHR Grand Chamber 17 January 2012), 143; *Ilnseher v. Germany* App nos 10211/12 and 27505/14 (ECtHR Grand Chamber 4 December 2018) 137; *Denis and Irvine v. Belgium* App nos 62819/17 and 63921/17 (ECtHR Grand Chamber 1 June 2021) 130. In their book, Van Dijk and colleagues also state that it should be examined whether less severe measures could have sufficed. They link this to the protection against arbitrariness. See: Van Dijk and others (n 107) 449. Murdoch states that the lawfulnenss requirement includes the two traditional requirements of 'necessary in a democratic society' and 'prescribed by law'. See: Murdoch (n 122) 499–500.

182 Sébastien Van Drooghenbroeck, 'Note relative à l'application des principes de proportionnalité et subsidiarité en matière pénale dans de droit de la Convention européenne des droits de l'Homme', Annex 2.7 to the Report on behalf of the Committee on Justice on the Bill on the Code of Criminal Procedure, *Parl.St.* Senaat 2005–06, no. 3–450/20, (1398) 1398; De Coensel, *Counter-Terrorism & Criminal Law: A Normative Legitimacy Test of Terrorism-Related Offences on Expression, Information and Movement* (n 1) 97 and 122; Gabriel Hallevy, *A Modern Treatise on the Principle of Legality in Criminal Law* (Springer Berlin Heidelberg 2010) 12.

183 See e.g.: *Chahal v. United Kingdom* App no 22414/93 (ECtHR Grand Chamber 15 November 1996) 112; *Čonka v. Belgium* App no 51564/99 (ECtHR 5 February 2002) 38; *Nasrulloyev v.*

44. Arbitrariness – As the purpose of Article 5 is protection against arbitrariness, those who allege Article 5 violations often claim that Member State regimes were arbitrary or allowed for arbitrary deprivations of liberty.[184]

Russia App no 656/06 (ECtHR 11 October 2007) 69; *Al Husin v. Bosnia and Herzegovina (no. 2)* App no 10112/16 (ECtHR 25 June 2019) 97. See also: Dhont (n 121) 328–329; Mueller (n 32) 329.

184 *Winterwerp v. Netherlands* App no 6301/73 (ECtHR 24 October 1979) 39; *Ashingdane v. United Kingdom* App no 8225/78 (ECtHR 28 May 1985) 44; *Bozano v. France* App no 9990/82 (ECtHR 18 December 1986) 54; *Bouamar v. Belgium* App no 9106/80 (ECtHR 29 February 1988) 47; *Van der Leer v. Netherlands* App no 12/1988/156/210 (ECtHR 21 February 1990) 22; *Wassink v. Netherlands* App no 12535/86 (ECtHR 27 September 1990) 24; *Kemmache v. France (no 3)* App no 17621/91 (ECtHR 24 November 1994) 37; *Benham v. United Kingdom* App no 19380/92 (ECtHR 10 June 1996) 40; *Amuur v. France* App no 19776/92 (ECtHR 25 June 1996) 50; *Chahal v. United Kingdom* App no 22414/93 (ECtHR Grand Chamber 15 November 1996) 118; *K.-F. v. Germany* App no 144/1996/765/962 (ECtHR 27 November 1997) 63; *Aerts v. Belgium* App no 61/1997/845/1051 (ECtHR 30 July 1998) 46; *Assenov and others v. Bulgaria* App no 90/1997/874/1086 (ECtHR 28 October 1998) 139; *Riera Blume and others v. Spain* App no 37680/97 (ECtHR 14 October 1999) 31; *Baranowski v. Poland* App no 28358/95 (ECtHR 28 March 2000) 51; *Witold Litwa v. Poland* App no 26629/95 (ECtHR 4 April 2000) 73; *Ječius v. Lithuania* App no 34578/97 (ECtHR 31 July 2000) 56; *Čonka v. Belgium* App no 51564/99 (ECtHR 5 February 2002) 39; *Stafford v. United Kingdom* App no 46295/99 (ECtHR Grand Chamber 28 May 2002) 63; *Vasileva v. Denmark* App no 52792/99 (ECtHR 25 September 2003) 32; *H.L. v. United Kingdom* App no 45508/99 (ECtHR 5 October 2004) 115; *Enhorn v. Sweden* App no 56529/00 (ECtHR 25 January 2005) 36; *Epple v. Germany* App no 77909/01 (ECtHR 24 March 2005) 33; *Ambruszkiewicz v. Poland* App no 38797/03 (ECtHR 4 May 2006) 27; *Nasrulloyev v. Russia* App no 656/06 (ECtHR 11 October 2007) 70; *Saadi v. United Kingdom* App no 13229/03 (ECtHR Grand Chamber 29 January 2008) 67; *Kafkaris v. Cyprus* App no 21906/04 (ECtHR Grand Chamber 12 February 2008) 116; *Ladent v. Poland* App no 11036/03 (ECtHR 18 March 2008) 48; *Varga v. Romania* App no 73957/01 (ECtHR 1 April 2008) 45; *Foka v. Turkey* App no 28940/95 (ECtHR 24 June 2008) 80; *Kandzhov v. Bulgaria* App no 68294/01 (ECtHR 6 November 2008) 55; *A. and others v. United Kingdom* App no 3455/05 (ECtHR Grand Chamber 19 February 2009) 164; *Krejčíř v. Czech Republic* App no 39298/04 and 8723/05 (ECtHR 26 March 2009) 76; *Stephens v. Malta (no. 1)* App no 11956/07 (ECtHR 21 April 2009) 61; *Oral and Atabay v. Turkey* App no 39686/02 (ECtHR 23 June 2009) 26; *Mooren v. Germany* App no 11364/03 (ECtHR Grand Chamber 9 July 2009) 72; *Abdolkhani and Karimnia v. Turkey* App no 30471/08 (ECtHR 22 September 2009) 130; *M. v. Germany* App no 19359/04 (ECtHR 17 December 2009) 91; *Rantsev v. Cyprus and Russia* App no 25965/04 (ECtHR 7 January 2010) 322; *Medvedyev and others v. France* App no 3394/03 (ECtHR Grand Chamber 29 March 2010) 79; *Garayev v. Azerbaijan* App no 53688/08 (ECtHR 10 June 2010) 95; *Gatt v. Malta* App no 28221/08 (ECtHR 27 July 2010) 40; *Iskandarov v. Russia* App no 17185/05 (ECtHR 23 September 2010) 145; *Osypenko v. Ukraine* App no 4634/04 (ECtHR 9 November 2010) 50; *Kharin v. Russia* App no 37345/03 (ECtHR 3 February 2011) 35; *Soare and others v. Romania* App no 24329/02 (ECtHR 22 February 2011) 232; *Sarigiannis v. Italy* App no 14569/05 (ECtHR 5 April 2011) 39; *Oshurko v. Ukraine* App no 33108/05 (ECtHR 8 September 2011) 97; *Kováčik v. Slovakia* App no 50903/06 (ECtHR 29 November 2011) 49; *Stanev v. Bulgaria* App no 36760/06 (ECtHR Grand Chamber 17 January 2012) 143; *Korneykova v. Ukraine* App no 39884/05 (ECtHR 19 January 2012) 33; *Reiner v. Germany* App no 28527/08 (ECtHR 19 January 2012) 83; *Lolova-Karadzhova v. Bulgaria* App no 17835/07 (ECtHR 27 March 2012) 28; *Creangă v. Romania* App no 29226/03 (ECtHR Grand Chamber 23 February 2012) 84; *Kakabadze and others v. Georgia* App no 1484/07 (ECtHR 2 October 2012) 63; *Yefimenko v. Russia* App no 152/04 (ECtHR 12 February 2013) 101; *Ostendorf v. Germany* App no 15598/08 (ECtHR 7 March 2013) 74; *M.A. v. Cyprus* App no 41872/10 (ECtHR 23 July 2013) 197; *Suso Musa v. Malta* App no 42337/12 (ECtHR 23 July 2013) 92; *H.W. v. Germany* App no 17167/11 (ECtHR 19 September 2013) 67; *Petkov*

Regarding the notion of arbitrariness, concrete elements or indicators have been developed in the case law, varying to some extent depending on the type of detention.[185] First, if detention has an element of bad faith or deception on the part of the authorities, it is arbitrary.[186] The same goes when the authorities have not attempted to apply the relevant legislation correctly.[187] Second, both the order to detain and the execution of the detention must genuinely conform with the purpose of the restrictions permitted by the relevant subparagraph of

and Profirov v. Bulgaria App nos 50027/08 and 50781/09 (ECtHR 24 June 2014) 41; *Ruslan Yakovenko v. Ukraine* App no 5425/11 (ECtHR 4 June 2015) 59; *Bergmann v. Germany* App no 23279/14 (ECtHR 7 January 2016) 101–102; *J.N. v. United Kingdom* App no 37289/12 (ECtHR 19 May 2016) 78; *Strogan v. Ukraine* App no 30198/11 (ECtHR 6 October 2016) 86; *Khlaifia and others v. Italy* App no 16483/12 (ECtHR Grand Chamber 15 December 2016) 91; *Ivan Todorov v. Bulgaria* App no 71545/11 (ECtHR 19 January 2017) 33; R*ozhkov v. Russia (No. 2)* App no 38898/04 (ECtHR 31 January 2017) 78; *Oravec v. Croatia* App no 51249/11 (ECtHR 11 July 2017) 48; *Merabishvili v. Georgia* App no 72508/13 (ECtHR Grand Chamber 28 November 2017) 186; *Mehmet Hasan Altan v. Turkey* App no 13237/17 (ECtHR 20 March 2018) 137; *Şahin Alpay v. Turkey* App no 16538/17 (ECtHR 20 March 2018) 116; *Paci v. Belgium* App no 45597/09 (ECtHR 17 April 2018) 66; *S., V. and A. v. Denmark* App nos 35553/23, 36678/23 and 36711/12 (ECtHR Grand Chamber 22 October 2018) 74; *Ilnseher v. Germany* App nos 10211/12 and 27505/14 (ECtHR Grand Chamber 4 December 2018) 136; *Al Husin v. Bosnia and Herzegovina (no. 2)* App no 10112/16 (ECtHR 25 June 2019) 97; *Kerem Çiftçi v. Turkey* App no 35205/09 (ECtHR 21 September 2021) 27.

185 *Saadi v. United Kingdom* App no 13229/03 (ECtHR Grand Chamber 29 January 2008) 68; *Mooren v. Germany* App no 11364/03 (ECtHR Grand Chamber 9 July 2009) 77; *Iskandarov v. Russia* App no 17185/05 (ECtHR 23 September 2010) 145; *James, Wells and Lee v. United Kingdom* App nos 25119/09, 57715/09 and 57877/09 (ECtHR 18 September 2012) 191; *Plesó v. Hungary* App no 41242/08 (ECtHR 2 October 2012) 57; *Ruslan Yakovenko v. Ukraine* App no 5425/11 (ECtHR 4 June 2015) 60; *J.N. v. United Kingdom* App no 37289/12 (ECtHR 19 May 2016) 79; *S., V. and A. v. Denmark* App nos 35553/23, 36678/23 and 36711/12 (ECtHR Grand Chamber 22 October 2018) 75. See also: Webber (n 95) 53.

186 *Bozano v. France* App no 9990/82 (ECtHR 18 December 1986) 54–60; *Benham v. United Kingdom* App no 19380/92 (ECtHR 10 June 1996) 47; *Čonka v. Belgium* App no 51564/99 (ECtHR 5 February 2002) 42; *Saadi v. United Kingdom* App no 13229/03 (ECtHR Grand Chamber 29 January 2008) 69; *Mooren v. Germany* App no 11364/03 (ECtHR Grand Chamber 9 July 2009) 78; *Iskandarov v. Russia* App no 17185/05 (ECtHR 23 September 2010) 146; *James, Wells and Lee v. United Kingdom* App nos 25119/09, 57715/09 and 57877/09 (ECtHR 18 September 2012) 192; *Kakabadze and others v. Georgia* App no 1484/07 (ECtHR 2 October 2012) 63; *Plesó v. Hungary* App no 41242/08 (ECtHR 2 October 2012) 58; *Ruslan Yakovenko v. Ukraine* App no 5425/11 (ECtHR 4 June 2015) 60; *J.N. v. United Kingdom* App no 37289/12 (ECtHR 19 May 2016) 80; *S., V. and A. v. Denmark* App nos 35553/23, 36678/23 and 36711/12 (ECtHR Grand Chamber 22 October 2018) 76. Specifically for subparagraph (f) see: *A. and others v. United Kingdom* App no 3455/05 (ECtHR Grand Chamber 19 February 2009) 164; *Azimov v. Russia* App no 67474/11 (ECtHR 18 April 2013) 161; *Suso Musa v. Malta* App no 42337/12 (ECtHR 23 July 2013) 93; *Aboya Boa Jean v. Malta* App no 62676/16 (ECtHR 2 April 2019) 55; *Al Husin v. Bosnia and Herzegovina (no. 2)* App no 10112/16 (ECtHR 25 June 2019) 97.

187 *Benham v. United Kingdom* App no 19380/92 (ECtHR 10 June 1996) 47; *LIU v. Russia* App no 42086/05 (ECtHR 6 December 2007) 82; *Marturana v. Italy* App no 63154 (ECtHR 4 March 2008) 80; *Mooren v. Germany* App no 11364/03 (ECtHR Grand Chamber 9 July 2009) 78; *Kakabadze and others v. Georgia* App no 1484/07 (ECtHR 2 October 2012) 63; *Ruslan Yakovenko v. Ukraine* App no 5425/11 (ECtHR 4 June 2015) 60; *S., V. and A. v. Denmark* App nos 35553/23, 36678/23 and 36711/12 (ECtHR Grand Chamber 22 October 2018) 76.

Article 5(1).[188] Third, there must be some relationship between the ground of permitted deprivation of liberty and the place and conditions of detention.[189] This can be relevant in the context of subparagraph (a) for example, when prisoners have served the punitive element of their sentence and are kept in detention as a form of risk prevention (see no. 46). In this case, special measures, instruments or institutions need to be in place, in addition to those available to ordinary long-term prisoners, aimed at reducing the danger they present and at limiting the duration of their detention to what is strictly necessary.[190] In this, a reasonable balance has to be struck between this requirement of Article 5 ECHR and the efficient management of public funds.[191] This search for a fair balance between the rights of individuals and the general interest of the community is inherent in the whole of the ECHR.[192] Protection against arbitrariness can also

188 *Winterwerp v. Netherlands* App no 6301/73 (ECtHR 24 October 1979) 39; *Ashingdane v. United Kingdom* App no 8225/78 (ECtHR 28 May 1985) 44; *Bouamar v. Belgium* App no 9106/80 (ECtHR 29 February 1988) 50; *Saadi v. United Kingdom* App no 13229/03 (ECtHR Grand Chamber 29 January 2008) 69; *Kafkaris v. Cyprus* App no 21906/04 (ECtHR Grand Chamber 12 February 2008) 117; *James, Wells and Lee v. United Kingdom* App nos 25119/09, 57715/09 and 57877/09 (ECtHR 18 September 2012) 193; *Plesó v. Hungary* App no 41242/08 (ECtHR 2 October 2012) 58; *Azimov v. Russia* App no 67474/11 (ECtHR 18 April 2013) 164; *J.N. v. United Kingdom* App no 37289/12 (ECtHR 19 May 2016) 80; *Merabishvili v. Georgia* App no 72508/13 (ECtHR Grand Chamber 28 November 2017) 186; *S., V. and A. v. Denmark* App nos 35553/23, 36678/23 and 36711/12 (ECtHR Grand Chamber 22 October 2018) 91; *Rooman v. Belgium* App no 18052/11 (ECtHR Grand Chamber 31 January 2019) 190; *Denis and Irvine v. Belgium* App nos 62819/17 and 63921/17 (ECtHR Grand Chamber 1 June 2021) 131. Specifically for subparagraph (f) see: *A. and others v. United Kingdom* App no 3455/05 (ECtHR Grand Chamber 19 February 2009) 164. Specifically for subparagraph (e) see: *Enhorn v. Sweden* App no 56529/00 (ECtHR 25 January 2005) 42. See also: Art. 18 ECHR. This is of course hard to verify in practice.

189 *Ashingdane v. United Kingdom* App no 8225/78 (ECtHR 28 May 1985) 44; *Bouamar v. Belgium* App no 9106/80 (ECtHR 29 February 1988) 50; *Aerts v. Belgium* App no 61/1997/845/1051 (ECtHR 30 July 1998) 46; *Hutchison Reid v. United Kingdom* App no 50272/99 (ECtHR 20 February 2003) 49; *Saadi v. United Kingdom* App no 13229/03 (ECtHR Grand Chamber 29 January 2008) 69; *Kallweit v. Germany* App no 17792/07 (ECtHR 13 January 2011) 46; *Stanev v. Bulgaria* App no 36760/06 (ECtHR Grand Chamber 17 January 2012), 147; *James, Wells and Lee v. United Kingdom* App nos 25119/09, 57715/09 and 57877/09 (ECtHR 18 September 2012) 194; *Plesó v. Hungary* App no 41242/08 (ECtHR 2 October 2012) 58; *J.N. v. United Kingdom* App no 37289/12 (ECtHR 19 May 2016) 80; *Ilnseher v. Germany* App nos 10211/12 and 27505/14 (ECtHR Grand Chamber 4 December 2018) 138; *Rooman v. Belgium* App no 18052/11 (ECtHR Grand Chamber 31 January 2019) 190. Specifically for subparagraph (f) see: *A. and others v. United Kingdom* App no 3455/05 (ECtHR Grand Chamber 19 February 2009) 164; *Azimov v. Russia* App no 67474/11 (ECtHR 18 April 2013) 161; *Suso Musa v. Malta* App no 42337/12 (ECtHR 23 July 2013) 93; *Aboya Boa Jean v. Malta* App no 62676/16 (ECtHR 2 April 2019) 55; *Al Husin v. Bosnia and Herzegovina (no. 2)* App no 10112/16 (ECtHR 25 June 2019) 97.

190 *M. v. Germany* App no 19359/04 (ECtHR 17 December 2009) 128; *Grosskopf v. Germany* App no 24478/03 (ECtHR 21 October 2010) 51; *James, Wells and Lee v. United Kingdom* App nos 25119/09, 57715/09 and 57877/09 (ECtHR 18 September 2012) 194.

191 *James, Wells and Lee v. United Kingdom* App nos 25119/09, 57715/09 and 57877/09 (ECtHR 18 September 2012) 194.

192 *Öcalan v. Turkey* app no 46221/99 (ECtHR Grand Chamber 12 May 2005) 88.

be linked to the rule of law and proportionality. This should come as no surprise, since this principle is at the core of Article 5 ECHR (see no. 90 and following).

45. Exceptions – For our purposes, the exceptions listed in subparagraphs (a), (b) and (c) are the most relevant. They are discussed in Subsections II to IV below. Subparagraph (d) focusses on the detention of minors, subparagraph (e) on detention for the prevention of the spreading of infectious diseases, of persons of unsound mind, alcoholics, drug addicts or vagrants[193] and (f) on detention in the context of immigration or extradition. Subsection V briefly touches upon the detention of persons of unsound mind, as a few parallels can be drawn between their situation and that of suspected terrorists. None of the other subparagraphs will feature in the analysis below, since they are less relevant for the topic of this book. Note that it is possible for detention to be justified under more than one subparagraph.[194] The same goes for different limbs of the same subparagraph.[195]

SUBSECTION II. SUBPARAGRAPH (A)

46. Conviction by competent court – Subparagraph (a) covers '*the lawful detention of a person after conviction by a competent court.*' In cases that fall under this subparagraph, the Court leaves a fair amount of leeway to Member States. The word 'conviction' signifies both a finding of guilt after an offence has been established[196] and the imposition of a penalty or other measure involving deprivation of liberty.[197] The term 'after' does not only have

193 In *Guzzardi* the Court ruled that this ground cannot be interpreted to *a fortiori* include the detention of people such as mafiosi. See: *Guzzardi v. Italy* App no 7367/76 (ECtHR Plenary 6 November 1980) 98.

194 *X. v. United Kingdom* App no 7215/75 (ECtHR 5 November 1981) 39; *Eriksen v. Norway* App no 17391/90 (ECtHR 27 May 1997) 76; *Witold Litwa v. Poland* App no 26629/95 (ECtHR 4 April 2000) 49; *Enhorn v. Sweden* App no 56529/00 (ECtHR 25 January 2005) 34; *M. v. Germany* App no 19359/04 (ECtHR 17 December 2009) 86; *Gatt v. Malta* App no 28221/08 (ECtHR 27 July 2010) 35; *Grosskopf v. Germany* App no 24478/03 (ECtHR 21 October 2010) 42; *Kharin v. Russia* App no 37345/03 (ECtHR 3 February 2011) 31; *Bergmann v. Germany* App no 23279/14 (ECtHR 7 January 2016) 95; *Klinkenbuß v. Germany* App no 53157/11 (ECtHR 25 February 2016) 45; *Ilnseher v. Germany* App nos 10211/12 and 27505/14 (ECtHR Grand Chamber 4 December 2018) 126; *McVeigh and others v. United Kingdom* App nos 8022/77, 8025/77 and 8027/77 (European Commission of Human Rights 18 March 1981) 163. Note that in a concurring opinion to the Eriksen case, judge Repik is of the opinion that subparagraph (a) and (c) are mutually exclusive. The majority did not share this view.

195 *Gatt v. Malta* App no 28221/08 (ECtHR 27 July 2010) 35.

196 *Guzzardi v. Italy* App no 7367/76 (ECtHR Plenary 6 November 1980) 100.

197 *X. v. United Kingdom* App no 7215/75 (ECtHR 5 November 1981) 39; *Van Droogenbroeck v. Belgium* App no 7906/77 (ECtHR 24 June 1982) 35; *B. v. Austria* App no 8/1989/168/224 (ECtHR 23 February 1990) 38; *Solmaz v. Turkey* App no 27561/02 (ECtHR 16 January 2007) 23; *M. v. Germany* App no 19359/04 (ECtHR 17 December 2009) 86; *Grosskopf v. Germany* App no 24478/03 (ECtHR 21 October 2010) 43; *Schwabe and M.G. v. Germany* App nos 8080/08 and 8577/08 (ECtHR 1 December 2011) 74; *Reiner v. Germany* App no 28527/08

a temporal meaning, but also a causal one. The detention must be the result of the conviction, or in other words there must be a sufficient causal connection between the two.[198] With the passage of time, the link between the conviction and the deprivation of liberty weakens and eventually the causal link might be broken,[199] meaning another ground for detention would be necessary. As long as the abovementioned general principles are adhered to and the detention follows and has a sufficient causal connection with a lawful conviction, the decision to impose a sentence and the length of that sentence are matters for the national authorities.[200] In other words the ECtHR does not judge the proportionality

(ECtHR 19 January 2012) 77; *James, Wells and Lee v. United Kingdom* App nos 25119/09, 57715/09 and 57877/09 (ECtHR 18 September 2012) 189; *Del Rio Prada v. Spain* App no 42750/09 (ECtHR Grand Chamber 21 October 2013) 123; *Ruslan Yakovenko v. Ukraine* App no 5425/11 (ECtHR 4 June 2015) 49. This means that if a person is not criminally responsible for reasons of e.g. mental illness, there can be no 'conviction' within the meaning of Art. 5(1)(a) ECHR (see: *Aerts v. Belgium* App no 61/1997/845/1051 (ECtHR 30 July 1998) 45).

198 *Van Droogenbroeck v. Belgium* App no 7906/77 (ECtHR 24 June 1982) 35; *Bozano v. France* App no 9990/82 (ECtHR 18 December 1986) 53; *Monnell and Morris v. United Kingdom* App nos 9562/81 and 9818/82 (ECtHR 2 March 1987) 40; *Weeks v. United Kingdom* App no 9787/82 (ECtHR 2 March 1987) 42; *B. v. Austria* App no 8/1989/168/224 (ECtHR 23 February 1990) 38; *Stafford v. United Kingdom* App no 46295/99 (ECtHR Grand Chamber 28 May 2002) 64; *Waite v. United Kingdom* App no 53236/99 (ECtHR 10 December 2002) 65; *Kafkaris v. Cyprus* App no 21906/04 (ECtHR Grand Chamber 12 February 2008) 117; *M. v. Germany* App no 19359/04 (ECtHR 17 December 2009) 88; *Grosskopf v. Germany* App no 24478/03 (ECtHR 21 October 2010) 44; *Reiner v. Germany* App no 28527/08 (ECtHR 19 January 2012) 77; *James, Wells and Lee v. United Kingdom* App nos 25119/09, 57715/09 and 57877/09 (ECtHR 18 September 2012) 189; *H.W. v. Germany* App no 17167/11 (ECtHR 19 September 2013) 102; *Del Rio Prada v. Spain* App no 42750/09 (ECtHR Grand Chamber 21 October 2013) 124; *Ruslan Yakovenko v. Ukraine* App no 5425/11 (ECtHR 4 June 2015) 50; *Klinkenbuß v. Germany* App no 53157/11 (ECtHR 25 February 2016) 46; *Ilnseher v. Germany* App nos 10211/12 and 27505/14 (ECtHR Grand Chamber 4 December 2018) 144; *Sy v. Italy* App no 11791/20 (ECtHR 24 January 2022) 101.

199 *Van Droogenbroeck v. Belgium* App no 7906/77 (ECtHR 24 June 1982) 40; *Weeks v. United Kingdom* App no 9787/82 (ECtHR 2 March 1987) 45; *Eriksen v. Norway* App no 17391/90 (ECtHR 27 May 1997) 78; *M. v. Germany* App no 19359/04 (ECtHR 17 December 2009) 88; *Grosskopf v. Germany* App no 24478/03 (ECtHR 21 October 2010) 44; *Reiner v. Germany* App no 28527/08 (ECtHR 19 January 2012) 77; *James, Wells and Lee v. United Kingdom* App nos 25119/09, 57715/09 and 57877/09 (ECtHR 18 September 2012) 189; *H.W. v. Germany* App no 17167/11 (ECtHR 19 September 2013) 102; *Klinkenbuß v. Germany* App no 53157/11 (ECtHR 25 February 2016) 46; *Sy v. Italy* App no 11791/20 (ECtHR 24 January 2022) 101.

200 *Weeks v. United Kingdom* App no 9787/82 (ECtHR 2 March 1987) 50; *T. v. United Kingdom* App no 24724/94 (ECtHR Grand Chamber 16 December 1999) 117; *V. v. United Kingdom* App no 24888/94 (ECtHR Grand Chamber 16 December 1999) 118; *Sawoniuk v. United Kingdom* App no 63716/00 (ECtHR Decision on admissibility 29 May 2001) 3; *Saadi v. United Kingdom* App no 13229/03 (ECtHR Grand Chamber 29 January 2008) 71; *James, Wells and Lee v. United Kingdom* App nos 25119/09, 57715/09 and 57877/09 (ECtHR 18 September 2012) 195; *Ruslan Yakovenko v. Ukraine* App no 5425/11 (ECtHR 4 June 2015) 61; *Khamtokhu and Aksenchik v. Russia* App nos 60367/08 and 961/11 (ECtHR Grand Chamber 24 January 2017) 55. See also, in the context of Art. 14 *j.* 5(1)(a) ECHR: *Aleksandr Aleksandrov v. Russia* App no 14431/06 (ECtHR 27 March 2018) 22. In the context of Art. 3 ECHR, see: *Vinter and others v. United Kingdom* App nos 66069/09, 130/10 and 3896/10 (ECtHR Grand Chamber 9 July 2013) 105.

of the sentence.[201] The term 'court' denotes a body which guarantees a judicial procedure[202] and exhibits certain fundamental features, the most important of which is independence from the executive and from the parties to the case.[203] In addition, a court is not 'competent' unless its composition is established by law.[204] A defendant is considered to be detained under subparagraph (a) once the judgment has been delivered at first instance, even when the judgment is not yet enforceable and remains amenable to appeal or when appeal is pending.[205] Preventive detention can constitute '*detention after conviction by a competent court*' if ordered by a sentencing court in accordance with domestic law.[206] In this case it is possible for the sentence to have a punitive part, which meets the requirements of retribution and deterrence and a preventive part, based on the detainee's dangerousness to society.[207] This second part of the sentence is preventive rather than punitive but can still fall under subparagraph (a). When the possible arbitrariness of this type of preventive detention is assessed, the Court identifies the purpose of the detention[208] and pursued a proportionality test, unlike for the punitive part.[209] When the preventive detention is for example based on the dangerousness of the detainee, the courts need to have up

---

201 Note that extremely harsh sentences could potentially violate other human rights. Think or example of long prison sentences for speech offences which may violate the freedom of speech (Art. 10 ECHR).

202 *Ţurcan and Ţurcan v. Moldova* App no 39835/05 (ECtHR 23 October 2007) 57.

203 *De Wilde, Ooms and Versyp v. Belgium* App nos 2832/66, 2835/66 and 2899/66 (ECtHR 18 June 1971) 78; *Weeks v. United Kingdom* App no 9787/82 (ECtHR 2 March 1987) 61; *A.D. v. Turkey* App no 29986/96 (ECtHR 22 December 2005) 21; *Dacosta Silva v. Spain* App no 69966/01 (ECtHR 2 November 2006) 43.

204 *Yefimenko v. Russia* App no 152/04 (ECtHR 12 February 2013) 109–111.

205 *Wemhoff v. Germany* App no 2122/64 (ECtHR 27 June 1968) 9; *B. v. Austria* App no 8/1989/168/224 (ECtHR 23 February 1990) 36; *I.A. v. France* App no 1/1998/904/1116 (ECtHR 23 September 1998) 98; *Piotr Baranowski v. Poland* App no 39742/05 (ECtHR 2 October 2007) 45; *Ruslan Yakovenko v. Ukraine* App no 5425/11 (ECtHR 4 June 2015) 46; *Stollenwerk v. Germany* App no 8844/12 (ECtHR 7 September 2017) 35.

206 *Van Droogenbroeck v. Belgium* App no 7906/77 (ECtHR 24 June 1982) 33–42; *Eriksen v. Norway* App no 17391/90 (ECtHR 27 May 1997) 78; *M. v. Germany* App no 19359/04 (ECtHR 17 December 2009) 96; *Grosskopf v. Germany* App no 24478/03 (ECtHR 21 October 2010) 47; *Reiner v. Germany* App no 28527/08 (ECtHR 19 January 2012) 85–87; *James, Wells and Lee v. United Kingdom* App nos 25119/09, 57715/09 and 57877/09 (ECtHR 18 September 2012) 197; *Ruslan Yakovenko v. Ukraine* App no 5425/11 (ECtHR 4 June 2015) 51. See also: Dhont (n 121) 294–295.

207 See e.g.: *Weeks v. United Kingdom* App no 9787/82 (ECtHR 2 March 1987) 46; *Hussain v. United Kingdom* App no 21928/93 (ECtHR 21 February 1996) 53–54; *James, Wells and Lee v. United Kingdom* App nos 25119/09, 57715/09 and 57877/09 (ECtHR 18 September 2012) 198; *H.W. v. Germany* App no 17167/11 (ECtHR 19 September 2013) 107–113.

208 *James, Wells and Lee v. United Kingdom* App nos 25119/09, 57715/09 and 57877/09 (ECtHR 18 September 2012) 205.

209 *Ruslan Yakovenko v. Ukraine* App no 5425/11 (ECtHR 4 June 2015) 61; *Klinkenbuß v. Germany* App no 53157/11 (ECtHR 25 February 2016) 59.

to date expert advice and the detainee must have access to the necessary means, e.g. therapy, to prove they are no longer dangerous.[210]

SUBSECTION III. SUBPARAGRAPH (B)

47. Noncompliance with court order or obligation prescribed by law – Under subparagraph (b), a person can be deprived of their liberty in the case of '*the lawful arrest or detention of a person for noncompliance with the lawful order of a court or in order to secure the fulfilment of any obligation prescribed by law.*' Under this subparagraph, detention is lawful if it is carried out after noncompliance with a lawful court order, such as the order to pay a fine,[211] or in order to compel the person to fulfil a specific and concrete obligation[212] already incumbent on them,[213] which they have not yet satisfied.[214] The detention must be aimed at or directly contribute to securing the fulfilment of that obligation and thus not be punitive.[215] Furthermore, the detention must be necessary to

---

210 *H.W. v. Germany* App no 17167/11 (ECtHR 19 September 2013) 103–116; *Klinkenbuß v. Germany* App no 53157/11 (ECtHR 25 February 2016) 47–48.

211 *Gatt v. Malta* App no 28221/08 (ECtHR 27 July 2010) 40. See also: Dhont (n 121) 297.

212 *A.D. v. Turkey* App no 29986/96 (ECtHR 22 December 2005) 20; *Soare and others v. Romania* App no 24329/02 (ECtHR 22 February 2011) 236.

213 *Ciulla v. Italy* App no 11152/84 (ECtHR Plenary 22 February 1989) 36; *Gatt v. Malta* App no 28221/08 (ECtHR 27 July 2010) 46; *Osypenko v. Ukraine* App no 4634/04 (ECtHR 9 November 2010) 57.

214 *Engel and others v. Netherlands* App nos 5100/71, 5101/71, 5102/71, 5354/72 and 5370/72 (ECtHR 8 June 1976) 69; *Epple v. Germany* App no 77909/01 (ECtHR 24 March 2005) 37; *A.D. v. Turkey* App no 29986/96 (ECtHR 22 December 2005) 20; *Sarigiannis v. Italy* App no 14569/05 (ECtHR 5 April 2011) 43; *Schwabe and M.G. v. Germany* App nos 8080/08 and 8577/08 (ECtHR 1 December 2011) 73; *Lolova-Karadzhova v. Bulgaria* App no 17835/07 (ECtHR 27 March 2012) 29; *Ostendorf v. Germany* App no 15598/08 (ECtHR 7 March 2013) 69; *Rozhkov v. Russia (No. 2)* App no 38898/04 (ECtHR 31 January 2017) 75; *I.S. v. Switzerland* App no 60202/15 (ECtHR 6 October 2020) 43; *McVeigh and others v. United Kingdom* App nos 8022/77, 8025/77 and 8027/77 (European Commission of Human Rights 18 March 1981) 172; *Johansen v. Norway* App no 10600/83 (European Commission of Human Rights 14 October 1985) 1. See also: Mueller (n 32) 327.

215 *Vasileva v. Denmark* App no 52792/99 (ECtHR 25 September 2003) 36; *Epple v. Germany* App no 77909/01 (ECtHR 24 March 2005) 37; *Gatt v. Malta* App no 28221/08 (ECtHR 27 July 2010) 46; *Osypenko v. Ukraine* App no 4634/04 (ECtHR 9 November 2010) 57; *Soare and others v. Romania* App no 24329/02 (ECtHR 22 February 2011) 236; *Schwabe and M.G. v. Germany* App nos 8080/08 and 8577/08 (ECtHR 1 December 2011) 73; *Lolova-Karadzhova v. Bulgaria* App no 17835/07 (ECtHR 27 March 2012) 29; *Ostendorf v. Germany* App no 15598/08 (ECtHR 7 March 2013) 71; *Göthlin v. Sweden* App no 8307/11 (ECtHR 16 October 2014) 57; *Rozhkov v. Russia (No. 2)* App no 38898/04 (ECtHR 31 January 2017) 76; *S., V. and A. v. Denmark* App nos 35553/23, 36678/23 and 36711/12 (ECtHR Grand Chamber 22 October 2018) 80; *I.S. v. Switzerland* App no 60202/15 (ECtHR 6 October 2020) 43; *McVeigh and others v. United Kingdom* App nos 8022/77, 8025/77 and 8027/77 (European Commission of Human Rights 18 March 1981) 172; *Johansen v. Norway* App no 10600/83 (European Commission of Human Rights 14 October 1985) 1.

achieve this aim.[216] A further requirement is that the nature of the obligation the fulfilment of which is sought, must be compatible with the Convention.[217] As soon as the relevant obligation has been fulfilled, the basis for detention disappears.[218] Finally, a balance must be struck between the importance in a democratic society of securing the immediate fulfilment of the obligation or the lawful court order in question and the importance of the right to liberty,[219] as imposed by the proportionality principle.[220] Relevant factors to strike this balance for obligations are: the nature of the obligation, including the underlying object and purpose, the person being detained, the particular circumstances leading to the detention and the duration of the detention.[221, 222] For example,

216 *Iliya Stefanov v. Bulgaria* App no 65755/01 (ECtHR 22 May 2008) 72; *S., V. and A. v. Denmark* App nos 35553/23, 36678/23 and 36711/12 (ECtHR Grand Chamber 22 October 2018) 77; *Aftanache v. Romania* App no 999/19 (ECtHR 26 May 2020) 91.

217 *Ostendorf v. Germany* App no 15598/08 (ECtHR 7 March 2013) 72; *Rozhkov v. Russia (No. 2)* App no 38898/04 (ECtHR 31 January 2017) 76; *S., V. and A. v. Denmark* App nos 35553/23, 36678/23 and 36711/12 (ECtHR Grand Chamber 22 October 2018) 81; *McVeigh and others v. United Kingdom* App nos 8022/77, 8025/77 and 8027/77 (European Commission of Human Rights 18 March 1981) 176; *Johansen v. Norway* App no 10600/83 (European Commission of Human Rights 14 October 1985) 1.

218 *Vasileva v. Denmark* App no 52792/99 (ECtHR 25 September 2003) 36; *Epple v. Germany* App no 77909/01 (ECtHR 24 March 2005) 37; *Osypenko v. Ukraine* App no 4634/04 (ECtHR 9 November 2010) 57; *Sarigiannis v. Italy* App no 14569/05 (ECtHR 5 April 2011) 43; *Soare and others v. Romania* App no 24329/02 (ECtHR 22 February 2011) 236; *Schwabe and M.G. v. Germany* App nos 8080/08 and 8577/08 (ECtHR 1 December 2011) 73; *Lolova-Karadzhova v. Bulgaria* App no 17835/07 (ECtHR 27 March 2012) 29; *Ostendorf v. Germany* App no 15598/08 (ECtHR 7 March 2013) 72; *Göthlin v. Sweden* App no 8307/11 (ECtHR 16 October 2014) 57; *Rozhkov v. Russia (No. 2)* App no 38898/04 (ECtHR 31 January 2017) 76; *S., V. and A. v. Denmark* App nos 35553/23, 36678/23 and 36711/12 (ECtHR Grand Chamber 22 October 2018) 81.

219 *Vasileva v. Denmark* App no 52792/99 (ECtHR 25 September 2003) 37; *Epple v. Germany* App no 77909/01 (ECtHR 24 March 2005) 37; *Iliya Stefanov v. Bulgaria* App no 65755/01 (ECtHR 22 May 2008) 72; *Gatt v. Malta* App no 28221/08 (ECtHR 27 July 2010) 40 and 46; *Osypenko v. Ukraine* App no 4634/04 (ECtHR 9 November 2010) 57; *Soare and others v. Romania* App no 24329/02 (ECtHR 22 February 2011) 236; *Sarigiannis v. Italy* App no 14569/05 (ECtHR 5 April 2011) 43; *Schwabe and M.G. v. Germany* App nos 8080/08 and 8577/08 (ECtHR 1 December 2011) 73; *Lolova-Karadzhova v. Bulgaria* App no 17835/07 (ECtHR 27 March 2012) 30; *Ostendorf v. Germany* App no 15598/08 (ECtHR 7 March 2013) 73; *Rozhkov v. Russia (No. 2)* App no 38898/04 (ECtHR 31 January 2017) 77.

220 *Vasileva v. Denmark* App no 52792/99 (ECtHR 25 September 2003) 41; *Saadi v. United Kingdom* App no 13229/03 (ECtHR Grand Chamber 29 January 2008) 70; *Gatt v. Malta* App no 28221/08 (ECtHR 27 July 2010) 40; *Osypenko v. Ukraine* App no 4634/04 (ECtHR 9 November 2010) 63; *Göthlin v. Sweden* App no 8307/11 (ECtHR 16 October 2014) 58 and 61; *S., V. and A. v. Denmark* App nos 35553/23, 36678/23 and 36711/12 (ECtHR Grand Chamber 22 October 2018) 82.

221 *Lolova-Karadzhova v. Bulgaria* App no 17835/07 (ECtHR 27 March 2012) 30.

222 *Vasileva v. Denmark* App no 52792/99 (ECtHR 25 September 2003) 38; *Epple v. Germany* App no 77909/01 (ECtHR 24 March 2005) 37; *Iliya Stefanov v. Bulgaria* App no 65755/01 (ECtHR 22 May 2008) 72; *Gatt v. Malta* App no 28221/08 (ECtHR 27 July 2010) 46; *Osypenko v. Ukraine* App no 4634/04 (ECtHR 9 November 2010) 57; *Soare and others v. Romania* App no 24329/02 (ECtHR 22 February 2011) 236; *Sarigiannis v. Italy* App no 14569/05 (ECtHR 5 April 2011) 43; *Ostendorf v. Germany* App no 15598/08 (ECtHR 7 March 2013) 73; *Göthlin*

in the *McVeigh* case, three men (aged between 31 and 58) arrived in Liverpool by boat, returning from a holiday in Ireland.[223] They were stopped by the police and, after initial questioning, taken to a police station, where they were detained for about 45 hours.[224] During this time they were questioned, photographed and their fingerprints were recorded. The European Commission of Human Rights held that this detention was justified under subparagraph (b) in order to fulfil the legal obligation to submit to further examination.[225] It considered the purpose of the detention, being the execution of security checks in order to combat terrorism, and the fact that detention was only employed in a small number of cases where prolonged examination was deemed necessary.[226] By contrast, in *Vasileva*, a detention of 13 and a half hours was deemed in violation of Article 5.[227] Although the detention was significantly shorter than the one in *McVeigh*, the nature and purpose of the obligation and person being detained tipped the scales in favour of the right to liberty. In *Vasileva*, the detention was imposed upon a 67-year-old woman who refused to identify herself to the police after she had had a dispute about a bus ticket. The Court held that the detention of the applicant in order to establish her identity was in accordance with Article 5 ECHR, but the length of the detention was not proportionate to the cause of the detention. During her detention, Ms. Vasileva was repeatedly asked to identify herself, but not during the period of 11 pm until 6:30 am, as the police wanted to let her sleep. The Court stated it '*would be reluctant to accept that such considerations could generally be given priority over the obligation to secure that the detention did not exceed a period proportionate to the cause of the detention.*'[228] In addition, the police neglected to have a doctor attend to the detainee, which might have broken the impasse in the communication, and her refusal to identify herself was a minor offence only carrying a fine. For these reasons, the Court found that extending the detention to 13 and a half hours did not strike a fair balance between the need to ensure the fulfilment of

---

v. Sweden App no 8307/11 (ECtHR 16 October 2014) 61; *Rozhkov v. Russia (No. 2)* App no 38898/04 (ECtHR 31 January 2017) 77; *S., V. and A. v. Denmark* App nos 35553/23, 36678/23 and 36711/12 (ECtHR Grand Chamber 22 October 2018) 82.

223 *McVeigh and others v. United Kingdom* App nos 8022/77, 8025/77 and 8027/77 (European Commission of Human Rights 18 March 1981) 50.

224 *McVeigh and others v. United Kingdom* App nos 8022/77, 8025/77 and 8027/77 (European Commission of Human Rights 18 March 1981) 55–56.

225 *McVeigh and others v. United Kingdom* App nos 8022/77, 8025/77 and 8027/77 (European Commission of Human Rights 18 March 1981) 196.

226 *McVeigh and others v. United Kingdom* App nos 8022/77, 8025/77 and 8027/77 (European Commission of Human Rights 18 March 1981) 191–195. Note that this case dates back to 1981. In 2024, presumably, much less time would be needed in order to run certain security checks as modern technology had made this much easier. Therefore, the Court might find that 45 hours would be too long as well.

227 *Vasileva v. Denmark* App no 52792/99 (ECtHR 25 September 2003) 43.

228 *Vasileva v. Denmark* App no 52792/99 (ECtHR 25 September 2003) 41.

the obligation and the right to liberty.[229] Regarding court orders, some of the relevant factors are the purpose of the order, the feasibility of compliance and the duration of the detention.[230] A wide interpretation of this subparagraph would entail consequences incompatible with the rule of law[231] and create the risk of arbitrary deprivations of liberty.[232] Article 5(1) (b) therefore does not justify, for example, administrative detention meant to compel a citizen to discharge their general duty of obedience to the law.[233] The obligation not to commit a criminal offence may only be considered sufficiently 'specific and concrete' for the purposes of this subparagraph if the place and time of the imminent commission of the offence and its potential victim(s) have been sufficiently specified, if the person concerned was made aware of the specific act which he or she was to refrain from committing, and if that person showed themselves not to be willing to refrain from committing that act.[234] The duty not to commit a criminal offence in the imminent future cannot be considered sufficiently concrete and specific to fall under Article 5(1)(b) ECHR, at least as long as no specific measures have been ordered which have not been complied with.[235]

SUBSECTION IV. SUBPARAGRAPH (C)

48. Distinct prongs? – Subparagraph (c) allows for '*the lawful arrest or detention of a person effected for the purpose of bringing him before the competent legal authority on reasonable suspicion of having committed an offence or when it is reasonably considered necessary to prevent his committing an offence or*

229 *Vasileva v. Denmark* App no 52792/99 (ECtHR 25 September 2003) 41–42.

230 *Gatt v. Malta* App no 28221/08 (ECtHR 27 July 2010) 40.

231 *Engel and others v. Netherlands* App nos 5100/71, 5101/71, 5102/71, 5354/72 and 5370/72 (ECtHR 8 June 1976) 69; *Iliya Stefanov v. Bulgaria* App no 65755/01 (ECtHR 22 May 2008) 72; *Schwabe and M.G. v. Germany* App nos 8080/08 and 8577/08 (ECtHR 1 December 2011) 82; *Ostendorf v. Germany* App no 15598/08 (ECtHR 7 March 2013) 70; R*ozhkov v. Russia (No. 2)* App no 38898/04 (ECtHR 31 January 2017) 76.

232 *S., V. and A. v. Denmark* App nos 35553/23, 36678/23 and 36711/12 (ECtHR Grand Chamber 22 October 2018) 83.

233 *Engel and others v. Netherlands* App nos 5100/71, 5101/71, 5102/71, 5354/72 and 5370/72 (ECtHR 8 June 1976) 69; *Schwabe and M.G. v. Germany* App nos 8080/08 and 8577/08 (ECtHR 1 December 2011) 73; *Ostendorf v. Germany* App no 15598/08 (ECtHR 7 March 2013) 70; R*ozhkov v. Russia (No. 2)* App no 38898/04 (ECtHR 31 January 2017) 76; *S., V. and A. v. Denmark* App nos 35553/23, 36678/23 and 36711/12 (ECtHR Grand Chamber 22 October 2018) 83; *McVeigh and others v. United Kingdom* App nos 8022/77, 8025/77 and 8027/77 (European Commission of Human Rights 18 March 1981) 171.

234 *Schwabe and M.G. v. Germany* App nos 8080/08 and 8577/08 (ECtHR 1 December 2011) 73 and 82; *Ostendorf v. Germany* App no 15598/08 (ECtHR 7 March 2013) 69–73 and 93–93; *S., V. and A. v. Denmark* App nos 35553/23, 36678/23 and 36711/12 (ECtHR Grand Chamber 22 October 2018) 83.

235 *Schwabe and M.G. v. Germany* App nos 8080/08 and 8577/08 (ECtHR 1 December 2011) 82; *S., V. and A. v. Denmark* App nos 35553/23, 36678/23 and 36711/12 (ECtHR Grand Chamber 22 October 2018) 83.

fleeing after having done so.' A first important question which arises is whether Article 5(1)(c) consists of several distinct prongs, or of one single ground of lawful detention. More specifically, is reasonably considering it necessary to prevent the commission of an offence (the second prong so to speak) a separate ground for lawful detention, independent of reasonable suspicion of having committed an offence (the first prong)?[236] The report of the Conference of Senior Officials on Human Rights to the Committee of Ministers on Article 5(1)(c) and 3 of the second draft of the Convention states that '*it may [...] be necessary in certain circumstances to arrest an individual in order to prevent his committing a crime, even if the facts which show his intention to commit the crime do not of themselves constitute a penal offence.*'[237] This seems to imply that the second prong is a separate ground for lawful detention.[238] The case law of the ECtHR, however, did not immediately support this conclusion. Note that if subparagraph (c) does exist of different prongs, there would then also be a third prong '*when it is reasonably considered necessary to prevent his [...] fleeing after having done so.*' However, in that case the person would also have committed an offence and thus fall under the first prong.[239] Therefore, this third prong will not be analysed further.

49. Lawless (1961) – In the *Lawless* case, which dates back to 1961, the Court recognised that subparagraph (c) allows for the lawful detention of a person '*when it is reasonably considered necessary to prevent his committing an offence*', as a distinct prong from the first one. It did so after explicitly finding there were no criminal charges against Mr. Lawless.[240] Therefore, by still analysing the application of subparagraph (c), the Court implied that this subparagraph is not necessarily limited to criminal proceedings. However, the Court also stated that the words '*effected for the purpose of bringing him before the competent legal authority*' did apply to this prong of subparagraph (c) as well.[241] Therefore,

---

236 *S., V. and A. v. Denmark* App nos 35553/23, 36678/23 and 36711/12 (ECtHR Grand Chamber 22 October 2018) 96. See also: Claire Macken, 'Preventive Detention and the Right to Personal Liberty and Security under Article 5 ECHR' (2006) 10 The International Journal of Human Rights 195, 197.

237 Preparatory work on Art. 5 of the Convention, bilingual version, 1967, *CDH* (67) 10, 32. See also: *S., V. and A. v. Denmark* App nos 35553/23, 36678/23 and 36711/12 (ECtHR Grand Chamber 22 October 2018) 42; Macken (n236) 201; Van Dijk and others (n 107) 456.

238 See also: Webber (n 95) 54.

239 For a slightly more detailed analysis, see: Dhont (n 121) 309–310; Van Dijk and others (n 107) 456–457.

240 *Lawless v. Ireland (no. 3)* App no 332/57 (ECtHR 1 July 1961) 12.

241 *Lawless v. Ireland (no. 3)* App no 332/57 (ECtHR 1 July 1961) 14. See also: *S., V. and A. v. Denmark* App nos 35553/23, 36678/23 and 36711/12 (ECtHR Grand Chamber 22 October 2018) 104–108; Partly dissenting opinion of judge Pinheiro Farinha to the Brogan case (*Brogan and others v. United Kingdom* App nos 11209/84, 11234/84, 11266/84 and 11386/85 (ECtHR Plenary 29 November 1988)). See also: Dhont (n 121) 308; Webber (n 95) 55. For an analysis of the arguments in favour and against, see: Macken (n 236) 204–208.

preventive (non-criminal) detention is in theory allowed, but can only be covered by subparagraph (c) if it is done for the purpose of bringing the person before the competent legal authority.

50. Ciulla (1989) and later case law – In its 1989 *Ciulla* judgment, the Court seems to depart from the *Lawless* case in one significant aspect. It stated that '*sub-paragraph (c) permits deprivation of liberty only in connection with criminal proceedings.*'[242] The Court reasoned that this follows from its wording, read in conjunction with subparagraph (a) and paragraph 3.[243] Preventive detention, which can be based on suspicion rather than proof, is thus not covered.[244] In later case law, the Court often refers back to the *Lawless* case, since the requirement that detention to prevent a person from committing an offence has as its purpose bringing that person before the competent legal authority is still present.[245] However, the analysis seems to be based much more on the *Ciulla* case, in the sense that the Court always explicitly limits the application of subparagraph (c) to criminal proceedings.[246] This is clearly demonstrated in the *Ostendorf* case, where the court held that '*Under its long-established case-law, the second alternative of Article 5 §1 (c) therefore only governs pre-trial detention and not custody for preventive purposes without the person concerned being suspected of having already committed a criminal offence.*'[247] In a concurring opinion to this case, judges Lemmens and Jäderblom disagreed with the majority on this point and instead they argued for a return to the *Lawless* case law. They were of the opinion that bringing the person 'before the competent legal authority' does not mean criminal proceedings have to be instituted. They pointed out that *Lawless* was not this narrow and that according to *Lawless* 'bringing before the competent legal authority' could also include a legal authority which examines the question of deprivation of liberty.

---

242 *Ciulla v. Italy* App no 11152/84 (ECtHR Plenary 22 February 1989) 38. See also: Macken (n 236) 198; Macken (n 95) 55–56; Sottiaux (n 27) 234; Webber (n 95) 55–56.

243 *Ciulla v. Italy* App no 11152/84 (ECtHR Plenary 22 February 1989) 38. See also: *Epple v. Germany* App no 77909/01 (ECtHR 24 March 2005) 35; *Ostendorf v. Germany* App no 15598/08 (ECtHR 7 March 2013) 68.

244 *Ciulla v. Italy* App no 11152/84 (ECtHR Plenary 22 February 1989) 39.

245 *Ječius v. Lithuania* App no 34578/97 (ECtHR 31 July 2000) 50–51; *Ostendorf v. Germany* App no 15598/08 (ECtHR 7 March 2013) 67; *Şahin Alpay v. Turkey* App no 16538/17 (ECtHR 20 March 2018) 103.

246 *Ječius v. Lithuania* App no 34578/97 (ECtHR 31 July 2000) 50; *Epple v. Germany* App no 77909/01 (ECtHR 24 March 2005), 35; *Schwabe and M.G. v. Germany* App nos 8080/08 and 8577/08 (ECtHR 1 December 2011) 72; *Ostendorf v. Germany* App no 15598/08 (ECtHR 7 March 2013) 68; *Mehmet Hasan Altan v. Turkey* App no 13237/17 (ECtHR 20 March 2018) 124; *Şahin Alpay v. Turkey* App no 16538/17 (ECtHR 20 March 2018) 103. See also, without referring back to *Lawless* explicitly: *Krejčíř v. Czech Republic* App no 39298/04 and 8723/05 (ECtHR 26 March 2009) 75; *Al Husin v. Bosnia and Herzegovina* App no 3727/08 (ECtHR 7 February 2012) 65; *Petkov and Profirov v. Bulgaria* App nos 50027/08 and 50781/09 (ECtHR 24 June 2014) 43. See also: Macken (n 236) 199; Mueller (n 32) 327.

247 *Ostendorf v. Germany* App no 15598/08 (ECtHR 7 March 2013) 82.

51. Steel (1998) – One case that stands out among the aforementioned case law is the *Steel* case. This case took place after *Ciulla* but before the case law which follows the *Ciulla* reasoning. Despite this, the *Steel* case is more reminiscent of the *Lawless* case. In this case people were deprived of their liberty for 'breach of the peace' and afterwards appeared before a national court.[248] 'Breach of the peace' was not a criminal offence under national law. Despite this fact, the ECtHR did consider it to be 'an offence' for the purposes of Article 5(1)(c) ECHR.[249] In other words, the Court did apply subparagraph (c) to non-criminal proceedings in this case.

52. S., V. and A. (2018) – Finally in the *S., V. and A. v. Denmark* case, the Grand Chamber seems to take a definitive stance on the issue. First it goes over its previous case law and then states that the second limb of subparagraph (c) is a distinct ground, separated from the first limb.[250] Provided that it complies with the underlying principle of Article 5, which is to protect the individual from arbitrariness, the lawful detention of a person outside the context of criminal proceedings can, as a matter of principle be permissible under Article 5(1)(c) of the Convention.[251] In doing so, the Court explicitly departs from the *Ciulla* and *Ostendorf* case law, finding support for its conclusion in the *Lawless* case and referring back to the concurring opinion of judges Lemmens and Jäderblom to the *Ostendorf* case.[252]

53. Purpose requirement – A follow-up question, which then arose, was whether the 'purpose' requirement in Article 5(1)(c) (the purpose of bringing the person before the competent legal authority) constituted an obstacle to preventive detention under the second limb. The Court found it did not. As already mentioned, in *Lawless* it stated that this requirement applies to all categories of cases.[253] However, this requirement is to be interpreted and applied

248 *Steel and others v. United Kingdom* App no 67/1997/851/1058 (ECtHR 23 September 1998) 6–24.

249 *Steel and others v. United Kingdom* App no 67/1997/851/1058 (ECtHR 23 September 1998) 46–49. See also: *S., V. and A. v. Denmark* App nos 35553/23, 36678/23 and 36711/12 (ECtHR Grand Chamber 22 October 2018) 109–113.

250 *S., V. and A. v. Denmark* App nos 35553/23, 36678/23 and 36711/12 (ECtHR Grand Chamber 22 October 2018) 114. In later case law, the Court takes this as a given. See: *I.S. v. Switzerland* App no 60202/15 (ECtHR 6 October 2020) 55–56. This was already established in the *Lawless* case and the preceding case law discussed above. See also e.g. the *De Jong, Baljet and Van den Brink* case, where the Court mentions '*three alternative circumstances*' (*De Jong, Baljet and Van den Brink v. the Netherlands* App nos 8805/79, 8806/79 and 9242/81 (ECtHR 22 May 1984) 44).

251 *S., V. and A. v. Denmark* App nos 35553/23, 36678/23 and 36711/12 (ECtHR Grand Chamber 22 October 2018) 116.

252 *S., V. and A. v. Denmark* App nos 35553/23, 36678/23 and 36711/12 (ECtHR Grand Chamber 22 October 2018) 102 and 115.

253 *Lawless v. Ireland (no. 3)* App no 332/57 (ECtHR 1 July 1961) 14. See also: Macken (n 95) 62–63.

with a certain flexibility when the intention which once existed of '*bringing the applicant before the competent legal authority*' does not materialise for some reason. The fact that an arrested person was neither charged nor brought before a judge does not necessarily mean that the purpose of their detention was not in accordance with Article 5(1)(c).[254] This had already been explicitly recognised in cases about the first limb.[255] There were several arguments to extend such flexibility to the second limb. If this were not the case, it would exclude any sort of short-term preventive detention, where the purpose is to release the detainee after a short period, as soon as the risk has passed.[256] If the police mean to release the person after a relatively short period of time when the risk has passed, and this would likely end before they can practically bring the person before a court, a strict interpretation may unduly prolong the detention.[257] Articles 2 and 3 of the Convention contain positive obligations for states (see no. 3) and too strict an interpretation would make it impracticable for the police to fulfil their duties.[258] Thus, the requirement implicitly depends on the cause of detention continuing long enough for the person to be brought before a court. If this is not the case, the person should have an enforceable right to compensation in accordance with Article 5(5) ECHR.[259] This flexibility is limited by the general requirements already elaborated (lawfulness, detention in keeping with the purpose of protecting from arbitrariness, etc.).[260]

54. Baş (2020) – Despite the very explicit stance on the issue in 2018, in the 2020 *Baş* case, the Court again states that '*a person may be detained under Article 5 §1 (c) of the Convention only in the context of criminal proceedings*', while referring back to the *Ciulla* line of cases.[261] How is this reconcilable with the *S., V. and A.* case? We believe the statement in the *Baş* case to be somewhat of an

254 *S., V. and A. v. Denmark* App nos 35553/23, 36678/23 and 36711/12 (ECtHR Grand Chamber 22 October 2018) 118.

255 *Brogan and others v. United Kingdom* App nos 11209/84, 11234/84, 11266/84 and 11386/85 (ECtHR Plenary 29 November 1988) 53; *Erdagöz v. Turkey* App no 127/1996/945/746 (ECtHR 22 October 1997) 51; *Petkov and Profirov v. Bulgaria* App nos 50027/08 and 50781/09 (ECtHR 24 June 2014) 43 and 52; *S., V. and A. v. Denmark* App nos 35553/23, 36678/23 and 36711/12 (ECtHR Grand Chamber 22 October 2018) 118–119. See also: Macken (n 236) 209–210.

256 *S., V. and A. v. Denmark* App nos 35553/23, 36678/23 and 36711/12 (ECtHR Grand Chamber 22 October 2018) 121.

257 *S., V. and A. v. Denmark* App nos 35553/23, 36678/23 and 36711/12 (ECtHR Grand Chamber 22 October 2018) 122.

258 *S., V. and A. v. Denmark* App nos 35553/23, 36678/23 and 36711/12 (ECtHR Grand Chamber 22 October 2018) 123–124. Note that in the *Ostendorf* case, the Court still dismissed this argument in similar circumstances (*Ostendorf v. Germany* App no 15598/08 (ECtHR 7 March 2013) 88–89).

259 *S., V. and A. v. Denmark* App nos 35553/23, 36678/23 and 36711/12 (ECtHR Grand Chamber 22 October 2018) 125–126.

260 *S., V. and A. v. Denmark* App nos 35553/23, 36678/23 and 36711/12 (ECtHR Grand Chamber 22 October 2018) 127.

261 *Baş v. Turkey* App no 66448/17 (ECtHR 3 March 2020) 170.

oversight on behalf of a Chamber of the Court.[262] Judging from the length and depth of the analysis in the *S., V. and A.* case, this point of the analysis was made very deliberately and after much consideration. By comparison, In the *Baş* case it is merely mentioned in one sentence. Furthermore, the *Baş* case did concern criminal proceedings, so this point of the analysis was by no means at the centre of the issue. Finally, the *S. V. and A.* case is a Grand Chamber case while the *Baş* case is not. We therefore believe the *S., V. and A.* case to be the deciding case.

55. First prong of subparagraph (c) – Subparagraph (c) under its first prong allows for the detention of a person on reasonable suspicion of having committed an offence. The Court holds that the requirement of reasonable suspicion that the person has committed an offence which must underlie an arrest or detention is an essential safeguard against arbitrary detention.[263] This presupposes the existence of facts or information which would satisfy an objective observer that the person may have committed the offence.[264] What is 'reasonable' depends on the circumstances, but the facts do not need to be of the same level as those necessary to justify a conviction or even the bringing of charges.[265] This is logical

262 Note that out of the 17 judges in *S., V. and A.* and seven judges in *Baş*, only one judge sat in both cases.

263 *Fox, Campbell and Hartley v. the UK* App nos 12244/86, 12245/86 and 12383/86 (ECtHR 30 August 1990) 32; *K.-F. v. Germany* App no 144/1996/765/962 (ECtHR 27 November 1997) 57; *O'Hara v. United Kingdom* App no 37555/97 (ECtHR 16 October 2001) 34; *İpek and others v. Turkey* App nos 17019/02 and 30070/02 (ECtHR 3 February 2009) 29; *Krejčíř v. Czech Republic* App no 39298/04 and 8723/05 (ECtHR 26 March 2009) 75; *Petkov and Profirov v. Bulgaria* App nos 50027/08 and 50781/09 (ECtHR 24 June 2014) 43; *Ali Osman Özmen v. Turkey* App no 42969/04 (ECtHR 5 October 2016) 63; *Merabishvili v. Georgia* App no 72508/13 (ECtHR Grand Chamber 28 November 2017) 184; *Şahin Alpay v. Turkey* App no 16538/17 (ECtHR 20 March 2018) 103; *Selahattin Demirtaş v. Turkey (no. 2)* App no 14305/17 (ECtHR Grand Chamber 22 December 2020) 314.

264 *Fox, Campbell and Hartley v. the UK* App nos 12244/86, 12245/86 and 12383/86 (ECtHR 30 August 1990) 32; *Erdagöz v. Turkey* App no 127/1996/945/746 (ECtHR 22 October 1997) 51; *K.-F. v. Germany* App no 144/1996/765/962 (ECtHR 27 November 1997) 57; *Labita v. Italy* App no 26772/95 (ECtHR Grand Chamber 6 April 2000) 155; *O'Hara v. United Kingdom* App no 37555/97 (ECtHR 16 October 2001) 34; *İpek and others v. Turkey* App nos 17019/02 and 30070/02 (ECtHR 3 February 2009) 29; *Krejčíř v. Czech Republic* App no 39298/04 and 8723/05 (ECtHR 26 March 2009) 75; *James, Wells and Lee v. United Kingdom* App nos 25119/09, 57715/09 and 57877/09 (ECtHR 18 September 2012) 193; *Urtāns v. Latvia* App no 16858/11 (ECtHR 28 October 2014) 35; *Ilgar Mammadov v. Azerbaijan* App no 15172/13 (ECtHR 22 May 2014) 88; *Petkov and Profirov v. Bulgaria* App nos 50027/08 and 50781/09 (ECtHR 24 June 2014) 43; *Mehmet Hasan Altan v. Turkey* App no 13237/17 (ECtHR 20 March 2018) 124; *Ali Osman Özmen v. Turkey* App no 42969/04 (ECtHR 5 October 2016) 63; *Şahin Alpay v. Turkey* App no 16538/17 (ECtHR 20 March 2018) 103; *S., V. and A. v. Denmark* App nos 35553/23, 36678/23 and 36711/12 (ECtHR Grand Chamber 22 October 2018) 91; *Baş v. Turkey* App no 66448/17 (ECtHR 3 March 2020) 171; *Selahattin Demirtaş v. Turkey (no. 2)* App no 14305/17 (ECtHR Grand Chamber 22 December 2020) 314. See also: F De Wael, "Ernstige aanwijzingen van schuld' uit de voorlopige hechteniswet gedefinieerd' (2021) 2021 Rechtspraak Antwerpen Brussel Gent (RABG) 1726, 1728–1729; Mueller (n 32) 333; Sottiaux (n 27) 204.

265 *Murray v. United Kingdom* App no 14310/88 (ECtHR Grand Chamber 28 October 1994) 55; *Erdagöz v. Turkey* App no 127/1996/945/746 (ECtHR 22 October 1997) 51; *K.-F. v. Germany*

since the purpose of questioning a suspect during detention under subparagraph (c) is to further the criminal investigation by confirming or dispelling the concrete suspicion grounding the arrest.[266] The purpose of the arrest or detention must be bringing the person concerned before a competent legal authority.[267] The existence of this purpose has to be considered independently of its achievement.[268] This loops back to the previous point that Article 5(1) (c) does not require the police to have sufficient evidence to bring charges at the time of arrest or while the applicant is in custody.[269] Similarly to detention under subparagraph (b), a deprivation of liberty in the context of subparagraph

App no 144/1996/765/962 (ECtHR 27 November 1997) 57; *Labita v. Italy* App no 26772/95 (ECtHR Grand Chamber 6 April 2000) 155; *O'Hara v. United Kingdom* App no 37555/97 (ECtHR 16 October 2001) 34–36; *Marturana v. Italy* App no 63154 (ECtHR 4 March 2008) 84; *Krejčíř v. Czech Republic* App no 39298/04 and 8723/05 (ECtHR 26 March 2009), 75; *Oral and Atabay v. Turkey* App no 39686/02 (ECtHR 23 June 2009) 29; *Urtāns v. Latvia* App no 16858/11 (ECtHR 28 October 2014) 35; *Ilgar Mammadov v. Azerbaijan* App no 15172/13 (ECtHR 22 May 2014) 87–88; *Petkov and Profirov v. Bulgaria* App nos 50027/08 and 50781/09 (ECtHR 24 June 2014) 43; *Ali Osman Özmen v. Turkey* App no 42969/04 (ECtHR 5 October 2016) 63; *Merabishvili v. Georgia* App no 72508/13 (ECtHR Grand Chamber 28 November 2017) 184; *Şahin Alpay v. Turkey* App no 16538/17 (ECtHR 20 March 2018) 103–104; *Baş v. Turkey* App no 66448/17 (ECtHR 3 March 2020) 171–172; *Selahattin Demirtaş v. Turkey (no. 2)* App no 14305/17 (ECtHR Grand Chamber 22 December 2020) 315. See also: Macken (n 236) 203.

266 *Brogan and others v. United Kingdom* App nos 11209/84, 11234/84, 11266/84 and 11386/85 (ECtHR Plenary 29 November 1988) 52–53; *Murray v. United Kingdom* App no 14310/88 (ECtHR Grand Chamber 28 October 1994) 55; *Erdagöz v. Turkey* App no 127/1996/945/746 (ECtHR 22 October 1997) 51; *O'Hara v. United Kingdom* App no 37555/97 (ECtHR 16 October 2001) 36; *İpek and others v. Turkey* App nos 17019/02 and 30070/02 (ECtHR 3 February 2009) 28; *Oral and Atabay v. Turkey* App no 39686/02 (ECtHR 23 June 2009) 29; *Ilgar Mammadov v. Azerbaijan* App no 15172/13 (ECtHR 22 May 2014) 87; *Mehmet Hasan Altan v. Turkey* App no 13237/17 (ECtHR 20 March 2018) 125; *Şahin Alpay v. Turkey* App no 16538/17 (ECtHR 20 March 2018) 104.

267 *Brogan and others v. United Kingdom* App nos 11209/84, 11234/84, 11266/84 and 11386/85 (ECtHR Plenary 29 November 1988) 52–53; *Murray v. United Kingdom* App no 14310/88 (ECtHR Grand Chamber 28 October 1994) 67–68; *K.-F. v. Germany* App no 144/1996/765/962 (ECtHR 27 November 1997) 60; *Merabishvili v. Georgia* App no 72508/13 (ECtHR Grand Chamber 28 November 2017) 185.

268 *Murray v. United Kingdom* App no 14310/88 (ECtHR Grand Chamber 28 October 1994) 67; *K.-F. v. Germany* App no 144/1996/765/962 (ECtHR 27 November 1997) 61; *Labita v. Italy* App no 26772/95 (ECtHR Grand Chamber 6 April 2000) 155; *İpek and others v. Turkey* App nos 17019/02 and 30070/02 (ECtHR 3 February 2009) 28; *Ilgar Mammadov v. Azerbaijan* App no 15172/13 (ECtHR 22 May 2014) 87; *Petkov and Profirov v. Bulgaria* App nos 50027/08 and 50781/09 (ECtHR 24 June 2014) 52.

269 *Brogan and others v. United Kingdom* App nos 11209/84, 11234/84, 11266/84 and 11386/85 (ECtHR Plenary 29 November 1988) 53; *Erdagöz v. Turkey* App no 127/1996/945/746 (ECtHR 22 October 1997) 51; *K.-F. v. Germany* App no 144/1996/765/962 (ECtHR 27 November 1997) 61; *İpek and others v. Turkey* App nos 17019/02 and 30070/02 (ECtHR 3 February 2009) 28; *Ilgar Mammadov v. Azerbaijan* App no 15172/13 (ECtHR 22 May 2014) 87; *Petkov and Profirov v. Bulgaria* App nos 50027/08 and 50781/09 (ECtHR 24 June 2014) 52; *Mehmet Hasan Altan v. Turkey* App no 13237/17 (ECtHR 20 March 2018) 125; *Selahattin Demirtaş v. Turkey (no. 2)* App no 14305/17 (ECtHR Grand Chamber 22 December 2020) 315.

(c) is arbitrary if it is not necessary in the circumstances[270] and other less serious measures have to be found insufficient.[271, 272] This is a proportionality requirement. The detention cannot be used as a form of coercion in order to elicit a confession or other information[273] and it must be a proportionate measure to achieve the stated aim.[274] A reasoned decision balancing relevant arguments for and against release is required.[275] The reasoning of the decision ordering a person's detention is therefore a relevant factor in determining whether the detention must be deemed arbitrary. The ECtHR has found that the absence of any grounds in the judicial authorities' decisions authorising detention for a prolonged period of time was incompatible with the principle of protection from arbitrariness.[276] Conversely, it has found that an applicant's detention on remand could not be said to have been arbitrary if the domestic court gave certain grounds justifying the continued detention, unless the reasons given were extremely laconic and did not refer to any legal provision which would have permitted the applicant's detention.[277] Detention ceases to be covered by this prong of subparagraph (c) once the person has been convicted or acquitted in first instance, even when this decision is not yet final.[278] From that point onward the detention falls under subparagraph (a) (see no. 46). In terrorism cases, states

270 *Ambruszkiewicz v. Poland* App no 38797/03 (ECtHR 4 May 2006) 31; *Korneykova v. Ukraine* App no 39884/05 (ECtHR 19 January 2012) 43; *Popoviciu v. Romania* App no 52942/09 (ECtHR 1 March 2016) 68; *Buzadji v. Republic of Moldova* App no 23755/07 (ECtHR Grand Chamber 5 July 2016) 122; *Strogan v. Ukraine* App no 30198/11 (ECtHR 6 October 2016) 86; *S., V. and A. v. Denmark* App nos 35553/23, 36678/23 and 36711/12 (ECtHR Grand Chamber 22 October 2018) 77; *Aftanache v. Romania* App no 999/19 (ECtHR 26 May 2020) 78 *Aftanache v. Romania* App no 999/19 (ECtHR 26 May 2020) 91.

271 *I.S. v. Switzerland* App no 60202/15 (ECtHR 6 October 2020) 54.

272 *Khayredinov v. Ukraine* App no 38717/04 (ECtHR 14 October 2010) 27–28.

273 *İpek and others v. Turkey* App nos 17019/02 and 30070/02 (ECtHR 3 February 2009) 29.

274 *Ambruszkiewicz v. Poland* App no 38797/03 (ECtHR 4 May 2006) 31–32; *Ladent v. Poland* App no 11036/03 (ECtHR 18 March 2008) 55–56; *Khayredinov v. Ukraine* App no 38717/04 (ECtHR 14 October 2010) 28; *Korneykova v. Ukraine* App no 39884/05 (ECtHR 19 January 2012) 43.

275 *Ladent v. Poland* App no 11036/03 (ECtHR 18 March 2008) 55; *Khayredinov v. Ukraine* App no 38717/04 (ECtHR 14 October 2010) 28; *Korneykova v. Ukraine* App no 39884/05 (ECtHR 19 January 2012) 43.

276 *Mooren v. Germany* App no 11364/03 (ECtHR Grand Chamber 9 July 2009) 79; *Urtāns v. Latvia* App no 16858/11 (ECtHR 28 October 2014) 28; *S., V. and A. v. Denmark* App nos 35553/23, 36678/23 and 36711/12 (ECtHR Grand Chamber 22 October 2018) 92.

277 *Mooren v. Germany* App no 11364/03 (ECtHR Grand Chamber 9 July 2009) 79; *Urtāns v. Latvia* App no 16858/11 (ECtHR 28 October 2014) 28; *S., V. and A. v. Denmark* App nos 35553/23, 36678/23 and 36711/12 (ECtHR Grand Chamber 22 October 2018) 92.

278 *B. v. Austria* App no 8/1989/168/224 (ECtHR 23 February 1990) 36; *Labita v. Italy* App no 26772/95 (ECtHR Grand Chamber 6 April 2000) 147; *Lavents v. Latvia* App no 58442/00 (ECtHR 28 November 2002) 66; *Solmaz v. Turkey* App no 27561/02 (ECtHR 16 January 2007) 25; *Piotr Baranowski v. Poland* App no 39742/05 (ECtHR 2 October 2007) 45; *Khayredinov v. Ukraine* App no 38717/04 (ECtHR 14 October 2010) 37; *Ruslan Yakovenko v. Ukraine* App no 5425/11 (ECtHR 4 June 2015) 46; *Buzadji v. Republic of Moldova* App no 23755/07 (ECtHR Grand Chamber 5 July 2016) 85; *I.S. v. Switzerland* App no 60202/15 (ECtHR 6 October 2020) 43.

cannot be required to establish the reasonableness of the suspicion grounding the arrest of a suspected terrorist by disclosing confidential sources of information and the standards of 'reasonableness' are not always the same as in other cases, as investigating and prosecuting terrorist offences is inherently difficult.[279, 280] However, these issues cannot justify stretching the notion of 'reasonableness' to the point of impairing the essence of the safeguards of Article 5(1)(c).[281]

56. Comparing IRA cases – In the context of Irish Republican Army (IRA) terrorism in Northern Ireland, the ECtHR has had to rule on several similar cases concerning the reasonableness of suspicion. In the *Brogan* case, Mr. Brogan and three others were arrested in their homes, questioned about their suspected involvement in the IRA and IRA attacks and detained for between four days and six hours and six days and 16 and a half hours.[282] None of them were brought before a judge or charged after their release.[283] In this case, the reasonableness of the suspicion did not play a part in the Court's reasoning. It was not even explicitly mentioned. The Court simply pointed out that the detainees were questioned concerning terrorism offences after their arrest. Although they do not explicitly state so, judges Walsh and Carrillo hinted at the lack of reasonable suspicion in a dissenting opinion to this case. Almost two years later, the reasonableness of the suspicion did become an element of analysis in the *Fox, Campbell and Hartley* case. Mr. Fox and Ms. Campbell, both of whom had previously been convicted for terrorism-related offences,[284] were stopped by the police and brought to the police station. Their vehicle was searched and they were both arrested on suspicion of terrorist activity.[285] After both had been questioned and detained for around 44 hours, they were released

279 *Selahattin Demirtaş v. Turkey (no. 2)* App no 14305/17 (ECtHR Grand Chamber 22 December 2020) 323.

280 *Fox, Campbell and Hartley v. United Kingdom* App nos 12244/86, 12245/86 and 12383/86 (ECtHR 30 August 1990) 32 and 34; *Murray v. United Kingdom* App no 14310/88 (ECtHR Grand Chamber 28 October 1994) 51; *O'Hara v. United Kingdom* App no 37555/97 (ECtHR 16 October 2001) 35; *Baş v. Turkey* App no 66448/17 (ECtHR 3 March 2020) 182. See also: Webber (n 95) 97–98.

281 *Fox, Campbell and Hartley v. United Kingdom* App nos 12244/86, 12245/86 and 12383/86 (ECtHR 30 August 1990) 32; *Murray v. United Kingdom* App no 14310/88 (ECtHR Grand Chamber 28 October 1994) 51; *O'Hara v. United Kingdom* App no 37555/97 (ECtHR 16 October 2001) 35; *Baş v. Turkey* App no 66448/17 (ECtHR 3 March 2020) 184; *Selahattin Demirtaş v. Turkey (no. 2)* App no 14305/17 (ECtHR Grand Chamber 22 December 2020) 323. See also: Sottiaux (n 27) 206.

282 *Brogan and others v. United Kingdom* App nos 11209/84, 11234/84, 11266/84 and 11386/85 (ECtHR Plenary 29 November 1988) 11–23. See also: Conte (n 10) 535; Macken (n 236) 202.

283 *Brogan and others v. United Kingdom* App nos 11209/84, 11234/84, 11266/84 and 11386/85 (ECtHR Plenary 29 November 1988) 24.

284 *Fox, Campbell and Hartley v. the UK* App nos 12244/86, 12245/86 and 12383/86 (ECtHR 30 August 1990) 12. See also: Dhont (n 121) 305–306.

285 *Fox, Campbell and Hartley v. the UK* App nos 12244/86, 12245/86 and 12383/86 (ECtHR 30 August 1990) 8–9.

without appearing before a judge and no charges were brought.[286] Mr. Hartley was arrested at home on suspicion of being a terrorist.[287] He was questioned and released after 30 hours and 15 minutes without appearing before a judge, nor were any charges brought.[288] The Court held that the mere fact that Mr. Fox and Ms. Campbell had already been convicted for acts of terrorism connected with the IRA cannot form the sole basis of reasonable suspicion seven years later.[289] All three applicants were questioned about specific terrorist acts after their arrest, but the Court now stated that this '*does no more than confirm that the arresting officers had a genuine suspicion that they had been involved in those acts, but it cannot satisfy an objective observer that the applicants may have committed these acts.*'[290] Therefore, the Court concluded there were insufficient elements to establish reasonable suspicion and there has been a breach of Article 5.[291] In a joint dissenting opinion judges Sir Vincent Evans, Bernhardt and Palm were of the opinion that the 'genuine suspicion' of the arresting officers must have had some basis in information held by the government, which it was unable to disclose for security reasons.[292] Therefore, they argued that there had been reasonable suspicion and Article 5 had not been violated. Some four years later, there was a Grand Chamber decision on a similar issue. In the *Murray* case Ms. Murray was arrested after her two brothers had already been convicted of arms offences related to the IRA in the US.[293] She was arrested by the army in her house in the early morning, taken to a base and questioned.[294] After a couple of hours she was released without charges.[295] The Court stated that the length of the detention could be material for the level of suspicion required.[296] It then continued by explaining that it did attach some credence to the government's assertions that reliable but confidential information existed.[297] Mrs. Murray

286 *Fox, Campbell and Hartley v. the UK* App nos 12244/86, 12245/86 and 12383/86 (ECtHR 30 August 1990) 10.

287 *Fox, Campbell and Hartley v. the UK* App nos 12244/86, 12245/86 and 12383/86 (ECtHR 30 August 1990) 13.

288 *Fox, Campbell and Hartley v. the UK* App nos 12244/86, 12245/86 and 12383/86 (ECtHR 30 August 1990) 14.

289 *Fox, Campbell and Hartley v. the UK* App nos 12244/86, 12245/86 and 12383/86 (ECtHR 30 August 1990) 35. See also: Sottiaux (n 27) 207.

290 *Fox, Campbell and Hartley v. the UK* App nos 12244/86, 12245/86 and 12383/86 (ECtHR 30 August 1990) 35. See also: De Wael (n 264) 1729.

291 *Fox, Campbell and Hartley v. the UK* App nos 12244/86, 12245/86 and 12383/86 (ECtHR 30 August 1990) 36. See also: Sottiaux (n 27) 207.

292 See also: Sottiaux (n 27) 209.

293 *Murray v. United Kingdom* App no 14310/88 (ECtHR Grand Chamber 28 October 1994) 10. See also: Dhont (n 121) 306.

294 *Murray v. United Kingdom* App no 14310/88 (ECtHR Grand Chamber 28 October 1994) 9–12.

295 *Murray v. United Kingdom* App no 14310/88 (ECtHR Grand Chamber 28 October 1994) 11–14.

296 *Murray v. United Kingdom* App no 14310/88 (ECtHR Grand Chamber 28 October 1994) 56. See also: Sottiaux (n 27) 207–208.

297 *Murray v. United Kingdom* App no 14310/88 (ECtHR Grand Chamber 28 October 1994) 59.

had visited the US and had had contacts with her brothers there. In addition, the offences for which her brothers were convicted implied collaboration with somebody trustworthy in Northern Ireland.[298] The ECtHR concluded by finding there was reasonable suspicion.[299] In a joint dissenting opinion judges Loizou, Morenilla and Makarczyk disagreed with this point.[300] They did not believe there was reasonable suspicion based on the abovementioned elements furnished by the government. They did not see a material difference between this case and the *Fox, Campbell and Hartley* case. In their opinion the government could have supplied additional information to establish the reasonableness of the suspicion without jeopardising the confidentiality of the source of the information. Finally, in the *O'Hara* case, Mr. O'Hara, a prominent member of Sinn Fein (a political party closely related to the IRA), was arrested in his home on suspicion of terrorist murder.[301] He was detained for six days and 13 hours.[302] During this time he was questioned but he refused to speak and in the end he was released.[303] The information on which the arrest was based, came from four separate informers, who according to the government, had in the past proved reliable and whose information was consistent.[304] The Court held that this information was sufficient to meet the standard of subparagraph (c).[305] In a partly dissenting opinion, judge Loucaides expressed the view that the aforementioned information was inadmissible since it was not produced before the domestic courts. He then concluded that since there was no information capable of satisfying the Court that the arrested person was reasonably suspected of having committed an offence, there was a violation of Article 5(1).[306]

57. Second prong of subparagraph (c) – Subparagraph (c) also allows for detention of a person when it is reasonably considered necessary to prevent their committing an offence. Here, a strict interpretation of the term 'offence' constitutes an important safeguard against arbitrariness. It does not permit a policy of general prevention directed against an individual or a category of individuals who are perceived by the authorities, rightly or wrongly, as being

298 *Murray v. United Kingdom* App no 14310/88 (ECtHR Grand Chamber 28 October 1994) 62. See also: Sottiaux (n 27) 207–208.

299 *Murray v. United Kingdom* App no 14310/88 (ECtHR Grand Chamber 28 October 1994) 63. See also: De Wael (n 264) 1731–1732; Sottiaux (n 27) 207–208.

300 See also: Sottiaux (n 27) 209. In a partly dissenting opinion, judge Jambrek elaborates his reasoning and by and large takes the same position.

301 *O'Hara v. United Kingdom* App no 37555/97 (ECtHR 16 October 2001) 8–15.

302 *O'Hara v. United Kingdom* App no 37555/97 (ECtHR 16 October 2001) 15.

303 *O'Hara v. United Kingdom* App no 37555/97 (ECtHR 16 October 2001) 37.

304 *O'Hara v. United Kingdom* App no 37555/97 (ECtHR 16 October 2001) 40. See also: Sottiaux (n 27) 208–209.

305 *O'Hara v. United Kingdom* App no 37555/97 (ECtHR 16 October 2001) 42 and 44. See also: Sottiaux (n 27) 208–209.

306 See also: Sottiaux (n 27) 209.

dangerous or having the propensity to commit unlawful acts.[307] This ground of detention does no more than afford states a means of preventing a concrete and specific offence,[308] as regards, in particular, the place and time of its commission and its victim(s).[309] This can be seen both from the use of the singular ('an offence') and from the object of Article 5, namely to ensure that no one should be deprived of their liberty in an arbitrary fashion.[310] According to the Court's case-law, however, the 'offence' does not have to be limited to conduct that has been characterised as an offence under national law.[311] For example, the UK concept 'breach of the peace', while not an offence under UK law, is an offence under Article 5(1)(c) ECHR. Finally, '*the Court is of the view that in order for a detention to be justified under the second limb of Article 5 §1 (c), the authorities must show convincingly that the person concerned would in all likelihood have been involved in the concrete and specific offence, had its commission not been prevented by the detention.*'[312] This prong does not allow for the continued detention of a convicted person for reasons of security after they have served their sentence.[313] In the *Eriksen* case, however, the Court did allow for a short period of detention under subparagraph (c) in order to determine whether the detainee should, after the termination of his sentence, be subject to a form of security detention on other grounds.[314]

---

307 *Shimovolos v. Russia* App no 30194/09 (ECtHR 21 June 2011) 54; *Al Husin v. Bosnia and Herzegovina* App no 3727/08 (ECtHR 7 February 2012) 65; *Ostendorf v. Germany* App no 15598/08 (ECtHR 7 March 2013) 66; *Urtāns v. Latvia* App no 16858/11 (ECtHR 28 October 2014) 33; *Ilnseher v. Germany* App nos 10211/12 and 27505/14 (ECtHR Grand Chamber 4 December 2018) 145.

308 *Ciulla v. Italy* App no 11152/84 (ECtHR Plenary 22 February 1989) 40; *Shimovolos v. Russia* App no 30194/09 (ECtHR 21 June 2011) 54; *Urtāns v. Latvia* App no 16858/11 (ECtHR 28 October 2014) 33. See also: Partly dissenting opinion of judge Pinto De Albuquerque to the *De Tommaso* judgment (*De Tommaso v. Italy* App no 43395/09 (ECtHR Grand Chamber 23 February 2017). See also: Macken (n 95) 53.

309 *Guzzardi v. Italy* App no 7367/76 (ECtHR Plenary 6 November 1980) 102; *M. v. Germany* App no 19359/04 (ECtHR 17 December 2009) 89 and 102; *Schwabe and M.G. v. Germany* App nos 8080/08 and 8577/08 (ECtHR 1 December 2011) 70; *Al Husin v. Bosnia and Herzegovina* App no 3727/08 (ECtHR 7 February 2012) 65; *Ostendorf v. Germany* App no 15598/08 (ECtHR 7 March 2013) 66; *S., V. and A. v. Denmark* App nos 35553/23, 36678/23 and 36711/12 (ECtHR Grand Chamber 22 October 2018) 89; *Ilnseher v. Germany* App nos 10211/12 and 27505/14 (ECtHR Grand Chamber 4 December 2018) 145. See also: Webber (n 95) 54.

310 *Guzzardi v. Italy* App no 7367/76 (ECtHR Plenary 6 November 1980) 102; *M. v. Germany* App no 19359/04 (ECtHR 17 December 2009) 89; *Schwabe and M.G. v. Germany* App nos 8080/08 and 8577/08 (ECtHR 1 December 2011) 70; *Ostendorf v. Germany* App no 15598/08 (ECtHR 7 March 2013) 66; *Urtāns v. Latvia* App no 16858/11 (ECtHR 28 October 2014) 33; *S., V. and A. v. Denmark* App nos 35553/23, 36678/23 and 36711/12 (ECtHR Grand Chamber 22 October 2018) 89.

311 *Steel and others v. United Kingdom* App no 67/1997/851/1058) (ECtHR 23 September 1998) 46–49; *S., V. and A. v. Denmark* App nos 35553/23, 36678/23 and 36711/12 (ECtHR Grand Chamber 22 October 2018) 90.

312 *S., V. and A. v. Denmark* App nos 35553/23, 36678/23 and 36711/12 (ECtHR Grand Chamber 22 October 2018) 91.

313 Van Dijk and others (n 107) 459.

314 *Eriksen v. Norway* App no 17391/90 (ECtHR 27 May 1997) 86; Dhont (n 121) 295–296 and 309; Van Dijk and others (n 107) 459.

SUBSECTION V. SUBPARAGRAPH (E)

58. Persons of unsound mind – Subparagraph (e) covers the detention of persons for the prevention of the spreading of infectious diseases, of persons of unsound mind, alcoholics, drug addicts or vagrants. In this subsection, we briefly discuss the detention of persons of unsound mind, as certain parallels can be drawn between them and suspected terrorists; and quite a few terrorist suspects and people convicted for terrorist offences suffer from mental health issues.

59. Public safety – Detention under subparagraph (e) has public safety and social policy as one of its foundations. The deprivation of liberty of people carrying infectious diseases or people of unsound mind has a clear public safety element. In this sense, there is an obvious parallel with preventive detention in a counter-terrorism context. However, subparagraph (e) also has a second underlying idea, being that the detention is necessary in the interest of the detainee themselves.[315] In this sense the situation of subparagraph (e) is quite different from preventive detention of terrorist suspects.

60. Scope of application – An exact definition of 'person of unsound mind' is very difficult to provide, as psychiatry is an evolving field, and therefore the Court cannot do so.[316] However, it has explicitly stated that the detention of a person is not allowed '*simply because his or her views or behaviour deviate from established norms.*'[317] The ECtHR requires that a 'true'[318] mental disorder exists, based on objective medical evidence.[319] In addition, the disorder must warrant compulsory confinement, meaning the deprivation of liberty is necessary under these circumstances, and the mental disorder must persist throughout the period

---

315 *Guzzardi v. Italy* App no 7367/76 (ECtHR Plenary 6 November 1980) 98; *Witold Litwa v. Poland* App no 26629/95 (ECtHR 4 April 2000) 60; *Enhorn v. Sweden* App no 56529/00 (ECtHR 25 January 2005) 34; *Saadi v. United Kingdom* App no 13229/03 (ECtHR Grand Chamber 29 January 2008) 43. Note that while this is usually the case for people carrying infectious diseases, as they need treatment, this is not always true. E.g. during the covid crisis quarantines were imposed for the protection of others more so than the treatment of the person who had covid.

316 *Glien v. Germany* App no 7345/12 (ECtHR 28 November 2013) 72; *Petschulies v. Germany* App no 6281/13 (ECtHR 2 June 2016) 59; *Denis and Irvine v. Belgium* App nos 62819/17 and 63921/17 (ECtHR Grand Chamber 1 June 2021) 134.

317 *Rakevich v. Russia* App no 58973/00 (ECtHR 28 October 2003) 26.

318 Requiring a certain seriousness. See: *Glien v. Germany* App no 7345/12 (ECtHR 28 November 2013) 85; *Petschulies v. Germany* App no 6281/13 (ECtHR 2 June 2016) 76; *Ilnseher v. Germany* App nos 10211/12 and 27505/14 (ECtHR Grand Chamber 4 December 2018) 129; *Denis and Irvine v. Belgium* App nos 62819/17 and 63921/17 (ECtHR Grand Chamber 1 June 2021) 106 and 136.

319 *Glien v. Germany* App no 7345/12 (ECtHR 28 November 2013) 72; *Petschulies v. Germany* App no 6281/13 (ECtHR 2 June 2016) 59; *Ilnseher v. Germany* App nos 10211/12 and 27505/14 (ECtHR Grand Chamber 4 December 2018) 152.

of detention.[320] Detention can be justified if necessary not only for treatment, therapy or medication but also for control and supervision, for example to prevent the detainee from harming themselves or others.[321] This implies that detention can be justified even if there is no treatment available to the psychiatric condition.[322] However, the ECtHR case law puts an increasing emphasis on the therapeutic aims of subparagraph (e) and the need to provide treatment. Thus, detention cannot be lawful if suitable therapy is not provided.[323] In addition, as far as possible, the detention under subparagraph (e) should take place with the permission of the detainee and therefore any measure taken without prior consultation of the person concerned requires a rigorous examination.[324] Finally, it is not required that the condition the person suffers excludes or diminishes criminal responsibility under domestic law[325] and the commission of previous offences is not a precondition.[326]

61. Possible application to terrorists – The preceding analysis of the case law on subparagraph (e) clearly shows that, while it may be relevant in certain specific instances, the detention of persons of unsound mind cannot be used as a general ground for justification of preventive detention in a counter-terrorism context. Subparagraph (e) is only applicable to situations of 'true' mental illness, requires suitable therapy and permission when possible. In addition, detention under subparagraph (e) must take place in a hospital or other appropriate institution and not in prison. It can take place in prisons only for a very short

320 *Winterwerp v. Netherlands* App no 6301/73 (ECtHR 24 October 1979) 39; *Varbanov v. Bulgaria* App no 31365/96 (ECtHR 5 October 2000) 45; *Hutchison Reid v. United Kingdom* App no 50272/99 (ECtHR 20 February 2003) 48; *Rakevich v. Russia* App no 58973/00 (ECtHR 28 October 2003) 27; *Shtukaturov v. Russia* App no 44009/05 (ECtHR 27 March 2008) 114; *Kallweit v. Germany* App no 17792/07 (ECtHR 13 January 2011) 45; *D.D. v. Lithuania* App no 13469/06 (ECtHR 14 February 2012) 156; *Stanev v. Bulgaria* App no 36760/06 (ECtHR Grand Chamber 17 January 2012) 145; *Glien v. Germany* App no 7345/12 (ECtHR 28 November 2013) 72; *Petschulies v. Germany* App no 6281/13 (ECtHR 2 June 2016) 59; *Ilnseher v. Germany* App nos 10211/12 and 27505/14 (ECtHR Grand Chamber 4 December 2018) 127; *Rooman v. Belgium* App no 18052/11 (ECtHR Grand Chamber 31 January 2019) 192; *Sy v. Italy* App no 11791/20 (ECtHR 24 January 2022) 104.

321 *Hutchison Reid v. United Kingdom* App no 50272/99 (ECtHR 20 February 2003) 52; *Stanev v. Bulgaria* App no 36760/06 (ECtHR Grand Chamber 17 January 2012) 146; *Glien v. Germany* App no 7345/12 (ECtHR 28 November 2013) 73; *Petschulies v. Germany* App no 6281/13 (ECtHR 2 June 2016) 61; *Ilnseher v. Germany* App nos 10211/12 and 27505/14 (ECtHR Grand Chamber 4 December 2018) 133; *Rooman v. Belgium* App no 18052/11 (ECtHR Grand Chamber 31 January 2019) 193; *Sy v. Italy* App no 11791/20 (ECtHR 24 January 2022) 108.

322 *Hutchison Reid v. United Kingdom* App no 50272/99 (ECtHR 20 February 2003) 51–55; *Rooman v. Belgium* App no 18052/11 (ECtHR Grand Chamber 31 January 2019) 193 and 205.

323 *Rooman v. Belgium* App no 18052/11 (ECtHR Grand Chamber 31 January 2019) 205–211.

324 *Sy v. Italy* App no 11791/20 (ECtHR 24 January 2022) 110.

325 *Glien v. Germany* App no 7345/12 (ECtHR 28 November 2013) 84; *Ilnseher v. Germany* App nos 10211/12 and 27505/14 (ECtHR Grand Chamber 4 December 2018) 149.

326 *Denis and Irvine v. Belgium* App nos 62819/17 and 63921/17 (ECtHR Grand Chamber 1 June 2021) 168.

amount of time and lack of spaces in appropriate institutions cannot justify continued detention in prison.[327]

SUBSECTION VI. OTHER SAFEGUARDS

62. Articles 5(2) to (5) – The remaining paragraphs of Article 5 contain additional safeguards for the person deprived of their liberty. We will discuss the relevant safeguards in this subsection, without falling into the rabbit hole of the intricacies of criminal procedure. Article 5 provides for the following rights: the right to be informed promptly of the reasons for an arrest,[328] the right to be brought promptly before a judge,[329] the right to have the lawfulness of detention speedily examined by a Court,[330] the right to trial within a reasonable time or to be released pending trial,[331] and the right to compensation for unlawful detention.[332] The first four will be discussed in varying degrees of detail, depending on their relevance. The last one is not relevant for our purposes as it does not really provide for a safeguard against arbitrary detention but aims to compensate after the fact and is therefore not discussed.

63. Article 5(2): the right to be informed promptly – The second Paragraph of Article 5 requires everybody who is arrested to be informed promptly of the reasons for their arrest and of any charge against them, in a language which they understand. This paragraph not only applies to detention under (1)(c) but also, for example, when a person is detained for extradition, medical treatment or after recalling a conditional release.[333] The purpose of the right to be informed is to enable people to effectively use their right to challenge their detention.[334] In order to be able to do so, they must be told, in simple, non-technical language that they can understand, the essential legal and factual

327 *Morsink v. Netherlands* App no 48865/99 (ECtHR 11 May 2004) 67–69; *Brand v. Netherlands* App no 49902/99 (ECtHR 11 May 2004) 64–66; *Pankiewicz v. Poland* App no 34151/04 (ECtHR 12 February 2008) 44–45; *Rooman v. Belgium* App no 18052/11 (ECtHR Grand Chamber 31 January 2019) 198; *Sy v. Italy* App no 11791/20 (ECtHR 24 January 2022) 135.

328 Art. 5(2) ECHR.

329 Which can be found in the first part of Art. 5(3) ECHR.

330 Art. 5(4) ECHR.

331 Which can be found in the second part of Art. 5(3) ECHR.

332 Art. 5(5) ECHR.

333 *X v. United Kingdom* App no 7215/75 (ECtHR 5 November 1981) 66; *Van der Leer v. the Netherlands* App no 11509/85 (ECtHR 21 February 1990) 27–28; *Shamayev and others v. Georgia and Russia* App no 36378/02 (ECtHR 12 April 2005) 414–415; *X. v. Belgium* App no 4741/71 (ECtHR Commission decision 2 April 1973).

334 *Van der Leer v. the Netherlands* App no 11509/85 (ECtHR 21 February 1990) 28; *Shamayev and others v. Georgia and Russia* App no 36378/02 (ECtHR 12 April 2005) 413; *Grubnyk v. Ukraine* App no 58444/15 (ECtHR 17 December 2020) 97 and 99.

grounds for the arrest.[335] Promptness must be assessed on a case-by-case basis, but it will be satisfied when the arrested person is informed of the reasons for their arrest within a few hours.[336]

64. Article 5(3): automatic judicial supervision and trial or release within reasonable time – Paragraph 3 of Article 5 is concerned with two different matters: first, the early stages following an arrest, when an individual is taken into the power of the authorities and second, the period pending any trial before a criminal court, during which the suspect may be detained or released with or without conditions.[337] This paragraph explicitly refers back to Article 5(1)(c) and thus only covers that subparagraph and not, for example, subparagraph (b) or (f).[338] The first part of the Article reads: '*Everyone arrested or detained in accordance with the provisions of paragraph 1 (c) of this Article shall be brought promptly before a judge or other officer authorised by law to exercise judicial power [...]*.'[339] The second part of Article 5(3) ECHR states that everyone detained under (1)(c) has the right to a trial within a reasonable time or to (conditional) release pending trial. This right requires the person to be conditionally released once continued detention pending trial ceases to be reasonable. The judicial supervision of detention which is required by the first part must be automatic and can therefore not be made dependent on a prior application by the detainee.[340] This is necessary to fulfil the purpose of the paragraph, as a person

335 *Fox, Campbell and Hartley v. the UK* App nos 12244/86, 12245/86 and 12383/86 (ECtHR 30 August 1990) 40; *Murray v. United Kingdom* App no 14310/88 (ECtHR Grand Chamber 28 October 1994) 72; *Khlaifia and others v. Italy* App no 16483/12 (ECtHR Grand Chamber 15 December 2016) 115; *J.R. and others v. Greece* App no 22696/16 (ECtHR 25 January 2018) 123–124.

336 *Fox, Campbell and Hartley v. United Kingdom* App nos 12244/86, 12245/86 and 12383/86 (ECtHR 30 August 1990) 40–42; *Kerr v. United Kingdom* App no 40451/98 (ECtHR Partial decision on the admissibility 7 December 1999).

337 *McKay v. United Kingdom* App no 543/03 (ECtHR Grand Chamber 3 October 2006) 31; *Ladent v. Poland* App no 11036/03 (ECtHR 18 March 2008) 71; *Krejčíř v. Czech Republic* App no 39298/04 and 8723/05 (ECtHR 26 March 2009) 89 and 101; *Medvedyev and others v. France* App no 3394/03 (ECtHR Grand Chamber 29 March 2010) 119; *Magee and others v. United Kingdom*, App nos 26289/12 and 2 others (ECtHR 12 May 2015) 75; *Buzadji v. Republic of Moldova* App no 23755/07 (ECtHR Grand Chamber 5 July 2016) 100. The second stage also requires provisional release once detention ceases to be reasonable. See: *De Jong, Baljet and Van den Brink v. Netherlands* App nos 8805/79, 8806/79 and 9242/81 (ECtHR 22 May 1984) 44; *T.W. v. Malta* App no 25644/94 (ECtHR Grand Chamber 29 April 1999) 41; *Khayredinov v. Ukraine* App no 38717/04 (ECtHR 14 October 2010) 39.

338 *B. v. Austria* App no 8/1989/168/224 (ECtHR 23 February 1990) 36; *Quinn v. France* App no 18580/91 (ECtHR 22 March 1995) 53; *Ječius v. Lithuania* App no 34578/97 (ECtHR 31 July 2000) 75; *Epple v. Germany* App no 77909/01 (ECtHR 24 March 2005), 42; *Shcherbina v. Russia* App no 41970/11 (ECtHR 26 June 2014) 63; Dhont (n 121) 336–337; Macken (n 95) 61; Murdoch (n 122) 507; Van Dijk and others (n 107) 472.

339 Art. 5(3) ECHR.

340 *Aquilina v. Malta* App no 25642/94 (ECtHR Grand Chamber 29 April 1999) 49; *T.W. v. Malta* App no 25644/94 (ECtHR Grand Chamber 29 April 1999) 43; *Niedbała v. Poland* App no 27915/95 (ECtHR 4 July 2000) 50; *McKay v. United Kingdom* App no 543/03 (ECtHR Grand

subjected to ill-treatment might be incapable of lodging an application asking for a judge to review their detention. The same might also be true for other vulnerable categories of detainees, such as the mentally frail or those ignorant of the language of the judicial officer.[341] This initial automatic review of arrest and detention must be capable of examining lawfulness issues and whether or not the reasonable suspicion that the arrested person has committed an offence persists.[342] Justifications for any period of detention must be convincingly demonstrated[343] and alternative means of ensuring that the person appears at trial must be considered.[344, 345] Quasi-automatic prolongation of detention violates (3).[346] The paragraph also includes a procedural requirement for the '*judge or other officer authorised by law*' to hear the individual brought before them in person,[347] and a substantive requirement for the same officer to review the circumstances militating for or against detention, meaning whether there are reasons to justify detention, and to order release if there are no such

Chamber 3 October 2006) 34; *Ladent v. Poland* App no 11036/03 (ECtHR 18 March 2008) 74; *Varga v. Romania* App no 73957/01 (ECtHR 1 April 2008) 52; *Oral and Atabay v. Turkey* App no 39686/02 (ECtHR 23 June 2009) 40; *Viorel Burzo v. Romania* App no 75109/01 and 12639/02 (ECtHR 30 June 2009) 107; *Medvedyev and others v. France* App no 3394/03 (ECtHR Grand Chamber 29 March 2010) 122; *Magee and others v. United Kingdom*, App nos 26289/12 and 2 others (ECtHR 12 May 2015) 79. See also: Macken (n 236) 210–211.

341 *Aquilina v. Malta* App no 25642/94 (ECtHR Grand Chamber 29 April 1999) 49; *T.W. v. Malta* App no 25644/94 (ECtHR Grand Chamber 29 April 1999) 43; *McKay v. United Kingdom* App no 543/03 (ECtHR Grand Chamber 3 October 2006) 34; *Ladent v. Poland* App no 11036/03 (ECtHR 18 March 2008) 74; *Medvedyev and others v. France* App no 3394/03 (ECtHR Grand Chamber 29 March 2010) 122; *Magee and others v. United Kingdom*, App nos 26289/12 and 2 others (ECtHR 12 May 2015) 79.

342 *McKay v. United Kingdom* App no 543/03 (ECtHR Grand Chamber 3 October 2006) 40; *Oral and Atabay v. Turkey* App no 39686/02 (ECtHR 23 June 2009) 41; *Buzadji v. Republic of Moldova* App no 23755/07 (ECtHR Grand Chamber 5 July 2016) 98–99; *S., V. and A. v. Denmark* App nos 35553/23, 36678/23 and 36711/12 (ECtHR Grand Chamber 22 October 2018) 128.

343 *Strogan v. Ukraine* App no 30198/11 (ECtHR 6 October 2016) 95.

344 See also: Sébastien Van Drooghenbroeck, 'Note relative à l'application des principes de proportionnalité et subsidiarité en matière pénale dans de droit de la Convention européenne des droits de l'Homme', Annex 2.7 to the Report on behalf of the Committee on Justice on the Bill on the Code of Criminal Procedure, *Parl.St.* Senaat 2005–06, no. 3–450/20, (1398) 1402.

345 *Jablonski v. Poland* App no 33492/96 (ECtHR 21 December 2000) 82–83; *Mamedova v. Russia* App no 7064/05 (ECtHR 1 June 2006) 77; *Ladent v. Poland* App no 11036/03 (ECtHR 18 March 2008) 55; *Khayredinov v. Ukraine* App no 38717/04 (ECtHR 14 October 2010) 28 and 38; *Osypenko v. Ukraine* App no 4634/04 (ECtHR 9 November 2010) 79; *Idalov v. Russia* App no 5826/03 (ECtHR Grand Chamber 22 May 2012) 140; *Buzadji v. Republic of Moldova* App no 23755/07 (ECtHR Grand Chamber 5 July 2016) 87; *S., V. and A. v. Denmark* App nos 35553/23, 36678/23 and 36711/12 (ECtHR Grand Chamber 22 October 2018) 77.

346 *Tase v. Romania* App no 29761/02 (ECtHR 10 September 2008) 40.

347 *De Jong, Baljet and Van den Brink v. the Netherlands* App nos 8805/79, 8806/79 and 9242/81 (ECtHR 22 May 1984) 51; *Aquilina v. Malta* App no 25642/94 (ECtHR Grand Chamber 29 April 1999) 50; *T.W. v. Malta* App no 25644/94 (ECtHR Grand Chamber 29 April 1999) 44.

reasons.[348, 349] This means that in absence of reasons to justify detention, the 'officer' must be able to make a binding order for the detainee's release.[350] The expression '*judge or other officer authorised by law to exercise judicial power*' is a synonym for the term '*competent legal authority*' in Article 5(1)(c).[351] While the 'officer' and the 'judge' are not identical, the former must have some of the latter's attributes, meaning they must satisfy certain conditions each of which constitutes a guarantee for the person arrested.[352] One such condition is independence of the executive and of the parties.[353] This does not mean that the officer may not be to some extent subordinate to other judges or officers on the condition that they themselves enjoy similar independence.[354] While a judicial officer who is competent to decide on detention may also carry out other duties, there is a risk of legitimate doubt concerning his impartiality on the part of those subject to his decisions, if the officer is entitled to intervene in the subsequent

348 *Aquilina v. Malta* App no 25642/94 (ECtHR Grand Chamber 29 April 1999) 47; *T.W. v. Malta* App no 25644/94 (ECtHR Grand Chamber 29 April 1999) 41; *Pantea v. Romania* App no 33343/96 (ECtHR 3 June 2003) 231; *Krejčíř v. Czech Republic* App no 39298/04 and 8723/05 (ECtHR 26 March 2009) 89.

349 *Schiesser v. Switzerland* App no 7710/76 (ECtHR 4 December 1979) 31; *Assenov and others v. Bulgaria* App no 90/1997/874/1086 (ECtHR 28 October 1998) 146; *Hood v. United Kingdom* App no 27267/95 (ECtHR 18 February 1999) 60; *Nikolova v. Bulgaria* App no 31195/96 (ECtHR Grand Chamber 25 March 1999) 49; *Niedbała v. Poland* App no 27915/95 (ECtHR 4 July 2000) 48–49; *Mamedova v. Russia* App no 7064/05 (ECtHR 1 June 2006) 81; *Medvedyev and others v. France* App no 3394/03 (ECtHR Grand Chamber 29 March 2010) 124; *Magee and others v. United Kingdom*, App nos 26289/12 and 2 others (ECtHR 12 May 2015) 81; *Buzadji v. Republic of Moldova* App no 23755/07 (ECtHR Grand Chamber 5 July 2016) 98. See also: Sottiaux (n 27) 212.

350 *De Jong, Baljet and Van den Brink v. the Netherlands* App nos 8805/79, 8806/79 and 9242/81 (ECtHR 22 May 1984) 47; *Assenov and others v. Bulgaria* App no 90/1997/874/1086 (ECtHR 28 October 1998) 146; *Nikolova v. Bulgaria* App no 31195/96 (ECtHR Grand Chamber 25 March 1999) 49; *Niedbała v. Poland* App no 27915/95 (ECtHR 4 July 2000) 49; *Pantea v. Romania* App no 33343/96 (ECtHR 3 June 2003) 236; *McKay v. United Kingdom* App no 543/03 (ECtHR Grand Chamber 3 October 2006) 40; *Krejčíř v. Czech Republic* App no 39298/04 and 8723/05 (ECtHR 26 March 2009) 89; *Oral and Atabay v. Turkey* App no 39686/02 (ECtHR 23 June 2009) 41; *Medvedyev and others v. France* App no 3394/03 (ECtHR Grand Chamber 29 March 2010) 124–125; *Magee and others v. United Kingdom*, App nos 26289/12 and 2 others (ECtHR 12 May 2015) 81; *Buzadji v. Republic of Moldova* App no 23755/07 (ECtHR Grand Chamber 5 July 2016) 99.

351 *Schiesser v. Switzerland* App no 7710/76 (ECtHR 4 December 1979) 29; *Medvedyev and others v. France* App no 3394/03 (ECtHR Grand Chamber 29 March 2010) 123; *Magee and others v. United Kingdom*, App nos 26289/12 and 2 others (ECtHR 12 May 2015) 80.

352 *Schiesser v. Switzerland* App no 7710/76 (ECtHR 4 December 1979) 31. See also: Sottiaux (n 27) 212.

353 *Schiesser v. Switzerland* App no 7710/76 (ECtHR 4 December 1979) 29 and 31; *Assenov and others v. Bulgaria* App no 90/1997/874/1086 (ECtHR 28 October 1998) 146; *Nikolova v. Bulgaria* App no 31195/96 (ECtHR Grand Chamber 25 March 1999) 49; *McKay v. United Kingdom* App no 543/03 (ECtHR Grand Chamber 3 October 2006) 35; *Magee and others v. United Kingdom*, App nos 26289/12 and 2 others (ECtHR 12 May 2015) 81; *Buzadji v. Republic of Moldova* App no 23755/07 (ECtHR Grand Chamber 5 July 2016) 98.

354 *Schiesser v. Switzerland* App no 7710/76 (ECtHR 4 December 1979) 31.

proceedings as a representative of the prosecuting authority.[355] In this respect, objective appearances at the time of the decision on detention are material: if it appears that the '*officer authorised by law to exercise judicial power*' may later intervene in subsequent criminal proceedings on behalf of the prosecuting authority, his independence and impartiality can be open to doubt.[356] In the context of paragraph 3 the Court has also held that investigations into terrorism present the authorities with special problems.[357] However, this does not mean the non-judicial authorities have carte blanche to act without supervision of courts, both nationally and internationally.[358] In addition to reasonable suspicion at the time of the arrest and initial detention, in cases of prolonged detention reasonable suspicion must also be shown to persist and to remain

---

355 *De Jong, Baljet and Van den Brink v. the Netherlands* App nos 8805/79, 8806/79 and 9242/81 (ECtHR 22 May 1984) 49; *Huber v. Switzerland* App no 12794/87 (ECtHR Plenary 23 October 1990) 43; *Brincat v. Italy* App no 13867/88 (ECtHR 26 November 1992) 20; *Assenov and others v. Bulgaria* App no 90/1997/874/1086 (ECtHR 28 October 1998) 146; *Medvedyev and others v. France* App no 3394/03 (ECtHR Grand Chamber 29 March 2010) 124; *Magee and others v. United Kingdom*, App nos 26289/12 and 2 others (ECtHR 12 May 2015) 81. In a dissenting opinion to the *Huber* case, judge Matscher questions whether this should be a requirement. He refers back to the *Schiesser* case, which does indeed not include this requirement (*Schiesser v. Switzerland* App no 7710/76 (ECtHR 4 December 1979) 34–35. Note that in dissenting opinions to this judgment judges Evrigenis and Ryssdal disagree with the majority on this exact point). However, subsequent case law (see above in this footnote) seems to consistently include this requirement. In this case law the Court ruled, based on this condition, that e.g. the Italian, Romanian and Bulgarian Public Prosecutors and the Swiss District Attorney are not 'officers' under Art. 5(3) ECHR (*Huber v. Switzerland* App no 12794/87 (ECtHR Plenary 23 October 1990) 43; *Brincat v. Italy* App no 13867/88 (ECtHR 26 November 1992) 21; *Assenov and others v. Bulgaria* App no 90/1997/874/1086 (ECtHR 28 October 1998) 149; *Nikolova v. Bulgaria* App no 31195/96 (ECtHR Grand Chamber 25 March 1999) 51; *I.I. v. Bulgaria* App no 44082/98 (ECtHR 9 June 2005) 96; *Năstase-Silivestru v. Romania* App no 74785/01 (ECtHR 4 October 2007) 29).

356 *Brincat v. Italy* App no 13867/88 (ECtHR 26 November 1992) 21; *Assenov and others v. Bulgaria* App no 90/1997/874/1086 (ECtHR 28 October 1998) 146; *Hood v. United Kingdom* App no 27267/95 (ECtHR 18 February 1999) 57; *Nikolova v. Bulgaria* App no 31195/96 (ECtHR Grand Chamber 25 March 1999) 49; *Niedbała v. Poland* App no 27915/95 (ECtHR 4 July 2000) 49; *Pantea v. Romania* App no 33343/96 (ECtHR 3 June 2003) 236.

357 *Brogan and others v. United Kingdom* App nos 11209/84, 11234/84, 11266/84 and 11386/85 (ECtHR Plenary 29 November 1988) 61; *Murray v. United Kingdom* App no 14310/88 (ECtHR Grand Chamber 28 October 1994) 58; *Aksoy v. Turkey* App no 21987/93 (ECtHR 18 December 1996) 78; *Öcalan v. Turkey* app no 46221/99 (ECtHR Grand Chamber 12 May 2005) 104; *Medvedyev and others v. France* App no 3394/03 (ECtHR Grand Chamber 29 March 2010) 126; *Magee and others v. United Kingdom*, App nos 26289/12 and 2 others (ECtHR 12 May 2015) 85. See also: Vanneste (n 27) 1670.

358 *Brogan and others v. United Kingdom* App nos 11209/84, 11234/84, 11266/84 and 11386/85 (ECtHR Plenary 29 November 1988) 61–62; *Murray v. United Kingdom* App no 14310/88 (ECtHR Grand Chamber 28 October 1994) 58; *Öcalan v. Turkey* app no 46221/99 (ECtHR Grand Chamber 12 May 2005) 104; *Medvedyev and others v. France* App no 3394/03 (ECtHR Grand Chamber 29 March 2010) 126; *Magee and others v. United Kingdom*, App nos 26289/12 and 2 others (ECtHR 12 May 2015) 85. See also: *Aksoy v. Turkey* App no 21987/93 (ECtHR 18 December 1996) 78; De Schutter (n 27) 123–124; Ludovic Hennebel and Hélène Tigroudja, 'Le Juge, Le Terroriste et l'état de Droit' in Ludovic Hennebel and Damien Vandermeersch (eds), *Juger le terrorisme dans l'État de droit* (Bruylant 2009) 123–124 and 141; Vanneste (n 27) 1670.

reasonable throughout the detention.[359] Circumstances can change and grounds for detention which may exist in the early stages of an investigation, may no longer be sufficient at a later stage, for example, the risk that the defendant would tamper with evidence.[360] Therefore, periodical review in which a judge decides that continued detention is justified, is an important aspect of judicial supervision. The case must thus be subject to judicial supervision at regular short intervals.[361] Furthermore, after *'a certain lapse of time'*, reasonable suspicion alone no longer suffices.[362] Then, the national judicial authorities must cite other grounds to continue justifying the deprivation of liberty.[363] If the ECtHR finds these grounds relevant and sufficient, it verifies whether the national authorities displayed 'special diligence' in the conduct of the proceedings.[364] Such grounds

359 *Stögmüller v. Austria* App no 1602/62 (ECtHR 10 November 1969) 4; *B. v. Austria* App no 8/1989/168/224 (ECtHR 23 February 1990) 42; *Toth v. Austria* App no 11894/85 (ECtHR 12 December 1991) 67; *Labita v. Italy* App no 26772/95 (ECtHR Grand Chamber 6 April 2000) 153; *Nikolova v. Bulgaria (no. 2)* App no 40896/98 (ECtHR 30 September 2004) 61; *McKay v. United Kingdom* App no 543/03 (ECtHR Grand Chamber 3 October 2006) 44; *Danov v. Bulgaria* App no 56796/00 (ECtHR 26 October 2006) 81; *Solmaz v. Turkey* App no 27561/02 (ECtHR 16 January 2007) 40; *Piotr Baranowski v. Poland* App no 39742/05 (ECtHR 2 October 2007) 44; *Prencipe v. Monaco* App no 43376/06 (ECtHR 16 July 2009) 74; *Ilgar Mammadov v. Azerbaijan* App no 15172/13 (ECtHR 22 May 2014) 90; *Urtāns v. Latvia* App no 16858/11 (ECtHR 28 October 2014) 32; *Buzadji v. Republic of Moldova* App no 23755/07 (ECtHR Grand Chamber 5 July 2016) 87; *Selahattin Demirtaş v. Turkey (no. 2)* App no 14305/17 (ECtHR Grand Chamber 22 December 2020) 320.

360 *Urtāns v. Latvia* App no 16858/11 (ECtHR 28 October 2014) 29.

361 *Urtāns v. Latvia* App no 16858/11 (ECtHR 28 October 2014) 29.

362 *Stögmüller v. Austria* App no 1602/62 (ECtHR 10 November 1969) 4; *Letellier v. France* App no 12369/86 (ECtHR 26 June 1991) 35; *Toth v. Austria* App no 11894/85 (ECtHR 12 December 1991) 67; *I.A. v. France* App no 1/1998/904/1116 (ECtHR 23 September 1998) 102; *Labita v. Italy* App no 26772/95 (ECtHR Grand Chamber 6 April 2000) 153; *Jablonski v. Poland* App no 33492/96 (ECtHR 21 December 2000) 80; *Nikolova v. Bulgaria (no. 2)* App no 40896/98 (ECtHR 30 September 2004) 61; *Mamedova v. Russia* App no 7064/05 (ECtHR 1 June 2006) 73; *McKay v. United Kingdom* App no 543/03 (ECtHR Grand Chamber 3 October 2006), 44; *Danov v. Bulgaria* App no 56796/00 (ECtHR 26 October 2006) 81; *Kučera v. Slovakia* App no 48666/99 (ECtHR 17 July 2007) 94; *Piotr Baranowski v. Poland* App no 39742/05 (ECtHR 2 October 2007) 44; *Prencipe v. Monaco* App no 43376/06 (ECtHR 16 July 2009) 74; *Idalov v. Russia* App no 5826/03 (ECtHR Grand Chamber 22 May 2012) 140; *Osmanović v. Croatia* App no 67604/10 (ECtHR 6 November 2012) 33; *Magee and others v. United Kingdom*, App nos 26289/12 and 2 others (ECtHR 12 May 2015) 88.

363 *Urtāns v. Latvia* App no 16858/11 (ECtHR 28 October 2014) 30; *Strogan v. Ukraine* App no 30198/11 (ECtHR 6 October 2016) 96.

364 *Stögmüller v. Austria* App no 1602/62 (ECtHR 10 November 1969) 5; *B. v. Austria* App no 8/1989/168/224 (ECtHR 23 February 1990) 41; *Letellier v. France* App no 12369/86 (ECtHR 26 June 1991) 35; *Clooth v. Belgium* App no 49/1990/240/311 (ECtHR 27 November 1991) 36; *Toth v. Austria* App no 11894/85 (ECtHR 12 December 1991) 67; *I.A. v. France* App no 1/1998/904/1116 (ECtHR 23 September 1998) 102; *Labita v. Italy* App no 26772/95 (ECtHR Grand Chamber 6 April 2000) 153; *Jablonski v. Poland* App no 33492/96 (ECtHR 21 December 2000) 80; *Nikolova v. Bulgaria (no. 2)* App no 40896/98 (ECtHR 30 September 2004) 61; *Mamedova v. Russia* App no 7064/05 (ECtHR 1 June 2006) 73; *McKay v. United Kingdom* App no 543/03 (ECtHR Grand Chamber 3 October 2006) 44; *Danov v. Bulgaria* App no 56796/00 (ECtHR 26 October 2006) 81; *Solmaz v. Turkey* App no 27561/02 (ECtHR 16 January 2007) 40; *Kučera v. Slovakia* App no 48666/99 (ECtHR 17 July 2007) 94; *Piotr*

include for example the risk of absconding,[365] reoffending,[366] influencing witnesses[367] or tampering with evidence.[368, 369] In the *Buzadji* case, the Court held that there were compelling arguments to '*synchronise the second limb of guarantees with the first one.*' Meaning that '*the requirement for the judicial officer to give relevant and sufficient reasons for the detention – in addition to the persistence of reasonable suspicion – applies already at the time of the first decision ordering detention on remand, that is to say 'promptly' after the arrest.*'[370]

65. Promptness – It follows directly from the wording of Article 5(3) that if the person is not arrested or detained, but has been 'promptly' released, there is no obligation to bring them promptly before a judge.[371] In order to determine whether release has taken place at a time before such prompt judicial control, the starting point should be the manner in which the requirement of 'promptness' in Article 5(3) has been applied in the Court's case-law. While promptness has to be assessed according to the special features of each case,[372] the strict time constraint imposed by this requirement leaves little flexibility in interpretation.[373] Any period in excess of four days is *prima facie* too long (even

---

Baranowski v. Poland App no 39742/05 (ECtHR 2 October 2007) 44; *Prencipe v. Monaco* App no 43376/06 (ECtHR 16 July 2009) 74; *Idalov v. Russia* App no 5826/03 (ECtHR Grand Chamber 22 May 2012) 140; *Gutsanovi v. Bulgaria* App no 34529/10 (ECtHR 15 October 2012) 162; *Magee and others v. United Kingdom*, App nos 26289/12 and 2 others (ECtHR 12 May 2015) 88; *Buzadji v. Republic of Moldova* App no 23755/07 (ECtHR Grand Chamber 5 July 2016) 87; *S., V. and A. v. Denmark* App nos 35553/23, 36678/23 and 36711/12 (ECtHR Grand Chamber 22 October 2018) 77.

365 *Wemhoff v. Germany* App no 2122/64 (ECtHR 27 June 1968) 14; *Stögmüller v. Austria* App no 1602/62 (ECtHR 10 November 1969) 14; *Toth v. Austria* App no 11894/85 (ECtHR 12 December 1991) 72.

366 *Stögmüller v. Austria* App no 1602/62 (ECtHR 10 November 1969) 15; *Toth v. Austria* App no 11894/85 (ECtHR 12 December 1991) 70.

367 *Labita v. Italy* App no 26772/95 (ECtHR Grand Chamber 6 April 2000) 162–163; *Kučera v. Slovakia* App no 48666/99 (ECtHR 17 July 2007) 95; *Piotr Baranowski v. Poland* App no 39742/05 (ECtHR 2 October 2007) 49.

368 *Wemhoff v. Germany* App no 2122/64 (ECtHR 27 June 1968) 14; *Labita v. Italy* App no 26772/95 (ECtHR Grand Chamber 6 April 2000) 162–163.

369 *Letellier v. France* App no 12369/86 (ECtHR 26 June 1991) 37–51; *Tomasi v. France* App no 12850/87 (ECtHR 27 August 1992) 85–99; *I.A. v. France* App no 1/1998/904/1116 (ECtHR 23 September 1998) 104–110; *Buzadji v. Republic of Moldova* App no 23755/07 (ECtHR Grand Chamber 5 July 2016) 88. See also: Dhont (n 121) 311–317.

370 *Buzadji v. Republic of Moldova* App no 23755/07 (ECtHR Grand Chamber 5 July 2016) 102.

371 *Brogan and others v. United Kingdom* App nos 11209/84, 11234/84, 11266/84 and 11386/85 (ECtHR Plenary 29 November 1988) 58; *S., V. and A. v. Denmark* App nos 35553/23, 36678/23 and 36711/12 (ECtHR Grand Chamber 22 October 2018) 129.

372 *De Jong, Baljet and Van den Brink v. Netherlands* App nos 8805/79, 8806/79 and 9242/81 (ECtHR 22 May 1984) 52.

373 *Brogan and others v. United Kingdom* App nos 11209/84, 11234/84, 11266/84 and 11386/85 (ECtHR Plenary 29 November 1988) 59; *Aquilina v. Malta* App no 25642/94 (ECtHR Grand Chamber 29 April 1999) 48; *T.W. v. Malta* App no 25644/94 (ECtHR Grand Chamber 29 April 1999) 42; *Pantea v. Romania* App no 33343/96 (ECtHR 3 June 2003) 240; *McKay v. United Kingdom* App no 543/03 (ECtHR Grand Chamber 3 October 2006) 33; *Ladent v.*

in terrorist investigations),[374] but in certain circumstances shorter periods can also be in breach of the promptness requirement.[375, 376] Under the first limb of

Poland App no 11036/03 (ECtHR 18 March 2008) 73; *Kandzhov v. Bulgaria* App no 68294/01 (ECtHR 6 November 2008) 65; *İpek and others v. Turkey* App nos 17019/02 and 30070/02 (ECtHR 3 February 2009) 34; *Medvedyev and others v. France* App no 3394/03 (ECtHR Grand Chamber 29 March 2010) *121; Gutsanovi v. Bulgaria* App no 34529/10 (ECtHR 15 October 2012) 153; *Magee and others v. United Kingdom*, App nos 26289/12 and 2 others (ECtHR 12 May 2015) 77; *S., V. and A. v. Denmark* App nos 35553/23, 36678/23 and 36711/12 (ECtHR Grand Chamber 22 October 2018) 130.

374 *McKay v. United Kingdom* App no 543/03 (ECtHR Grand Chamber 3 October 2006) 33; *Ladent v. Poland* App no 11036/03 (ECtHR 18 March 2008) 73; *İpek and others v. Turkey* App nos 17019/02 and 30070/02 (ECtHR 3 February 2009) 35; *Oral and Atabay v. Turkey* App no 39686/02 (ECtHR 23 June 2009) 43–44. See e.g. the *Brogan* case, which concerned terrorism suspects, in which 4 days and 6 hours was not considered 'prompt' by the majority of the Court (*Brogan and others v. United Kingdom* App nos 11209/84, 11234/84, 11266/84 and 11386/85 (ECtHR Plenary 29 November 1988) 62; Macken (n 95) 64–65.). In other terrorism cases, periods of 7 and 14 days were also not considered prompt (*Öcalan v. Turkey* app no 46221/99 (ECtHR Grand Chamber 12 May 2005) 104–105; *Aksoy v. Turkey* App no 21987/93 (ECtHR 18 December 1996) 66). See also: *O'Hara v. United Kingdom* App no 37555/97 (ECtHR 16 October 2001) 46. In a joint dissenting opinion to the *Brogan* case, however, judges Thór Vilhjálmsson, Bindschedler-Robert, Gölcüklü, Matscher and Valticos defend the view that this was prompt and even a longer period of six days and 16 and a half hours was also prompt, all considering the special circumstances of the case. The same goes for the partly dissenting opinion of judge sir Vincent Evans and the dissenting opinion of judge Martens to the *Brogan* case. See also: Sottiaux (n 27) 215–216. Also note that e.g. in *Medvedyev and others v. France*, a period of 13 days was still considered prompt. This was due to the specific circumstances of this case, which constituted 'wholly exceptional circumstances'. *In casu* the applicants were on a ship on the high seas very far removed from France and it was impossible for the government to bring the applicants before a judge any sooner. See: *Medvedyev and others v. France* App no 3394/03 (ECtHR Grand Chamber 29 March 2010) 130–132. For a similar case see: *Rigopoulos v. Spain* App no 37388/97 (European Commission of Human Rights 16 April 1998). However, in a partly dissenting opinion to the *Medvedyev* case, judges Tulkens, Bonello, Zupančič, Fura, Spielmann, Tsotsoria, Power and Poalelungi hold that there were important differences between *Medvedyev* and *Rigopoulos* and that the period of 13 days was not necessary in the case of *Medvedyev*.

375 See e.g. *İpek and others v. Turkey*, in which the Court ruled that detention for more than three days was arbitrary. Even though this was in a terrorism context, the Court found that the applicants were not brought promptly before a judge, due to the young age of the applicants, the lack of other safeguards (such as a lawyer) and the fact that the government did not undertake any other investigative measures during their detention. See: *İpek and others v. Turkey* App nos 17019/02 and 30070/02 (ECtHR 3 February 2009) 36–37. In the *Kandzhov v. Bulgaria* the Court found detention of three days and 23 hours before the applicant appeared in front of a judge to be not prompt. In this case, the charges were minor and non-violent, and no appropriate steps were taken to ensure the applicant's immediate appearance before a judge, while there were no special difficulties or exceptional circumstances. See: *Kandzhov v. Bulgaria* App no 68294/01 (ECtHR 6 November 2008) 66. In the *Gutsanovi v. Bulgaria* case three days and five and a half hours were deemed too long, in view of the psychological frailty of the defendant and the lack of investigatory measures after the first day of the detention. See: *Gutsanovi v. Bulgaria* App no 34529/10 (ECtHR 15 October 2012) 154–159. In a partly dissenting opinion to this case, judge Wojtyczek disagrees with the majority on this point. He believes the applicant was brought before a judge promptly because there are no good reasons to depart from the 4-day rule in this case.

376 *Năstase-Silivestru v. Romania* App no 74785/01 (ECtHR 4 October 2007) 32; *Oral and Atabay v. Turkey* App no 39686/02 (ECtHR 23 June 2009) 43; *Gutsanovi v. Bulgaria* App no 34529/10

subparagraph (c) a certain period between the arrest and the prompt appearance before the judge may be necessary for the investigating authorities to obtain evidence to substantiate that there are reasons to justify the detention.[377] Such considerations do not come into play for a detainee under the second limb.[378] The facts constituting the risk of committing an offence must already be established at the time when the person is detained in order to prevent their committing this offence. The period should therefore be shorter than in cases of pre-trial detention and should thus be significantly shorter than four days.[379] The Court finds that, generally speaking, release '*at a time before prompt judicial control*' in the context of preventive detention should be a matter of hours rather than days.[380] Finally, the second limb of Article 5(3) cannot apply to preventive detention where no criminal proceedings are initiated and no trial is to be held.[381]

66. ARTICLE 5(4): *HABEAS CORPUS* – In addition to the rights conferred in Article 5(3) ECHR, the Convention also contains the right for a detained person to actively seek a judicial review of their detention, also known as *habeas corpus*.[382] Unlike the one in paragraph 3, this right in paragraph 4, is applicable to detention under all subparagraphs of paragraph 1.[383] Paragraph 4 reads: '*Everyone who is deprived of his liberty by arrest or detention shall be entitled to take proceedings by which the lawfulness of his detention shall be decided speedily by a court and his release ordered if the detention is not lawful.*'[384] So every detainee has the right to request a judicial review and that review must take place 'speedily' (see no. 67). The existence of the review procedure must be sufficiently certain in practice.[385] The term lawfulness in paragraph 4 has the same meaning

(ECtHR 15 October 2012) 154; *Magee and others v. United Kingdom*, App nos 26289/12 and 2 others (ECtHR 12 May 2015) 78; *S., V. and A. v. Denmark* App nos 35553/23, 36678/23 and 36711/12 (ECtHR Grand Chamber 22 October 2018) 131.

377 *S., V. and A. v. Denmark* App nos 35553/23, 36678/23 and 36711/12 (ECtHR Grand Chamber 22 October 2018) 132.

378 *S., V. and A. v. Denmark* App nos 35553/23, 36678/23 and 36711/12 (ECtHR Grand Chamber 22 October 2018, 133.

379 *S., V. and A. v. Denmark* App nos 35553/23, 36678/23 and 36711/12 (ECtHR Grand Chamber 22 October 2018) 133.

380 *S., V. and A. v. Denmark* App nos 35553/23, 36678/23 and 36711/12 (ECtHR Grand Chamber 22 October 2018) 134.

381 *S., V. and A. v. Denmark* App nos 35553/23, 36678/23 and 36711/12 (ECtHR Grand Chamber 22 October 2018) 135. See also: Macken (n 236) 213–214.

382 *Rakevich v. Russia* App no 58973/00 (ECtHR 28 October 2003) 43; *Mooren v. Germany* App no 11364/03 (ECtHR Grand Chamber 9 July 2009) 106.

383 Dhont (n 121) 351.

384 Art. 5(4) ECHR.

385 *Kadem v. Malta* App no 55263/00 (ECtHR 9 January 2003) 41; *Nikolova v. Bulgaria (no. 2)* App no 40896/98 (ECtHR 30 September 2004) 75; *Zervudacki v. France* App no 73947/01 (ECtHR 27 July 2006) 76; *Abdolkhani and Karimnia v. Turkey* App no 30471/08 (ECtHR 22 September 2009) 139; *Garayev v. Azerbaijan* App no 53688/08 (ECtHR 10 June 2010) 103; *Louled Massoud v. Malta* App no 24340/08 (ECtHR 27 July 2010) 39; *Osmanović v. Croatia* App no 67604/10 (ECtHR 6 November 2012) 45; *Azimov v. Russia* App no 67474/11 (ECtHR

as in paragraph 1 (see no. 41).[386] The right also implies that the person must be informed of the reasons for the deprivation of liberty.[387] Otherwise the review would be deprived of all effective substance.[388] In general, Article 5(4) ECHR is applied to people still in detention, meaning it does not apply to people after release,[389] even if that release is on bail.[390, 391] However, in exceptional circumstances, it could also apply to an individual who is no longer detained during appeal proceedings the outcome of which is crucial in determining the lawfulness his detention.[392] This is for example the case when the detainee is released pending appeal proceedings during which their detention could be reconfirmed. In those cases, the guarantee of speediness has become irrelevant, but the guarantee of effectiveness of the review continues to apply.[393] On several occasions, the Court has held that when the detention is very brief and the detainee is released speedily, before review could take place, no issue arises under Article 5(4) ECHR.[394] In recent case law, however, the Court added that

---

18 April 2013) 150; *Suso Musa v. Malta* App no 42337/12 (ECtHR 23 July 2013) 51; *Petkov and Profirov v. Bulgaria* App nos 50027/08 and 50781/09 (ECtHR 24 June 2014) 66; *Khlaifia and others v. Italy* App no 16483/12 (ECtHR Grand Chamber 15 December 2016) 130.

386 *Brogan and others v. United Kingdom* App nos 11209/84, 11234/84, 11266/84 and 11386/85 (ECtHR Plenary 29 November 1988) 65; *E. v. Norway* App no 11701/85 (ECtHR 29 August 1990) 49; *Chahal v. United Kingdom* App no 22414/93 (ECtHR Grand Chamber 15 November 1996) 127; *Assenov and others v. Bulgaria* App no 90/1997/874/1086 (ECtHR 28 October 1998) 162; *Lavents v. Latvia* App no 58442/00 (ECtHR 28 November 2002) 81; *Zervudacki v. France* App no 73947/01 (ECtHR 27 July 2006) 74; *A. and others v. United Kingdom* App no 3455/05 (ECtHR Grand Chamber 19 February 2009) 202; *Krejčíř v. Czech Republic* App no 39298/04 and 8723/05 (ECtHR 26 March 2009) 116; *Louled Massoud v. Malta* App no 24340/08 (ECtHR 27 July 2010) 39; *Altınok v. Turkey* App no 31610/08 (ECtHR 29 November 2011) 45; *Korneykova v. Ukraine* App no 39884/05 (ECtHR 19 January 2012) 68; *Suso Musa v. Malta* App no 42337/12 (ECtHR 23 July 2013) 50; *M.H. v. United Kingdom* App no 11577/06 (ECtHR 22 October 2013) 74; *AM v. France* App no 56324/13 (ECtHR 12 July 2016) 40; *Khlaifia and others v. Italy* App no 16483/12 (ECtHR Grand Chamber 15 December 2016) 128; *Etute v. Luxembourg* App no 18233/16 (ECtHR 30 January 2018) 24; *Baş v. Turkey* App no 66448/17 (ECtHR 3 March 2020) 212; *Moustahi v. France* App no 9347/14 (ECtHR 25 June 2020) 100; *Dimo Dimov and others v. Bulgaria* App no 30044/10 (ECtHR 7 July 2020) 69.

387 *Khlaifia and others v. Italy* App no 16483/12 (ECtHR Grand Chamber 15 December 2016) 132. See also: Van Dijk and others (n 107) 483–484.

388 *Khlaifia and others v. Italy* App no 16483/12 (ECtHR Grand Chamber 15 December 2016) 132.

389 *X. v. Sweden* App no 10230/82 (European Commission of Human Rights 11 May 1983); *A.K. v. Austria* App no 20832/92 (European Commission of Human Rights 1 December 1993). Conditional release is also release. See: Murdoch (n 122) 501.

390 Art. 5(4) ECHR does not contain a right to unconditional release. See: *D.W. v. United Kingdom* App no 21387/93 (European Commission of Human Rights 21 October 1996) 6.

391 *Stephens v. Malta (no. 1)* App no 11956/07 (ECtHR 21 April 2009) 102. See also: Dhont (n 121) 351.The same goes for people for whom an arrest warrant has been issues but who are not yet in detention. See: *Guliyev v. Azerbaijan* App no 35584/02 (ECtHR Decision on admissibility 27 May 2005) 2.

392 *Oravec v. Croatia* App no 51249/11 (ECtHR 11 July 2017) 65.

393 *Kováčik v. Slovakia* App no 50903/06 (ECtHR 29 November 2011) 77; *Osmanović v. Croatia* App no 67604/10 (ECtHR 6 November 2012) 49.

394 *Fox, Campbell and Hartley v. United Kingdom* App nos 12244/86, 12245/86 and 12383/86 (ECtHR 30 August 1990) 45; *Slivenko v. Latvia* App no 48321/99 (ECtHR Grand Chamber

this is not the case if a judicial remedy is not available to individuals at all, in order to challenge the lawfulness of their detention; or the scope of the available judicial review was unduly limited.[395] In situations covered by subparagraph (a) of paragraph 1, the supervision required by Article 5(4) is incorporated in the decision by the court at the close of judicial proceedings and no further review is required.[396] This is not the case when the grounds for detention are susceptible to change over time[397] or new issues that affect the lawfulness of a detention arise after conviction.[398, 399] Where the Contracting States provide for procedures which go beyond the requirements of Article 5(4) of the Convention, the provision's guarantees have to be respected in these procedures as well.[400] This can for example be the case when domestic law treats a post-conviction

9 October 2003) 159; Rozhkov v. *Russia (No. 2)* App no 38898/04 (ECtHR 31 January 2017) 65; *Moustahi v. France* App no 9347/14 (ECtHR 25 June 2020) 101.

395 *Petkov and Profirov v. Bulgaria* App nos 50027/08 and 50781/09 (ECtHR 24 June 2014) 67–70. See e.g.: *AM v. France* App no 56324/13 (ECtHR 12 July 2016) 41–43; *Moustahi v. France* App no 9347/14 (ECtHR 25 June 2020) 103. Note that in a partly dissenting opinion to the *Moustahi* judgment judge Grozev, referring back to *Slivenko*, argues that Art. 5(4) does not deal with judicial review measures which may be used to review the lawfulness of a detention which has already ended.

396 *De Wilde, Ooms and Versyp v. Belgium* App nos 2832/66, 2835/66 and 2899/66 (ECtHR 18 June 1971) 76; *T. v. United Kingdom* App no 24724/94 (ECtHR Grand Chamber 16 December 1999) 118; *V. v. United Kingdom* App no 24888/94 (ECtHR Grand Chamber 16 December 1999) 119; *Waite v. United Kingdom* App no 53236/99 (ECtHR 10 December 2002) 56; *Gavril Yosifov v. Bulgaria* App no 74012/01 (ECtHR 6 November 2008) 57; *Kafkaris v. Cyprus* App no 9644/09 (ECtHR Decision on admissibility 21 June 2011) 58; *Ivan Todorov v. Bulgaria* App no 71545/11 (ECtHR 19 January 2017) 59; *Stollenwerk v. Germany* App no 8844/12 (ECtHR 7 September 2017) 36; *Etute v. Luxembourg* App no 18233/16 (ECtHR 30 January 2018) 25. Similarly, under subparagraph (e), see: *Sabeva v. Bulgaria* App no 44290/07 (ECtHR 10 June 2010) 63.

397 *Hussain v. United Kingdom* App no 21928/93 (ECtHR 21 February 1996) 54; *T. v. United Kingdom* App no 24724/94 (ECtHR Grand Chamber 16 December 1999) 118; *V. v. United Kingdom* App no 24888/94 (ECtHR Grand Chamber 16 December 1999) 119; *Waite v. United Kingdom* App no no 53236/99 (ECtHR 10 December 2002) 56; *Kafkaris v. Cyprus* App no 9644/09 (ECtHR Decision on admissibility 21 June 2011) 58. E.g. when a prisoner's tariff has expired and they are kept imprisoned. Their continued detention is only justified by their dangerousness, which is susceptible to change. For an example, under subparagraph (e), see: *Sabeva v. Bulgaria* App no 44290/07 (ECtHR 10 June 2010) 63.

398 *Gavril Yosifov v. Bulgaria* App no 74012/01 (ECtHR 6 November 2008) 58; *Ivan Todorov v. Bulgaria* App no 71545/11 (ECtHR 19 January 2017) 59; *Etute v. Luxembourg* App no 18233/16 (ECtHR 30 January 2018) 25. This is the case e.g. when a prisoner's release on licence is revoked or when the question was raised whether the sentence for a criminal offence imposed some 20 years earlier had become time barred. See respectively: *Etute v. Luxembourg* App no 18233/16 (ECtHR 30 January 2018) 33 and *Ivan Todorov v. Bulgaria* App no 71545/11 (ECtHR 19 January 2017) 60–61.

399 *Stollenwerk v. Germany* App no 8844/12 (ECtHR 7 September 2017) 36. See also: Dhont (n 121) 352–354; Nihal Jayawickrama (ed), 'The Right to Liberty', *The Judicial Application of Human Rights Law: National, Regional and International Jurisprudence* (Cambridge University Press 2002) 426. Van Dijk and colleagues state that '*Where a national court, after convicting a person of a criminal offence, imposes a fixed sentence of imprisonment for the purposes of punishment, the supervision required by Article 5(4) is incorporated in that court decision.*' (Van Dijk and others (n 107) 484.) See also: Murdoch (n 122) 519.

400 *Stollenwerk v. Germany* App no 8844/12 (ECtHR 7 September 2017) 36.

detention as detention on remand until the conviction is final.[401] Similarly, paragraph 4 does not include a right to appeal the decision concerning the lawfulness of the detention, but if the state provides such a right, the same guarantees apply.[402] The court providing the review does not necessarily have to be a court in the strict sense of the word, but, similarly to paragraph 3 must be a body of 'judicial character'[403] which is independent of the executive and the parties.[404] This body, which must be established by law,[405] must be able to review the procedural and substantive conditions which are essential for the lawfulness of the detention.[406] For detention under (1)(c), this means that the judicial body before which proceedings take place, must be able to examine whether sufficient evidence exists to give rise to a reasonable suspicion that the suspect

401 *Stollenwerk v. Germany* App no 8844/12 (ECtHR 7 September 2017) 36.

402 *Toth v. Austria* App no 11894/85 (ECtHR 12 December 1991) 84; *Navarra v. France* App no 13190/87 (ECtHR 23 November 1993) 28; *Kučera v. Slovakia* App no 48666/99 (ECtHR 17 July 2007) 107; *Piotr Baranowski v. Poland* App no 39742/05 (ECtHR 2 October 2007) 63; *Marturana v. Italy* App no 63154 (ECtHR 4 March 2008) 110; *Stephens v. Malta (no. 1)* App no 11956/07 (ECtHR 21 April 2009) 95; *Kováčik v. Slovakia* App no 50903/06 (ECtHR 29 November 2011) 67; *Ilgar Mammadov v. Azerbaijan* App no 15172/13 (ECtHR 22 May 2014) 115; *Oravec v. Croatia* App no 51249/11 (ECtHR 11 July 2017) 64; *Stollenwerk v. Germany* App no 8844/12 (ECtHR 7 September 2017) 37; *Ilnseher v. Germany* App nos 10211/12 and 27505/14 (ECtHR Grand Chamber 4 December 2018) 254.

403 *Nikolova v. Bulgaria (no. 2)* App no 40896/98 (ECtHR 30 September 2004) 75; *Öcalan v. Turkey* app no 46221/99 (ECtHR Grand Chamber 12 May 2005) 66; *Al Husin v. Bosnia and Herzegovina (no. 2)* App no 10112/16 (ECtHR 25 June 2019) 114.

404 *De Wilde, Ooms and Versyp v. Belgium* App nos 2832/66, 2835/66 and 2899/66 (ECtHR 18 June 1971) 77; *Winterwerp v. Netherlands* App no 6301/73 (ECtHR 24 October 1979) 56; *X. v. United Kingdom* App no 7215/75 (ECtHR 5 November 1981) 53; *Weeks v. United Kingdom* App no 9787/82 (ECtHR 2 March 1987) 61; *Benjamin and Wilson v. United Kingdom* App no 28212/95 (ECtHR 26 September 2002) 33; *Lavents v. Latvia* App no 58442/00 (ECtHR 28 November 2002) 81; *Gavril Yosifov v. Bulgaria* App no 74012/01 (ECtHR 6 November 2008) 56; *Ali Osman Özmen v. Turkey* App no 42969/04 (ECtHR 5 October 2016) 87; *Baş v. Turkey* App no 66448/17 (ECtHR 3 March 2020) 266–267. See also: Alati (n 95) 92.

405 *Lavents v. Latvia* App no 58442/00 (ECtHR 28 November 2002) 81.

406 *X. v. United Kingdom* App no 7215/75 (ECtHR 5 November 1981) 58; *Weeks v. United Kingdom* App no 9787/82 (ECtHR 2 March 1987) 59; *Brogan and others v. United Kingdom* App nos 11209/84, 11234/84, 11266/84 and 11386/85 (ECtHR Plenary 29 November 1988) 65; *E. v. Norway* App no 11701/85 (ECtHR 29 August 1990) 50; *Hussain v. United Kingdom* App no 21928/93 (ECtHR 21 February 1996) 57; *Niedbała v. Poland* App no 27915/95 (ECtHR 4 July 2000) 66; *Kadem v. Malta* App no 55263/00 (ECtHR 9 January 2003) 41; *Reinprecht v. Austria* App no 67175/01 (ECtHR 15 November 2005) 31; *Mamedova v. Russia* App no 7064/05 (ECtHR 1 June 2006) 89; *Stephens v. Malta (no. 1)* App no 11956/07 (ECtHR 21 April 2009) 94; *Louled Massoud v. Malta* App no 24340/08 (ECtHR 27 July 2010) 39; *Çatal v. Turkey* App no 26808/08 (ECtHR 17 April 2012) 32; *Idalov v. Russia* App no 5826/03 (ECtHR Grand Chamber 22 May 2012) 161; *Suso Musa v. Malta* App no 42337/12 (ECtHR 23 July 2013) 50; *M.H. v. United Kingdom* App no 11577/06 (ECtHR 22 October 2013) 74; *Ilgar Mammadov v. Azerbaijan* App no 15172/13 (ECtHR 22 May 2014) 113; *Khlaifia and others v. Italy* App no 16483/12 (ECtHR Grand Chamber 15 December 2016) 128; *Oravec v. Croatia* App no 51249/11 (ECtHR 11 July 2017) 64; *Baş v. Turkey* App no 66448/17 (ECtHR 3 March 2020) 212; *Moustahi v. France* App no 9347/14 (ECtHR 25 June 2020) 100. Specifically for Art. 5(1)(f), see: *AM v. France* App no 56324/13 (ECtHR 12 July 2016) 40–41; *Stollenwerk v. Germany* App no 8844/12 (ECtHR 7 September 2017) 36.

has committed an offence.[407] The judicial body must be empowered to order release in case of unlawfulness of the detention and it should therefore not have a merely advisory function.[408] The guarantees provided must be appropriate to the type of deprivation of liberty in question.[409] This means that the forms of review can differ from one domain to another and one type of deprivation of liberty to another.[410] If new factors emerge after the initial decision on deprivation of

407 *Nikolova v. Bulgaria* App no 31195/96 (ECtHR Grand Chamber 25 March 1999) 58; *I.I. v. Bulgaria* App no 44082/98 (ECtHR 9 June 2005) 102; *A. and others v. United Kingdom* App no 3455/05 (ECtHR Grand Chamber 19 February 2009), 204; *Ilgar Mammadov v. Azerbaijan* App no 15172/13 (ECtHR 22 May 2014) 113; *Sher and others v. United Kingdom* App no 5201/11 (ECtHR 20 October 2015) 148; *Dimo Dimov and others v. Bulgaria* App no 30044/10 (ECtHR 7 July 2020) 69–70.

408 *X. v. United Kingdom* App no 7215/75 (ECtHR 5 November 1981) 61; *Weeks v. United Kingdom* App no 9787/82 (ECtHR 2 March 1987) 61; *Chahal v. United Kingdom* App no 22414/93 (ECtHR Grand Chamber 15 November 1996) 130; *Benjamin and Wilson v. United Kingdom* App no 28212/95 (ECtHR 26 September 2002) 34; *Kadem v. Malta* App no 55263/00 (ECtHR 9 January 2003) 41; *Öcalan v. Turkey* app no 46221/99 (ECtHR Grand Chamber 12 May 2005) 66; *Gavril Yosifov v. Bulgaria* App no 74012/01 (ECtHR 6 November 2008) 56; *A. and others v. United Kingdom* App no 3455/05 (ECtHR Grand Chamber 19 February 2009) 202; *M.H. v. United Kingdom* App no 11577/06 (ECtHR 22 October 2013) 74; *Khlaifia and others v. Italy* App no 16483/12 (ECtHR Grand Chamber 15 December 2016) 128; *Ivan Todorov v. Bulgaria* App no 71545/11 (ECtHR 19 January 2017) 58; *Etute v. Luxembourg* App no 18233/16 (ECtHR 30 January 2018) 24. See also: Sottiaux (n 27) 230–231.

409 *De Wilde, Ooms and Versyp v. Belgium* App nos 2832/66, 2835/66 and 2899/66 (ECtHR 18 June 1971) 76–77; *Winterwerp v. Netherlands* App no 6301/73 (ECtHR 24 October 1979) 57; *X. v. United Kingdom* App no 7215/75 (ECtHR 5 November 1981) 53; *Weeks v. United Kingdom* App no 9787/82 (ECtHR 2 March 1987) 61; *Bouamar v. Belgium* App no 9106/80 (ECtHR 29 February 1988) 57; *Wassink v. Netherlands* App no 12535/86 (ECtHR 27 September 1990) 30; *Assenov and others v. Bulgaria* App no 90/1997/874/1086 (ECtHR 28 October 1998) 162; *Niedbała v. Poland* App no 27915/95 (ECtHR 4 July 2000) 66; *Benjamin and Wilson v. United Kingdom* App no 28212/95 (ECtHR 26 September 2002) 33; *Lavents v. Latvia* App no 58442/00 (ECtHR 28 November 2002) 81; *Reinprecht v. Austria* App no 67175/01 (ECtHR 15 November 2005) 31; *Mamedova v. Russia* App no 7064/05 (ECtHR 1 June 2006) 89; *A. and others v. United Kingdom* App no 3455/05 (ECtHR Grand Chamber 19 February 2009) 203; *Stephens v. Malta (no. 1)* App no 11956/07 (ECtHR 21 April 2009) 95; *Louled Massoud v. Malta* App no 24340/08 (ECtHR 27 July 2010) 40; *Altınok v. Turkey* App no 31610/08 (ECtHR 29 November 2011) 45; *Korneykova v. Ukraine* App no 39884/05 (ECtHR 19 January 2012) 68; *Çatal v. Turkey* App no 26808/08 (ECtHR 17 April 2012) 32; *Idalov v. Russia* App no 5826/03 (ECtHR Grand Chamber 22 May 2012) 161; *M.H. v. United Kingdom* App no 11577/06 (ECtHR 22 October 2013) 77; *Ilgar Mammadov v. Azerbaijan* App no 15172/13 (ECtHR 22 May 2014) 114; *Stollenwerk v. Germany* App no 8844/12 (ECtHR 7 September 2017) 37; *Al Husin v. Bosnia and Herzegovina (no. 2)* App no 10112/16 (ECtHR 25 June 2019) 114.

410 *De Wilde, Ooms and Versyp v. Belgium* App nos 2832/66, 2835/66 and 2899/66 (ECtHR 18 June 1971) 78; *X. v. United Kingdom* App no 7215/75 (ECtHR 5 November 1981) 52; *Weeks v. United Kingdom* App no 9787/82 (ECtHR 2 March 1987) 61; *Chahal v. United Kingdom* App no 22414/93 (ECtHR Grand Chamber 15 November 1996) 127; *A. and others v. United Kingdom* App no 3455/05 (ECtHR Grand Chamber 19 February 2009) 203; *M.H. v. United Kingdom* App no 11577/06 (ECtHR 22 October 2013) 75; *Ilgar Mammadov v. Azerbaijan* App no 15172/13 (ECtHR 22 May 2014) 114; *Sher and others v. United Kingdom* App no 5201/11 (ECtHR 20 October 2015) 147; *Khlaifia and others v. Italy* App no 16483/12 (ECtHR Grand Chamber 15 December 2016) 129; *Aboya Boa Jean v. Malta* App no 62676/16 (ECtHR 2 April 2019) 76.

liberty, the detainee must have a right to have the lawfulness of his detention speedily re-examined by a judicial body.[411] In general, the ECtHR has held that a remanded person should be able to challenge their detention at reasonable intervals.[412] In addition, a hearing of the person detained under subparagraph (c) is required.[413] It is not required that the person is heard every time they lodge an appeal but the possibility to exercise the right to be heard at regular intervals should be present.[414] In other cases, a hearing may also be required, depending on the context. For example, in the *Hussain* judgment, where a decision needed to be made about the detainee's continued detention after the expiration of his tariff, the Court stated that an oral hearing was required as well because a substantial term of imprisonment was at stake and characteristics pertaining to the detainee's personality and level of maturity were relevant in deciding on his dangerousness.[415] The proceedings must be adversarial and equality of arms between the parties must be ensured.[416, 417] For remanded detainees this

---

411 *Bezicheri v. Italy* App no 8/1988/152/206 (ECtHR 26 September 1989) 20; *Benjamin and Wilson v. United Kingdom* App no 28212/95 (ECtHR 26 September 2002) 33; *Azimov v. Russia* App no 67474/11 (ECtHR 18 April 2013) 151–152.

412 *Assenov and others v. Bulgaria* App no 90/1997/874/1086 (ECtHR 28 October 1998) 162; *Reinprecht v. Austria* App no 67175/01 (ECtHR 15 November 2005) 31; *Piotr Baranowski v. Poland* App no 39742/05 (ECtHR 2 October 2007) 63; *Aboya Boa Jean v. Malta* App no 62676/16 (ECtHR 2 April 2019) 76; *Dimo Dimov and others v. Bulgaria* App no 30044/10 (ECtHR 7 July 2020) 84. See also: Van Dijk and others (n 107) 487–488.

413 *Kampanis v. Greece* App no 17977/91 (ECtHR 13 July 1995) 47; *Assenov and others v. Bulgaria* App no 90/1997/874/1086 (ECtHR 28 October 1998) 162; *Nikolova v. Bulgaria* App no 31195/96 (ECtHR Grand Chamber 25 March 1999) 58; *Niedbała v. Poland* App no 27915/95 (ECtHR 4 July 2000) 66; *Nikolova v. Bulgaria (no. 2)* App no 40896/98 (ECtHR 30 September 2004) 75; *Öcalan v. Turkey* app no 46221/99 (ECtHR Grand Chamber 12 May 2005) 66–68; *Reinprecht v. Austria* App no 67175/01 (ECtHR 15 November 2005) 31; *Mamedova v. Russia* App no 7064/05 (ECtHR 1 June 2006) 89; *Ţurcan and Ţurcan v. Moldova* App no 39835/05 (ECtHR 23 October 2007) 58; *Gavril Yosifov v. Bulgaria* App no 74012/01 (ECtHR 6 November 2008) 56; *A. and others v. United Kingdom* App no 3455/05 (ECtHR Grand Chamber 19 February 2009) 204; *Krejčíř v. Czech Republic* App no 39298/04 and 8723/05 (ECtHR 26 March 2009) 116; *Stephens v. Malta (no. 1)* App no 11956/07 (ECtHR 21 April 2009) 95; *Altınok v. Turkey* App no 31610/08 (ECtHR 29 November 2011) 46; *Korneykova v. Ukraine* App no 39884/05 (ECtHR 19 January 2012) 69; *Idalov v. Russia* App no 5826/03 (ECtHR Grand Chamber 22 May 2012) 161; *Oravec v. Croatia* App no 51249/11 (ECtHR 11 July 2017) 66; *Baş v. Turkey* App no 66448/17 (ECtHR 3 March 2020) 212.

414 *Altınok v. Turkey* App no 31610/08 (ECtHR 29 November 2011) 49; *Çatal v. Turkey* App no 26808/08 (ECtHR 17 April 2012) 33; *Baş v. Turkey* App no 66448/17 (ECtHR 3 March 2020) 212.

415 *Hussain v. United Kingdom* App no 21928/93 (ECtHR 21 February 1996) 60. See also: Van Dijk and others (n 107) 491.

416 *Kampanis v. Greece* App no 17977/91 (ECtHR 13 July 1995) 47; *Niedbała v. Poland* App no 27915/95 (ECtHR 4 July 2000) 66.

417 *Sanchez-Reisse v. Switzerland* App no 9862/82 (ECtHR 21 October 1986) 51; *Nikolova v. Bulgaria* App no 31195/96 (ECtHR Grand Chamber 25 March 1999) 58; *Reinprecht v. Austria* App no 67175/01 (ECtHR 15 November 2005) 31; *Mamedova v. Russia* App no 7064/05 (ECtHR 1 June 2006) 89; *Ţurcan and Ţurcan v. Moldova* App no 39835/05 (ECtHR 23 October 2007) 57; *A. and others v. United Kingdom* App no 3455/05 (ECtHR Grand Chamber 19 February 2009), 204; *Mooren v. Germany* App no 11364/03 (ECtHR Grand

means they must be given an opportunity to effectively challenge the basis of the allegations against them.[418] This may require that witnesses whose testimony appears to have a bearing on the continuing lawfulness of the detention be heard or that the detainee (or their attorney) is given access to parts of the case file which contain essential information regarding the lawfulness of the detention.[419, 420] With regard to equality of arms, terrorism falls into a special category. For reasons of national security the threat of an imminent terrorist attack provides sufficient justifications for restrictions on the adversarial nature of the proceedings.[421] In these cases closed hearings, meaning hearings wherein confidential sources of information are submitted in the absence of the detainee or their lawyer, are allowed.[422] This is the case due to the risk of loss of lives and of human suffering; as well as the need to protect the sources of information.[423] One condition is that adequate information is disclosed to enable a detainee to know the nature of the allegations against them; to have the opportunity to refute the allegations, and to participate effectively in proceedings.[424]

Chamber 9 July 2009) 124; *Krejčíř v. Czech Republic* App no 39298/04 and 8723/05 (ECtHR 26 March 2009) 116; *Altınok v. Turkey* App no 31610/08 (ECtHR 29 November 2011) 45; *Korneykova v. Ukraine* App no 39884/05 (ECtHR 19 January 2012) 68; *Çatal v. Turkey* App no 26808/08 (ECtHR 17 April 2012) 32; *Ilgar Mammadov v. Azerbaijan* App no 15172/13 (ECtHR 22 May 2014) 114; *Oravec v. Croatia* App no 51249/11 (ECtHR 11 July 2017) 66; *Stollenwerk v. Germany* App no 8844/12 (ECtHR 7 September 2017) 37.

418 *Țurcan and Țurcan v. Moldova* App no 39835/05 (ECtHR 23 October 2007) 57–70; *A. and others v. United Kingdom* App no 3455/05 (ECtHR Grand Chamber 19 February 2009) 204; *Sher and others v. United Kingdom* App no 5201/11 (ECtHR 20 October 2015) 148.

419 *Nikolova v. Bulgaria* App no 31195/96 (ECtHR Grand Chamber 25 March 1999) 58; *Mooren v. Germany* App no 11364/03 (ECtHR Grand Chamber 9 July 2009) 124; *Korneykova v. Ukraine* App no 39884/05 (ECtHR 19 January 2012) 68; *Oravec v. Croatia* App no 51249/11 (ECtHR 11 July 2017) 66. Van Dijk and colleagues do not limit this rule to remanded prisoners, see: Van Dijk and others (n 107) 489–490.

420 *Țurcan and Țurcan v. Moldova* App no 39835/05 (ECtHR 23 October 2007) 59 and 68; *A. and others v. United Kingdom* App no 3455/05 (ECtHR Grand Chamber 19 February 2009) 204; *Krejčíř v. Czech Republic* App no 39298/04 and 8723/05 (ECtHR 26 March 2009) 116.

421 *Sher and others v. United Kingdom* App no 5201/11 (ECtHR 20 October 2015) 150. See *mutatis mutandis: Al Husin v. Bosnia and Herzegovina (no. 2)* App no 10112/16 (ECtHR 25 June 2019) 116–122. See also: Silvis (n 27) 669–670.

422 *Chahal v. United Kingdom* App no 22414/93 (ECtHR Grand Chamber 15 November 1996) 131; *Sher and others v. United Kingdom* App no 5201/11 (ECtHR 20 October 2015) 149; *Al Husin v. Bosnia and Herzegovina (no. 2)* App no 10112/16 (ECtHR 25 June 2019) 116–122. See also: De Schutter (n 27) 124–125. Note that in a dissenting opinion to the *Sher* case, judge Vehabović states that '*The decision in the present case to exclude the applicants and their representatives from even one part of the hearing implies that the police did not provide the applicants with adequate information about the reasons for their continued detention.*'

423 *Sher and others v. United Kingdom* App no 5201/11 (ECtHR 20 October 2015) 149.

424 *A. and others v. United Kingdom* App no 3455/05 (ECtHR Grand Chamber 19 February 2009) 218–220; *Sher and others v. United Kingdom* App no 5201/11 (ECtHR 20 October 2015) 149; *Al Husin v. Bosnia and Herzegovina (no. 2)* App no 10112/16 (ECtHR 25 June 2019) 115. See also: Van Dijk and others (n 107) 490.

67. Speediness – Article 5(4) ECHR includes the right to a speedy judicial decision concerning the lawfulness of detention and the ordering of its termination if it proves unlawful.[425] A lack of respect for the domestic law time-limits does not necessarily mean a breach of paragraph 4, if the requirement of speediness was met.[426] 'Speedily' does not imply the same urgency as the term 'promptly' in paragraph 3,[427] except for in situations where a decision to detain has been taken by a non-judicial authority. In those cases the standard of 'speediness' comes closer to the standard of 'promptness'.[428] The presumption of innocence also creates a special need for swiftness in cases of detention pending trial.[429] Conversely, when detention was imposed by a court in a procedure offering appropriate guarantees of due process, the requirement of speediness is less strict for the appeals procedure.[430] The starting point to assess speediness, is the moment that the application for release was made or the proceedings were instituted. The end point is the final determination of the legality of the detention, including appeal.[431] If an administrative remedy has to be exhausted before recourse can be had to a court, the starting point is the moment the

---

425 *Rehbock v. Slovenia* App no 29462/95 (ECtHR 28 November 2000) 84; *Jablonski v. Poland* App no 33492/96 (ECtHR 21 December 2000) 91; *Nasrulloyev v. Russia* App no 656/06 (ECtHR 11 October 2007) 86; *Baranowski v. Poland* App no 28358/95 (ECtHR 28 March 2000) 68; *Kučera v. Slovakia* App no 48666/99 (ECtHR 17 July 2007) 106; *Piotr Baranowski v. Poland* App no 39742/05 (ECtHR 2 October 2007) 62; *Marturana v. Italy* App no 63154 (ECtHR 4 March 2008) 110; *Mooren v. Germany* App no 11364/03 (ECtHR Grand Chamber 9 July 2009) 106; *Frasik v. Poland* App no 22933/02 (ECtHR 5 January 2010) 62; *Garayev v. Azerbaijan* App no 53688/08 (ECtHR 10 June 2010) 103; *Louled Massoud v. Malta* App no 24340/08 (ECtHR 27 July 2010) 39; *Idalov v. Russia* App no 5826/03 (ECtHR Grand Chamber 22 May 2012) 154; *Osmanović v. Croatia* App no 67604/10 (ECtHR 6 November 2012) 45; *Azimov v. Russia* App no 67474/11 (ECtHR 18 April 2013) 150; *Suso Musa v. Malta* App no 42337/12 (ECtHR 23 July 2013) 51; *Petkov and Profirov v. Bulgaria* App nos 50027/08 and 50781/09 (ECtHR 24 June 2014) 66; *Khlaifia and others v. Italy* App no 16483/12 (ECtHR Grand Chamber 15 December 2016) 131; *Mehmet Hasan Altan v. Turkey* App no 13237/17 (ECtHR 20 March 2018) 161; *Şahin Alpay v. Turkey* App no 16538/17 (ECtHR 20 March 2018) 133; *Ilnseher v. Germany* App nos 10211/12 and 27505/14 (ECtHR Grand Chamber 4 December 2018) 251; *Aboya Boa Jean v. Malta* App no 62676/16 (ECtHR 2 April 2019) 74.

426 *Aboya Boa Jean v. Malta* App no 62676/16 (ECtHR 2 April 2019) 80.

427 *Brogan and others v. United Kingdom* App nos 11209/84, 11234/84, 11266/84 and 11386/85 (ECtHR Plenary 29 November 1988) 59; *E. v. Norway* App no 11701/85 (ECtHR 29 August 1990) 64. See also: Sottiaux (n 27) 229.

428 *Shcherbina v. Russia* App no 41970/11 (ECtHR 26 June 2014) 65–70.

429 *Bezicheri v. Italy* App no 8/1988/152/206 (ECtHR 26 September 1989) 21; *Jablonski v. Poland* App no 33492/96 (ECtHR 21 December 2000) 93; *Piotr Baranowski v. Poland* App no 39742/05 (ECtHR 2 October 2007) 62; *Frasik v. Poland* App no 22933/02 (ECtHR 5 January 2010) 63; *Idalov v. Russia* App no 5826/03 (ECtHR Grand Chamber 22 May 2012) 155.

430 *Piotr Baranowski v. Poland* App no 39742/05 (ECtHR 2 October 2007) 63; *Shcherbina v. Russia* App no 41970/11 (ECtHR 26 June 2014) 65; *Ilnseher v. Germany* App nos 10211/12 and 27505/14 (ECtHR Grand Chamber 4 December 2018) 255.

431 *Sanchez-Reisse v. Switzerland* App no 9862/82 (ECtHR 21 October 1986) 54; *E. v. Norway* App no 11701/85 (ECtHR 29 August 1990) 64; *Shcherbina v. Russia* App no 41970/11 (ECtHR 26 June 2014) 66.

administrative authority is seized of the matter.[432] Speediness needs to be determined depending on the circumstances of each case.[433] The circumstances to be taken into account include the complexity of the proceedings, the conduct by the domestic authorities and by the applicant, what was at stake for the latter[434] and any specificities of the domestic procedure.[435, 436] The Court has strict standards, finding for example 17,[437] 23[438] or 26 days[439] too long.[440] While the complexity of the issues is relevant in determining what is reasonable[441] the complexity of the case can never fully absolve the authorities of their

---

432 *Sanchez-Reisse v. Switzerland* App no 9862/82 (ECtHR 21 October 1986) 54.

433 *Sanchez-Reisse v. Switzerland* App no 9862/82 (ECtHR 21 October 1986) 55; *R.M.D. v. Switzerland* App no 81/1996/700/892 (ECtHR 26 September 1997) 42; *Rehbock v. Slovenia* App no 29462/95 (ECtHR 28 November 2000) 84; *Jablonski v. Poland* App no 33492/96 (ECtHR 21 December 2000) 91; *Kadem v. Malta* App no 55263/00 (ECtHR 9 January 2003) 43; *Kučera v. Slovakia* App no 48666/99 (ECtHR 17 July 2007) 106; *Marturana v. Italy* App no 63154 (ECtHR 4 March 2008) 111; *Mooren v. Germany* App no 11364/03 (ECtHR Grand Chamber 9 July 2009) 106; *Louled Massoud v. Malta* App no 24340/08 (ECtHR 27 July 2010) 41; *Idalov v. Russia* App no 5826/03 (ECtHR Grand Chamber 22 May 2012) 154; *Shcherbina v. Russia* App no 41970/11 (ECtHR 26 June 2014) 62; *Khlaifia and others v. Italy* App no 16483/12 (ECtHR Grand Chamber 15 December 2016) 131; *Şahin Alpay v. Turkey* App no 16538/17 (ECtHR 20 March 2018) 134; *Ilnseher v. Germany* App nos 10211/12 and 27505/14 (ECtHR Grand Chamber 4 December 2018) 252; *Aboya Boa Jean v. Malta* App no 62676/16 (ECtHR 2 April 2019) 75; *Dimo Dimov and others v. Bulgaria* App no 30044/10 (ECtHR 7 July 2020) 78.

434 *Mooren v. Germany* App no 11364/03 (ECtHR Grand Chamber 9 July 2009) 106; *Mehmet Hasan Altan v. Turkey* App no 13237/17 (ECtHR 20 March 2018) 162; *Şahin Alpay v. Turkey* App no 16538/17 (ECtHR 20 March 2018) 134; *Ilnseher v. Germany* App nos 10211/12 and 27505/14 (ECtHR Grand Chamber 4 December 2018) 252; *Aboya Boa Jean v. Malta* App no 62676/16 (ECtHR 2 April 2019) 75.

435 *Mehmet Hasan Altan v. Turkey* App no 13237/17 (ECtHR 20 March 2018) 163; *Ilnseher v. Germany* App nos 10211/12 and 27505/14 (ECtHR Grand Chamber 4 December 2018) 270–271.

436 *Khlaifia and others v. Italy* App no 16483/12 (ECtHR Grand Chamber 15 December 2016) 131; *Dimo Dimov and others v. Bulgaria* App no 30044/10 (ECtHR 7 July 2020) 78.

437 *Kadem v. Malta* App no 55263/00 (ECtHR 9 January 2003) 44–45.

438 *Rehbock v. Slovenia* App no 29462/95 (ECtHR 28 November 2000) 85–86.

439 *Mamedova v. Russia* App no 7064/05 (ECtHR 1 June 2006) 96.

440 *Idalov v. Russia* App no 5826/03 (ECtHR Grand Chamber 22 May 2012) 157; *Suso Musa v. Malta* App no 42337/12 (ECtHR 23 July 2013) 52. For more examples, see: *Piotr Baranowski v. Poland* App no 39742/05 (ECtHR 2 October 2007) 64; *Ilnseher v. Germany* App nos 10211/12 and 27505/14 (ECtHR Grand Chamber 4 December 2018) 256; *Dimo Dimov and others v. Bulgaria* App no 30044/10 (ECtHR 7 July 2020) 78.

441 *Piotr Baranowski v. Poland* App no 39742/05 (ECtHR 2 October 2007) 66. E.g. in the *Mehmet Hasan Altan* and *Şahin Alpay* cases, the Court found proceedings before the Constitutional Court which took 14 months and three days and 16 months and three days respectively still speedy, taking into account the new and complex issues in light of the state of emergency which had arisen. See: *Mehmet Hasan Altan v. Turkey* App no 13237/17 (ECtHR 20 March 2018) 165–167; *Şahin Alpay v. Turkey* App no 16538/17 (ECtHR 20 March 2018) 137–139. Similarly, see *Ilnseher v. Germany* App nos 10211/12 and 27505/14 (ECtHR Grand Chamber 4 December 2018) 265–275. In this case a period of eight months and 23 days of proceedings before the Federal Constitutional Court was found reasonable, having regard in particular to the complexity of the issues raised by a new system of preventive detention.

obligation under paragraph 4.[442,443] Neither an excessive workload[444] nor a vacation period[445] can justify a period of inactivity on the part of the judicial authorities.[446]

SUBSECTION VII. PRACTICAL APPLICATION

68. Guzzardi (1980) – In the case of Mr. Guzzardi, the Court had found that he was deprived of his liberty (see no. *32*). It subsequently had to verify whether this deprivation was compatible with Article 5(1) ECHR. The Court considered all the subparagraphs as follows. Regarding subparagraph (a), the Court found that the measure was '*not a punishment for a specific offence but a preventive measure taken on the strength of indication of a propensity to crime.*'[447] The measure needs to be based on a conviction for an offence, which is not the case here.[448] Subparagraph (b) is not applicable either, since there was no court order which imposed a specific and concrete obligation on Mr. Guzzardi.[449] As far as subparagraph (c) was concerned, the Court acknowledged there was reasonable suspicion of an offence. However, the decision to impose the supervision had no connection in law with the investigation into the offence. His detention on remand was terminated. If the supervision was indeed an extension of his pre-trial detention, it was then not 'lawful' as required by the Convention. At first sight, it seems more likely it was '*reasonably considered necessary to prevent him committing an offence*' or '*fleeing after having done so.*' However, this would again raise questions of lawfulness. Furthermore, that phrase only covers means of preventing a concrete and specific offence, not a policy of general prevention.[450] Subparagraph (e) was the one the Italian government pleaded, claiming that Guzzardi was a vagrant since he had no apparent occupational activity. Furthermore, the government argued, if the Convention allows for vagrants to be deprived of their liberty, this should *a fortiori* be the case for mafiosi, who

442 *Baranowski v. Poland* App no 28358/95 (ECtHR 28 March 2000) 72–73; *Marturana v. Italy* App no 63154 (ECtHR 4 March 2008) 113.

443 *Jablonski v. Poland* App no 33492/96 (ECtHR 21 December 2000) 92; *Frasik v. Poland* App no 22933/02 (ECtHR 5 January 2010) 63; *Ilnseher v. Germany* App nos 10211/12 and 27505/14 (ECtHR Grand Chamber 4 December 2018) 253.

444 *Bezicheri v. Italy* App no 8/1988/152/206 (ECtHR 26 September 1989) 25.

445 *E. v. Norway* App no 11701/85 (ECtHR 29 August 1990) 66.

446 See also: Dhont (n 121) 362; Murdoch (n 122) 520.

447 *Guzzardi v. Italy* App no 7367/76 (ECtHR Plenary 6 November 1980) 100.

448 *Guzzardi v. Italy* App no 7367/76 (ECtHR Plenary 6 November 1980) 100. Note that Mr. Guzzardi did have prior convictions. However, the measure in question was not imposed as a punishment for any of these offences.

449 *Guzzardi v. Italy* App no 7367/76 (ECtHR Plenary 6 November 1980) 101.

450 *Guzzardi v. Italy* App no 7367/76 (ECtHR Plenary 6 November 1980) 102. See also: *Petkov and Profirov v. Bulgaria* App nos 50027/08 and 50781/09 (ECtHR 24 June 2014) 43 and 50; Macken (n 236) 198; Macken (n 95) 54.

are far more dangerous.[451] The Court, however, ruled that the exceptions in Article 5(1) should be narrowly interpreted (see no. 40). Mr. Guzzardi could not be considered a vagrant under the ordinary meaning of the word. In addition, the other categories in Article 5(1)(e) are persons of unsound mind, alcoholics and drug addicts. These are all people whose deprivation of liberty is partly in their own interest. Therefore, the *a fortiori* reasoning that the same reasons apply even stronger for mafiosi because they are more dangerous, does not hold.[452] The last two subparagraphs, being (d) and (f), were obviously not relevant and were dismissed out of hand.[453] In conclusion, the deprivation of liberty did not fall under any of the subparagraphs of Article 5(1) and could therefore not be justified. Of the dissenters in the Guzzardi case mentioned above (see no. 33), judges Bindschedler-Robert, Matscher, Teitgen and Garcia De Enterria found that even if the measure was a deprivation of liberty (which they doubted), it was justified under subparagraph (c).

69. CIULLA (1989) – Mr. Ciulla, an Italian national, was originally arrested in connection with drug offences and sentenced to jail time, a fine and a supervision order as a security measure.[454] The Court of Cassation however, annulled this judgment and Mr. Ciulla was released pending trial. A bit over two years later, Mr. Ciulla was convicted again. During the period between the two verdicts, the police and prosecution sought a compulsory residence order for Mr. Ciulla.[455] The national courts granted it and ordered that Mr. Ciulla be held in custody until this compulsory residence order was enforceable.[456] The ECtHR stated that this custody was unquestionably a deprivation of liberty.[457] This deprivation was not covered by subparagraph (b) since the obligation (the compulsory residence order) was not yet incumbent on Mr. Ciulla at the time of detention.[458] As explained above, it was not covered by subparagraph (c) either since the detention did not take place in the context of criminal proceedings (see no. 50).[459] Judges Valticos and Matscher dissented. They argued that the deprivation of liberty should not be severed from the whole body of judicial proceedings against Mr. Ciulla of which it formed a part. If that global context

451 *Guzzardi v. Italy* App no 7367/76 (ECtHR Plenary 6 November 1980) 97.
452 *Guzzardi v. Italy* App no 7367/76 (ECtHR Plenary 6 November 1980) 98.
453 *Guzzardi v. Italy* App no 7367/76 (ECtHR Plenary 6 November 1980) 103.
454 *Ciulla v. Italy* App no 11152/84 (ECtHR Plenary 22 February 1989) 11–12.
455 *Ciulla v. Italy* App no 11152/84 (ECtHR Plenary 22 February 1989) 15–16.
456 *Ciulla v. Italy* App no 11152/84 (ECtHR Plenary 22 February 1989) 16–17.
457 *Ciulla v. Italy* App no 11152/84 (ECtHR Plenary 22 February 1989) 34.
458 *Ciulla v. Italy* App no 11152/84 (ECtHR Plenary 22 February 1989) 36.
459 *Ciulla v. Italy* App no 11152/84 (ECtHR Plenary 22 February 1989) 37–42. Note that in a dissenting opinion, judge Valticos (approved by judge Matscher) argued that Art. 5(1) should be considered as a whole and that in light of the number of interwoven prosecutions and decisions which involved courts of different levels, it was unreasonable to conclude that there was a violation of Art. 5.

of Ciulla's situation was taken into account, it was in their view unreasonable to conclude there has been a violation of Article 5(1) ECHR.

70. Labita (2000) – Mr. Labita was suspected of being a member of a mafia-type organisation and of running a financial company on behalf of his brother-in-law, who was believed to be the leader of the main mafia gang in the area.[460] The accusations against Mr. Labita were mainly based on statements made by a so-called *pentito* (a former mafioso who has decided to cooperate with the authorities). In the context of these proceedings, an arrest warrant was issued against the applicant and he spent roughly two and a half years in prison pending trial. During this time, he lodged several appeals against the prolongation of his pre-trial detention, which were all dismissed.[461] While Mr. Labita was in pre-trail detention, the District Court also imposed a preventive measure upon him, placing him under special police supervision for three years, because he was considered dangerous. These preventive measures were suspended pending trial. At trial, Mr. Labita was acquitted and his release from pre-trial detention was ordered.[462] This judgment was delivered around 10 pm, but the applicant was only released at 8:30 am the next day.[463] Mr. Labita's acquittal was later upheld on appeal.[464] However, once he was acquitted and thus released from pre-trail detention, the special police supervision which had been imposed and suspended came into effect.[465] This special police supervision required Mr. Labita, among other things[466]:

- not to leave his home without informing the supervising authorities;
- to live an honest life and not to arouse suspicion;
- not to associate with persons who had a criminal record or who were subject to preventive or security measures;
- not to return home later than 8 pm or to leave home before 6 am, unless due cause could be shown and in all cases only after informing the authority responsible for supervising him;
- not to keep or carry weapons;
- not to go to bars or attend public meetings;
- to have on him at all times the card setting out his precise obligations under the preventive measures and a copy of the court order;
- to report to the relevant police station on Sundays between 9 am and 12 noon.

---

460 *Labita v. Italy* App no 26772/95 (ECtHR Grand Chamber 6 April 2000) 10.
461 *Labita v. Italy* App no 26772/95 (ECtHR Grand Chamber 6 April 2000) 10–23.
462 *Labita v. Italy* App no 26772/95 (ECtHR Grand Chamber 6 April 2000) 23.
463 *Labita v. Italy* App no 26772/95 (ECtHR Grand Chamber 6 April 2000) 24.
464 *Labita v. Italy* App no 26772/95 (ECtHR Grand Chamber 6 April 2000) 25–26.
465 *Labita v. Italy* App no 26772/95 (ECtHR Grand Chamber 6 April 2000) 69.
466 *Labita v. Italy* App no 26772/95 (ECtHR Grand Chamber 6 April 2000) 63.

Mr. Labita's appeal against The District Court's decision was dismissed.[467] The District Court denied his further applications to have the measure lifted.[468] The ECtHR had to decide on three questions relevant for our purposes. The first two related to the right to liberty and the third to freedom of movement. First, it ruled that Article 5(3) ECHR had been violated.[469] The national courts had refused to release Mr. Labita from pre-trial detention or prolonged his detention on the basis of the existence of serious evidence of his guilt, the danger of pressure being brought to bear on witnesses, the risk of evidence being tampered with, the fact that Mr. Labita was dangerous, the complexity of the case and the needs of the investigation.[470] The ECtHR noted that the allegations against the applicant came from a single source, a *pentito*.[471] Although the Court recognised the importance of *pentiti* in the fight against the mafia, the use of *pentiti* also gives rise to issues and in this case there was no corroborating evidence.[472] Therefore, very compelling reasons would have been required for Mr. Labita's lengthy detention to have been justified.[473] The Court found this not to be the case and therefore ruled that the detention infringed Article 5(3) ECHR.[474] Secondly, the question was whether Article (5)(c) ECHR had been violated due to the fact that it took 12 hours to release Mr. Labita from pre-trial detention after his release had been ordered. The Court answered this question in the affirmative, since the delay was caused by the absence of the registration officer and was therefore not just attributable to the need for the relevant administrative formalities to be carried out.[475]

71. Mancini (2001) – In *Mancini v. Italy* two applicants were suspected of involvement in two armed robberies.[476] They were both taken into pre-trial detention, a decision which they appealed. On appeal, the court decided to replace their pre-trial detention with house arrest.[477] This decision was filed with the registry and served on the applicants three days later. However, since no police officers were available to escort them from the prison to their home, this was not done the same day. Their transfer was delayed for another three days.[478] The Court points out that as a general rule Article 5(1) does not regulate

467 *Labita v. Italy* App no 26772/95 (ECtHR Grand Chamber 6 April 2000) 65–66.
468 *Labita v. Italy* App no 26772/95 (ECtHR Grand Chamber 6 April 2000) 71–72 and 74–75.
469 *Labita v. Italy* App no 26772/95 (ECtHR Grand Chamber 6 April 2000) 165.
470 *Labita v. Italy* App no 26772/95 (ECtHR Grand Chamber 6 April 2000) 154.
471 *Labita v. Italy* App no 26772/95 (ECtHR Grand Chamber 6 April 2000) 156.
472 *Labita v. Italy* App no 26772/95 (ECtHR Grand Chamber 6 April 2000) 157–160.
473 *Labita v. Italy* App no 26772/95 (ECtHR Grand Chamber 6 April 2000) 161.
474 *Labita v. Italy* App no 26772/95 (ECtHR Grand Chamber 6 April 2000) 162–165.
475 *Labita v. Italy* App no 26772/95 (ECtHR Grand Chamber 6 April 2000) 171–174.
476 *Mancini v. Italy* App no 44955/98 (ECtHR 2 August 2001) 7–10.
477 *Mancini v. Italy* App no 44955/98 (ECtHR 2 August 2001) 11.
478 *Mancini v. Italy* App no 44955/98 (ECtHR 2 August 2001) 12.

conditions of detention,[479] nor does it guarantee the right to be placed in a more lenient form of detention.[480] In this case, both imprisonment and house arrest amounted to a deprivation of liberty for the purposes of Article 5(1)(c).[481] The Court distinguished the case from *Ashingdane*,[482] stressing major differences. In *Ashingdane*, there was no alteration of the type of deprivation of liberty,[483] while in *Mancini* there was a change in the nature of the place of detention.[484] Therefore, contrary to *Ashingdane*, the situation in *Mancini* did fall within the scope of Article 5(1)(c).[485] While some delay in carrying out a decision to release a detainee is understandable and often inevitable,[486] this delay must be kept to a minimum.[487] A delay of more than a few hours cannot be justified.[488] In this case, the transfer was delayed for at least three days, which is too long. Hence, there had been a violation of Article 5.[489] In a short dissenting opinion, judges Conforti, Levits and Kovler, did not see a substantial difference between *Ashingdane* and *Mancani*. In their opinion, the analogies between the cases were far more important than the differences. They argued that in both cases there was a transition from a stricter form of detention to a more liberal one. This meant that in either case the detention did not cease to be a 'lawful detention' allowed under Article 5(1) (c).

72. S., V. and A. (2018) – The case of *S., V. and A. v. Denmark* involved three football fans/hooligans who were detained on the day of a match, all for around seven and a half hours.[490] The Danish Police Act, however, only allowed for administrative detention for a maximum period of six hours where possible. The Danish law allowed for detention when the person is causing a 'risk or danger',

---

479 *Lavents v. Latvia* App no 58442/00 (ECtHR 28 November 2002) 64; *Buzadji v. Republic of Moldova* App no 23755/07 (ECtHR Grand Chamber 5 July 2016) 113–114. See also: Dhont (n 121) 285.

480 *Mancini v. Italy* App no 44955/98 (ECtHR 2 August 2001) 16.

481 *Mancini v. Italy* App no 44955/98 (ECtHR 2 August 2001) 17.

482 *Ashingdane v. United Kingdom* App no 8225/78 (ECtHR 28 May 1985).

483 *Ashingdane v. United Kingdom* App no 8225/78 (ECtHR 28 May 1985) 47. See also: Dhont (n 121) 286.

484 *Mancini v. Italy* App no 44955/98 (ECtHR 2 August 2001) 19.

485 *Mancini v. Italy* App no 44955/98 (ECtHR 2 August 2001) 20.

486 *Quinn v. France* App no 18580/91 (ECtHR 22 March 1995) 42; *K.-F. v. Germany* App no 144/1996/765/962 (ECtHR 27 November 1997) 71.

487 *Mancini v. Italy* App no 44955/98 (ECtHR 2 August 2001) 24. See also: *Giulia Manzoni v. Italy* App no 19218/91 (ECtHR 1 July 1997) 25; *Labita v. Italy* App no 26772/95 (ECtHR Grand Chamber 6 April 2000) 171; *Ladent v. Poland* App no 11036/03 (ECtHR 18 March 2008) 81; *Oshurko v. Ukraine* App no 33108/05 (ECtHR 8 September 2011) 101.

488 *Ladent v. Poland* App no 11036/03 (ECtHR 18 March 2008) 81; *Oshurko v. Ukraine* App no 33108/05 (ECtHR 8 September 2011) 101; *Ruslan Yakovenko v. Ukraine* App no 5425/11 (ECtHR 4 June 2015) 68. See e.g. the *Quinn* case where a delay of 11 hours was deemed too long (*Quinn v. France* App no 18580/91 (ECtHR 22 March 1995) 42).

489 *Mancini v. Italy* App no 44955/98 (ECtHR 2 August 2001) 25–26.

490 *S., V. and A. v. Denmark* App nos 35553/23, 36678/23 and 36711/12 (ECtHR Grand Chamber 22 October 2018) 10–15.

meaning there was '*a concrete and imminent risk of disturbance of public order or of danger to the safety of individuals or public security.*'[491] The Court first briefly analysed the imposed measure under Article 5(1)(b) ECHR. It observed that the applicants were given no specific orders or clear warning of the consequences of their failure to comply with such an order. They were not told which specific act they were to refrain from either.[492] The case was therefore not covered by Article 5(1)(b).[493] The Court then focussed on Article 5(1)(c) and the additional safeguards of (3) and (5). First, the detention was covered by the second prong of subparagraph (c). The abovementioned conditions were met: they were released before it became necessary to bring them before a judge, they had the opportunity to bring the question of the lawfulness of their detention before the courts and could have been granted compensation if justified.[494] Second, the detention was lawful under domestic law. This is primarily for the national authorities to decide[495] and the domestic courts found the detention lawful. The ECtHR found no indication that their assessment was arbitrary or manifestly unreasonable.[496] Third, the detention was not arbitrary. This as well, is something the national authorities are better placed to evaluate.[497] Though the ECtHR is not bound by the findings of domestic courts and remains free to make its own appreciation in the light of all the material before it, in normal circumstances it requires cogent elements to lead it towards deviating from the findings of fact reached by the domestic courts.[498] The domestic courts found that the detention was based on sufficient reason to believe the applicants caused a concrete and imminent risk of disturbance of public order or of danger to the safety of individuals or public security. The ECtHR saw no reason to question this finding.[499] Regarding

---

491 *S., V. and A. v. Denmark* App nos 35553/23, 36678/23 and 36711/12 (ECtHR Grand Chamber 22 October 2018) 30.

492 *S., V. and A. v. Denmark* App nos 35553/23, 36678/23 and 36711/12 (ECtHR Grand Chamber 22 October 2018) 84.

493 *S., V. and A. v. Denmark* App nos 35553/23, 36678/23 and 36711/12 (ECtHR Grand Chamber 22 October 2018) 87.

494 *S., V. and A. v. Denmark* App nos 35553/23, 36678/23 and 36711/12 (ECtHR Grand Chamber 22 October 2018) 138–141.

495 *K.-F. v. Germany* App no 144/1996/765/962 (ECtHR 27 November 1997) 67; *Hilda Hafsteinsdóttir v. Iceland* App no 40905/98, (ECtHR 8 June 2004) 52; *Enhorn v. Sweden* App no 56529/00 (ECtHR 25 January 2005) 38; *Marturana v. Italy* App no 63154 (ECtHR 4 March 2008) 76.

496 *S., V. and A. v. Denmark* App nos 35553/23, 36678/23 and 36711/12 (ECtHR Grand Chamber 22 October 2018) 143–148.

497 *Winterwerp v. Netherlands* App no 6301/73 (ECtHR 24 October 1979) 40; *Weeks v. United Kingdom* App no 9787/82 (ECtHR 2 March 1987) 50; *Reiner v. Germany* App no 28527/08 (ECtHR 19 January 2012) 78.

498 *Austin and others v. United Kingdom* App nos 39692/09, 40713/09 and 41008/09 (ECtHR Grand Chamber 15 March 2012) 61; *S., V. and A. v. Denmark* App nos 35553/23, 36678/23 and 36711/12 (ECtHR Grand Chamber 22 October 2018) 154. In the context of Art. 2 ECHR, see: *Giuliani and Gaggio v. Italy* App no 23458/02 (ECtHR Grand Chamber 24 March 2011) 180.

499 *S., V. and A. v. Denmark* App nos 35553/23, 36678/23 and 36711/12 (ECtHR Grand Chamber 22 October 2018) 155.

the requirement in Article 5(1)(c) for the offence to be concrete and specific, relating in particular to the place and time of its commission and its victim(s), the Danish Police Act did not specify any acts the applicants should refrain from committing. However, other legislation did contain such offences, and the place and time could be very precisely described. Likewise, the victims could be identified as the public present.[500] Therefore, the offence was 'specific and concrete' and the applicants would in all likelihood have been involved in that offence had its commission not been prevented by their detention.[501] Fourth, the detention was necessary. It is required that less severe measures are considered and found to be insufficient to safeguard the individual or public interest which might require that the person concerned be detained.[502] A proper balance needs to be struck between the importance in a democratic society of preventing an imminent risk of an offence being committed and the importance of the right to liberty.[503] In order to be proportionate to such a serious measure as deprivation of liberty, the concrete and specific 'offence' referred to under the second limb of Article 5(1)(c) must also be of a serious nature, entailing danger to life and limb or significant material damage and the detention should cease as soon as the risk has passed.[504] This was the case[505] and the ECtHR saw no reason to disagree with the domestic courts' assessment that '*less radical measures could not be deemed sufficient to avert the risk of additional unrest in those circumstances*' and that the duration of the detention was justified.[506] In conclusion, there had been no violation of Article 5 of the convention.[507] In a joint partly dissenting opinion judges De Gaetano and Wojtyczek argued that in referring back to the original intent of the parties and the text of the treaty, the Court had turned its back on its usual evolutive interpretation. '*The result is that the Court has neither presented a coherent theory of treaty interpretation serving as a basis for its judgments nor explained its choices concerning the interpretative rules it applies.*' In addition, they did not agree with the interpretation given by the Court in this case.

---

500 *S., V. and A. v. Denmark* App nos 35553/23, 36678/23 and 36711/12 (ECtHR Grand Chamber 22 October 2018) 157–158.

501 *S., V. and A. v. Denmark* App nos 35553/23, 36678/23 and 36711/12 (ECtHR Grand Chamber 22 October 2018) 159–160.

502 *Witold Litwa v. Poland* App no 26629/95 (ECtHR 4 April 2000) 78; *Ladent v. Poland* App no 11036/03 (ECtHR 18 March 2008) 54. In the context of subparagraph (e), see: *Hilda Hafsteinsdóttir v. Iceland* App no 40905/98, (ECtHR 8 June 2004) 51; *Enhorn v. Sweden* App no 56529/00 (ECtHR 25 January 2005) 44.

503 *S., V. and A. v. Denmark* App nos 35553/23, 36678/23 and 36711/12 (ECtHR Grand Chamber 22 October 2018) 161.

504 *S., V. and A. v. Denmark* App nos 35553/23, 36678/23 and 36711/12 (ECtHR Grand Chamber 22 October 2018) 161.

505 *S., V. and A. v. Denmark* App nos 35553/23, 36678/23 and 36711/12 (ECtHR Grand Chamber 22 October 2018) 162–168.

506 *S., V. and A. v. Denmark* App nos 35553/23, 36678/23 and 36711/12 (ECtHR Grand Chamber 22 October 2018) 169–172.

507 *S., V. and A. v. Denmark* App nos 35553/23, 36678/23 and 36711/12 (ECtHR Grand Chamber 22 October 2018) 174.

73. Summary comparison to Ostendorf – As explained above (see no. 52), the *S., V. and A.* judgment explicitly departed from that in *Ostendorf*. A brief analysis of the facts suffices to show this. *Ostendorf* also concerned football hooliganism. Mr. Ostendorf was a football supporter registered in two databases of persons prepared to use violence in the context of sports events.[508] On the day of a football game, he was identified by the police as the 'gang leader' of a group of football fans who were found in the possession of a mouth protection device and several pairs of gloves filled with quartz sand.[509] The police surveilled the group as it went to a pub. When the group left the pub, Mr. Ostendorf tried to hide in the ladies' bathroom. However, he was found and arrested by the police.[510] He was detained for approximately four hours, until one hour after the game had ended and his phone was returned to him several days later.[511] While there are obvious similarities between the factual situation of the two cases, the Court's analysis was quite different. As discussed above, the Court in the *Ostendorf* case dismissed the idea that detention unconnected to criminal proceedings could be covered by subparagraph (c) and thus ruled it not applicable.[512] It did however apply subparagraph (b). It stated that the obligation to keep the peace by not committing a criminal offence was sufficiently specific and concrete in this case.[513] Furthermore, Mr. Ostendorf had taken clear and positive steps which indicated that he would not fulfil this obligation. He was ordered by the police, prior to his arrest, to stay with the group of football supporters and the consequences of non-compliance were made clear, but he still tried to arrange for a hooligan brawl by trying to evade the police and contacting hooligans from the opposing side.[514] The Court then analysed the other requirements of subparagraph (b) and concluded that the deprivation of liberty was justified under this subparagraph.[515]

SECTION III. FREEDOM OF MOVEMENT

SUBSECTION I. RESTRICTIONS

74. Article 2 of the Fourth Protocol – Article 2 of the Fourth Protocol to the ECHR, as quoted above (see no. 27), protects three related rights of people who are lawfully within a country: liberty of movement, the freedom to

---

508 *Ostendorf v. Germany* App no 15598/08 (ECtHR 7 March 2013) 6–7.
509 *Ostendorf v. Germany* App no 15598/08 (ECtHR 7 March 2013) 10.
510 *Ostendorf v. Germany* App no 15598/08 (ECtHR 7 March 2013) 11.
511 *Ostendorf v. Germany* App no 15598/08 (ECtHR 7 March 2013) 11–12.
512 *Ostendorf v. Germany* App no 15598/08 (ECtHR 7 March 2013) 68 and 77–89.
513 *Ostendorf v. Germany* App no 15598/08 (ECtHR 7 March 2013) 92–93.
514 *Ostendorf v. Germany* App no 15598/08 (ECtHR 7 March 2013) 94–96.
515 *Ostendorf v. Germany* App no 15598/08 (ECtHR 7 March 2013) 97–103.

choose one's residence and the freedom to leave any country.[516] As seen in the case law, all three of those rights can be relevant in restrictions of the freedom of movement to prevent terrorism. The focus will be on the first two, since limitations to the freedom to leave any country are often included in more strict limitations on the freedom of movement in our context. The Article also includes two restriction clauses.[517] Only the first one is relevant for our purposes. The second limitation clause allows states to implement specific policies in order to advance economic welfare or other social objectives.[518] Therefore, it is not applicable in our case. We will analyse restrictions under the third paragraph, which must be in accordance with law, pursue one of the legitimate aims referred to in the third paragraph of Article 2 of Protocol No. 4 and be necessary in a democratic society.[519]

75. Legality – The first requirement is that the measure is '*in accordance with law.*' This expression not only requires that the measure should have a basis in domestic law, but also refers to the quality of the law in question, requiring that it should be adequately accessible to the persons concerned and foreseeable as to its effects.[520] A norm cannot be regarded as a 'law' unless it is worded precisely

516 Art. 2 Prot. 4 ECHR, (1) and (2). See also: Gerards (n 114) 934; Todts (n 104) 57–58.

517 Art. 2 Prot. 4 ECHR, (3) and (4).

518 Explanatory Report to Protocol No. 4 to the Convention for the Protection of Human Rights and Fundamental Freedoms, securing certain rights and freedoms other than those already included in the Convention and in the first Protocol thereto, ETX No 46, 16 September 1963, 15 and 18; *Garib v. the Netherlands* App no 43494/09 (ECtHR Grand Chamber 6 November 2017) 85 and 109; Gerards (n 114) 941; Todts (n 104) 58–59.

519 *Raimondo v. Italy* App no 12954/87 (ECtHR 22 February 1994) 39; *Labita v. Italy* App no 26772/95 (ECtHR Grand Chamber 6 April 2000) 194–195; *Baumann v. France* App no 33592/96 (ECtHR 22 May 2001) 61; *Denizci and others v. Cyprus* App nos 25316–25321/94 and 27207/95 (ECtHR 23 May 2001) 405; *Luordo v. Italy* App no 32190/96 (ECtHR 17 July 2003) 93; *Timishev v. Russia* App nos 55762/00 and 55974/00 (ECtHR 13 December 2005) 45; *McKay v. United Kingdom* App no 543/03 (ECtHR Grand Chamber 3 October 2006) 30; *Bolat v. Russia* App no 14139/03 (ECtHR 5 October 2006) 67; *Földes And Földesné Hajlik v. Hungary* App no 41463/02 (ECtHR 31 October 2006) 32; *Bartik v. Russia* App no 55565/00 (ECtHR 21 December 2006) 38; *Sissanis v. Romania* App no 23468/02 (ECtHR 25 January 2007) 62; *Tatishvili v. Russia* App no. 1509/02 (ECtHR 22 February 2007) 47; *Marturana v. Italy* App no 63154 (ECtHR 4 March 2008) 190; *Villa v. Italy* App no 19675/06 (ECtHR 20 April 2010) 45; *Miażdżyk v. Poland* App no 23592/07 (ECtHR 24 January 2012) 30; *Khlyustov v. Russia* App no 28975/05 (ECtHR 11 July 2013) 64; *Battista v. Italy* App no 43978/09 (ECtHR 2 December 2014) 37; *Kerimli v. Azerbaijan* App no 3967/09 (ECtHR 16 July 2015) 47; *Popoviciu v. Romania* App no 52942/09 (ECtHR 1 March 2016) 85; *De Tommaso v. Italy* App no 43395/09 (ECtHR Grand Chamber 23 February 2017) 104; *Mursaliyev and others v. Azerbaijan* App nos 66650/13 and 10 others (ECtHR 13 December 2018) 30; *Stetsov v. Ukraine* App no 5170/15 (ECtHR 11 May 2021) 25.

520 *Sunday Times v. United Kingdom* App no 6538/74 (ECtHR 26 April 1979) 49; *Rotaru v. Romania* App no 28341/95 (ECtHR Grand Chamber 4 May 2000) 52; *Olivieira v. Netherlands* App no 33129/96 (ECtHR 4 June 2002) 47; *Sissanis v. Romania* App no 23468/02 (ECtHR 25 January 2007) 66; *Gochev v. Bulgaria* App no 34383/03 (ECtHR 26 November 2009) 46; *Khlyustov v. Russia* App no 28975/05 (ECtHR 11 July 2013) 68; *X. v. Latvia* App no 27853/09 (ECtHR Grand Chamber 26 November 2013) 58; *Battista v. Italy* App no 43978/09 (ECtHR

enough to enable citizens to regulate their conduct. In other words, they must be able to foresee, to a degree that is reasonable in the circumstances, the consequences which a given action may entail.[521] This may require appropriate advice. However, such consequences need not be foreseeable with absolute certainty: experience shows this to be unattainable.[522] Again, whilst it certainly is highly desirable, it may bring in its train excessive rigidity, and the law must be able to keep pace with changing circumstances. Accordingly, many laws are inevitably couched in terms which, to a greater or lesser extent, are vague and whose interpretation and application are questions of practice.[523] The level of precision required of domestic legislation – which cannot in any case provide for every eventuality – depends to a considerable degree on the content of the law in question, the field it is designed to cover and the number and status of those to whom it is addressed.[524] It is, moreover, primarily for the national authorities to interpret and apply domestic law.[525] The Court reiterates that a rule is 'foreseeable' when it affords a measure of protection against arbitrary

2 December 2014) 38; *De Tommaso v. Italy* App no 43395/09 (ECtHR Grand Chamber 23 February 2017) 106; *Berkovich and others v. Russia* App nos 5871/07 and 9 others (ECtHR 27 March 2018) 80; *Mursaliyev and others v. Azerbaijan* App nos 66650/13 and 10 others (ECtHR 13 December 2018) 31; *Rotaru v. Republic of Moldova* App no 26764/12 (ECtHR 8 December 2020) 24; *Pagerie v. France* App no 24203/16 (ECtHR 19 January 2023) 176.

521 *Sunday Times v. United Kingdom* App no 6538/74 (ECtHR 26 April 1979) 49; *Rekvényi v. Hungary* App no 25390/94 (ECtHR Grand Chamber 20 May 1999) 34; *Olivieira v. Netherlands* App no 33129/96 (ECtHR 4 June 2002) 52; *Sissanis v. Romania* App no 23468/02 (ECtHR 25 January 2007) 66; *Gochev v. Bulgaria* App no 34383/03 (ECtHR 26 November 2009) 46; *Khlyustov v. Russia* App no 28975/05 (ECtHR 11 July 2013) 68; *Battista v. Italy* App no 43978/09 (ECtHR 2 December 2014) 38; *De Tommaso v. Italy* App no 43395/09 (ECtHR Grand Chamber 23 February 2017) 107.

522 *Sunday Times v. United Kingdom* App no 6538/74 (ECtHR 26 April 1979) 49; *Rekvényi v. Hungary* App no 25390/94 (ECtHR Grand Chamber 20 May 1999) 34; *Khlyustov v. Russia* App no 28975/05 (ECtHR 11 July 2013) 68; *De Tommaso v. Italy* App no 43395/09 (ECtHR Grand Chamber 23 February 2017) 108.

523 *Sunday Times v. United Kingdom* App no 6538/74 (ECtHR 26 April 1979) 49; *Rekvényi v. Hungary* App no 25390/94 (ECtHR Grand Chamber 20 May 1999) 34; *Kokkinakis v. Greece* App no 14307/88 (ECtHR 25 May 1993) 40; *Khlyustov v. Russia* App no 28975/05 (ECtHR 11 July 2013) 68; *De Tommaso v. Italy* App no 43395/09 (ECtHR Grand Chamber 23 February 2017) 108.

524 *Vogt v. Germany* App no 17851/91 (ECtHR Grand Chamber 26 September 1995) 48; *Rekvényi v. Hungary* App no 25390/94 (ECtHR Grand Chamber 20 May 1999) 34; *RTBF v. Belgium* App no 50084/06 (ECtHR 29 March 2011) 104; *Khlyustov v. Russia* App no 28975/05 (ECtHR 11 July 2013) 69; *De Tommaso v. Italy* App no 43395/09 (ECtHR Grand Chamber 23 February 2017) 109.

525 *Winterwerp v. Netherlands* App no 6301/73 (ECtHR 24 October 1979) 46; *Kemmache v. France (no 3)* App no 17621/91 (ECtHR 24 November 1994) 37; *Quinn v. France* App no 18580/91 (ECtHR 22 March 1995) 47; *Vogt v. Germany* App no 17851/91 (ECtHR Grand Chamber 26 September 1995) 48; *Olivieira v. Netherlands* App no 33129/96 (ECtHR 4 June 2002) 49; *Öcalan v. Turkey* app no 46221/99 (ECtHR Grand Chamber 12 May 2005) 84; *Sissanis v. Romania* App no 23468/02 (ECtHR 25 January 2007) 75; *Khlyustov v. Russia* App no 28975/05 (ECtHR 11 July 2013) 69; *De Tommaso v. Italy* App no 43395/09 (ECtHR Grand Chamber 23 February 2017) 109.

interferences by the public authorities, as required by the rule of law.[526, 527] A law which confers a discretion must indicate the scope of that discretion, although the detailed procedures and conditions to be observed do not necessarily have to be incorporated in rules of substantive law.[528]

76. Proportionality – The second and third requirements are that the measure pursues one of the legitimate aims listed and that it is necessary in a democratic society. This necessity test implies that the measures are appropriate in achieving the aim[529] and requires a fair balance between the public interest and the individual's rights, which is a proportionality test.[530] The assessment of this issue must be based on all the special features of the case.[531] In this context the Court accepts that special measures might have to be taken to overcome an emergency situation in a specific area at a specific time.[532] For example, in an area where a lot of hard drugs are used and trafficked an emergency situation can exist.[533] In such a situation it is not disproportionate to impose a 14 day prohibition order on a person who did not live or work in the area, had already violated several shorter prohibition orders in order to use hard drugs in the area; and who was warned that further acts of such kind could lead to a 14

526 In its case law, the Court stresses the importance of the rule of law. See e.g.: *Olivieira v. Netherlands* App no 33129/96 (ECtHR 4 June 2002) 52.

527 *Khlyustov v. Russia* App no 28975/05 (ECtHR 11 July 2013) 70; *De Tommaso v. Italy* App no 43395/09 (ECtHR Grand Chamber 23 February 2017) 109; *Rotaru v. Republic of Moldova* App no 26764/12 (ECtHR 8 December 2020) 24; *Pagerie v. France* App no 24203/16 (ECtHR 19 January 2023) 176.

528 *Khlyustov v. Russia* App no 28975/05 (ECtHR 11 July 2013) 70; *De Tommaso v. Italy* App no 43395/09 (ECtHR Grand Chamber 23 February 2017) 109; *Rotaru v. Republic of Moldova* App no 26764/12 (ECtHR 8 December 2020) 24; *Pagerie v. France* App no 24203/16 (ECtHR 19 January 2023) 176.

529 *Bartik v. Russia* App no 55565/00 (ECtHR 21 December 2006) 46; *Berkovich and others v. Russia* App nos 5871/07 and 9 others (ECtHR 27 March 2018) 93; *Stetsov v. Ukraine* App no 5170/15 (ECtHR 11 May 2021) 31; *Pagerie v. France* App no 24203/16 (ECtHR 19 January 2023) 193.

530 *Luordo v. Italy* App no 32190/96 (ECtHR 17 July 2003) 96; *Riener v. Bulgaria* App no 46343/99 (ECtHR 23 May 2006) 109; *Földes And Földesné Hajlik v. Hungary* App no 41463/02 (ECtHR 31 October 2006) 32; *Gochev v. Bulgaria* App no 34383/03 (ECtHR 26 November 2009) 44; *Miażdżyk v. Poland* App no 23592/07 (ECtHR 24 January 2012) 35; *Khlyustov v. Russia* App no 28975/05 (ECtHR 11 July 2013) 84; *S.M. v. Italy* App no 18675/09 (ECtHR Decision on admissibility 8 October 2013) 25; *Kerimli v. Azerbaijan* App no 3967/09 (ECtHR 16 July 2015) 45; *Popoviciu v. Romania* App no 52942/09 (ECtHR 1 March 2016) 83 and 91. See also: Sébastien Van Drooghenbroeck, 'Note relative à l'application des principes de proportionnalité et subsidiarité en matière pénale dans de droit de la Convention européenne des droits de l'Homme', Annex 2.7 to the Report on behalf of the Committee on Justice on the Bill on the Code of Criminal Procedure, *Parl.St.* Senaat 2005–06, no. 3–450/20, (1398) 1402.

531 *Miażdżyk v. Poland* App no 23592/07 (ECtHR 24 January 2012) 35; *Popoviciu v. Romania* App no 52942/09 (ECtHR 1 March 2016) 91; *Pagerie v. France* App no 24203/16 (ECtHR 19 January 2023) 196.

532 *Olivieira v. Netherlands* App no 33129/96 (ECtHR 4 June 2002) 64.

533 *Olivieira v. Netherlands* App no 33129/96 (ECtHR 4 June 2002) 61.

day prohibition order.[534] The reasons given by the national authorities must be relevant and sufficient.[535] A measure is only justified as long as it can actually achieve the objective.[536] A measure which is automatically renewed for a long time can be disproportionate, even if it was justified at the outset.[537] The measure needs to be periodically re-examined.[538] The required frequency for these re-examinations depends on the measure and the facts of the specific case.[539] They should be carried out, at least as a last resort, by the courts, which offers the best guarantees of independence, impartiality and due process.[540] The scope of judicial review must allow the court to take into account all elements and thus review both proportionality[541] and legality.[542,543] The fact that domestic

---

534 *Olivieira v. Netherlands* App no 33129/96 (ECtHR 4 June 2002) 65. See also: Gerards (n 114) 939–940.

535 *Khlyustov v. Russia* App no 28975/05 (ECtHR 11 July 2013) 84.

536 *Riener v. Bulgaria* App no 46343/99 (ECtHR 23 May 2006) 122; *Gochev v. Bulgaria* App no 34383/03 (ECtHR 26 November 2009) 49; *Villa v. Italy* App no 19675/06 (ECtHR 20 April 2010) 47; *S.M. v. Italy* App no 18675/09 (ECtHR Decision on admissibility 8 October 2013) 27; *Battista v. Italy* App no 43978/09 (ECtHR 2 December 2014) 41; *Timofeyev and Postupkin v. Russia* App nos 45431/14 and 22769/15 (ECtHR 19 January 2021) 133.

537 *Luordo v. Italy* App no 32190/96 (ECtHR 17 July 2003) 96; *Riener v. Bulgaria* App no 46343/99 (ECtHR 23 May 2006) 121; *Földes And Földesné Hajlik v. Hungary* App no 41463/02 (ECtHR 31 October 2006) 35; *Gochev v. Bulgaria* App no 34383/03 (ECtHR 26 November 2009) 49; *Villa v. Italy* App no 19675/06 (ECtHR 20 April 2010) 47; *S.M. v. Italy* App no 18675/09 (ECtHR Decision on admissibility 8 October 2013) 27; *Battista v. Italy* App no 43978/09 (ECtHR 2 December 2014) 41; *Kerimli v. Azerbaijan* App no 3967/09 (ECtHR 16 July 2015) 56; *Rotaru v. Republic of Moldova* App no 26764/12 (ECtHR 8 December 2020) 28; *Timofeyev and Postupkin v. Russia* App nos 45431/14 and 22769/15 (ECtHR 19 January 2021) 133; *Stetsov v. Ukraine* App no 5170/15 (ECtHR 11 May 2021) 28.

538 *Gochev v. Bulgaria* App no 34383/03 (ECtHR 26 November 2009) 55; *Kerimli v. Azerbaijan* App no 3967/09 (ECtHR 16 July 2015) 56; *Popoviciu v. Romania* App no 52942/09 (ECtHR 1 March 2016) 95; *Rotaru v. Republic of Moldova* App no 26764/12 (ECtHR 8 December 2020) 25; *Pagerie v. France* App no 24203/16 (ECtHR 19 January 2023) 195. See also: Gerards (n 114) 939.

539 *Villa v. Italy* App no 19675/06 (ECtHR 20 April 2010) 48; *Timofeyev and Postupkin v. Russia* App nos 45431/14 and 22769/15 (ECtHR 19 January 2021) 133.

540 *Sissanis v. Romania* App no 23468/02 (ECtHR 25 January 2007) 70; *Gochev v. Bulgaria* App no 34383/03 (ECtHR 26 November 2009) 50; *Sarkizov and others v. Bulgaria* App nos 37981/06, 38022/06, 39122/06, and 44278/06 (ECtHR 17 April 2012) 69; *Battista v. Italy* App no 43978/09 (ECtHR 2 December 2014) 42; *Rotaru v. Republic of Moldova* App no 26764/12 (ECtHR 8 December 2020) 25; *Timofeyev and Postupkin v. Russia* App nos 45431/14 and 22769/15 (ECtHR 19 January 2021) 133; *Pagerie v. France* App no 24203/16 (ECtHR 19 January 2023) 196.

541 *Riener v. Bulgaria* App no 46343/99 (ECtHR 23 May 2006) 126; *Gochev v. Bulgaria* App no 34383/03 (ECtHR 26 November 2009) 54; *Popoviciu v. Romania* App no 52942/09 (ECtHR 1 March 2016) 92–93.

542 *Mursaliyev and others v. Azerbaijan* App nos 66650/13 and 10 others (ECtHR 13 December 2018) 34.

543 *Gochev v. Bulgaria* App no 34383/03 (ECtHR 26 November 2009) 50; *Sarkizov and others v. Bulgaria* App nos 37981/06, 38022/06, 39122/06, and 44278/06 (ECtHR 17 April 2012) 68–69; *Battista v. Italy* App no 43978/09 (ECtHR 2 December 2014) 42; *Timofeyev and Postupkin v. Russia* App nos 45431/14 and 22769/15 (ECtHR 19 January 2021) 133; *Rotaru v. Republic of Moldova* App no 26764/12 (ECtHR 8 December 2020) 25. See, *mutatis mutandis*: *Le Compte,*

law time limits were exceeded does not necessarily mean the measure was disproportionate.[544]

SUBSECTION II. PRACTICAL APPLICATION

77. RAIMONDO (1994) – Mr. Raimondo was suspected of belonging to a mafia-type organisation.[545] Criminal proceedings were brought against him, but he was acquitted both by the Catanzaro District Court in first instance and by the Catanzaro Court of Appeal on appeal.[546] During this time, the Catanzaro District Court imposed preventive measures on Mr. Raimondo. A number of his assets were seized, some of which were eventually confiscated. The day of his acquittal in first instance, he was also placed under special police supervision. This entailed a prohibition on leaving his house without informing the police, an obligation to report to the police on certain days and an obligation to stay in his house between 9 pm and 7 am, unless he had a valid reason and he had informed the authorities. He was also required pay a security of 2,000,000 lire (today that would amount to a little over 1,000 euros) as a guarantee.[547] Just over five months later (and before his criminal acquittal), at a private hearing, the Catanzaro Court of Appeal annulled the special supervision and ordered the restitution of the security and the seized and confiscated assets.[548] However, it took almost another five months for this decision to be filed with the registry and for the police to be informed, after which it took another 18 days for them to inform Mr. Raimondo.[549] In this case the ECtHR did not elaborately analyse the scope of application of Article 5 ECHR. It simply stated that the restrictions placed on Mr. Raimondo did not amount to a deprivation of liberty and thus moved on to the analysis of the freedom of movement.[550] It noted that the threat posed by the mafia made the measure necessary in a democratic society for the maintenance of public order and the prevention of crime. The Court also stated that the measure was proportionate to this aim up to the moment at which the Court of Appeal revoked it.[551] However, whether this is also the case for the period during which the measure continued after this decision, is less clear.

Van Leuven and De Meyere v. Belgium App nos 6878/75 and 7238/75 (ECtHR 23 June 1981) 60.

544 *S.M. v. Italy* App no 18675/09 (ECtHR Decision on admissibility 8 October 2013) 27.

545 *Raimondo v. Italy* App no 12954/87 (ECtHR 22 February 1994) 7.

546 *Raimondo v. Italy* App no 12954/87 (ECtHR 22 February 1994) 8–11.

547 *Raimondo v. Italy* App no 12954/87 (ECtHR 22 February 1994) 12–13.

548 *Raimondo v. Italy* App no 12954/87 (ECtHR 22 February 1994) 14–15.

549 *Raimondo v. Italy* App no 12954/87 (ECtHR 22 February 1994) 14.

550 *Raimondo v. Italy* App no 12954/87 (ECtHR 22 February 1994) 39. See also: Feldman (n 82) 5; Fenwick, 'Recalibrating ECHR Rights, and the Role of the Human Rights Act Post 9/11' (n 26) 168; Fenwick and Phillipson (n 25) 881.

551 *Raimondo v. Italy* App no 12954/87 (ECtHR 22 February 1994) 39.

The Court did not take an explicit stance on the period of almost five months between the decision and the filing with the registry. It did so concerning the 18 days between the filing and the notifying of Mr. Raimondo. Regarding this period the Court concluded the interference with his free movement was neither provided for by law, nor necessary and there thus had been a violation of Article 2 of Protocol No. 4.[552]

78. LABITA (2000) – As mentioned above (see no. 70), the *Labita* case also contained a free movement issue. The question was whether the special supervision imposed on Mr. Labita violated the right to free movement. The Court started by stating the restrictions on Mr. Labita's freedom of movement were '*very severe*' and '*undoubtedly amounted to an interference with his rights guaranteed by Article 2 of Protocol No. 4*.'[553] The measures had a legal basis and pursued a legitimate aim, being the maintenance of public order and the prevention of crime,[554] but according to the Court they were not necessary in a democratic society. The ECtHR '*considers that it is legitimate for preventive measures, including special supervision, to be taken against persons suspected of being members of the Mafia, even prior to conviction, as they are intended to prevent crimes being committed. Furthermore, an acquittal does not necessarily deprive such measures of all foundation, as concrete evidence gathered at trial, though insufficient to secure a conviction, may nonetheless justify reasonable fears that the person concerned may in the future commit criminal offences*.'[555] In Labita's case, the grounds relied on by the Italian courts for refusing to rescind the measure after the acquittal, were the *pentito*'s assertion that the applicant had contacts in the mafia clan as was proved by the fact that his deceased brother-in-law had been the head of the main clan and the fact that '*the applicant had not shown any real change in his lifestyle or genuine repentance*.'[556] The ECtHR found these reasons insufficient. Thus, the restrictions on Mr. Labita's freedom of movement were not necessary in a democratic society and therefore Article 2 of Protocol No. 4. had been violated.[557]

79. DE TOMMASO (2017) – In *De Tommaso* the Court found that the measures did not amount to a deprivation of liberty (see no. 38). It then continued to analyse the case under Article 2 of Protocol No. 4 since the restrictions imposed fell within the scope of this Article.[558] The Court found that the preventive

---

552 *Raimondo v. Italy* App no 12954/87 (ECtHR 22 February 1994) 40.
553 *Labita v. Italy* App no 26772/95 (ECtHR Grand Chamber 6 April 2000) 193.
554 *Labita v. Italy* App no 26772/95 (ECtHR Grand Chamber 6 April 2000) 194.
555 *Labita v. Italy* App no 26772/95 (ECtHR Grand Chamber 6 April 2000) 195.
556 *Labita v. Italy* App no 26772/95 (ECtHR Grand Chamber 6 April 2000) 196.
557 *Labita v. Italy* App no 26772/95 (ECtHR Grand Chamber 6 April 2000) 197.
558 *De Tommaso v. Italy* App no 43395/09 (ECtHR Grand Chamber 23 February 2017) 91 and 105.

measures had a legal basis in domestic law.[559] It then moved to analyse whether said law was accessible and foreseeable in its effects. In light of the significant impact on the liberty of movement, the Court deemed this very important.[560] The accessibility was not disputed.[561] The issue was the foreseeability. Referring to its earlier case law (see nos 37 and 77–78)[562] and the case law of the Italian Constitutional Court,[563] the Court observed that the imposition of preventive measures is linked to a prospective analysis by domestic courts. Neither the Italian legislation nor the Constitutional Court had clearly identified the 'factual evidence' or the specific types of behaviour which must be considered in order to assess the danger the individual poses to society and which may give rise to preventive measures. The European Court therefore considered that the Italian Act did not contain sufficiently detailed provisions as to what types of behaviour were to be regarded as posing a danger to society.[564] It observed that the court which imposed the measures *in casu* did not attribute any specific behaviour or criminal activity to Mr. De Tommaso and based its reasoning on the assumption of 'criminal tendencies', a criterion that the Italian Constitutional Court had already considered insufficient. Therefore, this section of the Act did not indicate with sufficient clarity the scope or manner of exercise of the very wide discretion conferred on the domestic courts. It was not worded with sufficient precision to provide protection against arbitrary interferences and to enable the applicant to regulate his conduct and foresee to a sufficiently certain degree the imposition of preventive measures.[565] Regarding two other sections of that same act which were also applied to Mr. De Tommaso, the Court observed they were worded in very general terms and their content was extremely vague and indeterminate. This applied in particular to the provisions concerning the obligations to 'lead an honest and law-abiding life' and to 'not give cause for suspicion'. The Italian Constitutional Court, however, found these provisions not to be in violation of the legality principle.[566] The ECtHR was not convinced. It found that the interpretation of the Italian Constitutional Court was just as indeterminate as the wording of the statute. In the Court's view, this interpretation did not provide sufficient guidance for the persons concerned. The Court therefore considered that this part of the Act had not been worded in sufficient detail and did not define with sufficient clarity the content of the preventive measures which could be imposed on an individual, even in the light of the Constitutional

559 *De Tommaso v. Italy* App no 43395/09 (ECtHR Grand Chamber 23 February 2017) 110.
560 *De Tommaso v. Italy* App no 43395/09 (ECtHR Grand Chamber 23 February 2017) 111.
561 *De Tommaso v. Italy* App no 43395/09 (ECtHR Grand Chamber 23 February 2017) 112.
562 *De Tommaso v. Italy* App no 43395/09 (ECtHR Grand Chamber 23 February 2017) 114.
563 *De Tommaso v. Italy* App no 43395/09 (ECtHR Grand Chamber 23 February 2017) 116.
564 *De Tommaso v. Italy* App no 43395/09 (ECtHR Grand Chamber 23 February 2017) 117.
565 *De Tommaso v. Italy* App no 43395/09 (ECtHR Grand Chamber 23 February 2017) 118.
566 *De Tommaso v. Italy* App no 43395/09 (ECtHR Grand Chamber 23 February 2017) 119.

Court's case-law.[567] The ECtHR concluded that the statute lacked sufficient precision and clarity and thus did not satisfy the foreseeability requirements.[568] There had therefore been a violation of Article 2 of Protocol No. 4.[569] Since the foreseeability required had not been met, the Court did not analyse whether the measures pursued one or more legitimate aims and were necessary in a democratic society.[570] Concurring judges Raimondi, Villiger, Šikuta, Keller and Kjølbro thought that the foreseeability requirement was met, so they continued the analysis. The aims pursued with the measure, the maintenance of public order and the prevention of crime, were legitimate. However, they found the measure not necessary in a democratic society, since the reasons on which the Italian authorities relied to impose the measure were irrelevant and insufficient. This was further aggravated by the lengthy delay between the lodging of the appeal against the measure and the decision. Judge Pinto De Albuquerque, who argued in a dissenting opinion that the measure did fall under Article 5 ECHR (see no. 38) was of the opinion that the measure did not fall under any of the subparagraphs of Article 5 and furthermore violated the legality principle.

80. TIMOFEYEV AND POSTUPKIN (2021) – As mentioned above (see no. 39) the Court found that the measures imposed on Mr. Timofeyev and Postupkin restricted their freedom of movement. Therefore, they had to be provided for by law, pursue a legitimate aim as referred to in the third paragraph of Article 2 of Protocol No. 4 and be necessary in a democratic society.[571] The Court analysed the Russian legislation and concluded that the measure was provided for by a law, which was sufficiently accessible and clear in its scope of application.[572] The aim of the legislation was to prevent offences and recidivism.[573] Then the Court analysed whether the measures were necessary in a democratic society, and in particular whether they were proportionate.[574] Under Russian law, the measure was imposed automatically and its duration was imposed by the legislation.[575] However, it was possible to request the courts to partially lift the measures. Those courts had to take into account all elements relating to the conduct of the person concerned. The legislation thus provided for the possibility of periodic

567 *De Tommaso v. Italy* App no 43395/09 (ECtHR Grand Chamber 23 February 2017) 122.
568 *De Tommaso v. Italy* App no 43395/09 (ECtHR Grand Chamber 23 February 2017) 125.
569 *De Tommaso v. Italy* App no 43395/09 (ECtHR Grand Chamber 23 February 2017) 126.
570 *De Tommaso v. Italy* App no 43395/09 (ECtHR Grand Chamber 23 February 2017) 127.
571 *Timofeyev and Postupkin v. Russia* App nos 45431/14 and 22769/15 (ECtHR 19 January 2021) 126.
572 *Timofeyev and Postupkin v. Russia* App nos 45431/14 and 22769/15 (ECtHR 19 January 2021) 127–131.
573 *Timofeyev and Postupkin v. Russia* App nos 45431/14 and 22769/15 (ECtHR 19 January 2021) 132.
574 *Timofeyev and Postupkin v. Russia* App nos 45431/14 and 22769/15 (ECtHR 19 January 2021) 132.
575 *Timofeyev and Postupkin v. Russia* App nos 45431/14 and 22769/15 (ECtHR 19 January 2021) 134.

review of all non-mandatory restrictions, such as the overnight curfew. Since the applicant had not requested such a review, it was impossible for the ECtHR to assess the practical application of this legislation *in casu*.[576] An application to lift the mandatory restrictions, such as the obligation to periodically report to the police, could also be made, but only after half of the period for administrative surveillance had ended.[577] If the application was rejected, another one could be filed after six months. *In casu* the applicant could file an application after three years. In light of the relatively low frequency with which the applicant had to report to the police station, the Court found that this was not incompatible with the requirement of periodic review.[578] In conclusion, the imposed measure was proportionate and did not violate the applicant's freedom of movement.[579]

81. Pagerie (2023) – Mr. Pagerie was a radical Muslim suspected of terrorist activity who received a MICAS, an administrative control and surveillance measure imposed by the Home Secretary. The measure imposed an obligation not to leave town, an overnight curfew between 10 pm and 6 am and a duty to report to the police station three times per day. Later the prohibition to contact a specific individual he knew from prison was added, as well as the prohibition to go to certain parts of town on one specific day because the Tour de France passed through town. After roughly nine months, a list of football stadium addresses and a hidden computer and phone containing IS propaganda were found in his house.[580] He had also violated the contact order. He was convicted for violating his MICAS and sentenced to prison. After his release, a new MICAS was imposed containing the same obligations as the previous one and his passport was confiscated. Five months later, he was arrested again after propaganda videos were found on his cell phone and he was convicted and imprisoned once more. After his release, yet another MICAS was imposed prohibiting him from leaving town and imposing the obligation to report to the police once every day. This MICAS was in place for nine months.[581] During the whole process, Mr. Pagerie filed several appeals, which were all dismissed.[582] Before the ECtHR he did not argue his right to liberty under Article 5 ECHR was violated. He focussed solely on his freedom of movement and private and family life. The Court

[576] *Timofeyev and Postupkin v. Russia* App nos 45431/14 and 22769/15 (ECtHR 19 January 2021) 135.

[577] *Timofeyev and Postupkin v. Russia* App nos 45431/14 and 22769/15 (ECtHR 19 January 2021) 136.

[578] *Timofeyev and Postupkin v. Russia* App nos 45431/14 and 22769/15 (ECtHR 19 January 2021) 137.

[579] *Timofeyev and Postupkin v. Russia* App nos 45431/14 and 22769/15 (ECtHR 19 January 2021) 138–139.

[580] *Pagerie v. France* App no 24203/16 (ECtHR 19 January 2023) 21–29.

[581] *Pagerie v. France* App no 24203/16 (ECtHR 19 January 2023) 45.

[582] *Pagerie v. France* App no 24203/16 (ECtHR 19 January 2023) 46–61.

acknowledged that the context of terrorism in France is a difficult one.[583] It held that his freedom of movement was restricted and considered the questions of legality, the aim of the measure and necessity.[584] The Court found no legality issues, as the legislation is clear enough when it requires serious grounds for believing that the behaviour constitutes a threat to public order and security.[585] In addition, it can only be applied in the context of a state of emergency and for measures exceeding 12 months, the threat needs to be of a particular gravity. It is not realistic to require an exhaustive list of situations in which a measure like this can be applied.[586] Furthermore, the procedure provides for sufficient guarantees against arbitrariness, such as the requirement of parliamentary assent within 12 days after the imposition of a state of emergency, the clear rules on the imposition of MICAS and their periodic review and the possibility to file a case for summary judgement.[587] The aims of the measure, to preserve national security and public safety and order, did not require much analysis.[588] In terms of proportionality, finally, the Court held that the restrictions were severe and restrictions such as these cannot be founded solely on past convictions or a person's religious practices.[589] However, in this case the combination of all elements did amount to serious reasons to think the person was a threat to public order and security, especially in the context at the time, being only a few days after the Paris terrorist attacks.[590] Secondly, the case was re-evaluated often and the measure only extended based on newly found elements.[591] Thirdly, the fact that he could move freely within the city, barring during curfew hours and when he had to report to the police station (which was very close to his residence), meant that he could have a social life and have contacts with the rest of the world.[592] Because of these reasons, the measure was proportionate and thus justified under Article 2 of the Fourth Protocol.[593]

---

583 *Pagerie v. France* App no 24203/16 (ECtHR 19 January 2023) 147–148.
584 *Pagerie v. France* App no 24203/16 (ECtHR 19 January 2023) 151–161.
585 *Pagerie v. France* App no 24203/16 (ECtHR 19 January 2023) 179.
586 *Pagerie v. France* App no 24203/16 (ECtHR 19 January 2023) 184.
587 *Pagerie v. France* App no 24203/16 (ECtHR 19 January 2023) 187–191.
588 *Pagerie v. France* App no 24203/16 (ECtHR 19 January 2023) 192.
589 *Pagerie v. France* App no 24203/16 (ECtHR 19 January 2023) 197–199.
590 *Pagerie v. France* App no 24203/16 (ECtHR 19 January 2023) 199–200.
591 *Pagerie v. France* App no 24203/16 (ECtHR 19 January 2023) 201.
592 *Pagerie v. France* App no 24203/16 (ECtHR 19 January 2023) 202.
593 *Pagerie v. France* App no 24203/16 (ECtHR 19 January 2023) 209.

CHAPTER II
APPLICATION IN THE CONTEXT OF TERRORISM PREVENTION

SECTION I. CRIMINAL LAW

82. Criminal vs. administrative – In this research on preventive counter-terrorism measures with a direct impact on the right to liberty, criminal law comes into play, as offences often entail imprisonment or house arrest. Criminal procedure law also allows for pre-trial detention. Administrative law has also been used in order to prevent terrorism in ways which have a direct impact on the right to liberty, for example, by way of TPIM's in the UK.

83. Sentences for terrorist offences – Terrorist offences are considered to be quite serious and therefore, the sentence will often be imprisonment. That is the most obvious example of a deprivation of liberty, which falls under Article 5 ECHR. Among the lighter sentences, full day house arrest would also be considered a deprivation of liberty. Other sentences would need to be analysed on a case-by-case basis; for example, probation measures with the obligation to report to the police at regular intervals and/or overnight house arrest. Looking at the case law of the ECtHR, we can try to draw a rough line. From *Guzzardi* we learn that the combination of a relocation order, a limited area to move about which is not frequented by many other people, overnight curfew between 10 pm and 7 am, the obligation to report twice a day and limitations on phone calls amount to a deprivation of liberty (see no. 33). On the other hand, the obligation to report to the police once a month, live at a specified address, not move away from the commune of residence and overnight curfew between 10 pm and 7 am did not amount to a deprivation of liberty (see no. 36 and 39 for a slightly shorter curfew). Similar obligations but with a slightly shorter overnight curfew and the obligation to report every week, were also no deprivation of liberty (see no. 37), even when the person was additionally not allowed to use mobile phones or radio communication devices (see no. 38).

84. Sentences under Article 5 ECHR – A sentence amounting to a deprivation of liberty, such as imprisonment, can be justified under Article 5(1)(a) ECHR if a causal relationship exists with a decision made by an independent court which has been established by law and follows a judicial procedure. In addition, the general principles need to be respected: the rule of law (and legal certainty in particular) and protection against arbitrariness. Sentences justified under subparagraph (a) can have a punitive and a preventive part. As far as the punitive part is concerned, the ECtHR does not judge the proportionality of the sentence,[594] while it does for the preventive part. When the punitive part of a sentence has ended and the preventive part begins, the grounds for detention have changed, meaning judicial review needs to be provided.

85. Sentences under Article 2 Prot. No. 4 ECHR – Sentences which do not amount to a deprivation of liberty need to be analysed under Article 2 of the Fourth Protocol to the ECHR (the freedom of movement). This freedom can be restricted if it is necessary in a democratic society, in accordance with law and pursues one of the legitimate aims referred to. In counter-terrorism cases, one or more of the following aims will be pursued: national security, public safety, the prevention of crime, the maintenance of public order. In addition, the protection of the rights and freedoms of others (right to life, etc.) may be at stake. In the context of a sentence for a criminal offence, chances also are that necessity in a democratic society will pose few problems.[595]

86. Pre-trial detention – Finally, before a sentence is imposed in criminal cases, it is possible for a person to be deprived of their right to liberty or for this to be restricted: this is pre-trial detention. Pre-trial detention will amount to a deprivation of liberty which has be justified under Article 5(1)(c) ECHR. In order for this to happen, there needs to be reasonable suspicion that the person has committed an offence and the detention must be necessary in the circumstances. In terrorism cases, states cannot be required to disclose confidential sources of information to establish the reasonableness of the suspicion, but they need to provide some elements establishing reasonable suspicion in addition to the confidential information (for practical applications see no. 56). Additionally, the pre-trial detention must be in accordance with the rule of law and the protection against arbitrariness. Furthermore, in cases of pre-trial detention prompt automatic judicial review must be provided, capable of examining the lawfulness of the detention. After '*a certain lapse of time*', which may already be at the time of the first judicial review, additional reasons for the pre-trial detention must be provided, such as the risk of absconding or reoffending.

---

594 As long as the sentence is not so disproportionate so as to amount to a violation of another Art. of the ECHR, such as e.g. Art. 3 (see fn 201). Note that the European Court of Justice does apply marginal testing.

595 The Court tends to give states more leeway in cases of terrorism than in other cases. See e.g. nos 55, 64 and 66.

SECTION II. ADMINISTRATIVE LAW

87. Measures under Article 5 ECHR – Preventive administrative measures which amount to a deprivation of liberty would have to be justified either under Article 5(1)(b) or (c) ECHR. Under both of those subparagraphs, detention must be compatible with the rule of law, including the principle of legal certainty, and the aim of protection against arbitrary detention must be respected. Additionally, under subparagraph (b) the detention must be necessary to achieve the fulfilment of a specific and concrete obligation incumbent on the person. The obligation not to commit a criminal offence is not sufficiently specific and concrete unless the place and time of the imminent commission of the offence and its potential victim(s) have been sufficiently specified; and the person concerned was made aware of the specific act they were to refrain from committing. Similarly, the Court held that subparagraph (c) is only applicable when preventing a concrete and specific offence, concerning, in particular, the place and time of its commission and its victim(s). In a counter-terrorism context, this will not be the case. Below we will establish that when the terrorist offence to be prevented is this specific already, the would-be perpetrator will have already committed one or several terrorist offences. Therefore, there is no reason to impose an administrative measure which would amount to a deprivation of liberty, since criminal law sanctions will be available.[596] In cases where the government would choose not to prosecute in order to protect sources of information, they will probably also not be willing to specify the time, place and victims of the administratively prevented attack in a sufficiently concrete manner. In addition, under subparagraph (c), the detainee needs to be brought before a judge promptly, which is an extra hurdle for administrative procedures. We can therefore conclude that preventive administrative law measures which amount to a deprivation of liberty are very hard to justify.

88. Administrative law measures under Article 2 Prot. No. 4 ECHR – Administrative law measures which amount to a restriction to the freedom of movement have to meet the requirements of Article 2 of the Fourth Protocol to the ECHR. This means they must be necessary in a democratic society, be in accordance with law and pursue one of the legitimate aims referred to. As was the case for criminal law measures, one or more of the following aims will be pursued: national security, public safety, the prevention of crime, the maintenance of public order and/or the protection of the rights and freedoms of others. The analysis will thus focus on whether the measures are necessary in a democratic society and are in accordance with the law.

[596] Note that in the UK, the prohibition of using intercept evidence in criminal trials (see no. 331) might make criminal prosecution difficult and therefore could be an incentive to use administrative law.

89. Note on the UK – Unlike Belgium (which did so in the seventies), the UK has not ratified Protocol No. 4 to the ECHR.[597] This means that the Protocol has not entered into force in the UK. However, this is not a major issue for the purposes of this book. The measures taken by each state will be evaluated in light of the framework set out in the next Chapter and any recommendations in Part IV will focus on Belgium, which is bound by the Protocol.

---

597 See chart of signatures and ratifications of Treaty 046, www.coe.int/en/web/conventions/full-list?module=signatures-by-treaty&treatynum=046. See also: *Gillow v. United Kingdom* App no 9063/80 (ECtHR 24 November 1986) 42; *Gillan and Quinton v. United Kingdom* App no 4158/05 (ECtHR 12 January 2010) 56; *Austin and others v. United Kingdom* App nos 39692/09, 40713/09 and 41008/09 (ECtHR Grand Chamber 15 March 2012) 55; Fenwick, 'Preventive Anti-Terrorist Strategies in the UK and ECHR: Control Orders, TPIMs and the Role of Technology' (n 25) 134; Fenwick and Phillipson (n 25) 879; Gerards (n 114) 937.

CHAPTER III

MAIN PRINCIPLES USED THROUGHOUT THIS BOOK

SECTION I. OPERATIONALISING MAIN PRINCIPLES

90. Right to liberty – As explained in the previous Chapter, deprivations of liberty relevant for our purposes will take place in the context of criminal proceedings rather than administrative measures. Specifically, subparagraphs (a) and (c) will be relevant. Looking at the case law of the ECtHR concerning the right to liberty, we can note that the Court is not always consistent when invoking principles. Judges do not always refer to the same principles and even when they do, they do not necessarily use the exact same terminology. The general principles referred to by the Court are the protection against arbitrariness, the rule of law (and specifically legal certainty) and proportionality. We would argue that the first principle, the ultimate goal of Article 5 ECHR, encompasses the other two. In several cases, the Court links avoiding the risk of arbitrariness back to respect for the rule of law and the principle of legal certainty,[598] and the principle of proportionality.[599] We would argue that these two principles are the core of the protection against arbitrariness: legal certainty (part of the legality principle) and proportionality.[600] The legality principle establishes the minimal conditions for a right, *in casu* the right to liberty, to be restricted but

598 See e.g.: *Medvedyev and others v. France* App no 3394/03 (ECtHR Grand Chamber 29 March 2010) 80; *Louled Massoud v. Malta* App no 24340/08 (ECtHR 27 July 2010) 62; *Khlyustov v. Russia* App no 28975/05 (ECtHR 11 July 2013) 70; *De Tommaso v. Italy* App no 43395/09 (ECtHR Grand Chamber 23 February 2017) 109; *Şahin Alpay v. Turkey* App no 16538/17 (ECtHR 20 March 2018) 118; *Rotaru v. Republic of Moldova* App no 26764/12 (ECtHR 8 December 2020) 24.

599 See e.g.: *James, Wells and Lee v. United Kingdom* App nos 25119/09, 57715/09 and 57877/09 (ECtHR 18 September 2012) 195; *Ruslan Yakovenko v. Ukraine* App no 5425/11 (ECtHR 4 June 2015) 61. Legal scholarship also does this, e.g. Van Dijk and others (n 107) 449. See also: fn. 181.

600 Regarding legality, see also: Erik Claes and Michal Krolikowski, 'The Limits of Legality in the Criminal Law' in Bert Keirsbilck, Wouter Devroe and Erik Claes (eds), *Facing the Limits of the Law* (Springer 2009) 90; Franklin Kuty, *Principes généraux du droit pénal Belge. Tome 1: La loi pénale* (3rd edn, Larcier 2018) 78–79; Peristeridou (n 171) 33; Michel van de Kerchove, 'Développements récents et paradoxaux du principe de la légalité criminelle et de ses corollaires essentiels' in Yves Poullet and Hendrik Vuye (eds), *Liber Amicorum Jean du Jardin* (Kluwer 2001) 312. It is interesting to note that recital 35 of the 2017 EU Directive explicitly

it does not refer to the substantial need to restrict that right. That is the role of the proportionality principle. So, while legality ensures foreseeability and – under the European vision on legality – democratic decision making in the process of restricting rights, it is proportionality which addresses the reasons why a right can be restricted and how far these restrictions can go.[601] Therefore, legal certainty and the proportionality principle will be the two main principles in our analysis. In legal scholarship, both principles are referred to when describing arbitrariness. For example, Jayawickrama states that arbitrariness includes elements of inappropriateness, injustice, lack of predictability and lack of due process of law, as well as elements of reasonableness, necessity and proportionality.[602] Hennebel and Tigroudja, referring to case law of the Human Rights Committee[603] state arbitrariness should be analysed from the point of view of what is appropriate, just and predictable.[604] Many of these principles can be brought back to either legal certainty (lack of predictability, lack of due process of law, etc.) or proportionality (inappropriateness, reasonableness, necessity, etc.).[605]

91. FREEDOM OF MOVEMENT – Freedom of movement and its restrictions can be relevant both in an administrative law and criminal law context. The three-prong test here is: necessity in a democratic society, accordance with the law and the pursuance of one of the legitimate aims referred to in the Article. As argued above, this last condition will not pose any issues in cases of terrorism. Therefore, we can simplify this test to the same two conditions as introduced above: legality (accordance with a law that meets European quality standards) and proportionality (necessity in a democratic society). It should not come as

---

states that the Directive respects, *i.a.* the right to liberty and the principles of legality and proportionality of criminal offences and penalties.

601 Erik Claes, *Legaliteit en rechtsvinding in het strafrecht: een grondslagentheoretische benadering* (Universitaire Pers Leuven 2003) 15; U De Vries and L Francot-Timmermans, 'As Good as It Gets: On Risk, Legality and the Precautionary Principle' in L Besselink, F Pennings and S Prechal (eds), *The Eclipse of the Legality Principle in the European Union* (Kluwer 2011) 26; J McBride, 'Proportionality and the European Convention on Human Rights' in E Ellis (ed), *The Principle of Proportionality in the Laws of Europe* (Hart Publishing 1999) 24; Dirk Van Zyl Smit and Andrew Ashworth, 'Disproportionate Sentences as Human Rights Violations' (2004) 67 The Modern Law Review 541, 543–544.

602 Jayawickrama (n 399) 375–376.

603 *Van Alphen v. Netherlands* Comm No 305/1988 (UN HRC 23 July 1990) 5.8; *Mr. Tai Wairiki Rameka et al. v. New Zealand* Comm No 1090/2002 (UN HRC 15 December 2003).

604 Hennebel and Tigroudja (n 358) 142.

605 Note that limitations of rights under the EU Charter of Fundamental Rights, including the right to liberty, also have to ensure legality and proportionality. Art. 52.1 of the Charter states: *'Any limitation on the exercise of the rights and freedoms recognised by this Charter must be provided for by law and respect the essence of those rights and freedoms. Subject to the principle of proportionality, limitations may be made only if they are necessary and genuinely meet objectives of general interest recognised by the Union or the need to protect the rights and freedoms of others.'*

a surprise that these principles are the same as under Article 5 ECHR. In its analysis of both Articles, the Court uses very similar wording regarding legal certainty: the legislation should be sufficiently accessible, precise and foreseeable in its application, meaning it is required that the person, if need be, with appropriate advice, can foresee the consequences of his actions to a reasonable degree. In those cases where the Court analyses the proportionality under Article 5 ECHR, it also uses similar wording as under Article 2 of the Fourth Protocol: detention should be necessary in the circumstances and other less serious measures should be found insufficient. The fact that the same principles are used does not mean that there is no difference. It is precisely in this proportionality/necessity test, that the difference is relevant. The more restrictive the measure, the more serious the situation has to be.

92. Other safeguards – These two main principles will be briefly elaborated upon in the next two Sections of this Chapter, since they will be recurring throughout the rest of this book. In addition to these main principles, the ECtHR has several other safeguards which can be relevant in specific situations: (1) the need for a link between the ground of permitted deprivation of liberty and the place and conditions of detention, (2) reasonable suspicion and prompt judicial review in cases of pre-trial detention and (3) the right to *habeas corpus* proceedings leading to a speedy decision. These safeguards are relevant in some cases and will be discussed when relevant, but are not part of the guiding principles as they cannot be universally applied. They do not apply to all cases and sometimes depend on the specific application of rules which in the abstract pose no problems in terms of the right to liberty or free movement.

93. Goal of this Chapter – Both the legality and proportionality principle have been elaborately discussed in legal scholarship.[606] It is not the goal of these two brief Sections, nor would it be possible, to redo all this work. Despite, or because of, this elaborate scholarship, the principles of legality and proportionality do not have one generally accepted definition.[607] The aim is to briefly discuss the two principles so as to get a better understanding of their importance in avoiding arbitrariness and in order clarify and operationalise them for the purposes of this book.

606 See among many examples: Petter Asp, 'Two Notions of Proportionality' in K Nuotio (ed), *Festschrift in honour of Raimo Lahti* (Forum Iuris 2007); Claes (n 601); Hallevy (n 182); Peristeridou (n 171).

607 For legality see: Claes (n 601) 439–443. For proportionality see: Asp (n 606) 207–219.

SECTION II. LEGAL CERTAINTY

94. Legality principle – It is widely accepted that the legality principle includes several subprinciples or corollaries, being the principle of non-retrospectivity, the principle of strict interpretation and the principle of clarity and foreseeability of the law.[608] Within civil law traditions, the legality principle also has a formal component, requiring that only 'the law', which has been created by a democratic assembly, can define offences and sentences.[609] The legality principle has a separate provision in the ECHR: Article 7, which the ECtHR also links to the rule of law.[610] After a cursory reading Article 7 very clearly incorporates the principle of non-retroactivity. It also states that only the law can define a criminal offence and prescribe a penalty for it. The Court links this to requirements of a clear definition in the law and accessibility and foreseeability of the law,[611] i.e. the principle of legal certainty. In an analysis

608 These underlying principles can be distilled from the literature and roughly encompass the 8 'Fuller criteria' or 8 elements of the rule of law, stating that statutes have to be general, promulgated, prospective, clear, non-contradictory, not ask the impossible, constant, and there must be a congruence between the laws and the way the officials enforce them. See: Peristeridou (n 171) 55. See also: L Besselink, F Pennings and S Prechal, 'Introduction: Legality in Multiple Legal Orders' in L Besselink, F Pennings and S Prechal (eds), *The Eclipse of the Legality Principle in the European Union* (Kluwer 2011) 6–7; Claes and Krolikowski (n 600) 89; De Coensel, *Counter-Terrorism & Criminal Law: A Normative Legitimacy Test of Terrorism-Related Offences on Expression, Information and Movement* (n 1) 135–136; De Vries and Francot-Timmermans (n 601) 26 and 30; Hallevy (n 182) 6–7; Keiran Hardy and George Williams, 'What Is Terrorism – Assessing Domestic Legal Definitions' (2011) 16 UCLA J. Intl. L. Foreign Aff. 77, 82; Kuty (n 600) 69; Peristeridou (n 171) 3–4 and 6–7; Jan Theunis, 'Le droit à la légalité des incriminations et des peines' in M Verdussen and N Bonbled (eds), *les droits consitutionnels en Belgique* (2nd edn, Bruylant 2011) 767; van de Kerchove (n 600) 311–320.

609 For an analysis of this formal component, see: Cesoni (n 15) 248–249; Tulkens and others (n 39) 237–242; van de Kerchove (n 600) 300–311; Van den Wyngaert, Vandromme and Traest (n 34) 84–87.

610 *S.W. v. United Kingdom* App no 20166/92 (ECtHR 22 November 1995) 34; *Kafkaris v. Cyprus* App no 21906/04 (ECtHR Grand Chamber 12 February 2008) 137; *Sud Fondi SRL and others v. Italy* App no 75909/01 (ECtHR 20 January 2009) 105; *Parmak and Bakir v. Turkey* App nos 22429/07 and 25195/07 (ECtHR 3 December 2019) 57; *Yüksel Yalçinkaya v. Türkiye* App no 15669/20 (ECtHR Grand Chamber 26 September 2023) 237. See also: De Coensel, *Counter-Terrorism & Criminal Law: A Normative Legitimacy Test of Terrorism-Related Offences on Expression, Information and Movement* (n 1) 134–135; Alain De Nauw, 'Nieuwe wendingen inzake het lex certa beginsel' in Frank Verbruggen and others (eds), *Strafrecht als roeping: Liber amicorum Lieven Dupont* (Universitaire Pers Leuven 2005) 757.

611 See e.g.: *Kokkinakis v. Greece* App no 14307/88 (ECtHR 25 May 1993) 52; *S.W. v. United Kingdom* App no 20166/92 (ECtHR 22 November 1995) 35; *Cantoni v. France* App no 17862/91 (ECtHR 11 November 1996) 29; *Streletz, Kessler and Krenz v. Germany* App no 34044/96 (ECtHR Grand Chamber 22 March 2001) 50; *Kafkaris v. Cyprus* App no 21906/04 (ECtHR Grand Chamber 12 February 2008) 140; *Sud Fondi SRL and others v. Italy* App no 75909/01 (ECtHR 20 January 2009) 107–108; *Parmak and Bakir v. Turkey* App nos 22429/07 and 25195/07 (ECtHR 3 December 2019) 58; *Yüksel Yalçinkaya v. Türkiye* App no 15669/20 (ECtHR Grand Chamber 26 September 2023) 238. See also: Conte (n 10) 290–291; De Nauw (n 610) 766–770; Jacqueline Hodgson and Victor Tadros, 'How to Make a Terrorist Out of Nothing' (2009) 72 Modern Law Review 984, 994; Mueller (n 32) 333; Peristeridou (n 171)

of the *lex certa* principle, Rozie concludes that the ECtHR is rather lenient.[612] Additionally, Article 7 ECHR requires that the law is not extensively construed to an accused's detriment.[613]

95. Legal certainty – As explained in the preceding paragraph, the legality principle has several sub-principles. The principle of non-retrospectivity forbids the application of a harsher criminal statute to facts which predate it.[614] Criminal procedural statutes and criminal statutes which are more lenient for the defendant can be applied retrospectively. The obligation of a strict interpretation includes for example the prohibition of analogous interpretations to the detriment of the accused.[615] The final subprinciple is legal certainty (*lex certa*).[616] This is the main principle the ECtHR refers to when it uses phrases such as '*sufficiently accessible, precise and foreseeable in its application*' and thus requires foreseeability. As legal scholars put it, the *lex certa* principle requires that everyone should be able to know for which conduct they can be held criminally liable and to what extent this is the case.[617] This requirement does take into account the interpretation given to legislation by the courts[618] and potentially

97; Joëlle Rozie, 'Beklaagde alwetend. Over het criterium van de redelijke voorzienbaarheid als maatstaf van het lex certa-principe in strafzaken' (2012–2013) 21 Rechtskundig Weekblad 802, 807.

612 Rozie, 'Beklaagde alwetend. Over het criterium van de redelijke voorzienbaarheid als maatstaf van het lex certa-principe in strafzaken' (n 611) 807.

613 *Kokkinakis v. Greece* App no 14307/88 (ECtHR 25 May 1993) 52; *S.W. v. United Kingdom* App no 20166/92 (ECtHR 22 November 1995) 35; *Streletz, Kessler and Krenz v. Germany* App no 34044/96 (ECtHR Grand Chamber 22 March 2001) 50; *Kafkaris v. Cyprus* App no 21906/04 (ECtHR Grand Chamber 12 February 2008) 138; *Sud Fondi SRL and others v. Italy* App no 75909/01 (ECtHR 20 January 2009) 106; *Parmak and Bakir v. Turkey* App nos 22429/07 and 25195/07 (ECtHR 3 December 2019) 58.

614 For a short analysis, see: Theunis (n 608) 783; van de Kerchove (n 600) 317–320.

615 For a short analysis, see: van de Kerchove (n 600) 314–317.

616 See also: De Nauw and Deruyck (n 39) 19.

617 Claes and Krolikowski (n 600) 92–93; Cesoni (n 15) 233; Dekrem (n 32) 162; De Nauw (n 610) 757; Hardy and Williams (n 608) 84–85; Kuty (n 600) 82–85; Christophe Marchand, 'Impact des nouvelles infractions terroristes quant à la qualification de participation à un groupe terroriste et à l'usage d'une preuve secrète devant le tribunal: commentaires d'un avocat' in Francesca Galli and Anne Weyembergh (eds), *EU counter-terrorism offences: What impact on national legislation and case-law?* (Editions de l'Université de Bruxelles 2012) 280; Rozie, 'Beklaagde alwetend. Over het criterium van de redelijke voorzienbaarheid als maatstaf van het lex certa-principe in strafzaken' (n 611) 803; Theunis (n 608) 774; Tulkens and others (n 39) 242–250; Van den Wyngaert, Vandromme and Traest (n 34) 82. This was also confirmed by the Court of Justice of the European Communities. See: *A.s.b.l. Advocaten voor de wereld v. Conseil des Ministres (Belgium)* Case C-303/05 (ECEJ 3 May 2007) 50.

618 Claes and Krolikowski (n 600) 96; van de Kerchove (n 600) 313–314; Van den Wyngaert, Vandromme and Traest (n 34) 82. Although as Rozie argues, it is not clear which courts are included in this and how realistic this requirement is. See: Rozie, 'Beklaagde alwetend. Over het criterium van de redelijke voorzienbaarheid als maatstaf van het lex certa-principe in strafzaken' (n 611) 811–813.

the need to seek legal advice.[619] The ECtHR itself and scholars alike realise that excessive rigidity in the application of this principle is not reconcilable with the concept of general laws applicable to a multitude of situations.[620] The focus of the ECtHR is rightfully on the principle of legal certainty as this is the most relevant sub-principle for our purposes. Therefore, the focus of this book will also be on legal certainty and thus the requirement that legislation is sufficiently precise, accessible and foreseeable in its application.[621] The other subprinciples of the legality principle will take somewhat of a back seat to the *lex certa* principle. These other subprinciples are automatically included as they overlap to an extent with the *lex certa* principle in criminal law. As Peristeridou explains, non-retrospectivity or the prohibition on extensive interpretations *in malam partem*, for example, also follow from the principle of legal certainty.[622] For our topic it is interesting to note at the outset that in legal scholarship the proliferation of inchoate offences is linked to a lack of predictability, and thus the principle of legal certainty.[623]

96. Operationalisation – In order to be able to use the principle of legal certainty as part of an evaluative and normative framework, it needs to be operationalised. This way, it can be applied more precisely. First, in order for legislation to be as foreseeable as possible, redundant wording and overlap should be avoided. Both redundant wording and overlap have no added value

---

619 De Nauw (n 610) 767–770; Peristeridou (n 171) 97–99; Rozie, 'Beklaagde alwetend. Over het criterium van de redelijke voorzienbaarheid als maatstaf van het lex certa-principe in strafzaken' (n 611) 807; Todts (n 104) 219–242.

620 See e.g.: *Kokkinakis v. Greece* App no 14307/88 (ECtHR 25 May 1993) 40; *Cantoni v. France* App no 17862/91 (ECtHR 11 November 1996) 31; *Kafkaris v. Cyprus* App no 21906/04 (ECtHR Grand Chamber 12 February 2008) 141; *Parmak and Bakir v. Turkey* App nos 22429/07 and 25195/07 (ECtHR 3 December 2019) 59. See also: Claes and Krolikowski (n 600) 101–102; De Coensel, *Counter-Terrorism & Criminal Law: A Normative Legitimacy Test of Terrorism-Related Offences on Expression, Information and Movement* (n 1) 136–137; De Nauw (n 610) 766–768; Peristeridou (n 171) 97; Rozie, 'Beklaagde alwetend. Over het criterium van de redelijke voorzienbaarheid als maatstaf van het lex certa-principe in strafzaken' (n 611) 805; Van den Wyngaert, Vandromme and Traest (n 34) 82.

621 For more on this, see: Juan Antonio García Amado, 'On the Principle of Criminal Legality and Its Scope: Foreseeability as a Component of Legality' in Mercedes Pérez Manzano, Juan Antonio Lascuraín Sánchez and Marina Mínguez Rosique (eds), *Multilevel Protection of the Principle of Legality in Criminal Law* (Springer International Publishing 2018); Hallevy (n 182) 138–141.

622 Peristeridou (n 171) 61. See also: Claes and Krolikowski (n 600) 92–93.

623 Amnesty International, 'Veiligheid & Mensenrechten: Maatregelen tegen terrorisme en radicalisering', Letter to the Belgian Chamber of Representatives following a hearing on 12 May 2015 (2015) 9; Asp and Cameron (n 10) 272; Claes and Krolikowski (n 600) 96; De Coensel, *Counter-Terrorism & Criminal Law: A Normative Legitimacy Test of Terrorism-Related Offences on Expression, Information and Movement* (n 1) 139; Sugman Stubbs and Galli (n 25) 299–300; Zedner, 'Fixing the Future? The Pre-Emptive Turn in Criminal Justice' (n 23) 50–51. Similarly, Vandromme and De Roy link the *lex certa* principle to the concept of risk liability (*risicoaansprakelijkheid*). See: Vandromme and De Roy (n 34) 547.

and only serve to create confusion. Second, while criminal legislation has to be general and thus often has to employ relatively broad and general terminology, if more precise terminology can reach the same goal, it should be preferred. Third, the *actus reus* of terrorism offences *sensu lato* is often very broad, making the *mens rea* the core of the offence. In such a case, the *mens rea* should be explicit in the offence and should not have to be implied. In addition, intent should be required. Offences with a broad *actus reus* in combination with a *mens rea* standard which does not require intention, create incredibly broad offences. Finally, in order to increase foreseeability, account should be taken of how far removed the perpetrator of the offence of terrorism *sensu lato* is from the offence of terrorism *sensu stricto* (see no. 6).

SECTION III. PROPORTIONALITY

97. Going beyond the ECtHR case law on Article 5 – When analysing subparagraph (c) and the preventive part of sentences under subparagraph (a), the ECtHR explicitly acknowledges the proportionality principle (see nos 46 and 55). However, in the context of the imposition of sentences and their retributive part, the Court has clearly stated that it does not concern itself with the proportionality of sentences under Article 5 ECHR. This is understandable in the context of the ECtHR and the political reality it operates in. However, we would argue that this should not hold us back to analyse the proportionality of these sentences. Proportionality of sentences is one of the cornerstones of criminal law in our society (in addition to legality[624]).[625] Moreover, a disproportionate response to terrorism can lead to radicalisation, making the numbers of terrorist organisations grow, and is thus counter-productive.[626] It is interesting to note that the Belgian Council of State at one point even stated that proportionality was implied by the legality principle.[627]

---

624 Claes and Krolikowski (n 600) 89; Peristeridou (n 171) 3 and 33; Kuty (n 600) 70; Rozie, 'Beklaagde alwetend. Over het criterium van de redelijke voorzienbaarheid als maatstaf van het lex certa-principe in strafzaken' (n 611) 817; Theunis (n 608) 763; Traest (n 168) 1190; Tulkens and others (n 39) 236; Van den Wyngaert, Vandromme and Traest (n 34) 81–82; Eric Wauters, 'Het Grondwettelijk Hof over het begrip "terrorisme"' [2007] Vigiles 176, 176. This was also confirmed by the Court of Justice of the European Communities. See: *A.s.b.l. Advocaten voor de wereld v. Conseil des Ministres (Belgium)* Case C-303/05 (ECEJ 3 May 2007) 49.

625 Besselink, Pennings and Prechal (n 608) 4; Lieven Dupont, *Beginselen van behoorlijke strafrechtsbedeling* (Kluwer 1979) 49–55 and 58–61; Traest (n 168) 1190–1207; Verbruggen, Prakken and Roef (n 25) 16–18.

626 Ahmed (n 21) 556–557; Meliá (n 25) 114 and 120.

627 Advies 34.379/3 van de Raad van State 14 november 2002, *Parl.St.* Kamer 2002–2003, no. 50-2176/1, 11 en no. 50-2124/12, 7. See also: Theunis (n 608) 786.

98. Different meanings – The proportionality principle does not have one sole meaning. Proportionality in the traditional criminal law sense refers to the abovementioned relationship between the seriousness of the conduct and the harshness of the sentence.[628] It is this type of proportionality the ECtHR does not judge but we will take into account (see no. 97). However, the term proportionality is often used in a broader sense. The most used framework for the proportionality principle goes beyond this and includes three elements or sub-principles: the principle of suitability, the principle of necessity and the principle of balancing (proportionality *sensu stricto*).[629] The suitability and necessity principles are related. They require that a measure is able to achieve a legitimate aim (suitability) and it should be necessary to achieve this aim, i.e. be the least restrictive means to achieve this aim.[630] This is a form of subsidiarity (see no. 43).[631] The balancing test is one of proportionality in the narrow sense since two interests are weighed against each other.[632] When it comes to criminal law measures, the punishment is balanced against the gravity of the offence and the culpability of the offender. However, in non-criminal preventive measures, this balancing exercise is aimed toward the dangerousness of the person.[633] The three aforementioned tests are to a certain extent intertwined. If a proportionality analysis *sensu stricto* shows that a measure is disproportionate, it

628 De Coensel, *Counter-Terrorism & Criminal Law: A Normative Legitimacy Test of Terrorism-Related Offences on Expression, Information and Movement* (n 1) 123–125; Carol S Steiker, 'Proportionality as a Limit on Preventive Justice: Promises and Pitfalls' in Andrew Ashworth, Lucia Zedner and Patrick Tomlin (eds), *Prevention and the limits of the criminal law* (Oxford University Press 2013) 195–196.

629 Sébastien Van Drooghenbroeck, 'Note relative à l'application des principes de proportionnalité et subsidiarité en matière pénale dans de droit de la Convention européenne des droits de l'Homme', Annex 2.7 to the Report on behalf of the Committee on Justice on the Bill on the Code of Criminal Procedure, *Parl.St.* Senaat 2005–06, no. 3-450/20, (1398) 1399; Yukata Arai-Takahashi, 'Proportionality' in D Shelton (ed), *The Oxford Handbook of International Human Rights Law* (Oxford University Press 2013) 451–452; Jonas Christoffersen, *Fair Balance: Proportionality, Subsidiarity and Primarity in the European Convention on Human Rights* (Brill | Nijhoff 2009) 69–70; Juan Cianciardo, 'The Principle of Proportionality: The Challenges of Human Rights' (2010) 3 Journal of Civil Law Studies 177, 179; De Coensel, *Counter-Terrorism & Criminal Law: A Normative Legitimacy Test of Terrorism-Related Offences on Expression, Information and Movement* (n 1) 125; S Feyen, 'Noodzakelijkheid als de schoonmoeder van het proportionaliteitsbeginsel' in R Leysen and others (eds), *Semper perseverans – Liber amicorum André Alen* (Intersentia 2020) 163–164; Sakari Melander, 'Ultima Ratio in European Criminal Law' (2013) 3 European Criminal Law Review 45, 54; Sottiaux (n 27) 45; Stavros Tsakyrakis, 'Proportionality: An Assault on Human Rights?' (2009) 7 International Journal of Constitutional Law 468, 474; Webber (n 95) 53.

630 Arai-Takahashi (n 629) 451–452; Christoffersen (n 629) 69–70; Cianciardo (n 629) 179–180; De Coensel, *Counter-Terrorism & Criminal Law: A Normative Legitimacy Test of Terrorism-Related Offences on Expression, Information and Movement* (n 1) 126; Melander (n 629) 55.

631 De Coensel, *Counter-Terrorism & Criminal Law: A Normative Legitimacy Test of Terrorism-Related Offences on Expression, Information and Movement* (n 1) 128.

632 Arai-Takahashi (n 629) 452; Cianciardo (n 629) 180; Conte (n 10) 292–295.

633 Steiker (n 628) 195–197.

might also have been unnecessary for example.[634] Proportionality has a cardinal or absolute dimension, meaning the actual balancing between the restrictiveness of the measure and the actions undertaken by the person subject to it.[635] Caeiro notes that in criminalising preparatory actions, this cardinal proportionality is sometimes threatened, with harsh sentences for quite harmless actions.[636] Proportionality also has an ordinal or comparative dimension, in which the proportionality of a measure or sentence is compared to other measures or sentences.[637] For example, an offence which is deemed more serious by the legislature and society than another should also have a harsher sentence.

99. Suitability and necessity included – In the case law of the ECtHR different subprinciples of proportionality are applied.[638] However, the Court does not always apply all three subprinciples and the application of the principle of proportionality is unsystematic.[639] In the cases discussed above, the ECtHR refers to the need for a measure to be necessary in the circumstances or necessary in a democratic society, which is the principle of necessity. The Court also requires a relationship of proportionality between the ground of detention relied upon and the detention in question or a fair balance between the public interest and the individual's rights. These tests refer more to the principle of balancing.[640] In this book, the term proportionality will be used to refer to the entirety of the different tests of necessity, suitability, and proportionality *sensu stricto*. The concept of balancing has been discussed in the literature and has received some criticism, especially in a preventive context.[641] We will therefore apply it with a degree of caution and usually limit ourselves to analysing ordinal

634 See also: Feyen (n 629) 166.
635 Steiker (n 628) 200.
636 Caeiro (n 21) 310.
637 Umar Azmeh, 'Exemplary Sentencing for Terrorist Offenders: The Counter- Terrorism and Sentencing Bill 2020' [2021] Criminal Law Review 5, 14; Smit and Ashworth (n 601) 555; Steiker (n 628) 200–201.
638 De Coensel, *Counter-Terrorism & Criminal Law: A Normative Legitimacy Test of Terrorism-Related Offences on Expression, Information and Movement* (n 1) 127–128.
639 Arai-Takahashi (n 629) 453–454; Sottiaux (n 27) 45; Todts (n 104) 330–331.
640 See also: Todts (n 104) 334–335.
641 See e.g.: Andrew Ashworth, 'Security, Terrorism and the Value of Human Rights' in B Goold and L Lazarus (eds), *Security and Human Rights* (Hart Publishing 2007); Barbara Hudson, 'Who Needs Justice? Who Needs Security?' in Barbara Hudson and Synnove Ugelvik (eds), *Justice in the Risk Society: Challenging and Re-affirming Justice in Late Modernity* (SAGE Publications Ltd 2012) 17–18; Tsakyrakis (n 629); Squires (n 25) 689–694; Steiker (n 628) 207–209; Thomas (n 92) 1207–1209; Jeremy Waldron, 'Security and Liberty: The Image of Balance' (2003) 11 Journal of Political Philosophy 191; Jessica Wolfendale, 'Terrorism, Security, and the Threat of Counterterrorism' (2007) 30 Studies in Conflict & Terrorism 77–80; Zedner, 'Securing Liberty in the Face of Terror: Reflections from Criminal Justice' (n 92) 512; Zedner, *Security* (n 8) 126–128 and 134–137.

proportionality.[642] As was the case for the principle of legal certainty, the proportionality of inchoate offences has been questioned. Scholars point out that the earlier on the *iter criminis* a perpetrator is, the smaller the risk for society. This should be reflected in the severity of the sentences, which they claim is not the case for terrorist offences.[643] Furthermore, many theories on the justification of non-penal prevention have the proportionality principle as one of their key features.[644]

100. Operationalisation – The first operationalisation of the proportionality principle can be found in ordinal proportionality. In the context of preventive counter-terrorism law this can often be expressed in how far the perpetrator is along the *iter criminis*. The closer to the terrorist offence *sensu stricto*, the higher on the scale the offender is. A second way to operationalise the proportionality principle is the application of a threshold for when legislation should intervene: *de minimis non curat praetor*. These two criteria link back to the final operationalisation element of the legal certainty principle (see no. 96). Criminalising conduct which is far removed from the terrorist offence *sensu stricto* can lead to legality issues, but also pose issues in terms of both ordinal proportionality and the *de minimis* reasoning.

642 It is very difficult to provide an objective basis for cardinal proportionality as well. See e.g. on the interpretation of gross disproportionality of sentences: Smit and Ashworth (n 601) 545–546.

643 Asp (n 4) 34; Florence Lee, 'Sentencing Cases of Preparation of Terrorist Acts (Terrorism Act 2006 s.5): A Call for Proportionality' [2018] Sentencing News 8; Vandromme and De Roy (n 34) 547; Zedner, 'Terrorizing Criminal Law' (n 45) 117.

644 See: Steiker (n 628) 195.

PART II
BELGIUM

INTRODUCTION

101. Overview of Part II – As explained in the methodology (see no. 18), in this Part we discuss the Belgian framework of preventive restrictions of physical liberty in a counter-terrorism context. Since Belgium has no administrative measures depriving or limiting the liberty of people to prevent terrorism, this Part is solely focussed on criminal law.[645] The rest of this introduction briefly outlines the Belgian criminal justice system and the country's context of terrorism. Chapters I through XII answer research question 2.1,[646] while Chapter XIII answers research question 2.2.[647] We will commence with a Chapter which focusses on the different possibilities for limitations to the right to liberty in Belgium. This Chapter is followed by nine other ones which each discuss one Article of the Belgian Criminal Code containing terrorist offences.[648] Chapter II covers terrorism *sensu stricto* and chapters III to X cover the offences of terrorism *sensu lato* (for the difference, see no. 7). In Chapter III the offences pertaining to terrorist groups are discussed. Some authors put these offences in the same category as the offences in Article 137 CC (terrorism *sensu stricto*).[649] However, the offences pertaining to terrorist groups are also based on a preventive rational.[650] It is not required that the group has already committed

645 Note that administrative detention does exist in Belgium. See: Art. 31 WPA. The legislation allows police officers to detain people who e.g. disturb public peace or endanger public safety. This detention is limited to 12 hours. It does not fall within the scope of this book as it is not a specific counter-terrorism measure, and its short maximum duration makes it impractical in most terrorism cases.

646 How has Belgium used direct restrictions to the right to liberty to attempt to prevent terrorism?

647 In which ways is the Belgian approach in line with our framework?

648 For a more condensed version of these chapters, see also: Ward Yperman, 'Terrorism Offences in Belgian Criminal Law: Is Less More?' [2021] Queen Mary Law Journal 150.

649 Delhaise (n 8) 44–45; Fransen and Kerkhofs (n 10) 18–49. The Council of State does something simliar, when it points to the preventive rationale of the offences in Art. 140*bis* to 140*septies* CC, but not 140 CC. See: Advies 59.147/3 van de Raad van State (II) 22 april 2016 bij wetsontwerp houdende diverse bepalingen ter bestrijding van terrorisme (III), *Parl.St.* Kamer 2015–2016, no. 54-1951/001, 25; Advies 59.789/3 van de Raad van State 19 juli 2016 bij wetsvoorstel 13 januari 2016 tot wijziging van het Strafwetboek wat betreft de bestraffing van terrorisme, *Parl.St. Kamer* 2015–2016, no. 54-1579/006, 10. See also: Gedr. St., Kamer, DOC 25-2502/001, 7 and DOC 54-1198/001, 6. Amnesty International on the other hand, explicitly refers to Art. 140 CC as an offence which is far removed from the 'main offence' (i.e. the act causing the harm). See: Amnesty International, 'Veiligheid & Mensenrechten: Maatregelen tegen terrorisme en radicalisering', Letter to the Belgian Chamber of Representatives following a hearing on 12 May 2015 (2015) 9.

650 Dekrem (n 32) 138; De La Serna (n 50) 213; Flore (n 10) 221–222; Thomas (n 50) 473.

terrorism *sensu stricto*. Having the intention suffices and therefore these offences allow for an intervention early on the *iter criminis*.[651] For this reason, we include them under the terrorism offences *sensu lato*. The other Belgian terrorism offences *sensu lato* are: public provocation to commit terrorism (Chapter IV), terrorist recruitment (Chapter V), providing training for terrorism (Chapter VI), receiving training for terrorism or self-study (Chapter VII), terrorist travel (Chapter VIII), preparing a terrorist attack (Chapter IX) and financing a terrorist (Chapter X). After all the current Belgian terrorist offences have been discussed, Chapter XI touches upon possible future changes in terms of an expansion of the current offences. Chapter XII covers the rules on pre-trial detention and the final Chapter (XIII) includes a preliminary analysis of the Belgian rules. This analysis builds upon the criticism, based on the normative framework established in Part I, voiced throughout the Part and discusses the current Belgian rules in isolation (although taking into account Belgium's international obligations). A more detailed comparative analysis of both the Belgian and UK rules, including recommendations, will be undertaken in the fourth and final Part of this book.

102. Belgian Criminal Justice: brief introduction – The Belgian criminal justice system is in many ways similar to the French one. Its basis is a Code of Criminal Procedure of 1808 (CCP) and a Criminal Code of 1867 (CC). It is a mix of an inquisitorial and an adversarial system.[652] In the investigation stage, there are two types of investigations. There is the preliminary investigation, which is led by the public prosecution service.[653] Over 90% of cases that go to the trial phase proceed from the preliminary investigation straight to the trial phase, usually via a direct summons.[654] In the other cases, a judiciary investigation is started. This investigation is led by the investigating judge, who has more investigatory powers than the public prosecution service.[655] Arrest warrants and search warrants for homes, for example, can only be issued by the investigating judge.[656] The trial phase takes place in front of the trial courts. There are four such types of courts, competent to preside over different types of offences at different stages. The police courts deal with contraventions, being the lightest offences, as well as all traffic offences.[657] The Correctional Courts are competent for standard offences and appeals against the police courts.[658] The Court of Appeal

---

651 Vandromme and De Roy (n 34) 536.

652 Van den Wyngaert, Vandromme and Traest (n 34) 602–603.

653 Van den Wyngaert, Vandromme and Traest (n 34) 609; Raf Verstraeten, *Handboek Strafvordering* (5de voll. herz. uitgave, Maklu 2012) 277.

654 Van den Wyngaert, Vandromme and Traest (n 34) 609.

655 Van den Wyngaert, Vandromme and Traest (n 34) 610; Verstraeten (n 653) 409–410.

656 Van den Wyngaert, Vandromme and Traest (n 34) 610; Verstraeten (n 653) 495 and 583.

657 Art. 137–138 CCP. See also: Van den Wyngaert, Vandromme and Traest (n 34) 688–689; Verstraeten (n 653) 812.

658 Art. 174 and 179 CCP. See also: De Nauw and Deruyck (n 39) 52; Van den Wyngaert, Vandromme and Traest (n 34) 687–688; Verstraeten (n 653) 813.

is responsible for appeals against the judgments of the Correctional Courts.[659] The Assize Courts, finally, judge felonies and all political and press offences.[660] An offence is a contravention when the principal penalty is a fine not exceeding 25 euros or an imprisonment which does not exceed seven days.[661] In modern Belgian criminal law, contraventions are rather rare. Note that all Belgian criminal fines have to be multiplied by a factor eight because of the application of so-called '10% surcharges'. Belgian law applies surcharges to criminal fines to adapt them to the real value of money without having to constantly change the criminal legislation. The idea is that this way the financial impact of a fine stays more or less the same over the years while the value of money changes. Since 2016, there are 70 10% surcharges, transforming a fine of 25 euros into one of 200 euros in practice.[662] Throughout this book the Belgian fines mentioned do not include these surcharges and still have to be multiplied by eight to know the actual fine applied in practice. Standard offences are all offences for which the prescribed principal penalty is imprisonment of more than seven days but not exceeding five years (possibly in combination with a fine) or a fine of more than 25 euros.[663] Felonies are all offences for which statutes prescribe so-called felony imprisonment, which has a minimum of five years and a maximum of life in prison.[664] Because of this relatively low threshold of five years, many offences in Belgian criminal law are felonies, which should be tried by the Assize Court. In the Assize Court however, jury trials take place. As the jury trial procedure is long and expensive, a technique called correctionalisation is often employed.[665] It is possible to try all but the most serious felonies in front of the Correctional Courts, if attenuating circumstances are invoked when referring the case to trial.[666] This is called correctionalisation based on attenuating circumstances and it has become standard practice for almost every felony for which the law allows it.[667] There is no list of what can be invoked as an attenuating circumstance, so

659 Art. 200 CCP. See also: Verstraeten (n 653) 815.

660 Art. 150 Belgian Constitution. See also: De Nauw and Deruyck (n 39) 52; Van den Wyngaert, Vandromme and Traest (n 34) 681; Verstraeten (n 653) 815.

661 Art. 28 and 38, section 1 CC; De Nauw and Deruyck (n 39) 46; Tulkens and others (n 39) 334 and 601–602; Van den Wyngaert, Vandromme and Traest (n 34) 195.

662 See: Art. 59 Programmawet 25 december 2016, *BS* 29 december 2016, 90879.

663 Art. 25, section 1 and 38, section 2 CC; De Nauw and Deruyck (n 39) 46; Tulkens and others (n 39) 334, 589 and 600; Van den Wyngaert, Vandromme and Traest (n 34) 195.

664 Art. 7, 1° CC; De Nauw and Deruyck (n 39) 45; Tulkens and others (n 39) 334 and 582–286; Van den Wyngaert, Vandromme and Traest (n 34) 195.

665 Brion and others (n 77) 59; Van den Wyngaert, Vandromme and Traest (n 34) 295 and 685.

666 De Nauw and Deruyck (n 39) 49–50; Vanessa Franssen, 'Algemeen' in M De Busscher and others (eds), *Strafrecht: duiding* (Larcier 2018) 162–163; Tulkens and others (n 39) 653; Van den Wyngaert, Vandromme and Traest (n 34) 295; Verstraeten (n 653) 697–698.

667 Brion and others (n 77) 59; Vanessa Franssen, 'Begrip Politiek Misdrijf' in M De Busscher and others (eds), *Strafrecht: duiding* (Larcier 2018) 29; Franssen (n 666) 163–164; Van den Wyngaert, Vandromme and Traest (n 34) 295.

the possibilities are near endless.[668] In practice, very few cases are tried by the Assize Courts. Murder and manslaughter are two of the few remaining felonies for which correctionalisation is not possible. Because correctionalisation is based on attenuating circumstances, the maximum sentence goes down slightly, but sentences can transcend five years imprisonment (the maximum for actual standard offences).[669] Felonies originally punishable with 20 to 30 years felony imprisonment or lifelong felony imprisonment, for example, (the two harshest sentences in Belgian criminal law[670]) are punishable with a maximum of 20 years imprisonment after correctionalisation.

103. Criminal offences – Belgian criminal law is so-called guilt-based criminal law. Criminal offences always require two elements: *actus reus* and *mens rea*.[671] This means on the one hand that offences solely consisting of an *actus reus* do not exist in Belgium (see also no. 193).[672] The required *mens rea* can be one of three main options: negligence, general intent or special intent.[673] General intent equals 'knowingly and willingly'.[674] Special intent goes one step further. The knowledge element ('knowingly') does not change, but the will element ('willingly') becomes more specific, requiring a particular intention, such as intent to harm or the intent to obtain an undue advantage.[675] Negligence, in turn, means that a person did not intend for the consequences to happen, but caused them by a lack of precaution or prudence.[676] It requires a comparison of one's actions with those of a hypothetical normally careful and circumspect person, the *bonus pater familias*, who is placed in the same position.[677] If this *bonus pater familias* would have acted in the same way as the would-be perpetrator, there is no criminal offence. On the other hand, Belgium always requires an *actus reus*, meaning that mere thoughts are free. The intention to do even the most heinous things, cannot be a criminal offence if the would-be perpetrator does not act on

---

668 Tulkens and others (n 39) 649–650; Van den Wyngaert, Vandromme and Traest (n 34) 294–295.

669 Art. 80 CC; Franssen (n 666) 162.

670 The Criminal Code also includes felony imprisonment of 30 to 40 years in its list of possible sentences. However, to date no offence has ever existed which actually imposes this sentence.

671 De Nauw and Deruyck (n 39) 36; Van den Wyngaert, Vandromme and Traest (n 34) 189–192.

672 N De Nil, F Deruyck and J Meese, 'Misdrijven', *Strafrecht geannoteerd* (die Keure 2020) 269; Tulkens and others (n 39) 474–475; Van den Wyngaert, Vandromme and Traest (n 34) 192.

673 De Nauw and Deruyck (n 39) 41.

674 De Nauw and Deruyck (n 39) 41; De Nil, Deruyck and Meese (n 672) 269; Tulkens and others (n 39) 463–464; Van den Wyngaert, Vandromme and Traest (n 34) 326.

675 Cesoni (n 15) 256; De Nauw and Deruyck (n 39) 42; Tulkens and others (n 39) 464; Van den Wyngaert, Vandromme and Traest (n 34) 328.

676 De Nauw and Deruyck (n 39) 43; Tulkens and others (n 39) 470; Van den Wyngaert, Vandromme and Traest (n 34) 337.

677 Bart Spriet, 'Elk misdrijf- ook dat uit het bijzonder strafrecht – vereist een moreel of schuldbestanddeel (noot onder Cass. 13 december 1994)' (1995) 1995–96 Rechtskundig Weekblad 533, 535–536; Van den Wyngaert, Vandromme and Traest (n 34) 338.

this intention. Belgium does not allow for the criminalisation of thoughts.[678] It is worth noting that although this basic rule still stands, Belgian case law seems to move to a more subjective doctrine. Belgian criminal law used to adhere to an objective doctrine: the need to punish was based on the objective harm of the act and not so much on the danger of the person of the offender.[679] However, this doctrine has been slowly shifting more towards the subjective, resulting in a mixed doctrine.[680] Under a subjective doctrine, more importance is given to the intentions and thus the dangerousness of the offender and less to the objective harm caused by the actions.[681] This shift could be seen as another step in the direction of a more preventive and risk averse criminal law.

104. Terrorism in Belgium – While the second half of the twentieth century was a time of high terrorist activity for some countries, this was not really the case for Belgium. There are a few exceptions. In the mid-eighties, the Cellules Communistes Combattantes (CCC), a far-left terrorist group, committed more than a dozen terrorist attacks, in total killing two people and injuring 28.[682] In the first half of that same decade the Brabant Killers had killed 28 and injured 40 in a series of bloody robberies.[683] The bloody nature and small score of these robberies, lead some to theorise this was a form of terrorism, but this was never proven and the perpetrators were never caught. In the wave of religiously inspired international terrorism of the last decades, this relative calm made way for higher terrorist activity in Belgium. Belgium was one of the countries with the highest number per capita of foreign terrorist fighters traveling to the conflict area in the Middle East[684] and several of the perpetrators of the 2015 Paris

678 Chris Van den Wyngaert, *Strafrecht, strafprocesrecht & internationaal strafrecht in hoofdlijnen* (Maklu 2003) 301.

679 Berkmoes, 'Algemeen' (n 39) 84–85; De Nauw and Deruyck (n 39) 68; Van den Wyngaert (n 678) 298–299; Van den Wyngaert, Vandromme and Traest (n 34) 360–361; Vandromme and De Roy (n 34) 1585.

680 Berkmoes, 'Algemeen' (n 39) 85; De Nauw and Deruyck (n 39) 68; Van den Wyngaert (n 678) 302; Van den Wyngaert, Vandromme and Traest (n 34) 362; Vandromme and De Roy (n 34) 1585.

681 Berkmoes, 'Algemeen' (n 39) 85; De Coensel, *Counter-Terrorism & Criminal Law: A Normative Legitimacy Test of Terrorism-Related Offences on Expression, Information and Movement* (n 1) 104; De Nauw and Deruyck (n 39) 68; Ten Voorde (n 45) 167–168; Van den Wyngaert (n 678) 299; Van den Wyngaert, Vandromme and Traest (n 34) 360–361; Vandromme and De Roy (n 34) 1585.

682 Sybille Smeets and Cedric Strebelle, 'Terrorisme, criminalité organisée et violence urbaine: L'expérience Belge' in Emmanuelle Bribosia and Anne Weyembergh (eds), *Lutte contre le terrorisme et droits fondamentaux* (Bruylant-Nemesis 2002) 198; Weyembergh and Kennes (n 58) 149.

683 Smeets and Strebelle (n 682) 198.

684 Philip Verwimp, 'Foreign Fighters in Syria and Iraq and the Socio-Economic Environment They Faced at Home: A Comparison of European Countries' (2016) 10 Perspectives on Terrorism 68, 72; Winants (n 8) 349; X., 'Meeste Syriëstrijders komen uit België' (*Het Laatste Nieuws* 23 August 2014) www.hln.be/buitenland/meeste-syriestrijders-komen-uit-belgie~ab5cbbc3/ (accessed 26 January 2021).

attacks were born and raised in Belgium. A number of attacks were perpetrated on Belgian soil as well.[685] The most infamous were the machine gun attack on the Jewish Museum in Brussels in 2014, killing four and the 2016 Brussels airport and metro bombings, killing 35 and injuring 340.

105. Introduction terrorist offences – Before 2003, there were no specific terrorist offences in Belgian criminal law.[686] Terrorism suspects, such as the members of the CCC, were prosecuted and convicted for other, 'ordinary' offences.[687] The introduction of terrorist offences into the Criminal Code was prompted by the international and European legal instruments discussed in the general introduction (see no. 2). The EU instruments provide for minimum harmonisation, which means they require Member States to criminalise certain conduct but allow states to go further if desired.[688] The Belgian legislature chose to expand some of the terrorism offences beyond the scope of the EU instruments, but overall, adhered quite closely to the wording of the EU instruments. The Belgian offences were therefore introduced in waves, in step with the international and European evolutions. The first wave came in 2003, adding a new title to the criminal code: Title I*ter*: Terrorist offences.[689] This new title contained Articles 137 to 140 and 141 to 141*ter* CC.[690] Roughly a decade later, the offences of Article 140*bis* to 140*quinquies* CC were added in what can be called a second big wave. Subsequently, Article 140*sexies* CC was introduced in 2015 and 140*septies* CC in the following year. That same piece of legislation in 2016 also rephrased the offence of Article 141 CC. A -for the time being- last wave of changes came in 2019, when the legislature did not introduce new Articles in Titel I*ter* but did introduce aggravating circumstances into many of the existing offences and added a new offence both to Article 140 and Article 140*quinquies* CC.

---

685 See the Europol Terrorism Situation and Trend Reports for data: 1 attack and 99 arrests in Belgium in 2019, 1 attack and 166 arrests in 2018, and 2 attacks and 50 arrests in 2017.

686 Frédéric Vanneste and Frank Verbruggen, 'Symboolstrafwet als vaandel van de strijd tegen terrorisme' [2004] Panopticon 80, 80; Stef Wittendorp and Edwin Bakker, 'Inventarisatie rechtszaken tegen jihadistische buitenlandse strijders: een vergelijking tussen Nederland, België, Denemarken, Duitsland, Frankrijk, het VK en de VS' (2017) ISGA Report 35.

687 De La Serna (n 8) 170 and 173; Masset (n 20) T60/8-T60/11; Martin Moucheron, 'Délit politique et terrorisme en Belgique : du noble au vil' [2006] Cultures & conflits 77, paras 1 and 15; Vanneste and Verbruggen (n 686) 80–81; Weyembergh and Kennes (n 58) 150; Weyembergh and Kennes (n 14) 103–104; Winants (n 8) 345; Wittendorp and Bakker (n 686) 35.

688 Art. 1 Directive (EU) 2017/541 of the European Parliament and of the Council of 15 March 2017 on combating terrorism and replacing Council Framework Decision 2002/475/JHA and amending Council Decision 2005/671/JHA [2017] *OJ* L88/6. See also: Caeiro (n 21) 306–307.

689 Weyembergh and Kennes (n 14) 102.

690 Masset (n 20) T60/1; Weyembergh and Kennes (n 58) 151.

106. Humanitarian law savings clause – The one Article of Title I*ter* CC which will not be discussed in this book, is Article 141*ter* CC. This Article contains a humanitarian law savings clause, excluding certain actions covered by international humanitarian law from the application of the terrorist offences. This Article has led to a good amount of discussion in the case law.[691] So much so, that it was amended in 2024.[692] The study of this Article would lead us much too far into a different field, that of international humanitarian law, and has moreover already been undertaken by Thomas Van Poecke in his PhD dissertation.[693]

107. Federal prosecution service – The Belgian prosecution service is divided into different districts, each responsible for offences committed in their designated area. However, in order to combat any issues of coordination in cases which span several districts or in cases requiring a certain specific expertise, a federal prosecution service was founded which is competent to act on the entire Belgian territory. If necessary for the good administration of justice, the federal prosecution service can take the prosecution of certain offences, including the terrorism offences, in hand.[694] In practice this usually happens[695] and local prosecutors have to report any possible terrorism case to the federal prosecution service.[696] However, it is possible for local prosecutors to be in charge of prosecution, in cases where the federal prosecution service does not take charge.[697]

---

691 See: Amendementen bij Wetsontwerp 14 december 2023 om Justitie menselijker, sneller en straffer te maken III, *Parl.St.* Kamer 2023–2024, no. 55-3322/014, 58–89; KI Brussel 14 september 2017, *RW* 2017–18, 1611, noot J. Wouters en T. Van Poecke; KI Brussel 8 maart 2019, *onuitg.*, 44; RK Brussel 3 november 2016, *onuitg.*, 11; Bjorn Ketels, 'Titel Iter Terroristische Misdrijven' in Martine De Busscher and others (eds), *Strafrecht: Duiding* (Larcier 2018) 242; Thomas Van Poecke, Frank Verbruggen and Ward Yperman, 'Terrorist Offences and International Humanitarian Law: The Armed Conflict Exclusion Clause' (2021) 103 International Review of the Red Cross 295; Jan Wouters and Thomas Van Poecke, 'Van strijdkrachten, terroristen en het belgisch strafrecht (noot onder KI Brussel 14 september 2017)' [2017–2018] Rechtskundig Weekblad 1616.

692 Art. 17 Wetsontwerp 5 januari 2024 om Justitie menselijker, sneller en straffer te maken III, *Parl.St.* Kamer 2023–2024, no. 55-3322/017.

693 See: Thomas Van Poecke, *Terrorism and Armed Conflict: A Transnational Criminal Law Framework* (PhD project funded by FWO, 2024).

694 Art. 144*ter*, §1, 2° Judicial Code (Gerechtelijk Wetboek). See also: De La Serna (n 8) 212; Flore (n 10) 225; Van den Wyngaert, Vandromme and Traest (n 34) 804–805; Verstraeten (n 653) 60–61; Weyembergh and Kennes (n 14) 123.

695 De La Serna (n 8) 212; Weyembergh and Kennes (n 58) 156; Weyembergh and Kennes (n 14) 123.

696 Art. 144*ter*, §2 Judicial Code. See also: Delmulle and Guenter (n 6) 5; Van den Wyngaert, Vandromme and Traest (n 34) 806; Verstraeten (n 653) 62.

697 Art. 144*ter*, §3 Judicial Code. See also: Weyembergh and Kennes (n 14) 123; Van den Wyngaert, Vandromme and Traest (n 34) 806; Verstraeten (n 653) 63.

108. Number of investigations and cases – In its 2021 yearly report, the terrorism section of the Federal Prosecution Service lists the following numbers[698]:

	2017	2018	2019	2020	2021	Total
New cases	251	155	86	95	64	651
New judicial investigations	67	73	43	28	25	236

During that same year, a total of 75 court decisions were made in terrorism cases while 172 cases were still ongoing and 98 were closed without a final court decision.

109. New criminal code and proposal for a new code of criminal procedure – The current Belgian Criminal Code and Code of Criminal Procedure being drafted in the 19th Century (see no. 102), several attempts have been made to modernise Belgian Criminal Law by introducing new codes.[699] In February 2024, a new Criminal Code was published, which should enter into force in April 2026, and the most recent draft of the Code of Criminal Procedure was under debate in parliament at the end of the last legislature.[700] The basic principles of Belgian criminal law are not changed in the new Criminal Code, the biggest change for our purposes being the introduction of eight levels of criminal sentences and of several new criminal sanctions.[701] One of these newly introduced sanctions is the treatment under deprivation of liberty. This is a sentence applicable to people suffering a mental or medical disorder, which is not so serious as to override their criminal liability, but does make them a danger to society.[702] It can last from six months to 20 years, depending on the level of

698 Federaal Parket, Jaarverslag 2021, 371–394. Note that this includes all cases handled by this section of the Federal Prosecution Service, which are not necessarily limited to prosecutions for terrorism offences but can include other offences committed by a terrorist group e.g..

699 Note that many clauses were amended over the years and few clauses are the exact same they were upon entry into force of the Code.

700 Wet 22 februari 2024 tot invoering van boek I van het Strafwetboek (1), *BS* 29 februari 2024, 40520; wet 22 februari 2024 tot invoering van boek II van het Strafwetboek (1), *BS* 29 februari 2024, 40548; Wetsontwerp (I) 23 mei 2023 tot invoering van Boek I van het Strafwetboek, *Parl.St.* Kamer 2022–2023, no. 55–3374/001; Wetsontwerp 24 juli 2023 tot invoering van Boek II van het Strafwetboek, *Parl.St.* Kamer 2022–2023, no. 55–3518/001.

701 See: Art. 36–37 Wetsontwerp (I) 23 mei 2023 tot invoering van Boek I van het Strafwetboek, *Parl.St.* Kamer 2022–2023, no. 55–3374/001.

702 Art. 42 Wetsontwerp (I) 23 mei 2023 tot invoering van Boek I van het Strafwetboek, *Parl.St.* Kamer 2022–2023, no. 55–3374/001. Note that a bill is also pending which would introduce a similar system in the current legislation, outside of the context of the new Criminal Code. See: Wetsvoorstel 7 januari 2021 betreffende de oplegging van een gevangenisstraf in combinatie met verplichte behandeling en tot invoering van de mogelijkheid van tijdelijke opvang in de psychiatrische afdeling van een gevangenis voor personen die niet volledig

the sentence and is linked to a substitute imprisonment in case the treatment is not undergone. The introduction of this new sentence raises important practical questions. Many perpetrators of offences suffer from mental or medical disorders, which makes the group of people this sentence could be applicable to substantial. Belgium has failed to provide sufficient spaces in specialised institutions for people subject to internment for the last several decades and the prison administration lacks means for even basic psychological care in regular prisons.[703] Without massive and continued investments in new infrastructure and staff, this new sentence will look good on paper but will remain just that, some words on a piece of paper. The change to a sentencing system with eight levels would alleviate some of the proportionality issues discussed throughout this Part, without, however, fully solving most of them. The terrorism offences stay virtually the same under the new Code, as they were only recently introduced and '*although many questions regarding these criminalisations are still pending, the drafters of the bill believe that these issues, given their challenges and their topicality, deserve a separate and specific debate that cannot be conducted in the context of this reform.*'[704] The new Code includes two new (variations on existing) offences, which will be briefly discussed in Chapter X of this Part (see nos 283–285) and changes the sentences for inciting terrorism and financing a terrorist, which will be discussed under those offence. This book is based on the Codes currently in force. It is not clear yet if and when the new Codes will enter into force. The new Criminal Code has been published and should enter into force in April 2026, but the new Code of Criminal Procedure has proven more difficult and politically sensitive and did not make it through parliament before its dissolution for the elections. The new Criminal Code provides for a transition period of minimum two years, but this may become longer if other legislation, such as the Code of Criminal Procedure, is not finished by then as it will be very difficult to implement the new Criminal Code without an updated criminal procedure. Reference will be made to (possible) future changes in the legislation where this is of particular relevance for our purposes.

110. Practical application – At the end of each Chapter discussing an offence, we will refer to the facts of some case law under a practical application Section. These Sections do not aim to be exhaustive. There is an extensive body of case law in Belgium on the terrorist offences, much of which has not been published. Many of those cases are not ground-breaking. These Sections will

ontoerekeningsvatbaar zijn, maar wel een gevaar kunnen zijn voor de maatschappij, *Parl.St.* Kamer 2020–2021, no. 55–1723/001.

703 See e.g.: *L.B. v. Belgium* App no 22831/08 (ECtHR 2 October 2012); *Claes v. Belgium* App no 43418/09 (ECtHR 10 January 2013); *Dufoort v. Belgium* App no 43653/09 (ECtHR 10 January 2013); *Swennen v. Belgium* App no 53448/10 (ECtHR 10 January 2013).

704 Own translation, original in Dutch and French, see: Wetsontwerp 24 juli 2023 tot invoering van Boek II van het Strafwetboek, *Parl.St.* Kamer 2022–2023, no. 55–3518/001, 300.

provide some examples of the practical application of the terrorist offences and of possible difficulties.

111. Quantitative analysis – When relevant, reference will be made to a quantitative case law analysis, undertaken by us in the context of a Belspo-funded research project called 'Reguide'.[705] That analysis included the large majority of Correctional Court and Court of Appeal trial cases concerning terrorism offences from their introduction in 2003 until the end of 2018. Since there is no central database for case law, it is very likely that not all cases which fit these parameters were included. In total 192 cases were analysed. Since the Reguide project was specifically focused on so-called foreign terrorist fighters, a selection of cases was made based on where the facts took place. If the list of charges did not include facts outside of the EU, the case was disregarded. This way a total of 94 Correctional Court and 22 Court of Appeal cases were identified as relevant. In those cases, a total of 336 people were prosecuted for terrorist offences. In addition, there were seven people whose case was retried, bringing the total to 343 individual judgments. On the total of 343 individual first instance judgments, one was declared inadmissible (approximately 0,3%), 27 people were acquitted (approximately 7,9%) and 315 people were convicted. In total 22 Court of Appeal cases were relevant concerning a total of 55 individual judgments. Of the total of 55 individual Court of Appeal decisions 30 confirmed the first instance decision, 14 imposed a higher sentence and 11 a lower sentence. A second case law analysis was made by members of the 'Affect' project, an interdisciplinary research project on Belgian de-radicalisation policies.[706] They analysed 179 cases between 2006 and 2019 covering a total of 540 individual judgments.[707] The results of that analysis were similar: with 0,3% of cases being inadmissible and 10,5% leading to acquittals in first instance.[708] The results of the analyses regarding prosecutions for specific terrorist offences are incorporated in the rest of this Part. One general take-away point seems to be that in both the Reguide and the Affect analysis, once prosecution for a terrorirst offences was brought, roughly nine people out of ten were found guilty.

---

705 For more information, see: https://reguide.be/.

706 For yet another analysis, which ranges until June 2017 and will be referenced in footnotes throughout the text, see: Wittendorp and Bakker (n 686) 35–40.

707 Brion and others (n 77) 17.

708 Brion and others (n 77) 68. The analysis did show a lower percentage of Court of Appeal decisions confirming the decision in first instance.

CHAPTER I

RESTRICTIONS TO THE RIGHT TO LIBERTY

INTRODUCTION

112. Possible limitations to liberty – The terrorist offences discussed in Chapters II to X of this Part can lead to a sentence after conviction, which would usually be a prison sentence. The exact duration of these prison sentences is discussed in the Chapters covering the different offences, but it is clear that a term of imprisonment constitutes a deprivation of liberty. Alternative sentences are possible as well. These alternatives can also severely limit a person's right to liberty and are discussed in Subsection I of Section I of this Chapter. Another option for Belgian judges is to impose a sentence with postponement of its enforcement or to suspend sentencing all together. This means the perpetrator does not go to prison but his right to liberty can be limited through conditions they have to abide by. These options are discussed in Subsection II of Section I. In Section II, two possible options to extend the limitation of the right to liberty beyond a prison sentence are discussed. Those two options are being placed under the supervision of the Sentence Enforcement Court, which is an additional criminal penalty that is currently in force, and the security measure for the protection of society, which is a security measure proposed in the context of the new Criminal Code. Finally, deprivations of liberty are possible before a conviction as well. These rules on pre-trial detention are discussed below in Chapter XII of this Part (see nos 286–309).

SECTION I. PRINCIPAL SENTENCES

SUBSECTION I. ALTERNATIVE SENTENCES

113. Alternative sentences – When convicting a person, judges have other options next to a prison sentence. Three alternative sentences exist in Belgium: electronic monitoring, community service and the autonomous probation sentence. These are principal criminal sanctions in Belgian criminal law,[709] which can only be imposed with the consent of the convicted person.[710] While consent is required, we could ask ourselves to what extent the consent given is informed enough. An accused person has to consent to the alternative sentence before knowing its duration, meaning consent has to be given before they know exactly what they are consenting to. As we will discuss in the following paragraphs, the duration of alternative sentences can vary quite a bit and perhaps the accused would have preferred for example a prison sentence of which the enforcement is postponed (see no. 119) over the maximum electronic monitoring or community service sentences.

114. Frequency – While alternative sentences are possible, the Reguide case law analysis shows that these alternative sentences are rarely used in cases of terrorism. In that analysis, not a single alternative sentence was imposed. During the analysis, one case was discovered in which a person was convicted to community service for the offence of participating in the activities of a terrorist group.[711] Family of the defendant had travelled to Syria to join IS and he had sent money to Turkey for them, for which he was convicted to community service. This case fell outside the scope of the Reguide analysis, since none of the facts committed by him took place outside of Belgium.

115. Electronic monitoring – The most intrusive of the alternative sentences is electronic monitoring. This sentence entails the obligation to be present at a set address for a certain period of time (authorised movements are possible), which is enforced by means of electronic monitoring.[712] A few general conditions are imposed (e.g. not committing new offences) and extra conditions can be added in the interest of the victim.[713] Electronic monitoring as a principal sentence is possible when the judge feels the offence is of such a nature that it should not be punished with more than one year imprisonment and the judge imposes electronic monitoring for the same amount of time as they would have imposed imprisonment.[714] This means that the maximum term for electronic

709 Electronic monitoring can also be a sentencing modality. This case is, however, not discussed since the execution of sentences falls outside of the scope of this book (see no. 14).

710 Tom Daems and Yana Magis, 'Elektronisch toezicht en autonome probatie nader bekeken' in P Traest, A Verhage and G Vermeulen (eds), *Strafrecht en strafprocesrecht: doel of middel in een veranderde samenleving?* (Wolters Kluwer 2017) 183; De Nauw and Deruyck (n 39) 128; Tulkens and others (n 39) 599; Van den Wyngaert, Vandromme and Traest (n 34) 431.

711 Corr. Oost Vlaanderen (afd. Dendermonde) 14 december 2018, *onuitg.*

712 Art. 37*ter*, §1, section 2 CC. See also: Daems and Magis (n 710) 180; De Nauw and Deruyck (n 39) 127; Todts (n 104) 240; Van den Wyngaert, Vandromme and Traest (n 34) 430.

713 Art.37*ter*, §5, section 3 CC. See also: Daems and Magis (n 710) 184; De Nauw and Deruyck (n 39) 129; Todts (n 104) 240; Tulkens and others (n 39) 599; Van den Wyngaert, Vandromme and Traest (n 34) 431.

714 Art. 37*ter*, §1, section 1 CC. See also: Cass. 28 juni 2023, P.23.0206.F, *RDPC* 2024, 75; Daems and Magis (n 710) 181; Tom Decaigny, 'Relatieve zwaarte, toepassingsgebied en duur' in M De

monitoring is one year. There is a minimum as well: one month.[715] The judge also imposes a substitute imprisonment for the same duration as the electronic monitoring, which will be executed if the convicted person does not abide by the imposed rules.[716] There is a short list of offences for which electronic monitoring can never be imposed. It is mainly made up out of sexual offences, but also includes murder and manslaughter.[717, 718] It is clear electronic monitoring will usually amount to a deprivation of liberty. In situations where a lot of movements are authorised, it would be possible for electronic monitoring not to reach the threshold of a deprivation of liberty, but it would still amount to a serious restriction of it.

116. Community service – Community service entails working unpaid during leisure time for a public service, non-profit organisation or foundation with a social, scientific or cultural goal.[719] The tasks involved cannot be those that would normally be undertaken by a paid worker.[720] Community service can be imposed for facts which would be punished by a police sentence or a correctional sentence, but some offences are explicitly excluded from the application of community service.[721] This is the case for all felonies punishable with 20 years felony imprisonment or more before correctionalisation, for several sexual

---

Busscher and others (eds), *Strafrecht: duiding* (Larcier 2018) 50; De Nauw and Deruyck (n 39) 127; Tulkens and others (n 39) 598; Van den Wyngaert, Vandromme and Traest (n 34) 430.

715 Art. 37*ter*, §2, section 1 CC. See also: Daems and Magis (n 710) 181; Decaigny, 'Relatieve zwaarte, toepassingsgebied en duur' (n 714) 51; De Nauw and Deruyck (n 39) 128; Todts (n 104) 240; Tulkens and others (n 39) 598; Van den Wyngaert, Vandromme and Traest (n 34) 431.

716 Daems and Magis (n 710) 182; Tom Decaigny, 'Vervangende Gevangenisstraf' in M De Busscher and others (eds), *Strafrecht: duiding* (Larcier 2018) 50; De Nauw and Deruyck (n 39) 129; Tulkens and others (n 39) 598; Van den Wyngaert, Vandromme and Traest (n 34) 431.

717 This is somewhat strange since even after applying attenuating circumstances to these offences, the minimum sentences are three years imprisonment, meaning electronic monitoring would not be possible either way. See: De Nauw and Deruyck (n 39) 128. The inclusion of these offences on the list would become relevant when grounds for remission of penalty are applied, the reasonable term has not been respected, the perpetrator turned government informant, in case attempted offences and/or aiding and abetting.

718 Art. 37*ter*, §1, section 3 CC. See also: Daems and Magis (n 710) 182; De Nauw and Deruyck (n 39) 128; Tulkens and others (n 39) 598; Van den Wyngaert, Vandromme and Traest (n 34) 430–431.

719 Art. 37*sexies*, §1, Section 1 CC. See also: Alain De Nauw and Filiep Deruyck, *Overzicht van het Belgisch algemeen strafrecht* (die Keure 2015) 129; Tulkens and others (n 39) 594; Yves Van Den Berge, 'Het Belgische strafrecht: veel aandacht voor de vrijheidsbeneming en de vrijheidsbeperking' [2019] Nullum Crimen 1, 10; Chris Van den Wyngaert, Philip Traest and Steven Vandromme, *Strafrecht en strafprocesrecht in hoofdlijnen* (Maklu 2017) 428.

720 Art. 37*sexies*, §1, Section 2 CC. See also: De Nauw and Deruyck (n 719) 129; Van den Wyngaert, Traest and Vandromme (n 719) 428–429.

721 Art. 37*quinquies*, §1, Section 1 CC. See also: MA Beernaert, 'L'individualisation dans le prononcé et l'exécution de la peine : machine arrière toute ?', *La loi " pot-pourri II " : un recul de civilisation ?* (Anthemis 2016) 182; De Nauw and Deruyck (n 719) 129; Tulkens and others (n 39) 591–592; Van den Wyngaert, Traest and Vandromme (n 719) 429.

offences and murder and manslaughter.[722, 723] In addition to the community service, the judge also imposes an alternative prison sentence or fine within the sentencing range of the offence.[724] Community services range from 20 to 300 hours, with a sentence of 45 hours or less being a police sentence and anything above being a correctional sentence.[725] The judge imposes the community service and can provide instructions as to its concrete implementation.[726] However, it is the justice assistant, under the supervision of the probation commission who decides on the concrete implementation.[727] Community service only has a small impact on the right to liberty, as no limitations are imposed upon the perpetrator outside of the hours they are expected to work.

117. Autonomous probation sentence – The autonomous probation sentence consists of the obligation to follow certain conditions during a certain period of time which ranges from six months to two years.[728] 12 months or less is a police sentence, anything above is a correctional sentence.[729] The judge decides on the duration of the sentence and gives indications on the possible conditions, but it is the probation commission and justice assistants who decide on the concrete conditions.[730] During the execution of the sentence, the probation

---

722 Which seems redundant since those offences are punishable with more than 20 years felony imprisonment. However, the list also includes the attempted offences and aiding and abetting in those offences (see: Cass. 15 november 2006, *Pas.* 2006, 2341). Therefore, this addition will be relevant in cases where the sentence is lowered below 20 years, e.g. attempted manslaughter or aiding and abetting manslaughter.

723 Art. 37*quinquies*, §1, Section 2 CC. See also: Beernaert, 'L'individualisation dans le prononcé et l'exécution de la peine : machine arrière toute ?' (n 721) 183–185; Jeroen De Herdt, 'Bijzonder strafrecht en straftoemeting na de Potpourri II-Wet' [2016] Nullum Crimen 189, 197; Van den Wyngaert, Traest and Vandromme (n 719) 429.

724 Art. 37*quinquies*, §1, Section 1 CC. See also: De Nauw and Deruyck (n 719) 130; Tulkens and others (n 39) 593; Van den Wyngaert, Traest and Vandromme (n 719) 430–431.

725 Art. 37*quinquies*, §2 CC. See also: De Nauw and Deruyck (n 719) 130; Tulkens and others (n 39) 593; Van den Wyngaert, Traest and Vandromme (n 719) 429.

726 Art. 37*quinquies*, §4 CC. See also: Van Den Berge (n 719) 10; Van den Wyngaert, Traest and Vandromme (n 719) 430.

727 Art. 37*septies*, §3 CC. See also: Van den Wyngaert, Traest and Vandromme (n 719) 430–431.

728 Art. 37*octies*, §1, Section 2 CC. See also: COL 18/2016 – Invoering van de probatie als autonome straf, 23 juni 2016, 8 and 11; Collectieve brief DG EPI no. 138 29 april 2016 over de probatie als autonome straf, 1; Daems and Magis (n 710) 191–192; Tom Decaigny, 'Nieuwe correctionele hoofdstraffen: de straf onder elektronisch toezicht en de autonome probatiestraf' [2014] Tijdschrift voor Strafrecht 211, 217; De Nauw and Deruyck (n 719) 132; Tulkens and others (n 39) 595–597; Van den Wyngaert, Traest and Vandromme (n 719) 432–433.

729 Art. 37*octies*, §2 CC. See also: COL 18/2016 – Invoering van de probatie als autonome straf, 23 juni 2016, 11; Collectieve brief DG EPI no. 138 29 april 2016 over de probatie als autonome straf, 1; Decaigny, 'Nieuwe correctionele hoofdstraffen: de straf onder elektronisch toezicht en de autonome probatiestraf' (n 728) 217; De Nauw and Deruyck (n 719) 132; Michel Rozie, 'De probatie kan voortaan ook op eigen vleugels vliegen' [2014] Nullum Crimen 349, 350; Van den Wyngaert, Traest and Vandromme (n 719) 433.

730 Art. 37*octies*, §4 and 37*novies*, §3 CC. See also: COL 18/2016 – Invoering van de probatie als autonome straf, 23 juni 2016, 14; Collectieve brief DG EPI no. 138 29 april 2016 over de

commission can also change, specify or suspend (parts of) the concrete measures. It can even decide that the sentence has been fully executed before the period imposed by the judge has ended or extend the period with maximum one year if it was impossible to fulfil the conditions during the original period.[731] It is possible to appeal the decisions of the probation commission in front of the Courts of First Instance.[732] In addition to the autonomous probation sentence, the judge imposes a prison sentence or fine which must be within the sentencing bracket for the offence and which will apply if the conditions are not met.[733] An autonomous probation sentence is possible for all offences for which a police or correctional sentence is possible, barring a short list of excluded offences.[734] This list contains all felonies punishable with more than 20 years felony imprisonment which are correctionalised and also for example murder and manslaughter.[735, 736] Almost all of the terrorist felonies can be correctionalised, so an autonomous probation sentence would be possible, barring for the excluded offences such as terrorist manslaughter. The legislation does not list possible conditions, allowing the judge and probation commission a lot of freedom. Conditions which are often imposed are: undergoing therapy, the prohibition of drinking alcohol or using drugs, and the prohibition to contact the victim or visit certain places.[737]

probatie als autonome straf, 2; Daems and Magis (n 710) 194; Decaigny, 'Nieuwe correctionele hoofdstraffen: de straf onder elektronisch toezicht en de autonome probatiestraf' (n 728) 214; Rozie, 'De probatie kan voortaan ook op eigen vleugels vliegen' (n 729) 354–355; Tulkens and others (n 39) 595; Van den Wyngaert, Traest and Vandromme (n 719) 433–434.

731 Art. 37*decies*, §1 CC. See also: COL 18/2016 – Invoering van de probatie als autonome straf, 23 juni 2016, 18–19; Collectieve brief DG EPI no. 138 29 april 2016 over de probatie als autonome straf, 2; Daems and Magis (n 710) 194; Decaigny, 'Nieuwe correctionele hoofdstraffen: de straf onder elektronisch toezicht en de autonome probatiestraf' (n 728) 219; Rozie, 'De probatie kan voortaan ook op eigen vleugels vliegen' (n 729) 357–358; Tulkens and others (n 39) 597; Van den Wyngaert, Traest and Vandromme (n 719) 434.

732 Art. 37*decies*, §2 CC. See also: COL 18/2016 – Invoering van de probatie als autonome straf, 23 juni 2016, 19; Daems and Magis (n 710) 194; Decaigny, 'Nieuwe correctionele hoofdstraffen: de straf onder elektronisch toezicht en de autonome probatiestraf' (n 728) 214–215; Rozie, 'De probatie kan voortaan ook op eigen vleugels vliegen' (n 729) 357–358; Tulkens and others (n 39) 597; Van den Wyngaert, Traest and Vandromme (n 719) 434.

733 Art. 37*octies*, §1, Section 3 CC. See also: COL 18/2016 – Invoering van de probatie als autonome straf, 23 juni 2016, 13; Daems and Magis (n 710) 194; Decaigny, 'Nieuwe correctionele hoofdstraffen: de straf onder elektronisch toezicht en de autonome probatiestraf' (n 728) 217; De Nauw and Deruyck (n 719) 132; Rozie, 'De probatie kan voortaan ook op eigen vleugels vliegen' (n 729) 351 and 355–356; Tulkens and others (n 39) 596; Van den Wyngaert, Traest and Vandromme (n 719) 433.

734 COL 18/2016 – Invoering van de probatie als autonome straf, 23 juni 2016, 10; De Nauw and Deruyck (n 719) 131; Van den Wyngaert, Traest and Vandromme (n 719) 433.

735 See above, fn. 722.

736 Art. 37*octies*, §1, Section 4 CC. See also: COL 18/2016 – Invoering van de probatie als autonome straf, 23 juni 2016, 10; Beernaert, 'L'individualisation dans le prononcé et l'exécution de la peine : machine arrière toute ?' (n 721) 183–185; Daems and Magis (n 710) 192; Decaigny, 'Nieuwe correctionele hoofdstraffen: de straf onder elektronisch toezicht en de autonome probatiestraf' (n 728) 217; Rozie, 'De probatie kan voortaan ook op eigen vleugels vliegen' (n 729) 351–352.

737 See e.g.: www.vlaanderen.be/autonome-probatiestraf.

Although it is uncommon in practice, nothing within the Belgian legislation prevents conditions such as curfews and house arrest to be imposed.[738] Full day house arrests could be argued to violate the legality principle, as imposing them would effectively circumvent the conditions for an electronic monitoring sentence and therefore it cannot have been the legislature's intention to allow this. However, shorter curfews, for example, overnight, could be envisaged for which this argument does not apply.

SUBSECTION II. SUSPENSION OF SENTENCING AND POSTPONEMENT OF ENFORCEMENT

118. Suspension of sentencing – Two so-called modalities of sentences can also be relevant. First there is the suspension of sentencing. This means that the judge finds a defendant guilty of an offence but does not impose a sentence.[739] The imposition of a sentence is suspended and a term is set ranging from one to five years.[740] A normal suspension can be revoked if the person commits an offence during this period for which a criminal sentence or a correctional sentence of more than one month is imposed and they will then also receive a sentence for the originally suspended offence. A suspension subject to probation is also possible, which means that there are additional conditions to abide by.[741] Suspension of sentence is not possible if the defendant has already been convicted for an offence to six months imprisonment or more.[742] The new offence cannot be of such a nature that the judge would deem it necessary to impose a sentence of more than five years.[743] Suspension of sentence is only

738 Decaigny, 'Nieuwe correctionele hoofdstraffen: de straf onder elektronisch toezicht en de autonome probatiestraf' (n 728) 214; Peter Hoet, 'Werkbare probatie en herroeping' in P Traest and others (eds), *Amicus Curiae* (Intersentia 2013) 207, www.jurisquare.be/en/book/9789400004306/werkbare-probatie-en-herroeping/.

739 Art. 1, §1 Probatiewet. See also: De Nauw and Deruyck (n 719) 179; Van den Wyngaert, Traest and Vandromme (n 719) 525; Kristien Vanderheiden, 'Opschorting, uitstel en probatie' (2016) O155 Postal Memorialis – Lexicon strafrecht, strafvordering en bijzondere wetten 1, 8.

740 Art. 3, Section 4 Probatiewet. See also: De Nauw and Deruyck (n 719) 180; Van den Wyngaert, Traest and Vandromme (n 719) 533.

741 COL7/2013 – De wet 27 december 2012 houdende diverse bepalingen betreffende Justitie, inzonderheid: TITEL VIII Wijziging van de wet 29 juni 1964 betreffende de opschorting, het uitstel en de probatie, 13 maart 2013, 2; De Nauw and Deruyck (n 719) 185; Van den Wyngaert, Traest and Vandromme (n 719) 525; Vanderheiden (n 739) 8.

742 Art. 3, Section 1 Probatiewet. See also: Beernaert, 'L'individualisation dans le prononcé et l'exécution de la peine : machine arrière toute ?' (n 721) 185; De Nauw and Deruyck (n 719) 180; Tulkens and others (n 39) 660–661; Van den Wyngaert, Traest and Vandromme (n 719) 530; Vanderheiden (n 739) 9.

743 Art. 3, Section 1 Probatiewet. See also: Beernaert, 'L'individualisation dans le prononcé et l'exécution de la peine : machine arrière toute ?' (n 721) 185; De Nauw and Deruyck (n 719) 180; Tulkens and others (n 39) 661; Vanderheiden (n 739) 10. In 2016, the legislature wanted to amend this to '*if the fact is not punishable by a correctional prison sentence of more than twenty years, and it does not appear to be of such a nature that it should be punished by a*

possible if the defendant agrees.[744] All trial courts can impose a suspension of sentence, except for the Assize Courts.[745] It is also possible for the investigation supervision courts to impose it, if they feel like the public debates which come with a trial would impede the rehabilitation of the defendant.[746]

119. Postponement of sentence enforcement – A second possibility is the postponement of sentence enforcement. This means that the judge does impose a sentence but that (a part of) this sentence does not have to be enforced as long as the convicted person abides by certain conditions.[747] Again, a normal postponement of enforcement is possible or the postponement of enforcement can be subject to probation, meaning there are additional conditions.[748] In the latter case, the agreement of the defendant is required.[749] Postponement of enforcement is only possible if the defendant has not been convicted yet to a sentence of more than 12 months imprisonment for a single offence.[750] There is no such threshold for postponement subject to probation.[751] Postponement of sentence enforcement is possible for sentences of up to five

principal sentence of more than five years imprisonment' (Art. 36 wet 5 februari 2016 tot wijziging van het strafrecht en de strafvordering en houdende diverse bepalingen inzake justitie, *BS* 19 februari 2016, 13130). This was part of a fairly large criminal law reform called 'Potpourri II'. Part of this reform was the elevation of sentences after correctionalisation and this specific change to the rules on postponement of sentence enforcement was made in this context. However, the Constitutional Court annulled the elevation of sentences after correctionalisation and thus also annulled this change to the rules on postponement of sentence enforcement. See: GwH 21 december 2017, 148/2017.

744 Art. 3, Section 1 Probatiewet; Cass. 31 mei 1995, P.94.868.F; Cass. 12 november 1996, P.95.0950.N. See also: De Nauw and Deruyck (n 719) 180; Tulkens and others (n 39) 659; Van den Wyngaert, Traest and Vandromme (n 719) 530; Vanderheiden (n 739) 9.

745 Art. 3, Section 1 Probatiewet. See also: Beernaert, 'L'individualisation dans le prononcé et l'exécution de la peine : machine arrière toute ?' (n 721) 185; De Nauw and Deruyck (n 719) 180; Tulkens and others (n 39) 659; Van den Wyngaert, Traest and Vandromme (n 719) 525; Vanderheiden (n 739) 8.

746 Art. 3, Section 2 Probatiewet. See also: De Herdt (n 723) 195; De Nauw and Deruyck (n 719) 180; Tulkens and others (n 39) 660; Van den Wyngaert, Traest and Vandromme (n 719) 525; Vanderheiden (n 739) 8.

747 De Nauw and Deruyck (n 719) 182; Van den Wyngaert, Traest and Vandromme (n 719) 525; Vanderheiden (n 739) 14–15.

748 COL7/2013 – De wet 27 december 2012 houdende diverse bepalingen betreffende Justitie, inzonderheid: TITEL VIII Wijziging van de wet 29 juni 1964 betreffende de opschorting, het uitstel en de probatie, 13 maart 2013, 2; De Nauw and Deruyck (n 719) 185; Tulkens and others (n 39) 665; Van den Wyngaert, Traest and Vandromme (n 719) 525; Vanderheiden (n 739) 15–16.

749 De Nauw and Deruyck (n 719) 183.

750 Art. 8, §1, Section 2 Probatiewet. See also: Beernaert, 'L'individualisation dans le prononcé et l'exécution de la peine : machine arrière toute ?' (n 721) 190; De Herdt (n 723) 196; De Nauw and Deruyck (n 719) 183; Tulkens and others (n 39) 666; Van den Wyngaert, Traest and Vandromme (n 719) 527; Vanderheiden (n 739) 15.

751 Art. 8, §1, section 1 Probatiewet. This threshold used to be three years but was deleted in 2022. See: Art. 114 wet 21 maart 2022 houdende wijzigingen aan het Strafwetboek met betrekking tot het seksueel strafrecht, *BS* 30 maart 2022, 25785.

years imprisonment.[752] It is not possible for electronic monitoring, community service or an autonomous probation sentence.[753] The term for suspension of a sentence is one to three years for fines and prison sentences of up to six months and one to five years for prison sentences up to five years.[754] Postponement of the enforcement of sentences can be imposed by all trial courts, including the Assize Courts.[755]

120. Case law analysis – In the Reguide case law analysis, a suspension of sentencing was granted in four cases, all of which were prosecutions for the offence of Article 140, §1 CC. The Affect analysis showed slightly higher percentages of suspension of sentencing (4,4%).[756] Postponement of sentence enforcement was granted 83 times in the cases analysed during the Reguide project. This postponement was for the full sentence in 16 cases and partial for the other cases. Not a single postponement was granted *in absentia* (although this is theoretically possible in case of postponement which is not subject to probation since in that case the agreement of the defendant is not required).

121. Restrictions of liberty – Suspension of sentencing and postponement of sentence enforcement have in common that the perpetrator does not have to serve prison time, as long as they abide by certain conditions. In case of suspension or postponement subject tot probation measures, these conditions can have an influence on the right to liberty of the perpetrator. They can for example be forced to search for employment, attend therapy, abstain from contacting certain people or going to certain places and informing the authorities of any change of address. As was discussed for the autonomous probation sentence (see no. 117), the legislation does not provide a list of possible conditions so in theory anything goes. Overnight curfews would therefore probably be allowed, but house arrests presumably would not be. The potential conditions do not amount to deprivations of liberty but can restrict the right to liberty of the convicted person.

---

752 Art. 8, §1, Section 1 Probatiewet. See also: De Nauw and Deruyck (n 719) 183; Tulkens and others (n 39) 666; Van den Wyngaert, Traest and Vandromme (n 719) 528; Vanderheiden (n 739) 15.

753 Art. 8, §1, Section 3 Probatiewet. See also: COL 18/2016 – Invoering van de probatie als autonome straf, 23 juni 2016, 7–10; Beernaert, 'L'individualisation dans le prononcé et l'exécution de la peine : machine arrière toute ?' (n 721) 187; Daems and Magis (n 710) 185–186 and 193; De Herdt (n 723) 196; Van den Wyngaert, Traest and Vandromme (n 719) 529; Vanderheiden (n 739) 15. Specifically for electronic tagging, see: COL 17/2016 – Elektronisch toezicht als autonome straf, updated version 18 oktober 2018, 7.

754 Art. 8, §1, Section 6 and 7 Probatiewet. See also: De Nauw and Deruyck (n 719) 183; Van den Wyngaert, Traest and Vandromme (n 719) 533; Vanderheiden (n 739) 16.

755 De Nauw and Deruyck (n 719) 183; Tulkens and others (n 39) 665; Van den Wyngaert, Traest and Vandromme (n 719) 525; Vanderheiden (n 739) 15.

756 Brion and others (n 77) 68–69.

SECTION II. ADDITIONAL LIMITATION OF LIBERTY

SUBSECTION I. SUPERVISION BY THE SENTENCE ENFORCEMENT COURT

122. Accessory penalty with a direct effect on physical liberty – Being at the disposal of the Sentence Enforcement Court is an accessory penalty,[757] meaning it is always imposed in combination with a principal penalty such as (felony) imprisonment.[758] It was introduced into the legislation in 2007, replacing the already existing sentence of 'being at the disposal of the government'.[759] This penalty starts at the end of the principal penalty.[760] When a person who is at the disposal of the Sentence Enforcement Court is still in prison at the end of their prison term, they are not automatically released.[761] Instead before the end of their term, they appear before the Sentence Enforcement Court, which can decide to either keep them incarcerated or release them (conditionally).[762] The Sentence Enforcement Court keeps them incarcerated

---

757 Art. 34*bis* CC. See also: COL17/2014 – De terbeschikkingstelling van de strafuitvoeringsrechtbank, 17 juli 2014, 3; Yves Van Den Berge, 'De terbeschikkingstelling van de strafuitvoeringsrechtbank: alweer een nieuwe straf, alweer een nieuwe uitvoering' [2013] Tijdschrift voor Strafrecht 222, 222; Van Den Berge (n 719) 12; Van den Wyngaert, Traest and Vandromme (n 719) 415; Fanny Vansiliette, 'Mise à la disposition du gouvernement des condamnés' (2014) M 140 Postal Memorialis – Lexicon strafrecht, strafvordering en bijzondere wetten 1, 10. The Court of Cassation already held in 1978 that being at the disposal of the government was a sentence, see: Cass. 4 april 1978, *Arr.Cass.* 1978, 884.

758 For the procedure and practical execution of this penalty, see Ministeriële omzendbrief no. 1813 18 november 2011 betreffende de terbeschikkingstelling van de strafuitvoeringsrechtbank.

759 Wet 26 april 2007 betreffende de terbeschikkingstelling van de strafuitvoeringsrechtbank, *BS* 13 juli 2007, 38299; Ministeriële omzendbrief no. 1813 18 november 2011 betreffende de terbeschikkingstelling van de strafuitvoeringsrechtbank, 1; COL17/2014 – De terbeschikkingstelling van de strafuitvoeringsrechtbank, 17 juli 2014, 3. See also: MA Beernaert, *Manuel de droit pénitentiaire* (Anthemis 2019) 353; Veerle Scheirs, 'Van binnen naar buiten. de externe rechtspositie van veroordeelde gedetineerden' in Kristel Beyens and Sonja Snacken (eds), *Straffen: Een penologisch perspectief* (Maklu 2017) 690–691.

760 Art. 95/2, §1 WERP. See also: Ministeriële omzendbrief no. 1813 18 november 2011 betreffende de terbeschikkingstelling van de strafuitvoeringsrechtbank, 37; COL17/2014 – De terbeschikkingstelling van de strafuitvoeringsrechtbank, 17 juli 2014, 10; Beernaert, *Manuel de droit pénitentiaire* (n 759) 354; Van Den Berge (n 757) 222; Van den Wyngaert, Traest and Vandromme (n 719) 415; Vansiliette (n 757) 10.

761 Verslag namens de commissie voor de Justitie 13 maart 2007 bij Wetsontwerp betreffende de terbeschikkingstelling van de strafuitvoeringsrechtbank, *Parl.St.* Senaat 2006–2007, no. 3-2054/4, 10; Van Den Berge (n 719) 12–14; Vansiliette (n 757) 14.

762 Verslag namens de commissie voor de Justitie 13 maart 2007 bij Wetsontwerp betreffende de terbeschikkingstelling van de strafuitvoeringsrechtbank, *Parl.St.* Senaat 2006–2007, no. 3-2054/4, 10; COL17/2014 – De terbeschikkingstelling van de strafuitvoeringsrechtbank, 17 juli 2014, 11–12; Beernaert, *Manuel de droit pénitentiaire* (n 759) 355; Van Den Berge (n 757) 226–227; Van Den Berge (n 719) 13–14; Vansiliette (n 757) 14–18.

when there is a risk the person will commit serious criminal offences, which affect the physical or psychological integrity of third parties, that, in the case of supervised release, cannot be overcome by the imposition of special conditions.[763] In this scenario, the Sentence Enforcement Court has to review the case every year.[764] If the detainee had already been conditionally released at the end of their principal penalty, the period of being at the disposal of the Sentence Enforcement Court is added to their probationary period.[765]

123. Terrorism *sensu stricto* – The sentence of being placed at the disposal of the Sentence Enforcement Court can only be imposed upon conviction for certain offences. In 2007, the law made it an obligatory sentence for convictions of terrorism *sensu stricto* to criminal sentences if the offence had caused the death of a victim.[766] In those cases the judge had to put the defendant at the disposal of the Sentence Enforcement Court for a period of five to 15 years.[767] In 2016, this provision was amended so that it is obligatory for defendants convicted for terrorism *sensu stricto* for a prison sentence of at least five years if the offence caused the death of a victim.[768] The change made it an obligatory sentence for those offences of terrorism *sensu stricto* which were correctionalised but are punished with more than five years imprisonment.[769] The requirement of the death of a victim is clearly meant to limit the additional sentence to the most

---

763 Art. 95/2, §3 WERP. See also: Ministeriële omzendbrief no. 1813 18 november 2011 betreffende de terbeschikkingstelling van de strafuitvoeringsrechtbank, 8; COL17/2014 – De terbeschikkingstelling van de strafuitvoeringsrechtbank, 17 juli 2014, 13; Beernaert, *Manuel de droit pénitentiaire* (n 759) 355; Van Den Berge (n 757) 226; Van den Wyngaert, Traest and Vandromme (n 719) 416–417; Vansiliette (n 757) 15–16.

764 Art. 95/21 and 95/25 WERP. See also: COL17/2014 – De terbeschikkingstelling van de strafuitvoeringsrechtbank, 17 juli 2014, 27–28; Beernaert, *Manuel de droit pénitentiaire* (n 759) 362; Van Den Berge (n 757) 233–234; Vansiliette (n 757) 16.

765 Art. 95/2, §2, section 2 WERP. See also: Verslag namens de commissie voor de Justitie 13 maart 2007 bij Wetsontwerp betreffende de terbeschikkingstelling van de strafuitvoeringsrechtbank, *Parl.St.* Senaat 2006–2007, no. 3–2054/4, 10; Ministeriële omzendbrief no. 1813 18 november 2011 betreffende de terbeschikkingstelling van de strafuitvoeringsrechtbank, 29; COL17/2014 – De terbeschikkingstelling van de strafuitvoeringsrechtbank, 17 juli 2014, 13; Beernaert, *Manuel de droit pénitentiaire* (n 759) 355; Van Den Berge (n 757) 227; Van Den Berge (n 719) 13–14; Vansiliette (n 757) 18.

766 Art. 34*ter* CC, as introduced by the wet 26 april 2007 betreffende de terbeschikkingstelling van de strafuitvoeringsrechtbank, *BS* 13 juli 2007, 38299. See also: COL17/2014 – De terbeschikkingstelling van de strafuitvoeringsrechtbank, 17 juli 2014, 5; Van Den Berge (n 757) 223; Van den Wyngaert, Traest and Vandromme (n 719) 416; Vansiliette (n 757) 12.

767 COL17/2014 – De terbeschikkingstelling van de strafuitvoeringsrechtbank, 17 juli 2014, 4; Scheirs (n 759) 691; Van Den Berge (n 719) 13; Van den Wyngaert, Traest and Vandromme (n 719) 416.

768 Art. 11 wet 5 februari 2016 tot wijziging van het strafrecht en de strafvordering en houdende diverse bepalingen inzake justitie, *BS* 19 februari 2016, 13130. See also: Scheirs (n 759) 691; Van Den Berge (n 719) 13.

769 MvT wetsontwerp 23 oktober 2015 houdende wijzigingen van het strafrecht en de strafvordering en houdende diverse bepalingen inzake justitie, *Parl.St.* Kamer 2015–2016, no. 54–1418/001, (4) 8.

dangerous offenders. However, it is possible for several people to participate in a criminal offence and for only one of them to be responsible for the death of a victim, or perhaps the death was unintended and resulted from unforeseen circumstances. Because it is an obligatory sentence, everybody involved will be subject to it. This issue could be resolved by making it a facultative additional sentence instead of an obligatory one, possibly in combination with an expansion of the scope by dropping the requirement of the death of a victim. This because the reasoning above can be applied in the other direction as well: perhaps an offender of a terrorist offence *sensu stricto* is extremely dangerous and has tried their hardest to cause the death of a victim but failed in doing so because of circumstances outside of their control. By focusing on the outcome of the offence and not on the intentions of individual perpetrators, the legislation does not quite hit the mark. This could be resolved by making it a facultative sentence with (slightly) larger scope and thus putting more faith in the ability of the courts to impose appropriate sentences.

124. Possibilities for the future – Currently, for the other terrorism offences, being put at the disposal of the Sentence Enforcement Court is not an option. One of the recommendations of the parliamentary research committee on the terrorist attacks of 22 March 2016 was to expand this sentence to the Articles 140 and 141 CC.[770] Four bills in that sense are pending. The first one wants to introduce the option for the judge to put the defendant at the disposal of the Sentence Enforcement Court for all terrorist offences which are not covered by the mandatory version of this sentence, with the exception of Article 140*septies* CC.[771] The parliamentarians who introduced this bill stated: '*That perpetrators of terrorism crimes must be regarded as criminals who pose a significant and constant threat to our society is beyond dispute.*'[772] The second

770 Derde tussentijds verslag over het onderdeel 'veiligheidsarchitectuur' 15 juni 2017 van de parlementaire onderzoekscommissie belast met het onderzoek naar de omstandigheden die hebben geleid tot de terroristische aanslagen 22 maart 2016 in de luchthaven Brussel-Nationaal en in het metrostation Maalbeek te Brussel, met inbegrip van de evolutie en de aanpak van de strijd tegen het radicalisme en de terroristische dreiging, *Parl.St.* Kamer 2016–2017, no. 54–1752/008, 412. See also: Toelichting bij wetsvoorstel 21 november 2019 tot wijziging van het Strafwetboek met het oog op de uitbreiding van de lijst met misdrijven die in aanmerking komen voor de facultatieve terbeschikkingstelling van de strafuitvoeringsrechtbank tot alle terrorismemisdrijven, *Parl.St.* Kamer 2019–2020, no. 55–0777/001, 3.

771 Art. 2. wetsvoorstel 21 november 2019 tot wijziging van het Strafwetboek met het oog op de uitbreiding van de lijst met misdrijven die in aanmerking komen voor de facultatieve terbeschikkingstelling van de strafuitvoeringsrechtbank tot alle terrorismemisdrijven, *Parl. St.* Kamer 2019–2020, no. 55–0777/001, 6. Note that the title of the bill states it will expand the disposal of the Sentence Enforcement Court to 'all terrorist offences', but the bill does not include Art. 140*septies* CC.

772 Own translation, original in Dutch and French: '*Dat daders van terrorismemisdrijven moeten beschouwd worden als delinquenten die een belangrijke en voortdurende dreiging vormen voor onze samenleving staat buiten kijf; Les auteurs d'infractions terroristes*

bill goes one step further and wants to introduce a mandatory disposal of the Sentence Enforcement Court. It only wants to do this for convictions to prison sentences of at least five years based on Articles 137, 140 and 141 CC.[773] This means that for Article 137 CC the requirement of the death of the victim is dropped and Articles 140 and 141 are added. It is odd, though, that the title of and explanation to the bill mentions 'all terrorist offences', while the actual bill does not include Articles 140*bis* to 140*septies* CC. The third bill wants to expand the mandatory disposal of the Sentence Enforcement Court to all terrorist offences and also raise the maximum term from 15 to 30 years.[774, 775] The fourth bill is the most draconian and wants to make it a mandatory sentence for all terrorist offences and raise the maximum period to life.[776] However, in light of the new Criminal Code, being at the disposal of the Sentence Enforcement Court would be phased out. The sentence would only keep existing temporarily until enough capacity exists outside of the prisons to implement a new sentence called the extended follow-up.[777] This extended follow-up would be a possibility for sentences of level three or higher for offences which seriously infringed the life, physical, sexual or psychological integrity of the victim or posed a serious threat to public safety. It would be mandatory for recidivists of offences of levels seven or eight and people convicted for sentences of level four or higher for a list of offences, including fatal terrorist offences *sensu stricto*.[778] If they are still imprisoned at the end of their prison sentence or treatment under deprivation of liberty, conditions are imposed upon perpetrators subject to an extended

doivent incontestablement être considérés comme des délinquants représentant une menace sérieuse et constante pour notre société.' See: Toelichting bij wetsvoorstel 21 november 2019 tot wijziging van het Strafwetboek met het oog op de uitbreiding van de lijst met misdrijven die in aanmerking komen voor de facultatieve terbeschikkingstelling van de strafuitvoeringsrechtbank tot alle terrorismemisdrijven, *Parl.St.* Kamer 2019–2020, no. 55–0777/001, 4.

773 Art. 2 wetsvoorstel 28 januari 2020 tot wijziging van het Strafwetboek, teneinde de terbeschikkingstelling van de strafuitvoeringsrechtbank uit te breiden tot alle terroristische misdrijven, *Parl.St.* Kamer 2019–2020, no. 55–0969/001, 8.

774 Note that yet another bill is pending which proposes to raise the maximum term to 20 years. See: Art. 2 wetsvoorstel 6 augustus 2019 tot wijziging van de artikelen 34*ter* en 34*quater* van het Strafwetboek en van artikel 95/7 van de wet 17 mei 2006 betreffende de externe rechtspositie van de veroordeelden tot een vrijheidsstraf en de aan het slachtoffer toegekende rechten in het raam van de strafuitvoeringsmodaliteiten, wat de terbeschikkingstelling van de strafuitvoeringsrechtbank betreft, *Parl.St.* Kamer 2019, no. 55–0212/001.

775 Art. 2 and 3 Wetsvoorstel 19 november 2019 tot wijziging van het Strafwetboek betreffende de terbeschikkingstelling van de strafuitvoeringsrechtbank, *Parl.St.* Kamer 2019–2020, no. 55–0768/001, 7.

776 Art. 2 Wetsvoorstel 14 maart 2022 tot wijziging van het Strafwetboek wat de terbeschikkingstelling van de strafuitvoeringsrechtbank betreft, *Parl.St.* Kamer 2021–2022, no. 55–2571/001.

777 MvT wetsontwerp (I) 23 mei 2023 tot invoering van Boek I van het Strafwetboek, *Parl.St.* Kamer 2022–2023, no. 55–3374/001, 10.

778 Art. 46 wetsontwerp (I) 23 mei 2023 tot invoering van Boek I van het Strafwetboek, *Parl.St.* Kamer 2022–2023, no. 55–3374/001.

follow-up. If they do not abide by these conditions, they can be deprived of their liberty again. This deprivation of liberty has to take place in specialised institutions and not in prison. The duration of the extended follow-up can be up to 15 years, depending on the level of the sentence.

125. Case law analysis – In the Reguide case law analysis, the additional sentence of being at the disposal of the Sentence Enforcement Court was only imposed upon one individual, which is not very surprising given its currently limited scope of application.

SUBSECTION II. SECURITY MEASURE FOR THE PROTECTION OF SOCIETY

126. Security measure – In the context of the introduction of a new Criminal Code, the government wants to create a new security measure. In order to do so, a bill was introduced together with the bill for Book I of the new Criminal Code.[779] An important caveat is that while the bill has become law, it has not entered into force yet. This may happen, but it is not clear when exactly it might (see no. 109). Contrary to the supervision by the Sentence Enforcement Court, the new measure is said to be a security measure and not a sentence.[780] This means that it could be applied retroactively (see however, no. 129).

127. Scope of application – The new security measure would be applicable to people sentenced to prison sentences of at least five years in combination with being at the disposal of the Sentence Enforcement Court, who are suffering from a serious psychiatric condition at the time of the decision for which no treatment is available. This psychiatric condition must have the effect of establishing a continuing serious risk of committing a new felony or standard offence seriously threatening the physical or psychological integrity of any third party and which may result in felony imprisonment or imprisonment for five years or more, but which is not of such a nature as to override cognitive function or control over their actions. Presumably, this last condition is included to make sure the measure does not create any overlap with the measure of internment. When the judge thinks these conditions may be met, they have to order a psychiatric evaluation to confirm their suspicions before they can impose the measure.

---

779 Wetsontwerp (I) 23 mei 2023 tot invoering van Boek I van het Strafwetboek en Wetsontwerp (II) tot invoering van een beveiligingsmaatregel ter bescherming van de maatschappij, *Parl. St.* Kamer no. 55–3374/001 and 55–3375/001.

780 Wetsontwerp (I) 23 mei 2023 tot invoering van Boek I van het Strafwetboek en Wetsontwerp (II) tot invoering van een beveiligingsmaatregel ter bescherming van de maatschappij, *Parl. St.* Kamer no. 55–3374/001 and 55–3375/001.

128. Application of the measure – The measure takes effect after the period of being at the disposal of the Sentence Enforcement Court has ended. If the person is still in detention one year before the end of their being at the disposal of the Sentence Enforcement Court, another psychiatric evaluation is conducted in order to ascertain whether the conditions are still met and whether it is necessary to impose specialised supervision. The chamber for the protection of society then has to decide whether or not to execute the measure. Doing so means the person is not released but is placed in a specialised institution. An appeal to the Court of Appeal is possible. Appeal to the Court of Cassation is also possible. For the execution of the measure and the modalities of its implementation, the same rules apply as for people who are subject to internment. The measure is lifted if the person no longer suffers from the psychiatric condition.

129. ECtHR: Security measure or penalty – The Belgian government is explicit about the fact that this is a security measure and not a criminal sentence. However, the question remains whether or not the ECtHR would agree with this assessment. A ruling of the ECtHR that it is in fact a sentence and not a security measure would block any retroactive application of the measure. In this respect, the ECtHR case law on German 'preventive detention' provides us with some guidance. Under German law preventive detention is a security measure imposed by the sentencing court in addition to a prison sentence if the offender has been shown to be a danger to the public. It used to have a maximum of ten years, but in 1998 the legislation was changed to remove this maximum limit. The German government applied this extension retroactively as it argued it was a security measure and not a criminal sentence. However, the ECtHR held that this form of detention was in fact a penalty under the ECHR and the extension could not be applied retroactively. It based this finding on the fact that the detention was ordered by the sentencing court following conviction for a criminal offence, took place in (separate wings of) prison without substantial differences to a prison sentence, and no special measures or institutions were in place to reduce the danger of the perpetrator and thus limit the duration of the preventive detention.[781] The German legislature subsequently (in 2013) changed the preventive detention system, having it take place in separate buildings under much better conditions than in prison, providing for medical and therapeutic care and adding the condition that preventive detention could only be retrospectively extended if the person subject to it suffered from a mental disorder. The ECtHR held that even after the changes, the measure in general was still a criminal penalty, as '*It finds that the more preventive nature and purpose of the revised form of preventive detention do not suffice to eclipse the fact that the measure, which entails a deprivation of liberty without a maximum duration, was*

781 *M. v. Germany* App no 19359/04 (ECtHR 17 December 2009) 122–137; *Glien v. Germany* App no 7345/12 (ECtHR 28 November 2013) 119–131.

imposed following conviction for a criminal offence and it is still determined by courts belonging to the criminal justice system.'[782] However, in cases where it is extended because of the need to treat a mental disorder, the criminal element is eclipsed to such an extent that it is no longer a criminal penalty.[783] Applying this case law to the Belgian security measure for the protection of society, we could assume the ECtHR would also consider it to be a security measure and not a criminal penalty. It is only applicable to people suffering from a psychiatric condition and cannot be executed in prison but has to take place in a specialised facility. Assuming therapeutic and medical care is also provided in these specialised facilities, we can with some confidence state that it would be considered a security measure under the current ECtHR case law.

130. Proportionality – A second question is whether the measure is proportionate. The measure can only be lifted when the person no longer suffers from the psychiatric condition, but one of the conditions for its imposition is that the psychiatric condition is one for which no treatment is available. Therefore, it is easy to see how people can get stuck within this measure without any real prospect of release. Finally, a practical question has to be raised. At this point Belgium already lacks the capacity to provide adequate facilities for all the people who are interned, leaving a portion of them in regular prisons (see also no. 109). The question of where the people subject to this new security measure would be placed therefore rises, as the legislation explicitly forbids their placement in (the psychiatric wing of) a prison.

782 *Bergmann v. Germany* App no 23279/14 (ECtHR 7 January 2016) 181.

783 *Bergmann v. Germany* App no 23279/14 (ECtHR 7 January 2016) 149–183; *W.P. v. Germany* App no 55594/13 (ECtHR 6 October 2016) 75–80; *Ilnseher v. Germany* App nos 10211/12 and 27505/14 (ECtHR Grand Chamber 4 December 2018) 202–239.

CHAPTER II
ARTICLE 137 CC

SECTION I. *ACTUS REUS*

131. Terrorist attacks –The first terrorist offence in Title I*ter* is terrorism *sensu stricto*: the actual terrorist attacks. This offence was introduced in 2003, implementing the original Framework Decision adopted by the EU in 2002.[784] The Belgian legislature adhered closely to the wording of the European instrument when transposing it to Belgian law.

132. Two lists – The *actus reus* of terrorism *sensu stricto* in Belgium consists of two lists. Article 137, §2 CC contains the first one. It consists of criminal offences that are also punishable outside of the context of terrorism, for example murder or hostage taking.[785] Article 137, §3 CC contains the second list, which describes actions that do not conform to the definition of other criminal offences outside of a terrorism context, for example, hijacking a vehicle other than an aircraft or a ship (hijacking those is a pre-existing offence featured in §2), or threatening to commit terrorism *sensu stricto*.[786] Note that this does not mean

---

784 Art. 1 Council Framework Decision 2002/475/JHA of 13 June 2002 on combating terrorism [2002] *OJ* L164/5; Art. 3 wet 19 december 2003 betreffende terroristische misdrijven, *BS* 29 december 2003, 61689. See also: Beernaert, 'La Loi du 19 Décembre 2003 relative aux infractions terroristes : Quand le droit pénal Belge évolue sous la dictée de l'Union Européenne' (n 20) 586; Ketels (n 691) 236; Tom Vander Beken, *From Brussels with Love: Bespiegelingen over de Invloed van de Europese Unie Op Het Belgische Strafrecht* (VVSR Preadvies 2002) 31. For a short analysis of this offence in the Framework Decision, see: Cesoni (n 64) 143–145; Stéphanie Bosly and Mathieu Van Ravenstein, 'L'harmonisation des incriminations' in Daniel Flore (ed), *Actualités de droit pénal Européen* (La Charte 2003) 47–48; Daniel Flore, *Droit Pénal Européen: Les enjeux d'une justice pénale Européenne* (Larcier 2008) 140–143.

785 Beernaert, 'La Loi du 19 Décembre 2003 relative aux infractions terroristes : Quand le droit pénal Belge évolue sous la dictée de l'Union Européenne' (n 20) 587; De La Serna (n 50) 207; Flore (n 10) 214–215; Delmulle and Guenter (n 6) 4; Hameeuw (n 8) 5; Ketels (n 691) 237; Traest (n 50) 257; Isabelle Wattier, 'Des infractions terroristes dans le Code Penal' (2004) Janvier Journal du Juriste 6; Weyembergh and Kennes (n 58) 152; Weyembergh and Kennes (n 14) 108; Winants (n 8) 347.

786 Beernaert, 'La Loi du 19 Décembre 2003 relative aux infractions terroristes : Quand le droit pénal Belge évolue sous la dictée de l'Union Européenne' (n 20) 587; Delhaise (n 8) 30; De La Serna (n 8) 167 and 180; De La Serna (n 50) 207; Delmulle and Guenter (n 6) 4; Alain De Nauw, 'Titel Iter: Terroristische misdrijven', *Inleiding tot het bijzonder Strafrecht* (sixth edition, Kluwer 2010) 7; Alain De Nauw and Franklin Kuty, *Manuel de Droit Pénal Spécial*

none of those actions could be punished outside of the context of terrorism since they might be included in other, broader, offences. Carjacking, for example, would constitute aggravated theft or extortion, depending on the circumstances. However, 'carjacking' as such is not a specific offence. After its introduction in 2003, Article 137 CC was amended three times. All three of those amendments added items to the lists. In 2009 piracy was added to the list of §2 of potential terrorist offences.[787] In 2013 the legislature changed the reference to the arms legislation (which had been replaced in 2006)[788] and added a §2, 11°, which adds to the list attempts of the standard offences on that list.[789] This mattered because attempted standard offences are only punishable in Belgium when the law explicitly states this (contrary to attempted felonies, which are always punishable).[790] Because of this general rule, certain attempted terrorist standard offences were not punishable, whereas the Framework Decision contained an obligation to include them.[791] The statute of 5 May 2019, thirdly, added a new §2, 4°/1, which adds the unlawful disturbance of (data in) an IT-system[792] to the list of possible terrorist offences. The same statute also expanded §3, 3° to radiological weapons.[793]

(Wolters Kluwer 2014) 17; Filiep Deruyck and Alain De Nauw, *Inleiding tot het bijzonder strafrecht* (Kluwer 2020) 8; Hameeuw (n 8) 5–6; Flore (n 10) 216; Fransen and Kerkhofs (n 10) 19–20; Ketels (n 691) 237; Masset (n 20) T60/18; Traest (n 50) 257; Weyembergh and Kennes (n 58) 152; Weyembergh and Kennes (n 14) 108; Winants (n 8) 347.

787 Art. 7 wet 30 december 2009 betreffende de strijd tegen piraterij op zee, *BS* 14 januari 2010, 1485. See also: Ketels (n 691) 236.

788 The 'Wet van 8 juni 2006 houdende regeling van economische en individuele activiteiten met wapens, *BS* 9 juni 2006, 29840' replaced the 'Wet op de vervaardiging van, de handel in en het dragen van wapens en op de handel in munitie, gewijzigd bij de wetten van 30 januari en 5 augustus 1991, 9 maart 1995, 24 juni 1996, 18 juli 1997, 10 januari 1999 en 30 maart 2000'. See also: Caroline Van Deuren, 'Nieuwe straffen bij terroristische misdrijven' (2013) 2013 Rechtspraak Antwerpen Brussel Gent 508, 508.

789 Art. 2 wet 18 februari 2013 tot wijziging van boek II, titel Iter van het Strafwetboek, *BS* 4 maart 2013, 13233. Art. 3 of this statute amended Art. 138 CC to set the sentence for these attempted standard offences. See also: Delhaise (n 8) 81; Fransen and Kerkhofs (n 10) 19; Ketels (n 691) 236; Van Deuren (n 788) 508–509.

790 Art. 53 CC; Henri Berkmoes, 'De niet-strafbare poging' in M De Busscher and others (eds), *Strafrecht: duiding* (Larcier 2018) 88; De La Serna (n 8) 207; Delhaise (n 8) 81; De Nauw and Deruyck (n 39) 51 and 72–73; Tulkens and others (n 39) 418–419; Chris Van den Wyngaert and Steven Vandromme, *Strafrecht en strafprocesrecht in hoofdlijnen* (Maklu 2014) 356; Van den Wyngaert, Vandromme and Traest (n 34) 197 and 367–368; Van Deuren (n 788) 509; Vandromme and De Roy (n 34) 512.

791 Art. 4.2 Council Framework Decision 2002/475/JHA of 13 June 2002 on combating terrorism, [2002] *OJ* L164/5. Now Art. 14(3) Directive (EU) 2017/541 of the European Parliament and of the Council of 15 March 2017 on combating terrorism and replacing Council Framework Decision 2002/475/JHA and amending Council Decision 2005/671/JHA, [2017] *OJ* L88/6. See also: MvT wetsontwerp 13 november 2012 tot wijziging van Titel 1*ter* van het Strafwetboek, *Parl.St.* Kamer 2012–2013, no. 53–2502/001, (4) 10; Bosly and Van Ravenstein (n 784) 49–50; Ketels (n 691) 238–239; Weyembergh and Kennes (n 58) 156; Winants (n 8) 350.

792 Art. 550*ter*, §1 – 3 CC.

793 Art. 74 wet 5 mei 2019 houdende diverse bepalingen in strafzaken en inzake erediensten, en tot wijziging van de wet 28 mei 2002 betreffende de euthanasie en van het Sociaal

133. Endangering human lives – Almost all the listed acts require that human lives are put in danger. However, for offences of large-scale destruction or damage, causing significant economic damage is sufficient.[794] It is always difficult to draw the line between terrorism and other offences. Some academics have stated that offences which do not constitute violence against people or at least the threat thereof, should not be labelled terrorism.[795] The label of 'terrorist' can have far-reaching consequences, both within criminal law and criminal procedure[796] and outside of it.[797] However, the requirement that significant economic damage must be caused, seems to suffice to us. Significant economic damage can have a large effect on the stability of a nation and can indirectly endanger human lives. In this sense the wording of the Article could have been clearer if it reflected that idea. The Constitutional Court did not find the current wording in violation of the principle of legality (see no. 157), nonetheless in our opinion a better alternative to 'significant damage' would have been 'damage that could endanger the stability of the country and the security of its citizens'.

134. Sexual offences – Delhaise points out that many sexual offences are not on the list, despite the fact that these offences, especially when committed

---

Strafwetboek (1), *BS* 24 mei 2019, 50023; Stéphanie De Coensel, 'De Wet Diverse Bepalingen in Strafzaken II: Terroristische misdrijven in lijn met de Europese verplichtingen?' (2019) 40 Panopticon 211, 212; Winants (n 8) 357.

794 Art. 137, §2, 4° CC; Fransen and Kerkhofs (n 10) 19.

795 B Ganor, 'Defining Terrorism: Is One Man's Terrorist Another Man's Freedom Fighter?' [2002] Police Practice and Research 287, 294; Hamilton (n 86) 212–213; B Hoffman, *Inside Terrorism, Revised and Expanded Edition* (Columbia University Press 2006) 40–41; R Jackson, 'In Defence of "Terrorism": Finding a Way through a Forest of Misconceptions' [2011] Behavioral Sciences of Terrorism and Political Aggression 116, 123; J Lutz and B Lutz, *Global Terrorism* (Routledge 2013) 8–9; Richards (n 21) 230.

796 Aggravated sentences, but also procedural exceptions. For an overview and analysis of some of these procedural consequence, see: Blaise and Delhaise (n 49); Ana Laura Claes and Ward Yperman, 'Overzicht(Elijk) – Recente ontwikkelingen in de contraterrorismewetgeving' [2022] Politie & Recht 69; Masset (n 20) T60/20-T60/22; Jan Roelandt, 'De strijd tegen het terrorisme: een overzicht van de recente wetgevende ingrepen in het straf(proces)recht' [2017] Nullum Crimen 10; Ward Yperman, 'De bestrijding van terrorisme en strafprocesrecht: vele kleintjes maken een grote' [2019] Tijdschrift voor Strafrecht 8.

797 In other branches of law, by e.g. the revocation of passports (for an analysis, see: Louise Reyntjens and Ward Yperman, 'Terrorisme en internationale mobiliteit: een coherent beleid of nattevingerwerk' [2019] Politie & Recht 99.) or asset freezing as an administrative measure (KB 28 december 2006 inzake specifieke beperkende maatregelen tegen bepaalde personen en entiteiten met het oog op de strijd tegen de financiering van het terrorisme, bekrachtigd door Art. 15 wet 25 april 2007 houdende diverse bepalingen (IV), *BS* 8 mei 2007, 25103), but also outside of the law, e.g. through stigmatisation (Matthias De Backer, 'Waarom we de term "radicalisering" beter weggooien' (*De Morgen* 24 August 2018) 24; Hale-Ross (n 1) 14; Hodgson and Tadros (n 611) 986; W Mucha, 'Polarization, Stigmatization, Radicalization. Counterterrorism and Homeland Security in France and Germany' [2017] Journal for deradicalization 230; G Mythen, S Walklate and F Khan, '"Why Should We Have to Prove We're Alright?": Counter-Terrorism, Risk and Partial Securities' [2012] Sociology 383; S Samuel Justin and A Daniel, *The Psychology of Terrorism Fears* (Oxford University Press 2012) 14; Tadros, 'Justice and Terrorism' (n 46) 685.

in a systematic manner and on a large scale, are used as a weapon by some terrorist organisations.[798] The only sexual offences on the list of possible terrorist offences are included in Article 409 CC. Article 409, §1 CC criminalises female genital mutilation. §2–5 of that Article contain aggravating circumstances for this offence, for example the genital mutilation of underage women or genital mutilation without the intention to kill but which causes death. In terms of consistency, it is strange that this offence would be included but no other sexual offences are. As Delhaise argues, sexual violence can be used by terrorist organisations to spread fear. Therefore, the inclusion of other offences such as rape and violations of sexual integrity would be logical.[799]

135. CONTEXTUAL ELEMENT? – Article 137 CC also requires that the offence may, given its nature or context, seriously damage a country or an international organisation. Legal doctrine calls this the 'contextual element' of the offence.[800] This requirement was copied from the Framework Decision.[801] The damage does not need to have set in already, the possibility for damage is sufficient.[802] This 'contextual element' takes into account not just the nature of the offence but also its wider consequences for the organisation and government of a country.[803] However, viewing contextual information as a separate element to be distinguished from the *actus reus*, is unnecessary. Taking into account

798 Delhaise (n 8) 30. Note that this is mainly the case in quasi-war situations outside of Europe (e.g. in the Middle East or Africa). It seems that the definition is to an extent shaped by the type of terrorism that we have so far experienced in Europe. Large scale sexual violence could also amount to a crime against humanity.

799 Art. 417/11 and 417/7 CC.

800 De La Serna (n 8) 177; De La Serna (n 50) 204–205; Delhaise (n 8) 28–29; Delhaise and Fievet (n 45) 118; Flore (n 10) 213; Flore (n 784) 142; Fransen and Kerkhofs (n 10) 21; Traest (n 50) 257; Winants (n 8) 347. Ketels does not do so and discusses it as part of the *actus reus*, see: Ketels (n 691) 237–238. Hameeuw states that the wording of what others call the contextual element is so broad that it cannot constitute a part of an offence. However, she seems to be the only one in the literature taking this stance. See: Hameeuw (n 8) 6. When, briefly, discussing the offence, Moucheron mentions what is usually called the contextual element as part of the *mens rea*. However, he seems to be the only one to do so. See: Moucheron (n 687) para 20.

801 Art. 1.1 Council Framework Decision 2002/475/JHA of 13 June 2002 on combating terrorism, [2002] *OJ* L164/4. Now Art. 3(1) Directive (EU) 2017/541 of the European Parliament and of the Council of 15 March 2017 on combating terrorism and replacing Council Framework Decision 2002/475/JHA and amending Council Decision 2005/671/JHA, [2017] *OJ* L88/6. See also: Masset (n 20) 18. Borgers, however, argues that it is not clear at all that the Framework Decision actually requires this. See: Matthias Borgers, 'Een gevaarzettingsvereiste voor terroristische misdrijven?' in Toine Sapens, Marc Groenhuijsen and Tijs Kooijmans (eds), *Universalis: Liber amicorum Cyrille Fijnaut* (Intersentia 2011).

802 Delhaise (n 8) 33; Ann Fransen and Jan Kerkhofs, 'Het materieel terrorismestrafrecht in België: De Misdrijven' (2018) 3 Tijdschrift voor Strafrecht 150, 21; Hameeuw (n 8) 6; Ketels (n 691) 238; Traest (n 50) 257; Vanneste and Verbruggen (n 686) 81. The decision on whether or not this is the case is made sovereignly by the judge(s). See: Cass. 8 november 2023, P.23.1218.F.

803 Verslag namens de commissie voor de Justitie 7 november 2003 bij wetsontwerp van 6 oktober 2003 betreffende terroristische misdrijven, *Parl.St.* Kamer 2003, no. 51-0258/004, 14; P De Hert and J Millen, 'Terrorisme' (2013) VIII.2013 Qualifications et Jurisprudence Penales 1, 3;

contextual information (legally relevant facts) when defining an offence is something that happens regularly and terrorism is in this respect not so special in comparison to other criminal offences. Contextual information is also part of the *actus reus* of other offences or serves as an aggravating circumstance. For example, for the offences of larceny, the fact that it is committed by night[804] is an aggravating circumstance,[805] for the offence of raping a person of less than 14 years old,[806] the age of the victim used to be part of the *actus reus* of the offence[807]; and for bankruptcy offences,[808] the fact that the company is bankrupt is part of the *actus reus* as well. Legal facts such as these are part of the *actus reus* and there is no need to create a new and special 'contextual element'.[809] The Parliamentary preparatory works themselves call it an additional 'objective element'.[810]

SECTION II. *MENS REA*

136. Special intent – The required *mens rea* is a form of special intent.[811] The offence needs to be committed '*with the aim of seriously intimidating a population, or unduly compelling a government or international organisation to perform or abstain from performing any act, or seriously destabilising or destroying the fundamental political, constitutional, economic or social structures of a country or an international organisation.*'[812] This phrasing is also a copy-

De La Serna (n 50) 204–205; Delmulle and Guenter (n 6) 3; Fransen and Kerkhofs (n 802) 21; Ketels (n 691) 237.

804 Art. 471 CC.

805 Patrick Arnou, 'Nacht', *Strafrecht en strafvordering. Artikelsgewijze commentaar met overzicht van rechtspraak en rechtsleer* (Wolters Kluwer 2010) 71–73; De Nauw and Kuty (n 786) 707–708.

806 Previously Art. 375, section 6 CC. Now this would fall under Art. 417/16 CC.

807 Cass. 10 maart 1930, *Pas.* 1930, I, 156; De Nauw and Kuty (n 786) 229; Gaëlle Marlier, *Familie in het straf- en strafprocesrecht: afbrokkelende hoeksteen van de samenleving?* (Wolters Kluwer 2018) 299.

808 Art. 489–489*sexies* CC.

809 A difference is that the age of the victim and the time of the offence are relatively easy to establish after the fact, while this may not be the case for the context. However, this difference does not change the finding that the context is a legal fact which can be part of the *actus reus*. Note in addition that it is possible for offences which include contextual information to have a different *mens rea* requirement for the actions and for the contextual information.

810 MvT wetsontwerp 6 oktober 2003 betreffende terroristische misdrijven, *Parl.St.* Kamer 2003, no. 51-0258/001, (4) 10.

811 Beernaert, 'La Loi du 19 Décembre 2003 relative aux infractions terroristes : Quand le droit pénal Belge évolue sous la dictée de l'Union Européenne' (n 20) 586; De La Serna (n 8) 179; De La Serna (n 50) 207; Delhaise and Fievet (n 45) 118; De Hert and Millen (n 803) 3; Fransen and Kerkhofs (n 10) 20; Hameeuw (n 8) 5; Ketels (n 691) 238; Vanneste and Verbruggen (n 686) 81; Wattier (n 785); Weyembergh and Kennes (n 14) 109; Winants (n 8) 347.

812 Own translation, original in Dutch: '*met het oogmerk om een bevolking ernstige vrees aan te jagen of om de overheid of een internationale organisatie op onrechtmatige wijze te dwingen*

paste from the Framework Decision.[813] The three options are not cumulative and a political, religious or philosophical motive is not required.[814] It is also not required that the aim has been reached and a population has for example been intimidated. The perpetrator's aim is what matters.[815] This means that for example oral threats do not have to be spread publicly (yet). The words 'international organisation' only refer to international organisations under public international law and not to NGOs, for example.[816] Belgium does not necessarily have to be a member of this organisation though. Legal doctrine states that the word 'a population' can refer to a nation's whole population, but to the populations of smaller areas such as a specific region or city as well.[817] It does imply that the aim of intimidating a single person or small group of people does not suffice.[818] 'Government', finally, not only refers to the Belgian government, but to any government, regardless of its democratic character.[819] For the offence of threatening a terrorist attack, it is irrelevant whether or not the perpetrator was planning to actually execute the attack.[820] What matters is whether the victims would reasonably feel threatened.[821]

tot het verrichten of het zich onthouden van een handeling, of om de politieke, constitutionele, economische of sociale basisstructuren van een land of een internationale organisatie ernstig te ontwrichten of te vernietigen' (Art. 137, §1 CC). See also: Delhaise (n 8) 31–33; Masset (n 20) 18; Traest (n 50) 256; Weyembergh and Kennes (n 14) 109; Winants (n 8) 347.

813 Art. 1.1 Council Framework Decision 2002/475/JHA of 13 June 2002 on combating terrorism, [2002] *OJ* L164/4. Now Art. 3(2) Directive (EU) 2017/541 of the European Parliament and of the Council of 15 March 2017 on combating terrorism and replacing Council Framework Decision 2002/475/JHA and amending Council Decision 2005/671/JHA, [2017] *OJ* L88/6. See also: Flore (n 784) 140; Hameeuw (n 8) 5; Wauters (n 624) 177; Weyembergh and Kennes (n 58) 153.

814 Delhaise (n 8) 31; Flore (n 10) 211; Fransen and Kerkhofs (n 10) 20; Hameeuw (n 8) 6; Ketels (n 691) 238; Traest (n 50) 256.

815 Cass. 8 november 2023, P.23.1218.F.

816 Verslag namens de commissie voor de Justitie 7 november 2003 bij wetsontwerp van 6 oktober 2003 betreffende terroristische misdrijven, *Parl.St.* Kamer 2003, no. 51–0258/004, 14; Beernaert, 'La Loi du 19 Décembre 2003 relative aux infractions terroristes : Quand le droit pénal Belge évolue sous la dictée de l'Union Européenne' (n 20) 587; De La Serna (n 8) 178; De La Serna (n 50) 206; Flore (n 10) 212; Flore (n 784) 141; Fransen and Kerkhofs (n 10) 21; Ketels (n 691) 237; Masset (n 20) T60/18.

817 De La Serna (n 8) 178; De La Serna (n 50) 206; Delhaise (n 8) 32; Flore (n 10) 212; Flore (n 784) 141; Fransen and Kerkhofs (n 10) 20. Hameeuw wonders where to draw the line though. When is a group of people too small to be a population? See: Hameeuw (n 8) 6.

818 De La Serna (n 8) 178; Flore (n 10) 212; Flore (n 784) 140.

819 See the GICM case: Corr. Brussel 16 februari 2006, *onuitg;* Brussel 19 januari 2007, *T.Strafr.* 2008, 281, noot F. Schuermans. See as well: Ignacio De La Serna, 'Des infractions terroristes' in Marie-Aude Beernaert and others, *Les infractions. 5: Les infractions contre l'ordre public* (Larcier 2013) 198–199; Fransen and Kerkhofs (n 10) 39; Ketels (n 691) 237; Marchand (n 617) 281; Traest (n 50) 257. For an analysis of this issue applied to the EU level, see: Asp and Cameron (n 10) 262–265.

820 Corr. West-Vlaanderen (afd. Brugge) (vakantiekamer) 14 juli 2016, *TGR-TWVR* 2016, afl. 5, 386; Ketels (n 691) 238.

821 Corr. West-Vlaanderen (afd. Brugge) (vakantiekamer) 14 juli 2016, *TGR-TWVR* 2016, afl. 5, 386; Ketels (n 691) 238.

137. A RIGHT TO RESIST? – As the Belgian definition of terrorism also covers actions which aim to compel non-democratic, authoritarian governments, it seems to have excluded the possibility of a right to rebel against or resist such governments. For example, the preamble to the Universal Declaration of Human Rights states '*Whereas it is essential, if man is not to be compelled to have recourse, as a last resort, to rebellion against tyranny and oppression, that human rights should be protected by the rule of law.*'[822] It therefore recognises that if human rights are not protected by the rule of law, people may be compelled to have recourse to violence against the government. International law does not, however, recognise a right to rebel and the existence and origin of such a right has been much discussed and written about.[823] The ECHR protects peaceful protest through the rights to free speech and assembly but also allows deprivation of life resulting from the use of absolutely necessary force in order to quell a riot or insurrection. It would therefore seem it does not recognise a right to rebel in a violent manner. However, this should be placed within its proper context, being one of a state which respects the ECHR and in our hypothesis, this is not the case, as we are assuming people violently resisting undemocratic, tyrannical governments. Regardless of whether a legal right to rebel exists, it could be argued that a moral one does exist and that it would be preferable for Belgium not to criminalise people who commit violence aimed at overthrowing autocratic, tyrannical regimes. In our opinion, their inclusion in the definition of terrorism should not be seen as problematic, on the condition that the rest of the definition is drafted properly. First, introducing some kind of exclusion for actions undertaken against undemocratic, tyrannical regimes would lead to the question which regimes qualify as undemocratic and tyrannical. Not only would this be a very difficult decision to make from a legal point of view, requiring some sort of weighing of regimes against a variety of different criteria which would be very hard to define. The ultimate decision would also inevitably lead to difficult political situations and might greatly influence Belgium's relationship with other states. Second, the *actus reus* of terrorism includes actions such as murder, kidnapping, etc. and we would argue that even if the goal is just, the ends do not justify all the possible means. Certain actions, such as murdering innocent civilians, should never be allowed, even in rebellion against an unjust regime. This is the key difference between what could be called

---

822 Preambule Universal Declaration of Human Rights, UN General Assembly, Paris, 10 December 1948 (GA Resolution 217 A).

823 See e.g.: Olivier Corten, *La Rébellion et Le Droit International: Le Principe de Neutralité En* Tension (Académie de droit international de La Haye 2014); Christopher Finlay, *Terrorism and the Right to Resist: A Theory of Just Revolutionary War* (Cambridge University Press 2015). Tony Honoré, 'The Right to Rebel' (1988) 8 Oxford J. Legal Stud. 34; Aleksandar Marsavelski,' The Crime of Terrorism and the Right of Revolution in International Law' (2012–2013) 28 Conn. J. Int'l L. 243; Chiara Redaelli, 'The Right to Rebel against Violations of Human Rights: A New Role for the Responsibility to Protect?' [2016] Palestine Yearbook of International Law 8.

rebellion, or in our case terrorism; and civil disobedience, the latter being non-violent.[824] However, we have to take into account the fact that the *actus reus* of terrorism is much broader than murder and kidnapping and also includes, for example, large scale economic damage. As argued above (see no. 133) we feel a more precise description would be preferable, but even under the current description, the damage must be large in scale, which does introduce a form of *de minimis* threshold which would exclude small scale damage resulting from otherwise peaceful civil disobedience or protests. Furthermore, the definition of terrorism does state 'unduly compelling a government' which implies that some forms of compelling a government are not covered, as long as they are not 'unduly'. It could be argued that, as a last resort, causing economic damage in order to compel a tyrannical government to for example not arbitrarily imprison its citizens, is not a form of undue pressure but is justified. However, this type of reasoning is in turn thwarted by the inclusion of the alternative for the *mens rea* of '*seriously destabilising or destroying the fundamental political, constitutional, economic or social structures of a country.*' In this case, perhaps the 'contextual element' could provide a solution. It could be argued that actions aimed at seriously destabilising the fundamental political, constitutional, economic or social structures of an unjust regime cannot in fact seriously damage the country but are beneficial to the country in the long run, as they aim to overthrow an unjust regime. While this reasoning might not convince everybody, it could provide a solution in those rare cases where the courts could feel potential perpetrators of an act of terrorism who target for example the economic structures of a state in opposition to a tyrannical regime, do not merit a conviction for terrorism.

138. (Too) vague? – The *mens rea* of terrorism *sensu stricto* is quite broad and vague.[825] For example, the 'aim of seriously intimidating a population' suffices and no further goal is required. While acts of terrorism often instrumentalise fear and aim to achieve their end goals through intimidating the population,[826] intimidation is rarely the end goal in itself. Furthermore, terminology such as 'seriously intimidating', 'unduly compelling', 'seriously destabilising' has an inherent vagueness about it. The broadness and vagueness of the *mens rea* is especially relevant because all of the terrorism offences *sensu lato*, which are discussed below, have a 'two stage' *mens rea*: their *mens rea* refers to terrorism *sensu stricto* (sometimes in addition to other terrorism offences *sensu lato* as well). Therefore, any broadness or vagueness in the offence of terrorism *sensu stricto*, has an effect on the scope and delineation of all terrorist offences. Since

---

824 Sergio Fiedler, 'The Right to Rebel: Social Movements and Civil Disobedience' (2009) 1 Cosmopolitan Civil Societies Journal 42, 44; John Rawls, *A Theory of Justice* (Harvard University Press 1978).

825 See also: Jespers (n 15) 12; Vanneste and Verbruggen (n 686) 82–83.

826 See e.g.: Hoffman (n 795) 40–41; Jackson (n 795) 123; Richards (n 21) 230.

the *mens rea* is a literal copy of the European instruments, it is up to the EU level to evaluate whether such broadness and vagueness is desired.

SECTION III. SENTENCES

139. ARTICLE 138 CC – Article 138 CC lists the sentences for terrorism *sensu stricto*. For the offences listed in Article 137, §2 CC, which are punishable outside of a terrorist context as well, terrorism serves as an aggravating circumstance.[827] The maximum imprisonment sentence is aggravated and standard offences with a maximum sentence of five years imprisonment become felonies with a sentence of five to ten years felony imprisonment.[828] For the terrorist standard offences, the preparatory works explicitly state that if the offence was originally punishable with a fine (as principal sentence or on top of the custodial sentence), the fine remains.[829] The sentences for felonies go up one step on the scale of Article 80 CC.[830] For the terrorist offences listed in Article 137, §3 CC, Article 138 CC imposes maximum sentences ranging from five years imprisonment to life felony imprisonment.[831] At first glance, this seems like a simple system of determining sentences but a more thorough analysis exposes issues in the wording of Article 138 CC.

140. DISPROPORTIONATE SENTENCE FOR THREATENING – The terrorist offences in Article 137, §3 CC are all felonies, with one exception. This exception is threatening to commit a terrorist standard offence.[832] The sentence for

[827] Beernaert, 'La Loi du 19 Décembre 2003 relative aux infractions terroristes : Quand le droit pénal Belge évolue sous la dictée de l'Union Européenne' (n 20) 587; De La Serna (n 8) 179 and 204; De La Serna (n 50) 207; Delhaise (n 8) 75; Flore (n 10) 214; Hameeuw (n 8) 7; Fransen and Kerkhofs (n 10) 22; Masset (n 20) T60/19; Wattier (n 785); Weyembergh and Kennes (n 14) 109; Weyembergh and Kennes (n 58) 153; Winants (n 8) 347.

[828] MvT wetsontwerp 6 oktober 2003 betreffende terroristische misdrijven, *Parl.St.* Kamer 2003, no. 51-0258/001, (4) 11 - 12; Delhaise (n 8) 76; Hameeuw (n 8) 7.

[829] MvT wetsontwerp 6 oktober 2003 betreffende terroristische misdrijven, *Parl.St.* Kamer 2003, no. 51-0258/001, (4) 11. See also: Ketels (n 691) 240.

[830] Hameeuw (n 8) 7. Art. 80 CC consists of a scale of sentences which is used when applying attenuating circumstances. This scale is used in Belgian criminal procedure for several purposes besides the application of attenuating circumstances. The sentences for attempted felonies or accessories to felonies e.g. are also derived from the scale of Art. 80 CC.

[831] Art. 138, §2 CC. See also: Flore (n 10) 220; Weyembergh and Kennes (n 14) 109.

[832] Beernaert, 'La Loi du 19 Décembre 2003 relative aux infractions terroristes : Quand le droit pénal Belge évolue sous la dictée de l'Union Européenne' (n 20) 587; De La Serna (n 8) 205–206; Delhaise (n 8) 77–78; Masset (n 20) 19; Weyembergh and Kennes (n 58) 153; Winants (n 8) 347. The original draft bill stated 'credible threat' and the parliamentary documents stated that the threat had to be serious (MvT wetsontwerp 6 oktober 2003 betreffende terroristische misdrijven, *Parl.St.* Kamer 2003, no. 51-0258/001, (4) 11). However, the Council of State pointed out that the word 'credible' was not part of the Framework Decision and wondered why it was included here (Advies 34.362/4 van de Raad van State bij wetsontwerp van

threatening with a terrorist felony is five to ten years felony imprisonment, making the offence of threatening a felony as well. The sentence for threatening a terrorist standard offence, however, is three months to five years imprisonment, which makes the threatening a standard offence.[833] This would be the case, for example, when threatening to destroy a monument and if this would endanger human lives or cause significant economic damage; or threatening intentional battery. However, the maximum principal sentence when these offences are actually committed is three years imprisonment.[834] This means that for these standard offences (and for some the other terrorist standard offences *sensu stricto*), threatening the offence has a higher maximum sentence than the offence itself. This seems a rather absurd consequence of careless legislating. Since the maximum principal sentence for threatening a terrorist standard offence (*sensu stricto*) is the maximum principal sentence for any standard offence, the sentence for threatening is per definition at least as high and sometimes higher than that for the actual offence. It is striking that the current wording, with a distinction between threatening a terrorist standard offence and a terrorist felony, is already a refinement of the original bill. In the proposal, threatening only had one sentence, being five to ten years felony imprisonment, regardless of the threatened offence. Some senators pointed out that this led some terrorist offences to have a lower sentence when committed than when merely threatened.[835] This prompted the change of the proposal to its current wording. However, the issue has not been fully solved and further refinement is required. The EU Directive furthermore requires that if the offence of threatening is committed by a person who is the leader of a terrorist group (see no. 191), the maximum sentence shall not be less than eight years.[836] The Belgian Criminal Code does not differentiate based on the capacity of the offender, so if the threatened offence is a standard offence, the maximum sentence is five years imprisonment. At first glance this does not meet the requirement of the Directive. However, per definition there is concurrence (see no. 183) and it is very likely there will be a collective offence (see no. 225). In this case, only the harshest sentence must be applied, which is the one for leadership. As discussed below, this sentence is well over eight years.

---

6 oktober 2003 betreffende terroristische misdrijven, *Parl.St.* Kamer 2003, no. 51-0258/001, (22) 39). After this, the word was deleted.

833 Art. 138, §3, 1° CC.

834 Respectively Art. 138, 3° and 2° CC.

835 Verslag namens de commissie voor de Justitie 3 december 2003 bij het wetsontwerp betreffende terroristische misdrijven, *Parl.St.* Senaat 2003-04, no. 3-332/3, 19.

836 Art. 15(3) Directive (EU) 2017/541 of the European Parliament and of the Council of 15 March 2017 on combating terrorism and replacing Council Framework Decision 2002/475/JHA and amending Council Decision 2005/671/JHA, [2017] *OJ* L88/6. This was also part of the original Framework Decision. See: Art. 5.3 Council Framework Decision 2002/475/JHA of 13 June 2002 on combating terrorism, [2002] *OJ* L164/5.

141. Attempted threatening – The fact that threatening to commit some offences is a felony and some others a standard offence, also influences the punishability of the attempt (see no. 132). Depending on the offence threatened, attempted threatening is punishable or not. Delhaise argues that for this offence, an attempt is simply not possible.[837] Once the execution of the offence has started, according to Delhaise, the offence has taken place. She reasons that it is hard to imagine attempting to threaten. Furthermore, through the terrorist offences, the legislature wanted to intervene as early as possible. Therefore, it would make no sense to have this attempt not punishable, and the offence must have taken place once the execution has started. While it is true the legislature has shown its willingness to intervene early, we believe expanding the offence in such a way that a start of execution equals the committed offence, would be in violation of the legality principle.

142. Imprisonment – An analysis of the aggravation of the sentences for the terrorist offences listed in Article 137, §2 CC raises several issues as well. First, the aggravation of the maximum imprisonment sentences is worded in an unclear way. The Code states that the sentences are substituted as follows:

1° a fine, by an imprisonment of one to three years;
2° imprisonment of no more than six months, by imprisonment of no more than three years;
3° imprisonment of no more than one year, by imprisonment of no more than three years;
4° imprisonment of no more than three years, by imprisonment of no more than five years;
5° imprisonment of no more than five years, by felony imprisonment of five to ten years; [...][838]

143. Unclear wording 'no more than' – A maximum imprisonment of six months, for example, can be substituted by a maximum imprisonment of three years. A literal reading of the Code, however, also shows that a maximum imprisonment of six months could be substituted by a maximum imprisonment of five years or even by felony imprisonment of five to ten years. A sentence of

837 Delhaise (n 8) 82.

838 Own translation, original in Dutch:
'*1° geldboete, door gevangenisstraf van een jaar tot drie jaar;*
2° gevangenisstraf van niet meer dan zes maanden, door gevangenisstraf van niet meer dan drie jaar;
3° gevangenisstraf van niet meer dan een jaar, door gevangenisstraf van niet meer dan drie jaar;
4° gevangenisstraf van niet meer dan drie jaar, door gevangenisstraf van niet meer dan vijf jaar;
5° gevangenisstraf van niet meer dan vijf jaar, door opsluiting van vijf jaar tot tien jaar;' (Art. 138, §1, 1°–5° CC).

six months is '*no more than six months*' but is also '*no more than three years*' or '*no more than five years*.' This was probably not the intention of the legislature. Whenever an uncertainty about the meaning of a statute arises, the judge can interpret the statute.[839] If we interpret this part of the statute according to the likely intention of the legislature,[840] we have to read '*imprisonment of no more than*' as '*a maximum imprisonment of*.' If we do so, the problem does not arise, since '*a maximum imprisonment of six months*' is not '*a maximum imprisonment of one year*', etc. The wording of 1° also leaves much to be desired, since it does not actually specify that the fine needs to be the principal sentence (as is the case for, for example, damaging, destroying, or impairing or preventing the functioning of any part of a public communications network, which endangers human lives or causes substantial economic damage[841]). However, it does not seem possible to apply the Article to fines which are accessory penalties. Doing so would lead to maximum imprisonment sentences of more than five years[842] or would force the judge to impose a combination of imprisonment and felony imprisonment. Finally, it is not entirely clear why the legislature distinguishes between 1°, 2° and 3°. All three lead to the same sentencing bracket.

144. CATEGORIES OF IMPRISONMENT NOT PRESENT IN ARTICLE 138, §1 CC – Second, a close analysis of the list of offences of Article 137, §2 CC shows that, for example, the offence of intentional battery which leads to illness or the incapacity to work, has a maximum sentence of two years imprisonment.[843] Two years is not on the list of Article 138, §1 CC. The categories go from one to three years. Unfortunately, this is not the only example of a standard offence on the list with a maximum sentence of two or four years imprisonment (for sentences of four years the same problem arises, since the categories go from three to five years).[844] Judges could apply a very strict interpretation, where for offences with maximum sentences of two or four years imprisonment, terrorism cannot lead

---

839 Cass. 22 december 1994, *Arr.Cass.* 1994, 1149; Claes (n 601) 28; Van den Wyngaert and Vandromme (n 790) 83.

840 Claes (n 601) 32–33; Van den Wyngaert and Vandromme (n 790) 85.

841 Art. 114, §4 wet 21 maart 1991 betreffende de hervorming van sommige economische overheidsbedrijven, *BS* 27 maart 1991, 6155.

842 Five years imprisonment was the traditional maximum sentence for standard offences. The widespread application of correctionalisation to felonies of ever-increasing seriousness, has led to the introduction of sentences of imprisonment which exceed five years. However, this is only the case after correctionalisation by the courts. The legislature has never introduced standard offences with sentences of more than five years. One can assume it did not have the intention to start at this point.

843 Art. 399, section 1 CC.

844 The following offences also have a maximum sentence of two years imprisonment: Art. 405*bis* 2° and 434 CC, Art. 5 and 7 wet 28 mei 1956 betreffende ontplofbare en voor de deflagratie vatbare stoffen en mengsels en de daarmee geladen tuigen, *BS* 9 juni 1956, 3990 and Art. 14 wet 5 juni 1928 houdende herziening van het Tucht- en Strafwetboek voor de koopvaardij en de zeevisserij. The following offences have a maximum sentence of four years imprisonment: Art. 405*bis* 3° and 513, *in fine* CC.

to an aggravation of the sentence. This would lead to absurd situations where, for example, the maximum sentence for terrorist battery which leads to illness or the incapacity to work would be lower than that for terrorist battery without illness or the incapacity to work. That result is obviously not to be desired. Another interpretation is called for, namely applying the aggravated sentence for offences punishable with '*imprisonment of no more than three years*' and '*imprisonment of no more than five years*' to offences with a maximum sentence of respectively two- and four-years imprisonment. This could be construed as a forbidden analogous interpretation *in malam partem*,[845] but it is not. When read literally, two years is '*no more than three years*', so an offence with a maximum sentence of two years imprisonment does fall in this category. In addition, the legislature intended for terrorism to aggravate the sentences for these offences as well. Otherwise, it would not have included them in the list. Furthermore, the EU Framework Decision (and now Directive) require higher sentences than those which are applicable to the same offences without terrorist intent.[846] Therefore, the second interpretation is definitely justifiable. This interpretation, however, goes directly against the interpretation that solved the first issue (see no. 143). If two years falls within the category of '*no more than three years*', then one year or six months also fall within this category. At present, therefore, the courts have to apply a double interpretation. For offences punishable by a maximum sentence of imprisonment of six months, one year, three years or five years, the case-law should read Article 138 §1 CC as '*a maximum sentence of.*' However, for offences with a maximum term of imprisonment of two and four years, the Article must be read literally ('*no more than*' three and five years) and those offences therefore fall under 4° and 5° respectively.

145. Felony imprisonment – The categories of felony imprisonment also lead to issues of interpretation. The Code states:

> [...]
>
> 6° felony imprisonment of five to ten years, by felony imprisonment of ten to fifteen years;
> 7° felony imprisonment of ten to fifteen years, by felony imprisonment of fifteen to twenty years;
> 8° felony imprisonment of ten to twenty years, by felony imprisonment of fifteen to twenty years;

---

845 Claes (n 601) 29; Kuty (n 600) 250–253; Van den Wyngaert and Vandromme (n 790) 89.

846 Art. 5.2 Council Framework Decision 2002/475/JHA of 13 June 2002 on combating terrorism, [2002] *OJ* L164/4. Now Art. 15(2) Directive (EU) 2017/541 of the European Parliament and of the Council of 15 March 2017 on combating terrorism and replacing Council Framework Decision 2002/475/JHA and amending Council Decision 2005/671/JHA, [2017] *OJ* L88/6.

9° felony imprisonment of fifteen to twenty years by felony imprisonment of twenty to thirty years;
10° felony imprisonment of twenty to thirty years, by felony imprisonment for life.[847]

146. Categories of felony imprisonment not present in Article 138, §1 CC – As discussed above (see no. 134), Article 409, §1 CC criminalises female genital mutilation and imposes a sentence of three to five years imprisonment. The second paragraph contains an aggravating circumstance, prescribing a sentence of five to seven years felony imprisonment. The list of Article 137, §1 CC explicitly includes both §1 and §2. It is not clear within which category the §2 felony falls. Five to seven years felony imprisonment is not a category in Article 138 CC and the wording does not allow for the easy solution of putting it in another category, as is the case for the standard offences. When analysing the problem in more detail, we find that a similar issue arises for this offence (outside of a terrorist context) with regard to correctionalisation. The application of attenuating circumstances which goes hand in hand with correctionalisation, also influences the sentencing bracket and Article 80 CC provides for the same sentencing ranges as Article 138, §1, 6°, 7°, 9° and 10° do for terrorism. In the legal doctrine on correctionalisation, Rozie states that 17 to 20 years felony imprisonment[848] before correctionalisation should be treated in the same manner as 15 to 20 years felony imprisonment (and should thus become one to 15 years imprisonment after correctionalisation).[849] The paramount difference, however, is that correctionalisation leads to an attenuation of the sentence and is therefore in favour of the defence, while terrorism serves as an aggravating circumstance and works to the detriment of the defence. The parallel between these two situations is therefore not quite right. We cannot simply do away with the issue by stating that five to seven years felony imprisonment falls within the category of five to ten years felony imprisonment. Doing so would be a forbidden analogous interpretation *in malam partem*. Interestingly, when creating the categories in Article 138 CC, the legislature did give special thought to Article 30 of the '*wet 27 juni 1937 houdende herziening van de wet van 16 november 1919 betreffende de regeling de luchtvaart.*' §1, 2° of this Article is on the list of Article 137 CC[850] and provides for a sentence of ten to 20 years

---

847 Own translation, original in Dutch:
'*6° opsluiting van vijf jaar tot tien jaar, door opsluiting van tien jaar tot vijftien jaar;*
7° opsluiting van tien jaar tot vijftien jaar, door opsluiting van vijftien jaar tot twintig jaar;
8° opsluiting van tien jaar tot twintig jaar door opsluiting van vijftien jaar tot twintig jaar;
9° opsluiting van vijftien jaar tot twintig jaar, door opsluiting van twintig jaar tot dertig jaar;
10° opsluiting van twintig jaar tot dertig jaar, door levenslange opsluiting.' (Art. 138, §1, 6°–10° CC).

848 In the context of the application of the rules on recidivism in Art. 55*bis*, *in fine* CC.

849 J Rozie, 'De recidivewet van 5 mei 2019: de vergiftigde kers op de repressieve taart' (2019) 14 Nullum Crimen 291, 295.

850 Art. 137, §2, 5° CC.

felony imprisonment for the high jacking of a plane. Article 138, §1, 8° CC includes an aggravation of the sentence for offences punishable with ten to 20 years felony imprisonment, specifically for this one offence.[851] If we were to bring 'five to seven years' within the category of 'five to ten years', any offence with a sentence of ten to 15 or 15 to 20 years felony imprisonment, would fall within the category of ten to 20 years felony imprisonment as well. This does not seem to be the intention of the legislature. On the other hand, stating that for the offence of Article 409, §2 CC, terrorism does not aggravate the sentence, may be at odds with the EU Directive on combatting terrorism. The Directive states that national legislation should ensure that terrorism offences '*are punishable by custodial sentences heavier than those imposable under national law for such offences in the absence of [terrorist] intent [...], except where the sentences imposable are already the maximum possible sentences under national law.*'[852] Therefore, the only option for current practice which is definitely in line with the Directive is to impose a more severe sentence. However, to avoid the prohibition on analogous interpretation *in malam partem*, we have to choose the category which is most favourable for the suspect. The only acceptable solution is to not apply the aggravating circumstance of the age of the victim or the aim of profit. In that case, the sentence for genital mutilation is three to five years imprisonment,[853] which would fall under Article 138, §1, 5° CC and in a terrorism context the sentencing bracket would be five to ten years felony imprisonment. In this case, it is odd the legislature explicitly included Article 409, §2 in the list of Article 137 CC and did not limit itself to Article 409, §1 CC, since we do not actually apply the second paragraph. The same problem arises for other felonies with certain aggravating circumstances that are on the list of Article 137 CC as well. Arson of an inhabited house where people are present, for example, is punishable with 15 to 20 years felony imprisonment.[854] When those people present are injured however, the sentence goes up to 15 to 22 years felony imprisonment, which is not listed in Article 138, §1 CC.[855] Other aggravating circumstances raise the minimum sentence with two years felony imprisonment,[856] because of which the sentence bracket does not fit neatly within the brackets that are listed in Article 138, §1 CC either. The latter problem had been noted in the Senate, specifically for Article 405*bis*, 11° CC. This Article contains an aggravating circumstance that increases the sentence

---

851 MvT wetsontwerp 6 oktober 2003 betreffende terroristische misdrijven, *Parl.St.* Kamer 2003, no. 51-0258/001, (4) 12.

852 Art. 15(2) Directive (EU) 2017/541 of the European Parliament and of the Council of 15 March 2017 on combating terrorism and replacing Council Framework Decision 2002/475/JHA and amending Council Decision 2005/671/JHA, [2017] *OJ* L88/6.

853 Art. 409, §1 CC.

854 Art. 510 CC.

855 Art. 518 CC.

856 See: Art. 405*ter*, Art. 409, §5 and Art. 410 CC.

for deliberately administering substances to somebody without the intention of killing them, but which results in their death, to 17 to 20 years imprisonment. The Secretary stated that this sentence should be treated the same as a sentence of 15 to 20 years imprisonment.[857] This is the same solution we arrived at, and it is relatively easy to justify. Normally, the aggravation of the sentence caused by terrorism is applied after other aggravating circumstances. The list of Article 137, §2 CC contains offences with aggravating circumstances which, therefore, are necessarily applied before terrorism is. However, the judge is obliged to qualify the facts as the highest possible offence.[858] Since terrorism leads to a harsher sentence, this harsher aggravating circumstance could absorb the lighter aggravating circumstance. The same goes for Article 518 CC for example. The judge then treats the sentencing bracket of 15 to 22 years as one of 15 to 20 years and increases it to 20 to 30 years felony imprisonment based on Article 138, §1, 9° CC.

147. The need for clear legislation – Many of the aforementioned issues can probably be resolved by interpreting the legislation in a logical manner. However, the legislature has to think more thoroughly about legislation. Especially when aggravating circumstances are present, a piece of legislation should be as clear as possible. All categories of sentences should therefore be included in Article 138 CC and confusing phrases such as 'no more than' are to be avoided in all but the lowest category. Following these principles, recommendations on what Article 138, §1, CC could look are included in Part IV below (see nos 624 and 648). In the end, it is the prerogative of the legislature to decide on which wording is best suited. In addition, it would be better to either exclude offences with aggravating circumstances which do not fall within the sentencing brackets of Article 138 CC from the list of Article 137, §2 CC or to further expand Article 138 CC to also include these situations (see also no. 619).

148. Decreased proportionality of sentences – In its current phrasing, the terrorist nature of an offence neutralises the effect of some of the other aggravating circumstances and decreases proportional differences between some of the offences. Since both fines as a principal penalty and imprisonment of 'no more than' six months and 'no more than' one year are replaced by

---

[857] Verslag namens de commissie voor de Justitie 3 december 2003 bij het wetsontwerp betreffende terroristische misdrijven, *Parl.St.* Senaat 2003–04, no. 3–332/3, 19.

[858] This is called '*sa plus haute expression pénale*'. See: Raoul Declercq, *Beginselen van Strafrechtspleging* (6de herwerkte ed., Kluwer 2014) 926; H Van Bavel and F Vandendriessche, 'Gunningsfraude en de strafrechtelijke bescherming van de vrijheid van opbod' [2013] Tijdschrift voor Strafrecht 283, 292; Fililp Van Volsem, 'Kwalificatieperikelen: Hij die als dief wordt vervolgd, kan worden veroordeeld als heler en omgekeerd (noot onder Cass. 9 december 2008)' [2009] Rechtspraak Antwerpen Brussel Gent 28, 28; Verstraeten (n 653) 833.

imprisonment of 'no more than' three years, the proportionality in the three lowest sentencing brackets disappears. The maximum sentence for terrorist battery, for example, is three years imprisonment, regardless whether or not there was premeditation.[859] This is striking because, premeditation doubles the maximum sentence for battery outside of a terrorist context.[860] Similar situations arise for other aggravating circumstances, such as the fact that the victim of the battery was a minor or someone in a vulnerable situation.[861] Finally, a strange situation arises because Article 138, §1 CC does not provide for a minimum sentence for the offences originally punishable with imprisonment, while it does so for offences originally punishable with a fine as a principal penalty. In the latter case the sentence becomes one to three years imprisonment. For offences originally punishable with a sentence of 'no more than' six months imprisonment, however, the Code only states that the sentence becomes 'no more than' three years. Since no new minimum sentence is mentioned, the application of the 'aggravating circumstance' of terrorism does not change the old minimum sentence.[862] By definition this sentence will be less than six months. Therefore, after the application of the 'aggravating circumstance' of terrorism, the principal sentence for an offence originally punishable with only a fine as principal sentence becomes one to three years while the principal sentence for an offence originally punishable with, for example, eight days to six months imprisonment becomes eight days to three years imprisonment. In other words, the principal sentence of the lighter offence has become heavier than the one for the more serious offence.[863] In order to avoid this, the legislature should have either provided for a minimum imprisonment for all categories originally punishable by imprisonment (which is now not the case for 2°, 3° and 4°), or it should have fixed the minimum sentence in 1° on eight days or omitted it all together.

149. Alternative sentences and modalities – Electronic monitoring as a principal sentence is possible when the judge feels the offence is of such a nature that it should not be punished with more than one year imprisonment

---

859 Delhaise states that premeditation is inherent to terrorism *sensu stricto* and that it will therefore always be present (Delhaise (n 8) 31.). Although in many cases there will indeed be premeditation, this is in our opinion not necessarily so. Premeditation is not part of the *actus reus* or *mens rea* of terrorism and it is therefore possible that these elements are present without premeditation. See for premeditation: Patrick Arnou, 'Voorbedachten Rade', *Strafrecht en strafvordering. Artikelsgewijze commentaar met overzicht van rechtspraak en rechtsleer* (Wolters Kluwer 1990) 2.

860 Art. 398 CC. We could also ask ourselves whether premeditation is not given too much weight outside a terrorism context, but that question falls outside the scope of this PhD.

861 Art. 398 *j.* 405*bis*, 1° CC.

862 Delhaise (n 8) 76.

863 Note that it is possible for a judge to impose a sentence below the minimum sentence if they are of the opinion attenuating circumstances are present. See: Art. 85 CC.

(see no. 115).[864] Therefore, it is possible for terrorism offences *sensu stricto* which are not originally punishable with more than 20 years felony imprisonment.[865] After correctionalisation the minimum sentence for offences punishable with 15 to 20 years felony imprisonment is one year imprisonment, which makes electronic monitoring a possibility. The electronic monitoring has a term equal to the term of imprisonment the judge would impose (so maximum one year) and a minimum of one month. In addition to this limit, electronic monitoring is impossible for certain terrorist offences *sensu stricto* as their base offences are explicitly excluded. This is the case for murder, manslaughter and poisoning.[866] Similar rules apply to community services and autonomous probation sentences (see nos 116 and 117). Both of those alternative sentences are applicable to terrorist standard offences and correctionalisation allows their imposition on terrorist felonies. However, all offences originally punishable with 20 years felony imprisonment or more, are explicitly excluded, as are the same listed offences as is the case for electronic monitoring.[867] In situations where the judge feels like a sentence of more than five years is not opportune and the perpetrator has not been convicted to a sentence of more than six months imprisonment before, a suspension of sentencing, possibly subject to probation measures, is also possible for terrorism *sensu stricto* (see no. 118). Postponement of sentence enforcement is also a possibility for sentences for terrorism *sensu stricto* of maximum five years imprisonment (see no. 119). In order for this to be possible without probation measure attached, the perpetrator cannot have been previously convicted to more than 12 months imprisonment.

150. Summary – Terrorism is an aggravating circumstance, which judges are obliged to impose once the conditions are met. However, as discussed in the previous paragraphs, the wording of the legislation creates issues when attempting to apply it to all of the different offences which could constitute terrorism. This is a clear legal certainty issue, and the legislature should ensure that the sentencing scales of Article 138 CC are adapted to the sentencing scales of all potential terrorist offences. In addition, Article 138 CC does provide for a form of ordinal proportionality, but still creates several situations in which proportionality is not guaranteed.

---

864 Art. 37*ter*, §1, section 1 CC. See also: Daems and Magis (n 710) 181; Decaigny, 'Relatieve zwaarte, toepassingsgebied en duur' (n 714) 50; De Nauw and Deruyck (n 39) 127; Tulkens and others (n 39) 598; Van den Wyngaert, Vandromme and Traest (n 34) 430.

865 Note that this is an application of the basic rule on correctionalisation. Other rules might interfere in order to lower a sentence further and result in the possibility of a sentence of less than one year imprisonment for offences originally punishable with more than 20 years felony imprisonment. This is the case, e.g., when grounds for remission of penalty are applied or the reasonable term has not been respected.

866 Art. 37*ter*, §1, section 2, 3° CC.

867 Art. 37*quinquies*, §1, section 2 and 37*octies*, §1, section 2 CC.

SECTION IV. POLITICAL OFFENCE?

151. Two types of political offences – The political offence exception is a well-known clause in international extradition law.[868] This clause is standard in extradition treaties and allows states to refuse extradition for political offences. Belgian law has a separate internal notion of political offences which is unrelated to the concept of political offences in extradition law. These Belgian political offences are the focus of this Section. They came into existence in the context of the creation of Belgium in the first half of the 19th Century. When the Belgian Constitution was written, the legislature feared that the state might not treat perpetrators of political (or press) offences fairly as their offences had targeted the state itself.[869] In order to avoid this possibility, the category of political offences was created, which were subjected to a special regime. The most important difference, especially for our purposes, is that political offences have to be tried by the Assize Courts, as the constitutional legislature assumed a jury would treat these political offenders more fairly.[870]

152. Belgian political offences – The Belgian system distinguishes two types of political offences. First, the pure political offences. They can be designated as such by the legislature by either explicitly making the Assize Courts competent for a standard offence or prescribing the sentence of detention instead of felony imprisonment.[871] If this is not the case, the qualification depends on the courts. An offence can still be a pure political offence if the offence necessarily is a direct attack on the political institutions in their existence, organisation, or functioning or a direct attack on the political rights of citizens.[872] The second category is that of the mixed political offences. The Court of Cassation has defined them as offences which are not necessarily a direct attack on the political institutions, etc. because of the nature of the offence but

868 See e.g.: Antje C Petersen, 'Extradition and the Political Offense Exception in the Suppression of Terrorism' (1992) 67 Indiana Law Journal 767; Christine Van den Wyngaert, 'The Political Offence Exception to Extradition: Defining the Issues and Searching a Feasible Alternative' [1983] Revue Belge de Droit International 741.

869 Sofie Royer, Ruben Vilain and Ward Yperman, 'Grondwetswijziging voor terrorismeprocessen is niet radicaal genoeg' [2020] De Juristenkrant 10.

870 Art. 150 Belgian Constitution; De La Serna (n 50) 201; Delhaise (n 8) 20; De Nauw and Deruyck (n 39) 54; Jan Kerkhofs, 'Noot onder corr. Hasselt 27 juli 1999' [1999] Limb. Rechtsl. 264, 265; Masset (n 20) T60/23; Tulkens and others (n 39) 342–343; Van den Wyngaert and Vandromme (n 790) 192 en 197; Van den Wyngaert, Vandromme and Traest (n 34) 207.

871 De Nauw and Deruyck (n 39) 53; Franssen (n 667) 30; Tulkens and others (n 39) 347; Van den Wyngaert, Vandromme and Traest (n 34) 203.

872 Cass. 18 november 2003, *Arr.Cass.* 2003, afl. 11, 2125, concl. M. Timperman; Cass. 9 november 2004, *JT* 2004, afl. 6157, 856, noot; Concl E.H. bij Cass. 15 februari 2006, P.05.1594; De Nauw and Deruyck (n 39) 54; Franssen (n 667) 30; J Huysmans and others, 'Grondwet (Uitreksel)', *Strafrecht geannoteerd* (die Keure 2020) 259; Kerkhofs (n 870) 265–266; Moucheron (n 687) para 9; Tulkens and others (n 39) 347; Van den Wyngaert and Vandromme (n 790) 194; Van den Wyngaert, Vandromme and Traest (n 34) 204.

which are committed with the intention of causing such an impairment of the political institutions and which, given the special circumstances in which they are committed, have or can have such a direct impairment as a consequence.[873]

153. Terrorism as a political offence? – As part of the *mens rea* of terrorism *sensu stricto* is the goal to unduly compel the government or to seriously destabilise or destroy fundamental structures of the state; and the contextual part of the *actus reus* requires serious damage to the state (or an international organisation) to be a possibility, terrorism *sensu stricto* seems to be eligible for the qualification of political offence.[874] The Belgian legislature, however, has not designated terrorism a pure political offence,[875] so this qualification is dependent on the case law.[876] The Court of Cassation states that a political offence is an offence '*that both because of the intent of the perpetrator and its effects, is a direct attack on the political institutions.*'[877] Political offences require a possible direct impairment of the political institutions. The Court of Cassation therefore ruled that the terrorist offences are not of such a nature that they can be a political offence because '*the damage the perpetrator wants to do to the political institutions is realised indirectly, by endangering random lives or economic interests, even though those lives or interests have nothing to do with the organisations or institutions the perpetrator claims to want to target.*'[878] So,

873 Cass. 24 maart 1908, *Pas.* 1908, 142; Cass. 7 september 1935, *Pas.* 1935, 334; Cass. 21 oktober 1981, *Arr.Cass.* 1981–82, 271; Cass. 18 november 2003, *Arr.Cass.* 2003, afl. 11, 2125, concl. M. Timperman; Cass. 9 november 2004, *JT* 2004, afl. 6157, 856, noot; Concl E.H. bij Cass. 15 februari 2006, P.05.1594; De La Serna (n 8) 168; De Nauw and Deruyck (n 39) 54; Franssen (n 667) 30; Huysmans and others (n 872) 259–260; Kerkhofs (n 870) 266; Moucheron (n 687) para 9; Tulkens and others (n 39) 348; Van den Wyngaert and Vandromme (n 790) 194–195; Van den Wyngaert, Vandromme and Traest (n 34) 204–205.

874 This is also briefly discussed in the preparatory documents, but without any real conclusion. See: Verslag namens de commissie voor de Justitie 3 december 2003 bij het wetsontwerp betreffende terroristische misdrijven, *Parl.St.* Senaat 2003–04, no. 3-332/3, 7, 10, 12 en 20. Looking at the historical roots of the political offence, terrorism *sensu stricto* is the type of offence the constitutional assembly of 1830 had in mind when it created the category of political offences. For an analysis, see: Moucheron (n 687).

875 The custodial penalties the Criminal Code imposes are felony imprisonment and imprisonment, not detention and the Assize Court has not been explicitly given competence over the standard offences.

876 Delmulle and Guenter (n 6) 4.

877 Own translation, original in French: '*qui, dans l'intention de son auteur et par ses effets, porte directement atteinte aux institutions politiques*' (Cass. 5 mei 1913, *Pas.* 1913, I, 207). See also: Cass. 21 november 1927, *Pas.* 1928, I, 20; Cass. 3 april 1984, *Arr.Cass.* 1983–84, 1023; Tulkens and others (n 39) 345–346; Van den Wyngaert and Vandromme (n 790) 193–194; Van den Wyngaert, Vandromme and Traest (n 34) 204.

878 Own translation, original in Dutch: '*de schade die de dader aan de werking van de politieke instellingen wil toebrengen wordt onrechtstreeks gerealiseerd, door willekeurige mensenlevens of economische belangen in gevaar te brengen, ook al hebben die niets te maken met de organisaties of instellingen die de dader beweert te willen treffen.*' (Cass. 27 juni 2007, P.07.0333.F). See also: Antwerpen 7 februari 2008, *onuitg.*, 34–35; De Hert and Millen (n 803) 3; Delhaise (n 8) 20; De Nauw and Deruyck (n 39) 53; De Nauw and Kuty (n 786) 17; Deruyck

the required political damage is not the direct and immediate consequence of the offences but only the indirect and hypothetical consequence.[879] This means that according to the Court of Cassation, terrorism *sensu stricto* is not a political offence. This does not seem quite accurate. Terrorism *sensu stricto* is not a pure political offence because it does not necessarily entail a direct impairment of the political institutions. Seriously intimidating a population suffices as well. Furthermore, acts against international organisation are eligible to be called terrorism *sensu stricto* while it is not clear whether they would be 'political institutions'.[880] However, terrorist attacks can also cause direct political damage, for example, by targeting political leaders.[881] In this case, it would be a mixed political offence.

154. Competent Court – The case law is very strict when it comes to the qualification of political offence.[882] The reasons of the Court of Cassation not to qualify terrorism as a political offence probably, at least partly, have to do with the competent court. As explained above (see no. 151), political offences have to be tried in front of the Assize Court. There is a general tendency to try as little cases as possible in front of the Assize Court.[883] In addition, it has been argued that in cases of terrorism the jury could on the one hand be intimidated into giving lenient sentences[884] or on the other hand impose very severe sentences because terrorism is a sensitive issue.[885] The trial of Nemmouche and Bendrer,

---

and De Nauw (n 786) 8; Ketels (n 691) 239; Tulkens and others (n 39) 349; Van den Wyngaert, Vandromme and Traest (n 34) 207; Weyembergh and Kennes (n 14) 123–124.

879 Cass. 27 juni 2007, P.07.0333.F; De La Serna (n 8) 213–214; De La Serna (n 50) 201.

880 There is no definition or exhaustive list. The Court of Cassation has stated that this includes among other things the constitutional regime of the state, the parliaments, the authority and constitutional prerogatives of the King, the order of succession to the throne, the exercise of ministerial powers and the political rights of citizens (Cass. 18 november 2003, Arr.Cass. 2003, afl. 11, 2125, concl. M. Timperman. See also: Tulkens and others (n 39) 346–347.).

881 De La Serna (n 8) 214; Moucheron (n 687) paras 21–22.

882 De La Serna (n 8) 168; De La Serna (n 50) 200–201; Delmulle and Guenter (n 6) 4; Franssen (n 667) 30; Kerkhofs (n 870) 266; Moucheron (n 687) para 12; Van den Wyngaert and Vandromme (n 790) 195.

883 MvT wetsontwerp 23 oktober 2015 houdende wijzigingen van het strafrecht en de strafvordering en houdende diverse bepalingen inzake justitie, *Parl.St.* Kamer 2015–16, no. 54 1418/001, (4) 112 – 113; Franssen (n 666) 161; Joëlle Rozie, 'Hof van assisen en correctionalisering na Potpourri II: kunst- en vliegwerk of dankbare ingreep van de wetgever?' [2016] Nullum Crimen (NC) 91, 92–93; Lientje Van Den Steen, 'De Potpourri II-Wet en de veralgemeende correctionaliseerbaarheid: een prefabbouwwerk met onstabiele fundamenten' [2015–2016] Rechtskundig Weekblad 1604, 1606; Ruben Vilain and Ward Yperman, 'Grondwettelijk Hof 21 december 2017: it came in like a wrecking ball' [2018] Nullum Crimen 1, 2–4.

884 Roach, *The 9/11 Effect: Comparative Counter-Terrorism* (n 79) 248.

885 MvT wetsontwerp 23 oktober 2015 houdende wijzigingen van het strafrecht en de strafvordering en houdende diverse bepalingen inzake justitie, *Parl.St.* Kamer 2015–16, no. 54 1418/001, (4) 113; F.V.G., 'Geen speciale rechtbank voor terroristen' (*De Standaard* 8 July 2009) www.standaard.be/cnt/j32cecet?utm_source=standaard&utm_medium=social&utm_campaign=send-to-a-friend&Articlehash=

the perpetrators of the terrorist attack in the Jewish museum in Brussels, took place in front of the Assize Court. The trial, which was wrought with issues, exacerbated by the massive media attention, shows that in this context jury trials are no easy task.[886] In this context, some people were worried about the jury trial for the terrorist attacks in Zaventem and Maelbeek. The federal prosecutor had warned against this[887] and a proposal to bring terrorism under the competence of the Correctional Courts was tabled in parliament, but later dismissed.[888] It would have been somewhat ironic to circumvent the constitutionally compulsory jury trial for practical reasons, while our constitutional order is one of the things we are trying to protect against terrorism. In the early stages of the trial in Zaventem and Maelbeek significant hurdles had to be overcome. It was postponed for several months because the boxes in which the defendants had to sit were deemed in violation of the rights of the defence; there was a summary judgment forbidding the police from systematically searching the defendants

Ecz8yweVh9P3D84sMy1iFrWup5M%2FeEb5Dy0Mzy6%2Bxlne%2BcKPmimlz9o%2BHeY ZNTNktKxocb46KnOHODmcu8qCd%2BGY6xKkSGRBtimfGJF5Dl334u5XwiBjo4llX8l2 tIuOWIeCwv%2BDABDLcdoR%2FBxWbMc1WqbpPIVFcjCcOqAleC4tP18cwk8PSxwp45 TH07B9n1vUj1wLeUO5Kvnvaxp0LJbmZgAzawgyX97neYiGeT2cmHDUlQx7sj%2Bkw0d5 nDxX1XutE0tOua%2Bx7xpoL%2FOF7VCtayab36Scp95uxiPMo7HoRTT5GEIbzsgwcEhY Y2yDpNrqlnaTF9JsPzWofp6dpA%3D%3D; Lore Gyselaers, 'La participation des citoyens à la fonction de juger en matière pénale. Etude comparative du droit Anglais, de droit Belge et de droit Français' (PhD thesis, KU Leuven 2011) 162; D Leestmans, 'Terrorisme blijft in strafrechtelijke termen deels onvatbaar, interview met Paul Ponsaers' [27 mei 2020] Juristenkrant 8, 8–9.

886 H. Decré, 'Rondleiding door slachtoffer', 'half doof' of 'skivakantie': excuses om niet in jury proces-Nemmouche te moeten zitten' (*vrtNWS* 7 January 2019) www.vrt.be/vrtnws/nl/2019/01/07/ik-ben-rondgeleid-door-een-slachtoffer-ik-ben-half-doof-of/; T.D., 'Juryleden proces Nemmouche bezorgd over veiligheid na diefstal dossier' (*Bruzz* 31 January 2019) www.bruzz.be/justitie/juryleden-proces-nemmouche-bezorgd-over-veiligheid-na-diefstal-dossier-2019-01-331; A. Vanrenterghem, 'Burgerlijke partijen en parket over complottheorie Mehdi Nemmouche: "Rookgordijn zonder bewijs, respectloos"' (*vrtNWS* 4 March 2019) www.vrt.be/vrtnws/nl/2019/03/04/proces-aanslag-joods-museum-replieken/; A.W., K.G. and H.A., 'Jurylid gewraakt op proces tegen Medhi Nemmouche na bizar gesprek met collega' (*Het Laatste Nieuws* 18 February 2019) www.hln.be/nieuws/binnenland/jurylid-gewraakt-op-proces-tegen-mehdi-nemmouche-na-bizar-gesprek-met-collega~add55bd1/; X., 'Opnieuw jurylid gewraakt op proces-Nemmouche' (*de standaard* 16 January 2019) www.standaard.be/cnt/dmf20190116_04107264; X., 'Zevende jurylid proces Nemmouche gewraakt na gesprek met collega' (*De Morgen* 18 February 2019) www.demorgen.be/binnenland/zevende-jurylid-proces-nemmouche-gewraakt-na-gesprek-met-collega-bff72490/.

887 See e.g.: Sandra Cardoen, 'Federaal procureur vindt proces aanslagen te complex voor jury: "Je vraagt niet aan iemand op straat om te opereren"' (*vrtNWS* 9 February 2020) www.vrt.be/vrtnws/nl/2020/02/09/aanslagen-assisen-versus-Correctionele/; Douglas De Coninck, 'Assisenproces ligt opnieuw onder vuur' (*De Morgen* 11 February 2020) www.demorgen.be/nieuws/assisenproces-ligt-opnieuw-onder-vuur~b84189c7/.

888 Voorstel tot herziening van artikel 150 van de Grondwet van 27 mei 2020 teneinde de juryrechtspraak voor terroristische misdaden af te schaffen, *Parl.St.* Kamer 2019–2020, no. 55–1287/001 and 003. For a brief analysis, see: Royer, Vilain and Yperman (n 869).

while naked; and several jurors had to be excused.[889] However, after this somewhat rocky start, the rest of the trial went relatively smoothly and resulted in well motivated and proportionate sentences.

SECTION V. CONSTITUTIONAL COURT

155. General legality analysis always included – The introduction of several of the terrorist offences was followed by an appeal for nullification to the Constitutional Court. In this Section, the Constitutional Court case regarding terrorism *sensu stricto* is discussed, but before doing so, one constant throughout the different Constitutional Court cases can already be explained: the legality principle. In virtually all the cases on the terrorist offences, the legality of the offences was questioned (in addition to other grounds, such as, for example, the freedom of speech or the principle of non-discrimination). Before analysing the legality of the offences, the Belgian Constitutional Court always refers to both the Belgian Constitution and the ECHR. It also states that the legality principle requires criminal law to be created by a democratically elected assembly. Additionally, it reiterates that the wording of the law should allow everybody to know whether behaviour is punishable at the moment they adopt it.[890] In order to achieve this, the wording of the legislation should be sufficiently precise, clear and legally certain so that the person can assess what the criminal consequences of their actions would be and that the judge is not left with too much discretion.[891] It is on this last point, legal certainty, that the analysis in the individual cases focusses.[892] The general rules the Constitutional Court invokes are very similar to the general principles of the ECtHR's case law. Rozie argues that although the Constitutional Court is slightly more demanding in its legality analysis than the ECtHR and the Court of Cassation, it is still quite

889 Denny Baert, 'Salah Abdeslam en jurylid door ziekte afwezig op terreurproces, proces niet geschorst' (*vrtNWS* 12 December 2022) www.vrt.be/vrtnws/nl/2022/12/12/terreurproces/; Douglas De Coninck, 'Rechter terreurproces: "Ik beveel afbraak glazen kooien"' (*De Morgen* 16 September 2022) www.demorgen.be/nieuws/rechter-terreurproces-ik-beveel-afbraak-glazen-kooien~b16551ac/; Mark Eeckhaut, '"Mensonterende" kooien op het proces van de aanslagen' (*De Standaard* 12 September 2022) www.standaard.be/cnt/dmf20220911_97613232; Stefan Grommen, 'Proces over aanslagen ligt opnieuw stil: voorzitter vordert politietopman om duidelijkheid te krijgen over nieuwe naaktfouilles' (*vrtNWS* 4 January 2023) www.vrt.be/vrtnws/nl/2023/01/04/proces-aanslagen–22-maart-zitting–4-januari–2023/.

890 See also: Todts (n 104) 221.

891 Arbitragehof 13 juli 2005, 125/2005, B.6.2; GwH 28 januari 2015, 9/2015, *TVW* 2015, B.13; GwH 18 januari 2018, 8/2018, B.7; GwH 14 maart 2019, 44/2019, B.9.1. This is not unique to terrorism cases, see: De Nauw (n 610) 758–763; Theunis (n 608) 776–777. The Court of Cassation also reiterates this in its case law. See: Cass. 3 mei 2022, P.22.0021.N, 3.

892 See also: Spreutels and Velu (n 95) 131.

lenient.[893] Over half a decade earlier De Nauw had also acknowledged the fact that the Constitutional Court was more demanding than the Court of Cassation and the ECtHR, but he seemed to assume the Constitutional Court was rather strict.[894] In general it can be asserted that the Constitutional Court became more lenient since 2004. After 2004 the Court found relatively few violations.[895] Let us now look at the specific application by the Belgian Constitutional Court in the context of terrorism.

156. Arbitration Court 13 July 2005 – An appeal for nullification was filed against part of the statute of 19 December 2003. The appeal focussed on the introduction of Articles 137 and 138 CC and the expansion of Belgium's territorial jurisdiction.[896] This appeal, which was based on the legality principle and the prohibition of discrimination, led to the judgment of 13 July 2005. The appeal came as no surprise since the introduction of the offence was criticised by the doctrine, defence lawyers and NGOs.[897] Back then, the Constitutional Court was still called the Court of Arbitration.

157. Legality principle – The introduction of Article 137 CC was challenged on the basis of the principle of legality. The applicants considered that terrorism *sensu stricto* was defined too broad and inaccurately, in particular because the contextual element and parts of the *mens rea* were not sufficiently clear.[898] The Arbitration Court, referring to the case law of the ECtHR,[899] stated that the legality principle does not prohibit the judge from having a margin of appreciation. Laws have a general character and the situations to which they are applied are diverse and changeable.[900] The Court reiterated that the definition of terrorism *sensu stricto* was inspired by the European Framework Decision. It

---

893 Rozie, 'Beklaagde alwetend. Over het criterium van de redelijke voorzienbaarheid als maatstaf van het lex certa-principe in strafzaken' (n 611) 807–809.

894 De Nauw (n 610) 770–773.

895 For an analysis, see: Theunis (n 608) 777–782.

896 The introduction of Art. 140 and 141 CC was not challenged in front of the Arbitration Court.

897 Hameeuw (n 8) 6; Traest (n 50) 256–257; Weyembergh and Kennes (n 58) 156. Flore, on the other hand, was of the opinion the offence did not violate the legality principle. See: Flore (n 10) 213–214.

898 Arbitragehof 13 juli 2005, no. 125/2005, B.4. See also: De Hert and Millen (n 803) 3; Benoit Dejemeppe and Marie-Françoise Rigaux, 'Lutte contre le terrorisme moderne : le contrôle des droits fondamentaux entre le marteau et l'enclume' in R Leysen and others (eds), *Semper perseverans – Liber amicorum André Alen* (Intersentia 2020) 758; Spreutels and Velu (n 95) 132–133; Traest (n 50) 257; Wauters (n 624) 178; Weyembergh and Kennes (n 14) 127.

899 *Müller v. Switzerland* App no 10737/84 (ECtHR 24 May 1988) 29; *Kokkinakis v. Greece* App no 14307/88 (ECtHR 25 May 1993) 40; *S.W. v. United Kingdom* App no 20166/92 (ECtHR 22 November 1995) 36; *Cantoni v. France* App no 17862/91 (ECtHR 11 November 1996) 31 and 35.

900 Arbitragehof 13 juli 2005, 125/2005, B.6.2–B.6.3. See e.g. as wel: Arbitragehof 30 juni 2005, 116/2005 B.3.2–B.3.3 and GwH 14 maart 2019, 44/2019, B.19.1–B.19.2. This is also reiterated in the case law of the Court of Cassation, see: Cass. 3 mei 2022, P.22.0021.N, 3.

admitted that the wording of the *mens rea* could, in certain cases give rise to difficulties of interpretation.[901] However, words such as 'serious', 'unlawful', and 'destroy' together with the obligation of a strict interpretation of criminal offences mean that a certain seriousness is required and therefore the definition is sufficiently clear.[902] The applicants had also claimed some of the *actus reus* in §3 was not sufficiently clear, but the Court similarly reasoned that words such as 'large-scale' or 'significant' ensure that it is impossible for judges to qualify acts of which the consequences are insignificant as terrorism. Finally, the Court referred to Articles 139, section 2 and 141*ter* CC, which are meant to keep the balance between efficiency and fundamental rights, before ruling that although the legislation leaves a wide margin of appreciation for the judge, it does not grant them an autonomous competence and therefore there is no legality issue.[903] This is in line with the opinion of the Council of State, which emphasised the importance of a restrictive interpretation.[904]

158. Equality and non-discrimination – The applicants also argued that terrorism *sensu stricto* violated the principle of equality and non-discrimination. This argument was based on the difference in treatment between terrorism and other offences. The difference is apparent throughout a criminal trial, starting in the investigation phase, where more investigatory measures are possible for terrorism, throughout the trial phase, where anonymous witness testimony can be a full-fledged piece of evidence, until sentencing.[905] These differences are mainly to do with the aggravated sentences. Pre-trial detention, investigative measures, the impossibility of out-of-court settlement with the prosecution, etc. all have thresholds of sentences that have to be met. By raising the sentences in cases of terrorism, these requirements are met in cases where they would not be in general criminal law. The Court of Arbitration stated that, taking into account Belgium's international obligations, it is not up to the Court to decide whether it is opportune to increase the sentences.[906] Furthermore, enabling certain investigatory measures to be used, is justified by the need to effectively fight terrorism. Finally, the Court refers to the constant care the legislature took not

901 Arbitragehof 13 juli 2005, 125/2005, B.7.2. See also: Wauters (n 624) 179.

902 Arbitragehof 13 juli 2005, 125/2005, B.7.2; Delhaise (n 8) 34–35; De La Serna (n 8) 175–176; Fransen and Kerkhofs (n 10) 21; Traest (n 50) 257.

903 Arbitragehof 13 juli 2005, 125/2005; De La Serna (n 8) 175–176; Delmulle and Guenter (n 6) 5; Ketels (n 691) 236; Masset (n 20) 18; Silvis (n 27) 132–133; Theunis (n 608) 776; Wauters (n 624) 179; Weyembergh and Kennes (n 58) 157; Weyembergh and Kennes (n 14) 128–129; Winants (n 8) 347 en 349. Despite this ruling, Comité T argues that Art. 137 CC does in fact violate the legality prinipcle. See: Comité T, 'Rapport 2019: Le respect des droits humains dans le cadre de la lutte contre le terrorisme: Un chantier en cours', 15.

904 Advies 34.362/4 van de Raad van State bij wetsontwerp 6 oktober 2003 betreffende terroristische misdrijven, *Parl.St.* Kamer 2003, no. 51–0258/001, 30–31. See also: Flore (n 10) 214; Weyembergh and Kennes (n 58) 156; Weyembergh and Kennes (n 14) 126.

905 Arbitragehof 13 juli 2005, 125/2005, B.9. See also: Weyembergh and Kennes (n 14) 127–128.

906 Arbitragehof 13 juli 2005, 125/2005 B.11.1. See also: De La Serna (n 8) 176.

to detract from fundamental rights, as shown by Article 139, section 2 and 141*ter* CC and the fact that the legislature decided not to introduce a system of sentence reduction in return for information on co-perpetrators, which was suggested by the Framework Decision.[907] Note that since 2018, Belgian legislation does include such rules so this last point is dated (see also no. 605).[908] The introduction of extraterritorial jurisdiction for terrorism based on passive personality was also non-problematic.[909] In conclusion, the Court did not see any problem in terms of equal treatment and discrimination.[910]

159. Lower courts – In subsequent cases in front of the lower courts, the defence has tried to argue that the legality principle was violated. However, lower courts have explicitly referred to this judgment of the Arbitration Court to support their conclusion that Article 137 CC does not violate the legality principle.[911]

SECTION VI. PRACTICAL APPLICATION

160. Assize Court or Correctional Court – In the Reguide case law analysis, a total of 28 people were prosecuted for terrorism *sensu stricto*. However, none of the cases analysed was tried by the Assize Courts.[912] As explained, many of the terrorist offences *sensu stricto* are felonies, which nominally fall within the competence of the Assize Courts. The statute on attenuating circumstances lists the offences which can be correctionalised.[913] The first two items on the list are general categories: all offences punishable by 20 years felony imprisonment or less and attempted felonies which were punishable with lifelong felony imprisonment (in which case the attempt is punishable with 20 to 30 years felony imprisonment). The third until fourteenth (and last item) on the list are specific offences which are punishable with more than 20 years felony imprisonment but

---

907 Arbitragehof 13 juli 2005, 125/2005, B.11.2.

908 Art. 216/1–216/8 CCP; wet 22 juli 2018 tot wijziging van het Wetboek van strafvordering betreffende toezeggingen in het kader van de strafvordering, de strafuitvoering of de hechtenis wegens het afleggen van een verklaring in het kader van de strijd tegen de georganiseerde criminaliteit en het terrorisme, *BS* 7 augustus 2018, 62054.

909 Arbitragehof 13 juli 2005, 125/2005, B.11.3.

910 Spreutels and Velu (n 95) 148–149; Winants (n 8) 349.

911 Antwerpen 8 januari 2014, *onuitg.*, 26–28, annulled by Cass. 16 december 2014, P.14.1048.N for violating Art. 40 Taalwet Gerechtszaken; Gent 26 januari 2016, *onuitg.*, 31, annulled by Cass. 13 september 2016, *RW* 2017–18, 421 for violating the right to contradiction; Corr. Mechelen 5 december 2012, *onuitg.*, 37–40. See also: Fransen and Kerkhofs (n 10) 21–22; Winants (n 8) 347.

912 Note that if prosecuted today, a few would have to be, but as explained in the rest of the paragraph, at the moment of their trials, these cases could be tried by the Correctional Courts.

913 Art. 2 wet 4 oktober 1867 op de verzachtende omstandigheden, *BS* 15 oktober 1867, 5505.

can still be correctionalised. This list does not contain Article 137 CC. Terrorism *sensu stricto* can therefore only be correctionalised when it is punishable by 20 years felony imprisonment or less, or if the offence was attempted but not completed.[914] If it is possible to correctionalise an offence (terrorist or other), it will almost always be done. Because of this, some terrorist offences *sensu stricto* can be tried by the Correctional Courts (e.g. terrorist kidnapping and attempted murder) and some have to be tried by the Assize Courts (e.g. terrorist murder and arson). There are a few exceptions to this rule. In 2016, a reform of criminal law and criminal procedure was implemented, which made it possible to correctionalise all felonies.[915] On 21 December 2017, however, the Constitutional Court annulled this part of the reform, but it decided that this annulment did not have retroactive effect.[916] At first, there was some confusion about what this meant in practice. In a second judgment, the Constitutional Court explained that cases which were already tried by the Correctional Courts or Courts of Appeal did not have to be retried.[917] In addition, cases which had already been brought before a Correctional Court in a valid way, could still be tried by that Correctional Court (and potentially the Court of Appeal and Court of Cassation afterwards). Because of this, a few cases of terrorist murder, which now would have to be tried by the Assize Court, were tried by the Correctional Courts (and Courts of Appeal).

161. Facts in Belgium – On 25 June 2013, the Correctional Court convicted a man to 17 years imprisonment for attempted terrorist murder.[918] The man had attacked three police officers with a knife in a metro station. The perpetrator stated he had wanted to avenge the Muslim community after acts of aggression by the local police caused by riots in Molenbeek (Brussels). Furthermore, he had previously attempted to travel to Somalia to join a terrorist group and was in contact with a known terrorist. In the Sharia4Belgium case, several members were convicted for threatening terrorist manslaughter or battery because they threatened to attack politicians or the Atomium, an important tourist attraction.[919] On 14 July 2016, a man was convicted to four years imprisonment

---

914 Delhaise (n 8) 84.

915 Wet 5 februari 2016 tot wijziging van het strafrecht en de strafvordering en houdende diverse bepalingen inzake justitie, *BS* 19 februari 2016, 13130 (Potpourri II). Art. 121 of this statute deleted the list of felonies which could be Correctionalised.

916 GwH 21 december 2017, 148/2017. For an analysis of this judgment, see: Vilain and Yperman (n 883).

917 GwH 9 maart 2018, 28/2018, *NjW* 2018, 581. For an analysis of this judgment, see: Ruben Vilain and Ward Yperman, 'Veralgemeende correctionaliseerbaarheid: Rechts(on)zekerheid na het interpretatief arrest van het Grondwettelijk Hof (no. 2018/28)' [2018] Nieuw Juridisch Weekblad 566.

918 Corr. Brussel 25 juni 2013, *onuitg.*, 19–22; Fransen and Kerkhofs (n 10) 23.

919 Corr. Antwerpen (afd. Antwerpen) 11 februari 2015, *NjW* 2015, 280, noot E. Vandebroek; Fransen and Kerkhofs (n 10) 24.

(two of which with postponement of enforcement subject to probation) for threatening terrorist arson.[920] He had claimed he was going to burn down a shop because it sold the *Charlie Hebdo* magazine. Only about a week after the terrorist attack on the building of that same magazine in Paris, a terrorist cell that wanted to commit attacks in Belgium was broken up in Verviers (a town in eastern Belgium, relatively close to the Dutch and German borders). Three of its members were later convicted for being co-perpetrators of attempted terrorist murder.[921] The following elements were taken into account to substantiate the conviction for attempted murder: the choice of means and perpetrators, training with explosives, making false documents, searching for a safe house, renting vehicles to transport jihadists, buying weapons and parts of explosives, buying phones, buying ingredients for bombs, buying police uniforms, choosing at least one target, etc. It was stated that these actions do not leave any doubt about the intention of the perpetrators and that the evidence made clear that they had not changed their minds and desisted from the plan. That the exact targets were not chosen yet, that the way of committing the offence was not completely clear or that not all the ingredients for explosives were bought yet, did not matter to the Court. Another well-known case is the one of Salah Abdeslam and Sofien Ayari. For a while, Abdeslam, who was involved in the Bataclan and Stade de France terror attacks in France, was one of the most wanted men in Belgium. During the manhunt following the Paris attacks, Abdeslam, Ayari and a third man, Mohamed Belkaid had a shootout with the police who tried to arrest them. Belkaid was killed and Abdeslam and Ayari escaped. After they were eventually caught, both men were tried for attempted terrorist murder of several police officers. Both were convicted to 20 years imprisonment.[922] The defence questioned the terrorist intent of their specific actions, but the Court argued that by shooting assault weapons at the police in a residential neighbourhood, the three IS members had the intention of intimidating the population.[923] In 2021, the Correctional Court of Antwerp convicted four people, one of whom was an Iranian diplomat, for attempted terrorist murder and participating in the activities of a terrorist organisation.[924] They intended to bomb a gathering of Iranian opposition parties and dissidents near Paris. Two of the defendants were intercepted while they were driving to the meeting with a bomb in their car, whereas the third defendant was arrested at the scene of the gathering. The fourth defendant, the Iranian diplomat, was the one who gave instructions and

---

920 Corr. West-Vlaanderen (afd. Brugge) (vakantiekamer) 14 juli 2016, *TGR-TWVR* 2016, afl. 5, 386; Fransen and Kerkhofs (n 10) 24.

921 Corr. Brussel 5 juli 2016, *onuitg*. This was confirmed by the Court of Appeal for one of them after he appealed (Brussel 31 maart 2017, *onuitg*., 34–36). See also: Fransen and Kerkhofs (n 10) 24–25.

922 Corr. Brussel 23 april 2018, *onuitg;* Fransen and Kerkhofs (n 10) 27.

923 Corr. Brussel 23 april 2018, *onuitg*., 47.

924 Corr. Antwerpen 4 februari 2021, *onuitg*.

planned the attack. It is a remarkable case in the sense that although the Court did not literally say so, this was quite clearly state sponsored terrorism.[925] The abovementioned case on the terrorist attacks at Brussels Airport and metro station Maelbeek (see no. 154) also led to convictions for terrorism *sensu stricto* (and several for offences under Article 140 CC (see nos 165–206).[926] Most of the terrorists present at the scene were dead, as it was a suicide attack, but two left the scenes and survived. In addition to them, four other people, including Abdeslam again, were convicted for terrorist murder and attempted terrorist murder.

162. Facts outside of Belgium – Some of the convictions for terrorism *sensu stricto* relate to facts that took place outside of Belgium. Such was the case for example for a man who had kidnapped two unidentified people in Syria. One was released after the ransom was paid and the other was killed because the ransom was not paid. The perpetrator was convicted to 28 years imprisonment for terrorist murder and terrorist kidnapping.[927] On 29 March 2018 the Correctional Court convicted a man to 30 years imprisonment for terrorist murder and participating in the activities of a terrorist group (see no. 170).[928] He featured in a video clip made by IS, where he beheaded a man in Syria.

163. Acquittal for terrorism – On 5 December 2014, the Assize Court acquitted a person for terrorist arson because the jury did not find the required *mens rea* and contextual element present.[929] The person had set fire to a mosque just before the evening prayers, killing the imam and wounding someone else. The jury stated that the person acted based on an indignation after seeing horrible images of violence in Syria. He wanted revenge for the death of Syrian children and did not want to commit a serious and symbolic terrorist attack. He was convicted to 27 years felony imprisonment for arson in an inhabited building, which caused the death of a person, but not for terrorism. In the Sharia4Belgium case, the Correctional Court convicted several members for terrorist kidnapping of another member in Syria. The victim wanted to return to Belgium and they feared he would tell on them. However, the Court of

925 Note that the Iranian diplomat was later part of a prison exchange. He was exchanged for a Belgian NGO worker who was arrested in Iran in 2022 on unclear charges. This exchange was preceded by a legal battle concerning the constitutionality of the statute which gave force to the extradition treaty between Belgium and Iran. See: GwH 8 december 2022, 163/2022; GwH 3 maart 2023, 36/2023.

926 Assisen Brussel 26 juli 2023, *JLMB* 2023, 1348.

927 Corr. Antwerpen (afd. Antwerpen) 13 februari 2017, *onuitg.*, 30–32; Fransen and Kerkhofs (n 10) 25–26; Wittendorp and Bakker (n 686) 37. This decision was appealed, but before ruling on the merits of the case, the Court of Appeal ordered the defendant to be put under observation in order to evaluate his mental state. See: Antwerpen 21 december 2017, *onuitg;* Antwerpen 24 oktober 2018, *onuitg.* We were unable to find a final decision on the merits in this case.

928 Corr. Antwerpen (afd. Mechelen) 29 maart 2018, *onuitg;* Fransen and Kerkhofs (n 10) 26.

929 Assisen Brussel 5 december 2014, *onuitg.*, 10; Fransen and Kerkhofs (n 10) 22.

Appeal stated that there was no terrorist intent.[930] Lastly, on 5 October 2016, a man attacked police officers in Schaarbeek (Brussels) with a knife. The Court of Appeal convicted him of several offences but found that he did not have terrorist intent.[931] He perpetrated the assault because of several events in his life he considered unjust, such as a traffic accident involving a police car.

164. Difficulty in ascertaining terrorist intent and contextual element of *actus reus* – Examples from the case law show that judging the terrorist intent and contextual element of the offence is no easy task. There have been several cases where the public prosecution service thought there was terrorism, but the courts did not see it that way. Furthermore, sometimes the courts derive terrorist intent from odd elements of the case. For example, in the Abdeslam and Ayari case, we think it is a stretch to say that the mere fact that they shot at the police with assault weapons is an expression of terrorist intent. If that were the case, many more criminals are in reality terrorists. While they were undoubtedly involved in a terrorist organisation, it is more likely that in this specific case, they shot at the police because they wanted to escape, instead of wanting to intimidate the population.

930 Antwerpen 27 januari 2016, *onuitg;* Antwerpen 8 december 2016, *onuitg.*, 38; Fransen and Kerkhofs (n 10) 23–24.

931 Brussel 20 april 2018, *onuitg;* Corr. Brussel 10 oktober 2017, *onuitg;* Fransen and Kerkhofs (n 10) 26.

CHAPTER III
ARTICLE 140 CC

SECTION I. TERRORIST GROUPS

165. Offences relating to terrorist groups – Article 140 CC contains three offences, all three of which criminalise conduct related to terrorist groups. An important question for these three offences therefore is, when is a group of people a terrorist group?

166. Definition terrorist group – Article 139 CC defines a terrorist group as '*any structured group of more than two persons, established over a period of time and acting in concert to commit terrorist offences, as meant in Article 137.*'[932] The preparatory works add that a structured group is a group that '*is not randomly formed and that does not need to have formally defined roles for its members, continuity of its membership or a developed structure.*'[933] Both the definition of a terrorist group in Article 139 CC and the definition of a structured group in the preparatory works, are almost literal copies of an Article of the Framework Decision.[934] While 'acting in concert' suggests a form of mutual deliberation and coherence of actions,[935] the extent of the collaboration required is uncertain. For

932 Own translation, original in Dutch: '*iedere gestructureerde vereniging van meer dan twee personen die sinds enige tijd bestaat en die in onderling overleg optreedt om terroristische misdrijven te plegen, als bedoeld in artikel 137*' (Art. 139, section 1 CC). See also: Delmulle and Guenter (n 6) 4; Wattier (n 785).

933 Own translation, original in Dutch: '*Zulks onderstelt dat de vereniging niet toevallig tot stand is gekomen, zonder dat evenwel sprake moet zijn van formeel afgebakende taken voor de leden van de vereniging, noch van continuïteit in de samenstelling van de leden van een uitgewerkte structuur.*' (MvT wetsontwerp 6 oktober 2003 betreffende terroristische misdrijven, *Parl.St.* Kamer 2003, no. 51-0258/001, (4) 12). See also: De Hert and Millen (n 803) 4; Delhaise (n 8) 36–37; Deruyck and De Nauw (n 786) 8; Hameeuw (n 8) 8; Ketels (n 691) 241; Vandromme and De Roy (n 34) 536; Winants (n 8) 347–348.

934 Art. 2 Council Framework Decision 2002/475/JHA of 13 June 2002 on combating terrorism, [2002] *OJ* L164/4. Now Art. 2(3) Directive (EU) 2017/541 of the European Parliament and of the Council of 15 March 2017 on combating terrorism and replacing Council Framework Decision 2002/475/JHA and amending Council Decision 2005/671/JHA, [2017] *OJ* L88/6. See also: Beernaert, 'La Loi du 19 Décembre 2003 relative aux infractions terroristes : Quand le droit pénal Belge évolue sous la dictée de l'Union Européenne' (n 20) 587; Bosly and Van Ravenstein (n 784) 49; De La Serna (n 8) 181–182; Delhaise (n 8) 35; Delhaise and Fievet (n 45) 118; Flore (n 10) 216–217; Flore (n 784) 144; Weyembergh and Kennes (n 58) 153; Weyembergh and Kennes (n 14) 106.

935 De La Serna (n 50) 211; Fransen and Kerkhofs (n 10) 28; Winants (n 8) 348.

example, not all members have to be informed about each other's actions or even know each other, as long as they all contribute to the existence of the group.[936] Nor does contact between members have to be in person, but can also be over the internet[937] or by other means of correspondence.[938] The legislature treats a terrorist group as a separate entity with its own intent, being the perpetration of terrorism *sensu stricto*. In the context of criminal organisations (see no. 167) Verbruggen has called this type of group with its own intent an 'illegal entity'.[939] To be able to judge the goal of a certain group, sometimes a good amount of geopolitical knowledge is required.[940] The situation on the ground can be chaotic and allegiances are not always clear, nor are the aims and origins of every group which is active in such areas. Furthermore, the fact that a group is part of a European or international list of terrorist organisations, does not automatically mean it qualifies as a terrorist group under Article 139 CC or *vice versa*.[941] While the goal of a terrorist group has to be the perpetration of terrorist offences *sensu stricto*, it is not required that these offences have actually been committed,[942] or even prepared already.[943] The mere act of conspiracy or collusion, or of making plans, is said to be sufficient. However, how do you prove that the intent of the illegal entity is the perpetration of a terrorist attack if the preparations for the attack have not even started yet? The danger of a broad interpretation arises where groups are labelled terrorist based on vague notions that they might intend to perpetrate a terrorist attack. Given that different types of involvement in the group constitute terrorist offences (see nos 170–194), this vague definition of a terrorist group can raise legal certainty issues.

167. Criminal organisations – We can also find the term 'structured group' in Article 324*bis* CC, which defines criminal organisations.[944] The Council of

936 De La Serna (n 8) 183; De La Serna (n 50) 209–211.

937 Which is used extensively. See: Sophie Lavaux, 'Terrorisme: la stratégie de l'union Européenne en matière de radicalisation et de recrutement (troisième partie)' [2015] Vigiles 114, 117–118.

938 De La Serna (n 8) 183.

939 In Dutch: '*strafrechtspersoon*'. See: Verbruggen (n 34) 195.

940 Brion and others (n 77) 62; De La Serna (n 8) 184 and 201; De La Serna (n 50) 211.

941 De La Serna (n 8) 186–187; De La Serna (n 50) 214; Fransen and Kerkhofs (n 10) 29. The Council Chamber and Indictment Chamber in Brussels e.g. ruled that the PKK was not a terrorist organisation, even though it is on the EU list of terrorist organisation. See: KI Brussel 14 september 2017, *RW* 2017–18, 1611, noot J. Wouters en T. Van Poecke; KI Brussel 8 maart 2019, *onuitg.*, 44; RK Brussel 3 november 2016, *onuitg.*, 11; Ketels (n 691) 242; Wouters and Van Poecke (n 691).

942 Delmulle and Guenter (n 6) 4.

943 Brussel 19 januari 2007, *T.Strafr.* 2008, 281, noot F. Schuermans; Gent 21 maart 2018, *RW* 2019–2020, 672; Corr. Brugge 28 februari 2006, *T.Strafr.* 2006, 159, noot P. De Hert; Dekrem (n 32) 140; De La Serna (n 8) 186; De La Serna (n 50) 212–213; Delhaise (n 8) 38; Deruyck and De Nauw (n 786) 8–9; Fransen and Kerkhofs (n 10) 29; Hameeuw (n 8) 8; Ketels (n 691) 241; Traest (n 50) 257; Weyembergh and Kennes (n 58) 159; Winants (n 8) 348.

944 Delhaise (n 8) 23; Hameeuw (n 8) 8; Inneke Onsea, 'Wet betreffende de criminele organisaties: een eerste effectieve stap in de strijd tegen georganiseerde criminaliteit?' [1999] Panopticon 278, 281; Traest (n 50) 250 and 257; Vandromme and De Roy (n 34) 530.

State remarked that there are many similarities between terrorist groups and organised crime.[945] Article 324*bis* CC defines criminal organisations as '*any structured group of more than two persons, established over a period of time and acting in concert to commit felonies or standard offences with a sentence of three years imprisonment or more, to directly or indirectly gain capital.*'[946]

168. Exclusion – The tenth recital of the Framework Decision states that '*nothing in this Framework Decision may be interpreted as being intended to reduce or restrict fundamental rights or freedoms such as the right to strike, freedom of assembly, of association or of expression, including the right of everyone to form and to join trade unions with others for the protection of his or her interests and the related right to demonstrate.*'[947] The legislature decided to include this recital in the legislation. First, the recital was copied into Article 139, section 2 CC but after some discussion, the commission for justice decided to move the recital to a new Article 141*ter* CC. This was done to make it clearer that the recital is applicable to the entire title of the Code.[948] In section two of Article 139 CC parliament then copied the second section of Article 324*bis* CC about the criminal organisation, since this was considered the '*least bad solution.*'[949] So, the second section of Article 139 CC now contains an exclusion clause for organisations whose factual goal is exclusively political, professional organisational, humanitarian, philosophical, or religious or that exclusively pursue any other lawful purpose.[950]

945 Advies 34.362/4 van de Raad van State bij wetsontwerp van 6 oktober 2003 betreffende terroristische misdrijven, *Parl.St.* Kamer 2003, no. 51–0258/001, (22) 33. See also: De La Serna (n 8) 182; Traest (n 50) 257; Verbruggen (n 34) 302–303.

946 Own translation, original in Dutch: '*iedere gestructureerde vereniging van meer dan twee personen die duurt in de tijd, met als oogmerk het in onderling overleg plegen van misdaden en wanbedrijven die strafbaar zijn met gevangenisstraf van drie jaar of een zwaardere straf, om direct of indirect vermogensvoordelen te verkrijgen*' (Art. 324*bis*, section 1 CC).

947 Recital 10 Council Framework Decision 2002/475/JHA of 13 June 2002 on combating terrorism [2002] *OJ* L164/3. Now Recital 35 Directive (EU) 2017/541 of the European Parliament and of the Council of 15 March 2017 on combating terrorism and replacing Council Framework Decision 2002/475/JHA and amending Council Decision 2005/671/JHA [2017] *OJ* L88/6.

948 Amendement no. 15 7 oktober 2003 bij het wetsontwerp betreffende terroristische misdrijven van 21 oktober 2003, *Parl.St.* Kamer 2003, no. 51–0258/003, 5; Verslag namens de commissie voor de Justitie 7 november 2003 bij wetsontwerp betreffende terroristische misdrijven van 6 oktober 2003, *Parl.St.* Kamer 2003, no. 51–0258/004, 16 – 20; Beernaert, 'La Loi du 19 Décembre 2003 relative aux infractions terroristes : Quand le droit pénal Belge évolue sous la dictée de l'Union Européenne' (n 20) 588; De La Serna (n 8) 197.

949 Amendement no. 14 7 oktober 2003 bij het wetsontwerp betreffende terroristische misdrijven van 21 oktober 2003, *Parl.St.* Kamer 2003, no. 51–0258/003, 4; Verslag namens de commissie voor de Justitie 7 november 2003 bij wetsontwerp betreffende terroristische misdrijven van 6 oktober 2003, *Parl.St.* Kamer 2003, no. 51–0258/004, 20; Delhaise (n 8) 23.

950 Art. 139, section 2 CC; Weyembergh and Kennes (n 14) 110.

169. Utility of the exclusion clause? – What purpose Article 139, section 2 CC serves, is unclear. According to the preparatory works '*this section aims to provide clarification and protection against the misuse of the statute.*'[951] Whether it succeeds in doing so is doubtful. The Council of State noted both for Article 324*bis*, section 2 CC[952] and Article 139, section 2 CC[953] that two interpretations were possible. Either this exclusion clause means that an organisation which pursues a legitimate aim has not been established for the purpose of committing offences in concert, or that investigating or prosecuting an organisation (also) pursuing a legitimate aim is not allowed. The latter interpretation would render the offences moot. The former interpretation therefore is the correct one,[954] but it is in turn stating the obvious and does not belong in a criminal code.[955] Although some members of parliament were of the same mind, the majority ignored this criticism, claiming that it was better to be needlessly expressive than dangerously mute.[956] This claim was unjustified, in our opinion. Because of the lack of added value and the possibility for confusion, the legislature would do better to delete Article 139, section 2 CC.[957] The same goes for Article 141*ter* CC, which has no added value either.[958]

SECTION II. PARTICIPATING IN THE ACTIVITIES OF A TERRORIST GROUP (§1)

SUBSECTION 1. *ACTUS REUS*

170. Open category of actions – The terrorist offence for which by far the most prosecutions are brought before the courts is participating in the activities

[951] Own translation, original in Dutch: '*is dit lid erop gericht een verduidelijking en een bescherming tegen verkeerd gebruik van de wet te bieden*' (MvT wetsontwerp 6 oktober 2003 betreffende terroristische misdrijven, *Parl.St.* Kamer 2003, no. 51-0258/001, (4) 12).

[952] Advies 28.026/2 van de Raad van State bij wetsontwerp 12 maart 1997 betreffende criminele organisaties, 96/97 no. 49-954/24, 2; Verbruggen (n 34) 307.

[953] Advies 34.362/4 van de Raad van State bij wetsontwerp van 6 oktober 2003 betreffende terroristische misdrijven, *Parl.St.* Kamer 2003, no. 51-0258/001, (22) 33; De La Serna (n 8) 197.

[954] De La Serna (n 8) 186; De La Serna (n 50) 213–214; Flore (n 10) 217–218; Fransen and Kerkhofs (n 10) 29–30; Winants (n 8) 348.

[955] Hameeuw (n 8) 8; Jespers (n 15) 13; Vandromme and De Roy (n 34) 531 and 536.

[956] Verslag namens de commissie voor de Justitie 7 november 2003 bij wetsontwerp van 6 oktober 2003 betreffende terroristische misdrijven, *Parl.St.* Kamer 2003, no. 51-0258/004, 11; Beernaert, 'La Loi du 19 Décembre 2003 relative aux infractions terroristes : Quand le droit pénal Belge évolue sous la dictée de l'Union Européenne' (n 20) 588; De La Serna (n 8) 197.

[957] See also: Onsea (n 944) 284.

[958] See also: De La Serna (n 8) 198; De La Serna (n 50) 228–230; Delhaise (n 8) 142; Hameeuw (n 8) 10; Traest (n 50) 258; Vandromme and De Roy (n 34) 538; Vanneste and Verbruggen (n 686) 83–84.

of a terrorist group.[959] Just like Article 137 CC, Article 140 CC was introduced in 2003[960] in response to the 2002 Framework Decision.[961] Article 140, §1 CC targets any person who participates in the activities of a terrorist group while they knew or should have known that their participation could contribute to the perpetration of a felony or standard offence by the terrorist group. The *actus reus* is the participation in any activity of a terrorist group. The Criminal Code, echoing the Directive, explicitly adds to this '*be it by providing data or material resources to a terrorist group or any form of financing of any activity of a terrorist group.*'[962] However, this enumeration of actions is not exhaustive.[963] According to Belgian case law, providing moral support for example, can also amount to participation in the activities of a terrorist group.[964] Furthermore, the contribution to the activities of the group does not need to be systematic, an occasional contribution suffices.[965] The action does not have to have a direct connection to the perpetration of the offence by the group either.[966]

---

959 Art. 140, §1 CC; Fransen and Kerkhofs (n 10) 16; Winants (n 8) 349; Wittendorp and Bakker (n 686) 36.

960 Art. 6 wet 19 december 2003 betreffende terroristische misdrijven, *BS* 29 december 2003, 61689.

961 Art. 2 Council Framework Decision 2002/475/JHA of 13 June 2002 on combating terrorism [2002] *OJ* L164/3. Now Art. 4 Directive (EU) 2017/541 of the European Parliament and of the Council of 15 March 2017 on combating terrorism and replacing Council Framework Decision 2002/475/JHA and amending Council Decision 2005/671/JHA [2017] *OJ* L88/6. See also: Vander Beken (n 784) 31.

962 Own translation, original in Dutch: '*zij het ook door het verstrekken van gegevens of materiële middelen aan een terroristische groep of door het in enigerlei vorm financieren van enige activiteit van een terroristische groep*' (Art. 140, §1 CC).

963 MvT wetsontwerp 6 oktober 2003 betreffende terroristische misdrijven, *Parl.St.* Kamer 2003, no. 51-0258/001, (4) 13; Corr. Brussel 3 mei 2016, 35, *onuitg;* De La Serna (n 8) 191; De La Serna (n 50) 219.

964 Brussel 2 juni 2017, *onuitg.*, 22; Corr. Brussel 3 mei 2016, *onuitg.*, 36; Corr. Brussel 8 mei 2017, *onuitg.*, 5; Fransen and Kerkhofs (n 10) 32; Fransen and Kerkhofs (n 802) 159; Deruyck and De Nauw (n 786) 9; Ward Yperman and Sofie Royer, 'Veroordeling Jihadibruid' [2017] Nieuw Juridisch Weekblad 813. Note that the idea of contributing to criminal behaviour through moral support is also present elsewhere in Belgian criminal law, namely in the figure of moral participation through omission. There is moral participation through omission when a person, by his intentional omission, unambiguously incites the commission of an offence. See: Cass. 17 december 2008, P.08.1233.F, *RW* 2010–11, 366, noot S. Van Overbeke; Cass. 2 september 2009, *RW* 2011–12, 1029, noot S. Van Overbeke; Van den Wyngaert and Vandromme (n 790) 380; Jan Vanheule, *Strafbare Deelneming* (Intersentia 2010) 556–560 and 582; S Van Overbeke, 'Aanwezigheid bij het misdrijf als vorm van strafbare deelneming: je was erbij dus je bent erbij? (noot onder Cass. 17 december 2008)' [2010–2011] Rechtskundig Weekblad 367, 369.

965 MvT wetsontwerp 6 oktober 2003 betreffende terroristische misdrijven, *Parl.St.* Kamer 2003, no. 51-0258/001, (4) 13; Corr. Luik (vakantiekamer) 19 juli 2017, *JLMB* 2017, 1391; Corr. Brussel 10 mei 2019, *NjW* 2019, 663, noot W. Yperman; De La Serna (n 8) 191; De La Serna (n 50) 219; Delhaise (n 8) 40; Fransen and Kerkhofs (n 10) 30; Hameeuw (n 8) 9; Ketels (n 691) 243; Weyembergh and Kennes (n 14) 111.

966 MvT wetsontwerp 6 oktober 2003 betreffende terroristische misdrijven, *Parl.St.* Kamer 2003, no. 51-0258/001, (4) 13; Corr. Brussel 10 mei 2019, *NjW* 2019, 663, noot W. Yperman;

171. Broad concept of 'participating in any activity' – The case law has given a broad interpretation to participating in any activity of a terrorist group, made possible by the broad wording of the legislation.[967] Article 140, §1 CC requires a concrete act of participation of a person (who, in addition, knows or should have known that they could contribute to the perpetration of a felony or standard offence by the terrorist group) but the case law considers almost anything a possible act of participation. This includes following military training with a terrorist group,[968] or fighting for a terrorist group in a war zone,[969] but also sending a package of civilian clothes to a family member who is a member of a terrorist group,[970] cooking for or being a driver for the group,[971] mentally encouraging fighters of the group by sending them messages from their families or promising them to join them[972] and marrying and having a sexual relationship with a fighter of the group.[973] If a suspect has travelled to Syria to join a terrorist group, it is not required that the exact assignments of the suspect for that group in Syria are to be identified.[974] Because of this very wide interpretation of the *actus reus*, Article 140, §1 CC has a very wide potential scope of application.[975] A mother who was being prosecuted under Article 140, §1 CC for sending money to her two sons in Syria, argued that this prosecution violated, among other Articles, Article 8 ECHR (right to private life) and Article 141*ter* CC. She also held that she was protecting the right to life of her sons. The Court of Cassation dismissed these arguments.[976] In a case on the execution of a European Arrest Warrant the Court of Cassation did hold that the simple fact of glorifying terrorism and humiliating its victims, while it can be relevant for the offences under Article 140, §1 and §1/1 CC, is in itself not sufficient to constitute these offences.[977]

Delhaise (n 8) 40–41; Delmulle and Guenter (n 6) 4; Deruyck and De Nauw (n 786) 9; Fransen and Kerkhofs (n 10) 30.

967 Brion and others (n 77) 63; Traest (n 50) 258; Weyembergh and Kennes (n 14) 129.

968 Brussel 28 mei 2015, *onuitg.*, 29.

969 Corr. Brussel 3 mei 2016, *onuitg.*, 52.

970 Corr. Brussel 14 mei 2014, *onuitg.*

971 Corr. Antwerpen (afd. Antwerpen) 11 februari 2015, *NjW* 2015, 280, noot E. Vandebroek; Corr. Antwerpen 30 maart 2015, *onuitg.*, 4; Corr. Antwerpen (afd. Antwerpen) 25 januari 2016, *onuitg.*, 3.

972 Corr. Brussel 3 mei 2016, *onuitg.*, 38–39.

973 Corr. Oost-Vlaanderen (afd. Gent) 16 oktober 2017, *NjW* 2017, 805, noot W. Yperman en S. Royer. The right to marry and the right to respect for private and family life are both human rights enshrined in the ECHR (respectively Art. 12 and 8 ECHR). These rights, however, are not absolute and can be limited. See e.g., the offence of bigamy (Art. 391 CC) which is not in violation with either Art. of the ECHR. See: *X. v. United Kingdom* App no 3898 (ECtHR 22 July 1970); *RB v. United Kingdom* App no 19628/92 (ECtHR 29 June 1992); Marlier (n 807) 409–410.

974 Corr. Brussel 10 mei 2019, *NjW* 2019, 663, noot W. Yperman.

975 Ketels also notes this, see: Ketels (n 691) 243.

976 Cass. 18 oktober 2023, *RABG* 2024, 136.

977 Cass. 18 januari 2022, P.21.1692.N, 15.

172. DIFFERENCE PARTICIPATING IN THE ACTIVITIES AND MEMBERSHIP GROUP – Article 324*ter* CC criminalises four types of conduct with regard to criminal organisations: knowingly being involved in the organisation, participating in legal activities of the organisation, participating in the taking any decision whatsoever within the organisation and leadership of the organisation. When these Articles were introduced in 1999, the definition of criminal organisations (see no. 167) included another part about the *modus operandi*: at which intimidation, threats, violence, deceit or corruption are used or commercial or other structures are used to conceal or facilitate the perpetration of the offences.[978] This part of the sentence was deleted in 2005, because the definition was seen as too restrictive and not covering certain situations that needed to be covered.[979] In 1999 Article 324*ter*, §1 CC stated: '*Every person who knowingly and willingly is part of a criminal organisation, is punished with imprisonment of one to three years and a fine of 100 to 5000 [euro] or one of those sentences alone, even though they do not have the intention to commit an offence in the context of the organisation or participate in the perpetration in one of the ways described in Article 66 and following.*'[980] In order not to change the level of involvement required for the offence, this was changed in 2005, together with the change in definition of a criminal organisation.[981] It now reads: '*When a criminal organisation uses intimidation, threats, violence, deceit or corruption, or commercial or other structures are used to conceal or facilitate the perpetration of the offences, any person who knowingly and willingly is part of it, is punished with imprisonment of one to three years and a fine of 100 to 5000 euro or one of those sentences alone, even though they do not have the intention to commit an offence in the context of the organisation or participate in the perpetration in one of the ways described in Article 66 to 99.*'[982] They did not want to change the offence,

---

978 Onsea (n 944) 281; Onsea (n 51) 39.

979 Art. 4 wet 10 Augustus 2005 tot wijziging van diverse bepalingen met het oog op de versterking van de strijd tegen mensenhandel en mensensmokkel en tegen praktijken van huisjesmelkers, *BS* 2 September 2005, 38454; Amendementen 9 maart 2005 bij wetsontwerp tot wijziging van diverse bepalingen met het oog op de versterking van de strijd tegen mensenhandel en mensensmokkel, *Parl.St.* Kamer 2004–2005, no. 51–1560/004, 4–7.

980 Own translation, original in Dutch: '*Iedere persoon die wetens en willens, deel uitmaakt van een criminele organisatie, wordt gestraft met gevangenisstraf van een jaar tot drie jaar en met geldboete van honderd frank tot vijfduizend frank of met een van die straffen alleen, ook al heeft hij niet de bedoeling een misdrijf in het raam van die organisatie te plegen of daaraan deel te nemen op één van die wijzen bedoeld in de artikelen 66 en volgende.*' (Art. 324*ter*, §1 CC, as introduced by Art. 3 wet 10 januari 1999 betreffende de criminele organisaties, *BS* 26 februari 1999, 5812).

981 Art. 5 wet 10 augustus 2005 tot wijziging van diverse bepalingen met het oog op de versterking van de strijd tegen mensenhandel en mensensmokkel en tegen praktijken van huisjesmelkers, *BS* 2 september 2005, 38454.

982 Own translation, original in Dutch: '*Wanneer de criminele organisatie gebruik maakt van intimidatie, bedreiging, geweld, listige kunstgrepen of Corruptie, of commerciële of andere structuren aanwendt om het plegen van de misdrijven te verbergen of te vergemakkelijken, wordt iedere persoon die wetens en willens daarbij betrokken is, gestraft met gevangenisstraf*

hence they changed Article 324*ter* CC together with Article 324*bis* CC.[983] So for criminal organisations mere involvement with the organisation is an offence, without it being required that the person participates in the activities of the organisation.[984] Involvement equals membership of the organisation (knowingly and willingly being part of it[985])[986] while participation in the activities requires an action. Consequently, for terrorist organisations an act of participation to the activities of the group is required and mere membership is not sufficient.[987] The Constitutional Court stated that this difference between criminal organisations and terrorist groups was justified because there is an objective difference in the nature of the offences the organisation or group aims to commit.[988] The aim of terrorist groups is to commit terrorist offences *sensu stricto* while that of criminal organisations is to commit offences punishable by three years' imprisonment or more, in order to obtain, directly or indirectly, financial benefits.

173. Illusory distinction – The offence of Article 140, §1 CC, however, is interpreted so expansively that the distinction between participating in the activities and mere membership is illusory. When discussing the offence of membership in Article 324*ter*, §1 CC, the representative of the Secretary of Justice gave the following examples when replying to the question of what knowingly and willingly being part of an organisation is: the driver, house staff,

---

van een jaar tot drie jaar en met geldboete van honderd euro tot vijfduizend euro of met een van die straffen alleen, ook al heeft hij niet de bedoeling een misdrijf in het raam van die organisatie te plegen of daaraan deel te nemen op één van de in de artikelen 66 tot 69 bedoelde wijzen.' (Art. 324*ter*, §1 CC).

983 Amendementen 9 maart 2005 bij wetsontwerp tot wijziging van diverse bepalingen met het oog op de versterking van de strijd tegen mensenhandel en mensensmokkel, *Parl.St.* Kamer 2004–2005, no. 51-1560/004, 7–8. See also: Vandromme and De Roy (n 34) 531–532.

984 Art. 324*ter*, §1 CC; De La Serna (n 8) 191.

985 This was the original phrasing of the statute. This phrasing was adapted in 2005 (Art. 5 wet 10 augustus 2005 tot wijziging van diverse bepalingen met het oog op de versterking van de strijd tegen mensenhandel en mensensmokkel en tegen praktijken van huisjesmelkers, *BS* 2 september 2005, 38454), but with the explicit intention to keep the content of the offence unaltered (Amendementen 9 maart 2005 bij wetsontwerp tot wijziging van diverse bepalingen met het oog op de versterking van de strijd tegen mensenhandel en mensensmokkel, *Parl.St.* Kamer 2004–2005, no. 51-1560/004, 7–8).

986 MvT wetsontwerp 12 maart 1997 betreffende criminele organisaties, 96/97 no. 49-954/1, 1–2; Amendementen 9 maart 2005 bij wetsontwerp tot wijziging van diverse bepalingen met het oog op de versterking van de strijd tegen mensenhandel en mensensmokkel, *Parl.St.* Kamer 2004–2005, no. 51-1560/004, 7–8; GwH 19 september 2014, 122/2014, *NjW* 2014, 840, B.4.2-B.4.3.

987 Corr. Antwerpen (afd. Antwerpen) 11 februari 2015, *NjW* 2015, 280, noot E. Vandebroek; Corr. Antwerpen 30 maart 2015, *onuitg.*, 4; Corr. Luik (vakantiekamer) 19 juli 2017, *JLMB* 2017, 1391; De La Serna (n 8) 191; De La Serna (n 50) 219; Delhaise (n 8) 40; Fransen and Kerkhofs (n 10) 30; Hameeuw (n 8) 9; Ketels (n 691) 243; Traest (n 50) 258; Weyembergh and Kennes (n 14) 111–112; Winants (n 8) 348.

988 GwH 19 september 2014, 122/2014, *NjW* 2014, 840, B.7.1-B.7.2. See also: Ketels (n 691) 246–247; Eef Vandebroek, 'Eenvoudig lidmaatschap van criminele vereniging' [2014] Nieuw Juridisch Weekblad 846, 847.

and security personnel of the leader of the organisation and '*the people who in are any form reimbursed by the criminal organisation to build a social network for the organisation, with the goal of apparent legitimate embedding and social implantation of the organisation in society.*'[989] Furthermore it is clarified that membership of a criminal organisation can be deduced from, for example, '*frequently being present at meetings of the criminal organisation or being a shareholder in the corporate law structure the organisation uses as a cover.*'[990] It is striking that the abovementioned examples of membership, when transposed to the context of a terrorist group, in all probability would fall under Article 140, §1 CC. It is safe to say that the alleged difference between the two does not actually exist in practice. The Council of State had in 1997 already stated that there is no difference between 'knowingly and willingly being a part of' and 'participating in'. As it explains '*only when a suspect has participated in an activity of the organisation, can it be assumed and proved that they know the organisation and know that it is a criminal organisation.*'[991] Once again, the Council of State seems to have been right. In order to be able to meaningfully apply the concept of membership, an act of participation will almost always be required, however minimal it may be. The fact that the Constitutional Court found the distinction justified, does not mean it is a meaningful distinction as well.

174. Strange analogy – This distinction between the concepts membership and participation has also led to a strange analogy made in some case law.[992] In several cases, the Brussels Correctional Court first refers to the preparatory

---

989 Own translation, original in French: '*personnes qui sont rémunérées sous une forme ou une autre par l'organisation pour constituer un cercle de relations sociales d'apparence licite*' (Advies van de Raad van State bij wetsontwerp 12 maart 1997 betreffende criminele organisaties, 96/97 no. 49–954/1, (13) 15–16). See as well: Arbitragehof 30 juni 2005, 116/2005, B.4.2; GwH 19 september 2014, 122/2014, *NjW* 2014, 840, B.4.3; Onsea (n 944) 282; Onsea (n 51) 39.

990 Own translation, original in Dutch: '*het geregeld aanwezig zijn op vergaderingen van de criminele organisatie of het aandeelhouderschap van een vennootschapsrechtelijke structuur die door een criminele organisatie als dekmantel wordt gebruikt*' (Verslag namens de commissie voor Justitie 29 mei 1997 bij wetsontwerp 12 maart 1997 betreffende criminele organisaties, 96/97 no. 49–954/6, 18). See also: Arbitragehof 30 juni 2005, 116/2005, B.4.2; GwH 19 september 2014, 122/2014, *NjW* 2014, 840, B.4.3.

991 Own translation, original in Dutch: '*Pas wanneer een verdachte aan een handeling van de organisatie heeft deelgenomen, kan ervan uit worden gegaan en worden bewezen dat hij de organisatie kent en weet dat het om een misdaadorganisatie gaat.*' (Advies van de Raad van State bij wetsontwerp 12 maart 1997 betreffende criminele organisaties, 96/97 no. 49–954/1, (13) 16).

992 Corr. Brussel 25 november 2015, *onuitg.*, 8; Corr. Brussel 3 mei 2016, *onuitg.*, 35–36; Corr. Brussel 8 mei 2017, *onuitg.*, 5; Corr. Brussel 29 maart 2018, *onuitg.*, 21. The Court states: '*Il faut néanmoins considérer que la participation au groupe terroriste est conçue plus largement que la participation à l'organisation criminelle dans la mesure où l'Article 324ter du Code pénal envisage une participation étroitement liée aux activités de l'organisation criminelle tandis que l'Article 140 vise toute forme de participation, pour autant que le participant soit conscient qu'il contribue à la commission d'un crime ou délit du groupe terroriste.*'

works of the legislation on criminal organisation 'by analogy'. After quoting the abovementioned examples of membership (being the driver, etc.) from these preparatory works, it then refers to the preparatory works that compare participation in any permitted activity of a criminal organisation to participation in a terrorist group. The court states that Article 324*ter* CC envisions participation closely linked to the organisation's activities while Article 140 CC targets all forms of participation, as long as the participant knows they will contribute to the commission of a standard offence or crime by the group. It is confusing that the court uses an analogy with an offence that is not comparable. The courts themselves state that mere membership of a terrorist organisation is not sufficient. This strange analogy, which is a recurring theme in the case law of the Brussels Correctional Court, shows the difficulty the courts have in clearly and consistently applying these concepts.

175. Continuous offence? – In 2019, the Brussels Correctional Court also ruled that the offence of participation in the activities of a terrorist group was a continuous offence.[993] The court decided so to solve an issue of the effect of legislative change over time (see no. 210).[994] However, since an act of participation is required, the offence in Article 140, §1 CC seems to be an immediate offence, which takes place the moment the act of participation is performed (in combination with the required *mens rea*). Therefore, other courts, including the Brussels Court of Appeal, have not held that participation in the activities of a terrorist offence is a continuous offence.[995] If several acts of participation succeed each other, they can constitute a continued or collective offence (see no. 225), but that does not make the participation a continuous one.

SUBSECTION 2. *MENS REA*

176. Which type of intent – The *mens rea* of Article 140, §1 CC is: '*while he knew or should have known that his participation could contribute to the perpetration of a felony or standard offence by the terrorist group.*'[996] This felony or standard offence does not necessarily have to be a terrorist offence, any felony or standard offence suffices and the participant does not need to know

993 Corr. Brussel 10 mei 2019, *NjW* 2019, 663, noot W. Yperman.

994 Since the new wording of the *mens rea* is broader, this new wording cannot be applied retroactively. See: Gent 21 maart 2018, *RW* 2019–2020, 672.

995 See e.g.: Brussel 21 december 2018, *onuitg;* Corr. Oost-Vlaanderen (afd. Dendermonde) 14 december 2018, *onuitg;* Corr. Antwerp 17 december 2018, *onuitg;* Corr. Luik 18 januari 2019, *onuitg.*

996 Own translation, original in Dutch: '*terwijl hij wist of moest weten dat zijn deelname zou kunnen bijdragen tot het plegen van een misdaad of wanbedrijf door de terroristische groep*' (Art. 140, §1 CC).

to which specific and concrete offence they are contributing.[997] Nor does the offence actually have to be committed.[998] The person also does not have to have the intention of committing this offence himself.[999] Nor do they have to be radicalised.[1000] Committing offences is the intention of the 'illegal entity' but not necessarily of the individual people participating in its activities. Their connection to the perpetration of the offence by the group does not have to be a direct one.[1001] When Article 140, §1 was introduced in 2003, the *mens rea* was '*while he knows that his participation contributes to the perpetration of a felony or standard offence by the terrorist group.*'[1002] This was copied from the Framework Decision and the Directive is still worded similarly.[1003] In December 2016 the Belgian legislature changed this to '*knew or should have known*' and '*could contribute.*'[1004] It did this to make the Article more repressive.[1005] This is remarkable since at the introduction of the Article in 2003, the explanatory memorandum still said that knowing that a person contributes to the perpetration of felonies and standard offences by the terrorist group was the decisive criterion.[1006] The change was made with the Dutch concept of '*mogelijkheidsbewustzijn*'[1007] in mind.[1008] This 'mogelijkheidsbewustzijn' is

---

997 MvT wetsontwerp 6 oktober 2003 betreffende terroristische misdrijven, *Parl.St.* Kamer 2003, no. 51-0258/001, (4) 13; Luik 18 oktober 2017, *JLMB* 2017, 1878; Corr. Luik (vakantiekamer) 19 juli 2017, *JLMB* 2017, 1391; De Hert and Millen (n 803) 5; De La Serna (n 8) 189; De La Serna (n 50) 216; De Nauw (n 786) 8; Deruyck and De Nauw (n 786) 8; Flore (n 10) 218; Flore (n 784) 144–145; Fransen and Kerkhofs (n 10) 30; Hameeuw (n 8) 9; Traest (n 50) 258; Vandromme and De Roy (n 34) 537; Weyembergh and Kennes (n 14) 111; Winants (n 8) 348.

998 Flore (n 10) 218.

999 De La Serna (n 8) 189; De La Serna (n 50) 213; Delhaise (n 8) 42–43; Flore (n 10) 218; Ketels (n 691) 243; Vandromme and De Roy (n 34) 537; Weyembergh and Kennes (n 14) 114.

1000 Gent 21 maart 2018, *RW* 2019–2020, 672.

1001 MvT wetsontwerp 6 oktober 2003 betreffende terroristische misdrijven, *Parl.St.* Kamer 2003, no. 51-0258/001, (4) 13; Delhaise (n 8) 40–41; Delmulle and Guenter (n 6) 4; Fransen and Kerkhofs (n 10) 30.

1002 Own translation, original in Dutch: '*terwijl hij weet dat zijn deelname bijdraagt tot het plegen van een misdaad of wanbedrijf door de terroristische groep*' (MvT wetsontwerp 6 oktober 2003 betreffende terroristische misdrijven, *Parl.St.* Kamer 2003, no. 51-0258/001, (4) 13). See also: Fransen and Kerkhofs (n 10) 28; Weyembergh and Kennes (n 14) 110–111; Winants (n 8) 348.

1003 Art. 4(b) Directive (EU) 2017/541 of the European Parliament and of the Council of 15 March 2017 on combating terrorism and replacing Council Framework Decision 2002/475/JHA and amending Council Decision 2005/671/JHA [2017] *OJ* L88/6.

1004 Art. 2 wet 14 december 2016 tot wijziging van het Strafwetboek wat betreft de bestraffing van terrorisme, *BS* 22 december 2016, 88017. See also: Gent 21 maart 2018, *RW* 2019–2020, 672; Deruyck and De Nauw (n 786) 8.

1005 As was acknowledged by the Correctional Court Limburg, see: Corr. Limburg (afd. Hasselt) 23 juni 2017, *Limburgs Rechtsleven* 2018, 51.

1006 MvT wetsontwerp 6 oktober 2003 betreffende terroristische misdrijven, *Parl.St.* Kamer 2003, no. 51-0258/001, (4) 7. See also: Cesoni (n 15) 240; De Hert and Millen (n 803) 5; Weyembergh and Kennes (n 58) 154; Winants (n 8) 348.

1007 Which literally translates to opportunity awareness. Another term for it can be translated as 'conditional intent'.

1008 Toelichting bij wetsvoorstel 13 januari 2016 tot wijziging van het Strafwetboek wat betreft de bestraffing van terrorisme, *Parl.St.* Kamer 2015–1026, no. 54-1579/001, 3; Fransen and Kerkhofs (n 10) 35; Winants (n 8) 355.

present when '*somebody intentionally acts or refrains from acting, and in doing so has imagined a consequence of that behaviour (which is not in itself intended) as [possible], but does not allow himself to be deterred by it. This possibility is accepted by the perpetrator.*'[1009] This closely resembles the Belgian concept of potential intent.[1010] Potential intent is a more flexible version of general intent ('knowingly and willingly', see no. 103) in two ways. First, the will element ('willingly') is relaxed to accepting the consequences instead of actually wanting them.[1011] Second, the knowledge element ('knowingly') is relaxed to knowledge of the possibility of consequences instead of certainty. How far this widening of the knowledge element exactly goes, is unclear. Some authors state that the possibility of consequences is enough, but others are more exacting and require the consequences to be probable or likely.[1012] For lack of statutory definition, the exact standard is unclear. Assuming the possibility of consequences suffices, Belgian potential intent fully equates to the Dutch '*mogelijkheidsbewustzijn*'. Even if a higher threshold would be required on paper, the question remains whether this would make any practical difference. A detailed analysis of the application in practice of both concepts would be needed in order to make any definitive statements on this point. Despite it being more flexible, legal doctrine

---

1009 Own translation, original in Dutch: '*iemand opzettelijk iets doet of nalaat en zich daarbij een (op zichzelf niet beoogd) gevolg van die gedraging heeft voorgesteld als [mogelijk], maar zich daardoor niet laat weerhouden. [...] Deze mogelijkheid neemt de dader op de koop toe*' (Conclusie A-G Berger bij Hoge Raad 30 mei 1975, ECLI:NL:PHR:1975:AC5594 (bierglasarrest)). See also: Gerechtshof Den Haag 27 October 2016, ECLI:NL:GHDHA:2016:3699; Gerechtshof Amsterdam 24 July 2018, ECLI:NL:GHAMS:2018:2580; JLM Boek, 'Een pleidooi voor het afschaffen van voorwaardelijk opzet' [2016] Strafblad 439, 439–444; J De Groote, 'De bovengrens der fout en de ondergrens van het opzet met bijzondere aandacht voor het eventueel opzet: een doctrinale en rechtsvergelijkende analyse' (2017) special number April 2017 Nullum Crimen (NC) 66, 90–92; AC 't Hart, 'Noot onder Hoge Raad 15 oktober 1996, ECLI:NL:HR:1996:ZD0139'; Nico Jörg, Constantijn Kelk and André Klip, *Strafrecht met mate* (14th edn, Wolters Kluwer 2019) 101–103; MJ Kronenberg and B de Wilde, *Grondtrekken van het Nederlandse strafrecht* (8th edn, Kluwer 2020) 60–62; AJ Machielsen, 'Materiële Verweren' in MF Attinger (ed), *Handboek Strafzaken* (2018) para 36.1.1.1; J Verboon and KAWM Schuurmans, 'Grenzen aan exonereren voor aansprakelijkheid' [2019] ORP 8, 15.

1010 De Coensel, *Counter-Terrorism & Criminal Law: A Normative Legitimacy Test of Terrorism-Related Offences on Expression, Information and Movement* (n 1) 105; De Groote (n 1009) 75–79; De Nauw and Deruyck (n 39) 42; Lieven Dupont, *Beginselen van Strafrecht, Deel I* (Acco 1983) 184; Bjorn Ketels, 'De strafrechtelijke context van risicovol seksueel gedrag' [2008] Tijdschrift voor Strafrecht 354, 361; Van den Wyngaert, Vandromme and Traest (n 34) 331–332; J Verhaegen, 'Le Dol éventuel et sa place en droit pénal Belge', *Liber Amicorum Hermann Bekaert* (Snoeck-Ducaju & Zoon 1977) 441–442; V Vereecke, 'Het eventueel opzet bij de beoordeling van het oogmerk om te doden' (2019) 2019 Rechtspraak Antwerpen Brussel Gent (RABG) 25, 26–27.

1011 Dupont states that potential intent is a weakening of the knowledge element and Vereecke states that it is a weakening of the will element. In our opinion both are correct and both elements are weakened.

1012 For an analysis of the different points of view, see: De Groote (n 1009) 75–77.

considers potential intent as a form of general intent.[1013] Regarding Article 140, §1 CC, however, commentators and the case law state that this is a form of special intent.[1014] The original *mens rea* seems to be a special intent indeed. Special intent requires the 'will-element' to be more specific (a specific goal or evil intention).[1015] Knowing that you are contributing to an offence by a terrorist group with your participation and still going ahead with it, implies the will to contribute to an offence by the group, which is more specific than just the will to participate in its activities. However, we still need to factor in the changes made in 2016. If we look at both changes to the *mens rea* separately, we see that the second change ('*could contribute*') is a part of '*mogelijkheidsbewustzijn*'/ potential intent indeed: the knowledge element is being relaxed to knowledge of the possibility. The first change ('*should have known*'), by contrast, is not a relaxation of the knowledge element, nor of the will element. The Council of State described it as a 'potential knowing' instead of a 'real knowing'.[1016] This 'potential knowing' can only be concluded based on concrete elements of the file and not from abstract criteria.[1017] It is a way to prove intent rather than a form of intent,[1018] a type of 'he should have known so he knew'-reasoning.[1019] If we combine both changes, we have a relaxation of the knowledge element and a rule of evidence. In 2016, the legislature made the *mens rea* broader so moved it further away from a special intent. A phrase such as '*should have known*' is even reminiscent of negligence. This issue has already been discussed in the context of other offences. The legislation on money laundering contains similar[1020]

1013 Dirk Dewandeleer, "Opzettelijk doden en opzettelijk toebrengen van lichamelijk letsel (Art. 392 t/m 417 Sw.), Algemeen', *Postal Memorialis – Lexicon strafrecht, strafvordering en bijzondere wetten* (2001) 8–10; Ketels (n 1010) 336 and 338; Marlier (n 807) 732; Verhaegen (n 1010) 445–446.

1014 Corr. Brussel 8 mei 2017, *onuitg.*, 5; Delhaise (n 8) 42; Fransen and Kerkhofs (n 10) 30; Fransen and Kerkhofs (n 802) 158; Fransen, Kerkhofs and Verrest (n 45) 46. The same goes for the pre-2016 version of the Art., see: Ketels (n 691) 244; Weyembergh and Kennes (n 14) 111.

1015 De Nauw and Deruyck (n 39) 42; Dupont (n 1010) 182; R Legros, *Opzet* (Larcier 1959) 13; Van den Wyngaert and Vandromme (n 790) 316–317.

1016 Advies 59.789/3 van de Raad van State 19 juli 2016 bij wetsvoorstel 13 januari 2016 tot wijziging van het Strafwetboek wat betreft de bestraffing van terrorisme, *Parl.St.* Kamer 2015–2016, no. 54-1579/006, 8.

1017 Advies 59.789/3 van de Raad van State 19 juli 2016 bij wetsvoorstel 13 januari 2016 tot wijziging van het Strafwetboek wat betreft de bestraffing van terrorisme, *Parl.St.* Kamer 2015–2016, no. 54-1579/006, 9; Fransen and Kerkhofs (n 10) 35; Winants (n 8) 355.

1018 For money laundering and the trade of animals in violation of the hormone regulation (both discussed below) see: De Nauw and Deruyck (n 39) 43.

1019 De Groote (n 1009) 96–67; W Devroe and A Rombouts, 'Wissel als witsel. de beteugeling van het witwassen van gelden via geldwissel in het Belgisch financieel en strafrecht (Noot onder corr. Antwerpen 23 februari 1993)' [1994] TRV 199, 204. Van den Wyngaert et al. wonder whether this actually does make difference in terms of proof, see: Van den Wyngaert, Vandromme and Traest (n 34) 336. This relaxation of the proof is criticised by Comité T in light of the presumption of innocence. See: Comité T, 'Rapport 2022: Évaluation des mesures visant à lutter contre le terrorisme à la lumière des droits humains', 51.

1020 In Dutch the wording is different, but the meaning is the same. Both Dutch phrases translate to the same thing in English: knew or should have known.

phrasing.[1021] This phrasing has its origins in a judgement of the Court of Cassation.[1022] Although the wording led to some confusion at first, it is by now generally accepted when it comes to the legislation on money laundering that general intent is required.[1023] In the preparatory works members of parliament even explicitly refer to the concept of potential intent.[1024] In the legislation on the trade of animals in violation of the hormone regulation, a similar wording is used to convey a heightened duty of care, which resembles negligence.[1025] However, it is clear from the preparatory works of the terrorism legislation that the legislature had the intention of using the same form of intent as in the money laundering legislation, which is general intent.[1026]

177. General intent – So, what type of intent does the post-2016 Article 140 CC require? The reasoning above, which infers the specificity of the will element from a more specific knowledge requirement, does not apply anymore. Acting while you know you could contribute to an offence does not seem to necessarily

1021 Art. 505, section 1, 2° and 4° CC; De Groote (n 1009) 77. Van Den Wyngaert and Vandromme call it a potential knowing or a 'should have known test', just as the Council of State did for the terrorism legislation (Van den Wyngaert and Vandromme (n 790) 323.).

1022 Cass. 13 november 1983, *Arr.Cass.* 1984–85, 363.

1023 Corr. Antwerpen 23 februari 1993, *T.R.V.* 1994, 195, noot W. Devroe en A. Rombouts; Corr. Antwerpen 14 april 1994, *T.R.V.* 1994, 285, noot F. Hellemans; Cesoni (n 15) 256–257; Filiep Deruyck, 'Witwassen', *Strafrecht en strafvordering. Artikelsgewijze commentaar met overzicht van rechtspraak en rechtsleer* (Wolters Kluwer) 245–247; Devroe and Rombouts (n 1019) 204; N Hustin-Denies, 'La législation Belge sur le blachiment de capiteaux d'origine criminelle: un instrument d'indemnisation des victimes et de lutte contre la criminalité organisée?' [1995] Ann dr Louv 53, 62–63; Bart Spriet and Kristel De Schepper, 'De nieuwe witwas(straf)wet – Een schematisch overzicht' [2009–2010] T Fin R 21, 21; Van den Wyngaert and Vandromme (n 790) 324; Van den Wyngaert, Vandromme and Traest (n 34) 335–336; Raf Verstraeten and Dirk Dewandeleer, 'Witwassen na de wet van 7 april 1995: kan het nog witter?' [1995] Rechtskundig Weekblad 689, 692–693 and 701. *Contra*: L Cornelis and R Verstraeten, 'Mag er nog witgewassen worden?' [1992] TBH 176, 203–204; D Devos, 'Le blanchiment des capitaux d'origine criminelle' [1992] Bank Fin 201, 202; F Hellemans, 'Witwassen: een strafbaar maar lonend misdrijf? (Noot onder corr. Antwerpen 14 april 1994)' [1994] TRV 287, 290.

1024 Verslag namens de commissie voor de Justitie 20 juni 1990 bij het ontwerp van wet tot wijziging van de artikelen 42, 43 en 505 van het Strafwetboek en tot invoeging van een artikel 43*bis* in hetzelfde Wetboek, *Gedr.St.* Senaat 1989–90, no. 890/2, 28; Cornelis and Verstraeten (n 1023) 193–205; Verstraeten and Dewandeleer (n 1023) 692–693.

1025 Antwerpen 18 oktober 1990, *RW* 1990–91, 856, noot B. Spriet; Bart Spriet, 'Het verhandelen van dieren waaraan stoffen met hormonale of antihormonale werking zijn toegediend (noot onder Antwerpen 18 oktober 1990)' [1990] Rechtskundig Weekblad 857, 858; M Sterkens, 'Hormonen: De Misdrijven', *Postal Memorialis – Lexicon strafrecht, strafvordering en bijzondere wetten* (2015) 8. The statute reads: '*of whom it is reasonable to assume that he knows or should know*' (original in Dutch: '*van wie men redelijkerwijze kan aannemen dat hij weet of moet weten*' (Art. 10, §1, 2°, b wet 15 juli 1985 betreffende het gebruik bij dieren van stoffen met hormonale, anti-hormonale, beta-adrenergische of produktie-stimulerende werking, *BS* 4 september 1985, 12669)).

1026 Verslag van de eerste lezing 20 oktober 2016 namens de tijdelijke commissie 'terrorismebestrijding' bij wetsvoorstel tot wijziging van het Strafwetboek wat betreft de bestraffing van terrorisme, *Parl.St.* Kamer 2015–2016, no. 54–1579/008, 9.

imply the will to contribute, since contribution is only a possibility and not a certainty anymore. Indeed, when knowingly and willingly participating in the activities of a terrorist group, should the person not always know they could contribute to an offence by that group? Therefore, Article 140, §1 CC has a general intent rather than a special one.[1027] Although potential intent, as already discussed, is seen as a form of general intent, the relaxation of the knowledge element it entails, is not without danger in this context. The concept '*contributing to the commission of a felony or standard offence by the group*' is an abstract one in any case and further relaxing the knowledge element to '*could contribute*' makes it even more abstract and thus vaguer.[1028]

178. Link with criminal actions of group – In 2016 another amendment to the *mens rea* was proposed, but it was not passed: '*while he knew or should have known that the group is a terrorist group.*'[1029] The Council of State was rather critical for this amendment because it would significantly broaden the offence and give a very wide margin of appreciation to the judge.[1030] This addition of a very broad *mens rea* to an already broad *actus reus*, which is mainly defined by the case law, could lead to legality issues, according to the Council of State.[1031] It thought that at the very least the legislation should make clear that involvement in the criminal activities of the terrorist group is required.[1032] The wording as it was eventually implemented, was less problematic in the eyes of the Council of State (see no. 171 above).[1033] However, it is striking that a recurring sentence in judgments of French speaking courts is that participation in the activities of a group is punishable '*provided that the participant is aware of the vocation of the movement*'[1034] With these words, the courts seem to refer to a lower threshold for the *mens rea* requirement which was not passed by the legislature.

1027 See also: Cesoni (n 15) 256.

1028 For similar criticism, see: Cesoni (n 15) 240–241.

1029 Own translation, original in Dutch: '*terwijl hij wist of moest weten dat de groep een terroristische groep is.*'

1030 Advies 59.789/3 van de Raad van State 19 juli 2016 bij wetsvoorstel 13 januari 2016 tot wijziging van het Strafwetboek wat betreft de bestraffing van terrorisme, *Parl.St.* Kamer 2015–2016, no. 54–1579/006, 5 – 7; Fransen and Kerkhofs (n 10) 35; Winants (n 8) 355. For an analysis, see also: Corr. Luik (vakantiekamer) 19 juli 2017, *JLMB* 2017, 1391.

1031 Advies 59.789/3 van de Raad van State 19 juli 2016 bij wetsvoorstel 13 januari 2016 tot wijziging van het Strafwetboek wat betreft de bestraffing van terrorisme, *Parl.St.* Kamer 2015–2016, no. 54–1579/006, 7; Winants (n 8) 355.

1032 Advies 59.789/3 van de Raad van State 19 juli 2016 bij wetsvoorstel 13 januari 2016 tot wijziging van het Strafwetboek wat betreft de bestraffing van terrorisme, *Parl.St.* Kamer 2015–2016, no. 54–1579/006, 7. See also: Cesoni (n 15) 241.

1033 Advies 59.789/3 van de Raad van State 19 juli 2016 bij wetsvoorstel 13 januari 2016 tot wijziging van het Strafwetboek wat betreft de bestraffing van terrorisme, *Parl.St.* Kamer 2015–2016, no. 54–1579/006, 8 – 9.

1034 Translated from French: '*pourvue que celui qui les apporte ait connaissance de la vocation du mouvement.*' See e.g.: Corr. Brussel 9 maart 2016, *onuitg.*, 14; Corr. Brussel 3 mei 2016, *onuitg;*

179. Extensive interpretation regardless – It is clear that even without the further expansion of the *mens rea* by the legislature, the Council of State's fear of too extensive an application has become reality. The *actus reus* of the offence is so broad it can encompass pretty much any action and the *mens rea* is very open and vague as well (see nos 176–178). As a result, people who in any way support a member of a terrorist group, without supporting the group itself and without wanting their actions to contribute to the perpetration of a felony or standard offence by the group, are being convicted anyway.[1035] Support to a member of the group is being fully equated to support to the group itself.[1036] This is regrettable because many of those people may not be supporters of a terrorist group. They could simply be people who want to help their brother, son, or lover, even though the latter have made very questionable choices. Employing the criminal justice system against a person whose only action is sending some clothes to their brother is not the best solution to say the least. An interesting case in this regard is the case of the vacation chamber of the Correctional Court of Liège of 19 July 2017.[1037] In this case the court explicitly compares the old and new wording of the *mens rea*, referring to the parliamentary documents and Council of State opinions. According to the court the old wording required a causal link between the actions of the would-be perpetrator and an offence by the group, while the new wording does not do so. The court concludes that the accused has not committed the offence as it was originally worded for lack of this causal link.

180. Legality – As the Council of State feared in 2016, all this leads to a legality issue: it grants very wide discretion to the judge and creates uncertainty in the minds of the person performing these actions about whether or not they are committing an offence.[1038] Therefore, it might be a good idea for the legislature to limit the *mens rea* again to its original wording, which is also what is required by the Directive. This will hopefully be a signal for the courts to require an actual link between the act of participation and the (potential/

Corr. Brussel 8 mei 2017, *onuitg;* Corr. Brussel 29 maart 2018, *onuitg;* Corr. Bergen 14 mei 2018, *onuitg;* Corr. Brussel 11 juni 2018, *onuitg.*

1035 See also, dating back as far as 2012: Marchand (n 617) 281–282; Moreau (n 47) 113–114.

1036 This reduces a person to one aspect of their identity: that of member of the group. However, it could be sensible to emphasise other aspects of their identity (father, brother, etc.) which are not shared with the group, in order to make them break away from the group. If all 'healthy contacts' of a member of a terrorist group are being forced to keep a distance under threat of criminal action, the group member only has the group and its sympathisers to fall back on. This just strengthens their bond with the group and their break with the rest of society.

1037 Corr. Luik (vakantiekamer) 19 juli 2017, *JLMB* 2017, 1391.

1038 Advies 59.789/3 van de Raad van State 19 juli 2016 bij wetsvoorstel 13 januari 2016 tot wijziging van het Strafwetboek wat betreft de bestraffing van terrorisme, *Parl.St.* Kamer 2015–2016, no. 54–1579/006, 7. This was also stated by Comité T in 2019, see: Comité T, 'Rapport 2019: Le respect des droits humains dans le cadre de la lutte contre le terrorisme: Un chantier en cours', 18–20. See also: Cesoni (n 15) 242; Moreau (n 47) 116.

envisaged) perpetration of a felony or standard offence by the group. These changes would bring the Belgian legislation back in line with the Directive and reduce the scope of the offence.

SUBSECTION 3. SENTENCES

181. Sentence – The Criminal Code provides for a sentence of five to ten years felony imprisonment and a fine of 100 to 5,000 euros for this offence, making it a felony.[1039] After correctionalisation, which is a standard procedure in this case,[1040] that becomes a principal sentence of one month to five years imprisonment.[1041] This means electronic monitoring as a principal sentence is possible, when the judge feels the offence is of such a nature that it should not be punished with more than one year imprisonment (see no. 115).[1042] The electronic monitoring has a term of one month to one year. Community service, with a term of 45 to 300 hours, and an autonomous probation sentence of one to two years are also possible (see nos 116 and 117).[1043] Finally, postponement of sentence enforcement subject to probation is an option, as is regular postponement of sentence enforcement and suspension of sentencing, possibly with probation measures as well, if the perpetrator does not have prior convictions which are too serious (see nos 118 and 119).

182. Possibly serious conduct with relatively low sentence – In 2016 the Council of State also warned that the proposed expansion of the *mens rea* (see no. 178) could cause a proportionality issue. It stated: '*Moreover, in view of the very diverse nature and degree of dangerousness of the acts potentially covered by the definition of the offence, it may be questioned whether the proposed change in the current wording is not at odds with the principle of the proportionality of sentences.*'[1044] Again, this criticism turned out to be relevant, even without the

---

1039 Delhaise (n 8) 78.

1040 J Rozie, 'De werking van verzachtende omstandigheden in strafzaken doorgelicht' (2013) 8 Nullum Crimen 1, 3–4 en 31; Rozie, 'De recidivewet van 5 mei 2019: de vergiftigde kers op de repressieve taart' (n 849) 295–296; Van Den Steen (n 883) 1615; Van den Wyngaert and Vandromme (n 790) 285.

1041 Art. 80, section 5 CC.

1042 Art. 37*ter*, §1, section 1 CC. See also: Daems and Magis (n 710) 181; Decaigny, 'Relatieve zwaarte, toepassingsgebied en duur' (n 714) 50; De Nauw and Deruyck (n 39) 127; Tulkens and others (n 39) 598; Van den Wyngaert, Vandromme and Traest (n 34) 430.

1043 Note that these minimum terms are an application of the basic rule on correctionalisation. Other rules might interfere in order to lower a sentence further and result in the possibility of community service of less than 45 hours (the absolute minimum being 20) or an autonomous probation sentence of less than one year (the absolute minimum being six months). This is the case, e.g., when grounds for remission of penalty are applied or the reasonable term has not been respected.

1044 Own translation, original in Dutch: '*Gelet op de zeer diverse aard en gevaarlijkheidsgraad van daden die mogelijk onder de delictsomschrijving vallen, kan bovendien de vraag worden*

proposed expansion of the *mens rea*. The abovementioned sentencing bracket of one month to five years imprisonment is relatively narrow for the very wide spectrum of activities that is prosecuted as participation in the activities of a terrorist group,[1045] from the man who sends some clothes to the man who is fighting in Syria and everything in between. For people who actual took up arms in Syria for example, five years imprisonment is a relatively light sentence. This issue is illustrated by a 2019 judgment of the Brussels Correctional Court.[1046] In this case five people were convicted for participating in the activities of a terrorist group. Four of them had travelled to Syria and fought for IS over there. They were convicted to five years imprisonment. The fifth suspect had not travelled to Syria himself, but carried out propaganda, helped organise the trip to Syria and provided moral support. Contrary to the other four suspects, the fifth suspect had a clean criminal record and for him the reasonable time period for prosecution had been exceeded. He was convicted to 30 months imprisonment. So, the sentence for a person without a criminal record for whom the reasonable time limit was exceeded and who had limited himself to providing moral and practical support from Belgium, was 30 months. The others received double this sentence, but they actually travelled to Syria and fought for a terrorist organisation, had a criminal record and the reasonable time limit was not exceeded for them.[1047] This relatively small difference in sentence for a very different situation shows that the maximum sentence of five years is probably too low. It is striking as well that in the Reguide analysis, the maximum sentence of five years imprisonment was imposed in 158 cases, which is almost 60%. The new Criminal Code should remedy this issue. Systematic correctionalisation should be a thing of the past under the new system. In the new Criminal Code participating in the activities of a terrorist group is a level four offence, meaning the sentence is five to ten years imprisonment.[1048]

183. Participating in activities group punished harsher than actual terrorist attack – The proportionality of the sentence in Article 140, §1 CC has been called into question for other reasons too. Participating in the activities of a terrorist group has a higher maximum sentence than some of the terrorist offences *sensu stricto*.[1049] It is therefore possible that the terrorist offence the

gesteld of de voorgenomen wijziging in de huidige formulering niet op gespannen voet staat met het beginsel van de evenredigheid van de straffen.' (Advies 59.789/3 van de Raad van State 19 juli 2016 bij wetsvoorstel 13 januari 2016 tot wijziging van het Strafwetboek wat betreft de bestraffing van terrorisme, *Parl.St.* Kamer 2015–2016, no. 54-1579/006, 6).

1045 See also: Brion and others (n 77) 64.

1046 Corr. Brussel 10 mei 2019, *NjW* 2019, 663, noot W. Yperman.

1047 See also: Ward Yperman, 'Breed concept van deelname met smalle strafschaal' [2019] Nieuw Juridisch Weekblad 673.

1048 Art. 376 wetsontwerp 24 juli 2023 tot invoering van Boek II van het Strafwetboek, *Parl.St.* Kamer 2022–2023, no. 55-3518/001, 1013–1014.

1049 A similar argument can be made regarding the *mens rea* of the participant: the participant knows or should have known they could contribute to a standard offence or felony. It is

terrorist group aims to commit has a lighter sentence than participating in the activities of that same terrorist group.[1050] According to the Secretary of Justice at the time, Laurette Onkelinx, this was not a problem, since this would only be the case for '*as good as risk-free terrorist acts*', and concurrence between offences is possible.[1051] There are two types of concurrence[1052]: ideal concurrence, which means that one act constitutes more than one offence and material concurrence, which means that a person has committed an offence before being convicted for another offence previously committed.[1053] Often these offences will then be tried simultaneously. With the words '*as good as risk-free*', she referred to offences such as intentional battery, potentially with premeditation[1054]; intentionally damaging part of a public telecommunications network, destroying it, or obstructing or preventing its proper functioning, when this offence endangers human lives or causes significant economic damage[1055]; and maliciously or fraudulently submerging someone else's yard, when this offence endangers human lives.[1056, 1057] All these acts can hardly be called risk-free, especially because for many

possible that the standard offence they know or should have known they could contribute to has a lower sentence than the one for participating in the activities of the group. See: Flore (n 10) 221.

1050 Advies 59.789/3 van de Raad van State 19 juli 2016 bij wetsvoorstel 13 januari 2016 tot wijziging van het Strafwetboek wat betreft de bestraffing van terrorisme, *Parl.St.* Kamer 2015–2016, no. 54–1579/006, 7–8; Delhaise (n 8) 77; Vanneste and Verbruggen (n 686) 84.

1051 Verslag namens de commissie voor de Justitie 7 november 2003 bij wetsontwerp van 6 oktober 2003 betreffende terroristische misdrijven, *Parl.St.* Kamer 2003, no. 51–0258/004, 22.

1052 A third option is that of a collective offence, in case the different offences are part of one single criminal project (see no. 225). In this scenario, only the harshest sentence is applied as well. According to Delhaise, in a terrorism context, there will often be collective offences. See: Delhaise (n 8) 85–86.

1053 Cass. 9 mei 1995, P.95.0266.N, *Arr.Cass.* 1995, 46; Decaigny, 'Relatieve zwaarte, toepassingsgebied en duur' (n 714) 114; De Nauw and Deruyck (n 39) 173; Tulkens and others (n 39) 631–640; Van den Wyngaert, Vandromme and Traest (n 34) 519.

1054 Art. 398 CC.

1055 Art. 114, §4 wet 21 maart 1991 betreffende de hervorming van sommige economische overheidsbedrijven, *BS* 27 maart 1991, 6155.

1056 Art. 549 CC.

1057 Other offences that fall within this category are: destroying or damaging graves, monuments, etc. when this offence endangers human lives or causes substantial economic loss (Art. 526 CC); intentionally destroying, rendering unusable or abandoning ship's equipment when this offence endangers human lives or causes substantial economic loss (Art. 15 wet 5 juni 1928 houdende herziening van het Tucht- en Strafwetboek voor de koopvaardij en de zeevisserij); lending out firearms without due respect for the conditions for doing so (except for arms dealers e.g.) (Art. 12/1 *j.* 23, section 4 wet 8 juni 2006 houdende regeling van economische en individuele activiteiten met wapens, *BS* 9 juni 2006, 29840); failure to comply with safety requirements to which the storage, transport, possession and collection of fire arms, ammunition and magazines are subject (except for arms dealers e.g.) (Art. 35, 1° *j.* 23, section 4 wet 8 juni 2006 houdende regeling van economische en individuele activiteiten met wapens, *BS* 9 juni 2006, 29840); developing, producing, stockpiling, acquiring, possessing or transferring of weapons, equipment or the means for proliferation specially designed to use agents or toxins for hostile purposes or in an armed conflict (Art. 2, 2° wet houdende goedkeuring van het Verdrag tot verbod van de ontwikkeling, de productie en de aanleg van

of them the Code itself states that they have to endanger human lives. Hence, the justification of the Secretary on this point makes no sense. The argument about concurrence makes a bit more sense. The Secretary stated that individual actions are less dangerous than actions executed by a group.[1058] Thus, a person who individually commits one of the 'lighter' terrorist offences, only risks the lower sentence for that offence. For a person who commits this offence as part of a terrorist group, there will be ideal concurrence between the terrorist offence *sensu stricto* and participation in the activities of the terrorist group. In case of ideal concurrence, only the sentence for the more severe offence is applicable,[1059] *in casu* the participation in the activities of the terrorist group. Although this line of reasoning is better than that of the risk-free terrorism, it is still only mildly convincing. An action of a group is not per definition more dangerous than an action of an individual[1060] and it is strange the sentence for the exact same set of actions is higher if those actions were committed by a group than by an individual. Furthermore, the group has not necessarily committed a terrorist offence yet (see no. 166) so simply planning the offence as a group would carry a higher maximum sentence than actually committing the offence as an individual.

184. Directive requirement – Article 15.3 of the EU Directive requires that participation in the activities of a terrorist group is punishable with a maximum sentence of not less than eight years.[1061] The Belgian Criminal Code meets this requirement with a maximum sentence of ten years felony imprisonment.[1062] However, as explained above, correctionalisation is standard practice in these cases. In concrete cases, the maximum sentence will therefore usually be five years imprisonment. When practically applied, the Belgian offence thus falls three years short. Again, this issue should be resolved in the new Criminal Code (see no. 181).

---

voorraden van bacteriologische (biologische) en toxinewapens en inzake de vernietiging van deze wapens, opgemaakt te Londen, Moskou en Washington op 10 april 1972).

1058 Verslag namens de commissie voor de Justitie 7 november 2003 bij wetsontwerp van 6 oktober 2003 betreffende terroristische misdrijven, *Parl.St.* Kamer 2003, no. 51–0258/004, 22. Delhaise is also of this opinion: Delhaise (n 8) 77.

1059 Art. 65, section 1 CC. See also: De Nauw and Deruyck (n 39) 175; Tulkens and others (n 39) 634; Van den Wyngaert, Vandromme and Traest (n 34) 522.

1060 The Council of State asked that same question with regard to Art. 140*septies* CC, pointing out that a terrorist offence committed by a person acting alone is not necessarily less serious than an offence committed by a group. See: Advies 59.789/3 van de Raad van State 19 juli 2016 bij wetsvoorstel 13 januari 2016 tot wijziging van het Strafwetboek wat betreft de bestraffing van terrorisme, *Parl.St.* Kamer 2015–2016, no. 54–1579/006, 16; Advies 59.147/3 van de Raad van State (II) 22 april 2016 bij wetsontwerp houdende diverse bepalingen ter bestrijding van terrorisme (III), *Parl.St.* Kamer 2015–2016, no. 54–1951/001, 31.

1061 This was also part of the original Framework Decision. See: Art. 5.3 Council Framework Decision 2002/475/JHA of 13 June 2002 on combating terrorism [2002] *OJ* L164/5.

1062 De La Serna (n 8) 204.

SECTION III. PARTICIPATING IN THE TAKING OF ANY DECISION REGARDING THE ACTIVITIES OF A TERRORIST GROUP (§1/1)

SUBSECTION I. *ACTUS REUS*

185. Between participation and leadership – With the statute of 5 May 2019, the legislature added a new paragraph to Article 140 CC. This paragraph was placed in between §1 and §2 and its sentence also neatly fits in between the sentences for those offences.[1063] The legislature even explicitly stated that it wanted to create an intermediate sentencing level.[1064] This was an attempt to solve the issue of the relatively low maximum sentence of Article 140, §1 CC while it can cover serious terrorist activities. Article 140, §1/1 punishes the participation in the taking of any decision in the context of the activities of the terrorist group with a principal sentence of ten to 15 years felony imprisonment.[1065] As a result of this new offence, judges have more options when it comes to sentencing. Once more, the legislature was inspired by the pre-existing offences concerning the criminal organisation.[1066]

186. Too wide – We have to ask ourselves whether this new category targets the right people. In the context of the offence of participating in the making of any decision in the framework of the activities of a criminal organisation, Verbruggen states that 'taking any decision' is not a suitable *actus reus* for an offence.[1067] The same criticism can be levelled against Article 140, §1/1 CC. We make a plethora of decisions every single day, making this criterion void. Deciding what to drink during a meeting, whether or not to open the window, where to sit, etc. Those are all decisions, which will lead a person to commit this offence when they are made in the context of the activities of a terrorist group. Since making a decision is almost inevitable, anyone who came within the ambit of the offence of participating in the activities of the group, will now come within the ambit of this new offence. As we have seen, this is a very broad category of people. The man who sent clothes to his brother the terrorist fighter decided

1063 Cesoni (n 15) 239; De Coensel, 'De Wet Diverse Bepalingen in Strafzaken II: Terroristische misdrijven in lijn met de Europese verplichtingen?' (n 793) 214; Winants (n 8) 357.

1064 Wetsvoorstel 6 februari 2019 houdende diverse bepalingen in strafzaken en inzake erediensten, *Parl.St.* Kamer 2018–2019, no. 54-3515/001, 102–103.

1065 Art. 75 wet 5 mei 2019 houdende diverse bepalingen in strafzaken en inzake erediensten, en tot wijziging van de wet 28 mei 2002 betreffende de euthanasie en van het Sociaal Strafwetboek, *BS* 24 mei 2019, 50023.

1066 Art. 324*ter*, §3 CC; Wetsvoorstel 6 februari 2019 houdende diverse bepalingen in strafzaken en inzake erediensten, *Parl.St.* Kamer 2018–2019, no. 54-3515/001, 102–103; De Coensel, 'De Wet Diverse Bepalingen in Strafzaken II: Terroristische misdrijven in lijn met de Europese verplichtingen?' (n 793) 214; Winants (n 8) 357.

1067 Verbruggen (n 34) 347–348.

to send those clothes, the woman who married the terrorist fighter decided to marry him, etc. Furthermore, not only making decisions is punishable, but also participating in the making of a decision. This means that a member of the group who voted against committing a terrorist attack, participated in the making of this decision and would therefore be liable for the higher sentence. Even an outsider, non-member, who tries to convince his friend who is a member of a group not to do something stupid, is participating in the making of this decision. Therefore, it is clear the offence is too broad. While the legislature attempted to create an offence which targets members of terrorist organisations higher up the ladder, it created one with an *actus reus* which is almost as broad as the offence of participating in the activities of the group. This offence with its exceedingly broad *actus reus*, which is not part of the Directive, runs afoul of the legality principle and the legislature would do well to delete it again. The federal prosecution service has stated in the media that in future situations of foreign terrorist fighters, they will prosecute for the offence of Article 140, §1/1 CC.[1068] Statements such as these clearly show this offence fails to target people higher up the ladder of the group.

SUBSECTION II. *MENS REA*

187. Same as §1 – The *mens rea* of Article 140, §1/1 CC is the exact same as the one in §1. The same questions can therefore be asked (see nos 176–179).

SUBSECTION III. SENTENCES

188. Possible sentences – The legislation provides for a sentence of felony imprisonment of ten to 15 years and a fine. After correctionalisation ten to 15 years felony imprisonment becomes six months to ten years imprisonment.[1069] This means electronic monitoring as a principal sentence is possible, when the judge feels the offence is of such a nature that it should not be punished with more than one year imprisonment (see no. 115).[1070] The electronic monitoring

---

1068 G.V.V., 'België gaat terroristen dubbel zo zwaar proberen te straffen: dit zijn de plannen' (*De Morgen* 16 November 2021) www.demorgen.be/nieuws/belgie-gaat-terroristen-dubbel-zo-zwaar-proberen-te-straffen-dit-zijn-de-plannen~b4c41f42/; Guy Van Vlierden, 'België gaat terroristen dubbel zo zwaar proberen te straffen: van 5 naar 10 jaar voor 'welke beslissing dan ook'' (*Het Laatste Nieuws* 16 November 2021) www.hln.be/binnenland/belgie-gaat-terroristen-dubbel-zo-zwaar-proberen-te-straffen-van-5-naar-10-jaar-voor-welke-beslissing-dan-ook~a4c41f42/.

1069 Art. 80 CC.

1070 Art. 37*ter*, §1, section 1 CC. See also: Daems and Magis (n 710) 181; Decaigny, 'Relatieve zwaarte, toepassingsgebied en duur' (n 714) 50; De Nauw and Deruyck (n 39) 127; Tulkens and others (n 39) 598; Van den Wyngaert, Vandromme and Traest (n 34) 430.

has a term of six months to one year. Community service, with a term of 45 to 300 hours, and an autonomous probation sentence of one to two years are also possible (see nos 116 and 117). Finally, postponement of sentence enforcement subject to probation is an option, as is regular postponement of sentence enforcement and suspension of sentencing, possibly with probation measures as well, if the perpetrator does not have prior convictions which are too serious (see nos 118 and 119).

189. Fines as a principal sentence – The legislature overlooked one thing when creating this new offence. The sentences for Article 140, §1 and §2 are respectively '*felony imprisonment of five years to ten years and a fine of one hundred to five thousand euros*' and '*felony imprisonment of fifteen years to twenty years and a fine of one thousand euros to two hundred thousand euros.*'[1071] The sentence in Article 140, §1/1 CC, however, is drafted as follows: '*felony imprisonment for ten years to fifteen years and a fine of one thousand to two hundred thousand euros, or one of those sentences by itself.*'[1072] Because of the last part of this phrase, it is possible to punish the taking of any decision in the context of the activities of a terrorist group with a fine as a principal sentence, while this is not the case for participating in the activities of the group.[1073] Since the latter offence is supposed to be the lighter offence, this was not the intention of the legislature.[1074] As a consequence, a bill was proposed on 23 January 2020 to remedy this by deleting '*or one of those sentences by itself*' from Article 140, §1/1 CC.[1075]

190. Proportionality issue resolved? – While the legislature did create an extra sentencing option for judges, the question remains whether it is not disproportionate to convict somebody who sends clothing to a family member for participating in the activities of a terrorist group. Maybe it would have been better (perhaps in addition to the creation of a new category) to limit the lowest category. People who perform minimal and sporadic 'acts of participation' and who often do this for reasons entirely alien to the terrorist intentions of the group, should not be prosecuted. Even if they themselves are showing signs of

---

1071 Own translation, original in Dutch: '*opsluiting van vijf jaar tot tien jaar en met geldboete van honderd euro tot vijfduizend euro*' (Art. 140, §1 CC) and '*opsluiting van vijftien jaar tot twintig jaar en met geldboete van duizend euro tot tweehonderdduizend euro*' (Art. 140, §2 CC).

1072 Own translation, original in Dutch: '*opsluiting van tien jaar tot vijftien jaar en met een geldboete van duizend euro tot tweehonderdduizend euro of met een van die straffen alleen*' (Art. 140, §1/1 CC).

1073 Barring any exceeding of a reasonable time period, which allows for a decrease of the sentence below the legal minimum.

1074 Wetsvoorstel 23 januari 2020 tot wijziging van het Strafwetboek wat de strafmaat voor misdrijven door terroristische groepen betreft, *Parl.St.* Kamer 2019–20, no. 55–0962/001, 3.

1075 Wetsvoorstel 23 januari 2020 tot wijziging van het Strafwetboek wat de strafmaat voor misdrijven door terroristische groepen betreft, *Parl.St.* Kamer 2019–20, no. 55–0962/001.

radicalisation, which is not necessarily the case, both they and our society would benefit more from an intelligent deradicalisation policy than from criminal penalties.

SECTION IV. LEADERSHIP OF A TERRORIST GROUP

SUBSECTION I. *ACTUS REUS*

191. Leadership – The second paragraph of Article 140 CC criminalises leadership of a terrorist group. While the Directive imposes on Member States the obligation to criminalise directing a terrorist group, the definition of leadership and directing is ambiguous. The preparatory works define leaders as '*the people who take upon themselves the more important responsibilities within the group.*'[1076] On top of that, they are '*because of their central role within the terrorist group, better informed than anyone about the offences and take the final decisions.*'[1077] The Council of State thought that the legislature should clarify the Article so that it reflected this intention more clearly.[1078] Despite this advice, the legislature decided not the change the Article. With the introduction of the offence in §1/1, the question now also arises as to what the difference is between a final decision (taken by a leader) and any other decision. The offence of leadership does not require that the person themselves had the intention of committing a terrorist offence or that they were involved in committing it.[1079] Nor does it require that the person is the one, absolute leader of the entire group.[1080] Having a central role, being able to speak for the group, coordinating actions, raising funds, etc. suffices.[1081] The size and importance of the group are irrelevant as well, as long as it is a terrorist group.[1082]

1076 Own translation, original in Dutch: '*de personen die binnen de groep de belangrijkste verantwoordelijkheden op zich nemen*' (MvT wetsontwerp 6 oktober 2003 betreffende terroristische misdrijven, *Parl.St.* Kamer 2003, no. 51–0258/001, (4) 14). See also: Ketels (n 691) 244.

1077 Own translation, original in Dutch: '*zij wegens hun centrale rol in de terroristische groep beter dan wie ook op de hoogte van de misdrijven en nemen ze de eindbeslissingen*' (MvT wetsontwerp 6 oktober 2003 betreffende terroristische misdrijven, *Parl.St.* Kamer 2003, no. 51–0258/001, (4) 14). See also: De Hert and Millen (n 803) 6; De La Serna (n 50) 215; Fransen and Kerkhofs (n 10) 35–36; Weyembergh and Kennes (n 14) 112; Winants (n 8) 348.

1078 Advies 34.362/4 van de Raad van State bij wetsontwerp van 6 oktober 2003 betreffende terroristische misdrijven, *Parl.St.* Kamer 2003, no. 51–0258/001, (22) 40–41.

1079 Cass. 24 juni 2008, P.08.0408.N, *Arr.Cass.* 2008, 1654, *T.Strafr.* 2009, 20; De Hert and Millen (n 803) 6; De La Serna (n 8) 188; De La Serna (n 50) 215–216; Delhaise (n 8) 44; De Nauw (n 786) 8; De Nauw and Kuty (n 786) 18; Deruyck and De Nauw (n 786) 9; Ketels (n 691) 244–245.

1080 Ketels (n 691) 244.

1081 De La Serna (n 8) 187–188; De La Serna (n 50) 215; Delhaise (n 8) 41; Fransen and Kerkhofs (n 10) 37; Winants (n 8) 348.

1082 Winants (n 8) 348.

192. (Too) broad interpretation – In practice, the jurisprudence interprets 'leadership' quite broadly. For the Court of Appeal in Antwerp for example, close involvement in several meetings and not excluding that one would commit an attack themself, was enough to be a leader.[1083] The fact that two other people were designated as respectively leader of the cell and spiritual leader, did not change this. The Court of Appeal in Brussels, in turn, convicted a person for leadership who provided material support to terrorist fighters in Syria (who were departing or already on-site); who was an intermediary and facilitated communication between jihadists, jihadist candidates and their families; and who was an advisor when it came to indoctrination and exfiltration to Syria.[1084] In our opinion, these actions make them active members of the group, but not necessarily leaders as well. The ambiguity of this definition is also evidenced by the Court of Appeal's jurisprudence which frequently overturns convictions for participation and converts them into leadership and *vice versa*.[1085] All of this is caused by the lack of definition of leadership in Article 140, §2 CC. The legislature should have probably thought twice before ignoring the advice of the Council of State. A possible (partial) explanation for the stretching of the definition of leadership is that for some people the maximum sentence of five years imprisonment for participation was seen as too low (see also no. 182). The introduction of the new intermediate category of Article 140, §1/1 CC might resolve this issue.

SUBSECTION II. *MENS REA*

193. Not explicit – Article 140, §2 CC contains no explicit *mens rea*. However, this does not mean there is no *mens rea*. Under Belgian criminal law, offences always require both *actus reus* and *mens rea*.[1086] There are two possible solutions. The general rule is that if a felony does not explicitly mention the *mens rea*, then a general intent is required.[1087] A second option would be to require the same

---

1083 Antwerpen 8 januari 2014, *onuitg.*, 42.

1084 Brussel 2 juni 2017, *onuitg.*, 26–30.

1085 Brussel 19 januari 2007, *T.Strafr.* 2008, 281; Antwerpen 8 januari 2014, *onuitg;* Brussel 18 november 2016, *onuitg;* Brussel 31 maart 2017, *onuitg.*

1086 Cass. 12 mei 1987, *Arr.Cass.* 1986–87, 1194, concl. Du Jardin; Cass. 13 december 1994, *RW* 1995–96, 533, noot B. Spriet; De Nil, Deruyck and Meese (n 672) 269; Spriet, 'Elk misdrijf- ook dat uit het bijzonder strafrecht – vereist een moreel of schuldbestanddeel (noot onder Cass. 13 december 1994)' (n 677); Tulkens and others (n 39) 474–475; Van den Wyngaert, Vandromme and Traest (n 34) 192; Winants (n 8) 359. In special criminal statues, it is possible, however, that indications of the existence of the *mens rea* are derived from the proven existence of the *actus reus*. See: Cass. 24 februari 2014, S.13.0031.N; Cass. 8 april 2008, P.08.0006.N; Cass. 12 mei 1987, *Arr.Cass.* 1986–87, 1194, concl. Du Jardin; Spriet, 'Elk misdrijf- ook dat uit het bijzonder strafrecht – vereist een moreel of schuldbestanddeel (noot onder Cass. 13 december 1994)' (n 677) 536–537.

1087 Hans Van Bavel, 'De strafrechtelijke aansprakelijkheid van vennootschappen en leidinggevenden: de lege lata, de lege ferenda' [2017] Tijdschrift voor Strafrecht 3, 8. This is

mens rea as the other two paragraphs of the same Article, being '*while he knew or should have known that his participation could contribute to the perpetration of a felony or standard offence by the terrorist group.*' As explained above (see no. 177), this is also a general intent. Therefore, we can say a general intent is required. In the literature this is not stressed very often, probably because this intent will never cause any issues. It is hard to see how one could be a leader of a group out of negligence. Leadership always implies a certain knowledge and will.

SUBSECTION III. SENTENCES

194. Harsher sentence – The sentence for leadership is another step up the ladder compared to the previous paragraph: 15 to 20 years felony imprisonment and a fine of 1,000 to 200,000 euros.[1088] This is more than what is required by the EU Directive, which states that Member States should ensure a maximum sentence of not less than 15 years.[1089] Even after correctionalisation, the maximum sentence under Belgian law is 15 years imprisonment. The minimum sentence after correctionalisation is one year imprisonment. This means that electronic monitoring as a principal sentence is possible when the judge feels the offence is of such a nature that it should not be punished with more than this minimum sentence (see no. 115).[1090] Instead of one year imprisonment, they could then also impose one year electronic monitoring.[1091] Community service, with a term of 45 to 300 hours, and an autonomous probation sentence of one to two years are also possible (see nos 116 and 117). Finally, postponement of sentence enforcement subject to probation is an option, as is regular postponement of sentence enforcement and suspension of sentencing, possibly with probation measures as well, if the perpetrator does not have prior convictions which are too serious (see nos 118 and 119).

---

also the case for the comparable offence in the context of criminal organisations. See: Frederic Vroman, 'Criminele Organisaties' (2014) C80 Postal Memorialis – Lexicon strafrecht, strafvordering en bijzondere wetten 46, 28.

1088 Art. 140, §2 CC.

1089 Art. 15(3) Directive (EU) 2017/541 of the European Parliament and of the Council of 15 March 2017 on combating terrorism and replacing Council Framework Decision 2002/475/JHA and amending Council Decision 2005/671/JHA [2017] *OJ* L88/6. This was also part of the original Framework Decision. See: Art. 5.3 Council Framework Decision 2002/475/JHA of 13 June 2002 on combating terrorism [2002] *OJ* L164/5. See also: De La Serna (n 8) 204.

1090 Art. 37*ter*, §1, section 1 CC. See also: Daems and Magis (n 710) 181; Decaigny, 'Relatieve zwaarte, toepassingsgebied en duur' (n 714) 50; De Nauw and Deruyck (n 39) 127; Tulkens and others (n 39) 598; Van den Wyngaert, Vandromme and Traest (n 34) 430.

1091 Art. 37*ter*, §1, section 1 CC. See also: Daems and Magis (n 710) 181; Decaigny, 'Relatieve zwaarte, toepassingsgebied en duur' (n 714) 50; De Nauw and Deruyck (n 39) 127; Tulkens and others (n 39) 598; Van den Wyngaert, Vandromme and Traest (n 34) 430.

SECTION V. PRACTICAL APPLICATION

195. Case law analysis – As mentioned above, in practice, the variety of existing terrorist offences is not reflected in prosecutions. Of the 343 individual first instance judgments part of the case law analysis, only six did not include prosecution for one of the offences in Article 140 CC.[1092] These six concerned a case in which six people were prosecuted for terrorism *sensu stricto* and one person for terrorism *sensu stricto* and participation in the activities of a terrorist group. The former six people were all acquitted and the latter was convicted on both counts (see no. 162, footnote 927). This means that not a single case was brought under Articles 140*bis* to 141 CC which was not also prosecuted under Article 140 CC. In total 266 people were prosecuted for the offence in Article 140, §1 CC, ten for the attempt to this offence and 65 for leadership. The numbers of the case law analysis clearly show that because of the broadness of the offences relating to terrorist groups, the other terrorist offences *sensu lato* have very limited added value. They were only invoked a total of 19 times (or roughly 5,5% of cases) and never without being in conjunction with Article 140 CC. The Affect analysis painted a similar picture, with 86% of cases analysed being prosecuted under Article 140 CC and only 2,3% under other terrorist offences (the analysis also included 8,3% of cases prosecuted exclusively for non-terrorist offences).[1093]

196. GICM – A first noteworthy case is that of the GICM, a terrorist group aimed at overthrowing the regime in Morocco. Ten of its members were convicted for participating in the activities or leadership of a terrorist group.[1094] This case clearly illustrates that terrorist groups in Belgium do not necessarily have to be aimed at overthrowing the Belgian government.

197. Iraqi network – The so-called 'Iraqi network' was a terrorist group operating out of Belgium. For its leader, the following actions were considered acts of leadership: having international contacts to facilitate the activities of the group, coordinating the activities of the group and organising how members can infiltrate in or exfiltrate from the war zone. People who financed the activities of the group, forged documents, helped exfiltrate a wounded person from Syria, etc. were convicted for participating in the activities of the group.[1095] Another man was not found guilty of participating in the activities of a terrorist group.

1092 Being Art. 140, §1 and/or §2 CC, since §1/1 did not exist yet.

1093 Brion and others (n 77) 61.

1094 Corr. Brussel 16 februari 2006, *onuitg*; Brussel 19 januari 2007, 33–37 and 63–67, *T.Strafr.* 2008, 281, noot F. Schuermans, struck down by Cass. 11 december 2013 (P.13.1150.F-P.13.1153.F) for three defendants after a conviction by the ECtHR on 25 September 2012. See also: De La Serna (n 8) 198–199; Fransen and Kerkhofs (n 10) 39; Weyembergh and Kennes (n 58) 159–160; Weyembergh and Kennes (n 14) 112–114.

1095 Brussel 26 juni 2008, *onuitg*; Fransen and Kerkhofs (n 10) 39.

He had rendered services for a friend who had left for Iraq. The former had emptied the latter's apartment, stockpiling part and selling another part of the household effects. The court found that it could not be excluded the man acted out of friendship and not with the aim of supporting the terrorist group and therefore he was acquitted.[1096]

198. DHKP-C – The DHKP-C is a Turkish communist organisation. Two members of the group were tried under Article 140 CC for their involvement in the DHKP-C, for example, by translating and disseminating a communiqué containing apologies for civilian victims in a so-called failed retaliation against Turkey. First they were convicted by the Court of Appeal of Ghent.[1097] Subsequently, this conviction was annulled by the Court of Cassation for violating the right to a fair trial.[1098] The Court of Appeal of Antwerp, to which the case was referred, then acquitted them because it found insufficient evidence that they were part of a terrorist group.[1099] The Court ruled that it was not proven that the defendants intended to unite for the purpose of committing terrorist offences. The Court thought it clear that they do not disapprove of such things but '*the Court should not judge the thinking of the defendants*.'[1100] However, this judgment was again annulled by the Court of Cassation.[1101] The Court of Cassation struck it down on several grounds, one of which concerned terrorism. The highest Court pointed out that to convict somebody for leadership of a terrorist group, it is not required that the defendant themself had the intention to commit a terrorist offence *sensu stricto*. In focussing on what the defendants intended to do, the Court of Appeal of Antwerp seemed to have insufficiently motivated its decision. The Court of Cassation referred the case to the Court of Appeal of Brussels, which acquitted the defendants for leadership or participating in the activities of a terrorist organisation. According to the Court, their actions did not contribute to the perpetration of an offence by a terrorist group and furthermore the information provided was covered by the right to free speech.[1102]

199. Afghan network – The 'Afghan network' refers to a group of people who wanted to join Al Qaida. They held regular meetings, had calls, etc. and wanted to send jihadists to Pakistan or Afghanistan to be trained there. The Court stated

---

1096 Brussel 26 juni 2008, 77–78, *onuitg*; De La Serna (n 8) 190; Fransen and Kerkhofs (n 10) 39; Weyembergh and Kennes (n 58) 163; Weyembergh and Kennes (n 14) 118.

1097 Gent 7 november 2006, 125–127, *juristenkrant* 2007, afl. 148, 4.

1098 Cass. 19 april 2007, *T.Strafr.* 2007, 376, noot P. De Hert en J. Millen.

1099 Antwerpen 7 februari 2008, *onuitg.*, 149–159.

1100 Antwerpen 7 februari 2008, *onuitg.*, 159.

1101 Cass. 24 juni 2008, P.08.0408.N, *Arr.Cass.* 2008, 1654, *T.Strafr.* 2009, 20.

1102 Brussel 23 december 2009, *onuitg.*, 31–32. For a description of the case, see as well: De La Serna (n 8) 199–201; Fransen and Kerkhofs (n 10) 39–41; Marchand (n 617) 282–284; Weyembergh and Kennes (n 58) 160–162; Weyembergh and Kennes (n 14) 114–117.

that Al Qaida was a terrorist group, but also contained within itself many other terrorist groups, such as this one. A woman was convicted as a leader of the group because she, among other things, recruited people, created and managed the website and was in charge of the goal and direction of the organisation.[1103] It was in this context that another man was convicted for sending a parcel containing two pairs of shoes, T-shirts and shoelaces to his brother who was in Afghanistan (see no. 171).[1104]

200. Blood and Honour Flanders – In a high-profile case of right-wing terrorism, several people were convicted for participating in the activities of a terrorist group or leadership of such a group. Blood and Honour Flanders was a far-right group that wanted to destabilise the national order and, among other things, provided paramilitary training for its members. People were convicted for leadership of the group because they had written a manifesto and journal, recruited and trained members, had recorded a propaganda video, procured, and stockpiled material, organised concerts and meetings to finance the group, etc. Acts of membership were the participation in close combat training, shooting drills and survival training, and being present at meetings. Furthermore, the Correctional Court stated that the defendants had the required *mens rea*.[1105] For some of them, however, the Court of Appeal disagreed. The Court stated that although they knew the organisation was extreme-right or even fascist and committed offences, there was no proof that all of them knew that the group was a terrorist group.[1106]

201. Sharia4Belgium – In the abovementioned Sharia4Belgium case, 37 people were convicted for participating in the activities of a terrorist group and another seven for leadership of the group. Sharia4Belgium in itself was considered a terrorist group. It was well organised and wanted to violently overthrow the existing political regime to install a Caliphate or totalitarian Islamic state based on sharia law.[1107] Accepted as acts of participation were, among other things, following mental and physical training, participating in violent actions in Belgium and combat in Syria.

1103 Brussel 1 december 2010, *onuitg.*, 21–34; Corr. Brussel 10 mei 2010, *onuitg.*, 37–43; De La Serna (n 8) 192; Fransen and Kerkhofs (n 10) 41–42; Weyembergh and Kennes (n 58) 164; Weyembergh and Kennes (n 14) 118–119.

1104 Corr. Brussel 14 mei 2014, *onuitg;* Fransen and Kerkhofs (n 10) 42.

1105 Corr. Dendermonde 7 februari 2014, *onuitg.*

1106 Gent 4 november 2014, *onuitg.*, 92–93, Fransen and Kerkhofs (n 10) 42–43.

1107 Antwerpen 27 januari 2016, *onuitg.*, 47; Antwerpen 8 december 2016, *onuitg.*, 36; Corr. Antwerpen (afd. Antwerpen) 11 februari 2015, *NjW* 2015, 280, noot E. Vandebroek. For a description of the case, see as well: Fransen and Kerkhofs (n 10) 44–46; Wittendorp and Bakker (n 686) 36.

202. ISIS, JABHAT AL NUSRA, ETC. – The courts have stated on several occasions that groups such as ISIS, Jabhat Al Nusra, Katiba Al Khattab and Majlis Shura Al Mujahidin were terrorist groups.[1108] Noteworthy is that in one of these cases, the Court of Appeal of Brussels decided that financially supporting the family of combatants in Syria, arrested jihadists or their families, was not in itself participation in the activities of a terrorist group, because those people themselves do not participate in the activities of a terrorist group (anymore).[1109] In another case the following actions were seen as participation in the activities of a terrorist group, *i.a.*: helping people leave for Syria by giving them coordinates of smugglers, giving advice on the best route to follow, doing certain purchases for them, driving them to the airport, booking plane tickets, as well as following religious sessions or military training in Syria or financially supporting terrorist fighters or spreading propaganda.[1110] In that same case, acts of leadership included repeatedly putting potential jihadists in contact with fighters who are already in Syria to exchange information, helping potential jihadists by accompanying them to purchase material, saving money, transporting them to the airport, being a go-between for fighters in Syria and their families, creating a Facebook profile to allow them to communicate, managing the bank account of a fighter, etc.[1111] The Court hereby stated that because of the frequency of the actions, it was no matter of simply helping a friend, regardless of existing friendships.[1112] In the same case, the Court of Appeal convicted a person who was acquitted in first instance for participation because he transported a potential jihadist to the airport, knowing that person wanted to join a terrorist group.[1113] An extra passenger in the car was acquitted because he did not execute an action himself.

1108 Luik 30 juni 2016, *onuitg;* Brussel 18 november 2016, *onuitg.*, 15–23; Antwerpen 22 december 2016, *onuitg;* Luik 30 maart 2017, *onuitg;* Brussel 2 juni 2017, *onuitg;* Antwerpen 13 december 2017, *onuitg.*, 28–29; Corr. Antwerpen 20 maart 2015, *onuitg;* Corr. Brussel 29 juli 2015, *onuitg;* Corr. Brussel 6 november 2015, *onuitg;* Corr. Antwerpen 7 december 2015, *onuitg;* Corr. Brussel 27 januari 2016, *onuitg;* Corr. Brussel 29 januari 2016, *onuitg.*, 42–66; Corr. Brussel 3 maart 2016, *onuitg;* Corr. Brussel 3 mei 2016, *onuitg.*, 33–34; Bergen 29 juni 2016, *onuitg;* Corr. Brussel 15 december 2016, *onuitg;* Corr. Luik (afd. Luik) 20 januari 2017, *onuitg;* Corr. Brussel 9 maart 2017, *onuitg;* Corr. Antwerpen (afd. Antwerpen) 13 maart 2017, *onuitg;* Corr. Brussel 8 mei 2017, *onuitg;* Corr. Brussel 31 mei 2017, *onuitg;* Bergen 20 juni 2017, *onuitg;* Corr. Luik (vakantiekamer) 19 juli 2017, *JLMB* 2017, 1391; Corr. West-Vlaanderen (afd. Brugge) 19 juli 2017, *onuitg;* Corr. Antwerpen (afd. Mechelen) 7 september 2017, *onuitg;* Corr. Brussel 27 oktober 2017, *onuitg;* Corr. Antwerpen (afd. Mechelen) 4 januari 2018, *onuitg;* Corr. Luik 16 februari 2018, *onuitg;* Corr. Antwerpen (afd. Antwerpen) 19 februari 2018, *onuitg;* Corr. Brussel 1 maart 2018, *onuitg;* Corr. Antwerpen (afd. Antwerpen) 19 maart 2018, *onuitg;* Corr. Antwerpen (afd. Antwerpen) 16 april 2018, *onuitg.* See also: Fransen and Kerkhofs (n 10) 46–49.

1109 Brussel 18 november 2016, *onuitg.*, 18.

1110 Corr. Brussel 3 mei 2016, *onuitg.*, 38, 51, 52, 58, 61, 75 and 84. See also: Fransen and Kerkhofs (n 10) 47.

1111 Brussel 2 juni 2017, *onuitg.*, 24–30 and 50–55.

1112 Corr. Brussel 3 mei 2016, *onuitg.*, 93–101 and 199–207.

1113 Brussel 2 juni 2017, *onuitg.*, 48 and 50.

203. Verviers cell – In the case of the terrorist cell in Verviers (see no. 161), 12 members were convicted for participation in the activities of a terrorist group, being the cell itself. The three people convicted for attempted terrorism *sensu stricto*, were also convicted for leadership in first instance. One of them appealed and his conviction was overturned, after which he was convicted for participation in the activities instead. According to the Court of Appeal, there was insufficient proof of his central role and authority over the other members.[1114]

204. Department 312 of MOIS – In the case involving the Iranian diplomat (see no. 161), the Court held that within a department of the Iranian intelligence service, there was a group which it considered to be a terrorist group.[1115] While the Court did not hold that the Iranian intelligence service itself was a terrorist group, it is noteworthy that it did say that a number of Iranian intelligence officers banded together to form a terrorist group.

205. Doomsday preppers – Finally, in a recent case of 'doomsday preppers', several people had formed a group in which they prepared for the end of civilisation, which included amassing a large amount of firearms.[1116] In addition, they had a deep distrust for the government and wanted to take up arms against it, although they had not made any concrete plans for an attack yet. When the police arrested them, the leader of the group started a firefight which ended in his death. Three other members of the group were prosecuted for participation in the activities of a terrorist group and two of them were convicted for this offence.

206. Sentences – As discussed above, the maximum sentence after correctionalisation for Article 140, §1 CC is quite low. This means that the sentences in the vast majority of cases are relatively close together. This was also clear from the Reguide case law analysis. The maximum sentence (barring recidivism) of five years imprisonment was imposed in 158 cases, which is almost 60% (see no. 181). In a few cases of recidivism, the sentence was as high as ten years, being the maximum in cases of recidivism. Sentences for Article 140, §2 CC are often, although not always, higher, with several sentences of 15 years

---

1114 Brussel 31 maart 2017, *onuitg.*, 37. See also: Fransen and Kerkhofs (n 10) 49.

1115 Corr. Antwerpen 4 februari 2021, *onuitg.*, 45.

1116 Joren Wollants, 'Zaak tegen "preppers", vrienden van doodgeschoten Yannick, wordt in november behandeld' (*Het Laatste Nieuws* 26 September 2023) www.hln.be/antwerpen/zaak-tegen-preppers-vrienden-van-doodgeschoten-yannick-wordt-in-november-behandeld~a88106cc/; Mark Eeckhaut, '"Preppers" met arsenaal van honderden wapens staan terecht voor plannen terreuraanslag: "Uit de hand gelopen hobby"' (*De Standaard* 15 November 2023) www.standaard.be/cnt/dmf20231114_97724612; Hanne Decré, 'Celstraffen tot 5 jaar (deels met uitstel) voor "doomsday preppers" die zich voorbereidden op einde van de wereld met voedsel, geld en veel wapens' (*vrtNWS* 12 December 2023) www.vrt.be/vrtnws/nl/2023/12/12/uitspraak-doomsday-preppers-antwerpen/.

imprisonment being its maximum. Sentences for attempted participation ranged from three years to five years imprisonment. As the maximum sentence is most often imposed for Article 140, §1 CC, it is no surprise that it was usually imposed when this offence was combined with another offence *sensu lato*.[1117]

[1117] This was not so in only three out of 19 cases.

CHAPTER IV
ARTICLE 140*BIS* CC

SECTION I. *ACTUS REUS*

207. Introduction 2013 – Article 140*bis* CC was introduced in 2013, in response to the Council of Europe Convention on the Prevention of Terrorism[1118] and the Council Framework Decision 2008/919/JHA.[1119, 1120] At the moment of its introduction, the *actus reus* of the offence was the following: disseminating or otherwise making available to the public a message when such conduct, whether or not directly aimed at the commission of some terrorist offences (see no. 213), carries a risk that one or more of these offences may be committed.[1121] With this offence the legislature wanted to criminalise both direct and indirect incitement to commit a terrorist offence, as required by the EU Directive.[1122] The general rules on public incitement, which are applicable

1118 Warsaw, 16 May 2005. Art. 5 of which states that parties should criminalise public provocation to commit a terrorist offence.

1119 Council Framework Decision 2008/919/JHA of 28 November 2008 amending Framework Decision 2002/475/JHA on combating terrorism [2008] *OJ* 330/21–23. For an analysis of this offence in the Framework Decision and Directive, see: Stéphanie De Coensel, 'Incitement to Terrorism: The Nexus Between Causality and Intent and the Question of Legitimacy – A Case Study of the European Union, Belgium and the United Kingdom' in Christophe Paulussen and Martin Scheinin (eds), *Human Dignity and Human Security in Times of Terrorism* (TMC Asser Press 2020) 283, http://link.springer.com/10.1007/978-94-6265-355-9_1, accessed 14 September 2023; De Coensel, *Counter-Terrorism & Criminal Law: A Normative Legitimacy Test of Terrorism-Related Offences on Expression, Information and Movement* (n 1) 197–206; Flore (n 784) 147–149. Currently it is Art. 5 of the Directive.

1120 Corr. Luik (vakantiekamer) 19 juli 2017, *JLMB* 2017, 1391; Sophie Lavaux, 'Recente Overheidsmaatregelen i.v.m. de "Foreign Fighters"' [2016] Panopticon 352, 352.

1121 Olivier Bonfond, 'Incitation au terrorisme: qui trop embrasse, mal étreint' (2018) 26 Jurisprudence de Liege, Mons et Bruxelles 1237, 1237–1238.

1122 MvT wetsontwerp 13 november 2012 tot wijziging van Titel 1*ter* van het Strafwetboek, *Parl. St.* Kamer 2012–2013, no. 53-2502/001, (4) 11; Delhaise (n 8) 48; Ketels (n 691) 250–251; Winants (n 8) 350. See for the Directive: European Union Agency for Fundamental Rights, *Directive (EU) 2017/541 on combatting terrorism: Impact on fundamental rights and freedoms*, 2021, 51. This criminalisation of indirect incitement is criticised by Comité T for endangering both the legality and proportionality principles and the freedom of expression. See: Comité T, 'Rapport 2020: Evaluation des mesures visant à lutter contre le terrorisme à la lumière des droits humains', 17.

to all felonies and standard offences, only criminalise direct incitement.[1123] Several factors are important for the analysis of whether or not there is a risk that terrorist offences may be committed. These factors are: the perpetrator (e.g. whether they are a person of influence and charisma), the receiver (e.g. the amount of people who receive the message and how easy they are to influence), the nature of the message (e.g. whether the words themselves call for violence or hatred) and the context (e.g. political tension).[1124] In the original bill, the risk that one or more terrorist offences is committed was not required.[1125] However, the Council of State pointed out that this risk requirement was part of the Convention and Framework Decision and that omitting it might lead the offence to violate the freedom of speech.[1126] The legislature amended the bill to remedy this issue, stating that '*it is imperative to specify that the criminalisation of public incitement to commit terrorist acts must not lead to the punishment of acts which have no connection whatsoever with terrorism and would thus create the danger of restricting the freedom of speech. Therefore, it is important to stress that these offences may only be aimed at those situations in which there are serious indications that a danger exists that a terrorist offence would be committed.*'[1127]

208. Amendment in 2016 – Three years later, however, the legislature changed its mind again. In 2016, vaguely referring to the altered security situation, the foreign terrorist fighter problem and the role of social media in radicalisation, it decided to delete the risk requirement because it made it too difficult to provide the evidence required.[1128] The Council of State suggested that because the new

---

1123 Art. 66 CC; MvT wetsontwerp 13 november 2012 tot wijziging van Titel 1*ter* van het Strafwetboek, *Parl. St.* Kamer 2012–2013, no. 53–2502/001, (4) 11; Weyembergh and Kennes (n 58) 151–152.

1124 MvT wetsontwerp 13 november 2012 tot wijziging van Titel 1*ter* van het Strafwetboek, *Parl. St.* Kamer 2012–2013, no. 53–2502/001, (4) 12–13; Delhaise (n 8) 51; Fransen and Kerkhofs (n 10) 52–53; Ketels (n 691) 251; Sofie Royer, 'De strijd tegen terroristische propaganda op social media' [2021] Tijdschrift voor Strafrecht 26, 27; Van Deuren (n 788) 509; Winants (n 8) 350.

1125 MvT wetsontwerp 13 november 2012 tot wijziging van Titel 1*ter* van het Strafwetboek, *Parl. St.* Kamer 2012–2013, no. 53–2502/001, (19) 19–20; Winants (n 8) 354.

1126 Advies 51.806/3 van de Raad van State 18 september 2012 bij wetsontwerp 13 november 2012 tot wijziging van Titel 1*ter* van het Strafwetboek, *Parl.St.* Kamer 2012–2013, no. 53–2502/001, (22) 25–27. See also: Cesoni (n 15) 246; Velaers (n 27) 778–779; Winants (n 8) 354.

1127 Own translation, original in Dutch: '*Er moet absoluut nader worden bepaald dat de strafbaarstelling van de publieke aanzetting tot het plegen van terroristische handelingen niet mag leiden tot de bestraffing van handelingen die geen enkel verband hebben met het terrorisme en waardoor de vrijheid van meningsuiting gevaar loopt aangetast te worden. Daarom is het belangrijk te beklemtonen dat deze strafbaarstelling slechts die situatie mag beogen waarin er ernstige aanwijzingen zijn dat een gevaar bestaat dat een terroristisch misdrijf gepleegd zou worden.*' (MvT wetsontwerp 13 november 2012 tot wijziging van Titel 1*ter* van het Strafwetboek, *Parl.St.* Kamer 2012–2013, no. 53–2502/001, (4) 12).

1128 MvT wetsontwerp 6 juli 2016 houdende diverse bepalingen ter bestrijding van terrorisme (III), *Parl.St.* Kamer 2015–2016, no. 54–1951/001, (4) 8; Bonfond (n 1121) 1238–1239; Cesoni (n 15) 245; De Coensel, 'Incitement to Terrorism' (n 1119) 282–283; Delhaise (n 8) 49; Deruyck and De Nauw (n 786) 12; Fransen and Kerkhofs (n 10) 51; Winants (n 8) 353–354.

wording also included less serious cases, the legislature should verify whether the minimum sentence should not be lowered.[1129] The legislature refused this because it thought it necessary to tackle the problem of public incitement to terrorism, especially in light of the development of social media.[1130]

209. Constitutional Court – When Article 140*bis* CC was introduced into the Criminal Code, an appeal for annulment was filed with the Constitutional Court (see nos 219 and 220 for the legality and freedom of speech analysis). One of the arguments made for annulment was based on freedom of speech. The Constitutional Court stated that freedom of expression is one of the pillars of a democratic society and therefore exceptions need to be interpreted strictly.[1131] Article 140*bis* CC is one of those exceptions and must comply with Article 10(2) ECHR.[1132] It must thus be demonstrated that the restrictions are necessary in a democratic society, that they correspond to an overriding societal need and that they remain proportionate to the legitimate objectives they pursue.[1133] The Court stated that it is necessary to protect society against those who would undercut it through violence and terrorism. The government may limit freedom of expression to attain that goal. The legislature had stated it did not aim to punish actions that are not connected to terrorism. This, in combination with the special intent required and the fact that the judge must take into account the person who spreads the message, the person who receives it, and the nature and the context of the message, makes that although the judge has a wide margin of appreciation, Article 140*bis* CC does not violate the freedom of expression.[1134] After the deletion of the risk requirement, however, the Article was brought before the Constitutional Court again. The Court made the same analysis of limitations to the freedom of expression. However, this time around the Court's conclusion was that Article 140*bis* CC did violate the freedom of expression and the Article deleting the risk requirement was annulled.[1135] The

1129 Advies 59.147/3 van de Raad van State 22 april 2016 bij wetsontwerp van 6 juli 2016 houdende diverse bepalingen ter bestrijding van terrorisme (III), *Parl.St.* Kamer 2015–2016, no. 54–1951/001, (19) 24–25; Bonfond (n 1121) 1240; Fransen and Kerkhofs (n 10) 52.

1130 MvT wetsontwerp 6 juli 2016 houdende diverse bepalingen ter bestrijding van terrorisme (III), *Parl.St.* Kamer 2015–2016, no. 54–1951/001, (4) 8; Deruyck and De Nauw (n 786) 11; Fransen and Kerkhofs (n 10) 52.

1131 GwH 28 januari 2015, 9/2015, *TVW* 2015, 179, B.24.

1132 GwH 28 januari 2015, 9/2015, *TVW* 2015, 179, B.25.3.

1133 GwH 28 januari 2015, 9/2015, *TVW* 2015, 179, B.24 and B.25.3.

1134 GwH 28 januari 2015, 9/2015, *TVW* 2015, 179, B.25.4-B.25.5. See also: Bonfond (n 1121) 1238; Dejemeppe and Rigaux (n 898) 765–766; Ketels (n 691) 252–253; Spreutels and Velu (n 95) 141–142; Velaers (n 27) 779; Comité T, 'Rapport 2019: Le respect des droits humains dans le cadre de la lutte contre le terrorisme: Un chantier en cours', 16.

1135 GwH 15 maart 2018, 31/2018, *NjW* 2018, 477, B.8. See also: De Coensel, *Counter-Terrorism & Criminal Law: A Normative Legitimacy Test of Terrorism-Related Offences on Expression, Information and Movement* (n 1) 207; Dejemeppe and Rigaux (n 898) 765–766; Deruyck and De Nauw (n 786) 12; Fransen and Kerkhofs (n 10) 53–54; Ketels (n 691) 248–250; Royer (n 1124) 27; Winants (n 8) 354; Comité T, 'Rapport 2019: Le respect des droits humains dans le cadre de la

need to facilitate the proof of the offence does not justify the imposition of an imprisonment and fine when there are no serious indications that there is a risk of a terrorist offence. Therefore, Article 140*bis* CC, without the risk requirement is not necessary in a democratic society and limits the freedom of expression unduly.[1136] In closing the Court remarks that both the Framework Decision and the new Directive include such a risk requirement.[1137] Because of the annulment of the part of the Article that deleted it, the risk requirement was revived and is part of Article 140*bis* CC again.[1138] As was mentioned under Article 140 CC (see no. 171), the Court of Cassation held that glorifying terrorism and humiliating its victims is not in itself a criminal offence in Belgium and is only punishable if it falls under Article 140*bis*, with the required special intent and risk requirement.[1139]

210. Effect of legislative changes in time – The principle of non-retroactivity is enshrined within the legality principle (see no. 94).[1140] It entails that new legislation which elevates sentences, creates new offences or expands the scope of an existing offence cannot be applied to facts that took place before this legislation was in force, even if it is in force when those facts are tried.[1141] For Article 140*bis* CC, this means that the deletion of the risk requirement should not work retroactively. Annulment, on the other hand, works retroactively. Once annulled, a piece of legislation disappears from the legal order *ex tunc*. Anybody who was convicted under this legislation, can start a procedure of repeal.[1142]

---

lutte contre le terrorisme: Un chantier en cours', 16; European Union Agency for Fundamental Rights, *Directive (EU) 2017/541 on combatting terrorism: Impact on fundamental rights and freedoms*, 2021, 59. Amnesty International had warned for the effect of this deletion on the freedom of expression. See: Amnesty International report, 'Dangerously disproportionate, the ever-expanding national security state in Europe'(2017) 39.

1136 GwH 15 maart 2018, 31/2018, *NjW* 2018, 477, B.7.6. See also: Bonfond (n 1121) 1239–1240; Cesoni (n 15) 246; De Coensel, 'Incitement to Terrorism' (n 1119) 283; Delhaise (n 8) 49; Spreutels and Velu (n 95) 143; Winants (n 8) 354; Ward Yperman, 'Terro III dan toch een stap te ver' [2018] Nieuw Juridisch Weekblad 480. There is an ECtHR case on the application of Art. 10 ECHR to a similar French offence, namely that of indirect incitement to terrorism through the public glorification of terrorist offences. In this case, the Court held that while punishment was possible in that specific case, the sentence of 18 months imprisonment (of which ten with postponement of execution) was disproportionate. See: *Rouillan v. France* App no 28000/19 (ECtHR 23 September 2022); Olivier Wouters, 'Vrijheidsstraf voor het verheerlijken van terrorisme in overeenstemming met artikel 10 EVRM? (noot onder EHRM 23 september 2022)' [2023] Nieuw Juridisch Weekblad 170.

1137 GwH 15 maart 2018, 31/2018, *NjW* 2018, 477, B.7.7. See also: Bonfond (n 1121) 1240; Cesoni (n 15) 246; Delhaise (n 8) 50; Winants (n 8) 354.

1138 Ketels (n 691) 250; Petersen (n 12) 56.

1139 Cass. 18 januari 2022, P.21.1692.N, 20.

1140 De Nauw and Deruyck (n 39) 22; Kuty (n 600) 69; Tulkens and others (n 39) 274.

1141 De Nauw and Deruyck (n 39) 22–23; De Nil, Deruyck and Meese (n 672) 273–274; Kuty (n 600) 297–301; Tulkens and others (n 39) 274–280; Van den Wyngaert, Vandromme and Traest (n 34) 110–118.

1142 Declercq (n 858) 1839–1845; Yperman, 'Terro III dan toch een stap te ver' (n 1136) 481.

211. Concrete nor personal – The Criminal Code criminalises the dissemination or otherwise making available of a message to the public. This implies a positive action and refraining from undertaking a certain action can therefore not suffice.[1143] In order to be punishable, the incitement does not have to be aimed at a specific person or group of people (*intuitu personae*).[1144] Therefore, incitement can easily happen over the internet as well, as long as it is public.[1145] Any mode of dissemination can be punishable.[1146] The message has to be made available to the public, which means that a conversation between two people is probably not covered.[1147] According to the case law, however, even individual messages to people can be public because the internet allows them to spread and multiply quickly.[1148] In addition, the incitement does not have to be aimed at the perpetration of a concrete offence.[1149] Nor does the incited offence actually have to take place.[1150] The term 'message' is not defined, so must be interpreted in its general sense: a form of communication that is transmitted, be that orally or written.[1151]

212. Without prejudice to the application of Article 140 CC – Article 140*bis* CC, as do Articles 140*ter* to 140*sexies* CC, explicitly states that it applies '*without prejudice to the application of Article 140.*'[1152] The legislature acknowledged that (some of) the actions being criminalised by these Articles were already being prosecuted under Article 140 CC and it wanted to alleviate all doubt about the fact that concurrence of offences is possible. Indeed, the Antwerp Correctional Court, for example, had a case of a woman who was very active on Facebook in support of IS. She was convicted for participation in the activities of a terrorist group and for incitement for one specific Facebook message.[1153] The

---

1143 Delhaise (n 8) 50.

1144 Corr. Luik (vakantiekamer) 19 juli 2017, *JLMB* 2017, 1391; Fransen and Kerkhofs (n 10) 55; Ketels (n 691) 253; Winants (n 8) 350.

1145 MvT wetsontwerp 13 november 2012 tot wijziging van Titel 1*ter* van het Strafwetboek, *Parl. St.* Kamer 2012–2013, no. 53-2502/001, (4) 13; Deruyck and De Nauw (n 786) 11; Fransen and Kerkhofs (n 10) 55; Winants (n 8) 350.

1146 Delhaise (n 8) 50.

1147 Corr. Luik (vakantiekamer) 19 juli 2017, *JLMB* 2017, 1391; Delhaise (n 8) 50–51.

1148 Corr. West-Vlaanderen (afd. Brugge) 26 juli 2018, *onuitg.*, 10; Fransen and Kerkhofs (n 10) 60–61.

1149 Delhaise (n 8) 52; Fransen and Kerkhofs (n 10) 55–56; Ketels (n 691) 253; Winants (n 8) 350.

1150 Amendement no. 1 7 juli 2016 bij wetsvoorstel 13 januari 2016 tot wijziging van het Strafwetboek wat betreft de bestraffing van terrorisme, *Parl.St.* Kamer 2015–2016, no. 54-1579/005, 6; Deruyck and De Nauw (n 786) 11; Van Deuren (n 788) 508; Winants (n 8) 350.

1151 According to Van Dale, the official Dutch dictionary: *boodschap: mondeling of schriftelijk bericht; bericht: overgebrachte mededeling, inlichting.* According to Delhaise, the French definition is: '*une information, une nouvelle transmise à une persone*' (Delhaise (n 8) 51.). These two definitions match and are translated above.

1152 Own translation, original in Dutch: '*Onverminderd de toepassing van artikel 140*' (Art. 140*bis*, section 1 CC). See also: De La Serna (n 50) 221; Van Deuren (n 788) 508.

1153 Corr. Antwerp 7 december 2015, *onuitg.*

practical application of these offences has taught us that they are almost always prosecuted in concurrence with Article 140 CC. So the question as to their added value presents itself in many cases. The addition of this phrase could raise questions about the concurrence of the terrorism offences *sensu lato* amongst each other. By only referring to Article 140 CC, the legislature has created the possibility for confusion. Concurrence of felonies is possible so for clarity's sake either the legislature should have added the other terrorism offences *sensu lato*, or it should have deleted this part of the sentence all together.[1154] As the addition only reiterates a general rule and therefore has no added value, the deletion of this part of the sentence should be preferred as a solution.

SECTION II. *MENS REA*

213. Special intent – A special intent is required, being '*the intention of inciting the commission of one of the offences referred to in Article 137 or 140sexies, with the exception of the offence referred to in Article 137, §3, 6°.*'[1155] The Article thus refers to terrorism sensu stricto, with the exception of threatening a terrorist offence, and the offence of traveling for terrorist purposes (see nos 252–263). This corresponds to the Directive, except for traveling, which is not part of the *mens rea* in the Directive. Traveling for terrorist purposes was not part of the original *mens rea* in the Belgian legislation either, since the offence did not exist yet in 2013. It was added when the offence was amended in 2016.[1156] In doing so, the Belgian legislature took a more repressive approach than the Directive. Since the traveling offence has a very broad *mens rea* itself (see nos 253–254), the *mens rea* of Article 140*bis* CC is broad too, and significantly broader than required by the Directive. In 2016, the legislature also added the words '*directly or indirectly*' after the word intention. The reference to indirect incitement was originally part of the risk requirement, which included the words '*when such conduct, whether or not directly aimed at the commission of terrorist offences.*' When deleting the risk requirement, this reference to indirect incitement was also deleted. To clarify indirect incitement was still covered by the offence, the legislature explicitly inserted it into the *mens rea* by adding the words '*directly*

[1154] Delhaise (n 8) 67.

[1155] Own translation, original in Dutch: '*met het oogmerk aan te zetten tot het plegen van één van de in de artikelen 137 of 140sexies bedoelde misdrijven, met uitzondering van het in artikel 137, §3, 6°, bedoelde misdrijf*' (Art. 140*bis* CC). See also: MvT wetsontwerp 13 november 2012 tot wijziging van Titel 1*ter* van het Strafwetboek, *Parl.St.* Kamer 2012–2013, no. 53–2502/001, (4) 13; Delhaise (n 8) 52; Fransen and Kerkhofs (n 10) 56; Ketels (n 691) 251; Royer (n 1124) 27; Winants (n 8) 350.

[1156] MvT wetsontwerp 6 juli 2016 houdende diverse bepalingen ter bestrijding van terrorisme (III), *Parl.St.* Kamer 2015–2016, no. 54–1951/001, (4) 7; De Coensel, 'Incitement to Terrorism' (n 1119) 282–283; Delhaise (n 8) 49; Deruyck and De Nauw (n 786) 12; Fransen and Kerkhofs (n 10) 51; Petersen (n 12) 56.

or indirectly'.[1157] However, after the Constitutional Court judgment which reinstated the risk requirement, this idea of 'direct or indirect incitement' was part of the offence twice.[1158] Therefore, the legislature deleted it from the *mens rea* again in 2019, returning to the original text of 2013.[1159]

SECTION III. SENTENCES

214. Felony – The legislature wished to introduce a sentence comparable to Articles 140 and 141 CC, making the offence a felony. It justified the severity of the sentence by referring to the possibilities of the internet and audiovisual media, allowing for a wide distribution of the messages.[1160] Therefore, the sentence is five to ten years felony imprisonment and a fine of 100 to 5,000 euros.[1161] This is the exact same sentence as prescribed by Article 140, §1 CC. Here as well, correctionalisation will always be used, making the maximum sentence five years imprisonment. This sentence of five to ten years (again, in practice one month to five years), is higher than the sentence for some of the terrorism offences *sensu stricto*.[1162] Due to this, the sentence of for example inciting somebody to commit terrorist battery, is higher than the sentence for the terrorist battery itself (maximum three years imprisonment).[1163] The same goes for the other terrorist offences *sensu lato*.[1164]

215. Aggravating circumstance – The EU Directive states that Member States should take measures to ensure that when the offences of recruitment or providing training for terrorism (see nos 230 and 238) are directed towards

1157 MvT wetsontwerp 6 juli 2016 houdende diverse bepalingen ter bestrijding van terrorisme (III), *Parl.St.* Kamer 2015–2016, no. 54–1951/001, (4) 8; Delhaise (n 8) 49; Fransen and Kerkhofs (n 10) 57.

1158 Fransen and Kerkhofs (n 10) 54–55; Winants (n 8) 354; Yperman, 'Terro III dan toch een stap te ver' (n 1136).

1159 Art. 76 wet 5 mei 2019 houdende diverse bepalingen in strafzaken en inzake erediensten, en tot wijziging van de wet 28 mei 2002 betreffende de euthanasie en van het Sociaal Strafwetboek (1), *BS* 24 mei 2019, 50023; Toelichting bij wetsvoorstel 6 februari 2019 houdende diverse bepalingen in strafzaken en inzake erediensten, *Parl.St.* Kamer 2018–2019, no. 54–3515/001, (3) 103; Deruyck and De Nauw (n 786) 13; Winants (n 8) 357.

1160 MvT wetsontwerp 13 november 2012 tot wijziging van Titel 1*ter* van het Strafwetboek, *Parl. St.* Kamer 2012–2013, no. 53–2502/001, (4) 13–14. See also: Ketels (n 691) 251.

1161 Delhaise (n 8) 78.

1162 Delhaise (n 8) 78–79.

1163 See also: Dekrem (n 32) 155. As Delhaise points out, terrorists will often have the intention to kill, making them guilty of attempted manslaughter or murder, raising the sentence above the one for the terrorist offence *sensu lato*. Then applying the rules for concurrence, the higher sentence will be applied. See: Delhaise (n 8) 79.

1164 Delhaise (n 8) 78–79.

children, this may be taken into account when sentencing.[1165] The Directive does not state this for incitement to terrorism, however the Belgian legislature decided to also create an aggravating circumstance for this offence.[1166] It reasoned that minors can also be the specific target group of perpetrators of incitement, who know that minors are more vulnerable and easier to manipulate and influence.[1167] Since 2019, Article 140*bis* CC therefore has a second section, stating that '*the sentence is felony imprisonment of ten to fifteen years and a fine of 5000 to 10000 euros if the dissemination or the act of making public meant in section one is specifically aimed at minors.*'[1168] This aggravating circumstance elevates the principal sentence to the same level as the one in Article 140, §1/1 CC. The maximum fine stays well below the maximum of 200,000 euros in Article 140, §1/1 CC though. Cesoni points out that the aggravating circumstance refers to 'minors'. The age of majority is 18 in Belgium, but Cesoni asks what happens if the youth in question is not Belgian and the age of majority is different in their state.[1169] However, it seems the legislature has answered this question. Article 100*ter* CC states that for the purposes of the offences in the Criminal Code, the term 'minor' means anybody under the age of 18 years old.[1170] The incitement needs to be aimed at them specifically, but not necessarily exclusively, for example, messages spread on online forums mainly used by minors or in the vicinity of schools,[1171] or propaganda images of minors or young adults.[1172] The Belgian legislature's choice for an aggravating circumstance, is a repressive one.[1173] The Directive states that the minority may be taken into account, but the application of an aggravating circumstance is obligatory for the judge, leaving

1165 Art. 15(4) Directive (EU) 2017/541 of the European Parliament and of the Council of 15 March 2017 on combating terrorism and replacing Council Framework Decision 2002/475/JHA and amending Council Decision 2005/671/JHA [2017] *OJ* L88/6 – L88/21.

1166 Cesoni (n 15) 244; De Coensel, 'De Wet Diverse Bepalingen in Strafzaken II: Terroristische misdrijven in lijn met de Europese verplichtingen?' (n 793) 213; Winants (n 8) 357.

1167 Toelichting bij wetsvoorstel 6 februari 2019 houdende diverse bepalingen in strafzaken en inzake erediensten, *Parl.St.* Kamer 2018–2019, no. 54-3515/001, (3) 103.

1168 Own translation, original in Dutch: '*De straf is opsluiting van tien jaar tot vijftien jaar en een geldboete van vijfduizend euro tot tienduizend euro indien de verspreiding of de publiekelijke terbeschikkingstelling bedoeld in het eerste lid specifiek gericht is op minderjarigen.*' (Art. 140*bis*, section 2 CC).

1169 Cesoni (n 15) 245.

1170 Art. 100*ter* CC. See also: De Nauw and Deruyck (n 39) 112; Tulkens and others (n 39) 444; Van den Wyngaert, Vandromme and Traest (n 34) 305. This is the case, even for extraterritorial offences, see *mutatis mutandis*: Ivo Delbrouck, 'Niet-consensuele seksuele misdrijven – bijzondere strafrechtelijke en strafprocesrechtelijke aspecten' [2023] Postal Memorialis – Lexicon strafrecht, strafvordering en bijzondere wetten N31/1, 37.

1171 Cesoni criticises these examples. See: Cesoni (n 15) 244–245.

1172 Toelichting bij wetsvoorstel 6 februari 2019 houdende diverse bepalingen in strafzaken en inzake erediensten, *Parl.St.* Kamer 2018–2019, no. 54-3515/001, (3) 104; Winants (n 8) 357.

1173 De Coensel, 'De Wet Diverse Bepalingen in Strafzaken II: Terroristische misdrijven in lijn met de Europese verplichtingen?' (n 793) 213.

no choice.[1174] Hence Belgian law choses the most restrictive option. More so, the recitals to the Directive state: '*When recruitment and training for terrorism are directed towards a child, Member States should ensure that judges can take this circumstance into account when sentencing offenders, although there is no obligation on judges to increase the sentence. It remains within the discretion of the judge to assess that circumstance together with the other facts of the particular case.*'[1175] By making it an aggravating circumstance, the Belgian legislature seems to have gone against this recital.

216. Alternative sentences and modalities – As the sentence after correctionalisation is sufficiently low, electronic monitoring as a principal sentence is possible, when the judge feels the offence is of such a nature that it should not be punished with more than one year imprisonment (see no. 115).[1176] The electronic monitoring has a term of one month to one year. Community service, with a term of 45 to 300 hours, and an autonomous probation sentence of one to two years are also possible (see nos 116 and 117). Finally, postponement of sentence enforcement subject to probation is an option, as is regular postponement of sentence enforcement and suspension of sentencing, possibly with probation measures as well, if the perpetrator does not have prior convictions which are too serious (see nos 118 and 119).

217. New Criminal Code – Contrary to the other terrorist offences (barring the current offence of Article 141 CC, see no. 281), the new Criminal Code changes the sentences for the incitement offence. It provides for a sentence of level 3 (imprisonment of three to five years) if the incitement relates to a terrorist offence punishable by a sentence of level 2 or more and a level 4 sentence (imprisonment of five to ten years) if the incitement offence relates to a terrorist offence punishable by a sentence of level 5 or more. The sentence for the aggravated offence is one of level 5 (ten to 15 years imprisonment). Therefore, compared to the current situation, the sentence for the aggravated offence is the same as the current one pre-correctionalisation, as is the sentence for non-aggravated inciting of a terrorism offence punishable with a sentence of level 5 or more. However, for incitement of terrorist offences punishable by sentences of level 2, 3 or 4 has a lower sentence than is currently the case.

1174 Cesoni (n 15) 244; De Nauw and Deruyck (n 39) 65; Tulkens and others (n 39) 627; Van den Wyngaert, Vandromme and Traest (n 34) 296.

1175 Recital 19 Directive (EU) 2017/541 of the European Parliament and of the Council of 15 March 2017 on combating terrorism and replacing Council Framework Decision 2002/475/JHA and amending Council Decision 2005/671/JHA [2017] *OJ* L88/6 – L88/21.

1176 Art. 37*ter*, §1, section 1 CC. See also: Daems and Magis (n 710) 181; Decaigny, 'Relatieve zwaarte, toepassingsgebied en duur' (n 714) 50; De Nauw and Deruyck (n 39) 127; Tulkens and others (n 39) 598; Van den Wyngaert, Vandromme and Traest (n 34) 430.

SECTION IV. CONSTITUTIONAL COURT

218. Constitutional Court 28 January 2015 – Two appeals were lodged against the statute of 18 February 2013 and more specifically against the introduction of Articles 140*bis* to 140*quinquies* CC.[1177] These appeals led to the Constitutional Court judgment of 28 January 2015. In their appeals, the applicants had requested the Court to petition the Court of Justice of the European Union for a preliminary ruling. The Constitutional Court refused this request, deeming a preliminary ruling unnecessary.[1178]

219. Legality principle – Article 140*bis* CC was claimed not to be in line with the legality principle and the freedoms of speech and association. After a general analysis of the legality principle (see no. 155), the Constitutional Court applied it to the offence in question. The applicants thought that words such as 'indirectly incite', 'indirectly provoke' and 'risk' were insufficiently clear.[1179] The Constitutional Court explained the legality principle and reiterated that it does allow for the judge to have a margin of appreciation.[1180] The Court then noted that the wording of Article 140*bis* CC is identical to that of the Framework Decision on which the Article is based.[1181] It is true that the legislature did not define the aforementioned terms. The Court of Cassation had already stated that if that is the case, terms need to be interpreted according to their usual meaning.[1182] The Constitutional Court explained that the usual meanings of 'incite', 'aim' and 'risk' are clear.[1183] Finally, once more referring to Articles 139, section 2 and 141*ter* CC as proof of the constant care the legislature takes to protect fundamental freedoms when fighting terrorism, the Court stated that Article 140*bis* CC grants judges a large margin of appreciation, but no

1177 The 2013 statute also amended Art. 141*ter* CC, by requiring the limitation or hindrance to the rights listed was not justified and by referring explicitly to the freedom of the printing press and other media. An appeal for nullification was lodged against the introduction of the words 'not justified'. However, by the time the Court ruled on this appeal, another statute had already deleted those words again, making the appeal moot on this point. See: GwH 28 januari 2015, 9/2015, *TVW* 2015, 179, B.4–.5; Winants (n 8) 351.

1178 GwH 28 januari 2015, 9/2015, *TVW* 2015, 179, B.55. The Constitutional Court is not the only high court in Belgium applying this type of reasoning. In a case regarding the application of Art. 141*bis* CC, the Court of Cassation also refused a request to refer a question about the scope of application of the EU Framework Decision to the Court of Justice of the European Union for a preliminary ruling. See: Cass. 28 januari 2020, P.19.0310.N.

1179 GwH 28 januari 2015, 9/2015, *TVW* 2015, 179, B.9.

1180 GwH 28 januari 2015, 9/2015, *TVW* 2015, 179, B.13.

1181 GwH 28 januari 2015, 9/2015, *TVW* 2015, 179, B.15 – B.16. Even though in its own case law, the Court had stated that the fact that the legislator implements a European Directive does not exempt him from respecting the principle of legality. See: GwH 10 mei 2006, 71/2006, B.20. See also: Theunis (n 608) 782.

1182 Cass. 27 april 1999, *Arr.Cass.* 1999, 568; Cass. 8 oktober 2014, P.14.0955.F.

1183 GwH 28 januari 2015, 9/2015, *TVW* 2015, 179, B.17.1–B.17.3.

autonomous competence.[1184] Therefore, the legality principle had not been violated.[1185]

220. Freedom of speech and association – Next to alleging a breach of the legality principle, the applicants also alleged a violation of the freedom of speech and freedom of association. This claim was dismissed as well. For a more detailed analysis, see no. 209.

221. Constitutional Court 15 March 2018 – In 2016, the so-called 'Terro III' statute made three changes to Article 140*bis* CC.[1186] It introduced the words 'directly or indirectly' in the *mens rea* (1°), added the offence of Article 140*sexies* CC to the *mens rea* (2°) and deleted the risk requirement (3°). The introduction of Article 140*sexies* CC into the *mens rea* (2°) was not challenged by the appellants and therefore, the Court did not rule on this part of the Article. The other two sections (1° and 3°) were challenged. The deletion of the risk requirement was found in violation of the freedom of expression and therefore annulled (see no. 209). The appellant had also alleged a violation of the freedom of association, but since the section (3°) of the Article was already annulled based on the freedom of expression, the Court did not analyse the freedom of association.[1187] Breaches of the legality principle and proportionality principle were also put forward, but the Court likewise ruled that they required no analysis since the section (3°) had already been annulled.[1188] The applicants also claimed that the section of the Article that introduced 'directly or indirectly' into the *mens rea* (1°) violated the legality principle. The Court, however, stated that it was only a formal adjustment which did not change the interpretation of the Article (see no. 213). Therefore, the legality principle had not been violated.[1189]

SECTION V. PRACTICAL APPLICATION

222. Scarce – The case law on Article 140*bis* CC is rather limited. There is often concurrence with the offence of participation in the activities of a terrorist group.[1190] In the Reguide case law analysis only four people were prosecuted

1184 GwH 28 januari 2015, 9/2015, *TVW* 2015, 179, B.18–B.19.

1185 GwH 28 januari 2015, 9/2015, *TVW* 2015, 179, B.20. See also: Dejemeppe and Rigaux (n 898) 762–763; Ketels (n 691) 252; Spreutels and Velu (n 95) 133–135; Winants (n 8) 351. For criticism on this conclusion, see: Cesoni (n 15) 234–235.

1186 Wet 3 augustus 2016 houdende diverse bepalingen ter bestrijding van terrorisme (III), *BS* 11 augustus 2016, 50973.

1187 GwH 15 maart 2018, 31/2018, *NjW* 2018, 477, B.9.

1188 GwH 15 maart 2018, 31/2018, *NjW* 2018, 477, B.12 and B.15.

1189 GwH 15 maart 2018, 31/2018, *NjW* 2018, 477, B.13.2–B.14.

1190 Fransen and Kerkhofs (n 10) 57.

for the offence in Article 140*bis* CC and always in concurrence with one of the offences related to terrorist groups.

223. Acquittal – In a case concerning a group called the 'Kamikaze Riders', two suspects were prosecuted but acquitted for incitement to terrorism.[1191] They had posted several messages on Facebook, but the court decided there was no risk that a terrorist offence would actually be committed. Furthermore, the Facebook posts did not meet the publicity requirement. The suspects were convicted for the offences of Article 140, §1 CC and Article 140*ter* CC (see nos 226–234).

224. Convictions – Other suspects have been convicted for incitement on social media.[1192] For example, a woman who called for the murdering of people in Facebook posts;[1193] and a brother and sister who (among other things) translated texts from English to Bosnian so they could be published in a Bosnian version of DABIQ,[1194] posted videos and messages of IS and self-made images of fighters with inspiring religious texts on social media, and who praised martyrdom and actions of IS on social media accounts.[1195]

225. Effect of legislative changes in time – A woman was prosecuted for incitement to terrorism for facts spanning from before the deletion of the risk requirement until after that deletion. The court convicted her for a collective offence, meaning that there were several separate instances of incitement, but they were seen as intrinsically linked because they were part of a single criminal project.[1196] In that case, they are tried as one fact, only imposing the sentence for the most serious offence (i.e. the one with the highest sentence[1197]).[1198] If a collective offence spans a change in legislation, the most recent legislation is applicable.[1199] In this case, that was Article 140*bis* CC without the risk

---

1191 Corr. Brussel 20 oktober 2016, *onuitg;* Fransen and Kerkhofs (n 10) 57–58; Royer (n 1124) 27.

1192 See also: Royer (n 1124) 27.

1193 Corr. Antwerpen 7 december 2015, *onuitg;* Fransen and Kerkhofs (n 10) 58.

1194 This is a magazine published by IS.

1195 Corr. Limburg (afd. Hasselt) 23 juni 2017, *Limburgs Rechtsleven* 2018 51; Fransen and Kerkhofs (n 10) 59. They also helped in translating the IS propaganda magazine DABIQ, wrote texts and poems with IS propaganda and incited people to go fight in Syria.

1196 Art. 65, section 1 CC. See also: Tom Decaigny, in M De Busscher and others (eds), *Strafrecht: duiding* (Larcier 2018) 116; De Nauw and Deruyck (n 39) 174; Kuty (n 600) 385; Tulkens and others (n 39) 634; Van den Wyngaert, Vandromme and Traest (n 34) 522–523; Patrick Waeterinckx, 'Samenloop van verscheidene misdrijven', *Strafrecht geannoteerd* (die Keure 2020) 355–357.

1197 Art. 63 CC. See also: De Nil, Deruyck and Meese (n 672) 277; Waeterinckx (n 1196) 353–354.

1198 Cass. 21 juni 1983, *Arr.Cass.* 1982–83, 1302, noot; Decaigny (n 1196) 116; De La Serna (n 8) 208; De Nauw and Deruyck (n 39) 175; Tulkens and others (n 39) 634–635; Van den Wyngaert, Vandromme and Traest (n 34) 523; Waeterinckx (n 1196) 357.

1199 Cass. 17 mei 1983, AR 7915, *Arr.Cass.* 1982–83, 1143; Cass. 7 mei 2002, P.02.0308.N, *Arr. Cass.* 2002, 1235; Cass. 10 oktober 2006, P.06.0836.N, *Arr.Cass.* 2006, 1967. See also: De

requirement. The woman was thus convicted of incitement, without the risk requirement being applied.[1200] After the annulment by the Constitutional Court she decided to file a claim for a repeal. The case was brought before the Correctional Court again, which decided to repeal the decision. However, the Correctional Court took her case under consideration again and once more convicted her of incitement, this time after considering that the risk requirement was met.[1201]

Nil, Deruyck and Meese (n 672) 271; Kuty (n 600) 385; Patrick Waeterinckx, 'Het collectief misdrijf – De verhouding tussen artikel 65 Sw. en artikel 2, tweede lid Sw.' in M De Busscher and others (eds), *Strafrecht: duiding* (Larcier 2018) 8; Waeterinckx (n 1196) 357.

1200 Corr. West-Vlaanderen (afd. Brugge) 19 februari 2018, *onuitg;* Fransen and Kerkhofs (n 10) 59.

1201 Corr. West-Vlaanderen (afd. Brugge) 26 juli 2018, *onuitg;* Fransen and Kerkhofs (n 10) 59–60.

CHAPTER V
ARTICLE 140*TER* CC

SECTION I. *ACTUS REUS*

226. Recruitment – Article 140*ter* CC criminalises recruitment for terrorist purposes. It was also introduced in 2013, in the wake of the Council of Europe Convention and the update of the Framework Decision.[1202] The Article criminalises anybody who recruits another person to commit or contribute to the commission of one of the offences in Article 137, 140 or 140*sexies* CC, with the exception of Article 137, §3, 6° CC. So this is terrorism *sensu stricto*, with the exception of threatening terrorism, the offences relating to terrorist groups, and traveling for terrorist purposes (see nos 252–263).[1203] The preparatory works talk about recruitment to become a member of a terrorist group.[1204] However, membership in itself is not punishable under Article 140 CC (see nos 172–173). The reference to Article 140*sexies* CC was added after its creation in 2016.[1205] As was the case for Article 140*bis* CC, with this addition the Belgian legislature went beyond the obligations of the Directive. The part reading '*or contribution to the commission*', was added in 2019.[1206] This wording is part of the Directive

---

1202 Art. 6 Council of Europe Convention on the Prevention of Terrorism of 16 May 2005, Warsaw. Art. 5 of which states that parties should criminalise public provocation to commit a terrorist offence. Council Framework Decision 2008/919/JHA of 28 November 2008 amending Framework Decision 2002/475/JHA on combating terrorism [2008] *OJ* 330/21–23; MvT wetsontwerp 13 november 2012 tot wijziging van Titel 1*ter* van het Strafwetboek, *Parl.St.* Kamer 2012–2013, no. 53-2502/001, (4) 14; Ketels (n 691) 254; Lavaux, 'Recente Overheidsmaatregelen i.v.m. de 'Foreign Fighters'' (n 1120) 352. For a short analysis of this offence in the Framework Decision, see: Flore (n 784) 149–150.

1203 Delhaise (n 8) 55; Fransen and Kerkhofs (n 10) 61; Winants (n 8) 351. It is now Art. 6 of the Directive.

1204 MvT wetsontwerp 13 november 2012 tot wijziging van Titel 1*ter* van het Strafwetboek, *Parl. St.* Kamer 2012–2013, no. 53-2502/001, (4) 14. See also: De La Serna (n 50) 223.

1205 Art. 3 wet 3 augustus 2016 houdende diverse bepalingen ter bestrijding van terrorisme (III), *BS* 11 augustus 2016, 50973; Deruyck and De Nauw (n 786) 12; Fransen and Kerkhofs (n 10) 62; Ketels (n 691) 256; Winants (n 8) 353.

1206 Art. 77, 1° wet 5 mei 2019 houdende diverse bepalingen in strafzaken en inzake erediensten, en tot wijziging van de wet 28 mei 2002 betreffende de euthanasie en van het Sociaal Strafwetboek, *BS* 24 mei 2019, 50023; De Coensel, 'De Wet Diverse Bepalingen in Strafzaken II: Terroristische misdrijven in lijn met de Europese verplichtingen?' (n 793) 212.

on combatting terrorism, but was not part of the Belgian legislation yet.[1207] If necessary, these actions could be prosecuted under Article 140 CC or as aiding and abetting.[1208] However, since 2016 it was part of the offence in Article 141 CC (see nos 274–276) and to maintain uniformity, the legislature decided to also introduce it in Article 140*ter* CC.[1209] This addition maintained uniformity at the cost of increased overlap.[1210] There will be very few situations in which a person is recruited to contribute to the commission of a terrorist offence, that are not already covered by Article 140 CC. This situation will always involve three people (the recruiter, the contributor to the ultimately intended offence and its perpetrator) and three people is the threshold for a terrorist group. Even if there is no terrorist group, the rules on aiding and abetting apply both to the recruitment offence and to the ultimately intended terrorist offence. Instead of criminalising new situations, the addition of this phrase predominantly brought situations within the ambit of this offence which were already covered by other terrorist offences, therefore reducing clarity and simplicity. An exact definition of recruitment has not been provided by the legislature. In the context of human trafficking, the Court of Cassation has stated that recruitment is enlisting recruits or getting someone to join a group.[1211] For the offence of recruitment to take place, it is not required that the recruited person actually commit one of the offences they were recruited for.[1212] What is required, is that the recruiter successfully approaches the other person, meaning they have convinced them to

---

1207 Art. 6 Directive (EU) 2017/541 of the European Parliament and of the Council of 15 March 2017 on combating terrorism and replacing Council Framework Decision 2002/475/JHA and amending Council Decision 2005/671/JHA [2017] *OJ* L88/6 – L88/21; Winants (n 8) 357. Note that Belgium was not alone in this, the lack of transposition of this element was noted as a transposition of particular concern by the European Commission. See: Report from the Commission to the European Parliament and the Council based on Art. 29(1) of Directive (EU) 2017/541 of the European Parliament and of the Council of 15 March 2017 on combating terrorism and replacing Council Framework Decision 2002/475/JHA and amending Council Decision 2005/671/JHA, Brussels 30 September 2020, COM(2020) 619, 3–4.

1208 Toelichting bij wetsvoorstel 6 februari 2019 houdende diverse bepalingen in strafzaken en inzake erediensten, *Parl.St.* Kamer 2018–2019, no. 54-3515/001, (3) 104; Comité T, 'Rapport 2020: Evaluation des mesures visant à lutter contre le terrorisme à la lumière des droits humains', 15.

1209 Toelichting bij wetsvoorstel 6 februari 2019 houdende diverse bepalingen in strafzaken en inzake erediensten, *Parl.St.* Kamer 2018–2019, no. 54-3515/001, (3) 104–105; Comité T, 'Rapport 2020: Evaluation des mesures visant à lutter contre le terrorisme à la lumière des droits humains', 15.

1210 See also: Cesoni (n 15) 246–247.

1211 Cass. 8 oktober 2014, P.14.0955.F; Delhaise (n 8) 55.

1212 MvT wetsontwerp 13 november 2012 tot wijziging van Titel 1*ter* van het Strafwetboek, *Parl. St.* Kamer 2012–2013, no. 53-2502/001, (4) 14; Amendement no. 1 7 juli 2016 bij wetsvoorstel 13 januari 2016 tot wijziging van het Strafwetboek wat betreft de bestraffing van terrorisme, *Parl.St.* Kamer 2015–2016, no. 54-1579/005, 6; De La Serna (n 50) 223; Delhaise (n 8) 55; Deruyck and De Nauw (n 786) 11; Fransen and Kerkhofs (n 10) 61; Van Deuren (n 788) 508; Winants (n 8) 351.

perpetrate the offence.[1213] Just as Article 140*bis* CC (see no. 212), Article 140*ter* also states it is applicable without prejudice to the application of Article 140 CC.

227. Useless inclusion – The usefulness of including Article 140 CC in the list of offences the recruitment of which is punishable, can be questioned. Will recruiting somebody to join a terrorist group not always be a participation in the activities of that group? This inclusion therefore seems a bit pointless. The Court of Appeal of Liège for example had a case of recruitment to join a terrorist group (taking place after 2013), which was only prosecuted under Article 140 CC.[1214]

SECTION II. *MENS REA*

228. Not explicit – Article 140*ter* CC does not explicitly include a *mens rea*. As explained above, this does not mean there is no *mens rea* (see nos 103 and 193). The Directive states the offence must be committed intentionally but the Belgian legislation requires special intent for almost all of the terrorist offences, so it would be logical to also require special intent here. It is therefore generally accepted that 'recruitment to commit' one of the offences mentioned above, actually means 'recruitment with the aim of seeing one of these offences being committed'.[1215] This is form of special intent.[1216] As was explained above, the traveling offence was added to the *mens rea* in 2016, expanding it beyond the scope of the offence defined in the Directive. The Belgian offence is therefore broader than the one in the Directive.

SECTION III. SENTENCES

229. Felony – The sentence for recruitment is five to ten years felony imprisonment and a fine of 100 to 5,000 euros. This is the exact same sentence as for incitement and participation in the activities of a terrorist group (see nos 181 and 214).[1217] Therefore, this offence is also a felony, which will also almost always be correctionalised, making the maximum imprisonment five years. This means electronic monitoring as a principal sentence is possible, when the judge feels

1213 MvT wetsontwerp 13 november 2012 tot wijziging van Titel 1*ter* van het Strafwetboek, *Parl. St.* Kamer 2012–2013, no. 53-2502/001, (4) 14; De La Serna (n 50) 223–224; Fransen and Kerkhofs (n 10) 61; Deruyck and De Nauw (n 786) 11; Ketels (n 691) 254; Winants (n 8) 351. Delhaise talks about the proposal being received ('*la proposition du recruteur est accueillie par la personne approchée*' (Delhaise (n 8) 55.)).

1214 Luik 18 oktober 2017, *JLMB* 2017, 1878.

1215 Delhaise (n 8) 56; Fransen and Kerkhofs (n 10) 62–63; Winants (n 8) 351.

1216 Ketels (n 691) 256.

1217 Delhaise (n 8) 78.

the offence is of such a nature that it should not be punished with more than one year imprisonment (see no. 115).[1218] The electronic monitoring has a term of one month to one year. Community service, with a term of 45 to 300 hours, and an autonomous probation sentence of one to two years are also possible (see nos 116 and 117). Finally, postponement of sentence enforcement subject to probation is an option, as is regular postponement of sentence enforcement and suspension of sentencing, possibly with probation measures as well, if the perpetrator does not have prior convictions which are too serious (see nos 118 and 119).

230. Aggravating circumstance – As explained above (see no. 215), the Directive states that it should be possible to take into account that the offence of recruitment is aimed at a minor when sentencing.[1219] In 2019, the legislature introduced such an aggravating circumstance into the second section of Article 140*ter* CC.[1220] This section states that the sentence becomes ten to 15 years felony imprisonment and a fine of 5,000 to 10,000 when the recruitment is aimed specifically at minors.

SECTION IV. CONSTITUTIONAL COURT

231. Legality principle – In its judgment of 28 January 2015 the Constitutional Court judgment also had to rule on Article 140*ter* CC. After a general analysis of the legality principle (see no. 155), the Constitutional Court applied it to the offence in question. With regard to Article 140*ter* CC, the applicants claimed it violated the legality principle for two reasons. Firstly, the wording was not clear enough. Secondly, sentencing was unforeseeable because an offence of recruiting people for foreign armies already existed with a sentence of three months to two years imprisonment.[1221] The Constitutional Court first referred to the Council of Europe Treaty and the Framework Decision on which the Article is based. It then reiterated that Article 140*ter* CC requires that the proposal was accepted by the person being recruited. Therefore, the Article does not make it possible to convict every person who approaches another

1218 Art. 37*ter*, §1, section 1 CC. See also: Daems and Magis (n 710) 181; Decaigny, 'Relatieve zwaarte, toepassingsgebied en duur' (n 714) 50; De Nauw and Deruyck (n 39) 127; Tulkens and others (n 39) 598; Van den Wyngaert, Vandromme and Traest (n 34) 430.

1219 Toelichting bij wetsvoorstel 6 februari 2019 houdende diverse bepalingen in strafzaken en inzake erediensten, *Parl.St.* Kamer 2018–2019, no. 54–3515/001, (3) 105.

1220 Art. 77, 2° wet 5 mei 2019 houdende diverse bepalingen in strafzaken en inzake erediensten, en tot wijziging van de wet 28 mei 2002 betreffende de euthanasie en van het Sociaal Strafwetboek, *BS* 24 mei 2019, 50023; De Coensel, 'De Wet Diverse Bepalingen in Strafzaken II: Terroristische misdrijven in lijn met de Europese verplichtingen?' (n 793) 213; Deruyck and De Nauw (n 786) 12–13; Winants (n 8) 357.

1221 Art. 1 wet 1 augustus 1979 betreffende diensten bij een vreemde leger- of troepenmacht die zich op het grondgebied van een vreemde Staat bevindt, *BS* 24 augustus 1979, 9272.

person with a discourse that is considered unlawful, radical or extreme by the prosecuting authority.[1222] Article 140*ter* CC is sufficiently accurate and clear so anyone can know which conduct is punishable and which sentence is provided for. The fact that it can be difficult for the prosecuting authorities to furnish the evidence does not change this, nor does the fact that the same conduct can be punished under a different Article of the Criminal Code.[1223] Hence, there is no violation of the legality principle.[1224] The second argument does not change this. The circumstances of the two offences are different and even then, concurrence is possible.[1225] A person who recruits another person for a foreign army in circumstances that fall within the scope of Article 140*ter* CC, can therefore know they can be sentenced to the higher sentence.

232. Freedom of speech and association – The applicants also alleged that Article 140*ter* CC violated both the freedom of speech and the freedom of association. The Court stated that the Article did not even restrict the freedom of speech and therefore did not need to be analysed in this regard.[1226] As to the freedom of association, while it is restricted by the Article, this restriction is necessary in a democratic society in order to protect national security, public safety and public order, to prevent criminal offences, or to protect the rights and freedoms of others.[1227] The Court was thus of the opinion that the restriction of the right to association is justified.[1228]

SECTION V. PRACTICAL APPLICATION

233. Attempted recruitment – The Correctional Court of Brussels convicted a man for attempted recruitment for financing terrorism.[1229] He had contacted people on social media and encouraged them to commit offences to finance the jihad. In his defence he claimed to be addicted to drugs and that he was conning people out of their money to buy drugs, without the intention to finance terrorism. Since he was known to have been in Syria, the court did not believe this defence.

1222 GwH 28 januari 2015, 9/2015, *TVW* 2015, 179, B.30.1.
1223 GwH 28 januari 2015, 9/2015, *TVW* 2015, 179, B.30.2.
1224 GwH 28 januari 2015, 9/2015, *TVW* 2015, 179, B.33. See also: Ketels (n 691) 254–255; Spreutels and Velu (n 95) 136; Winants (n 8) 351.
1225 GwH 28 januari 2015, 9/2015, *TVW* 2015, 179, B.31.2–B.31.3.
1226 GwH 28 januari 2015, 9/2015, *TVW* 2015, 179, B.36.
1227 GwH 28 januari 2015, 9/2015, *TVW* 2015, 179, B.37. See also: Ketels (n 691) 255–256.
1228 Spreutels and Velu (n 95) 144; Winants (n 8) 351–352.
1229 Corr. Brussel 26 juni 2015, *onuitg;* Fransen and Kerkhofs (n 10) 63.

234. RECRUITMENT – The same court convicted another man for recruitment for convincing people over Facebook to go to Syria to fight.[1230] The defendant posted propaganda on a Facebook profile, which he followed up with private messages to potential jihadists. The Youth Court of Brussels also convicted a minor for recruitment.[1231] She was in Syria and during Skype sessions and text messages she convinced two other girls to join her in Syria to marry jihadist fighters.

1230 Corr. Brussel 20 oktober 2016, *onuitg*; Fransen and Kerkhofs (n 10) 63.

1231 Jeugdrechtbank Brussel 4 juli 2016, *onuitg*.

CHAPTER VI
ARTICLE 140*QUATER* CC

SECTION I. *ACTUS REUS*

235. Providing training – Article 140*quater* CC was also introduced in 2013, in the wake of the Council of Europe Convention and the update of the Framework Decision.[1232] For both the *actus reus* and *mens rea* of this offence, the Belgian legislature used wording very similar to that of the European instruments.[1233] The *actus reus* of Article 140*quater* CC is to instruct or provide training in the manufacturing or use of explosives, firearms or other weapons or harmful or dangerous substances or in other specific methods and techniques.[1234] This is a non-exhaustive list, so any training or instruction that are provided with the required *mens rea* (see no. 236) can fall within the scope of this Article. The preparatory works provide as extra examples of training in the sense of Article *140quater* CC flying or driving lessons, or lessons on how to hack a website.[1235] However, as discussed below (see no. 239) the Constitutional Court has introduced some doubt on whether the offence actually goes so far as to potentially criminalise driving lessons and the like. The training provided can be theoretic or practical.[1236] Both 'instruct' and 'provide' imply an action on behalf of the perpetrator.[1237] The Criminal Code also states that Article 140*quater* is applicable without prejudice to the application of Article 140 CC (for comments on this, see no. 212).

[1232] Art. 1 Council Framework Decision 2008/919/JHA of 28 November 2008 amending Framework Decision 2002/475/JHA on combating terrorism [2008] *OJ* 330/21–23; Art. 7 Council of Europe Convention on the Prevention of Terrorism of 16 May 2005, Warsaw; Ketels (n 691) 256; Lavaux, 'Recente Overheidsmaatregelen i.v.m. de "Foreign Fighters"' (n 1120) 352.

[1233] Art. 7 Directive (EU) 2017/541 Directive (EU) 2017/541 of the European Parliament and of the Council of 15 March 2017 on combating terrorism and replacing Council Framework Decision 2002/475/JHA and amending Council Decision 2005/671/JHA [2017] *OJ* L88/6. See also: Fransen and Kerkhofs (n 10) 63.

[1234] Art. 140*quater* CC. See also: Flore (n 784) 150.

[1235] MvT wetsontwerp 13 november 2012 tot wijziging van Titel 1*ter* van het Strafwetboek, *Parl. St.* Kamer 2012–2013, no. 53–2502/001, (4) 15; De La Serna (n 50) 224; Deruyck and De Nauw (n 786) 11; Fransen and Kerkhofs (n 10) 64; Ketels (n 691) 257; Winants (n 8) 351.

[1236] Delhaise (n 8) 58.

[1237] Delhaise (n 8) 57.

SECTION II. *MENS REA*

236. Special intent – The *mens rea* is a special intent: acting with a view to commit or contribute to the perpetration of one of the offences referred to in Article 137, with the exception of the offence referred to in Article 137, §3, 6° CC.[1238] So the training has to be provided with the view to commit or contribute to the commission of terrorism *sensu stricto*, once more with the exception of threatening a terrorist attack. This is the same as in the Framework Decision.[1239] Here too, the part '*or contribute to the commission of*' was added in 2019,[1240] because this is part of the wording of the Directive and the legislature wanted to increase coherence (see no. 226).[1241] Concreteness is not required, so the person providing the training does not need to know the exact terrorist offence for which they are providing training.[1242] They do need to know, however, that the aim is to perpetrate one of the aforementioned offences.[1243] Then again, it is not required that the offence for which the training was provided, actually takes place.[1244]

SECTION III. SENTENCES

237. Felony – Once again, the sentence is five to ten years felony imprisonment and a fine of 100 to 5,000 euros. This is the exact same sentence as for incitement and recruitment[1245] and the offence of participating in the activities of a terrorist group. This means electronic monitoring as a principal sentence is possible, when the judge feels the offence is of such a nature that it should not be punished with more than one year imprisonment (see no. 115).[1246] The electronic monitoring

---

1238 Art. 140*quater* CC; MvT wetsontwerp 13 november 2012 tot wijziging van Titel 1*ter* van het Strafwetboek, *Parl.St.* Kamer 2012–2013, no. 53-2502/001, (4) 15; De La Serna (n 50) 224; Delhaise (n 8) 58; Fransen and Kerkhofs (n 10) 65; Ketels (n 691) 257.

1239 Fransen and Kerkhofs (n 10) 64.

1240 Art. 78, 1° wet 5 mei 2019 houdende diverse bepalingen in strafzaken en inzake erediensten, en tot wijziging van de wet 28 mei 2002 betreffende de euthanasie en van het Sociaal Strafwetboek, *BS* 24 mei 2019, 50023; De Coensel, 'De Wet Diverse Bepalingen in Strafzaken II: Terroristische misdrijven in lijn met de Europese verplichtingen?' (n 793) 212.

1241 Art. 7 Directive (EU) 2017/541 of the European Parliament and of the Council of 15 March 2017 on combating terrorism and replacing Council Framework Decision 2002/475/JHA and amending Council Decision 2005/671/JHA [2017] *OJ* L88/6 – 21; Toelichting bij wetsvoorstel 6 februari 2019 houdende diverse bepalingen in strafzaken en inzake erediensten, *Parl.St.* Kamer 2018–2019, no. 54-3515/001, (3) 104–105; Winants (n 8) 357.

1242 Delhaise (n 8) 58 and 78; Fransen and Kerkhofs (n 10) 65; Winants (n 8) 351.

1243 GwH 28 januari 2015, 9/2015, *TVW* 2015, B.41.3; Ketels (n 691) 257.

1244 Deruyck and De Nauw (n 786) 11; Van Deuren (n 788) 508.

1245 MvT wetsontwerp 13 november 2012 tot wijziging van Titel 1*ter* van het Strafwetboek, *Parl. St.* Kamer 2012–2013, no. 53-2502/001, (4) 15.

1246 Art. 37*ter*, §1, section 1 CC. See also: Daems and Magis (n 710) 181; Decaigny, 'Relatieve zwaarte, toepassingsgebied en duur' (n 714) 50; De Nauw and Deruyck (n 39) 127; Tulkens and others (n 39) 598; Van den Wyngaert, Vandromme and Traest (n 34) 430.

has a term of one month to one year. Community service, with a term of 45 to 300 hours, and an autonomous probation sentence of one to two years are also possible (see nos 116 and 117). Finally, postponement of sentence enforcement subject to probation is an option, as is regular postponement of sentence enforcement and suspension of sentencing, possibly with probation measures as well, if the perpetrator does not have prior convictions which are too serious (see nos 118 and 119).

238. Aggravating circumstance – In 2019, the legislature added an aggravating circumstance to this offence as well.[1247] The sentence goes up to 10 to 15 years felony imprisonment and a fine of 5,000 to 10,000 euros if the instructions or training are specifically aimed at minors. Here as well, this is the consequence of the Directive.[1248]

SECTION IV. CONSTITUTIONAL COURT

239. Legality principle – In its judgment of 28 January 2015 the Constitutional Court judgment also had to rule on Article *140quater* CC. After a general analysis of the legality principle (see no. 155), the Constitutional Court applied it to the offence in question. The applicants also deemed the wording of Article 140*quater* CC unclear. The Court again started by referring to the Council of Europe Treaty and the Framework decision.[1249] It noted that the preparatory works stated that the Article does not only cover providing training for methods specific for terrorist purposes, such as weapons training, but also other methods such as flying or driving lessons or hacking websites. The Framework Decision, however, only targets training for specific methods and techniques, meaning, according to the Court, methods and techniques specific to committing terrorist offences. The Court considered the wording of the Article: '*training in the manufacturing or use of explosives, firearms or other weapons or harmful or dangerous substances or in other specific methods and techniques, with a view to commit or contribute to the commission of one of the offences referred to in Article 137, with the exception of the offence referred to in Article 137, §3, 6° CC.*' It found the *actus reus* sufficiently accurate and clear, since

1247 Art. 77, 2° wet 5 mei 2019 houdende diverse bepalingen in strafzaken en inzake erediensten, en tot wijziging van de wet 28 mei 2002 betreffende de euthanasie en van het Sociaal Strafwetboek, *BS* 24 mei 2019, 50023; Deruyck and De Nauw (n 786) 12–13.

1248 Art. 15(4) Directive (EU) 2017/541 of the European Parliament and of the Council of 15 March 2017 on combating terrorism and replacing Council Framework Decision 2002/475/JHA and amending Council Decision 2005/671/JHA [2017] *OJ* L88/6 – 21; Toelichting bij wetsvoorstel 6 februari 2019 houdende diverse bepalingen in strafzaken en inzake erediensten, *Parl.St.* Kamer 2018–2019, no. 54-3515/001, (3) 104–105; De Coensel, 'De Wet Diverse Bepalingen in Strafzaken II: Terroristische misdrijven in lijn met de Europese verplichtingen?' (n 793) 213.

1249 GwH 28 januari 2015, 9/2015, *TVW* 2015, 179, B.40.1–B.40.3.

the potential ambiguity of the preparatory works, cannot have precedence over the clear wording of the statute.[1250] This clarification is never discussed in detail by commentators and has not been relevant to lower case law so it is hard to judge how far its implications go. However, the Constitutional Court does seem to have limited the *actus reus* of the offence to an extent and has overruled the statement in the preparatory works that the offence can cover driving lessons, etc. as these are everyday actions and not techniques specific to committing terrorist offences. The *mens rea* is also sufficiently accurate and clear. The offence only exists when the person providing the training knows the training is provided with the intention to commit one of the offences mentioned.[1251] The Court concludes that as long as this last interpretation is adhered to, there is no violation of the legality principle.[1252]

240. Freedom of speech and association – Regarding the alleged violation of the freedom of speech and freedom of association, the Court followed the same reasoning as for Article 140*ter* CC. It stated that Article 140*quater* CC does not make it possible to convict every person who approaches another person with a discourse that is considered unlawful, radical or extreme by the prosecuting authority.[1253] Therefore, Article 140*quater* does not restrict the freedom of speech.[1254] It does restrict the freedom of association, but this restriction is necessary in a democratic society in order to protect national security, public safety and public order, to prevent criminal offences, or to protect the rights and freedoms of others.[1255] Therefore, there is no violation of the freedom of association.[1256]

SECTION V. PRACTICAL APPLICATION

241. Convictions – The Correctional Court convicted a man for providing training because he had undertaken practice in the use of weapons and the like.[1257] He was considered the trainer because during this practice he had taken on an instructive and corrective roll towards his companion. The Correctional Court of Hainaut convicted another man for leading shooting and weapons

1250 GwH 28 januari 2015, 9/2015, *TVW* 2015, 179, B.41.2.
1251 GwH 28 januari 2015, 9/2015, *TVW* 2015, 179, B.42.3.
1252 GwH 28 januari 2015, 9/2015, *TVW* 2015, 179, B.42. See also: Ketels (n 691) 257; Spreutels and Velu (n 95) 137–138; Winants (n 8) 351.
1253 GwH 28 januari 2015, 9/2015, *TVW* 2015, 179, B.44.
1254 GwH 28 januari 2015, 9/2015, *TVW* 2015, 179, B.45. See also: Ketels (n 691) 257–258.
1255 GwH 28 januari 2015, 9/2015, *TVW* 2015, 179, B.46.
1256 Ketels (n 691) 257–258; Spreutels and Velu (n 95) 144–145; Winants (n 8) 351–352.
1257 Corr. Oost-Vlaanderen (afd. Dendermonde) 25 januari 2016, *onuitg*; Fransen and Kerkhofs (n 10) 65.

practice in the combat zone.[1258] In the Reguide case law analysis a total of five people was prosecuted for providing training.

242. Acquittal – In the so-called Kamikaze Riders case, a man was acquitted of providing training.[1259] He had organised paintball and airsoft activities. The court found there was no evidence for the narrative put forward by the public prosecutor that these activities were military training practices to prepare recruits for battle.

1258 Corr. Henegouwen (afd. Charleroi) 27 september 2017, *onuitg.*, 6; Fransen and Kerkhofs (n 10) 66.

1259 Corr. Brussel 20 oktober 2016, *onuitg*; Fransen and Kerkhofs (n 10) 65–66.

CHAPTER VII
ARTICLE 140*QUINQUIES* CC

SECTION I. *ACTUS REUS*

243. Receiving training – Together with the offence of providing instruction or training, the legislature introduced the offence of receiving training for terrorism.[1260] It stated that it made operational and logical sense to also criminalise the person who receives the training.[1261] The wording of this offence also closely resembles that of the Directive.[1262] Article 140*quinquies* CC criminalises anybody who, in Belgium or abroad, receives instruction or training as described in Article 140*quater* CC. The Article explicitly refers to Article 140*quater* CC with regard to the type of instruction or training, so anything said there (see no. 235) is also applicable here.[1263] The training can be in person or via the internet for example.[1264] Once more, the Criminal Code states this Article is applicable without prejudice to the application of Article 140 CC.

244. Self-study – The legislature added a new section to Article 140*quinquies* CC in 2019.[1265] While for the Articles 140*bis*, 140*ter* and 140*quater* CC, it added an aggravating circumstance, in Article 140*quinquies* CC, it added a second offence. The *actus reus* of this offence is: in Belgium or abroad, acquiring knowledge yourself or educating yourself in the matters referred to in Article 140*quater* CC. Because of the wording of the first section, it is

---

1260 Art. 7 wet 18 februari 2013 tot wijziging van boek II, titel Iter van het Strafwetboek, *BS* 4 maart 2013, 13233. See also: De La Serna (n 50) 225.

1261 MvT wetsontwerp 13 november 2012 tot wijziging van Titel 1*ter* van het Strafwetboek, *Parl. St.* Kamer 2012–2013, no. 53–2502/001, (4) 16; Fransen and Kerkhofs (n 10) 67.

1262 Art. 8 Directive (EU) 2017/541 of the European Parliament and of the Council of 15 March 2017 on combating terrorism and replacing Council Framework Decision 2002/475/JHA and amending Council Decision 2005/671/JHA [2017] *OJ* L88/6 – 21.

1263 Delhaise (n 8) 60; Winants (n 8) 351.

1264 Delhaise and Fievet (n 45) 118.

1265 Art. 79, 2° wet 5 mei 2019 houdende diverse bepalingen in strafzaken en inzake erediensten, en tot wijziging van de wet 28 mei 2002 betreffende de euthanasie en van het Sociaal Strafwetboek, *BS* 24 mei 2019, 50023. A similar proposal was already tabled once before, in 2018. See: wetsvoorstel 18 januari 2018 tot wijziging van het Strafwetboek teneinde zelfinstructie in het kader van terrorisme strafbaar te stellen, *Parl.St.* Kamer 2017–2018, no. 54–2900/001.

generally accepted that its scope only covers people receiving training from somebody else.[1266] Because the recitals to the Directive state that training should also include self-study,[1267] the legislature decided to introduce this second section, focusing on just that.[1268] In the preparatory works, it emphasises that occasionally visiting a website, or visiting it for academic purposes does not suffice to be punishable. There needs to be an active and conscious action of the perpetrator.[1269] Cesoni argues that this is insufficient and warns for a reversal of the burden of proof, violations of the presumption of innocence and the possibility of thought police.[1270]

245. In Belgium or abroad – Both sections explicitly state that the training is received or undertaken in Belgium or abroad.[1271] This is not specified in the offence of providing training, nor in many of the other terrorist offences. It is unclear why the legislature decided to specify this in Article 140*quinquies* CC.[1272] It is highly unlikely that the Belgian legislature wanted to imply that the other offences, such as providing training, are not punishable if they did not take place on Belgian soil. As imposed by the Framework Decision[1273] and the Directive,[1274] Belgian legislation includes grounds of extraterritorial jurisdiction for terrorism.[1275] The Preceding Title to the Code of Criminal Procedure (PT

1266 Toelichting bij wetsvoorstel 6 februari 2019 houdende diverse bepalingen in strafzaken en inzake erediensten, *Parl.St.* Kamer 2018–2019, no. 54-3515/001, (3) 106; Bounjoua (n 14) 672; Delhaise (n 8) 60–61; Winants (n 8) 357.

1267 Recital 11 Directive (EU) 2017/541 of the European Parliament and of the Council of 15 March 2017 on combating terrorism and replacing Council Framework Decision 2002/475/JHA and amending Council Decision 2005/671/JHA [2017] *OJ* L88/6–21; Toelichting bij wetsvoorstel 6 februari 2019 houdende diverse bepalingen in strafzaken en inzake erediensten, *Parl. St.* Kamer 2018–2019, no. 54-3515/001, (3) 106; European Union Agency for Fundamental Rights, *Directive (EU) 2017/541 on combatting terrorism: Impact on fundamental rights and freedoms*, 2021, 79. Cesoni argues that this is not binding upon Member States, however. See: Cesoni (n 15) 238.

1268 Cesoni (n 15) 237–238; De Coensel, 'De Wet Diverse Bepalingen in Strafzaken II: Terroristische misdrijven in lijn met de Europese verplichtingen?' (n 793) 213–214.

1269 Toelichting bij wetsvoorstel 6 februari 2019 houdende diverse bepalingen in strafzaken en inzake erediensten, *Parl.St.* Kamer 2018–2019, no. 54-3515/001, (3) 106. See also: Deruyck and De Nauw (n 786) 13; Winants (n 8) 357; Comité T, 'Rapport 2019: Le respect des droits humains dans le cadre de la lutte contre le terrorisme: Un chantier en cours', 17.

1270 Cesoni (n 15) 238–239.

1271 Bounjoua (n 14) 671–672; Ketels (n 691) 258; Winants (n 8) 351.

1272 Fransen and Kerkhofs (n 10) 67.

1273 Art. 9 Council Framework Decision 2002/475/JHA of 13 June 2002 on combating terrorism [2002] *OJ* L164/3. See also: Beernaert, 'La Loi du 19 Décembre 2003 relative aux infractions terroristes : Quand le droit pénal Belge évolue sous la dictée de l'Union Européenne' (n 20) 588; Gless (n 14) 938.

1274 Art. 19 Directive (EU) 2017/541 of the European Parliament and of the Council of 15 March 2017 on combating terrorism and replacing Council Framework Decision 2002/475/JHA and amending Council Decision 2005/671/JHA [2017] *OJ* L88/6 – 21.

1275 See: De La Serna (n 8) 209; De Nauw (n 786) 8–9; Hameeuw (n 8) 10–11; R Malagnini, 'La poursuite en Belgique des infractions terroristes commises à l'étranger' [2018] Revue de Jurisprudence de Liège, Mons et Bruxelles (JLMB) 1423; Weyembergh and Kennes (n 58)

CCP) states that any Belgian or person who has their main residence in Belgium can be prosecuted in Belgium when they commit a terrorist offence (*sensu lato* or *sensu stricto*) outside of Belgium (active personality principle).[1276] Furthermore, it also states that anybody who commits a terrorist offence (*sensu stricto* or *sensu lato*) outside of Belgium can be prosecuted in Belgium if this offence was aimed at a Belgian subject[1277] or institution or against an institution of the European Union or of a body established in accordance with the Treaty establishing the European Community or the Treaty on the European Union, which is located in Belgium.[1278] Furthermore, as a general rule, to prosecute a person who commits an extraterritorial offence for which the statute allows prosecution in Belgium, it is required that the suspect can be found in Belgium.[1279] However, in case of prosecutions for terrorism *sensu stricto*,[1280] this rule does not apply.[1281]

155; Weyembergh and Kennes (n 14) 122–123. In addition, an offence is a territorial offence as soon as one constituent element of the offence took place in Belgium (see among other cases: Cass. 4 februari 1986, *Pas.*, 1986, I, 671; Cass. 4 oktober 2017, *NC* 2018, 303). So e.g. a Frenchman residing in France recruiting a Frenchman residing in Belgium over the internet for a terrorist attack in France, would commit a Belgian territorial offence. In a recent case, the Court of Cassation went even further and stated that a material act which prepares one of the constituent elements of the offence taking place in Belgium is sufficient for the offence to be a Belgian territorial offence. (Cass. 10 maart 2021, P.20.1295.F, *JLMB* 2021, 1122, noot F. Kuty).

1276 Art. 6, 1°*ter* PT CCP. See also: Beernaert, 'La Loi du 19 Décembre 2003 relative aux infractions terroristes : Quand le droit pénal Belge évolue sous la dictée de l'Union Européenne' (n 20) 588; De Hert and Millen (n 803) 11–12; De La Serna (n 8) 209; Deruyck and De Nauw (n 786) 16; Flore (n 10) 222; Hameeuw (n 8) 10; Kuty (n 600) 455; Malagnini (n 1275) 1425–1426; Tulkens and others (n 39) 302–303; Van den Wyngaert, Vandromme and Traest (n 34) 170; Wattier (n 785); Winants (n 8) 349.

1277 The European Commission noted that this does not seem to cover residents who are not nationals. See: Report from the Commission to the European Parliament and the Council based on Art. 29(1) of Directive (EU) 2017/541 of the European Parliament and of the Council of 15 March 2017 on combating terrorism and replacing Council Framework Decision 2002/475/JHA and amending Council Decision 2005/671/JHA, Brussels 30 September 2020, COM(2020) 619, 14.

1278 Art. 10*ter*, section 1, 4° PT CCP. See also: Beernaert, 'La Loi du 19 Décembre 2003 relative aux infractions terroristes : Quand le droit pénal Belge évolue sous la dictée de l'Union Européenne' (n 20) 588; De Hert and Millen (n 803) 12; De La Serna (n 8) 209; Deruyck and De Nauw (n 786) 16; Flore (n 10) 222; Hameeuw (n 8) 10; Kuty (n 600) 457–458; Malagnini (n 1275) 1425; Tulkens and others (n 39) 303–304; Van den Wyngaert, Vandromme and Traest (n 34) 170; Wattier (n 785); Winants (n 8) 349.

1279 Art. 12, section 1 PT CPP. See also: Beernaert, 'La Loi du 19 Décembre 2003 relative aux infractions terroristes : Quand le droit pénal Belge évolue sous la dictée de l'Union Européenne' (n 20) 588; Kuty (n 600) 447; Tulkens and others (n 39) 301.

1280 Some commentators suggest that this is the case for all terrorist offences. See: Deruyck and De Nauw (n 786) 16; Malagnini (n 1275) 1426–1428. However, other commentators do not agree.

1281 Art. 12, 1° and 4° PT CCP. See also: Deruyck and De Nauw (n 786) 16; Kuty (n 600) 449; Van den Wyngaert, Vandromme and Traest (n 34) 170. Before this statute was adapted in 2012, there was discussion about whether or not this general rule applied to terrorism offences. See: Weyembergh and Kennes (n 14) 123. The majority of commentators seemed to think the rule did apply. E.g.: Beernaert, 'La Loi du 19 Décembre 2003 relative aux infractions terroristes : Quand le droit pénal Belge évolue sous la dictée de l'Union Européenne' (n 20) 588; De La Serna (n 8) 210; Delmulle and Guenter (n 6) 5; Flore (n 10) 222–223; Hameeuw (n 8) 11.

In this case, if the suspect is not Belgian and cannot be found on Belgian soil, the prosecution can only take place after the complaint has been evaluated by the public prosecution service.[1282] In addition to the grounds of extraterritorial jurisdiction, it is noteworthy that one of the examples in the preparatory works of Article 140*quater* (see no. 247) explicitly refers to training provided abroad.[1283]

SECTION II. *MENS REA*

246. Special intent – The *mens rea* for both offences in Article 140*quinquies* CC is a form of special intent: with a view to commit or contribute to the commission of one of the offences referred to in Article 137, with the exception of the offence referred to in Article 137, §3, 6°.[1284] So here too the training has to be received or undertaken with the view to commit or contribute to the commission of terrorism *sensu stricto*, with the exception of threatening a terrorist attack. In section 1 of the Article, the part '*or contribute to the commission of*' was added in 2019,[1285] because this is part of the wording of the Directive and the legislature wanted to increase coherence (see no. 226).[1286] Section 2 of the Article was only introduced in 2019, with this phrase already in it. Concreteness is not required, so the person receiving or undertaking the training does not need to know the exact terrorist offence for which they are training, nor does this offence actually have to be committed.[1287]

SECTION III. SENTENCES

247. Felony – The sentences for both variants of Article 140*quinquies* CC are five to ten years felony imprisonment and a fine of 100 to 5,000 euros. This is the same sentence as for incitement, recruitment, providing training[1288] and

1282 Art. 10*ter*, section 2 PT CCP. See also: Van den Wyngaert, Vandromme and Traest (n 34) 170.

1283 MvT wetsontwerp 13 november 2012 tot wijziging van Titel 1*ter* van het Strafwetboek, *Parl. St.* Kamer 2012–2013, no. 53-2502/001, (4) 16; Fransen and Kerkhofs (n 10) 67–68.

1284 Art.140*quinquies* CC; Delhaise (n 8) 62; Delhaise and Fievet (n 45) 118; Fransen and Kerkhofs (n 10) 68; Ketels (n 691) 258–259.

1285 Art. 79, 1° wet 5 mei 2019 houdende diverse bepalingen in strafzaken en inzake erediensten, en tot wijziging van de wet 28 mei 2002 betreffende de euthanasie en van het Sociaal Strafwetboek, *BS* 24 mei 2019, 50023; De Coensel, 'De Wet Diverse Bepalingen in Strafzaken II: Terroristische misdrijven in lijn met de Europese verplichtingen?' (n 793) 212; Winants (n 8) 357.

1286 Art. 8 Directive (EU) 2017/541 of the European Parliament and of the Council of 15 March 2017 on combating terrorism and replacing Council Framework Decision 2002/475/JHA and amending Council Decision 2005/671/JHA [2017] *OJ* L88/6–21; Toelichting bij wetsvoorstel 6 februari 2019 houdende diverse bepalingen in strafzaken en inzake erediensten, *Parl.St.* Kamer 2018–2019, no. 54-3515/001, (3) 106.

1287 Delhaise (n 8) 62; Fransen and Kerkhofs (n 10) 68; Ketels (n 691) 259; Van Deuren (n 788) 508; Winants (n 8) 351.

1288 De La Serna (n 50) 225; Delhaise (n 8) 78; Ketels (n 691) 258.

participating in the activities of a terrorist group (see nos 181, 214, 229 and 237). After correctionalisation, which is standard in this case, the maximum imprisonment is five years. When the Article was introduced in 2013, the Council of State reasoned that having the same sentence for the person providing the training (Art. 140*quater* CC) and for the person receiving the training (Art. 140*quinquies* CC) could be discriminatory because it is treating two different situations in the same way.[1289] The legislature replied that both actions are serious, with the perpetrators having the same intent, and both should be felonies because of how dangerous they are.[1290] It gave the example of someone who goes abroad to receive training for terrorism and returns to Belgium to put that knowledge into practice. Both the trainer and trainee have the same goal, being the commission of a terrorist attack. Therefore, the legislature reasoned, it is justified they are punishable with the same sentence.[1291]

248. Alternative sentences and modalities – Because the sentence after correctionalisation is one month to five years imprisonment, electronic monitoring as a principal sentence is possible. This is the case when the judge feels the offence is of such a nature that it should not be punished with more than one year imprisonment (see no. 115).[1292] The electronic monitoring has a term of one month to one year. Community service, with a term of 45 to 300 hours, and an autonomous probation sentence of one to two years are also possible (see nos 116 and 117). Finally, postponement of sentence enforcement subject to probation is an option, as is regular postponement of sentence enforcement and suspension of sentencing, possibly with probation measures as well, if the perpetrator does not have prior convictions which are too serious (see nos 118 and 119).

SECTION IV. CONSTITUTIONAL COURT

249. Legality principle, and freedom of speech and association – The final Article that was challenged and had to be discussed by the Constitutional Court in its judgment of 28 January 2015, was Article 140*quinquies* CC. After a general analysis of the legality principle (see no. 155), the Constitutional Court applied it to the offence in question. Regarding Article 140*quinquies* CC, a

1289 Advies 51.806/3 van de Raad van State 18 September 2012 bij wetsontwerp 13 november 2012 tot wijziging van Titel 1*ter* van het Strafwetboek, *Parl.St.* Kamer 2012–2013, no. 53-2502/001, (22) 27; Delhaise (n 8) 62; Fransen and Kerkhofs (n 10) 68.

1290 MvT wetsontwerp 13 november 2012 tot wijziging van Titel 1*ter* van het Strafwetboek, *Parl. St.* Kamer 2012–2013, no. 53-2502/001, (4) 16; Delhaise (n 8) 62–63; Ketels (n 691) 258.

1291 MvT wetsontwerp 13 november 2012 tot wijziging van Titel 1*ter* van het Strafwetboek, *Parl. St.* Kamer 2012–2013, no. 53-2502/001, (4) 16; Fransen and Kerkhofs (n 10) 67–68.

1292 Art. 37*ter*, §1, section 1 CC. See also: Daems and Magis (n 710) 181; Decaigny, 'Relatieve zwaarte, toepassingsgebied en duur' (n 714) 50; De Nauw and Deruyck (n 39) 127; Tulkens and others (n 39) 598; Van den Wyngaert, Vandromme and Traest (n 34) 430.

violation of the principle of legality and the freedoms of speech and association was alleged. However, the Court referred to the inextricable link between Articles 140*quinquies* and 140*quater* CC and referred to its reasoning for the latter Article (see nos 239–240) to conclude that the former also does not violate the legality principle.[1293] It then did the same for the freedom of speech and freedom of association.[1294]

SECTION V. PRACTICAL APPLICATION

250. Conviction – In one case, a man who had travelled to Syria was acquitted in first instance. He travelled there to find and visit his sister in IS-controlled territory. While he was there, he had stayed in an IS military camp, where he participated in physical training, studied the Quran and shot a Kalashnikov. The Correctional Court however acquitted him because there was doubt about his intent.[1295] He had to stay in the IS camp to visit his sister and the fact that he participated in the daily activities of the camp, does not mean he had the intention to commit a terrorist attack, according to the Correctional Court. The Court of Appeal, however, convicted him.[1296] It found that he did have the required intent because he knew IS was a terrorist group and knew about the terrorist offences the group wanted to commit. Furthermore, it specified that the fact that he was not a member of IS himself, was irrelevant. The Court of Appeal discussed participation in the activities of IS and following training together. However, while their *actus reus* may coincide, they have a different *mens rea*, which the court did not sufficiently take into account.

251. Acquittals – In the abovementioned Kamikaze Riders case, the person who participated in the paintball and airsoft activities was acquitted, for the same reason the person organising the activities was (see no. 242).[1297] In another case that was already mentioned under Article 140*quater* CC, the Correctional Court of Hainaut convicted a man for providing training for terrorism (see no. 241). He was also prosecuted for receiving training, but the court could only find proof he provided training, not that he received any. Therefore, he was acquitted for the charge of receiving training.[1298] This was the only case in the Reguide case law analysis in which a defendant was prosecuted for receiving training.

1293 GwH 28 januari 2015, 9/2015, *TVW* 2015, 179, B.49. See also: Ketels (n 691) 259; Spreutels and Velu (n 95) 138; Winants (n 8) 351.

1294 GwH 28 januari 2015, 9/2015, *TVW* 2015, 179, B.53. See also: Ketels (n 691) 259; Winants (n 8) 351–352.

1295 Corr. Antwerpen 2 november 2015, *onuitg*; Fransen and Kerkhofs (n 10) 68.

1296 Antwerpen 2 maart 2016, *onuitg*; Fransen and Kerkhofs (n 10) 68–69.

1297 Corr. Brussel 20 oktober 2016, *onuitg*; Fransen and Kerkhofs (n 10) 69.

1298 Corr. Henegouwen (afd. Charleroi) 27 september 2017, *onuitg.*, 6; Fransen and Kerkhofs (n 10) 69.

CHAPTER VIII
ARTICLE 140*SEXIES* CC

SECTION I. *ACTUS REUS*

252. Traveling for terrorist purposes – When the issue of foreign terrorist fighters took the foreground, the UN Security Council stated in a resolution '*that all States shall ensure that their domestic laws and regulations establish serious criminal offences sufficient to provide the ability to prosecute and to penalize in a manner duly reflecting the seriousness of the offence: (a)their nationals who travel or attempt to travel to a State other than their States of residence or nationality, and other individuals who travel or attempt to travel from their territories to a State other than their States of residence or nationality, for the purpose of the perpetration, planning, or preparation of, or participation in, terrorist acts, or the providing or receiving of terrorist training.*'[1299] After this resolution, the Council of Europe included a similar provision in an additional protocol to the Convention on the Prevention of Terrorism.[1300] The EU also included a comparable provision in its Directive on Combating Terrorism.[1301] However, on top of outbound travel, the Directive also covers inbound travel. With regard

---

1299 UN Security Council Resolution S/RES/2178 (24 September 2014) 6(a), http://unscr.com/en/resolutions/2178. See also: MvT wetsontwerp 22 juni 2015 tot versterking van de strijd tegen terrorisme, *Parl.St.* Kamer 2014–15, no. 54–1198/001, 5; Blaise and Delhaise (n 49) 173–174; Tarik Gherbaoui, 'Criminalising Foreign Fighter Travel in Order to Prevent Terrorism in Europe: An Illegitimate Assault on Human Dignity?' in Christophe Paulussen and Martin Scheinin (eds), *Human Dignity and Human Security in Times of Terrorism* (TMC Asser Press 2020) 245–247; Lavaux, 'Terrorisme: La stratégie de l'union Européenne en matière de radicalisation et de recrutement (troisième partie)' (n 937) 124; Mitsilegas (n 25) 184–185.

1300 Art. 4 Additional Protocol to the Council of Europe Convention on the Prevention of Terrorism, 2015, CETS 217; European Union Agency for Fundamental Rights, *Directive (EU) 2017/541 on combatting terrorism: Impact on fundamental rights and freedoms*, 2021, 67; Gherbaoui (n 1299) 249–250; Mitsilegas (n 25) 187; Alejandro Sánchez Frías, 'Public Security Derogations to the Free Movement of EU Citizens and Preventive Criminal Law: A Collision between Ever-Expanding Concepts?' [2019] European Journal of Crime, Criminal Law and Criminal Justice 293, 298–303; Guy Stessens, 'Terroristen op reis: over de strafbaarstelling van reizen met terroristisch oogmerk en andere maatregelen ter beperking van de reisvrijheid van (vermeende) terroristen' in Steven Dewulf (ed), *La [CVDW] Liber Amicorum Chris Van den Wyngaert* (Maklu 2017) 443–445.

1301 Art. 9 Directive (EU) 2017/541 of the European Parliament and of the Council of 15 March 2017 on combating terrorism and replacing Council Framework Decision 2002/475/JHA and amending Council Decision 2005/671/JHA [2017] *OJ* L88/6–21. See also: Bounjoua (n 14) 666–667; Gherbaoui (n 1299) 251–257; Mitsilegas (n 25) 187.

to inbound travel the Member States have two options: to criminalise inbound travel as the mirror image of outbound travel or to criminalise preparatory acts undertaken by a person entering the Member State with the intention to commit or contribute to the commission of terrorism *sensu stricto*.[1302] The second option thus requires a stronger link between the inbound travel and the intended terrorist offence (*sensu stricto*). The Belgian legislature went with the first option and fulfilled its international obligations by introducing Article 140*sexies* into the Criminal Code.[1303] The *actus reus* of this offence is leaving[1304] or entering[1305] the national territory. This is an everyday action, which makes the *mens rea* the core of this offence.[1306] The wording of the Article implies the *actus reus* is present once the person crosses the Belgian border, not when they start or end their journey.[1307] In addition, Belgian merchant ships, war ships and airplanes are considered fictional Belgian territory.[1308] Presumably, the offence can therefore also be committed when a person boards or disembarks a Belgian ship or plane. Article 140*sexies* CC, states that it is applicable without prejudice to the application of Article 140 CC as well (see no. 212).

SECTION II. *MENS REA*

253. Special intent –The *mens rea* is the aim to commit or contribute to the commission, in Belgium or abroad, of one of the offences meant in Article 137,

---

1302 Art. 9(2) Directive (EU) 2017/541 of the European Parliament and of the Council of 15 March 2017 on combating terrorism and replacing Council Framework Decision 2002/475/JHA and amending Council Decision 2005/671/JHA [2017] *OJ* L88/6–21; De Coensel, *Counter-Terrorism & Criminal Law: A Normative Legitimacy Test of Terrorism-Related Offences on Expression, Information and Movement* (n 1) 245; Stessens (n 1300) 446–448; European Union Agency for Fundamental Rights, *Directive (EU) 2017/541 on combatting terrorism: Impact on fundamental rights and freedoms*, 2021, 67.

1303 Art. 2 wet 20 juli 2015 tot versterking van de strijd tegen het terrorisme, *BS* 5 augustus 2015, 49326; MvT wetsontwerp 22 juni 2015 tot versterking van de strijd tegen terrorisme, *Parl. St.* Kamer 2014–15, no. 54–1198/001, 5; Beernaert, 'Renforcement de l'arsenal législatif anti-terroriste: entre symboles et prévention' (n 50) 834; Deruyck and De Nauw (n 786) 13; Lavaux, 'Recente Overheidsmaatregelen i.v.m. de "Foreign Fighters"' (n 1120) 352–353; Velaers (n 27) 786–787. De Coensel points out that when applied to a Belgian national, this offence violates the right to enter that person's own country. See: De Coensel, *Counter-Terrorism & Criminal Law: A Normative Legitimacy Test of Terrorism-Related Offences on Expression, Information and Movement* (n 1) 264.

1304 Art. 140*sexies*, 1° CC.

1305 Art. 140*sexies*, 2° CC.

1306 Advies 57.127/AV van de Raad van State 24 maart 2015 bij wetsontwerp 22 juni 2015 tot versterking van de strijd tegen het terrorisme, *Parl.St.* Kamer 2014–15, no. 54–1198/001, (13) 17; Beernaert, 'Renforcement de l'arsenal législatif anti-terroriste: entre symboles et prévention' (n 50) 834; Delhaise (n 8) 65; Ward Yperman, 'Heiligt het doel de middelen?' [2018] Nieuw Juridisch Weekblad 304.

1307 Delhaise (n 8) 63–64.

1308 Herman Fransen, 'Strafwet' [2017] Postal Memorialis – Lexicon strafrecht, strafvordering en bijzondere wetten S180/01, 58–59.

140 to 140*quinquies* and 141 CC, with the exception of the offence in Article 137, §3, 6°. This covers all terrorist offences under Belgian law, except for threatening a terrorist offence (*sensu stricto*)[1309] and preparing a terrorist offence (*sensu stricto*)[1310] (see nos 264–273). This is broader than the Directive, which does not include incitement and recruitment but at the same time it is also slightly narrower, since the Directive does not exclude threatening. This aim, which is a special intent, needs to be present simultaneously with the *actus reus*, meaning at the time of leaving or entering the national territory.[1311] Concreteness is not required, so the traveller does not need to know exactly which terrorist offence they will commit.[1312] *A fortiori* it is not required that the intended offence is actually committed.[1313] The danger in the case of an offence that revolves almost exclusively around the *mens rea* is that mere thoughts become punishable, whereas in Belgium the principle is that only acts are punishable.[1314] The Council of State noted in this respect that the offence is situated on the border between the material and the intentional by criminalising an everyday action.[1315] The Council pointed towards the need for sufficient concrete, objective and material indications for the intention of the perpetrator.[1316] The use of stereotypes and presumptions has to be avoided.[1317] The explanatory memorandum explicitly states that the evidence and the facts of the case will be of crucial importance for the assessment of the *mens rea*.[1318]

1309 Art. 137, §3, 6° CC. See also: Ketels (n 691) 259.

1310 Art. 140*septies* CC.

1311 Advies 57.127/AV van de Raad van State 24 maart 2015 bij wetsontwerp 22 juni 2015 tot versterking van de strijd tegen het terrorisme, *Parl.St.* Kamer 2014–15, no. 54–1198/001, (13) 18; Delhaise (n 8) 65; Deruyck and De Nauw (n 786) 13; Fransen and Kerkhofs (n 802) 179–180; Fransen and Kerkhofs (n 10) 70–71; Ketels (n 691) 260; Winants (n 8) 352.

1312 Bounjoua (n 14) 676; Fransen and Kerkhofs (n 802) 180; Fransen and Kerkhofs (n 10) 72; Ketels (n 691) 260; Winants (n 8) 352.

1313 MvT wetsontwerp 22 juni 2015 tot versterking van de strijd tegen terrorisme, *Parl.St.* Kamer 2014–15, no. 54–1198/001, 6; Beernaert, 'Renforcement de l'arsenal législatif anti-terroriste: entre symboles et prévention' (n 50) 834; Blaise and Delhaise (n 49) 174; Bounjoua (n 14) 675–676; Delhaise (n 8) 65; Deruyck and De Nauw (n 786) 13; Fransen and Kerkhofs (n 10) 70; Moreau (n 47) 107; Winants (n 8) 352.

1314 Fransen and Kerkhofs (n 802) 179; Fransen and Kerkhofs (n 10) 71; Gherbaoui (n 1299) 261.

1315 Advies 57.127/AV van de Raad van State 24 maart 2015 bij wetsontwerp 22 juni 2015 tot versterking van de strijd tegen het terrorisme, *Parl.St.* Kamer 2014–15, no. 54–1198/001, (13) 17; Blaise and Delhaise (n 49) 174; Bounjoua (n 14) 676; Velaers (n 27) 787–788; Winants (n 8) 352.

1316 Advies 57.127/AV van de Raad van State 24 maart 2015 bij wetsontwerp 22 juni 2015 tot versterking van de strijd tegen het terrorisme, *Parl.St.* Kamer 2014–15, no. 54–1198/001, (13) 17. See also: Bounjoua (n 14) 676; Fransen and Kerkhofs (n 802) 179; Moreau (n 47) 107–108; Velaers (n 27) 787–788.

1317 Beernaert, 'Renforcement de l'arsenal législatif anti-terroriste: entre symboles et prévention' (n 50) 834; Delhaise (n 8) 65–66; Moreau (n 47) 107–108; Velaers (n 27) 787–788.

1318 MvT wetsontwerp 22 juni 2015 tot versterking van de strijd tegen terrorisme, *Parl.St.* Kamer 2014–15, no. 54–1198/001, 5.

254. Extension in 2019 – In 2019, the scope of Article 140*sexies* CC was further extended. As with the other terrorist offences (see no. 226), the Directive requires Member States to criminalise not only travel to commit a terrorist offence, but also travel to contribute to the commission of such an offence.[1319] As a result, the legislature inserted the words '*or contributing to the commission*' twice (both for leaving and for entering the national territory) in Article 140*sexies* CC.[1320] Many, if not all, of these actions are already punishable under (attempted) Article 140 CC or (participation in) one of the other terrorist offences *sensu lato*. Nevertheless, the legislature wanted to increase coherence and legal certainty and therefore thought the addition necessary.[1321] Again, while increasing coherence, this also increased overlap and this while the Belgian traveling offence is broader already than required by the Directive. Bearing in mind the aforementioned danger of a broad application, it might have been better not to formulate Article 140*sexies* CC even more broadly. Comité T called the Article 140*sexies* offence an offence of pure intent which violated the legality principle and presumption of innocence.[1322]

SECTION III. SENTENCES

255. Felony – As with the offences of Article 140*bis* to 140*quinquies* CC,[1323] the sentence for traveling for terrorist purposes is five to ten years felony imprisonment, which becomes one month to five years imprisonment after correctionalisation, and a fine of 100 to 5,000 euros. This means electronic monitoring as a principal sentence is possible, when the judge feels the offence is of such a nature that it should not be punished with more than one year imprisonment (see no. 115).[1324] The electronic monitoring has a term of one month to one year. Community service, with a term of 45 to 300 hours, and an

1319 Art. 9 Directive (EU) 2017/541 of the European Parliament and of the Council of 15 March 2017 on combating terrorism and replacing Council Framework Decision 2002/475/JHA and amending Council Decision 2005/671/JHA [2017] *OJ* L88/6–21.

1320 Art. 80 wet 5 mei 2019 houdende diverse bepalingen in strafzaken en inzake erediensten, en tot wijziging van de wet 28 mei 2002 betreffende de euthanasie en van het Sociaal Strafwetboek, *BS* 24 mei 2019, 50023; MvT wetsvoorstel 6 februari 2019 houdende diverse bepalingen in strafzaken en inzake erediensten, *Parl.St.* Kamer 2018–2019, no. 54–3515/001, (3) 106–107; De Coensel, 'De Wet Diverse Bepalingen in Strafzaken II: Terroristische misdrijven in lijn met de Europese verplichtingen?' (n 793) 212; Winants (n 8) 357.

1321 Toelichting bij wetsvoorstel 6 februari 2019 houdende diverse bepalingen in strafzaken en inzake erediensten, *Parl.St.* Kamer 2018–2019, no. 54–3515/001, (3) 104–105.

1322 Comité T, 'Rapport 2019: Le respect des droits humains dans le cadre de la lutte contre le terrorisme: Un chantier en cours', 17.

1323 Delhaise (n 8) 78.

1324 Art. 37*ter*, §1, section 1 CC. See also: Daems and Magis (n 710) 181; Decaigny, 'Relatieve zwaarte, toepassingsgebied en duur' (n 714) 50; De Nauw and Deruyck (n 39) 127; Tulkens and others (n 39) 598; Van den Wyngaert, Vandromme and Traest (n 34) 430.

autonomous probation sentence of one to two years are also possible (see nos 116 and 117). Finally, postponement of sentence enforcement subject to probation is an option, as is regular postponement of sentence enforcement and suspension of sentencing, possibly with probation measures as well, if the perpetrator does not have prior convictions which are too serious (see nos 118 and 119).

SECTION IV. CONSTITUTIONAL COURT

256. Constitutional Court 18 January 2018 – The introduction of Article 140*sexies* CC was appealed as well. This appeal was based on the principle of legality and the free movement of persons but was rejected by the Constitutional Court.[1325] The argumentation resembles the discussion that had already taken place before the Council of State.

257. Legality principle: accuracy and clarity – Firstly, the question was raised as to whether Article 140*sexies* CC complies with the principle of legality. After a general analysis of the legality principle (see no. 155), the Constitutional Court analysed the specific offence and replied that the provision was drafted in a sufficiently precise and clear manner and thus provided sufficient legal certainty.[1326] With regard to the *mens rea*, the Court stressed that a person can reasonably determine whether they intend to commit one of the listed offences and that the court must consider objective elements, taking into account the specific circumstances of each case.[1327] The fact that the *mens rea* refers to another offence, with its own particular special intent, does not prevent a person from assessing what the criminal consequence of their conduct will be.[1328] All this is in line with what the Council of State had said.

258. Legality principle: overlap – Subsequently, it was argued that Article 140*sexies* CC did not criminalise anything that was not already punishable. On this point, the explanatory memorandum had already clarified that not all terrorists travel to follow a training course before committing an attack (Art. 140*quinquies* CC) or to join a terrorist group (Art. 140 CC).[1329]

1325 GwH 18 januari 2018, 8/2018, *NjW* 2018, 299–304, noot W. Yperman. See also: Spreutels and Velu (n 95) 138–139; Winants (n 8) 352–353.

1326 GwH 18 januari 2018, 8/2018, *NjW* 2018, 300–301, B.7; Dejemeppe and Rigaux (n 898) 763–764; Delhaise (n 8) 67; Moreau (n 47) 115–116.

1327 GwH 18 januari 2018, 8/2018, *NjW* 2018, 301–302, B.9.1; Blaise and Delhaise (n 49) 174; Delhaise (n 8) 67; European Union Agency for Fundamental Rights, *Directive (EU) 2017/541 on combatting terrorism: Impact on fundamental rights and freedoms*, 2021, 69.

1328 GwH 18 januari 2018, 8/2018, *NjW* 2018, 302–303, B.9.3.

1329 MvT wetsontwerp 22 juni 2015 tot versterking van de strijd tegen terrorisme, *Parl.St.* Kamer 2014–15, no. 54-1198/001, 6–7; See also: Blaise and Delhaise (n 49) 175; Delhaise (n 8) 66; Ketels (n 691) 261.

Either way, concurrence is possible,[1330] so any potential overlap would not be a problem.[1331] The Council of State had inquired about this overlap too and had stated that the government had not given a concrete example of a situation that does not fall under other terrorist offences (and specifically Art. 140 CC).[1332] However, the Council of State had agreed that from a legal point of view this was not a problem. Wanting absolute certainty that all the targeted situations would be punishable is a sufficient reason to introduce a new offence.[1333] In line with its judgment of 28 January 2015 (see no. 231), the Constitutional Court ruled that the principle of legality has not been violated if two provisions criminalise the same conduct.[1334]

259. Free movement of persons – Secondly, the applicant stated that Article 140*sexies* CC is contrary to the free movement of persons. The Constitutional Court did not agree with this argument either. Without further explanation, the Court referred to the fact that the provision was introduced to combat terrorism within the framework of UN Security Council Resolution no. 2178 and therefore does not violate the free movement of persons.[1335] The Council of State, however, had explicitly stated in its opinion, referring to European case law,[1336] that this does not exempt states from their obligations to

1330 There is ideal concurrence when several qualifications are applicable to the same set of facts. In such cases, only the most severe penalty is applied (Art. 65, section 1 CC). See no. 183.

1331 MvT wetsontwerp 22 juni 2015 tot versterking van de strijd tegen terrorisme, *Parl.St.* Kamer 2014–15, no. 54–1198/001, 7; Blaise and Delhaise (n 49) 173; Bounjoua (n 14) 677.

1332 Advies 57.137/AV van de Raad van State bij wetsontwerp houdende diverse bepalingen ter bestrijding van terrorisme, *Parl.St.* Kamer 2014–2015, no. 54–1198/001, (13) 18–19; Fransen and Kerkhofs (n 10) 70–71.

1333 Advies 57.137/AV van de Raad van State 24 maart 2015 bij wetsontwerp houdende diverse bepalingen ter bestrijding van terrorisme, *Parl.St.* Kamer 2014–15, no. 54–1198/001, (13) 19.

1334 GwH 18 januari 2018, 8/2018, *NjW* 2018, 302–303, B.9.3; Blaise and Delhaise (n 49) 175; Delhaise (n 8) 66–67. Moreover, both the sentences and the procedural regime are the same.

1335 GwH 18 januari 2018, 8/2018, *NjW* 2018, 304, B.13.4. See also: Spreutels and Velu (n 95) 145; Winants (n 8) 353. On this point the comparison with the UN Human Rights Committee case Sayadi can prove interesting. In this case the Committee did analyse Belgium's compliance with human rights and found it lacking, despite the fact that the measures were based on a UN Security Council resolution. See: *Sayadi v. Belgium* UN Doc CCPR/C/94/D/1472/2006 (Official Case No) IHRL 3216 (UN HRC 2008). See also: F Krenc, 'La Belgique "condamnée" pour la première fois par le Comité Des Droits de l'homme sur fond de lutte contre le terrorisme – Cap sur Genève!' [2009] Journal des tribunaux 621, 622–624.

1336 *Al-Jedda v. United Kingdom* App no 27021/08 (ECtHR Grand Chamber 7 July 2011) 101–102; *Nada v. Switzerland* App no 10593/08 (ECtHR Grand Chamber 12 September 2012) 168–171; *Al-Dulimi and Montana Management Inc v. Switzerland* App no 5809/08 (ECtHR Grand Chamber 21 June 2016) 95–96; *Yassin Abdullah Kadi and Al Barakaat International Foundation v. Council of the European Union and Commission of the European Communities* Case C-402/05 and C-415/05 [2008] CJEU ECLI:EU:C:2008:461; *European Commission et al v. Yassin Abdullah Kad*i Case C-584/10, C-593/10 and C-595/10 [2013] CJEU ECLI:EU:C:2013:518;.

protect fundamental rights.[1337] Article 2 of the Fourth Protocol to the ECHR, which protects the free movement of persons, states that restrictions on free movement must be provided for by law, be necessary in a democratic society and be proportionate to the objective pursued (see no. 74 and following).[1338] For the assessment of whether the restriction is provided for by law, the Council of State had referred to the discussion of the principle of legality.[1339] The Council had furthermore stated that the restriction is necessary for national security, public safety, the maintenance of public order and the protection of the rights and freedoms of others and is therefore necessary in a democratic society.[1340] The proportionality analysis is less straightforward. The sentence in Article 140*sexies* CC is the same as for many other terrorist offences. The Council of State had stated that the compatibility with the principle of proportionality '*must be assessed and justified in a comprehensive manner, in the light of the possible coherence of that Article with other draft legislative provisions aimed at restricting, in a similar manner but by other means, the free movement of persons in the context of the fight against terrorism*.'[1341] The Council of State referred to the legislation governing the refusal, withdrawal or invalidation of passports, travel documents and identity cards. This way, however, the Council of State did not address the specific situation of Article 140*sexies* CC and therefore did not actually give its opinion on the issue of proportionality.

260. Proportionality – This is a shame, since the question of proportionality is essential. The principal penalty under Article 140*sexies* CC is five to ten years imprisonment. Because this is a felony, the attempt is also punishable.[1342] Article 140*sexies* CC furthermore criminalises not only travelling to commit an attack, but also, for example, travelling to follow a training course (Art. 140*quinquies* CC). Therefore, a start of execution (attempt) of an act of

---

1337 Advies 57.127/AV van de Raad van State 24 maart 2015 bij wetsontwerp 22 juni 2015 tot versterking van de strijd tegen het terrorisme, *Parl.St.* Kamer 2014–15, no. 54–1198/001, (13) 14–15.

1338 Art. 2 ECHR Fourth Protocol; Advies 57.127/AV van de Raad van State 24 maart 2015 bij wetsontwerp 22 juni 2015 tot versterking van de strijd tegen het terrorisme, *Parl.St.* Kamer 2014–15, no. 54–1198/001, (13) 20.

1339 Advies 57.127/AV van de Raad van State 24 maart 2015 bij wetsontwerp 22 juni 2015 tot versterking van de strijd tegen het terrorisme, *Parl.St.* Kamer 2014–15, no. 54–1198/001, (13) 20.

1340 Advies 57.127/AV van de Raad van State 24 maart 2015 bij wetsontwerp 22 juni 2015 tot versterking van de strijd tegen het terrorisme, *Parl.St.* Kamer 2014–15, no. 54–1198/001, (13) 20; Blaise and Delhaise (n 49) 175; Velaers (n 27) 787.

1341 Advies 57.127/AV van de Raad van State 24 maart 2015 bij wetsontwerp 22 juni 2015 tot versterking van de strijd tegen het terrorisme, *Parl.St.* Kamer 2014–15, no. 54–1198/001, (13) 21. Original quote in Dutch: "*op een alomvattende manier beoordeeld en gerechtvaardigd [moet] worden, in het licht van de mogelijke samenhang van dat artikel met andere ontworpen wetgevende bepalingen die op een soortgelijke wijze maar met andere middelen het vrij verkeer van personen in het kader van de strijd tegen het terrorisme beogen te beperken.*"

1342 Art. 52 CC; GwH 18 januari 2018, 8/2018, *NjW* 2018, 302, B.9.2.

preparation (travelling) for an act of preparation (attending training) for an actual attack can be punished.[1343] The Constitutional Court stated, referring to a statement by the Secretary of Justice in the House of Representatives, that, for example, buying an airplane ticket after having openly announced the intention to kill people is sufficient.[1344] We can ask ourselves whether this should be punishable. *A fortiori*, the question arises as to whether a custodial sentence is proportionate for these offences.

SECTION V. PRACTICAL APPLICATION

261. Overlap – There is a lot of overlap between Article 140*sexies* CC and the other terrorist offences, mainly Article 140 CC.[1345] For this reason, there has not been any case yet which we know of in which a person was convicted for traveling for terrorist purposes and not also for one of the offences from Article 140 CC.[1346] In the Reguide case law analysis, a total of seven people were prosecuted for traveling, in concurrence with one of the group offences.

262. Attempted travel – On 21 April 2016, a man was convicted for attempted travel for terrorist purposes because he wanted to go to Syria.[1347] He claimed he just wanted to get news about his son and convince him to come home. However, the Court, referring among other things to the amount and type of clothing he packed, the financial means he gathered and the logistics of his travel, stated he wanted to fight for IS and/or die a martyr. The Court did state it did not know exactly which terrorist offence the man wanted to commit. In a different case, a woman was acquitted for attempted travel for terrorist purposes because she had shown that she wanted to travel on to her family in Kazakhstan.[1348] A third case where a person was prosecuted for attempted travel also led to an acquittal on this charge.[1349] The Court held that while the accused supported IS, had started saving money to finance his trip and had started looking for contacts to aid him in his travels, this did not amount to a start of execution of the offence (see no. 266). Therefore, there was no criminal attempt.

1343 Yperman, 'Heiligt het doel de middelen?' (n 1306) 304–305.

1344 GwH 18 januari 2018, 8/2018, *NjW* 2018, 302, B.9.2.

1345 Moreau (n 47) 112–113.

1346 De Coensel, *Counter-Terrorism & Criminal Law: A Normative Legitimacy Test of Terrorism-Related Offences on Expression, Information and Movement* (n 1) 248; Fransen and Kerkhofs (n 802) 180; Fransen and Kerkhofs (n 10) 74. See also: European Union Agency for Fundamental Rights, *Directive (EU) 2017/541 on combatting terrorism: Impact on fundamental rights and freedoms*, 2021, 68 and 74.

1347 Corr. Brussel 21 april 2016, *onuitg*; Fransen and Kerkhofs (n 10) 72–73.

1348 Corr. Henegouwen (afd. Bergen) 14 mei 2018, *onuitg.*, 26–27; Fransen and Kerkhofs (n 10) 74.

1349 Corr. Luik (vakantiekamer) 19 juli 2017, *JLMB* 2017, 1391.

263. Travel – On 31 May 2017 man was convicted for travel because he had left Belgium to join IS.[1350] He was arrested in Turkey, but had left the national territory of Belgium, so the offence had taken place. Another man travelled to Sudan, with the intention of then traveling on to Libya to join IS. The Correctional Court of Antwerp and Court of Appeal of Antwerp found this sufficient for a conviction under Article 140*sexies* CC, without knowing exactly which terrorist offence the suspect wanted to commit.[1351] In Dendermonde, the Correctional Court convicted a man for traveling for terrorist purposes for traveling to Syria.[1352] He claimed he wanted to go live in the Caliphate to teach religion, without wanting to commit a (concrete) terrorist offence. The Court convicted him, not going into which concrete terrorist offence he would have wanted to commit.

1350 Corr. Brussel 31 mei 2017, *onuitg*; Fransen and Kerkhofs (n 10) 73.

1351 Corr. Antwerpen 19 september 2016, *onuitg*; Antwerpen 22 december 2016, *onuitg;* Fransen and Kerkhofs (n 10) 73.

1352 Corr. Oost-Vlaanderen (afd. Dendermonde) 26 februari 2018, *onuitg.*, 77; Fransen and Kerkhofs (n 10) 73–74.

CHAPTER IX

ARTICLE 140*SEPTIES* CC

SECTION I. *ACTUS REUS*

264. Preparation – In 2016, the legislature wanted to crack down further on terrorism.[1353] In this context, it decided to criminalise preparatory actions, because a terrorist offence is often impossible without these actions.[1354] The Directive does not contain a similar offence. Indeed, it simply states that criminalising preparatory acts undertaken by a person entering a Member State with the intention to commit or contribute to the commission of terrorism *stricto sensu* is a way to respond to terrorist travel (see no. 252).[1355] Article 140*septies* CC criminalises anybody who prepares a terrorist offence meant in Article 137 CC, with the exception of Article 137, §3, 6°. This means every terrorist offence *sensu stricto* except for threatening terrorism. The second paragraph of the Article includes a list of actions that can be preparation:

1° Gathering information on locations, occurrences, events or people which makes it possible to carry out an action on those locations or during those occurrences or events or to cause damage to those people, and observe those locations, occurrences, events or people;

2° The possession, purchase, transport or manufacture of or search for objects or substances which are of such a nature that they can be dangerous to other people or cause substantial economic damage;

3° The possession, purchase, transport or manufacture of or search for financial or material resources, false or illegally obtained documents, information carriers, means of communication, means of transport;

4° The possession or acquisition of or search for premises that acts as a hideout, meeting place, place for gathers or shelter;

1353 Samenvatting van wetsvoorstel 13 januari 2016 tot wijziging van het Strafwetboek wat betreft de bestraffing van terrorisme, *Parl.St.* Kamer 2015–2016, no. 54–1579/001, 1. See also: Cesoni (n 15) 251–252.

1354 Toelichting bij wetsvoorstel 13 januari 2016 tot wijziging van het Strafwetboek wat betreft de bestraffing van terrorisme, *Parl.St.* Kamer 2015–2016, no. 54–1579/001, (3) 4. Note that this is true for more elaborate terrorist attacks, but not necessarily for lone wolf attacks with vehicles or knives. These types of attacks can be committed without much preparation at all.

1355 Art. 9(2)(b) Directive (EU) 2017/541 Directive (EU) 2017/541 of the European Parliament and of the Council of 15 March 2017 on combating terrorism and replacing Council Framework Decision 2002/475/JHA and amending Council Decision 2005/671/JHA [2017] *OJ* L88/6–21.

5° The prior claiming of a terrorist offence, with the exception of the offence of Article 137, §3, 6° CC, regardless of the form or means of the claim.

265. Non-exhaustive – The Criminal Code states that preparation can mean these five things 'among others'. In other words, this list is non-exhaustive.[1356] Anything can be preparation, including an omission.[1357] The Council of State found that a non-exhaustive list does not necessarily violate the legality principle, on the condition that the general description of the offence is sufficiently detailed, clear and predictable.[1358] On the one hand the list needed to be non-exhaustive because terrorism is a changeable form of criminality.[1359] On the other hand, a kind of list was needed in order to delimit the offence and to indicate the type of conduct particularly intended.[1360] The preparatory works state that it is not the intention to target people who provide limited and non-decisive help.[1361] However, that help can be considered as aiding and abetting the preparation of a terrorist offence or financing terrorism (see nos 274–282).[1362] In the preparatory works, it is also explained that point 1° on the list is mainly aimed at observing people or locations, including via the internet.[1363] As an example for point 2°, purchasing explosives, or materials to create explosives is cited.[1364] The words 'means of communication' in point 3° cover

1356 Advies 59.147/3 van de Raad van State (II) 22 april 2016 bij wetsontwerp houdende diverse bepalingen ter bestrijding van terrorisme (III), *Parl.St.* Kamer 2015–2016, no. 54–1951/001, 26; Delhaise (n 8) 69; Deruyck and De Nauw (n 786) 14–15; Fransen and Kerkhofs (n 10) 75; Winants (n 8) 356.

1357 Amendement no. 1 7 juli 2016 bij wetsvoorstel 13 januari 2016 tot wijziging van het Strafwetboek wat betreft de bestraffing van terrorisme, *Parl.St.* Kamer 2015–2016, no. 54–1579/005, 10; Deruyck and De Nauw (n 786) 15; Fransen and Kerkhofs (n 10) 76; Winants (n 8) 356.

1358 Advies 59.789/3 van de Raad van State 19 juli 2016 bij wetsvoorstel 13 januari 2016 tot wijziging van het Strafwetboek wat betreft de bestraffing van terrorisme, *Parl.St.* Kamer 2015–2016, no. 54–1579/006, 13; Advies 59.147/3 van de Raad van State (II) 22 april 2016 bij wetsontwerp houdende diverse bepalingen ter bestrijding van terrorisme (III), *Parl.St.* Kamer 2015–2016, no. 54–1951/001, 28; Delhaise (n 8) 69; Fransen and Kerkhofs (n 10) 75.

1359 Fransen and Kerkhofs (n 10) 75.

1360 Amendement no. 1 7 juli 2016 bij wetsvoorstel 13 januari 2016 tot wijziging van het Strafwetboek wat betreft de bestraffing van terrorisme, *Parl.St.* Kamer 2015–2016, no. 54–1579/005, 10.

1361 Amendement no. 1 7 juli 2016 bij wetsvoorstel 13 januari 2016 tot wijziging van het Strafwetboek wat betreft de bestraffing van terrorisme, *Parl.St.* Kamer 2015–2016, no. 54–1579/005, 3; Fransen and Kerkhofs (n 10) 75.

1362 Amendement no. 1 7 juli 2016 bij wetsvoorstel 13 januari 2016 tot wijziging van het Strafwetboek wat betreft de bestraffing van terrorisme, *Parl.St.* Kamer 2015–2016, no. 54–1579/005, 3.

1363 Amendement no. 1 7 juli 2016 bij wetsvoorstel 13 januari 2016 tot wijziging van het Strafwetboek wat betreft de bestraffing van terrorisme, *Parl.St.* Kamer 2015–2016, no. 54–1579/005, 9; Fransen and Kerkhofs (n 10) 76.

1364 Amendement no. 1 7 juli 2016 bij wetsvoorstel 13 januari 2016 tot wijziging van het Strafwetboek wat betreft de bestraffing van terrorisme, *Parl.St.* Kamer 2015–2016, no. 54–1579/005, 9; Fransen and Kerkhofs (n 10) 76.

new technologies and their evolutions and an example of point 5° can be a video claiming an attack yet to be committed.[1365]

266. Preparation vs. attempt – Preparation is not to be confused with an attempted offence. Under Belgian criminal law, there is an attempted offence, if the intention to commit the offence has been manifested by external acts which constitute the beginning of the commission of that offence and which have ceased or have missed their effect solely as a result of circumstances beyond the control of the perpetrator.[1366] In general criminal law, preparatory actions that are not the beginning of the commission of the offence are not punishable.[1367] To ascertain the difference between a mere act of preparation and the beginning of the commission of the offence, one must ask whether the action is susceptible to multiple interpretations. If there can be no doubt about the intention of the perpetrator and the act will necessarily lead to the commission of the offence, the action is the beginning of the commission of the offence.[1368] The fact that actions are required that constitute the beginning of the commission of the offence, is an expression of the traditional objective doctrine within Belgian criminal law.[1369] The idea behind criminalising preparatory acts, is to not wait for the

1365 Amendement no. 1 7 juli 2016 bij wetsvoorstel 13 januari 2016 tot wijziging van het Strafwetboek wat betreft de bestraffing van terrorisme, *Parl.St.* Kamer 2015–2016, no. 54-1579/005, 9; Fransen and Kerkhofs (n 10) 76.

1366 Art. 51 CC; Cass. 3 november 2004, *RW* 2005–06, 1583, noot C. De Roy; Henri Berkmoes, 'Bestanddelen van de strafbare poging' in M De Busscher and others (eds), *Strafrecht: duiding* (Larcier 2018) 85–88; Delhaise (n 8) 81; De Nauw and Deruyck (n 39) 69–71; C De Roy, 'De strafbare poging als klassiek leerstuk in het raam van de hedendaagse strijd tegen het terrorisme (noot onder Cass. 3 november 2004)' (2005–2006) 69 Rechtskundig Weekblad 1584, 1585; Onsea (n 51) 41; Bart Spriet, 'Poging tot misdaad of tot wanbedrijf', *Strafrecht geannoteerd* (die Keure 2020) 336–338; Tulkens and others (n 39) 420–424; Van den Wyngaert, Vandromme and Traest (n 34) 362–367; Vandromme and De Roy (n 34) 511.

1367 Berkmoes, 'Bestanddelen van de strafbare poging' (n 1366) 86; De Nauw and Deruyck (n 39) 67 and 70; Onsea (n 51) 41; Spriet, 'Poging tot misdaad of tot wanbedrijf' (n 1366) 337; Tulkens and others (n 39) 421; Van den Wyngaert, Vandromme and Traest (n 34) 363; Winants (n 8) 355. Other statutes that criminalise preparatory actions are the statute on combating piracy at sea and the statute on the trade of narcotics. See: Art. 3, §1, c) wet 30 december 2009 betreffende de strijd tegen piraterij op zee, *BS* 14 januari 2010, 1485; Art. 2*bis*, §6 and 2*quater*, 6° wet 7 februari 2014 tot wijziging van de wet 24 februari 1921 betreffende het verhandelen van gifstoffen, slaapmiddelen en verdovende middelen, psychotrope stoffen, ontsmettingsstoffen en antiseptica en van de stoffen die kunnen gebruikt worden voor de illegale vervaardiging van verdovende middelen en psychotrope stoffen, *BS* 6 maart 1921, 1834; Amendement no. 1 7 juli 2016 bij wetsvoorstel 13 januari 2016 tot wijziging van het Strafwetboek wat betreft de bestraffing van terrorisme, *Parl.St.* Kamer 2015–2016, no. 54-1579/005, 6.

1368 Cass. 3 november 2004, *RW* 2005–06, 1583, noot C. De Roy; Berkmoes, 'Bestanddelen van de strafbare poging' (n 1366) 86; Dekrem (n 32) 138; De Nauw and Deruyck (n 39) 70; De Roy (n 1366) 1585; Tulkens and others (n 39) 421–422; Van den Wyngaert, Vandromme and Traest (n 34) 364; Vandromme and De Roy (n 34) 514.

1369 Van den Wyngaert, Vandromme and Traest (n 34) 364; Vandromme and De Roy (n 34) 513.

beginning of the commission of the offence but intervene sooner.[1370] However, the preparatory works explain that sometimes actions listed as preparation can be a beginning of the commission of the offence as well, depending on the circumstances of the case.[1371] An excellent example of this is the Verviers case (see no. 161).[1372] In that case, acts such as forging documents, searching a safe house, renting vehicles to transport jihadists, weapons and parts of explosives, buying phones, buying ingredients for bombs, and buying weapons and police uniforms were ruled to be attempted terrorism *sensu stricto*, although they are all listed as possible acts of preparation in Article 140*septies* CC as well.

267. Delicate – The criminalisation of preparatory actions is a delicate offence. This is another offence with an open-ended and broad *actus reus* and therefore there is a strong importance on the *mens rea*.[1373] It is a prime example of preventive criminal law as it can criminalise actions which in themselves are not 'wrong' at all, but become an offence in combination with the *mens rea*.[1374] The same can be said of Article 140*sexies* CC and many of the other terrorist offences. This evolution of our criminal law is deemed necessary.[1375] Comité T

1370 Amendement no. 1 7 juli 2016 bij wetsvoorstel 13 januari 2016 tot wijziging van het Strafwetboek wat betreft de bestraffing van terrorisme, *Parl.St.* Kamer 2015–2016, no. 54–1579/005, 5; Advies 59.147/3 van de Raad van State (II) 22 april 2016 bij wetsontwerp houdende diverse bepalingen ter bestrijding van terrorisme (III), *Parl.St.* Kamer 2015–2016, no. 54–1951/001, 25; Fransen and Kerkhofs (n 10) 76; Ketels (n 691) 262; Moreau (n 47) 109–110; Onsea (n 51) 41–42; Comité T, 'Rapport 2019: Le respect des droits humains dans le cadre de la lutte contre le terrorisme: Un chantier en cours', 18.

1371 Amendement no. 1 7 juli 2016 bij wetsvoorstel 13 januari 2016 tot wijziging van het Strafwetboek wat betreft de bestraffing van terrorisme, *Parl.St.* Kamer 2015–2016, no. 54–1579/005, 5; Fransen and Kerkhofs (n 10) 76; Ketels (n 691) 262.

1372 Moreau (n 47) 114–115.

1373 MvT wetsontwerp 5 juli 2016 houdende diverse bepalingen ter bestrijding van terrorisme (III), *Parl.St.* Kamer 2015–16, no. 54–1951/001, (4) 25–26 and 29; Amendementen 7 juli 2016 bij wetsvoorstel 13 januari 2016 tot wijziging van het Strafwetboek wat betreft de bestraffing van terrorisme, *Parl.St.* Kamer 2015–2016, no. 54–1579/005, 6; Advies 59.789/3 van de Raad van State 19 juli 2016 bij wetsvoorstel 13 januari 2016 tot wijziging van het Strafwetboek wat betreft de bestraffing van terrorisme, *Parl.St.* Kamer 2015–2016, no. 54–1579/006, 10; Delhaise (n 8) 69; Fransen and Kerkhofs (n 10) 75; Winants (n 8) 355.

1374 Amendementen 7 juli 2016 bij wetsvoorstel 13 januari 2016 tot wijziging van het Strafwetboek wat betreft de bestraffing van terrorisme, *Parl.St.* Kamer 2015–2016, no. 54–1579/005, 6; Advies 59.789/3 van de Raad van State 19 juli 2016 bij wetsvoorstel 13 januari 2016 tot wijziging van het Strafwetboek wat betreft de bestraffing van terrorisme, *Parl.St.* Kamer 2015–2016, no. 54–1579/006, 10; Advies 59.147/3 van de Raad van State (II) 22 april 2016 bij wetsontwerp houdende diverse bepalingen ter bestrijding van terrorisme (III), *Parl.St.* Kamer 2015–2016, no. 54–1951/001, 25; Comité T, 'Rapport 2019: Le respect des droits humains dans le cadre de la lutte contre le terrorisme: Un chantier en cours', 18; Delhaise (n 8) 69; Fransen and Kerkhofs (n 10) 75; Winants (n 8) 355.

1375 Amendementen 7 juli 2016 bij wetsvoorstel 13 januari 2016 tot wijziging van het Strafwetboek wat betreft de bestraffing van terrorisme, *Parl.St.* Kamer 2015–2016, no. 54–1579/005, 6; Advies 59.789/3 van de Raad van State 19 juli 2016 bij wetsvoorstel 13 januari 2016 tot wijziging van het Strafwetboek wat betreft de bestraffing van terrorisme, *Parl.St.* Kamer 2015–2016, no. 54–1579/006, 10; Advies 59.147/3 van de Raad van State (II) 22 april 2016 bij

however, stated that '*[...] this provision poses obvious evidentiary problems and seriously endangers the presumption of innocence. Moreover, as soon as concrete evidence shows the beginning of the execution of acts of terrorism by means of these instruments, one will be within the framework of the attempt, which makes this offense unnecessary.*'[1376]

SECTION II. *MENS REA*

268. Special intent – Once more, the *mens rea* is not explicit in the text of the Article. The preparatory works explain that next to the *actus reus,* the intention to commit a terrorist offence as described in Article 137 CC is necessary.[1377] The action in itself never suffices. This intention is a form of special intent[1378] and for this offence there is a requirement of concreteness: the prosecution has to prove which offence was intended.[1379] The Council of State emphasised the importance of concrete and consistent factual elements that provide proof of the intention to commit a terrorist offence.[1380] However, this intent was not quite clear. On the one hand, the preparatory works state that an offence prepared by one person can also be executed by another.[1381] On the other hand, they say that the *mens rea* is the intention to commit a terrorist offence. If someone prepares a terrorist offence for somebody else, they do not have the intention of committing one themselves. The Council of State pointed towards this inconsistency and asked

wetsontwerp houdende diverse bepalingen ter bestrijding van terrorisme (III), *Parl.St.* Kamer 2015–2016, no. 54–1951/001, 25–26.

1376 Own translation, original in French. See: Comité T, 'Rapport 2019: Le respect des droits humains dans le cadre de la lutte contre le terrorisme: Un chantier en cours', 18.

1377 Amendement no. 1 7 juli 2016 bij wetsvoorstel 13 januari 2016 tot wijziging van het Strafwetboek wat betreft de bestraffing van terrorisme, *Parl.St.* Kamer 2015–2016, no. 54–1579/005, 8; Fransen and Kerkhofs (n 10) 77.

1378 Ketels (n 691) 262.

1379 Advies 59.789/3 van de Raad van State 19 juli 2016 bij wetsvoorstel 13 januari 2016 tot wijziging van het Strafwetboek wat betreft de bestraffing van terrorisme, *Parl.St.* Kamer 2015–2016, 54–1579/006, 14; Advies 59.147/3 van de Raad van State (II) 22 april 2016 bij wetsontwerp houdende diverse bepalingen ter bestrijding van terrorisme (III), *Parl. St.* Kamer 2015–2016, no. 54–1951/001, 29; Verslag van de eerste lezing 20 oktober 2016 namens de tijdelijke commissie 'terrorismebestrijding' bij wetsvoorstel tot wijziging van het Strafwetboek wat betreft de bestraffing van terrorisme, *Parl.St.* Kamer 2015–2016, no. 54–1579/008, 5–6; Delhaise (n 8) 71; Fransen and Kerkhofs (n 10) 77.

1380 Advies 59.789/3 van de Raad van State 19 juli 2016 bij wetsvoorstel 13 januari 2016 tot wijziging van het Strafwetboek wat betreft de bestraffing van terrorisme, *Parl.St.* Kamer 2015–2016, no. 54–1579/006, 12; Advies 59.147/3 van de Raad van State (II) 22 april 2016 bij wetsontwerp houdende diverse bepalingen ter bestrijding van terrorisme (III), *Parl.St.* Kamer 2015–2016, no. 54–1951/001, 27; Fransen and Kerkhofs (n 10) 77.

1381 Amendement no. 1 7 juli 2016 bij wetsvoorstel 13 januari 2016 tot wijziging van het Strafwetboek wat betreft de bestraffing van terrorisme, *Parl.St.* Kamer 2015–2016, no. 54–1579/005, 3.

for clarification.[1382] The legislature did not change the Article, but did explain to the Council of State that Article 140*septies* CC is only meant to target people who prepare their own terrorist offence.[1383] People preparing another person's terrorist offence, are potentially liable as accomplices.[1384] This however raises an interesting question under the proportionality principle. The sentences for accomplices are higher than the sentences for preparation in Article 140*septies* CC. Accomplices are sentenced to the sentence that is one step down from the actual offence on the scale of Article 80 CC (see no. 146).[1385] So preparing a terrorist offence to be committed by somebody else is punished harsher than preparing your own.[1386] As the legislature points out in the preparatory works, it is impossible to punish preparation less harshly than attempt without also punishing it less harshly than aiding and abetting, since attempt and aiding and abetting have the same sentence.[1387] Furthermore, prosecution for aiding and abetting an offence implies that the offence (or at least its attempt) has actually taken place,[1388] which is not the case for preparatory actions.[1389] It is possible to aid and abet the attempted offence, but then the sentence goes down another level compared to the aiding and abetting of the offence itself. The limitation of the *mens rea* to people who prepare their own terrorist offence *sensu stricto*,

---

1382 Advies 59.789/3 van de Raad van State 19 juli 2016 bij wetsvoorstel 13 januari 2016 tot wijziging van het Strafwetboek wat betreft de bestraffing van terrorisme, *Parl.St.* Kamer 2015–2016, no. 54–1579/006, 12; Advies 59.147/3 van de Raad van State State bij wetsontwerp van 6 juli 2016 houdende diverse bepalingen ter bestrijding van terrorisme (III), *Parl.St.* Kamer 2015–16, no. 54–1951/001, (19) 27–28.

1383 Advies 59.789/3 van de Raad van State 19 juli 2016 bij wetsvoorstel 13 januari 2016 tot wijziging van het Strafwetboek wat betreft de bestraffing van terrorisme, *Parl.St.* Kamer 2015–2016, no. 54–1579/006, 17; Verslag van de eerste lezing 20 oktober 2016 namens de tijdelijke commissie 'terrorismebestrijding' bij wetsvoorstel tot wijziging van het Strafwetboek wat betreft de bestraffing van terrorisme, *Parl.St.* Kamer 2015–2016, no. 54–1579/008, 5; Dekrem (n 32) 157; Deruyck and De Nauw (n 786) 14; Fransen and Kerkhofs (n 10) 75; Winants (n 8) 356. *Contra*: Delhaise (n 8) 70–71.

1384 Art. 67 CC; De Nauw and Deruyck (n 39) 95–96; Tulkens and others (n 39) 511–512; Jan Vanheule, 'Daden van deelneming die worden omschreven in artikel 67 Sw.' in M De Busscher and others (eds), *Strafrecht: duiding* (Larcier 2018) 139–141; Van den Wyngaert, Vandromme and Traest (n 34) 388–389; Waeterinckx (n 1196) 376–377.

1385 Art. 69 CC. See also: De Nauw and Deruyck (n 39) 96; Tulkens and others (n 39) 512–513; Van den Wyngaert, Vandromme and Traest (n 34) 394.

1386 Advies 59.789/3 van de Raad van State 19 juli 2016 bij wetsvoorstel 13 januari 2016 tot wijziging van het Strafwetboek wat betreft de bestraffing van terrorisme, *Parl.St.* Kamer 2015–2016, no. 54–1579/006, 19–20.

1387 Verslag van de eerste lezing 20 oktober 2016 namens de tijdelijke commissie 'terrorismebestrijding' bij wetsvoorstel tot wijziging van het Strafwetboek wat betreft de bestraffing van terrorisme, *Parl.St.* Kamer 2015–2016, no. 54–1579/008, 6.

1388 Delhaise (n 8) 85; Tulkens and others (n 39) 505–506; Jan Vanheule, 'Stelsel van de onzelfstandige strafbare deelneming en de voorwaarden voor de strafbare deelneming' in M De Busscher and others (eds), *Strafrecht: duiding* (Larcier 2018) 124; Van den Wyngaert, Vandromme and Traest (n 34) 386.

1389 Verslag van de eerste lezing 20 oktober 2016 namens de tijdelijke commissie 'terrorismebestrijding' bij wetsvoorstel tot wijziging van het Strafwetboek wat betreft de bestraffing van terrorisme, *Parl.St.* Kamer 2015–2016, no. 54–1579/008, 7.

can be applauded, although the legislature should have made this limitation clearer in the Code. For an offence with as broad an *actus reus* as the one in Article 140*septies* CC, the *mens rea* should be as precise and narrow as possible in order to exclude the misapplication of the offence.[1390]

SECTION III. SENTENCES

269. Dependent on prepared offence – The sentence for preparation depends on the sentence for the prepared offence. The Criminal Code sets out the following sentences:

- Imprisonment of eight days to a year, if the prepared offence is punishable with imprisonment of maximum five years;
- Imprisonment of maximum three years, if the prepared offence is punishable with five to ten years felony imprisonment;
- Imprisonment of maximum five years, if the prepared offence is punishable with ten to fifteen years or fifteen to twenty years felony imprisonment;
- Felony imprisonment of five to ten years, if the prepared offence is punishable with twenty to thirty years or lifelong felony imprisonment.

The Code also adds that the accessory penalties, for example the fines, are the same as for the prepared offence. Note that in theory this could also apply to supervision by the Sentence Enforcement Court, which is an accessory penalty. However, the legislation as it currently stands only allows this for terrorist offences *sensu stricto* which caused the death of a victim. Because of this requirement, it would be impossible to apply it to the preparation offence as this requirement implies the offence has actually been committed. If future changes to the legislation expand the scope of the supervision by the Sentence Enforcement Court (see no. 124), it could become a possibility for 140*septies* CC offences as well.

270. Proportionality – As with Article 138 CC, this seems like a fairly straightforward system. Preparation of terrorism is a standard offence, unless the prepared terrorist offence is punishable with 20 to 30 years felony imprisonment or lifelong felony imprisonment. In that case, preparation is a felony. The system is also created in such a way that the maximum sentence for attempt will be higher than the maximum sentence for preparation.[1391] In the Article as

---

1390 Note that Delhaise sees things differently. She states that the legislature should have included the other terrorist offences *sensu lato* in the *mens rea* of Art. 140*septies* CC. See: Delhaise (n 8) 69–70. We disagree, as this inclusion would have made the offence much too broad.

1391 Amendement no. 1 7 juli 2016 bij wetsvoorstel 13 januari 2016 tot wijziging van het Strafwetboek wat betreft de bestraffing van terrorisme, *Parl.St.* Kamer 2015–2016, no. 54-1579/005, 8.

originally proposed, there was one sentence for the preparation of any terrorist offence: two to five years imprisonment and a fine of 26 to 1,000 euros.[1392] This was changed after the Council of State pointed out that this could lead to proportionality and discrimination issues, providing for harsher sentences for the preparation of some offences than for their actual commission.[1393] The system as adopted is more proportionate than the one originally proposed. However, three remarks can still be made regarding proportionality. The first is very similar to one of the comments made regarding the sentencing of Article 140, §1 CC compared to terrorism *sensu stricto*. Most of the sentences for preparing terrorism *sensu stricto* are more lenient than the ones for participating in the activities of a terrorist group. This means that when terrorism *sensu stricto* is prepared in the context of a terrorist group, the defendants will be liable for the harsher sentence for participating in the activities of a terrorist group, while an individual preparing that same terrorist offence, is only liable for the lower sentence for preparation. The Council of State raised this question. The reply was that offences in group are more dangerous than offences committed by individuals, an explanation the Council of State doubted.[1394] Second, the category of felony preparation will normally be correctionalised, which makes it into a standard offence punishable with one month to five years imprisonment. This puts the maximum sentence on the same level as for preparation of offences punishable with ten to 15 years or 15 to 20 years felony imprisonment. So, in practice the maximum sentence for the preparation of an offence originally punishable with ten to 15 years felony imprisonment will be the same as for preparation of an offence originally punishable with lifelong felony imprisonment. Third, because of the combination of Article 138 and 140*septies* CC, the preparation of a terrorist offence originally punishable with only a fine is punishable with up to a year imprisonment. So outside of a terrorist context, this offence only warrants a fine, but merely preparing that same offence within a terrorist context can lead to up to a year in prison.

271. ATTEMPT – Since most of the penalties in Article 140*septies* CC are imprisonment, most of the offences of preparation are standard offences. This

1392 Art. 3 wetsvoorstel 13 januari 2016 tot wijziging van het Strafwetboek wat betreft de bestraffing van terrorisme, *Parl.St.* Kamer 2015–2016, no. 54–1579/001, (5) 5; Fransen and Kerkhofs (n 10) 77.

1393 Advies 59.789/3 van de Raad van State 19 juli 2016 bij wetsvoorstel 13 januari 2016 tot wijziging van het Strafwetboek wat betreft de bestraffing van terrorisme, *Parl.St.* Kamer 2015–2016, no. 54–1579/006, 14–15; Advies 59.147/3 van de Raad van State (II) 22 april 2016 bij wetsontwerp houdende diverse bepalingen ter bestrijding van terrorisme (III), *Parl.St.* Kamer 2015–2016, no. 54–1951/001, 29–30; Amendement no. 1 7 juli 2016 bij wetsvoorstel 13 januari 2016 tot wijziging van het Strafwetboek wat betreft de bestraffing van terrorisme, *Parl.St.* Kamer 2015–2016, no. 54–1579/005, 7; Moreau (n 47) 111.

1394 Advies 59.147/3 van de Raad van State (II) 22 april 2016 bij wetsontwerp houdende diverse bepalingen ter bestrijding van terrorisme (III), *Parl.St.* Kamer 2015–2016, no. 54–1951/001, 30–31.

means that under the general rule, an attempt of these offences is not punishable (see no. 132). As with the offence of threatening terrorism, Delhaise argues that it is impossible to attempt the preparation and that once the execution of the offence has started, the offence has taken place (see no. 141). As stated above, in principle we think this would violate the legality principle and the attempts are simply not punishable. That being said, while attempted threatening is something which could be imagined, it is much more difficult to ascertain what attempted preparation would look like in practice. As preparation is such a broad and nebulous concept, the threshold of the offence itself will easily be achieved and there seems to be little practical room for an attempted offence.

272. Alternative sentences and modalities – Most of the preparation offences are standard offences and even the one category which is a felony can be correctionalised. This means electronic monitoring as a principal sentence is possible, when the judge feels the offence is of such a nature that it should not be punished with more than one year imprisonment (see no. 115).[1395] The electronic monitoring has a term of one month to one year. Community service, with a term of 45 to 300 hours, and an autonomous probation sentence of one to two years are also possible (see nos 116 and 117). Finally, postponement of sentence enforcement subject to probation is an option, as is regular postponement of sentence enforcement and suspension of sentencing, possibly with probation measures as well, if the perpetrator does not have prior convictions which are too serious (see nos 118 and 119).

SECTION IV. PRACTICAL APPLICATION

273. Only case yet – For a long time, there were no cases in which a person was prosecuted for the preparation of a terrorist attack under Article 140*septies* CC.[1396] As explained above, there was the case of the Verviers cell, but the offence did not exist yet (see no. 161). At the end of 2022, a man was convicted to 80 months imprisonment, of which 60 with postponement of the execution of the sentence for preparing a terrorist attack.[1397] A half finished pipe bomb was found in his attic, providing proof for the preparation of a terrorist attack, but the Court also held that the man was not a member of a terrorist group.

1395 Art. 37*ter*, §1, section 1 CC. See also: Daems and Magis (n 710) 181; Decaigny, 'Relatieve zwaarte, toepassingsgebied en duur' (n 714) 50; De Nauw and Deruyck (n 39) 127; Tulkens and others (n 39) 598; Van den Wyngaert, Vandromme and Traest (n 34) 430.

1396 Fransen and Kerkhofs (n 10) 77; Moreau (n 47) 114; Comité T, 'Rapport 2022: Évaluation des mesures visant à lutter contre le terrorisme à la lumière des droits humains', 52.

1397 Corr. Brugge, zoals geciteerd in F. Martinez, '80 maanden cel voor man die terroristische aanslag voorbereidt op zolder in Roeselare', *vrtNWS* 12 december 2022, www.vrt.be/vrtnws/nl/2022/12/12/80-maanden-cel-voor-man-die-terroristische-aanslag-voorbereidt-o/.

CHAPTER X
ARTICLE 141 CC

SECTION I. *ACTUS REUS*

274. Evolution – This is a first generation terrorist offence, introduced in 2003.[1398] It was not included in the Framework Decision but in the International Convention for the Suppression of the Financing of Terrorism, signed by Belgium on 27 September 2001.[1399] It was not part of the first draft bill of the 2003 statute either, because Article 140, §1 CC already explicitly refers to the financing of terrorism. However, the Council of State noted that Article 140 CC only covered a certain form of financing, namely the financing of a terrorist group.[1400] The legislature also wanted to tackle the financing of individual terrorists and therefore added Article 141 CC to plug this gap.[1401] Prosecuting the financer for aiding and abetting the (attempted) commission of a terrorist offence *sensu stricto* was possible, but requires the terrorist offence *sensu stricto* to at least have been attempted and the preparation offence did not exist yet. The offence introduced in 2003 criminalised '*[a]ny person who except in the cases referred to in Article 140, provides material resources, including financial assistance, with*

1398 Art. 7 wet 19 december 2003 betreffende terroristische misdrijven, *BS* 29 december 2003, 61689.

1399 Art. 2 International Convention for the Suppression of the Financing of Terrorism of 9 December 1999, New York; Beernaert, 'La Loi du 19 Décembre 2003 relative aux infractions terroristes : Quand le droit pénal Belge évolue sous la dictée de l'Union Européenne' (n 20) 588; De Hert and Millen (n 803) 10; De La Serna (n 8) 193; De La Serna (n 50) 225–226; Flore (n 10) 219; Hameeuw (n 8) 9; Ketels (n 691) 263; Traest (n 50) 258; Weyembergh and Kennes (n 58) 154; Weyembergh and Kennes (n 14) 120; Winants (n 8) 349. Currently, Art. 11 of the Directive includes the offence of terrorist financing.

1400 Advies 34.362/4 van de Raad van State bij wetsontwerp van 6 oktober 2003 betreffende terroristische misdrijven, *Parl.St.* Kamer 2003, no. 51–0258/001, (22) 40. See also: Delhaise and Fievet (n 45) 119.

1401 MvT wetsontwerp 6 oktober 2003 betreffende terroristische misdrijven, *Parl.St.* Kamer 2003, no. 51–0258/001, (4) 9 and 14–15; Verslag namens de commissie voor de Justitie 7 november 2003 bij wetsontwerp van 6 oktober 2003 betreffende terroristische misdrijven, *Parl.St.* Kamer 2003, no. 51–0258/004, 23; Beernaert, 'La Loi du 19 Décembre 2003 relative aux infractions terroristes : Quand le droit pénal Belge évolue sous la dictée de l'Union Européenne' (n 20) 588; De La Serna (n 8) 192–193; De La Serna (n 50) 225; Deruyck and De Nauw (n 786) 10; Hameeuw (n 8) 9; Ketels (n 691) 263; Weyembergh and Kennes (n 58) 154; Weyembergh and Kennes (n 14) 120; Winants (n 8) 348.

a view to committing a terrorist offence referred to in Article 137.'[1402] However, in its recommendations, the Financial Action Task Force (FATF) stressed that terrorist financing offences should not require that the funds are linked to a specific terrorist act.[1403] According to the FATF, collecting or providing funds to one or two people (i.e. outside of the situation of Art. 140 CC) does not seem to be covered by Article 141 CC, if the connection to a specific terrorist offence cannot be established. Therefore, Article 141 did not fully comply with this recommendation.[1404] In order to resolve this, the Article was replaced in 2016.[1405] Three slightly different amendments were proposed, but in the end the third one made it, because it resembled the EU Directive, which does include a similar offence, the closest.[1406]

275. *Actus Reus* – The current version of Article 141 CC criminalises the direct or indirect provision or collection of material resources, including financial assistance, by any means.[1407] Compared to the original Article, Article 141 is now not only aimed at people who provide resources but also those who collect them.[1408] The legislature noted that the wording of the new Article is broader than the original one, but that this does not necessarily mean

---

1402 Own translation, original in Dutch: '*Iedere persoon die, behalve in de gevallen bedoeld in artikel 140, materiële middelen verstrekt, daaronder begrepen financiële hulp, met het oog op het plegen van een terroristisch misdrijf bedoeld in artikel 137.*' (Art. 141 CC as introduced by Art. 7 wet 19 december 2003 betreffende terroristische misdrijven, *BS* 29 December 2003, 61689). See also: Fransen and Kerkhofs (n 10) 78.

1403 Recommendation 5 FATF international standards on combating money laundering and the financing of terrorism & proliferation, updated June 2019, 11, www.fatf-gafi.org/media/fatf/documents/recommendations/pdfs/FATF%20Recommendations%202012.pdf. See in the original recommendations as well: FATF IX Special Recommendations, October 2001, 5, www.fatf-gafi.org/media/fatf/documents/reports/FATF%20Standards%20-%20IX%20Special%20Recommendations%20and%20IN%20rc.pdf. Note that Belgium and the European Commission (and the UK) are members of the FATF and by joining have consented to carry out its recommendations. There is some form of democratic deficit as the FATF mandate is established by the executive of its member states.

1404 FATF, *Anti-money laundering and counter-terrorist financing measures -Belgium, Fourth Round Mutual Evaluation Report* (2015) 160, www.fatf-gafi.org/publications/mutualevaluations/documents/mer-belgium-2015.html.

1405 Amendement no. 2 7 juli 2016 bij wetsvoorstel 13 januari 2016 tot wijziging van het Strafwetboek wat betreft de bestraffing van terrorisme, *Parl.St.* Kamer 2015–2016, no. 54–1579/005, 11–12. See also: Deruyck and De Nauw (n 786) 10; Ketels (n 691) 263.

1406 Verslag van de eerste lezing 20 oktober 2016 namens de tijdelijke commissie 'terrorismebestrijding' bij wetsvoorstel tot wijziging van het Strafwetboek wat betreft de bestraffing van terrorisme, *Parl.St.* Kamer 2015–2016, no. 54–1579/008, 14; Amendement no. 3 6 oktober 2016 bij wetsvoorstel tot wijziging van het Strafwetboek wat betreft de bestraffing van terrorisme, *Parl.St.* Kamer 2015–2016, no. 54–1579/007, 2–3; Fransen and Kerkhofs (n 10) 79; Winants (n 8) 356.

1407 Art. 141 CC; Delhaise (n 8) 72.

1408 Amendement no. 3 6 oktober 2016 bij wetsvoorstel tot wijziging van het Strafwetboek wat betreft de bestraffing van terrorisme, *Parl.St.* Kamer 2015–2016, no. 54–1579/007, 4; Deruyck and De Nauw (n 786) 10; Fransen and Kerkhofs (n 10) 79; Winants (n 8) 356.

that the original Article did not encompass the elements that were made more specific in the new wording.[1409] For example, the Directive includes providing or collecting funds, by '*any means, directly or indirectly.*'[1410] The legislature copied this to the new Article 141 CC, but explicitly stated that this does not mean it was not already covered in the original Article.[1411] The words '*material resources, including financial assistance*' were not altered. According to the FATF they were already sufficiently broad.[1412] It is not required that the resources are actually used to commit or contribute to the commission of an offence.[1413] The new Criminal Code makes one addition to this offence, being the explicit inclusion of the provision of 'data'.

SECTION II. *MENS REA*

276. Intent with two options – The *mens rea* allows for two options. The resources have to be provided or collected with the intention that they be used, or in the knowledge that they are to be used, in full or in part, (1°) to commit or contribute to the commission of a terrorist offence *sensu stricto* or *sensu lato*, or (2°) by another person when the person providing or collecting the resources knows that this other person is committing or will commit terrorism *sensu stricto*.[1414] This is significantly broader than the *mens rea* from 2003 (see no. 274). 1° is a copy from the EU Directive.[1415] Compared to the original Article, it expanded the offences of which the financing is criminalised from terrorism *sensu stricto* to all terrorist offences, including participating in the activities of a terrorist group and preparing a terrorist offence.[1416] Furthermore, the legislature

---

1409 Amendement no. 3 6 oktober 2016 bij wetsvoorstel tot wijziging van het Strafwetboek wat betreft de bestraffing van terrorisme, *Parl.St.* Kamer 2015–2016, no. 54–1579/007, 3–4.

1410 Art. 11(1) Directive (EU) 2017/541 of the European Parliament and of the Council of 15 March 2017 on combating terrorism and replacing Council Framework Decision 2002/475/JHA and amending Council Decision 2005/671/JHA [2017] *OJ* L88/6–21.

1411 Amendement no. 3 6 oktober 2016 bij wetsvoorstel tot wijziging van het Strafwetboek wat betreft de bestraffing van terrorisme, *Parl.St.* Kamer 2015–2016, no. 54–1579/007, 4; Fransen and Kerkhofs (n 10) 79.

1412 FATF, *Anti-money laundering and counter-terrorist financing measures -Belgium, Fourth Round Mutual Evaluation Report* (2015) 159, www.fatf-gafi.org/publications/mutualevaluations/documents/mer-belgium-2015.html. See also: Fransen and Kerkhofs (n 10) 79; Winants (n 8) 356.

1413 Fransen and Kerkhofs (n 802) 184; Ketels (n 691) 263–264.

1414 Art. 141 CC. See also: Deruyck and De Nauw (n 786) 10.

1415 Art. 11(1) Directive (EU) 2017/541 of the European Parliament and of the Council of 15 March 2017 on combating terrorism and replacing Council Framework Decision 2002/475/JHA and amending Council Decision 2005/671/JHA [2017] *OJ* L88/6–21; Amendement no. 3 6 oktober 2016 bij wetsvoorstel tot wijziging van het Strafwetboek wat betreft de bestraffing van terrorisme, *Parl.St.* Kamer 2015–2016, no. 54–1579/007, 5.

1416 Amendement no. 3 6 oktober 2016 bij wetsvoorstel tot wijziging van het Strafwetboek wat betreft de bestraffing van terrorisme, *Parl.St.* Kamer 2015–2016, no. 54–1579/007, 5; Fransen and Kerkhofs (n 10) 80.

wanted to make sure no connection with a specific terrorist act was required. The new wording had to make clearer that it is not necessary the resources are actually used or that the perpetrator knows which specific offences they will be used for.[1417] This is explicitly required by the Directive when the financing concerns terrorism *sensu stricto*, terrorist offences relating to a terrorist group or traveling for terrorist purposes.[1418] Belgium, however, thought this was too restrictive and the legislature made clear that this also applies for the other terrorist offences.[1419] In 2° the legislature wanted to emphasise that helping an individual terrorist is also an offence, as required by the FATF.[1420] Strangely enough the legislature hereby stated that the Council of State had not expressed any objections about this.[1421] This is strange because the Council of State had questioned the distinction between 1° and 2°. According to the Council, 1° already includes financing an individual terrorist.[1422] The legislature never replied to this observation. Despite this lack of reply, the Council of State had a point. Providing resources in the knowledge that they are to be used to commit a terrorist offence *sensu stricto* (1°) or providing them in the knowledge that they are to be used by another person when the person providing or collecting the resources knows that this other person is committing or will commit terrorism *sensu stricto* (2°) is the same thing.[1423] Therefore, 1° includes 2°, making the latter moot. By not adhering to the wording of the Directive, but unnecessarily adding 2°, the Belgian legislature created confusion about 1°, making the scope of the offence less clear.

1417 Amendement no. 3 6 oktober 2016 bij wetsvoorstel tot wijziging van het Strafwetboek wat betreft de bestraffing van terrorisme, *Parl.St.* Kamer 2015–2016, no. 54–1579/007, 5–6; Deruyck and De Nauw (n 786) 10; Fransen and Kerkhofs (n 10) 79; Winants (n 8) 356. Although under the old wording, it was not required that the terrorist act was committed either. See: De La Serna (n 8) 194.

1418 Art. 11(2) Directive (EU) 2017/541 of the European Parliament and of the Council of 15 March 2017 on combating terrorism and replacing Council Framework Decision 2002/475/JHA and amending Council Decision 2005/671/JHA [2017] *OJ* L88/6–21.

1419 Amendement no. 3 6 oktober 2016 bij wetsvoorstel tot wijziging van het Strafwetboek wat betreft de bestraffing van terrorisme, *Parl.St.* Kamer 2015–2016, no. 54–1579/007, 6.

1420 Amendement no. 3 6 oktober 2016 bij wetsvoorstel tot wijziging van het Strafwetboek wat betreft de bestraffing van terrorisme, *Parl.St.* Kamer 2015–2016, no. 54–1579/007, 6; Amendement no. 1 7 juli 2016 bij wetsvoorstel 13 januari 2016 tot wijziging van het Strafwetboek wat betreft de bestraffing van terrorisme, *Parl.St.* Kamer 2015–2016, no. 54–1579/005, 12.

1421 Amendement no. 3 6 oktober 2016 bij wetsvoorstel tot wijziging van het Strafwetboek wat betreft de bestraffing van terrorisme, *Parl.St.* Kamer 2015–2016, no. 54–1579/007, 6.

1422 Advies 59.789/3 van de Raad van State 19 juli 2016 bij wetsvoorstel 13 januari 2016 tot wijziging van het Strafwetboek wat betreft de bestraffing van terrorisme, *Parl.St.* Kamer 2015–2016, no. 54–1579/006, 21–22; Advies 59.147/3 van de Raad van State 22 april 2016 bij wetsontwerp van 6 juli 2016 houdende diverse bepalingen ter bestrijding van terrorisme (III), *Parl. St.* Kamer 2015–2016, no. 54–1951/001, (19) 31–32; Delhaise (n 8) 73; Fransen and Kerkhofs (n 10) 80.

1423 Delhaise (n 8) 73.

277. Special intent – Most literature simply states the *mens rea* is a special intent.[1424] This seems to be the case but is not as obvious as the literature makes it out to be. The Article states '*the intention that they be used, or in the knowledge that they are to be used.*' The part about the intention would be a special intent, since this is a specification of the will element. However, the Article also provides another option since it uses 'or'. At first glance, the knowledge part does not entail a special intent since it is a specification of the knowledge element and not of the will at all.[1425] This observation in turn, needs to be nuanced. Similarly to the reasoning for Article 140 CC, if somebody provides means in the knowledge that they will be used to perpetrate a certain terrorist attack, it would seem they also provide those means with the intention that they be used for this goal. Since they have the knowledge of the goal and act regardless, the intention is implied. Therefore, Article 141 CC does require a special intent and the wording that seems to refer to a kind of general intent is redundant and slightly confusing.

SECTION III. SENTENCES

278. Felony – The sentence for financing is five to ten years felony imprisonment and a fine of 100 to 5,000 euros. This is the same sentence as many of the other terrorist offences *sensu lato*. The FATF stated that the maximum pecuniary penalty of 30,000 euros does not seem dissuasive.[1426] Belgian law applies surcharges to criminal fines to adapt them to the real value of money (see no. 102). Back in 2015, there were 50 10% surcharges, effectively increasing every criminal fine with a factor 6. Hence, the actual maximum fine being 30,000 euros in 2015. The legislature never increased the maximum fines the Criminal Code prescribes for the offence. However, in 2016 it did increase the 10% surcharges to 70, making the maximum fine for this terrorist offence 40,000 euros in practice.[1427]

1424 Delhaise (n 8) 72–73; Winants (n 8) 356; Yperman, 'Terrorism Offences in Belgian Criminal Law' (n 648) 177. Note that Comité T does question whether this is a general or a special intent, without answering the question. See: Comité T, 'Rapport 2022: Évaluation des mesures visant à lutter contre le terrorisme à la lumière des droits humains', 52.

1425 See also: Cesoni (n 15) 254. Note that Cesoni states that the combination of the intention to 2° reverts back to a general intent. However, as explained above we feel 2° is redundant as it is fully part of 1°.

1426 FATF, *Anti-money laundering and counter-terrorist financing measures -Belgium, Fourth Round Mutual Evaluation Report* (2015) 160, www.fatf-gafi.org/publications/mutualevaluations/documents/mer-belgium-2015.html.

1427 Art. 59 programmawet 25 december 2016, *BS* 29 december 2016, 90879.

279. Aggravating circumstance – In 2019, the legislature introduced an aggravating circumstance for this offence as well.[1428] Section 2 of the Article states that the sentence is 10 to 15 years felony imprisonment and a fine of 5,000 to 10,000 euros if the provision or collection of the material resources takes place with a view to their full or partial use by a minor for the purpose of committing or contributing to the commission of a terrorist offence *sensu stricto*.[1429] This elevation of the sentence is not required by the Directive, but the legislature saw fit to include it here as well.[1430] The legislature explains that the aggravating circumstance only covers part of the situation of 1°. Financing a minor with a view to the commission of terrorism *sensu lato* does not fall within the scope of the aggravating circumstance.[1431] Nor does, according to the legislature financing a minor knowing that they are committing or will commit terrorism *sensu stricto* (2°).[1432] However, as explained above we believe the Council of State is correct in arguing that this falls within the scope of 1° and therefore the aggravating circumstance could be applicable.

280. Alternative sentences and modalities – Electronic monitoring as a principal sentence is possible, when the judge feels the offence is of such a nature that it should not be punished with more than one year imprisonment (see no. 115).[1433] The electronic monitoring has a term of one month to one year. Community service, with a term of 45 to 300 hours, and an autonomous probation sentence of one to two years are also possible (see nos 116 and 117). Finally, postponement of sentence enforcement subject to probation is an option, as is regular postponement of sentence enforcement and suspension of sentencing, possibly with probation measures as well, if the perpetrator does not have prior convictions which are too serious (see nos 118 and 119).

281. New Criminal Code – The new Criminal Code makes a change to the sentences for this offence. It introduces a difference between the sentence

---

1428 Art. 81 wet 5 mei 2019 houdende diverse bepalingen in strafzaken en inzake erediensten, en tot wijziging van de wet 28 mei 2002 betreffende de euthanasie en van het Sociaal Strafwetboek (1), *BS* 24 mei 2019, 50023.

1429 Art. 141, section 2 CC.

1430 Wetsvoorstel 6 februari 2019 houdende diverse bepalingen in strafzaken en inzake erediensten, *Parl.St.* Kamer 2018–2019, no. 54-3515/001, 107; De Coensel, 'De Wet Diverse Bepalingen in Strafzaken II: Terroristische misdrijven in lijn met de Europese verplichtingen?' (n 793) 213.

1431 Wetsvoorstel 6 februari 2019 houdende diverse bepalingen in strafzaken en inzake erediensten, *Parl.St.* Kamer 2018–2019, no. 54-3515/001, 107; Deruyck and De Nauw (n 786) 10; Winants (n 8) 358.

1432 Wetsvoorstel 6 februari 2019 houdende diverse bepalingen in strafzaken en inzake erediensten, *Parl.St.* Kamer 2018–2019, no. 54-3515/001, 107; Winants (n 8) 358.

1433 Art. 37*ter*, §1, section 1 CC. See also: Daems and Magis (n 710) 181; Decaigny, 'Relatieve zwaarte, toepassingsgebied en duur' (n 714) 50; De Nauw and Deruyck (n 39) 127; Tulkens and others (n 39) 598; Van den Wyngaert, Vandromme and Traest (n 34) 430.

for the current 1° and 2° (which become two Articles). The sentence for the current 1° becomes: a level 3 sentence (three to five years imprisonment) if the provision is linked to an offence punishable by a level 4 sentence (five to ten years imprisonment) or lower and a level 4 sentence if the provision is linked to an offence punishable by a level 5 sentence (ten to 15 years imprisonment) or higher. The current 2°, however, becomes punishable by a level 4 sentence if the provision is linked to an offence punishable by a level 4 sentence or lower and a level 5 sentence (ten to 15 years imprisonment) if the provision is linked to an offence punishable by a level 5 sentence or higher. What prompted this change is unclear, as this is not explained in the explanatory memorandum.

SECTION IV. PRACTICAL APPLICATION

282. No case law yet – To our knowledge, there is yet to be a case in which a person is convicted of terrorist financing under Article 141 CC.[1434] In the case that led to the judgment of the Correctional Court of Brussels of 10 March 2017, a man was prosecuted for financing under Article 141 CC. However, the Court judged there was a terrorist group and convicted him for participating in the activities of that terrorist group and not for financing an individual terrorist under Article 141 CC.[1435]

[1434] Fransen and Kerkhofs (n 10) 81.

[1435] Corr. Brussel 10 maart 2017, *onuitg*; Fransen and Kerkhofs (n 10) 81.

CHAPTER XI
PROPOSED NEW OFFENCES

283. Two new variations to offences – As explained in the introduction to this Chapter (see no. 109) the new Criminal Code includes the same terrorist offences as the current Criminal Code, to which two new variations of offences would be added, being glorification and facilitating travel.

284. Glorification – The new Code includes a new paragraph in the incitement offence which criminalises glorification.[1436] The new offence consists of publicly, denying, grossly minimising, attempting to justify or condone the traveling offences or any of the offences of terrorism *sensu stricto*, excluding the threatening offence, when this behaviour poses a serious and real risk that one or more of these offences may be committed and the behaviour was committed with that intention.[1437] This new offence would not have any added value compared to the already existing incitement offence, as it is simply a subcategory of the existing offence (see no. 576).

285. Facilitating travel – A new paragraph would also be introduced in the traveling offence. This new paragraph criminalises organising or in any other way facilitating a trip from or to Belgium for a person with a view to committing or contributing to the commission of terrorism *sensu stricto*, barring the threatening offence, and terrorism *sensu lato*, barring the preparation offence.[1438] Such acts should be punishable as per Article 10 of the EU Directive. However, they would be already covered by aiding and abetting the (attempted) traveling offence. The addition of a separate offence was suggested by the College of Prosecutors-General and the legislature just went with it.[1439] This is a shame

---

1436 Note that another, earlier proposal, proposed to introduce a new Art. 140*octies* CC with a specific glorification offence. This proposal is still pending, but in light of the proposal for the new Criminal Code, it seems unlikely this would be passed. See: wetsvoorstel 11 maart 2021 tot wijziging van het Strafwetboek, teneinde de verheerlijking van terrorisme in het openbaar en op het internet te bestraffen, *Parl.St.* Kamer 2020–2021, no. 55–1847/001.

1437 Wetsontwerp 24 juli 2023 tot invoering van Boek II van het Strafwetboek, *Parl.St.* Kamer 2022–2023, no. 55–3518/001, 1014.

1438 Wetsontwerp 24 juli 2023 tot invoering van Boek II van het Strafwetboek, *Parl.St.* Kamer 2022–2023, no. 55–3518/001, 1016.

1439 Wetsontwerp 24 juli 2023 tot invoering van Boek II van het Strafwetboek, *Parl.St.* Kamer 2022–2023, no. 55–3518/001, 310.

as the extra offence has no real added value. The only situation in which it would criminalise actions not yet covered by aiding and abetting the traveling offence is the situation in which the traveling offence was not even attempted (see no. 588).

CHAPTER XII
PRE-TRIAL DETENTION

SECTION I. NUMBERS

286. Parliamentary research committee numbers – In one of its reports the Parliamentary research committee on the Brussels terrorist attacks lists the following numbers concerning pre-trial detention[1440]:

	2012	2013	2014	2015	2016	Total	2017 (until 13 March)
In pre-trial detention	13	16	40	93	105	267	8
Released immediately	2	0	1	12	26	41	3
Released (total)	8	10	22	54	60	154	3
Not released	5	6	18	39	45	113	4

SECTION II. INITIAL DEPRIVATION OF LIBERTY

287. Deprivation of liberty before conviction – The aforementioned criminal offences can lead to a deprivation of liberty in the form of a conviction to a prison sentence or electronic monitoring. However, within the criminal justice system, deprivations of liberty before a final conviction are possible as well. Suspects can be taken into pre-trial detention, which can also take the form of imprisonment or electronic monitoring.[1441] Electronic monitoring in

1440 Derde tussentijds verslag over het onderdeel 'veiligheidsarchitectuur' 15 juni 2017 van de parlementaire onderzoekscommissie belast met het onderzoek naar de omstandigheden die hebben geleid tot de terroristische aanslagen 22 maart 2016 in de luchthaven Brussel-Nationaal en in het metrostation Maalbeek te Brussel, met inbegrip van de evolutie en de aanpak van de strijd tegen het radicalisme en de terroristische dreiging, *Parl.St.* Kamer 2016–2017, no. 54-1752/008, 392.

1441 Art. 16, §1, section 2 Statute on pre-trial detention (wet 20 juli 1990 betreffende de voorlopige hechtenis, *BS* 14 augustus 1990, 15779). See also: P Daeninck, 'De impact van een beschikking van de onderzoeksrechter tot ET [elektronisch toezicht] op een hangend hoger beroep inzake voorlopige hechtenis' (2021) 2021 Tijdschrift voor Strafrecht 2, 3; Van den Wyngaert, Vandromme and Traest (n 34) 1198–1199; Filip Van Volsem and others, *Voorlopige hechtenis: commentaar* (Daniel De Wolf ed, INNI publishers 2014) 132–133.

this context means the suspect has to stay at a specific address the whole time, unless they are explicitly granted the right to leave for certain reasons, and this house arrest is enforced with an electronic tag.[1442] Furthermore, a provisional release from pre-trial detention is possible too, meaning suspects are released but have to observe conditions. Posting a bail sum can be one of the conditions imposed.[1443] It is up to the judge to decide which conditions they deem appropriate. However, the conditions need to relate to the reasons for absolute necessity for the public security (see no. 294).[1444] Furthermore, the preparatory works state that the conditions cannot amount to custodial measures, such as 24 hour house arrest.[1445] More recently, the Court of Cassation stated several times that the judge may not impose conditions which are, in principle, contrary to provisions of supranational treaties which have a direct effect in the internal legal order, such as the ECHR, or which are, in principle, contrary to the Constitution, national laws or general principles of law, unless they justify their absolute necessity.[1446] It is therefore possible that one of the conditions for a provisional release is, for example, overnight house arrest, which limits the suspect's right to free movement, but only if the judge can justify the absolute necessity of this condition.[1447]

288. Police agent vs. police officer – As explained above (see no. 102), investigatory measures in a criminal investigation will usually be ordered by either the public prosecutor during a preliminary investigation or the investigating judge during a judicial investigation. While the police often execute these measures,[1448] they only have very limited independent investigatory

1442 Daeninck, 'De impact van een beschikking van de onderzoeksrechter tot ET [elektronisch toezicht] op een hangend hoger beroep inzake voorlopige hechtenis' (n 1441) 3; P Tersago, 'Hoofdstuk II. Voorlopige Hechtenis' in T De Meester and others, *Potpourri II - Strafrecht en strafprocesrecht* (Intersentia 2016) 17; Laurens Van Puyenbroeck and Laurens Claes, 'Actualia Voorlopige Hechtenis' in P Traest, A Verhage and G Vermeulen (eds), *Strafrecht en strafprocesrecht: doel of middel in een veranderde samenleving?* (Wolters Kluwer 2017) 282; Van Volsem and others (n 1441) 133.

1443 Philip Daeninck, 'Voorlopige hechtenis: over de omvang en andere vraagstukken van de borgsom' [2023] Tijdschrift voor Strafrecht 207.

1444 K Beirnaert, 'Vrijheid en invrijheidstelling onder voorwaarden versus vrijheid van meningsuiting en vrijheid van vergadering' (2004) 2004 Tijdschrift voor Strafrecht 69, 73–74; Daeninck, 'Voorlopige hechtenis: over de omvang en andere vraagstukken van de borgsom' (n 1443) 208; Van den Wyngaert, Vandromme and Traest (n 34) 1234; Van Volsem and others (n 1441) 373; Verstraeten (n 653) 644–645.

1445 Verslag namens de commissie voor de Justitie 5 juni 1990 bij ontwerp van wet betreffende de voorlopige hechtenis, *Parl.St.* Senaat 1988–1989, 658–2, 108; Senator Lallemand, *Hand.* Senaat 3 juli 1990, 2423. See also: Beirnaert (n 1444) 70; Van Volsem and others (n 1441) 374; Verstraeten (n 653) 645.

1446 Cass. 18 maart 2003, *T.Strafr.* 2004, 68, noot K. Beirnaert; Cass. 1 oktober 2019, P.19..0958.N, *RW* 2020–21, 538; Cass. 24 december 2019, P.19.1281.N. See also: Van den Wyngaert, Vandromme and Traest (n 34) 1234–1235; Verstraeten (n 653) 645.

1447 Cass. 1 oktober 2019, P.19.0958.N, *RW* 2020–21, 538.

1448 Art. 28*ter*, §3 CCP; Verstraeten (n 653) 280–281.

powers themselves. In this context, a difference can be made between two types of policemen: police agents and police officers. Police agents have much less independent investigatory powers, while police officers have some more.[1449] This distinction is important in the context of pre-trial detention for it means that when a suspect is caught in the act, a police officer has to make a decision around the first stage of the initial deprivation of liberty of a suspect (see no. 289).

289. Maximum 48 hours – An initial deprivation of liberty can last up to 48 hours.[1450] If an arrest warrant is not issued by the investigating judge within those 48 hours, the suspect has to be released. The actual pre-trial detention only starts at the arrest warrant, so this period of 48 hours before the arrest warrant is issued is not technically part of the pre-trial detention. The public prosecutor or investigating judge can order the deprivation of liberty of any person for whom there are serious indications of guilt of a felony or standard offence.[1451] If the person tries to flee, they can be forcefully detained.[1452] The time limit of 48 hours starts from the moment the person was informed of the decision to deprive them of their liberty, or when physical restraint is necessary, the moment they are actually deprived of their liberty.[1453] If a suspect is caught in the act by the police, they can immediately deprive them of their liberty, without an order being issued by the prosecutor or investigating judge. In that case, a police agent has to immediately give custody of the person to a police officer, who in turn notifies the public prosecutor or investigating judge without delay.[1454] In this case, the time limit of 48 hours starts when the suspect has lost their liberty at the hands of the police agent.[1455] If a suspect is caught in the act by another citizen while committing a felony or standard offence, this citizen can deprive the suspect of their liberty. They then have to notify the police as soon as possible, and the time limit of 48 hours starts at the moment the police are notified.[1456]

1449 Verstraeten (n 653) 270.

1450 Art. 1, 1° and 2, section 1 Statute on pre-trial detention. See also: Filiep Deruyck, 'De impact van het arrest no. 148/2017 van het Grondwettelijk Hof van 21 december 2017 op de voorlopige hechtenis' [2017] Nullum Crimen 54, 54; Van den Wyngaert, Vandromme and Traest (n 34) 1195.

1451 Art. 2 Statute on pre-trial detention. See also: Van Volsem and others (n 1441) 50; Van den Wyngaert, Vandromme and Traest (n 34) 1190; Verstraeten (n 653) 565.

1452 Art. 2, 2° and 6° Statute on pre-trial detention. See also: Van Volsem and others (n 1441) 51–52; Verstraeten (n 653) 565.

1453 Art. 2, 5° Statute on pre-trial detention. See also: Van Volsem and others (n 1441) 52; Van den Wyngaert, Vandromme and Traest (n 34) 1196.

1454 Art. 1, 2° and 4° Statute on pre-trial detention. See also: Van Volsem and others (n 1441) 41–42; Van den Wyngaert, Vandromme and Traest (n 34) 1190; Verstraeten (n 653) 561.

1455 Van Volsem and others (n 1441) 39; Van den Wyngaert, Vandromme and Traest (n 34) 1196; Verstraeten (n 653) 562–563.

1456 Art. 1, 3° Statute on pre-trial detention. See also: Van den Wyngaert, Vandromme and Traest (n 34) 1196; Van Volsem and others (n 1441) 46; Verstraeten (n 653) 561–563.

290. From 24 to 48 hours – Traditionally, the time limit for this initial period of deprivation of liberty was 24 hours.[1457] Since 2011, it was possible for the investigating judge to issue a so-called extension order, extending the initial 24 hour period with an extra 24 hours.[1458] In 2017, this system was abolished and the time limit of 24 hours was extended to 48 hours instead.[1459] This change was, by necessity, preceded by an amendment to the Belgian Constitution, Article 12 of which protects the right to liberty.[1460] Nonetheless, these changes were deemed necessary for several reasons. Because of the right for suspects to an attorney during interrogations, 24 hours was deemed rather short and the system of extension orders was cumbersome to apply in practice.[1461] A second reason was the increasing complexity of criminal case and the growing threat of terrorism and organised crime.[1462] Although the threat of terrorism and

---

1457 Yves Liégeois and Bart De Smet, 'Verlenging termijn van arrestatie van 24 uur naar 48 uur' (2018) 20 Rechtskundig Weekblad 762; Marie Horseele and others, 'Recente wijzigingen in het straf(proces)recht: consequent incoherent?', *Recht in beweging – 25ste VRG-Alumnidag* (Gompel&Svacina 2018) 119; Van den Wyngaert, Vandromme and Traest (n 34) 1195; Verstraeten (n 653) 562–563.

1458 *Ex*-art. 15*bis* Statute on pre-trial detention; Verslag namens de commissie voor de Justitie 8 juni 2011 bij het wetsontwerp tot wijziging van de wet 20 juli 1990 betreffende de voorlopige hechtenis en van het Wetboek van Strafvordering, om aan elkeen die wordt verhoord en aan elkeen die van zijn vrijheid wordt beroofd rechten te verlenen, waaronder het recht om een advocaat te raadplegen en door hem te worden bijgestaan, *Parl.St.* Kamer 2010–11, no. 53–1279/005, 11; Liégeois and De Smet (n 1457); Horseele and others (n 1457) 119; Van den Wyngaert and Vandromme (n 790) 1140–1141; Van den Wyngaert, Vandromme and Traest (n 34) 1195; Van Volsem and others (n 1441) 91–100; Verstraeten (n 653) 575–579.

1459 Art. 5 wet 31 oktober 2017 tot wijziging van de wet van 20 juli 1990 betreffende de voorlopige hechtenis, de wet 7 juni 1969 tot vaststelling van de tijd gedurende welke geen opsporing ten huize, huiszoeking of aanhouding mag worden verricht, de wet van 5 augustus 1992 op het politieambt en de wet van 19 december 2003 betreffende het Europees aanhoudingsbevel, *BS* 29 november 2017, 104136. See also: H Bosly, 'Révision de la Constitution : le délai de «garde à vue» porté à 48 heures maximum en droit Belge' (2018) 2 Revue de droit pénal et de criminologie 167; Liégeois and De Smet (n 1457). A different bill, which kept the extension order for terrorist offences, was not passed (wetsvoorstel 28 september 2016 tot wijziging van de wet van 20 juli 1990 betreffende de voorlopige hechtenis, *Parl.St.* Kamer 2015–16, no. 54–2057/001 and voorstel 28 september 2016 tot herziening van artikel 12 van de Grondwet, *Parl.St.* Kamer 2015–16, no. 54–2056/001).

1460 Herziening van art. 12 van de Grondwet, 24 oktober 2017, *BS* 29 november 2017, 104076.

1461 Toelichting bij voorstel 13 juli 2017 tot herziening van artikel 12 van de Grondwet, *Parl.St. Kamer* 2016–17, no. 54 2611/001, 3 – 6; Toelichting bij wetsvoorstel 13 juli 2017 tot wijziging van de wet van 20 juli 1990 betreffende de voorlopige hechtenis wat de termijn betreft, *Parl.St. Kamer* 2016–17, no. 54 2612/001, 3. See also: Horseele and others (n 1457) 120; Velaers (n 27) 784.

1462 Toelichting bij voorstel 13 juli 2017 tot herziening van artikel 12 van de Grondwet, *Parl.St. Kamer* 2016–17, no. 54 2611/001, 3–4; Toelichting bij wetsvoorstel 13 juli 2017 tot wijziging van de wet van 20 juli 1990 betreffende de voorlopige hechtenis wat de termijn betreft, *Parl.St. Kamer* 2016–17, no. 54 2612/001, 3; Bosly (n 1459) 167–168; Horseele and others (n 1457) 120; Velaers (n 27) 784. The measure was first announced in a list of counter-terrorism measures. See: Lijst van contra-terrorismemaatregelen, plenaire sessie Kamer van Volksvertegenwoordigers, 19 november 2015. According to Hennebel and Tigroudja this is a relatively common reaction to terrorism. See: Hennebel and Tigroudja (n 358) 140.

organised crime was invoked as a reason for the change, the rules were amended for all offences and not just for terrorism and organised crime.[1463] Several proposals were tabled to extend the time limit just for terrorism and not for all offences, but in the end the proposal extending the time limit for all offences made it.[1464] While doubling the time limit for all offences may seem like a very big change, it has to be looked at in a wider context. Judicial supervision after a very short period of time is necessary in order to avoid undue pressure on or even physical abuse of the suspect. The right to have an attorney present during interrogations does counter this to a degree.

291. Order to appear before investigating judge – Next to the oral order of a deprivation of liberty, given by the public prosecutor or investigating judge, Belgian criminal procedure also contains the option of a written order to appear before the investigating judge. This is a written, more formal procedure which is possible during a judicial investigation. The investigating judge can order any person against whom there are serious indications that they committed a felony or standard offence and who is not already at their disposal, to appear before them so they can be questioned.[1465] This order can also be imposed upon witnesses who refuse to appear after being summoned.[1466] Since this is the whole point of the order, the statute declares that the investigating judge has to interrogate the person without unnecessary delay after the order has been served.[1467] When imposed upon a suspect, the suspect can be deprived of their liberty for up to 48 hours.[1468] When the order is imposed upon a witness,

1463 Bosly (n 1459) 168.

1464 Van Cauwenberghe (n 92) 13; Yperman, 'De bestrijding van terrorisme en strafprocesrecht: vele kleintjes maken een grote' (n 796) 11. E.g. by extending the time limit to 48 hours just for terrorism (voorstel tot herziening van Art. 12, derde lid, van de Gw. 21 september 2016, *Parl.St.* Kamer 2015–16, no. 54-2047/001) or by making a second extension order possible for terrorism (voorstel tot herziening van Art. 12, derde lid, van de Gw. 4 april 2016, *Parl. St.* Kamer 2015–16, no. 54-1741/001). Another proposal entailed extending the time limit to 72 hours for a limited number of offences, including terrorism (Voorstel tot herziening van Artikel 12 van de Grondwet 16 december 2015 teneinde voor bepaalde misdrijven een aanhoudingstermijn van tweeënzeventig uren mogelijk te maken, *Parl.St.* Kamer 2015–16, no. 54-1529/001. See also: Velaers (n 27) 783–786.). For an analysis, see: Henri Bosly, 'Constitution, garde à vue et lutte contre le terrorisme' in Steven Dewulf (ed), *La [CVDW] Liber Amicorum Chris Van den Wyngaert* (Maklu 2017).

1465 Art. 3, section 1 Statute on pre-trial detention. See also: Van den Wyngaert, Vandromme and Traest (n 34) 1197–1198; Van Volsem and others (n 1441) 80; Verstraeten (n 653) 579–580.

1466 Art. 4 Statute on pre-trial detention. See also: Van den Wyngaert, Vandromme and Traest (n 34) 1197; Van Volsem and others (n 1441) 80.

1467 Art. 5 Statute on pre-trial detention. See also: Van den Wyngaert, Vandromme and Traest (n 34) 1198; Verstraeten (n 653) 582.

1468 Art. 3, section 2 Statute on pre-trial detention. See also: Bosly (n 1459) 167; Horseele and others (n 1457) 121; Liégeois and De Smet (n 1457); Van den Wyngaert, Vandromme and Traest (n 34) 1198.

that witness can be deprived of their liberty for up to 24 hours.[1469] These time limits start from the moment the suspect or witness has been deprived of their liberty.[1470] It is possible that an order to appear before the investigating judge is issued for a person whose deprivation of liberty has already been ordered by the prosecutor or by another investigating judge. In this case, however, the original time limit of 48 hours is not extended.

SECTION III. ARREST WARRANT

292. Start pre-trial detention – The arrest warrant is the start of the actual pre-trial detention.[1471] It can only be issued by the investigating judge[1472] and requires a judicial investigation. While the initial deprivation of liberty is possible in a preliminary investigation, actual pre-trial detention is only possible in a judicial investigation. No appeal is possible against the issuing of an arrest warrant or the refusal to do so.[1473]

293. Conditions – The legislation explicitly states that an arrest warrant should not be issued as a form of immediate punishment or as a kind of coercion (e.g. to force a confession).[1474] Furthermore, an arrest warrant is only possible when there are serious indications of guilt of an offence for which the maximum penalty equals or exceeds one year imprisonment.[1475] These serious indications

1469 Art. 12 Statute on pre-trial detention. See also: Bosly (n 1459) 167; Horseele and others (n 1457) 121; Liégeois and De Smet (n 1457); Van den Wyngaert, Vandromme and Traest (n 34) 1198.

1470 Art. 3, section 2 Statute on pre-trial detention. See also: Horseele and others (n 1457) 121; Van den Wyngaert, Vandromme and Traest (n 34) 1198; Van Volsem and others (n 1441) 86.

1471 Verstraeten (n 653) 559; Yperman, 'De bestrijding van terrorisme en strafprocesrecht: vele kleintjes maken een grote' (n 796) 9.

1472 Art. 16, §1, section 1 Statute on pre-trial detention. See also: Van Volsem and others (n 1441) 107–108; Verstraeten (n 653) 583.

1473 Art. 17, section 2 and Art. 19, §1 Statute on pre-trial detention. See also: Daeninck, 'De impact van een beschikking van de onderzoeksrechter tot ET [elektronisch toezicht] op een hangend hoger beroep inzake voorlopige hechtenis' (n 1441) 4–5; P Daeninck, 'De voorafgaande ondervraging van de verdachte door de onderzoeksrechter' (2021) 2021 Tijdschrift voor Strafrecht 234, 234; Verstraeten (n 653) 583 and 599.

1474 Art. 16, §1, section 3 Statute on pre-trial detention. See also: Art. 10 Basiswet 12 januari 2005 betreffende het gevangeniswezen en de rechtspositie van de gedetineerden, *BS* 1 februari 2005, 2815; Verslag namens de commissie voor de Justitie 5 juni 1990 bij ontwerp van wet betreffende de voorlopige hechtenis, *Parl.St.* Senaat 1988–1989, 658–2, 17–18; Van Volsem and others (n 1441) 109–110; Verstraeten (n 653) 584; Yperman, 'De bestrijding van terrorisme en strafprocesrecht: vele kleintjes maken een grote' (n 796) 9. The Court of Cassation has ruled that this is a core condition, a violation of which cannot be Corrected later in the procedure. See: Cass. 10 februari 2021, P.20.163.F, described by P. Vanwalleghem, *Juristenkrant* 2021, afl. 426, 1.

1475 Art. 16, §1, section 1 and §5, section 1 Statute on pre-trial detention. See also: Tersago (n 1442) 11; Van den Wyngaert, Vandromme and Traest (n 34) 1199–1200; Van Volsem and others (n 1441) 110–112; Verstraeten (n 653) 584–585.

of guilt need to be based on information which would convince an objective observer that it is possible that the suspect committed an offence.[1476] Non-objectifiable and vague suspicions or police information the source of which is unclear are insufficient.[1477] Unless the suspect is a fugitive or there is force majeure,[1478] the investigating judge has to interrogate the suspect before they can issue an arrest warrant.[1479] Finally, an arrest warrant is only possible when it is absolutely necessary for public security.[1480]

294. Absolute necessity for public security – The requirement of absolute necessity for public security is either an open-ended category or not, depending on the offence. The standard rule is that for offences for which the maximum penalty does not exceed 15 years felony imprisonment, there is a limitative list of situations in which there is an absolute necessity for public security. This is the case when there are serious reasons to believe that the suspect would commit new felonies or standard offences,[1481] they would try to flee, or that they would try to make evidence disappear or conspire with others.[1482] When the maximum sentence for the offence exceeds 15 years felony imprisonment, the investigating judge is not bound by this list.[1483] There is an exception for terrorist offences (*sensu stricto* and *sensu lato*), which fixes this threshold at five years instead of

---

1476 Cass. 7 april 2021, P.21.0453.N, *RW* 2021–2022, 868. See also: De Wael (n 264) 1728.

1477 Cass. 7 april 2021, P.21.0453.N, *RW* 2021–2022, 868. See also: De Wael (n 264) 1728–1730.

1478 E.g., the Court of Cassation has accepted that the fact that the suspect was hearing impaired and a medical examination had to take place before the interrogation, constituted force majeur. See Cass. 24 november 2020, P.20.1143.N, *T.Strafr.* 2020, 226; Daeninck, 'De voorafgaande ondervraging van de verdachte door de onderzoeksrechter' (n 1473) 236.

1479 Art. 16, §2 Statute on pre-trial detention; Cass. 24 november 2020, P.20.1143.N, *T.Strafr.* 2020, 226; Daeninck, 'De voorafgaande ondervraging van de verdachte door de onderzoeksrechter' (n 1473).

1480 Art. 16, §1, section 1 Statute on pre-trial detention. See also: Ivo Mennes, 'De Wet van 31 mei 2005: een face-lift van de voorlopige hechtenis?', *Strafrecht en Strafprocesrecht* (Wolters Kluwer 2006) 300; Van den Wyngaert, Vandromme and Traest (n 34) 1200–1201; Van Volsem and others (n 1441) 113–114; Verstraeten (n 653) 585–586.

1481 Note that this motive requires a tricky balancing exercise between Art. 5 and Art. 6 ECHR. In order to comply with Art. 5, the risk of recidivism needs to be motivated in a concrete and clear manner. However, while doing so, the investigating judge needs to be careful not to violate the presumption of innocence. E.g., they cannot state that it is highly likely that the suspect has commited the offence or even imply it, for risk of violating this presumption. See: Cass. 8 September 2020, P.20.0906.N, *T.Strafr.* 2021, 85; P Tersago, 'Het recidiverisico bij de voorlopige hechtenis: de vreemde eend in de bijt (noot onder Cass. 8 september 2020)' [2021] Tijdschrift voor Strafrecht 85.

1482 Art. 16, §1, section 4 Statute on pre-trial detention. See also: Van Volsem and others (n 1441) 113–116; Horseele and others (n 1457) 126; Mennes (n 1480) 301; Van den Wyngaert and Vandromme (n 790) 1144–1145; Van den Wyngaert, Vandromme and Traest (n 34) 1200; Van Volsem and others (n 1441) 114–117; Verstraeten (n 653) 585; Yperman, 'De bestrijding van terrorisme en strafprocesrecht: vele kleintjes maken een grote' (n 796) 10.

1483 Horseele and others (n 1457) 127; Van den Wyngaert and Vandromme (n 790) 1144; Van den Wyngaert, Vandromme and Traest (n 34) 1200; Verstraeten (n 653) 585–586; Yperman, 'De bestrijding van terrorisme en strafprocesrecht: vele kleintjes maken een grote' (n 796) 10.

15.[1484] As we have explained above, the penalties for almost all of the terrorist offences exceed five years, so in most terrorism cases this will be an open ended condition.

295. Constitutional Court 15 March 2018 – In the same case in which the deletion of the risk requirement from Article 140*bis* was challenged (see nos 209, 219 and 220), the appellants also alleged a violation of the right to liberty by the introduction of the terrorism exception for the motivation requirements of an arrest warrant. The Court is mindful of the fundamental importance of *habeas corpus* and stressed that all restrictions to individual freedom have to be interpreted restrictively.[1485] However, the Court referred to the ECtHR case *Prencipe v. Monaco*, in which the ECtHR stated that certain serious offences can lead to societal unrest because of the public reaction they invoke.[1486] This can justify the use of pre-trial detention, if the detention is explicitly motivated by a concrete and current threat to public order.[1487] The Constitutional Court, as the Council of State did before it,[1488] considered that the other substantive and procedural conditions for pre-trial detention remained unchanged. Moreover, the investigating judge is never obligated to issue an arrest warrant and the statute which introduced the exception does not change anything about the requirement that pre-trial detention has to be absolutely necessary for public safety.[1489] Hence, the Constitutional Court found that there is no violation of the right to liberty.[1490]

296. Usefulness exception? – The preparatory works state that the lowering of the threshold for terrorism is justified by the need to prevent terrorist attacks (i.e. the need for prevention).[1491] This justification is remarkable, since one of the three criteria under which pre-trial detention is also possible for non-terrorist offences punishable with less than 15 years is the situation where there are serious grounds for fearing that the suspect, if released, would commit new standard offences or felonies. The prevention of new attacks can therefore be achieved as effectively within the three limitative criteria.[1492] Therefore, the question

1484 Art. 16, §1, section 4 Statute on pre-trial detention. See also: Bonfond (n 1121) 1241; Horseele and others (n 1457) 127.

1485 GwH 15 maart 2018, 31/2018, *NjW* 2018, 477, B.18.2.

1486 *Prencipe v. Monaco* App no 43376/06 (ECtHR 16 July 2009) 79.

1487 GwH 15 maart 2018, 31/2018, *NjW* 2018, 477, B.19.2.

1488 Advies 58.946/3 van de Raad van State (I) 9 maart 2016 bij wetsontwerp houdende diverse bepalingen ter bestrijding van terrorisme (III), *Parl.St.* Kamer 2015–2016, no. 54–1951/001, 16.

1489 GwH 15 maart 2018, 31/2018, *NjW* 2018, 477, B.19.2.

1490 See also: Spreutels and Velu (n 95) 145–146.

1491 MvT wetsontwerp 5 juli 2016 houdende diverse bepalingen ter bestrijding van terrorisme (III), *Parl.St. Kamer* 2015–16, no. 54 1951/001, 12; Horseele and others (n 1457) 127.

1492 Yperman, 'De bestrijding van terrorisme en strafprocesrecht: vele kleintjes maken een grote' (n 796) 10.

remains why this exception for terrorism was really necessary.[1493] Unfortunately, when finding the change in legislation constitutional, the Constitutional Court did not comment on the grounds for the change.[1494]

297. Deprivation of liberty for maximum five days or conditional freedom for maximum three months – Based on an arrest warrant, a suspect can be deprived of their liberty for maximum five days.[1495] This means the suspect can be imprisoned[1496] for that time, but electronic monitoring is possible as well.[1497] Instead of issuing an arrest warrant, the investigating judge can also decide on a provisional release.[1498] The conditions can apply for a maximum of three months.[1499] A provisional release is only possible in situations where an arrest warrant would also be possible.[1500] During the judicial investigation, the investigating judge can impose new conditions and also change, lift or extend the existing conditions.[1501] These extensions also have maximum time limit of three months.[1502] If they neglect to extend the conditions before the time limit expires, the conditions extinguish.

SECTION IV. FURTHER PRE-TRIAL DETENTION

298. Council Chamber – In order to allow the pre-trial detention to continue, the suspect has to appear before the Council Chamber within five days.[1503] This time limit can only be extended when the suspect requests so themself.[1504] The Council Chamber will verify the legality and regularity of the

---

1493 See also: Bonfond (n 1121) 1241–1242.
1494 Bonfond (n 1121) 1242.
1495 Art. 21, §1, section 1 Statute on pre-trial detention. See also: Deruyck (n 1450) 55; Van Volsem and others (n 1441) 158; Verstraeten (n 653) 609.
1496 Art. 19, §5 Statute on pre-trial detention.
1497 Art. 16, §1 section 2 Statute on pre-trial detention. See also: Daeninck, 'De impact van een beschikking van de onderzoeksrechter tot ET [elektronisch toezicht] op een hangend hoger beroep inzake voorlopige hechtenis' (n 1441) 5; Van Puyenbroeck and Claes (n 1442) 283; Van Volsem and others (n 1441) 132–135.
1498 Daeninck, 'De impact van een beschikking van de onderzoeksrechter tot ET [elektronisch toezicht] op een hangend hoger beroep inzake voorlopige hechtenis' (n 1441) 5; Verstraeten (n 653) 642.
1499 Mennes (n 1480) 320; Van den Wyngaert, Vandromme and Traest (n 34) 1233; Verstraeten (n 653) 646.
1500 Art. 35, §1 Statute on pre-trial detention. See also: Van den Wyngaert, Vandromme and Traest (n 34) 1232–1233; Verstraeten (n 653) 643.
1501 Art. 36, §1, section 1 Statute on pre-trial detention.
1502 Art. 36, §1, section 2 Statute on pre-trial detention. See also: Verstraeten (n 653) 646.
1503 Art. 21, §1, section 2 Statute on pre-trial detention. See also: Deruyck (n 1450) 55; Mennes (n 1480) 306; Tersago (n 1442) 12; Van den Wyngaert, Vandromme and Traest (n 34) 1213; Van Volsem and others (n 1441) 158–159.
1504 Art. 32 Statute on pre-trial detention. See also: Verstraeten (n 653) 609–610.

arrest warrant and also decide whether it is necessary for the pre-trial detention to continue.[1505] The Council Chamber can decide to extend the pre-trial detention for one month.[1506] It can also decide to convert a pre-trial detention in prison into electronic monitoring or *vice versa*.[1507] If the Council Chamber decides to extend the pre-trial detention, the suspect has to appear before the Council Chamber again within the month.[1508] At that moment, the Council Chamber will once more verify the necessity of the pre-trial detention and can extend it with another month.[1509] This continues until the fourth decision by the Council Chamber, at which point it can extend the pre-trial detention for a maximum of two months.[1510] From that point onward, the Council Chamber can extend the pre-trial detention with two months at a time.[1511] During any of its interventions, the Council Chamber can decide on a provisional release as well.[1512] If the suspect is at liberty but subject to conditions, they can at any

---

1505 Art. 21, §4 Statute on pre-trial detention. See also: Van den Wyngaert, Vandromme and Traest (n 34) 1214; Van Volsem and others (n 1441) 159–165; Verstraeten (n 653) 614–616.

1506 Art. 21, §6 Statute on pre-trial detention. See also: Deruyck (n 1450) 55; Verstraeten (n 653) 616.

1507 Daeninck, 'De impact van een beschikking van de onderzoeksrechter tot ET [elektronisch toezicht] op een hangend hoger beroep inzake voorlopige hechtenis' (n 1441) 3; Tersago (n 1442) 18; Van den Wyngaert, Vandromme and Traest (n 34) 1206; Van Puyenbroeck and Claes (n 1442) 284.

1508 Art. 21, §6 Statute on pre-trial detention. See also: Van Puyenbroeck and Claes (n 1442) 276; Van den Wyngaert, Vandromme and Traest (n 34) 1217–1218; Van Volsem and others (n 1441) 176.

1509 Art. 22, section 1 Statute on pre-trial detention. Van den Wyngaert, Vandromme and Traest (n 34) 1217–1219; Van Puyenbroeck and Claes (n 1442) 276; Verstraeten (n 653) 622–623.

1510 Art. 22, section 2 Statute on pre-trial detention. Until 2016, there was a differentiation in the system. For standard offences and felonies for which correctionalisation was possible, there was a monthly intervention by the Council Chamber. For felonies for which correctionalisation was not possible, the Council Chamber only had to intervene every three months, after the second confirmation of the pre-trial detention. In addition, it was possible for the suspect to petition the Council Chamber for provisional release every month (see: Mennes (n 1480) 307–310; Horseele and others (n 1457) 122; Van den Wyngaert, Vandromme and Traest (n 34) 1216–1217; Van Volsem and others (n 1441) 178–179 and 189–191; Verstraeten (n 653) 618–619.). The legislature changed this to the current system in 2016, although the two-month period started from the third decision onward (Art. 128 and 129 wet 5 februari 2016 tot wijziging van het strafrecht en de strafvordering en houdende diverse bepalingen inzake justitie, *BS* 19 februari 2016, 13130 (Potpourri II); MvT wetsontwerp 23 oktober 2015 houdende wijzigingen van het strafrecht en de strafvordering en houdende diverse bepalingen inzake justitie, *Parl.St.* Kamer 2015–16, no. 54 1418/001, (4) 120–122; Deruyck (n 1450) 55; Horseele and others (n 1457) 122; Tersago (n 1442) 12–13; Van den Wyngaert, Vandromme and Traest (n 34) 1216–1218; Van Puyenbroeck and Claes (n 1442) 275–276.). In 2017, the Constitutional Court rendered a judgment, finding the new system not unconstitutional (GwH 21 december 2017, 148/2017; Deruyck (n 1450) 56; Vilain and Yperman (n 883) 15.). In 2023, the duration of the third decision to extend the pre-trial detention was shortened to one month. See: Art. 11 and 12 wet 31 juli 2023 om justitie menselijker, sneller en straffer te maken IV, *BS* 9 augustus 2023, 66557.

1511 Deruyck (n 1450) 55; Horseele and others (n 1457) 122; Tersago (n 1442) 12–13.

1512 Art. 35, §5 Statute on pre-trial detention. See also: Van den Wyngaert, Vandromme and Traest (n 34) 1232–1233; Van Volsem and others (n 1441) 372–373; Verstraeten (n 653) 643.

time ask the Council Chamber to lift the conditions.[1513] After this request, the Council Chamber has to render a judgment within five days.[1514]

299. INDICTMENT CHAMBER – An appeal against the decisions of the Council Chamber regarding the pre-trial detention is possible. The suspect remains in custody until the end of the appeal period and in case of an appeal, until it has been decided, even if the Council Chamber decided to release them from pre-trial detention.[1515] The deadline for appeal is 24 hours after the original decision when the public prosecution wants to file an appeal and 24 hours after the decision has been served (which happens within 24 hours after the decision)[1516] when the suspects wants to file an appeal.[1517] The Indictment Chamber has to decide within 15 days after the appeal was filed.[1518] If the Indictment Chamber decides to extend the pre-trial detention, it can do so for one month if it delivers a judgment on appeal against the first, second or third decision of the Council Chamber, or for two months if it delivers a judgment on appeal against the following judgments of the Council Chamber.[1519] This means that the suspect has to appear before the Council Chamber again within either one or two months after the judgment of the Indictment Chamber in order to have their pre-trial detention reviewed. As is the case for the Council Chamber, the Indictment Chamber can decide to conditionally release the suspect[1520] or convert their pre-trial detention in jail to one by way of electronic monitoring or *vice versa*[1521] whenever it has to render a judgment on the pre-trial detention.[1522]

1513 Van den Wyngaert, Vandromme and Traest (n 34) 1236.

1514 Art. 36, §1, section 5 Statute on pre-trial detention.

1515 Art. 30, §3, section 2 Statute on pre-trial detention. See also: Van Volsem and others (n 1441) 307; Verstraeten (n 653) 626.

1516 Art. 30, §2, section 2 Statute on pre-trial detention. See also: Van Volsem and others (n 1441) 271; Verstraeten (n 653) 623.

1517 Art. 30, §2, section 1 Statute on pre-trial detention. See also: Van den Wyngaert, Vandromme and Traest (n 34) 1222–1223; Van Volsem and others (n 1441) 271; Verstraeten (n 653) 626.

1518 Art. 30, §3, section 2 Statute on pre-trial detention. See also: Van den Wyngaert, Vandromme and Traest (n 34) 1223; Van Volsem and others (n 1441) 307; Verstraeten (n 653) 630.

1519 Art. 30, §4, section 1 Statute on pre-trial detention. See also: Deruyck (n 1450) 55; Tersago (n 1442) 13; Van den Wyngaert, Vandromme and Traest (n 34) 1224–1225.

1520 Art. 35, §5 Statute on pre-trial detention. See also: Van den Wyngaert, Vandromme and Traest (n 34) 1232–1233; Van Volsem and others (n 1441) 372–373; Verstraeten (n 653) 643.

1521 Daeninck, 'De impact van een beschikking van de onderzoeksrechter tot ET [elektronisch toezicht] op een hangend hoger beroep inzake voorlopige hechtenis' (n 1441) 3–4; Van den Wyngaert, Vandromme and Traest (n 34) 1206 and 1224; Van Puyenbroeck and Claes (n 1442) 284.

1522 Note, however, that if the suspect is the only party that filed for an appeal, it is impossible for the Indictment Chamber to convert pre-trial detention by way of electronic monitoring to pre-trial detention in jail. This decision would be detrimental to the suspect, which is not allowed if they are the only party who appealed. See: Cass. 14 mei 2019, P.19.0486.N; Daeninck, 'De impact van een beschikking van de onderzoeksrechter tot ET [elektronisch toezicht] op een hangend hoger beroep inzake voorlopige hechtenis' (n 1441) 4.

300. Court of Cassation – It is possible to file an appeal to the Court of Cassation against all judgments of the Indictment Chamber that extend the pre-trial detention.[1523] This appeal will usually be filed by the suspect, but there is nothing stopping the public prosecution service from doing so if they would feel so inclined.[1524] No appeal to the Court of Cassation is possible against judgments of the Indictment Chamber that do not extend the pre-trial detention.[1525] Appeals to the Court of Cassation do not suspend the execution of the appealed judgment. In the case of a release, this means that even if an appeal would be possible, the suspect would be released pending the appeal, making the appeal moot. Again, the deadline for appeal is 24 hours after the original decision when the public prosecution wants to file an appeal and 24 hours after the decision has been served (which happens within 24 hours after the decision)[1526] when the suspects wants to file an appeal.[1527] The Court of Cassation has to judge the case within 15 days after the appeal was filed.[1528] If the Court of Cassation annuls the judgment of the Indictment Chamber, the Indictment Chamber has to rule on the case again within 15 days.[1529] If the Indictment Chamber extends the pre-trial detention again, this extension lasts for one month in case of the first, second or third decision or two months for the fourth decision onward.[1530] If the Court of Cassation does not annul the judgment of the Indictment Chamber, the suspect stays in pre-trial detention until they appear before the Council Chamber again, at latest one or two months after the judgment of the Court of

---

1523 Art. 31, §2 Statute on pre-trial detention. See also: Van Volsem and others (n 1441) 319; Verstraeten (n 653) 633. In 2016, the legislature wanted the Court of Cassation to be able to focus more on its core business, being deciding on final judgments in cases (MvT wetsontwerp 23 oktober 2015 houdende wijzigingen van het strafrecht en de strafvordering en houdende diverse bepalingen inzake justitie, *Parl.St.* Kamer 2015–16, no. 54 1418/001, (4) 127–128; Horseele and others (n 1457) 123; Van Puyenbroeck and Claes (n 1442) 274; Vilain and Yperman (n 883) 7.). In order to achieve that, it limited the possibility for an immediate appeal to the Court of Cassation to the decision by the Indictment Chamber on the pre-trial detention concerning the first extension, being the one within five days after the arrest warrant (Art. 127 Potpourri II; Deruyck (n 1450) 57; Horseele and others (n 1457) 123; Tersago (n 1442) 16–17; Van Puyenbroeck and Claes (n 1442) 275.). However, this change was annulled by the Constitutional Court in 2017, making immediate appeals to the Court of Cassation against all pre-trial detention judgments of the Indictment Chamber possible again (GwH 21 december 2017, 148/2017; Deruyck (n 1450) 57–59; Horseele and others (n 1457) 124; Van den Wyngaert, Vandromme and Traest (n 34) 1225; Vilain and Yperman (n 883) 8.).

1524 Verstraeten (n 653) 633.

1525 Van den Wyngaert, Vandromme and Traest (n 34) 1226; Verstraeten (n 653) 633.

1526 Art. 31, §1 Statute on pre-trial detention.

1527 Art. 31, §2 Statute on pre-trial detention. See also: Van den Wyngaert, Vandromme and Traest (n 34) 1225–1226; Van Volsem and others (n 1441) 328; Verstraeten (n 653) 634.

1528 Art. 31, §3, section 2 Statute on pre-trial detention. See also: Van den Wyngaert, Vandromme and Traest (n 34) 1225; Verstraeten (n 653) 635.

1529 Art. 31, §4, section 1 Statute on pre-trial detention. See also: Van Volsem and others (n 1441) 337; Verstraeten (n 653) 636.

1530 Art. 31, §4, section 3 Statute on pre-trial detention. This used to always be one month, see: Verstraeten (n 653) 637.

Cassation, depending on whether the appeal was against one of the first three Council Chamber decisions or one of the following.[1531]

301. Investigating judge – At any point in time during the investigation, the investigating judge can decide to release a suspect from pre-trial detention.[1532] The public prosecution service does not have a right to appeal this decision (nor does the defence or the victim).[1533] The investigating judge can also at any point decide to conditionally release the suspect,[1534] or that a pre-trial detention in prison is being converted to a pre-trial detention by way of electronic monitoring.[1535] They can also decide that pre-trial detention by way of electronic monitoring will be converted to pre-trial detention in prison, but only in the following cases: the suspect did not appear when their case was being judged, they violated the standard rules regarding electronic monitoring, they violated certain prohibitions which can accompany electronic monitoring (e.g. the prohibition of receiving visits from certain people), there are new and serious circumstances which necessitate their imprisonment, or the continuation of the electronic monitoring proves technically impossible.[1536] The suspect cannot appeal this decision.[1537]

SECTION V. DETENTION DURING AND AFTER TRIAL

302. Detention during trial – At the end of the investigation phase and the start of the trial phase, the basic rule on pre-trial detention is that the suspect is released.[1538] However, it is possible for the Council Chamber or Indictment

---

1531 Art. 31, §5 Statute on pre-trial detention. This used to be 15 days, see: Van Volsem and others (n 1441) 341; Verstraeten (n 653) 636.

1532 Art. 25, §1 and 2 Statute on pre-trial detention. See also: Daeninck, 'De impact van een beschikking van de onderzoeksrechter tot ET [elektronisch toezicht] op een hangend hoger beroep inzake voorlopige hechtenis' (n 1441) 2 and 5; Mennes (n 1480) 315–317; Van den Wyngaert, Vandromme and Traest (n 34) 1209; Van Volsem and others (n 1441) 210–213; Verstraeten (n 653) 599.

1533 Mennes (n 1480) 317; Tersago (n 1442) 14; Van den Wyngaert, Vandromme and Traest (n 34) 1209; Van Volsem and others (n 1441) 212.

1534 Verstraeten (n 653) 642.

1535 Art. 24*bis*, §2 Statute on pre-trial detention. See also: Daeninck, 'De impact van een beschikking van de onderzoeksrechter tot ET [elektronisch toezicht] op een hangend hoger beroep inzake voorlopige hechtenis' (n 1441) 2; Tersago (n 1442) 18; Van den Wyngaert, Vandromme and Traest (n 34) 1206; Van Puyenbroeck and Claes (n 1442) 283.

1536 Art. 24*bis*, §1 Statute on pre-trial detention. See also: Tersago (n 1442) 18; Van den Wyngaert, Vandromme and Traest (n 34) 1206; Van Puyenbroeck and Claes (n 1442) 284; Van Volsem and others (n 1441) 204–208.

1537 Van Volsem and others (n 1441) 208.

1538 Van Volsem and others (n 1441) 219.

Chamber to decide that the pre-trial detention will be extended during trial.[1539] They can also extend a pre-trial detention by way of electronic monitoring, convert a pre-trial detention in prison to one by way of electronic monitoring[1540] or conditionally release the defendant.[1541] If they decide to (conditionally) release the defendant, the prosecution service can appeal this decision.[1542] This appeal suspends the defendant's release. If their pre-trial detention is extended (regardless whether it is detention in prison or through electronic monitoring), the defendant can petition the trial court for a provisional release.[1543] The Court has to decide within five days, lest the defendant be released from detention.[1544] The Court can also decide to conditionally release the defendant.[1545] If their request for provisional release is denied, the defendant can submit a new one after one month has passed.[1546] When the suspect is subject to electronic monitoring, the trial court can only decide to convert this to detention in prison under the same circumstances this is possible for the investigating judge (see no. 301).[1547] This needs to happen at the request of the public prosecutor.[1548] Whether it can also convert a pre-trial detention in prison to one by way of electronic monitoring is unclear.[1549]

303. Provisional release during trial – If the Council Chamber or Indictment Chamber create or extend a situation of conditional freedom at the end of the investigation stage, they can do so for a maximum of three

1539 Art. 26, §3 Statute on pre-trial detention. See also: Van den Wyngaert, Vandromme and Traest (n 34) 1228; Van Volsem and others (n 1441) 221–222; Verstraeten (n 653) 1055.

1540 This follows from a Constitutional Court judgement in which the Constitutional Court ruled that the fact that the electronic monitoring of the suspect who was already subject to it during the investigation, could be extended, while a suspect's pre-trial detention in jail could not be converted to pre-trial detention by way of electronic monitoring was unconstitutional. See: GwH 21 december 2017, 148/2017. See also: Cass. 29 oktober 2019, P.19.1036.N, *AC* 2019, 2031–2035; Deruyck (n 1450) 60–61; Horseele and others (n 1457) 124–125; Vilain and Yperman (n 883) 8–9.

1541 Verstraeten (n 653) 643.

1542 Art. 26, §4 Statute on pre-trial detention. This is not the case when the pre-trial detention is extended, regardless of whether that is in prison or by way of electronic monitoring. See: Cass. 29 oktober 2019, P.19.1036.N, *AC* 2019, 2031–2035.

1543 Art. 27, §1 Statute on pre-trial detention. See also: Tersago (n 1442) 15; Van den Wyngaert, Vandromme and Traest (n 34) 1226; Van Volsem and others (n 1441) 233–235; Verstraeten (n 653) 1056.

1544 Art. 27, §3, section 3 Statute on pre-trial detention. See also: Van den Wyngaert, Vandromme and Traest (n 34) 1227; Van Volsem and others (n 1441) 237; Verstraeten (n 653) 1060.

1545 Art. 35, §5 Statute on pre-trial detention. See also: Van den Wyngaert, Vandromme and Traest (n 34) 1233; Van Volsem and others (n 1441) 372; Verstraeten (n 653) 1059.

1546 Art. 27, §4 Statute on pre-trial detention. See also: Tersago (n 1442) 15; Van den Wyngaert, Vandromme and Traest (n 34) 1227; Van Puyenbroeck and Claes (n 1442) 278.

1547 Art. 24*bis*, §3 *j.* §1 Statute on pre-trial detention. See also: Tersago (n 1442) 19; Van den Wyngaert, Vandromme and Traest (n 34) 1208.

1548 Tersago (n 1442) 19; Van Puyenbroeck and Claes (n 1442) 286.

1549 *Pro*: Tersago (n 1442) 19. *Contra*: Van den Wyngaert, Vandromme and Traest (n 34) 1227; Van Puyenbroeck and Claes (n 1442) 286.

months.[1550] During trial it is up to the trial court to extend the conditions, again for maximum three months at a time. The trial court can also revoke some or all of the conditions.[1551] They cannot, however, add new conditions.

304. DETENTION POST-TRIAL – If a defendant is convicted to a prison sentence, they will be deprived of their liberty in execution of this sentence. However, this execution does not start the moment the judgment is rendered. A judgment can only be executed if it has force of *res judicata*.[1552] If the convicted defendant was already in detention for those offences, however, they remain in detention, as long as they were convicted to a prison sentence which is longer than three years and longer than the time they already spent in (pre-trial) detention.[1553] For terrorist offences, however, this threshold is one year instead of three.[1554] If the defendant was not in detention yet, they remain at liberty even after the judgment, until it gains force or *res judicata* and can be executed.

305. IMMEDIATE ARREST – It is possible, however, for the trial court to order the immediate arrest of the convicted defendant who was not detained yet. This is not an early execution of the sentence, but a form of remand in custody, just like the pre-trial detention or detention during trial.[1555] This is possible if the defendant was convicted to a sentence of minimum three years imprisonment.[1556] When the defendant was convicted for terrorism (*sensu strico* or *sensu lato*) or certain sexual offences, however, their immediate arrest can be ordered if his sentence is minimum one year imprisonment.[1557] In addition, an immediate arrest can only be ordered when the trial court fears (in a

---

1550 Verstraeten (n 653) 1055. This limitation does not apply to bail. See: Daeninck, 'Voorlopige hechtenis: over de omvang en andere vraagstukken van de borgsom' (n 1443) 207–208.

1551 Art. 36, §3 Statute on pre-trial detention. See also: Verstraeten (n 653) 1055.

1552 Van den Wyngaert, Vandromme and Traest (n 34) 1230; Verstraeten (n 653) 1192.

1553 Art. 33, §1 Statute on pre-trial detention. See also: Van den Wyngaert, Vandromme and Traest (n 34) 1230; Verstraeten (n 653) 1170–1171.

1554 This is also the case for certain sexual offences. In addition, if the convicted person does not have an address in Belgium, they will not be released, unless the court is of the opinion there is no risk of him absconding.

1555 Van Volsem and others (n 1441) 352; Verstraeten (n 653) 1171.

1556 Art. 33, §2 Staute on pre-trial detention. See also: Horseele and others (n 1457) 125; Van den Wyngaert, Vandromme and Traest (n 34) 1230.

1557 Art. 33, §2 Statute on pre-trial detention. See also: Van den Wyngaert, Vandromme and Traest (n 34) 1230. It used to be one year for all offences (Verstraeten (n 653) 1171–1172.). In 2017 the legislature raised this threshold to three years for all offences, except for terrorism and certain sexual offences (Art. 7 wet 21 december 2017, tot wijziging van diverse bepalingen met het oog op de invoering van een beveiligingsperiode en tot wijziging van de wet van 20 juli 1990 betreffende de voorlopige hechtenis voor wat de onmiddellijke aanhouding betreft, *BS* 11 januari 2018, 1185). This was done without really motivating the differentiation between terrorism and sexual offences on the one hand and all other offences on the other hand. See: Horseele and others (n 1457) 125–126; Yperman, 'De bestrijding van terrorisme en strafprocesrecht: vele kleintjes maken een grote' (n 796) 10–11.

substantiated manner) the convicted defendant might try to evade the execution of their sentence or might commit new standard offences or felonies.[1558] When a suspect is in detention after an immediate arrest (e.g. while awaiting their appeal), they can request their provisional release from the court where their case is pending.[1559] No appeal is possible against a decision from this court in this matter.[1560] This technique of immediate arrest warrants is often combined with a trial *in absentia* for defendants suspected of terrorist offences who are believed to still be in Syria or Iraq.[1561] This means that the convicted foreign terrorist fighter can be arrested immediately upon returning to Belgium in execution of this immediate arrest warrant and can be kept in detention while a possible retrial takes place. This was clear from the Reguide case law analysis as well. In 152 cases an immediate arrest warrant was issued and of these 152 immediate arrest warrants 135 followed a trial *in absentia*. This means only 17 immediate arrest warrants were issued with the defendant present. In cases not *in absentia*, immediate arrest warrants were sometimes requested, but the chances of it being granted were much lower, a refusal being very rare *in absentia*.

SECTION VI. ARTICLE 5 SAFEGUARDS

306. Safeguards of Article 5(1)(c), (3) and (4) ECHR – In this Section, we will verify whether the Belgian rules on pre-trial detention meet the standards

---

[1558] Art. 33, §2 Statute on pre-trial detention. Until 2019, an immediate arrest was only possible in case of risk of evasion of the execution of the sentence (Verstraeten (n 653) 1172.) The reasoning was that the suspect had been at liberty up until that point and had not committed other offences during the investigation and procedure (or tried to manipulate the evidence or conspired with others). The judgment did, however, give them an extra reason to flee. Therefore, an immediate arrest was possible when there were reasons to believe they would do so. After a highly mediatised case of a murder committed by a man who had already been convicted for previous offences but who appealed his conviction and whose immediate arrest was not ordered because there was no risk he would flee, the legislature decided to make an immediate arrest also possible in case there is a risk of new offences being committed. See: wetsvoorstel 1 oktober 2019 tot wijziging van de wet van 20 juli 1990 betreffende de voorlopige hechtenis aangaande de onmiddellijke aanhouding, *Parl.St.* Kamer 2019, no. 55-0489/001, 3–4; Amendement no. 3 5 november 2019 bij tot wijziging van de wet van 20 juli 1990 betreffende de voorlopige hechtenis aangaande de onmiddellijke aanhouding, *Parl.St.* Kamer 2019, 55-0489/005, 2. This addition was challenged before the Constitutional Court, which found it to be constitutional. See: GwH 10 juni 2021, 86/2021, *Rechtskundig Weekblad* 2021–2022, 755.

[1559] Art. 27, §1, 2° and §2 Statute on pre-trial detention; Cass. 5 januari 2021, P.20.1338.N, *T.Strafr.* 2021, 232, noot P. Daeninck; Van Volsem and others (n 1441) 235.

[1560] Cass. 5 januari 2021, P.20.1338.N, *T.Strafr.* 2021, 232, noot P. Daeninck; P Daeninck, 'Over het verzoekschrift tot voorlopige invrijheidstelling na het instellen van hoger beroep tegen de beslissing ten gronde' (2021) 2021 Tijdschrift voor Strafrecht 232.

[1561] See e.g.: Corr. Brussel 21 mei 2014, *onuitg;* Corr. Brussel 25 november 2015, *onuitg;* Corr. Brussel 3 mei 2016, *onuitg;* Corr. Charleroi 22 november 2017, *onuitg;* Corr. Mechelen 4 januari 2018, *onuitg;* Corr. Brussel 1 maart 2018, *onuitg;* Corr. Antwerpen 18 maart 2018, *onuitg.*.

of Article 5 ECHR. Within Article 5, the first prong of (1)(c), (3) and (4) are the most relevant in this context. Belgian law seems to meet all the requirements under Article 5 ECHR.

307. Article 51(c) ECHR – Reasonable suspicion that the person has committed an offence is required. In this context, the Court of Cassation has specified that the information needs to be able to satisfy an objective observer,[1562] which is the same standard the ECtHR uses. In addition, the requirement of absolute necessity for public security of pre-trial detention covers the necessity in the circumstances. Belgian law explicitly states that pre-trial detention cannot be a form of coercion and the courts deciding on pre-trial detention need to give their grounds for justifying the continued detention.

308. Article 5(3) ECHR – The requirement of automatic and periodic judicial review is met as well, first by the investigating judge and then by the Council Chamber and Indictment Chamber, which are capable of examining the lawfulness of the detention and the (continued) presence of reasonable suspicion. The ECtHR has held, in relation to France, that investigating judges certainly are '*judge[s] or other officer[s] authorised by law to exercise judicial power*',[1563] so it is safe to assume that the same goes for Belgium. The legislation also requires the investigating judge to hear the individual before issuing an arrest warrant and the arrest warrant has to be issued within 48 hours after arrest, which would be considered prompt.

309. Article 5(4) ECHR – The Belgian system of automatic period review in pre-trial detention also meets the *habeas corpus* requirements of (4). The detainee has a right to access to the criminal file, the procedure is adversarial, and the review takes place at reasonable intervals.[1564] When a defendant is in remand during the trial phase, they have the right to request review from the courts, again at reasonable intervals.

1562 Cass. 7 april 2021, P.21.0453.N, *RW* 2021–2022, 868.

1563 *Medvedyev and others v. France* App no 3394/03 (ECtHR Grand Chamber 29 March 2010) 128.

1564 Regarding monthly review, see: Murdoch (n 122) 518.

CHAPTER XIII
ANALYSIS

SECTION I. OFFENCES

SUBSECTION I. THE GOAL OF THIS CHAPTER

310. Analysing existing offences – Throughout Chapters I to IX of this Part, we have described the Belgian terrorism offences and their application. It is clear from these Chapters that, when given options, the Belgian legislature has often chosen for the most repressive one, for example by choosing for an aggravating circumstance if minors are involved; by including it in more offences than mentioned in the Directive; or by choosing to criminalise inbound travel.[1565] However, Chapters I to IX did more than just describe. Throughout the text, issues in the legislation in light of the framework set up in Part I have been highlighted. This final Chapter of this Part will serve as a summary of the most important of these issues and offer preliminary remedies. These remedies are preliminary because their goal is to provide answers for the most pressing issues without fundamentally altering the Belgian response to terrorism. Attempting to answer the main research question in full would be premature at this stage. How the Belgian legislation can be improved, is a question which will be answered in the fourth and final Part of this book, after a thorough comparison of the Belgian and UK jurisdictions.

SUBSECTION II LEGAL CERTAINTY

a) *Constitutional Court 19 March 2019*

311. Lenient Court – As discussed above (see nos 155–159, 209, 218–221, 231–232, 239–240, 249 and 256–260), several of the terrorist offences were challenged before the Constitutional Court for potentially violating the legality principle. The Court always took a rather lenient approach and only ever found no violations of the legality principle. One remarkable judgment which we have not discussed yet, is the Constitutional Court judgment of 19 March

1565 For a short analysis, see: Stessens (n 1300) 447–448.

2019. This judgment does not directly concern the terrorist offences. Instead, it is a judgement on an appeal for nullification of a procedural rule regarding the professional secrecy of staff members of the OCMW/CPAS, the municipal welfare offices.[1566] Its relevance for our analysis is explained below.

312. Duty to report – In 2017, the legislature found that the flow of information between OCMW staff members and the public prosecutor's office was poor and that this made terrorism investigations more difficult. According to the legislature, one reason for this was that some OCMW staff members were 'hiding' behind their professional secrecy.[1567] That is why, among other things, it introduced an active reporting obligation for OCMW staff. If they came across information that could constitute serious indications of a terrorist offence *sensu stricto* or *sensu lato*, they had to report this to the public prosecution service.[1568] This was an exception to their professional secrecy.

313. Legality principle – This duty to report was nullified by the Constitutional Court on the basis of the principle of legality.[1569] The Court stated that, because of the duty to report, OCMW staff members had to assess a complex factual situation with criminal consequences (possible violation of professional secrecy) and that there was a real risk of error. This presupposed that they attributed a legal qualification to the conduct of a third party (the recipient of benefits or the socially insured person). Moreover, the Court stated, terrorist offences are complex and require several conditions to be met, including criminal intent. For these reasons, the duty to report violated the principle of legality.

314. Difference? – The difference between this judgment and previous judgments on the principle of legality of terrorist offences is that the OCMW staff had to assess the conduct of a third party while they do not have the expertise or the necessary means to do so. However, a large part of the Court's reasoning can also apply to perpetrators of terrorist offences. Terrorist offences have different conditions and are complex, especially with regard to the *mens rea*. Nor do the potential perpetrators have any special expertise or resources

1566 These 'Public Centres for Social Welfare' are present in every Belgian town. They offer a variety of services to increase the social welfare of citizens such as financial aid, housing, debt mediation, etc.

1567 Wetsvoorstel 22 september 2016 tot wijziging van het Wetboek van Strafvordering om de strijd tegen het terrorisme te bevorderen, *Parl.St.* Kamer 2015–16, no. 54–2050/001, 3–5.

1568 Art. 46*bis*/1, §3 CCP, as introduced by Art. 2 wet 17 mei 2017 tot wijziging van het Wetboek van strafvordering om de strijd tegen het terrorisme te bevorderen, *BS* 3 juli 2017, 69494.

1569 For an analysis, see also: Dejemeppe and Rigaux (n 898) 771–772; Lucien Nouwynck, 'Institutions de sécurité sociale, travailleus sociaux, secret professionnel et terrorisme: La Cour Constitutionelle remet les pendules à l'heure (noot onder GwH 19 maart 2019)' [2019] Revue de droit communal 21; Spreutels and Velu (n 95) 139–140.

for this assessment. The judgment of 19 March 2019 at least shows that the Constitutional Court is aware that it is not easy to know when a person commits a terrorist offence. Terrorist offences are therefore not self-evident in the light of the principle of legality.

b) Analysis

315. Focus on the *mens rea* – While the Directive sets out a broad range of acts that should be punishable in Member States, Member States are free to choose how it is implemented. Belgium chose to create new offences for every act the Directive lists while relatively closely adhering to the wording of the Directive. This is supported by the fact that the European Commission made no comments regarding the transposition of the offences from the Directive into Belgian law.[1570] Offences such as participating in the activities of a terrorist group, traveling for terrorist purposes, or self-study, have a very broad *actus reus* which includes daily neutral actions. This makes the *mens rea* the core element of the offence.[1571] The *mens rea* is internal and always has to be inferred.[1572] Therefore, it has an inherent vagueness and offences with a strong focus on the *mens rea* are inevitably also quite vague.[1573] The danger in having broad offences with a focus on the *mens rea* is that mere thoughts become punishable, whereas (in Belgium and many other states) the principle is that only acts are punishable.[1574] Criminalising mere thoughts invades an individual's private world and fails to treat them as a moral agent capable of changing their mind.[1575] Regarding the offence of traveling, for example, the Belgian Council of State

1570 Report from the Commission to the European Parliament and the Council based on Art. 29(1) of Directive (EU) 2017/541 of the European Parliament and of the Council of 15 March 2017 on combating terrorism and replacing Council Framework Decision 2002/475/JHA and amending Council Decision 2005/671/JHA, Brussels 30 September 2020, COM(2020) 619, 4–11.

1571 See also: Cesoni (n 15) 235; Mitsilegas (n 25) 188; Vandromme and De Roy (n 34) 547. European Union Agency for Fundamental Rights, *Directive (EU) 2017/541 on combatting terrorism: Impact on fundamental rights and freedoms*, 2021, 7 and 34.

1572 RA Duff, *Intention, Agency and Criminal Liability: Philosophy of Action and the Criminal Law* (Blackwell 1990) 117., European Union Agency for Fundamental Rights, *Directive (EU) 2017/541 on combatting terrorism: Impact on fundamental rights and freedoms*, 2021, 7–8.

1573 For the group offences, see: Marchand (n 617) 282. For traveling see: Advies 57.127/AV van de Raad van State 24 maart 2015 bij wetsontwerp van 22 juni 2015 tot versterking van de strijd tegen het terrorisme, *Parl.St.* Kamer 2014–15, no. 54–1198/001, (13) 17; Delhaise (n 8) 65; Mitsilegas (n 25) 188; Moreau (n 47) 115; Yperman, 'Heiligt het doel de middelen?' (n 1306).

1574 Fransen and Kerkhofs (n 802) 179; Fransen and Kerkhofs (n 10) 71; Gherbaoui (n 1299) 61–63; Meliá and Petzsche (n 45) 205; Vandromme and De Roy (n 34) 547.

1575 Ashworth and Zedner (n 18) 110; Ohana (n 41) 31–32; Zedner, 'Securing Liberty in the Face of Terror: Reflections from Criminal Justice' (n 92) 524; L Zedner, 'Preventive Justice or Pre-Punishment? The Case of Control Orders' (2007) 60 Current Legal Problems 174, 197. See also, in the context of control orders: Squires (n 25) 688; Tadros, 'Controlling Risk' (n 88) 144–148.

noted that it is situated on the border between the material and the intentional by criminalising an everyday action.[1576] Proving the *mens rea* is no easy task.[1577] On the one hand, there is the risk that the evidence is so difficult to provide in practice that the Article turns out to be an empty box. On the other hand, there is the risk of an overly broad application if the principle that there must be sufficient concrete, objective and material evidence for the *mens rea* is weakened.[1578] In general the motivation of Belgian court judgments often does not go into the *mens rea* in much detail and the presence of *mens rea* seems to be assumed rather easily. For 'traditional' offences (see no. 5) this is not a major issue as the *mens rea* is often relatively easy to infer from the *actus reus*. For example, the action of pointing a gun at somebody's head and then pulling the trigger, thereby shooting them in the head is a clear indication of the intention to kill. In the case of terrorism offences *sensu lato*, however, the *actus reus* is often so broad, one cannot infer the *mens rea* quite as easily. Too easily accepting the existence of a *mens rea* in that scenario, can violate the legality principle. This is seen in the ECtHR case of Yüksel Yalcinkaya. In this case the defendant was convicted for membership of an armed terrorist organisation in Turkey and the *mens rea* was established solely based on the fact that he had a specific app (ByLock) on his phone. The ECtHR held that assuming the existence of the *mens rea* of the offence solely based on this fact was a violation of the legality principle. All elements of the offence were not established in an individualised manner.[1579] Perhaps Belgian courts are sometimes too quick to assume the existence of the *mens rea* in cases of terrorism offences *sensu lato* as well. The issue of the focus of the offences on the *mens rea* is further exacerbated by the fact that this *mens rea* not only includes the perpetration of terrorist offences, but also the contributing to their perpetration; and refers to other terrorist offences *sensu lato* as well. This makes the *mens rea* broader and even more complicated to analyse. Some authors have dubbed this 'double preparation' as this means that offences can be linked together through their *mens rea*. For example, traveling in order to contribute to a terrorist offence; or inciting somebody to travel in order to commit a terrorist offence *sensu stricto*, is punishable.[1580] However, with a little

[1576] Advies 57.127/AV van de Raad van State 24 maart 2015 bij wetsontwerp van 22 juni 2015 tot versterking van de strijd tegen het terrorisme, *Parl.St.* Kamer 2014–15, no. 54–1198/001, (13) 17; Blaise and Delhaise (n 49) 174; Cesoni (n 15) 235–236; Winants (n 8) 352.

[1577] Delhaise and Fievet (n 45) 120.

[1578] Comité T, 'Rapport 2019: Le respect des droits humains dans le cadre de la lutte contre le terrorisme: Un chantier en cours', 17; Blaise and Delhaise (n 49) 177. Asp argues that this is most likely to be the case. See: Asp (n 4) 35–36.

[1579] *Yüksel Yalçinkaya v. Türkiye* App no 15669/20 (ECtHR Grand Chamber 26 September 2023) 255–268.

[1580] De Coensel, 'De Wet Diverse Bepalingen in Strafzaken II: Terroristische misdrijven in lijn met de Europese verplichtingen?' (n 793) 212 and 215; Delhaise (n 8) 64; Anne Ponseille, 'Les infractions de prévention, argonautes de la lutte contre le terrorisme' [2017] Revue des droits et libertés fondamentaux.

creativity it is possible to expand this to 'triple', 'quadruple', etc. preparation. For example, attempting to incite a person to travel in order to receive training in order to contribute to a terrorism offence *sensu stricto* would be punishable and is five steps removed from the actual terrorism offence *sensu stricto*. The Belgian legislature has shown it is aware of the broadness of the terrorist offences. In the preparatory works of the Act on civilian infiltration, it is stated that it is almost impossible for an informant to operate in terrorism investigations. Informants are not allowed to commit criminal offences, and the terrorism offences are so broad that an informant who moves in those circles is almost always committing one.[1581] These broad and vague offences have to be applied cautiously because this broadness and vagueness does not sit well with the requirement of legal certainty that offences are clearly defined in the law.[1582] Part of this is due to the broadness and vagueness of the actions the Directive requires the Member States to criminalise. In a report published in 2021 on the impact of the EU Directive on fundamental rights and freedoms, the European Union Agency for Fundamental Rights (FRA) comes to a similar conclusion. It points out that the definitions of terrorism *sensu stricto* and of a terrorist group are broad, making the scope of newer offences which refer to them unclear.[1583] It also states that '*offences that encompass a wide range of loosely defined behaviours are frequently applied – such as various forms of participation in a terrorist organisation. This reduces legal clarity.*'[1584] As we have seen, this is the case for Belgium. Finally, the FRA points to existing overlap between the definitions of different offences in national law before concluding that all this reduces foreseeabiltiy of what is criminalised and under what offence.[1585] In a second point, the FRA expresses concern about lawful activities being criminalised through preparatory offences.[1586]

316. GOING BEYOND THE DIRECTIVE – Belgium, however, chose to go further still, in several cases. By rather carelessly transposing these offences, they became even broader and vaguer.[1587] For example, Belgium expanded the *mens rea* of the offence of participating in the activities of a terrorist group, while

[1581] MvT wetsontwerp 19 februari 2018 tot wijziging van het Wetboek van Strafvordering met het oog op het invoeren van de bijzondere opsporingsmethode burgerinfiltratie, *Parl.St.* Kamer 2017–18, no. 54-2940/001, 12–15.

[1582] Art. 7 ECtHR; *Cantoni v. France* App no 17862/91 (ECtHR 11 November 1996) 29; *Del Rio Prada v. Spain* App no 42750/09 (ECtHR Grand Chamber 21 October 2013) 79.

[1583] European Union Agency for Fundamental Rights, Directive (EU) 2017/541 on combatting terrorism: Impact on fundamental rights and freedoms, 2021, 6.

[1584] European Union Agency for Fundamental Rights, Directive (EU) 2017/541 on combatting terrorism: Impact on fundamental rights and freedoms, 2021, 6.

[1585] European Union Agency for Fundamental Rights, Directive (EU) 2017/541 on combatting terrorism: Impact on fundamental rights and freedoms, 2021, 6–7.

[1586] European Union Agency for Fundamental Rights, Directive (EU) 2017/541 on combatting terrorism: Impact on fundamental rights and freedoms, 2021, 7.

[1587] Murphy (n 13) 227.

the offence in the Framework Decision was already criticised for being too far removed from actual terrorism.[1588] This already was an offence with a very broad *actus reus* and the focus mainly on the *mens rea*. The legislature expanded this *mens rea* and we have seen that the case law goes even further, interpreting it quite loosely. This led to convictions for sending clothes to siblings or trying to marry.[1589] However, it seems that the case law went beyond what the legislature intended, thereby violating the *lex certa* principle. By reverting back to the wording of the Directive, the legislature could give a signal to the courts that they are going too far. The Belgian legislature also created offences which are not part of the Directive. The first one being preparing a terrorist offence. The core of this offence is also the *mens rea* but this *mens rea* is not even explicit in the Article. The legislature would do well to explicitly include this, it being the most important part of the offence. Another expansion upon the Directive is the offence of participating in the making of a decision in the context of a terrorist group. This is a poorly worded offence, which encompasses almost everybody who has had any relation with the group and which should be deleted again. In the incitement offence, as well as the recruitment offence, the legislature added the traveling offence to the *mens rea*. Since the traveling offence itself has a broad *mens rea*, this addition makes these offences significantly broader than the ones in the Directive. In addition, it creates a strange distinction: inciting or recruiting somebody to travel to another country to receive or provide terrorist training there is punishable under Articles 140*bis* or 140*ter* CC; while inciting or recruiting them to do so in Belgium is not. The Belgian legislature also expanded the *mens rea* of the traveling offence itself compared to the Directive. This allows for offences of triple, quadruple, etc. preparation and thus causes actions that are very far removed from an actual terrorist attack to be punishable. Criminalising conduct that early on the *iter criminis* also reduces the incentive of the perpetrator to abandon their plans, since they are already punishable and the proverbial die has been cast.

317. Clearly defining core concepts – The offence which is at the core of it all is terrorism *sensu stricto*. It is therefore vital that this offence is defined as clearly as possible. In Section I of Chapter I, we have already suggested a change in the wording of the *actus reus* of '*significant economic damage*'. The *mens rea* also includes several vague terms, which could be further defined and narrowed down.[1590] These terms are copied from the Directive, so part of the responsibility for this lies at the EU level. Furthermore, the phrasing of the sentences in Article 138 CC is very poor. These can be rephrased in a clearer way,

1588 Cesoni (n 64) 145–148.

1589 Corr. Brussel 14 mei 2014; Corr. Oost-Vlaanderen (afd. Gent) 16 oktober 2017, *NjW* 2017, 805, noot W. Yperman en S. Royer.

1590 See also: Cesoni (n 15) 233.

as suggested above (see no. 147). Other core concepts which could be further defined are 'leadership' in the context of Article 140, §2 CC and the definition of a terrorist group in Article 139 CC, more specifically regarding the question of how to prove the group is a terrorist group if it has not even started preparing or planning a terrorist attack.

318. Overlap – Due to the aforementioned broadness and vagueness, there is a fair amount of overlap between many of the terrorist offences.[1591] For example, a message on social media calling for people to travel to Syria could be recruitment, inciting and participation in the travelling offence. Looking up certain information online could be self-study and preparation and, if accompanied by other actions, perhaps even an attempted terrorist offence *stricto sensu*. On top of that, if either of those things happen within the context of a terrorist group, they also fall under participation in the activities of a terrorist group.

319. Redundancy can lead to confusion – The Belgian legislature is aware of this overlap, thus Articles 140*bis* to 140*sexies* CC state that they apply '*without prejudice to the application of Article 140*.'[1592] The legislature therefore acknowledged that (some of) the actions being criminalised by these Articles were already being prosecuted under Article 140 CC. It intended to alleviate all doubt about the fact that concurrent offences are possible. The practical application of these offences demonstrates that they are not prosecuted that often and even if they are, the prosecution is in concurrence with Article 140 CC.[1593] Therefore, they have minimal added value.[1594] The question also arises regarding the impact of the overlap between Articles 140*bis* to 140*sexies*. By only referring to Article 140 CC, the legislature has created the possibility for confusion. Under the general rules of Belgian criminal law, concurrence between

---

1591 See related to different terrorism offences: MvT wetsontwerp 13 november 2012 tot wijziging van Titel I*ter* van het Strafwetboek, *Parl.St.* Kamer 2012–2013, no. 53–2502/001, 8–9; Amendement no. 1 7 juli 2016 bij wetsvoorstel 13 januari 2016 tot wijziging van het Strafwetboek wat betreft de bestraffing van terrorisme, *Parl.St.* Kamer 2015–2016, no. 54–1579/005, 4; Advies 59.789/3 van de Raad van State 19 juli 2016 bij wetsvoorstel 13 januari 2016 tot wijziging van het Strafwetboek wat betreft de bestraffing van terrorisme, *Parl.St. Kamer* 2015–2016, no. 54–1579/006, 13; Delhaise (n 8) 52; Fransen and Kerkhofs (n 10) 63–64 and 66.

1592 Own translation, original in Dutch and French.

1593 For examples of concurrent prosecution, see: Antwerpen 2 maart 2016, *onuitg;* Antwerpen 22 december 2016, *onuitg;* Corr. Brussel 26 juni 2015, *onuitg;* Corr. Antwerpen 7 december 2015, *onuitg;* Corr. Oost-Vlaanderen (afd. Dendermonde) 25 januari 2016, *onuitg;* Corr. Brussel 20 oktober 2016, *onuitg;* Corr. Brussel 9 maart 2017, *onuitg;* Corr. Brussel 31 mei 2017, *onuitg;* Corr. Henegouwen (afd. Charleroi) 27 september 2017, *onuitg;* Corr. Oost-Vlaanderen (afd. Dendermonde) 26 februari 2018, *onuitg.* See also: Brion and others (n 77) 62; Fransen and Kerkhofs (n 10) 57, 63–64, 74 and 81.

1594 Note that Moreau also makes this point for Art. 140*septies* CC. See: Moreau (n 47) 115.

offences is possible without this explicitly being acknowledged in the Articles containing the individual offences.[1595] Why then did the legislature explicitly refer to Article 140 CC but not to the other terrorist offences? One could think the legislature implicitly wanted to exclude concurrence with the other terrorist offences, but that is doubtful considering the current climate of extensive criminalisation. What is more likely is that the legislature did not have a specific reason for including this clause, and for clarity's sake, it should either have included all the other Articles in this clause or omitted it altogether.[1596] This is not the only example of redundant phrases in the offences. Other redundancies include the the phrase '*in Belgium or abroad*' in Article 140*quinquies* CC and the second section of Article 139 CC. Finally, the Belgian legislature created a second prong to the *mens rea* of the offence of financing a terrorist, which is not part of the Directive. This second prong, however, is already encompassed by the first prong, thus making it pointless. While these redundancies may not have had substantial impact so far, they are examples of thoughtless legislating and can lead to unnecessary confusion.

320. Legal certainty in danger – In general it is safe to conclude that the Belgian terrorism offences pose several major issues in terms of legal certainty.[1597] They are very broad and sometimes vague, which is the exact thing the legal certainty principle seeks to avoid.[1598] In addition, they overlap and contain redundant wording which makes the entire situation even less clear. It is noteworthy that upon the introduction of the first terrorism offences, some members of parliament were afraid of the implications of the terrorism offences for rights and liberties and thought judges were given too much leeway.[1599] In response to their concerns, some formal safeguards such as section 2 of Article 139 and Article 141*ter* CC were further developed but these have turned out to be paper tigers. Compared to the current situation, the 2003 offences were not nearly as broad and vague, while most of the expansions have not received the same level of criticism, clearly showing how the legislature has been influenced by the changing security situation and the perception of insecurity.

1595 Art. 58–65 CC.

1596 Delhaise (n 8) 67.

1597 See also: Comité T, 'Rapport 2019: Le respect des droits humains dans le cadre de la lutte contre le terrorisme: Un chantier en cours', 14–15.

1598 See also: Delhaise (n 8) 54.

1599 Verslag namens de commissie voor de Justitie 7 november 2003 bij wetsontwerp betreffende terroristische misdrijven, *Parl.St.* Kamer 2003–04, no. 51–0258/004; Verslag namens de commissie voor de Justitie 3 december 2003 bij wetsontwerp betreffende terroristische misdrijven *Parl.St.* Senaat 2003–04, no. 3–332/3. See also: Weyembergh and Kennes (n 14) 127. Certain academics in 2004 also argued that the offences were too broad, see e.g.: Beernaert, 'La Loi du 19 Décembre 2003 relative aux infractions terroristes : Quand le droit pénal Belge évolue sous la dictée de l'Union Européenne' (n 20) 589–590.

SUBSECTION III. PROPORTIONALITY

321. General issue – Before going into some of the specific offences, one general proportionality issue can be raised. The sentences for the terrorism offences *sensu lato* (excluding Article 140*septies* CC) are harsher than the lowest sentences for terrorism *sensu stricto*. This was explained in detail for Article 140, §1 CC, but applies to the other offences as well. For example, the sentencing bracket for recruiting or training somebody for terrorist battery is higher than for terrorist battery itself. The same goes for undergoing training, incitement, traveling and financing.[1600] Specifically for the incitement and financing offences, the legislature has somewhat alleviated this issue in the new Criminal Code (see nos 217 and 281) as the sentence for inciting and providing data or material resources in the knowledge that they are to be used to commit or contribute to the commission of the least serious terrorist offences *sensu stricto* has been lowered. It is unclear if this was the intention of the legislature in making these changes, as the parliamentary documents do not explain them. Whatever the reasoning, the issue has not been entirely solved, as, for example, inciting a level 2 offence is punishable with a level 3 sentence.

322. Article 138 CC – Differentiation between the lowest sentences in Article 138 CC to reflect some of the proportionality which is present outside of a terrorism context could be a good step. When making changes, the legislature should ensure that the minimum sentence for offences originally punishable with a fine is not higher than lowest category of imprisonment. The sentence for threatening terrorism *sensu stricto* should probably be made dependent on the threatened offence for standard offences to avoid threatening being punished harsher than the actual offence.

[1600] Note that in the context of the drug legislation a similar issue arose, which was challenged before the Constitutional Court. In the drug legislation, the preparation of certain drug offences is punished with the same sentence as the actual offence and thus more harshly than the attempt to those offences (see: Art. 2*bis*, §6 wet 24 februari 1921 betreffende het verhandelen van gifstoffen, slaapmiddelen en verdovende middelen, psychotrope stoffen, ontsmettingsstoffen en antiseptica en van de stoffen die kunnen gebruikt worden voor de illegale vervaardiging van verdovende middelen en psychotrope stoffen, *BS* 6 maart 1921, 1834). This was brought before the Constitutional Court, which ruled that it was not discriminatory. The Court deferred to the legislature in terms of which facts are reprehensible, what should be offences, the seriousness of offences and the harshness of the punishment. The Court limits itself to cases of obvious unreasonability and obviously disproportionate sentences (see: GwH 20 oktober 2022, 132/2022, *JLMB* 2023/7, 276). This judgment is logical in light of the Constitutional Court's role and the separation of powers. It is safe to assume a similar case concerning the terrorism offences would end in a similar judgment. However, as was mentioned before in the context of the ECtHR, this should not deter us from commenting on the proportionality of sentences as we are not encumbered by the same limitations the Constitutional Court is.

323. Article 140 CC – If the scope of the offence would be limited as suggested above (see no. 316), that would already introduce a form of *de minimis* threshold by narrowing the spectrum of the punishable activities. In addition to this and to deleting §1/1 from the Article, the maximum sentences for §1 could be raised to 15-year felony imprisonment, making it ten years imprisonment after correctionalisation. This way, jihadist fighters can be punished more harshly, and it would bring Belgian practice in line with what the Directive requires. This, however, would further exacerbate the issue of participation in the activities of a group being punished more harshly than the offence the group aims to commit. One possible solution could be to differentiate between categories of terrorist groups, but this could become overly complex. Another option would be to limit the definition of a terrorist group to a group which aims to commit only the more serious terrorist offences (see no. 650). This does raise the question of whether or not this is allowed under the Directive.

324. Incoherence compared to 'general' offences – Because of the broad and often overlapping offences, the Belgian Criminal Code lacks coherence as well. It is striking that a woman who helps her husband hide the body of a person he has murdered[1601] or a man who helps his brother go into hiding, knowing that this brother has committed a murder,[1602] go unpunished, since the legislation provides for a ground for impunity for blood relatives and spouses in these cases.[1603] However, these same people commit an offence when they cook for their husband or send their brother clothes if that husband or brother happen to be IS fighters. For terrorism and terrorist groups the legislature seems to want to be extra strict which can cause proportionality issues. Perhaps, judges would consider an analogous application of the abovementioned ground of impunity, but this argument has not been made in court (yet).

SECTION II. SUPERVISION BY THE SENTENCE ENFORCEMENT COURT

325. Court of Cassation: disposal of the government no violation of Article 5 ECHR – Being at the disposal of the Sentence Enforcement Court has a clear preventive rationale, being mainly focussed on recidivists. However, as explained in Part I, preventive detention can constitute 'detention after conviction by a competent court' if ordered by a sentencing court in accordance

1601 For which the sentence normally is three months to two years imprisonment and a fine of 50 to 600 euros (Art. 340 CC).

1602 For which the sentence normally is eight days to two years imprisonment and a fine of 26 to 500 euros (Art. 339 CC).

1603 Art. 341 CC. For an analysis of these two offences and the ground for impunity, see: Marlier (n 807) 718–725.

with domestic law. This is the case for being placed at the disposal of the Sentence Enforcement Court. In a 1978 case concerning being at the disposal of the government, the Court of Cassation held that this penalty was not in violation of Article 5 ECHR.[1604] The Court pointed out that the sentence was imposed by a judge with all the legal safeguards and possibilities of appeal that it entails. Therefore, the judicial supervision required by Article 5(4) ECHR was already present in the judgment imposing the sentence. Furthermore, the sentence had a set and clear term.

326. ECtHR: DISPOSAL OF THE GOVERNMENT VIOLATION OF ARTICLE 5(4) ECHR – In the *Van Droogenbroeck* case the ECtHR also came to the conclusion that being at the disposal of the government did not violate Article 5(1) ECHR. The Court held that it fell under Article 5(1)(a) ECHR.[1605] It also clarified that this sentence is a deprivation of liberty, regardless of how the sentence is implemented.[1606] These deprivations of liberty, however, were imposed after a conviction by a competent court and the detention resulted from the conviction.[1607] Since the Secretary's discretion whether or not to detain was exercised within the framework set out by the act and by the sentence pronounced by the court, there was a sufficient connection between the judgment and the deprivation of liberty.[1608] The Court did state that '*The link might eventually be broken if a position were reached in which those decisions were based on grounds that had no connection with the objectives of the legislature and the court or on an assessment that was unreasonable in terms of those objectives.*'[1609] However, in the *Van Droogenbroeck* case, this was not so. In the case of *De Schepper*, the ECtHR also found being at the disposal of the government to be in line with Article 5(1)ECHR.[1610] In that case Mr. Van Droogenbroeck argued that the decision by the Secretary to intern him in prison had sufficient causal connection to the original court decision. On the issue of judicial supervision in the *Van Droogenbroeck* case, the ECtHR did differ in opinion to the Court of Cassation. The ECtHR disagreed that the supervision incorporated in the original judgment is sufficient. The individual must be able to apply to a court during the course of their detention, once a certain period of time has elapsed and after that at regular intervals.[1611] The government held that this option was present, referring to several procedures including the juge de référés. The ECtHR

1604 Cass. 4 april 1978, *Arr.Cass.* 1978, 884.

1605 *Van Droogenbroeck v. Belgium* App no 7906/77 (ECtHR 24 June 1982) 33–34.

1606 *Van Droogenbroeck v. Belgium* App no 7906/77 (ECtHR 24 June 1982) 34.

1607 *Van Droogenbroeck v. Belgium* App no 7906/77 (ECtHR 24 June 1982) 35. See also: Dhont (n 121) 294–295.

1608 *Van Droogenbroeck v. Belgium* App no 7906/77 (ECtHR 24 June 1982) 39.

1609 *Van Droogenbroeck v. Belgium* App no 7906/77 (ECtHR 24 June 1982) 40.

1610 *De Schepper v. Belgium* App no 27428/07 (ECtHR 13 October 2009) 35–50. See also: Van Den Berge (n 757) 237.

1611 *Van Droogenbroeck v. Belgium* App no 7906/77 (ECtHR 24 June 1982) 48.

however, ruled that these remedies were either not judicial, not sufficiently certain or did not have the authority to end the detention.[1612] Therefore, the Court found the sentence of being at the disposal of the government, at that point in time, in violation of Article 5(4) ECHR.

327. Application to being at the disposal of the Sentence Enforcement Court – Since the sentence of being at the disposal of the government was found to be in line with Article 5(1)(a) ECHR it stands to reason that the same applies for its successor.[1613] The relevant points of the sentence have stayed the same. Furthermore, a crucial innovation is the introduction of a yearly review by the Sentence Enforcement Court. It is likely that this review suffices in light of Article 5(4) ECHR, meaning that being at the disposal of the Sentence Enforcement Court is not in violation of Article 5 ECHR.

1612 *Van Droogenbroeck v. Belgium* App no 7906/77 (ECtHR 24 June 1982) 51–56.

1613 See also: Van Den Berge (n 757) 238.

PART III

THE UK

INTRODUCTION

328. Criminal law and administrative law – As was the case for Belgium, most restrictions to the right to liberty in the UK take place within the context of the criminal justice system. Contrary to Belgium, however, the UK also has a system of preventatively restricting physical liberty on an administrative law basis. For our purposes the indefinite detention of suspected international terrorists in Belmarsh prison and the subsequent control order and TPIM regimes are the most relevant (see nos 496–519).

329. Overview of Part III – This Part of the book aims to do the same as Part II did for Belgium, but now for the UK. This introduction briefly presents the UK legal system and its context of (counter-)terrorism. The rest of the Part contains three Chapters, the first two of which cover research question 3.1[1614] and the third of which covers research question 3.2.[1615] The first Chapter focusses on criminal law; the second on restrictions of liberty within administrative law; and the third contains a preliminary analysis of the UK rules. The first Chapter is divided into 16 Sections. Section II discusses the definition of terrorism in UK law, Section III focusses on terrorism *sensu stricto* and Sections IV to XIV on the offences of terrorism *sensu lato* (see no. 7). These, often very broad, terrorism offences *sensu lato* are offences related to proscribed organisations (Section IIII), offences related to terrorist property (Section V), training offences (Section VI), directing a terrorist organisation (Section VII), possession for terrorist purposes and collection of information (Section VIII), not disclosing certain information on terrorism (Section IX), eliciting, publishing or communicating information on members of the armed forces (Section X), a designated area offence (Section XI), encouraging terrorism and the dissemination of terrorist publications (Section XII), the preparation of terrorist acts (Section XIII) and offences involving radioactive devices and materials (Section XIV). The final two Sections deal with extraterritorial offences and pre-trial detention respectively. As was the case for Belgium, near the end of most Sections discussing (an) offence(s), we refer to case law where possible. These practical application Subsections serve to provide examples and point to specific issues which arise in the case law, but do not aim to be exhaustive. In addition, the Sections on the offences which have received the most criticism will end with a criticism Subsection, in which this

---

1614 How has the UK used direct restrictions to the right to liberty to attempt to prevent terrorism?
1615 In which ways is the UK approach in line with our framework?

criticism is discussed, with reference to relevant ECtHR cases where possible. In Chapter II the relevant administrative law measures are discussed. This Chapter is divided into three Sections, covering the three main administrative law regimes which succeeded each other. This means Section I covers detention under the Anti-Terrorism, Crime and Security Act 2001, Section II the control orders regime and Section III TPIMs. The third and final Chapter of this Part contains some conclusions on the right to liberty in the UK under the ECHR and a preliminary analysis of the UK rules using the framework set out in Part I of this book. As was the case for Belgium (see Part II), this analysis builds upon the criticism voiced throughout the Part and discusses the current UK legislation. A more detailed comparative analysis of both the Belgian and UK rules, including recommendations for Belgium, will be undertaken in the fourth and final Part of this book.

330. Focus on England and Wales – Within UK criminal law, a division should be made between England and Wales, Northern Ireland, and Scotland. These three parts of the UK have (slightly) diverging criminal legislation.[1616] For simplicity's sake, we will chose one jurisdiction to focus on, but the text is to a significant extent also applicable to the other two since in counter-terrorism the differences between the three parts are largely a matter of terminology and details.[1617] Considering the history of (Northern-)Ireland, this seems like a good candidate or the position of jurisdiction of choice. However, at the beginning of the 21st Century, the UK counter-terrorism legislation was explicitly detached from the Northern-Irish situation (see no. 335). Therefore, our focus will be on the legislation applicable to England and Wales, as this is by far the largest part of the three.

331. UK Criminal Justice: brief introduction – In England and Wales, there are three types of criminal offences, being summary offences, triable either-way offences and indictable-only offences. The first are tried by Magistrates' Courts and the second can be tried either by the Magistrates' Courts or the

1616 Anthony Amatrudo and Leslie William Blake, *Human Rights and the Criminal Justice System* (Routledge 2015) 34–38; John R Spencer, '"No Thank You, We've Already Got One!" Why EU Anti-Terrorist Legislation Has Made Little Impact on the Law of the UK' in Francesca Galli and Anne Weyembergh (eds), *EU counter-terrorism offences: What impact on national legislation and case-law?* (Editions de l'Université de Bruxelles 2012) 119.

1617 Spencer (n 1616) 119. Special powers, and other special provisions, for dealing with terrorism are so-called 'reserved matters' for Scotland, as is the case for terrorist financing in Northern Ireland. See: s. B8 Schedule 5 Scotland Act 1998; s. 25 Schedule 3 Northern Ireland Act 1998. See also: Florence Lee and Clive Walker, 'The Counter-Terrorism and Sentencing Act 2021 and the Advance of Intensified Terrorism Punishment' [2022] Criminal Law Review 864, 872; Roger Masterman and Collin Murray, *Constitutional and Administrative Law* (3rd edn, Cambridge University Press 2022) 445–471.

Crown Courts.[1618] In those cases it is either the defendant who insists upon a trial in a Crown Court or the Magistrate may send the case on to a Crown Court if they consider it to be of sufficient seriousness.[1619] Over 90% of all criminal cases are tried by a Magistrates' Court.[1620] The maximum sentence for summary offences is 12 months imprisonment. Indictable-only offences, which are the most serious offences, have to be tried by the Crown Courts.[1621] Crown Courts also deal with appeals against decisions by the Magistrates' Courts. In a Crown Court, the verdict on matters of fact is rendered by a jury.[1622] Defendants who were convicted on indictment (i.e. by the Crown Court) can appeal to the Court of Appeal.[1623] A final appeal to the Supreme Court is possible under certain circumstances.[1624] The Supreme Court is the highest court in the country since 2009, when it replaced the House of Lords in this capacity. Despite the broad spectrum of terrorist offences (see Chapter I of this Part), obtaining criminal convictions is no easy task. This is mainly due to two factors. First, jury trials are expensive and concerns have been voiced about their reliability, as was the case in Belgium (see nos 102 and 154).[1625] Second, the use of intercepted phone calls or letters (intercept evidence) as evidence is prohibited, which can be a severe handicap to obtaining convictions.[1626] In England and Wales, the age of legal

---

1618 Michael Allen and Ian Edwards, *Criminal Law* (Sixteenth edition, Oxford University Press 2021) 23; Steven Cammiss, 'Courts and the Trial Process' in Anthea Hucklesby and Azrini Wahidin (eds), *Criminal Justice* (Second edition, Oxford University Press); Janet Loveless, Mischa Allen and Caroline Derry, *Complete Criminal Law* (Seventh edition, Oxford University Press 2020) 16–17; Jacqueline Martin, *Criminal Law* (Routledge 2014) 3; John Sprack and Michael Engelhardt-Sprack, *A Practical Approach to Criminal Procedure* (Oxford University Press 2019) 8–9; Lucy Welsh, Layla Skinns and Andrew Sanders, 'Summary Justice in the Magistrates' Court' in Lucy Welsh, Layla Skinns and Andrew Sanders, *Sanders & Young's Criminal Justice* (Oxford University Press 2021) 390.

1619 Allen and Edwards (n 1618) 24; Cammiss (n 1618); Loveless, Allen and Derry (n 1618) 17; Sprack and Engelhardt-Sprack (n 1618) 115–119.

1620 Loveless, Allen and Derry (n 1618) 17; Welsh, Skinns and Sanders, 'Summary Justice in the Magistrates' Court' (n 1618) 390.

1621 Allen and Edwards (n 1618) 23; Cammiss (n 1618); Loveless, Allen and Derry (n 1618) 17; Martin (n 1618) 3; Spencer (n 1616) 126; Sprack and Engelhardt-Sprack (n 1618) 7–9; Welsh, Skinns and Sanders, 'Summary Justice in the Magistrates' Court' (n 1618) 390.

1622 Allen and Edwards (n 1618) 28–29; Cammiss (n 1618); Loveless, Allen and Derry (n 1618) 17; Spencer (n 1616) 126; Sprack and Engelhardt-Sprack (n 1618) 7–8.

1623 S. 1 (1) Criminal Appeal Act 1968. See also: Allen and Edwards (n 1618) 30–31; Loveless, Allen and Derry (n 1618) 17; Sprack and Engelhardt-Sprack (n 1618) 425 and 459.

1624 S. 33 Criminal Appeal Act 1968. See also: Amatrudo and Blake (n 1616) 37–38; Sprack and Engelhardt-Sprack (n 1618) 455.

1625 Cammiss (n 1618); Spencer (n 1616) 126–128.

1626 Anderson, 'Shielding the Compass: How to Fight Terrorism without Defeating the Law' (n 25) 9; Brice Dickson, 'Terrorism Laws and Legal Accountability' in Genevieve Lennon and Clive Walker (eds), *Routledge Handbook of Law and Terrorism* (Routledge 2015) 122; Stuart Macdonald and Lord Carlile, 'Disrupting Terrorist Activity: What Are the Limits to Criminal Methods of Disruption?' in Satvinder S Juss (ed), *Beyond human rights and the war on terror* (Routledge, Taylor & Francis Group 2019) 126; Spencer (n 1616) 128–129. Lord Lloyd of Berwick recommended making intercept evidence admissible in cases affecting national security, such as terrorism cases. See: Lord Lloyd of Berwick, *Inquiry into legislation against*

responsibility is ten.[1627] The standard rule for minors (under 18) is that they can only be convicted to detention and training orders, which last for maximum 24 months.[1628] However, if the offence is punishable with imprisonment of at least 14 years, a sentence of detention can be imposed with the same maximum sentence as an adult offender.[1629]

332. Criminal offences – Criminal offences in the UK consist of three elements: *actus reus*, *mens rea*, and the absence of a valid defence.[1630] For the *mens rea* often recklessness suffices, but for some offences, intent is required.[1631] Although terms such as intent and recklessness are not always interpreted in precisely the same manner depending on the context, we will set out what their generally accepted meaning is in most cases.[1632] The defendant intended the action if they either intended it in the ordinary, core sense of 'intention' (direct intention) or recognised that the result was a virtually certain consequence of their actions (indirect or oblique intention).[1633] Regarding direct intention, Child and colleagues state that a person intends an action if three conditions are met:

---

terrorism (Cm 3420, 1996) 33–38. Note, however, that according to the UK Government and the Independent Reviewer, the impact of this is often overstated. See: Carlile of Berriew, 'Sixth Report of the Independent Reviewer Pursuant to Section 14(3) of the Prevention of Terrorism Act 2005' (2011) Independent Reviewer of Terrorism Legislation paras 6 and 66; Secretary of State for the Home Department, *Review of Counter-Terrorism and Security Powers* (Cm 8004, 2011) 37–38; Secretary of State for the Home Department, *The Government Response to the Report by Lord Carlile of Berriew Q.C. Sixth Report of the Independent Reviewer Pursuant to Section 14(3) of the Prevention of Terrorism Act 2005* (Cm 8095, 2011) 13. See also: Ben Middleton, 'Rebalancing, Reviewing or Rebranding the Treatment of Terrorist Suspects: The Counter-Terrorism Review 2011' (2011) 75 The Journal of Criminal Law 225, 229. For an analysis of the discussions in this regard, see: JCHR, *Counter-Terrorism Policy and Human Rights (Seventeenth Report): Bringing Human Rights Back* (HL paper 23, HC paper 111, 2010) para 90–102.

1627 Allen and Edwards (n 1618) 152; Catherine Elliott and Frances Quinn, *Criminal Law* (Eleventh edition, Pearson Education Limited 2016) 350–351; Jonathan Herring, *Criminal Law: Text, Cases and Materials* (Ninth edition, Oxford University Press 2020) 701; Loveless, Allen and Derry (n 1618) 374; Martin (n 1618) 89.

1628 S. 234 (1) (a) and 236 (1) SA 2020.

1629 S. 249 and 252 (2) SA 2020. See also: Joint Committee on Consolidation Bills, *Drafter's notes on the Sentencing Bill* (21 July 2020) para 143–156.

1630 JJ Child and others, *Simester and Sullivan's Criminal Law: Theory and Doctrine* (Eight, Hart Publishing 2022) 106; Martin (n 1618) 5; William Wilson, *Criminal Law* (Sixth Edition, Pearson Education Limited 2017) 71. Specifically for the defence of duress, see: *DPP for Northern Ireland v. Lynch* [1975] AC 653, 679–80.

1631 Duff, *Intention, Agency and Criminal Liability: Philosophy of Action and the Criminal Law* (n 1572) 142.

1632 Findley Stark, 'It's Only Words: On Meaning and Mens Rea' (2013) 72 Cambridge Law Journal 155; Findlay Stark, *Culpable Carelessness: Recklessness and Negligence in the Criminal Law* (Cambridge University Press 2016) 33; Victor Tadros, 'The System of the Criminal Law' (2002) 22 Legal Studies 448, 451–455.

1633 *R v. Woollin* [1999] 1 AC 82, 96; *R v. Nedrick* [1986] 1 WLR 1025 (CA), 1028; Allen and Edwards (n 1618) 86–94; Child and others (n 1630) 199; RA Duff, *Criminal Attempts* (Oxford University Press 1997) 17–21; Elliott and Quinn (n 1627) 23; Herring (n 1627) 130–132 and

a. He wants to do that action (or to bring about that consequence), or
b. He believes it is possible for him to achieve something he wants by doing that action (or by bringing about that consequence); and
c. He behaves as he does because of his desire in (a) or his belief in (b).[1634]

Recklessness means that the person ran a foreseen unreasonable risk.[1635] How this reasonableness ought to be judged led to a lot of discussion but by now it has been accepted that this reasonableness is judged subjectively.[1636] Negligence is a lower standard still,[1637] which does not require that the defendant foresee the risk. The test for negligence is that a reasonable person in the same circumstances would have been aware of the risk and would not have taken it.[1638] Negligence has two subcategories: ordinary negligence and gross negligence, the difference being one of degree. If the defendant's actions fall short of the standard by a considerable margin, they are grossly negligent.[1639] Some statutes contain other forms of *mens rea* still, such as 'knowingly', 'wilfully' or 'with a view to'.[1640] Offences of strict liability (also sometimes called absolute offences)[1641] exist as well and are quite prevalent in UK law.[1642] However, when the legislature has

---

174–177; Loveless, Allen and Derry (n 1618) 90–93; Martin (n 1618) 33–35; Stark, 'It's Only Words: On Meaning and Mens Rea' (n 1632) 156; Wilson (n 1630) 128–140. For an elaborate analysis, see: Duff, *Intention, Agency and Criminal Liability: Philosophy of Action and the Criminal Law* (n 1572) 74–98.

1634 Child and others (n 1630) 200.

1635 *R v. G and Another* [2003] UKHL 50, [2004] 1 A.C. 1034, 41; *R v. Ian Beckenridge* [1984] 79 Cr. App. R. 244; Allen and Edwards (n 1618) 103; Child and others (n 1630) 207–208; Duff, *Intention, Agency and Criminal Liability: Philosophy of Action and the Criminal Law* (n 1572) 142–144; Elliott and Quinn (n 1627) 23; Herring (n 1627) 142–144; Loveless, Allen and Derry (n 1618) 114–115; Martin (n 1618) 35; Stark, 'It's Only Words: On Meaning and Mens Rea' (n 1632) 158; Stark, *Culpable Carelessness: Recklessness and Negligence in the Criminal Law* (n 1632) 27; Wilson (n 1630) 140–148.

1636 *R v. G and Another* [2003] UKHL 50, [2004] 1 A.C. 1034; Allen and Edwards (n 1618) 103–108; Elliott and Quinn (n 1627) 23–30; Herring (n 1627) 142 and 146–150; Loveless, Allen and Derry (n 1618) 114–126; Martin (n 1618) 36; Wilson (n 1630) 144–146.

1637 Whether or not it qualifies as a form of *mens rea* under UK law is disputed among scholars.

1638 Allen and Edwards (n 1618) 126 and 129; Child and others (n 1630) 214; Elliott and Quinn (n 1627) 30; Herring (n 1627) 150–152; Douglas Husak, 'Negligence, Belief, Blame and Criminal Liability: The Special Case of Forgetting' (2011) 5 Criminal Law and Philosophy 199, 200; Loveless, Allen and Derry (n 1618) 130; Martin (n 1618) 37; Wilson (n 1630) 151–152.

1639 *Percy Bateman* (1927) 19 Cr. App. R. 8, 11–12; *R v. Sellu* [2016] EWCA Crim 1716, [2017] 4 WLR 64, 150–152; Child and others (n 1630) 215; Elliott and Quinn (n 1627) 118–119; Loveless, Allen and Derry (n 1618) 130–131; Martin (n 1618) 37; Wilson (n 1630) 152.

1640 Allen and Edwards (n 1618) 99–102 and 108–110; Herring (n 1627) 161–162; Loveless, Allen and Derry (n 1618) 158–161; Wilson (n 1630) 148–150.

1641 Note that in some jurisdictions a difference exists between absolute offences and strict liability offences. In those jurisdictions an absolute offence is an offence for which lack of guilty knowledge does not lead to acquittal while strict liability offences are offences where it suffices for the prosecution to establish a *prima facie* case after which the defendant has to prove lack of guilty knowledge (see: *Sweet v. Parsley* [1970] AC 132, 141). However, in England and Wales, this distinction is not made. See: Child and others (n 1630) 149–150.

1642 Herring (n 1627) 211; Loveless, Allen and Derry (n 1618) 140; Martin (n 1618) 48.

not explicitly included a *mens rea*, the offence is not automatically assumed to be one of strict liability. Instead, the courts apply the presumption of a *mens rea*. Under this presumption, the words of the legislation are considered and only if these show a clear intention of creating an absolute offence, is it interpreted this way.[1643] This will depend on the nature of the offence and the language and scheme of the legislation.[1644] If the words give no clear indication either way, it is presumed that parliament intended the offence to have a *mens rea*.[1645] Even if the offence is one of strict liability, sometimes some limited form of *mens rea* might be applicable through the absence of a defence, such as a due diligence defence.[1646] Finally, if an offence is presumed to have a *mens rea* under the aforementioned presumption, the question is which *mens rea*. This will be determined case by case. In *Sweet v Parsley* the Court stated that it can be a full *mens rea* (criminal intent), but also gross negligence.[1647] Herring on the other hand states that the presumed *mens rea* is the defence that the defendant believed an aspect of the *actus reus* did not exist.[1648]

333. Human rights law in the UK – The UK is a Member State of the Council of Europe and is therefore a party to the ECHR. However, the ECHR is not directly applicable in the UK legal order. Instead, it is applied through the Human Rights Act 1998 (HRA 1998).[1649] This Act does not have a higher status than other statutes however, which implies parliament can enact laws which do not align with it.[1650] In addition, the Act does not include all convention

---

1643 *Pwr v. Director of Public Prosecutions, Akdogan and another v. Director of Public Prosecutions* [2022] UKSC 2, 27–34; *R v. Sally Lane and John Letts (AB and CD)* [2018] UKSC 36, 2018 WL 03368388, 8; *Attorney-General's Reference (No. 1 of 2020)* [2020] EWCA Crim 1665, [2021] QB 441, 42; *Sweet v. Parsley* [1970] AC 132, 148; *Nurse v. Trinidad and Tobago* [2019] UKPC 43, [2021] AC 1, 20–24; Allen and Edwards (n 1618) 133–134; Child and others (n 1630) 241; Elliott and Quinn (n 1627) 41–42; Herring (n 1627) 214; Loveless, Allen and Derry (n 1618) 142–148; Martin (n 1618) 48–49; Wilson (n 1630) 160–161.

1644 *Nurse v. Trinidad and Tobago* [2019] UKPC 43, [2021] AC 1, 31. For a more detailed analysis of what this means, see: Allen and Edwards (n 1618) 133–142; Child and others (n 1630) 241–245; Elliott and Quinn (n 1627) 42–47; Herring (n 1627) 214; Loveless, Allen and Derry (n 1618) 142–148; Wilson (n 1630) 161–164.

1645 *R v. Sally Lane and John Letts (AB and CD)* [2018] UKSC 36, 2018 WL 03368388, 8; *Sweet v. Parsley* [1970] AC 132, 148–149; Loveless, Allen and Derry (n 1618) 142–148.

1646 Allen and Edwards (n 1618) 146; Wilson (n 1630) 164–165.

1647 *Sweet v. Parsley* [1970] AC 132, 150.

1648 Herring (n 1627) 215.

1649 Amatrudo and Blake (n 1616) 46; Helen Fenwick, *Fenwick on Civil Liberties and Human Rights* (Taylor & Francis Group 2016) 135–136; David Hoffman and John Rowe, *Human Rights in the UK: An Introduction to the Human Rights Act 1998* (Third edition, Pearson Education Limited 2010) 3; Irene Khan, 'Human Rights in an Age of Terror' in Nicolas Kang-Riou, Jo Milner and Suryia Nayak (eds), *Confronting the Human Rights Act: contemporary themes and perspectives* (Routledge 2012) 104.

1650 S. 3 (2) (b) and (c) HRA 1998. See also: Amatrudo and Blake (n 1616) 48; Helen Fenwick, 'Replacing the Human Rights Act with a British Bill of Rights: Creating Greater Parliamentary Autonomy on Human Rights Matters?' in Nicolas Kang-Riou, Jo Milner and Suryia Nayak

and protocol rights.[1651] Most notably for us, it does not include the freedom of movement under Article 2 to the Fourth Protocol of the ECHR, as this protocol was not ratified by the UK (see no. 89). The HRA 1998 has been controversial and repealing/replacing it has been a topic of political debate.[1652] S. 3 of the Act states that as far as possible all legislation has to be interpreted consistently with the rights set out in it.[1653] This means that if the wording of the statute allows it, it is 'read down' so as to be HRA 1998 (and thus ECHR) compliant. In addition, when interpreting legislation, the domestic courts should 'take into account' the case law of the ECtHR.[1654] This means, that they have to consider the ECtHR case law, but can then decide not to apply it.[1655] This latter course of action could put the UK in breach of its obligations under the ECHR, but nothing in UK domestic law forbids it. In the *Ullah* case, the House of Lords seemed to have given quite a strong interpretation to the obligation to take into account ECtHR case law, stating that in the absence of special circumstances UK courts should follow clear and consistent ECtHR case law.[1656] However, since this case, there

(eds), *Confronting the Human Rights Act : contemporary themes and perspectives* (Routledge 2012) 296; Fenwick, *Fenwick on Civil Liberties and Human Rights* (n 1649) 136 and 147; Ian Leigh and others, *Making Rights Real : The Human Rights Act in Its First Decade* (Bloomsbury Publishing Plc 2008) 18.

1651 S. 1 HRA 1998. See also: Fenwick, *Fenwick on Civil Liberties and Human Rights* (n 1649) 141; Hoffman and Rowe (n 1649) 109–113; Leigh and others (n 1650) 6; Richard Stone, *Textbook on Civil Liberties & Human Rights* (Tenth edition, Oxford University Press 2016) 38.

1652 Alan DP Brady, *Proportionality and Deference under the UK Human Rights Act: An Institutionally Sensitive Approach* (Cambridge University Press 2012) 5; Fenwick, 'Replacing the Human Rights Act with a British Bill of Rights: Creating Greater Parliamentary Autonomy on Human Rights Matters?' (n 1650) 291–296; Helen Fenwick, 'The Human Rights Act or a British Bill of Rights: Creating a down-Grading Recalibration of Rights against the Counter-Terror Backdrop?' [2012] Public Law 468, 468; Fenwick, *Fenwick on Civil Liberties and Human Rights* (n 1649) 137; Helen Fenwick and Roger Masterman, 'The Conservative Project to "Break the Link between British Courts and Strasbourg": Rhetoric or Reality?' (2017) 80 The Modern Law Review 1111; Khan (n 1649) 103 and 114; Leigh and others (n 1650) 3–5; Stone (n 1651) 78–81. For a critical analysis of the Act in the counter-terrorism context, see: KD Ewing, 'The Futility of the Human Rights Act' [2004] Public Law 829.

1653 S. 3 HRA 1998. See also: Brady (n 1652) 117; Ewing (n 1652) 841; Fenwick, *Fenwick on Civil Liberties and Human Rights* (n 1649) 146–147; Conor Gearty, 'The Human Rights Act – an Academic Sceptic Changes His Mind but Not His Heart' [2010] European Human Rights Law Review 582, 583; Peter Halstead, *Human Rights* (Routledge 2014) 35; Herring (n 1627) 38; Hoffman and Rowe (n 1649) 65–66; Leigh and others (n 1650) 88–89; Stone (n 1651) 54.

1654 S. 2 (1) HRA 1998.

1655 Fenwick, 'Replacing the Human Rights Act with a British Bill of Rights: Creating Greater Parliamentary Autonomy on Human Rights Matters?' (n 1650) 304; Fenwick, 'The Human Rights Act or a British Bill of Rights: Creating a down-Grading Recalibration of Rights against the Counter-Terror Backdrop?' (n 1652) 477–478; Fenwick, *Fenwick on Civil Liberties and Human Rights* (n 1649) 157; Fenwick and Masterman (n 1652) 1113; Hoffman and Rowe (n 1649) 62; Leigh and others (n 1650) 51–52.

1656 R (Ullah) v. Special Adjudicator [2004] UKHL 26, 20. See also: *R (Alconbury Developments Ltd) v. Secretary of State for the Environment, Transport and the Regions* [2001] UKHL 23, [2003] 2 AC 295, 26; Fenwick, 'Replacing the Human Rights Act with a British Bill of Rights: Creating Greater Parliamentary Autonomy on Human Rights Matters?' (n 1650)

has been a tempering of this stance, with UK courts veering off the path set by the ECtHR, for example stating there is no 'clear and consistent case law', that the application of ECtHR case law would be inconsistent with fundamental aspects of UK law or that there is conflicting domestic precedent.[1657] In general though, the UK courts tend to, sometimes reluctantly, follow the ECtHR.[1658] Finally, s. 4 HRA 1998 allows higher courts to issue declarations of incompatibility if they find legislation to be incompatible with a human right. These declarations are, however, not legally binding.[1659] This system has been hailed as striking a good balance between parliamentary sovereignty and human rights law.[1660]

334. Terrorism in the UK – Sadly, the UK has quite a long history of terrorism[1661] and is sometimes viewed as a model for how to respond to it.[1662] Irish republican groups have resorted to terrorism since the second half of the 19th century.[1663] In the wave of Islamic inspired terrorism of the early 21st century, the UK was not spared either. Between 11 September 2001 and 31 March 2016 there were 54 deaths in Great Britain as a direct result of terrorist

304; Fenwick, 'The Human Rights Act or a British Bill of Rights: Creating a down-Grading Recalibration of Rights against the Counter-Terror Backdrop?' (n 1652) 478; Fenwick, *Fenwick on Civil Liberties and Human Rights* (n 1649) 157–159; Fenwick and Masterman (n 1652) 1113–1114; Hoffman and Rowe (n 1649) 63; Leigh and others (n 1650) 59–62.

1657 See e.g.: *R (Hicks) v. Commissioner of the Police of the Metropolis* [2014] EWCA Civ 3, [2014] 1 WLR 2152; *AG's Reference No 69 of 2013, R v. McLoughlin, R v. Newell* [2014] EWCA Crim 188, [2014] 1 WLR 3964, 14–37; *Manchester City Council v. Pinnock* [2010] UKSC 45, [2011] 1 All ER 285, 48–49; *R v. Horncastle* [2009] UKSC 14, [2010] 2 AC 373; *R (Animal Defenders International) v. Secretary of State for Culture, Media and Sport* [2008] UKHL 15; *Kay and others v. Lambeth London Borough Council, Leeds City Council v. Price and others* [2006] UKHL 10, 43–44. See also: Fenwick, *Fenwick on Civil Liberties and Human Rights* (n 1649) 158; Fenwick and Masterman (n 1652) 1117–1120; Hoffman and Rowe (n 1649) 64–65; Leigh and others (n 1650) 71–75.

1658 See e.g.: *Secretary of State for the Home Department v. AF (FC) and another and one other action* [2009] UKHL 28, 70. See also: Alati (n 95) 100–101; Fenwick, 'Replacing the Human Rights Act with a British Bill of Rights: Creating Greater Parliamentary Autonomy on Human Rights Matters?' (n 1650) 304–305.

1659 S. 4 HRA 1998. See also: Brady (n 1652) 117; Ewing (n 1652) 841; Fenwick, 'Replacing the Human Rights Act with a British Bill of Rights: Creating Greater Parliamentary Autonomy on Human Rights Matters?' (n 1650) 296–297; Fenwick, 'The Human Rights Act or a British Bill of Rights: Creating a down-Grading Recalibration of Rights against the Counter-Terror Backdrop?' (n 1652) 483; Fenwick, *Fenwick on Civil Liberties and Human Rights* (n 1649) 147; Dickson (n 1626) 126; Gearty (n 1653) 583; Conor Gearty, 'Human Rights in an Age of Counter-Terrorism: Injurious, Irrelevant or Indispensable?' (2005) 58 Current Legal Problems 25, 38; Halstead (n 1653) 35; Hoffman and Rowe (n 1649) 72–74; Khan (n 1649) 105; Leigh and others (n 1650) 89–92; Stone (n 1651) 63–64; Walker, 'Counterterrorism within the Rule of Law?' (n 171) 344.

1660 Fenwick and Masterman (n 1652) 1135–1136; Gearty (n 1653).

1661 Lord Lloyd of Berwick, *Inquiry into legislation against terrorism* (Cm 3420, 1996) Appendix F 7–37; Alati (n 95) 58; Conte (n 10) 219; Demirsu (n 56) 69; Halstead (n 1653) 152–154; Spencer (n 1616) 117.

1662 Walker, 'Counterterrorism within the Rule of Law?' (n 171) 339.

1663 Spencer (n 1616) 118.

acts (excluding the perpetrators).[1664] The vast majority of these deaths happened in 2005, due to what was probably the most well-known in a long series of (attempted) terrorist attacks, the London bombings on 7 July 2005 (also called the 7/7 bombings).[1665] 2017 also saw several major terrorist attacks, with the Manchester arena attack and several attacks in London.[1666] The abovementioned numbers are luckily relatively low compared to numbers of casualties caused by terrorism from the seventies to the mid-nineties. Peak years were 1972 with 344 deaths in Northern Ireland and 1988 with 271 deaths due to the Lockerbie bombing.[1667]

335. Introduction of terrorist offences – Because of its long history of terrorism, the UK already had some form of terrorist legislation dating back to the 19th century.[1668] This legislation was mainly focussed on Northern Ireland. In 1995 the government asked Lord Lloyd of Berwick to write a report on the need for specific counter-terrorism legislation in the UK in case of a lasting peace in Ireland.[1669] In 2,000 this report led the UK government to overhaul the terrorism legislation, with the creation of the Terrorism Act 2,000 which replaced the temporary and fragmented measures which were in place before.[1670] In

---

1664 Grahame Allen and Noel Dempsey, 'Terrorism in Great Britain: The Statistics' (2017) 7613 Commons Library Briefing Paper 25, 5; Anderson, 'Shielding the Compass: How to Fight Terrorism without Defeating the Law' (n 25) 3–4.

1665 Alati (n 95) 64; Halstead (n 1653) 154; Spencer (n 1616) 118.

1666 Home Office, *Counter-Terrorism And Border Security Bill: Explanatory Notes (Bill 219-EN, 2018)* para 3; Max Hill, 'The Terrorism Acts in 2017' (2018) Report of the Independent Reviewer of Terrorism Legislation on the Operation of the Terrorism Acts 2000 and 2006, the Terrorism Prevention and Investigation Measures Act 2011, and the Terrorist Asset Freezing Etc Act 2010 para 4.1. For the Manchester arena report, see also: Report of the Public Inquiry into the Attack on Manchester Arena on 22nd May 2017 (HC paper 1137) Presented to Parliament pursuant to section 26 of the Inquiries Act 2005.

1667 Spencer (n 1616) 118.

1668 For a brief analysis of some of this legislation, see: Leandro Martínez-Peñas and Manuela Fernández-Rodríguez, 'Evolution of British Law on Terrorism: From Ulster to Global Terrorism (1970–2010)' in Aniceto Masferrer (ed), *Post 9/11 and the State of Permanent Legal Emergency: Security and Human Rights in Countering Terrorism*, vol 14 (Springer Netherlands 2012) 201–209; Roach, *The 9/11 Effect: Comparative Counter-Terrorism* (n 79) 244–255.

1669 Lord Lloyd of Berwick, *Inquiry into legislation against terrorism* (Cm 3420, 1996); Secretary of State for the Home Department and Secretary of State for Northern Ireland, *Legislation Against Terrorism: A consultation paper* (Cm 4178, 1998) para 1–8.

1670 Terrorism Act 2000 (hereinafter: TA 2000): www.legislation.gov.uk/ukpga/2000/11/contents. See also: Alati (n 95) 58–59; Allen and Dempsey (n 1664) 3; Anderson, 'Shielding the Compass: How to Fight Terrorism without Defeating the Law' (n 25) 2; David Anderson, 'Independent Review of Terrorism Laws: Searchlight or Veil?' [2014] SSRN Electronic Journal 5, www.ssrn.com/abstract=2400656, accessed 4 March 2023; Conte (n 10) 220; Fenwick, *Fenwick on Civil Liberties and Human Rights* (n 1649) 1047; Daniel Greenberg, 'Terrorism' [2022] Westlaw UK 14, 1; Hardy and Williams (n 608) 113; Masset (n 20) 3; Roach, *The 9/11 Effect: Comparative Counter-Terrorism* (n 79) 242; JJ Rowe, 'The Terrorism Act 2000' [2001] Criminal Law Review 527, 527; Tadros, 'Justice and Terrorism' (n 46) 664; Clive Walker, *Blackstone's Guide to the Anti-Terrorism Legislation* (Oxford University Press 2002) 1–3; Wittendorp and Bakker (n 686) 60–61; Wood (n 25) 11.

response to 9/11 the UK passed the Anti-Terrorism, Crime and Security Act 2001 (ATCSA 2001) which made significant changes in the fight against terrorism, including a regime of administrative detention and a few changes to the terrorist offences.[1671] Because of this pre-existing legislation the UK did not need to make any changes when the 2002 EU Framework Decision[1672] came into force.[1673] The regime of administrative detention was overhauled and further relatively minor changes to criminal law were made by the Prevention of Terrorism Act 2005 (PTA 2005). In response to the 7/7 bombings and the creation of the 2005 Council of Europe Convention, a larger expansion of the terrorism offences was undertaken with the Terrorism Act 2006 which added extra offences.[1674] This meant that once again, the 2008 update to the EU Framework Decision[1675] did not require any changes to the UK legislation.[1676] Since then the UK terrorist legislation has steadily expanded, for example through the Counter-Terrorism Act 2008 (CTA 2008) and the Counter-Terrorism and Security Act 2015 (CTSA 2015).[1677] The most recent changes include (but are not limited to) the 2019 Counter-Terrorism and Border Security Act (CTBSA 2019)[1678] and the Counter-Terrorism and Sentencing Act 2021 (CTSA 2021).[1679] As this book focusses on preventive restrictions to liberty, certain offences which are technically terrorist offences are not discussed in detail. This is the case for offences more focussed on internet service providers and financial institutions. The TA 2000 contains disclosure duties and related offences for example.[1680] In addition, the CTSA 2015 added an offence to the TA 2000 which can only be committed by insurers. It is an offence for them to knowingly make a payment in response to a demand made for terrorist purposes.[1681] Furthermore, if the offence is committed by a body corporate with the consent, connivance or attributable to the neglect of a manager, etc. that person is also guilty.[1682] The Terrorism Act 2006 (TA 2006)

1671 Martínez-Peñas and Fernández-Rodríguez (n 1668) 211–213.
1672 Council Framework Decision 2002/475/JHA of 13 June 2002 on combating terrorism [2002] *OJ* L164/5.
1673 Spencer (n 1616) 118–119.
1674 Terrorism Act 2006 (hereinafter: TA 2006): www.legislation.gov.uk/ukpga/2006/11/contents. See also: Conte (n 10) 239; Roach, *The 9/11 Effect: Comparative Counter-Terrorism* (n 79) 243; Martínez-Peñas and Fernández-Rodríguez (n 1668) 213–217; Tadros, 'Justice and Terrorism' (n 46) 664.
1675 Council Framework Decision 2008/919/JHA of 28 November 2008 amending Framework Decision 2002/475/JHA on combating terrorism [2008] *OJ* 330/21.
1676 Spencer (n 1616) 120.
1677 Counter-Terrorism Act 2008 (hereinafter: CTA 2008): www.legislation.gov.uk/ukpga/2008/28/contents. See also: Conte (n 10) 242.
1678 Counter-Terrorism and Border Security Act 2019 (hereinafter: CTBSA 2019): www.legislation.gov.uk/ukpga/2019/3/contents.
1679 Counter-Terrorism and Sentencing Act 2021 (hereinafter: CTSA 2021): www.legislation.gov.uk/ukpga/2021/11/contents.
1680 S. 19–22A TA 2000. See also: Rowe (n 1670) 537–539; Walker, *Blackstone's Guide to the Anti-Terrorism Legislation* (n 1670) 70–74 and 100–108.
1681 S. 17A (1) TA 2000.
1682 S. 17A (2) TA 2000.

also introduced a system of notices for internet activities, the breach of which is a criminal offence as well. This system provides for a notice which can be given[1683] by a constable and which declares that in their opinion, a statement, article or record is unlawfully terrorism-related.[1684] This notice warns the recipient that within two working days, they have to make sure the statement, article or record is no longer available to the public; or is modified so it is not terrorism-related anymore.[1685] Failure to do so will lead to the statement, article or record being regarded as having their endorsement.[1686] Conte criticises this system as giving too much power to police constables without a requirement that their opinion is reasonably held or based upon reviewable factors.[1687]

336. Numbers – Between 9/11 and 2017 a total of 945 people were charged for terrorism related offences. Against 772 (82%) proceedings were started which led to 646 (84%) convictions.[1688] According to Allen and Dempsey, on 31 March 2017 there were 186 detainees which were classed as terrorist or extremist prisoners.[1689] At the end of that same year, the Independent Reviewer for Terrorism Legislation counted 224 people in custody for terrorism-related offences.[1690] In his 2017 report, the independent reviewer stated that 77 people were convicted for terrorism-related offences during that year, with the following sentences[1691]:

a. 6 received life sentences.
b. 7 received sentences of between 10 and 20 years.
c. 32 received sentences of between 4 and 10 years.
d. 23 received sentences of between 1 and 4 years.
e. 3 received sentences of less than a year.
f. 6 received non-custodial sentences.

In his 2020 report his successor stated that: '*In England and Wales, statistics from December 2011 to 2020 reveal 944 charges under terrorism legislation, of which 151 related to information collection, 84 to membership, 82 to possession of articles, and 192 to attack-planning; and 392 terrorist-related charges under non-terrorism legislation including 47 relating to homicide and 31 relating to explosives.*'[1692]

1683 For explanation on how this can be given, see: S. 4 TA 2006.
1684 S. 3 (3) (a) TA 2006; Conte (n 10) 646; Stone (n 1651) 463.
1685 S. 3 (3) (b) and (c) TA 2006.
1686 S. 3 (2)TA 2006; Conte (n 10) 646.
1687 Conte (n 10) 646.
1688 Allen and Dempsey (n 1664) 18.
1689 Allen and Dempsey (n 1664) 19.
1690 Hill (n 1666) para 10.3.
1691 Hill (n 1666) para 10.2.
1692 Jonathan Hall, 'The Terrorism Acts in 2020' (2020) Report of the Independent Reviewer of Terrorism Legislation on the Operation of the Terrorism Acts 2000 and 2006, and the Terrorism Prevention and Investigation Measures Act 2011 para 7.1.

CHAPTER I
CRIMINAL LAW

SECTION I. RESTRICTIONS TO THE RIGHT TO LIBERTY

337. Deprivation of liberty – As was the case for Belgium, deprivations of liberty in a counter-terrorism context will most often be imposed within a criminal law framework. When a person is suspected of a criminal offence, they can be taken into pre-trial detention if certain conditions are met (see nos 486–495). After conviction for a terrorism offence a prison sentence, depriving the convicted person of their liberty for a substantial period of time, is the most likely outcome.

338. Sentencing Act 2020 – In 2020, UK parliament acknowledged that the existing rules on sentencing had become too difficult to apply and even to find.[1693] Therefore, the rules were amended and consolidated in 2020 by the Sentencing (Pre-consolidation Amendments) Act 2020 and the Sentencing Act 2020 (SA 2020).

339. Sentencing: serious terrorist sentences – When imposing a custodial sentence, a court must impose the shortest possible sentence commensurate with the seriousness of the offence or the combination of the offence and other offences associated with it.[1694] This rule does not apply when the sentence is fixed by law, including mandatory life sentences.[1695] Another exception, which was introduced by the CTSA 2021 (and only applies to offences committed after its entry into force)[1696] are the serious terrorist sentences. Certain terrorist offences are considered serious terrorist offences by the SA 2020, being: the offences in s. 54, 56, and 59 TA 2000 and s. 5, 6, 9, 10, and 11 TA 2006 (see nos 399–403, 412–414 and 463–483), any of their inchoate offences, and a list of other offences including murder, kidnapping and hijacking if they

---

1693 Joint Committee on Consolidation Bills, *Drafter's notes on the Sentencing Bill* (21 July 2020) para 3.

1694 S. 231 (2) SA 2020.

1695 S. 231 (3) SA 2020.

1696 S. 4–14 CTSA 2021.

have a terrorist connection (see no. 360).[1697] Under certain conditions, courts have to convict the perpetrator of a serious terrorist offence to a serious terrorist sentence. These conditions are[1698]:

a. The offender is aged 18 or older.
b. The court does not impose a life sentence and is of the opinion that:
   i. there is a significant risk to members of the public of serious harm occasioned by the commission by the offender of further serious terrorist offences or other specified offences (see no. 340); and
   ii. the serious terrorist offence (potentially in combination with associated offences) was very likely to result in or contribute (directly or indirectly) to the deaths of two or more people as a result of terrorism and the offender was, or should have been, aware of this. It is irrelevant whether any deaths actually occurred.

If these conditions are met, a serious terrorist sentence is obligatory, unless there are exceptional circumstances which relate to the offence or offender which justify not imposing one.[1699] A serious terrorist sentence consists of a custodial sentence of at least 14 years or longer if the term of imprisonment that would be imposed if the court did not impose a serious terrorist sentence would have been longer, and an extension period.[1700] During this extension period the offender is subject to a licence.[1701] The period must be of the length considered necessary by the Court for the protection of members of the public from serious harm caused by the commission by the offender of further serious terrorist offences or other specified offences. In addition, the period has a minimum term of seven years and a maximum term of 25 years.[1702] If the offender is not 21 years old yet at the time of conviction, the same rules apply, but the detention takes

[1697] S. 306 (2) and Schedule 17A SA 2020. See also: Home Office, *Counter-Terrorism And Sentencing Bill: Explanatory Notes* (Bill 129–EN, 2020) para 83; Azmeh (n 637) 8; Rory Kelly, 'Reforming the Sentencing and Release of Terrorist Offenders' [2023] Criminal Law Review 639, 643; Lee and Walker (n 1617) 877.

[1698] S. 268 B (1), (3), and (4) and 282B (1), (3), and (4) SA 2020. See also: Home Office, *Counter-Terrorism And Sentencing Bill: Explanatory Notes* (Bill 129–EN, 2020) para 95; Azmeh (n 637) 8; Kelly (n 1697) 643–644; Florence Lee and Clive Walker, 'The Sentencing of Precursor Terrorism Crimes in the United Kingdom' in Clive Walker, Mariona Llobet Anglí and Manuel C Meliá (eds), *Precursor Crimes of Terrorism: The Criminalisation of Terrorism Risk in Comparative Perspective* (Edward Elgar Publishing 2022) 323; Lee and Walker (n 1617) 877.

[1699] S. 268B (2) and 282B (2) SA 2020. See also: Home Office, *Counter-Terrorism And Sentencing Bill: Explanatory Notes* (Bill 129–EN, 2020) para 96; Azmeh (n 637) 8–9; Kelly (n 1697) 644; Lee and Walker (n 1617) 878.

[1700] S. 268C (2) and 282C (2) SA 2020. See also: Home Office, *Counter-Terrorism And Sentencing Bill: Explanatory Notes* (Bill 129–EN, 2020) para 94; Azmeh (n 637) 9; Lee and Walker (n 1698) 323; Lee and Walker (n 1617) 878.

[1701] S. 268A (b) and 282A (b) SA 2020. See also: Azmeh (n 637) 9; Lee and Walker (n 1617) 878.

[1702] S. 268C (3) and (4), and 282C (3) and (4) SA 2020. See also: Home Office, *Counter-Terrorism And Sentencing Bill: Explanatory Notes* (Bill 129–EN, 2020) para 99; Azmeh (n 637) 9–10; Kelly (n 1697) 644; Lee and Walker (n 1698) 323; Lee and Walker (n 1617) 878.

place in a young offender institution.[1703] This is the case since courts may not impose imprisonment upon offenders who are aged under 21 at the time of conviction.[1704] If the Court is imposing a discretionary life sentence upon the offender who would otherwise be sentenced to a serious terrorist sentence, the minimum term of the tariff is 14 years, barring exceptional circumstances.[1705] In his note on the Bill, the independent reviewer pointed out that the minimum sentence of 14 years imprisonment will in practice not make much difference in cases where multiple deaths are likely, as is required.[1706] In addition, he wonders why the minima of 14 years and seven years for the term have been chosen.[1707] Commentators on the other hand criticise the 14 year minimum custodial term of the serious terrorist sentence, pointing out that it may cause proportionality issues because it could restrict the judge in taking into account mitigating factors such as age.[1708] In addition, they criticise the very existence of the serious terrorist sentence as unnecessary and overly complicating the sentencing.[1709]

340. Sentencing: extended sentences – The SA 2020 also expanded upon the sentencing rules related to extended sentences for terrorism which were introduced in 2019 (for terrorism *sensu lato*, a similar regime already existed for terrorism *sensu stricto* before as these offences were covered by the 'specified violent offences' category).[1710] When the conditions for a serious terrorist sentence are not met, in certain circumstances, courts can still impose extended sentences. These circumstances are[1711]:

a. The offence is a specified violent, sexual or terrorist offence: the terrorism offences *sensu stricto* discussed in Section III of the book are included in the 'specified violent offences' category.[1712] The terrorism offences *sensu lato* discussed in the Sections IV to XIV are all included, as are their inchoate offences, in the 'specified terrorist offences' category, barring the offences

1703 Home Office, *Counter-Terrorism And Sentencing Bill: Explanatory Notes* (Bill 129-EN, 2020) para 85–92; Azmeh (n 637) 10.

1704 S. 262 and 277 (1) SA 2020. See also: Sprack and Engelhardt-Sprack (n 1618) 369–370.

1705 S. 323, (3)–(5) SA 2020. See also: Home Office, *Counter-Terrorism And Sentencing Bill: Explanatory Notes* (Bill 129-EN, 2020) para 126–129; Azmeh (n 637) 10–11; Lee and Walker (n 1617) 873.

1706 Jonathan Hall, 'Note on Counter-Terrorism and Sentencing Bill: Sentencing Reforms (1)' (2020) Independent Reviewer of Terrorism Legislation para 8. See also: Jacqueline Beard and Joanne Dawson, 'Counter-Terrorism and Sentencing Bill 2019–21' (2020) 8771 House of Commons Library Briefing Paper 30; Kelly (n 1697) 644.

1707 Hall, 'Note on Counter-Terrorism and Sentencing Bill: Sentencing Reforms (1)' (n 1706) para 12.

1708 Azmeh (n 637) 14–15; Lee and Walker (n 1617) 879.

1709 Lee and Walker (n 1617) 879–882. See also on the complicated nature of the sentencing rules for terrorists: Kelly (n 1697) 645–646.

1710 S. 9 CTBSA 2019. See also: Kelly (n 1697) 641.

1711 S. 267 (1), (3), (4) and 280 (1), (3), (4) SA 2020.

1712 Part 1 Schedule 18 SA 2020.

related to uniform and publication of images, the offences related to terrorist property and the offence of not disclosing information about acts of terrorism (see nos. 378–398 and 432–437).[1713]

b. The Court
   i. is not required to impose a serious terrorism sentence (added by CTSA 2021 when introducing serious terrorism sentences);
   ii. believes there to be a significant risk to members of the public of serious harm caused by the commission by the offender of further specified offences;
   iii. is not required to impose a life sentence; and
   iv. would impose a custodial sentence of at least four years or the offender has a prior conviction for an offence listed in Schedule 14. This Schedule contains a list of offences including serious offences against people such as manslaughter or murder, offences involving explosives or firearms and a good amount of terrorist offences such as weapons training or directing a terrorist organisation.

The term 'members of the public' does not only cover the UK public but also the public in other countries.[1714] If the conditions are met, the court can impose an extended sentence, meaning that, as was the case for serious terrorism sentences, in addition to the custodial sentence, a further period is determined for which the offender will be subject to a licence.[1715] The extension period must be of the length necessary to protect members of the public, with a minimum of one year.[1716] The maximum term is eight years for specified terrorism offences or ten years in case of serious terrorist offences.[1717] This last maximum term was added in 2021 and only applies to offences committed after the entry into force of the CTSA 2021.[1718] The term of the extended sentence must not exceed the maximum term of imprisonment for the offence.[1719] The exact same rules apply to offenders aged 18 to 21 who can be sentenced to extended detention in a young offender institution. Minors can also be convicted to an extended sentence under the same conditions, with two changes.[1720] First, since they cannot receive a serious terrorist sentence, the absence of one is not a condition. Second, the prior conviction for a listed offence is not an alternative to the four-year term

1713 Part 3 Schedule 18 SA 2020.

1714 *R v. Abdalraouf Abdallah and Stephen Gray and an application under s.36 of the Criminal Justice Act 1986 by Hm Attorney General (No. 323 of 2016), Junead Khan and Shazib Khan, Ayman Shaukat and Lorna Moore* [2016] EWCA Crim 1868, 12–17.

1715 S. 254, 266 and 279 SA 2020.

1716 S. 256 (3) and (4) (a), 268 (3) and (4) (a) and 281 (3) and (4) (a) SA 2020. See also: Sprack and Engelhardt-Sprack (n 1618) 379.

1717 S. 256 (4) (b), 268 (4) (b) and 281 (4) (b) SA 2020. See also: Lee and Walker (n 1617) 882.

1718 S. 16, 17 and 18 CTSA 2021. See also: Home Office, *Counter-Terrorism And Sentencing Bill: Explanatory Notes* (Bill 129-EN, 2020) para 147–148; Azmeh (n 637) 11; Kelly (n 1697) 644.

1719 S. 281 (5) SA 2020. See also: Sprack and Engelhardt-Sprack (n 1618) 379.

1720 S. 255 SA 2020.

condition. For offenders who are under 21 (including minors), the term of the extended sentence can never exceed the maximum custodial sentence set for the offence when committed by a person aged 21 or over.[1721] The main difference between extended sentences and serious terrorist sentences, in addition to the latter having much longer minimum terms both custodial and for the extension period, is that serious terrorist sentences are mandatory while extended sentences are not.[1722]

341. Sentencing: special custodial sentences for offenders of particular concern – Finally, in situations where neither the serious terrorist sentences nor the extended sentences apply (and the Court does not impose a life sentence), most terrorist offenders can receive 'special custodial sentences'. These sentences consist of the appropriate custodial term, and a further period of one year for which the offender is on licence, but they should not exceed the maximum term of imprisonment for the offence.[1723] They have to be imposed if the Court wants to impose a prison sentence upon adult offenders (at the time of conviction) for any terrorism offence *sensu lato*, including their inchoate offences or any offence with a terrorist connection, but excluding the uniform and publication offences related to proscribed organisations (see nos 378–383).[1724] For offenders aged 18 to 21 at the time of conviction, the detention takes place in a young offender institution. The CTSA 2021 introduced a similar system for underage offenders, only applicable to offences committed after its entry into force.[1725] For offences committed before this date, the offender had to have been at least 18 years old at the time of the offence in order to be able to receive a special custodial sentence. For offences committed after this date, this is no longer a requirement, as long as the Court would impose a custodial sentence.[1726] As was the case for serious terrorist sentences but contrary to extended sentences, the special custodial sentences for offenders of particular concern are mandatory once the conditions are met. The independent reviewer found the special custodial sentences for offenders of particular concern for terrorism offenders a sensible reform as it avoids a 'cliff-edge' upon release,[1727] meaning the detainee does not go from imprisonment to full freedom. On the other hand, as Harris points out, the fact that the courts have to decide the

1721 S. 256 (5) and 268 (5) SA 2020.
1722 Azmeh (n 637) 9.
1723 S. 252A (4), 265 (2) and 278 (2) SA 2020. See also: Sprack and Engelhardt-Sprack (n 1618) 379.
1724 S. 265 (1), 278 (1) and Part 1 Schedule 13 SA 2020.
1725 S. 21–22 CTSA 2021. See also: Home Office, *Counter-Terrorism And Sentencing Bill: Explanatory Notes* (Bill 129–EN, 2020) para 152–156; Azmeh (n 637) 12.
1726 S. 252A SA 2020. See also: Home Office, *Counter-Terrorism And Sentencing Bill: Explanatory Notes* (Bill 129–EN, 2020) para 157.
1727 Jonathan Hall, 'Note on Counter-Terrorism and Sentencing Bill: Sentencing Reforms (2)' (2020) Independent Reviewer of Terrorism Legislation para 14. See also: Lee and Walker (n 1617) 883.

custodial term as they would usually and then add a licence period, leads to disproportionately severe sentences.[1728]

342. Community orders – For some less serious offences, a community order is also an option. A community order is possible for offenders over 18 years old when convicted if the offence is punishable with imprisonment, as long as no mandatory sentence requirements apply and the Court does not impose a suspended sentence.[1729] A community order can include many different requirements to be imposed upon an offender, some of which can seriously limit a person's right to liberty, such as a curfew which can be monitored electronically.[1730] The curfew period can extend to maximum 112 hours per week, which can differ both in length and even in location on different days of the week.[1731] The maximum curfew per day was 16 hours[1732] before 2022 and is 20 hours since.

343. Suspended sentence orders – Another sentencing option is a suspended sentence order. This entails a sentence of imprisonment which will not take immediate effect but can be activated if the person subject to the order commits another offence or breaches any of the requirements which can be imposed in the order.[1733] A suspended sentence order is available for sentences of 14 days to two years imprisonment.[1734] The operational period during which the suspended sentence can become effective if another offence is committed ranges from six months to two years.[1735] The supervision period during which requirements must be observed also ranges from six months to two years and cannot be longer than the operational period.[1736] The requirements which can be imposed are the same as can be imposed under a community order (see no. 342). According to the sentencing council guidelines, courts should only impose a suspended sentence order after having already decided to impose a custodial sentence.[1737]

1728 Lyndon Harris, 'Commentary: R. v LF; R. v DS' [2016] Criminal Law Review 676, 680.

1729 S. 202 and 203 SA 2020.

1730 S. 201 and Parts 5 and 14 Schedule 9 SA 2020. See also: Andrew Ashworth (ed), *Sentencing and Criminal Justice* (5th edn, Cambridge University Press 2010) 341–351, www.cambridge.org/core/product/E3B5572348E4CE06260FE6CD92455D90.

1731 S. 9 (3) and (4) Schedule 9 SA 2020.

1732 S. 9 (4A) Schedule 9 SA 2020; s. 150 Police, Crime, Sentencing and Courts Act 2022.

1733 S. 286 (1)–(3) SA 2020. See also: Ashworth, *Sentencing and Criminal Justice* (n 1730) 301.

1734 S. 277 SA 2020. See also: Eleanor Curzon and Julian V Roberts, 'The Suspended Sentence Order in England and Wales' [2021] Sentencing Academy 16, 5.

1735 S. 288 (2) SA 2020. See also: Ashworth, *Sentencing and Criminal Justice* (n 1730) 301; Curzon and Roberts (n 1734) 5.

1736 S. 288 (4) SA 2020. See also: Ashworth, *Sentencing and Criminal Justice* (n 1730) 301; Curzon and Roberts (n 1734) 5–6.

1737 www.sentencingcouncil.org.uk/publications/item/imposition-of-community-custodial-sentences-definitive-guideline/. See also: Ashworth, *Sentencing and Criminal Justice* (n 1730) 301–302; Curzon and Roberts (n 1734) 6.

344. Sentencing guidelines – In sentencing or exercising functions related to sentencing, courts must follow any relevant sentencing guidelines unless they are satisfied it would be contrary to the interests of justice to do so.[1738] The sentencing guidelines for terrorism offences date to 27 April 2018 and have to be applied to all sentencing of adult offenders on or after that date.[1739] Note, however, that these guidelines do not cover all terrorist offences. Soon after their introduction, the guidelines already predated some major changes to the sentencing regimes, such as the serious terrorist sentences.[1740] This meant that in some cases, what the judge might consider a just and proportionate sentence under the guidelines could not be imposed because of the changed legislation and in those cases the guidelines could not be applied.[1741] Another issue which arose in some cases was that the guidelines were introduced before changes in the maximum sentences. In those cases where the guidelines had not been updated yet, the Court of Appeal held that Courts should apply the guidelines system of structured steps, but without being constrained by the sentence ranges and starting points established by the guidelines.[1742] The guidelines have since been updated to reflect these changes (most recent version in force since 1 October 2022).[1743] The guidelines contain eight or ten steps, depending on the offence.[1744] In step one, the offence category has to be determined based on an exhaustively listed number of factors related to culpability (ranging from category A with the highest culpability to category C or D) and harm (ranging from category 1 with the highest harm to category 2 or 3).[1745] The factors differ from offence to offence. In terms of culpability, depending on the offence, the fact that an offender acted alone or in a leading role will lead to higher culpability as will the fact they abused a position of trust, authority or influence. For offences which have several *mens rea* options, the greater *mens rea* will usually lead to a higher category. In terms of harm the likeliness of deaths or of other intended purposes (encouragement, contributions to a terrorist cause made by money or property, etc.) will influence the harm categories. In step two the Court has to determine a starting point and category range based on the harm and culpability categories. In addition, the guidelines provide for a non-exhaustive list of extra factual elements which could result in an upward or downward adjustment of the sentence. This list also varies for each offence but typically includes, for example, previous convictions, failure to respond to warnings and age and/or

1738 S. 59–62 SA 2020. See also: Sentencing Council, *Terrorism Offences: Definitive Guideline* (2018) 4.
1739 Sentencing Council, Terrorism Offences: Definitive Guideline (2018) 4.
1740 Azmeh (n 637) 15–17.
1741 Azmeh (n 637) 15–17.
1742 *R v. Michael Nugent* [2021] EWCA Crim 1535, 2021 WL 04950303, 24.
1743 See also: Lee and Walker (n 1617) 869.
1744 See also: Lee and Walker (n 1698) 327–328.
1745 See also: Rory Kelly, 'Sentencing Terrorism Offences: No Harm Intended?' [2019] Criminal Law Review 764, 764–765.

lack of maturity where it affects the responsibility of the offender. In step three any factors which indicate a reduction for assistance to the prosecution should be considered and in step four a reduction for guilty pleas is awarded. Step five is the totality principle, meaning the Court has to consider whether the overall sentence is just and proportionate in case of sentencing for more than one offence or sentencing an offender already serving a sentence. In step six courts have to consider whether to make ancillary orders. Finally, in step seven courts have to give the reasons for and explain the effect of the sentence and in step eight must consider time spent on bail. For offences for which these are a possibility, courts have to consider the dangerousness of the offender to assess the need for a life sentence or an extended sentence and apply the rules on special custodial sentences for certain offenders of particular concern. Where needed these rules take the place of steps five and six, pushing the usual steps five to eight back, making them steps seven to ten. For each terrorism offence *sensu lato* included in the guidelines, we will provide the table of starting points and categories, which gives a good overview of the sentencing possibilities. However, the lists of harm and culpability factors and aggravating and mitigating circumstances will not be copied as it would take up too much space. Those who wish to have more information are referred to the sentencing guidelines.[1746]

SECTION II. DEFINING TERRORISM

345. Definition in 2000 – The very first thing the Terrorism Act 2000 did was defining terrorism. This definition did not create a new offence but is important because many other terrorist offences refer to it and it is used to allow for special investigatory measures and other procedural exceptions.[1747] The first section of the TA 2000 as it stands today defines terrorism as '*the use or threat of action where:*

(a) the action
  (i) involves serious violence against a person,
  (ii) involves serious damage to property,
  (iii) endangers a person's life, other than that of the person committing the action,

[1746] www.sentencingcouncil.org.uk/.

[1747] *R v. F* [2007] EWCA Crim 243, 2007 WL 434775, 13; Carlile of Berriew, 'The Definition of Terrorism' (2007) Independent Reviewer of Terrorism Legislation Cm 7052 12; Hall, 'The Terrorism Acts in 2020' (n 1692) para 1.2; Conte (n 10) 692; Fenwick, *Fenwick on Civil Liberties and Human Rights* (n 1649) 1049–1050; Jacqueline S Hodgson and Victor Tadros, 'The Impossibility of Defining Terrorism' (2013) 16 New Criminal Law Review 494, 497–498; Rowe (n 1670) 532; Andrew Staniforth, *Preventing Terrorism and Violent Extremism* (Oxford University Press 2014) 34.

(iv) creates a serious risk to the health or safety of the public or a section of the public, or
(v) is designed seriously to interfere with or seriously to disrupt an electronic system.

And

(b) the use or threat is designed to influence the government or an international governmental organisation or to intimidate the public or a section of the public, and
(c) the use or threat is made for the purpose of advancing a political, religious, racial or ideological cause.'[1748]

In addition, the use or threat of a listed action which involves the use of firearms or explosives is terrorism whether or not it is designed to influence the government or to intimidate the public or a section of the public.[1749] In the case of R *(Miranda)*, the Court of Appeal clarified that the actions listed in the definition all imply a mental element and exclude unwitting or accidental behaviour.[1750] The TA 2000 also specifies that 'actions' can take place outside of the UK, references to people or property include any person or any property wherever situated, 'public' does not only mean the UK public and 'government' is not limited to the UK government.[1751] In a case concerning acts aimed against the Gaddafi government Libya, the Court of Appeal further clarified that the term 'government' is not limited to democratic governments.[1752] In addition, there is no implicit international humanitarian law savings clause, meaning military attacks by non-state armed groups in the context of a non-international

1748 S. 1 TA 2000. See also: Carlile of Berriew, 'The Definition of Terrorism' (n 1747) 11; Conte (n 10) 229–230; Demirsu (n 56) 74; Fenwick, *Fenwick on Civil Liberties and Human Rights* (n 1649) 1049; Daniel Greenberg, 'Terrorist Offences' [2022] Westlaw UK 1–2; Hale-Ross (n 1) 15; Hardy and Williams (n 608) 111–112; Paye (n 79) 14; Roach, *The 9/11 Effect: Comparative Counter-Terrorism* (n 79) 255–256; Staniforth (n 1747) 35; Walker, *Blackstone's Guide to the Anti-Terrorism Legislation* (n 1670) 20–21.

1749 See also: Carlile of Berriew, 'The Definition of Terrorism' (n 1747) 73; Conte (n 10) 432; Ian Cram, 'Regulating the Media: Some Neglected Freedom of Expression Issues in the United Kingdom's Counter-Terrorism Strategy' (2006) 18 Terrorism and Political Violence 335, 339; Fenwick, *Fenwick on Civil Liberties and Human Rights* (n 1649) 1049; Hale-Ross (n 1) 15; Halstead (n 1653) 155; Stone (n 1651) 442.

1750 Regina (Miranda) v. Secretary of State for the Home Department and another (Liberty and others intervening) [2016] EWCA Civ 6, 53–54.

1751 Anderson, 'Shielding the Compass: How to Fight Terrorism without Defeating the Law' (n 25) 15; Cram (n 1749) 339; Fenwick, 'The Anti-Terrorism, Crime and Security Act 2001' (n 92) 734; Fenwick, *Fenwick on Civil Liberties and Human Rights* (n 1649) 1049; Halstead (n 1653) 155; Roach, *The 9/11 Effect: Comparative Counter-Terrorism* (n 79) 256.

1752 *R v. F* [2007] EWCA Crim 243, 2007 WL 434775, 19–32; Anderson, 'Shielding the Compass: How to Fight Terrorism without Defeating the Law' (n 25) 15; Conte (n 10) 432; Fenwick, *Fenwick on Civil Liberties and Human Rights* (n 1649) 1050; Hale-Ross (n 1) 34–35; Hardy and Williams (n 608) 115–116; Hodgson and Tadros (n 1747) 503; Stone (n 1651) 443–444; Tadros, 'Justice and Terrorism' (n 46) 674; Clive Walker, 'Commentary: R v AY' [2010] Criminal Law Review 882, 884. This was also the approach supported by the independent reviewer of terrorism legislation, see: Carlile of Berriew, 'The Definition of Terrorism' (n 1747) 78–82.

armed conflict can be included in the definition.[1753] Finally, '*a reference to action taken for the purposes of terrorism includes a reference to action taken for the benefit of a proscribed organisation.*'

346. Changes in 2006 and 2008 – Both the TA 2006 and the CTA 2008 slightly expanded the definition. The TA 2006 added the words '*or an international governmental organisation*' to point number (b), in order to bring the UK definition closer to some international ones.[1754] The CTA 2008 added the term 'racial' to the listed causes in point number (c).[1755] This addition was not done out of belief it would widen the scope of the definition but more for clarity's sake.[1756]

347. Legal certainty: UK Court – In 2007, the England and Wales High Court was confronted with the question of whether the UK definition was in breach of the legal certainty principle. The case concerned a man who was subject to a control order (see nos 501–510), legislation that relied on the definition in the TA 2000. The Court held that the definition did not infringe upon the principle of legal certainty. While it is broad, it is also accessible, detailed, specific and unambiguous, according to the Court.[1757]

348. Criticism – Despite this ruling, the definition of terrorism has been widely criticised for its broadness and vagueness.[1758] It is criticised as being overly broad because it includes serious damage to property, serious risk to the health or safety of the public or a section of the public and serious interference with or serious disruption of an electronic system.[1759] Lord Carlile, as the

1753 *R v. Gul (Mohammed)* [2013] UKSC 64. See also: Hale-Ross (n 1) 34.

1754 See also: Hardy and Williams (n 608) 114; Roach, *The 9/11 Effect: Comparative Counter-Terrorism* (n 79) 256.

1755 See also: Fenwick, *Fenwick on Civil Liberties and Human Rights* (n 1649) 1050; Hardy and Williams (n 608) 114; Roach, *The 9/11 Effect: Comparative Counter-Terrorism* (n 79) 256.

1756 Hansard (House of Lords) Vol.704, 21 October 2008, col.1064. See also: Greenberg, 'Terrorism' (n 1670) 3.

1757 *Secretary of State for the Home Department v. E* [2007] EWHC 233 (Admin), 144; See also: Hardy and Williams (n 608) 114–115.

1758 See e.g.: Amnesty International report, "Dangerously disproportionate, the ever-expanding national security state in Europe" (2017) 26; Art. 19, *The Impact of UK Anti-Terror Laws on Freedom of Expression: Submission to ICJ Panel of Eminent Jurists on Terrorism, Counter-Terrorism and Human Rights*, London, April 2006, 4–5; Ashworth and Zedner (n 18) 173–174; Fenwick, 'The Anti-Terrorism, Crime and Security Act 2001' (n 92) 734; Rowe (n 1670) 532; Fenwick, *Fenwick on Civil Liberties and Human Rights* (n 1649) 1049–1050; Zedner, 'Securing Liberty in the Face of Terror: Reflections from Criminal Justice' (n 92) 512; Zedner, 'Terrorizing Criminal Law' (n 45) 113. The case law also underlines the breadth of the definition. See e.g.: *R v. Gul (Mohammed)* [2013] UKSC 64, 26–29 and 62–63. See also: JCHR, *Counter-Terrorism Policy and Human Rights: Terrorism Bill and related matters* (HL paper 75, HC paper 561, 2005) para 13.

1759 Ashworth and Zedner (n 18) 173; Conte (n 10) 461; Hardy and Williams (n 608) 119–120; Hodgson and Tadros (n 1747) 510; Kent Roach, 'The Case for Defining Terrorism With

independent reviewer, defended the inclusion of these parts. On property damage he argued that it can induce a sense of terror for the future.[1760] While this is undoubtedly true, these situations would already be covered by other parts of the definition, such as threatening further action or endangering people's lives. Regarding interference with electronic systems, he points to potentially enormous economic damage and the potential for injury as a result.[1761] Indeed, this seems to be the reasoning for its inclusion in the definition.[1762] This is a logical point to make, which does, however, lead to the same remark as it did for Belgium (see no. 133). If these are the situations that are supposed to be targeted, then it would have been preferable to explicitly include this in the definition. Conte argues that with these inclusions, the definition goes beyond what is required by the Security Council and suggested by the Special Rapporteur and '*may capture effects of conduct which are not truly 'terrorist' in nature*.'[1763] In this conclusion, he is supported by many other commentators.[1764] Even Lord Carlile contended that the definition was so broad it included non-terrorist activities. He, however, did not find this problematic because of his trust in prosecutorial discretion.[1765] This seems to us to be flawed reasoning. Trust in discretion is no excuse under the legality principle for drafting overly wide legislation.[1766] It is the task of the legislature to clearly define statutes. Many commentators add that the intention to 'influence' a government or international organisation is a low threshold and, for example, 'compel' or 'intimidate' would have been preferable.[1767] David Anderson, who succeeded Lord Carlile as the independent reviewer, seems to be a bit more critical of the definition than his predecessor. In his 2013 report as the independent reviewer for terrorism legislation, Anderson

Restraint and Without Reference to Political or Religious Motive' in Andrew Lynch, Edwina Macdonald and George Williams (eds), *Law and Liberty in the war on terror* (The Federation Press 2007) 40; Kent Roach, 'Must We Trade Rights for Security? The Choice Between Smart, Harsh, or Proportionate Security Strategies in Canada and Britain' in David Dyzenhaus (ed), *Civil rights and security* (Ashgate 2009) 281; Stone (n 1651) 443.

1760 Carlile of Berriew, 'The Definition of Terrorism' (n 1747) 50.

1761 Carlile of Berriew, 'The Definition of Terrorism' (n 1747) 71.

1762 Secretary of State for the Home Department and Secretary of State for Northern Ireland, *Legislation Against Terrorism: A consultation paper* (Cm 4178, 1998) para 3.16–3.17; Walker, *Blackstone's Guide to the Anti-Terrorism Legislation* (n 1670) 24–25.

1763 Conte (n 10) 461.

1764 Art. 19, The Impact of UK Anti-Terror Laws on Freedom of Expression: Submission to ICJ Panel of Eminent Jurists on Terrorism, Counter-Terrorism and Human Rights, London, April 2006, 4–5; Ashworth and Zedner (n 18) 173–174; Fenwick, 'The Anti-Terrorism, Crime and Security Act 2001' (n 92) 734; Fenwick, *Fenwick on Civil Liberties and Human Rights* (n 1649) 1050; Gearty (n 1659) 42; Hardy and Williams (n 608) 100–101; Hodgson and Tadros (n 1747) 501; Stone (n 1651) 443.

1765 Carlile of Berriew, 'The Definition of Terrorism' (n 1747) 34 and 60–64. See also: Hardy and Williams (n 608) 117–118.

1766 See also: Fenwick, *Fenwick on Civil Liberties and Human Rights* (n 1649) 1050.

1767 Ashworth and Zedner (n 18) 173; Carlile of Berriew, 'The Definition of Terrorism' (n 1747) 58–59; Fenwick, 'The Anti-Terrorism, Crime and Security Act 2001' (n 92) 734; Hale-Ross (n 1) 29–33; Hardy and Williams (n 608) 119.

questions the inclusion of property damage as well as whether the bar of 'serious violence against a person' is not too low.[1768] He also questions the need for the underlying purpose and even the target to be included, but does not argue for their abolition because of their limiting effect.[1769] The issues with the definition are only exacerbated and reverberate throughout the other offences since the definition forms the basis for many of these other terrorism offences.[1770]

SECTION III. TERRORISM *SENSU STRICTO*

SUBSECTION I. VARIOUS PIECES OF LEGISLATION

349. 2002 Framework Decision – The UK has no specific terrorism offence *sensu stricto* the same way Belgium does. As was the case in Belgium before 2003 (see no. 105), the UK uses general criminal law offences such as murder to prosecute acts of terrorism *sensu stricto*.[1771] In addition, some pieces of legislation were introduced to tackle specific instances of terrorism *sensu stricto* because this was required by international conventions (see no. 2).[1772] These offences mainly focus on explosives, biological, chemical and nuclear material and aviation security. A fair amount of them have never been applied in practice.[1773] All these offences cover actions which fall under the list of actions in s. 1 of the TA 2000. In this Section we will give a brief overview of some of those offences. Afterwards, sentences are discussed. The 2002 Framework Decision requires enhanced penalties for certain offences in terrorism context, unless they are already punishable with life imprisonment.[1774] Originally, there was no need to transpose this since almost all of the aforementioned UK offences already carried the maximum sentence of life imprisonment.[1775] One notable exception was terrorist threatening, which was not always punishable. It was already punishable in the most obvious cases, but not all.[1776]

1768 Anderson, 'Shielding the Compass: How to Fight Terrorism without Defeating the Law' (n 25) 13–14.

1769 Anderson, 'Shielding the Compass: How to Fight Terrorism without Defeating the Law' (n 25) 14–15.

1770 Ashworth and Zedner (n 18) 173; Zedner, 'Terrorizing Criminal Law' (n 45) 114.

1771 Lord Lloyd of Berwick, *Inquiry into legislation against terrorism* (Cm 3420, 1996) ix; Anderson, 'Shielding the Compass: How to Fight Terrorism without Defeating the Law' (n 25) 4–5; Jessie Blackbourn, Deniz Kayis and Nicola McGarrity, *Anti-Terrorism Law and Foreign Terrorist Fighters* (Routledge 2018) 10–11; Walker, *Blackstone's Guide to the Anti-Terrorism Legislation* (n 1670) 165.

1772 Lord Lloyd of Berwick, *Inquiry into legislation against terrorism* (Cm 3420, 1996) 15–17.

1773 Lee and Walker (n 1617) 873.

1774 Art. 1 Council Framework Decision 2002/475/JHA of 13 June 2002 on combating terrorism [2002] *OJ* L164/5.

1775 Spencer (n 1616) 119.

1776 Spencer (n 1616) 119.

350. Murder, assault, etc. – Often, terrorist attacks will revolve around (attempted) homicides, i.e. killing a person or persons. A homicide consists of the death of a human being who is under the queen's peace being caused through an act or omission of one or more other human beings (or exceptionally, a corporation or organisation).[1777] The requirement of the queen's peace excludes alien enemies in the course of war and rebels engaged in hostile operations against the crown.[1778] Murder is homicide with the intent to cause death or grievous bodily harm (i.e. really serious but not necessarily life-threatening or permanent harm).[1779, 1780] In three situations an act which is a *prima facie* murder will not amount to murder but to voluntary manslaughter. This is the case when the act is committed in response to some incident or event which constitutes loss of control, in pursuance of a suicide pact or with some form of diminished responsibility.[1781, 1782] In cases of terrorism, these situations will not be applicable and the offence committed or attempted will usually constitute murder. When there is no intention to kill and no casualties were caused, offences such as assault, malicious wounding or infliction of grievous bodily harm will be applicable.[1783] Depending on the context, other offences such as arson might also be relevant.

1777 Allen and Edwards (n 1618) 360–361; Child and others (n 1630) 384–385; Elliott and Quinn (n 1627) 57–64; Herring (n 1627) 231–233; Loveless, Allen and Derry (n 1618) 230–239; Martin (n 1618) 150–151; Peter Rowe, 'The Criminal Liability of a British Soldier Merely for Participating in the Iraq War 2003: A Response to Chilcot Evidence' [2010] Criminal Law Review 752, 753.

1778 *R v. Page* [1954] 1 QB 170; Allen and Edwards (n 1618) 361; Child and others (n 1630) 390; Herring (n 1627) 232; Loveless, Allen and Derry (n 1618) 238–239; Rowe (n 1777) 753–754. Note that a prison of war is under the queen's peace. See: *Maria v. Hall* (1807) 1 Taunt 33, 127 ER 741. Some scholars doubt whether the inclusion of this element has additional value to the definition. See: Elliott and Quinn (n 1627) 64; Michael Hirst, 'Murder under the Queen's Peace' [2008] Criminal Law Review 541.

1779 *R v. Ashman* (1858) 1 Foster and Finlason 88; *Director of Public Prosecutions v. Smith* [1961] AC 290, 334–335; *R v. Bollom* [2003] EWCA Crim 2846, 53. Note that in the *Sidhu* case the Court of Appeal did state there are degrees of 'serious' harm and for murder, a higher degree of serious harm was required than was the case. See: *R v. Sidhu (Ryandeep Singh)* [2019] EWCA Crim 1034, 19.

1780 *R v. Rahman and others* [2008] UKHL 45, 8, 35 and 51; *R v. Vickers* [1957] 2 QB 664, 670–671; *Hyam v. Director of Public Prosecutions* [1975] AC 55, 93–98; *R v. Cunningham* [1982] AC 566; *R v. Nedrick* [1986] 1 WLR 1025 (CA), 1027; *Attorney-General's Reference (No. 3 of 1994)* [1998] AC 245, 258; *R v. Woollin* [1999] 1 AC 82, 90; *R v. Powell, Daniels and English* [1999] 1 AC 1, 12 and 14–15; Allen and Edwards (n 1618) 363–364; Child and others (n 1630) 390–391; Duff, *Intention, Agency and Criminal Liability: Philosophy of Action and the Criminal Law* (n 1572) 8; Elliott and Quinn (n 1627) 65–70; Herring (n 1627) 233–234; Loveless, Allen and Derry (n 1618) 241–243; Martin (n 1618) 151; Rowe (n 1777) 753; Stark, 'It's Only Words: On Meaning and Mens Rea' (n 1632) 160; Wilson (n 1630) 366–368.

1781 S. 2 Homicide Act 1957.

1782 Allen and Edwards (n 1618) 366–392; Child and others (n 1630) 395; Elliott and Quinn (n 1627) 82–104; Herring (n 1627) 234–270; Loveless, Allen and Derry (n 1618) 249–285; Martin (n 1618) 152–156; Wilson (n 1630) 371–390.

1783 S. 18, 20 and 47 Offences against the Person Act 1861 (OAPA 1861). For a discussion of these offences and some other potentially relevant offences, see: Child and others (n 1630) 441–452;

351. Explosive Substances Act 1883 – The oldest piece of counter-terrorism legislation still in force in the UK is the Explosive Substances Act 1883.[1784] This act criminalises the unlawful and malicious causing of an explosion of a nature likely to endanger life or to cause serious injury to property.[1785] This is an offence regardless of the explosive substance used and regardless of whether any injury to person or property has actually been caused. In addition, the Act criminalises the attempt to cause explosion or making or keeping explosives with intent to endanger life or property or under suspicious circumstances.[1786] Finally, the act criminalises anybody who procures, counsels, aids, abets, or is accessory to, the commission of any offence under the Act.[1787]

352. Biological Weapons Act 1974 – A second piece of legislation which criminalises acts which could constitute terrorism *sensu stricto* is the Biological Weapons Act 1974. This act criminalises the development, production, stockpiling, acquiring, retaining or transferring of biological agents or toxins or their delivery agents.[1788] The Act was already in place since 1974 and was expanded by the ATCSA 2001.[1789]

353. Chemical Weapons Act 1996 – Similarly, the Chemical Weapons Act 1996 makes it an offence to use, develop, have in possession, participate in the transfer or engage in preparations of a military nature for the use of chemical weapons.[1790]

354. Nuclear material, facilities and weapons – The Nuclear Material (Offences) Act 1983 provides that for a certain list of offences such as murder and manslaughter the sentence (so far as this was not already the case) can be life imprisonment if the acts were done in relation to or by means of nuclear material or the act was directed against a nuclear facility or resulted in the emission of radiation.[1791] Secondly, it is an offence to receive, hold or deal with nuclear materials; to do an act directed at a nuclear facility; or to do an act which interferes with the operation of such a facility, if the person either intends to cause or is reckless as to whether damage would be caused to the environment.[1792] Thirdly, another offence is introduced, being the unlawful

Elliott and Quinn (n 1627) 151–161; Herring (n 1627) 322–418; Loveless, Allen and Derry (n 1618) 452–514; Martin (n 1618) 177–196; Wilson (n 1630) 283–306.

1784 Conte (n 10) 221.
1785 S. 2 Explosive Substances Act 1883.
1786 S. 3 and 4 Explosive Substances Act 1883.
1787 S. 5 Explosive Substances Act 1883.
1788 S. 1 (1) and (1A) Biological Weapons Act 1974.
1789 See also: Conte (n 10) 237–238.
1790 S. 2 (1) Chemical Weapons Act 1996.
1791 S. 1A Nuclear Material (Offences) Act 1983.
1792 S. 1B Nuclear Material (Offences) Act 1983.

export, import or shipment as stores from one country to another of nuclear material.[1793] It is also an offence for a person to receive, hold or deal with nuclear material or perform an act directed at a nuclear facility, or that interferes with the operation of such a facility intending to cause or being reckless as to the causing of relevant injury or damage.[1794] Finally, it is an offence to threaten to cause injury, damage or damage to the environment by means of nuclear material or the emission of ionising radiation or the release of radioactive material resulting from an act which is directed at a nuclear facility, or which interferes with the operation of such a facility, with the intention that the person to whom the threat is made shall fear that it will be carried out.[1795] The same goes for threatening the obtaining of nuclear material by an act which is an offence in order to compel a state, international organisation or person to do, or abstain from doing, any act.[1796] The ATCSA 2001 introduced two further offences, related to nuclear weapons. The first is to knowingly cause a nuclear explosion or to develop, produce (or participate in the development or production),[1797] have, participate in the transfer of[1798] or engage in military preparations, or in preparations of a military nature, intending to use, or threaten to use, a nuclear weapon.[1799] The ATCSA 2001 also contains exceptions and defences for this offence.[1800] Second, it is an offence to aid, abet, counsel, procure or incite a person who commits an offence related to chemical, biological or nuclear weapons outside of UK jurisdiction.[1801]

355. Aviation and maritime security – Three different Acts deal with aviation and maritime security, being the Civil Aviation Act 1982 (CAA 1982), the Aviation Security Act 1982 (ASA 1982) and the Aircraft and Maritime Security Act 1990 (AMSA 1990). The ASA 1982 contains several offences related to safety of aircraft, such as hijacking, destroying, damaging or endangering the safety of aircraft and destroying or damaging any property used for the provision of air navigation facilities.[1802] The AMSA 1990 added a long list of additional offences, such as endangering the safety at aerodromes, hijacking ships or seizing or exercising control of fixed platforms.[1803] In addition to these offences, the CAA 1982 provides jurisdiction for any act or omission on board a

1793 S. 1C Nuclear Material (Offences) Act 1983.
1794 S. 2 (2) and (3) Nuclear Material (Offences) Act 1983.
1795 S. 2 (4) – (6) Nuclear Material (Offences) Act 1983. See also: Conte (n 10) 228.
1796 S. 2 (7) Nuclear Material (Offences) Act 1983.
1797 As defined by S. 47 (3) ATCSA 2001.
1798 As defined by S. 47 (4) ATCSA 2001.
1799 S. 47 (1) ATCSA 2001.
1800 S. 48 and 49 ATCSA 2001.
1801 S. 50 ATCSA 2001. See also: Conte (n 10) 238.
1802 S. 1–3 ASA 1982. For a brief overview, see: Conte (n 10) 224.
1803 S. 1, 5 and 9–15 AMSA 1990. For a brief overview, see: Conte (n 10) 224–226.

British-controlled aircraft or foreign aircraft which will land in the UK if the act or omission is also an offence under the law of the registering state.[1804]

356. The protection of persons – The Internationally Protected Persons Act 1978 introduced several offences related to protected persons. A second relevant Act is the Taking of Hostages Act 1982. This Act criminalises the detaining of another person and threatening to kill, injure or continue to detain them '*in order to compel a State, international governmental organisation or person to do or abstain from doing any act.*'[1805]

357. Use or threat of noxious substances – The ATCSA 2001 introduced another specific offence of terrorism *sensu stricto*, this one relating to noxious substances. It is an offence to take any action involving noxious substances or things which (does or is likely to) '*(a)causes serious violence against a person anywhere in the world; (b)causes serious damage to real or personal property anywhere in the world; (c)endangers human life or creates a serious risk to the health or safety of the public or a section of the public; or (d)induces in members of the public the fear that the action is likely to endanger their lives or create a serious risk to their health or safety*' and '*is designed to influence the government or an international governmental organisation or to intimidate the public or a section of the public.*'[1806] Any effect on the person taking the action is to be disregarded.[1807] Again, the terms 'government' and 'public' are not limited to the UK.[1808] It is also an offence to threaten any of the above-mentioned actions with the intention to induce the fear the threat is likely to be carried out (in a person anywhere in the world).[1809] An additional offence is included concerning hoaxes involving noxious substances or things.[1810]

SUBSECTION II. SENTENCES

358. Life imprisonment – The sentences for the abovementioned offences vary slightly, but the majority carries a sentence of life imprisonment. The sentence for any of the offences under the Explosive Substances Act 1883, is life imprisonment on indictment.[1811] The same goes for the offences under the Biological Weapons Act 1974,[1812] the Chemical Weapons Act 1996,[1813] the aviation and maritime

1804 S. 91 (1) and (1A) CAA 1982.
1805 S. 1 (1) Taking of Hostages Act 1982.
1806 S. 113 (1) and (2) ACTSA 2001.
1807 S. 113 (2) ACTSA 2001.
1808 S. 113 (5) ACTSA 2001.
1809 S. 113 (3) ACTSA 2001.
1810 S. 114 ACTSA 2001.
1811 See also: Conte (n 10) 221.
1812 S. 1 (3) Biological Weapons Act 1974.
1813 S. 2 (8) Chemical Weapons Act 1996.

security Acts, the Taking of Hostages Act,[1814] and the offences under the Nuclear Facilities and Weapons Act.[1815] The exception in the last Act is the unlawful export, import or shipment as stores of nuclear material which carries a sentence of maximum 14 years imprisonment on indictment. This same sentence is also applicable to the noxious substances offences in the ATCSA 2001 (or six months on summary conviction).[1816] The maximum sentence for hoaxes is only seven years imprisonment on indictment (or six months on summary conviction).[1817] The sentence for murder is a mandatory life sentence.[1818] When imposing a life sentence, courts also have to determine the minimum tariff to be served. Relevant in cases of terrorism is that the legislation states the starting point for this determination is a whole life tariff in case the offence was committed for the purpose of advancing a political, religious, racial or ideological cause.[1819]

359. Discretionary life sentences – As mentioned above, the life sentence for murder is a mandatory one. However, for most of the terrorist offences discussed in this book for which a life sentence is possible this sentence is not mandatory but discretionary. In those cases, the SA 2020 obliges courts to impose a life sentence in two situations. First, when there is significant risk to the public of serious harm on the commission of further offending.[1820] Second, when the defendant is convicted of his second offence.[1821] Outside of these cases, the courts will have the freedom to impose a sentence within the sentencing bracket of the specific offence. They do, however, have to take into account the existence of an aggravating factor for terrorism.

360. Aggravating factor – In his 2007 report on the definition of terrorism, Lord Carlile proposed special sentencing powers for offences connected with terrorism.[1822] He suggested that any offence punishable with five years imprisonment or more should be able to receive an additional term of up to five years if it was '*aggravated by the intention to facilitate or assist a terrorist, a terrorist group, or a terrorist purpose.*' The next year a system was actually put in place, but it did not go quite as far as Lord Carlile had suggested, introducing an aggravating factor, but not raising the maximum sentence. The CTA 2008 imposed upon courts the obligation to take 'a terrorist connection' into account

1814 S. 1 (2) Taking of Hostages Act 1982.
1815 S. 2 (8) Nuclear Material (Offences) Act 1983; s. 47 (5) ATCSA 2001.
1816 S. 113 (4) ACTSA 2001.
1817 S. 114 (3) ACTSA 2001.
1818 S. 1 (1) Murder (Abolition of Death Penalty) Act 1965. See also: Allen and Edwards (n 1618) 362; Elliott and Quinn (n 1627) 72; Loveless, Allen and Derry (n 1618) 243–244.
1819 S. 2 (2) (d) Schedule 21 Sentencing Act 2020 (SA 2020). See also: Lee and Walker (n 1617) 873–874.
1820 S. 258 and 285 and schedule 19 SA 2020. See also: Lee and Walker (n 1617) 873.
1821 S. 283 and 284 and schedule 15 SA 2020.
1822 Carlile of Berriew, 'The Definition of Terrorism' (n 1747) 44–45.

as an aggravating factor in sentencing.[1823] This rule was replaced by a nearly identical one in the SA 2020,[1824] which also imposes the obligation on courts to take into account 'a terrorist connection' as an aggravating factor (and stating so in open court).[1825] Schedule 1 of the Act lists offences for which this was originally the case, covering mainly the offences discussed in this Section of this book.[1826] The CTSA 2021 expanded this to all offences punishable on indictment for more than two years (committed after it came into force),[1827] barring terrorist offences *sensu lato*, since they already are terrorist offences.[1828] The eligible offences have a terrorist connection if they are, or take place in the course of an act of terrorism or are committed for the purposes of terrorism (using the TA 2000 definition of terrorism). The 2021 amendment of the SA 2020 greatly expanded the scope of the aggravating factor. A terrorist connection also has consequences for other rules such as early release and notification requirements, which fall outside of the scope of this book.[1829]

361. Alternative sentences – For less serious terrorist offences *sensu stricto*, sometimes alternatives to actual imprisonment will be available. Community orders (see no. 342) are a possibility as long as the offence does not have a mandatory life sentence and a serious terrorist sentence is not required either (see no. 339). A suspended sentence order is also possible in situations where the Court finds a sentence of maximum two years appropriate (see no. 343). In cases of terrorism *sensu stricto*, however, these situations might be rather rare.

362. Explosive substances guideline – We cannot include sentencing guidelines for all the above-mentioned terrorism offences *sensu stricto* since many of them do not have guidelines (yet).[1830] The terrorism sentencing guidelines only include guidelines for the offence of causing an explosion likely to endanger life or property and attempting to cause explosion or making or keeping explosives with intent to endanger life or property. The categories for these offences are[1831]:

1823 S. 30 CTA 2008. See also: Azmeh (n 637) 7; Lee and Walker (n 1698) 320.

1824 Joint Committee on Consolidation Bills, *Drafter's notes on the Sentencing Bill* (21 July 2020) para 9 and 63–66.

1825 S. 69 SA 2020. See also: Lee and Walker (n 1698) 320; Lee and Walker (n 1617) 874.

1826 Schedule 1 SA 2020.

1827 Note that the entry into force of different sections of the CTSA 2021 varies. Three options are available, being entry into force from the day after the day on which the Act is passed, entry into force two months after the day on which the act is passed or entry into force on a day appointed by regulations of the Secretary of State. See: s. 50 CTSA 2021.

1828 S. 1 CTSA 2021; Home Office, *Counter-Terrorism And Sentencing Bill: Explanatory Notes* (Bill 129-EN, 2020) para 61–64; Azmeh (n 637) 7; Kelly (n 1697) 645; Lee and Walker (n 1698) 323; Lee and Walker (n 1617) 874.

1829 Azmeh (n 637) 7–8; Lee and Walker (n 1617) 874–875.

1830 Lee and Walker (n 1698) 327.

1831 www.sentencingcouncil.org.uk/.

Culpability				
Harm	A	B	C	D
Category 1	**Starting point** Life imprisonment – minimum term 35 years' custody	**Starting point** Life imprisonment – minimum term 25 years' custody	**Starting point** Life imprisonment – minimum term 15 years' custody	**Starting point** 15 years' custody
	Category range Life imprisonment – minimum term 30–40 years' custody	**Category range** Life imprisonment – minimum term 20–30 years' custody	**Category range** Life imprisonment – minimum term 10–20 years' custody	**Category range** 10–20 years' custody
Category 2	**Starting point** Life imprisonment – minimum term 25 years' custody	**Starting point** Life imprisonment – minimum term 15 years' custody	**Starting point** 15 years' custody	**Starting point** 8 years' custody
	Category range Life imprisonment – minimum term 20–30 years' custody	**Category range** Life imprisonment – minimum term 10–20 years' custody	**Category range** 10–20 years' custody	**Category range** 6–10 years' custody
Category 3	**Starting point** 16 years' custody	**Starting point** 12 years' custody	**Starting point** 8 years' custody	**Starting point** 4 years' custody
	Category range 12–20 years' custody	**Category range** 8–16 years' custody	**Category range** 6–10 years' custody	**Category range** 3–6 years' custody

363. Grievous bodily harm guidelines – By way of example we also include the guidelines for the offences of inflicting grievous bodily harm and unlawful wounding:

Culpability			
Harm	A	B	C
Category 1	**Starting point** 4 years' custody	**Starting point** 3 years' custody	**Starting point** 2 years' custody
	Category range 3–4 years' 6 months' custody	**Category range** 2–4 years' custody	**Category range** 1–3 years' custody

Culpability			
Harm	A	B	C
Category 2	**Starting point** 3 years' custody	**Starting point** 2 years' custody	**Starting point** 1 years' custody
	Category range 2–4 years' custody	**Category range** 1–3 years' custody	**Category range** High level community order – 2 years' custody
Category 3	**Starting point** 2 years' custody	**Starting point** 1 years' custody	**Starting point** 26 weeks' custody
	Category range 1–3 years' custody	**Category range** High level community order – 2 years' custody	**Category range** Medium level community order – 1 year's custody

SUBSECTION III. PRACTICAL APPLICATION

364. Conspiracy to murder or cause explosions – A fairly large amount of uncovered terrorist plots which are relatively far advanced, is prosecuted as conspiracy to murder or cause explosion (for a brief explanation on conspiracy, see no. 452). In a well-known case concerning an attempted bombing using a detonator called the 'hifidigimonster' five people were convicted to life imprisonment with varying minimum terms for conspiracy to cause explosion likely to endanger life.[1832] Two co-accused were acquitted. In another case a group planned to blow up transatlantic airliners with IEDs and to put this plan in motion they were in the process of building the bombs and detonators. Eight people were convicted for conspiracy to murder (together with some other defendants for other offences).[1833] All of them received a life sentence with minimum terms ranging from 18 to 40 years. In another plot, four men even further along in their plans, were arrested.[1834] They had boarded London public transport with bombs, but three of the four bombs failed to explode upon detonation, and the fourth person abandoned their bomb without activating it. The first three received life sentences with minimum terms of 40 years. The fourth defendant received a sentence of 33 years imprisonment. The plans do not have to have advanced that far, however. In the *Barot* case a man was convicted for conspiracy to murder while no bomb-making materials had been acquired

1832 *R v. Omar Khyam, Salahuddin Amin, Jawed Akbar, Anthony Garcia, Waheed Mahmood* [2008] EWCA Crim 1612, 2008 WL 2821519.

1833 *R v. Abdulla Ahmed Ali and others* [2011] EWCA Crim 1260, 2011 WL 1151813.

1834 *R v. Ibrahim, Omar, Osman (aka Hamdi), Mohamed* [2008] EWCA Crim 880, 2008 WL 1771443; R *v. Asiedu (Manfo Kwaku)* [2008] EWCA Crim 1725, 2008 WL 5683938.

yet.[1835] He had attended terrorist training camps on two occasions and had scouted possible locations for an attack in the US and made plans for other attacks in the UK. It was accepted that he did not plan to take part in the attacks himself. He was convicted to imprisonment for life with a minimum term of 40 years in first instance but on appeal his minimum term was amended to 30 years.

365. Taking into account age and mental issues – In the *Nadeem* case, a man was stopped in an airport with an IED in his luggage. He claimed it was planted there without his knowledge but the jury held that he planned to detonate it on the plane and he was convicted of possession of an explosive substance with intent to endanger life or cause serious injury to property (s. 3(1)(b) Explosive Substances Act 1883). No clear terrorist connection could be established, which was taken into account at sentencing. In first instance he received an extended sentence of 23 years comprising a custodial term of 18 years and an extension period of five years but this was changed on appeal to 27 years (five of which were the extension period).[1836] In the *Damon Smith* case, a man was convicted for the same offence.[1837] The defendant was only 19 years old at the time of the facts and was diagnosed with Asperger's syndrome. He had constructed an IED after getting the instructions from *Inspire*, a magazine published by Al Qaeda, and left it on an underground train in London. Luckily, the device did not explode and the perpetrator claimed it had been a prank. This was not believed by the jury. Despite the defendant having an interest in Islam and the Koran, the evidence could not establish a terrorist connection. He was convicted to an extended sentence of 20 years, of which 15 years were the custodial term and five years extended license period. The *Nadeem* and *Damon Smith* cases are strikingly similar in several ways. Both men made IEDs and planned to detonate them on modes of transport (plane or underground train). No terrorist connection could be established for either of them. If anything the offence of *Damon Smith* was a bit more serious, his IED being larger and him already having planted it and left the train. However, the Courts clearly took into account the age and mental illness of the offender in handing down a significantly lower sentence to *Damon Smith*.

SECTION IV. OFFENCES RELATED TO PROSCRIBED ORGANISATIONS

SUBSECTION I. PROSCRIBED ORGANISATIONS

366. List – Schedule 2 of the TA 2000 contains a list of proscribed organisations. This list is drafted and amended by the Secretary of State. They may only add organisations they believe are involved in terrorism. This means the organisation

1835 *R v. Barot (Dhiren)* [2007] EWCA Crim 1119, Crim. L.R. 2007, Sep, 741–744.
1836 *R v. Nadeem Muhammed* [2017] EWCA Crim 1832, 2017 WL 05598509.
1837 *R v. Damon Smith* [2018] EWCA Crim 528, 2018 WL 01471413.

'commits or participates in acts of terrorism, prepares for terrorism, promotes or encourages terrorism, or is otherwise concerned in terrorism.'[1838] In 2006 the legislature added that *'the cases in which an organisation promotes or encourages terrorism include any case in which activities of the organisation (a)include the unlawful glorification of the commission or preparation (whether in the past, in the future or generally) of acts of terrorism; or (b)are carried out in a manner that ensures that the organisation is associated with statements containing any such glorification.'*[1839] The JCHR questioned the compatibility of this extension with Articles 10 and 11 ECHR.[1840] Glorification is only covered *'if there are persons who may become aware of it who could reasonably be expected to infer that what is being glorified, is being glorified as (a)conduct that should be emulated in existing circumstances, or (b)conduct that is illustrative of a type of conduct that should be so emulated.'*[1841] The legislation states that *'"glorification" includes any form of praise or celebration, and cognate expressions are to be construed accordingly; "statement" includes a communication without words consisting of sounds or images or both.'*[1842] Groups or their members receive no advance warning when the group is about to be proscribed.[1843] The fact a group is on the EU or US list of terrorist organisations does not necessarily mean it will be proscribed in the UK as well.[1844] There is a procedure, including appeals, in order to have an organisation deproscribed.[1845] In 2017 and 2018, there were 74 international organisations and 14 in Northern Ireland proscribed under the TA 2000.[1846] In 2020 and 2021 that was 78 international organisations and 14 in Northern Ireland.[1847]

1838 S. 3 (5) TA 2000. See also: Conte (n 10) 230 and 593; Fenwick, *Fenwick on Civil Liberties and Human Rights* (n 1649) 1054; Greenberg, 'Terrorist Offences' (n 1748) 2; David Lowe, *Terrorism: Law and Policy* (Routledge 2018) 65; Macdonald and Carlile (n 1626) 128; Tanveer Qureshi, 'Support for Proscribed Organisations' [2022] Westlaw UK 7, paras 4–6; Stone (n 1651) 445; Walker, *Blackstone's Guide to the Anti-Terrorism Legislation* (n 1670) 50.

1839 S. 3 (5A) TA 2000. See also: Fenwick, *Fenwick on Civil Liberties and Human Rights* (n 1649) 1054; Stone (n 1651) 445.

1840 JCHR, Counter-Terrorism Policy and Human Rights: Terrorism Bill and related matters (HL paper 75, HC paper 561, 2005) para 63.

1841 S. 3 (5B) TA 2000.

1842 S. 3 (5C) TA 2000.

1843 Fenwick, *Fenwick on Civil Liberties and Human Rights* (n 1649) 1056.

1844 Fenwick, *Fenwick on Civil Liberties and Human Rights* (n 1649) 1056.

1845 S. 4–7 TA 2000. See also: HM Government, *Counter-terrorism Disruptive Powers Report 2021* (CP 779, 2023), www.gov.uk/government/publications/counter-terrorism-disruptive-powers-report-2021/hm-government-counter-terrorism-disruptive-powers-report-2021-accessible-version; Conte (n 10) 230; Fenwick, *Fenwick on Civil Liberties and Human Rights* (n 1649) 163–167; Macdonald and Carlile (n 1626) 128; Roach, *The 9/11 Effect: Comparative Counter-Terrorism* (n 79) 258; Rowe (n 1670) 539–540; Stone (n 1651) 446; Walker, *Blackstone's Guide to the Anti-Terrorism Legislation* (n 1670) 50–61.

1846 Home Office, Counter-Terrorism And Border Security Bill: Explanatory Notes (Bill 219–EN, 2018) para 28; Art. 19, House of Commons Public Bill Committee – Counter-Terrorism and Border Security Bill 2018: Art. 19 written evidence (2018) para 6; Hill (n 1666) para 5.2. The list of proscribed organisations can be found here: www.gov.uk/government/publications/proscribed-terror-groups-or-organisations--2/proscribed-terrorist-groups-or-organisations-accessible-version#list-of-proscribed-international-terrorist-groups.

1847 HM Government, *Counter-terrorism Disruptive Powers Report 2021* (CP 779, 2023), www.gov.uk/government/publications/counter-terrorism-disruptive-powers-report–2021/hm-government-

SUBSECTION II. MEMBERSHIP AND SUPPORT

a) S. 11 TA 2000: Membership

367. ACTUS REUS – Belonging or professing to belong to a proscribed organisation is a criminal offence.[1848] Lord Bingham pointed out that 'professing' is not defined in the legislation and he stated the scope of the term is so uncertain it may lead to convictions of people who have not undertaken any blameworthy conduct.[1849] 'Belonging to' needs to be given its ordinary meaning and means membership. No formality or participation in the activities of the organisation is required.[1850] Belonging to a splinter group of a proscribed organisation is also covered.[1851]

368. *MENS REA* – The offence requires no *mens rea* and proving that the defendant did not know that the organisation was proscribed or that it was engaged in terrorist activities is no defence.[1852] This offence is therefore one of strict liability.

369. DEFENCE – The legislation does provide for a defence. It is a defence to prove '*that the organisation was not proscribed on the last (or only) occasion on which he became a member or began to profess to be a member, and that he has not taken part in the activities of the organisation at any time while it was proscribed.*'[1853] This defence is close to reversing the burden of proof and is especially relevant since members receive no warning of the organisation being proscribed.[1854] The burden of proof for this defence was originally intended to be one to civil standards,[1855] but the House of Lords read down the provision so that it did not violate the right to a fair trial and held that it was an evidential

counter-terrorism-disruptive-powers-report–2021-accessible-version; Hall, 'The Terrorism Acts in 2020' (n 1692) para 3.2.

1848 S. 11 (1) TA 2000. See also: Conte (n 10) 231; Fenwick, *Fenwick on Civil Liberties and Human Rights* (n 1649) 1058; Walker, *Blackstone's Guide to the Anti-Terrorism Legislation* (n 1670) 61.

1849 *Attorney General's Reference (No. 4 of 2002)* [2004] UKHL 48.

1850 *R v. Ahmed (Rangzieb) and Ahmed (Habib)* [2011] EWCA Crim 184, 82–89. See also: Greenberg, 'Terrorist Offences' (n 1748) 3; Clive Walker, 'Terrorist Offences: R. v Ahmed (Rangzieb); R. v Ahmed (Habib) – Defendant Charged with Terrorist Offences Claiming That Tortured during Detention in Pakistan' [2011] Criminal Law Review 734, 737.

1851 *R v. Z* [2005] UKHL 35. See also: C.P.W., 'Commentary: R v Z' [2005] Criminal Law Review 985, 987–991; Lowe (n 1838) 65.

1852 *R v. Hundal and Dhaliwal* [2004] EWCA Crim 389; Fenwick, *Fenwick on Civil Liberties and Human Rights* (n 1649) 1059; Walker, 'Commentary: R v AY' (n 1752) 886.

1853 S. 11 (2) TA 2000. See also: Fenwick, *Fenwick on Civil Liberties and Human Rights* (n 1649) 1058; Stone (n 1651) 446; Walker, *Blackstone's Guide to the Anti-Terrorism Legislation* (n 1670) 61–62.

1854 Fenwick, *Fenwick on Civil Liberties and Human Rights* (n 1649) 1058.

1855 Walker, *Blackstone's Guide to the Anti-Terrorism Legislation* (n 1670) 62.

burden only.[1856] This means the defence only has to raise the issue after which the prosecution has to prove beyond a reasonable doubt that the defence is not applicable.[1857] What is not a defence according to the case law, is to prove the involvement in the organisation took place abroad in a state where the organisation was not proscribed.[1858]

b) S. 12 TA 2000: Offences related to support

370. Inviting support – In addition to membership, '*a person commits an offence if he invites support for a proscribed organisation, and the support is not, or is not restricted to, the provision of money or other property.*'[1859] Financial support is excluded since it falls under the s. 15 offence (see nos 387–388).[1860] Non-financial support includes for example the provision of clothing, medical assistance or tools.[1861] Support can be both tangible and practical, but does not need to be and could thus be intellectual or moral support such as approval or endorsement.[1862] This offence is broad, and although it does not explicitly include an element of *mens rea*, the support must be invited knowingly.[1863] It is not required for the person accused of inviting support to also be engaged in providing support for the organisation or intending to do so.[1864] The person does not have to personally provide support, since the offence is in the inviting.

1856 *Attorney General's Reference (No. 4 of 2002)* [2004] UKHL 43, 51–53. See also: Fenwick, *Fenwick on Civil Liberties and Human Rights* (n 1649) 1059; Macdonald and Carlile (n 1626) 141; Stone (n 1651) 446; Tadros, 'Justice and Terrorism' (n 46) 671; Victor Tadros, 'Rethinking the Presumption of Innocence' (2007) 1 Criminal Law and Philosophy 193, 201; Walker, 'The Impact of Contemporary Security Agendas Against Terrorism on the Substantive Criminal Law' (n 45) 137.

1857 *Attorney General's Reference (No. 4 of 2002)* [2004] UKHL 43, 1; Allen and Edwards (n 1618) 27; Elliott and Quinn (n 1627) 350; Tadros, 'Rethinking the Presumption of Innocence' (n 1856) 201; Wilson (n 1630) 10.

1858 *R v. Hundal and Dhaliwal* [2004] EWCA Crim 389, 12. See also: Walker, 'Commentary: R v AY' (n 1752) 886.

1859 S. 12 (1) TA 2000. See also: Conte (n 10) 231; Fenwick, *Fenwick on Civil Liberties and Human Rights* (n 1649) 1060; Walker, *Blackstone's Guide to the Anti-Terrorism Legislation* (n 1670) 62.

1860 *Anjem Choudary, Mohammed Mizanur Rahman v. R* [2016] EWCA Crim 61, 54; Walker, *Blackstone's Guide to the Anti-Terrorism Legislation* (n 1670) 62.

1861 Qureshi (n 1838) para 8.

1862 *Anjem Choudary, Mohammed Mizanur Rahman v. R* [2016] EWCA Crim 61, 46; *Anjem Choudary, Mohammed Mizanur Rahman v. R* [2017] EWCA Crim 1606; Liberty's Briefing on the Counter-Terrorism and Border Security Bill for Second Reading in the House of Lords (October 2018) 4; Qureshi (n 1838) para 20.

1863 *Pwr v. Director of Public Prosecutions, Akdogan and another v. Director of Public Prosecutions* [2022] UKSC 2, 39; *Anjem Choudary, Mohammed Mizanur Rahman v. R* [2016] EWCA Crim 61, 48; Fenwick, *Fenwick on Civil Liberties and Human Rights* (n 1649) 1060; Fenwick and Fenwick (n 56) 29.

1864 *Anjem Choudary, Mohammed Mizanur Rahman v. R* [2016] EWCA Crim 61, 44–45; *Anjem Choudary, Mohammed Mizanur Rahman v. R* [2017] EWCA Crim 1606; Qureshi (n 1838) paras 25–30.

371. Arranging meetings – A person also commits an offence, '*if he arranges, manages or assists in arranging or managing a meeting which he knows is (a)to support a proscribed organisation, (b)to further the activities of a proscribed organisation, or (c)to be addressed by a person who belongs or professes to belong to a proscribed organisation.*'[1865] The second part of this offence is the *mens rea*, providing for three options in terms of knowledge. This offence means that one person who professes to belong to a proscribed organisation speaking at a meeting which is almost exclusively non-terrorist, would render the organisers liable for criminal prosecution.[1866] A meeting must include three or more persons, regardless of whether the public are admitted.[1867] A meeting is private if the public are not admitted.[1868] It is a defence for a person charged with the offence under point number (c) to prove that they had no reasonable cause to believe that the address would support a proscribed organisation or further its activities.[1869] If the defence can provide sufficient evidence to raise doubt about whether they had cause to believe this, it is up to the prosecution to prove beyond reasonable doubt that this was the case.[1870] Fenwick points out that this defence is very narrow.[1871]

372. Addressing a meeting – A person also commits an offence '*if he addresses a meeting and the purpose of his address is to encourage support for a proscribed organisation or to further its activities.*'[1872] Presumably the *mens rea* is the intention to encourage support for a proscribed organisation or to further its activities as this is implied in the purpose of the address.

373. Expressing supportive opinions – In the *Choudhary* case, the Court of Appeal made it clear that simply expressing an opinion or belief is not sufficient to commit the aforementioned offences, since they require inviting support.[1873] Therefore, in 2019 the legislature also made it an offence to '*express an opinion or*

1865 S. 12 (2) TA 2000. See also: Fenwick, *Fenwick on Civil Liberties and Human Rights* (n 1649) 1060; Walker, *Blackstone's Guide to the Anti-Terrorism Legislation* (n 1670) 62.

1866 Fenwick, *Fenwick on Civil Liberties and Human Rights* (n 1649) 1062.

1867 S. 12 (5) TA 2000. See also: Fenwick, *Fenwick on Civil Liberties and Human Rights* (n 1649) 1060; Stone (n 1651) 446; Qureshi (n 1838) para 35; Walker, *Blackstone's Guide to the Anti-Terrorism Legislation* (n 1670) 63.

1868 S. 12 (5) TA 2000.

1869 S. 12 (4) TA 2000. See also: Fenwick, *Fenwick on Civil Liberties and Human Rights* (n 1649) 1060; Walker, *Blackstone's Guide to the Anti-Terrorism Legislation* (n 1670) 62.

1870 S. 118 TA 2000. See also: Fenwick, *Fenwick on Civil Liberties and Human Rights* (n 1649) 1060; Rowe (n 1670) 540–541; Stone (n 1651) 446; Walker, *Blackstone's Guide to the Anti-Terrorism Legislation* (n 1670) 62–63.

1871 Fenwick, *Fenwick on Civil Liberties and Human Rights* (n 1649) 1060.

1872 S. 12 (3) TA 2000. See also: Fenwick, *Fenwick on Civil Liberties and Human Rights* (n 1649) 1060; Walker, *Blackstone's Guide to the Anti-Terrorism Legislation* (n 1670) 63.

1873 *Anjem Choudary, Mohammed Mizanur Rahman v. R* [2016] EWCA Crim 61, 49. See also: Home Office, *Counter-Terrorism And Border Security Bill: Explanatory Notes (Bill 219-EN, 2018)* para 30; Qureshi (n 1838) para 23.

belief that is supportive of a proscribed organisation, and in doing so being reckless as to whether a person to whom the expression is directed will be encouraged to support a proscribed organisation.'[1874]

c) Sentences

374. Triable either way – These offences are triable either-way. They were originally punishable with a maximum of ten years imprisonment, a fine or both,[1875] but the prison sentence was raised to maximum 14 years in 2021.[1876] On summary conviction, they are punishable with imprisonment for a term not exceeding six months, a fine or both.[1877] Note that on indictment or on summary conviction for offences which are triable either-way, there are no maximum fines.[1878] The offences are specified offences for which an extended sentence is possible if the other conditions are met (see no. 340). Community orders (see no. 342) are also a possibility, as is a suspended sentence order, in situations where the Court finds a sentence of maximum two years appropriate (see no. 343).

375. Guidelines membership – The sentencing guideline categories for the membership offence are slightly simpler than the other ones since they have no variation in the level of harm caused, as the membership is 'inherently harmful'.[1879]

	Culpability		
Harm	A	B	C
Category 1	**Starting point** 10 years' custody	**Starting point** 7 years' custody	**Starting point** 3 years' custody
	Category range 8–13 years' custody	**Category range** 5–9 years' custody	**Category range** High level community order – 4 years' custody

1874 S. 12 (1A) TA 2000. See also: Fenwick and Fenwick (n 56) 33.

1875 See: Conte (n 10) 231; Greenberg, 'Terrorist Offences' (n 1748) 2; Walker, *Blackstone's Guide to the Anti-Terrorism Legislation* (n 1670) 63.

1876 S. 11 (3)(a) and 12 (6)(a) TA 2000; s. 26 (1) CTSA 2021. See also: Azmeh (n 637) 12; Kelly (n 1697) 645; Lee and Walker (n 1698) 323; Lee and Walker (n 1617) 885; Qureshi (n 1838) para 41; Walker, *Blackstone's Guide to the Anti-Terrorism Legislation* (n 1670) 63.

1877 S. 11 (3)(b) and 12 (6)(b) TA 2000.

1878 Sentencing Council, *Approach to the assessment of fines, 9. Maximum fines*, www.sentencingcouncil.org.uk/explanatory-material/magistrates-court/item/fines-and-financial-orders/approach-to-the-assessment-of-fines-2/9-maximum-fines/; Sprack and Engelhardt-Sprack (n 1618) 396–397.

1879 www.sentencingcouncil.org.uk/.

376. GUIDELINES SUPPORT – The guidelines for the support offences on the other hand do include harm categories. They are the following[1880]:

	Culpability		
Harm	A	B	C
Category 1	**Starting point** 10 years' custody	**Starting point** 7 years' custody	**Starting point** 3 years' custody
	Category range 8–13 years' custody	**Category range** 5–9 years' custody	**Category range** 2–5 years' custody
Category 2	**Starting point** 8 years' custody	**Starting point** 4 years' custody	**Starting point** 2 years' custody
	Category range 6–9 years' custody	**Category range** 3–7 years' custody	**Category range** 1–3 years' custody
Category 3	**Starting point** 6 years' custody	**Starting point** 3 years' custody	**Starting point** 1 year's custody
	Category range 4–7 years' custody	**Category range** 2–4 years' custody	**Category range** High level community order – 2 years' custody

d) *Practical application*

377. EXAMPLES – In the case of *R v Alamgir and others*, several members of a group of people in Luton were convicted for the support offences.[1881] They spoke at meetings and held classes for the members of the group the main purpose of which was the encouragement and support of ISIS. These speeches included calls for an end to 'procrastination', glorification of IS fighters and atrocities, encouraging people 'stepping forward to carry the banner', etc. The defendants denied their purpose was to encourage support for ISIS, but this was not believed. At that time, the maximum sentence was still ten years imprisonment and there were no sentencing guidelines yet for these offences. Three defendants were convicted to respectively six years, four and a half years and five years imprisonment for the offence of inviting support, with an additional sentence of 18 months imprisonment for the third defendant for the offence of arranging a

1880 www.sentencingcouncil.org.uk/.

1881 *R v. Alamgir and others* [2018] EWCA Crim 21; *R v. Mohammed Alamgir, Yousaf Bashir, Rajib Khan* [2018] EWCA Crim 1553.

meeting contrary to s. 12. These sentences were confirmed on appeal. The Court of Appeal stated that the following factors should be taken into account: the position of the offender, whether they had a position of authority or influence, the persistence of their efforts, the type of activity involved, in the context of live meetings the size and nature of the target audience and finally the extent of support (likely to be) gained.[1882]

SUBSECTION III. UNIFORM AND PUBLICATION OF IMAGES

a) *S. 13 TA 2000: Wearing uniforms or insignia*

378. Actus reus – In addition to the membership and support offences, it is also an offence for a person to wear an item of clothing, or wear, carry or display an article, '*in such a way or in such circumstances as to arouse reasonable suspicion that he is a member or supporter of a proscribed organisation.*'[1883] This suspicion does not need to be precise in terms of factions of specific groups.[1884]

379. No *mens rea* – These are offences of strict liability, meaning no knowledge or intention to arouse suspicion of membership of the group is required.[1885] According to the courts, the presumption of *mens rea* cannot be applied since the text of the Act is clear and unambiguous.[1886] The person does, however, need to know they are wearing or displaying the item (i.e. it cannot be attached to their backpack without their knowledge for example), which is a

---

1882 *R v. Alamgir and others* [2018] EWCA Crim 21, 34–35.

1883 S. 13 (1) TA 2000. See also: Conte (n 10) 231; Demirsu (n 56) 75; Fenwick, *Fenwick on Civil Liberties and Human Rights* (n 1649) 1060; Walker, *Blackstone's Guide to the Anti-Terrorism Legislation* (n 1670) 63.

1884 *Barr v. Public Prosecution Service* [2020] NICA 46, 36; Greenberg, 'Terrorist Offences' (n 1748) 2; Stone (n 1651) 445–446.

1885 *Pwr v. Director of Public Prosecutions, Akdogan and another v Director of Public Prosecutions* [2022] UKSC 2; *Rahman PWR, Ismail Akdogan, Rotinda Demir v. Director of Public Prosecutions* [2020] EWHC 798 (Admin); Fenwick, *Fenwick on Civil Liberties and Human Rights* (n 1649) 1060–1061; Jonathan Hall, 'The Terrorism Acts in 2021' (2021) Report of the Independent Reviewer of Terrorism Legislation on the Operation of the Terrorism Acts 2000 and 2006, and the Terrorism Prevention and Investigation Measures Act 2011 para 3.22; Hall, 'The Terrorism Acts in 2020' (n 1692) para 3.3. See also: Greenberg, 'Terrorist Offences' (n 1748) 5–6; Hall, 'The Terrorism Acts in 2021' para 3.22. The case law relates to the offence of wearing uniform or insignia and not to the publication of images, but the Supreme Court stated that the same applies to the latter offence. See: Pwr v. Director of Public Prosecutions, Akdogan and another v. Director of Public Prosecutions [2022] UKSC 2, 49–50.

1886 *Pwr v. Director of Public Prosecutions, Akdogan and another v. Director of Public Prosecutions* [2022] UKSC 2, 35–58; *Rahman PWR, Ismail Akdogan, Rotinda Demir v. Director of Public Prosecutions* [2020] EWHC 798 (Admin), 48–61.

limited form of *mens rea*.[1887] They do not have to know of the importance of the item or its capacity to arouse the required suspicion.

380. Defence – No defence is provided for, but Fenwick draws the analogy with the s. 11 offence and the *Attorney General's Reference (No 4 of 2002)* case. In that case (see no. 369) the House of Lords reasoned that if a person who had not engaged in any blameworthy conduct could commit an offence under the Act, the presumption of innocence was infringed by requiring them to disprove a significant element of the offence. Under the wording of the offence, it would be possible to prosecute a person even if the organisation were not proscribed at the time they for example wore the uniform. In such a case the defendant would not have engaged in any blameworthy conduct. Therefore, as Fenwick points out, the section should be read as 'currently proscribed'.[1888]

b) S. 13 (1A): Publication of images

381. Actus reus – In 2019 another subsection was added which states that '*[a] person commits an offence if the person publishes an image of an item of clothing, or any other article, in such a way or in such circumstances as to arouse reasonable suspicion that the person is a member or supporter of a proscribed organisation.*'[1889] This refers to a still or moving image produced by any means.[1890] As an example, the government gave the publication of a picture taken in one's bedroom which included an IS flag.[1891]

382. No *mens rea* – Again no (explicit) *mens rea* is provided for. For this offence, it is hard to see how a person could inadvertently publish something, so the knowledge that the image was published could be assumed to be included in the term 'publish'.

c) Sentences

383. Summary offences – These offences are the only summary offences in the TA 2000. People committing these offences are liable on summary conviction to imprisonment for a term not exceeding six months, a fine not

---

1887 *Pwr v. Director of Public Prosecutions, Akdogan and another v. Director of Public Prosecutions* [2022] UKSC 2, 26; *Rahman PWR, Ismail Akdogan, Rotinda Demir v. Director of Public Prosecutions* [2020] EWHC 798 (Admin), 50.

1888 Fenwick, *Fenwick on Civil Liberties and Human Rights* (n 1649) 1061.

1889 S. 13 (1A) TA 2000.

1890 S. 13 (1B) TA 2000.

1891 Home Office, Counter-Terrorism And Border Security Bill: Explanatory Notes (Bill 219–EN, 2018) para 33.

exceeding level five on the standard scale (i.e. 5000 GBP),[1892] or both.[1893] These are the only terrorism offences *sensu lato* which are not eligble for a special sentence for offenders of particular concern. Community orders (see no. 342) are a possibility, as is a suspended sentence order (see no. 343). There appear to be no sentencing guidelines (yet) for these offences.[1894]

SUBSECTION IV. CRITICISM

384. Proscription – The procedure for proscription is criticised as giving the executive too much leeway in deciding on the proscription of organisations.[1895] This is a very valid point, especially considering the fact the executive also has the administrative track available to them, as TPIMs are imposed by the Home Secretary (see no. 513). In addition, Fenwick criticises the whole range of offences related to proscribed organisations as potentially violating the freedom of expression. They can seriously hamper the freedom to protest and assemble peacefully.[1896] It is easy to see how the offence of membership of a proscribed organisation and offences related to organising and addressing meetings limit the freedom of assembly. Freedom of assembly, as is the case for freedom of expression, is a right which can be limited under the ECHR.[1897] However, these limitations have to be prescribed by law, have a legitimate aim and be necessary in a democratic society. This first requirement also includes a reference to the quality of the law and legal certainty (see no. 75).[1898] The offences do include some vague terms such as 'professing to belong' and are very broad, which could lead to legal certainty issues. In a counter-terrorism context, several of the legitimate aims listed in the ECHR can be applicable, such as the prevention of crime or disorder and the protection of the rights of others. However, the main point of criticism can be levelled against the necessity in a democratic society. This criterion requires a pressing social need and proportionality to the legitimate aim.[1899] The nature and severity of the sanctions imposed are taken into account when assessing this proportionality, with criminal sanctions

1892 S. 122 SA 2020.

1893 S. 13 (3) TA 2000. See also: Walker, *Blackstone's Guide to the Anti-Terrorism Legislation* (n 1670) 63.

1894 Lee and Walker (n 1698) 327.

1895 Fenwick, *Fenwick on Civil Liberties and Human Rights* (n 1649) 1051–1052; Macdonald and Carlile (n 1626) 130.

1896 Fenwick, *Fenwick on Civil Liberties and Human Rights* (n 1649) 1062–1063. See also: Macdonald and Carlile (n 1626) 129.

1897 Art. 10 and 11 ECHR.

1898 See e.g.: *N.F. v. Italy* App no 37119/97 (ECtHR 2 August 2001) 26 and 29; *Djavit An v. Turkey* App no 20652/92 (ECtHR 20 February 2003) 65; *Kudrevičius and others v. Lithuania* App no 37553/05 (ECtHR Grand Chamber 15 October 2015) 108–110.

1899 *Kudrevičius and others v. Lithuania* App no 37553/05 (ECtHR Grand Chamber 15 October 2015) 142–146.

requiring particular justification.[1900] In light of this, the sentences for the membership and support offences, with a maximum of 14 years imprisonment are extremely high. Especially considering these are offences of strict liability or where recklessness suffices.[1901] Therefore, the questions on their compatibility with the abovementioned Articles of the ECHR seem justified.

385. Criticism of human rights organisations on new offences – The offence of expressing supportive opinions was criticised by Liberty and Article 19 as being in violation of the freedom of speech.[1902] Liberty argued that this was the case because of both the broadening of the *actus reus* to cover mere expression, without even clarifying what this constitutes, and the *mens rea* to recklessness.[1903] Article 19 stated that the term 'support' and the offence in general were too wide.[1904] Walker argues that the offence overlaps to a considerable degree with s. 1 and 2 of the TA 2006 (see nos 447–462) and is too close to thought crime.[1905] The Home Office, however, stated that the offence does not violate the ECHR as it is necessary in a democratic society, for among other aims, the protection of national security and public safety.[1906] This may well be the case, but as discussed in the previous paragraph regarding Article 11 ECHR, the freedom of expression also requires the lawfulness of the interference and its proportionality.[1907] This means that the Home Office's response only covered one part of the equation and was therefore lacking. The introduction of the offence of publishing images was also criticised by Liberty and Article 19 for having a potential chilling effect on journalists and researchers and allowing for criminalisation of conduct not intended to incite criminality.[1908] Walker

1900 *Rai and Evans v. United Kingdom* App nos 26258/07 and 26255/07 (ECtHR decision on admissibility 17 November 2009); *Kudrevičius and others v. Lithuania* App no 37553/05 (ECtHR Grand Chamber 15 October 2015) 146; *Ekrem Can and others v. Turkey* App no 10613/10 (ECtHR 5 September 2022) 89–92.

1901 Note that the uniform and publication of images offences also have limited *mens rea*, but as their sentences are relatively low, proportionality is less of an issue.

1902 Art. 19, *House of Commons Public Bill Committee – Counter-Terrorism and Border Security Bill 2018: ARTICLE 19 written evidence* (2018) para 4–8; Liberty's Briefing on the Counter-Terrorism and Border Security Bill for Second Reading in the House of Lords (October 2018) 4–6.

1903 Liberty's Briefing on the Counter-Terrorism and Border Security Bill for Second Reading in the House of Lords (October 2018) 5.

1904 Art. 19, House of Commons Public Bill Committee – Counter-Terrorism and Border Security Bill 2018: ARTICLE 19 written evidence (2018) para 5–7.

1905 Clive Walker, Written evidence (CBS001) in response to the Joint Committee for Human Rights' call for evidence in connection with the Counter Terrorism & Border Security Bill 2017–19 (2018) 2–3.

1906 Home Office, Counter-Terrorism And Border Security Bill: ECHR Memorandum (2018) para 8–19.

1907 See e.g.: *Stoll v. Switzerland* App no 69698/01 (ECtHR Grand Chamber 10 December 2007) 48–112; *Morice v. France* App no 29369/10 (ECtHR Grand Chamber 23 April 2015) 124–127; *Perinçek v. Switzerland* App no 27510/08 (ECtHR Grand Chamber 15 October 2015) 125–197.

1908 Liberty's Briefing on the Counter-Terrorism and Border Security Bill for Second Reading in the House of Lords (October 2018) 6–8; Art. 19, *House of Commons Public Bill Committee – Counter-Terrorism and Border Security Bill 2018: ARTICLE 19 written evidence* (2018) para 9–10.

on the other hand doubts its added value.[1909] The government stated the belief that the offence did not violate the ECHR.[1910] This remains to be seen as the offence is in fact very broad both in its *actus reus* and its *mens rea*, which can raise legality issues. In terms of proportionality, it does appear to be significantly less problematic than the membership and support offences since the sentence is much lower.

SECTION V. OFFENCES RELATED TO TERRORIST PROPERTY

SUBSECTION I. TERRORIST PROPERTY

386. Definition – The TA 2000 defines terrorist property as follows[1911]:

(a) Money or other property which is likely to be used for the purposes of terrorism (including any resources of a proscribed organisation),
(b) proceeds of the commission of acts of terrorism, and
(c) proceeds of acts carried out for the purposes of terrorism.

In addition[1912]:

(a) a reference to proceeds of an act includes a reference to any property which wholly or partly, and directly or indirectly, represents the proceeds of the act (including payments or other rewards in connection with its commission), and
(b) the reference to an organisation's resources includes a reference to any money or other property which is applied or made available, or is to be applied or made available, for use by the organisation.

SUBSECTION II. OFFENCES

a) S. 15 TA 2000: Fund-raising

387. Actus reus – The TA 2000 defines three fund-raising offences.[1913] The *actus reus* of the first is inviting another to provide money or other property. The second covers receiving money or other property.[1914] The third consists of

[1909] Clive Walker, Written evidence (CBS001) in response to the Joint Committee for Human Rights' call for evidence in connection with the Counter Terrorism & Border Security Bill 2017–19 (2018) 3–4.
[1910] Home Office, Counter-Terrorism And Border Security Bill: ECHR Memorandum (2018) para 20–25.
[1911] S. 14 (1) TA 2000. See also: Conte (n 10) 231–232; Rowe (n 1670) 536.
[1912] S. 14 (2) TA 2000.
[1913] See also: Conte (n 10) 232.
[1914] S. 15 (2) TA 2000. See also: Walker, *Blackstone's Guide to the Anti-Terrorism Legislation* (n 1670) 69.

providing money or other property.[1915] The Act also explains that a reference to the provision of money or property refers to giving, lending or otherwise making available, regardless of consideration.[1916] Consideration is a concept of common law contract law entailing reciprocity. It requires that for a promise to be enforceable as a contract, the other party has to provide something in exchange (consideration).[1917] For the fundraising offences, no consideration is required.

388. *Mens rea* – The *mens rea* of the first two offences is that the person '*intends that it should be used, or has reasonable cause to suspect that it may be used, for the purposes of terrorism.*'[1918] With regards to the third offence, it is required that he '*knows or has reasonable cause to suspect that it will or may be used for the purposes of terrorism.*'[1919] Therefore, the *mens rea* of the offences is intent or reasonable (so not subjective) awareness.[1920]

b) S. 16 TA 2000: Use and possession

389. Actus reus and *mens rea* – In the next section, the TA 2000 criminalises use and possession. It states that '*a person commits an offence if he uses money or other property for the purposes of terrorism.*'[1921] or he '*possesses money or other property, and intends that it should be used, or has reasonable cause to suspect that it may be used, for the purposes of terrorism.*'[1922]

c) S. 17 TA 2000: Funding arrangements

390. Actus reus – The TA 2000 also states that '*[a] person commits an offence if he enters into or becomes concerned in an arrangement as a result of which money or other property is made available or is to be made available to another.*'[1923]

1915 S. 15 (3) TA 2000. See also: Walker, *Blackstone's Guide to the Anti-Terrorism Legislation* (n 1670) 69.
1916 S. 15 (4) TA 2000. See also: Walker, *Blackstone's Guide to the Anti-Terrorism Legislation* (n 1670) 69.
1917 Hugh Beale, *Chitty on Contracts* (34th edn, Sweet & Maxwell 2022) ch 6.2; Daniel Greenberg, 'Formation of Contract: Consideration' [2023] Westlaw UK paras 2–7.
1918 S. 15 (1) TA 2000. See also: Walker, *Blackstone's Guide to the Anti-Terrorism Legislation* (n 1670) 69.
1919 S. 15 (3) TA 2000. See also: Walker, *Blackstone's Guide to the Anti-Terrorism Legislation* (n 1670) 69.
1920 Walker, *Blackstone's Guide to the Anti-Terrorism Legislation* (n 1670) 69.
1921 S. 16 (1) TA 2000. See also: Walker, *Blackstone's Guide to the Anti-Terrorism Legislation* (n 1670) 69.
1922 S. 16 (2) TA 2000. See also: Conte (n 10) 232; Walker, *Blackstone's Guide to the Anti-Terrorism Legislation* (n 1670) 69.
1923 S. 17 TA 2000. See also: Conte (n 10) 232; Walker, *Blackstone's Guide to the Anti-Terrorism Legislation* (n 1670) 69.

391. *Mens rea* – The *mens rea* for this offence is knowledge or reasonable cause to suspect the money or property will or may be used for the purposes of terrorism. The question arose whether the phrase 'reasonable cause to suspect' meant the defendant actually suspected it and their suspicion was for reasonable cause or that the information they had, should have, assessed objectively, given them reasonable cause to suspect. The Supreme Court held unanimously that this latter interpretation was the correct one.[1924] This means that the offence can actually be committed without the convicted person knowing or suspecting that the money or property may be used for the purposes of terrorism. It suffices that '*on the information available to the accused, a reasonable person would (not might or could) suspect that the money might be used for terrorism.*'[1925] Laird points out that this approach can be very detrimental for people who due to psychiatric conditions cannot attain the standard of a reasonable person.[1926]

d) S. 18 TA 2000: Money laundering

392. Actus reus – Finally, the TA 2000 contains a specific money laundering offence.

> A person commits an offence if he enters into or becomes concerned in an arrangement which facilitates the retention or control by or on behalf of another person of terrorist property
> (a) by concealment,
> (b) by removal from the jurisdiction,
> (c) by transfer to nominees, or
> d) in any other way.[1927]

'Arrangements' can include concealment of the money.[1928]

393. *Mens rea* and Defence – Proving they did not know and had no reasonable cause to suspect that the arrangement related to terrorist property, is a defence.[1929] This is a reversal of the burden of proof, with it being a strict liability offence.[1930] However, in light of the right to a fair trial, the same reasoning as in

---

1924 *R v. Sally Lane and John Letts (AB and CD)* [2018] UKSC 36, 2018 WL 03368388, 6 and 25. See also: *Regina v. Salim Wakil* [2019] EWCA Crim 1351, 2019 WL 03457705, 6–7; Deborah Colbran Espanda, 'Sentence: New Cases: Particular Offences Terrorism' CLW/19/46/27; Karl Laird, 'Commentary: R v Lane (Sally)' [2019] Criminal Law Review 178, 180.

1925 *R v. Sally Lane and John Letts (AB and CD)* [2018] UKSC 36, 2018 WL 03368388, 24. Underlining by the UKSC.

1926 Laird (n 1924) 180.

1927 S. 18 (1) TA 2000. See also: Conte (n 10) 232.

1928 Walker, *Blackstone's Guide to the Anti-Terrorism Legislation* (n 1670) 69.

1929 S. 18 (2) TA 2000. See also: Walker, *Blackstone's Guide to the Anti-Terrorism Legislation* (n 1670) 69–70.

1930 Tadros, 'Justice and Terrorism' (n 46) 671; Walker, *Blackstone's Guide to the Anti-Terrorism Legislation* (n 1670) 69–70.

the *Attorney General's Reference (No 4 of 2002)* case could probably be applied, meaning the burden for this defence is an evidential burden only.[1931]

e) Sentences

394. Triable either-way – The sentence for these offences is a maximum imprisonment of 14 years, a fine or both. On summary conviction, it is imprisonment for a term not exceeding six months, a fine or both.[1932] Community orders (see no. 342) are also a possibility, as is a suspended sentence order, in situations where the Court finds a sentence of maximum two years appropriate (see no. 343).

395. Guidelines – The sentencing guidelines for the terrorist property offences are the following[1933]:

Culpability			
Harm	A	B	C
Category 1	**Starting point** 12 years' custody	**Starting point** 9 years' custody	**Starting point** 7 years' custody
	Category range 10–13 years' custody	**Category range** 8–10 years' custody	**Category range** 6–8 years' custody
Category 2	**Starting point** 9 years' custody	**Starting point** 7 years' custody	**Starting point** 4 years' custody
	Category range 8–10 years' custody	**Category range** 6–8 years' custody	**Category range** 2–5 years' custody
Category 3	**Starting point** 7 years' custody	**Starting point** 4 years' custody	**Starting point** 2 years' custody
	Category range 6–8 years' custody	**Category range** 2–5 years' custody	**Category range** High level community order – 3 years' custody

[1931] Fenwick, *Fenwick on Civil Liberties and Human Rights* (n 1649) 1069.
[1932] See also: Walker, *Blackstone's Guide to the Anti-Terrorism Legislation* (n 1670) 70.
[1933] www.sentencingcouncil.org.uk/.

f) Practical application

396. *Mens rea* AFFECTING SENTENCE – In the case of *Wakil*, a person was convicted for entering into a funding arrangement for the purposes of terrorism. The defendant had sent money via Western Union to a contact in Lebanon upon request of his sister who was in Syria with IS.[1934] The defendant himself did not share her beliefs but had been warned not to send money since that would be an offence. However, he did so anyway after requests from his sister who claimed to be unwell and hungry and in need of money to leave Syria, which she did not end up doing despite the money being sent. Medical evidence showed the defendant to be of low IQ and heightened suggestibility.[1935] The starting point in the sentencing guidelines for this case was four years (category 3B). The judge then took into account the failure to heed the given warnings and the defendant's mental health disorder and imposed a sentence of 30 months imprisonment.[1936] On appeal, however, this sentence was commuted to 20 months.[1937] The Court of Appeal noted that the defendant was within the lowest category of culpability of the offence. It pointed out there are three broad categories of *mens rea*: (1) the defendant knows the money will be or may be used for terrorism, (2) they actually suspect this for reasonable cause or (3) the information known to the defendant, objectively, gives reasonable cause to suspect this.[1938] Since the defendant was in the third category and taking into account his mental illness, the Court of Appeal found the sentence imposed in first instance excessive. This case shows that for offences such as this, with quite widely differing possibilities for the *mens rea*, while the perpetrators commit the same offence, the difference is taken into account when sentencing. This is important since in this case, the defendant did not even suspect the money would be used for terrorism.

397. REASON FOR REQUEST – In the *Mutegombwa* case a man had asked an undercover officer for 256 GBP to travel abroad and commit a suicide bombing attack.[1939] He was sentenced to ten years imprisonment. The low amount of money requested was offset by the degree of gravity for which it was requested.

g) Criticism

398. OBJECTIVE REASONABLENESS – Fenwick points out that the offences relating to terrorist property are broad and have the ability to draw in members

---

1934 *Regina v. Salim Wakil* [2019] EWCA Crim 1351, 2019 WL 03457705, 10.

1935 *Regina v. Salim Wakil* [2019] EWCA Crim 1351, 2019 WL 03457705, 19.

1936 *Regina v. Salim Wakil* [2019] EWCA Crim 1351, 2019 WL 03457705, 25–27.

1937 *Regina v. Salim Wakil* [2019] EWCA Crim 1351, 2019 WL 03457705, 35.

1938 *Regina v. Salim Wakil* [2019] EWCA Crim 1351, 2019 WL 03457705, 8.

1939 *R v. Mutegombwa* [2009] EWCA Crim 684 as described in The Court of Appeal Criminal Division, *Review of the Legal Year 2008 / 2009*, 5.8.

of the public who are only marginally related to terrorism activities.[1940] The main issue for these offences is the *mens rea*, which has the option of intent, but also of objective reasonableness. This inclusion of 'reasonable cause to suspect' has been criticised as it is very broad and does not require the person to actually suspect anything.[1941] This means a person who did not actually suspect the funds were going to be used for terrorist purposes, can still be convicted for a terrorist offence with a maximum penalty of 14 years imprisonment. As seen in the *Wakil* case (see no. 396), the courts take the level of *mens rea* into account in sentencing, but even so the final result in that case was a sentence of 20 months imprisonment. Espanda rightfully criticises this outcome, arguing that people who do not believe they are funding terrorism should not be subject to custodial sentences.[1942] This *mens rea* standard becomes extra problematic if you consider the broadness of some of the *actus rei* such as, for example, 'possessing money or other property'.

SECTION VI. TRAINING

SUBSECTION I. S. 54 TA 2000: PROVIDING OR RECEIVING WEAPONS TRAINING

399. Actus reus – Both providing and receiving instructions or training in the making or use of certain weapons are offences in the TA 2000.[1943] This is the case for instructions or training in the making or use of '*(a) firearms, (aa) radioactive material or weapons designed or adapted for the discharge of any radioactive material, (b) explosives, or (c) chemical, biological or nuclear weapons.*'[1944] Point (aa) was added to the TA 2000 by the ATCSA 2001.[1945] The legislation also defines 'biological weapon', 'chemical weapon' and 'radioactive material'.[1946] In addition, it is an offence to invite another to receive instruction or training, if this receipt would either be a terrorist offence as described in this paragraph or would be if it had taken place in the UK.[1947] The legislation further

---

1940 Fenwick, *Fenwick on Civil Liberties and Human Rights* (n 1649) 1069.

1941 Roach, *The 9/11 Effect: Comparative Counter-Terrorism* (n 79) 259; Tadros, 'Justice and Terrorism' (n 46) 671.

1942 Espanda (n 1924).

1943 See also: Conte (n 10) 232–233; Walker, *Blackstone's Guide to the Anti-Terrorism Legislation* (n 1670) 166.

1944 S. 54 (1) and (2) TA 2000. See also: Walker, *Blackstone's Guide to the Anti-Terrorism Legislation* (n 1670) 166.

1945 S. 120 ATCSA 2001. See also: Walker, *Blackstone's Guide to the Anti-Terrorism Legislation* (n 1670) 166.

1946 S. 55 TA 2000. See also: Walker, *Blackstone's Guide to the Anti-Terrorism Legislation* (n 1670) 166.

1947 S. 54 (3) TA 2000.

clarifies that providing instruction includes making it available generally or to (one or more) specific person(s) and likewise an invitation to receive instruction can be general or addressed to (one or more) specific person(s).[1948]

400. *Mens rea* – Again, no explicit *mens rea* is provided for, but it is difficult to see how one can provide or receive weapons training without knowing it. In addition, the defence provides some form of *mens rea*.

401. Defence – If the accused can prove that his involvement was '*wholly for a purpose other than assisting, preparing for or participating in terrorism*', this is a defence.[1949] The burden of proof for this defence is an evidential one.[1950] This defence means that the terrorist purpose must exist and is actually a form of *mens rea*, with the difference being the burden of proof.

SUBSECTION II. S. 6 TA 2006: PROVIDING OR RECEIVING TRAINING FOR TERRORISM

402. Actus reus – The TA 2006 added further training offences by criminalising both the providing and receiving of training for terrorism. In doing so, it assured the UK's compliance with the 2008 update to the EU Framework Decision well before the Framework Decision was created.[1951] The *actus reus* of these offences is providing or receiving instruction or training in any of the listed skills.[1952] These skills are:

(a) the making, handling or use of a noxious substance,[1953] or of substances of a description of such substances;
(b) the use of any method or technique for doing anything else that is capable of being done for the purposes of terrorism, in connection with the commission or preparation of an act of terrorism or Convention offence or in connection with assisting the commission or preparation by another of such an act or offence; and
(c) the design or adaptation for the purposes of terrorism, or in connection with the commission or preparation of an act of terrorism or Convention offence, of any method or technique for doing anything.[1954]

1948 S. 54 (4) TA 2000.
1949 S. 54 (5) TA 2000.
1950 S. 118 TA 2000. See also: Rowe (n 1670) 540–541.
1951 Spencer (n 1616) 121.
1952 S. 6 (1) (a) and (2) (a) TA 2006. See also: Conte (n 10) 240.
1953 For a definition, see: S. 6 (7) TA 2006.
1954 S. 6 (3) TA 2006. See also: Stone (n 1651) 464.

This summing up, especially part (b) was claimed to be too broad and therefore in violation of the legality principle. The Court of Appeal, however, conceded the wording was very broad, but not unclear.[1955]

403. *Mens rea* – The *mens rea* is respectively the knowledge these skills are intended or the intention to use the skills '*(i) for or in connection with the commission or preparation of acts of terrorism or Convention offences; or (ii) for assisting the commission or preparation by others of such acts or offences.*'[1956] It is irrelevant whether the training is provided generally or to (one or more) people in particular.[1957] However, the trainer has to know (at least) one of the trainees intends to use the skills for terrorism.[1958] Similarly, the assistance a person intends to provide to others can be to particular people or to people whose identity is not yet known.[1959] Finally, the intended acts can concern particular acts, or terrorism acts in general.[1960]

SUBSECTION III. S. 8 TA 2006: ATTENDANCE AT A PLACE USED FOR TERRORIST TRAINING

404. Actus reus – The *actus reus* of the third training offence is attending any place, in the UK or abroad, where instruction or training as defined in the TA 2000 (see no. 399) or TA 2006 (see no. 402) are provided[1961] wholly or partly for purposes connected with the commission or preparation of terrorist acts.[1962] Once again, the training or instruction can be provided for purposes connected to one or more particular acts of terrorism or terrorism generally.[1963]

405. *Mens rea* – The *mens rea* has two options: '*(a) he knows or believes that instruction or training is being provided there wholly or partly for purposes connected with the commission or preparation of acts of terrorism or Convention offences; or (b) a person attending at that place throughout the period of that person's attendance could not reasonably have failed to understand that instruction or training was being provided there wholly or partly for such*

1955 *R v. Kibley Da Costa, Muhammed Al-Figari, Kader Ahmed, Mohammed Hamid, Atilla Ahmet* [2009] EWCA Crim 482, 24.

1956 S. 6 (1) (b) and (2) (b) TA 2006. See also: Conte (n 10) 241.

1957 S. 6 (4) (a) TA 2006.

1958 *R v. Kibley Da Costa, Muhammed Al-Figari, Kader Ahmed, Mohammed Hamid, Atilla Ahmet* [2009] EWCA Crim 482. *Contra*: Greenberg, 'Terrorist Offences' (n 1748) 13.

1959 S. 6 (4) (c) TA 2006.

1960 S. 6 (4) (b) TA 2006.

1961 This includes instruction or training being made available. See: S. 8 (6) TA 2006.

1962 S. 8 (1) TA 2006. See also: Conte (n 10) 241; Helen Fenwick, 'Redefining the Role of TPIMs in Combatting "Home-Grown" Terrorism within the Widening Counter-Terror Framework' [2015] European human rights law review 41.

1963 S. 8 (3) (b) TA 2006.

purposes.'[1964] Contrary to the previous offence, for this offence it is not necessary that the provider of the training knew that at least one of those receiving it intended to use the skills for terrorist purposes.[1965] The person attending does not need to have the intention to put training into practice.[1966] More so, it is immaterial whether the person receives this training themself.[1967]

SUBSECTION IV. SENTENCES

406. TA 2000 – The TA 2000 weapons training offence is triable either way. People guilty of a weapons training offence can be sentenced to up to life imprisonment, a fine or both.[1968] This used to be ten years imprisonment, but was elevated to imprisonment for life in 2015.[1969] On summary conviction, they can be sentenced to imprisonment not exceeding six months, a fine or both.[1970] This is a serious terrorist offence, meaning that if the other conditions are met, courts have to impose a serious terrorist sentence (see no. 339). When this is not the case, the offence still is a specified offence for which an extended sentence is possible if the other conditions are met (see no. 340). Community orders (see no. 342) are also a possibility if the conditions for serious terrorist sentences or extended sentences are not met. A suspended sentence order is possible as well, in situations where the Court finds a sentence of maximum two years appropriate (see no. 343).

407. TA 2006 – Both training offences in the TA 2006 are triable either way. The sentence for the training offence is lifelong imprisonment, a fine or both on indictment.[1971] This used to be ten years imprisonment, but was significantly elevated to imprisonment for life in 2015.[1972] On summary conviction it is maximum 12 months imprisonment,[1973] a fine or both.[1974] The TA 2006 training offence is a serious terrorist offence as well, meaning that if the other conditions are met, courts have to impose a serious terrorism sentence (see no.

1964 S. 8 (2) TA 2006. See also: Conte (n 10) 241; Fenwick, *Fenwick on Civil Liberties and Human Rights* (n 1649) 1070; Roach, *The 9/11 Effect: Comparative Counter-Terrorism* (n 79) 300.

1965 The Court of Appeal Criminal Division, *Review of the Legal Year 2008 / 2009*, para 5.7.

1966 *R v. Kibley Da Costa, Muhammed Al-Figari, Kader Ahmed, Mohammed Hamid, Atilla Ahmet* [2009] EWCA Crim 482, 21.

1967 S. 8 (3) (a) TA 2006. See also: Conte (n 10) 241.

1968 S. 54 (6) (a) TA 2000. See also: Greenberg, 'Terrorist Offences' (n 1748) 9.

1969 S. 1 (2) Criminal Justice and Courts Act 2015 (CJCA 2015) See also: Lee and Walker (n 1698) 320.

1970 S. 54 (6) (b) TA 2000.

1971 S. 6 (5) (a) TA 2006.

1972 S. 1 (3) CJCA 2015. See also: Conte (n 10) 241; Lee and Walker (n 1698) 320.

1973 For Scotland and Northern Ireland, this is six months. See: S. 6 (5) (c) TA 2006. The same goes for offences committed before 2 May 2022 in England and Wales. See: S. 6 (6) TA 2006.

1974 S. 6 (5) (b) TA 2006.

339). The sentence for the attendance at a training camp offence on indictment is maximum 14 years imprisonment, a fine or both.[1975] This used to be ten years but was elevated in 2021.[1976] On summary conviction it is maximum 12 months imprisonment,[1977] a fine or both.[1978] Both offences are specified offences for which an extended sentence is possible if the other conditions are met (see no. 340). Community orders (see no. 342) are also a possibility if the conditions for serious terrorism sentences or extended sentences are not met. A suspended sentence order is possible as well, in situations where the Court finds a sentence of maximum two years appropriate (see no. 343).

408. Sentencing guidelines – There appear to be no sentencing guidelines (yet) for these offences.[1979]

SUBSECTION V. CRITICISM

409. Providing or receiving weapons training – Conte and Walker note that while this offence is part of the TA 2000, it is not limited in its application to the context of terrorism.[1980] In addition, in his review, Lord Lloyd noted that a pre-existing similar offence in Northern Ireland had never been prosecuted and he therefore recommended not including such an offence in the legislation.[1981] The government decided to include it anyway and to expand it to types of weapons not previously included being nuclear, chemical or biological weapons.[1982]

410. Attendance at a place used for terrorist training – Several authors criticise the *mens rea* for not requiring intent and allowing somebody to be convicted for this offence based on what amounts to negligence,[1983] which is problematic. The JCHR also considered the offence to be disproportionate.[1984]

1975 S. 8 (4) (a) TA 2006.

1976 S. 26 (2) CTSA 2021. See also: Azmeh (n 637) 12; Conte (n 10) 241; Kelly (n 1697) 645; Lee and Walker (n 1698) 323; Lee and Walker (n 1617) 885.

1977 For Scotland and Northern Ireland, this is six months. See: S. 8 (4) (c) TA 2006. The same goes for offences committed before 2 May 2022 in England and Wales. See: S. 8 (5) TA 2006.

1978 S. 8 (4) (b) TA 2006.

1979 Lee and Walker (n 1698) 327.

1980 Conte (n 10) 444; Walker, *Blackstone's Guide to the Anti-Terrorism Legislation* (n 1670) 167.

1981 Lord Lloyd of Berwick, *Inquiry into legislation against terrorism* (Cm 3420, 1996) 95. See also: Walker, *Blackstone's Guide to the Anti-Terrorism Legislation* (n 1670) 166.

1982 Secretary of State for the Home Department and Secretary of State for Northern Ireland, *Legislation Against Terrorism: A consultation paper* (Cm 4178, 1998) para 12.11–12.13.

1983 Roach, *The 9/11 Effect: Comparative Counter-Terrorism* (n 79) 300; Stone (n 1651) 464; Walker, 'The Impact of Contemporary Security Agendas Against Terrorism on the Substantive Criminal Law' (n 45) 130.

1984 JCHR, Counter–Terrorism Policy and Human Rights: Terrorism Bill and related matters (HL paper 75, HC paper 561, 2005) para 59.

411. Broadness and overlap – It is clear these offences are very broad and overlap to a substantial degree. The *actus reus* of the TA 2006 training offence includes training in '*any method or technique for doing anything else*' and in '*the design or adaptation [...] of any method or technique for doing anything.*' The offence is then narrowed down by the purpose of the training, but it is hard to imagine a broader description for an *actus reus*. This also means that any weapons training for terrorist purposes is covered by both training offences.

SECTION VII. DIRECTING A TERRORIST ORGANISATION

412. Offence separate from proscribed organisation – Directing the activities of an organisation which is concerned in the commission of acts of terrorism, at any level, is also a terrorist offence.[1985] This offence is not confined to the proscribed organisations. This was done because of the width of the power to proscribe. It was felt that directing organisations which were 'simply promoting or encouraging terrorism' should not be covered by the offence, while those organisations can be proscribed.[1986] Roach and Walker point out that this offence can be applied to directions which are in themselves lawful, including for example directing people not to commit a terrorist attack.[1987] Fenwick on the other hand makes the point that no actual action on behalf of the defendant is required, the offence consists of having their position in the organisation.[1988]

413. 2002 Framework Decision – Yet again, the UK legislation did not need to be changed to be in line with the 2002 EU Framework Decision. Both membership and leadership were already punishable with an adequately high sentence.[1989]

414. Sentence – The sentence provided is life imprisonment on indictment.[1990] The very high maximum sentence was criticised for potentially being out of line

1985 S. 56 (1) TA 2000. See also: Conte (n 10) 233; Roach, *The 9/11 Effect: Comparative Counter-Terrorism* (n 79) 260; Walker, *Blackstone's Guide to the Anti-Terrorism Legislation* (n 1670) 169.

1986 Hansard (House of Commons) Vol.187, 6 March 1991, cols 403 and 405. Note that this discussion applies to the pre-TA 2000 offence. However, the reasoning stands as the offence and the power to proscribe are worded very similarly. See also: Walker, *Blackstone's Guide to the Anti-Terrorism Legislation* (n 1670) 170.

1987 Roach, *The 9/11 Effect: Comparative Counter-Terrorism* (n 79) 260; Walker, *Blackstone's Guide to the Anti-Terrorism Legislation* (n 1670) 170.

1988 Fenwick, *Fenwick on Civil Liberties and Human Rights* (n 1649) 1068.

1989 Spencer (n 1616) 119–120.

1990 S. 56 (2) TA 2000.

with other precursor offences and devaluing the sentence for homicides.[1991] This is a serious terrorist offence, meaning that if the other conditions are met, courts have to impose a serious terrorism sentence (see no. 339). If this is not the case, it is still a specified offence for which an extended sentence is possible if the other conditions are met (see no. 340). Community orders (see no. 342) are also a possibility if the conditions for serious terrorism sentences or extended sentences are not met. A suspended sentence order is possible as well, in situations where the Court finds a sentence of maximum two years appropriate (see no. 343). There appear to be no sentencing guidelines (yet) for this offence.[1992]

SECTION VIII. POSSESSION FOR TERRORIST PURPOSES AND COLLECTION OF INFORMATION

SUBSECTION I. S. 57 TA 2000: POSSESSION

415. Actus reus – It is an offence to '*possess an article in circumstances which give rise to a reasonable suspicion that the possession is for a purpose connected with the commission, preparation or instigation of an act of terrorism.*'[1993] The legislation goes one step further still and defines two situations in which the accused is assumed to have possessed an article. These situations are when '*an article (a) was on any premises at the same time as the accused, or (b) was on premises of which the accused was the occupier or which he habitually used otherwise than as a member of the public.*'[1994] In order to rebut this assumption, the accused has to prove they did not know of the presence of the article on the premises or that they had no control over it. The Court of Appeal originally held that 'articles' could not include documents and records since that would make s. 58 (see nos 418–421) largely redundant.[1995] However, in a later landmark case it held that 'articles' can also include written material, which does create overlap with the offence in s. 58 but this line of reasoning was later confirmed by the House of Lords.[1996] The inclusion of offences like this (and s. 58) in the TA 2000

1991 Hansard (House of Commons) Vol.187, 6 March 1991, cols 401–406; Lee and Walker (n 1698) 318.

1992 Lee and Walker (n 1698) 327.

1993 S. 57 (1) TA 2000. See also: Conte (n 10) 233; Antje Du Bois-Pedain, 'Terrorist Possession Offences: Curiosity Kills the Cat?' (2009) 68 The Cambridge Law Journal 261, 261; Sugman Stubbs and Galli (n 25) 297; Walker, *Blackstone's Guide to the Anti-Terrorism Legislation* (n 1670) 171.

1994 S. 57 (3) TA 2000. See also: Walker, *Blackstone's Guide to the Anti-Terrorism Legislation* (n 1670) 171.

1995 *R v. M, Z, I, R, B* [2007] EWCA Crim 218, 2007 WL 261181, 36. See also: C.P.W., 'Commentary: R v Rowe' [2008] Criminal Law Review 72, 75–76.

1996 *Rowe v. R* [2007] EWCA Crim 635, [2007] QB 975. See also: *R v. G, R v. J* [2009] UKHL 13, [2010] 1 AC 43, 59; C.P.W (n 1995) 76–77; D.C.O., 'Commentary: R v G; R v J' [2009] Criminal

was suggested by Lord Lloyd of Berwick in his 1996 review.[1997] However, he gave a few very specific examples: all related to the possession of household materials which could be used to manufacture bombs.[1998] The eventual wording and application of s. 57 is much broader.

416. *Mens rea* – The offence requires reasonable suspicion of the purpose of the possession. Reasonable suspicion is a low threshold, so the offence does not require proof of the possessor actually having a terrorist purpose.[1999] The question arose what 'a purpose connected with the commission, preparation or instigation of an act of terrorism' actually means. The Court of Appeal held that a direct connection between the object and the act of terrorism is required. A correct interpretation is: '*reasonable suspicion that he intends it to be used for the purpose of the commission, preparation or instigation of an act of terrorism.*'[2000] This does narrow down the offence, but it is still quite broad. For example, the purpose of inciting somebody to commit terrorism is also included, as this is included in 'instigate'.[2001] In addition, the articles do not need to be possessed for the sole purpose of terrorism.[2002]

417. Defence – The legislation provides for the defence of proving '*that his possession of the article was not for a purpose connected with the commission, preparation or instigation of an act of terrorism.*'[2003] The burden on the defence is an evidential one only.[2004] Therefore, here as well, if the defence adduces evidence to the application of this defence, it is up to the prosecution to prove the defence is not satisfied.[2005]

Law Review 679, 683; Alistair Richardson and Alex Chalk, 'Possession of Terrorist Materials' [2014] Westlaw UK 3.

1997 Lord Lloyd of Berwick, *Inquiry into legislation against terrorism* (Cm 3420, 1996) 91–92.

1998 Lord Lloyd of Berwick, *Inquiry into legislation against terrorism* (Cm 3420, 1996) 91. See also: *R v. G, R v. J* [2009] UKHL 13, [2010] 1 AC 43, 41; Secretary of State for the Home Department and Secretary of State for Northern Ireland, *Legislation Against Terrorism: A consultation paper* (Cm 4178, 1998) para 12.3–12.4; Richardson and Chalk (n 1996) 2.

1999 Sugman Stubbs and Galli (n 25) 297; Walker, *Blackstone's Guide to the Anti-Terrorism Legislation* (n 1670) 171.

2000 *Aitzaz Zafar, Akbar Butt, Awaab Iqbal, Mohammed Raja, Usman Malik v. R* [2008] EWCA Crim 184, 2008 WL 370958, 29. See also: Richardson and Chalk (n 1996) 3; Stone (n 1651) 461.

2001 Aitzaz Zafar, Akbar Butt, Awaab Iqbal, Mohammed Raja, Usman Malik v. R [2008] EWCA Crim 184, 2008 WL 370958, 31.

2002 *R v. Altimimi* [2008] EWCA Crim 2829 as described in The Court of Appeal Criminal Division, *Review of the Legal Year 2008 / 2009*, para 5.2; Richardson and Chalk (n 1996) 3.

2003 S. 57 (2) TA 2000. See also: Du Bois-Pedain (n 1993) 261; Tadros, 'Justice and Terrorism' (n 46) 671; Walker, *Blackstone's Guide to the Anti-Terrorism Legislation* (n 1670) 171.

2004 S. 118 TA 2000; *R v. G, R v. J* [2009] UKHL 13, [2010] 1 AC 43, 63; Richardson and Chalk (n 1996) 3; Rowe (n 1670) 540–541; Walker, *Blackstone's Guide to the Anti-Terrorism Legislation* (n 1670) 173–174; Zedner, 'Terrorizing Criminal Law' (n 45) 115.

2005 *R v. G, R v. J* [2009] UKHL 13, [2010] 1 AC 43, 68; *The Queen v. AY* [2010] EWCA Crim 762, [2010] 1 WLR 2644, 4.

SUBSECTION II. S. 58 TA 2000: COLLECTION OF INFORMATION

418. Actus reus – The TA 2000 also states that

> a person commits an offence if
> (a) he collects or makes a record of information of a kind likely to be useful to a person committing or preparing an act of terrorism,
> (b) he possesses a document or record containing information of that kind, or
> (c) the person views, or otherwise accesses, by means of the internet a document or record containing information of that kind.[2006]

Contrary to the s. 57 offence, which focusses on the circumstances of the possession of the article, the s. 58 offence focusses on the nature of the information.[2007] Subsections (a) and (b) were present at the introduction of the legislation in 2000 while subsection (c) was added in 2019.[2008] In the original bill on this addition, the viewing needed to take place on three or more occasions, since the legislature wanted to target a certain 'pattern'.[2009] However, this 'three click' offence was deemed arbitrary and unworkable and therefore this part was deleted.[2010] In 2019 the legislature also clarified that subsection (a) includes collecting or making records by means of the internet, by downloading or otherwise.[2011] 'Record' includes photographs and electronic recordings.[2012] In order to 'view by means of the internet' it is not required that the person was in control of the computer.[2013] From the lack of paragraph equivalent to s. 57 (3), the House of Lords deduced that in order for the possession to be punishable under s. 58 the prosecution must prove beyond a reasonable doubt that the defendant knew they were in possession of the document and had control over

---

2006 S. 58 (1) TA 2000. See also: Conte (n 10) 233; Andrew Cornford, 'Terrorist Precursor Offences: Evaluating the Law in Practice' [2020] Criminal Law Review 663, 678; Du Bois-Pedain (n 1993) 361; Tadros, 'Justice and Terrorism' (n 46) 671.

2007 *R v. G, R v. J* [2009] UKHL 13, [2010] 1 AC 43; D.C.O. (n 1996) 683; Du Bois-Pedain (n 1993) 262.

2008 See also: Cornford (n 2006) 678; De Coensel, *Counter-Terrorism & Criminal Law: A Normative Legitimacy Test of Terrorism-Related Offences on Expression, Information and Movement* (n 1) 229.

2009 Home Office, *Counter-Terrorism And Border Security Bill: Explanatory Notes* (Bill 219–EN, 2018) para 37; Home Office, *Counter-Terrorism And Border Security Bill: ECHR Memorandum* (2018) para 29; Fenwick and Fenwick (n 56) 33.

2010 Liberty's Briefing on the Counter-Terrorism and Border Security Bill for Second Reading in the House of Lords (October 2018) 8; Art. 19, *House of Commons Public Bill Committee – Counter-Terrorism and Border Security Bill 2018: ARTICLE 19 written evidence* (2018) para 12; Hill (n 1666) para 3.19.

2011 S. 58 (1A) TA 2000.

2012 S. 58 (2) TA 2000. See also: Greenberg, 'Terrorist Offences' (n 1748) 10; Walker, *Blackstone's Guide to the Anti-Terrorism Legislation* (n 1670) 174.

2013 Home Office, Counter-Terrorism And Border Security Bill: Explanatory Notes (Bill 219–EN, 2018) para 37.

it.[2014] In addition, it must be proved they were aware of the kind of information, assuming the defendant did not deliberately fail to enquire about it in order to avoid the knowledge.[2015]

419. *Mens rea* – The *mens rea* of the offence used to be knowledge of the nature of the information.[2016] However, with the introduction of the defence that the defendant did not know and had no reason to believe the information was terrorist information (see no. 420), this seems to not be the case anymore. Therefore, this offence does not have a *mens rea* and is one of strict liability.[2017] The reasonable excuse provides for a weak form of *mens rea* instead.[2018]

420. Defence – A reasonable excuse for the action or possession is a defence.[2019] This reasonable excuse cannot be the legitimate resistance against a tyrannical government.[2020] Since 2019, the legislation gives two (non-exhaustive) examples of such an excuse: '*(a) at the time of the person's action or possession the person did not know, and had no reason to believe, that the document or record in question contained, or was likely to contain, information of a kind likely to be useful to a person committing or preparing an act of terrorism, or (b) the person's action or possession was for the purposes of – (i) carrying out work as a journalist, or (ii) academic research.*'[2021] The burden for this defence is an evidential one only.[2022] Originally, the Court of Appeal held in the *R v K* case that 'a reasonable excuse' simply meant possession for any other (i.e. non-terrorist) purpose, even if that purpose infringes some other legal provision.[2023] However, this view was overruled by the House of Lords in the *R*

2014 *R v. G, R v. J* [2009] UKHL 13, [2010] 1 AC 43, 46. See also: Lowe (n 1838) 61.

2015 *R v. G, R v. J* [2009] UKHL 13, [2010] 1 AC 43, 47.

2016 Cornford (n 2006) 678; Hale-Ross (n 1) 107.

2017 Fenwick, *Fenwick on Civil Liberties and Human Rights* (n 1649) 1074.

2018 *R v. Brown (Terence Roy)* [2011] EWCA Crim 2751, 2011 WL 5828783, 22; Liberty's Briefing on the Counter-Terrorism and Border Security Bill for Second Reading in the House of Lords (October 2018) 10.

2019 S. 58 (3) TA 2000. See also: Cornford (n 2006) 679; De Coensel, *Counter-Terrorism & Criminal Law: A Normative Legitimacy Test of Terrorism-Related Offences on Expression, Information and Movement* (n 1) 229; Du Bois-Pedain (n 1993) 261; Walker, *Blackstone's Guide to the Anti-Terrorism Legislation* (n 1670) 174.

2020 *R v. F* [2007] EWCA Crim 243, 2007 WL 434775; Tadros, 'Justice and Terrorism' (n 46) 675; Walker, 'The Impact of Contemporary Security Agendas Against Terrorism on the Substantive Criminal Law' (n 45) 137.

2021 S. 58 (3A) TA 2000. See also: Cornford (n 2006) 679. Before the introduction of this paragraph, commentators had expressed concern about the section's potential application (and chilling effect) on journalists and academics. See e.g.: Cram (n 1749) 242–243; Walker, *Blackstone's Guide to the Anti-Terrorism Legislation* (n 1670) 174–175.

2022 S. 118 TA 2000. See also: Fenwick, *Fenwick on Civil Liberties and Human Rights* (n 1649) 1074–1075; Hodgson and Tadros (n 611) 985; Rowe (n 1670) 540–541; Tadros, 'Justice and Terrorism' (n 46) 676–677; Walker, *Blackstone's Guide to the Anti-Terrorism Legislation* (n 1670) 174.

2023 *R v. K* [2008] EWCA Crim 185, [2008] Q.B. 827S, 15. See also: Andrew Cornford, 'Narrowing the Scope of Absurdly Broad Offences: The Case of Terrorist Possession' (2016) 38 Statute Law Review 286, 290; Cornford (n 2006) 684; D.C.O. (n 1996) 683; Du Bois-Pedain (n 1993) 261.

v G case (see no. 426). The House of Lords held that, contrary to the offence in s. 57, the excuse in s. 58 does not reference the purpose of the person, making it irrelevant. This means that the mere fact the defendant did not intend to commit an act of terrorism does not matter.[2024] The defendant must offer a good reason for the possession of the information which cannot be other criminal plans or mental illness.[2025] This narrow interpretation of the defence seems to be contrary to what Lord Lloyd had argued.[2026] Interestingly, the Court of Appeal in *R v K* had held that the offence did not violate the legality principle, if it was interpreted 'in accordance with that judgment',[2027] which is not completely the case anymore. An application was brought before the ECtHR to verify whether the interpretation of the reasonable excuse violated the legality principle under Article 7 ECHR. The ECtHR held that it did not.[2028] Similarly, the UK Court of Appeal had to decide whether the uncertainty deriving from the overruling of the Court of Appeal by the House of Lords resulted in a violation of the legality principle. It decided this was not the case.[2029]

421. Broadness – If read literally, the s. 58 offence is incredibly broad. Case law has stated that the information does not need to be useful only to a terrorist.[2030] Hodgson and Tadros point out that virtually any information of general use can be useful to a terrorist, who also needs to eat (cook books), clothe himself (washing machine instructions), etc.[2031] On this issue, the House of Lords stated that '*parliament cannot have intended to criminalise the possession of information of a kind which is useful to people for all sorts of everyday purposes and which many members of the public regularly obtain for use, simply because that information could also be useful to someone who was preparing an act of terrorism.*'[2032] It added that '*the information must, of its very nature, be designed to provide practical assistance to a person committing*

2024 *R v. G, R v. J* [2009] UKHL 13, [2010] 1 AC 43, 79; *Sultan Muhammed v. The Crown* [2010] EWCA Crim 227, 2010 WL 517086, 42. See also: Cornford (n 2023) 290; Cornford (n 2006) 679; D.C.O. (n 1996) 683; Du Bois-Pedain (n 1993) 262; Greenberg, 'Terrorist Offences' (n 1748) 11; Hall, 'The Terrorism Acts in 2020' (n 1692) para 7.27; Hodgson and Tadros (n 611) 991; Stone (n 1651) 462; Walker, 'The Impact of Contemporary Security Agendas Against Terrorism on the Substantive Criminal Law' (n 45) 137–138.

2025 Cornford (n 2006) 680–681.

2026 See also: Cornford (n 2023) 292; Hodgson and Tadros (n 611) 991.

2027 *R v. K* [2008] EWCA Crim 185, [2008] Q.B. 827S, 16.

2028 *Jobe v. United Kingdom* App no 48278/09 (ECtHR decision as to the admissibility 14 June 2011). See also: Lowe (n 1838) 61.

2029 *R v. Brown (Terence Roy)* [2011] EWCA Crim 2751, 2011 WL 5828783, 27–29.

2030 *R v. G, R v. J* [2009] UKHL 13, [2010] 1 AC 43, 43; *Sultan Muhammed v. The Crown* [2010] EWCA Crim 227, 2010 WL 517086; Richardson and Chalk (n 1996) 4.

2031 Hodgson and Tadros (n 611) 985; Cornford (n 2023) 287.

2032 *R v. G, R v. J* [2009] UKHL 13, [2010] 1 AC 43, 42. See also: Cornford (n 2023) 288–289; Cornford (n 2006) 679; Hodgson and Tadros (n 611) 986.

or preparing an act or terrorism.'[2033] This is in line with what Lord Lloyd stated in his Inquiry into Legislation against Terrorism, when he gave the example of targeting lists, and the government's response to his inquiry.[2034] However, it is not required that the information is useful to just terrorists.[2035] Hodgson and Tadros doubt that the first clarification will be applied strictly, especially since it seems to be contradicted by the second.[2036] They propose taking into account the ease with which the information can be obtained and the range of uses it might have.[2037] The explanation itself is not entirely clear, causing more confusion in the case law.[2038] The Court of Appeal stated it excludes information which is in everyday use by ordinary members of the public (e.g. train timetables), but does not exclude information which might be useful to anyone wishing to commit any offence (e.g. bomb making instructions to be used to blow a bank vault).[2039] Then again, in the *Amjad* case the s. 58 offence was held to cover the 'Mujahid minimum training', which was a hand written fitness regime even though a fitness regime is presumably also in everyday use by ordinary people (the only thing particular about it being the 'Mujahid' in the title).[2040] On the other hand, the Court has held that a document containing propaganda or theological material or simply encouraging terrorism is not included in this.[2041] Finally, extrinsic evidence cannot convert an item which does not fall within this definition into one that does.[2042] This is again a very broad offence, with Cornford even calling it 'absurdly broad',[2043] dependent on prosecutorial discretion to narrow it.[2044]

2033 *R v. G, R v. J* [2009] UKHL 13, [2010] 1 AC 43, 43. See also: Cornford (n 2006) 679; Hale-Ross (n 1) 107. For a practical application, see: *R v. Samina Hussain Malik* [2008] EWCA Crim 1450, 2008 WL 2311341.

2034 Lord Lloyd of Berwick, *Inquiry into legislation against terrorism* (Cm 3420, 1996) 92; Secretary of State for the Home Department and Secretary of State for Northern Ireland, *Legislation Against Terrorism: A consultation paper* (Cm 4178, 1998) para 12.4. See also: Hodgson and Tadros (n 611) 986.

2035 See also: Kajsa Dinesson, '(Un)Reasonable Excuses – On R v Dunleavy, R v Copeland, and Section 58' (2022) 85 Modern Law Review 1550, 1554.

2036 Hodgson and Tadros (n 611) 988.

2037 Hodgson and Tadros (n 611) 988–989.

2038 Cornford (n 2023) 189; Cornford (n 2006) 679–680.

2039 *Sultan Muhammed v. The Crown* [2010] EWCA Crim 227, 2010 WL 517086.

2040 *R v. Adeel Amjad* [2016] EWCA Crim 1618, 2016 WL 06397476. See also: Cornford (n 2006) 680; Fenwick and Fenwick (n 56) 31–32.

2041 *R v. Samina Hussain Malik* [2008] EWCA Crim 1450, 2008 WL 2311341, 9; *R v. K* [2008] EWCA Crim 185, [2008] Q.B. 827S, 13. See also: Hale-Ross (n 1) 107; Tanveer Qureshi, 'Preparation of Terrorist Acts' [2016] Westlaw UK 5, para 18.

2042 *R v. G, R v. J* [2009] UKHL 13, [2010] 1 AC 43, 44; *Sultan Muhammed v. The Crown* [2010] EWCA Crim 227, 2010 WL 517086, 39–40. See also: Hodgson and Tadros (n 611) 988.

2043 Cornford (n 2023) 287.

2044 Liberty's Briefing on the Counter-Terrorism and Border Security Bill for Second Reading in the House of Lords (October 2018) 9.

SUBSECTION III. SENTENCES

422. Triable either-way – People convicted of either of these offences are liable to conviction on indictment to imprisonment for maximum 15 years, a fine or both, or on summary conviction imprisonment for maximum six months, a fine or both.[2045] At the introduction of these offences in 2000, the maximum sentence was ten years imprisonment. However, this sentence was raised in respectively 2006 and 2019.[2046] In general, the sentences imposed for s. 58 seem to be lower than for s. 57, as also indicated by the sentencing guidelines.[2047] These offences are specified offences for which an extended sentence is possible if the other conditions are met (see no. 340). Community orders (see no. 342) are also a possibility but for the s. 57 offence they seem unlikely considering the sentencing guidelines (see no. 423). A suspended sentence order is possible as well, in situations where the Court finds a sentence of maximum two years appropriate (see no. 343).

423. Guidelines possession for terrorist purposes – The guidelines for the s. 57 offence are the following[2048]:

	Culpability		
Harm	A	B	C
Category 1	**Starting point** 12 years' custody	**Starting point** 7 years' custody	**Starting point** 4 years' custody
	Category range 9–14 years' custody	**Category range** 6–9 years' custody	**Category range** 3–6 years' custody
Category 2	**Starting point** 8 years' custody	**Starting point** 6 years' custody	**Starting point** 3 years' custody
	Category range 7–9 years' custody	**Category range** 4–7 years' custody	**Category range** 2–4 years' custody
Category 3	**Starting point** 6 years' custody	**Starting point** 4 years' custody	**Starting point** 2 years' custody
	Category range 4–7 years' custody	**Category range** 2–5 years' custody	**Category range** 1–3 years' custody

2045 S. 57 (4) and 58 (4) TA 2000.
2046 S. 13 TA 2006 and s. 7 (3) CTBSA 2019. See also: C.P.W. (n 1995) 78; Kelly (n 1697) 640; Lee and Walker (n 1698) 320; Sugman Stubbs and Galli (n 25) 297.
2047 Richardson and Chalk (n 1996) 5.
2048 www.sentencingcouncil.org.uk/.

424. Guidelines collection of terrorist information – The guidelines for the s. 58 offence are the following[2049]:

Culpability			
Harm	A	B	C
Category 1	**Starting point** 10 years' custody	**Starting point** 7 years' custody	**Starting point** 3 years' custody
	Category range 8–14 years' custody	**Category range** 5–9 years' custody	**Category range** 1–5 years' custody
Category 2	**Starting point** 7 years' custody	**Starting point** 4 years' custody	**Starting point** 1 year 6 months' custody
	Category range 5–9 years' custody	**Category range** 3–5 years' custody	**Category range** 6 months – 3 years' custody
Category 3	**Starting point** 5 years' custody	**Starting point** 3 years' custody	**Starting point** 1 year's custody
	Category range 3–6 years' custody	**Category range** 2–5 years' custody	**Category range** High level community order – 2 years' custody

SUBSECTION IV. PRACTICAL APPLICATION

425. Lower sentences for s. 58 – In the *R v Sultan Muhammed, Aabid Hassain Khan* case, the second defendant was convicted to 12 years imprisonment and the first to eight for the offence in s. 57.[2050] They were both found in possession of hard drives and CDs with large amounts of terrorist materials. The difference in sentence stemmed from the fact that the information showed the second defendant to be actively engaged in giving advice and in the recruitment of other more vulnerable people.[2051] In fact, in first instance the first defendant received a ten year sentence, which was found to be excessive on appeal because of this difference.[2052] For comparison, the first defendant

2049 www.sentencingcouncil.org.uk/.

2050 *R v. Sultan Muhammed, Aabid Hassain Khan* [2009] EWCA Crim 2653, 2009 WL 4666923.

2051 *R v. Sultan Muhammed, Aabid Hassain Khan* [2009] EWCA Crim 2653, 2009 WL 4666923, 8–15.

2052 *R v. Sultan Muhammed, Aabid Hassain Khan* [2009] EWCA Crim 2653, 2009 WL 4666923, 16–23.

was also convicted for the offence in s. 58, for which he received a (concurrent) sentence of two years imprisonment, which was brought down from four by the Court of Appeal.[2053]

426. Young offenders with psychological disorders – A striking line of case law deals with young men, often with psychological disorders. In the *R v G* case, an incarcerated young man who suffered from paranoid schizophrenia had gathered a variety of information, such as text books on explosives, a plan of an army centre and extremist materials. His illness made him think the guards were antagonising him and he claimed he had gathered the information to annoy the guards.[2054] The House of Lords did not deem this excuse to be reasonable and he was convicted anyway.[2055] In the *Dunleavy* case, a young man was found in possession of digital copies of books on firearms, explosives and military tactics as well as weapons.[2056] The defendant also visited extreme right wing online forums. He claimed all of it was done out of boyish curiosity, he just wanted to boast online about having the items and knowledge, and a psychologist had diagnosed him with high functioning autism spectrum disorder (ASD).[2057] The Court held that this was not a reasonable excuse.[2058] In the *John (Ben)* case, a 19 year old was convicted for the offence under s. 58 for the possession of a large quantity of extreme far right material in combination with the anarchist cookbook. The boy claimed he had downloaded the items between the ages of 12 and 14 and there was no evidence this was false.[2059] In the *Mansha* case a young man was arrested with the personal information, including the (old) address, of a UK soldier on his person. The police also found DVDs with Jihadist propaganda and other information on terrorist attacks, and a (non-functional, although attempts were made to make it functional) gun.[2060] At first instance the defendant was convicted to six years imprisonment. Despite the defendant's youth and low intelligence and educational level, this sentence was upheld on appeal.[2061] In the *Bel* case the defendant was a young man who was also diagnosed with autism.[2062] He frequented far right online forums and had expressed far right ideas online. In his room a

---

2053 *Sultan Muhammed v. The Crown* [2010] EWCA Crim 227, 2010 WL 517086, 50.

2054 *R v. G, R v. J* [2009] UKHL 13, [2010] 1 AC 43, 8–13. See also: Du Bois-Pedain (n 1993) 261; Hodgson and Tadros (n 611) 984.

2055 *R v. G, R v. J* [2009] UKHL 13, [2010] 1 AC 43, 87; Greenberg, 'Terrorist Offences' (n 1748) 11; Richardson and Chalk (n 1996) 5; Stone (n 1651) 462.

2056 *Paul Dunleavy v. R* [2021] EWCA Crim 39, 2021 WL 00202849, 8–16.

2057 *Paul Dunleavy v. R* [2021] EWCA Crim 39, 2021 WL 00202849, 13–18. See also: Dinesson (n 2035) 1551–1552.

2058 *Paul Dunleavy v. R* [2021] EWCA Crim 39, 2021 WL 00202849, 47–49. See also: Dinesson (n 2035) 1552.

2059 *R v. Ben John* [2022] EWCA Crim 54, 2022 WL 00286378, 3–4.

2060 *R v. Mansha* [2006] EWCA Crim 2051, 2006 WL 2629774, 2–5.

2061 *R v. Mansha* [2006] EWCA Crim 2051, 2006 WL 2629774, 11.

2062 *R v. Oliver Bel* [2021] EWCA Crim 1461, 2021 WL 04710515.

copy of the anarchist's cookbook was found, which he claimed he had out of academic interest. The defendant was convicted for s. 58 and sentenced to a special custodial sentence for an offender of particular concern of three years, being two years imprisonment and a one-year license period. The anarchist's cookbook is a document which often recurs in these types of cases but usually offenders have this in their possession together with other information or other items such as bomb making ingredients. It is striking in the *Bel* case that these additional elements were not present, and the conviction was based exclusively on the possession of the one book (freely available on Amazon).

427. Lawful object defence preferable? – In a case quite similar to *Dunleavy*, a boy diagnosed with ASD was found in possession of homemade explosives, manuals and videos on how to make them and videos of him experimenting with homemade explosives.[2063] He was prosecuted under s. 4 of the Explosive Substances Act 1883 (see no. 351) instead of s. 58. A key difference is that s. 4 provides for a defence of lawful object contrary to s. 58's reasonable excuse. The defence stated that because of his mental illness the boy had an obsessive interest in military things and an obsessive need to understand the workings of explosives. The Supreme Court held that personal experimentation or private education can be regarded as a lawful object, absent an ulterior unlawful purpose and the boy was acquitted.[2064] In a case note, Dinesson compares this case to the *Dunleavy* case and argues that the reasonable excuse defence under s. 58 is lacking in clarity.[2065] This is so because it is judged objectively, not taking into account for example mental illness, and it is left to the jury to decide on a case-by-case basis.[2066] Instead she argues for a lawful object defence similar to the one in s. 4 Explosive Substances Act 1883.

428. Information for defensive purposes – In the *R v AY* case, a Somali man was prosecuted for the offence under s. 58 for being in possession of the Mujahideen Terrorist Handbook, the Mujahideen Explosives Handbook, and videos of instructions on how to make explosive devices.[2067] He invoked the excuse that he had that material in the belief that the Somali people were the victims of unlawful and disproportionate force and needed to defend themselves.[2068] The Court explicitly rejected the idea of one side of the conflict being 'better' than the other.[2069] Accepting this would have put the idea that

2063 *R v. Copeland* [2020] UKSC 8, 4–8. See also: Dinesson (n 2035) 1553.
2064 *R v. Copeland* [2020] UKSC 8, 33–43. See also: Dinesson (n 2035) 1553.
2065 Dinesson (n 2035) 1556.
2066 Dinesson (n 2035) 1556–1558.
2067 *The Queen v. AY* [2010] EWCA Crim 762, [2010] 1 WLR 2644, 4.
2068 *The Queen v. AY* [2010] EWCA Crim 762, [2010] 1 WLR 2644, 7. See also: Hodgson and Tadros (n 1747) 505.
2069 *The Queen v. AY* [2010] EWCA Crim 762, [2010] 1 WLR 2644, 27.

terrorism can also target non-democratic states on uneven ground (see nos 345 and 420). As the Court in the *R v F* case also held, the goal of changing an allegedly undemocratic or illegal regime cannot serve as a reasonable excuse.[2070] However, the Court in the *R v AY* case held that if he could prove the information was to be used only for defensive purposes, it could constitute a reasonable excuse.[2071] Hodgson and Tadros criticise the Court's reasoning and argue that the distinction between defensive and offensive is impossible to make.[2072] They link this to the lack of exception for struggle against non-democratic governments in the definition of terrorism and conclude that the distinction between the two cases is arbitrary.[2073]

SUBSECTION V. CRITICISM

429. Broad offences – The two possession offences are among the most discussed, and criticised, of all terrorist offences. Both offences have been criticised for being overly broad and vague.[2074] De Coensel, for example, states that both offences are too broad and she specifically denounces the lack of intent requirement.[2075] Neither the offence of possession nor that of collecting information requires proof that the person actually has the intention to commit a terrorist act.[2076] In 2021, the independent reviewer noted that because of the wide availability of information on the internet, these offences are easier to commit than ever (especially s. 58 which does not require intent), calling upon prosecutors and police to be careful in their employment.[2077] Both offences indeed seem to be overly broad. The fact that the possession of one freely available book can lead to the commission of the s. 58 offence clearly shows this. The most obvious reason for this broadness can be found in the *mens rea*. Reasonable suspicion in s. 57 is a very low threshold and s. 58 even has no real *mens rea*. A defence cannot provide the same amount of protection as an actual *mens rea* as this partly reverses the burden of proof. In addition to this lack of

2070 *R v. F* [2007] EWCA Crim 243, 2007 WL 434775.

2071 *The Queen v. AY* [2010] EWCA Crim 762, [2010] 1 WLR 2644, 14 and 27. See also: *Rowe v. R* [2007] EWCA Crim 635, [2007] QB 975; Walker, 'Commentary: R v AY' (n 1752) 885.

2072 Hodgson and Tadros (n 1747) 505–506.

2073 Hodgson and Tadros (n 1747) 508.

2074 See e.g.: Du Bois-Pedain (n 1993) 263; Hale-Ross (n 1) 107. For s. 57, see: Tadros, 'Justice and Terrorism' (n 46) 671. For s. 58, see: Cornford (n 2006) 681–684; Dinesson (n 2035) 1550; Hodgson and Tadros (n 611) 984; Tadros, 'Justice and Terrorism' (n 46) 671.

2075 De Coensel, *Counter-Terrorism & Criminal Law: A Normative Legitimacy Test of Terrorism-Related Offences on Expression, Information and Movement* (n 1) 229. Hodgson and Tadros also recommend introducing some kind of fault requirement. See: Hodgson and Tadros (n 611) 995.

2076 Roach, *The 9/11 Effect: Comparative Counter-Terrorism* (n 79) 262.

2077 Hall, 'The Terrorism Acts in 2021' (n 1885) para 7.17–7.19.

proper *mens rea*, both offences have a very broad *actus reus* which overlaps, especially as s. 57 also can include written materials. All this does give a very wide margin of appreciation to prosecutors, police and courts, which violates the legality principle in our opinion (see no. 522 and following). For example, concerning the definition of purposes 'connected to' terrorism in s. 57 the courts narrowed down the offence through their interpretation, but this should not have been necessary as it is up to the legislature to create clear offences. Other parts of the offences are still not clear, such as for example the exact meaning of 'information likely to be useful'. Not only do both offences overlap with each other, but also with other offences (such as the preparation offence, see no. 463–467) or with the possibility of imposing a TPIM (see nos 511–519).

430. Criticism on online offence – The online variant of s. 58 was criticised extensively upon its introduction. In a submission on the amending clause which introduced the online offence, Max Hill, the then independent reviewer, and Clive Walker extensively criticised the offence, the same criticism was largely echoed by Liberty and Article 19. They questioned the clarity of the term 'viewing' and wondered whether a page would be considered viewed if merely appearing as a pop up spam advert, even if immediately closed; and what amount of a document would need to be viewed, especially in the case of those containing terrorist propaganda mixed with other types of information.[2078] More generally, they criticised the broadness of 'information likely to be useful' and would prefer a focus on information which directly encourages or facilitates terrorism.[2079] All this, argues Article 19, could lead to a chilling effect on journalists and researchers.[2080] Regarding the *mens rea*, they point out, the offence could be narrowed by specifying proof of intent to commit terrorism by the viewer.[2081] Originally, a *mens rea* of knowing or having reason to believe that the records contain terrorist material was

2078 Max Hill and Clive Walker, *Counter Terrorism And Border Security Bill: Submission In Relation To Clause 3* (2018) 2(d); Liberty's Briefing on the Counter-Terrorism and Border Security Bill for Second Reading in the House of Lords (October 2018) 9.

2079 Max Hill and Clive Walker, *Counter Terrorism And Border Security Bill: Submission In Relation To Clause 3* (2018) 4(a); Liberty's Briefing on the Counter-Terrorism and Border Security Bill for Second Reading in the House of Lords (October 2018) 9; Art. 19, *House of Commons Public Bill Committee – Counter-Terrorism and Border Security Bill 2018: ARTICLE 19 written evidence* (2018) para 13. See also: Clive Walker, *Written evidence (CBS001) in response to the Joint Committee for Human Rights' call for evidence in connection with the Counter Terrorism & Border Security Bill 2017–19* (2018) 7.

2080 Art. 19, House of Commons Public Bill Committee – Counter-Terrorism and Border Security Bill 2018: ARTICLE 19 written evidence (2018) para 12–13.

2081 Max Hill and Clive Walker, *Counter Terrorism And Border Security Bill: Submission In Relation To Clause 3* (2018) 4(b); Liberty's Briefing on the Counter-Terrorism and Border Security Bill for Second Reading in the House of Lords (October 2018) 12. See also: Clive Walker, *Written evidence (CBS001) in response to the Joint Committee for Human Rights' call for evidence in connection with the Counter Terrorism & Border Security Bill 2017–19* (2018) 7.

included in the bill. This was the case since the government acknowledged it is easier to inadvertently download material on the internet.[2082] However, as was the case for the other s. 58 offences, this *mens rea* was replaced by the reasonable excuse.

431. NARROWNESS OF THE S. 58 DEFENCE – The s. 58 reasonable excuse defence has also been criticised. Hodgson and Tadros criticise the House of Lords' approach to this defence, arguing that an explanation should suffice and that the House of Lords allows for terrorist convictions even it is clear the person had nothing to do with terrorism.[2083] Therefore, the offence is entirely reliant on prosecutorial and police discretion.[2084] In light of all this, Hodgson and Tadros argue that the offence is in fact in violation of the legality principle.[2085] Cornford also argues against the broad interpretation of the offence by the House of Lords and advances several arguments why a more narrow interpretation, such as the one of the Court of Appeal, would have been preferable.[2086] We fully agree with their arguments. The reasonable excuse defence is interpreted much too narrowly. The standard of reasonableness employed is an objective one, but a lot of people are not reasonable. This can easily be seen in the case law on young offenders suffering from mental illness. People might just be curious, and researching topics of interest should not be limited to academics and journalists. What constitutes a reasonable excuse is vague and unclear, which can be seen in the case law on the 'defensive purposes'. It is completely unclear what exactly 'defensive purposes' entail and how this is different from an exception for undemocratic regimes, which was explicitly rejected.

SECTION IX. INFORMATION ABOUT ACTS OF TERRORISM

SUBSECTION I. OFFENCE S.38B TA 2000

432. INTRODUCED IN 2001 – Even though the TA 2000 was still relatively new at the time, the ATCSA 2001 added another offence. It is striking that in

2082 Home Office, Counter-Terrorism And Border Security Bill: Explanatory Notes (Bill 219–EN, 2018) para 36; Home Office, Counter-Terrorism And Border Security Bill: ECHR Memorandum (2018) para 28.

2083 Hodgson and Tadros (n 611) 991–992.

2084 Cornford (n 2023) 290–291; Hodgson and Tadros (n 611) 992–993.

2085 Hodgson and Tadros (n 611) 993–995. For the same argument concerning the definition of terrorism, see: Hardy and Williams (n 608) 103.

2086 Cornford (n 2023) 291–294.

his review, Lord Lloyd had explicitly recommended that an offence such as this should not be included.[2087]

433. Actus reus – Since 2001 it is an offence not to disclose certain information to a constable as soon as reasonably practicable.[2088] This means that the offence can be committed through complete inactivity, or by providing only partial or false information.[2089]

434. *Mens rea* – This is the case for information '*which he knows or believes might be of material assistance (a) in preventing the commission by another person of an act of terrorism, or (b) in securing the apprehension, prosecution or conviction of another person, in the United Kingdom, for an offence involving the commission, preparation or instigation of an act of terrorism.*'[2090] Rumours or gossip are not covered by this.[2091] While option (a) may concern an act of terrorism abroad, option (b) does require some prospect of legal proceedings in the UK.[2092] In regards to option (b), Walker argues that based on case law on a pre-existing similar Northern Irish offence, proof that an actual terrorist offence had been committed was required.[2093] He adds that while this is not necessarily the case for option (a), it would be desirable to limit the offence as requiring that a terrorist offence was being committed or would have been committed, so as not to make the offence overly broad.[2094] The addition of 'belief' is only relevant

---

2087 Lord Lloyd of Berwick, *Inquiry into legislation against terrorism* (Cm 3420, 1996) 93–94. See also: Secretary of State for the Home Department and Secretary of State for Northern Ireland, *Legislation Against Terrorism: A consultation paper* (Cm 4178, 1998) para 12.5–12.7; Walker, *Blackstone's Guide to the Anti-Terrorism Legislation* (n 1670) 108; Clive Walker, 'Conscripting the Public in Terrorism Policing: Towards Safer Communities or a Police State?' [2010] Criminal Law Review 441, 443.

2088 S. 38B (2) and (3) TA 2000. See also: Julian Roberts, 'Sentencing Cases of Failure to Disclose Information about Acts of Terrorism (Terrorism Act 2000 (Section 38B)): A Plea in Mitigation' [2018] Sentencing News 9, 9; Walker, *Blackstone's Guide to the Anti-Terrorism Legislation* (n 1670) 108.

2089 Walker, 'Conscripting the Public in Terrorism Policing: Towards Safer Communities or a Police State?' (n 2087) 444.

2090 S. 38B (1) TA 2000. See also: Demirsu (n 56) 77; Roach, *The 9/11 Effect: Comparative Counter-Terrorism* (n 79) 268; Walker, *Blackstone's Guide to the Anti-Terrorism Legislation* (n 1670) 108–109; Walker, 'Conscripting the Public in Terrorism Policing: Towards Safer Communities or a Police State?' (n 2087) 443.

2091 Walker, 'Conscripting the Public in Terrorism Policing: Towards Safer Communities or a Police State?' (n 2087) 444.

2092 Walker, 'Conscripting the Public in Terrorism Policing: Towards Safer Communities or a Police State?' (n 2087) 444.

2093 Walker, 'Conscripting the Public in Terrorism Policing: Towards Safer Communities or a Police State?' (n 2087) 444.

2094 Walker, 'Conscripting the Public in Terrorism Policing: Towards Safer Communities or a Police State?' (n 2087) 444.

in cases where the offender believes their information to be relevant even though it may be immaterial or inaccurate.[2095]

435. Defence – Proving a reasonable excuse is a defence.[2096] Here as well, Fenwick argues that based on the House of Lords case law, it would be a human rights violation for the burden for the defence to be anything but an evidential burden only.[2097]

SUBSECTION II. SENTENCE

436. Triable either-way – The sentence for this offence is maximum ten years on indictment, a fine or both. This used to be five years but was doubled by the CTBSA 2019.[2098] On summary conviction the maximum sentence is six months, a fine or both.[2099] In determining the sentence (pre-guidelines), the Court of Appeal held that it is the seriousness of the terrorist activity to which the information related and not the extent of the information which is of importance.[2100] However, in the sentencing guidelines (see no. 437) the only factor determining the culpability, is the significance of the information.[2101] Because of the difficulties experienced by would-be offenders for example in terms of family relations or ambiguity of information, Roberts suggests paying special attention to pleas in mitigation in order to avoid disproportionate punishments.[2102] Community orders (see no. 342) are a possibility, as is a suspended sentence order, in situations where the Court finds a sentence of maximum two years appropriate (see no. 343).

437. Guidelines – The sentencing guidelines provide for the following categories[2103]:

2095 *R v. Sherif (Abdul)* [2008] EWCA Crim 2653, [2008] 11 WLUK 567; Walker, 'Conscripting the Public in Terrorism Policing: Towards Safer Communities or a Police State?' (n 2087) 444–445.

2096 S. 38B (4) TA 2000. See also: *Shiv Malik v. Manchester Crown Court, Chief Constable of Greater Manchester Police v. Constable and Robinson Ltd, Attorney General* [2008] EWHC 1362 (Admin), [2008] 4 All E.R. 403, 70; Greenberg, 'Terrorist Offences' (n 1748) 9; Walker, *Blackstone's Guide to the Anti-Terrorism Legislation* (n 1670) 109; Walker, 'Conscripting the Public in Terrorism Policing: Towards Safer Communities or a Police State?' (n 2087) 445.

2097 Fenwick, *Fenwick on Civil Liberties and Human Rights* (n 1649) 1074.

2098 S. 7 (2) CTBSA 2019. See also: Kelly (n 1697) 640; Lee and Walker (n 1698) 320.

2099 S. 38B (5) TA 2000.

2100 *R v. Sherif (Abdul)* [2008] EWCA Crim 2653, [2008] 11 WLUK 567, 45. See also: Greenberg, 'Terrorist Offences' (n 1748) 9; Walker, 'Conscripting the Public in Terrorism Policing: Towards Safer Communities or a Police State?' (n 2087) 450.

2101 www.sentencingcouncil.org.uk/offences/crown-court/item/failure-to-disclose-information-about-acts-of-terrorism/. See also: Roberts (n 2088) 10.

2102 Roberts (n 2088).

2103 www.sentencingcouncil.org.uk/.

Culpability			
Harm	A	B	C
Category 1	**Starting point** 7 years' custody	**Starting point** 5 years' custody	**Starting point** 2 years' custody
	Category range 6–9 years' custody	**Category range** 4–6 years' custody	**Category range** 6 months – 3 years' custody
Category 2	**Starting point** 4 years' custody	**Starting point** 2 years' custody	**Starting point** 1 years 6 months' custody
	Category range 3–5 years' custody	**Category range** 6 months – 3 years' custody	**Category range** High level community order – 2 years' custody

SUBSECTION III. PRACTICAL APPLICATION

438. Family – Case law shows that this offence is used to prosecute family members of terrorists.[2104] A close personal relationship cannot be a reasonable excuse.[2105] For example, in the *Chowdhury* case, a woman was convicted for this offence for not informing on her brother who was planning a terrorist attack. Her brother had used her bank account to buy training equipment and training swords and she participated in his knife stabbing practice.[2106] In the *Girma* case the wife of a man who had attempted to detonate explosives on London public transport (see no. 364) was convicted for this offence, together with her brother and sister.[2107] The three of them had helped the husband flee London after his bomb had failed to go off and helped him afterwards, without contacting the police even though they were after him. In addition, the wife had known of the impending attack (shortly) beforehand and had not contacted the police.

2104 Lord Lloyd of Berwick, *Inquiry into legislation against terrorism* (Cm 3420, 1996) 94; Roach, *The 9/11 Effect: Comparative Counter-Terrorism* (n 79) 268; Roberts (n 2088) 10; Walker, *Blackstone's Guide to the Anti-Terrorism Legislation* (n 1670) 110; Walker, 'Conscripting the Public in Terrorism Policing: Towards Safer Communities or a Police State?' (n 2087) 445–446.

2105 Walker, 'Conscripting the Public in Terrorism Policing: Towards Safer Communities or a Police State?' (n 2087) 445–446; Walker, 'The Impact of Contemporary Security Agendas Against Terrorism on the Substantive Criminal Law' (n 45) 140.

2106 *R v. Sneha Chowdhury* [2020] EWCA Crim 1421, 2020 WL 06565151.

2107 *R v. Yeshiembert Girma, Esayas Girma, Mulumebet Girma, Mohamed Kabashi* [2009] EWCA Crim 912.

SUBSECTION IV. CRITICISM

439. Broad and unclear scope – Fenwick points out that since the definition of terrorism is very broad, this offence is also very broad and can easily target spouses or children of, for example, activists who might fall under the definition of terrorism.[2108] Walker adds to this that due to the broadness of the definition, a person could be unaware that their knowledge could be considered relevant and thus unwittingly commit the offence.[2109] However, since the offence calls for the person to know or believe it, we do not think its application in this respect stretches quite as far as feared. However, the offence does raise several issues. It can lead to mistrust and strained relationships within families and communities. In addition, it can cause problems in terms of privileged information, the privilege against self-incrimination, and problems for journalists.[2110] They may have to produce journalistic materials for investigations or can be scared off from investigating certain topics,[2111] which can lead to less public debate.[2112] In some of these situations, the reasonable excuse defence could be used, but there is much uncertainty on these matters. If a lawyer argues that they did not disclose certain information because it was privileged; or a journalist refrains from doing so because the information was obtained from a journalistic source they want to protect, this would in our opinion be covered by the reasonable excuse defence. However, as there is no legislation or case law explicitly confirming this point, there is no certainty, which may lead specific information to be disclosed out of fear for prosecution even though there are good reasons not to disclose it.

SECTION X. ELICITING, PUBLISHING OR COMMUNICATING INFORMATION ABOUT MEMBERS OF ARMED FORCES

SUBSECTION I. OFFENCE S. 58A TA 2000

440. Constitutive elements. – In 2008, yet another offence was introduced into the TA 2000. Since then it is also an offence to

2108 Fenwick, 'The Anti-Terrorism, Crime and Security Act 2001' (n 92) 726.

2109 Walker, 'Conscripting the Public in Terrorism Policing: Towards Safer Communities or a Police State?' (n 2087) 443–444.

2110 Walker, 'Conscripting the Public in Terrorism Policing: Towards Safer Communities or a Police State?' (n 2087) 446–450.

2111 Fenwick, *Fenwick on Civil Liberties and Human Rights* (n 1649) 1073. See e.g.: *Shiv Malik v. Manchester Crown Court, Chief Constable of Greater Manchester Police v. Constable and Robinson Ltd, Attorney General* [2008] EWHC 1362 (Admin), [2008] 4 All E.R. 403.

2112 Cram (n 1749) 339–340; Greenberg, 'Terrorist Offences' (n 1748) 8; Walker, *Blackstone's Guide to the Anti-Terrorism Legislation* (n 1670) 116; Walker, 'Conscripting the Public in Terrorism Policing: Towards Safer Communities or a Police State?' (n 2087) 449–450.

(a) elicit or attempt to elicit information about an individual who is or has been
  (i) a member of Her Majesty's forces,
  (ii) a member of any of the intelligence services, or
  (iii) a constable, which is of a kind likely to be useful to a person committing or preparing an act of terrorism, or
(b) publish or communicate any such information.[2113]

Here as well, a reasonable excuse is a defence,[2114] but the legislation does not provide examples. The term 'intelligence services' means the Security Service, the Secret Intelligence Service and GCHQ.[2115]

SUBSECTION II. SENTENCE

441. Triable either-way – On indictment the sentence is imprisonment not exceeding 15 years, a fine or both.[2116] Here as well, this was originally ten years but was raised in 2019.[2117] On summary conviction the sentence is imprisonment of maximum 12 months,[2118] a fine or both.[2119] This offence is a specified offence for which an extended sentence is possible if the other conditions are met (see no. 340). Community orders (see no. 342) are also a possibility if the conditions for extended sentences are not met. A suspended sentence order is possible as well, in situations where the Court finds a sentence of maximum two years appropriate (see no. 343).

442. Sentencing guidelines – There appear to be no sentencing guidelines (yet) for these offences.[2120]

SECTION XI. DESIGNATED AREA OFFENCE

SUBSECTION I. OFFENCE S. 58B TA 2000

443. Designated areas – The CTBSA 2019 also added a new offence to the TA 2000, that of entering or remaining in a designated area. For this offence, the Secretary of State can designate an area outside the UK if they are '*satisfied that it is necessary, for the purpose of protecting members of the public from a risk*

2113 S. 58A (1) TA 2000. See also: Demirsu (n 56) 87.
2114 S. 58A (2) TA 2000.
2115 S. 58A (4) TA 2000.
2116 S. 58A (3) (a) TA 2000.
2117 See also: Kelly (n 1697) 640.
2118 This is six months for Northern Ireland. See: S. 58A (3) (b) (ii) TA 2000.
2119 S. 58A (3) (b) (i) TA 2000.
2120 Lee and Walker (n 1698) 327.

of terrorism, to restrict United Kingdom nationals and United Kingdom residents from entering, or remaining in, the area.'[2121] 'The public' is not limited to the UK public.[2122] The Secretary of State must keep under review whether the conditions continue to be met and after three years the regulation for a specific area ceases to have effect.[2123] This does not prevent the making of new regulations to the same or similar effect.[2124] This scrutiny by the Secretary themselves has been criticised as being insufficient.[2125] In 2021 no areas had been designated yet.[2126]

444. Entering or remaining – When an area has been designated so, it is an offence for any UK national or resident to enter it or remain there.[2127] A reasonable excuse can be a defence.[2128] People who are already traveling to or are already in the area when it is designated, have one month to leave the area.[2129] In addition, entering or remaining involuntarily or doing so for specific purposes is not an offence either.[2130] These purposes include, among others[2131]: providing humanitarian aid,[2132] carrying out work[2133] for another government or the UN and attending the funeral of a relative.[2134, 2135] But in order for this to not constitute an offence, the person must enter or remain in the area exclusively for these purposes.[2136]

2121 S. 58C (3) TA 2000. See also: De Coensel, *Counter-Terrorism & Criminal Law: A Normative Legitimacy Test of Terrorism-Related Offences on Expression, Information and Movement* (n 1) 260.
2122 S. 58C (1) and (2) TA 2000.
2123 S. 58C (4) and (5) TA 2000.
2124 S. 58C (6) TA 2000.
2125 Liberty's Briefing on the Counter-Terrorism and Border Security Bill for Second Reading in the House of Lords (October 2018) 12.
2126 Hall, 'The Terrorism Acts in 2021' (n 1885) para 7.10.
2127 S. 58B (1) TA 2000.
2128 S. 58B (2) TA 2000.
2129 S. 58B (3) TA 2000.
2130 S. 58B (4) TA 2000. See also: De Coensel, *Counter-Terrorism & Criminal Law: A Normative Legitimacy Test of Terrorism-Related Offences on Expression, Information and Movement* (n 1) 261.
2131 They are listed in the TA 2000. The Secretary of State can by regulation add or remove purposes. See: S. 58B (7) TA 2000.
2132 This '*does not include the provision of aid in contravention of internationally recognised principles and standards applicable to the provision of humanitarian aid.*' See: S. 58B (8) (a) TA 2000.
2133 This does '*not include the carrying out of any act which constitutes an offence in a part of the United Kingdom or would do so if the act occurred in a part of the United Kingdom.*' See: S. 58B (8) (b) TA 2000.
2134 Meaning '*a spouse or civil partner, brother, sister, ancestor or lineal descendant.*' See: S. 58B (10) TA 2000.
2135 S. 58B (5) TA 2000.
2136 S. 58B (6) TA 2000.

SUBSECTION II. SENTENCE

445. Indictable only offence – The sentence for entering or remaining in a designated area is imprisonment for maximum ten years, a fine or both, on indictment.[2137] This offence is a specified offence for which an extended sentence is possible if the other conditions are met (see no. 340). There appear to be no sentencing guidelines (yet) for these offences.[2138]

SUBSECTION III. CRITICISM

446. No added value – The introduction of this offence was criticised by Liberty. They argued that the UK already had so many terrorist offences that any wrongful conduct would already fall under (one or several of) these offences.[2139] Therefore, if the offence is needed to prosecute somebody who cannot be prosecuted for any other offence, it is incompatible with the presumption of innocence.[2140] In addition, the offence leads to a chilling effect on legitimate travel.[2141] Both of these are valid points and it is telling that so far no areas have been designated. As the Secretary of State already has the power to proscribe organisations, they could simply proscribe the most important organisations active in a certain area instead of designating that area itself.

SECTION XII. ENCOURAGING TERRORISM AND DISSEMINATION OF TERRORIST PUBLICATIONS

SUBSECTION I. S. 1 TA 2006: ENCOURAGEMENT OF TERRORISM

447. Actus reus – The first offence included in the TA 2006 is the encouragement of terrorism. According to the Act, encouragement is '*a statement that is likely to be understood by a reasonable person as a direct or indirect encouragement or other inducement, to some or all of the members of the public to whom it is published, to the commission, preparation or instigation of acts of terrorism or Convention offences.*'[2142] Convention offences are offences

2137 S. 58B (9) TA 2000.

2138 Lee and Walker (n 1698) 327.

2139 Liberty's Briefing on the Counter-Terrorism and Border Security Bill for Second Reading in the House of Lords (October 2018) 12–13.

2140 Liberty's Briefing on the Counter-Terrorism and Border Security Bill for Second Reading in the House of Lords (October 2018) 13.

2141 Liberty's Briefing on the Counter-Terrorism and Border Security Bill for Second Reading in the House of Lords (October 2018) 13.

2142 S. 1 (1) TA 2006. See also: Hale-Ross (n 1) 108–109.

defined in 12 counter-terrorism conventions related to explosives, chemical weapons, etc. while 'acts of terrorism' refers back to the TA 2000 definition (see nos 345–348).[2143] This definition was originally worded differently, but was amended by the CTBSA 2019.[2144] The original test was not that of the understanding of the 'reasonable person' but that of 'some or all of the members of the public to whom it is published'.[2145] This was changed out of worry that the original wording excluded statements directed at children or vulnerable people who would not understand the statement to be an encouragement.[2146] According to Walker, however, this rephrasing had little practical impact.[2147] The *actus reus* of the offence of encouraging terrorism consists of publishing or causing another to publish a statement as described above. A statement can also be a description and does not have to contain words, but can be solely sounds and/or images.[2148] 'Publishing' includes the provision of a statement via electronic means.[2149] Hunt points out that because of this, the offence also covers internet service providers.[2150] The legislation then lists two types of statements which are always covered, being statements which glorify the commission or preparation of such acts and statements which '*members of the public could reasonably be expected to infer that what is being glorified is being glorified as conduct that should be emulated by them in existing circumstances.*'[2151] In order to determine how a statement is likely to be understood and what members of the public could reasonably be expected to infer, regard must be had for the

2143 Adrian Hunt, 'Criminal Prohibitions on Direct and Indirect Encouragement of Terrorism' [2007] Criminal Law Review 441, 445–446.

2144 For the original wording, see also: Roach, *The 9/11 Effect: Comparative Counter-Terrorism* (n 79) 299; Zedner, 'Fixing the Future? The Pre-Emptive Turn in Criminal Justice' (n 23) 49.

2145 See e.g.: Hunt (n 2143) 441; Roach, 'Must We Trade Rights for Security? The Choice Between Smart, Harsh, or Proportionate Security Strategies in Canada and Britain' (n 1759) 288; Anneke Petzsche, 'The Penalization of Public Provocation to Commit a Terrorist Offence – Evaluating Different National Implementation Strategies of the International and European Legal Framework in Light of Freedom of Expression' (2017) 7 European Criminal Law Review 241, 247.

2146 Home Office, *Counter-Terrorism And Border Security Bill: Explanatory Notes* (Bill 219–EN, 2018) para 42; Fenwick and Fenwick (n 56) 33.

2147 Clive Walker, Written evidence (CBS001) in response to the Joint Committee for Human Rights' call for evidence in connection with the Counter Terrorism & Border Security Bill 2017–19 (2018) 8.

2148 S. 20 (6) TA 2006. See also: Conte (n 10) 643; Hall, 'The Terrorism Acts in 2021' (n 1885) para 7.34.

2149 S. 20 (4) TA 2006; Home Office, *Counter-Terrorism And Border Security Bill: Explanatory Notes (Bill 219–EN, 2018)* para 41; Conte (n 10) 643; Fenwick and Fenwick (n 56) 28; Hall, 'The Terrorism Acts in 2021' (n 1885) para 7.43; Hunt (n 2143) 444.

2150 Hunt (n 2143) 444.

2151 S. 1 (3) TA 2006; Conte (n 10) 643; Cram (n 1749) 343; De Coensel, 'Incitement to Terrorism' (n 1119) 283–284; De Coensel, *Counter-Terrorism & Criminal Law: A Normative Legitimacy Test of Terrorism-Related Offences on Expression, Information and Movement* (n 1) 208; Demirsu (n 56) 83; Hale-Ross (n 1) 110; Hunt (n 2143) 448; Stone (n 1651) 462–463; Zedner, 'Fixing the Future? The Pre-Emptive Turn in Criminal Justice' (n 23) 49.

contents of the statement and the circumstances and manner of publication.[2152] As was the case for the TA 2000, the TA 2006 states that glorification includes '*any form of praise or celebration, and cognate expressions.*'[2153] Hunt argues that beyond the inclusion of glorification, the definition of indirect incitement is not clear at all, since some form of indirect incitement is already covered by the general encouragement offence (see no. 451).[2154] In fact, he argues that it may be impossible to define it in a way which has added value and is still compatible with the ECHR. The encouragement can relate both to particular acts of terrorism as to acts of terrorism generally.[2155] Whether or not any person actually commits, prepares or instigates any such act is irrelevant is well.[2156] Nor is an imminent risk of terrorism required.[2157]

448. *Mens rea* – The *mens rea* of the offence is '*he – (i) intends members of the public to be directly or indirectly encouraged or otherwise induced by the statement to commit, prepare or instigate acts of terrorism or Convention offences; (ii) is reckless as to whether members of the public will be directly or indirectly encouraged or otherwise induced by the statement to commit, prepare or instigate such acts or offences.*'[2158] 'Members of the public' includes a meeting which is open to the public (even after payment), even if it takes place in a private setting.[2159] With this offence, the UK legislation complies with the 2008 EU Framework Decision, which requires the criminalisation of public provocation to commit a terrorist offence.[2160] The UK legislation even goes beyond the Framework Decision since mere recklessness suffices and no intent is required.[2161]

2152 S. 1 (4) TA 2006; Conte (n 10) 644; Cram (n 1749) 343; De Coensel, 'Incitement to Terrorism' (n 1119) 283–284; De Coensel, *Counter-Terrorism & Criminal Law: A Normative Legitimacy Test of Terrorism-Related Offences on Expression, Information and Movement* (n 1) 208; Hunt (n 2143) 448.

2153 S. 20 (2) TA 2006. See also: Hunt (n 2143) 448; Petzsche (n 2145) 248.

2154 Hunt (n 2143) 453–456.

2155 S. 1 (5) (a) TA 2006; Conte (n 10) 643; De Coensel, 'Incitement to Terrorism' (n 1119) 283–284; Hall, 'The Terrorism Acts in 2021' (n 1885) para 7.33.

2156 S. 1 (5) (b) TA 2006; Conte (n 10) 643; Cram (n 1749) 343; De Coensel, *Counter-Terrorism & Criminal Law: A Normative Legitimacy Test of Terrorism-Related Offences on Expression, Information and Movement* (n 1) 208.

2157 Roach, *The 9/11 Effect: Comparative Counter-Terrorism* (n 79) 299.

2158 S. 1 (2) TA 2006. See also: Conte (n 10) 240; De Coensel, 'Incitement to Terrorism' (n 1119) 284; Fenwick and Fenwick (n 56) 28; Hale-Ross (n 1) 109.

2159 S. 20 (3) TA 2006; Hall, 'The Terrorism Acts in 2021' (n 1885) para 7.35.

2160 Art. 3(2)(a) Council Framework Decision 2008/919/JHA of 28 November 2008 amending Framework Decision 2002/475/JHA on combating terrorism [2008] *OJ* 330/21. See also: Petzsche (n 2145) 245.

2161 Hunt (n 2143) 452–453; Petzsche (n 2145) 248; Spencer (n 1616) 121–122.

449. Defence – It is a defence to prove the statement did not express the views of the accused, nor was it endorsed by them, if this was clear in all the circumstances of the statement's publication.[2162]

450. Secondary participation – It is important to note that the UK criminal legislation contains several other ways of dealing with forms of incitement. First, secondary participation to an offence is possible. This means that when an offence is committed, not only the principal offender (the person actual carrying out the offence) is punishable, but also people who assist or encourage the offence.[2163] Note that as a general rule, the actual commission of the offence (or its attempt) is required for secondary participation to be possible.[2164] The statute states that anybody aiding, abetting, counselling or procuring the commission of any indictable offence is liable to be punished as a principal offender.[2165] These four actions (or omissions) overlap to a degree and can be used in combination.[2166] They can be briefly described as follows. Aiding is assisting, helping or giving material support (at the time of the offence); abetting is mainly encouraging in any form (at the time of the offence)[2167]; counselling is either giving advice or information or urging somebody to commit the offence (both of which overlap with one of the other three forms); procurement requires the secondary participant to induce or influence the principal to commit the offence.[2168, 2169] These actions must be connected to the commission of the offence and the secondary participant must intend to aid, abet, counsel or procure, meaning they know that acts and circumstances constituting an offence would exist and acted voluntarily.[2170]

2162 S. 1 (6) TA 2006; Conte (n 10) 644; De Coensel, *Counter-Terrorism & Criminal Law: A Normative Legitimacy Test of Terrorism-Related Offences on Expression, Information and Movement* (n 1) 208.

2163 *R v. Jogee, Ruddock v. The Queen (Jamaica)* [2016] UKSC 8, 1; Allen and Edwards (n 1618) 258–259; Dennis Baker, *Reinterpreting Criminal Complicity and Inchoate Participation Offences* (1st edn, Routledge 2016); Child and others (n 1630) 262; Elliott and Quinn (n 1627) 306; Herring (n 1627) 849; Loveless, Allen and Derry (n 1618) 184–226; Martin (n 1618) 58–60; Wilson (n 1630) 562.

2164 *Omar Scott v. DPP* [2022] EWHC 91 (Admin), [2022] 1 WLR 2231, 15; Child and others (n 1630) 285–286; Elliott and Quinn (n 1627) 307; Herring (n 1627) 849; Loveless, Allen and Derry (n 1618) 185; Martin (n 1618) 58.

2165 S. 8 Accessories and Abettors Act 1861. See also: Elliott and Quinn (n 1627) 306; Wilson (n 1630) 562.

2166 *Ferguson v. Weaving* [1951] 1 KB 814, 819; Child and others (n 1630) 265; Elliott and Quinn (n 1627) 308; Loveless, Allen and Derry (n 1618) 186; Wilson (n 1630) 564.

2167 *R v. Clarkson, R v. Carroll, R v. Dodd* [1971] 1 WLR 1402.

2168 *A-G's reference (no 1 of 1975)* [1975] QB 773, 779–780.

2169 Allen and Edwards (n 1618) 261–263; Child and others (n 1630) 265–267; Elliott and Quinn (n 1627) 308–309; Herring (n 1627) 849–852; Loveless, Allen and Derry (n 1618) 186–194; Martin (n 1618) 59–60; Wilson (n 1630) 564.

2170 *R v. Jogee, Ruddock v. The Queen (Jamaica)* [2016] UKSC 8, 10 and 15–17; Allen and Edwards (n 1618) 267–272; Child and others (n 1630) 270; Elliott and Quinn (n 1627) 310–312; Herring

451. General encouragement offence – Second, general offences of encouraging and assisting exists. These two, together with conspiracy and attempt (see nos 452 and 465) constitute the four inchoate offences in UK criminal law.[2171] These are independent offences which do not require the 'main' offence to be committed.[2172] There used to be a common law incitement offence but this was abolished in 2007.[2173] The same Act created the inchoate offence of encouraging or assisting offences. The Act introduced three offences with almost the same *actus reus*,[2174] being an act capable of encouraging or assisting the commission of an offence, but different *mens rea*. The *mens rea* options are: intent to encourage or assist, believing the offence will be committed and that the act will encourage or assist, or where the act is capable of encouraging or assisting the commission of one or more of a number of principal offences, believing that one or more of those offences will be committed and that their act will encourage or assist one or more of them.[2175] The maximum penalty is the same as for the anticipated offence (barring for murder where the mandatory life sentence becomes a discretionary one).[2176] For lack of definition, encouragement is defined based on the case law on the abolished common law incitement offence.[2177] This means that encouragement is some communication or gesture which might persuade, induce or influence another to commit an offence.[2178] Assistance is conduct which makes the substantive offence easier to be committed, which may

(n 1627) 859–863; Loveless, Allen and Derry (n 1618) 195–202; Martin (n 1618) 60; Wilson (n 1630) 571–578.

2171 Allen and Edwards (n 1618) 310; Child and others (n 1630) 326; Elliott and Quinn (n 1627) 277; Herring (n 1627) 782–783; Loveless, Allen and Derry (n 1618) 681; Martin (n 1618) 72; Wilson (n 1630) 510.

2172 Child and others (n 1630) 326; Elliott and Quinn (n 1627) 277; Herring (n 1627) 800. Specifically for encouragement, see: *Omar Scott v. DPP* [2022] EWHC 91 (Admin), [2022] 1 WLR 2231, 14.

2173 S. 59 Serious Crime Act 2007. See also: Allen and Edwards (n 1618) 310; Child and others (n 1630) 326–327; Elliott and Quinn (n 1627) 295; Herring (n 1627) 783; Loveless, Allen and Derry (n 1618) 709–710; Martin (n 1618) 72; David Ormerod and Rudi Fortson, 'Serious Crime Act 2007: The Part 2 Offences' [2009] Criminal Law Review 389, 389; John Spencer and Graham Virgo, 'Encouraging and Assisting Crime: Legislate in Haste, Repent at Leisure' [2008] Arch. News 7, 7. For the common law offence, see: *The King v. Higgins* (1801) 2 East 5, 102 ER 269.

2174 While the wording of the *actus reus* in the offences is the same, they are in practice not exactly the same since s. 49 (4) and (5) exclude certain offences from the *actus reus* of the s. 45 and 46 offences but not of the s. 44 offence. See also: Spencer and Virgo (n 2173) 7.

2175 S. 44–46 Serious Crime Act 2007. See also: Allen and Edwards (n 1618) 313–316; Baker (n 2163) 212–292; Child and others (n 1630) 327; Elliott and Quinn (n 1627) 295–297; Herring (n 1627) 801–806; Loveless, Allen and Derry (n 1618) 711–713; Martin (n 1618) 73; Ormerod and Fortson (n 2173) 389–390; Spencer and Virgo (n 2173) 7; Wilson (n 1630) 549–553.

2176 S. 58 Serious Crime Act 2007. See also: Child and others (n 1630) 327–328; Elliott and Quinn (n 1627) 298; Ormerod and Fortson (n 2173) 392.

2177 Elliott and Quinn (n 1627) 296; Loveless, Allen and Derry (n 1618) 713; Ormerod and Fortson (n 2173) 401.

2178 Child and others (n 1630) 328.

also be provided indirectly.[2179, 2180] The encouragement offences cover both public and private incitement, direct and indirect incitement[2181] and general incitement suffices.[2182, 2183] In addition, the *actus reus* is quite broad since the act needs to be 'capable' of encouraging or assisting, but no actual encouragement or assistance is required.[2184] Therefore, commentators argue the added value of the new terrorism encouragement offence is limited.[2185] Roach and Fenwick point out that several extremists had already been convicted for soliciting murder[2186] or racial hatred and thereby question the introduction of the specific encouragement offence.[2187] Hunt, however, argues that the encouragement offence does criminalise forms of incitement not previously covered, because of its reference to the vague definition of terrorism and coverage of general incitement.[2188] Roach also points to potential counter-productive effects of increased radicalisation of people who feel like the UK government does not understand or care about them.[2189]

452. Conspiracy – Third, the inchoate offence of conspiracy can be relevant in cases of encouragement. This offence is committed when people agree to pursue a course of conduct which, when carried out, will amount to the commission of an offence, or would do so if not for facts which render it impossible.[2190] There must be an agreement, in the sense that they have a common, shared design (without this necessarily requiring direct communication between all the participants).[2191] Conspiracy is to quite a large extent included in encouraging,

---

2179 S. 66 Serious Crime Act 2007.

2180 Child and others (n 1630) 329; Ormerod and Fortson (n 2173) 403.

2181 S. 66 Serious Crime Act 2007; Allen and Edwards (n 1618) 313.

2182 See e.g.: *The Queen v. Most* (1881) 7 QBD 244; *Invicta plastics Ltd and Another v. Clare* [1976] RTR 251; *R v. Michael David Marlow* [1997] Crim LR 897 (CA); *R v. Ian Anthony Jones* [2007] EWCA Crim 1118, [2008] QB 460, 14–16. See also: Elliott and Quinn (n 1627) 296. *Contra*: JCHR, *Counter-Terrorism Policy and Human Rights: Terrorism Bill and related matters* (HL paper 75, HC paper 561, 2005) para 21.

2183 Child and others (n 1630) 328–329; Spencer (n 1616) 121.

2184 Allen and Edwards (n 1618) 313; Child and others (n 1630) 327–328; Elliott and Quinn (n 1627) 296; Herring (n 1627) 801; Loveless, Allen and Derry (n 1618) 710; Ormerod and Fortson (n 2173) 391; Wilson (n 1630) 550.

2185 Cram (n 1749) 344.

2186 See e.g.: *R v. Abdullah Ibrahim El-Faisal* [2004] EWCA Crim 343, 2004 WL 229347; *R v. EL-Faisal* [2004] EWCA Crim 456, 2004 WL 413053. See also: JCHR, *Counter-Terrorism Policy and Human Rights: Terrorism Bill and related matters* (HL paper 75, HC paper 561, 2005) para 23–24.

2187 Fenwick, *Fenwick on Civil Liberties and Human Rights* (n 1649) 1076; Roach, *The 9/11 Effect: Comparative Counter-Terrorism* (n 79) 299. See e.g.: *R v. Abu Hamza* [2006] EWCA Crim 2918, 2006 WL 3390045.

2188 Hunt (n 2143).

2189 Roach, *The 9/11 Effect: Comparative Counter-Terrorism* (n 79) 300.

2190 S. 1 (1) Criminal Law Act 1977. See also: Allen and Edwards (n 1618) 319–333; Child and others (n 1630) 338; Elliott and Quinn (n 1627) 285; Herring (n 1627) 809–819; Loveless, Allen and Derry (n 1618) 696–705; Martin (n 1618) 74–75; Wilson (n 1630) 535–546.

2191 *R v. Ardalan and others* [1972] 1 W.L.R. 463, 468–469; *Subhash Mehta v. R* [2012] EWCA Crim 2824, 36; *Wayne Lee Shillam v. R* [2013] EWCA Crim 160, 18–19; Child and others (n

assisting or even attempt.[2192] It is, however, clear it could be applied to some situations which would fall under the encouragement of terrorism offences.

SUBSECTION II. S. 2 TA 2006: DISSEMINATION OF TERRORIST PUBLICATIONS

453. Actus reus – The *actus reus* of the offence of dissemination consists of a list of possible actions:

(a) distributing or circulating a terrorist publication;
(b) giving, selling or lending such a publication;
(c) offering such a publication for sale or loan;
(d) providing a service to others that enables them to obtain, read, listen to or look at such a publication, or to acquire it by means of a gift, sale or loan;
(e) transmitting the contents of such a publication electronically; or
(f) having such a publication in possession with a view to its becoming the subject of conduct falling within any of paragraphs (a) to (e).[2193]

According to the Courts 'with a view to' in subparagraph (f) should be read as 'with intent that'.[2194] A publication '*includes any article capable of storing data, or any record (permanent or otherwise) containing matter to be read, looked at, or listened to.*'[2195] An important question which then arises is what a terrorist publication is. The TA 2006 also provides a definition. A publication is a terrorist publication '*if matter contained in it is likely – (a) to be understood by a reasonable person as a direct or indirect encouragement or other inducement, to some or all of the persons to whom it is or may become available as a result of that conduct, to the commission, preparation or instigation of acts of terrorism; or (b) to be useful in the commission or preparation of such acts and to be understood, by some or all of those persons, as contained in the publication, or made available to them, wholly or mainly for the purpose of being so useful to them.*'[2196] Originally, subparagraph (a) was phrased differently, not focussing on the 'reasonable person' but instead stating: '*by some or all of the persons to*

1630) 339; Ian Dennis, 'The Rationale of Criminal Conspiracy' (1977) 93 The Law Quarterly review 39, 40; Elliott and Quinn (n 1627) 285–286; Herring (n 1627) 810–813; Loveless, Allen and Derry (n 1618) 697–699; Martin (n 1618) 74; Wilson (n 1630) 535–536.

2192 Child and others (n 1630) 353–354; Dennis (n 2191).

2193 S. 2 (2) TA 2006. See also: Cornford (n 2006) 671; Demirsu (n 56) 84.

2194 *Ahmed Raza Faraz v. R* [2012] EWCA Crim 2820, 49.

2195 S. 2 (13) and 20 (2) TA 2006; Conte (n 10) 644; Fenwick and Fenwick (n 56) 28.

2196 S. 2 (3) TA 2006. See also: Home Office, *Counter-Terrorism And Border Security Bill: Explanatory Notes (Bill 219-EN, 2018)* para 46; Conte (n 10) 240 and 644; Cornford (n 2006) 671; De Coensel, 'Incitement to Terrorism' (n 1119) 284; De Coensel, *Counter-Terrorism & Criminal Law: A Normative Legitimacy Test of Terrorism-Related Offences on Expression, Information and Movement* (n 1) 208–209; Hunt (n 2143) 443.

whom it is or may become available as a consequence of that conduct, as a direct or indirect encouragement or other inducement to them.' This was changed in 2019 to the 'reasonable person' test for the same reason as was the case for the encouragement offence (see no. 447).[2197] The fact that a publication has been found in the possession of people convicted for terrorist offences is relevant to the issue of whether some of them would understand the publication to be an encouragement to commit terrorist acts.[2198] However, this does not mean that fact can be considered as evidence that people who had read it were in fact encouraged to commit terrorist offences.[2199] According to the courts, 'likely' means 'probable' and a minimum requirement of indirect encouragement is that the publication encourages by 'necessary implication'.[2200] In practice, however, the offence seems to cover mere depictions or descriptions of terrorism, which Cornford convincingly argues is too wide an interpretation.[2201] The legislature further clarifies that a matter is likely to be understood by a reasonable person as indirect encouragement in case of glorification of the commission or preparation of terrorist acts and a person could reasonably be expected to infer that they should emulate this conduct.[2202] This specific variation of the offence is slightly more narrowly defined since it requires that the member of the audience themself might emulate the conduct and it must be possible in the present context.[2203] Whether or not a publication is terrorist in relation to particular conduct, must be determined at the time of the conduct and having regard to the contents of the publication and the circumstances of the conduct.[2204] As was the case for encouragement, it is irrelevant for the dissemination of terrorist publications whether they relate to the commission, preparation or instigation of particular acts of terrorism or acts of terrorism in general.[2205] The same goes for the question of whether the encouragement or inducement is successful.[2206]

2197 S. 5 (6) CTBSA 2019; Home Office, *Counter-Terrorism And Border Security Bill: Explanatory Notes* (Bill 219–EN, 2018) para 47.

2198 *Ahmed Raza Faraz v. R* [2012] EWCA Crim 2820, 43.

2199 *Ahmed Raza Faraz v. R* [2012] EWCA Crim 2820, 44.

2200 *Ahmed Raza Faraz v. R* [2012] EWCA Crim 2820, 49. Note, however, that when directing the jury, the judge does not have to replace these words. See: *R v. Ali (Humza)* [2018] EWCA Crim 547, [2018] 3 WLUK 454, 22.

2201 Cornford (n 2006) 672 and 677–678.

2202 S. 2 (4) TA 2006. See also: De Coensel, *Counter-Terrorism & Criminal Law: A Normative Legitimacy Test of Terrorism-Related Offences on Expression, Information and Movement* (n 1) 208–209; Fenwick, *Fenwick on Civil Liberties and Human Rights* (n 1649) 1077.

2203 Fenwick, *Fenwick on Civil Liberties and Human Rights* (n 1649) 1077.

2204 S. 2 (5) TA 2006.

2205 S. 2 (7) TA 2006. See also: *R v. Rahman (Abdul)* [2008] EWCA Crim 1465, Crim. L.R. 2008, 11, 906–908; De Coensel, *Counter-Terrorism & Criminal Law: A Normative Legitimacy Test of Terrorism-Related Offences on Expression, Information and Movement* (n 1) 208–209.

2206 S. 2 (8) TA 2006; *R v. Rahman (Abdul)* [2008] EWCA Crim 1465, Crim. L.R. 2008, 11, 906–908; Conte (n 10) 644; De Coensel, *Counter-Terrorism & Criminal Law: A Normative Legitimacy Test of Terrorism-Related Offences on Expression, Information and Movement* (n 1) 208–209; Fenwick, *Fenwick on Civil Liberties and Human Rights* (n 1649) 1077.

It is not even required that a person actually read the statement, nor that access to it was easy.[2207] Holding offensive views in itself is not an offence, the offence consists of the dissemination of publications.[2208]

454. *Mens rea* – The *mens rea* of the offence consists of three options:

(a) he intends an effect of his conduct to be a direct or indirect encouragement or other inducement to the commission, preparation or instigation of acts of terrorism;
(b) he intends an effect of his conduct to be the provision of assistance in the commission or preparation of such acts; or
(c) he is reckless as to whether his conduct has an effect mentioned in paragraph (a) or (b).[2209]

455. Defence – For this offence as well, it is a defence to prove the publication did not express the views of the accused, nor was it endorsed by them, if this was clear in all the circumstances of the conduct.[2210] This is only the case, however, if two conditions are met. First the conduct must be terrorist because matter contained in it is likely to be understood by a reasonable person as a direct or indirect encouragement or other inducement, to some or all of the persons to whom it is or may become available as a result of that conduct, to the commission, preparation or instigation of acts of terrorism. Second, the accused cannot have intended an effect of his conduct to be a direct or indirect encouragement or other inducement to the commission, preparation, or instigation of acts of terrorism.[2211] Cornford notes that this defence is not used in practice, perhaps because it is too difficult to prove all elements.[2212]

SUBSECTION III. SENTENCES

456. Triable either-way – The sentence for the offences in this Section on indictment is imprisonment of up to 15 years, a fine or both.[2213] This used to be

2207 Hall, 'The Terrorism Acts in 2021' (n 1885) para 7.44.

2208 *R v. Ali (Humza)* [2018] EWCA Crim 547, [2018] 3 WLUK 454, 17–20; Greenberg, 'Terrorist Offences' (n 1748) 12.

2209 S. 2 (1) TA 2006. See also: Cornford (n 2006) 672; De Coensel, 'Incitement to Terrorism' (n 1119) 284; De Coensel, *Counter-Terrorism & Criminal Law: A Normative Legitimacy Test of Terrorism-Related Offences on Expression, Information and Movement* (n 1) 208; Fenwick, *Fenwick on Civil Liberties and Human Rights* (n 1649) 1077.

2210 S. 2 (9) TA 2006. See also: Cornford (n 2006) 672; De Coensel, *Counter-Terrorism & Criminal Law: A Normative Legitimacy Test of Terrorism-Related Offences on Expression, Information and Movement* (n 1) 209.

2211 S. 2 (10) TA 2006.

2212 Cornford (n 2006) 676–677.

2213 S. 1 (7) (a) and 2 (11) (a) TA 2006.

seven years but was changed in 2019.[2214] On summary conviction the sentence is maximum 12 months[2215] imprisonment, a fine or both.[2216] These offences are specified offences for which an extended sentence is possible if the other conditions are met (see no. 340). Community orders (see no. 342) are also a possibility if the conditions for extended sentences are not met. A suspended sentence order is possible as well, in situations where the Court finds a sentence of maximum two years appropriate (see no. 343). The Court of Appeal pointed out that offences under s. 2 could vary widely in seriousness, as is reflected by the wide possible sentencing bracket.[2217]

457. Guidelines – The applicable sentencing guidelines provide for the following categories[2218]:

Culpability			
Harm	A	B	C
Category 1	**Starting point** 10 years' custody	**Starting point** 7 years' custody	**Starting point** 3 years' custody
	Category range 7–14 years' custody	**Category range** 4–9 years' custody	**Category range** 2–4 years' custody
Category 2	**Starting point** 7 years' custody	**Starting point** 4 years' custody	**Starting point** 2 years' custody
	Category range 4–9 years' custody	**Category range** 3–5 years' custody	**Category range** 1–3 years' custody
Category 3	**Starting point** 4 years' custody	**Starting point** 2 years' custody	**Starting point** 1 year's custody
	Category range 3–5 years' custody	**Category range** 1–3 years' custody	**Category range** High level community order – 2 years' custody

2214 S. 7 (6) and (7) CTBSA 2019. See also: Conte (n 10) 240; Kelly (n 1697) 640; Lee and Walker (n 1698) 320; Zedner, 'Fixing the Future? The Pre-Emptive Turn in Criminal Justice' (n 23) 49.

2215 Six months in Scotland and Northern Ireland. See: S. 1 (7) (c) and 2 (11) (c) TA 2006. The same is the case for offences committed in England or Wales before 2 May 2022. See: S. 1 (8) and 2 (12) TA 2006.

2216 S. 1 (7) (b) and 2 (11) (b) TA 2006.

2217 *R v. Rahman (Abdul)* [2008] EWCA Crim 1465, Crim. L.R. 2008, 11, 906–908.

2218 www.sentencingcouncil.org.uk/.

SUBSECTION IV. PRACTICAL APPLICATION

458. ENCOURAGEMENT – In the *Deghayes* case, a man gave a speech in a mosque for about 50 people, including young men and boys. In this speech he said things such as '*Jihad, jihad, jihad is compulsory. Jihad by fighting by sword means jihad is a compulsory obligation upon you.*'[2219] He was convicted for the encouragement of terrorism, based on recklessness rather than intent. The judge qualified the defendant under the old sentencing guidelines (before the raising of the maximum sentence for the offence) as category B2, with a starting point of three years and a range of two to four years imprisonment.[2220] The Court of Appeal, however, stated that the critical factor in terms of seriousness was '*the extent to which the chances of the statement or publication influencing the actions of an adherent to the cause were increased by the circumstances in which it was published.*'[2221] In this case the mosque was respectable and the audience was not selected for radicalism. On the other hand, the defendant did abuse a religious gathering and the audience contained young men and boys. All this considered, the Court of Appeal judged this to be a case of category C2. Therefore, his sentence was reduced from a special custodial sentence for offenders of particular concern of five years (including one year licence) to one of four years (including one year licence).

459. DISSEMINATING – In the *Hamza* case, a man was convicted for encouragement for posts on Facebook regarding terrorism in Bangladesh.[2222] He received a special custodial sentence of four years for an offender of particular concern, consisting of a three-year custodial term and a one year licence period. In the *Nugent* case, a man was convicted for both disseminating terrorist publications and collecting information likely to be useful to a terrorist. He had a large amount of material including instructions for making weapons and explosives and he was active in encouraging others online to take action in the context of right-wing extremism.[2223] The defendant had a history of mental illness which was made worse by the COVID crisis. When it came to sentencing, the Court of Appeal pointed out that right wing terrorist groups are not any less dangerous than other types of terrorism and no distinction should be made between different groups.[2224] It classified the offending as category A2 for the dissemination offence (and B2 for the collection offence). In first instance he was convicted to a special custodial sentence of 54 months (42 months custodial term and one year licence period). This sentence was raised on appeal to a special

[2219] *R v. Abubaker Deghayes* [2023] EWCA Crim 97, 2023 WL 02139667, 7–8.
[2220] *R v. Abubaker Deghayes* [2023] EWCA Crim 97, 2023 WL 02139667, 14.
[2221] *R v. Abubaker Deghayes* [2023] EWCA Crim 97, 2023 WL 02139667, 24.
[2222] *R v. Munna Hamza* [2021] EWCA Crim 1460, 2021 WL 04710555.
[2223] *R v. Michael Nugent* [2021] EWCA Crim 1535, 2021 WL 04950303, 11.
[2224] *R v. Michael Nugent* [2021] EWCA Crim 1535, 2021 WL 04950303, 26.

custodial sentence of six years (five years custodial term and one year licence period).[2225]

SUBSECTION V. CRITICISM

460. ENCOURAGEMENT – The scope of the encouragement offence is very broad.[2226] Article 19 argues that since this offence uses the broad definition of terrorism of the TA 2000 and combines it with broad terms such as 'inducement' or 'glorification', it violates the legality principle.[2227] This could lead to a chilling effect[2228] and potential marginalisation.[2229] Other commentators also criticise the inclusion of an imprecise term such as 'glorification'.[2230] Hunt adds his own similar criticism, but does nuance this by adding he does not believe this means the offence violates the legality principle.[2231] Ashworth and Zedner also point out that the offence is more widely defined than what is expected based on its justification which allows for criminalisation of people with little normative involvement in actual terrorism.[2232] Finally, the legislation does not require the intention to incite, which is said to violate free speech.[2233]

461. DISSEMINATION – The dissemination offence has been criticised for potentially violating free speech, including by the JCHR.[2234] The courts, however, have dismissed this argument.[2235] De Coensel criticises both this offence and the offence of encouragement of terrorism for being too broad both in terms of

2225 *R v. Michael Nugent* [2021] EWCA Crim 1535, 2021 WL 04950303, 37–38.

2226 Cram (n 1749) 344; Tadros, 'Justice and Terrorism' (n 46) 671; Zedner, 'Fixing the Future? The Pre-Emptive Turn in Criminal Justice' (n 23) 49.

2227 Art. 19, The Impact of UK Anti-Terror Laws on Freedom of Expression: Submission to ICJ Panel of Eminent Jurists on Terrorism, Counter-Terrorism and Human Rights, London, April 2006, 7–8.

2228 See also: Hunt (n 2143) 457–458; Petzsche (n 2145) 248; Stone (n 1651) 463.

2229 Art. 19, The Impact of UK Anti-Terror Laws on Freedom of Expression: Submission to ICJ Panel of Eminent Jurists on Terrorism, Counter-Terrorism and Human Rights, London, April 2006, 7.

2230 Amnesty International report, 'Dangerously disproportionate, the ever-expanding national security state in Europe' (2017) 42–43; Fenwick, *Fenwick on Civil Liberties and Human Rights* (n 1649) 1076; Petersen (n 12) 66; Petzsche (n 2145) 248.

2231 Hunt (n 2143) 449–452.

2232 Ashworth and Zedner (n 18) 113 and 180.

2233 Art. 19, The Impact of UK Anti-Terror Laws on Freedom of Expression: Submission to ICJ Panel of Eminent Jurists on Terrorism, Counter-Terrorism and Human Rights, London, April 2006, 8–9; Hunt (n 2143) 456–457.

2234 JCHR, *Counter-Terrorism Policy and Human Rights: Terrorism Bill and related matters* (HL paper 75, HC paper 561, 2005) para 34–37; Cram (n 1749) 344–347; Demirsu (n 56) 84; Fenwick, *Fenwick on Civil Liberties and Human Rights* (n 1649) 1078; Hale-Ross (n 1) 110–111; Stone (n 1651) 463.

2235 *R v. Brown (Terence Roy)* [2011] EWCA Crim 2751, 2011 WL 5828783, 23–24; *Ahmed Raza Faraz v. R* [2012] EWCA Crim 2820.

actus reus and *mens rea* (which is broader than the EU Directive requires).[2236] She, together with others,[2237] states that the standard of recklessness is too low, especially in cases of glorification where objective recklessness seems to suffice. The JCHR also advocated a threshold of intent and if it were to be recklessness, then subjective recklessness.[2238] In addition, the lack of risk requirement is also pointed out by several commentators.[2239] Hunt and Petzsche argue that the UK offence is likely to violate Article 10 ECHR.[2240] The UN Human Rights Committee (as well as the JCHR) also 'noted with concern' that the offence of encouragement was broad and vague and did not require intent.[2241] Conte, on the other hand argues that inclusion of recklessness is not as problematic as it seems at first glance. Recklessness does require proof of foresight of dangerous consequences and the intention to continue regardless. In addition, the legislation provides for a defence. For these two reasons he considers the offences to require adequate levels of unlawful and intentional behaviour.[2242] In his analysis of the dissemination offence in practice, Cornford concludes that the offence is applied very broadly due to the wide range of publications covered in combination with the fact that recklessness suffices.[2243] It covers conduct which creates little risk of encouraging terrorism and interferes with the freedom of speech and of religion. The offence risks creating a chilling effect while discussing controversial views that can have great value in free speech terms.

462. Broadness and lack of added value – Both offences are very broad. Recklessness suffices for both and no risk of the commission of the incited offence is required. The combination of this makes for broad offences which may violate the freedom of speech. Limitations to this right have to be proportionate (see no. 209) and the question can be asked whether a reckless encouragement or dissemination which creates no real risk that offences will be committed should be punishable, especially considering the high maximum penalty of 15 years imprisonment for these offences. Furthermore, the existence of a relatively broad inchoate encouragement offence also raises the question of the added

2236 De Coensel, 'Incitement to Terrorism' (n 1119) 290–291; De Coensel, *Counter-Terrorism & Criminal Law: A Normative Legitimacy Test of Terrorism-Related Offences on Expression, Information and Movement* (n 1) 209.

2237 Cornford (n 2006) 677; Demirsu (n 56) 85; Hunt (n 2143); Petzsche (n 2145) 247–248.

2238 JCHR, Counter-Terrorism Policy and Human Rights: Terrorism Bill and related matters (HL paper 75, HC paper 561, 2005) para 30–33 and 46–49.

2239 Demirsu (n 56) 85; Hunt (n 2143) 456–457; Petzsche (n 2145) 248.

2240 Hunt (n 2143) 456–457; Petzsche (n 2145) 255–256.

2241 United Nations Human Rights Committee (2008) Concluding Observations of the Human Rights Committee: United Kingdom of Great Britain and Northern Ireland, Ninety Third Session, 7–25 July, para 26; JCHR, Counter-Terrorism Policy and Human Rights: Terrorism Bill and related matters (HL paper 75, HC paper 561, 2005) para 34–37. See also: Fenwick, *Fenwick on Civil Liberties and Human Rights* (n 1649) 1078–1079.

2242 Conte (n 10) 647–648.

2243 Cornford (n 2006) 673–678.

value of these terrorist offences. Much of the conduct covered by the terrorist encouragement and dissemination offences will be covered by the general inchoate encouragement offence. This means that the terrorist offences will only have added value in those situations where the general encouragement offence is not applicable. Punishing those situations with sentences of up to 15 years imprisonment seems disproportionate, while the terrorist offences are of little added value in other situations as these situations were already punishable.

SECTION XIII. PREPARATION OF TERRORIST ACTS

SUBSECTION I. S. 5 TA 2006: PREPARATION

463. Actus reus – The TA 2006 also criminalises the preparation of a terrorist act. Interesting to note is that the government rejected the idea of introducing such an offence in the TA 2000 as was suggested by Lord Lloyd,[2244] but apparently changed its mind some years later. The offence covers any conduct in preparation for giving effect to the intention of committing an act of terrorism or assisting another in doing so.[2245] Once more, it is irrelevant whether this relates to particular acts of terrorism or terrorism in general.[2246] The preparation in the UK for offences which are to take place abroad is also covered.[2247]

464. *Mens rea* – The *mens rea* of the offence is the intention to commit or assist one or more acts of terrorism.[2248]

465. Preparation vs. attempt – Preparation has to be distinguished from an attempted offence, which is one of the four inchoate offences in UK law (see no. 451). A person commits a criminal attempt when they undertake an action which is more than merely preparatory to the commission of an indictable offence, and they have the intent to commit this offence.[2249] The statute does not provide for a test as to when an action is more than merely preparatory. It

---

2244 Secretary of State for the Home Department and Secretary of State for Northern Ireland, *Legislation Against Terrorism: A consultation paper* (Cm 4178, 1998) para 7.15.

2245 S. 5 (1) TA 2006. See also: Conte (n 10) 240; Cornford (n 2006) 665; Lee (n 643) 9; Qureshi (n 2041) paras 2–3; Roach, *The 9/11 Effect: Comparative Counter-Terrorism* (n 79) 300; Zedner, 'Terrorizing Criminal Law' (n 45) 114.

2246 S. 5 (2) TA 2006. See also: Cornford (n 2006) 665; Fenwick, *Fenwick on Civil Liberties and Human Rights* (n 1649) 1071.

2247 *R v. Abbas Niazi Iqbal, Ilyas Niazi Iqbal* [2010] EWCA Crim 3215, 2010 WL 5625104, 27.

2248 Cornford (n 2006) 665.

2249 S. 1 (1) Criminal Attempts Act 1981. See also: *R v. Ian John Gullefer* (1990) 91 Cr App R 356, 357; *R v. Ian Anthony Jones* [2007] EWCA Crim 1118, [2008] QB 460, 39; Allen and Edwards (n 1618) 340; Child and others (n 1630) 354; CMV Clarkson, 'Attempt: The Conduct Requirement' (2009) 29 Oxford Journal of Legal Studies 25, 25; Elliott and Quinn (n 1627) 278; Herring (n 1627) 783; Loveless, Allen and Derry (n 1618) 682–683; Martin (n 1618) 78–79.

just states that if there is sufficient evidence, the question of whether the act is more than merely preparatory is one for the jury to decide.[2250] Case law has stated that the person must at least 'try' to commit the offence, meaning they broach commission of the *actus reus* or that they have 'embarked on the crime proper'.[2251] These clarifications are of some help, but the test remains difficult to apply.[2252] Clarkson concluded, after an analysis of the case law, that the threshold is whether or not there has been a confrontation between defendant and the victim or property.[2253] Voluntary withdrawal or desistence is not provided for by the legislation as a defence and there is no clear case law allowing it either.[2254] In addition to the action, the perpetrator of the attempt must have intent to commit (the central aspects of)[2255] the offence, even if the offence itself does not require intent.[2256] The possible sentence for an attempted offence is the sentence for the completed offence, be that on indictment or in case of triable either-way offences on summary conviction.[2257] In practice, however, courts often tend to impose lighter sentences than for the completed offence.[2258] In case of attempted murder or another offence with a fixed sentence, the sentence is imprisonment for life, but discretionary instead of mandatory.[2259]

2250 S. 4 (3) Criminal Attempts Act 1981. See also: Allen and Edwards (n 1618) 346–347; Child and others (n 1630) 355; Duff, *Criminal Attempts* (n 1633) 58; Elliott and Quinn (n 1627) 278; Wilson (n 1630) 519.

2251 *R v. Tony Campbell* [1990] 93 Cr App R 350 (CA), 354; *R v. Kenneth Henry Jones* (1990) 91 Cr App R 351 (CA), 354–356; *R v.Ian John Gullefer* (1990) 91 Cr App R 356, 358; *A-G's reference (no 1 of 1992)* [1993] 1 W.L.R. 274, 284–285;*R v. Tosti (Andre)* [1997] Crim LR 746 (CA), 747; *R v. Geddes* [1996] Crim LR 894, 895; *Mason v. DPP* [2009] EWHC 2198 (Admin), 19–20; *Application By Prosecution for Leave to Appeal Under Section 58 Criminal Justice Act 2003 (MS)* [2021] EWCA Crim 600, 2021 WL 01616966, 22–28. See also: Allen and Edwards (n 1618) 347–351; Child and others (n 1630) 356; Clarkson (n 2249) 26; Elliott and Quinn (n 1627) 278–279; Herring (n 1627) 790–793; Loveless, Allen and Derry (n 1618) 683–686; Macdonald and Carlile (n 1626) 136; Martin (n 1618) 78–79; Wilson (n 1630) 518–521.

2252 *R v. Tosti (Andre)* [1997] Crim LR 746 (CA), 747.

2253 Clarkson (n 2249) 26–28.

2254 Child and others (n 1630) 363–364; Herring (n 1627) 798; Wilson (n 1630) 528–529. For a discussion on its relevance and workings, see: Duff, *Criminal Attempts* (n 1633) 66–75. See e.g.: *R v. Lankford* [1959] Crim. L.R. 209.

2255 For an analysis, see: Duff, *Criminal Attempts* (n 1633) ch 1. E.g. for the offence of attempted rape intent is required for the sexual intercourse but for the lack of consent, recklessness suffices, since it also suffices for the actual offence. See: *R v. Ian Beckenridge* [1984] 79 Cr. App. R. 244; *R v. Khan (Mohammed Iqbal), R v. Dhokia, R v. Banga, R v. Faiz* [1990] 1 WLR 813, 819. Note that there is uncertainty in the case law about the intent requirement for circumstances or consequences. See: Herring (n 1627) 784–789.

2256 Allen and Edwards (n 1618) 341–346; Duff, *Criminal Attempts* (n 1633) 5; Elliott and Quinn (n 1627) 280–281; Herring (n 1627) 783–789; Loveless, Allen and Derry (n 1618) 689–693; Martin (n 1618) 79; Wilson (n 1630) 523–528.

2257 S. 4 (1) Criminal Attempts Act 1981. See also: Elliott and Quinn (n 1627) 282; Wilson (n 1630) 511.

2258 Duff, *Criminal Attempts* (n 1633) 116–117.

2259 S. 4 (1) Criminal Attempts Act 1981. See also: Wilson (n 1630) 511.

SUBSECTION II. SENTENCE

466. Indictable only offence – The sentence for the preparation offence is imprisonment for life on indictment.[2260] This leaves a very wide sentencing range for a very broad offence,[2261] which has led to some inconsistency in sentencing.[2262] In the *Kahar* case, which was later referred to and confirmed in the *Abdallah* case,[2263] the Court of Appeal attempted to introduce some guidelines on this topic. The Court devised a system with different categories based on eight factors (some only applicable in cases of terrorism abroad): sophistication of plans and route, duration of involvement, depth of radicalisation, indoctrination and involvement of others, equipment and funds, activity in the conflict zone and reasons and methods of return.[2264] In addition to these factors, the number, nature and gravity of the intended terrorist act(s) played a role and the system led to six scales of criminality.[2265] The Court also dismissed the idea of 'good' and 'bad' terrorism (i.e. terrorism for noble causes or not) or the fact that the acts were planned in the UK or abroad having an influence on sentencing.[2266] This system led to increased consistency in sentencing, but still remained rather complicated. The categories of wrongdoing overlap sometimes and the focus is on cases involving multiple offenders and complex planning.[2267] In addition, some of the sentences proposed are very high even for preparations which are short of attempted murder or conspiracy to murder.[2268] This is a serious terrorist offence, meaning that if the other conditions are met, courts have to impose a

---

2260 S. 5 (3) TA 2006. See also: Conte (n 10) 240; Lazarus, Goold and Goss (n 30) 464; Lee (n 643) 9; Zedner, 'Terrorizing Criminal Law' (n 45) 114.

2261 Clive Walker, 'Foreign Terrorist Fighters and UK Counter Terrorism Laws' in Javaid Rehman and Ayesha Shahid (eds), *The Asian Yearbook of Human Rights and Humanitarian Law: Volume 2* (Brill | Nijhoff 2018) 188.

2262 Qureshi (n 2041) para 4.

2263 *R v. Abdalraouf Abdallah and Stephen Gray and an application under s.36 of the Criminal Justice Act 1986 by HM Attorney General (No. 323 of 2016), Junead Khan and Shazib Khan, Ayman Shaukat and Lorna Moore* [2016] EWCA Crim 1868, 3.

2264 *R v. Mohammed Abdul Kahar (Reference by the Attorney General under s.36 of the Criminal Justice Act 1988) R v. Brusthom Ziamani, Abdurraouf Eshati, Yahya Rashid, Silhan Ozcelik, Sana Khan* [2016] EWCA Crim 568, 2016 WL 02771996, 14–28. See also: Lee and Walker (n 1698) 325; Qureshi (n 2041) paras 13–14; Walker, 'Foreign Terrorist Fighters and UK Counter Terrorism Laws' (n 2261) 188.

2265 *R v. Mohammed Abdul Kahar (Reference by the Attorney General under s.36 of the Criminal Justice Act 1988) R v. Brusthom Ziamani, Abdurraouf Eshati, Yahya Rashid, Silhan Ozcelik, Sana Khan* [2016] EWCA Crim 568, 2016 WL 02771996, 30–35. See also: Andrew Ashworth, 'R. v Kahar Case Comment' [2016] Criminal Law Review 670, 672–673; Lee and Walker (n 1698) 325; Qureshi (n 2041) paras 14–15. Rob Dacre, 'Greater Threats to Society' – The New Draft Guidelines for Terrorism Offences, www.2harecourt.com/training-knowledge/greater-threats-society-new-draft-guidelines-terrorism-offences/.

2266 *R v. Mohammed Abdul Kahar (Reference by the Attorney General under s.36 of the Criminal Justice Act 1988) R v. Brusthom Ziamani, Abdurraouf Eshati, Yahya Rashid, Silhan Ozcelik, Sana Khan* [2016] EWCA Crim 568, 2016 WL 02771996, 8–13. See also: Ashworth, 'R. v Kahar Case Comment' (n 2265) 672; Qureshi (n 2041) paras 8–10.

2267 Lee and Walker (n 1698) 329.

2268 Ashworth, 'R. v Kahar Case Comment' (n 2265) 675; Lee and Walker (n 1698) 329.

serious terrorism sentence (see no. 339). In addition, it is a specified offence for which an extended sentence is possible if the other conditions are met (see no. 340). Community orders (see no. 342) are also a possibility if the conditions for serious terrorism sentences or extended sentences are not met, but considering the sentencing guidelines, they seem unlikely. A suspended sentence order is possible as well, in situations where the Court finds a sentence of maximum two years appropriate (see no. 343). Again though, two years falls below the sentencing range of the lowest category of sentences in the sentencing guidelines so a suspended sentence order will be rare as well.

467. GUIDELINES – A few years after the Court of Appeal's attempt to create more consistent sentencing, the Sentencing Council issued the terrorism sentencing guidelines (see no. 344), which also included the s. 5 offence, thereby making the system devised by the Court of Appeal unnecessary. The categories provided for s. 5, which are identical to the ones for Explosive substances (see no. 362), are the following[2269]:

	Culpability			
Harm	A	B	C	D
Category 1	**Starting point** Life imprisonment – minimum term 35 years' custody	**Starting point** Life imprisonment – minimum term 25 years' custody	**Starting point** Life imprisonment – minimum term 15 years' custody	**Starting point** 15 years' custody
	Category range Life imprisonment – minimum term 30–40 years' custody	**Category range** Life imprisonment – minimum term 20–30 years' custody	**Category range** Life imprisonment – minimum term 10–20 years' custody	**Category range** 10–20 years' custody
Category 2	**Starting point** Life imprisonment – minimum term 25 years' custody	**Starting point** Life imprisonment – minimum term 15 years' custody	**Starting point** 15 years' custody	**Starting point** 8 years' custody
	Category range Life imprisonment – minimum term 20–30 years' custody	**Category range** Life imprisonment – minimum term 10–20 years' custody	**Category range** 10–20 years' custody	**Category range** 6–10 years' custody

2269 www.sentencingcouncil.org.uk/. For a brief analysis, see: Umar Azmeh, 'Comment on the Terrorism Offences Definitive Guideline' [2018] Sentencing News 6.

Culpability				
Harm	A	B	C	D
Category 3	**Starting point** 16 years' custody	**Starting point** 12 years' custody	**Starting point** 8 years' custody	**Starting point** 4 years' custody
	Category range 12–20 years' custody	**Category range** 8–16 years' custody	**Category range** 6–10 years' custody	**Category range** 3–6 years' custody

SUBSECTION III. PRACTICAL APPLICATION

468. Used to prosecute FTFs – In an analysis of cases relating to Foreign Terrorist Fighters in 2015 and 2016 (until 19 July), Walker notes all five of the attempted departures were prosecuted under this offence and six out of the eight actual departures were.[2270] In their case law analysis, Wittendorp and Bakker counted 27 out of the 31 FTF cases in the UK between March 2011 and June 2017 as being prosecuted under s. 5 TA 2006.[2271] Interestingly, however, Walker notes only about a quarter of FTFs was being prosecuted.[2272] In the Wittendorp and Bakker analysis this is even less. The reason most FTFs were not prosecuted at all was apparently lack of evidence.[2273]

469. Examples of preparation – The *Khan et al* case concerned three groups of men, situated in Stoke, Cardiff and London, who were in contact with each other.[2274] The Cardiff and London groups wanted to carry out explosive attacks in London. The Stoke group wanted to undertake training abroad with the aim of further attacks in the future, together with men they were going to recruit. They had met several times, discussed plans, and were starting to discuss how to construct a pipe bomb. All involved were prosecuted and convicted for preparation of a terrorist attack (barring one who was prosecuted for possession for terrorist purposes). The defendants received extended sentences ranging from 22 years and eight months (including the five-year extension period) to

2270 Walker, 'Foreign Terrorist Fighters and UK Counter Terrorism Laws' (n 2261) 186.

2271 Wittendorp and Bakker (n 686) 61–62. See e.g.: *R v. Khalil Maher, R v. Patrick Kabele, R v. Jabed Hussain* and *R v. Shamin Ahmed* as described in Hill (n 1666) 98–103. For an analysis and overview of cases prosecuted for a range of different offences, see: Blackbourn, Kayis and McGarrity (n 1771) 20–27.

2272 Walker, 'Foreign Terrorist Fighters and UK Counter Terrorism Laws' (n 2261) 187. See also: Blackbourn, Kayis and McGarrity (n 1771) 21.

2273 Walker, 'Foreign Terrorist Fighters and UK Counter Terrorism Laws' (n 2261) 187.

2274 *Usman Khan, Mohibur Rahman, Omar Sharif Latif, Abdul Bosher Mohammed Shahjahan, Nazam Hussain v. The Queen* [2013] EWCA Crim 468, 2013 WL 618129. See also: Cornford (n 2006) 666–667.

15 years and four months. In the *Tabbakh* case a man who suffered from PTSD was prosecuted for the preparation offence.[2275] He had compiled bomb making instructions and had started to assemble the necessary ingredients. He was found guilty and convicted to seven years imprisonment. Similarly, in the *Roddis* case, a man was convicted for preparation because he had done research on how to make a bomb and had started to collect ingredients.[2276] As explained above, the preparation offence covers both preparation of a specific terrorist act as well as preparation in general. This led to a man being convicted to life imprisonment for preparation in the *farooqi* case without the prosecution being able to prove involvement in any particular plot.[2277] He had tried to radicalise others to travel abroad and fight jihad, but nobody had actually done so.

470. More than one leading role possible – In the *Boular* case, two sisters (young adults) were convicted for preparation and sentenced to life imprisonment with minimum tariffs of 11 and 16 years.[2278] One had first planned to commit a suicide bombing abroad and when she failed to travel abroad had planned an attack with firearms and/or grenades in the British Museum. After she had been arrested, her older sister planned to use knives to attack members of the public around parliament. In sentencing them, the judge categorised the second sister in category A2 and the first one in B2, both having a leading role and multiple deaths being risked but not likely. The difference was, however, that for the second sister the preparations were complete or very close to completion while for the first one they were only 'advanced'. The overall effect of the different category was a five-year difference in the tariff. This difference was increased by the Court of Appeal from three to five years when it lowered the tariff for the younger sister from 13 to 11 years due to her young age and history of grooming. In this case the judge also reiterated that there can be more than one leading role per offence.

SUBSECTION IV. CRITICISM

471. Broadness offence – This offence is very broad and overlaps with other terrorist offences. According to the courts this is not an issue and it is up to the prosecution to decide which offence(s) it wants to prosecute.[2279] Several

2275 *R v. Hassan Tabbakh* [2009] EWCA Crim 464, 2009 WL 392237. See also: Cornford (n 2006) 670.

2276 *R v. Nicholas Roddis* [2009] EWCA Crim 585, 2009 WL 648870. See also: Cornford (n 2006) 669.

2277 *R v. Munir Ahmed Farooqi, Matthew Newton, Israr Hussain Malik* [2013] EWCA Crim 1649, 2013 WL 5328717. See also: Cornford (n 2006) 668.

2278 *R v. Rizlaine Boular, Safaa Boular* [2019] EWCA Crim 798, 2019 WL 02162983.

2279 *R v. Mohammed Abdul Kahar (Reference by the Attorney General under s.36 of the Criminal Justice Act 1988) R v. Brusthom Ziamani, Abdurraouf Eshati, Yahya Rashid, Silhan Ozcelik,*

commentators point out that the *actus reus* of this offence is so broad it '*risks creating what is, in effect, a thought crime.*'[2280] The fact that such a broad range of situations is covered and that early intervention is possible, is helpful for prosecutors who will have to once again use their discretion wisely.[2281] In his case law analysis, Cornford notes that the extreme cases which in theory are covered by the offence have in practice not yet been prosecuted. Even taking this into account, however, the conduct caught by s. 5 varies widely in types of conduct and culpability, ranging from merely discussing things to undertaking military training and gathering weapons.[2282] He concludes that the offence is too broad, catching too many early-stage preparations. This is problematic for several reasons. The dangerousness and culpability of these acts tends to be low, and we do not know which type of conduct actually indicates an attack will follow. The offence focusses on the *mens rea* and proof of this *mens rea* is often circumstantial making it very hard to know if the person actually intended to cause harm. The investigative methods used to try to ascertain this are sometimes very intrusive, causing a chilling effect among certain communities where people avoid raising any suspicion to avoid this type of treatment.[2283] The offence is in fact very broad, with its *actus reus* including conduct which merely assists others in their preparation and conduct related to terrorism in general instead of to a specific act of terrorism. This last point also applies to the *mens rea*, which leads to a very broad offence in general, as can be seen in the *farooqi* case.

472. SENTENCES – Dacre points out that the sentences on the high end of the spectrum in the guidelines are similar to the ones in *Kahar*, but for the low categories they are higher than they were in *Kahar*.[2284] It is difficult to exactly compare though, since the categories do not match precisely. This means that

---

Sana Khan [2016] EWCA Crim 568, 2016 WL 02771996, 6–7; *R v. Abbas Niazi Iqbal, Ilyas Niazi Iqbal* [2010] EWCA Crim 3215, 2010 WL 5625104, 29. The JCHR also pointed to overlap, but concluded the new offence was necessary as well. See: JCHR, Counter-Terrorism Policy and Human Rights: Terrorism Bill and related matters (HL paper 75, HC paper 561, 2005) para 50–54.

2280 Zedner, 'Terrorizing Criminal Law' (n 45) 114. See also: Ashworth, 'Criminal Law, Human Rights and Preventative Justice' (n 27) 90; Fenwick, *Fenwick on Civil Liberties and Human Rights* (n 1649) 1070–1071; Stone (n 1651) 463; Walker, 'The Impact of Contemporary Security Agendas Against Terrorism on the Substantive Criminal Law' (n 45) 130.

2281 Fenwick, *Fenwick on Civil Liberties and Human Rights* (n 1649) 1070; Stone (n 1651) 463; Walker, 'Foreign Terrorist Fighters and UK Counter Terrorism Laws' (n 2261) 188. On the breadth of the offence, see also: *Usman Khan, Mohibur Rahman, Omar Sharif Latif, Abdul Bosher Mohammed Shahjahan, Nazam Hussain v. The Queen* [2013] EWCA Crim 468, 2013 WL 618129, 76.

2282 Cornford (n 2006) 665.

2283 Cornford (n 2006) 667–671.

2284 Rob Dacre, *'Greater Threats to Society' – The New Draft Guidelines for Terrorism Offences*, www.2harecourt.com/training-knowledge/greater-threats-society-new-draft-guidelines-terrorism-offences/.

a level six offender (lowest level) under *Kahar* will probably not be a category D3 offender under the sentencing guidelines, but fall in one of the higher categories.[2285] Compared to the *Kahar* system, the sentencing guidelines do have the benefit of greater clarity, consistency and coverage (since they include other offences).[2286] However, Lee and Walker list several issues with the guidelines.[2287] First, the guidelines were created in a short time, being rushed. Second, the methodology with its eight or ten steps and lists of exhaustive and non-exhaustive elements is complicated, especially in relation to the uncertain anticipatory nature of the wrongdoing, with Lee and Walker calling it '*riddled with conceptual and practical problems when assessing culpability and harm.*'[2288] This leads to legality (rule of law) and proportionality issues. The former stem from the complex boundaries of categories with new uncertainties, the latter from the focus on utilitarian deterrence or incapacitation with too little emphasis on culpability.[2289] The starting points are very high, with categories 1C–1A having life sentences with minimum terms of 15 to 35 years. Lee and Walker compare this to murder which has a life sentence with a minimum term between 12 and 30 years.[2290] Second, the closer to completion of the preparations, the higher the level of culpability, which means that the time of arrest has an influence on the sentence, although this is out of the perpetrator's control.[2291] Similarly, having a lesser role in a plot which is far advanced puts one at the same level as having a leading role in a plot which is not advanced as far, meaning that again factors outside of the control of the perpetrator have an influence instead of what they did.[2292] Finally, Lee and Walker criticise the (lack of) inclusion and the wording of certain aggravating and mitigating factors.[2293] In general it is striking that the maximum sentence for preparation is life imprisonment. This means that the maximum sentence of the preparation offence is at least as high and sometimes higher than the sentence for the prepared offence. For offences punishable with a life sentence, the legislature does not differentiate in terms of sentence between preparation, attempt, and the completed offence. For offences with a lower sentence, the sentences for preparation are actually higher than for the attempted or completed offence. This is a serious proportionality issue for the preparation offence.

2285 Rob Dacre, *'Greater Threats to Society' – The New Draft Guidelines for Terrorism Offences*, www.2harecourt.com/training-knowledge/greater-threats-society-new-draft-guidelines-terrorism-offences/.

2286 Lee and Walker (n 1698) 327.

2287 Lee and Walker (n 1698) 326.

2288 Lee and Walker (n 1698) 327–328.

2289 Lee and Walker (n 1698) 328–330.

2290 Lee (n 643) 10; Lee and Walker (n 1698) 330.

2291 Lee (n 643) 9; Lee and Walker (n 1698) 330.

2292 Lee (n 643) 9; Lee and Walker (n 1698) 330.

2293 Lee (n 643) 10; Lee and Walker (n 1698) 331–332.

473. Evaluating harm – In addition to the criticism above, commentators pointed out that the analysis of harm is difficult for an offence of preparation where no harm has actually occurred yet. This was applied in practice to the preparation offence but is also applicable to the other terrorism offences *sensu lato* for which guidelines exist. Originally, the sentencing council planned to use the intended harm as a way to measure harm, but after consultation it decided to use the likelihood of harm instead, as this is a better indicator.[2294] However, in cases of undercover operations, for example, no harm is likely because of the interference of the security services for example making sure the bombs are inert. In those cases, courts shifted from likelihood of harm to the intended harm and in doing so went against the guidelines.[2295] The sentencing council then reacted, not by amending the specific guidelines, but by adding a general note on culpability and harm to the guidelines. This note states that if an undercover law enforcement officer is involved, culpability has to be assessed as if that person was a genuine conspirator. In those situations, the harm category should be identified based on the intended harm and viability of the plan disregarding the involvement of the undercover agent. Lee and Walker point out that this approach makes the preparation offence closer to a thought crime.[2296]

SECTION XIV. OFFENCES INVOLVING RADIOACTIVE DEVICES AND MATERIALS AND NUCLEAR FACILITIES AND SITES

SUBSECTION I. MIXTURE OF TERRORISM *SENSU STRICTO* AND *SENSU LATO*

474. *Sensu lato* and/or *sensu stricto* – Finally, the TA 2006 also contains several offences related to radioactive devices and materials or nuclear facilities and sites. Some of these offences span both actions which would be considered terrorism *sensu stricto* and other actions of terrorism *sensu lato*. The offences will be discussed in the next subsections. The making or possessing offence is terrorism *sensu lato*, as is the offence of threats for access to nuclear facilities or the supply of radioactive materials. These actions clearly precede a terrorism offence *sensu stricto* and are thus preventive in this sense. The offence of threatening the use of radioactive materials, however, is a terrorist offence *sensu stricto*. The misuse and damage offences are most obviously categorised as terrorism *sensu stricto* but could in fact also be terrorism *sensu lato* depending on the circumstances, as they are very broad.

2294 Kelly (n 1745) 766; Lee and Walker (n 1698) 330–331.

2295 Kelly (n 1745) 767–768; Lee and Walker (n 1698) 330–331. For an example of this issue, see: *R v. Rizlaine Boular, Safaa Boular* [2019] EWCA Crim 798, 2019 WL 02162983, 51–52.

2296 Lee and Walker (n 1698) 330–331.

SUBSECTION II. S. 9 TA 2006: MAKING OR POSSESSING RADIOACTIVE DEVICES OR MATERIALS

475. *Actus reus* and *mens rea* – Making or having in possession a radioactive device[2297] or having in possession radioactive material can be an offence. This is the case if combined with the *mens rea* of '*the intention of using the device or material in the course of or in connection with the commission or preparation of an act of terrorism or for the purposes of terrorism, or of making it available to be so used.*'[2298] Again, it is irrelevant whether the act of terrorism is a particular act of terrorism or terrorism in general.[2299]

SUBSECTION III. S. 10 TA 2006: MISUSE AND DAMAGE

476. *Actus reus* and *mens rea* – The next offence is using a radioactive device or radioactive material, or the use or damaging of a nuclear facility[2300] in a manner which causes the release or creates or increases the risk of release of radioactive material and this happens '*in the course of or in connection with the commission of an act of terrorism or for the purposes of terrorism.*'[2301] The offence includes no clear *mens rea* but the word 'use' does imply a conscious action.

SUBSECTION IV. S. 11 TA 2006: THREATS

477. *Actus reus* and *mens rea* – A final pair of offences is related to threatening. First,

> a person commits an offence if, in the course of or in connection with the commission of an act of terrorism or for the purposes of terrorism
> (a) he makes a demand
>   i. for the supply to himself or to another of a radioactive device or of radioactive material;
>   ii. for a nuclear facility to be made available to himself or to another; or
>   iii. for access to such a facility to be given to himself or to another;
> (b) he supports the demand with a threat that he or another will take action if the demand is not met; and
> (c) the circumstances and manner of the threat are such that it is reasonable for the person to whom it is made to assume that there is real risk that the threat will be carried out if the demand is not met.[2302]

[2297] As defined by the TA 2006. See: S. 9 (4) and (5) TA 2006.
[2298] S. 9 (1) TA 2006. See also: Conte (n 10) 241.
[2299] S. 9 (2) TA 2006.
[2300] As defined by the TA 2006. See: S. 10 (4) and (5) TA 2006.
[2301] S. 10 (1) and (2) TA 2006. See also: Conte (n 10) 241–242.
[2302] S. 11 (1) TA 2006. See also: Conte (n 10) 242. Note that the terms 'nuclear facility', 'radioactive device' and 'radioactive material' have the same meanings as defined earlier in the TA 2006. See: S. 11 (5) TA 2006.

478. Additional terrorism offence *sensu stricto* – In addition, it is an offence to threaten the use of radioactive material or radioactive devices or threaten the use or damaging of a nuclear facility in a manner that releases radioactive material or creates or increases a risk that such material will be released '*in the course of or in connection with the commission of an act of terrorism or for the purposes of terrorism.*'[2303] This is only the case, however, '*if the circumstances and manner of the threat are such that it is reasonable for the person to whom it is made to assume that there is real risk that the threat will be carried out, or would be carried out if demands made in association with the threat are not met.*'[2304] This final offence is an offence of terrorism *sensu stricto.*

SUBSECTION V. SENTENCES

479. Indictable only offences – The sentence for these offences is imprisonment for life, on indictment.[2305] These are serious terrorist offences, meaning that if the other conditions are met, courts have to impose a serious terrorism sentence (see no. 339). In addition, they are specified offences for which an extended sentence is possible if the other conditions are met (see no. 340). Community orders (see no. 342) are also a possibility if the conditions for serious terrorism sentences or extended sentences are not met. A suspended sentence order is possible as well, in situations where the Court finds a sentence of maximum two years appropriate (see no. 343). There appear to be no sentencing guidelines (yet) for these offences.[2306]

SUBSECTION VI. CRITICISM

480. Added value – Once more, the added value of these offences can be questioned. They do not appear to have been used yet and the chances of them ever being used are small. Even if actions are undertaken which could constitute one of these offences, they would almost certainly also constitute at least one other terrorist offence. The making or possessing of radioactive devices or materials and misuse and damage offences will surely always constitute the preparation offence, the possession offence and/or attempted murder. The threatening offence was already covered partly by the Nuclear Material (Offences) Act 1983 (see no. 354). If anything, it would have been more logical to extend that offence where necessary. The sentence for this offence also raises

---

2303 S. 11 (2) (a) and (3) TA 2006.
2304 S. 11 (2) (b) TA 2006. See also: Conte (n 10) 242.
2305 S. 9 (3), 10 (3) and 11 (4) TA 2006.
2306 Lee and Walker (n 1698) 327.

the question of proportionality in terms of the sentence. A maximum sentence of life imprisonment seems disproportionately high for merely threatening to do something.

SECTION XV. EXTRATERRITORIAL OFFENCES

SUBSECTION I. INCITING TERRORISM OVERSEAS

481. S. 59 TA 2000 – S. 59 of the TA 2000 criminalises inciting terrorism overseas.[2307] This could be considered an offence in its own right, or an extraterritorial application of the general incitement offence (see no. 451). The 'offence' is committed if a person '*incites another person to commit an act of terrorism wholly or partly outside the United Kingdom, and the act would, if committed in England and Wales, constitute one of the offences listed in subsection (2).*'[2308] Subsection (2) then lists the following offences: murder, wounding with intent, poisoning, explosions and endangering life by damaging property.[2309] Finally, it is immaterial whether the person inciting is in the UK at the time.[2310] The Act does not include some kind of freedom fighter exception.[2311]

482. Same sentence as incited person – The person inciting the offence is liable to any penalty to which they would be liable if they committed the offence they are inciting.[2312] The choice of offences means that for example if somebody incites another to commit grievous bodily harm abroad,[2313] they are liable to life imprisonment, but if they incite the person to commit serious bodily harm (which is not included),[2314] they have not committed an offence.[2315] With the exception of poisoning, inciting terrorism overseas is a serious terrorist offence, meaning that if the other conditions are met, courts have to impose a serious terrorism sentence (see no. 339). All of them (including poisoning) are specified offences for which an extended sentence is possible if the other conditions are met (see no. 340).

2307 Roach, *The 9/11 Effect: Comparative Counter-Terrorism* (n 79) 260.

2308 S. 59 (1) TA 2000. See also: Fenwick, *Fenwick on Civil Liberties and Human Rights* (n 1649) 1075; Walker, *Blackstone's Guide to the Anti-Terrorism Legislation* (n 1670) 175.

2309 S. 59 (2) TA 2000. See also: Fenwick, *Fenwick on Civil Liberties and Human Rights* (n 1649) 1075; Walker, *Blackstone's Guide to the Anti-Terrorism Legislation* (n 1670) 175.

2310 S. 59 (4) TA 2000. See also: Walker, *Blackstone's Guide to the Anti-Terrorism Legislation* (n 1670) 176.

2311 Roach, *The 9/11 Effect: Comparative Counter-Terrorism* (n 79) 260.

2312 S. 59 (3) TA 2000. See also: Conte (n 10) 233; Fenwick, *Fenwick on Civil Liberties and Human Rights* (n 1649) 1075.

2313 S. 18 OAPA 1861.

2314 S. 20 OAPA 1861.

2315 Fenwick, *Fenwick on Civil Liberties and Human Rights* (n 1649) 1075.

483. Case law example – Three young men who made websites were convicted for inciting terrorism overseas.[2316] They had purchased, constructed, and maintained a large number of websites and online forums on which material was published which incited acts of terrorist murder in Iraq. This material included films made by Al-Qaeda, calls to fight armed jihad and kill, and practical information useful for these purposes. In first instance they received sentences of ten, seven and a half and six and a half years imprisonment. The Court of Appeal, however, found these sentences to be unduly lenient. They were raised to respectively 16, 12 and ten years.

SUBSECTION II. OTHER EXTRATERRITORIAL JURISDICTION

484. Terrorism *sensu stricto* – For offences under the Explosive Substances Act 1883,[2317] Biological Weapons Act 1974 and the Chemical Weapons Act 1996, the TA 2000 explicitly states they are also punishable if they take place outside of the UK if they are done as an act of terrorism or for the purposes of terrorism.[2318] The TA 2000 also contains a second list of offences for which this is the case:

(a) murder, manslaughter, culpable homicide, rape, assault causing injury, assault to injury, kidnapping, abduction or false imprisonment,
(b) an offence under section 4, 16, 18, 20, 21, 22, 23, 24, 28, 29, 30 or 64 of the Offences against the Person Act 1861,
(c) an offence under any of sections 1 to 5 of the Forgery and Counterfeiting Act1981,
(d) the uttering of a forged document or an offence under section 46A of the Criminal Law (Consolidation) (Scotland) Act 1995,
(e) an offence under section 1 or 2 of the Criminal Damage Act 1971,
(f) an offence under Article 3 or 4 of the Criminal Damage (Northern Ireland) Order 1977,
(g) malicious mischief,
(h) wilful fire-raising.[2319]

For the offences listed in (a) to (d), with the exception of Section 5 (2) of the Forgery and Counterfeiting Act 1981, the TA 2000 also includes extraterritorial jurisdiction based on the passive personality principle. This is the case if these actions are undertaken as an act of terrorism or for the purposes of terrorism,

2316 Attorney General's References (Nos 85, 86 & 87 of 2007) [2007] EWCA Crim 3300.
2317 Barring s. 4 of the Explosive Substances Act 1883.
2318 S. 62 TA 2000. See also: Conte (n 10) 233–234; Walker, *Blackstone's Guide to the Anti-Terrorism Legislation* (n 1670) 177–178.
2319 S. 63B (2) TA 2000.

and the victim is a UK national, UK resident or a protected person.[2320] The legislation lists which categories of people are protected. This includes members of diplomatic missions and consular posts.[2321] The noxious substances offences in the ATCSA 2001 have extraterritorial jurisdiction both based on active and passive personality if they are done for the purpose of advancing a political, religious, racial or ideological cause.[2322] Finally, there are grounds for extraterritorial jurisdiction based on passive personality if certain terrorist offences are undertaken or threatened against premises or vehicles where protected persons are present and which are ordinarily used by these people.[2323] In order to start proceedings based on any of the aforementioned sections,[2324] the consent of the Attorney General is required.[2325] In addition to this, the Internationally Protected Persons Act 1978 establishes universal jurisdiction for attacks against protected persons, their property or vehicles or threats thereof.[2326] The same goes for attempted offences and aiding and abetting, counselling or procuring.[2327] Finally, the Nuclear Material (Offences) Act 1983 establishes universal jurisdiction for a list of offences such as murder and manslaughter if they are committed in relation to or by means of nuclear material.[2328] It also provides for universal jurisdiction for several of the newly added offences by the Act, such as acts directed against nuclear facilities or which interfere with their operation if they cause death, injury or damage resulting from the emission of ionising radiation or the release of radioactive material.[2329] The Criminal Justice and Immigration Act 2008 made several changes to this legislation, which were inserted in 2009. Since 2009 the Act also contains grounds for universal jurisdiction for attempting, conspiring, inciting or aiding, abetting, counselling or procuring the commission of a nuclear offence.[2330]

485. Terrorism *sensu lato* – The UK legislation also provides for extraterritoriality for many of the terrorism offences *sensu lato*.[2331] The TA 2000 specifies that a person doing anything outside of the UK that would have constituted an offence related to terrorist property if done in the UK,

2320 S. 63C (1) and (2) TA 2000.
2321 S. 63C (3) and (4) TA 2000.
2322 S. 113A ATCSA 2001.
2323 S. 63D TA 2000.
2324 Except for proceedings based on the Internationally Protected Persons Act 1978, the Suppression of Terrorism Act 1978, the Nuclear Material (Offences) Act 1983 or the United Nations Personnel Act 1997.
2325 S. 63E TA 2000; s. 113B ATCSA 2001.
2326 S. 1 (1), (1A) an d (3) Internationally Protected Persons Act 1978. For a brief overview, see: Conte (n 10) 227.
2327 S. 1 (3) Internationally Protected Persons Act 1978.
2328 S. 1 (1) Nuclear Material (Offences) Act 1983.
2329 S. 1 (1A) Nuclear Material (Offences) Act 1983.
2330 S. 2A Nuclear Material (Offences) Act 1983.
2331 Conte (n 10) 234; Roach, *The 9/11 Effect: Comparative Counter-Terrorism* (n 79) 260.

is also an offence.[2332] Since 2003, the TA 2000 also includes a ground for extraterritorial jurisdiction based on active personality for the offences of directing a terrorist organisation, possession for terrorist purpose, collection of information, eliciting, etc. information about members of the armed forces, entering or remaining in a designated area and inciting terrorism overseas.[2333] This appears somewhat strange for the offences of inciting terrorism overseas and the designated area offences, since the offences themself already contain a large element of extraterritoriality. In addition, the TA 2006 provides for extraterritorial jurisdiction[2334] based on universality for certain offences. This is the case for:

> (a) an offence under section 1 or 2 of this Act;
> (b) an offence under section 5 or 6 or any of sections 8 to 11 of this Act;
> (c) an offence under section 11(1) of the Terrorism Act 2000 (c. 11) (membership of proscribed organisations);
> (d) an offence under section 54 of that Act (weapons training);
> (da) an offence under section 4 of the Explosive Substances Act 1883 (making or possessing explosives under suspicious circumstances) so far as committed for the purposes of an act of terrorism;
> (e) conspiracy to commit an offence falling within this subsection;
> (f) inciting a person to commit such an offence;
> (g) attempting to commit such an offence;
> (h) aiding, abetting, counselling or procuring the commission of such an offence.[2335]

For two other offences the TA 2006 provides for extraterritorial jurisdiction based on active personality.[2336] This is the case for: '*(ca) an offence under section 12(1) or (1A) of that Act (inviting or expressing support for proscribed organisation); and (cb) an offence under section 13 of that Act (uniform etc. associated with proscribed organisation).*'[2337] Any prosecution referred to in this section can only go ahead with the consent of the Director of Public Prosecutions who in turn needs the permission of the Attorney General.[2338]

2332 S. 63 TA 2000.

2333 S. 63A TA 2000. See also: Conte (n 10) 234; Roach, *The 9/11 Effect: Comparative Counter-Terrorism* (n 79) 260.

2334 Note once again that there is an section detailing the consequences for managers, etc. if the offence is committed by a body corporate. See: S. 18 TA 2006.

2335 S. 17 (1), (2) and (3) TA 2006.

2336 Based on the nationality or residence of the perpetrator. See: S. 17 (3B) TA 2006.

2337 S. 17 (3) and (3A) TA 2006.

2338 S. 19 (1) (a) and (2) (a) TA 2006.

SECTION XVI. INVESTIGATIVE AND PRE-TRIAL DETENTION

SUBSECTION I. GENERAL RULES ON ARREST AND DETENTION

486. Arrest with warrant – There are several statutes which allow for arrest with a warrant, the most important being s. 1 of the Magistrates' Courts Act 1980.[2339] Under this Act, a Justice of the Peace can issue a written arrest warrant in order to bring a person before a Magistrate's Court. This person must be at least 18 years old and the offence must be indictable or punishable with imprisonment or the person must not have a sufficiently established address for a summons to be served on them.[2340] However, in light of the broad possibilities for arrest without a warrant under PACE 1984 (see next paragraph), the option of arrest with a warrant is seldom used.[2341]

487. General rules: arrest without warrant – The Police and Criminal Evidence Act 1984 (PACE 1984) sets out the general rules for arrest and detention without a warrant. According to this Act a constable can arrest without a warrant, any person who (they have reasonable grounds for suspecting) is about to commit an offence, is in the act of committing one or has committed an offence.[2342] This is only possible if the constable has reasonable grounds for believing that any of the following reasons are present:

(a) to enable the name of the person in question to be ascertained (in the case where the constable does not know, and cannot readily ascertain, the person's name, or has reasonable grounds for doubting whether a name given by the person as his name is his real name);
(b) correspondingly as regards the person's address;
(c) to prevent the person in question
 (i) causing physical injury to himself or any other person;
 (ii) suffering physical injury;
 (iii) causing loss of or damage to property;
 (iv) committing an offence against public decency where members of the public going about their normal business cannot reasonably be expected to avoid the person in question; or

[2339] Fenwick, *Fenwick on Civil Liberties and Human Rights* (n 1649) 877; Stone (n 1651) 112.
[2340] S. 1 (1)–(4) Magistrates' Courts Act 1980.
[2341] Fenwick, *Fenwick on Civil Liberties and Human Rights* (n 1649) 877; Alpa Parmar, 'Arrest' in Lucy Welsh, Layta Skinns and Andrew Sanders, *Sanders & Young's Criminal Justice* (Oxford University Press 2021) 119; Stone (n 1651) 112.
[2342] S. 24 (1)–(3) PACE 1984. See also: Richard Clayton and Hugh Tomlinson, 'Arrest and Reasonable Grounds for Suspicion' (1988) 85 Law Society Gazette 22, 22; Conte (n 10) 496; Fenwick, *Fenwick on Civil Liberties and Human Rights* (n 1649) 877; Parmar (n 2341) 120; Sprack and Engelhardt-Sprack (n 1618) 23–24; Stone (n 1651) 113.

(v) causing an unlawful obstruction of the highway;
(d) to protect a child or other vulnerable person from the person in question;
(e) to allow the prompt and effective investigation of the offence or of the conduct of the person in question;
(f) to prevent any prosecution for the offence from being hindered by the disappearance of the person in question.[2343]

The arresting officer must believe the arrest is necessary in relation to one of these purposes and this belief must be objectively justified.[2344] Regular citizens can also make arrests without a warrant. However, they can only do so to people who are, or they have reasonable grounds for suspecting to be, in the process of committing an indictable offence or who (they have reasonable grounds for suspecting) have committed an indictable offence.[2345] In addition, they can only do so if it appears to not be reasonably practicable for a constable to make the arrest instead and they have reasonable grounds for believing it necessary to prevent the other person from:

(a) causing physical injury to himself or any other person;
(b) suffering physical injury;
(c) causing loss of or damage to property; or
(d) making off before a constable can assume responsibility for him.[2346]

488. Reasonable suspicion – As regards the standard of reasonable suspicion required for an arrest, the UK courts use phrasing similar to that of the ECtHR (see no. 55), requiring that it would be apparent for an objective observer.[2347] However, they seem to be quite lax in applying it.[2348] In addition, a constable

---

2343 S. 24 (5) and (6) PACE 1984. See also: Fenwick, *Fenwick on Civil Liberties and Human Rights* (n 1649) 877–878; Parmar (n 2341) 120; Sprack and Engelhardt-Sprack (n 1618) 24; Stone (n 1651) 113–115.

2344 *Edwards (Deborah) v. DPP* (1993) 97 Cr App R 301, 306–307; *Scott Hayes v. Chief Constable of Merseyside Police* [2011] EWCA Civ 911, 30–35; Clayton and Tomlinson (n 2342) 22; Fenwick, *Fenwick on Civil Liberties and Human Rights* (n 1649) 889; Christopher Ryan and Katherine Williams, 'Police Discretion' [1986] Public Law 285, 288; Stone (n 1651) 116–117; Walker, *Blackstone's Guide to the Anti-Terrorism Legislation* (n 1670) 121.

2345 S. 24A (1) and (2) PACE 1984. See also: Parmar (n 2341) 129; Sprack and Engelhardt-Sprack (n 1618) 23; Stone (n 1651) 117–118.

2346 S. 24A (3) and (4) PACE 1984. See also: Fenwick, *Fenwick on Civil Liberties and Human Rights* (n 1649) 878; Parmar (n 2341) 129; Stone (n 1651) 117–118.

2347 *Dallison v. Caffrey* [1965] 1 Q.B. 348, 371; *Ward v. Chief Constable of Somerset and Avon Constabulary* 1986 WL 408352; *Anna Castorina v. The Chief Constable of Surrey* 1988 WL 622865. See also: Fenwick, *Fenwick on Civil Liberties and Human Rights* (n 1649) 883; Ryan and Williams (n 2344) 288.

2348 Clayton and Tomlinson (n 2342); Fenwick, *Fenwick on Civil Liberties and Human Rights* (n 1649) 884; Parmar (n 2341) 131–132; Ryan and Williams (n 2344) 306–310. E.g., the following amounted to reasonable suspicion of theft: the fact that Easter eggs had been stolen, that the quantity of eggs found was too much to buy for one child according to the arresting officer, that the eggs did not have a price tag and that the purchase price stated by the suspect was considered to be too low (*Ward v. Chief Constable of Somerset and Avon Constabulary* 1986

can also arrest a person who is about to commit an offence, is in the act of committing one or has committed an offence without reasonable suspicion being required. This leads commentators to conclude that if the officer has a hunch, they can act upon it and they will be covered by PACE if the hunch turns out to be correct.[2349] If the hunch turns out to be wrong, the arrest cannot be justified on the grounds that reasonable suspicion did in fact (objectively) exists, since it has to be shown that the arresting officer actually suspected it.[2350] This interpretation could be at odds with the ECHR as Article 5(1)(c) explicitly requires reasonable suspicion an offence has been committed.

489. Investigative Detention – Upon arrest, the arrested person needs to be given certain information and must be taken to a designated police station as soon as practicable.[2351] In these police stations one or more custody officers are appointed.[2352] This custody officer, who is independent of the investigation, has to determine whether there is sufficient evidence to charge the person.[2353] When not charging yet, police bail is a possibility,[2354] as is detention without charge under the conditions they have '*reasonable grounds for believing that the person's detention without being charged is necessary to secure or preserve evidence relating to an offence for which the person is under arrest or to obtain such evidence by questioning the person.*'[2355] Commentators note that in practice, at this stage arrests are mostly just rubber stamped.[2356] Detention without charge

WL 408352). For other examples, see: *Castorina v. The Chief Constable of Surrey* 1988 WL 622865; *Anna Julie Ann Clarke v. Chief Constable of North Wales Police* 2000 WL 345127.

2349 Fenwick, *Fenwick on Civil Liberties and Human Rights* (n 1649) 877 and 883; Parmar (n 2341) 131.

2350 Fenwick, *Fenwick on Civil Liberties and Human Rights* (n 1649) 887. See e.g.: *Siddiqui v. Swain* [1979] RTR 454; *Chapman v. DPP* (1989) Cr App R 190, [1988] Crim LR 843.

2351 S. 28 and 30 (1) and (1A) PACE 1984. See also: Conte (n 10) 497; Fenwick, *Fenwick on Civil Liberties and Human Rights* (n 1649) 890–893; Gibson-Morgan (n 163) 123; Sprack and Engelhardt–Sprack (n 1618) 25–26; Stone (n 1651) 119 and 126. In certain circumstances the constable can bring the arrested person to any police station. In that case they have to be taken to a designated police station or released within six hours. See: S. 30 (3)–(6) PACE 1984. See also: Stone (n 1651) 119.

2352 S. 35 and 36 PACE 1984; Sprack and Engelhardt–Sprack (n 1618) 26; Stone (n 1651) 125–126. On the role of custody officers, see: Fenwick, *Fenwick on Civil Liberties and Human Rights* (n 1649) 900–901.

2353 Gibson-Morgan (n 163) 124; Stone (n 1651) 127; Sprack and Engelhardt–Sprack (n 1618) 27; Lucy Welsh, Layla Skinns and Andrew Sanders, 'Detention in the Police Station' in Lucy Welsh, Layla Skinns and Andrew Sanders, *Sanders & Young's Criminal Justice* (Oxford University Press 2021) 157.

2354 Gibson-Morgan (n 163) 125; Welsh, Skinns and Sanders, 'Detention in the Police Station' (n 2353) 165; Lucy Welsh, Layla Skinns and Andrew Sanders, 'Prosecutions and Constructing Guilt' in Lucy Welsh, Layla Skinns and Andrew Sanders, *Sanders & Young's Criminal Justice* (Oxford University Press 2021) 330–331.

2355 S. 37 (3) PACE 1984. See also: Fenwick, *Fenwick on Civil Liberties and Human Rights* (n 1649) 895; Sprack and Engelhardt–Sprack (n 1618) 27; Stone (n 1651) 127.

2356 David Dixon and others, 'Safeguarding the Rights of Suspects in Police Custody' (1990) 115 Policing and Society 115, 130; Fenwick, *Fenwick on Civil Liberties and Human Rights* (n

may last for a maximum of 24 hours.[2357] During this period, the detention has to be reviewed by a review officer, in principle after six hours and then every nine hours.[2358] The detention without charge can be extended to maximum 36 hours by a police superintendent, but only for investigations into indictable offences which are being conducted diligently and expeditiously; and for which the detention is necessary to secure or preserve evidence or to obtain such evidence through questioning.[2359] Before any extension can be authorised, the person or their solicitor have to be given the opportunity to make representations about the detention.[2360] For further detention after those 36 hours a warrant is required. This warrant can be issued by a Magistrates' Court if, after the person being brought before the Court, it is satisfied that there are reasonable grounds for believing that the further detention is justified.[2361] A warrant can only be justified under the same conditions a superintended can extend pre-charge detention.[2362] A warrant of further detention is also valid for maximum 36 hours.[2363] The warrant can be extended for another period of maximum 36 hours, if there are reasonable grounds for believing this is justified.[2364] The detention can be further extended, as long as the total period of detention does not exceed 96 hours.[2365] Again, according to commentators, the application of

1649) 895; Mike McConville, Andrew Sanders and Roger Leng, *The Case for the Prosecution* (Routledge 1991) 41–44; Welsh, Skinns and Sanders, 'Detention in the Police Station' (n 2353) 174–175.

2357 S. 41 (1) PACE 1984. See also: Fenwick, *Fenwick on Civil Liberties and Human Rights* (n 1649) 895; Gibson-Morgan (n 163) 124; Sprack and Engelhardt-Sprack (n 1618) 28; Stone (n 1651) 131; Welsh, Skinns and Sanders, 'Detention in the Police Station' (n 2353) 167. When this period of 24 hours starts, depends on the concrete situation. See: S. 41 (2) and (3) PACE 1984; Stone (n 1651) 129–131.

2358 S. 40 (3) PACE 1984. See also: Sprack and Engelhardt-Sprack (n 1618) 27–28; Stone (n 1651) 131–132.

2359 S. 42 (1) PACE 1984. See also: Lord Lloyd of Berwick, *Inquiry into legislation against terrorism* (Cm 3420, 1996) 43; Fenwick, *Fenwick on Civil Liberties and Human Rights* (n 1649) 895; Gibson-Morgan (n 163) 124; Sprack and Engelhardt-Sprack (n 1618) 28; Stone (n 1651) 133–135; Welsh, Skinns and Sanders, 'Detention in the Police Station' (n 2353) 167.

2360 S. 42 (6) PACE 1984. See also: Dixon and others (n 2356) 130; Stone (n 1651) 134; Welsh, Skinns and Sanders, 'Detention in the Police Station' (n 2353) 167.

2361 S. 43 (1) and (2) (b) PACE 1984. See also: Fenwick, *Fenwick on Civil Liberties and Human Rights* (n 1649) 895; Sprack and Engelhardt-Sprack (n 1618) 28; Stone (n 1651) 135.

2362 S. 43 (4) PACE 1984. See also: Sprack and Engelhardt-Sprack (n 1618) 28; Stone (n 1651) 135.

2363 S. 43 (12) PACE 1984. See also: Sprack and Engelhardt-Sprack (n 1618) 28; Stone (n 1651) 135; Welsh, Skinns and Sanders, 'Detention in the Police Station' (n 2353) 168.

2364 S. 44 (1)–(3) PACE 1984. See also: Stone (n 1651) 135; Welsh, Skinns and Sanders, 'Detention in the Police Station' (n 2353) 168.

2365 S. 44 (4) PACE 1984. See also: Lord Lloyd of Berwick, *Inquiry into legislation against terrorism* (Cm 3420, 1996) 43; Ashworth and Zedner (n 18) 189; Conte (n 10) 502; Fenwick, *Fenwick on Civil Liberties and Human Rights* (n 1649) 896; Sprack and Engelhardt-Sprack (n 1618) 28–29; Welsh, Skinns and Sanders, 'Detention in the Police Station' (n 2353) 168; Zedner, 'Terrorizing Criminal Law' (n 45) 116.

these rules is routinised and they are only formally adhered to.[2366] According to Stone and Conte, the arrangement is in line with Article 5(3) ECHR since it provides for judicial review.[2367]

490. Post-charge detention – In principle suspects are released after they have been charged. However, the custody officer can decide not to order their release if:

(a) the detainee has refused to give his name and address; or
(b) there are reasonable grounds for the custody officer to believe:
  (i) the name and address furnished are not genuine; or
  (ii) the detainee will not answer bail; or
  (iii) if the offence charged is imprisonable, the detention is necessary to prevent him committing a further offence; or
  (iv) if the offence charged is non-imprisonable, his detention is necessary to prevent him causing injury to another or loss of or damage to property; or
  (v) his detention is necessary to prevent him from interfering with the administration of justice or the investigation of an offence; or
  (vi) his detention is necessary for his own protection; or
(c) The offence charged is murder.[2368]

If the suspect is kept in detention, they must be brought before a Magistrates' Court as soon as practicable.[2369] Any hearing prior to trial or sentencing must conclude with a decision on the continuation of pre-trail detention.[2370]

491. Bail – When the accused person appears before the Magistrates' Court, they in principle have a right to bail.[2371] This presumption of bail can only be defeated for people accused of imprisonable offences in a set of listed circumstances. The most relevant for us are: if '*there are substantial grounds for believing that the defendant, if released on bail would (a) fail to surrender to*

2366 Dixon and others (n 2356) 130–131; Fenwick, *Fenwick on Civil Liberties and Human Rights* (n 1649) 896.

2367 Conte (n 10) 502; Stone (n 1651) 133.

2368 S. 38 (1) PACE 1984. See also: Sprack and Engelhardt-Sprack (n 1618) 29–30.

2369 S. 46 (1) and (2) PACE 1984. See also: Sprack and Engelhardt-Sprack (n 1618) 30.

2370 S. 5 (1), 10 (4), 18 (4), and 128 (1) Magistrates' Courts Act 1980; S. 81 Senior Courts Act 1981; S. 52 (5) Crime and Disorder Act 1998; Tom Smith, 'The Practice of Pre-Trial Detention in England & Wales – Changing Law and Changing Culture' (2022) 28 European Journal on Criminal Policy and Research 435, 436; Tom Smith, '"Rushing Remand"? Pretrial Detention and Bail Decision Making in England and Wales' (2021) 60 The Howard Journal of Crime and Justice 46, 52.

2371 S. 4 Bail Act 1976 (BA 1976). See also: Pollly Dyer, 'Bail: Criminal Proceedings' [2021] Westlaw UK 11, para 3; Smith, 'The Practice of Pre-Trial Detention in England & Wales – Changing Law and Changing Culture' (n 2370) 436; Smith, '"Rushing Remand"?' (n 2370) 52; Sprack and Engelhardt-Sprack (n 1618) 91; Welsh, Skinns and Sanders, 'Summary Justice in the Magistrates' Court' (n 1618) 405; Wood (n 25) 149.

custody, or (b) commit an offence while on bail, or (c) interfere with witnesses or otherwise obstruct the course of justice, whether in relation to himself or any other person' or if necessary for their own protection.[2372] Bail can be accompanied by a variety of conditions and requirements, including electronic monitoring requirements.[2373] A refusal of bail by the Magistrates' Court can be appealed to the Crown Court.[2374]

SUBSECTION II. TERRORISM SPECIFIC RULES ON ARREST AND DETENTION

492. Terrorism specific arrest rules – In addition to the general rules mentioned in the previous Subsection, UK law has terrorism-specific rules concerning arrest and detention. The TA 2000 states that any constable may arrest a person without a warrant, if they reasonably suspect them to be a terrorist.[2375] A 'terrorist' is in this context defined by the legislation as '*a person who has committed an offence under any of sections 11, 12, 15 to 18, 54 and 56 to 63, or is or has been concerned in the commission, preparation or instigation of acts of terrorism.*'[2376] The latter part '*includes a reference to a person who has been, whether before or after the passing of this Act, concerned in the commission, preparation or instigation of acts of terrorism within the meaning given by section 1.*'[2377] Note that there is no additional requirement of certain goals for the arrest such as preventing the person from causing injury or from hindering prosecution.[2378] The power of arrest was criticised as being overly broad for several reasons.[2379] First, it does not require the constable to have a particular offence in mind since the definition uses the vague 'acts of terrorism'.[2380] For this

2372 S. 2 (1) and (3) Schedule 1 BA 1976. See also: Duff, 'Pre-Trial Detention and the Presumption of Innocence' (n 96) 117; Dyer (n 2371) paras 4–14; Smith, 'The Practice of Pre-Trial Detention in England & Wales – Changing Law and Changing Culture' (n 2370) 436; Smith, '"Rushing Remand"?' (n 2370) 52; Sprack and Engelhardt-Sprack (n 1618) 91–92; Welsh, Skinns and Sanders, 'Summary Justice in the Magistrates' Court' (n 1618) 406.

2373 S. 3 (6)–(6F) BA 1976. See also: Dyer (n 2371) 15–22; Welsh, Skinns and Sanders, 'Summary Justice in the Magistrates' Court' (n 1618) 408–410.

2374 S. 60 Criminal Justice Act 1982. See also: Dyer (n 2371) para 36; Welsh, Skinns and Sanders, 'Summary Justice in the Magistrates' Court' (n 1618) 415.

2375 S. 41 (1) TA 2000. See also: Allen and Dempsey (n 1664) 10; Anderson, 'Shielding the Compass: How to Fight Terrorism without Defeating the Law' (n 25) 7; Conte (n 10) 235 and 498; Fenwick, *Fenwick on Civil Liberties and Human Rights* (n 1649) 879; Hill (n 1666) para 9.1; Parmar (n 2341) 122; Rowe (n 1670) 532; Spencer (n 1616) 124; Staniforth (n 1747) 140; Stone (n 1651) 450; Walker, *Blackstone's Guide to the Anti-Terrorism Legislation* (n 1670) 120.

2376 S. 40 (1) TA 2000. See also: Conte (n 10) 498; Fenwick, *Fenwick on Civil Liberties and Human Rights* (n 1649) 879; Hall, 'The Terrorism Acts in 2021' (n 1885) para 5.2; Stone (n 1651) 450.

2377 S. 40 (2) TA 2000.

2378 Fenwick, *Fenwick on Civil Liberties and Human Rights* (n 1649) 879.

2379 See also: Conte (n 10) 498; Hill (n 1666) para 9.1.

2380 Fenwick, *Fenwick on Civil Liberties and Human Rights* (n 1649) 879; Stone (n 1651) 450; Stephen Vladeck and Clive Walker, 'Detention and Interrogation in Law and War' in

reason, some commentators doubt it is justifiable under Article 5(1)(c) ECHR. They refer to the *Brogan* case (see no. 56), in which the Court held that an arrest based on a similar statute definition of acts of terrorism was justifiable because the definition of terrorism was 'well in keeping with the idea of an offence' and after arrest the applicants were asked about specific offences.[2381] Fenwick expresses doubt as to whether the current legislation would pass this test. Walker on the other hand seemed to have more fate in the ability of the legislation to withstand this test.[2382] Second, the person only needs to be 'concerned in the commission, preparation or instigation', which is broader than being a principal or a party to an offence.[2383] During detention under the TA 2000, the detainee has the right to make representations, to certain information, etc. as is the case under PACE 1984.[2384]

493. Duration of detention – The person arrested under the TA 2000 can be detained for the first 48 hours on the authority of the police.[2385] Afterwards, a warrant for further detention issued by a Magistrates' Court is necessary.[2386] The police do have until six hours after the 48 hours have lapsed to actually apply for this supervision if it was not reasonably practical to do so earlier, without needing to release the suspect (this is not a terrorism specific rule, which also applies for other arrestees).[2387] Within the original 48 hours, a review officer has to authorise the detention every 12 hours.[2388] Originally, after a warrant for further detention was issued, suspects could be detained for maximum seven days (including the original 48 hours).[2389] This was already higher than

---

Genevieve Lennon and Clive Walker (eds), *Routledge Handbook of Law and Terrorism* (Routledge 2015) 172; Walker, *Blackstone's Guide to the Anti-Terrorism Legislation* (n 1670) 121; Webber (n 95) 97.

2381 Fenwick, *Fenwick on Civil Liberties and Human Rights* (n 1649) 880–881; Rowe (n 1670) 533.

2382 Walker, *Blackstone's Guide to the Anti-Terrorism Legislation* (n 1670) 121–123.

2383 Stone (n 1651) 450; Rowe (n 1670) 533.

2384 See e.g. s. 26–28, 31 and 33–34 Schedule 8 TA 2000.

2385 S. 41 (3) TA 2000. See also: Staniforth (n 1747) 144; Stone (n 1651) 453; Vladeck and Walker (n 2380) 172; Walker, *Blackstone's Guide to the Anti-Terrorism Legislation* (n 1670) 123; Webber (n 95) 98.

2386 Secretary of State for the Home Department, *Review of Counter-Terrorism and Security Powers* (Cm 8004, 2011) 7; Conte (n 10) 503; Hill (n 1666) para 9.1; Roach, *The 9/11 Effect: Comparative Counter-Terrorism* (n 79) 259; Rowe (n 1670) 533–534; Spencer (n 1616) 124; Stone (n 1651) 453; Vladeck and Walker (n 2380) 172–173; Walker, *Blackstone's Guide to the Anti-Terrorism Legislation* (n 1670) 123.

2387 S. 30 (1) (b) Schedule 8 TA 2000; Fenwick, *Fenwick on Civil Liberties and Human Rights* (n 1649) 899; Stone (n 1651) 453; Walker, *Blackstone's Guide to the Anti-Terrorism Legislation* (n 1670) 125.

2388 S. 21–28 Schedule 8 TA 2000. See also: Fenwick, *Fenwick on Civil Liberties and Human Rights* (n 1649) 899; Stone (n 1651) 453; Walker, *Blackstone's Guide to the Anti-Terrorism Legislation* (n 1670) 128–129; Webber (n 95) 98.

2389 Roach, 'Must We Trade Rights for Security? The Choice Between Smart, Harsh, or Proportionate Security Strategies in Canada and Britain' (n 1759) 307; Rowe (n 1670) 533; Stone (n 1651) 453; Walker, *Blackstone's Guide to the Anti-Terrorism Legislation* (n 1670) 123.

the four days recommended by Lord Lloyd in his review.[2390] However, after 9/11 the period of seven days was further raised to 14.[2391] In the aftermath of the 7/7 bombings, the government wanted to extend the period drastically again, to 90 days.[2392] However, this proposal did not make it through parliament and a compromise of 28 days was reached.[2393] This extension had to be renewed every year and in 2010 it was decided not to do so.[2394] This decision was reached after a review showed that prolonged periods of pre-charge detention were not used often anyway and that when used, their utility was questioned.[2395] Since

2390 Lord Lloyd of Berwick, *Inquiry into legislation against terrorism* (Cm 3420, 1996) 45–48. See also: Secretary of State for the Home Department and Secretary of State for Northern Ireland, *Legislation Against Terrorism: A consultation paper* (Cm 4178, 1998) para 8.22–8.24; Walker, *Blackstone's Guide to the Anti-Terrorism Legislation* (n 1670) 123.

2391 S. 306 Criminal Justice Act 2003. See also: JCHR, *Counter-Terrorism Policy and Human Rights: Terrorism Bill and related matters* (HL paper 75, HC paper 561, 2005) para 65–68; Allen and Dempsey (n 1664) 16; Conte (n 10) 498 and 502; Fenwick, *Fenwick on Civil Liberties and Human Rights* (n 1649) 898; Hill (n 1666) para 9.7; Middleton (n 1626) 241; Roach, 'Must We Trade Rights for Security? The Choice Between Smart, Harsh, or Proportionate Security Strategies in Canada and Britain' (n 1759) 307; Spencer (n 1616) 124; Sprack and Engelhardt-Sprack (n 1618) 58; Stone (n 1651) 453; Welsh, Skinns and Sanders, 'Detention in the Police Station' (n 2353) 170.

2392 JCHR, *Counter-Terrorism Policy and Human Rights: Terrorism Bill and related matters* (HL paper 75, HC paper 561, 2005) para 64; Amnesty International report, 'Dangerously disproportionate, the ever-expanding national security state in Europe' (2017) 47; Anderson, 'Shielding the Compass: How to Fight Terrorism without Defeating the Law' (n 25) 17; Anderson, 'Independent Review of Terrorism Laws' (n 1670) 6; D Cole, 'English Lessons: A Comparative Analysis of UK and US Responses to Terrorism' (2009) 62 Current Legal Problems 136, 142; Conte (n 10) 504; Demirsu (n 56) 83; John Ip, 'Terrorism Laws and Constitutional Accountability' in Genevieve Lennon and Clive Walker (eds), *Routledge Handbook of Law and Terrorism* (Routledge 2015) 102; Middleton (n 1626) 241; Roach, *The 9/11 Effect: Comparative Counter-Terrorism* (n 79) 299; Spencer (n 1616) 124; Stone (n 1651) 453; Welsh, Skinns and Sanders, 'Detention in the Police Station' (n 2353) 170. Another proposal was made for 42 days. This proposal was criticised as well. See e.g.: United Nations Human Rights Committee (2008) *Concluding Observations of the Human Rights Committee: United Kingdom of Great Britain and Northern Ireland*, Ninety Third Session, 7–25 July, para 15. See also: Cole 142; Kenneth O Morgan, 'The Politics of Pre-Trial Detention in the United Kingdom since 2000' in Marion Charret-Del Bove and Fabrice Mourlon (eds), *Pre-trial detention in 20th and 21st Century Common Law and Civil Law Systems* (Cambridge Scholars Publishing 2014) 19–20.

2393 S. 23 TA 2006. See also: JCHR, *Counter-Terrorism Policy and Human Rights: Terrorism Bill and related matters* (HL paper 75, HC paper 561, 2005) para 64; Allen and Dempsey (n 1664) 16; Ashworth, 'Criminal Law, Human Rights and Preventative Justice' (n 27) 90; Cole (n 2392) 142; Conte (n 10) 498 and 502; Demirsu (n 56) 83; Fenwick, *Fenwick on Civil Liberties and Human Rights* (n 1649) 898; Ip (n 2392) 102; Middleton (n 1626) 241; Morgan (n 2392) 19; Roach, 'Must We Trade Rights for Security? The Choice Between Smart, Harsh, or Proportionate Security Strategies in Canada and Britain' (n 1759) 307; Roach, *The 9/11 Effect: Comparative Counter-Terrorism* (n 79) 244; Stone (n 1651) 453; Tadros, 'Justice and Terrorism' (n 46) 664–665; Webber (n 95) 99; Welsh, Skinns and Sanders, 'Detention in the Police Station' (n 2353) 170.

2394 See: S. 25 TA 2006; House of Commons 'Counter-terrorism Review' 2010–2012 (Hansard) 26 January 2011, 522–106: 306–326, 307; Spencer (n 1616) 124; Stone (n 1651) 453; Vladeck and Walker (n 2380) 171.

2395 Lord MacDonald, Review Of Counter-Terrorism And Security Powers (Cm 8003, 2011) 4; Secretary of State for the Home Department, *Review of Counter-Terrorism and Security*

January 2011, therefore, the period is back to 14 days.[2396] At that time, though, two draft bills were also introduced which would reintroduce the maximum of 28 days for a period of three months.[2397] These bills have received pre-legislative scrutiny and can be made law quickly in emergency situations.[2398] A warrant for further detention is valid for seven days (starting at the time of arrest) and is issued by a District Judge (Magistrates' Courts).[2399] This warrant is issued if there are reasonable grounds for believing it necessary to obtain or preserve relevant evidence or pending the results of the examination or analysis of evidence.[2400] The warrant can be further extended by the judicial authority for maximum seven days at a time up to the (current) total maximum of 14 days.[2401] The longer period was said to be important since under UK law, a suspect cannot be questioned once criminal proceedings have formally been instituted against them.[2402] In order to remedy this problem, the CTA 2008[2403] allowed for 'post-charge questioning' in terrorist cases if this is necessary in the interest of justice.[2404] A Crown Court judge may allow post-charge questioning for terrorism offences or offences which appear to have a terrorist connection.[2405] In his report on the year 2020, the independent reviewer stated that the power had only been used a total of four times (none of which were in 2020) and in the 2021 report he mentions that during that year this power was only utilised once, meaning the total at the end of 2021 was only at five.[2406]

Powers (Cm 8004, 2011) 7–14; Stone (n 1651) 453; Webber (n 95) 99. For criticism, see also: JCHR, *Counter-Terrorism Policy and Human Rights (Seventeenth Report): Bringing Human Rights Back* (HL paper 23, HC paper 111, 2010) para 65–80.

2396 Anderson, 'Shielding the Compass: How to Fight Terrorism without Defeating the Law' (n 25) 7–8; Anderson, 'Independent Review of Terrorism Laws' (n 1670) 6; Ashworth and Zedner (n 18) 189; Fenwick, *Fenwick on Civil Liberties and Human Rights* (n 1649) 896; Morgan (n 2392) 21; Staniforth (n 1747) 144; Zedner, 'Terrorizing Criminal Law' (n 45) 114.

2397 Draft Detention of Terrorist Suspects (Temporary Extension) Bills (Cm 8018, 2011). See also: Hill (n 1666) para 9.9; Webber (n 95) 99. This was recommended by the Secretary's review. See: Secretary of State for the Home Department, *Review of Counter-Terrorism and Security Powers* (Cm 8004, 2011) 14. In addition, in 2012 the power to make a temporary extension order was granted to the Secretary of State in case parliament is dissolved. See: S. 38 Schedule 8 TA 2000. See also: Amnesty International report, 'Dangerously disproportionate, the ever-expanding national security state in Europe' (2017) 47.

2398 Joint Committee on the Draft Detention of Terrorist Suspects (Temporary Extension) Bills, *Draft Detention of Terrorist Suspects (Temporary Extension) Bills: Report* (HL paper 161, HC paper 893, 2011).

2399 S. 29 Schedule 8 TA 2000. See also: Stone (n 1651) 455; Vladeck and Walker (n 2380) 172–173.

2400 S. 32 Schedule 8 TA 2000. See also: Webber (n 95) 99.

2401 S. 36 Schedule 8 TA 2000. See also: Vladeck and Walker (n 2380) 172; Webber (n 95) 99.

2402 Gibson-Morgan (n 163) 124; Spencer (n 1616) 125; Stone (n 1651) 459.

2403 The relevant part entering into force in 2012. See: Counter-Terrorism Act 2008 (Commencement No.6) Order 2012.

2404 S. 22–27 CTA 2008. See also: Hall, 'The Terrorism Acts in 2021' (n 1885) para 4.66; Middleton (n 1626) 241; Spencer (n 1616) 125; Webber (n 95) 98–99.

2405 S. 22 (2) CTA 2008. See also: Stone (n 1651) 459.

2406 Hall, 'The Terrorism Acts in 2021' (n 1885) para 4.67; Hall, 'The Terrorism Acts in 2020' (n 1692) para 4.18.

494. Bail – No police bail is possible for people detained under schedule 8 of the TA 2000.[2407] This is criticised by Liberty and some commentators because they feel police bail would be a better alternative to TPIMs (see nos 511–519).[2408]

495. Numbers – According to Allen and Dempsey (2017), there had been 3514 terrorism related arrests since 11 September 2001, 1855 (53%) of which were made under section 41 of the TA 2000.[2409] During the early years of this legislation, the vast majority of the arrests was made under section 41. More recently, this shifted in favour of other legislation.[2410] The peak was in 2016–2017 with 304 terrorism related arrests. The majority of arrests were classified as relating to international terrorism.[2411] Hill and the Home Office even count 412 terrorism related arrests in 2017.[2412] Regarding the duration of detention, Allen and Dempsey state the following:

> Of the 1,855 people arrested under section 41 of the Terrorism Act 2000 since 11 September 2001, the majority (90%) have been detained for fewer than 7 days; 739 people (40%) have been held for less than one day, and 925 (50%) for between one and seven days. Only 11 people have been detained for longer than 14 days, 10 in 2006/07 and one in 2007/08. Six people were detained for the 28 day maximum period in 2006/07.[2413]

Only 39% of those arrested have been charged and of those, 32% were charged for non-terrorism offences.[2414] In 2021, 186 terrorism-related arrests took place, of which only 32 (17%) were under section 41.[2415] 57 (31%) of those total arrests resulted in a charge, 49 (86%) of which were considered to be terrorism-related.[2416]

2407 Secretary of State for the Home Department, *Review of Counter-Terrorism and Security Powers* (Cm 8004, 2011) 11.

2408 Liberty's Report Stage Briefing on the Terrorism Prevention and Investigation Measures Bill in the House of Commons (August 2011), 5. See also: Wood (n 25) 151–153.

2409 Allen and Dempsey (n 1664) 10.

2410 Allen and Dempsey (n 1664) 11.

2411 Allen and Dempsey (n 1664) 11–12.

2412 Home Office, *Counter-Terrorism And Border Security Bill: Explanatory Notes (Bill 219–EN, 2018)* para 4; Hill (n 1666) para 9.4.

2413 Allen and Dempsey (n 1664) 17.

2414 Hill (n 1666) para 9.15.

2415 HM Government, *Counter-terrorism Disruptive Powers Report 2021* (CP 779, 2023), www.gov.uk/government/publications/counter-terrorism-disruptive-powers-report-2021/hm-government-counter-terrorism-disruptive-powers-report-2021-accessible-version; Hall, 'The Terrorism Acts in 2021' (n 1885) para 5.1 and 5.4.

2416 HM Government, *Counter-terrorism Disruptive Powers Report 2021* (CP 779, 2023), www.gov.uk/government/publications/counter-terrorism-disruptive-powers-report-2021/hm-government-counter-terrorism-disruptive-powers-report-2021-accessible-version.

CHAPTER II
ADMINISTRATIVE LAW

INTRODUCTION

496. Evolution of the legislation – The UK also employed administrative detention as a tool in its struggle with terrorism in the 20th Century. When originally consolidating and restructuring its counter-terrorism legislation in the TA 2000, the UK legislature did not include administrative detention. However, in response to 9/11, a version of administrative detention was introduced as a counter-terrorism measure.[2417] This administrative detention was controversial from the outset and after a declaration of incompatibility by the House of Lords, it was replaced by control orders. Control orders were also widely criticised and led to legal challenges and extensive case law. Due to this case law and a change in government, control orders were in turn abolished and replaced by Terrorism Prevention and Investigation Measures (TPIMs). The TPIM legislation is currently still in force. At the outset TPIMs were significantly more lenient than control orders in several respects, but several changes to the legislation have made them stricter again and at this point, the practical difference between a TPIM and what used to be a control order is minimal. This Chapter discusses the evolution from administrative detention under the ATCSA 2001 to the current TPIMs and analyses the current legislation.

SECTION I. ANTI-TERRORISM, CRIME AND SECURITY ACT 2001

497. Administrative detention of foreigners – The ATCSA 2001 made it possible to indefinitely detain foreign terrorism suspects who would have been deported if not for issues such as the risk of torture or killing in their country of origin.[2418] The system was introduced for lack of other option to deal with

2417 *A v. Secretary of State for the Home Department* [2004] UKHL 56, [2005] 2 WLR 87, 7.

2418 Anderson, 'Shielding the Compass: How to Fight Terrorism without Defeating the Law' (n 25) 8; Ashworth and Zedner (n 18) 183; Cole (n 2392) 140; Demirsu (n 56) 78; Fenwick, 'The Anti-Terrorism, Crime and Security Act 2001' (n 92) 731; Fenwick, *Fenwick on Civil Liberties and Human Rights* (n 1649) 1081–1082; Fenwick and Phillipson (n 25) 873; Gearty (n 1659) 27–28;

these people. On the one hand the government could not convict them for lack of admissible evidence due to (among other things) the prohibition of the use of intercept evidence and the fact that the information on them often came from intelligence sources.[2419] On the other hand they could not be detained for long periods of time under immigration law because detention in that context is only allowed with a view to deportation, which was impossible.[2420] Therefore, the ATCSA 2001 allowed for indefinite detention on the order of the Home Secretary on reasonable conviction that a person's presence in the UK presented a risk for national security and reasonable suspicion of involvement in the commission, preparation or instigation of acts of international terrorism or of being members of or having links with an international terrorist group.[2421, 2422] 'Links' in this context meant assisting or supporting such a group.[2423] According to Fenwick, the wording of the legislation was too broad and allowed for too many people to be detained.[2424] The person was released if they agreed to leave the country voluntarily.[2425] The statute provided for a possibility to appeal to the Special Immigration Appeals Commission (SIAC) and for automatic

---

Adrian Hunt, 'From Control Orders to TPIMs: Variations on a Number of Themes in British Legal Responses to Terrorism' (2014) 62 Crime, Law and Social Change 289, 290; Lazarus, Goold and Goss (n 30) 469; Paye (n 79) 15; Roach, *The 9/11 Effect: Comparative Counter-Terrorism* (n 79) 271; Spencer (n 1616) 129–130; Stone (n 1651) 465; Tadros, 'Justice and Terrorism' (n 46) 666; Thomas (n 92) 1218; Walker, 'Keeping Control of Terrorists without Losing Control of Constitutionalism' (n 26) 1404. For the landmark case on this issue, see: *Chahal v. United Kingdom* App no 22414/93 (ECtHR Grand Chamber 15 November 1996).

2419 See e.g.: Walker, 'The Impact of Contemporary Security Agendas Against Terrorism on the Substantive Criminal Law' (n 45) 128.

2420 *A v. Secretary of State for the Home Department* [2004] UKHL 56, [2005] 2 WLR 87, 8; *R v. Governor of Durham prison ex p Singh* [1984] 1 WLR 704; Conte (n 10) 537–538; Fenwick, 'Recalibrating ECHR Rights, and the Role of the Human Rights Act Post 9/11' (n 26) 158; Fenwick, 'The Anti-Terrorism, Crime and Security Act 2001' (n 92) 737–738; Fenwick, *Fenwick on Civil Liberties and Human Rights* (n 1649) 1081–1083; Fenwick and Phillipson (n 25) 873–874; Gearty (n 1659) 27–28; Walker, *Blackstone's Guide to the Anti-Terrorism Legislation* (n 1670) 218–223; Wood (n 25) 115–116.

2421 Being a group which '*is subject to the control or influence of persons outside the United Kingdom, and the Secretary of State suspects that it is concerned in the commission, preparation or instigation of acts of international terrorism.*' See: S. 21 (3) ATCSA 2001.

2422 S. 21 (1) and (2) ATCSA 2001. See also: Fenwick, 'The Anti-Terrorism, Crime and Security Act 2001' (n 92) 733; Fenwick, *Fenwick on Civil Liberties and Human Rights* (n 1649) 1084; Paye (n 79) 14; Stone (n 1651) 465; Walker, *Blackstone's Guide to the Anti-Terrorism Legislation* (n 1670) 225; Walker, 'Keeping Control of Terrorists without Losing Control of Constitutionalism' (n 26) 1405.

2423 S. 21 (4) ATCSA 2001. See also: Fenwick, 'The Anti-Terrorism, Crime and Security Act 2001' (n 92) 733; Roach, *The 9/11 Effect: Comparative Counter-Terrorism* (n 79) 272; Walker, *Blackstone's Guide to the Anti-Terrorism Legislation* (n 1670) 226.

2424 Fenwick, 'The Anti-Terrorism, Crime and Security Act 2001' (n 92) 736–737; Fenwick, *Fenwick on Civil Liberties and Human Rights* (n 1649) 1084–1086.

2425 Demirsu (n 56) 78; Gearty (n 1659) 28; Paye (n 79) 15; Roach, *The 9/11 Effect: Comparative Counter-Terrorism* (n 79) 275; Walker, *Blackstone's Guide to the Anti-Terrorism Legislation* (n 1670) 224. See e.g.: *A v. Secretary of State for the Home Department* [2004] UKHL 56, [2005] 2 WLR 87, 2. Note, however, that Fenwick points out that the legislation made no express

review.[2426] However, this procedure included the use of secret evidence and special advocates.[2427] For lack of information about their detention on the side of the detainee, both Fenwick and Tadros argue that this procedure did not offer the necessary rights.[2428] In addition, the Commission only automatically reviewed a case after six months and even if it cancelled a detention certificate, the Secretary of State could issue another one.[2429] The regime was accompanied by a derogation from Article 5(1) ECHR (see no. 28).[2430] Numbers are not easy to come by, but not many people were subject to this regime. In total about 17 people were detained under this Act during the period it was in force.[2431]

498. Criticism – The regime was heavily criticised. Critics stated that no real state of emergency existed upon which the derogation could be based. They pointed to the lack of immediate intelligence regarding a specific terrorist threat

provision for this. See: Fenwick, 'The Anti-Terrorism, Crime and Security Act 2001' (n 92) 736.

2426 S. 25 ATCSA 2001. See also: Demirsu (n 56) 78; Donkin (n 56) 27; Ewing (n 1652) 841; Fenwick, 'The Anti-Terrorism, Crime and Security Act 2001' (n 92) 730; Fenwick, *Fenwick on Civil Liberties and Human Rights* (n 1649) 1086; Paye (n 79) 15; Roach, *The 9/11 Effect: Comparative Counter-Terrorism* (n 79) 273; Stone (n 1651) 465; Tadros, 'Justice and Terrorism' (n 46) 666; Thomas (n 92) 1218–1219.

2427 *A. and others v. United Kingdom* App no 3455/05 (ECtHR Grand Chamber 19 February 2009) 215; Demirsu (n 56) 78; Fenwick, 'The Anti-Terrorism, Crime and Security Act 2001' (n 92) 740; Gearty (n 1659) 31; Hunt (n 2418) 290; Thomas (n 92) 1219; Walker, *Blackstone's Guide to the Anti-Terrorism Legislation* (n 1670) 229; Walker, 'Keeping Control of Terrorists without Losing Control of Constitutionalism' (n 26) 1405; Welsh, Skinns and Sanders, 'Detention in the Police Station' (n 2353) 171.

2428 Fenwick, 'The Anti-Terrorism, Crime and Security Act 2001' (n 92) 741; Tadros, 'Justice and Terrorism' (n 46) 666. Note that SIAC did in fact overrule the Secretary of State on occasion, herein supported by the Court of Appeal. See e.g.: *The Secretary of State for the Home Department v. 'M'* [2004] EWCA Civ 324, 2004 WL 412985.

2429 S. 27 (9) ATCSA 2001; Fenwick, 'The Anti-Terrorism, Crime and Security Act 2001' (n 92) 738; Fenwick, *Fenwick on Civil Liberties and Human Rights* (n 1649) 1086; Roach, *The 9/11 Effect: Comparative Counter-Terrorism* (n 79) 273; Walker, *Blackstone's Guide to the Anti-Terrorism Legislation* (n 1670) 228.

2430 *A. and others v. United Kingdom* App no 3455/05 (ECtHR Grand Chamber 19 February 2009) 9–12; *A v. Secretary of State for the Home Department* [2004] UKHL 56, [2005] 2 WLR 87, 11; Allen and Dempsey (n 1664) 21; Conte (n 10) 237 and 537; Demirsu (n 56) 78–79; Fenwick, 'The Anti-Terrorism, Crime and Security Act 2001' (n 92) 730–731; Fenwick, 'Preventive Anti-Terrorist Strategies in the UK and ECHR: Control Orders, TPIMs and the Role of Technology' (n 25) 130; Fenwick and Fenwick (n 56) 17; Fenwick, *Fenwick on Civil Liberties and Human Rights* (n 1649) 1083–1084; Fenwick and Phillipson (n 25) 873; Gearty (n 1659) 31–32; Khan (n 1649) 108; Paye (n 79) 15; Roach, *The 9/11 Effect: Comparative Counter-Terrorism* (n 79) 271; Stone (n 1651) 465; Tadros, 'Justice and Terrorism' (n 46) 666; Thomas (n 92) 1217; Walker, *Blackstone's Guide to the Anti-Terrorism Legislation* (n 1670) 233–234; Walker, 'Keeping Control of Terrorists without Losing Control of Constitutionalism' (n 26) 1406.

2431 Ashworth and Zedner (n 18) 183; Demirsu (n 56) 78; Khan (n 1649) 108; Walker, 'Keeping Control of Terrorists without Losing Control of Constitutionalism' (n 26) 1406. Allen and Dempsey put the number at 16. See: Allen and Dempsey (n 1664) 21. Anderson at 15. See: Anderson, 'Shielding the Compass: How to Fight Terrorism without Defeating the Law' (n 25) 8.

and the fact that no other European state had requested a derogation.[2432] Second, the rules were said to be discriminatory and third, disproportionate.[2433] Fenwick even raised the question whether the whole scheme did not violate Article 3 ECHR.[2434]

499. Declaration of incompatibility – Several people subject to the regime challenged its lawfulness as well. This led to a House of Lords case in which the regime was declared incompatible with Articles 5 and 14 ECHR, with Lord Walker of Gestingthorpe being the only one dissenting.[2435] The Human Rights Act did not incorporate Article 15 ECHR, but the Attorney General accepted that the conditions of Article 15 ECHR (see no. 152) had to be met for a derogation to be permissible.[2436] The majority of the House of Lords held that there was a public emergency, allowing for derogation under Article 15 ECHR.[2437] They reasoned the decision was mainly a political one in which great weight should be given to the judgment of the Home Secretary, his colleagues and parliament.[2438] However, measures taken in derogation of ECHR rights under Article 15 should be '*strictly required by the exigencies of the situation*' (see also no. 28), which is a proportionality test.[2439] In applying this test, the House showed less deference

2432 Conte (n 10) 540–541; Roach, *The 9/11 Effect: Comparative Counter-Terrorism* (n 79) 274. For an analysis, see also: Fenwick, 'The Anti-Terrorism, Crime and Security Act 2001' (n 92) 743–750.

2433 Conte (n 10) 539–540; Ip (n 2392) 104–105; Paye (n 79) 15.

2434 Fenwick, 'The Anti-Terrorism, Crime and Security Act 2001' (n 92) 755–756.

2435 *A v. Secretary of State for the Home Department* [2004] UKHL 56, [2005] 2 WLR 87, 73. See also: Allen and Dempsey (n 1664) 21; Anderson, 'Shielding the Compass: How to Fight Terrorism without Defeating the Law' (n 25) 8; Conte (n 10) 237 and 540; Duff, 'Pre-Trial Detention and the Presumption of Innocence' (n 96) 115; Fenwick, 'Recalibrating ECHR Rights, and the Role of the Human Rights Act Post 9/11' (n 26) 159; Fenwick, 'Preventive Anti-Terrorist Strategies in the UK and ECHR: Control Orders, TPIMs and the Role of Technology' (n 25) 130; Hele Fenwick, 'Designing ETPIMs around ECHR Review or Normalisation of "Preventive" Non-Trial-Based Executive Measures?' (2013) 76 Modern Law Review 876, 879; Fenwick, 'Terrorism and the Control Orders/TPIMs Saga: A Vindication of the Human Rights Act or a Manifestation of "Defensive Democracy"?' (n 45) 612; Fenwick and Fenwick (n 56) 17–18; Fenwick, *Fenwick on Civil Liberties and Human Rights* (n 1649) 1090; Fenwick and Phillipson (n 25) 866; Stone (n 1651) 466; Tadros, 'Controlling Risk' (n 88) 134; Walker, 'Keeping Control of Terrorists without Losing Control of Constitutionalism' (n 26) 1406; Walker, 'Counterterrorism within the Rule of Law?' (n 171) 341–342; Zedner, 'Preventive Justice or Pre-Punishment?' (n 1575) 176; Zedner, 'Terrorizing Criminal Law' (n 45) 105.

2436 Tadros, 'Justice and Terrorism' (n 46) 666.

2437 *A v. Secretary of State for the Home Department* [2004] UKHL 56, [2005] 2 WLR 87, 26–29. Note that Lord Hoffman disagreed on this point and argued there was no such emergency. See: *A v. Secretary of State for the Home Department* [2004] UKHL 56, [2005] 2 WLR 87, 96. See also: Alati (n 95) 63 and 95–96; Fenwick, *Fenwick on Civil Liberties and Human Rights* (n 1649) 1087–1088; Fenwick and Fenwick (n 56) 17–18; Gearty (n 1659) 32–33; Stone (n 1651) 466.

2438 *A v. Secretary of State for the Home Department* [2004] UKHL 56, [2005] 2 WLR 87, 29, 116 and 154.

2439 Art. 15 ECHR. See also: *A v. Secretary of State for the Home Department* [2004] UKHL 56, [2005] 2 WLR 87, 30.

to the executive and parliament, making its own proportionality analysis.[2440] The measure in question was found to be discriminatory and irrational and thus disproportionate.[2441] First, there were nationals who also posed a threat but the measure only applied to foreigners and did not affect these nationals.[2442] The prohibition of discrimination is enshrined in Article 14 ECHR and the UK did not derogate from this Article.[2443] The Attorney General argued the relevant comparison was between non-nationals suspected of terrorism who could be deported and those who could not and that in this comparison there was a relevant ground of distinction.[2444] The House of Lords, however, followed the applicants reasoning that the relevant comparison was between UK nationals suspected of terrorism and suspected non-UK nationals who could not be removed as both groups share the most relevant characteristics.[2445] In an immigration context the distinction between nationals and non-nationals might be pertinent, but not in a security context and therefore the measure was found to be discriminatory. It is on this point that Lord Walker dissented, arguing that these two categories were distinctly different.[2446] Second, the measure did not sufficiently address the threat posed by foreign nationals either, as it let terrorist suspects leave the UK to potentially plot terrorist attacks abroad.[2447] This is a consequence of the fact that the detention was framed as an immigration power, which shows the weakness of using immigration rules to tackle security problems.[2448] Based on these arguments, the House of Lords issued a declaration of incompatibility of the detention with Articles 5 and 14 of the ECHR.

2440 *A v. Secretary of State for the Home Department* [2004] UKHL 56, [2005] 2 WLR 87, 131.

2441 *A v. Secretary of State for the Home Department* [2004] UKHL 56, [2005] 2 WLR 87, 73. See also: Alati (n 95) 62; Ashworth and Zedner (n 18) 183; Donkin (n 56) 28; Fenwick, *Fenwick on Civil Liberties and Human Rights* (n 1649) 1088–1090; Fenwick and Fenwick (n 56) 17–18; Craig Forcese and Kent Roach, *False Security: The Radicalization of Canadian Anti-Terrorism* (Irwin Law 2015) 212; Khan (n 1649) 108; Roach, 'Must We Trade Rights for Security? The Choice Between Smart, Harsh, or Proportionate Security Strategies in Canada and Britain' (n 1759) 301; Stone (n 1651) 466; Walker, 'Keeping Control of Terrorists without Losing Control of Constitutionalism' (n 26) 1407; Webber (n 95) 100.

2442 *A v. Secretary of State for the Home Department* [2004] UKHL 56, [2005] 2 WLR 87, 32–34. See also: Cole (n 2392) 141; Fenwick and Phillipson (n 25) 874; Stone (n 1651) 466; Tadros, 'Justice and Terrorism' (n 46) 666.

2443 *A v. Secretary of State for the Home Department* [2004] UKHL 56, [2005] 2 WLR 87, 48 and 157.

2444 *A v. Secretary of State for the Home Department* [2004] UKHL 56, [2005] 2 WLR 87, 52.

2445 *A v. Secretary of State for the Home Department* [2004] UKHL 56, [2005] 2 WLR 87, 53.

2446 *A v. Secretary of State for the Home Department* [2004] UKHL 56, [2005] 2 WLR 87, 212–216.

2447 *A v. Secretary of State for the Home Department* [2004] UKHL 56, [2005] 2 WLR 87, 8; 32–34. See also: Alati (n 95) 63 and 95–97; Demirsu (n 56) 79–80; Fenwick, 'Recalibrating ECHR Rights, and the Role of the Human Rights Act Post 9/11' (n 26) 158–159; Fenwick, *Fenwick on Civil Liberties and Human Rights* (n 1649) 1088–1090; Gearty (n 1659) 34–37; Roach, *The 9/11 Effect: Comparative Counter-Terrorism* (n 79) 242 and 277; Walker, 'Keeping Control of Terrorists without Losing Control of Constitutionalism' (n 26) 1407; Walker, 'Counterterrorism within the Rule of Law?' (n 171) 341–342; Wood (n 25) 117.

2448 *A v. Secretary of State for the Home Department* [2004] UKHL 56, [2005] 2 WLR 87, 43.

500. ECtHR confirmation – The matter went on to the ECtHR Grand Chamber, which unanimously held that the detention violated the rights enshrined in Article 5(1), Article 5(4) and Article 5(5) ECHR.[2449] The ECtHR found the House of Lords' decision on the existence of but disproportionate response to the emergency under Article 15 to be not manifestly unreasonable and not misinterpreting the Convention or case law and thus followed it.[2450] In addition, the measure could not be justified under (1) subparagraph (f) since no actual deportation proceedings were being pursued and the exceptions listed in Article 5(1) ECHR are exhaustive and there can be no appeal to the need to balance the interests of the state against those of the detainee.[2451] Regarding Article 5(4), the Court reiterated that detention based '*solely or to a decisive degree on closed material*' violates procedural fairness guarantees and suspects need sufficient information in order to be able to instruct their attorney.[2452]

SECTION II. CONTROL ORDERS

501. Introduction – As discussed above (see no. 333), UK courts cannot overturn or annul legislation.[2453] They have to interpret it in a Human Rights compatible manner and if this is impossible, the most they can do is issue a declaration of incompatibility under s. 4 of the HRA 1998, which is what happened in the case of detention under the ATCSA 2001. Although the government was not bound to respond to the finding of non-compatibility to the ECHR, it decided to do so by revoking the existing scheme, including the derogation from Article 5 ECHR.[2454] The government concurrently introduced

2449 See also: Alati (n 95) 66–67 and 99–100; Ashworth and Zedner (n 18) 183–184; Cole (n 2392) 141.

2450 *A. and others v. United Kingdom* App no 3455/05 (ECtHR Grand Chamber 19 February 2009) 173–190. See also: Alati (n 95) 66–67.

2451 *A. and others v. United Kingdom* App no 3455/05 (ECtHR Grand Chamber 19 February 2009) 169–171. See also: Fenwick and Phillipson (n 25) 887–888.

2452 *A. and others v. The United Kingdom* App no 3455/05 (ECtHR Grand Chamber 19 February 2009) 220. See also: JCHR, Counter-Terrorism Policy and Human Rights (Sixteenth Report): Annual Renewal of Control Orders Legislation (HL paper 64, HC paper 395, 2010) 8; Alati (n 95) 67.

2453 *A. and others v. United Kingdom* App no 3455/05 (ECtHR Grand Chamber 19 February 2009) 94; *A v. Secretary of State for the Home Department* [2004] UKHL 56, [2005] 2 WLR 87, 90; Demirsu (n 56) 70–71; Fenwick, 'Preventive Anti-Terrorist Strategies in the UK and ECHR: Control Orders, TPIMs and the Role of Technology' (n 25) 139.

2454 Conte (n 10) 540; Duff, 'Pre-Trial Detention and the Presumption of Innocence' (n 96) 115; Fenwick, 'Recalibrating ECHR Rights, and the Role of the Human Rights Act Post 9/11' (n 26) 159–160; Fenwick, 'Preventive Anti-Terrorist Strategies in the UK and ECHR: Control Orders, TPIMs and the Role of Technology' (n 25) 130; Fenwick, *Fenwick on Civil Liberties and Human Rights* (n 1649) 1090; Fenwick and Phillipson (n 25) 867; Roach, *The 9/11 Effect: Comparative Counter-Terrorism* (n 79) 280; Wood (n 25) 119.

a new scheme of administrative detention, called control orders.[2455] A control order consisted of a non-specified number of limitations upon the freedoms of the suspected terrorist, the most drastic of which was house arrest.[2456] These orders did not just apply to foreigners, but to UK nationals as well, thereby solving the discrimination problem which led to the declaration of incompatibility in the Belmarsh case (see no. 499).[2457] The government claimed the measures had a dual goal, being prevention and investigation, but in practice the emphasis was on prevention. The PTA 2005 contained a procedure for consultation with the police regarding possible prosecution of a person for whom the Secretary intended to make a control order.[2458] However, this was not a qualifying condition, meaning that not following this procedure did not lead to an invalid control order.[2459] Despite this procedure being in place, control orders did not do anything to further criminal investigations. The measures imposed, such as limits on electronic communications, even hampered any potential investigations.[2460]

2455 Anderson, 'Shielding the Compass: How to Fight Terrorism without Defeating the Law' (n 25) 8; Ashworth and Zedner (n 18) 184; Carlile of Berriew, 'First Report Of The Independent Reviewer Pursuant To Section 14(3) Of The Prevention Of Terrorism Act 2005' (2006) Independent Reviewer of Terrorism Legislation para 2; Demirsu (n 56) 79; Duff, 'Pre-Trial Detention and the Presumption of Innocence' (n 96) 115; Fenwick, 'Recalibrating ECHR Rights, and the Role of the Human Rights Act Post 9/11' (n 26) 160; Fenwick, 'Preventive Anti-Terrorist Strategies in the UK and ECHR: Control Orders, TPIMs and the Role of Technology' (n 25) 130; Fenwick, 'Terrorism and the Control Orders/TPIMs Saga: A Vindication of the Human Rights Act or a Manifestation of "Defensive Democracy"?' (n 45) 612; Fenwick and Fenwick (n 56) 18; Fenwick and Phillipson (n 25) 867; Hunt (n 2418) 290; Khan (n 1649) 108; Roach, *The 9/11 Effect: Comparative Counter-Terrorism* (n 79) 242–243; Stone (n 1651) 466; Tadros, 'Justice and Terrorism' (n 46) 663–664; Tadros, 'Controlling Risk' (n 88) 134; Walker, 'Keeping Control of Terrorists without Losing Control of Constitutionalism' (n 26) 1408; Zedner, 'Preventive Justice or Pre-Punishment?' (n 1575) 176.

2456 S. 1 (4) PTA 2005; Allen and Dempsey (n 1664) 22; Demirsu (n 56) 90; Spencer (n 1616) 130; Tadros, 'Controlling Risk' (n 88) 134.

2457 Ashworth and Zedner (n 18) 184; Carlile of Berriew, 'First Report Of The Independent Reviewer Pursuant To Section 14(3) Of The Prevention Of Terrorism Act 2005' (n 2455) para 4; Donkin (n 56) 28; Fenwick, *Fenwick on Civil Liberties and Human Rights* (n 1649) 1091; Fenwick and Fenwick (n 56) 18; Fenwick and Phillipson (n 25) 875; Hunt (n 2418) 290; Khan (n 1649) 108–109; Roach, 'Must We Trade Rights for Security? The Choice Between Smart, Harsh, or Proportionate Security Strategies in Canada and Britain' (n 1759) 301; Walker, 'Keeping Control of Terrorists without Losing Control of Constitutionalism' (n 26) 1408.

2458 S. 8 PTA 2005. See also: Carlile of Berriew, 'The Definition of Terrorism' (n 1747) paras 142–143; Donkin (n 56) 29; Christopher Forsyth, 'Control Orders, Conditions, Precedent and Compliance with Article 6(1)' (2008) 67 The Cambridge Law Journal 1, 2; Walker, 'Keeping Control of Terrorists without Losing Control of Constitutionalism' (n 26) 1429; Wood (n 25) 126; Zedner, 'Preventive Justice or Pre-Punishment?' (n 1575) 194.

2459 *Secretary of State for the Home Department v. E and another* [2007] UKHL 47, 15. See also: Forsyth (n 2458) 2–3.

2460 Lord MacDonald, Review Of Counter-Terrorism And Security Powers (Cm 8003, 2011) 9 and 12–15; Secretary of State for the Home Department, *Review of Counter-Terrorism and Security Powers* (Cm 8004, 2011) 37; Fenwick, 'Preventive Anti-Terrorist Strategies in the UK and ECHR: Control Orders, TPIMs and the Role of Technology' (n 25) 132; Fenwick, 'Designing ETPIMs around ECHR Review or Normalisation of "Preventive" Non-Trial-Based Executive

502. Derogating vs. non-derogating control orders – The legislation provided for two types of control orders. First, derogating control orders which amounted to a deprivation of liberty and therefore would require a derogation from Article 5 ECHR, and second, non-derogating ones which did not.[2461] When imposing the order, the Secretary of State had to declare whether they considered it a derogating or non-derogating order, but it was the High Court which made the final decision on whether or not the order was in line with Article 5 ECHR.[2462] During the time the control order regime was in force, no derogation from Article 5 ECHR was applied for and no derogating control orders were ever imposed.[2463]

503. Derogating control orders – While no derogating control orders were ever issued, the legislation did provide for a procedure in order to be able to do so. Derogating control orders were to be imposed by the High Court on application of the Home Secretary.[2464] After a preliminary hearing in which the Court decided on the imposition of the order, a full hearing had to be organised.[2465] At that hearing, the order was only confirmed if the Court, on the

---

Measures?' (n 2435) 906; Fenwick, 'Redefining the Role of TPIMs in Combatting "Home-Grown" Terrorism within the Widening Counter-Terror Framework' (n 1962); Fenwick, *Fenwick on Civil Liberties and Human Rights* (n 1649) 1108–1109; Middleton (n 1626) 235.

2461 S. 1 (10) PTA 2005; *Secretary of State for the Home Department v. JJ and others* [2007] UKHL 45, 7; Ashworth and Zedner (n 18) 184; Carlile of Berriew, 'Sixth Report of the Independent Reviewer Pursuant to Section 14(3) of the Prevention of Terrorism Act 2005' (n 1626) para 13; Conte (n 10) 238 and 552; Donkin (n 56) 29; Fenwick, 'Preventive Anti-Terrorist Strategies in the UK and ECHR: Control Orders, TPIMs and the Role of Technology' (n 25) 130; Fenwick, *Fenwick on Civil Liberties and Human Rights* (n 1649) 1091; Fenwick and Phillipson (n 25) 875; Lynch, Tulich and Welsh (n 63) 8; Spencer (n 1616) 130; Stone (n 1651) 466; Tadros, 'Justice and Terrorism' (n 46) 667; Walker, 'Keeping Control of Terrorists without Losing Control of Constitutionalism' (n 26) 1415; Webber (n 95) 103; Welsh, Skinns and Sanders, 'Detention in the Police Station' (n 2353) 171; Wood (n 25) 119; Zedner, 'Preventive Justice or Pre-Punishment?' (n 1575) 177–178.

2462 *Secretary of State for the Home Department v. JJ and others* [2006] EWCA Civ 1141; *Secretary of State for the Home Department v. E* [2007] EWHC 233 (Admin), 150; JCHR, Counter-Terrorism Policy and Human Rights (Twelfth Report): Draft Prevention of Terrorism Act 2005 (Continuance in force of sections 1 to 9) Order 2006 (HL paper 122, HC paper 915, 2006) para 38; Fenwick and Phillipson (n 25) 875–876; Tadros, 'Justice and Terrorism' (n 46) 668–669.

2463 Secretary of State for the Home Department, *Review of Counter-Terrorism and Security Powers* (Cm 8004, 2011) 41; Allen and Dempsey (n 1664) 22; Ashworth and Zedner (n 18) 184; Donkin (n 56) 29; Fenwick, 'Terrorism and the Control Orders/TPIMs Saga: A Vindication of the Human Rights Act or a Manifestation of "Defensive Democracy"?' (n 45) 613; Fenwick and Fenwick (n 56) 18; Hunt (n 2418) 312; Spencer (n 1616) 131; Stone (n 1651) 466; Webber (n 95) 103; Wood (n 25) 119.

2464 S. 4 (1) PTA 2005. See also: *Secretary of State for the Home Department v. JJ and others* [2007] UKHL 45, 8; Feldman (n 82) 4; Lynch, Tulich and Welsh (n 63) 8; Tadros, 'Justice and Terrorism' (n 46) 667; Tadros, 'Controlling Risk' (n 88) 134; Walker, 'Keeping Control of Terrorists without Losing Control of Constitutionalism' (n 26) 1424; Wood (n 25) 121.

2465 S. 4 (1) (b) and (2) PTA 2005; Anderson, 'Shielding the Compass: How to Fight Terrorism without Defeating the Law' (n 25) 9; Conte (n 10) 553; Fenwick and Phillipson (n 25) 878;

balance of probabilities, was satisfied that the controlee was an individual who is or has been involved in terrorism-related activity, if it was necessary for purposes connected with protecting members of the public from a risk of terrorism and the risk was associated with the derogation from Article 5 ECHR.[2466] The use of the civil standard of 'balance of probabilities' in order to deprive someone of their liberty has been criticised.[2467] A derogating control order was to be valid for six months, but could be renewed.[2468] The reason why no attempt was made to introduce any derogating control orders remains up for debate, but it is very likely there was simply no need for them. In terms of restrictions on the right to liberty, there was no clear cut-off point between derogating and non-derogating control orders.[2469] As will be discussed in the next paragraphs, the government tried to push the boundaries of what was permissible under a non-derogating control order and when the lines had been drawn, it in all likelihood decided non-derogating control orders were sufficiently strict not to warrant a derogation from Article 5 ECHR.

504. Non-derogating control orders – Non-derogating control orders were imposed by the Home Secretary themself, but subject to court permission by the High Court.[2470] Non-derogating control orders were valid for 12 months, subject to renewal. A continual internal review of the imposed control orders

Forsyth (n 2458) 3; Hunt (n 2418) 290; Lazarus, Goold and Goss (n 30) 467; Roach, *The 9/11 Effect: Comparative Counter-Terrorism* (n 79) 240; Squires (n 25) 687; Tadros, 'Justice and Terrorism' (n 46) 670; Tadros, 'Controlling Risk' (n 88) 137; Walker, 'Keeping Control of Terrorists without Losing Control of Constitutionalism' (n 26) 1440–1441; Webber (n 95) 103–104; Wood (n 25) 128.

2466 S. 4 (7) PTA 2005. See also: Conte (n 10) 575; Walker, 'Keeping Control of Terrorists without Losing Control of Constitutionalism' (n 26) 1425; Wood (n 25) 121.

2467 See e.g.: JCHR, Counter-Terrorism Policy and Human Rights (Twelfth Report): Draft Prevention of Terrorism Act 2005 (Continuance in force of sections 1 to 9) Order 2006 (HL paper 122, HC paper 915, 2006) para 64; Zedner, 'Preventive Justice or Pre-Punishment?' (n 1575) 178. See also: Walker, 'Keeping Control of Terrorists without Losing Control of Constitutionalism' (n 26) 1424 and 1426.

2468 S. 4 (8) PTA 2005. See also: Conte (n 10) 553; Tadros, 'Justice and Terrorism' (n 46) 669; Walker, 'Keeping Control of Terrorists without Losing Control of Constitutionalism' (n 26) 1427; Welsh, Skinns and Sanders, 'Detention in the Police Station' (n 2353) 171.

2469 *Secretary of State for the Home Department v. JJ and others* [2007] UKHL 45, 22; Fenwick, 'Recalibrating ECHR Rights, and the Role of the Human Rights Act Post 9/11' (n 26) 160; Fenwick and Phillipson (n 25) 875; Walker, 'Keeping Control of Terrorists without Losing Control of Constitutionalism' (n 26) 1428; Wood (n 25) 120; Zedner, 'Preventive Justice or Pre-Punishment?' (n 1575) 178; Zedner, 'Fixing the Future? The Pre-Emptive Turn in Criminal Justice' (n 23) 49.

2470 S. 1 (3) and 3 (1) (a) PTA 2005. See also: *Secretary of State for the Home Department v. JJ and others* [2007] UKHL 45, 8; Allen and Dempsey (n 1664) 22; Donkin (n 56) 30; Feldman (n 82) 5; Fenwick, 'Recalibrating ECHR Rights, and the Role of the Human Rights Act Post 9/11' (n 26) 160; Fenwick, 'Preventive Anti-Terrorist Strategies in the UK and ECHR: Control Orders, TPIMs and the Role of Technology' (n 25) 130; Fenwick, *Fenwick on Civil Liberties and Human Rights* (n 1649) 1091; Fenwick and Phillipson (n 25) 875; Forsyth (n 2458) 1; Lynch, Tulich and Welsh (n 63) 8; Spencer (n 1616) 130; Tadros, 'Controlling Risk' (n 88) 134;

took place. In order to impose them, the Secretary had to '*have reasonable grounds for suspecting that the individual is or has been involved in terrorism-related activity*' and the order had to be '*necessary for purposes connected with protecting members of the public from a risk of terrorism.*'[2471] Involvement in terrorism-related activity was defined as the commission, preparation or instigation of acts of terrorism, conduct which facilitates or gives encouragement to this or which gives support or assistance to individuals who are known or believed to be involved in terrorism-related activity.[2472] This applied to specific acts of terrorism and terrorism generally.[2473] Zedner points out that this covers a wide range of conduct going from people who have committed very serious criminal offences to people on the periphery.[2474] Since non-derogating orders only required reasonable grounds for suspicion and derogating orders required a balance of probability, the threshold for non-derogating orders was lower.[2475] A balance of probability is the civil standard (the criminal standard being 'beyond a reasonable doubt'), making the reasonable suspicion standard quite a low one.[2476] There were two situations in which no court permission was required,

---

Walker, 'Keeping Control of Terrorists without Losing Control of Constitutionalism' (n 26) 1420; Wood (n 25) 114–115; Zedner, 'Preventive Justice or Pre-Punishment?' (n 1575) 176–177.

2471 S. 1 (3) and PTA 2005. See also: *Secretary of State for the Home Department v. MB and others* [2006] EWCA Civ 1140, 2006 WL 2133149, 9; *AP v. Secretary of State for the Home Department* [2009] EWCA Civ 731, 2009 WL 1949565, 10; Ashworth and Zedner (n 18) 184; Conte (n 10) 238 and 552; Donkin (n 56) 30; Fenwick, 'Recalibrating ECHR Rights, and the Role of the Human Rights Act Post 9/11' (n 26) 160; Fenwick, 'Preventive Anti-Terrorist Strategies in the UK and ECHR: Control Orders, TPIMs and the Role of Technology' (n 25) 130; Fenwick and Phillipson (n 25) 876; Forsyth (n 2458) 1; Middleton (n 1626) 233; Roach, *The 9/11 Effect: Comparative Counter-Terrorism* (n 79) 280; Spencer (n 1616) 130; Tadros, 'Justice and Terrorism' (n 46) 668; Adam Tomkins, 'National Security and the Role of the Court: A Changed Landscape?' [2010] Law Quarterly Review 543, 552; Walker, 'Keeping Control of Terrorists without Losing Control of Constitutionalism' (n 26) 1416; Webber (n 95) 102–103; Wood (n 25) 121; Zedner, 'Terrorizing Criminal Law' (n 45) 106.

2472 S. 2 (1) PTA 2005. See also: *Secretary of State for the Home Department v. MB and others* [2006] EWCA Civ 1140, 2006 WL 2133149, 9; Carlile of Berriew, 'Sixth Report of the Independent Reviewer Pursuant to Section 14(3) of the Prevention of Terrorism Act 2005' (n 1626) para 102; Conte (n 10) 552; Walker, 'Keeping Control of Terrorists without Losing Control of Constitutionalism' (n 26) 1412; Zedner, 'Preventive Justice or Pre-Punishment?' (n 1575) 193.

2473 S. 1 (9) PTA 2005. See also: Walker, 'Keeping Control of Terrorists without Losing Control of Constitutionalism' (n 26) 1412.

2474 Zedner, 'Preventive Justice or Pre-Punishment?' (n 1575) 193–194.

2475 JCHR, Counter-Terrorism Policy and Human Rights (Twelfth Report): Draft Prevention of Terrorism Act 2005 (Continuance in force of sections 1 to 9) Order 2006 (HL paper 122, HC paper 915, 2006) para 57–58; Donkin (n 56) 28; Lazarus, Goold and Goss (n 30) 467; Webber (n 95) 103; Wood (n 25) 121.

2476 JCHR, Counter-Terrorism Policy and Human Rights (Twelfth Report): Draft Prevention of Terrorism Act 2005 (Continuance in force of sections 1 to 9) Order 2006 (HL paper 122, HC paper 915, 2006) para 59; Fenwick and Phillipson (n 25) 876; Walker, 'Keeping Control of Terrorists without Losing Control of Constitutionalism' (n 26) 1418; Welsh, Skinns and Sanders, 'Detention in the Police Station' (n 2353) 172; Wood (n 25) 121; Zedner, 'Preventive Justice or Pre-Punishment?' (n 1575) 176.

being urgency or people designated as 'suspected international terrorists' under the ATCSA 2001.[2477] In those scenarios, court supervision was required to begin within seven days.[2478]

505. Court supervision and special advocates – The abovementioned initial court review was limited to considering whether the decision to impose the control order and the specific obligations was 'obviously flawed'.[2479] The danger of such a standard is that it does not allow for effective judicial oversight, while giving the control order the semblance of legality because there was court involvement.[2480] At this point, the person subject to them did not know the order had been requested.[2481] Further judicial review was also included, but it was a closed hearings system with special advocates.[2482] Following the ECtHR (see no. 500),[2483] the House of Lords did specify that the controlee had the right to sufficient information in order to challenge the case against them by instructing the special advocate.[2484] Disclosure of information could be refused

---

2477 S. 3 (1) (b) and (c) PTA 2005, the latter as repealed by s. 100(5), Sch. 9 Pt. 5 CTA 2008. See also: Conte (n 10) 553; Fenwick, *Fenwick on Civil Liberties and Human Rights* (n 1649) 1092; Walker, 'Keeping Control of Terrorists without Losing Control of Constitutionalism' (n 26) 1420.

2478 S. 3 (3) and (4) PTA 2005. See also: Allen and Dempsey (n 1664) 22; Carlile of Berriew, 'First Report Of The Independent Reviewer Pursuant To Section 14(3) Of The Prevention Of Terrorism Act 2005' (n 2455) para 12; Carlile of Berriew, 'Sixth Report of the Independent Reviewer Pursuant to Section 14(3) of the Prevention of Terrorism Act 2005' (n 1626) para 23; Conte (n 10) 553; Donkin (n 56) 30; Fenwick, *Fenwick on Civil Liberties and Human Rights* (n 1649) 1092; Walker, 'Keeping Control of Terrorists without Losing Control of Constitutionalism' (n 26) 1421.

2479 S. 3 (2) PTA 2005. See also: *Secretary of State for the Home Department v. JJ and others* [2007] UKHL 45, 8; Donkin (n 56) 30; Fenwick and Fenwick (n 56) 18; Lynch, Tulich and Welsh (n 63) 8–9; Roach, *The 9/11 Effect: Comparative Counter-Terrorism* (n 79) 281; Tadros, 'Controlling Risk' (n 88) 137; Tomkins (n 2471) 557; Walker, 'Keeping Control of Terrorists without Losing Control of Constitutionalism' (n 26) 1421; Wood (n 25) 126; Zedner, 'Preventive Justice or Pre-Punishment?' (n 1575) 177.

2480 Roach, *The 9/11 Effect: Comparative Counter-Terrorism* (n 79) 281. For the same argument in a more general context, see: Fenwick and Phillipson (n 25) 871.

2481 Walker, 'Keeping Control of Terrorists without Losing Control of Constitutionalism' (n 26) 1422; Wood (n 25) 121. The same goes for TPIMs, see: Macdonald and Carlile (n 1626) 126.

2482 S. 3 PTA 2005. See also: Carlile of Berriew, 'Sixth Report of the Independent Reviewer Pursuant to Section 14(3) of the Prevention of Terrorism Act 2005' (n 1626) para 24; Donkin (n 56) 30; Lynch, Tulich and Welsh (n 63) 9; Middleton (n 1626) 233–234; Welsh, Skinns and Sanders, 'Detention in the Police Station' (n 2353) 171; Zedner, 'Preventive Justice or Pre-Punishment?' (n 1575) 177.

2483 *A. and others v. United Kingdom* App no 3455/05 (ECtHR Grand Chamber 19 February 2009) 220.

2484 *Secretary of State for the Home Department v. AF (FC) and another and one other action* [2009] UKHL 28, 59. See also: JCHR, Counter-Terrorism Policy and Human Rights (Sixteenth Report): Annual Renewal of Control Orders Legislation (HL paper 64, HC paper 395, 2010) 9; Alati (n 95) 66; David Anderson, *Terrorism Prevention and Investigation Measures in 2012: First Report of the Independent Reviewer on the Operation of the Terrorism Prevention and Investigation Measures Act 2011* (Stationery Office 2013) 23; Ashworth and Zedner (n 18) 185–186; Dickson (n 1626) 123; Donkin (n 56) 52; Hunt (n 2418) 304; Ip (n 2392) 114; Lynch,

if it was likely to harm the public interest, which is a low bar.[2485] Exactly how far the courts could go in their review was unclear at first. The court had to verify whether the decision of the Secretary was flawed in light of the two conditions for imposition of the order (see previous paragraph) and whether each of the obligations imposed was necessary.[2486] Some commentators interpreted the standard as not being substantially different from that of 'obviously flawed', stating that courts were limited to recognised grounds for review,[2487] and that they could not substitute their own judgment on the merits for that of the Secretary.[2488, 2489] However, in applying the test, the courts themselves went further and they gave the cases quite a high degree of scrutiny.[2490] As Tomkins argues, this was probably not what the legislature envisioned upon enacting the Statute.[2491] In the *MB* case, the Court of Appeal stated that it could '*substitute its own judgment for that of the decision maker, if that is what Article 6 [ECHR]*

Tulich and Welsh (n 63) 12; Macdonald and Carlile (n 1626) 132; Middleton (n 1626) 234–235; Roach, *The 9/11 Effect: Comparative Counter-Terrorism* (n 79) 285; Squires (n 25) 687; Stone (n 1651) 467–468; Tadros, 'Controlling Risk' (n 88) 137; Tomkins (n 2471) 550–551; Webber (n 95) 105–106. For an analysis of the issue and the case, see: JCHR, Counter-Terrorism Policy and Human Rights (Sixteenth Report): Annual Renewal of Control Orders Legislation (HL paper 64, HC paper 395, 2010) 17–31; Fenwick, 'Recalibrating ECHR Rights, and the Role of the Human Rights Act Post 9/11' (n 26) 202–228; Fenwick, *Fenwick on Civil Liberties and Human Rights* (n 1649) 1028–1033; Aileen Kavanagh, 'Special Advocates, Control Orders and the Right to a Fair Trial'; Daniel Kelman, 'Closed Trials and Secret Allegations: An Analysis of the "Gisting" Requirement' (2016) 80 The Journal of Criminal Law 264; Lynch, Tulich and Welsh (n 63); A Tomkins, 'National Security and the Due Process of Law' (2011) 64 Current Legal Problems 215.

2485 *Secretary of State for the Home Department v. MB and others* [2006] EWCA Civ 1140, 2006 WL 2133149, 18; Fenwick and Phillipson (n 25) 898; Lynch, Tulich and Welsh (n 63) 10.

2486 S. 3 (10) PTA 2005. See also: Tomkins (n 2471) 552; Walker, 'Keeping Control of Terrorists without Losing Control of Constitutionalism' (n 26) 1422.

2487 Being irrationality, illegality, procedural error and proportionality. See: *Council of Civil Service Unions and Others Appellants v. Minister for the Civil Service* [1985] A.C. 374 (H.L.), 410–411; *R v. Secretary of State for the Home Department, Ex parte Brind and Others* [1991] 1 A.C. 696 (H.L.), 721, 750.

2488 This was in line with the original decision of the High Court in the *MB* case which stated that it could not engage in a merits review (*Secretary of State for the Home Department v. MB* [2006] EWHC (Admin) 1,000, 28–29 and 79). This was, however overruled by the Court of Appeal (see fn. 2492). See also e.g.: *R (Daly) v. Secretary of State for the Home Department* [2001] UKHL 26, 28, [2001] 2 A.C. 532, 548.

2489 Walker, 'Keeping Control of Terrorists without Losing Control of Constitutionalism' (n 26) 1423.

2490 Tomkins (n 2471) 554–555; Walker, 'Keeping Control of Terrorists without Losing Control of Constitutionalism' (n 26) 1447–1450. See e.g.: *Secretary of State for the Home Department v. AP* [2010] UKSC 24, 2010 WL 2131699; *R (on the application of Secretary of State for the Home Department) v. Bullivant* [2008] EWHC 337, 2008 WL 678090; *Secretary of State for the Home Department v. Al Saadi* [2009] EWHC 3390 (Admin), 2009 WL 4872782; *Secretary of State for the Home Department v. NN sub nom. Secretary of State for the Home Department v. GG* [2009] EWHC 142 (Admin), 2009 WL 364285 upheld by the Court of Appeal in *Secretary of State for the Home Department v. GG* [2009] EWCA Civ 786, 2009 WL 2173225; *Secretary of State for the Home Department v. AV* [2009] EWHC 902 (Admin), 2009 WL 1096180.

2491 Tomkins (n 2471) 554–555.

requires.'[2492] This meant that, regarding the reasonable suspicion, the Court must decide for itself, as a question of objective fact, whether the facts relied upon by the Secretary of State amount to reasonable grounds for suspicion.[2493] In terms of the necessity of the control order to protect the public, intense scrutiny is applied, yet a degree of deference is to be given to the Secretary of State since they are better placed to decide on this.[2494] In executing this supervision, the courts must not limit themselves to the situation at the time of imposition, but also take account of the situation at the time of supervision.[2495] An appeal to the Court by the controlee was also possible upon renewal or modification of the order or when the Secretary made a decision on an application for revocation or modification.[2496] In case of modification however, the court review was limited to the necessity of the modification.[2497]

506. Administrative measures backed up by criminal sanctions – The contravention of a control order was a criminal offence punishable with five years imprisonment, a fine or both on indictment.[2498] The obstruction of

---

2492 *Secretary of State for the Home Department v. MB and others* [2006] EWCA Civ 1140, 2006 WL 2133149, 48.

2493 *Secretary of State for the Home Department v. MB and others* [2006] EWCA Civ 1140, 2006 WL 2133149, 58–60. See also: *R (on the application of Secretary of State for the Home Department) v. Bullivant* [2008] EWHC 337, 2008 WL 678090, 11; *Secretary of State for the Home Department v. NN sub nom. Secretary of State for the Home Department v. GG* [2009] EWHC 142 (Admin), 2009 WL 364285, 10; *Secretary of State for the Home Department v. Al Saadi* [2009] EWHC 3390 (Admin), 2009 WL 4872782, 7; *Secretary of State for the Home Department v. CC and CF* [2012] EWHC 2837 (Admin), 2012 WL 4866832, 15. See also: Carlile of Berriew, 'Sixth Report of the Independent Reviewer Pursuant to Section 14(3) of the Prevention of Terrorism Act 2005' (n 1626) para 116.

2494 *Secretary of State for the Home Department v. MB and others* [2006] EWCA Civ 1140, 2006 WL 2133149, 64–65. See also: *Secretary of State for the Home Department v. AP* [2008] EWHC 2001 (Admin), 2008 WL 3819438, 21; *R (on the application of Secretary of State for the Home Department) v. Bullivant* [2008] EWHC 337, 2008 WL 678090, 13; *Secretary of State for the Home Department v. Al Saadi* [2009] EWHC 3390 (Admin), 2009 WL 4872782, 7–8; *Secretary of State for the Home Department v. NN sub nom. Secretary of State for the Home Department v. GG* [2009] EWHC 142 (Admin), 2009 WL 364285, 10; *Secretary of State for the Home Department v. CC and CF* [2012] EWHC 2837 (Admin), 2012 WL 4866832, 16. See also: Carlile of Berriew, 'Sixth Report of the Independent Reviewer Pursuant to Section 14(3) of the Prevention of Terrorism Act 2005' (n 1626) para 116.

2495 *Secretary of State for the Home Department v. MB and others* [2006] EWCA Civ 1140, 2006 WL 2133149, 40; *R (on the application of Secretary of State for the Home Department) v. Bullivant* [2008] EWHC 337, 2008 WL 678090, 11; *Secretary of State for the Home Department v. Al Saadi* [2009] EWHC 3390 (Admin), 2009 WL 4872782, 6; *Secretary of State for the Home Department v. NN sub nom. Secretary of State for the Home Department v GG* [2009] EWHC 142 (Admin), 2009 WL 364285, 10; *Secretary of State for the Home Department v. CC and CF* [2012] EWHC 2837 (Admin), 2012 WL 4866832, 12. See also: Carlile of Berriew, 'Sixth Report of the Independent Reviewer Pursuant to Section 14(3) of the Prevention of Terrorism Act 2005' (n 1626) para 22.

2496 S. 10 (1) and (3) PTA 2005. See also: Donkin (n 56) 31; Walker, 'Keeping Control of Terrorists without Losing Control of Constitutionalism' (n 26) 1437.

2497 Tomkins (n 2471) 558.

2498 S. 9 (4) PTA 2005; *Secretary of State for the Home Department v. JJ and others* [2007] UKHL 45, 6; Ashworth and Zedner (n 18) 184; Carlile of Berriew, 'Sixth Report of the Independent

its service was an offence as well, punishable on summary conviction.[2499] This looming sword of Damocles required the person subject to the control order to regulate their behaviour and apply self-surveillance to ensure compliance with the order.[2500]

507. Restrictions – A control order could impose any obligations '*the Home Secretary or a court considers necessary for purposes connected with preventing or restricting the involvement of that individual in terrorism-related activity.*'[2501] The legislation set out a non-exhaustive list including for example restrictions concerning a place of residence, restrictions on movements to, from or within (part of) the UK and the requirement to report to a specified person at specified times.[2502] The choice of the restrictions in specific cases was up to the Home Secretary.[2503] Wood points out that the level of involvement with terrorism of the person was not necessarily taken into account, which could lead to disproportionate orders.[2504] In addition, Zedner points to inconsistencies in the restrictions.[2505] Important restrictions included house arrest for a certain

Reviewer Pursuant to Section 14(3) of the Prevention of Terrorism Act 2005' (n 1626) 147; Conte (n 10) 238–239 and 555; Donkin (n 56) 28; Duff, 'Pre-Trial Detention and the Presumption of Innocence' (n 96) 115; Fenwick, 'Preventive Anti-Terrorist Strategies in the UK and ECHR: Control Orders, TPIMs and the Role of Technology' (n 25) 132; Fenwick and Phillipson (n 25) 876; Roach, *The 9/11 Effect: Comparative Counter-Terrorism* (n 79) 282; Welsh, Skinns and Sanders, 'Detention in the Police Station' (n 2353) 171; Wood (n 25) 122; Zedner, 'Preventive Justice or Pre-Punishment?' (n 1575) 180; Zedner, 'Terrorizing Criminal Law' (n 45) 106. It was also punishable on summary conviction to imprisonment of 12 months, a fine or both in England and Wales or imprisonment of six months, a fine or both in Scotland and Northern Ireland.

2499 S. 9 (7) PTA 2005. See also: Walker, 'Keeping Control of Terrorists without Losing Control of Constitutionalism' (n 26) 1436. The sentence was maximum 51 weeks imprisonment, a fine of maximum level 5 or both in England and Wales and maximum six months imprisonment and/or the same fine in Scotland and Northern Ireland.

2500 Wood (n 25) 123; Zedner, 'Preventive Justice or Pre-Punishment?' (n 1575) 180–181.

2501 *Secretary of State for the Home Department v. MB and others* [2006] EWCA Civ 1140, 2006 WL 2133149, 9; Carlile of Berriew, 'First Report Of The Independent Reviewer Pursuant To Section 14(3) Of The Prevention Of Terrorism Act 2005' (n 2455) para 30; Conte (n 10) 553; Fenwick, 'Recalibrating ECHR Rights, and the Role of the Human Rights Act Post 9/11' (n 26) 164; Fenwick, 'Terrorism and the Control Orders/TPIMs Saga: A Vindication of the Human Rights Act or a Manifestation of "Defensive Democracy"?' (n 45) 615–616; Fenwick, *Fenwick on Civil Liberties and Human Rights* (n 1649) 1091; Hunt (n 2418) 312; Zedner, 'Preventive Justice or Pre-Punishment?' (n 1575) 177.

2502 *Secretary of State for the Home Department v. JJ and others* [2007] UKHL 45, 6; Ashworth and Zedner (n 18) 184; Conte (n 10) 554; Fenwick, 'Preventive Anti-Terrorist Strategies in the UK and ECHR: Control Orders, TPIMs and the Role of Technology' (n 25) 132; Fenwick and Phillipson (n 25) 877; Hunt (n 2418) 290; Lazarus, Goold and Goss (n 30) 467; Walker, 'Keeping Control of Terrorists without Losing Control of Constitutionalism' (n 26) 1412–1413; Wood (n 25) 122; Zedner, 'Preventive Justice or Pre-Punishment?' (n 1575) 179–180; Zedner, 'Terrorizing Criminal Law' (n 45) 106.

2503 Donkin (n 56) 29; Fenwick and Phillipson (n 25) 875; Wood (n 25) 122.

2504 Wood (n 25) 122.

2505 Zedner, 'Preventive Justice or Pre-Punishment?' (n 1575) 181 and 190–191. See also: Wood (n 25) 124.

amount of hours every day, relocation orders and restrictions on the use of telecommunications.

508. The right to liberty – As explained in Part I. (see nos 30–39), a deprivation of liberty is not limited to detention in prison.[2506] House arrest for example can also amount to a deprivation of liberty. In 2006, the independent reviewer explicitly acknowledged that 24-hour house arrest required a derogation from the right to liberty (see no. 28).[2507] That same year the JCHR expressed doubts about whether the restrictions being imposed under non-derogating control orders were mere restrictions of the right to liberty and not deprivations, which would have required derogating control orders.[2508] Their doubts would turn out to be justified. In several cases the House of Lords set out guidelines for deciding whether a control order deprived the controlee of their liberty. In the first case, *Secretary of State for the Home Department v JJ and others*, Lord Bingham mirrored the ECtHR in stating that the concrete situation of the individual is of importance, taking into account a range of factors such as nature, duration, effect and manner of execution or implementation of the measure.[2509] In this case six people were subject to a non-derogating (according to the government) control order which imposed house arrest in their one bedroom flats between 4 pm and 10 am (being 18 hours per day) and a limited area they could move about during their six hours outside of the flat. This was enforced by electronic tagging. In addition, they could only meet (inside or outside the flat) with authorised people, were subject to spot checks and could not use communications equipment, but for one monitored phone line.[2510] The government implied that given the special circumstances of the terrorism threat, Article 5 ECHR should be interpreted more narrowly.[2511] The majority

---

2506 See also: Conte (n 10) 569.

2507 Carlile of Berriew, 'First Report Of The Independent Reviewer Pursuant To Section 14(3) Of The Prevention Of Terrorism Act 2005' (n 2455) para 31; Conte (n 10) 569.

2508 JCHR, Counter-Terrorism Policy and Human Rights (Twelfth Report): Draft Prevention of Terrorism Act 2005 (Continuance in force of sections 1 to 9) Order 2006 (HL paper 122, HC paper 915, 2006) para 38.

2509 *Secretary of State for the Home Department v. JJ and others* [2007] UKHL 45, 15–16. See also: Conte (n 10) 570; Fenwick, 'Recalibrating ECHR Rights, and the Role of the Human Rights Act Post 9/11' (n 26) 173; Fenwick, 'Preventive Anti-Terrorist Strategies in the UK and ECHR: Control Orders, TPIMs and the Role of Technology' (n 25) 132–133; Fenwick and Phillipson (n 25) 880; Webber (n 95) 105; Wood (n 25) 131.

2510 *Secretary of State for the Home Department v. JJ and others* [2007] UKHL 45, 20; *Secretary of State for the Home Department v. JJ and others* [2006] EWCA Civ 1141, 4. See also: Conte (n 10) 570; Feldman (n 82) 5–6; Fenwick, 'Recalibrating ECHR Rights, and the Role of the Human Rights Act Post 9/11' (n 26) 172; Fenwick, 'Preventive Anti-Terrorist Strategies in the UK and ECHR: Control Orders, TPIMs and the Role of Technology' (n 25) 132; Fenwick and Phillipson (n 25) 879; Stone (n 1651) 466–467; Walker, 'Keeping Control of Terrorists without Losing Control of Constitutionalism' (n 26) 1450.

2511 Fenwick, 'Recalibrating ECHR Rights, and the Role of the Human Rights Act Post 9/11' (n 26) 156, 165 and 172; Fenwick, 'The Human Rights Act or a British Bill of Rights: Creating

of the House of Lords held, as had the High Court and Court of Appeal, that the combination of these measures amounted to a deprivation of liberty.[2512] Note that the other members of the majority did not consider the duration of the house arrest in isolation of other factors, but Lord Brown did state that he thought 18 hours was too long, but 16 would be acceptable.[2513] His strong focus on the duration of the house arrest contrasts with the ECtHR's holistic approach (see nos 30–31).[2514] Lady Hale explicitly refused to do the same as Lord Brown and stated '*As such situations may be many and various I would hesitate to suggest, in the abstract, what length of curfew would fall on the other side of the line.*'[2515] Lords Hoffmann and Carswell dissented, pleading for a more narrow interpretation of the right to liberty which only covers paradigm cases of deprivations of liberty, being actual imprisonment, and situations which very closely resemble it.[2516] In other words, they followed the government's argument of the need for a strict interpretation of the right to liberty. It is of interest to note that while Lord Carswell dissented on the point that there was a deprivation of liberty, he also stated he would not enter into discussion on the length of a curfew which would amount to a deprivation of liberty since it depended too much on the facts of specific cases.[2517] In the second case, *Secretary of State v E and another*, the principles set out in the first case were affirmed. The non-derogating control order in question imposed similar restrictions as in the

---

a down-Grading Recalibration of Rights against the Counter-Terror Backdrop?' (n 1652) 473; Fenwick, 'Designing ETPIMs around ECHR Review or Normalisation of "Preventive" Non-Trial-Based Executive Measures?' (n 2435) 892; Fenwick, *Fenwick on Civil Liberties and Human Rights* (n 1649) 1099; Fenwick and Phillipson (n 25) 879.

2512 *Secretary of State for the Home Department v. JJ and others* [2007] UKHL 45. See also: Alati (n 95) 65; Cole (n 2392) 141; Conte (n 10) 570–571; Donkin (n 56) 49; Feldman (n 82) 6; Fenwick, 'Recalibrating ECHR Rights, and the Role of the Human Rights Act Post 9/11' (n 26) 172–175; Fenwick, 'Preventive Anti-Terrorist Strategies in the UK and ECHR: Control Orders, TPIMs and the Role of Technology' (n 25) 133; Fenwick, 'Designing ETPIMs around ECHR Review or Normalisation of "Preventive" Non-Trial-Based Executive Measures?' (n 2435) 892; Forsyth (n 2458) 1–2; Halstead (n 1653) 159; Hunt (n 2418) 315–316; Roach, *The 9/11 Effect: Comparative Counter-Terrorism* (n 79) 243; Stone (n 1651) 467; Tadros, 'Controlling Risk' (n 88) 138–139; Webber (n 95) 105; Wood (n 25) 131.

2513 *Secretary of State for the Home Department v. JJ and others* [2007] UKHL 45, 105. See also: *AP v. Secretary of State for the Home Department* [2009] EWCA Civ 731, 2009 WL 1949565, 24; Donkin (n 56) 50; Feldman (n 82) 6; Fenwick, 'Recalibrating ECHR Rights, and the Role of the Human Rights Act Post 9/11' (n 26) 174; Fenwick, 'Preventive Anti-Terrorist Strategies in the UK and ECHR: Control Orders, TPIMs and the Role of Technology' (n 25) 133; Fenwick, 'Designing ETPIMs around ECHR Review or Normalisation of "Preventive" Non-Trial-Based Executive Measures?' (n 2435) 893; Fenwick and Phillipson (n 25) 880; Hunt (n 2418) 316; Middleton (n 1626) 234.

2514 Feldman (n 82) 6; Fenwick, 'Preventive Anti-Terrorist Strategies in the UK and ECHR: Control Orders, TPIMs and the Role of Technology' (n 25) 133; Hunt (n 2418) 316.

2515 *Secretary of State for the Home Department v. JJ and others* [2007] UKHL 45, 63.

2516 *Secretary of State for the Home Department v. JJ and others* [2007] UKHL 45, 36–45 and 69–84; See also: Feldman (n 82) 7; Fenwick, 'Recalibrating ECHR Rights, and the Role of the Human Rights Act Post 9/11' (n 26) 174; Fenwick and Phillipson (n 25) 880.

2517 *Secretary of State for the Home Department v. JJ and others* [2007] UKHL 45, 84.

first case, but with a curfew of only 12 hours instead of 18. In first instance this control order was quashed as well, but this was overturned on appeal. The House of Lords followed the Court of Appeal. It reasoned that while the other restrictions were stringent, the significantly more limited curfew was the core element and the total effect on the right to liberty was not a deprivation.[2518] In doing so, Lord Bingham referred to ECtHR case *Trijonis* and stated that if the core element of the measure (house arrest) was insufficiently strict, other elements could not in themselves amount to a deprivation of liberty.[2519] In the third case, *Secretary of State v MB and AF*, the curfew was 14 hours per day, enforced by electronic tagging. Outside his curfew hours AF was restricted to a limited zone, communications devices were forbidden, and his flat was liable to be searched at any time. In addition, he was not to communicate with certain specified persons. This was not found to be a deprivation of liberty by the House of Lords either.[2520] These decisions seem to align with Lord Brown's opinion in the *JJ* case in their relatively strong focus on the duration of the curfew. As different authors point out, it is difficult to set a threshold for deprivations of liberty based on the duration of the curfew alone, since other factors also play a role, but if a threshold were established based on this case law, it would probably be around 16 hours, including the normal hours of sleep.[2521] The government interpreted the House of Lords case law similarly and went as far as to increase the curfews of some existing control orders from 12 or 14 to 16 hours.[2522] The

2518 *Secretary of State for the Home Department v. E and another* [2007] UKHL 47, 11. See also: Conte (n 10) 571–572; Feldman (n 82) 6; Fenwick, 'Recalibrating ECHR Rights, and the Role of the Human Rights Act Post 9/11' (n 26) 176; Fenwick, 'Preventive Anti-Terrorist Strategies in the UK and ECHR: Control Orders, TPIMs and the Role of Technology' (n 25) 133; Fenwick, *Fenwick on Civil Liberties and Human Rights* (n 1649) 1100; Fenwick and Phillipson (n 25) 880; Stone (n 1651) 467; Wood (n 25) 131–132.

2519 Feldman (n 82) 6; Fenwick, 'Recalibrating ECHR Rights, and the Role of the Human Rights Act Post 9/11' (n 26) 176; Fenwick, 'Designing ETPIMs around ECHR Review or Normalisation of "Preventive" Non-Trial-Based Executive Measures?' (n 2435) 893.

2520 *Secretary of State for the Home Department v. MB and AF* [2007] UKHL 46. See also: Conte (n 10) 573; Donkin (n 56) 50; Feldman (n 82) 6–7; Fenwick, 'Recalibrating ECHR Rights, and the Role of the Human Rights Act Post 9/11' (n 26) 176; Fenwick, 'Preventive Anti-Terrorist Strategies in the UK and ECHR: Control Orders, TPIMs and the Role of Technology' (n 25) 133; Fenwick and Phillipson (n 25) 880; Roach, *The 9/11 Effect: Comparative Counter-Terrorism* (n 79) 243; Wood (n 25) 133.

2521 Conte (n 10) 573–574; Fenwick, 'Recalibrating ECHR Rights, and the Role of the Human Rights Act Post 9/11' (n 26) 177; Fenwick, 'Preventive Anti-Terrorist Strategies in the UK and ECHR: Control Orders, TPIMs and the Role of Technology' (n 25) 133; Fenwick, 'Designing ETPIMs around ECHR Review or Normalisation of "Preventive" Non-Trial-Based Executive Measures?' (n 2435) 893; Wood (n 25) 133.

2522 Alati (n 95) 65; Fenwick, 'Recalibrating ECHR Rights, and the Role of the Human Rights Act Post 9/11' (n 26) 178; Fenwick, 'Preventive Anti-Terrorist Strategies in the UK and ECHR: Control Orders, TPIMs and the Role of Technology' (n 25) 133; Fenwick and Phillipson (n 25) 880–881; Hunt (n 2418) 316. See e.g.: *Secretary of State for the Home Department v. NN sub nom. Secretary of State for the Home Department v. GG* [2009] EWHC 142 (Admin), 2009 WL 364285, 4–7.

line set out by the House of Lords was further built upon by its successor, the Supreme Court. In the *Secretary of State for the Home Department v AP* case, a person was subject to a 16-hour curfew and relocation order to a location over 240 km away. The Court of Appeal had held there was no breach of Article 5 ECHR, overruling the High Court, but the Supreme Court in turn unanimously overruled the Court of Appeal.[2523] The combination of the curfew with the relocation order made it impossible to live life as he might otherwise do.[2524] This case, with the judgment written by lord Brown, affirmed that while the UK Supreme Court considers the duration of the 'core' restriction, being the curfew, to be the most important element, in borderline cases other restrictions, such as a relocation order can push a control order over the threshold if they were '*unusually destructive of the life the controlee might otherwise have been living.*'[2525]

509. Criticism – The control order regime also led to a lot of criticism, both from scholars and from institutions such as the UN Human Rights Committee.[2526] This criticism related, among other things, to the low standard of proof.[2527] Wood for example points out that measures like control orders are prone to creating miscarriages of justice because of this low threshold while breaching them is a criminal offence.[2528] In addition, the controlee has to challenge information and intelligence they have no access to.[2529] Furthermore, control orders have a collateral impact on the family and community of the suspect.[2530] The risk is that communities become disillusioned and vulnerable to

2523 *Secretary of State for the Home Department v. AP* [2010] UKSC 24, 2010 WL 2131699; *AP v. Secretary of State for the Home Department* [2009] EWCA Civ 731, 2009 WL 1949565, 30–33; *Secretary of State for the Home Department v. AP* [2008] EWHC 2001 (Admin), 2008 WL 3819438, 97.

2524 *Secretary of State for the Home Department v. AP* [2010] UKSC 24, 2010 WL 2131699. See also: Fenwick, 'Recalibrating ECHR Rights, and the Role of the Human Rights Act Post 9/11' (n 26) 233–234; Fenwick, 'Preventive Anti-Terrorist Strategies in the UK and ECHR: Control Orders, TPIMs and the Role of Technology' (n 25) 133–134; Fenwick, 'Designing ETPIMs around ECHR Review or Normalisation of "Preventive" Non-Trial-Based Executive Measures?' (n 2435) 893; Fenwick and Phillipson (n 25) 881; Hunt (n 2418) 317; Roach, *The 9/11 Effect: Comparative Counter-Terrorism* (n 79) 284; Wood (n 25) 133–134.

2525 *Secretary of State for the Home Department v. AP* [2010] UKSC 24, 2010 WL 2131699, 4. See also: Fenwick, 'Recalibrating ECHR Rights, and the Role of the Human Rights Act Post 9/11' (n 26) 233–234; Fenwick, *Fenwick on Civil Liberties and Human Rights* (n 1649) 1100; Fenwick and Phillipson (n 25) 881–882.

2526 United Nations Human Rights Committee (2008) *Concluding Observations of the Human Rights Committee: United Kingdom of Great Britain and Northern Ireland*, Ninety Third Session, 7–25 July, para 17; Donkin (n 56) 7; Gearty (n 1659) 43; Khan (n 1649) 109; Tadros, 'Justice and Terrorism' (n 46) 670; Zedner, 'Terrorizing Criminal Law' (n 45) 106.

2527 JCHR, Counter-Terrorism Policy and Human Rights (Twelfth Report): Draft Prevention of Terrorism Act 2005 (Continuance in force of sections 1 to 9) Order 2006 (HL paper 122, HC paper 915, 2006) para 61; Ashworth and Zedner (n 18) 184; Zedner, 'Preventive Justice or Pre-Punishment?' (n 1575) 176.

2528 Wood (n 25) 140–141.

2529 Wood (n 25) 156.

2530 *Secretary of State for the Home Department v. E* [2007] EWHC 233 (Admin), 133; JCHR, Counter-Terrorism Policy and Human Rights (Twelfth Report): Draft Prevention of Terrorism

radicalisation. Fenwick and Phillipson also comment extensively on the House of Lords/Supreme Court case law, arguing that the Court implicitly went along with the government's argument of the need of a more narrow interpretation of a deprivation of liberty, contrary to the one of the ECtHR.[2531] They argue too much emphasis is placed on the duration of the curfew and not enough on the overall impact and that if there would be a 'cut-off point', it would be closer to 12 hours rather than 16 hours, based on the ECtHR case law.[2532] In addition, the (indefinite) duration of the control orders[2533] and the coercion caused by the threat of criminal sentence upon breach was not taken into account.[2534]

510. Abolishment – The control order regime included a sunset clause, requiring it to be reviewed every year.[2535] This did not lead to extensive parliamentary debate, however.[2536] Eventually, after sustained criticism, including from the JCHR,[2537] and a change in government, the scheme was abolished in order to be replaced (see no. 511). In total, 52 non-derogating control orders were imposed.[2538] The abolishment came after the Labour government,

---

Act 2005 (Continuance in force of sections 1 to 9) Order 2006 (HL paper 122, HC paper 915, 2006) para 85; JCHR, Counter-Terrorism Policy and Human Rights (Seventeenth Report): Bringing Human Rights Back (HL paper 23, HC paper 111, 2010) para 106; JCHR, Counter-Terrorism Policy and Human Rights (Sixteenth Report): Annual Renewal of Control Orders Legislation (HL paper 64, HC paper 395, 2010) 14–15; Squires (n 25) 686–687; Wood (n 25) 142; Walker, 'Keeping Control of Terrorists without Losing Control of Constitutionalism' (n 26) 1414; Zedner, 'Preventive Justice or Pre-Punishment?' (n 1575) 181–182. Similarly for TPIMs, see: Joint Committee on the Draft Enhanced Terrorism Prevention and Investigation Measures Bill, Draft Enhanced Terrorism Prevention and Investigation Measures Bill: Oral Evidence (24 October 2012), reply of Sophie Farthing to Q139 and 140.

2531 Fenwick, 'Designing ETPIMs around ECHR Review or Normalisation of "Preventive" Non-Trial-Based Executive Measures?' (n 2435); Fenwick and Phillipson (n 25) 882 and 886–887.

2532 Fenwick, 'Recalibrating ECHR Rights, and the Role of the Human Rights Act Post 9/11' (n 26) 184–187; Fenwick and Phillipson (n 25) 885–886. Note that in the cases discussed in Part I. (see nos 34–39) where the ECtHR held there was no deprivation of liberty, the longest curfew (in the *Trijonis* case) was 12 hours on week days and full weekends.

2533 See also: Squires (n 25) 686; Walker, 'Keeping Control of Terrorists without Losing Control of Constitutionalism' (n 26) 1458.

2534 Fenwick, 'Recalibrating ECHR Rights, and the Role of the Human Rights Act Post 9/11' (n 26) 180–182 and 187–190; Fenwick, 'Designing ETPIMs around ECHR Review or Normalisation of "Preventive" Non-Trial-Based Executive Measures?' (n 2435) 896–898; Fenwick and Phillipson (n 25) 886.

2535 JCHR, Counter-Terrorism Policy and Human Rights (Twelfth Report): Draft Prevention of Terrorism Act 2005 (Continuance in force of sections 1 to 9) Order 2006 (HL paper 122, HC paper 915, 2006) para 7; Ashworth and Zedner (n 18) 184–185; Walker, 'Keeping Control of Terrorists without Losing Control of Constitutionalism' (n 26) 1443.

2536 Ip (n 2392) 103.

2537 JCHR, Counter-Terrorism Policy and Human Rights (Sixteenth Report): Annual Renewal of Control Orders Legislation (HL paper 64, HC paper 395, 2010).

2538 Anderson, 'Shielding the Compass: How to Fight Terrorism without Defeating the Law' (n 25) 8; Anderson, *Terrorism Prevention and Investigation Measures in 2012* (n 2484) 8; Forcese and Roach (n 2441) 212; Hunt (n 2418) 294; Webber (n 95) 103; Wood (n 25) 113. Note that Spencer puts the number at 38 instead of 52. See: Spencer (n 1616) 131.

which had been in power since 1997, was replaced by a coalition of Conservatives and Liberal Democrats in 2010. Part of this coalition's programme was to '*reverse the substantial erosion of civil liberties and roll back state intrusion.*'[2539] In order to achieve this, the government organised a review of six key counter-terrorism powers, including control orders. Regarding control orders, this review concluded that their usefulness was limited (not in the least by the courts)[2540] and they were too intrusive and widely defined.[2541] Therefore, the control order regime was to be abolished and replaced by another regime of measures which were similar to control orders, but less intrusive and more 'light touch'.

SECTION III. TERRORISM PREVENTION AND INVESTIGATION MEASURES (TPIMS)

511. Introduction – In December 2011 TPIMs were introduced as a replacement to control orders.[2542] TPIMs are very similar to control orders and have been criticised for this.[2543] However, in comparison to control orders, TPIMs in their original iteration were much less invasive in several ways. First,

2539 Secretary of State for the Home Department, *Review of Counter-Terrorism and Security Powers* (Cm 8004, 2011) 4.

2540 See e.g. on the special advocates procedure: *A. and others v. United Kingdom* App no 3455/05 (ECtHR Grand Chamber 19 February 2009); *Secretary of State for the Home Department v. AF (FC) and another and one other action* [2009] UKHL 28. On the duration of the curfew and relocation, see: *Secretary of State for the Home Department v. AP* [2010] UKSC 24, 2010 WL 2131699. On the standard of judicial scrutiny, see: *Secretary of State for the Home Department v. MB and others* [2006] EWCA Civ 1140, 2006 WL 2133149.

2541 Secretary of State for the Home Department, *Review of Counter-Terrorism and Security Powers* (Cm 8004, 2011) 36–43. See also: Fenwick, 'Redefining the Role of TPIMs in Combatting "Home-Grown" Terrorism within the Widening Counter-Terror Framework' (n 1962); Hunt (n 2418) 291; Spencer (n 1616) 131; Welsh, Skinns and Sanders, 'Detention in the Police Station' (n 2353) 172.

2542 S. 1 TPIMA 2011; Alati (n 95) 69; Allen and Dempsey (n 1664) 23; Anderson, 'Shielding the Compass: How to Fight Terrorism without Defeating the Law' (n 25) 9; Anderson, *Terrorism Prevention and Investigation Measures in 2012* (n 2484) 9; Demirsu (n 56) 89–90; Duff, 'Pre-Trial Detention and the Presumption of Innocence' (n 96) 115; Fenwick, 'Preventive Anti-Terrorist Strategies in the UK and ECHR: Control Orders, TPIMs and the Role of Technology' (n 25) 131; Fenwick, 'Terrorism and the Control Orders/TPIMs Saga: A Vindication of the Human Rights Act or a Manifestation of "Defensive Democracy"?' (n 45) 615; Forcese and Roach (n 2441) 212; Hunt (n 2418) 290; Tadros, 'Controlling Risk' (n 88) 135; Wood (n 25) 113 and 208; Zedner, 'Terrorizing Criminal Law' (n 45) 106.

2543 House of Commons 'Counter-terrorism Review' 2010–2012 (Hansard) 26 January 2011, 522–106: 306–326, 311; Liberty's Report Stage Briefing on the Terrorism Prevention and Investigation Measures Bill in the House of Commons (August 2011), 3; Ashworth and Zedner (n 18) 186–187; Demirsu (n 56) 90; Fenwick, 'Preventive Anti-Terrorist Strategies in the UK and ECHR: Control Orders, TPIMs and the Role of Technology' (n 25) 131; Fenwick, 'Designing ETPIMs around ECHR Review or Normalisation of "Preventive" Non-Trial-Based Executive Measures?' (n 2435) 882; Hunt (n 2418); Webber (n 95) 106; Welsh, Skinns and Sanders, 'Detention in the Police Station' (n 2353) 172; Wood (n 25) 210; Zedner, 'Terrorizing Criminal Law' (n 45) 106.

instead of 'reasonable suspicion', 'reasonable belief' is required.[2544] Second, TPIMs are restricted to exhaustively listed measures.[2545] Third, TPIMs were originally limited to two years (with a duration of one year which was renewable once), unless there was evidence of new[2546] terrorist activity.[2547]

512. Time limit – While TPIMs were originally limited to two years, the time limit did not take into account any time spent under a control order and the same activities that were the basis for the control order, could form the basis for a TPIM.[2548] In addition, in his 2020 report, the independent reviewer notes two cases of men who were on their second TPIMs because of new terrorism activity after the imposition of their original TPIM.[2549] The two year time limit was seen by some as providing an incentive for the authorities to try to secure a criminal conviction, but this has never materialised (see no. 515).[2550] On the other

---

2544 JCHR, *Legislative Scrutiny: Terrorism Prevention and Investigation Measures Bill: Sixteenth Report of Session 2010–12* (HL paper 180, HC paper 1432, 2011), 6; Ashworth and Zedner (n 18) 186–187; Demirsu (n 56) 90; Fenwick, 'Preventive Anti-Terrorist Strategies in the UK and ECHR: Control Orders, TPIMs and the Role of Technology' (n 25) 131; Fenwick and Fenwick (n 56) 20; Spencer (n 1616) 131; Zedner, 'Terrorizing Criminal Law' (n 45) 106.

2545 S. 2 (1) TPIMA 2011; Home Office, *Terrorism Prevention and Investigation Measures Act 2011: Explanatory Notes* (2011) 20; Allen and Dempsey (n 1664) 23; Anderson, *Terrorism Prevention and Investigation Measures in 2012* (n 2484) 8; Demirsu (n 56) 90; Hunt (n 2418) 312; Macdonald and Carlile (n 1626) 126–127; Staniforth (n 1747) 151–152.

2546 As defined by s. 3 (6) TPIMA 2011 as follows: '*(a) if no TPIM notice relating to the individual has ever been in force, terrorism-related activity occurring at any time (whether before or after the coming into force of this Act); (b) if only one TPIM notice relating to the individual has ever been in force, terrorism-related activity occurring after that notice came into force; or (c) if two or more TPIM notices relating to the individual have been in force, terrorism-related activity occurring after such a notice came into force most recently.*' See also: Staniforth (n 1747) 151.

2547 *Secretary of State for the Home Department v. AM* [2012] EWHC 1854 (Admin), 2012 WL 2,500,050, 5; JCHR, Legislative Scrutiny: Terrorism Prevention and Investigation Measures Bill: Sixteenth Report of Session 2010–12 (HL paper 180, HC paper 1432, 2011), 7; Anderson, *Terrorism Prevention and Investigation Measures in 2012* (n 2484) 8 and 19; Demirsu (n 56) 90; Fenwick, 'Preventive Anti-Terrorist Strategies in the UK and ECHR: Control Orders, TPIMs and the Role of Technology' (n 25) 131; Fenwick, 'Designing ETPIMs around ECHR Review or Normalisation of "Preventive" Non-Trial-Based Executive Measures?' (n 2435) 885; Fenwick, 'Terrorism and the Control Orders/TPIMs Saga: A Vindication of the Human Rights Act or a Manifestation of "Defensive Democracy"?' (n 45) 616; Fenwick, *Fenwick on Civil Liberties and Human Rights* (n 1649) 1095–1096; Fenwick and Fenwick (n 56) 21; Forcese and Roach (n 2441) 212; Hunt (n 2418) 308; Spencer (n 1616) 131–132; Staniforth (n 1747) 152; Stone (n 1651) 470; Tadros, 'Controlling Risk' (n 88) 138; Wood (n 25) 236.

2548 *Secretary of State for the Home Department v. BM* [2012] EWHC 714 (Admin), 2012 WL 609334, 17; *Secretary of State for the Home Department v. AM* [2012] EWHC 1854 (Admin), 2012 WL 2,500,050, 13; *Secretary of State for the Home Department v. CC and CF* [2012] EWHC 2837 (Admin), 2012 WL 4866832, 20–21. See also: Fenwick, 'Designing ETPIMs around ECHR Review or Normalisation of "Preventive" Non-Trial-Based Executive Measures?' (n 2435) 885; Fenwick, *Fenwick on Civil Liberties and Human Rights* (n 1649) 1096; Stone (n 1651) 468.

2549 Hall, 'The Terrorism Acts in 2020' (n 1692) para 8.18.

2550 Joint Committee on the Draft Enhanced Terrorism Prevention and Investigation Measures Bill, *Draft Enhanced Terrorism Prevention and Investigation Measures Bill: Oral Evidence*

hand, critics pointed out that this time limit overrides the analysis of whether the person is still dangerous to the public, which then leads to the question of the utility of the TPIMs in the first place.[2551] In his last review, Lord Carlile suggested raising the evidentiary threshold to a balance of probabilities when a second TPIM is imposed based on new terrorist activity,[2552] but the government was not persuaded.[2553] In 2021, the legislature increased the one time renewal limit to four times, meaning a TPIM can now last five years.[2554] They did so for fear of suspects 'biding their time' and just waiting out their two years.[2555]

513. TPIMs: STANDARD OF PROOF – TPIMs are imposed by the Home Secretary, after court permission (see no. 518).[2556] They can do so upon reasonable belief that the individual is, or has been, involved in terrorism-related activity; and when they reasonably consider it necessary for purposes connected with protecting members of the public from a risk of terrorism and with preventing or restricting the individual's involvement in terrorism-related activity.[2557] The Act also defines 'involvement in terrorism-related activity'. This

(24 October 2012), reply of professor Fenwick to Q137 and reply of Sophie Farthing to Q165; Fenwick, *Fenwick on Civil Liberties and Human Rights* (n 1649) 1096 and 1109; Wood (n 25) 237.

2551 See: Hunt (n 2418) 309.

2552 Carlile of Berriew, 'Sixth Report of the Independent Reviewer Pursuant to Section 14(3) of the Prevention of Terrorism Act 2005' (n 1626) paras 55–56.

2553 Secretary of State for the Home Department, The Government Response to the Report by Lord Carlile of Berriew Q.C. Sixth Report of the Independent Reviewer Pursuant to Section 14(3) of the Prevention of Terrorism Act 2005 (Cm 8095, 2011) 11–12.

2554 S. 5 TPIMA 2011; S. 35 (3) CTSA 2021. See also: HM Government, *Counter-terrorism Disruptive Powers Report 2021* (CP 779, 2023), www.gov.uk/government/publications/counter-terrorism-disruptive-powers-report-2021/hm-government-counter-terrorism-disruptive-po wers-report-2021-accessible-version; Hall, 'The Terrorism Acts in 2021' (n 1885) para 8.13; Hall, 'The Terrorism Acts in 2020' (n 1692) para 8.24. Note that the original idea was to just abolish the time limit, but this was amended in the House of Lords. See: Home Office, *Counter-Terrorism And Sentencing Bill: Explanatory Notes* (Bill 129–EN, 2020) para 224–225; Home Office, *Counter-Terrorism And Sentencing Bill: Explanatory Notes on Lords Amendments* (Bill 274–EN, 2020) para 22; The counter-terrorism and sentencing bill changes to TPIM standard of proof and time limit, January 2021, 6–10; Beard and Dawson (n 1706) 28.

2555 The counter-terrorism and sentencing bill changes to TPIM standard of proof and time limit, January 2021, 8. See also: Ashworth and Zedner (n 18) 187; Fenwick, 'Redefining the Role of TPIMs in Combatting "Home-Grown" Terrorism within the Widening Counter-Terror Framework' (n 1962); Hill (n 1666) para 5.13. Note that the fact sheet uses an example where a gap of 16 months was created between the end of a TPIM (because it reached its two-year limit) and the imposition of a new one. However, in this case, if the person has not committed any acts of terrorism in those 16 months, one could wonder whether the second TPIM was necessary.

2556 Allen and Dempsey (n 1664) 23; Anderson, *Terrorism Prevention and Investigation Measures in 2012* (n 2484) 8; Fenwick, 'Designing ETPIMs around ECHR Review or Normalisation of "Preventive" Non-Trial-Based Executive Measures?' (n 2435) 883; Fenwick, *Fenwick on Civil Liberties and Human Rights* (n 1649) 1094; Forcese and Roach (n 2441) 212; Middleton (n 1626) 236; Staniforth (n 1747) 150.

2557 S. 3 (1), (3) and (4) TPIMA 2011. See also: *Secretary of State for the Home Department v. AM* [2012] EWHC 1854 (Admin), 2012 WL 2,500,050, 3; Anderson, *Terrorism Prevention and Investigation Measures in 2012* (n 2484) 18; Fenwick, 'Designing ETPIMs around ECHR

covers the commission, preparation or instigation of acts of terrorism, conduct which facilitates or encourages this or is intended to, or supporting or assisting people who are known or believed to be involved in the commission, preparation or instigation of acts of terrorism.[2558] This last option used to be broader and also included supporting or assisting people who are known or believed to be involved in facilitating or encouraging the commission, preparation or instigation of such acts, but this was narrowed in 2015.[2559] Regarding this last option, Hunt wonders whether '*the support or assistance must be materially connected to conduct about which the individual concerned may know or believe the person being supported or assisted may be engaged in.*'[2560] It does not matter whether any of this concerns specific acts of terrorism or acts of terrorism in general.[2561] Compared to the control order standard of reasonable suspicion, the standard of reasonable belief is said to be more requiring.[2562] As was explained in the *R v CC and CF* case: '*Belief is a state of mind by which the person in question thinks that X is the case. Suspicion is a state of mind by which the person in question thinks that X may be the case.*'[2563] However, courts have held that the difference is small[2564] and Lords Carlile and Lloyd of Berwick stated that though there is a real distinction, it would make little difference in practice.[2565] It therefore comes as no surprise that scholars find the difference between the two unclear and/or too minimal and

---

Review or Normalisation of "Preventive" Non-Trial-Based Executive Measures?' (n 2435) 884; Hunt (n 2418) 292; Lowe (n 1838) 80; Staniforth (n 1747) 150; Tadros, 'Controlling Risk' (n 88) 135; Wood (n 25) 220.

2558 S. 4 (1) TPIMA 2011. See also: Hunt (n 2418) 293; Lowe (n 1838) 80; Staniforth (n 1747) 150–151; Stone (n 1651) 468–469.

2559 S. 20 (2) CTSA 2015. See also: Blackbourn, Kayis and McGarrity (n 1771) 56; Fenwick and Fenwick (n 56) 22–23; Macdonald and Carlile (n 1626) 134.

2560 Hunt (n 2418) 293.

2561 S. 4 (1) TPIMA 2011.

2562 See e.g.: *Secretary of State for the Home Department v. CD* [2012] EWHC 3026 (Admin), 2012 WL 4867182, 8; *Secretary of State for the Home Department v. BM* [2012] EWHC 714 (Admin), 2012 WL 609334, 4; Home Office, Terrorism Prevention and Investigation Measures Bill: ECHR Memorandum (2011) 17; Home Office, Terrorism Prevention and Investigation Measures Act 2011: Explanatory Notes (2011) 19; Ryan and Williams (n 2344) 295.

2563 *A and others v. Secretary of State for the Home Department* [2004] EWCA Civ 1123 2004 WL 1640297, 229; *Secretary of State for the Home Department v. CC and CF* [2012] EWHC 2837 (Admin), 2012 WL 4866832, 24. See also: *Secretary of State for the Home Department v. CD* [2012] EWHC 3026 (Admin), 2012 WL 4867182, 8; Anderson, *Terrorism Prevention and Investigation Measures in 2012* (n 2484) 25; Fenwick, 'Designing ETPIMs around ECHR Review or Normalisation of "Preventive" Non-Trial-Based Executive Measures?' (n 2435) 885; Hunt (n 2418) 300; Wood (n 25) 221.

2564 *Her Majesty's Treasury v. Ahmed and others* [2010] UKSC 2, 172. Note that this was in a case concerning asset freezing. However, the threshold is the same and the change of threshold between control orders and TPIMs was explicitly made to ensure consistency with asset freezing. Sophie Farthing of Liberty called the change from suspicion to belief a 'tweak around the edges'. See: Joint Committee on the Draft Enhanced Terrorism Prevention and Investigation Measures Bill, *Draft Enhanced Terrorism Prevention and Investigation Measures Bill: Oral Evidence* (24 October 2012), reply of Sophie Farthing to Q136.

2565 Carlile of Berriew, 'Sixth Report of the Independent Reviewer Pursuant to Section 14(3) of the Prevention of Terrorism Act 2005' (n 1626) paras 28–30. Lord Lloyd of Berwick, Hansard

some recommend the use of the civil standard of 'a balance of probabilities'.[2566] Tadros stands out, being of the view that the reasonable belief standard is actually higher than the balance of probabilities one.[2567] This view is not supported by the case law or for example the ETPIM Bill though.[2568] If anything, this discussion shows the opacity of the standard. The government eventually intervened, but in a rather unhelpful way. In 2015, they changed the standard from 'reasonable belief' to 'is satisfied, on the balance of probabilities'.[2569] The threshold was heightened because the same Act made TPIMs stricter (see no. 514) and according to the Home Secretary, all existing TPIMs would have met that threshold anyway.[2570] However, in 2021, they changed it back to 'reasonable belief'.[2571] This was done to increase flexibility in light of online radicalisation and was argued not to raise human rights issue since the control order regime was found to be compatible.[2572] The original Bill even proposed to lower the standard to the control order standard of 'reasonable grounds for suspecting', but the House of lords was doubtful on the influence of the changes on human rights and as a compromise this was changed to reasonable belief.[2573] Tadros also

---

(House of Lords), 25 October 2010, col. 1037. See also: Hunt (n 2418) 300–301; Middleton (n 1626) 236–237.

2566 Joint Committee on the Draft Enhanced Terrorism Prevention and Investigation Measures Bill, *Draft Enhanced Terrorism Prevention and Investigation Measures Bill: Oral Evidence* (24 October 2012), reply of professor Fenwick to Q153; Anderson, *Terrorism Prevention and Investigation Measures in 2012* (n 2484) 97–98; Fenwick, 'Designing ETPIMs around ECHR Review or Normalisation of "Preventive" Non-Trial-Based Executive Measures?' (n 2435) 884; Fenwick, *Fenwick on Civil Liberties and Human Rights* (n 1649) 1094–1095; Hunt (n 2418) 296–301; Macdonald and Carlile (n 1626) 131; Middleton (n 1626) 236–237; Tadros, 'Controlling Risk' (n 88) 135–136; Wood (n 25) 221–222; Zedner, 'Fixing the Future? The Pre-Emptive Turn in Criminal Justice' (n 23) 48.

2567 Tadros, 'Controlling Risk' (n 88) 136. Note that Amnesty International also states that the standard was lowered from reasonable belief to balance of probabilities. See: Amnesty International report, 'Dangerously disproportionate, the ever-expanding national security state in Europe' (2017) 53.

2568 Commentary on Clauses 29, *Draft Enhanced Terrorism Prevention and Investigation Measures Bill* (Cm 8166, 2011) (hereinafter ETPIM Bill). See also: Anderson, *Terrorism Prevention and Investigation Measures in 2012* (n 2484) 32.

2569 S. 20 (1) CTSA 2015. See also: Blackbourn, Kayis and McGarrity (n 1771) 56; Fenwick, 'Terrorism and the Control Orders/TPIMs Saga: A Vindication of the Human Rights Act or a Manifestation of "Defensive Democracy"?' (n 45) 618–619; Fenwick and Fenwick (n 56) 22; Macdonald and Carlile (n 1626) 130.

2570 Blackbourn, Kayis and McGarrity (n 1771) 56; Fenwick, *Fenwick on Civil Liberties and Human Rights* (n 1649) 1103.

2571 S. 34 CTSA 2021. See also: Home Office, *Counter-Terrorism And Sentencing Bill: Explanatory Notes* (Bill 129–EN, 2020) para 224; HM Government, *Counter-terrorism Disruptive Powers Report 2021* (CP 779, 2023), www.gov.uk/government/publications/counter-terrorism-disruptive-powers-report–2021/hm-government-counter-terrorism-disruptive-powers-report-2021-accessible-version; Hall, 'The Terrorism Acts in 2021' (n 1885) para 8.14; Hall, 'The Terrorism Acts in 2020' (n 1692) para 8.37.

2572 The counter-terrorism and sentencing bill changes to TPIM standard of proof and time limit, January 2021, 2, 4 and 5.

2573 Home Office, *Counter-Terrorism And Sentencing Bill: Explanatory Notes on Lords Amendments* (Bill 274–EN, 2020) para 21; House of Lords Select committee on the

points out that terms such as 'necessary' and 'risk' are ambiguous and unclear and that any risk, however miniscule would suffice.[2574] Failure to comply with the measures imposed by a TPIM is a criminal offence punishable on indictment with five years imprisonment, a fine or both.[2575] The use of TPIMs, which was never extensive, seems to be on the decline. In 2012, ten people were subject to a TPIM,[2576] on 31 March 2017, there were six TPIMs in force,[2577] and in February 2022 only two.[2578] Regarding this last number it is important to note that four more TPIMs would have been in force, but were revoked because of breaches, which led to criminal prosecutions.[2579]

514. TPIMs: MEASURES – As mentioned above, there is an exhaustive list of potential measures, which includes travel restrictions, curfews, and exclusion zones.[2580] One of the most controversial obligations, forced relocation, was not originally included on this list.[2581] What was included, were measures restricting the use of telecommunications devices. However, these measures have been made less stringent than they were under the control order regime since now a complete ban on electronic communications is not allowed, as the individual must have access to a landline, a mobile phone (without internet)

Constitution, *Counter-Terrorism and Sentencing Bill* (HL paper 134) 16th Report of Session 2019–21, para 13; Beard and Dawson (n 1706) 17–18; Joanna Dawson and Jacqueline Beard, 'Counter-Terrorism and Sentencing Bill 2019–2021: Lords amendments' (2021) 9169 House of Commons Library Briefing Paper 7.

2574 Tadros, 'Controlling Risk' (n 88) 136.

2575 S. 23 TPIMA 2011. See also: Home Office, *Terrorism Prevention and Investigation Measures Act 2011: Explanatory Notes* (2011) 121; Anderson, *Terrorism Prevention and Investigation Measures in 2012* (n 2484) 23; Ashworth and Zedner (n 18) 187; Wood (n 25) 215. On summary conviction this is 12 months, a fine or both in England and Wales or Scotland for offences committed after 2 May 2022 and six months, a fine or both in Northern Ireland or for offences committed before 2 May 2022. The maximum sentence on indictment is raised to 10 years if the offence consists of contravening a travel measure.

2576 Squires (n 25) 694.

2577 Allen and Dempsey (n 1664) 23; Hill (n 1666) para 5.8; Walker, 'Foreign Terrorist Fighters and UK Counter Terrorism Laws' (n 2261) 198.

2578 Hall, 'The Terrorism Acts in 2021' (n 1885) para 8.20.

2579 Hall, 'The Terrorism Acts in 2021' (n 1885) para 8.26.

2580 Anderson, *Terrorism Prevention and Investigation Measures in 2012* (n 2484) 19–20; Blackbourn, Kayis and McGarrity (n 1771) 52; Hunt (n 2418) 312–313; Lowe (n 1838) 81–82; Stone (n 1651) 469–470; Wood (n 25) 219.

2581 JCHR, Legislative Scrutiny: Terrorism Prevention and Investigation Measures Bill: Sixteenth Report of Session 2010–12 (HL paper 180, HC paper 1432, 2011), 7; Home Office, Terrorism Prevention and Investigation Measures Act 2011: Explanatory Notes (2011) 45; Ashworth and Zedner (n 18) 186; Blackbourn, Kayis and McGarrity (n 1771) 52–53; Fenwick, 'Preventive Anti-Terrorist Strategies in the UK and ECHR: Control Orders, TPIMs and the Role of Technology' (n 25) 136; Fenwick, 'Terrorism and the Control Orders/TPIMs Saga: A Vindication of the Human Rights Act or a Manifestation of "Defensive Democracy"?' (n 45) 616; Fenwick and Fenwick (n 56) 21; Hunt (n 2418) 313; Tadros, 'Controlling Risk' (n 88) 138; Wood (n 25) 219; Zedner, 'Terrorizing Criminal Law' (n 45) 106.

and a computer (with internet).[2582] This facilitates the gathering of evidence concerning people under a TPIM and also affects the likelihood of the measures amounting to a deprivation of liberty.[2583] In a memorandum on the bill of the Act which introduced TPIMs, the Home Office stated that TPIMs which interfere with ECHR rights will be assessed as being necessary and proportionate.[2584] For this proportionality assessment, Wood refers to the *de Freitas* case of the Privy Council, which includes the following proportionality test: '*whether: (i) the legislative objective is sufficiently important to justify limiting a fundamental right; (ii) the measures designed to meet the legislative objective are rationally connected to it; and (iii) the means used to impair the right or freedom are no more than is necessary to accomplish the objective.*'[2585] The Supreme Court has used the same analysis, with one more added step: '*do the measures strike a fair balance between the rights of the individual and the interests of the community?*'[2586] In 2015, the government introduced several new possible restrictions as a response to the foreign fighters problem and reintroduced the relocation orders, but in a slightly modified form.[2587] The main difference is that a person cannot be relocated more than 200 miles (approximately 322 km) from their residence without their consent.[2588] In 2017

2582 Home Office, *Terrorism Prevention and Investigation Measures Bill: ECHR Memorandum* (2011) 17; Anderson, *Terrorism Prevention and Investigation Measures in 2012* (n 2484) 20; Fenwick, 'Preventive Anti-Terrorist Strategies in the UK and ECHR: Control Orders, TPIMs and the Role of Technology' (n 25) 136; Fenwick, *Fenwick on Civil Liberties and Human Rights* (n 1649) 1097; Hunt (n 2418) 313; Wood (n 25) 223–230.

2583 Fenwick, 'Preventive Anti-Terrorist Strategies in the UK and ECHR: Control Orders, TPIMs and the Role of Technology' (n 25) 136; Wood (n 25) 223–230.

2584 Home Office, *Terrorism Prevention and Investigation Measures Bill: ECHR Memorandum* (2011) 17. See also: Wood (n 25) 234.

2585 *Elloy de Freitas v. Permanent Secretary of Ministry of Agriculture, Fisheries, Lands and Housing* [1991] 1 AC 69, [1998] 3 W.L.R. 675, 9. See also: Gearty (n 1659) 34; Lowe (n 1838) 82–83; Wood (n 25) 235.

2586 *Beghal v. Director of Public Prosecutions* [2015] UKSC 49, 2015 WL 4401455, 53–56. See also: *Austin v. Commissioner of Police of the Metropolis* [2009] UKHL 5, [2009] 1 AC 564, 120; *Regina (Aguilar Quila and another) v. Secretary of State for the Home Department (AIRE Centre and others intervening) Regina (Bibi and another) v. Same (Same intervening)* [2011] UKSC 45 [2012] 1 A.C. 621, 45; *Bank Mellat v. HM Treasury (No 2)* [2013] UKSC 38 and 39 [2014] AC 700, 20; Fenwick, 'The Human Rights Act or a British Bill of Rights: Creating a down-Grading Recalibration of Rights against the Counter-Terror Backdrop?' (n 1652) 474.

2587 Blackbourn, Kayis and McGarrity (n 1771) 53; Fenwick, 'Terrorism and the Control Orders/TPIMs Saga: A Vindication of the Human Rights Act or a Manifestation of "Defensive Democracy"?' (n 45) 618–619; Fenwick, *Fenwick on Civil Liberties and Human Rights* (n 1649) 1102–1103; Fenwick and Fenwick (n 56) 22; Forcese and Roach (n 2441) 213; Welsh, Skinns and Sanders, 'Detention in the Police Station' (n 2353) 172.

2588 S. 1 (3A) and (5) Schedule 1 TPIMA 2011. See also: HM Government, *Counter-terrorism Disruptive Powers Report 2021* (CP 779, 2023), www.gov.uk/government/publications/counter-terrorism-disruptive-powers-report-2021/hm-government-counter-terrorism-disruptive-powers-report-2021-accessible-version; Blackbourn, Kayis and McGarrity (n 1771) 53; Fenwick, 'Terrorism and the Control Orders/TPIMs Saga: A Vindication of the Human Rights Act or a Manifestation of "Defensive Democracy"?' (n 45) 620; Fenwick, *Fenwick on Civil Liberties and Human Rights* (n 1649) 1103; Fenwick and Fenwick (n 56) 23.

the independent reviewer observed that this relocation measure was part of every TPIM he reviewed.[2589]

515. Prosecution – As was the case for detention under the ATCSA 2001 and for control orders, the point of TPIMs is to impose them upon people who cannot be prosecuted or deported.[2590] However, since the word 'investigation' is in the name 'TPIM', the government made it clear it wanted TPIMs to aid investigations in order to facilitate prosecution.[2591] This change was welcomed by the JCHR and Lord MacDonald, who emphasised the importance of prosecutions.[2592] They proposed a review of the potential measures in light of their ability to facilitate or hamper the collection of evidence and an added condition for TPIMs that a criminal investigation into the person is justified.[2593] This approach was rejected by the government.[2594] Instead, a similar but slightly strengthened procedure as was the case for control orders, was put in place, which obliges the Secretary of State to consult with the police regarding possible prosecution before imposing a TPIM, and the prospect of prosecution

---

2589 Hill (n 1666) para 5.17. See also: Blackbourn, Kayis and McGarrity (n 1771) 54–55.

2590 Secretary of State for the Home Department, *Review of Counter-Terrorism and Security Powers* (Cm 8004, 2011) 36; The Government Reply To The Sixteenth Report From The Joint Committee On Human Rights (Cm 8167, 2011) 1 and 4; The counter-terrorism and sentencing bill changes to TPIM standard of proof and time limit, January 2021, 1. See also: Anderson, *Terrorism Prevention and Investigation Measures in 2012* (n 2484) 8 and 19; Fenwick, 'Redefining the Role of TPIMs in Combatting "Home-Grown" Terrorism within the Widening Counter-Terror Framework' (n 1962); Hunt (n 2418) 294–295; Zedner, 'Preventive Justice or Pre-Punishment?' (n 1575) 177.

2591 House of Commons 'Counter-terrorism Review' 2010–2012 (Hansard) 26 January 2011, 522–106: 306–326, 307–308; JCHR, *Legislative Scrutiny: Terrorism Prevention and Investigation Measures Bill: Sixteenth Report of Session 2010–12* (HL paper 180, HC paper 1432, 2011), 7–8; Secretary of State for the Home Department, *The Government Response to the Report by Lord Carlile of Berriew Q.C. Sixth Report of the Independent Reviewer Pursuant to Section 14(3) of the Prevention of Terrorism Act 2005* (Cm 8095, 2011) 12–13; Fenwick, 'Designing ETPIMs around ECHR Review or Normalisation of "Preventive" Non-Trial-Based Executive Measures?' (n 2435) 905–906; Fenwick, 'Redefining the Role of TPIMs in Combatting "Home-Grown" Terrorism within the Widening Counter-Terror Framework' (n 1962); Fenwick, *Fenwick on Civil Liberties and Human Rights* (n 1649) 1108. In its memorandum on human rights e.g., the Home Office explicitly states that '*prosecution through the criminal courts remains the government's priority.*' See: Home Office, *Terrorism Prevention and Investigation Measures Bill: ECHR Memorandum* (2011) 17.

2592 Lord MacDonald, Review Of Counter-Terrorism And Security Powers (Cm 8003, 2011) 9–10; JCHR, *Legislative Scrutiny: Terrorism Prevention and Investigation Measures Bill: Sixteenth Report of Session 2010–12* (HL paper 180, HC paper 1432, 2011), 7–8. They are not alone in this emphasis, see e.g.: Liberty's Report Stage Briefing on the Terrorism Prevention and Investigation Measures Bill in the House of Commons (August 2011), 4.

2593 Lord MacDonald, Review Of Counter-Terrorism And Security Powers (Cm 8003, 2011) 10–11; JCHR, *Legislative Scrutiny: Terrorism Prevention and Investigation Measures Bill: Sixteenth Report of Session 2010–12* (HL paper 180, HC paper 1432, 2011), 8–9.

2594 The Government Reply To The Sixteenth Report From The Joint Committee On Human Rights (Cm 8167, 2011) 4–7. See also: Fenwick, 'Redefining the Role of TPIMs in Combatting "Home-Grown" Terrorism within the Widening Counter-Terror Framework' (n 1962).

must be kept under review.[2595] In his one year review of TPIMs, Anderson, the independent reviewer, stated that for the ten TPIMs in place the decision not to prosecute was taken on the basis of insufficient evidence.[2596] Scholars and the independent reviewer, however, are sceptical about the possibility of TPIMs to further prosecutions.[2597] Wood points out that in light of the complete lack of prosecutions under the control order regime, this seems unlikely and Ashworth and Zedner also criticise the procedure as being 'watered down'.[2598] Fenwick for example states that the only way TPIMs have managed to aid in prosecution, is that the perceived ineffectiveness of the TPIMs may incentivise prosecution.[2599]

516. Deprivation or restriction? – TPIMs are in general less intrusive than control orders and will therefore be less likely to amount to a deprivation of liberty. However, the length of the curfew is not explicitly limited, barring the fact that originally, it had to be 'overnight'.[2600] The explanatory notes to the Terrorism Prevention and Investigation Measures Act 2011 (TPIMA 2011) state that while the term 'overnight' is not defined in the Act, '*the period would need to fall between hours which a reasonable person would consider "overnight"*.'[2601] In the *BM* case, the Court held that 'overnight' '*should bear some relationship to the hours between which most people would regard it as reasonable to think that people might be at home, the evening having come to an end*' and that

2595 S. 10 TPIMA 2011. See also: Anderson, *Terrorism Prevention and Investigation Measures in 2012* (n 2484) 19; Fenwick, 'Designing ETPIMs around ECHR Review or Normalisation of "Preventive" Non-Trial-Based Executive Measures?' (n 2435) 906; Fenwick, 'Redefining the Role of TPIMs in Combatting "Home-Grown" Terrorism within the Widening Counter-Terror Framework' (n 1962); Fenwick, *Fenwick on Civil Liberties and Human Rights* (n 1649) 1109; Staniforth (n 1747) 152.

2596 Anderson, *Terrorism Prevention and Investigation Measures in 2012* (n 2484) 60.

2597 See: Anderson, *Terrorism Prevention and Investigation Measures in 2012* (n 2484) 70; Ashworth and Zedner (n 18) 187; Fenwick, 'Designing ETPIMs around ECHR Review or Normalisation of "Preventive" Non-Trial-Based Executive Measures?' (n 2435) 906–907; Fenwick, 'Redefining the Role of TPIMs in Combatting "Home-Grown" Terrorism within the Widening Counter-Terror Framework' (n 1962); Fenwick, *Fenwick on Civil Liberties and Human Rights* (n 1649) 1109; Fenwick and Fenwick (n 56) 34; Zedner, 'Terrorizing Criminal Law' (n 45) 108 and 112. See also: Joint Committee on the Draft Enhanced Terrorism Prevention and Investigation Measures Bill, *Draft Enhanced Terrorism Prevention and Investigation Measures Bill: Oral Evidence* (24 October 2012), reply of Sophie Farthing to Q137.

2598 Ashworth and Zedner (n 18) 189; Wood (n 25) 290.

2599 Fenwick, 'Terrorism and the Control Orders/TPIMs Saga: A Vindication of the Human Rights Act or a Manifestation of "Defensive Democracy"?' (n 45) 622–623.

2600 *Secretary of State for the Home Department v. BM* [2012] EWHC 714 (Admin), 2012 WL 609334, 51–52; Fenwick, 'Preventive Anti-Terrorist Strategies in the UK and ECHR: Control Orders, TPIMs and the Role of Technology' (n 25) 135; Fenwick, 'Terrorism and the Control Orders/TPIMs Saga: A Vindication of the Human Rights Act or a Manifestation of "Defensive Democracy"?' (n 45) 616; Fenwick and Fenwick (n 56) 21; Hunt (n 2418) 313; Stone (n 1651) 469; Wood (n 25) 241.

2601 Home Office, Terrorism Prevention and Investigation Measures Act 2011: Explanatory Notes (2011) 42.

it does not reasonably stretch beyond 9 pm to 7 am (which was the curfew in that case).[2602] Numbers included by Hunt show that the last three years of the control order regime, the average length of the curfew was between 12 and 11,1 hours (in a downward trend, probably influenced by the *AP* case).[2603] This means that control orders were evolving in that direction anyway. The point about the practical significance of the difference became a moot one in 2021, when the legislature deleted the word 'overnight'.[2604] In addition to all this, there is no limit on the amount of measures which can be combined within the same TPIM.[2605] After the 2021 changes, the difference between control orders and TPIMs has become negligible. It is therefore not impossible for a TPIM to amount to a deprivation of liberty. In its memorandum on ECHR compliance, the Home Office stated that the relevant assessment was that of '*the length of the period for which the individual is confined to their residence.*'[2606] This view is not in line with the ECtHR analysis of Article 5 ECHR as discussed in Part I, as it puts too much emphasis on the idea of physical confinement.[2607] The Memorandum does refer to the UK *MB and AF* and *AP v. Secretary of State* cases, which put more emphasis on this element.[2608] In addition, the fact that violation of a TPIM can lead to up to five years imprisonment and the duration of the measures, which has a maximum of five years but can be renewed (or an ETPIM could be imposed) are of importance in the analysis.[2609]

2602 *Secretary of State for the Home Department v. BM* [2012] EWHC 714 (Admin), 2012 WL 609334, 52. See also: *Secretary of State for the Home Department v. CC and CF* [2012] EWHC 2837 (Admin), 2012 WL 4866832, 64; Anderson, *Terrorism Prevention and Investigation Measures in 2012* (n 2484) 75; Fenwick, 'Designing ETPIMs around ECHR Review or Normalisation of "Preventive" Non-Trial-Based Executive Measures?' (n 2435) 895; Fenwick, *Fenwick on Civil Liberties and Human Rights* (n 1649) 1101; Hunt (n 2418) 314.

2603 Hunt (n 2418) 314–315. See also: Anderson, *Terrorism Prevention and Investigation Measures in 2012* (n 2484) 52; Middleton (n 1626) 238. Lord Carlile notes that in 2009 the average was 12 hours and in 2010 11,9 hours. See: Carlile of Berriew, 'Sixth Report of the Independent Reviewer Pursuant to Section 14(3) of the Prevention of Terrorism Act 2005' (n 1626) para 19.

2604 S. 37 CTSA 2021. See also: Home Office, *Counter-Terrorism And Sentencing Bill: Explanatory Notes* (Bill 129–EN, 2020) para 231; HM Government, *Counter-terrorism Disruptive Powers Report 2021* (CP 779, 2023), www.gov.uk/government/publications/counter-terrorism-disruptive-powers-report–2021/hm-government-counter-terrorism-disruptive-powers-report–2021-accessible-version; Hall, 'The Terrorism Acts in 2021' (n 1885) para 8.14.

2605 Home Office, *Terrorism Prevention and Investigation Measures Act 2011: Explanatory Notes* (2011) 41; Wood (n 25) 241.

2606 Home Office, *Terrorism Prevention and Investigation Measures Bill: ECHR Memorandum* (2011) 22. See also: Wood (n 25) 242.

2607 See also: Fenwick, 'Preventive Anti-Terrorist Strategies in the UK and ECHR: Control Orders, TPIMs and the Role of Technology' (n 25) 137; Wood (n 25) 242.

2608 Home Office, *Terrorism Prevention and Investigation Measures Bill: ECHR Memorandum* (2011) 22; Fenwick, 'Preventive Anti-Terrorist Strategies in the UK and ECHR: Control Orders, TPIMs and the Role of Technology' (n 25) 137.

2609 Fenwick, 'Preventive Anti-Terrorist Strategies in the UK and ECHR: Control Orders, TPIMs and the Role of Technology' (n 25) 137; Fenwick, 'Designing ETPIMs around ECHR Review or Normalisation of "Preventive" Non-Trial-Based Executive Measures?' (n 2435) 896–898; Wood (n 25) 243–245.

517. ETPIMs – Relatively soon after the introduction of TPIMs, the government introduced the idea of ETPIMs, which allow for more restrictions, moving even more in the direction of control orders. These ETPIMs are emergency powers which can only be activated in exceptional circumstances.[2610] It is unclear which exact circumstances would trigger this, but it needs to be apparent from the circumstances that normal TPIMs would not suffice.[2611] The bill introducing ETPIMs is published and has undergone parliamentary scrutiny but still requires to be voted on and to receive royal assent in order to enter into force.[2612] This practice of preparing draft emergency legislation (also applied for example with the maximum duration of investigative detention, see no. 493) was suggested by Lord Lloyd of Berwick in his 1996 *Inquiry into the Legislation on Terrorism*.[2613] In addition to this bill, the TPIM Act contains a provision allowing the government to enforce temporary ETPIMs for up to 90 days when parliament is not in session.[2614] The ETPIM bill contains many rules similar to the regular TPIMs. One main difference between TPIMs and ETPIMs in terms of the measures imposed, is that under the ETPIM regime, a relocation order is possible without the 200 mile limit, as well as other more stringent measures.[2615]

2610 Fenwick, 'Designing ETPIMs around ECHR Review or Normalisation of "Preventive" Non-Trial-Based Executive Measures?' (n 2435) 904–905; Fenwick, 'Redefining the Role of TPIMs in Combatting "Home-Grown" Terrorism within the Widening Counter-Terror Framework' (n 1962); Fenwick, *Fenwick on Civil Liberties and Human Rights* (n 1649) 1110; Fenwick and Fenwick (n 56) 24; Webber (n 95) 108; Wood (n 25) 214.

2611 Joint Committee on the Draft Enhanced Terrorism Prevention and Investigation Measures Bill, *Draft Enhanced Terrorism Prevention and Investigation Measures Bill: Oral Evidence* (24 October 2012), reply of Sophie Farthing to Q143; Fenwick, 'Designing ETPIMs around ECHR Review or Normalisation of "Preventive" Non-Trial-Based Executive Measures?' (n 2435) 904–905; Fenwick, 'Terrorism and the Control Orders/TPIMs Saga: A Vindication of the Human Rights Act or a Manifestation of "Defensive Democracy"?' (n 45) 617; Fenwick, *Fenwick on Civil Liberties and Human Rights* (n 1649) 1110. Fenwick expressed concern about the possibility of ETPIMs being used against people whose two-year period for a TPIM had ended. This seems not to have materialised. See: Fenwick, 'Designing ETPIMs around ECHR Review or Normalisation of "Preventive" Non-Trial-Based Executive Measures?' (n 2435) 882–883; Fenwick and Fenwick (n 56) 24.

2612 Anderson, *Terrorism Prevention and Investigation Measures in 2012* (n 2484) 29; Fenwick, 'Designing ETPIMs around ECHR Review or Normalisation of "Preventive" Non-Trial-Based Executive Measures?' (n 2435) 877; Fenwick, *Fenwick on Civil Liberties and Human Rights* (n 1649) 1110; Fenwick and Fenwick (n 56) 24.

2613 Lord Lloyd of Berwick, *Inquiry into legislation against terrorism* (Cm 3420, 1996) 109–112. See also: Anderson, *Terrorism Prevention and Investigation Measures in 2012* (n 2484) 29–30.

2614 S. 26 TPIMA 2011. See also: Home Office, *Terrorism Prevention and Investigation Measures Act 2011: Explanatory Notes* (2011) 33 and 134; Anderson, *Terrorism Prevention and Investigation Measures in 2012* (n 2484) 30; Fenwick, 'Designing ETPIMs around ECHR Review or Normalisation of "Preventive" Non-Trial-Based Executive Measures?' (n 2435) 877; Fenwick, 'The Human Rights Act or a British Bill of Rights: Creating a down-Grading Recalibration of Rights against the Counter-Terror Backdrop?' (n 1652) 472; Fenwick, *Fenwick on Civil Liberties and Human Rights* (n 1649) 1110; Fenwick and Fenwick (n 56) 24; Wood (n 25) 214.

2615 For an overview, see Part 1 Schedule 1 ETPIM Bill. See also: Anderson, *Terrorism Prevention and Investigation Measures in 2012* (n 2484) 31; Fenwick and Fenwick (n 56) 24.

The standard for an ETPIM is '*the balance of probabilities that the individual is, or has been, involved in terrorism-related activity.*'[2616] Regarding the duration of an ETPIM, the bill refers to the TPIMA 2011, meaning that when the maximum limit for a TPIM was increased from two to five years, the same happened for the ETPIMs.[2617] The attached commentary on the clauses, however, does refer explicitly to the two year limit.[2618]

518. Oversight – In order for the Secretary of State to be able to impose a TPIM, they have to receive prior court permission, unless they reasonably consider that the urgency of the case requires the TPIM to be imposed without obtaining such permission.[2619] However, as was the case for control orders, this first court decision is limited to determining whether the decision of the Secretary of State was 'obviously flawed'.[2620] This standard received criticism from the JCHR.[2621] The Court then automatically starts the process of a full review.[2622] During this review, the special advocates procedure in place for control orders remains the same, which led to criticism, and the same case law also applies (see no. 505).[2623] Tadros points out that the TPIMA 2011 does not

2616 S. 2 (1) ETPIM Bill. See also: Home Office, *Terrorism Prevention and Investigation Measures Act 2011: Explanatory Notes* (2011) 133; Anderson, *Terrorism Prevention and Investigation Measures in 2012* (n 2484) 32; Fenwick, 'Designing ETPIMs around ECHR Review or Normalisation of "Preventive" Non-Trial-Based Executive Measures?' (n 2435) 885; Fenwick, 'Terrorism and the Control Orders/TPIMs Saga: A Vindication of the Human Rights Act or a Manifestation of "Defensive Democracy"?' (n 45) 617; Wood (n 25) 222.

2617 S. 3 (1) (a) ETPIM Bill. For the previous limit of two years, see: Anderson, *Terrorism Prevention and Investigation Measures in 2012* (n 2484) 31; Fenwick, 'Terrorism and the Control Orders/TPIMs Saga: A Vindication of the Human Rights Act or a Manifestation of "Defensive Democracy"?' (n 45) 617.

2618 33 Commentary on Clauses ETPIM Bill.

2619 S. 3 (5) TPIMA 2011. See also: JCHR, *Legislative Scrutiny: Terrorism Prevention and Investigation Measures Bill: Sixteenth Report of Session 2010–12* (HL paper 180, HC paper 1432, 2011), 12; Anderson, *Terrorism Prevention and Investigation Measures in 2012* (n 2484) 8 and 18; Webber (n 95) 106–107.

2620 S. 6 (3) TPIMA 2011. See also: JCHR, *Legislative Scrutiny: Terrorism Prevention and Investigation Measures Bill: Sixteenth Report of Session 2010–12* (HL paper 180, HC paper 1432, 2011), 12; Hunt (n 2418) 303; Lowe (n 1838) 80.

2621 JCHR, Legislative Scrutiny: Terrorism Prevention and Investigation Measures Bill: Sixteenth Report of Session 2010–12 (HL paper 180, HC paper 1432, 2011), 12–13.

2622 Secretary of State for the Home Department v. CD [2012] EWHC 3026 (Admin), 2012 WL 4867182, 3; Secretary of State for the Home Department v. AM [2012] EWHC 1854 (Admin), 2012 WL 2,500,050, 3; JCHR, Legislative Scrutiny: Terrorism Prevention and Investigation Measures Bill: Sixteenth Report of Session 2010–12 (HL paper 180, HC paper 1432, 2011), 12; The Government Reply To The Sixteenth Report From The Joint Committee On Human Rights (Cm 8167, 2011) 8; HM Government, Counter-terrorism Disruptive Powers Report 2021 (CP 779, 2023), www.gov.uk/government/publications/counter-terrorism-disruptive-powers-report–2021/hm-government-counter-terrorism-disruptive-powers-report–2021-accessible-version; Anderson, *Terrorism Prevention and Investigation Measures in 2012* (n 2484) 8 and 21; Macdonald and Carlile (n 1626) 127; Stone (n 1651) 469.

2623 See: Schedule 4 TPIMA 2011. See also: JCHR, *Legislative Scrutiny: Terrorism Prevention and Investigation Measures Bill: Sixteenth Report of Session 2010–12* (HL paper 180, HC paper

require a summary of the relevant information to be provided in all cases,[2624] meaning it might not fully comply with the rules set out in the *A and others* and *AF* cases (see no. 505).[2625] The TPIM legislation did incorporate the practice of the courts for control orders (see no. 505) in which they verify whether the conditions for a TPIM were met and continue to be met.[2626] In addition, courts apply the same level of scrutiny as they did for control orders.[2627] Whenever a TPIM is extended or made stricter or when the individual has asked the Secretary of State to change or revoke the TPIM, the individual can also appeal to the Court.[2628] Next to this judicial oversight, a few other oversight measures are in place. There is the legislative reviewing process which aims to determine whether a suspect can be prosecuted (see no. 515).[2629] Second, quarterly reports are provided to parliament, but they are quantitative in nature and do not provide a real opportunity for debate.[2630] Parliament does have to renew the TPIMA every five years.[2631] This is, however, quite a big step down from the annual renewal of control orders. The original idea was not to require any renewal by parliament for the TPIMA, but the JCHR insisted upon annual renewal, which eventually led to the current five year renewal.[2632] In November

1432, 2011), 13–15; Ashworth and Zedner (n 18) 188; Fenwick, 'Designing ETPIMs around ECHR Review or Normalisation of "Preventive" Non-Trial-Based Executive Measures?' (n 2435) 902–903; Fenwick, 'Terrorism and the Control Orders/TPIMs Saga: A Vindication of the Human Rights Act or a Manifestation of "Defensive Democracy"?' (n 45) 620; Fenwick, *Fenwick on Civil Liberties and Human Rights* (n 1649) 1106–1108; Forcese and Roach (n 2441) 212; Hunt (n 2418) 290; Webber (n 95) 104. For criticism, see: Hunt (n 2418) 303–308; Macdonald and Carlile (n 1626) 133–134.

2624 S. 4 (1) Schedule 4 TPIMA 2011.

2625 Tadros, 'Controlling Risk' (n 88) 137.

2626 Home Office, Terrorism Prevention and Investigation Measures Bill: ECHR Memorandum (2011) 25–26.

2627 *Secretary of State for the Home Department v. CC and CF* [2012] EWHC 2837 (Admin), 2012 WL 4866832, 17.

2628 S. 16 TPIMA 2011. See also: HM Government, *Counter-terrorism Disruptive Powers Report 2021* (CP 779, 2023), www.gov.uk/government/publications/counter-terrorism-disruptive-powers-report-2021/hm-government-counter-terrorism-disruptive-powers-report-2021-accessible-version; Anderson, *Terrorism Prevention and Investigation Measures in 2012* (n 2484) 22; Webber (n 95) 107.

2629 S. 10 (4)–(8) TPIMA 2011. See also: Home Office, Terrorism Prevention and Investigation Measures Act 2011: Explanatory Notes (2011) 83–84.

2630 S. 19 TPIMA 2011; Home Office, *Terrorism Prevention and Investigation Measures Act 2011: Explanatory Notes* (2011) 115; Webber (n 95) 107; Wood (n 25) 290.

2631 Anderson, *Terrorism Prevention and Investigation Measures in 2012* (n 2484) 26; Ashworth and Zedner (n 18) 194; Fenwick, 'Designing ETPIMs around ECHR Review or Normalisation of "Preventive" Non-Trial-Based Executive Measures?' (n 2435) 903–904; Fenwick, 'Terrorism and the Control Orders/TPIMs Saga: A Vindication of the Human Rights Act or a Manifestation of "Defensive Democracy"?' (n 45) 619; Fenwick and Fenwick (n 56) 23; Webber (n 95) 107.

2632 JCHR, Renewal of Control Orders Legislation 2011 (Eighth Report of Session 2010–11) (HL paper 106, HC paper 838, 2011) 10; JCHR, Legislative Scrutiny: Terrorism Prevention and Investigation Measures Bill: Sixteenth Report of Session 2010–12 (HL paper 180, HC paper 1432, 2011), 15–16; The Government Reply To The Sixteenth Report From The Joint

2021, the scheme was renewed for another five years.[2633] Third, the independent reviewer might provide some oversight.[2634] The original Act did not provide for deadlines for his reviews.[2635] However, since 2021, the Act states that '*The independent reviewer must carry out a review under this section in respect of each calendar year starting with 2022 and ending with 2026.*'[2636]

519. Current TPIMs as the result of a long evolution – TPIMs in their current iteration result from a long process of interplay between the government and courts, set against the background of the changing terrorism threat. The traditional focus of UK counter-terrorism policy was Northern Ireland, but 9/11 initiated a shift towards international terrorism which led to the introduction of detention under the ATCSA 2001. However, the *A and others* House of Lords case showed that immigration law was not a suitable tool to achieve the government's aims and therefore it was replaced by control orders. Control orders started out very strict, but case law tempered the most extreme cases and strengthened certain safeguards. Even then, control orders remained an intrusive tool. As the political climate shifted, the government decided to replace control orders by TPIMs, which originally were less strict than control orders in several ways. TPIMs had a maximum time limit of two years, the threshold for imposing a TPIM was (slightly) higher and TPIMs were limited to a certain number of measures, which did not include relocation and limited house arrest to overnight curfews. In case of emergency, however, draft legislation was prepared to introduce ETPIMs, which were basically control orders. After several changes to the TPIMs regime, the differences between TPIMs and control orders have become negligible. The two year limit was increased to five years, the 'overnight' part of the curfews has been deleted and relocation orders have been reintroduced (in a slightly more limited form). The current TPIMs regime allows for the same types of measures to be imposed as was the case at the end of the control order regime. This means that the chances of ETPIMs being introduced are very slim for the same reasons no derogating control orders were ever imposed: there simply is no need for them as the general regime allows for sufficiently strict measures. One main difference between control orders

---

Committee On Human Rights (Cm 8167, 2011) 12. See also: Liberty's Report Stage Briefing on the Terrorism Prevention and Investigation Measures Bill in the House of Commons (August 2011), 6; Fenwick, *Fenwick on Civil Liberties and Human Rights* (n 1649) 1108.

2633 Terrorism Prevention and Investigation Measures Act 2011 (Continuation) Order 2021. See also: Hall, 'The Terrorism Acts in 2021' (n 1885) para 8.11.

2634 HM Government, *Counter-terrorism Disruptive Powers Report 2021* (CP 779, 2023), www.gov.uk/government/publications/counter-terrorism-disruptive-powers-report–2021/hm-government-counter-terrorism-disruptive-powers-report–2021-accessible-version. Note that this supervision, as well as the quarterly reports were also present for control orders. See: S. 14 PTA 2005.

2635 Fenwick and Fenwick (n 56) 23; Wood (n 25) 290.

2636 S. 20 (1A) TPIMA 2011; S. 41 CTSA 2021.

and TPIMs is that the TPIMs regime is more entrenched than the control order regime ever was. The one-year sunset clause for control orders has become five years. In addition, TPIMs were originally introduced as a way to stop the erosion of liberties and increase human rights protection compared to the control order regime. Because of this, they have less of a negative connotation to them, although at this point, they are in practice no different from control orders.

CHAPTER III
ANALYSIS

SECTION I. THE GOAL OF THIS CHAPTER

520. ANALYSING THE EXISTING LEGISLATION – Throughout the first two Chapters of this Part, the UK legislation has been described in detail. The UK uses both criminal justice and administrative law to try to counter terrorism. Within the criminal justice system, we see terrorism offences *sensu stricto* as well as a large amount of terrorism offences *sensu lato*. In addition to this description, criticism sections highlighted the most important criticism on the legal framework. As was the case for the Belgian Part (see no. 310–327), the final Chapter of this Part will serve as a summary of the most important of these issues. This analysis is, however, relatively short as it just seeks to touch upon the main points of the UK legislation and the main criticisms. A thorough and more detailed analysis will be included in the next Part of this book, which compares the Belgian and UK legal frameworks and aims to answer the main research question of this book.

SECTION II. THE RIGHT TO LIBERTY IN THE UK

521. DOMESTIC INTERPRETATION OF ARTICLE 5 ECHR – In their interpretation of Article 5 ECHR, the UK domestic courts largely follow the case law of the ECtHR. However, several commentators argue that a domestic recalibration of Article 5 took place, narrowing its scope.[2637] This became clear in the control order case law, as UK courts put more focus on the paradigm element of deprivations of liberty. While paying lip service to the ECtHR system, the UK courts moved slowly towards an analysis which put (too) much emphasis on the duration of the house arrest, moving away from the more holistic ECtHR approach. This narrowing scope is also apparent from other cases unrelated to control orders or TPIMs, for example in the context of stop and searches or cordoning. As Edwards points out, the UK courts add two meaningful limitations to the European case law. First, the UK courts added a *de minimis*

2637 Fenwick, 'Recalibrating ECHR Rights, and the Role of the Human Rights Act Post 9/11' (n 26) 190–193; Fenwick and Fenwick (n 56) 19.

test to the *Guzzardi* principles.[2638] In certain cases, the UK courts held that the deprivation was too minor to be within the scope of Article 5 ECHR.[2639] Second, when deciding whether or not a deprivation of liberty occurred, the purpose of the measure is taken into account.[2640] This implies a balancing exercise between the purpose of the measure (public interest considerations) and the individual's rights.[2641] In general, Ashworth points out that English judges apply a broader balancing test when applying Article 5 than allowed for under the ECHR.[2642] Although the ECtHR has always explicitly refused to introduce a balancing exercise into Article 5 ECHR (see no. 40), Edwards and Fenwick argue that in *Austin* the ECtHR did in fact do so. In that case the Court decided that the purpose of the measure was relevant by reading another element into the Guzzardi test, being that of context.[2643] Because of the specific context, the Court held there was no deprivation of liberty. Edwards and Fenwick make a good point here. The Court decided the measure in question was not a deprivation of liberty and thus did not fall into the scope of Article 5 ECHR because of the context, i.e. the purpose for which the measure was taken. In doing so, the Court did accept some form of balancing between public interest and individual liberty.[2644] It is important to note, however, that the Court emphasised the decision was based on the 'specific and exceptional facts' of the case.[2645] In addition, since then, no major shift in the ECtHR case law on this point can be seen, so the *Austin* case may have been a one off.

2638 Edwards (n 106) 337–340.

2639 *R (Gillan) v. The Commissioner of Police for the Metropolis* [2006] UKHL 12, 2006 WL 502934, 25; *Beghal v. Director of Public Prosecutions* [2015] UKSC 49, 2015 WL 4401455, 53–56. See also: *Austin v. Commissioner of Police of the Metropolis* [2009] UKHL 5, [2009] 1 AC 564, 17.

2640 See: *Austin v. Commissioner of Police of the Metropolis* [2009] UKHL 5, [2009] 1 AC 564, 26–34; *R (Hicks) v. Commissioner of the Police of the Metropolis* [2017] UKSC 9, [2017] AC 256, 31; Edwards (n 106) 340–343; Fenwick, 'Recalibrating ECHR Rights, and the Role of the Human Rights Act Post 9/11' (n 26) 193–194.

2641 *Austin v. Commissioner of Police of the Metropolis* [2009] UKHL 5, [2009] 1 AC 564, 34; Fenwick, 'Recalibrating ECHR Rights, and the Role of the Human Rights Act Post 9/11' (n 26) 194.

2642 Andrew Ashworth, *Human Rights, Serious Crime and Criminal Procedure* (Sweet & Maxwell 2002) 127.

2643 *Austin and others v. United Kingdom* App nos 39692/09, 40713/09 and 41008/09 (ECtHR Grand Chamber 15 March 2012) 57–60; Edwards (n 106) 341–342; Fenwick, 'Designing ETPIMs around ECHR Review or Normalisation of "Preventive" Non-Trial-Based Executive Measures?' (n 2435) 898–899.

2644 For criticism, see also the joint dissenting opinion of judges Tulkens, Spielmann and Garlicki to the *Austin* case.

2645 *Austin and others v. United Kingdom* App nos 39692/09, 40713/09 and 41008/09 (ECtHR Grand Chamber 15 March 2012) 68.

SECTION III. OFFENCES

SUBSECTION I. LEGALITY

522. Very broad offences – It is clear from the analysis in Chapter I of this Part that the UK has (too?) many terrorist offences. In addition, many of these offences are exceedingly broad. Cornford sees this as only one emanation of the UK parliament's recent tendency to legislate absurdly broad legislation. He refers to s. 58 TA 2000 and the definition of terrorism in s. 1 TA 2000 as examples of this.[2646] It is true that the s. 58 offence is very broad and quite vague. It is still not clear when something is 'useful' to a terrorist. In addition, the offence has no *mens rea* in the usual sense of the word and the defendant's state of mind is irrelevant unless they have a reasonable excuse. The idea behind the offence seems to be to have the defendant explain their possession of certain information, which is very practical for the prosecution but does raise questions under the right to silence. Its 'sister offence' in s. 57 TA 2000 is equally as broad. Reasonable suspicion is a low threshold and possession is assumed. Again, the *ratio legis* seems to be to facilitate police work more than anything.[2647] It is an offence which could provide a relatively easy ability to search premises and require the defendant to explain themself in order to invoke the defence.[2648] This again does not always sit right with the right to silence.[2649] These are but two concrete examples of the broadness of the terrorist offences, but similar arguments can be, and indeed have been (see nos 384–385, 398, 409–411, 439, 446, 460–462 and 471), developed for many of the other terrorism offences *sensu lato*.[2650]

523. Reversal of burden of proof – As was already alluded to in the previous paragraph, the use of offences with strict liability or very low *mens rea* requirements, relying to a large extent on defences in order to provide a little bit of balance, shifts the burden of proof to the defendant.[2651] The imposition of an evidential burden only, which was probably not always the original intention of parliament but was imposed by the case law regardless, does alleviate the issue somewhat. It is, however, by no means a perfect solution.

2646 Cornford (n 2023) 297.

2647 Lowe states in this regard '*In the UK two offences were introduced to assist investigators in preventing acts of terrorism.*' See: Lowe (n 1838) 60.

2648 Sugman Stubbs and Galli (n 25) 297.

2649 C.P.W. (n 1995) 75; Du Bois-Pedain (n 1993) 263.

2650 See also: Macdonald and Carlile (n 1626) 137–139; Zedner, *Security* (n 8) 131–132.

2651 Spencer (n 1616) 122–123; Sugman Stubbs and Galli (n 25) 297; Vladeck and Walker (n 2380) 174.

524. Clearly defining core concepts – Core concepts of offences are not always clearly defined. Not in the least this applies to the definition of terrorism in the TA 2000 which is central to many terrorist offences. Many commentators rightly point out parts of the definition which are unclear (see no. 348). Several other criticisms can be added to this, such as for example the question whether violence or damage being 'serious' is a clear enough threshold. Especially for the damage to property, as well as for interference with IT systems, it would have been much better to explicitly require certain possible consequences such as the death of people or the widespread disruption of the economic or governmental system. Other terms in the terrorism offences *sensu lato* also lack clarity, such as for example 'professing to belong' to a proscribed organisation or 'view or access' terrorist information on the internet.

525. Overlap – The use of many broad and vague offences leads to much overlap between those offences.[2652] Examples of situations which are covered by many different offences are easy to come by. Following training in an IS training camp for example could, depending on the concrete situation, amount to any (or several) of the three training offences, membership of a proscribed organisation and preparation of a terrorist act. If any areas are ever designated, this offence could be added to the list if the camp is located in such an area, which is not unlikely. Recruitment for terrorism online can amount to either of the encouragement offences, to inciting a criminal offence, to preparation of a terrorist offence and depending on the propaganda material used perhaps the possession of terrorist material offence. In addition, if a terrorist group is involved which is proscribed, it would also be membership of proscribed organisation.[2653] Several of the offences mentioned have never been used in practice and at this point only serve to clutter the legislation and confuse people.

526. Children and people with mental illness – As the age of criminal responsibility in the UK is set at only ten years old, many children are at risk of being prosecuted. This issue is only rising in prominence.[2654] The low age of criminal responsibility causes problems for example when judging the reasonable excuse under s. 57 or 58 TA 2000. It is a simple fact that children are not always reasonable. One commentator on the *Rowe* case put it rather poignantly when they stated: '*foolish or impressionable young Muslim men have their immature scribblings poured over by the terrorism police as if they were plans set in stone rather than the fantasies of wannabes, such as 17-year-old schoolboys whose realistic ambitions encompass a trip to Bradford rather than*

[2652] Hill (n 1666) para 1.21; Middleton (n 1626) 228.

[2653] See also: Spencer (n 1616) 121.

[2654] Hall, 'The Terrorism Acts in 2021' (n 1885) para 5.8–5.14 and 7.2.

Baghdad.'[2655] This quote illustrates the aforementioned issue. This is perhaps most pronounced in the possession offences but is certainly not limited to them. For example, the terrorist property offences require 'reasonable cause to suspect' and the attendance of a place of terrorist training offence requires that a person 'could not have reasonably failed to understand'. Another striking feature of the case law is that often (possibly in combination with young age) defendants have some sort of psychological disorder. These issues are often not severe enough to amount to criminal insanity but do show that the 'reasonable' standard cannot be easily applied to everyone. This results in convictions for terrorism offences of people who did not actually realise or understand that what they were doing was supporting terrorism, even if a reasonable person would have realised in that situation. This can be contrasted to the general evolution in UK law on the interpretation of the standard of recklessness. This has been a debated topic (see no. 332) but recent case law clearly shows that the standard for recklessness is subjective instead of objective, meaning the perpetrator has to actually have foreseen the risk. The use of a 'reasonableness' standard in the abovementioned terrorist offences stands in stark contrast to this evolution.

527. High pace of changes – In general, the legislation changes very rapidly. The sentences are a clear example of this. Many of the current terrorist offences were only introduced in 2000 or 2006. Even though these offences are only about 20 years old, most of their sentences have been elevated since (barring the ones already punishable with life imprisonment from the start). In addition to this raise in sentences, many terrorist offences could receive sentences of imprisonment for public protection from 2005 until the abolition of this sentence in 2012. Then, in 2015 sentences for offenders of particular concern (including terrorist offenders) were introduced and in 2019 extended sentences for terrorist offences (which already existed for certain violent and sexual offences) were added. Further changes were made in 2020 and then again in 2021 when serious terrorism sentences were introduced.[2656]

528. Accessibility – The main reason for introducing the TA 2000 was to establish a permanent, clear, and structured framework. Twenty years later only the 'permanent' part of this goal has been achieved. What started off as one Act with counter-terrorism rules quickly devolved into a situation with a number of Acts containing different offences and amending previous legislation. In addition, the TA 2000 framework only covered terrorism *sensu lato* while the rules on terrorism *sensu stricto* were still scattered around a large number of different pieces of legislation. The final result is a clutter of legislation which takes a while to untangle and fully comprehend.

2655 C.P.W. (n 1995) 79.

2656 See also: Kelly (n 1697) 645–646.

529. Influence of the executive – As has been discussed in Chapter II and will be discussed further in Section IV of this Chapter, administrative law is an option used to prevent terrorism where the executive is very much in the driver's seat. Despite this, the Secretary of State also has a relatively extensive influence on some criminal offences. By proscribing an organisation or designating an area, the Secretary has a direct influence on when these offences are committed as the legislation only provides for a framework for the offence while the most important part of the offence in concrete cases is dependent upon a decision by the Secretary of State.

530. The need for restraint by decision makers – As Anderson states in his 2013 report, the UK legislation leaves wide discretion to decision makers (police, Home Secretary, CPS, etc.).[2657] While he praises the decision making so far, he also points out, quoting Lord Bingham,[2658] that this discretion does not sit well with the rule of law.[2659] This is the core of the issue. The offences are so broad the police and CPS have much discretion in whether or not to arrest, prosecute, etc. The Secretary of State has discretion in whether or not to proscribe an organisation or designate an area, and the courts have large discretion in interpreting offences and their defences and in sentencing. Some form of discretion is inevitable and indeed necessary, but it is clear the current legislation has gone over the line of how much discretion is acceptable. The whole system relies on the restraint and common sense of the people applying the legislation as the legislation itself often does not provide any meaningful boundaries. This is in no way an indictment of the large number of people who are called upon every day to make these, often difficult, decisions; and if anything, the fact that the system continues to function is a testament to their good decision making. It is, however, clear that the legislature has not done the job expected of it and the current system is not foreseeable, nor clear, and therefore in violation of the legality principle.

SUBSECTION II. PROPORTIONALITY

531. No easy task – The broadness and vagueness of the offences makes it rather difficult to analyse the proportionality of the sentences. A clear example of this can be found in two different cases of the Court of Appeal when comparing the severity of the sentence for the encouragement offence to that of inviting support for a proscribed organisation. Before both sentences were raised to

2657 Anderson, 'Shielding the Compass: How to Fight Terrorism without Defeating the Law' (n 25) 16. See also: Hale-Ross (n 1) 40–41.

2658 *R v. K* [2001] UKHL 41, 2001 WL 825055, 24.

2659 Anderson, 'Shielding the Compass: How to Fight Terrorism without Defeating the Law' (n 25) 17.

respectively 15- and 14-years imprisonment, the encouragement offence carried a maximum sentence of seven years imprisonment while the offence of inviting support carried a maximum sentence of ten years imprisonment. It is already striking in terms of ordinal proportionality that when raising the sentences the legislature seems to have flipped the seriousness of these offences without the offences themselves being meaningfully changed. Perhaps it should come as no surprise then that the Court of Appeal gave mixed signals concerning the seriousness of both offences. In one case, expressing itself cautiously, it referred to the fact that inviting moral support for proscribed organisation had a higher sentence than encouraging terrorism as potentially being 'an anomaly'.[2660] In a case two years later, however, the Court of Appeal stated that the higher sentence for inviting support compared to encouraging is logical, since the act of proscribing makes the offence more serious.[2661] Whatever the 'correct' interpretation of the ordinal proportionality of these two offences may be, the difference between these two cases very clearly shows the difficulty of the task of comparing these broad pre-inchoate offences. This issue being kept in mind, we still attempt to analyse the proportionality of the offences to a certain degree, focussing on the most pronounced potential problems.

532. Almost all terrorist defendants are of particular concern – Quite a few terrorist offenders will fall in the category receiving a serious terrorist sentence and the majority of those who do not, can receive an extended sentence. For the small number who do not qualify for either of these regimes, the 'catch all' special custodial sentence for offenders of particular concern still applies. 'Regular' sentences have become the exception for terrorist offenders (for the one exception, see no. 383). This raises the question whether they are really all of particular concern, keeping in mind the broadness of the terrorist offences and the relative ease with which a defendant is caught within the scope of one of them. This restricts judges in their ability to impose a proportionate sentence in cases on the lower end of the spectrum.[2662]

533. High sentences without actual harm – In the pre-inchoate offences, no real harm has occurred yet. However, the possible sentences are high, with well over ten years imprisonment or even life imprisonment as a possibility.[2663] For example membership or inviting support for a proscribed organisation, the property offences, and attendance of a place of terrorist training carry sentences of up to 14 years, while the possession and encouragement offences have a maximum sentence of 15 years. These sentences have only ever been

2660 *Anjem Choudary, Mohammed Mizanur Rahman v. R* [2016] EWCA Crim 61, 58.
2661 *R v. Alamgir and others* [2018] EWCA Crim 21, 33.
2662 Kelly (n 1697) 652–653.
2663 Kelly (n 1697) 655; Zedner, 'Terrorizing Criminal Law' (n 45) 117.

raised over the years.[2664] In 2019 when some were increased, Walker argued this should not have happened without a stronger evidential basis and pleaded for a holistic review of sentencing.[2665] We can only agree. Because of the high sentences, there is little difference between many offences in the sentences provided for by the legislation. The sentence for a murder or bombing for example is life imprisonment, but the sentence for attempting these offences is also life imprisonment. One step further, the preparation of those same offences (assuming they are terrorist offences) or weapons training in order to execute the murder carries a maximum sentence of, once again, life imprisonment. The only difference being that the life sentence is mandatory for murder rather than discretionary. However, life imprisonment is already a possibility from the preparation stages. All this is rather odd in terms of proportionality. In general, it can be questioned whether any terrorist offences *sensu lato* should ever carry a life imprisonment sentence, as is currently the case for the terrorist training, weapons training, preparation offences and directing a terrorist organisation. This means their maximum sentence is as high as murder and significantly higher than some other possible terrorist offences *sensu stricto* such as for example inflicting grievous bodily harm, which carries a maximum sentence of five years imprisonment.[2666]

534. Sentencing guidelines – The sentences imposed by the legislation are only one part of the equation, however. These sentences still have to be applied to concrete cases. For some offences the courts are assisted in this exercise by the sentencing guidelines. However, there are no guidelines for all offences and even if guidelines are available, they leave a large discretion to the courts. The guidelines themselves are not always conducive to proportionate sentencing. The guidelines for both the preparation offence and explosive substances offences (causing an explosion likely to endanger life or property and attempting to cause explosion or making or keeping explosives with intent to endanger life or property) propose life sentences with minimum terms of respectively 35, 25 and 15 years for category 1A, 1B and 1C offences. The SA 2020 provides for a starting point for murder of a whole life tariff in cases of exceptionally high seriousness (for example the murder of two or more people where each murder involved abduction or sexual or sadistic conduct).[2667] However, for all other murders, the starting points range from from 12 years (offenders aged under 18) to 30 years (for example the murder of two or more people or murder involving

2664 See also: Kelly (n 1697).

2665 Clive Walker, Written evidence (CBS001) in response to the Joint Committee for Human Rights' call for evidence in connection with the Counter Terrorism & Border Security Bill 2017–19 (2018) 10 and 13.

2666 See s. 20 Offences against the Person Act 1861.

2667 S. 2 Schedule 21 SA 2020.

a firearm).[2668] As was argued by Ashworth, Lee and Walker (see no. 467–473), the guidelines for preparation seem to be disproportionate, knowing that the most serious category of the preparation offence has a starting point which is five years higher than the actual murder of two or more people. Considering the fact that even in case of a very serious preparation offence, no victims have died yet, the starting point is much too high in comparison.

SECTION IV. ADMINISTRATIVE LAW

535. Derogations – The road travelled has been a long one for the administrative measures. TPIMs, the current iteration, however, seem to be here to stay. Contrary to the situation under the ATCSA 2001, no derogation of Article 5 ECHR was provided for in the cases of control orders and TPIMs. A derogation could possibly have avoided much costly litigation and legal uncertainty, so why did the government not go that route? This question is impossible to answer definitively, but we can think of a few possible reasons. It might have been politically difficult. The *A and others* case was a bit of a shock to the system and the government might have wanted to avoid a second derogation being found incompatible.[2669] In addition, a second derogation may have led to the renewed criticism of being the only state to derogate from its Convention obligations in response to terrorism,[2670] although in more recent years France did so as well. Finally, the whole idea of the TA 2000 and the legislation which built upon it, was to have permanent counter-terrorism legislation instead of relying on temporary measures. A derogation would have once again been temporary and thus go against this underlying idea. The lack of derogation could be applauded as a derogation implies that human rights will not be fully respected for a certain amount of time. However, the key is in that temporal limitation.[2671] Instead of a derogation, we have seen a narrowing of the scope of the right to liberty in UK law. This adverse human rights effect is not temporary in the way a derogation is, and in that regard, another derogation might have been preferable.[2672]

536. Prosecution – TPIMs, as was the case for control orders and detention under ATCSA 2001, are imposed upon people who cannot be prosecuted for lack of admissible evidence. They are supposed to help investigations in uncovering

2668 S. 3–6 Schedule 21 SA 2020; Sentencing Council, *Murder Sentencing Leaflet.*
2669 See also, for ETPIMs: Fenwick and Fenwick (n 56) 25.
2670 See: Walker, 'The Impact of Contemporary Security Agendas Against Terrorism on the Substantive Criminal Law' (n 45) 127.
2671 See also: Galli (n 25) 170–171.
2672 As Zedner argues, emergency powers tend to become permanent and expand in scope of application. See: Zedner, *Security* (n 8) 123–125.

that evidence, but this hope has very much turned out to be vain. As explained above, the UK has many and very broad pre-inchoate offences. The behaviours which could lead to the imposition of a TPIM are often the same which could be prosecuted under these terrorist offences, think for example about s. 57 and 58 of the TA 2000. If the choice is made to impose a TPIM instead of prosecuting, we can only assume that is because of the inability of the authorities to prove the existence of an offence beyond a reasonable doubt. The argument could be made that if it is not possible to prosecute a person even for these broad pre-inchoate offences, then maybe no restrictions of liberty should be imposed at all. In addition, the time limits of TPIMs, while they are a welcome recognition of the fact that the TPIM situation is not sustainable long term, do mean that the issue of whether or not to prosecute a person is just postponed. The issue is postponed further in the case of 'new' terrorist activity after the imposition of a first TPIM since this allows for a second TPIM to be imposed. We do wonder why prosecution is not the preferred possibility in that case. This new terrorist activity must amount to a breach of the original TPIM and/or another of the many broad terrorist offences. The question thus arises why to chose for a new TPIM instead of prosecution.

537. Practical value – One of the constants throughout the different administrative regimes is their low frequency of use. Throughout their entire existence less than 20 people and only just over 50 people were subject to respectively detention under ATCSA 2001 and control orders. TPIMs are not used more frequently, as in February 2022 only two TPIMs were in force. Compared to the number of criminal prosecutions for terrorist offences, these numbers are very small. Despite their infrequent use, the measures have been widely discussed and much time and effort has been spent on crafting, criticising, and amending them. All this leads to the question whether the game is worth the candle. The UK government and legislature for their part do seem to think so, as in 2023 they introduced 'Prevention and Investigation Measures' applicable to threats relating to foreign powers which are nearly identical to TPIMs.[2673]

538. The right to liberty – TPIMs were originally introduced to be more human rights compliant than control orders were. However, TPIMs in their current iteration are almost as likely to amount to deprivations of liberty as control orders were. TPIMs offer wide discretion to the Home Secretary, but this discretion is likely to be exercised with the control orders' case law in mind. This means that house arrests should be shorter than when control orders were originally introduced. In addition, the forced relocation measure is slightly less stringent. These changes are attempts to address the issue of social isolation caused by control orders/TPIMs. While they do provide for some limitations,

[2673] S. 39–62 and Schedule 7 National Security Act 2023.

they are only relevant in the most extreme cases and still leave a lot of leeway. Following the current line of UK case law (see no. 508), individual measures such as 16 hour house arrest or a forced relocation would not amount to a deprivation of liberty. However, the combination of those measures (possibly in addition to other measures such as restrictions on telecommunications) could amount to a deprivation of liberty if they were *'unusually destructive of the life the controlee might otherwise have been living.'*[2674]

[2674] *Secretary of State for the Home Department v. AP* [2010] UKSC 24, 2010 WL 2131699, 4. See also: Fenwick, 'Recalibrating ECHR Rights, and the Role of the Human Rights Act Post 9/11' (n 26) 233–234; Fenwick, *Fenwick on Civil Liberties and Human Rights* (n 1649) 1100; Fenwick and Phillipson (n 25) 881–882.

PART IV

COMPARATIVE ANALYSIS AND RECOMMENDATIONS

INTRODUCTION

539. Overview of Part IV – This final Part of the book is divided into three Chapters. The first contains the comparative analysis of the two jurisdictions. In this Chapter, the Belgian and UK systems are systematically compared on all relevant points. In doing so, this Chapter answers research questions 4.1[2675] and 4.2.[2676] The second Chapter contains general remarks which set the stage for the final Chapter. In this third and final Chapter recommendations are made for changes which can be made to create a system where the risk of arbitrariness is as small as possible and it thus answers the final research question, question 4.3.[2677]

540. Jurisdictions and relevance – The first Chapter of this Part, the comparative analysis, focusses on Belgian and UK law. The second Chapter, however, contains general remarks which transcend any one specific jurisdiction. Examples given in this Chapter are drawn from the rest of the book, which means they focus on Belgium and the UK, but the issues touched upon are wider than just the Belgian or UK context and can be relevant for different states around the globe. The third and final Chapter zooms back in on Belgium and provides concrete recommendations for Belgian law.

2675 How do the Belgian and UK legal systems compare in the ways they directly restrict the right to liberty to prevent terrorism?

2676 Which of these attempts is most in line with our framework?

2677 Which changes can be made to the Belgian legislation to create a system where the risk of arbitrariness is as small as possible without unduly hindering the government's ability to prevent terrorism?

CHAPTER I
COMPARATIVE ANALYSIS

SECTION I. GENERAL COMPARISON

541. Belgian vs. UK criminal law – In the introductions to Parts II and III, some general observations are made and basic rules explained with regard to Belgian and UK law. Comparing these two introductions, many small differences immediately catch the eye. However, none of these differences are so marked as to make comparison impossible. Even so, a few points have to be kept in mind. In terms of criminal law, both jurisdictions in principle require *actus reus* and *mens rea* for an offence to exist, but the UK also has strict liability offences and a system of defences, which depend on the specific offence. This system does not exist in Belgium and sometimes makes the construction of the elements of the offence more complicated in the UK, as the defence can be a form of *mens rea* for which the burden of proof is shifted. Regarding sentencing, Belgian criminal law provides lower maximum sentences for inchoate offences than for the actual offence, which is not the case in the UK. At first glance, UK criminal law allows judges more leeway when sentencing in general, because it only provides for (often relatively high) maximum sentences and no minima. However, this first reading is deceptive. Belgian judges are authorised to lower the sentences well below the minimum sentence when applying attenuating circumstances, which is something that very frequently happens. In addition, when comparing sentences, we also need to take into account the sentencing guidelines in the UK, which provide some guidance for judges (see no. 344), as no equivalent exists in Belgium. All this means that in practice Belgian judges do not have less freedom to impose the sentence they deem appropriate.

542. Belgian vs. UK criminal procedure – In Belgium, the ECHR has direct application, while in the UK it does not and it has to be applied through the HRA 1998 (see no. 333). In addition, the Belgian Constitutional Court has the ability to suspend or annul legislation, which is unconstitutional or violates human rights, while the UK Supreme Court can only issue non-binding declarations of incompatibility. Furthermore, Belgium has ratified the protocol to the ECHR that contains the free movement of persons and the UK has not (see no. 89). These differences mean that in the UK the government is often given slightly more leeway by the courts when it comes to human rights. Also, once a measure does not amount to a deprivation of liberty, the UK government has less restrictions than in Belgium, as the UK government does not need to comply with the free movement of persons under the ECHR, because the UK has not ratified the protocol including this right. This does not mean the UK government has free reign, however, as it still has to comply with other human rights and international obligations. Another UK specific rule which also needs to be kept in mind is the prohibition on the use of intercept evidence (see no. 331). This can thwart the possibility of prosecution in situations where Belgian prosecutors would not have the same issues and could use intercept evidence in court. A final influential difference is the position of the prosecution services and certain judges. In the UK, the police can conduct investigations under their own authority while in Belgium they are always directed by either the prosecution service or the investigating judge. The UK Crown Prosecution Service only really takes the foreground when cases have to go to trial, while at this point the Belgian prosecution service has already played a very important role in the investigation. This could create situations where Belgian prosecutors have more personal stakes in a case than their UK counterparts and also gives much more power to the Belgian prosecution service, as it means they were able to conduct the investigation entirely as they saw fit. When it comes to the courts, the UK has broader possibilities for jury trials, because while Belgian criminal law has many cases which in theory require a jury trial, the construct of correctionalisation has allowed the vast majority of cases to be diverted away from the jury. In addition, the UK has a system of lay Magistrates, while all Belgian judges are professional judges with law degrees and usually many years of legal experience. These are the general differences which are most relevant for our comparison. Whenever they, or any other small yet significant differences, come into play, this will be pointed out throughout the analysis.

SECTION II. ADMINISTRATIVE LAW

543. No need for administrative measures – One of the main differences between the UK approach and the Belgian approach to countering terrorism through direct restrictions of liberty is the use of administrative measures. The UK has used some form of administrative preventive measures which impose direct restrictions on the right to liberty for a long time (see no. 496 and following). In Belgium, such measures have been discussed but at this point in time they do not feature in the Belgian legal system. The first question therefore is whether Belgium should introduce them. These administrative measures, such as TPIMs, would not preclude the use of criminal law as well, but would be an addition to the existing framework. As was discussed in the previous Part (see no. 519), finding the right balance for these measures has proven an arduous task for the UK and even now the question remains whether the TPIMs system is fully 'ECtHR proof'. The interpretation of the right to liberty in the UK seems to have shifted in the direction of less protection, which is an undesirable result in terms of human rights (see no. 521). In Belgium, the situation would be even more difficult as Belgium is bound by the free movement of people which is part of the second Article of the Fourth Protocol to the ECHR. As explained in Part I, the main analysis remains that of legal certainty and proportionality and administrative measures can be challenged on both grounds. In light of all this, we must consider the question of the added value of administrative measures. Although they have been in force in the UK over the last 23 years, very few of these measures have actually been imposed (see no. 537). The consensus is that prosecution is the preferable option and therefore administrative measures are used only in these situations where no prosecution is possible. However, as will be discussed below, the existing terrorism offences are exceedingly broad, both in Belgium and in the UK. Therefore, there are only few situations which do not come within the scope of any of the terrorist offences and people for whom the prosecution cannot prove any of these broad offences, should not be subject to a measure which restricts their liberty. In the UK context, such measures might be relevant because of the inability to use intercept evidence and the subsequent reliance on intelligence information, but this is not the case for Belgium. Therefore, there are no reasons for Belgium to actually introduce such measures.

544. Reminder on the scope – The result of the analysis is clear on this point: there is no need for administrative measures (see no. 543). That is, no need for administrative measures which have a direct impact on the right to liberty of the person. Of course, other administrative measures can still remain useful. For example, an eye can still be kept on people who are at liberty; or they could receive certain guidance or counselling. Institutions which clearly spread radicalising ideology could still be monitored or closed down, etc. All these types of measures fall outside of the scope of this research (see nos 12–13). The same goes for measures within the context of immigration law, which were explicitly excluded from our scope as well (see no. 13). While these measures can still prove useful, they must be handled with care so that their cumulative effect is not disproportionate. For example, confiscating passport and ID card, in combination with extensive asset freezing and surveillance could prove very detrimental to both the free movement and private lives of the people subject to them. Therefore, a system in which many administrative measures which individually seem acceptable, are combined *at infinitum* is not the answer. Any measures imposed must be well-reasoned and their combination cannot disproportionately limit a person's rights.

545. Criminal justice more suited to long-term goals – The criminal justice process, if it functions completely as intended, is better suited to provide long-term prevention. Immediate incapacitation can be provided through pre-trial detention if necessary, the entire process is built around the required safeguards in terms of fundamental rights, and sentences are supposed to prepare perpetrators for their reintegration into society. In theory, services are provided for offenders after conviction in order to improve themselves, work on their place in society and avoid recidivism. All those things would lead to long-term prevention. However, we must say that in practice these goals sadly remain far from being reached and a lot of work has still to be done to make this ideal situation a reality. The current state of affairs has even had the opposite effect, due to poor prison conditions, no psychological support and lack of useful ways to pass the time in prison. Several terrorists started out as petty criminals and were radicalised in prison.[2678] Nowadays, authorities are more aware of this danger and are actively trying to counter it, but this is still a long cry from actually providing sufficient therapy, suitable living conditions, etc. This being said, the idea of long-term prevention through rehabilitation is part of criminal law, while administrative measures tend to become too fixated on short-term prevention without any real long-term plan.

SECTION III. CRIMINAL LAW

SUBSECTION I. RESTRICTIONS OF LIBERTY

a) Principal sentences

546. Imprisonment – The most common principal sentence for terrorism offences in both Belgium and the UK is imprisonment. The exact duration of this sentence can vary wildly depending on the offence and it is therefore discussed in the Subsections below covering the different offences.

547. Alternative sentences – Both jurisdictions also provide alternatives to a prison sentence. While Belgium has three alternative non-custodial sentences which could nevertheless restrict a person's right to liberty, the UK has only one. Of the three Belgian ones, community service (see no. 116) is the least relevant as its restrictions to physical liberty are very limited. Autonomous probation sentences (see no. 117) provide for more options in terms of restricting liberty and electronic monitoring (see no. 115) can actually amount to a deprivation of liberty. In the UK, community orders (see no. 342) allow for similar measures as is the case under the three Belgian sentences.[2679] The unpaid work requirement

---

2678 See: Cyriel Fijnaut, *De samenhang tussen georganiseerde misdaad en terrorisme en de aanslagen in Parijs en Brussel in 2015–2016* (Intersentia 2020); R Kats, B De Graaf and P Jacobs, 'Terroristen in detentie: een overzicht van de ontwikkeling en discussie over de terroristenafdelingen in Nederland, 2004–2022' [2022] Justitiele Verkenningen 10.

2679 See Schedule 9 SA 2020.

is similar to a Belgian community service sentence. The Belgian minimum of 25 hours is lower than the UK minimum of 40 hours but the maximum in both countries is 300 hours. Community orders also allow for curfews and electronic monitoring, which compares to the Belgian electronic monitoring sentence. The UK system provides for a maximum of 112 hours of curfew per week (which equates to a daily curfew of 16 hours if the curfew is the same every day). The Belgian legislation does not provide for a maximum amount of hours per week so in theory 24 hour curfews are possible. However, if for example the perpetrator has a job, they will usually be allowed to go to work, meaning their curfew will be maximum around 16 hours per day as well. The UK requirements can last for two years while in Belgium the maximum term is one year. This means the UK curfew and electronic tagging could be in place twice as long, which more than balances the possibility of slightly shorter curfews. Finally, the other UK requirements, such as rehabilitation activity requirements, programme requirements, exclusion requirements, etc. are possible within a Belgian autonomous probation sentence. Even curfews should be possible within this sentence. The Belgian autonomous probation sentence also has a maximum of two years, which puts that at the same level as is the case for the UK. A major difference between the three Belgian sentences and the UK community order is that when imposing any of the three, the Belgian judge also imposes a replacement sentence which can be executed if the perpetrator does not abide by the rules. In the UK, the breach of a community order can lead to a summons to appear before the court and a re-sentencing.[2680] So in the UK, a second court intervention is required. In general, both systems are similar, with the UK system being slightly more onerous as it provides for a possibly longer period of electronic monitoring, a longer minimum unpaid work requirement, etc. In addition, the three Belgian sentences cannot be combined, while it would be possible in the UK to for example impose a work requirement and an electronic monitoring requirement in the same community order. On the other hand, Belgian legislation provides for a list of offences for which alternative sentences are not a possibility, which is not the case in the UK. In general, the UK system seems to be preferable in terms of clarity. It has one single sentence which provides for the same possibilities as the three Belgian sentences. In addition, the possible requirements are provided for by law in quite a lot of detail, contrary to the situation in Belgium.

548. Suspension and postponement – The Belgian system of suspension of sentencing (see no. 118) does not have a UK equivalent. In fact, the closest equivalent is again the community order. A suspension of sentencing with probation requirements is not too dissimilar from a community order in the sense that the perpetrator is found guilty but does not receive a custodial

[2680] S. 6–15 Schedule 9 SA 2020.

sentence. Instead, they have to abide by certain requirements and if they fail to do so, they can receive (another) sentence. Suspension of sentencing without probation, however, would not be covered by a community sentence as the requirements are too light. The Belgian system of postponement of sentence enforcement (see no. 119) does have a UK equivalent, being the suspended sentence orders (see no. 343). The concept is the same: imposing a sentence of imprisonment which is not executed as long as the perpetrator does not commit new offences and abides by certain conditions, but the practical rules differ. First, Belgian legislation does not allow for a postponement of sentence enforcement without probation if the perpetrator has prior convictions to more than 12 months imprisonment. The UK has no such requirement for suspended sentence orders, but neither does Belgium for postponement of sentence enforcement with probation. Second, postponement of sentence enforcement in Belgium is possible for sentences of up to five years imprisonment, while this threshold in the UK is only two years. Third, the operational and supervisory period in the UK is maximum two years as well, while it is three or five years in Belgium, depending on the sentence for which the enforcement is postponed. Finally, in the UK extensive curfews and electronic monitoring are allowed under suspended sentence orders. The Belgian legislation does not explicitly exclude this, but presumably this is not an option in Belgium as this would circumvent the electronic monitoring sentence. In general, the UK rules are stricter as more stringent requirements are possible and a suspended sentence order is only possible for sentences of up to two years. However, this is counter-balanced slightly by the shorter duration of the operational and supervisory period. The existence of the Belgian autonomous probation sentence does raise the question whether separate systems of probation suspension of sentencing and postponement of sentence enforcement are still necessary. They further add to the opaqueness of the Belgian legislation created by the existence of three different alternative sentences compared to the one in the UK.

b) Additional restrictions of liberty

549. Supervision by Sentence Enforcement Court vs. different extended sentences – In Belgium, supervision by the Sentence Enforcement Court can add five to 15 years to a prison sentence (see nos 122–123). However, it is only possible for offences of terrorism *sensu stricto* which caused the death of a victim and are punished with at least five years imprisonment. The extended follow-up which would eventually replace the supervision of the Sentence Enforcement Court in the new Criminal Code, would also be mandatory for terrorism *sensu stricto* if the death of a victim is caused (see nos 126–129). A relatively recent addition to the UK counter-terrorism arsenal are different types of extended sentences. At this point, three are relevant for our purposes: serious terrorist sentences (see no. 339), extended sentences (see no.

340) and special custodial sentences for offenders of particular concern (see no. 341). They have in common that they consist of a normal prison sentence and an extension period during which the convicted person is subject to a license. The custodial part has to be of the same length as the sentence the judge would normally impose. For serious terrorism sentences, the minimum custodial part is 14 years, and the extension period is 7 to 25 years. For extended sentences, the extension period is minimum one year and maximum eight for specified terrorism offences or ten for serious terrorist offences. Finally, special custodial sentences for offenders of particular concern have an extension period of one year. Serious terrorism sentences can be imposed for serious terrorist offences, which include murder, but also the weapons and terrorism training offences, directing a terrorist organisation, and preparing a terrorist offence, if those offences were likely to result in multiple deaths and there is a risk of further harm to the public. Extended sentences are applicable to most terrorist offences *sensu lato* (see no. 340) if the judge would impose a sentence of at least four years or the defendant is a recidivist and there is a significant risk for serious harm to the public. Special custodial sentences for offenders of particular concern, finally, have to be imposed if the judge wants to impose a prison sentence upon people convicted for any terrorist offence *sensu lato*, except for the uniform and publication offences related to proscribed organisations, which do not receive a serious terrorism sentence or an extended sentence.

550. Scope and impact – Comparing the Belgian and UK situations, three things must be noted. First, the scope of the UK system of sentences with extension periods is much broader than the scope of the Belgian supervision by the Sentence Enforcement Court system. In Belgium this is applicable to only some of the most serious terrorist offences *sensu stricto* while in the UK almost all terrorist offenders will be subject to a sentence with an extension period. Second, supervision of the Sentence Enforcement Court lasts for five to 15 years, while the extension periods in the UK can range from one year as part of a special custodial sentence for offenders of particular concern or an extended sentence to a maximum of 25 years as part of a serious terrorist sentence. Considering the fact that the scope of application of the UK sentences is much broader, the lower minimum is logical, but the maximum of 25 years is significantly higher than the 15-year maximum in Belgium. This is counter-balanced to a degree by the third difference. In Belgium, the period of supervision by the Sentence Enforcement Court is added to the prison sentence but is not included in it. For example, for an offence with a maximum sentence of 15 years imprisonment, the Court can impose 15 years imprisonment and 15 years supervision by the Sentence Enforcement Court. In the UK, the total of the custodial sentence and the extension period combined cannot exceed the maximum custodial sentence for the offence. This is not the case in Belgium, meaning the supervision by the Sentence Enforcement Court can raise the time spent in custody substantially above the maximum sentence provided for the offence. In addition, in the UK no extension periods are possible for people convicted to life sentences while in Belgium supervision by the Sentence Enforcement Court can be combined with a life sentence. So while the scope of application for the sentences allowing for extension periods in the UK is significantly broader and for serious terrorism sentences the extension period can be much longer than supervision by the Sentence Enforcement Court, the extension periods in the UK can never lead to a deprivation of liberty which exceeds the maximum sentence provided in the legislation. This is the case for supervision by the Sentence Enforcement Court. This observation in turn can be nuanced by the fact that maximum sentences in the UK are much higher than in Belgium to begin with, so their capacity to act as a proportionate maximum threshold is limited.

c) Pre-trial detention

551. Two UK regimes of detention – The UK has different regimes for arrest and detention, the main ones being the PACE 1984 regime which is applicable to all offences and the TA 2000 regime which is only applicable to terrorist offences. Under the PACE regime, the absolute maximum a person can be deprived of their liberty before being brought before a judge is 36 hours (see no. 489). Within this time frame the arrestee has to be brought before a Magistrates' Court which can issue a warrant for further detention valid for another 36 hours. This can be repeated but the total detention cannot exceed 96 hours. The TA arrest and detention regime allows for a bit more leeway. First, the standard for arresting a suspect is that they are reasonably suspected to 'be a terrorist' (see no. 492). Second, the arrestee can be detained for 48 hours before a warrant for further detention has to be issued (see no. 493). This warrant, issued by a Magistrates' Court is valid for seven days starting at the time of arrest. It can be renewed to a total maximum of 14 days. So compared to the PACE regime, under the TA regime, the arrestee can be detained for an additional 12 hours before having to be brought before a judge and then for ten days longer (14 instead of four days) under warrants for further detention. After this period of maximum four or 14 days (depending on the grounds for arrest), the regimes converge and for further detention the suspect has to be charged. In principle they are released upon charge, but under certain circumstances they can be kept in detention (see no. 490), in which case they have to be brought before the Magistrates' Court again.

552. Compared to Belgium – Belgium does not have a different regime for terrorism than it has for other offences, but there are some minor differences, the main one being that the threshold for the motivation of the absolute necessity for public security (see nos 294–296). Compared to the UK system, Belgian pre-trial detention has a tendency to last longer. The suspect can be detained for an initial 48 hours without an arrest warrant (see no. 289), which is the same as

detention under the TA 2000 in the UK. A Belgian arrest warrant is valid for five days, which only start at the time of the issuing of the warrant (see no. 297). This puts the maximum duration of the detention at the same length as arrest under the TA 2000 for the first warrant for further detention. This warrant is valid for seven days, starting at the time of arrest, while in Belgium the detention after arrest can last for two days, after which an additional five can be added on the basis of the arrest warrant, bringing the total to seven days as well. A major difference then is that the Belgian arrest warrant cannot be extended by the same judge, as is the case in the UK, but the arrestee has to be brought before a different judge, the Council Chamber. At that point the Belgian system of automatic periodic review comes into play (see nos 298–300). For the first seven days, the Belgian pre-trial detention system is thus roughly similar to the UK TA 2000 system, meaning it is significantly stricter to the arrestee than the general UK pre-charge detention. An important addition to this, is that while both Belgian and UK law provide or judicial supervision after 48 hours, the position of the judge is different. In the UK, the Magistrate only intervenes punctually in order to decide on the warrant. In Belgium, the investigating judge is in charge of the whole investigation. While they are judges, who are (supposed to be) impartial and independent, their direct and close involvement in the case is bound to change their approach to it. This could be perceived as an issue but also as a strength, as the investigating judge should be better acquainted with the details and intricacies of the case, which means they should be less under the influence of the prosecution/police when making their decision. This is part of a wider debate, which is also being had in the context of a proposal for a new Belgian Code of Criminal Procedure (see no. 109). Arguments can be made for both sides, but our personal belief is that the situation of a judge who intervenes punctually, as is the case in the UK, is preferable. It would however be best if the judge in question were a legally trained, professional judge with access to all possible tools needed to correctly interpret the case file and legislation; and able to reduce the power of the prosecution and police by providing adequate scrutiny. Once the UK arrestee is charged, they are released. Further detention can be decided in certain situations, which are similar in some ways to – but wider than the possibilities for – an arrest warrant in Belgium if the offence is not punishable with 15 years imprisonment or more, being: the suspect would flee, interfere with the administration of justice or commit new offences. But furthermore, in the UK, detention is possible for the protection of the suspect; and it is always possible if the offence charged is murder (see no. 490). It is also possible for non-imprisonable offences if the detention is necessary to prevent them causing injury to another or loss of or damage to property. In Belgium, pre-trial detention is not possible for non-imprisonable offences, which is a major difference. In terrorism cases, however, the other two scenarios would not pose any difficulty in Belgium either, as the threshold for the motivation based on the abovementioned factors is lowered to five years, which covers almost all of the terrorism offences.

553. Bail – In Belgium, bail is issued under the system of provisional release, which has the same conditions of application as pre-trial detention (see no. 287 and 297). This is not the case in the UK where the presumption of bail when appearing before the Magistrates' Court can only be defeated in certain circumstances (see no. 491), which are virtually the same ones which are required for the protection of public safety when issuing an arrest warrant in Belgium. This means that in theory, in situations not covered by those circumstances, bail is granted to a person in the UK while in Belgium pre-trial detention nor bail are possible for offences with sentences under 15 years or terrorist offences with sentences under five years.

SUBSECTION II. TERRORISM *SENSU STRICTO*

554. Specific offence or not – The first major difference between Belgium and the UK in terms of terrorist offences, is that Belgium has one specific terrorism offence *sensu stricto* while the UK does not. The UK approach has the advantage of not singling terrorism out as different at this level and not adding extra legislation. The Belgian approach on the other hand does help with coherence and clarity and could therefore be preferable under the legal certainty principle. In his review of the definition of terrorism, Lord Carlile argued for a system of aggravated sentences for terrorism (see no. 360). This looked very much like what is currently in place in Belgium. A major difference, however, was that Lord Carlile's proposal was not limited to an exhaustive list of offences: it used a sentence cap of all offences punishable with five years or more. However, this proposal was not adopted by parliament and the UK still uses different general criminal law offences to tackle terrorism *sensu* stricto. Although Belgian criminal law provides for an aggravating circumstance in situations of terrorism *sensu stricto*, the sentences are not higher than the UK ones, mainly because of the general tendency in the UK to provide for relatively high sentences.

555. Murder – The most common terrorist offence *sensu stricto* is murder. In general, Belgian criminal law, murder is punishable with life felony imprisonment, but it does require premeditation. Manslaughter, which does not require premeditation, is punishable with 20 to 30 years felony imprisonment. However, after application of the aggravating circumstance of terrorism, this sentence becomes life felony imprisonment as well. In the UK, premeditation is not required in order to qualify a homicide as murder. Once a homicide is committed with the intent to cause death or grievous bodily harm, it constitutes murder under UK law and is punishable with life imprisonment (see no. 350).

In terms of maximum sentence, there is no difference between Belgium and the UK. However, an action undertaken with the intent to cause grievous bodily harm which causes the victim's death would under Belgian law not be qualified as manslaughter. In Belgium, this offence is punishable with five to ten years felony imprisonment, or ten to 15 years in case of premeditation.[2681] After applying the aggravating circumstance of terrorism, this offence is punishable with ten to 15 years felony imprisonment or 15 to 20 years felony imprisonment in case of premeditation.[2682] This does not take into account the potential of correctionalisation which would lower the sentence again to respectively six months to ten years imprisonment and one to 15 years imprisonment. In those situations, UK criminal law is significantly stricter than Belgian criminal law. We can therefore conclude that in the straightforward situations of terrorist killing with intent, the sentences in both jurisdictions are the same, but in the more complicated situation of terrorist killing without intent to kill but with intent to cause grievous bodily harm, UK criminal law is stricter.

556. Other offences – A similar situation arises for other offences of terrorism *sensu stricto*. In some respects, the sentences are similarly high. This is the case, for example, for endangering life by releasing noxious substances or owning, producing, or transporting nuclear or chemical weapons, which are punishable with life imprisonment in both jurisdictions. However, UK law does not differentiate, for example, between causing explosions endangering life or making or keeping explosives with intent to endanger life (see nos 351 and 358). Both are punishable with life imprisonment. Similarly, the development, production, stockpiling, acquiring, retaining, or transferring of biological agents or toxins is punishable with life imprisonment in the UK. In Belgium, keeping, selling, etc. of explosives with the intent to commit a crime against people or property as a terrorist offence is punishable with ten to 15 years felony imprisonment (six months to ten years imprisonment after correctionalisation).[2683] The Belgian sentence for developing, stockpiling, owning, transferring, etc. of bacteriological agents or toxins or weapons, equipment or means of their spreading in a terrorist context and with terrorist intent is only three years imprisonment.[2684] Once again we see that in the more extreme cases, the sentences in both jurisdictions are the same, but that Belgian law is more lenient towards perpetrators of offences which it deems somewhat less serious.

2681 Art. 401 CC.

2682 Art. 138 *j.* 401 CC.

2683 Art. 137, §2 7° CC *j.* Art. 138, §1 6° CC *j.* Art. 6 wet 28 mei 1956 betreffende ontplofbare en voor de deflagratie vatbare stoffen en mengsels en de daarmede geladen tuigen, *BS* 9 juni 1956, 3990.

2684 Art. 137, §2 10° CC *j.* Art. 138, §1 3° CC *j.* Art. 2 wet 10 juli 1978 houdende goedkeuring van het Verdrag tot verbod van de ontwikkeling, de produktie en de aanleg van voorraden van bacteriologische (biologische) en toxinewapens en inzake de vernietiging van deze wapens, opgemaakt te Londen, Moskou en Washington op 10 april 1972, *BS* 6 juli 1979.

557. Inchoate offences – The same observation can be made in relation to the inchoate offences. While in Belgium attempt and aiding and abetting are punishable with lower sentences than the actual offences (see no. 266), the sentences for the UK inchoate offences of attempt, encouragement, assistance and conspiracy are the same as for the offences themselves (see nos 451, 452 and 465). Some Acts reiterate this, such as for example the explosive substances act 1883, which explicitly includes attempting, procuring, counselling, aiding, abetting, or being accessory to the offences under the Act (see no. 351).

558. Definition of terrorism for other terrorist offences – Another major difference between the two jurisdictions is that in Belgium the offence of terrorism *sensu stricto* is used in the *mens rea* of the terrorism offences *sensu lato*. Since the UK does not have a specific terrorism offence *sensu stricto*, this was not possible, so the TA 2000 includes a definition of terrorism which is used when terrorism offences *sensu lato* refer to the term. Both the UK and Belgian definition cover roughly the same actions which can constitute terrorism, the only difference being that the UK definition is articulated in more general terms, while the Belgian definition includes a more detailed and more extensive list of actions (see nos 131–138 and 345–348). Because of this approach, it is possible for the UK definition to cover certain actions which are not covered by the Belgian one. As the Belgian list is quite extensive such situations will be relatively rare, but for example rape is not included on the Belgian list (see no. 134). This offence, especially in a terrorist context, will often 'involve serious violence against a person', meaning it is covered by the UK definition. Similarities between the definitions include the fact that neither are limited to acts aimed at their respective governments or even democratic governments, nor to acts which endanger human lives. In terms of *mens rea* the UK definition is broader in several respects but also slightly narrower in others. It covers all actions which are designed to:

- influence the government or an international governmental organisation or
- to intimidate (a section of) the public.

The Belgian definition by comparison requires the action to have the aim of:

- seriously intimidating a population, or
- unduly compelling a government or international organisation to perform or abstain from performing any act,
- or seriously destabilising or destroying the fundamental political, constitutional, economic or social structures of a country or an international organisation.

The Belgian definition is more exacting because it uses qualifying terms such as 'seriously intimidating' the population or 'unduly compelling' instead of just 'intimidating' or 'influencing'. In this respect the Belgian definition is narrower and the inclusion of these qualifying terms was in fact the reason the Belgian Constitutional Court ruled that the definition was not in violation of the legality principle (see no. 156–157). We could therefore (cautiously) assume the UK definition would not have passed this test. Important to note, however, is that the UK definition does not in itself constitute an offence but is only part of other offences, while the Belgian definition defines an offence in itself. In addition, the UK definition assumes the presence of the *mens rea* for any use or threat of a listed action which involves the use of firearms or explosives (see no. 345), while in Belgium there is no such assumption.[2685] The Belgian definition is broader on other points, however, as it provides for a third *mens rea* option while the UK definition does not. Marchand specifically criticises this third *mens rea* option as being too vague.[2686] In addition, the UK definition is a two tier *mens rea*. It also requires the act to be made for the purpose of advancing a political, religious, racial or ideological cause. The Belgian definition (as well as the EU definition on which it is based), does not include this and only consists of a one tier *mens rea*.[2687] In the preparatory works, Belgian parliament even explicitly excluded this from the definition (see no. 136). The inclusion of a two tier *mens rea* is a bit more demanding for the prosecution, as they have to prove an extra step. The Belgian definition does include the so-called contextual element (see no. 135), which also provides for an extra step and thus narrows down the definition slightly, but in a different sense. In conclusion, it is impossible to state one definition is broader than the other, as they are both broad in certain ways but less so in others. However, the Belgian definition does seem to have a higher threshold in terms of *mens rea*, as all three options include qualifying terms which require a certain seriousness. The contextual element also requires further seriousness. Therefore, the UK definition seems to be broader in the sense that it catches more actions which are not as serious or dangerous. For example, hindering traffic in order to protest against certain government policies could endanger lives and is designed to influence the government or could even intimidate the public in some scenarios. This would suffice in qualifying as terrorism under the UK definition, while we would argue it is insufficient in Belgium, as the Belgian definition requires the population to be seriously intimidated or the government to be unduly compelled. However, a lot depends on the application of these provisions in practice as they are both very broad, and terms such as 'seriously' can also be interpreted more or less strictly. However,

[2685] Note, however, that in the Abdeslam and Ayari case, the Court did find that the fact they shot at the police using assault weapons in a residential neighbourhood was proof of the required *mens rea* (see no. 161).

[2686] Marchand (n 617) 281.

[2687] Hale-Ross (n 1) 18–19.

as argued several times throughout this book, the legality principle requires the offences to be as clearly and narrowly defined as possible.

559. Evaluation: legality – The Belgian situation, while far from ideal, seems to be the preferable one under the legality principle, although both approaches have pros and cons. First, the approach of including all terrorist offences *sensu stricto* in one Article which deals with this type of offences, enhances the accessibility of the legislation compared to using all sorts of different offences in different legislation. Second, the definition of terrorism in Belgium is worded in a way that excludes more mundane 'low harm' actions. This also means the Belgian definition is less likely to include actions which could be considered legitimate resistance against undemocratic, tyrannical regimes. As argued above (see no. 137), we believe the definition of terrorism should not include a 'right to rebel', but it should allow for non-violent protest against (unjust) regimes. Even so, the Belgian legislation still poses several legality issues. The wording of the offence could still be improved, especially in terms of sentencing (see nos 142–147). The possible application of the concept of political offences should also be clarified (see nos 151–154).

560. Evaluation: proportionality – The UK terrorism offences *sensu stricto* are notable for their harsh sentences, with many carrying a maximum sentence of life imprisonment. Problematic in terms of ordinal proportionality, is the UK legislation's tendency not to lower the maximum sentence for inchoate offences.[2688] In that sense, the Belgian legislature has made a valiant attempt to differentiate between the varying sentences but as explained (see nos 140 and 148), it did not succeed in introducing a system without any proportionality flaws.

SUBSECTION III. TERRORISM SENSU LATO

a) *Offences relating to terrorist groups*

561. Defining terrorist groups – In Belgium, the Criminal Code defines a terrorist group to be any structured group of more than two persons, established over a period of time and acting in concert to commit terrorist offences (see no. 166). Under UK law, two types of groups are relevant. First, an organisation can be prescribed by the Secretary of State if it commits or participates in

[2688] Note that during the drafting process of the new Belgian Criminal Code, the idea was floated to have the same maximum sentence for an attempted offence as for the completed offence. The Council of State, however, was against this for proportionality reasons and the idea was abandoned. See: Toelichting bij wetsvoorstel 13 maart 2019 tot invoering van een nieuw Strafwetboek – Boek 1 en Boek 2, *Parl.St.* Kamer 2018–2019, no. 54-3651/001, 48–50.

acts of terrorism, prepares for terrorism, promotes or encourages terrorism (including glorification), or is otherwise concerned in terrorism. Second, the offence of directing a terrorist organisation uses a different definition of 'terrorist organisation', which is an organisation concerned in the commission of acts of terrorism. This definition is narrower than the one that provides for the possibility of proscription. The second UK definition is the most similar to the Belgian one, only including organisations which aim to commit terrorism *sensu stricto* (for a comparison of this definition, see nos 558–559). The Belgian definition goes into more detail on what a 'group' is. Although this definition is not always crystal clear, the additional information does provide some insights and enhances foreseeability. This is preferable in terms of legality. The definition of terrorist organisations which is supposed to delineate the power to proscribe, is extremely broad. Indeed, this was the main reason not to use that same definition for the offence of directing a terrorist organisation (see no. 412). This must be nuanced slightly, as the fact that an organisation could be proscribed, does not mean this is automatically the case. The Secretary needs to intervene and actually proscribe the organisation. This again provides much discretion to the Secretary to decide which organisations they want to proscribe amid the plethora of possibilities provided by the very broad definition.

562. Power of the executive to influence criminal offences – The Affect project actually stated as one of their recommendations '*To examine the possibility of entrusting the identification of a group as terrorist to a body other than the judiciary.*'[2689] This is the case in the UK for the proscribed organisations (see no. 366). The advantage of entrusting this decision to the government, for example, is that it is better placed to take into account geostrategic or economic reasons as to why certain groups should perhaps not be considered terrorist groups. We do not agree this would be the best way forward for Belgium. Entrusting this decision to the executive could be argued to be problematic in terms of the separation of powers. There is no need to have a political decision which influences criminal offences, especially in a sensitive context such as terrorism. Geostrategic or economic reasons should not have a decisive influence on this matter. Legally speaking they are irrelevant in establishing whether or not a group is a terrorist group; and morally speaking they should not matter either. If governments make these decisions, the danger of a system where 'anybody who is against us, is a terrorist' arises (see also no. 604). We need an independent and objective decision maker, which is exactly what the judiciary is intended to be.

563. General comparison of *mens rea* – Before going into the specific offences and their *mens rea*, it is helpful to compare the general framework.

2689 Brion and others (n 77) 72.

Belgian general intent and UK intention are similar. The UK concept of indirect or oblique intention (see no. 332) can be roughly equated to Belgian potential intent. However, the threshold of potential intent seems to be a bit lower than for oblique intention. Potential intent requires the perpetrator to accept the possible or probable consequences before acting (see no. 176). The UK oblique intention requires the result to not just be possible or probable, but to be a virtually certain consequence. Therefore, it seems the threshold for oblique intention is a bit higher, although, again (see no. 176), a detailed analysis of the application in practice of both concepts would be needed in order to make any definitive statements about this. We can assume they are roughly similar, but some situations of Belgian potential intent in which the consequences are not certain enough to amount to oblique intention, would be considered recklessness in the UK. Most situations of UK recklessness, however, are part of what would be considered negligence in Belgium. Those situations of UK recklessness equate to Belgian conscious negligence.[2690] UK negligence, finally, equates to Belgian unconscious negligence. As argued in Part II (see no. 177), the *mens rea* in the Belgian offences of Article 140 CC, '*while he knew or should have known that his participation could contribute to the perpetration of a felony or standard offence by the terrorist group*', is a general intent. Under UK law this would amount to an intentional offence and not a reckless one. The wording 'should have known' seems to hint towards recklessness or even negligence, but it has been established that the person actually knew and the 'should have known' is a kind of rule of evidence. Therefore, if we were to literally transpose the Belgian offences relating to terrorist groups to UK law, they would have to be committed intentionally in the sense of UK law.

564. Membership vs. participating in the activities – The first UK offence related to proscribed organisations is membership, defined as belonging or professing to belong to the organisation (see no. 367). Under Belgian law, mere membership has been explicitly excluded from the scope of the participation offence, which requires an act of participation in the activities of the group. However, the case law interprets this very broadly and virtually anything can be an act of participation (see nos 170–173). In terms of *actus reus,* we would therefore argue that the difference is negligible. Under the current Belgian case law, you could argue that any way that membership is proven, also meets the *actus reus* requirement of participation. This does however not go both ways. Situations are conceivable, and have in fact occurred, where a person is not a member of a terrorist group but does participate in its activities under Belgian law. Despite appearances, the UK membership offence could therefore be interpreted as being less broad in terms of *actus reus* than the Belgian offence. As for the *mens rea*, however, the UK membership offence is problematic. The

2690 See also: De Groote (n 1009) 95.

UK offence of membership is one of strict liability (see no. 368), while in Belgium general intent is required. This is a major issue for the UK offence, which has a very broad *actus reus* and no real *mens rea*. The defence which the legislation provides for this offence (see no. 369) also does not offer any real protection, as it could be argued that a person who can successfully invoke the defence was not actually a member of a proscribed organisation in the first place. In addition to this absence of a *mens rea*, the maximum sentence in the UK is 14 years imprisonment, while in Belgium this is only ten years, which is in practice almost always reduced to five years maximum through correctionalisation (see no. 181). The UK offence is problematic both in terms of broadness and proportionality, with a high maximum sentence combined with an offence of strict liability without *mens rea*. The Belgian offence is preferable in the sense that it includes a *mens rea* and has a lower sentence but is still far from perfect. The *actus reus* of the Belgian offence is actually broader than the UK offence and the presence of the *mens rea* is established very quickly.

565. Participating in the activities vs. support offences – The *actus reus* of the UK offences of inviting support, arranging meetings, and addressing meetings are definitely covered by the *actus reus* of the Belgian participation offence. Regarding the *mens rea*, the inviting of support has to occur knowingly (see no. 370), which is similar to the *mens rea* of the Belgian offence. Similarly, the UK offence of addressing a meeting requires the intention to encourage (see no. 372), which would also be needed under the Belgian offence. The offence of arranging meetings is slightly more complicated. It provides for three *mens rea* options (see no. 371), the first two of which are always covered by the Belgian offence. Arranging a meeting while knowing the meeting is to support a proscribed organisation or to further the activities of a proscribed organisation would be included in knowingly and willingly participating in the activities of the organisation. The third option, however, arranging meetings knowing to be addressed by a person who belongs or professes to belong to a proscribed organisation is not always covered. Arranging such a meeting does not imply the person knowingly and willingly participates in the activities of the terrorist organisation. The UK offence of expressing supportive opinions, finally, also does not always fall under the Belgian participation offence. In certain situations such actions might be construed as moral support of a group, which can be covered by the Belgian offence, but this is not necessarily the case as the Court of Cassation held that the simple fact of glorifying terrorism and humiliating its victims is in itself not sufficient (see no. 171). The main question will be whether or not the perpetrator acted with intent to further terrorist goals. Expressing supportive opinions with the intention that the recipient will be encouraged to support a terrorist organisation will under the current case law in all likelihood be considered participation in the activities of the group. The supportive opinion

offence, however, can be committed recklessly (see no. 373). This is broader than the general intent *mens rea* in Belgium which at least requires the acceptance of the possible consequences. Therefore, the supportive opinions offence covers situations which would not fall under the Belgian participation offence, being situations of reckless support. As the sentences for the offences discussed in this paragraph are the same as the ones in the last paragraph, the same applies here.

566. Participating in the activities vs. uniform and publication of images offences – The *actus reus* of the UK uniform and publication of images offences would in all likelihood be covered by the Belgian participation offence. However, as the UK offences are strict liability offences (see no. 379) and the Belgian offence requires intent, the UK offences are significantly broader than the Belgian one. They are summary offences punishable with maximum six months imprisonment, so their sentence is significantly lower than the maximum sentence for the Belgian participation offence.

567. Leadership and decision-making offences – The final offences concerning terrorist groups, are the ones of greatest involvement: directing the group. In Belgium two such offences exist, one of leadership of the group and one of participating in the making of any decision in the context of the group. As argued in Part II (see no. 186), this second offence is much too broad. The UK only has one offence of directing a terrorist organisation at any level (see nos 412–414). This offence largely compares to the Belgian leadership offence, which is broader than just the top leadership of the group and also covers directing at lower levels. The UK offence is not quite as wide as the Belgian participating in the making of any decision offence since the word 'direct' implies a certain level of commanding obedience.[2691] This is not required for the Belgian participating in the making of any decision offence, as this applies to everybody who participates in the making of the decision and it does not specify that the person has to have a key role in that decision. The UK offence can be applied to directions which are in themselves lawful (see no. 412). This seems to be less of an issue for the Belgian leadership offence as this offence does not focus as much on individual decisions but rather on the position of the perpetrator, the offence criminalising 'any leading person'. The same does not apply to the participating in any decision offence, which can be applied to lawful decisions. Regarding the sentence, the UK offence again stands out as having a very high maximum sentence, being life imprisonment (see no. 414). The Belgian leadership offence carries a sentence of 15 to 20 years felony imprisonment (one to 15 years imprisonment after correctionalisation) and the participating in any decision offence a sentence of ten to 15 years felony imprisonment (six months to ten years imprisonment after correctionalisation). The sentence for the UK offence is

[2691] Walker, *Blackstone's Guide to the Anti-Terrorism Legislation* (n 1670) 170.

therefore significantly higher than for the Belgian offences and as argued in Part III (see no. 414) the maximum sentence of life imprisonment could be deemed disproportionate for preventive offences.

b) Financing

568. Actus reus – Under Belgian criminal law, the financing of terrorist activities can be prosecuted under Article 140, §1 or 141 CC, depending on the situation. Article 140, §1 CC provides as an explicit example of participating in the activities of a terrorist group '*providing [...] material resources to a terrorist group or any form of financing of any activity of a terrorist group.*' This is quite a broad description but does always require the existence of a terrorist group. Article 141 does not require a terrorist group to exist and its *actus reus* is also quite broad, being the direct or indirect provision or collection of material resources, including financial assistance, by any means (see no. 275). The UK has four terrorist property offences, which use more detailed descriptions of their *actus reus* than is the case in Belgium. The UK definition of terrorist property is very broad and includes not only money or property to be used for terrorism but also all resources of proscribed organisations and the proceeds of acts of terrorism (see no. 386). The *actus reus* of the UK fund-raising and funding arrangement offences would undoubtedly be covered by the Belgian offences. Receiving or providing money, inviting others to provide money or entering into arrangements to provide money will be covered by participation in the activities of a terrorist group, if a group exists, or by the direct or indirect provision or collection of material resources under Article 141 CC. Any action which is covered by the UK terrorist money laundering offence (see nos 392–393) will be covered by the Belgian participation in the activities offence, if a terrorist group exists. However, if this is not the case, it is doubtful Article 141 CC will cover most of the money laundering activities, as Article 141 focusses on the provision or collection of funds and not on their retention or control. Of course, Belgium has a general money laundering offence which could be used in certain situations.[2692] In order for this offence to apply, the funds do have to be illegally obtained. This could therefore cover the proceeds of terrorism or the proceeds of other offences used to finance terrorism. However, a person who enters into an arrangement to facilitate the retention by another person of money likely to be used for terrorism (where no terrorist group exists) where this money has been obtained legally, does not commit the Belgian offences of Article 140, 141 or money laundering. It is possible for that person to be charged with aiding and abetting any of the other terrorism offences or their attempt though, depending on what exactly the money is for and how advanced the other person's plans are already. Finally, the UK use and possession offence (see no. 389) creates a similar

[2692] Art. 505 CC.

situation in Belgium. If a terrorist group exists, these actions will constitute participation in its activities. If no group exists, the use of funds for the purposes of terrorism should amount to an attempted terrorism offence. The possession could so as well, but this *actus reus* (possessing money or other property) is so broad, it is virtually meaningless, which brings us to the *mens rea* of these offences.

569. *Mens rea* – The *mens rea* of the UK offences is the intention that the property should be used for the purposes of terrorism, or reasonable cause to suspect that this is the case. Some of the offences do not use the word 'intention' but state 'the knowledge that the property will be used'. This makes no practical difference, because if a person knows this is the case and acts regardless, this amounts to (oblique) intention. The money laundering offence is one of strict liability, but proving the person did not know and had no reasonable cause to suspect that the arrangement related to terrorist property, is a defence (see no. 393). In other words, this is a *mens rea* requirement, but the burden of proof is on the defence. The reasonable cause to suspect has to be judged objectively, meaning that the defendant does not actually have to suspect anything (see no. 398). This means a person can negligently commit these offences in the UK. In Belgium the *mens rea* for the participation in the activities offence is general intent (see no. 177). The wording of 'should have known' in Article 140 CC could be interpreted as a form of negligence as well, which would put it on par with the UK 'reasonable cause to suspect' standard, but as explained (see nos 176–177), it has been generally accepted this is not the case and Belgium requires intent. The *mens rea* in Article 141 CC is also intent, be it a special intent this time, as it is required the perpetrator acts with the intention or knowledge that the funds are to be used, in full or in part to commit or contribute to the commission of a terrorist offence (*sensu stricto* or *senu lato*). The Belgian situation in which intent is required, is preferable to the UK one where negligence suffices. Considering the broadness of the *actus reus* of these offences, only requiring negligence could violate the legality principle. On the other hand, the UK *mens rea* is limited to terrorism *sensu stricto* while the Belgian *mens rea* in Article 141 CC covers all terrorist offences *sensu lato* as well. Considering the broadness of the other terrorist offences, this is quite an expansion of the *mens rea* in Belgium.

570. Sentences – The sentence for the UK offences is maximum 14 years imprisonment (see no. 394) while for the Belgian offences the sentence is five to ten years felony imprisonment and there is an aggravating circumstance for Article 141 (see nos 181–184 and 278–279). If the provision or collection of the material resources takes place with a view to their full or partial use by a minor for the purpose of committing or contributing to the commission of a terrorist offence *sensu stricto*, the sentence goes up to ten to 15 years felony imprisonment. At first glance, these sentences do not seem too dissimilar, but in Belgium correctionalisation has to be taken into account, as it is applied in the vast majority of cases and lowers the maximum sentences to respectively five- and ten-years imprisonment. This means that outside of the situation of the aggravating circumstance, in most cases the maximum sentence in Belgium is only roughly one third of that in the UK. This is a remarkable difference considering that the UK offences can be committed negligently.

c) Recruitment and inciting

571. Actus reus: encouraging – Belgian Article 140*bis* CC criminalises disseminating a message or otherwise making it available to the public when such conduct, whether or not directly aimed at the commission of a terrorist offence *sensu stricto* or the traveling offence, carries a risk that one or more of these offences may be committed (see nos 207–213). This offence is comparable to the UK s. 1 TA 2006 offence of publishing or causing another to publish a statement that is likely to be understood by a reasonable person as a direct or indirect encouragement or other inducement, to some or all of the members of the public to whom it is published, to the commission, preparation or instigation of acts of terrorism (see nos 447–449). In addition, the TA 2006 also criminalises the dissemination of terrorist publications (see nos 453–455). The UK offences are slightly narrower than the Belgian offence in one respect, as they refer to terrorism *sensu stricto* and the Belgian offence also includes the encouragement of the traveling offence. The s. 1 offence does refer to encouragement to the preparation of an act of terrorism, so some scenarios of traveling could be included in this. The UK offences are significantly broader than the Belgian offence in several other respects. First, the Belgian offence includes a risk requirement, without which the offence was held to be in violation of the freedom of expression (see no. 209). The UK offences do not require the risk that a terrorist offence may be committed. Their compatibility with the ECHR can therefore be seriously questioned. The JCHR also noted the lack of risk requirement.[2693] Second, the dissemination offence of s. 2 TA 2006 defines a terrorist publication to be such not only when it contains encouragement to terrorism, but also if it is likely to be useful in the commission or preparation of terrorism and is likely to be understood, as contained in the publication, or made available, wholly or mainly for the purpose of being so useful. These types of publications may not be covered by the Belgian encouragement offence. In certain situations, the dissemination of some of them may amount to aiding and abetting the Belgian self-study offence (see no. 244) or participating in the activities of a terrorist group. Third, the *mens rea* of the UK offences is broader.

[2693] JCHR, Counter-Terrorism Policy and Human Rights: Terrorism Bill and related matters (HL paper 75, HC paper 561, 2005) para 34–37 and 47–49.

572. *Mens rea*: encouraging – The Belgian encouragement offence requires the intention of inciting the commission of one of the offences. The UK offences, however, require either the intention to encourage or provide assistance or recklessness to this same effect. The UK offences include defences, but they are quite narrow. The inclusion of recklessness broadens the offences to a significant degree and further exacerbates the abovementioned freedom of speech issue.[2694] The fact that unintentionally encouraging may be a criminal offence could lead to a chilling effect.

573. Recruitment – The Belgian criminal code also includes a specific offence of recruiting another person to commit or contribute to the commission of terrorism *sensu stricto*, the offences related to terrorist groups or the traveling offence (see nos 226–228). The UK legislation does not include a specific recruitment offence. Some of the situations may be covered by the encouragement offences discussed in the paragraphs above. UK criminal law does, contrary to Belgium, have a general encouragement offence. It is an offence in the UK to act in any way capable of encouraging or assisting the commission of an offence, including the terrorist offences (see no. 451). This could be compared to the Belgian aiding and abetting, were it not that the Belgian legislation requires the main offence (or its attempt) to be committed before aiding and abetting can be punishable. This is not the case in the UK, meaning prosecution is allowed in pretty much any scenario to which the Belgian recruitment offence could be applicable and more, since it is not limited to only the three abovementioned terrorist offences but can be applied to all UK terrorist offences.

574. Sentences – Both Belgian offences are punishable with five to ten years felony imprisonment, becoming one month to five years imprisonment after correctionalisation (see nos 214 and 229). Both also include an aggravating circumstance if the offence is specifically aimed at minors which increases the sentence to ten to 15 years felony imprisonment (six months to ten years imprisonment after correctionalisation) (see nos 215 and 230). The two UK encouragement offences are punishable with maximum 15 years imprisonment (see no. 456). Therefore, the UK offences are both broader and have a higher maximum sentence. The general encouragement offence under UK criminal law can be punished with the same sentence as the anticipated offence. This means that encouraging someone to commit terrorist murder would be punishable with a maximum of life imprisonment in the UK.

575. Reasonable person and risk – Since the change to the legislation in 2019, the standard of the UK encouragement and dissemination of terrorist publications offences is not the understanding of the person to whom

[2694] See also: Petersen (n 12) 66 and 73.

the statement or publication is made available but that of the 'reasonable person' (see nos 447 and 453). The legislature did so to include statements or publications aimed at children or vulnerable people who would not understand it as encouragement. The Belgian legislation, on the other hand, explicitly includes a risk requirement. This means that messages aimed at people who would not understand them as encouragement, could not be punishable under Article 140*bis* CC. No risk could exist if the people who receive the messages do not understand they are being encouraged to do something. Therefore, the standard of the 'reasonable person' in the UK legislation could be argued to violate the freedom of speech and in order to be in line with this right, the UK legislature should either explicitly include a risk requirement, or at least return to the previous standard of the recipient of the message.

576. Glorification – Both UK offences include a reference to glorification as part of the *actus reus* of the offence stating that glorification is covered by the offences. In Belgium this is not the case yet. In the new Criminal Code, a new paragraph would be introduced into the incitement offence which would explicitly criminalise glorification (see no. 284). However, the offence would still require the behaviour to pose a serious and real risk that one or more of the glorified offences (i.e. traveling or terrorism *sensu stricto*) may be committed and the glorifying happened with that intention. Since there is a risk requirement and the *mens rea* is the same as the *mens rea* for the existing incitement offence in Article 140*bis* CC, the addition would be pointless. The only difference is that the new section would define the action of glorification as '*publicly, denying, grossly minimising, attempting to justify or condone the offence*' but these actions are already covered by the more general '*disseminating a message or otherwise making it available to the public.*' Therefore, this addition would be of no added value.

d) Training

577. Actus reus – The UK has two training offences. The *actus reus* of both covers providing and receiving instructions or training in certain skills. The first offence focusses on instructions or training in the making or use of firearms, explosives or nuclear, chemical or biological weapons (the 'weapons training' offence) (see nos 399–401). The second offence (the 'terrorism training' offence) lists three skills, the first relating to noxious substances. The second and third are incredibly broad, being catch-all provisions for any methods or techniques capable of being done for the purposes or terrorism (see no. 402). Belgium also has two training offences, the first one focusing on providing training and the second one on receiving it (see nos 235–251). The Belgian offences also list certain skills, being the manufacturing or use of explosives, firearms or other weapons or harmful or dangerous substances. The Belgian list roughly covers

the same actions as the UK weapons training offence and the first listed skills in the terrorism training offence. However, the Belgian legislation makes it clear this list is non-exhaustive. The Constitutional Court did emphasise the offences only apply to methods and techniques specific to committing terrorist offences (see no. 239). On a basic level, the UK offences seem less broad because they include an exhaustive list of skills while the Belgian ones only include a non-exhaustive list, but the listed items in the UK are so broad this makes no difference. In fact, the UK wording 'any act which is capable of being done for the purposes of terrorism or in connection with the commission or preparation of an act of terrorism' seems broader than the wording 'specific methods and techniques'. Teaching somebody how an internet browser works, for example, could definitely be considered instructions in '*the use of any method or technique for doing anything else that is capable of being done [...], in connection with the commission or preparation of an act of terrorism.*' Therefore, this could fall under the ambit of the UK terrorist training offence while it might not be considered a method or techniques specific to committing terrorist offences. We say 'might' because it is not entirely clear what the Constitutional Court means when it states this. Commentators or case law have not meaningfully engaged with what this actually means, so all we can do is make an educated guess. In conclusion, in terms of *actus reus*, if there is a major difference between the two jurisdictions at all, this is the case, in the sense that the UK offences are broader than the Belgian ones.

578. Self-study – Belgium has another offence in §2 of Article 140*quinquies* CC dealing with self-study (see no. 244). The UK training offences both use the term 'receiving' training or instructions. If we use the same reasoning as was applied to the Belgian offence, this wording does not include self-study. Therefore, the UK does not seem to have a self-study offence. This is not an issue however, as other offences, such as the preparation offence and the information offences, are available (see nos 415–431 and 463–473). The case law on the information offences clearly shows its application to situations which could be termed 'self-study' (see no. 425–428).

579. *Mens rea* – *Mens rea* for all Belgian training offences is a view to commit or contribute to the commission of terrorism *sensu stricto*. The UK terrorist training offence has a similar *mens rea* being the knowledge these skills are intended (for the teaching) or the intention to use (for the receiving) the skills for or in connection with the commission or preparation of acts of terrorism or for assisting the preparation or commission of these offences by others. Although worded differently, this *mens rea* covers the same situations as the Belgian one. The weapons training offence, on the other hand, has no explicit *mens rea*. However, a defence exists of proving the training was '*wholly for a* *purpose other than assisting, preparing for or participating in terrorism*' (see no. 401). This implies a *mens rea*, as the purpose of the training has to at least partly be assisting, preparing for or participating in terrorism. The inclusion of this requirement as a defence, does provide for a partial shift in the burden of proof. The lack of explicit *mens rea* for the weapons training offence in the UK is in line with the idea that no terrorist intent has to be proven under the definition of terrorism of the TA 2000 when the action involves the use of firearms or explosives (see no. 345). The UK legislature seems to be willing to accept a sort of implied terrorist intent in those cases. While this greatly facilitates the prosecution service's task, it is a stretch to assume that the use of firearms or explosives is always linked to terrorism. A lot of drug related crime for example also includes this.[2695]

580. Attendance at a place used for terrorist training – A third training offence in the UK is the attendance at a place used for terrorist training (see nos 404–405). Belgium has no equivalent offence. However, this does not mean that situations covered by this offence in the UK would not be punishable in Belgium. The UK offence targets attendance at any place, in the UK or abroad, where training is provided. Usually, a terrorist group will exist which provides this training, which would then allow Belgian prosecutors to prosecute this offence as participation in the activities of that group. For training provided abroad, the Belgian traveling offence (see nos 252–263 and 586–588) could be used. While the *actus reus* of these offences overlaps considerably, a notable difference is that the UK attendance offence can be committed negligently as the *mens rea* of the offence has two options, the second of which is that the person could not reasonably have failed to understand that instruction or training was being provided there. All Belgian terrorist offences require intent, so the UK *mens rea* is once again broader.

581. Sentences – The Belgian sentence for the training offences is in line with the Belgian sentences for other offences of terrorism *sensu lato*, meaning five to ten years felony imprisonment (becoming one month to five years imprisonment after correctionalisation) (see nos 237 and 247). The offence of providing training also has an aggravating circumstance when the training is specifically aimed at minors (see no. 238). The UK sentences are comparatively very high, with life imprisonment for both training offences (see nos 406–407). At its introduction, the weapons training offence had a sentence of 'only' ten years, but this was raised a lot to the current maximum of life imprisonment in 2015. The sentence for attendance at a place used for terrorist training is 14 years imprisonment (see no. 407). This is significantly lower than the life imprisonment for the actual

2695 The use of hand grenades and firearms is a common occurrence in the Antwerp drug scene, e.g..

training offences, which is a logical difference to make in terms of ordinal proportionality, as the prosecution cannot actually prove the perpetrator of the attendance offence has undertaken any training themselves. Compared to the Belgian sentences, this is still a very high maximum sentence, however. The maximum for attendance is almost three times the practical maximum sentence the same person would face in Belgium for actually receiving or providing the training themselves.

e) Preparation

582. Actus reus – Both Belgium and the UK have a specific terrorist preparation offence. The *actus reus* of these offences is very broad. The Belgian provision includes a non-exhaustive list of preparatory actions, but anything can be an act of preparation (see nos 264–265). The UK provision does not include such a list but simply targets any conduct in preparation for giving effect to the intention of committing an act of terrorism or assisting another in doing so (see no. 463). The *actus reus* of both offences is therefore equally broad.

583. *Mens rea* – While the *actus reus* is the same, the Belgian and UK offences differ in *mens rea*. Once more, the Belgian offence is defined more narrowly. First, the Belgian *mens rea* is the intention to commit terrorism *sensu stricto* (see no. 268). The UK *mens rea* is the intention to commit or assist one or more acts of terrorism (see no. 464). This may seem similar, but the addition of the words 'or assist' in the UK makes it considerably broader. In Belgium, preparation of another person's terrorist offence does not fall under the preparation offence, while in the UK it does, as a person preparing another's offence does not have the intention to commit terrorism *sensu stricto* but does have the intention to assist it. Second, the Belgian offence has a requirement of concreteness, meaning the prosecution has to prove which exact terrorist offence the offender is preparing. The UK does not have this requirement and the preparation can relate to particular acts of terrorism or terrorism in general (see no. 463). This again substantially broadens the offence. For the prosecution to be able to prove the concrete terrorist offence in preparation, the offender's preparations must have advanced considerably further. Considering the broadness of the *actus reus*, the very broad UK *mens rea* is problematic as it could cause legality issues. The Belgian narrower *mens rea* should therefore be preferred. Some preparatory acts which do not fall within the scope of the Belgian *mens rea* can be prosecuted as other terrorist offences *sensu lato* or participation in an (attempted) terrorist offence *sensu stricto*. If none of these options are available and the prosecution would have to fall back on a kind of catch all offence of preparation, the conduct should not be punishable as it is clearly too far removed from the commission of the actual terrorist offence *sensu stricto*.

584. Sentences – While the Belgian Criminal Code provides for a sentencing system in which the sentence for the preparation offence depends on the prepared offence (see no. 269), the UK legislation simply provides for a maximum sentence: life imprisonment (see no. 466). This is a very high sentence, knowing that the highest category of preparation in Belgium, preparing an offence punishable with life imprisonment, is punishable with five to ten years felony imprisonment (one month to five years imprisonment after correctionalisation). The Belgian system provides for some form of ordinal proportionality when comparing the actual offence which was being prepared to the preparation offence. In the UK this is not the case, as the sentence for preparation is at least as high and sometimes higher than the sentence for the prepared offence. This is highly problematic in terms of proportionality. The sentencing guidelines do provide some guidance for judges (see no. 467), but they are only guidelines and also still provide for very high sentences, with the starting points for categories A1, B1, C1, A2 and B2 being life imprisonment. The lowest category of preparation in the UK (C3) has a starting point of four years imprisonment, which would put it in the second highest of the four categories Belgium has. So once more, the UK combines a broader offence with a stricter punishment.

585. Acting alone or in group – One striking point in the UK sentencing guidelines for this offence is the position of acting alone versus acting in a group. Under the UK sentencing guidelines, acting alone is put at a higher level of culpability than acting in a significant role within a terrorist group and is put in the same category as having a leading role in a group.[2696] This is in line with the ideas of lord Lloyd of Berwick, who stated in his review of the terrorism legislation: '*Why should the existence of other like-minded terrorists make any difference? It cannot be because terrorist organisations are likely to be more dangerous than individuals.*'[2697] In the UK, it therefore seems to be accepted that acting as a group is not more dangerous than acting alone. This differs from the opinion of the Belgian legislature, which used the argument that acting alone is less dangerous than acting as a group, as a response to several proportionality issues being raised (see nos 183 and 270), concerning the participation in the activities of a terrorist group, and the preparation offence on the one hand and offence of terrorism *sensu stricto* on the other. The important distinction to make here, is the one between possible harm and culpability. The UK guidelines make this distinction and evaluate them separately: the question of whether the person acted individually or as part of a group (and then in which capacity within the group) is considered under culpability. The Belgian approach seems to mix them. The potential harm is already taken into account as the preparation of

2696 Azmeh (n 2269) 7; Lee (n 643) 9.

2697 Lord Lloyd of Berwick, *Inquiry into legislation against terrorism* (Cm 3420, 1996) 30. For further counter-arguments to this idea, see: Dennis (n 2191) 49–51.

different offences in Belgium leads to different maximum sentences. As the level of possible harm is a given once this is established, it is illogical to then consider groups more dangerous than individuals. In terms of individual culpability, it would take a more determined and arguably more dangerous person to prepare a terrorist attack by themselves than it would to do so as a part of a group.

f) Traveling

586. Traveling offence vs. designated area – Belgium has a specific terrorist traveling offence (see nos 252–263) and the UK does not. The closest thing it does have, is the designated area offence (see nos 443–446). Under this offence, it is punishable to voluntarily enter or remain in an area which is designated by the Secretary of State. It is noteworthy that, as was the case for proscription of organisations, the Secretary of State is given a direct role in the decision on the scope of a criminal offence. However, the Secretary has not designated any areas yet (contrary to the power to proscribe organisations, which has been used). The designated area offence is much more specific than the Belgian offence in this regard, as it provides a clear definition of the area a person cannot enter or remain in. Under the Belgian offence, the *actus reus* is much broader, as it covers leaving or entering the Belgian national territory (see no. 252). In terms of *mens rea*, the Belgian offence does require a terrorist intent (see no. 253) and the UK offence only requires that the action is taken voluntarily (see no. 444). Entering or remaining in the area is allowed for a few listed purposes, but this leaves it up to the defence to prove they entered or remained exclusively for those purposes, or they had a reasonable excuse for doing so. The UK *mens rea* is therefore significantly broader than the Belgian one, but is counterbalanced by the more narrow and clearer *actus reus*. As long as the Secretary of State remains cautious in his approach to designating areas, the UK offence seems to be preferable in light of the legality principle, as it does not allow for the same amount of uncertainty the Belgian offence does. In addition, the sentence for the designated area offence is comparatively low for UK standards, with a maximum sentence of ten years imprisonment.

587. Response to foreign terrorist fighters – The Belgian traveling offence was introduced as a direct response to the foreign terrorist fighter phenomenon (see no. 252). The UK, not having such an offence and not having designated any areas, has chosen to prosecute foreign terrorist fighters under other offences, mainly the preparation offence (see no. 468).[2698] This approach led to a much lower rate of prosecution for people who travelled to Syria or Iraq. In the UK only around a quarter of FTFs was prosecuted. Belgium has prosecuted more FTFs. Wittendorp and Bakker counted 97 prosecutions of

[2698] Wittendorp and Bakker (n 686) 21.

FTFs in Belgium between March 2011 and June 2017.[2699] This is roughly 38,6% of all FTFs in that period while during the same period only about 3,8% of FTFs was being prosecuted in the UK. The sentences in the UK for those who were convicted, were significantly higher than in Belgium with an average of 77,6 months imprisonment versus 53 months imprisonment. One reason for the much higher percentage of FTFs prosecuted in Belgium is the possibility of *in absentia* judgments. The Reguide analysis shows a total of 180 judgments were made *in absentia*, this being more than half of the total of 343 individual judgments.[2700] Of the Affect cases 41% were tried *in absentia*.[2701] The slightly lower percentage of trials *in absentia* compared to the Reguide analysis could be explained by the focus of the research. The Reguide analysis focussed specifically on cases in which the listed charges included facts taking place outside of the EU while the Affect analysis did not. This corroborates the idea that *in absentia* procedures contribute to the amount of FTFs prosecuted. Despite the fact that Belgium has a traveling offence (and had it for part of the period analysed by Wittendorp and Bakker) which was introduced specifically to deal with FTFs, they are not prosecuted for that traveling offence very often and if they are, it is in concurrence with one of the group offences (see no. 261). This should come as no surprise considering the broadness of the Belgian group offences (see nos 171–180) and the overlap between the traveling offence and the other terrorist offences (see no. 261). This situation raises the question of the necessity of the traveling offence. In the UK, only one FTF was prosecuted for membership of a proscribed organisation.[2702]

588. New addition – Despite the fact the Belgian traveling offence is rarely used and has little to no added value, the legislature wants to introduce an additional offence in the new Criminal Code. This would be the offence of organising or in any other way facilitating a trip from or to Belgium, with the same *mens rea* as the current traveling offence (see no. 285). Adding another offence to an Article which is already barely in use, seems a bit redundant. If the travel was actually attempted or succeeded, the perpetrator of the new offence would be liable to be prosecuted for aiding and abetting (attempted) traveling. Other iterations of the new offence would be covered by recruiting to travel under Article 140*ter* CC. If a terrorist group exists, which is almost always the case, the

2699 Wittendorp and Bakker (n 686) 20–21.

2700 In addition, out of the total of 343 individual first instance judgments eight were retrials after a trial *in absentia*, divided into five cases. The punishment cannot be increased upon retrial. For four defendants the sentence stayed the same, for two it went down and in one case a conviction was turned into an acquittal. For one case the original *in absentia* decision could not be found, making it impossible to compare. One Court of Appeal judgment concerned a retrial after an appeal trial *in absentia*, which imposed the same sentence as the trial *in absentia*.

2701 Brion and others (n 77) 61.

2702 Wittendorp and Bakker (n 686) 63.

offence of participating in its activities comes into play for the person organising or facilitating the travel the same way it does for the person traveling. Therefore, as was argued for the new glorification offence (see no. 576), the addition of this new offence would be of no value and the idea should be dropped.

g) Possession and information offences

589. No specific information offences in Belgium – The UK has several offences which could be termed possession or information offences. These offences are the possession of articles for terrorist purposes (see nos 415–417), the collection of information useful to a terrorist (see nos 418–421), the non-disclosure of terrorist information (see nos 432–439), eliciting, publishing or communicating information about members of the armed forces (see nos 440–441) and the offences involving radioactive devices and materials or nuclear facilities and sites (the ones which do not amount to terrorism *sensu stricto*, see no. 474). These offences relate to certain articles or information which the perpetrators possess, collect or (refuse to) communicate. Especially the possession of articles and collection of information offence have been widely criticised for their broadness and vagueness (see nos 429–431). Belgium has no similar offences. Under the right circumstances some of these offences could be prosecuted for participation in the activities of a terrorist group, but then a group has to exist, and the person has to have undertaken an act of participation. Although this is interpreted in an extensive manner, simply having certain information on a computer would probably not be regarded as participation in the activities of a terrorist group.

590. Possession for terrorist purposes and collection of information – In Belgium, an offence relating to consulting internet websites which incite or glorify terrorism, regularly and without a legal reason, was proposed in parliament. However, the analysis by the Council of State pointed to several issues in terms of legality and the freedom of information, and the proposal was not accepted by parliament.[2703] The closest thing to an information offence in Belgium, is the self-study offence in Article 140*quinquies*, section 2 CC (see no. 244). This offence can be applied to people visiting certain websites or accessing certain information. However, the intent to commit or contribute to the commission of terrorism *sensu stricto* is required (see no. 246). This is different from the UK offences. The possession of articles offence does require the intention of the perpetrator to be that the use of information is intended for

[2703] Advies 52.522/AV van de Raad van State 19 februari 2013 bij wetsvoorstel tot wijziging van de wet 29 juli 1934 waarbij de private milities verboden worden, wat het verbod van ondemocratische groeperingen betreft, *Parl.St.* Kamer 2012–2013, no. 53-0809/008, 35–38. See also: Velaers (n 27) 779–881.

the purpose of the commission, preparation or instigation of an act of terrorism (see no. 416). This is already broader than the Belgian *mens rea* and in addition, it only has to be proven to a standard of reasonable suspicion. The collection of information offence is even a strict liability offence with the reasonable excuse providing a weak *mens rea*, requiring even less in terms of *mens rea* (see nos 419–420). One of the two reasonable excuses explicitly provided for is that the possession was for academic or journalistic purposes. This shows UK parliament had similar concerns as the Belgian parliament, which emphasised in the preparatory works that occasionally visiting a website, or visiting it for academic purposes does not suffice in being punishable.[2704]

591. Not disclosing information – The UK offence of withholding information also has no Belgian equivalent. Belgium does have a general offence of culpable negligence. This is applicable when a person fails to provide assistance to someone in great danger, which could be provided without serious danger to themselves or others.[2705] The UK offence has two options, the non-disclosure of information which they know or believe might be of material assistance: (a) in preventing the commission by another person of an act of terrorism, or (b) in securing the apprehension, prosecution or conviction of another person for an offence involving the commission, preparation or instigation of an act of terrorism (see nos 433–434). Option (a) of not disclosing information which they know or believe might be of material assistance in preventing the commission by another person of an act of terrorism, could be prosecuted as culpable negligence in many cases. Option (b) however, could not as in this scenario the danger has already passed.

592. Eliciting, publishing or communicating information about members of the armed services – The offence on information about members of the armed services does not have a clear Belgian equivalent either. However, the *actus reus* can be covered by different offences. Eliciting the information could be preparation of a terrorist offence and publishing or communicating it could be incitement to a terrorist offence. If an actual attack is committed, then any of those actions could be aiding and abetting it. However, all of these Belgian offences require a *mens rea*. This is not the case in the UK. The UK offence is one of strict liability with a reasonable excuse defence (see no. 440). This is a major difference, making the UK offence much broader than the Belgian offences.

2704 Toelichting bij wetsvoorstel 6 februari 2019 houdende diverse bepalingen in strafzaken en inzake erediensten, *Parl.St.* Kamer 2018–2019, no. 54-3515/001, (3) 106. See also: Deruyck and De Nauw (n 786) 13; Winants (n 8) 357; Comité T, 'Rapport 2019: Le respect des droits humains dans le cadre de la lutte contre le terrorisme: Un chantier en cours', 17.

2705 Art. 422*bis* CC.

593. Radioactive devices and materials and nuclear facilities and sites – The UK offences of terrorism *sensu lato* related to radioactive devices and materials or nuclear facilities and sites could all be covered by the Belgian preparation offence (the same could be said in relation to the UK preparation offence, see nos 463–473) or the group offences if a group exists. For example, making or possessing radioactive devices or materials requires the intention of using it for terrorism, which is a clear act of preparation.

SUBSECTION IV. CONCLUSIONS

594. Administrative law – Belgium does not have administrative counter-terrorism measures which directly restrict the right to liberty. The UK does, and the question around whether Belgium should introduce them as well has to be answered. The conclusion of this book is a resounding no. The use of administrative measures creates too much risk for arbitrary deprivations of liberty and the gains are minimal. Belgium would be better off focussing on improving its criminal law system instead of making it more complicated and opaque by introducing a parallel administrative system.

595. (Too) broad – At the end of the comparative analysis, we can draw a few conclusions about the systems in Belgium and the UK. The counter-terrorism criminal law framework in both countries has become very broad. As was noted for both jurisdictions, the core of the offences is the *mens rea* (see nos 315, 411 and 471). Taking a step back, this should come as no surprise. The idea behind preventive offences is to intervene before the offence which the legislature seeks to prevent (i.e. terrorism *sensu strico*) has even been attempted. In both jurisdictions an attempt requires an act which is more than merely preparatory. In Belgium, this requirement is interpreted as the person committing acts which are not open to multiple interpretations (see no. 266). As Belgian criminal law intervenes before this point, the person's actions will by definition be open to multiple interpretations, meaning that it is almost inevitable that the *mens rea* is the core of the offence, as the *actus reus* can be interpreted in a harmless way as well. In the UK the interpretation is slightly different, requiring the person to have broached the commission of the *actus reus* (see no. 465). It stands to reason that any act preceding this will again be open to harmless interpretations, meaning the core of the preparatory offence has to lie in the *mens rea*. The broad and vague framework gives a lot of leeway to judges and (in the UK) other actors to make decisions.

596. Legality – While the offences are extremely broad in both states, the UK offences tend to be even broader than the Belgian ones. Often the *actus reus* of the offences is equally broad, but the Belgian offences always require intent

and some of the UK offences can be committed recklessly or negligently. In addition, the UK has more offences. Sometimes it is simply the case that the *actus reus* of several UK offences is covered by the same Belgian offence, such as for example the two UK training offences or the financing offences. This is not the case, however, for the UK possession and information offences, which are extremely broad. These offences do not have a Belgian counterpart. One of the Belgian offences which covers several UK offences is the participation in the activities of a terrorist group. This Belgian offence most closely resembles the UK membership of a proscribed organisation offence but is actually broader in terms of *actus reus*. This may seem counterintuitive, but the Belgian offence does not require the person to be a member and pretty much anything can be an act of participation. This means that some minor acts of people who are not members of the group would not be covered by the UK offence but can amount to participation in the activities of a terrorist group under Belgian law due to the extremely broad interpretation given to this offence by the courts.

597. Proportionality – The UK offences also have significantly higher sentences. As discussed elaborately in the Belgian Chapter, the Belgian legislature has sometimes struggled with the wording and ordinal proportionality of the sentences; but at least it tried to create a layered system with proportionate sentences. In the UK, the maximum sentences are often so high we must ask ourselves whether they are still proportionate. In addition, almost all UK terrorist offenders fall within one of the special sentencing regimes. The ordinal proportionality of the UK sentences should also be questioned with many preventive offences having sentences as high as the completed offences they aim to prevent. The existence of sentencing guidelines for some of the offences provides courts with a bit of guidance on the sentencing but cannot solve the issue entirely. There are no guidelines for many of the offences and they remain guidelines. In addition, the guidelines themselves sometimes have very high starting points.

598. Pre-trial detention – Although it does not appear so at first glance, the systems of pre-trial detention for terrorist suspects are not too dissimilar in Belgium and the UK. In the UK, bail can only be refused under certain circumstances, which are roughly the same as the circumstances in which an arrest warrant can be issued and detention maintained in Belgium. This would mean that in situations which are not covered by these circumstances, the defendant would be out on bail in the UK while they would be simply released without conditions or bail in Belgium. However, the presumption of bail also points towards bail being much more common in the UK than it is in Belgium and Belgian judges indeed have shown themselves quite willing to impose pre-trial detention.

CHAPTER II
GENERAL OBSERVATIONS

599. The issue of prevention – As established in the very beginning of this book, in the field of counter-terrorism, prevention is considered a must (see no. 3). Governments all over the world, the Belgian and UK governments included, have undertaken a myriad of initiatives in order to prevent terrorist attacks. Government intervention has indeed succeeded in apprehending certain people who had nefarious plans which, if left unchecked, would have caused civilian casualties and could have spread terror. However, prevention in itself is almost impossible to measure. It is extremely difficult to assess whether actions undertaken to avoid events taking place did actually succeed in their goal, as the fact that something did not happen does not mean the preventative action was successful. An infinite number of other factors may have played a role; establishing causality between a preventative government policy and the fact that terrorist attacks did not happen is therefore near impossible. This means that the exact impact and efficacy of a policy and especially of individual policy decisions is, and will most likely always remain, unknown. In this book we have assumed that restrictions to physical liberty can have a preventative effect, which seems to be a relatively safe assumption in general; but the inherent vagueness of prevention should always be kept in mind. Prevention is used by governments as the impetus to introduce many and far-reaching powers. Once introduced, these powers tend to be very hard to challenge because it is impossible to prove they do not work, and the ever-present looming shadow of a catastrophic terrorist attack creates a 'better safe than sorry' attitude. This leads to a situation in which terrorism legislation is always expanding without any real discussion on the usefulness of specific measures; and on whether or not existing measures should be kept in place.

600. The need for specialised legislation – This leads to a first general question: Should terrorism be treated as an exception, with special procedural rules and offences, or should it be an offence like any other, so the same rules would apply? The answer to this question has to be: It depends. The basic premise must be to apply the same rules to terrorism as to other criminal offences. Sometimes, the issues which are experienced in terrorism cases can even lead to logical changes to those general rules, such as, for example, the change the maximum period of detention without a warrant applied in Belgium (from 24 to 48 hours); and the accompanying simplification of this part of criminal procedure (see no. 290). However, other times terrorism does require something different or extra. This is the case for the very concept of terrorism offences *sensu lato*. Because of the possible catastrophic effects of a terrorist attack, elaborate rules on prevention are necessary, while this is not the case for larceny, for example. Criminalising the preparation of larceny or the participation in the activities of a group which aims to commit larceny is a step too far (or several steps too far). However, every time an exception is made for terrorism, the legislature must ask itself whether this exception is necessary. This is where the pendulum has swung too far. For example the Belgian terrorism exceptions for arrest warrants and immediate arrests (see nos 296 and 305) are useless, or we could question whether nearly every perpetrator of a terrorist offence in the UK is 'of particular concern' (see no. 532). This point actually applies to the very existence of several of the terrorism offences *sensu lato* (see Chapter III of this Part).

601. Exceptional becoming standard – This mindless application of exceptions creates the danger of a situation in which the 'exceptional' measures are so omnipresent they start to overshadow the general rules in place for everybody. A classic argument used in the case of terrorism legislation is that it is an exceptional phenomenon. The rules which are introduced have a specific target and these scenarios are said to be so extreme that more extreme measures are justified to counter them. However, it has become clear that the exceptional rules for extreme circumstances tend to spill over into other areas. The exceptional rules can slowly erode liberties and safeguards not just for the specific group they target, but for society as a whole (see no. 535). They slowly but surely move the line of what can be considered acceptable in any situation. The mere existence of preventive offences is an example of this. Criminal law traditionally intervenes after the legal asset has been damaged (see no. 5). At their inception, the rules on criminal attempts and aiding and abetting were exceptions to this. Nowadays, these rules have become standard and are themselves becoming less relevant as more and more preventive offences, which are even broader and intervene even earlier, are introduced (see no. 6).

602. Sunset clauses? – One way to try to avoid exceptional rules becoming standard ones, is to include sunset clauses. These have been used for administrative measures in the UK (see nos 510 and 518), but are not something commonly seen in criminal law. The UK's experience with control orders has taught us that the mere existence of a sunset clause does not guarantee any meaningful debate in parliament. In issues as sensitive as terrorism, parliamentarians do not have much incentive to scrutinise rules meant to prevent a terrorist attack. Keeping the rules in place does not cost them much, as the erosion of rights and liberties is a slow (but steady) process with no immediate response from their constituents, while a terrorist attack is a sudden, violent outburst which always raises loud questions. One way to strengthen the effect of sunset clauses would be to require an ever-increasing majority for each renewal of the legislation. This would lower the threshold for a meaningful discussion as gradually less people who are willing to actually critically assess the legislation are required in order to force the issue. Still, the concept of sunset clauses for criminal offences seems slightly strange. Either society deems certain actions worthy of punishment and then they should permanently be criminal offences; or it does not, in which case they should never be criminal offences. Stating something is a criminal offence now but will stop being one in a number of years is odd. It is of course possible for societal norms to change and for the idea of what is a criminal offence to change with it, as we have seen, for example, with cases concerning sexual offences within a marriage. However, this is rarely an evolution which takes place within a few years, and it is one which is impossible to predict and could never require sunset clauses. A better way forward for criminal law would be to critically assess any new legislation before introducing it, and to undertake an extensive review of the legality and proportionality of the existing legislation. Criminal offences are permanent, and every offence should be scrutinised extensively with this in mind. In the next Chapter of this Part, we will make several concrete recommendations for Belgium in this respect.

603. How to define criminal offences – Before going into these detailed recommendations, we can ask ourselves what went wrong for the terrorist offences in general. The creation of the offences clearly started as a reaction to a phenomenon which, while it did exist before, suddenly skyrocketed in importance. This prompted an immediate response which did not leave much time for reflection. The terrorist offences read more like criminological descriptions of the phenomenon of terrorism than criminal offences.[2706] This is in stark contrast with the best practice for drafting criminal offences, being to define a (or several) very concrete action(s) which is (are) forbidden. For example, one could define sexual violence as in any way forcing another person to perform any sexual act. However, this would be a poor definition for a criminal offence and a better way to approach this from a legal perspective would be to criminalise a series of very concrete actions which are forbidden, such as penetration without consent (i.e. rape). This will not solve all possible issues of interpretation and application, because questions will always remain such as: what is penetration and what is consent? However, it is a huge step forward from the very vague description of sexual violence. The one thing the general description does, is to provide judges with enormous freedom to decide what is and is not sexual violence to them, thereby creating a lot of legal uncertainty. This

2706 See also, in the context of criminal organisations: Verbruggen (n 34) 350–351.

is the main issue with the terrorist offences in general. In addition, the terrorism offences *sensu lato* are based too much on describing what 'terrorists' do and not on which actions are harmful. This means that terrorists can relatively easily adapt their behaviour to avoid being criminalised by these specific offences, at which point the legislation needs to be adapted (i.e. expanded) again. Clear examples of this are the designated area offence in the UK (see nos 443–446) and the traveling offence in Belgium (see nos 252–263). These offences were introduced in order to prevent people from traveling to jihadist zones to join terrorist groups. They were therefore based on specific actions taken by people who were considered to be terrorists and did not define any intrinsically harmful conduct. For several reasons, people stopped traveling to jihadist zones and the offences have remained unused. All this leads to one question: how broad should the terrorist offences be and what are they trying to achieve? It is a very difficult question, which probably does not have one single correct answer, but it is an important one to keep asking.

604. Why it matters – Throughout this book, one of the main points made is the broadness of the offences and how this is an issue under the legality principle (see nos 595–596). As discussed in Part I, the legality principle is an important part of both the right to liberty and the free movement of persons. Broad offences give a large amount of discretion to investigators, prosecutors and judges and could lead to arbitrary detention. However, neither the Belgian, nor the UK criminal justice systems have come crashing down around us, so why does this matter? The problem with broad offences which could lead to arbitrary detention is that they rely on the individual investigators, prosecutors, judges and on the state's authorities in general, not to abuse the broad powers given to them. As we are used to the system functioning more or less how it is supposed to, we seem to lose the ability to imagine anything else happening in our respective countries. However, we could ask ourselves: if other states, perhaps Russia, China or Turkey, would introduce offences which are this broad, would we condemn them for being autocratic, undemocratic, etc.? The answer is probably yes, because offences such as these can be abused in order to imprison political enemies and other undesirables. Especially in the context of terrorism legislation, which has been used in different places around the world to curtail political opposition and rights and freedoms. The fact that these powers have not been abused yet in our society does not mean they cannot be abused in the future, and it would be a mistake to think otherwise. In addition, the shift of power to individuals provides more room for cultural and other biases to come into play. Although the text of the terrorism offences does not target specific groups, the offences have been applied disproportionately to a specific group. This in itself is not proof of any bias or discrimination, but bias or discrimination is clearly a possibility. Even unconscious biases can come into play. Looking at the Belgian case law, for example, we see the group offences are often applied to family members. We could ask whether the role of family and family ties within certain cultures are sufficiently understood and taken into account. Some cultures have much closer family ties than we do, which are poorly understood, and which could be misinterpreted as criminal ties instead. This does not mean family members should never be prosecuted, but it does mean prosecutors and judges may not fully understand the situation and could misapply certain offences, which the current, very broad legislation enables them to do.

605. Short-term thinking – Much of the terrorism legislation came into existence as an immediate reaction to an acute problem (see also no. 603). This can lead to a focus on short-term solutions which loses track of what is best long-term (see also no. 545). This type of response is typical for the counter-terrorism legislation of the first two decades of this century. Harsh legislation which does not respect human rights can have many negative side effects in the long run (see no. 24), which are ignored. In addition, this type of flashlight politics tends to lead to statutes which do not fit well within the general legal framework. Take for example the Belgian group offences. They are so broad they could for example cover an attorney who negotiates on behalf of a client who is a member of a terrorist organisation, and want to turn themselves in. Under the current Belgian case law, that attorney could be said to participate in the activities of a terrorist group. This is an example of probably unintended consequences of this type of legislation, but it also shows that this legislation fits poorly within the broader legal framework and even clashes with other counter-terrorism legislation. In 2018 the legislature introduced a system of perpetrators collaborating with the prosecution in return for certain advantages such as reduced sentences.[2707] Such a system had been considered in the past but because of the terrorism threat and the hope that it would be useful in certain organised crime cases, the decision was made to finally introduce it.[2708] The introduction of this system is very clearly meant to encourage perpetrators of less important offences to turn informant against others higher up the ladder of a terrorist group, for example. The idea that the attorney of a member of a terrorist group is committing a terrorist offence when facilitating this process is therefore in direct conflict with this goal. This is but one concrete example of how short-term thinking can lead to illogical consequences and long-term issues.

2707 Wet 22 juli 2018 tot wijziging van het Wetboek van strafvordering betreffende toezeggingen in het kader van de strafvordering, de strafuitvoering of de hechtenis wegens het afleggen van een verklaring in het kader van de strijd tegen de georganiseerde criminaliteit en het terrorisme, *BS* 7 augustus 2018, 62054.

2708 MvT wetsontwerp 3 april 2018 tot wijziging van het Wetboek van strafvordering met het oog op het invoeren van een wettelijke regeling inzake spijtoptanten, *Parl.St.* Kamer 2017–18, no. 54-3016/001, 5–7.

606. Prisons – A terrorist conviction will usually lead to some form of prison sentence. This is not necessarily problematic because prison provides both short-term prevention as well as the possibility for long-term prevention, since it creates an opportunity to actively work on rehabilitation (see no. 545). This means criminal justice is more suited to long-term prevention than administrative measures, but this is only the case if adequate resources are provided. In theory, prison is a place where detainees can work on themselves and overcome their personal issues in order to avoid recidivism. However, the situation in practice rarely allows for this. Prison infrastructure is often poor and funding for sufficient therapy is lacking. Belgium is a clear example of this, with very old and overcrowded prisons and barely any funds for psychological treatment or even for a useful way to spend time (for example by learning a trade). Serious investments in the prison system are required in order for it to achieve its potential. At this point in time, prison in most countries does not help avoid reoffending at all. At most, it focusses the reoffending within the prison walls for the duration of the sentence, after which the detainee is released without anything having fundamentally changed for the better. The only way to break this cycle is to invest a substantial amount of funds and use this money not just to increase security in prisons but to improve living conditions, provide meaningful therapeutic options and teach detainees the skills they need to become functioning members of society. This type of spending is not very popular and therefore rarely happens. Although no causation can be established without extensive research on this topic, it is remarkable that for example Norway, a country known for its humane and well-funded prisons, has very low recidivism rates.[2709] Therefore, we believe investment in the prison system is necessary, which could lead to less recidivism. This in turn will make society safer and, in that sense, have a preventive effect, as well as reduce the long-term costs of the prison system as less recidivism also means less inmates. However, these are all long-term effects which take a while to achieve. Legislatures seem more interested in short-term policies regardless of their long-term impact.

607. Alternative sentences – A related issue is that of alternative sentences. Seeing as Belgian prisons are overcrowded and poorly equipped, one could assume alternative sentences would be in frequent use. The Reguide analysis has shown this not to be the case for terrorism offences. At most, prison sentences are imposed with (partial) postponement of enforcement. Considering the broad terrorist offences and poor prison conditions, this should be somewhat of a surprise. Considering the current state of prisons, alternative sentences should be used as much as possible. Especially when criminal offences are so broad

---

[2709] Denis Yukhnenko, Leen Farouki and Seena Fazel, 'Criminal Recidivism Rates Globally: A 6-Year Systematic Review Update – ScienceDirect' (2023) 88 Journal of Criminal Justice, www.sciencedirect.com/science/article/pii/S0047235223000867#s0020, accessed 23 January 2024.

they catch a lot of low-level involvement, an alternative sentence might be a very useful tool.

608. The need for specialists – As we have discussed, in some situations exceptional measures are required (see nos 600–601). We could ask ourselves whether we also need specialised people to handle terrorism cases. Belgian criminal procedure has seen a push for specialisation when it comes to investigating and prosecuting terrorism. The vast majority of the cases is handled by the federal prosecution service (see no. 107) and there are special investigating judges who are specialised in terrorism cases. In the UK, we see a similar situation at the level of the police, where specialised units exist. This specialisation has obvious advantages, mainly greater knowledge and understanding of the problem and ways to tackle it. However, this specialisation could also lead to a form of tunnel vision, vying for resources and could further cement prejudices. While these are real dangers, we believe the benefits far outweigh them and specialisation is the way forward. At the trial stage, this is no longer the case. During the investigation, specific knowledge about terrorism, how terrorist groups operate, etc. is invaluable for the people leading the investigation. However, at the trial stage this becomes less important, as all relevant information for the case in question should be available in the case file and from the conclusions of the parties. On the other hand, having a judge who is not specialised specifically in terrorism cases has added value because they will look at a terrorism case from a different angle, in a different, uninhibited manner. Therefore, while specialisation of investigators has more benefits than disadvantages, the reverse is true for specialised judges. However, these judges should still be legally trained professionals. Jury trials are expensive, disruptive for the organisation of the rest of the legal system and some jurors can be too easily influenced by well-spoken attorneys, because they do not fully understand the law or legal implications of certain actions. The final result of the Belgian jury trial on the Zaventem and Maelbeek terrorist attacks cannot be criticised on this last point, as the judgment is well-reasoned. However, one swallow does not make a summer. Lay Magistrates, in turn, are relatively inexpensive and help with organising of the rest of the legal system. While these are good arguments for lay Magistrates, they are outweighed by the fact that a lack of legal knowledge inevitably must lead to judgments of lesser quality, especially when difficult and convoluted legislation such as the terrorist legislation is at play. Therefore, while we advocate for non-specialised judges, we do mean non-specialised professional judges; and non-specialised means they are not specialised in cases of terrorism but are in criminal law in general.

609. Offences with far reaching consequences – When discussing the general conclusions of this research from a birds-eye perspective, it is also important to note that counter-terrorism legislation goes far beyond the offences and rules discussed in this book.[2710] The qualification of an offence as a terrorist offence or of an offender as a terrorist offender has a ripple effect throughout the entire criminal process and beyond. For example in Belgium, extended confiscation is possible for some terrorist offences,[2711] the Belgian nationality of some terrorist convicts can be revoked,[2712] and criminal procedure contains numerous procedural exceptions for terrorism.[2713] In the UK, for example, there is a separate regime for pre-trial detention and post-charge questioning is allowed (see nos 492–494), there are supplementary powers of forfeiture[2714] and a separate procedure for search warrants exists.[2715] Many of these competences and exceptions depend on an investigation into – or conviction for – a terrorist offence. The broader the terrorist offences, the quicker these powers can be used.[2716] Some Belgian authors even argue that this expansion of the reach of investigatory powers is the main reason why the legislature has expanded the offences.[2717]

610. EU INSTRUMENTS – The Belgian legislation is to a large extent based on EU instruments (see no. 2). As these instruments are binding upon Belgium, the recommendations made in the next Chapter are made in such a way that their implementation would not lead to Belgium violating its EU obligations (see no. 618). However, these EU instruments are not without their flaws either. Some remarks made so far in this Chapter (see nos 599–605) apply to them as well. They themselves are the consequence of shocks to the system and were conceived in difficult times. There are clear advantages in terms of cooperation between Member States in having similar terrorism offences. However, Member States manage to cooperate in other parts of criminal law without this harmonisation. Some form of harmonisation creates no real issues, such as the criminalisation of terrorism *sensu stricto*. However, the EU instruments go much further and require the criminalisation of broad and vague conduct in order to prevent terrorism. Therefore, the questions of what exactly legislatures are trying to achieve and how broad the offence should be, have to be asked at the EU level

---

2710 Cesoni (n 64) 141–142; Fransen and Kerkhofs (n 10) 16.

2711 Art.43*quater*, §1, 1°, b) CC.

2712 Art. 23/2 Code of Belgian Nationality. For an analysis, see: Reyntjens and Yperman (n 797).

2713 E.g. Art. 90*ter*, §5 and 112*quater*–112*undecies* CCP; Art. 1, section 2, 6° and 2, section 2, 5° Huiszoekingswet. For an analysis of some of these measures, see: Blaise and Delhaise (n 49) 173–177; De La Serna (n 8) 210–212; Roelandt (n 796) 10–21; Yperman, 'De bestrijding van terrorisme en strafprocesrecht: vele kleintjes maken een grote' (n 796).

2714 S. 120A TA 2000.

2715 Schedule 5 TA 2000.

2716 Vandromme and De Roy (n 34) 562.

2717 See: Cesoni (n 64) 148–149; De Roy (n 1366); Masset (n 20) T60/13; G Mols and T De Roos, 'Naar een algemene strafbaarheid van voorbereidingshandelingen' [1992] N.J.B. 221–225; Paye (n 14) 12–13; Van den Wyngaert (n 678) 333; Vandromme and De Roy (n 34) 550–551; Verbruggen, Prakken and Roef (n 25) 117–118 and 192–193. Onsea made a similar argument for the offences regarding criminal organisations. See: Onsea (n 51) 465.

as well. In general, criminal legislation tends to become broader as it is added to; but unless a large reform happens, it is rarely narrowed down again. This is clear from the evolution of the EU instruments on counterterrorism but also for example from the EU rules on money laundering, where the EU is already on its fifth Directive.[2718] This is extra important because of the concept of minimum harmonisation. While expanding offences in EU Directives obliges Member States to ensure the same actions are punishable, narrowing them down does not have that same effect. So even if the EU would decide to thoroughly rewrite its Directive on Combatting Terrorism in a way which narrows down the criminal offences, this would not lead to any obligation on Member States to do the same.

611. National responsibility – The fact that legislation is based on international instruments does not mean that states have no say whatsoever in which offences need to be created. Conventions are negotiated and signed by states and Framework Decisions such as the Council Framework Decision of 13 June 2002 on combating terrorism were adopted by unanimity.[2719] It is the case, however, that the unanimity required for Framework Decisions was unanimity in the Council of Ministers, which includes members of the executive power of each Member State. The European Parliament only had a consultative role, and the national parliaments are bound by the result of the Framework Decision. Therefore, although individual Member States had a say, there was a form of democratic deficit.[2720] This is not the case for Directives anymore, as the European Parliament now has a more prominent role in the legislative process. However, as the majority of the offences included in the EU Directive were already included in the 2008 Framework Decision, one might ask to what extent the European Parliament actually seriously considered the need for their inclusion in the Directive. None of this diminishes the main point that although the counter-terrorism legislation of many states is heavily influenced by international and European instruments, states cannot hide behind the international origins of the legislation and plead powerlessness.[2721] These

[2718] Directive (EU) 2018/843 of the European Parliament and of the Council of 30 May 2018 amending Directive (EU) 2015/849 on the prevention of the use of the financial system for the purposes of money laundering or terrorist financing, and amending Directives 2009/138/EC and 2013/36/EU [2018] *OJ* L156.

[2719] See: M Wasmeier and N Thwaites, 'The "Battle of the Pillars": Does the European Community Have the Power to Approximate National Criminal Laws?' [2004] European Law Review 613, 615.

[2720] Beernaert, 'La Loi du 19 Décembre 2003 relative aux infractions terroristes : Quand le droit pénal Belge évolue sous la dictée de l'Union Européenne' (n 20) 586; Caeiro (n 21) 309; Cesoni (n 64) 151–152; Yulia Chistyakova, 'Democratic Legitimacy, Effectiveness and Impact of EU Counter-Terrorism Measures' in Fiona de Londras and Josephine Doody (eds), *The Impact, Legitimacy and Effectiveness of EU Counter-Terrorism* (1st edn, Routledge 2015); Galli and Weyembergh (n 13) 17 and 20; Thomas (n 50) 477; Vander Beken (n 784) 19–21; Vanneste and Verbruggen (n 686) 82.

[2721] For an analysis of this issue, see also: Cesoni (n 15) 248–251.

international instruments are created by those very same states and therefore cannot provide an excuse for overly broad or poorly written legislation.

612. EU AS BEACON OF RIGHTS AND DEMOCRACY – On the world stage, the EU has a tendency to profile itself as a beacon of human rights and democracy. This makes it somewhat ironic that some of the more draconian counter-terrorism measures which are imposed in EU Member States, such as the broad offences discussed in this book, started their life as part of EU instruments. This alone should give the EU an incentive to exercise some caution in imposing obligations on Member States in this field.

613. THE ORIGINS OF MANY DEMOCRATIC STATES – Belgium and the UK do not exclude actions against undemocratic and/or dictatorial regimes from their definition of terrorism, as the EU does not require this either. This raises another question: should the EU not recognise some sort of right to rebel against dictatorial regimes which violate the human rights of their citizens? If the EU is serious about being a protector of human rights, it is odd to criminalise people who fight for those human rights in their countries. They might not use the methods we would prefer, but then again neither did many of the founders of modern EU countries. The EU was only able to become what it is today, human rights included, through a lot of actions it would now label terrorism. As explained above (see no. 137), we do not support the explicit recognition of a right to rebel. We believe the concept of using violence against innocent civilians is always wrong and even a just cause cannot legitimise such a tactic. Non-violent civil disobedience, however, should be allowed, especially against unjust regimes. It is true that the founders of many modern EU countries might be considered terrorists in today's context, but the fact that the end result (contemporary democratic nation states which (attempt to) respect human rights) is positive, does not mean that the road taken to this result was the only correct one. Perhaps there are better ways to achieve similar goals. In addition, the global context is different; every state is different, and so are its issues. Therefore, the EU should not be apprehensive to include violence aimed at undemocratic regimes in its definition of terrorism.

CHAPTER III
RECOMMENDATIONS

SECTION I. INTRODUCTION

614. BELGIUM – Contrary to the more general remarks in the previous Chapter, the recommendations made in this Chapter focus on Belgian law (see also no. 540). Some points might be relevant for the UK or third countries, but that will not be the case for all of the recommendations. Many of them depend upon the specificities of the Belgian legal system and are therefore difficult to generalise for other jurisdictions. The recommendations also build upon the Belgian legal system as it is at this moment in time. For the reasons mentioned above (see no. 109), abstraction will be made of possible future reforms of the Belgian system, including the new Criminal Code.

615. CRIMINAL LAW – As noted above (see no. 543), we do not recommend introducing administrative measures such as TPIMs in Belgium. Therefore, the recommendations will only cover criminal law. There is no need to introduce administrative measures in the Belgian system as Belgian criminal law is sufficiently equipped to deal with the issue and administrative measures tend to be difficult to reconcile with Article 5 ECHR.

616. THE NEED FOR REFORM – It is clear that the current Belgian criminal law framework to counter terrorism lacks coherence.[2722] It has been added to without first analysing whether the expansion of the offences was needed, and how new offences would fit into the framework.[2723] In addition, the Articles often needlessly restate general rules. The fact that the legislature decided not to reform the terrorist offences in the context of the new Criminal Code is therefore a missed opportunity. The preparatory works state: '*Although many questions relating to these criminal offences are still pending, the drafters believe that, given their challenges and their topical value, these issues deserve a separate and specific debate that cannot be conducted within the framework of this*

2722 See also: Delhaise (n 8) 143.

2723 More generally, a report on the EU Policies on Counter-Terrorism also recommended to properly and thoroughly scrutinise calls for new measures. See: Directorate-General for Internal Policies, *The European Union's Policies on Counter-Terrorism: Relevance, Coherence and Effectiveness* (2017) Study for the LIBE Committee, 81.

reform.'[2724] We disagree. These offences are topical and important, and it is a shame the legislature did not rise to the challenge of reforming these offences as reform is sorely needed. In a similar vein the EU Directorate-General for Internal Policies recommended '*that the EU set up monitoring, evaluation and oversight mechanisms of existing measures before adopting new ones.*'[2725] This is in line with our own observations. As the Belgian offences are based on the EU ones, the need for monitoring and evaluation at the EU level should come as no surprise. However, as this research only focussed on two states, one of which is not an EU Member State anymore, it would be presumptuous to make EU-wide recommendations based on it.

617. Two sets of recommendations – As we strongly believe the aforementioned reform to be necessary, we will make recommendations which could assist any future decision maker in this process. They are divided into two sets. A first set, which we termed 'minimal changes', takes the current legislation as a starting point and attempts to make it more in line with the principles of legal certainty and proportionality; and thus, with the right to liberty and the right to free movement under the ECHR. These recommendations are minimal in the sense they assume the current structure of the offences and the current amount of offences has to remain unchanged. The only Article in Title I*ter* not discussed is 141*bis* CC, for the same reasons it has not been discussed throughout this whole book (see no. 106). The second set are recommendations for a more thorough reform to bring the system more in line with the legality and proportionality principles and thus Articles 5 ECHR and 2 Fourth Protocol ECHR. This goal is achieved by simplifying the offences and limiting them to a minimum, while still providing the prosecution with enough possibilities to effectively prosecute terrorism *sensu lato*.

618. Supranational framework – What has to also be taken into account is that Belgium has obligations under the EU Directive and several international treaties. As the EU Directive has already taken into account the Council of Europe and UN obligations, ensuring conformity with the EU Directive will suffice in ensuring Belgium meets its international and supranational obligations. Therefore, the recommendations made in this Chapter explicitly include references to the minimum standards imposed by the EU Directive. Even within these boundaries, it is possible to devise a system which is clearer and more proportionate than the current one.

2724 Own translation, original in Dutch and French. See: MvT Wetsontwerp 24 juli 2023 tot invoering van Boek II van het Strafwetboek, *Parl.St.* Kamer 2022–2023, no. 55-3501/001, 300. See also: wetsvoorstel 12 februari 2020 tot instelling van een nieuw Strafwetboek (boek 1 en 2) Deel II, *Parl.St.* Kamer 2019–2020, no. 55-1011/001, 510.

2725 Directorate-General for Internal Policies, The European Union's Policies on Counter-Terrorism: Relevance, Coherence and Effectiveness (2017) Study for the LIBE Committee, 83.

SECTION II. MINIMAL CHANGES

SUBSECTION I. ARTICLE 137 CC

619. Delete useless additions to *actus reus* – The list of Article 137, §2 CC contains several useless additions, such as for example Articles 409, §2 or 518 CC. These Articles contain aggravated offences and have sentences which do not fit the list of Article 138 CC (see nos 144 and 146). Instead of adding a plethora of options to Article 138, it makes most sense to just delete the aggravated offences which are punishable with for example five to seven years or 15 to 22 years felony imprisonment. That way it is clear only the aggravating circumstance of terrorism has to be applied to the base offence, which is the situation which should occur in practice already.

620. Add sexual offences – While some aggravated offences should be deleted from the list, other offences could be added to it. The main category of offences which is currently missing concerns sexual offences (see no. 134). A very simple addition would be to add the entire first section of the chapter on sexual offences to the list.[2726] A slightly more nuanced solution would be to limit the addition to the offences of violation of sexual integrity and rape, and the aggravated offences of non-consensual sexual actions.[2727] This would exclude the offences of voyeurism and non-consensual spreading of sexual content, which are not typically associated with terrorism.

621. Specify significant economic damage – Wherever the *actus reus* uses the term 'significant economic damage', the legislature should specify what this means (see no. 133). An obvious solution would be to change it to 'economic damage that could endanger the stability of the country and the security of its citizens'. Another option would be to list the protected legal assets more concretely. For example: 'damage to critical infrastructure, the monetary stability or the credit rating of the state'. This second option has the advantage of being even more concrete than the first. It does create a small risk of certain actions being excluded because they created significant damage to another legal asset not included in the limitative list of assets. However, this risk seems negligible because of the sufficiently broad terminology of critical infrastructure and monetary stability. Therefore, the second option is preferable.

2726 Being: Section 1. Violation of sexual integrity, voyeurism, non-consensual spreading of sexual content and rape of Chapter I/1. Offences against sexual integrity, sexual right to self-determination and good morals of Title VIII. Offences and standard offences against people of Book II. of the Criminal Code (Art. 417/5–417/23).

2727 Art. 417/7 and 417/11–417/22 CC.

622. WOULD A GENERAL AGGRAVATING CIRCUMSTANCE BE BETTER? – Another way to simplify Article 137 CC would be to simply delete the list of actions constituting the *actus reus*. In this situation terrorism would become an aggravating circumstance applicable to any criminal offence committed with the required *mens rea* and contextual element. This would avoid any discussions around which exact offences should be included in the list. However, this advantage is outweighed by the disadvantages. First, it would create a whole lot of new terrorist offences, which keeping in mind the broad procedural and other consequences (see no. 609) and the negative label of 'terrorism' is not something to aspire to. Second, some actions which are currently part of the list in §3 would be decriminalised. Think for example about threatening or attempted standard offences currently on the list. This could be problematic as their criminalisation is required by the EU Directive. Third, it would require very extensive changes to the sentencing scales of Article 138 CC, which would make the Article very complicated. It would require every possible felony sentence for any offence in the Criminal Code to be included in Article 138 CC in order to avoid the issues discussed above (see nos 145–146).

623. WHAT ABOUT POLITICAL OFFENCES? – One question which remains, is whether or not terrorism can be a political offence. As explained, we believe it can be under the current legislation (see nos 153–154). However, there is an easier way to avoid the whole discussion. We need to take a step back and ask ourselves whether the concept of political offences within Belgian criminal law still has added value. The original reasoning behind political offences was sound, but almost two centuries later, this original reasoning does not apply anymore. Modern day judges can be trusted to remain impartial and independent and as explained above, jury trials have several important downsides. In the original spirit of the rules on political offences, terrorist offences are a shoe-in to receive this qualification; and the fact the Court of Cassation had to intervene the way it did, shows that the concept is dated. Therefore, we would recommend abolishing the whole concept of political offences within Belgian criminal law (not including the political offence exception in international law, which has a different *ratio legis* entirely, see no. 151).

SUBSECTION II. ARTICLE 138 CC

624. WORDING IMPRISONMENT – The categories of Article 138, §1, 1°–5° should be reworded to avoid the wording 'no more than' (see nos 142–143). In addition, to increase proportionality 1° should not include a minimum sentence. The categories could therefore be worded as follows:

1° a fine as a principal penalty or a maximum imprisonment of no more than a year by a maximum imprisonment of three years;
2° a maximum imprisonment of more than a year but no more than three years, by a maximum imprisonment of five years;
3° a maximum imprisonment of more than three years but no more than five years, by a felony imprisonment of five years to ten years;

625. THREATENING – In order to ensure the proportionality of the threatening offence (see no. 140), Article 138, § 2, 1° CC should have three categories, which could be worded as:

- Five to ten years felony imprisonment for threatening felonies with sentences of more than ten years felony imprisonment.
- Three months to five years imprisonment for threatening felonies with a sentence of up to ten years felony imprisonment.
- A maximum sentence of one year less than the maximum sentence for the threatened offence for threatening standard offences.

SUBSECTION III. ARTICLE 139 CC

626. DELETING PARAGRAPH 2 – The exclusion clause in the second paragraph of Article 139 CC has no added value and should therefore be deleted (see nos 168–169).

627. ONLY TERRORIST FELONIES – In addition, in order to avoid the proportionality issue of participation in the activities of a terrorist group being punished harsher than the offence the group aims to commit (see no. 183), the definition should specify that a terrorist group is a group that aims to commit terrorist felonies. This would exclude groups which specifically aim to commit one or more terrorist standard offences. In addition to solving the aforementioned proportionality issue, this change would also act as a *de minimis* threshold for the offences in Article 140 CC. As certain groups which only aim to commit standard offences would not be terrorist groups anymore, the participation in their activities would also, no longer an offence. For example, a group which aims to take to the street and damage cars and/or statues or monuments[2728]; or a group which threatens to beat up people,[2729] could be a terrorist group under the current legislation. But if the definition of a group is amended as proposed, that would no longer be the case.

[2728] Art. 137, §2, 4° *j.* 138, §1, 3° and 4° and 521, Section 3 and 526 CC.
[2729] Art. 137, §3, 6° *j.* 138, §2, 1° CC *j.* 398 CC.

SUBSECTION IV. ARTICLE 140 CC

628. *Mens rea* – The *mens rea* of the offences in Article 140 CC is unclear and too broad. It should be narrowed down to its original wording in order to emphasise the necessity of a connection between the *actus reus* and the criminal activities of the terrorist group. In the explanatory memorandum of this legislation, the legislature would also do well to clearly explain the current interpretation of Article 140 CC is too broad.

629. Paragraph 1/1 – The offence in paragraph 1/1 should be narrowed down significantly. It should require some form of authority from the decision maker. In terms of wording 'the participation in the taking of any decision in the context of the activities of the terrorist group' could be reworded in several ways. As is the case for the leadership offence, it should focus not on the act of participating in the making of a decision but on the position of the decision maker. Something along the lines of 'Being a member of the group who has a meaningful influence on important decisions within the group'. For the sentence of §1/1 the words '*or one of these sentences by itself*' should be deleted.

630. Leadership – The leadership offence, finally, should explicitly include a definition of leadership, which differentiates between them and the people targeted by §1/1. The current wording included in the explanatory memorandum could be updated and inserted in the legislation. For example: 'the people who have a central role within the terrorist group, take upon themselves the more important responsibilities within the group and take the final decisions.'

SUBSECTION V. ARTICLE 140*BIS* CC

631. No need for additions – The risk requirement is part of the legislation again due to the case law of the Constitutional Court (see no. 209). The future addition of glorification does not change anything so it should not be introduced (see no. 284).

632. Room for deletions – Two parts of the offence could be deleted because they both lack added value. First, the part '*Without prejudice to the application of Article 140*' (see no. 212) should be deleted as this is already covered by the general rules on concurrence. Second, a simple way of reducing overlap between this offence and the group offences is to delete the 2019 addition of '*or contribute to.*' This can be done without decriminalising many, if any, situations. Inciting with a goal of contributing to another offence necessarily includes three people: the inciter plus the person who is incited to contribute to the offence they are incited to commit (the 'actual' offence) and then the perpetrator of the actual offence. This means a terrorist group should exist and the offences in Article 140 CC would apply. In addition, different types of perpetrators, for example those providing necessary help, are already covered by the concept of being a (co-)perpetrator of the incitement offence so would be punishable under Article 140*bis* even after deleting these few words.

SUBSECTION VI. ARTICLE 140*TER* CC

633. Clarify wording – As was the case for Article 140*bis* CC, the part '*Without prejudice to the application of Article 140*' should be deleted for lack of added value. What would have, on the other hand, been valuable, is an explicit inclusion of the *mens rea* (see no. 228). For clarity's sake, the legislature should include 'with the aim of seeing one of these offences being committed' in the offence.

634. Delete Article 140 CC and 'or contribute to' from Article 140*ter* – To decrease overlap, the recruitment to commit the offences in Article 140 CC should not be punishable under Article 140*ter* as it is already covered by Article 140 itself (see no. 227). Therefore, Article 140 CC could be deleted from the offence of Article 140*ter* without lifting punishability of any situations which are punishable at this point in time. This would decrease overlap and thereby increase clarity. In addition, the same argument can be made towards deleting the words '*or contribute to*' as was made for Article 140*bis*. Recruiting with a goal of contributing to another offence necessarily includes three people: the recruiter plus the person who is recruited to contribute to the actual offence and then the perpetrator of the actual offence, which means a terrorist group would exist.

SUBSECTION VII. ARTICLE 140*QUATER* CC

635. Deleting words – Again, the part '*Without prejudice to the application of Article 140*' should be deleted for lack of added value. Again, the part 'or contribute to' could be deleted for the same reasons explained above.

636. Clarification in explanatory memorandum – While the text of the offence is clear in that it states '*other specific methods and techniques*', the original explanatory memorandum of the offence does muddy the waters by giving very general examples. The memorandum of any new legislation which alters this offence should explicitly refer to the Constitutional Court case of 28 January 2015 (see no. 239) and emphasise the word 'specific' to clarify the examples in the original explanatory memorandum were too broad.

SUBSECTION VIII. ARTICLE 140*QUINQUIES* CC

637. Redundant wording – Article 140*quinquies* CC contains redundant wording on three points. First, once more the '*Without prejudice to the application of Article 140*' is redundant. Second, '*in Belgium or abroad*' is a redundant addition (see no. 245). Both should therefore be deleted. Third, in the first paragraph, the words '*or contribute to*' could once again be deleted without decriminalising situations.

SUBSECTION IX. ARTICLE 140*SEXIES* CC

638. Wording: without prejudice – In this offence as well, the part '*Without prejudice to the application of Article 140*' should be deleted for lack of added value.

639. Exclusion of threatening – The Belgian offence excludes the threatening offence from its scope, while this is not the case in the Directive. This should be added in order to ensure full compliance with the Directive.

640. No need for new offence – The newly proposed offence of facilitating travel would have no added value and should therefore not be introduced (see no. 285).

SUBSECTION X. ARTICLE 140*SEPTIES* CC

641. Explicitly include *mens rea* – The *mens rea* of the preparation offence should explicitly be added to the offence. This would increase clarity in general, as well as provide a less opaque confirmation that the offence only covers preparation of one's own terrorist offence (see no. 268). An addition as simple as 'with the intention to commit this offence' would suffice.

642. Proportionality – If the definition of a terrorist group is limited to groups aiming to commit terrorist felonies as suggested above, the proportionality issue of preparation by oneself having lower sentences than preparation in group only arises for a specific category of terrorist offences, being those punishable with five to ten years felony imprisonment. For groups aiming to commit terrorist standard offences it poses no issue anymore as participation in their activities is not an offence. For groups aiming to commit terrorist felonies punishable with more than ten years felony imprisonment, it does not either as the sentence for preparation of those offences is maximum five years imprisonment or more and the maximum sentence for participation in the activities after correctionalisation is also five years. It seems impossible to solve the proportionality issue fully, as raising the sentence of preparation of an offence punishable with a sentence of five to ten years felony imprisonment would put the sentence at the same level of an attempted offence. This would create inconsistency in the ordinal proportionality which now exists between preparation, attempt, and the committed offence. Changing the sentence on the other end and lowering the sentence for participation in the activities of the group would create proportionality issues when comparing Article 140 with other terrorist offences *sensu lato*. This is because for example, participating in the activities of a terrorist group which aims to commit such an offence would be sentenced lower than traveling for it, providing training for it, etc. while the participation in the activities of the group could be as close or closer to the actual commission of the offence. In addition, such a change would greatly complicate the sentencing for the offence of participation in the activities of a terrorist group. Therefore, this proportionality issue seems to be unavoidable, but by making the small change proposed in this paragraph, it can be limited to only one, relatively small, category of offences.

SUBSECTION XI. ARTICLE 141 CC

643. Simplifying *mens rea* – The current *mens rea* of Article 141 CC is needlessly complicated with the addition of a useless second option (see nos 276–277). This 2° is redundant and should be deleted.

SUBSECTION XII. ARTICLE 141*TER* CC

644. Deleting Article 141*ter* CC – As was the case for Article 139, §2 CC, Article 141*ter* CC is redundant. It states that no provision of title I*ter* may be read as limiting or impeding fundamental freedoms. This is redundant as any limitations of human rights which are caused, have to be (and indeed have been) judged in light of Belgium's human rights obligations, mainly under the ECHR and the Belgian Constitution. This is a general obligation which is not in any way changed by Article 141*ter* CC.

SUBSECTION XIII. PRE-TRIAL DETENTION

645. Needless exception – The Belgian pre-trail detention rules have a few exceptions for terrorism cases, but in general the same rules apply to terrorism cases as do to other cases. One of the few exceptions is the lower threshold for the motivation of absolute necessity for public security (see nos 294–296). This exception should be deleted. The *ratio legis* does not match up with the legislation and the same goals can be reached without the exception.

SUBSECTION XIV. BEING AT THE DISPOSAL OF THE SENTENCE ENFORCEMENT COURT

646. Redefining scope – At this point, the scope of the sentence of being at the disposal of the Sentence Enforcement Court fails to target the most dangerous offenders (see no. 123). First, it is obligatory in some cases where it is not needed and other cases where it might be needed are excluded from its scope. The first issue can be resolved by making it a facultative sentence. This can be achieved by removing Article 137 CC from Article 34*ter*, 3° CC and adding a new °5 to Article 34*quater* CC. This new °5 should reference convictions to sentences of at least five years imprisonment for offences in Article 137 CC without requiring the death of the victim, thereby resolving the second issue mentioned above.

SECTION III. THOROUGH REFORM

647. Recommendations from previous section – In this final Section of the book we will go one step further and make recommendations for a more thorough reform. Some of these recommendations overlap with ones from the previous Section, making the latter unnecessary. However, this is not the case all of the previous recommendations. The recommendations from the previous Section which are made unnecessary because they are superseded by larger changes in this Section are the changes to Articles 140, §1/1 (see no. 629), 140*ter* (see nos 633–634), 140*quater* (see nos 635–636), 140*quinquies* (see no. 637), 140*sexies* (see nos 638–640) and 141 CC (see no. 643). These proposals from the previous Section should therefore be disregarded, but all other recommendations should be applied in addition to the recommendations in this Section.

648. Proportionality of terrorism *sensu stricto* – With regard to the sentencing brackets in Article 138 CC, it is possible to go one step further than proposed in the last Section and differentiate between the three lowest categories in order to increase proportionality. The categories would then be worded as follows:

1° a fine as a principal sentence, by an imprisonment of maximum one year;
2° imprisonment of no more than six months, by imprisonment of no more than two years;

3° maximum imprisonment of more than six months but no more than one year, by imprisonment of no more than three years;
4° maximum imprisonment of more than one year but no more than three years, by imprisonment of no more than five years;
5° maximum imprisonment of more than three years but no more than five years, by felony imprisonment of five to ten years.

649. And threatening? – The proposal made above to impose a maximum sentence for threatening terrorist standard offences of one year imprisonment less than the threatened offence (see no. 625), still works with the new sentencing scales proposed in the previous paragraph, barring 1°. Applying this to the new scales above would lead threatening a standard offence in 1° to have a maximum sentence of zero years imprisonment. This is in itself not a bad outcome, threatening a terrorist offence, which if that same offence is committed outside a terrorist context only has a fine as a principal sentence, should not be punishable under the *de minimis* rule. Therefore, Article 138, §2, 1° CC should explicitly state that threatening terrorist offences which fall under Article 138, §1, 1° CC is not punishable.

650. Article 140 CC: *de minimis* and proportionality – In addition to reverting the *mens rea* of Article 140 CC to its original iteration, a further *de minimis* change could be made. Instead of just criminalising participation in the activities of a terrorist group, a quantifier could be added, such as for example 'substantial' participation. This would further increase the threshold of the offence and exclude the people who are the furthest removed from the offence of terrorism *sensu stricto*. This change would be combined with an increase in sentence for §1 to ten to 15 years felony imprisonment and a deletion of §1/1. This would avoid the issues of the very broad wording of §1/1 and the differentiation between that §1/1 and §2. At the same time, it would ensure the option of a more proportionate sentence of people who are higher up on the level of the terrorist group (i.e. whose participation is more substantial). It would also create a situation in which Article 140, §1 CC is not just technically in accordance with the Directive requirement of a sentence of eight years or more for the offence but also making it so in practice as after correctionalisation that sentence would become six months to ten years imprisonment. The Directive requires states to criminalise participating in the activities of a terrorist group but does not define participation. Therefore, adding a qualifier to it could be argued not to be a violation of the Directive as it is not clear what exactly is covered by the Directive.

651. Expanding the definition of a terrorist group – The Directive defines a terrorist group in the same words as the Belgian legislation, meaning it is '*a structured group of more than two persons [...]*'. It is possible to change

Article 139 CC to 'a structured group of at least two persons'. This would not violate the Directive, which provides for a minimum norm and expanding it is allowed. This change would mean that two people who act in concert to commit a terrorist offence can constitute a terrorist group. This change would allow for the deletion and simplification of several other offences (see following paragraphs). Defining a group as constituted of at least two people is not far-fetched. According to Merriam-Webster dictionary and Black's Law Dictionary, a group consists of two or more.[2730] In addition, the group offences are in essence an extension of the theory of conspiracy and there is no reason to limit this to groups of more than two people. The UK theory of criminal conspiracy for example only requires two people (see no. 452). The requirement of at least three people for a terrorist group was copied from the legislation on criminal organisations. In Belgium, forming a gang is a criminal offence as well, and was already so before the offences of terrorist groups or criminal organisations came into existence.[2731] When introducing the offences related to criminal organisations, the question was asked what the difference was between a criminal organisation and a gang. After much discussion, the reply was that a criminal organisation requires at least three people while for a gang two suffice.[2732] As pointed out by Verbruggen in this context, this is a completely arbitrary distinction and it was not even clear why a minimum of three people was required for criminal organisations.[2733] This question was raised in the Senate, but never answered.[2734] The only relevant information stated is that the requirement of at least three people was copied from an inter-EU working group on drugs and organised crime on 4 January 1996. In conclusion, there seems to be no real reason why at least three people are required for a terrorist group. It is a requirement which has been mindlessly copied since the 1990s while it has no real added value.

652. Deleting the recruitment offence – The offence which has the least added value is the recruitment offence in Article 140*ter* CC. As explained above, it adds nothing with respect to recruiting to participate in the activities of a terrorist group and the reference to Article 140 CC should be deleted (see no. 634). However, we could go one step further and simply delete the offence altogether. Recruitment for terrorism *sensu stricto* would be covered by the group offences if the threshold for a terrorist group is lowered to two people. In addition, many situations would also be covered by the incitement offence in

2730 See: www.merriam-webster.com/dictionary/group and https://thelawdictionary.org/group/.

2731 Art. 322–324 CC.

2732 Verslag 24 maart 1998 namens de commissie voor de Justitie bij wetsontwerp betreffende criminele organisaties, *Parl.St.* Senaat 1997–1998, no. 1–662/4.

2733 Verbruggen (n 34) 327 and 335–336.

2734 Verslag 24 maart 1998 namens de commissie voor de Justitie bij wetsontwerp betreffende criminele organisaties, *Parl.St.* Senaat 1997–1998, no. 1–662/4.

Article 140*bis* CC and if the offence for which the person is recruited is attempted or committed, the recruiter would be punishable for aiding and abetting the (attempted) offence. Recruiting people to travel also could be covered by the group offences as there will be a terrorist group. Important to note here as well, is that the criminalisation of recruitment to travel is not required by the EU Directive. In summary, the recruitment offence is only relevant in situations where no terrorist group exists, no other terrorist offence has been attempted and there has been no public incitement of terrorism *sensu stricto* in the sense of Article 140*bis* CC. This situation is very niche, especially if we lower the threshold for a terrorist group, and far removed from the actual terrorist offence, making its deletion possible under the *de minimis* rule. This deletion would not put Belgium in violation of its EU obligations as the EU does not require recruitment to travel to be an offence and recruitment to commit terrorism *sensu stricto* is sufficiently covered by other offences.

653. Deleting the training offences – Similarly, lowering the threshold for a terrorist group would make the training offences in Article 140*quater* and 140*quinquies*, §1 redundant. A person providing training or receiving training to commit terrorism *sensu stricto* would then automatically be part of a terrorist group, being two people working in concert to commit terrorism *sensu stricto*. This means that they would be covered by the participation offence of Article 140, §1 CC and the training offences would thus become moot. That would only leave the self-study offence in Article 140*quinquies*, §2 CC. Self-study is a clear form of preparation and could easily be a sub-category of a preparation offence. The main different in Belgian law is that the preparation offence requires concreteness while the self-study offence does not. In situations where the self-study can be linked to a concrete terrorist offence *sensu stricto*, this would amount to preparation, if this cannot be done, it would not be possible to prosecute as preparation. We would argue that the self-study offence can be deleted. The cases of self-study which would not fall under the preparation offence are simply too far removed from the terrorist offence *sensu stricto* to prosecute. The offence creates a real danger of a chilling-effect on people who have harmless intentions but for whatever reason are just curious. Once their study is linked to an actual terrorist attack they are preparing, it can be prosecuted as preparation, if not, then it should not be a criminal offence. This also poses no real issues under the EU Directive, as the only reference to self-study is made in a recital, which is not binding.

654. Deleting the traveling offence – Probably the most controversial terrorist offence when it was introduced, was the terrorist traveling offence of Article 140*sexies* CC. After the changes proposed above, this offence could be deleted as it would lose what little added value it had. Currently it criminalises

traveling to commit terrorism *sensu stricto*, the group offences, incitement, recruitment, the training offences and the financing offence. As we propose to delete the recruitment and training offences, as well as the financing offence (see no. 655), they should be deleted from the *mens rea* anyway. We would also delete the incitement offence from the *mens rea* for two reasons. First, every offence (other from terrorism *sensu stricto*) included in the *mens rea* creates more opportunity for double, triple, etc. preparation (see no. 315). Second, considering the context and *ratio legis* of the traveling offence, the FTF phenomenon,[2735] criminalising traveling to incite is not the focus of the offence. There is no need to add the incitement offence in order to be able to tackle the FTF phenomenon and there have been no cases in which this was a useful addition. Finally, traveling to commit a group offence could be deleted from the *mens rea* as well, since this in itself constitutes an attempted group offence, as seen in the case law. This would leave us with just traveling to commit or contribute to terrorism *sensu stricto*. The '*or contribute to*' could be deleted because lowering the threshold for the group offences would create a situation in which this would always be a group offence, since it would always include two people, and therefore make up a terrorist group. Finally, traveling to commit terrorism *sensu stricto* could be prosecuted as attempted terrorism *sensu stricto* or preparation. Again, this would require a link with the actual terrorist offence *sensu stricto*, but this is perfectly acceptable under the *de minimis* rule. Deleting the traveling offence would also not cause any issues under the EU Directive. The Directive does not include traveling for the purposes of inciting or recruiting. The offences which are required by the Directive, being traveling to commit terrorism *sensu stricto*, a group offence or a training offence. As explained, these situations are adequately covered by the preparation offence, attempted terrorist offences and the group offences themselves.

655. Deleting the financing offence – The changes proposed so far, also make the financing offence in Article 141 CC virtually moot. By lowering the threshold for a terrorist group, any form of financing another person with terrorist intent can be prosecuted under Article 140 CC. The situation of a person collecting funds or resources for their own terrorist attack could be prosecuted under the preparation offence or attempted terrorism *sensu stricto*, depending on how far along the preparations are. The only situations which would be decriminalised, are those in which the prosecution cannot link the gathering of funds to a terrorist attack which the perpetrator aims to commit. Again, those cases should not be prosecuted.

[2735] See e.g.: Directorate-General for Internal Policies, *The European Union's Policies on Counter-Terrorism: Relevance, Coherence and Effectiveness* (2017) Study for the LIBE Committee, 62–63.

656. Sentences for preparation – The proposal for new sentencing scales for terrorist standard offences *sensu stricto* (see no. 648), also has consequences for the preparation offence. As the new scales for Article 138 would have a lowest category of one year imprisonment, this would put them at the same level as the first category of preparation. This means that preparing those standard offences would have the same sentence as actually committing them, which is not ideal in terms of ordinal proportionality. Therefore, Article 140*septies* CC should include a new category, stating that the sentence is eight days to six months if the prepared offence is punished with maximum one year imprisonment. In addition, the current first category (preparing terrorist standard offences) should be reworded to avoid overlap, it could become: 'Imprisonment of maximum one year, if the prepared offence is punishable with one to five years imprisonment.'

657. Summary – In summary, the proposal for thorough reform would leave us with the following Articles: 137, 138, 139, §1, 140, §1 and §2, 140*bis* and 140*septies*. Provided these Articles are amended as proposed (and presumably renumbered as well), this would greatly simplify the Belgian legislation in order to ensure respect for the principle of legal certainty and it would increase proportionality. These changes also keep in mind the EU Directive and would not lead to Belgium violating its European obligations.

GENERAL CONCLUSION

658. Main research question –

> Is the Belgian or the UK approach to prevention of terrorism through direct restrictions to the right to liberty preferable in light of this right; and how could the Belgian approach be improved?

This is the main research question that was set out to be answered. The question has two facets. First, which jurisdiction has the preferable approach in terms of the right to liberty. Second, how the Belgian approach could be improved. However, before any meaningful answer could be formulated for either of these facets, several terms had to be defined and operationalised.

659. Restrictions of liberty – The first Part of this book does exactly that. The right to liberty and the free movement of persons under the ECHR were analysed in detail. This provides a detailed and nuanced answer to the question what a 'restriction of liberty' is. Part I focussed first on the ECtHR case law related to the scope of application of the right to liberty and the possibilities to limit this right. Next, the case law on the free movement of persons was discussed.

660. Evaluative and normative framework – The main goal of the right to liberty is the prevention of arbitrary detention. Two main principles which aim to achieve this goal were identified: legal certainty and proportionality. The analysis also showed that those same principles are at the core of restrictions to the free movement of persons. Therefore, they were used as the framework for the analysis throughout the rest of the book. The principle of legal certainty was operationalised through several basic rules: avoiding overlap and redundancies, using precise terminology, explicitly requiring intent and avoiding intervention based on conduct very far removed from the actual act of terrorism. The principle of proportionality was operationalised through the concept of ordinal proportionality and a *de minimis* rule.

661. Belgium – The second Part of the book focussed on the question of whether there is a risk of arbitrariness in the Belgian restrictions of liberty. In Belgium, these restrictions are imposed within a criminal law framework. Therefore, the Part analysed all Belgian terrorist offences in detail, with a focus on proportionality and legal certainty. Furthermore, the rules on pre-trial detention and additional deprivations of liberty were discussed. This analysis resulted in the conclusion that the Belgian legislation was lacking in several respects. The Belgian offences are marked by redundancies and overlap. The terminology is not always as precise as could be and while intent is always necessary, the requirement is not explicitly included in all offences. The legislation also allows very early intervention. In terms of proportionality, the legislature has attempted to introduce ordinal proportionality, but has not always succeeded in doing so. Finally, the application of the offences raises *de minimis* concerns.

662. The UK: criminal law – A similar analysis was made for the UK in the third Part. A major difference is that the UK also employs measures which directly restrict the right to liberty outside of the context of criminal law. The first Chapter of Part III, however, discussed the UK criminal offences and pre-trial detention. In the UK as well, the offences overlap and contain some redundancies. The terminology is again rather vague at times and some offences do not require intent, or a *mens rea* at all. The legislature intervenes very early, has made little to no attempt to ensure ordinal proportionality and has included no *de minimis* thresholds.

663. The UK: administrative law – The evolution of UK administrative measures was discussed in the second Chapter of Part III. These measures have undergone a long series of amendments and have led to a limiting shift in the scope of application of the right to liberty in the UK. Their potential scope is broad, and they allow for very early intervention, based on secret evidence. In practice, however, they are applied very sparingly. As prosecution is the preferred option, administrative measures are only imposed upon people who cannot be prosecuted. Keeping in mind the broadness of the criminal offences, this raises a *de minimis* point: if none of the broad early intervention criminal offences can be proven, no restrictions of liberty should be imposed. Therefore, these administrative measures possibly do more harm than good.

664. Comparative analysis – The fourth and final Part started with a comparative analysis of both jurisdictions. As Belgium does not have administrative measures, this analysis focussed solely on criminal law. This analysis showed that the UK has more offences than Belgium does, and that they are broader as well. Especially the weak *mens rea* requirements and partial reversal of the burden of proof by using defences are problematic in the UK. The sentences are also higher and do not take into account ordinal proportionality. Therefore, the Belgian system is more in line with our framework than the UK's.

665. Minimal recommendations – This does not mean, however, that there is no room for improvement in Belgium. Chapter II of Part IV contained general observations on the prevention of terrorism through criminal law and administrative law, based on the rest of the book preceding it. Chapter III then made recommendations on how to improve the Belgian system. First, it must be noted that because of their lack of added value and potential issues, administrative measures need not be introduced in Belgium. Criminal law should suffice, and the recommendations thus focused on the Belgian criminal offences. These recommendations can be split up into two categories. Taking the current Belgian legislation as a starting point, the first set of recommendations contains minimal changes. These changes do not fundamentally alter anything within the Belgian framework but aim to decrease overlap and redundancies through omitting or slightly altering certain phrases. In addition, some simple changes can make certain wording more precise or clearer and increase ordinal proportionality.

666. Recommendations for thorough reform – The second set of recommendations goes one step further. Several offences could be deleted as their scope overlaps to a very large extent with other offences. If the definition of a terrorist group is expanded slightly, the deletion of these offences would not decriminalise any situations. In addition, a couple of the other offences could be narrowed down further and a few tweaks to the sentences would increase proportionality. These recommendations would go a long way in increasing legal certainty and proportionality of the terrorist offences, while still respecting Belgium's supranational obligations.

667. Answer to the main research question – The first facet of the main research question was answered by the comparative analysis between Belgium and the UK. It has shown that the current Belgian legislation provides better safeguards in terms of legal certainty and proportionality and therefore in terms of the right to liberty and free movement. The analysis also showed administrative measures which have a direct impact on the right to liberty are not needed to prevent terrorism, and criminal law suffices. The second facet – how the Belgian approach can be improved, has been answered by the recommendations in Part IV. The proposed changes to the Belgian offences would further increase legal certainty and proportionality and therefore limit the risk of arbitrariness.

BIBLIOGRAPHY

LEGISLATION

INTERNATIONAL AND SUPRANATIONAL

EUROPEAN UNION INSTRUMENTS

Treaty on the Functioning of the European Union 2007 [2012] *OJ* C 326/47. (TFEU).

Charter of Fundamental Rights of the European Union (2000/C 364/01) [2000] *OJ* C364.

Council Framework Decision 2002/475/JHA of 13 June 2002 on combating terrorism [2002] *OJ* L164.

Directive 2004/38/EC of the European Parliament and of the Council of 29 April 2004 on the right of citizens of the Union and their family members to move and reside freely within the territory of the Member States amending Regulation (EEC) No 1612/68 and repealing Directives 64/221/EEC, 68/360/EEC, 72/194/EEC, 73/148/EEC, 75/34/EEC, 75/35/EEC, 90/364/EEC, 90/365/EEC and 93/96/EEC (Text with EEA relevance) [2004] *OJ* L158.

Council Framework Decision 2008/919/JHA of 28 November 2008 amending Framework Decision 2002/475/JHA on combating terrorism [2008] *OJ* 330.

Directive (EU) 2017/541 of the European Parliament and of the Council of 15 March 2017 on combating terrorism and replacing Council Framework Decision 2002/475/JHA and amending Council Decision 2005/671/JHA [2017] *OJ* L88.

Directive (EU) 2018/843 of the European Parliament and of the Council of 30 May 2018 amending Directive (EU) 2015/849 on the prevention of the use of the financial system for the purposes of money laundering or terrorist financing, and amending Directives 2009/138/EC and 2013/36/EU [2018] *OJ* L156.

CONVENTIONS

European Convention of Human Rights 1950 (ECHR).

Protocol no. 4 to the Convention for the Protection of Human Rights and Fundamental Freedoms securing certain rights and freedoms other than those already included in the Convention and in the First Protocol thereto of 16 September 1963, Strasbourg (ECHR Fourth Protocol).

Convention on Offences and Certain Other Acts Committed On Board Aircraft of 14 September 1963, Tokyo, *United Nations Treaty Series* 1969, 220.

European Convention on the Suppression of Terrorism of 27 January 1977, *ETS* 90, Strasbourg.

International Convention for the Suppression of Terrorist Bombings of 15 December 1997, New York, *United Nations Treaty Series* 2001, 256.

International Convention for the Suppression of the Financing of Terrorism of 9 December 1999, New York.
Council of Europe Convention on the Prevention of Terrorism of 16 May 2005, Warsaw, [2018] *Pb. EU* 159/3.
Additional Protocol to the Council of Europe Convention on the Prevention of Terrorism, 2015, CETS 217.

OTHER

Universal Declaration of Human Rights, UN General Assembly, Paris, 10 December 1948 (GA Resolution 217 A).
Explanatory Report to Protocol No. 4 to the Convention for the Protection of Human Rights and Fundamental Freedoms, securing certain rights and freedoms other than those already included in the Convention and in the first Protocol thereto, ETX No 46, 16 September 1963.
Preparatory work on Article 5 of the Convention, bilingual version, 1967, *CDH* (67) 10.
Council Common Position 2001/931/CFSP of 27 December 2001 on the application of specific measures to combat terrorism [2001] *OJ* L344/93.
UN Security Council Resolution S/RES/2178 (24 September 2014).
Declaration contained in a letter from the Permanent Representative of France to the Council of Europe, dated 24 November 2015, registered at the Secretariat General on 24 November 2015.
Directorate-General for Internal Policies, *The European Union's Policies on Counter-Terrorism: Relevance, Coherence and Effectiveness* (2017) Study for the LIBE Committee.
European Parliament Research Service, 'The fight against terrorism' PE 621.817 May 2018.
European Union Agency for Fundamental Rights, *Directive (EU) 2017/541 on combatting terrorism: Impact on fundamental rights and freedoms*, 2021.

BELGIUM

STATUTES

Gecoördineerde Grondwet 17 februari 1994, *BS* 17 februari 1994, 4054.
Herziening Art. 12 Grondwet, 24 oktober 2017, *BS* 29 november 2017, 104076
Wetboek van Strafvordering 17 november 1808, *BS* 27 november 1808.
Strafwetboek 8 juni 1867, *BS* 9 juni 1867, 3133.
Wet 4 oktober 1867 op de verzachtende omstandigheden, *BS* 15 oktober 1867, 5505.
Wet 17 april 1887 houdende de voorafgaande titel van het wetboek van strafvordering, *BS* 25 april 1887, 1265.
Wet 24 februari 1921 betreffende het verhandelen van gifstoffen, slaapmiddelen en verdovende middelen, psychotrope stoffen, ontsmettingsstoffen en antiseptica

en van de stoffen die kunnen gebruikt worden voor de illegale vervaardiging van verdovende middelen en psychotrope stoffen, *BS* 6 maart 1921, 1834.

Wet 5 juni 1928 houdende herziening van het Tucht- en Strafwetboek voor de koopvaardij en de zeevisserij.

Wet 28 mei 1956 betreffende ontplofbare en voor de deflagratie vatbare stoffen en mengsels en de daarmede geladen tuigen, *BS* 9 juni 1956, 3990.

Gerechtelijk Wetboek 10 oktober 1967, *BS* 31 oktober 1967, 11360.

Wet 29 juni 1964 betreffende de opschorting, het uitstel en de probatie, *BS* 17 juli 1964, 7812 (Probatiewet).

Wet 7 juni 1969 tot vaststelling van de tijd gedurende welke geen opsporing ten huize, huiszoeking of vrijheidsbeneming mag worden verricht, *BS* 28 juni 1969, 6470 (Huiszoekingswet).

Wet houdende goedkeuring van het Verdrag tot verbod van de ontwikkeling, de productie en de aanleg van voorraden van bacteriologische (biologische) en toxinewapens en inzake de vernietiging van deze wapens, opgemaakt te Londen, Moskou en Washington op 10 april 1972.

Wet 10 juli 1978 houdende goedkeuring van het Verdrag tot verbod van de ontwikkeling, de produktie en de aanleg van voorraden van bacteriologische (biologische) en toxinewapens en inzake de vernietiging van deze wapens, opgemaakt te Londen, Moskou en Washington op 10 april 1972, *BS* 6 juli 1979.

Wet 1 augustus 1979 betreffende diensten bij een vreemde leger- of troepenmacht die zich op het grondgebied van een vreemde Staat bevindt, *BS* 24 augustus 1979, 9272.

Wetboek van de Belgische nationaliteit 28 juni 1984, *BS* 12 juli 1984, 10100.

Wet 15 juli 1985 betreffende het gebruik bij dieren van stoffen met hormonale, anti-hormonale, beta-adrenergische of produktie-stimulerende werking, *BS* 4 september 1985, 12669.

Wet 20 juli 1990 betreffende de voorlopige hechtenis, *BS* 14 augustus 1990, 15779.

Wet op de vervaardiging van, de handel in en het dragen van wapens en op de handel in munitie, gewijzigd bij de wetten van 30 januari en 5 augustus 1991, 9 maart 1995, 24 juni 1996, 18 juli 1997, 10 januari 1999 en 30 maart 2000'.

Wet 21 maart 1991 betreffende de hervorming van sommige economische overheidsbedrijven, *BS* 27 maart 1991, 6155.

Wet 5 augustus 1992 op het politieambt, *BS* 22 december 1992, 27124.

Wet 10 januari 1999 betreffende de criminele organisaties, *BS* 26 februari 1999, 5812.

Wet 19 december 2003 betreffende terroristische misdrijven, *BS* 29 december 2003, 61689.

Basiswet 12 januari 2005 betreffende het gevangeniswezen en de rechtspositie van de gedetineerden, *BS* 1 februari 2005, 2815.

Wet 10 augustus 2005 tot wijziging van diverse bepalingen met het oog op de versterking van de strijd tegen mensenhandel en mensensmokkel en tegen praktijken van huisjesmelkers, *BS* 2 september 2005, 38454.

Wet 17 mei 2006 betreffende de externe rechtspositie van de veroordeelden tot een vrijheidsstraf en de aan het slachtoffer toegekende rechten in het raam van de strafuitvoeringsmodaliteiten, *BS* 15 juni 2006, 30455.

Wet 8 juni 2006 houdende regeling van economische en individuele activiteiten met wapens, *BS* 9 juni 2006, 29840.

Wet 25 april 2007 houdende diverse bepalingen (IV), *BS* 8 mei 2007, 25103.

Wet 26 april 2007 betreffende de terbeschikkingstelling van de strafuitvoeringsrechtbank, *BS* 13 juli 2007, 38299.

Wet 30 december 2009 betreffende de strijd tegen piraterij op zee, *BS* 14 januari 2010, 1485.

Wet 18 februari 2013 tot wijziging van boek II, titel Iter van het Strafwetboek, *BS* 4 maart 2013, 13233.

Wet 7 februari 2014 tot wijziging van de wet van 24 februari 1921 betreffende het verhandelen van gifstoffen, slaapmiddelen en verdovende middelen, psychotrope stoffen, ontsmettingsstoffen en antiseptica en van de stoffen die kunnen gebruikt worden voor de illegale vervaardiging van verdovende middelen en psychotrope stoffen, *BS* 6 maart 1921, 1834.

Wet 20 juli 2015 tot versterking van de strijd tegen het terrorisme, *BS* 5 augustus 2015, 49326.

Wet 5 februari 2016 tot wijziging van het strafrecht en de strafvordering en houdende diverse bepalingen inzake justitie, *BS* 19 februari 2016, 13130 (Potpourri II).

Wet 3 augustus 2016 houdende diverse bepalingen ter bestrijding van terrorisme (III), *BS* 11 augustus 2016, 50973.

Wet 14 december 2016 tot wijziging van het Strafwetboek wat betreft de bestraffing van terrorisme, *BS* 22 december 2016, 88017.

Programmawet 25 december 2016, *BS* 29 december 2016, 90879.

Wet 17 mei 2017 tot wijziging van het Wetboek van strafvordering om de strijd tegen het terrorisme te bevorderen, *BS* 3 juli 2017, 69494.

Wet 31 oktober 2017 tot wijziging van de wet van 20 juli 1990 betreffende de voorlopige hechtenis, de wet van 7 juni 1969 tot vaststelling van de tijd gedurende welke geen opsporing ten huize, huiszoeking of aanhouding mag worden verricht, de wet van 5 augustus 1992 op het politieambt en de wet van 19 december 2003 betreffende het Europees aanhoudingsbevel, *BS* 29 november 2017, 104136.

Wet 21 december 2017, tot wijziging van diverse bepalingen met het oog op de invoering van een beveiligingsperiode en tot wijziging van de wet van 20 juli 1990 betreffende de voorlopige hechtenis voor wat de onmiddellijke aanhouding betreft, *BS* 11 januari 2018, 1185.

Wet 22 juli 2018 tot wijziging van het Wetboek van strafvordering betreffende toezeggingen in het kader van de strafvordering, de strafuitvoering of de hechtenis wegens het afleggen van een verklaring in het kader van de strijd tegen de georganiseerde criminaliteit en het terrorisme, *BS* 7 augustus 2018, 62054.

Wet 5 mei 2019 houdende diverse bepalingen in strafzaken en inzake erediensten, en tot wijziging van de wet van 28 mei 2002 betreffende de euthanasie en van het Sociaal Strafwetboek (1), *BS* 24 mei 2019, 50023.

Wet 21 maart 2022 houdende wijzigingen aan het Strafwetboek met betrekking tot het seksueel strafrecht, *BS* 30 maart 2022, 25785.

Wet 31 juli 2023 om justitie menselijker, sneller en straffer te maken IV, *BS* 9 augustus 2023, 66557.

Wet 22 februari 2024 tot invoering van boek I van het Strafwetboek (1), *BS* 29 februari 2024, 40520.

Wet 22 februari 2024 tot invoering van boek II van het Strafwetboek (1), *BS* 29 februari 2024, 40548.

KB 28 december 2006 inzake specifieke beperkende maatregelen tegen bepaalde personen en entiteiten met het oog op de strijd tegen de financiering van het terrorisme, *BS* 17 januari 2007, 1898.

PARLIAMENTARY AND OTHER DOCUMENTS

Verslag namens de commissie voor de Justitie 5 juni 1990 bij ontwerp van wet betreffende de voorlopige hechtenis, *Parl.St.* Senaat 1988–1989, 658–2.

Verslag namens de commissie voor de Justitie 20 juni 1990 bij het ontwerp van wet tot wijziging van de artikelen 42, 43 en 505 van het Strafwetboek en tot invoeging van een artikel 43*bis* in hetzelfde Wetboek, *Gedr.St.* Senaat 1989–90, no. 890/2.

Senator Lallemand, *Hand.* Senaat 3 juli 1990, 2423.

MvT wetsontwerp 12 maart 1997 betreffende criminele organisaties, 96/97 no. 49–954/1.

Verslag namens de commissie voor de Justitie 29 mei 1997 bij wetsontwerp van 12 maart 1997 betreffende criminele organisaties, 96/97 no. 49–954/6.

Advies van de Raad van State bij wetsontwerp van 12 maart 1997 betreffende criminele organisaties, 96/97 no. 49–954/1, 13.

Verslag 24 maart 1998 namens de commissie voor de Justitie bij wetsontwerp betreffende criminele organisaties, *Parl.St.* Senaat 1997–1998, no. 1–662/4.

Advies 28.026/2 van de Raad van State bij wetsontwerp van 12 maart 1997 betreffende criminele organisaties, 96/97 no. 49–954/24.

Advies 34.379/3 van de Raad van State van 14 november 2002, *Parl.St.* Kamer 2002–2003, no. 50–2176/1, 11 en no. 50–2124/12, 7.

MvT wetsontwerp 6 oktober 2003 betreffende terroristische misdrijven, *Parl.St.* Kamer 2003, no. 51–0258/001, 4.

Advies 34.362/4 van de Raad van State bij wetsontwerp van 6 oktober 2003 betreffende terroristische misdrijven, *Parl.St.* Kamer 2003, no. 51–0258/001, 22.

Amendementen 7 oktober 2003 bij het wetsontwerp betreffende terroristische misdrijven van 21 oktober 2003, *Parl.St.* Kamer 2003, no. 51–0258/003.

Verslag namens de commissie voor de Justitie 7 november 2003 bij wetsontwerp van 6 oktober 2003 betreffende terroristische misdrijven, *Parl.St.* Kamer 2003, no. 51–0258/004.

Verslag namens de commissie voor de Justitie 3 december 2003 bij wetsontwerp betreffende terroristische misdrijven *Parl.St.* Senaat 2003–04, no. 3–332/3.

Amendementen 9 maart 2005 bij wetsontwerp tot wijziging van diverse bepalingen met het oog op de versterking van de strijd tegen mensenhandel en mensensmokkel, *Parl.St.* Kamer 2004–2005, no. 51–1560/004.

Sébastien Van Drooghenbroeck, 'Note relative à l'application des principes de proportionnalité et subsidiarité en matière pénale dans de droit de la Convention européenne des droits de l'Homme', Annex 2.7 to the Report on behalf of the Committee on Justice on the Bill on the Code of Criminal Procedure, *Parl.St.* Senaat 2005–06, no. 3–450/20, 1398.

Verslag namens de commissie voor de justitie 13 maart 2007 bij wetsontwerp betreffende de terbeschikkingstelling van de strafuitvoeringsrechtbank, *Parl.St.* Senaat 2006-2007, no. 3-2054/4.

Advies 52.522/AV van de Raad van State 19 februari 2013 bij wetsvoorstel tot wijziging van de wet 29 juli 1934 waarbij de private milities verboden worden, wat het verbod van ondemocratische groeperingen betreft, *Parl.St.* Kamer 2012-2013, no. 53-0809/008.

Verslag namens de commissie voor de Justitie 8 juni 2011 bij het wetsontwerp tot wijziging van de wet van 20 juli 1990 betreffende de voorlopige hechtenis en van het Wetboek van Strafvordering, om aan elkeen die wordt verhoord en aan elkeen die van zijn vrijheid wordt beroofd rechten te verlenen, waaronder het recht om een advocaat te raadplegen en door hem te worden bijgestaan, *Parl.St.* Kamer 2010-11, no. 53-1279/005.

MvT wetsontwerp 13 november 2012 tot wijziging van Titel I*ter* van het Strafwetboek, *Parl.St.* Kamer 2012-2013, no. 53-2502/001.

Advies 51.806/3 van de Raad van State 18 September 2012 bij wetsontwerp van 13 november 2012 tot wijziging van Titel 1*ter* van het Strafwetboek, *Parl.St.* Kamer 2012-2013, no. 53-2502/001, 22.

MvT wetsontwerp 13 november 2012 tot wijziging van Titel 1*ter* van het Strafwetboek, *Parl.St.* Kamer 2012-2013, no. 53-2502/001, 4.

Gedr. St. Kamer, DOC 25-2502/001, 7 and DOC 54-1198/001.

MvT wetsontwerp 22 juni 2015 tot versterking van de strijd tegen terrorisme, *Parl.St.* Kamer 2014-15, no. 54-1198/001.

Advies 57.127/AV van de Raad van State 24 maart 2015 bij wetsontwerp van 22 juni 2015 tot versterking van de strijd tegen het terrorisme, *Parl.St.* Kamer 2014-15, no. 54-1198/001, 13.

MvT wetsontwerp 23 oktober 2015 houdende wijzigingen van het strafrecht en de strafvordering en houdende diverse bepalingen inzake justitie, *Parl.St.* Kamer 2015-16, no. 54-1418/001, 4.

Lijst van contra-terrorismemaatregelen, plenaire sessie Kamer van Volksvertegenwoordigers, 19 november 2015.

Voorstel tot herziening van Artikel 12 van de Grondwet 16 december 2015 teneinde voor bepaalde misdrijven een aanhoudingstermijn van tweeënzeventig uren mogelijk te maken, *Parl.St.* Kamer 2015-16, no. 54-1529/001.

Wetsvoorstel 13 januari 2016 tot wijziging van het Strafwetboek wat betreft de bestraffing van terrorisme, *Parl.St.* Kamer 2015-2016, no. 54-1579/001.

Samenvatting van wetsvoorstel 13 januari 2016 tot wijziging van het Strafwetboek wat betreft de bestraffing van terrorisme, *Parl.St.* Kamer 2015-2016, no. 54-1579/001, 1.

Toelichting bij wetsvoorstel 13 januari 2016 tot wijziging van het Strafwetboek wat betreft de bestraffing van terrorisme, *Parl.St.* Kamer 2015-1026, no. 54-1579/001, 3.

Amendementen 7 juli 2016 bij wetsvoorstel van 13 januari 2016 tot wijziging van het Strafwetboek wat betreft de bestraffing van terrorisme, *Parl.St.* Kamer 2015-2016, no. 54-1579/005.

Advies 59.789/3 van de Raad van State 19 juli 2016 bij wetsvoorstel van 13 januari 2016 tot wijziging van het Strafwetboek wat betreft de bestraffing van terrorisme, *Parl.St.* Kamer 2015-2016, no. 54-1579/006.

Amendementen 6 oktober 2016 bij wetsvoorstel tot wijziging van het Strafwetboek wat betreft de bestraffing van terrorisme, *Parl.St.* Kamer 2015–2016, no. 54–1579/007.

Verslag van de eerste lezing namens de tijdelijke commissie 'terrorismebestrijding' 20 oktober 2016 bij wetsvoorstel tot wijziging van het Strafwetboek wat betreft de bestraffing van terrorisme, *Parl.St* Kamer 2015–2016, no. 54–1579/008.

Voorstel tot herziening van Art. 12, derde lid, van de Gw. 4 april 2016, *Parl.St.* Kamer 2015–16, no. 54–1741/001.

Derde tussentijds verslag over het onderdeel 'veiligheidsarchitectuur' 15 juni 2017 van de parlementaire onderzoekscommissie belast met het onderzoek naar de omstandigheden die hebben geleid tot de terroristische aanslagen van 22 maart 2016 in de luchthaven Brussel-Nationaal en in het metrostation Maalbeek te Brussel, met inbegrip van de evolutie en de aanpak van de strijd tegen het radicalisme en de terroristische dreiging, *Parl.St.* Kamer 2016–2017, no. 54–1752/008.

MvT wetsontwerp 5 juli 2016 houdende diverse bepalingen ter bestrijding van terrorisme (III), *Parl.St.* Kamer 2015–16, no. 54–1951/001, 4.

Advies 58.946/3 van de Raad van State (I) 9 maart 2016 bij wetsontwerp houdende diverse bepalingen ter bestrijding van terrorisme (III), *Parl.St.* Kamer 2015–2016, no. 54–1951/001, 16.

Advies 59.147/3 van de Raad van State (II) 22 april 2016 bij wetsontwerp houdende diverse bepalingen ter bestrijding van terrorisme (III), *Parl.St.* Kamer 2015–2016, no. 54–1951/001, 31.

Voorstel tot herziening van Art. 12, derde lid, van de Gw. 21 september 2016, *Parl.St.* Kamer 2015–16, no. 54–2047/001.

Wetsvoorstel 22 september 2016 tot wijziging van het Wetboek van Strafvordering om de strijd tegen het terrorisme te bevorderen, *Parl.St.* Kamer 2015–16, no. 54–2050/001.

Voorstel tot herziening van artikel 12 van de Grondwet 28 september 2016, *Parl.St.* Kamer 2015–16, no. 54–2056/001

Wetsvoorstel 28 september 2016 tot wijziging van de wet van 20 juli 1990 betreffende de voorlopige hechtenis, *Parl.St.* Kamer 2015-16, no. 54–2057/001.

Toelichting bij voorstel 13 juli 2017 tot herziening van artikel 12 van de Grondwet, *Parl. St. Kamer* 2016–17, no. 54–2611/001.

Toelichting bij wetsvoorstel 13 juli 2017 tot wijziging van de wet van 20 juli 1990 betreffende de voorlopige hechtenis wat de termijn betreft, *Parl.St. Kamer* 2016–17, no. 54 2612/001, 3.

Wetsvoorstel 18 januari 2018 tot wijziging van het Strafwetboek teneinde zelfinstructie in het kader van terrorisme strafbaar te stellen, *Parl.St.* Kamer 2017–2018, no. 54–2900/001.

MvT wetsontwerp 19 februari 2018 tot wijziging van het Wetboek van Strafvordering met het oog op het invoeren van de bijzondere opsporingsmethode burgerinfiltratie, *Parl.St.* Kamer 2017–18, no. 54–2940/001.

MvT wetsontwerp 3 april 2018 tot wijziging van het Wetboek van strafvordering met het oog op het invoeren van een wettelijke regeling inzake spijtoptanten, *Parl.St.* Kamer 2017–18, no. 54–3016/001.

Wetsvoorstel 6 februari 2019 houdende diverse bepalingen in strafzaken en inzake erediensten, *Parl.St.* Kamer 2018–2019, no. 54–3515/001.

Toelichting bij wetsvoorstel 6 februari 2019 houdende diverse bepalingen in strafzaken en inzake erediensten, *Parl.St.* Kamer 2018–2019, no. 54–3515/001, 3.

Toelichting bij wetsvoorstel 13 maart 2019 tot invoering van een nieuw Strafwetboek – Boek 1 en Boek 2, *Parl.St.* Kamer 2018–2019, no. 54–3651/001.

Amendementen 5 november 2019 bij tot wijziging van de wet van 20 juli 1990 betreffende de voorlopige hechtenis aangaande de onmiddellijke aanhouding, *Parl.St.* Kamer 2019, 55–0489/005.

Wetsvoorstel 6 augustus 2019 tot wijziging van de artikelen 34*ter* en 34*quater* van het Strafwetboek en van artikel 95/7 van de wet van 17 mei 2006 betreffende de externe rechtspositie van de veroordeelden tot een vrijheidsstraf en de aan het slachtoffer toegekende rechten in het raam van de strafuitvoeringsmodaliteiten, wat de terbeschikkingstelling van de strafuitvoeringsrechtbank betreft, *Parl.St.* Kamer 2019, no. 55–0212/001.

Wetsvoorstel 1 oktober 2019 tot wijziging van de wet van 20 juli 1990 betreffende de voorlopige hechtenis aangaande de onmiddellijke aanhouding, *Parl.St.* Kamer 2019, no. 55–0489/001.

Wetsvoorstel 19 november 2019 tot wijziging van het Strafwetboek betreffende de terbeschikkingstelling van de strafuitvoeringsrechtbank, *Parl.St.* Kamer 2019-2020, no. 55–0768/001.

Wetsvoorstel 21 november 2019 tot wijziging van het Strafwetboek met het oog op de uitbreiding van de lijst met misdrijven die in aanmerking komen voor de facultatieve terbeschikkingstelling van de strafuitvoeringsrechtbank tot alle terrorismemisdrijven, *Parl.St.* Kamer 2019–2020, no. 55–0777/001.

Toelichting bij wetsvoorstel 21 november 2019 tot wijziging van het Strafwetboek met het oog op de uitbreiding van de lijst met misdrijven die in aanmerking komen voor de facultatieve terbeschikkingstelling van de strafuitvoeringsrechtbank tot alle terrorismemisdrijven, *Parl.St.* Kamer 2019–2020, no. 55–0777/001, 3.

Wetsvoorstel 23 januari 2020 tot wijziging van het Strafwetboek wat de strafmaat voor misdrijven door terroristische groepen betreft, *Parl.St.* Kamer 2019–20, no. 55–0962/001.

Wetsvoorstel 28 januari 2020 tot wijziging van het Strafwetboek, teneinde de terbeschikkingstelling van de strafuitvoeringsrechtbank uit te breiden tot alle terroristische misdrijven, *Parl.St.* Kamer 2019–2020, no. 55–0969/001.

Wetsvoorstel 12 februari 2020 tot instelling van een nieuw Strafwetboek (boek 1 en 2) Deel II, *Parl.St.* Kamer 2019–2020, no. 55–1011/001.

Voorstel tot herziening van artikel 150 van de Grondwet 27 mei 2020 teneinde de juryrechtspraak voor terroristische misdaden af te schaffen, *Parl.St.* Kamer 2019–2020, no. 55–1287/001 and 003.

Wetsvoorstel 7 januari 2021 betreffende de oplegging van een gevangenisstraf in combinatie met verplichte behandeling en tot invoering van de mogelijkheid van tijdelijke opvang in de psychiatrische afdeling van een gevangenis voor personen die niet volledig ontoerekeningsvatbaar zijn, maar wel een gevaar kunnen zijn voor de maatschappij, *Parl.St.* Kamer 2020–2021, no. 55–1723/001.

Wetsvoorstel 11 maart 2021 tot wijziging van het Strafwetboek, teneinde de verheerlijking van terrorisme in het openbaar en op het internet te bestraffen, *Parl.St.* Kamer 2020–2021, no. 55–1847/001.

Wetsvoorstel 14 maart 2022 tot wijziging van het Strafwetboek wat de terbeschikkingstelling van de strafuitvoeringsrechtbank betreft, *Parl.St.* Kamer 2021–2022, no. 55-2571/001.

Wetsontwerp (I) 23 mei 2023 tot invoering van Boek I van het Strafwetboek, *Parl.St.* Kamer 2022–2023, no. 55-3374/001.

MvT wetsontwerp (I) 23 mei 2023 tot invoering van Boek I van het Strafwetboek, *Parl.St.* Kamer 2022–2023, no. 55-3374/001.

Wetsontwerp (II) tot invoering van een beveiligingsmaatregel ter bescherming van de maatschappij, *Parl.St.* Kamer no. 55-3374/001 and 55-3375/001.

MvT Wetsontwerp 24 juli 2023 tot invoering van Boek II van het Strafwetboek, *Parl.St.* Kamer 2022–2023, no. 55-3501/001.

Wetsontwerp 24 juli 2023 tot invoering van Boek II van het Strafwetboek, *Parl.St.* Kamer 2022–2023, no. 55-3518/001.

Amendementen bij Wetsontwerp 14 december 2023 om Justitie menselijker, sneller en straffer te maken III, *Parl.St.* Kamer 2023–2024, no. 55-3322/014.

Wetsontwerp 5 januari 2024 om Justitie menselijker, sneller en straffer te maken III, *Parl. St.* Kamer 2023–2024, no. 55-3322/017.

Ministeriële omzendbrief no. 1813 van 18 november 2011 betreffende de terbeschikkingstelling van de strafuitvoeringsrechtbank.

COL7/2013 – De wet 27 december 2012 houdende diverse bepalingen betreffende Justitie, inzonderheid: TITEL VIII Wijziging van de wet van 29 juni 1964 betreffende de opschorting, het uitstel en de probatie, 13 maart 2013.

COL17/2014 – De terbeschikkingstelling van de strafuitvoeringsrechtbank, 17 juli 2014.

Collectieve brief DG EPI no. 138 van 29 april 2016 over de probatie als autonome straf.

COL 17/2016 – Elektronisch toezicht als autonome straf, updated version 18 oktober 2018.

COL 18/2016 – Invoering van de probatie als autonome straf, 23 juni 2016.

UK

STATUTES

Accessories and Abettors Act 1861.

Offences against the Person Act 1861 (OAPA 1861).

Explosive Substances Act 1883.

Homicide Act 1957.

Murder (Abolition of Death Penalty) Act 1965.

Criminal Appeal Act 1968.

Biological Weapons Act 1974.

Bail Act 1976 (BA 1976).

Criminal Law Act 1977.

Internationally Protected Persons Act 1978.

Magistrates' Courts Act 1980.

Criminal Attempts Act 1981.

Senior Courts Act 1981.

Taking of Hostages Act 1982.
Criminal Justice Act 1982.
Aviation Security Act 1982 (ASA 1982).
Civil Aviation Act 1982 (CAA 1982).
Nuclear Material (Offences) Act 1983.
Police and Criminal Evidence Act 1984 (PACE 1984).
Aircraft and Maritime Security Act 1990 (AMSA 1990).
Chemical Weapons Act 1996.
Crime and Disorder Act 1998.
Human Rights Act 1998 (HRA 1998).
Northern Ireland Act 1998.
Scotland Act 1998.
Regulation of Investigatory Powers Act 2000.
Terrorism Act 2000 (TA 2000).
Anti-Terrorism, Crime and Security Act 2001 (ACTSA 2001).
Criminal Justice Act 2003.
Prevention of Terrorism Act 2005 (PTA 2005).
Terrorism Act 2006 (TA 2006).
Serious Crime Act 2007.
Counter-Terrorism Act 2008 (CTA 2008).
Counter-Terrorism Act 2008 (Commencement No.6) Order 2012.
Terrorism Prevention and Investigation Measures Act 2011 (TPIMA 2011).
Counter-Terrorism and Security Act 2015 (CTSA 2015).
Criminal Justice and Courts Act 2015 (CJCA 2015).
Counter-Terrorism and Border Security Act 2019 (CTBSA 2019).
Sentencing Act 2020 (SA 2020).
Counter-Terrorism and Sentencing Act 2021 (CTSA 2021).
Terrorism Prevention and Investigation Measures Act 2011 (Continuation) Order 2021.
Police, Crime, Sentencing and Courts Act 2022.
National Security Act 2023.

PARLIAMENTARY AND OTHER DOCUMENTS

Lord Lloyd of Berwick, *Inquiry into legislation against terrorism* (Cm 3420, 1996).

Secretary of State for the Home Department and Secretary of State for Northern Ireland, *Legislation Against Terrorism: A consultation paper* (Cm 4178, 1998).

Lord MacDonald, Review Of Counter-Terrorism And Security Powers (Cm 8003, 2011).

Secretary of State for the Home Department, *Review of Counter-Terrorism and Security Powers* (Cm 8004, 2011).

Draft Detention of Terrorist Suspects (Temporary Extension) Bills (Cm 8018, 2011).

Secretary of State for the Home Department, *The Government Response to the Report by Lord Carlile of Berriew Q.C. Sixth Report of the Independent Reviewer Pursuant to Section 14(3) of the Prevention of Terrorism Act 2005* (Cm 8095, 2011).

Commentary on Clauses 29, *Draft Enhanced Terrorism Prevention and Investigation Measures Bill* (Cm 8166, 2011) (ETPIM Bill).

The Government Reply To The Sixteenth Report From The Joint Committee On Human Rights (Cm 8167, 2011).

Hansard (House of Commons) Vol.187, 6 March 1991.

Hansard (House of Lords) Vol.704, 21 October 2008, col.1064.

Lord Lloyd of Berwick, Hansard (House of Lords), 25 October 2010, col. 1037.

House of Commons 'Counter-terrorism Review' 2010–2012 (Hansard) 26 January 2011, 522–106: 306–326.

Home Office, *Terrorism Prevention and Investigation Measures Act 2011: Explanatory Notes* (2011).

Home Office, *Terrorism Prevention and Investigation Measures Bill: ECHR Memorandum* (2011).

Home Office, *Counter-Terrorism And Border Security Bill: Explanatory Notes* (Bill 219–EN, 2018).

Home Office, *Counter-Terrorism And Border Security Bill: ECHR Memorandum* (2018).

Home Office, *Counter-Terrorism And Sentencing Bill: Explanatory Notes* (Bill 129–EN, 2020).

Home Office, *Counter-Terrorism And Sentencing Bill: Explanatory Notes on Lords Amendments* (Bill 274–EN, 2020).

HM Government, *Counter-terrorism Disruptive Powers Report 2021* (CP 779, 2023).

JCHR, *Counter–Terrorism Policy and Human Rights: Terrorism Bill and related matters* (HL paper 75, HC paper 561, 2005).

JCHR, *Counter-Terrorism Policy and Human Rights (Twelfth Report): Draft Prevention of Terrorism Act 2005 (Continuance in force of sections 1 to 9) Order 2006* (HL paper 122, HC paper 915, 2006).

JCHR, *Counter-Terrorism Policy and Human Rights (Sixteenth Report): Annual Renewal of Control Orders Legislation* (HL paper 64, HC paper 395, 2010).

JCHR, *Counter-Terrorism Policy and Human Rights (Seventeenth Report): Bringing Human Rights Back* (HL paper 23, HC paper 111, 2010).

JCHR, *Renewal of Control Orders Legislation 2011 (Eighth Report of Session 2010–11)* (HL paper 106, HC paper 838, 2011).

Joint Committee on the Draft Detention of Terrorist Suspects (Temporary Extension) Bills, *Draft Detention of Terrorist Suspects (Temporary Extension) Bills: Report* (HL paper 161, HC paper 893, 2011).

JCHR, *Legislative Scrutiny: Terrorism Prevention and Investigation Measures Bill: Sixteenth Report of Session 2010–12* (HL paper 180, HC paper 1432, 2011), 13–15

Joint Committee on the Draft Enhanced Terrorism Prevention and Investigation Measures Bill, *Draft Enhanced Terrorism Prevention and Investigation Measures Bill: Oral Evidence* (24 October 2012).

Report of the Public Inquiry into the Attack on Manchester Arena on 22nd May 2017 (HC paper 1137) Presented to Parliament pursuant to section 26 of the Inquiries Act 2005.

House of Lords Select committee on the Constitution, *Counter-Terrorism and Sentencing Bill* (HL paper 134) 16th Report of Session 2019–21.

Joint Committee on Consolidation Bills, *Drafter's notes on the Sentencing Bill* (21 July 2020).

Liberty's Report Stage Briefing on the Terrorism Prevention and Investigation Measures Bill in the House of Commons (August 2011).

Article 19, *House of Commons Public Bill Committee – Counter-Terrorism and Border Security Bill 2018: ARTICLE 19 written evidence* (2018).

Clive Walker, *Written evidence (CBS001) in response to the Joint Committee for Human Rights' call for evidence in connection with the Counter Terrorism & Border Security Bill 2017–19* (2018).

Max Hill and Clive Walker, *Counter Terrorism And Border Security Bill: Submission In Relation To Clause 3* (2018) 2(d).

Liberty's Briefing on the Counter-Terrorism and Border Security Bill for Second Reading in the House of Lords (October 2018).

The counter-terrorism and sentencing bill changes to TPIM standard of proof and time limit, January 2021.

CASE LAW

EUROPEAN COURT OF HUMAN RIGHTS

A and others v. United Kingdom App no (ECtHR Grand Chamber 19 February 2009).
A. and others v. United Kingdom App no 3455/05 (ECtHR Grand Chamber 19 February 2009).
A.D. v. Turkey App no 29986/96 (ECtHR 22 December 2005).
A.K. v. Austria App no 20832/92 (European Commission of Human Rights 1 December 1993).
Abdolkhani and Karimnia v. Turkey App no 30471/08 (ECtHR 22 September 2009).
Aboya Boa Jean v. Malta App no 62676/16 (ECtHR 2 April 2019).
Aerts v. Belgium App no 61/1997/845/1051 (ECtHR 30 July 1998).
Aftanache v. Romania App no 999/19 (ECtHR 26 May 2020).
Aksoy v. Turkey App no 21987/93 (ECtHR 18 December 1996).
Al Husin v. Bosnia and Herzegovina (no. 2) App no 10112/16 (ECtHR 25 June 2019).
Al-Dulimi and Montana Management Inc v. Switzerland App no (ECtHR Grand Chamber 21 June 2016).
Aleksandr Aleksandrov v. Russia App no 14431/06 (ECtHR 27 March 2018).
Ali Osman Özmen v. Turkey App no 42969/04 (ECtHR 5 October 2016).
Al-Jedda v. United Kingdom App no (ECtHR Grand Chamber 7 July 2011).
Altınok v. Turkey App no 31610/08 (ECtHR 29 November 2011).
AM v. France App no 56324/13 (ECtHR 12 July 2016).
Ambruszkiewicz v. Poland App no 38797/03 (ECtHR 4 May 2006).
Amuur v. France App no 19776/92 (ECtHR 25 June 1996).
Aquilina v. Malta App no 25642/94 (ECtHR Grand Chamber 29 April 1999).
Ashingdane v. United Kingdom App no 8225/78 (ECtHR 28 May 1985).
Assenov and others v. Bulgaria App no 90/1997/874/1086 (ECtHR 28 October 1998).
Austin and others v. United Kingdom App nos 39692/09, 40713/09 and 41008/09 (ECtHR Grand Chamber 15 March 2012).
Azimov v. Russia App no 67474/11 (ECtHR 18 April 2013).
B. v. Austria App no 8/1989/168/224 (ECtHR 23 February 1990).
Baranowski v. Poland App no 28358/95 (ECtHR 28 March 2000).
Bartik v. Russia App no 55565/00 (ECtHR 21 December 2006).
Baş v. Turkey App no 66448/17 (ECtHR 3 March 2020).
Battista v. Italy App no 43978/09 (ECtHR 2 December 2014).
Baumann v. France App no 33592/96 (ECtHR 22 May 2001).
Benham v. United Kingdom App no 19380/92 (ECtHR 10 June 1996).
Benjamin and Wilson v. United Kingdom App no 28212/95 (ECtHR 26 September 2002).
Bergmann v. Germany App no 23279/14 (ECtHR 7 January 2016).

Berkovich and others v. Russia App nos 5871/07 and 9 others (ECtHR 27 March 2018).
Bezicheri v. Italy App no 8/1988/152/206 (ECtHR 26 September 1989).
Bolat v. Russia App no 14139/03 (ECtHR 5 October 2006).
Bouamar v. Belgium App no 9106/80 (ECtHR 29 February 1988).
Bozano v. France App no 9990/82 (EctHR 18 December 1986).
Brand v. Netherlands App no 49902/99 (ECtHR 11 May 2004).
Brannigan and McBride v. United Kingdom App nos 14553/89 and 14554/89 (ECtHR 25 May 1993).
Brincat v. Italy App no 13867/88 (ECtHR 26 November 1992).
Brogan and others v. United Kingdom App nos 11209/84, 11234/84, 11266/84 and 11386/85 (ECtHR Plenary 29 November 1988).
Buzadji v. Republic of Moldova App no 23755/07 (ECtHR Grand Chamber 5 July 2016).
Cantoni v. France App no 17862/91 (ECtHR 11 November 1996).
Çatal v. Turkey App no 26808/08 (ECtHR 17 April 2012).
Chahal v. United Kingdom App no 22414/93 (ECtHR Grand Chamber 15 November 1996).
Ciulla v. Italy App no 11152/84 (ECtHR Plenary 22 February 1989).
Claes v. Belgium App no 43418/09 (ECtHR 10 January 2013).
Clooth v. Belgium App no 49/1990/240/311 (ECtHR 27 November 1991).
Čonka v. Belgium App no 51564/99 (ECtHR 5 February 2002).
Creangă v. Romania App no 29226/03 (ECtHR Grand Chamber 23 February 2012).
D.D. v. Lithuania App no 13469/06 (ECtHR 14 February 2012).
D.W. v. United Kingdom App no 21387/93 (European Commission of Human Rights 21 October 1996).
Dacosta Silva v. Spain App no 69966/01 (ECtHR 2 November 2006).
Danov v. Bulgaria App no 56796/00 (ECtHR 26 October 2006).
De Jong, Baljet and Van den Brink v. Netherlands App nos 8805/79, 8806/79 and 9242/81 (ECtHR 22 May 1984).
De Schepper v. Belgium App no 27428/07 (ECtHR 13 October 2009).
De Tommaso v. Italy App no 43395/09 (ECtHR Grand Chamber 23 February 2017).
De Wilde, Ooms and Versyp v. Belgium App nos 2832/66, 2835/66 and 2899/66 (ECtHR 18 June 1971).
Del Rio Prada v. Spain App no 42750/09 (ECtHR Grand Chamber 21 October 2013).
Denis and Irvine v. Belgium App nos 62819/17 and 63921/17 (ECtHR Grand Chamber 1 June 2021).
Denizci and others v. Cyprus App nos 25316–25321/94 and 27207/95 (ECtHR 23 May 2001).
Dimo Dimov and others v. Bulgaria App no 30044/10 (ECtHR 7 July 2020).
Djavit An v. Turkey App no 20652/92 (ECtHR 20 February 2003).
Dufoort v. Belgium App no 43653/09 (ECtHR 10 January 2013).
E. v. Norway App no 11701/85 (ECtHR 29 August 1990).
Ekrem Can and others v. Turkey App no 10613/10 (ECtHR 5 September 2022).
Engel and others v. Netherlands App nos 5100/71, 5101/71, 5102/71, 5354/72 and 5370/72 (ECtHR 8 June 1976).
Enhorn v. Sweden App no 56529/00 (ECtHR 25 January 2005).
Epple v. Germany App no 77909/01 (ECtHR 24 March 2005).

Erdagöz v. Turkey App no 127/1996/945/746 (ECtHR 22 October 1997).
Eriksen v. Norway App no 17391/90 (ECtHR 27 May 1997).
Etute v. Luxembourg App no 18233/16 (ECtHR 30 January 2018).
Foka v. Turkey App no 28940/95 (ECtHR 24 June 2008).
Földes And Földesné Hajlik v. Hungary App no 41463/02 (ECtHR 31 October 2006).
Fox, Campbell and Hartley v. the UK App nos 12244/86, 12245/86 and 12383/86 (ECtHR 30 August 1990).
Frasik v. Poland App no 22933/02 (ECtHR 5 January 2010).
Garayev v. Azerbaijan App no 53688/08 (ECtHR 10 June 2010).
Garib v. the Netherlands App no 43494/09 (ECtHR Grand Chamber 6 November 2017).
Gatt v. Malta App no 28221/08 (ECtHR 27 July 2010).
Gavril Yosifov v. Bulgaria App no 74012/01 (ECtHR 6 November 2008).
Gillan and Quinton v. United Kingdom App no 4158/05 (ECtHR 12 January 2010).
Gillow v. United Kingdom App no 9063/80 (ECtHR 24 November 1986).
Giulia Manzoni v. Italy App no 19218/91 (ECtHR 1 July 1997).
Giuliani and Gaggio v. Italy App no 23458/02 (ECtHR Grand Chamber 24 March 2011).
Glien v. Germany App no 7345/12 (ECtHR 28 November 2013).
Gochev v. Bulgaria App no 34383/03 (ECtHR 26 November 2009).
Göthlin v. Sweden App no 8307/11 (ECtHR 16 October 2014).
Grosskopf v. Germany App no 24478/03 (ECtHR 21 October 2010).
Grubnyk v. Ukraine App no 58444/15 (ECtHR 17 December 2020).
Guliyev v. Azerbaijan App no 35584/02 (ECtHR Decision on admissibility 27 May 2005).
Gutsanovi v. Bulgaria App no 34529/10 (ECtHR 15 October 2012).
Guzzardi v. Italy App no 7367/76 (ECtHR Plenary 6 November 1980).
H.L. v. United Kingdom App no 45508/99 (ECtHR 5 October 2004).
H.M. v. Switzerland App no 39187/98 (ECtHR 26 February 2002).
H.W. v. Germany App no 17167/11 (ECtHR 19 September 2013).
Hilda Hafsteinsdóttir v. Iceland App no 40905/98, (ECtHR 8 June 2004).
Hood v. United Kingdom App no 27267/95 (ECtHR 18 February 1999).
Huber v. Switzerland App no 12794/87 (ECtHR Plenary 23 October 1990).
Hussain v. United Kingdom App no 21928/93 (ECtHR 21 February 1996).
Hutchison Reid v. United Kingdom App no 50272/99 (ECtHR 20 February 2003).
I.A. v. France App no 1/1998/904/1116 (ECtHR 23 September 1998).
I.I. v. Bulgaria App no 44082/98 (ECtHR 9 June 2005).
I.S. v. Switzerland App no 60202/15 (ECtHR 6 October 2020).
Idalov v. Russia App no 5826/03 (ECtHR Grand Chamber 22 May 2012).
Ilgar Mammadov v. Azerbaijan App no 15172/13 (ECtHR 22 May 2014).
Iliya Stefanov v. Bulgaria App no 65755/01 (ECtHR 22 May 2008).
Ilnseher v. Germany App nos 10211/12 and 27505/14 (ECtHR Grand Chamber 4 December 2018).
İpek and others v. Turkey App nos 17019/02 and 30070/02 (ECtHR 3 February 2009).
Ireland v. United Kingdom App no (ECtHR 18 January 1978).
Iskandarov v. Russia App no 17185/05 (ECtHR 23 September 2010).
Ivan Todorov v. Bulgaria App no 71545/11 (ECtHR 19 January 2017).
J.N. v. United Kingdom App no 37289/12 (ECtHR 19 May 2016).
J.R. and others v. Greece App no 22696/16 (ECtHR 25 January 2018).

Jablonski v. Poland App no 33492/96 (ECtHR 21 December 2000).
James, Wells and Lee v. United Kingdom App nos 25119/09, 57715/09 and 57877/09 (ECtHR 18 September 2012).
Järvinen v. Finland App no 30408/96 (European Commission of Human Rights 15 January 1998).
Ječius v. Lithuania App no 34578/97 (ECtHR 31 July 2000).
Jobe v. United Kingdom App no 48278/09 (ECtHR decision as to the admissibility 14 June 2011).
Johansen v. Norway App no 10600/83 (European Commission of Human Rights 14 October 1985).
K.-F. v. Germany App no 144/1996/765/962 (ECtHR 27 November 1997).
Kadem v. Malta App no 55263/00 (ECtHR 9 January 2003).
Kafkaris v. Cyprus App no 21906/04 (ECtHR Grand Chamber 12 February 2008).
Kakabadze and others v. Georgia App no 1484/07 (ECtHR 2 October 2012).
Kallweit v. Germany App no 17792/07 (ECtHR 13 January 2011).
Kampanis v. Greece App no 17977/91 (ECtHR 13 July 1995).
Kandzhov v. Bulgaria App no 68294/01 (ECtHR 6 November 2008).
Kemmache v. France (no 3) App no 17621/91 (ECtHR 24 November 1994).
Kerem Çiftçi v. Turkey App no 35205/09 (ECtHR 21 September 2021).
Kerimli v. Azerbaijan App no 3967/09 (ECtHR 16 July 2015).
Kerr v. United Kingdom App no 40451/98 (ECtHR Partial decision on the admissibility 7 December 1999).
Khamtokhu and Aksenchik v. Russia App nos 60367/08 and 961/11 (ECtHR Grand Chamber 24 January 2017).
Kharin v. Russia App no 37345/03 (ECtHR 3 February 2011).
Khayredinov v. Ukraine App no 38717/04 (ECtHR 14 October 2010).
Khlaifia and others v. Italy App no 16483/12 (ECtHR Grand Chamber 15 December 2016).
Khlyustov v. Russia App no 28975/05 (ECtHR 11 July 2013).
Klass and others v. Germany App no 5029/71 (ECtHR 6 September 1978).
Klinkenbuß v. Germany App no 53157/11 (ECtHR 25 February 2016).
Kokkinakis v. Greece App no 14307/88 (ECtHR 25 May 1993).
Korneykova v. Ukraine App no 39884/05 (ECtHR 19 January 2012).
Kováčik v. Slovakia App no 50903/06 (ECtHR 29 November 2011).
Krejčíř v. Czech Republic App no 39298/04 and 8723/05 (ECtHR 26 March 2009).
Kučera v. Slovakia App no 48666/99 (ECtHR 17 July 2007).
Kudrevičius and others v. Lithuania App no 37553/05 (ECtHR Grand Chamber 15 October 2015).
L.B. v. Belgium App no 22831/08 (ECtHR 2 October 2012).
L.C.B. v. United Kingdom App no 14/1997/798/1001 (ECtHR 9 June 1998).
Labita v. Italy App no 26772/95 (ECtHR Grand Chamber 6 April 2000).
Ladent v. Poland App no 11036/03 (ECtHR 18 March 2008).
Lavents v. Latvia App no 58442/00 (ECtHR 28 November 2002).
Lawless v. Ireland (no. 3) App no 332/57 (ECtHR 1 July 1961).
Le Compte, Van Leuven and De Meyere v. Belgium App nos 6878/75 and 7238/75 (ECtHR 23 June 1981).

Letellier v. France App no 12369/86 (ECtHR 26 June 1991).
LIU v. Russia App no 42086/05 (ECtHR 6 December 2007).
Lolova-Karadzhova v. Bulgaria App no 17835/07 (ECtHR 27 March 2012).
Louled Massoud v. Malta App no 24340/08 (ECtHR 27 July 2010).
Luordo v. Italy App no 32190/96 (ECtHR 17 July 2003).
M. v. Germany App no 19359/04 (ECtHR 17 December 2009).
M.A. v. Cyprus App no 41872/10 (ECtHR 23 July 2013).
M.H. v. United Kingdom App no 11577/06 (ECtHR 22 October 2013).
Magee and others v. United Kingdom, App nos 26289/12 and 2 others (ECtHR 12 May 2015).
Mamedova v. Russia App no 7064/05 (ECtHR 1 June 2006).
Mancini v. Italy App no 44955/98 (ECtHR 2 August 2001).
Marturana v. Italy App no 63154 (ECtHR 4 March 2008).
McKay v. United Kingdom App no 543/03 (ECtHR Grand Chamber 3 October 2006).
McVeigh and others v. United Kingdom App nos 8022/77, 8025/77 and 8027/77 (European Commission of Human Rights 18 March 1981).
Medvedyev and others v. France App no 3394/03 (ECtHR Grand Chamber 29 March 2010).
Mehmet Hasan Altan v. Turkey App no 13237/17 (ECtHR 20 March 2018).
Merabishvili v. Georgia App no 72508/13 (ECtHR Grand Chamber 28 November 2017).
Miażdżyk v. Poland App no 23592/07 (ECtHR 24 January 2012).
Monnell and Morris v. United Kingdom App nos 9562/81 and 9818/82 (ECtHR 2 March 1987).
Mooren v. Germany App no 11364/03 (ECtHR Grand Chamber 9 July 2009).
Morice v. France App no 29369/10 (ECtHR Grand Chamber 23 April 2015).
Morsink v. Netherlands App no 48865/99 (ECtHR 11 May 2004).
Moustahi v. France App no 9347/14 (ECtHR 25 June 2020).
Müller v. Switzerland App no (ECtHR 24 May 1988).
Murray v. United Kingdom App no 14310/88 (ECtHR Grand Chamber 28 October 1994).
Mursaliyev and others v. Azerbaijan App nos 66650/13 and 10 others (ECtHR 13 December 2018).
N.C. v. Italy App no 24952/94 (ECtHR 11 January 2001).
N.F. v. Italy App no 37119/97 (ECtHR 2 August 2001).
Nada v. Switzerland App no 10593/08 (ECtHR Grand Chamber 12 September 2012).
Nasrulloyev v. Russia App no 656/06 (ECtHR 11 October 2007).
Năstase-Silivestru v. Romania App no 74785/01 (ECtHR 4 October 2007).
Navarra v. France App no 13190/87 (ECtHR 23 November 1993).
Niedbała v. Poland App no 27915/95 (ECtHR 4 July 2000).
Nikolova v. Bulgaria (no. 2) App no 40896/98 (ECtHR 30 September 2004).
Nikolova v. Bulgaria App no 31195/96 (ECtHR Grand Chamber 25 March 1999).
Ninescu v. Republic of Moldova App no 47306/07 (ECtHR 15 July 2014).
Novotka v. Slovakia App no 47244/99 (ECtHR Decision on admissibility 4 November 2003).
Nurse v. Trinidad and Tobago [2019] UKPC 43, [2021] AC 1.
O'Hara v. United Kingdom App no 37555/97 (ECtHR 16 October 2001).
Öcalan v. Turkey app no 46221/99 (ECtHR Grand Chamber 12 May 2005).

Olivieira v. Netherlands App no 33129/96 (ECtHR 4 June 2002).
Opuz v. Turkey App no 33401/02 (ECtHR 9 June 2009).
Oral and Atabay v. Turkey App no 39686/02 (ECtHR 23 June 2009).
Oravec v. Croatia App no 51249/11 (ECtHR 11 July 2017).
Oshurko v. Ukraine App no 33108/05 (ECtHR 8 september 2011).
Osman v. United Kingdom App no 87/1997/871/1083 (ECtHR 28 October 1998).
Osmanović v. Croatia App no 67604/10 (ECtHR 6 November 2012).
Ostendorf v. Germany App no 15598/08 (ECtHR 7 March 2013).
Osypenko v. Ukraine App no 4634/04 (ECtHR 9 November 2010).
Paci v. Belgium App no 45597/09 (ECtHR 17 April 2018).
Pagerie v. France App no 24203/16 (ECtHR 19 January 2023).
Paladi v. Moldova App no 39806/05 (ECtHR Grand Chamber 10 March 2009).
Pankiewicz v. Poland App no 34151/04 (ECtHR 12 February 2008).
Pantea v. Romania App no 33343/96 (ECtHR 3 June 2003).
Parmak and Bakir v. Turkey App nos 22429/07 and 25195/07 (ECtHR 3 December 2019).
Perinçek v. Switzerland App no 27510/08 (ECtHR Grand Chamber 15 October 2015).
Petkov and Profirov v. Bulgaria App nos 50027/08 and 50781/09 (ECtHR 24 June 2014).
Petschulies v. Germany App no 6281/13 (ECtHR 2 June 2016).
Piotr Baranowski v. Poland App no 39742/05 (ECtHR 2 October 2007).
Plesó v. Hungary App no 41242/08 (ECtHR 2 October 2012).
Popoviciu v. Romania App no 52942/09 (ECtHR 1 March 2016).
Prencipe v. Monaco App no 43376/06 (ECtHR 16 July 2009).
Quinn v. France App no 18580/91 (ECtHR 22 March 1995).
R.M.D. v. Switzerland App no 81/1996/700/892 (ECtHR 26 September 1997).
Rai and Evans v. United Kingdom App nos 26258/07 and 26255/07 (ECtHR decision on admissibility 17 November 2009).
Raimondo v. Italy App no 12954/87 (ECtHR 22 February 1994).
Rakevich v. Russia App no 58973/00 (ECtHR 28 October 2003).
Rantsev v. Cyprus and Russia App no 25965/04 (ECtHR 7 january 2010).
RB v. United Kingdom App no 19628/92 (ECtHR 29 June 1992).
Rehbock v. Slovenia App no 29462/95 (ECtHR 28 November 2000).
Reiner v. Germany App no 28527/08 (ECtHR 19 January 2012).
Reinprecht v. Austria App no 67175/01 (ECtHR 15 November 2005).
Rekvényi v. Hungary App no 25390/94 (ECtHR Grand Chamber 20 May 1999).
Riener v. Bulgaria App no 46343/99 (ECtHR 23 May 2006).
Riera Blume and others v. Spain App no 37680/97 (ECtHR 14 October 1999).
Rigopoulos v. Spain App no 37388/97 (European Commission of Human Rights 16 April 1998).
Rooman v. Belgium App no 18052/11 (ECtHR Grand Chamber 31 January 2019) 190.
Rotaru v. Republic of Moldova App no 26764/12 (ECtHR 8 December 2020).
Rotaru v. Romania App no 28341/95 (ECtHR Grand Chamber 4 May 2000).
Rouillan v. France App no 28000/19 (ECtHR 23 september 2022).
Rozhkov v. Russia (No. 2) App no 38898/04 (ECtHR 31 January 2017).
RTBF v. Belgium App no 50084/06 (ECtHR 29 March 2011).
Ruslan Yakovenko v. Ukraine App no 5425/11 (ECtHR 4 June 2015).

S., V. and A. v. Denmark App nos 35553/23, 36678/23 and 36711/12 (ECtHR Grand Chamber 22 October 2018).
S.M. v. Italy App no 18675/09 (ECtHR Decision on admissibility 8 October 2013).
S.W. v. United Kingdom App no 20166/92 (ECtHR 22 November 1995).
Saadi v. United Kingdom App no 13229/03 (ECtHR Grand Chamber 29 January 2008).
Sabeva v. Bulgaria App no 44290/07 (ECtHR 10 June 2010).
Şahin Alpay v. Turkey App no 16538/17 (ECtHR 20 March 2018).
Sanchez-Reisse v. Switzerland App no 9862/82 (EctHR 21 October 1986).
Sarigiannis v. Italy App no 14569/05 (ECtHR 5 April 2011).
Sawoniuk v. United Kingdom App no 63716/00 (ECtHR Decision on admissibility 29 May 2001).
Schiesser v. Switzerland App no 7710/76 (ECtHR 4 December 1979).
Schwabe and M.G. v. Germany App nos 8080/08 and 8577/08 (ECtHR 1 December 2011).
Selahattin Demirtaş v. Turkey (no. 2) App no 14305/17 (ECtHR Grand Chamber 22 December 2020).
Shamayev and others v. Georgia and Russia App no 36378/02 (ECtHR 12 April 2005).
Shcherbina v. Russia App no 41970/11 (ECtHR 26 June 2014).
Sher and others v. United Kingdom App no 5201/11 (ECtHR 20 October 2015).
Shimovolos v. Russia App no 30194/09 (ECtHR 21 June 2011).
Shtukaturov v. Russia App no 44009/05 (ECtHR 27 March 2008).
Simons v. Belgium App no 71407/10 (ECtHR 28 August 2012).
Sissanis v. Romania App no 23468/02 (ECtHR 25 January 2007).
Slivenko v. Latvia App no 48321/99 (ECtHR Grand Chamber 9 October 2003).
Soare and others v. Romania App no 24329/02 (ECtHR 22 February 2011).
Solmaz v. Turkey App no 27561/02 (ECtHR 16 January 2007).
Stafford v. United Kingdom App no 46295/99 (ECtHR Grand Chamber 28 May 2002).
Stanev v. Bulgaria App no 36760/06 (ECtHR Grand Chamber 17 January 2012).
Steel and others v. United Kingdom App no 67/1997/851/1058 (ECtHR 23 September 1998).
Stephens v. Malta (no. 1) App no 11956/07 (ECtHR 21 April 2009).
Stetsov v. Ukraine App no 5170/15 (ECtHR 11 May 2021).
Stögmüller v. Austria App no 1602/62 (ECtHR 10 November 1969).
Stoll v. Switzerland App no 69698/01 (ECtHR Grand Chamber 10 December 2007).
Stollenwerk v. Germany App no 8844/12 (ECtHR 7 September 2017).
Storck v. Germany App no 61603/00 (ECtHR 16 June 2005).
Streletz, Kessler and Krenz v. Germany App no 34044/96 (ECtHR Grand Chamber 22 March 2001).
Strogan v. Ukraine App no 30198/11 (ECtHR 6 October 2016).
Sud Fondi SRL and others v. Italy App no 75909/01 (ECtHR 20 January 2009).
Sunday Times v. United Kingdom App no 6538/74 (ECtHR 26 April 1979).
Suso Musa v. Malta App no 42337/12 (ECtHR 23 July 2013).
Swennen v. Belgium App no 53448/10 (ECtHR 10 January 2013).
Sy v. Italy App no 11791/20 (ECtHR 24 January 2022).
T. v. United Kingdom App no 24724/94 (ECtHR Grand Chamber 16 December 1999).
T.W. v. Malta App no 25644/94 (ECtHR Grand Chamber 29 April 1999).
Tagayeva and others v. Russia App no 26562/07 and 6 others (ECtHR 13 April 2017).

Tase v. Romania App no 29761/02 (ECtHR 10 September 2008).
Tatishvili v. Russia App no. 1509/02 (ECtHR 22 February 2007).
Timishev v. Russia App nos 55762/00 and 55974/00 (EctHR 13 December 2005).
Timofeyev and Postupkin v. Russia App nos 45431/14 and 22769/15 (ECtHR 19 January 2021).
Tomasi v. France App no 12850/87 (ECtHR 27 August 1992).
Toth v. Austria App no 11894/85 (ECtHR 12 December 1991).
Trijonis v. Lithuania App no 2333/02 (ECtHR 15 december 2005).
Trijonis v. Lithuania App no 2333/02 (ECtHR Decision on admissibility 17 March 2005).
Ţurcan and Ţurcan v. Moldova App no 39835/05 (ECtHR 23 October 2007).
Urtāns v. Latvia App no 16858/11 (ECtHR 28 October 2014).
V. v. United Kingdom App no 24888/94 (ECtHR Grand Chamber 16 December 1999).
Van der Leer v. Netherlands App no 12/1988/156/210 (ECtHR 21 February 1990).
Van Droogenbroeck v. Belgium App no 7906/77 (ECtHR 24 June 1982).
Varbanov v. Bulgaria App no 31365/96 (ECtHR 5 October 2000).
Varga v. Romania App no 73957/01 (ECtHR 1 April 2008).
Vasileva v. Denmark App no 52792/99 (ECtHR 25 September 2003).
Villa v. Italy App no 19675/06 (ECtHR 20 April 2010).
Vinter and others v. United Kingdom App nos 66069/09, 130/10 and 3896/10 (ECtHR Grand Chamber 9 July 2013).
Viorel Burzo v. Romania App no 75109/01 and 12639/02 (ECtHR 30 June 2009).
Vito Ciancimino v. Italy App no 12541/86 (European Commission of Human Rights Decision on admissibility 27 May 1991).
Vogt v. Germany App no 17851/91 (ECtHR Grand Chamber 26 September 1995).
W.P. v. Germany App no 55594/13 (ECtHR 6 October 2016).
Waite v. United Kingdom App no 53236/99 (ECtHR 10 December 2002).
Wassink v. Netherlands App no 12535/86 (ECtHR 27 September 1990).
Weeks v. United Kingdom App no 9787/82 (ECtHR 2 March 1987).
Wemhoff v. Germany App no 2122/64 (ECtHR 27 June 1968).
Winterwerp v. Netherlands App no 6301/73 (ECtHR 24 October 1979).
Witold Litwa v. Poland App no 26629/95 (ECtHR 4 April 2000).
X. v. United Kingdom App no 7215/75 (ECtHR 5 November 1981).
X. v. United Kingdom App no 7215/75 (ECtHR 5 November 1981).
X. v. Belgium App no 4741/71 (ECtHR Commission decision 2 April 1973).
X. v. Latvia App no 27853/09 (ECtHR Grand Chamber 26 November 2013).
X. v. Sweden App no 10230/82 (European Commission of Human Rights 11 May 1983).
X. v. United Kingdom App no 3898 (ECtHR 22 July 1970).
Yefimenko v. Russia App no 152/04 (ECtHR 12 February 2013).
Yüksel Yalçinkaya v. Türkiye App no 15669/20 (ECtHR Grand Chamber 26 September 2023).
Z. and others v. United Kingdom App no 29392/95 (ECtHR Grand Chamber 10 May 2001).
Zelčs v. Latvia App no 65367/16 (ECtHR 20 February 2020).
Zervudacki v. France App no 73947/01 (ECtHR 27 July 2006).

BELGIUM

Arbitragehof 30 juni 2005, 116/2005
Arbitragehof 13 juli 2005, 125/2005.
GwH 10 mei 2006, 71/2006.
GwH 19 september 2014, 122/2014, *NjW* 2014, 840.
GwH 28 januari 2015, 9/2015, *TVW* 2015, 179.
GwH 21 december 2017, 148/2017.
GwH 18 januari 2018, 8/2018, *NjW* 2018, 299–304, noot W. Yperman.
GwH 9 maart 2018, 28/2018, *NjW* 2018, 581.
GwH 15 maart 2018, 31/2018, *NjW* 2018, 477.
GwH 14 maart 2019, 44/2019.
GwH 10 juni 2021, 86/2021, *Rechtskundig Weekblad* 2021–2022, 755.
GwH 20 oktober 2022, 132/2022, *JLMB* 2023/7, 276.
GwH 8 december 2022, 163/2022.
GwH 3 maart 2023, 36/2023.
Cass. 24 maart 1908, *Pas.* 1908, 142.
Cass. 5 mei 1913, *Pas.* 1913, I, 207.
Cass. 21 november 1927, *Pas.* 1928, I, 20.
Cass. 10 maart 1930, *Pas.* 1930, I, 156.
Cass. 7 september 1935, *Pas.* 1935, 334.
Cass. 4 april 1978, *Arr.Cass.* 1978, 884.
Cass. 21 oktober 1981, *Arr.Cass.* 1981–82, 271.
Cass. 17 mei 1983, AR 7915, *Arr.Cass.* 1982–83, 1143.
Cass. 21 juni 1983, *Arr.Cass.* 1982–83, 1302, noot.
Cass. 13 november 1983, *Arr.Cass.* 1984–85, 363.
Cass. 3 april 1984, *Arr.Cass.* 1983–84, 1023.
Cass. 4 februari 1986, *Pas.*, 1986, I, 671.
Cass. 12 mei 1987, *Arr.Cass.* 1986–87, 1194, concl. Du Jardin.
Cass. 13 december 1994, *RW* 1995–96, 533, noot B. Spriet.
Cass. 22 december 1994, *Arr.Cass.* 1994, 1149.
Cass. 9 mei 1995, P.95.0266.N, *Arr.Cass.* 1995, 46.
Cass. 31 mei 1995, P.94.868.F.
Cass. 12 november 1996, P.95.0950.N.
Cass. 27 april 1999, *Arr.Cass.* 1999, 568.
Cass. 7 mei 2002, P.02.0308.N, *Arr.Cass.* 2002, 1235.
Cass. 18 maart 2003, *T.Strafr.* 2004, 68, noot K. Beirnaert.
Cass. 18 november 2003, *Arr.Cass.* 2003, afl. 11, 2125, concl. M. Timperman.
Cass. 3 november 2004, *RW* 2005–06, 1583, noot C. De Roy.
Cass. 9 november 2004, *JT* 2004, afl. 6157, 856, noot.
Cass. 10 oktober 2006, P.06.0836.N, *Arr.Cass.* 2006, 1967.
Cass. 15 november 2006, *Pas.* 2006, 2341
Cass. 19 april 2007, *T.Strafr.* 2007, 376, noot P. De Hert en J. Millen.
Cass. 27 juni 2007, P.07.0333.F.
Cass. 8 april 2008, P.08.0006.N.
Cass. 24 juni 2008, P.08.0408.N, *Arr.Cass.* 2008, 1654, *T.Strafr.* 2009, 20.

Cass. 17 december 2008, P.08.1233.F, *RW* 2010–11, 366, noot S. Van Overbeke.
Cass. 2 september 2009, *RW* 2011–12, 1029, noot S. Van Overbeke.
Cass. 11 december 2013, P.13.1150.F-P.13.1153.F.
Cass. 24 februari 2014, S.13.0031.N.
Cass. 8 oktober 2014, P.14.0955.F
Cass. 16 december 2014, P.14.1048.N.
Cass. 13 september 2016, *RW* 2017–18, 421.
Cass. 4 oktober 2017, *NC* 2018, 303.
Cass. 14 mei 2019, P.19.0486.N.
Cass. 1 oktober 2019, P.19..0958.N, *RW* 2020–21, 538.
Cass. 29 oktober 2019, P.19.1036.N, *AC* 2019, 2031.
Cass. 24 december 2019, P.19.1281.N.
Cass. 28 januari 2020, P.19.0310.N.
Cass. 8 September 2020, P.20.0906.N, *T.Strafr.* 2021, 85.
Cass. 24 november 2020, P.20.1143.N, *T.Strafr.* 2020, 226.
Cass. 5 januari 2021, P.20.1338.N, *T.Strafr.* 2021, 232, noot P. Daeninck.
Cass. 10 februari 2021, P.20.163.F, described by P. Vanwalleghem, *Juristenkrant* 2021, afl. 426, 1.
Cass. 10 maart 2021, P.20.1295.F, *JLMB* 2021, 1122, noot F. Kuty.
Cass. 7 april 2021, P.21.0453.N, *RW* 2021–2022, 868.
Cass. 18 januari 2022, P.21.1692.N.
Cass. 3 mei 2022, P.22.0021.N.
Cass. 28 juni 2023, P.23.0206.F, *RDPC* 2024, 75.
Cass. 18 oktober 2023, RABG 2024, 136.
Cass. 8 november 2023, P.23.1218.F.
Antwerpen 18 oktober 1990, *RW* 1990–91, 856, noot B. Spriet.
Gent 7 november 2006, 125–127, *juristenkrant* 2007, afl. 148, 4.
Brussel 19 januari 2007, 33–37 and 63–67, *T.Strafr.* 2008, 281, noot F. Schuermans.
Antwerpen 7 februari 2008, *onuitg.*
Brussel 26 juni 2008, *onuitg.*
Brussel 23 december 2009, *onuitg.*
Brussel 1 december 2010, *onuitg.*
Antwerpen 8 januari 2014, *onuitg.*
Gent 4 november 2014, *onuitg.*
Brussel 28 mei 2015, *onuitg.*
Gent 26 januari 2016, *onuitg.*
Antwerpen 27 januari 2016, *onuitg.*
Antwerpen 2 maart 2016, *onuitg.*
Bergen 29 juni 2016, *onuitg.*
Luik 30 juni 2016, *onuitg.*
Brussel 18 november 2016, *onuitg.*
Antwerpen 8 december 2016, *onuitg.*
Antwerpen 22 december 2016, *onuitg.*
Luik 30 maart 2017, *onuitg.*
Brussel 31 maart 2017, *onuitg.*
Brussel 2 juni 2017, *onuitg.*

Bergen 20 juni 2017, *onuitg.*
Luik 18 oktober 2017, *JLMB* 2017, 1878.
Antwerpen 13 december 2017, *onuitg.*
Antwerpen 21 december 2017, *onuitg.*
Gent 21 maart 2018, *RW* 2019–2020, 672.
Brussel 20 april 2018, *onuitg.*
Antwerpen 24 oktober 2018, *onuitg.*
Brussel 21 december 2018, *onuitg.*
KI Brussel 14 september 2017, *RW* 2017–18, 1611, noot J. Wouters en T. Van Poecke.
KI Brussel 8 maart 2019, *onuitg.*
Assisen Brussel 5 december 2014, *onuitg.*
Assisen Brussel 26 juli 2023, *JLMB* 2023, 1348.
Corr. Antwerpen 23 februari 1993, *T.R.V.* 1994, 195, noot W. Devroe en A. Rombouts.
Corr. Antwerpen 14 april 1994, *T.R.V.* 1994, 285, noot F. Hellemans.
Corr. Brussel 16 februari 2006, *onuitg.*
Corr. Brugge 28 februari 2006, *T.Strafr.* 2006, 159, noot P. De Hert.
Corr. Brussel 10 mei 2010, *onuitg.*
Corr. Mechelen 5 december 2012, *onuitg.*
Corr. Brussel 25 juni 2013, *onuitg.*
Corr. Dendermonde 7 februari 2014, *onuitg.*
Corr. Brussel 14 mei 2014, *onuitg.*
Corr. Brussel 21 mei 2014, *onuitg.*
Corr. Antwerpen (afd. Antwerpen) 11 februari 2015, *NjW* 2015, 280, noot E. Vandebroek.
Corr. Antwerpen 20 maart 2015, *onuitg.*
Corr. Antwerpen 30 maart 2015, *onuitg.*
Corr. Brussel 26 juni 2015, *onuitg.*
Corr. Brussel 29 juli 2015, *onuitg.*
Corr. Antwerpen 2 november 2015, *onuitg.*
Corr. Brussel 6 november 2015, *onuitg.*
Corr. Brussel 25 november 2015, *onuitg.*
Corr. Antwerp 7 december 2015, *onuitg.*
Corr. Antwerpen (afd. Antwerpen) 25 januari 2016, *onuitg.*
Corr. Oost-Vlaanderen (afd. Dendermonde) 25 januari 2016, *onuitg.*
Corr. Brussel 27 januari 2016, *onuitg.*
Corr. Brussel 29 januari 2016, *onuitg.*
Corr. Brussel 3 maart 2016, *onuitg.*
Corr. Brussel 21 april 2016, *onuitg.*
Corr. Brussel 3 mei 2016, *onuitg.*
Corr. Brussel 5 juli 2016, *onuitg.*
Corr. West-Vlaanderen (afd. Brugge) (vakantiekamer) 14 juli 2016, *TGR-TWVR* 2016, afl. 5, 386.
Corr. Antwerpen 19 september 2016, *onuitg.*
Corr. Brussel 20 oktober 2016, *onuitg.*
Corr. Brussel 15 december 2016, *onuitg.*
Corr. Luik (afd. Luik) 20 januari 2017, *onuitg.*
Corr. Antwerpen (afd. Antwerpen) 13 februari 2017, *onuitg.*

Corr. Brussel 9 maart 2017, *onuitg.*
Corr. Brussel 10 maart 2017, *onuitg.*
Corr. Antwerpen (afd. Antwerpen) 13 maart 2017, *onuitg.*
Corr. Brussel 8 mei 2017, *onuitg.*
Corr. Brussel 31 mei 2017, *onuitg.*
Corr. Limburg (afd. Hasselt) 23 juni 2017, *Limburgs Rechtsleven* 2018, 51.
Corr. Luik (vakantiekamer) 19 juli 2017, *JLMB* 2017, 1391.
Corr. West-Vlaanderen (afd. Brugge) 19 juli 2017, *onuitg.*
Corr. Antwerpen (afd. Mechelen) 7 september 2017, *onuitg.*
Corr. Henegouwen (afd. Charleroi) 27 september 2017, *onuitg.*
Corr. Brussel 10 oktober 2017, *onuitg.*
Corr. Oost-Vlaanderen (afd. Gent) 16 oktober 2017, *NjW* 2017, 805, noot W. Yperman en S. Royer.
Corr. Brussel 27 oktober 2017, *onuitg.*
Corr. Charleroi 22 november 2017, *onuitg.*
Corr. Antwerpen (afd. Mechelen) 4 januari 2018, *onuitg.*
Corr. Mechelen 4 januari 2018, *onuitg.*
Corr. Luik 16 februari 2018, *onuitg.*
Corr. Antwerpen (afd. Antwerpen) 19 februari 2018, *onuitg.*
Corr. West-Vlaanderen (afd. Brugge) 19 februari 2018, *onuitg.*
Corr. Oost-Vlaanderen (afd. Dendermonde) 26 februari 2018, *onuitg.*
Corr. Brussel 1 maart 2018, *onuitg.*
Corr. Antwerpen 18 maart 2018, *onuitg.*
Corr. Antwerpen (afd. Antwerpen) 19 maart 2018, *onuitg.*
Corr. Antwerpen (afd. Mechelen) 29 maart 2018, *onuitg.*
Corr. Brussel 29 maart 2018, *onuitg.*
Corr. Antwerpen (afd. Antwerpen) 16 april 2018, *onuitg.*
Corr. Brussel 23 april 2018, *onuitg.*
Corr. Bergen 14 mei 2018, *onuitg.*
Corr. Henegouwen (afd. Bergen) 14 mei 2018, *onuitg.*
Corr. Brussel 11 juni 2018, *onuitg.*
Corr. West-Vlaanderen (afd. Brugge) 26 juli 2018, *onuitg.*
Corr. Oost-Vlaanderen (afd. Dendermonde) 14 december 2018, *onuitg.*
Corr. Antwerp 17 december 2018, *onuitg.*
Corr. Luik 18 januari 2019, *onuitg.*
Corr. Brussel 10 mei 2019, *NjW* 2019, 663, noot W. Yperman.
Corr. Antwerpen 4 februari 2021, *onuitg.*
Corr. Brugge, zoals geciteerd in F. Martinez, '80 maanden cel voor man die terroristische aanslag voorbereidt op zolder in Roeselare', *vrtNWS* 12 december 2022.
Jeugdrechtbank Brussel 4 juli 2016, *onuitg.*
RK Brussel 3 november 2016, *onuitg.*
Concl E.H. bij Cass. 15 februari 2006, P.05.1594.

UK

A and others v. Secretary of State for the Home Department [2004] EWCA Civ 1123 2004 WL 1640297.
A v. Secretary of State for the Home Department [2004] UKHL 56, [2005] 2 WLR 87.
A-G's reference (no 1 of 1975) [1975] QB 773.
A-G's reference (no 1 of 1992) [1993] 1 W.L.R. 274, 284–285.
AG's Reference No 69 of 2013, R v. McLoughlin, R v. Newell [2014] EWCA Crim 188, [2014] 1 WLR 3964.
Ahmed Raza Faraz v. R [2012] EWCA Crim 2820.
Aitzaz Zafar, Akbar Butt, Awaab Iqbal, Mohammed Raja, Usman Malik v. R [2008] EWCA Crim 184, 2008 WL 370958.
Anjem Choudary, Mohammed Mizanur Rahman v. R [2016] EWCA Crim 61.
Anna Castorina v. The Chief Constable of Surrey 1988 WL 622865.
Anna Julie Ann Clarke v. Chief Constable of North Wales Police 2000 WL 345127.
AP v. Secretary of State for the Home Department [2009] EWCA Civ 731, 2009 WL 1949565.
Application By Prosecution for Leave to Appeal Under Section 58 Criminal Justice Act 2003 (MS) [2021] EWCA Crim 600, 2021 WL 01616966.
Attorney General's Reference (No. 4 of 2002) [2004] UKHL 48.
Attorney General's References (Nos. 85, 86 & 87 of 2007) [2007] EWCA Crim 3300.
Attorney-General's Reference (No. 1 of 2020) [2020] EWCA Crim 1665, [2021] QB 441.
Attorney-General's Reference (No. 3 of 1994) [1998] AC 245.
Austin v. Commissioner of Police of the Metropolis [2009] UKHL 5, [2009] 1 AC 564.
Bank Mellat v. HM Treasury (No 2) [2013] UKSC 38 and 39 [2014] AC 700.
Barr v. Public Prosecution Service [2020] NICA 46.
Beghal v. Director of Public Prosecutions [2015] UKSC 49, 2015 WL 4401455.
Castorina v. The Chief Constable of Surrey 1988 WL 622865.
Chapman v. DPP (1989) Cr App R 190, [1988] Crim LR 843.
Council of Civil Service Unions and Others Appellants v. Minister for the Civil Service [1985] A.C. 374 (H.L.).
Dallison v. Caffrey [1965] 1 Q.B. 348.
Director of Public Prosecutions v. Smith [1961] AC 290, 334–335.
DPP for Northern Ireland v. Lynch [1975] AC 653, 679–80.
Edwards (Deborah) v. DPP (1993) 97 Cr App R 301, 306–307.
Elloy de Freitas v. Permanent Secretary of Ministry of Agriculture, Fisheries, Lands and Housing [1991] 1 AC 69, [1998] 3 W.L.R. 675, 9.
Ferguson v. Weaving [1951] 1 KB 814, 819.
Her Majesty's Treasury v. Ahmed and others [2010] UKSC 2, 172.
Hyam v. Director of Public Prosecutions [1975] AC 55, 93–98.
Invicta plastics Ltd and Another v. Clare [1976] RTR 251.
Kay and others v. Lambeth London Borough Council, Leeds City Council v. Price and others [2006] UKHL 10.
Manchester City Council v. Pinnock [2010] UKSC 45, [2011] 1 All ER 285, 48–49.
Maria v. Hall (1807) 1 Taunt 33, 127 ER 741.
Mason v. DPP [2009] EWHC 2198 (Admin).

Omar Scott v. DPP [2022] EWHC 91 (Admin), [2022] 1 WLR 2231.
Paul Dunleavy v. R [2021] EWCA Crim 39, 2021 WL 00202849.
Percy Bateman (1927) 19 Cr. App. R. 8.
Pwr v. Director of Public Prosecutions, Akdogan and another v Director of Public Prosecutions [2022] UKSC 2.
R (Alconbury Developments Ltd) v. Secretary of State for the Environment, Transport and the Regions [2001] UKHL 23, [2003] 2 AC 295.
R (Animal Defenders International) v. Secretary of State for Culture, Media and Sport [2008] UKHL 15.
R (Daly) v. Secretary of State for the Home Department [2001] UKHL 26, 28, [2001] 2 A.C. 532.
R (Gillan) v. The Commissioner of Police for the Metropolis [2006] UKHL 12, 2006 WL 502934.
R (Hicks) v. Commissioner of the Police of the Metropolis [2014] EWCA Civ 3, [2014] 1 WLR 2152.
R (Hicks) v. Commissioner of the Police of the Metropolis [2017] UKSC 9, [2017] AC 256.
R (on the application of Secretary of State for the Home Department) v. Bullivant [2008] EWHC 337, 2008 WL 678090.
R (Ullah) v. Special Adjudicator [2004] UKHL 26.
R v.Ian John Gullefer (1990) 91 Cr App R 356.
R v. Abbas Niazi Iqbal, Ilyas Niazi Iqbal [2010] EWCA Crim 3215, 2010 WL 5625104.
R v. Abdalraouf Abdallah and Stephen Gray and an application under s.36 of the Criminal Justice Act 1986 by Hm Attorney General (No. 323 of 2016), Junead Khan and Shazib Khan, Ayman Shaukat and Lorna Moore [2016] EWCA Crim 1868.
R v. Abdulla Ahmed Ali and others [2011] EWCA Crim 1260, 2011 WL 1151813.
R v. Abdullah Ibrahim El-Faisal [2004] EWCA Crim 343, 2004 WL 229347.
R v. Abu Hamza [2006] EWCA Crim 2918, 2006 WL 3390045.
R v. Abubaker Deghayes [2023] EWCA Crim 97, 2023 WL 02139667.
R v. Adeel Amjad [2016] EWCA Crim 1618, 2016 WL 06397476.
R v. Ahmed (Rangzieb) and Ahmed (Habib) [2011] EWCA Crim 184.
R v. Alamgir and others [2018] EWCA Crim 21.
R v. Ali (Humza) [2018] EWCA Crim 547, [2018] 3 WLUK 454.
R v. Altimimi [2008] EWCA Crim 2829 as described in The Court of Appeal Criminal Division, *Review of the Legal Year 2008 / 2009*.
R v. Ardalan and others [1972] 1 W.L.R. 463.
R v. Ashman (1858) 1 Foster and Finlason 88.
R *v. Asiedu (Manfo Kwaku)* [2008] EWCA Crim 1725, 2008 WL 5683938.
R v. Barot (Dhiren) [2007] EWCA Crim 1119, Crim. L.R. 2007, Sep, 741–744.
R v. Ben John [2022] EWCA Crim 54, 2022 WL 00286378.
R v. Bollom [2003] EWCA Crim 2846.
R v. Brown (Terence Roy) [2011] EWCA Crim 2751, 2011 WL 5828783.
R v. Clarkson, R v. Carroll, R v. Dodd [1971] 1 WLR 1402.
R v. Copeland [2020] UKSC 8.
R v. Cunningham [1982] AC 566.
R v. Damon Smith [2018] EWCA Crim 528, 2018 WL 01471413.
R v. EL-Faisal [2004] EWCA Crim 456, 2004 WL 413053.

R v. F [2007] EWCA Crim 243, 2007 WL 434775.
R v. G and Another [2003] UKHL 50, [2004] 1 A.C. 1034.
R v. G, R v. J [2009] UKHL 13, [2010] 1 AC 43.
R v. Geddes [1996] Crim LR 894.
R v. Governor of Durham prison ex p Singh [1984] 1 WLR 704.
R v. Gul (Mohammed) [2013] UKSC 64.
R v. Hassan Tabbakh [2009] EWCA Crim 464, 2009 WL 392237.
R v. Horncastle [2009] UKSC 14, [2010] 2 AC 373.
R v. Hundal and Dhaliwal [2004] EWCA Crim 389.
R v. Ian Anthony Jones [2007] EWCA Crim 1118, [2008] QB 460.
R v. Ian Beckenridge [1984] 79 Cr. App. R. 244.
R v. Ian John Gullefer (1990) 91 Cr App R 356.
R v. Ibrahim, Omar, Osman (aka Hamdi), Mohamed [2008] EWCA Crim 880, 2008 WL 1771443.
R v. Jogee, Ruddock v. The Queen (Jamaica) [2016] UKSC 8.
R v. K [2001] UKHL 41, 2001 WL 825055.
R v. K [2008] EWCA Crim 185, [2008] Q.B. 827S.
R v. Kenneth Henry Jones (1990) 91 Cr App R 351 (CA).
R v. Khalil Maher, R v. Patrick Kabele, R v. Jabed Hussain and *R v. Shamin Ahmed* as described in M. Hill, *Report of the Independent Reviewer of Terrorism Legislation on the Operation of the Terrorism Acts 2000 and 2006, the Terrorism Prevention and Investigation Measures Act 2011, and the Terrorist Asset Freezing Etc Act 2010*, October 2018.
R v. Khan (Mohammed Iqbal), R v. Dhokia, R v. Banga, R v. Faiz [1990] 1 WLR 813.
R v. Kibley Da Costa, Muhammed Al-Figari, Kader Ahmed, Mohammed Hamid, Atilla Ahmet [2009] EWCA Crim 482.
R v. Lankford [1959] Crim. L.R. 209.
R v. M, Z, I, R, B [2007] EWCA Crim 218, 2007 WL 261181.
R v. Mansha [2006] EWCA Crim 2051, 2006 WL 2629774.
R v. Michael David Marlow [1997] Crim LR 897 (CA).
R v. Michael Nugent [2021] EWCA Crim 1535, 2021 WL 04950303.
R v. Mohammed Abdul Kahar (Reference by the Attorney General under s.36 of the Criminal Justice Act 1988) R v. Brusthom Ziamani, Abdurraouf Eshati, Yahya Rashid, Silhan Ozcelik, Sana Khan [2016] EWCA Crim 568, 2016 WL 02771996.
R v. Mohammed Alamgir, Yousaf Bashir, Rajib Khan [2018] EWCA Crim 1553.
R v. Munir Ahmed Farooqi, Matthew Newton, Israr Hussain Malik [2013] EWCA Crim 1649, 2013 WL 5328717.
R v. Munna Hamza [2021] EWCA Crim 1460, 2021 WL 04710555.
R v. Mutegombwa [2009] EWCA Crim 684 as described in The Court of Appeal Criminal Division, *Review of the Legal Year 2008 / 2009.*
R v. Nadeem Muhammed [2017] EWCA Crim 1832, 2017 WL 05598509.
R v. Nedrick [1986] 1 WLR 1025 (CA).
R v. Nicholas Roddis [2009] EWCA Crim 585, 2009 WL 648870.
R v. Oliver Bel [2021] EWCA Crim 1461, 2021 WL 04710515.
R v. Omar Khyam, Salahuddin Amin, Jawed Akbar, Anthony Garcia, Waheed Mahmood [2008] EWCA Crim 1612, 2008 WL 2821519.

R v. Page [1954] 1 QB 170.
R v. Powell, Daniels and English [1999] 1 AC 1.
R v. Rahman (Abdul) [2008] EWCA Crim 1465, Crim. L.R. 2008, 11.
R v. Rahman and others [2008] UKHL 45.
R v. Rizlaine Boular, Safaa Boular [2019] EWCA Crim 798, 2019 WL 02162983.
R v. Sally Lane and John Letts (AB and CD) [2018] UKSC 36, 2018 WL 03368388.
R v. Samina Hussain Malik [2008] EWCA Crim 1450, 2008 WL 2311341.
R v. Secretary of State for the Home Department, Ex parte Brind and Others [1991] 1 A.C. 696 (H.L.), 721.
R v. Sellu [2016] EWCA Crim 1716, [2017] 4 WLR 64.
R v. Sherif (Abdul) [2008] EWCA Crim 2653, [2008] 11 WLUK 567.
R v. Sidhu (Ryandeep Singh) [2019] EWCA Crim 1034, 19.
R v. Sneha Chowdhury [2020] EWCA Crim 1421, 2020 WL 06565151.
R v. Sultan Muhammed, Aabid Hassain Khan [2009] EWCA Crim 2653, 2009 WL 4666923.
R v. Tony Campbell [1990] 93 Cr App R 350 (CA).
R v. Tosti (Andre) [1997] Crim LR 746 (CA).
R v. Vickers [1957] 2 QB 664.
R v. Woollin [1999] 1 AC 82.
R v. Yeshiembert Girma, Esayas Girma, Mulumebet Girma, Mohamed Kabashi [2009] EWCA Crim 912.
R v. Z [2005] UKHL 35.
Rahman PWR, Ismail Akdogan, Rotinda Demir v. Director of Public Prosecutions [2020] EWHC 798 (Admin).
Regina (Aguilar Quila and another) v. Secretary of State for the Home Department (AIRE Centre and others intervening) Regina (Bibi and another) v. Same (Same intervening) [2011] UKSC 45 [2012] 1 A.C. 621.
Regina (Miranda) v. Secretary of State for the Home Department and another (Liberty and others intervening) [2016] EWCA Civ 6.
Regina v. Salim Wakil [2019] EWCA Crim 1351, 2019 WL 03457705.
Rowe v. R [2007] EWCA Crim 635, [2007] QB 975.
Scott Hayes v. Chief Constable of Merseyside Police [2011] EWCA Civ 911.
Secretary of State for the Home Department v. AF (FC) and another and one other action [2009] UKHL 28.
Secretary of State for the Home Department v. Al Saadi [2009] EWHC 3390 (Admin), 2009 WL 4872782.
Secretary of State for the Home Department v. AM [2012] EWHC 1854 (Admin), 2012 WL 2500050.
Secretary of State for the Home Department v. AP [2008] EWHC 2001 (Admin), 2008 WL 3819438.
Secretary of State for the Home Department v. AP [2010] UKSC 24, 2010 WL 2131699.
Secretary of State for the Home Department v. AV [2009] EWHC 902 (Admin), 2009 WL 1096180.
Secretary of State for the Home Department v. BM [2012] EWHC 714 (Admin), 2012 WL 609334.

Secretary of State for the Home Department v. CC and CF [2012] EWHC 2837 (Admin), 2012 WL 4866832.
Secretary of State for the Home Department v. CD [2012] EWHC 3026 (Admin), 2012 WL 4867182.
Secretary of State for the Home Department v. E [2007] EWHC 233 (Admin).
Secretary of State for the Home Department v. E and another [2007] UKHL 47.
Secretary of State for the Home Department v. GG [2009] EWCA Civ 786, 2009 WL 2173225.
Secretary of State for the Home Department v. JJ and others [2006] EWCA Civ 1141.
Secretary of State for the Home Department v. JJ and others [2007] UKHL 45.
Secretary of State for the Home Department v. MB [2006] EWHC (Admin) 1,000.
Secretary of State for the Home Department v. MB and others [2006] EWCA Civ 1140, 2006 WL 2133149.
Secretary of State for the Home Department v. MB and AF [2007] UKHL 46.
Secretary of State for the Home Department v. NN sub nom. Secretary of State for the Home Department v. GG [2009] EWHC 142 (Admin), 2009 WL 364285.
Shiv Malik v. Manchester Crown Court, Chief Constable of Greater Manchester Police v. Constable and Robinson Ltd, Attorney General [2008] EWHC 1362 (Admin), [2008] 4 All E.R. 403.
Siddiqui v. Swain [1979] RTR 454.
Subhash Mehta v. R [2012] EWCA Crim 2824.
Sultan Muhammed v. The Crown [2010] EWCA Crim 227, 2010 WL 517086.
Sweet v. Parsley [1970] AC 132.
The King v. Higgins (1801) 2 East 5, 102 ER 269.
The Queen v. AY [2010] EWCA Crim 762, [2010] 1 WLR 2644.
The Queen v. Most (1881) 7 QBD 244.
The Secretary of State for the Home Department v. 'M' [2004] EWCA Civ 324, 2004 WL 412985.
Usman Khan, Mohibur Rahman, Omar Sharif Latif, Abdul Bosher Mohammed Shahjahan, Nazam Hussain v. The Queen [2013] EWCA Crim 468, 2013 WL 618129.
Ward v. Chief Constable of Somerset and Avon Constabulary 1986 WL 408352.
Wayne Lee Shillam v. R [2013] EWCA Crim 160.

OTHER

A.s.b.l. Advocaten voor de wereld v. Conseil des Ministres (Belgium) Case C-303/05 (ECEJ 3 May 2007).
Yassin Abdullah Kadi and Al Barakaat International Foundation v. Council of the European Union and Commission of the European Communities Case C-402/05 and C-415/05 [2008] CJEU ECLI:EU:C:2008:461.
*European Commission et al v. Yassin Abdullah Kad*i Case C-584/10, C-593/10 and C-595/10 [2013] CJEU ECLI:EU:C:2013:518.
JZ v. Prokuratura Rejonowa Lodz C-294/16 (CJEU 28 July 2016).
Van Alphen v. Netherlands Comm No 305/1988 (UN HRC 23 July 1990).

Mr. Tai Wairiki Rameka et al. v. New Zealand Comm No 1090/2002 (UN HRC 15 December 2003).

Sayadi v. Belgium UN Doc CCPR/C/94/D/1472/2006 (Official Case No) IHRL 3216 (UN HRC 2008).

Gerechtshof Den Haag 27 October 2016.

Gerechtshof Amsterdam 24 July 2018, ECLI:NL:GHAMS:2018:2580.

Conclusie A-G Berger bij Hoge Raad 30 mei 1975, ECLI:NL:PHR:1975:AC5594 (bierglasarrest).

LEGAL DOCTRINE

Ahmed S, 'The "emotionalization of the 'War on Terror'": Counter-Terrorism, Fear, Risk, Insecurity and Helplessness' (2015) 15 Criminology & Criminal Justice 545.

Alati D, *Domestic Counter-Terrorism in a Global World: Post-9/11 Institutional Structures and Cultures in Canada and the United Kingdom* (1st edn, Routledge 2017).

Alexander L and Ferzan KK, 'Risk and Inchoate Crimes: Retribution or Prevention?' in GR Sullivan and Ian Dennis (eds), *Seeking Security : Pre-Empting the Commission of Criminal Harms* (Bloomsbury Publishing 2012).

Allen G and Dempsey N, 'Terrorism in Great Britain: The Statistics' (2017) 7613 Commons Library Briefing Paper 25.

Allen M and Edwards I, *Criminal Law* (Sixteenth edition, Oxford University Press 2021).

Amado JAG, 'On the Principle of Criminal Legality and Its Scope: Foreseeability as a Component of Legality' in Mercedes Pérez Manzano, Juan Antonio Lascuraín Sánchez and Marina Mínguez Rosique (eds), *Multilevel Protection of the Principle of Legality in Criminal Law* (Springer International Publishing 2018).

Amatrudo A and Blake LW, *Human Rights and the Criminal Justice System* (Routledge 2015).

Anderson D, *Terrorism Prevention and Investigation Measures in 2012: First Report of the Independent Reviewer on the Operation of the Terrorism Prevention and Investigation Measures Act 2011* (Stationery Office 2013).

Anderson D, 'Shielding the Compass: How to Fight Terrorism without Defeating the Law' (2013) Independent Reviewer of Terrorism Legislation.

Anderson D, 'Independent Review of Terrorism Laws: Searchlight or Veil?' [2014] SSRN Electronic Journal www.ssrn.com/abstract=2400656 accessed 4 March 2023.

Aradau C and Van Munster R, 'Governing Terrorism Through Risk: Taking Precautions, (Un)Knowing the Future' (2007) 13 European Journal of International Relations 89.

Arai-Takahashi Y, 'Proportionality' in D Shelton (ed), *The Oxford Handbook of International Human Rights Law* (Oxford University Press 2013).

Arnou P, 'Voorbedachten Rade', *Strafrecht en strafvordering. Artikelsgewijze commentaar met overzicht van rechtspraak en rechtsleer* (Wolters Kluwer 1990).

Arnou P, 'Nacht', *Strafrecht en strafvordering. Artikelsgewijze commentaar met overzicht van rechtspraak en rechtsleer* (Wolters Kluwer 2010).

Ashworth A, *Human Rights, Serious Crime and Criminal Procedure* (Sweet & Maxwell 2002).

Ashworth A, 'Security, Terrorism and the Value of Human Rights' in B Goold and L Lazarus (eds), *Security and Human Rights* (Hart Publishing 2007).

Ashworth A, 'Criminal Law, Human Rights and Preventative Justice' in B McSherry, A Norrie and S Bronitt (eds), *Regulating deviance: The redirection of criminalisation and the futures of criminal law* (Hart Publishing 2009).

Ashworth A (ed), *Sentencing and Criminal Justice* (5th edn, Cambridge University Press 2010) www.cambridge.org/core/product/E3B5572348E4CE06260FE6CD92455D90.

Ashworth A, 'The Unfairness of Risk-Based Possession Offences' (2011) 5 Criminal Law and Philosophy 237.

Ashworth A, 'R. v Kahar Case Comment' [2016] Criminal Law Review 670.

Ashworth A and Zedner L, *Preventive Justice* (Oxford University Press 2014).

Ashworth A, Zedner L and Tomlin P, 'Introduction' in Andrew Ashworth, Lucia Zedner and Patrick Tomlin (eds), *Prevention and the Limits of the Criminal Law* (Oxford University Press 2013).

Asp P, 'Two Notions of Proportionality' in K Nuotio (ed), *Festschrift in honour of Raimo Lahti* (Forum Iuris 2007).

Asp P, 'Preventionism and Criminalization of Nonconsummate Offences' in Andrew Ashworth, Lucia Zedner and Patrick Tomlin (eds), *Prevention and the Limits of the Criminal Law* (Oxford University Press 2013).

Asp P and Cameron I, 'Terrorism and Legal Security – a Swedish and European Perspective' in Mattias Dahlberg (ed), *Uppsala-Minnesota Colloquium: Law, Culture and Values* (Iustus förlag 2009).

Azmeh U, 'Comment on the Terrorism Offences Definitive Guideline' [2018] Sentencing News 60.

Azmeh U, 'Exemplary Sentencing for Terrorist Offenders: The Counter- Terrorism and Sentencing Bill 2020' [2021] Criminal Law Review 5.

Baker D, *Reinterpreting Criminal Complicity and Inchoate Participation Offences* (1st edn, Routledge 2016).

Beale H, *Chitty on Contracts* (34th edn, Sweet & Maxwell 2022).

Beard J and Dawson J, 'Counter-Terrorism and Sentencing Bill 2019–21' (2020) 8771 House of Commons Library Briefing Paper.

Beck U, *Risk Society: Towards a New Modernity* (SAGE Publications 1992).

Beck U, 'The Terrorist Threat: World Risk Society Revisited' (2002) 19 Theory, Culture & Society 39.

Beernaert M-A, 'La Loi du 19 Décembre 2003 relative aux infractions terroristes : Quand le droit pénal Belge évolue sous la dictée de l'Union Européenne' (2004) 24 Journal des tribunaux 585.

Beernaert M-A, 'Renforcement de l'arsenal législatif anti-terroriste: entre symboles et prévention' [2015] Journal des tribunaux 833.

Beernaert M-A, 'L'individualisation dans le prononcé et l'exécution de la peine : machine arrière toute ?', *La loi "pot-pourri II" : un recul de civilisation ?* (Anthemis 2016).

Beernaert M-A, *Manuel de droit pénitentiaire* (Anthemis 2019).

Beirnaert K, 'Vrijheid en invrijheidstelling onder voorwaarden versus vrijheid van meningsuiting en vrijheid van vergadering' (2004) 2004 Tijdschrift voor Strafrecht 69.

Berkmoes H, 'Algemeen' in M De Busscher and others (eds), *Strafrecht: duiding* (Larcier 2018).

Berkmoes H, 'Bestanddelen van de strafbare poging' in M De Busscher and others (eds), *Strafrecht: duiding* (Larcier 2018).

Berkmoes H, 'De niet-strafbare poging' in M De Busscher and others (eds), *Strafrecht: duiding* (Larcier 2018).

Besselink L, Pennings F and Prechal S, 'Introduction: Legality in Multiple Legal Orders' in L Besselink, F Pennings and S Prechal (eds), *The Eclipse of the Legality Principle in the European Union* (Kluwer 2011).

Billiet CM, De Smedt P and Van Landeghem H, 'Vlaamse milieuhandhaving nieuwe stijl' [2009] Tijdschrift voor Milieurecht 326.

Blackbourn J, Kayis D and McGarrity N, *Anti-Terrorism Law and Foreign Terrorist Fighters* (Routledge 2018).

Blaise N and Delhaise E, 'La répression des voyages à visée terroriste à l'aune des droits fondamentaux' [2019] Journal Tribunaux 173.

Boek JLM, 'Een pleidooi voor het afschaffen van voorwaardelijk opzet' [2016] Strafblad 439.

Bonfond O, 'Incitation au terrorisme: qui trop embrasse, mal étreint' (2018) 26 Jurisprudence de Liege, Mons et Bruxelles 1237.

Borgers M, 'Een gevaarzettingsvereiste voor terroristische misdrijven?' in Toine Sapens, Marc Groenhuijsen and Tijs Kooijmans (eds), *Universalis: Liber amicorum Cyrille Fijnaut* (Intersentia 2011).

Bosly H, 'Constitution, garde à vue et lutte contre le terrorisme' in Steven Dewulf (ed), *La [CVDW] Liber Amicorum Chris Van den Wyngaert* (Maklu 2017).

Bosly H, 'Révision de la Constitution : le délai de " garde à vue " porté à 48 heures maximum en droit Belge' (2018) 2 Revue de droit pénal et de criminologie 167.

Bosly S and Van Ravenstein M, 'L'harmonisation des incriminations' in Daniel Flore (ed), *Actualités de droit pénal Européen* (La Charte 2003).

Bounjoua A, 'L'harmonisation des infractions de " l'entraînement au terrorisme " et du " voyage à des fins de terrorisme " en droit pénal Européen à l'aune des départs et des retours de zones de conflits au sein d'états tiers à l'Union Européenne' [2022] Revue de droit international et de droit comparé 645.

Brady ADP, *Proportionality and Deference under the UK Human Rights Act: An Institutionally Sensitive Approach* (Cambridge University Press 2012).

Braum S, 'Are We Heading towards a European Form of "Enemy Criminal Law"? On the Compatibility of Jakob's Conception of "an Enemy Criminal Law" and European Criminal Law' in Francesca Galli and Anne Weyembergh (eds), *EU counter-terrorism offences: What impact on national legislation and case-law?* (Editions de l'Université de Bruxelles 2012).

Brion F and others, 'Impact Assessment of Belgian De-"Radicalisation" Policies Upon Social Cohesion and Liberties' (2022) AFFECT.

Caeiro P, 'Concluding Remarks' in Francesca Galli and Anne Weyembergh (eds), *EU counter-terrorism offences: What impact on national legislation and case-law?* (Editions de l'Université de Bruxelles 2012).

Cammiss S, 'Courts and the Trial Process' in Anthea Hucklesby and Azrini Wahidin (eds), *Criminal Justice* (Second edition, Oxford University Press).

Carlile of Berriew, 'First Report Of The Independent Reviewer Pursuant To Section 14(3) Of The Prevention Of Terrorism Act 2005' (2006) Independent Reviewer of Terrorism Legislation.

Carlile of Berriew, 'The Definition of Terrorism' (2007) Independent Reviewer of Terrorism Legislation Cm 7052.

Carlile of Berriew, 'Sixth Report of the Independent Reviewer Pursuant to Section 14(3) of the Prevention of Terrorism Act 2005' (2011) Independent Reviewer of Terrorism Legislation.

Cesoni ML, 'Terrorisme et involutions démocratiques' [2002] Rev Dr Pén Crim 141.

Cesoni ML, 'Les "infractions terroristes": de la répression des actes à la police de la pensée' in Christian De Valkeneer and Henri D Bosly (eds), *Actualités en droit pénal 2019* (Larcier 2019).

Chalk P, 'The Response to Terrorism as a Threat to Liberal Democracy' in Alan O'Day (ed), *War on terrorism* (Ashgate 2004).

Child J and others, *Simester and Sullivan's Criminal Law: Theory and Doctrine* (Eight, Hart Publishing 2022).

Chistyakova Y, 'Democratic Legitimacy, Effectiveness and Impact of EU Counter-Terrorism Measures' in Fiona de Londras and Josephine Doody (eds), *The Impact, Legitimacy and Effectiveness of EU Counter-Terrorism* (1st edn, Routledge 2015).

Christoffersen J, *Fair Balance: Proportionality, Subsidiarity and Primarity in the European Convention on Human Rights* (Brill | Nijhoff 2009).

Cianciardo J, 'The Principle of Proportionality: The Challenges of Human Rights' (2010) 3 Journal of Civil Law Studies 177.

Claes AL and Yperman W, 'Overzicht(Elijk) – Recente ontwikkelingen in de contraterrorismewetgeving' [2022] Politie & Recht 69.

Claes E, *Legaliteit en rechtsvinding in het strafrecht: een grondslagentheoretische benadering* (Universitaire Pers Leuven 2003).

Claes E and Krolikowski M, 'The Limits of Legality in the Criminal Law' in Bert Keirsbilck, Wouter Devroe and Erik Claes (eds), *Facing the Limits of the Law* (Springer 2009).

Clarkson CMV, 'Attempt: The Conduct Requirement' (2009) 29 Oxford Journal of Legal Studies 25.

Clayton R and Tomlinson H, 'Arrest and Reasonable Grounds for Suspicion' (1988) 85 Law Society Gazette 22.

Cole D, 'English Lessons: A Comparative Analysis of UK and US Responses to Terrorism' (2009) 62 Current Legal Problems 136.

Cole D, 'The Difference Prevention Makes: Regulating Preventive Justice' (2015) 9 Crim Law and Philos 501.

Conte A, *Human Rights in the Prevention and Punishment of Terrorism* (Springer Berlin Heidelberg 2010).

Cornelis L and Verstraeten R, 'Mag er nog witgewassen worden?' [1992] TBH 176.

Cornford A, 'Narrowing the Scope of Absurdly Broad Offences: The Case of Terrorist Possession' (2016) 38 Statute Law Review 286.

Cornford A, 'Terrorist Precursor Offences: Evaluating the Law in Practice' [2020] Criminal Law Review 663.

Corten O, *La Rébellion et Le Droit International: Le Principe de Neutralité En Tension* (Académie de droit international de La Haye 2014)

C.P.W., 'Commentary: R v Z' [2005] Criminal Law Review 985.

C.P.W., 'Commentary: R v Rowe' [2008] Criminal Law Review 72.

Cram I, 'Regulating the Media: Some Neglected Freedom of Expression Issues in the United Kingdom's Counter-Terrorism Strategy' (2006) 18 Terrorism and Political Violence 335.

Curzon E and Roberts JV, 'The Suspended Sentence Order in England and Wales' [2021] Sentencing Academy 16.

Daems T and Magis Y, 'Elektronisch toezicht en autonome probatie nader bekeken' in P Traest, A Verhage and G Vermeulen (eds), *Strafrecht en strafprocesrecht: doel of middel in een veranderde samenleving?* (Wolters Kluwer 2017).

Daeninck P, 'De impact van een beschikking van de onderzoeksrechter tot ET [elektronisch toezicht] op een hangend hoger beroep inzake voorlopige hechtenis' (2021) 2021 Tijdschrift voor Strafrecht 2.

Daeninck P, 'De voorafgaande ondervraging van de verdachte door de onderzoeksrechter' (2021) 2021 Tijdschrift voor Strafrecht 234.

Daeninck P, 'Over het verzoekschrift tot voorlopige invrijheidstelling na het instellen van hoger beroep tegen de beslissing ten gronde' (2021) 2021 Tijdschrift voor Strafrecht 232.

Daeninck P, 'Voorlopige hechtenis: over de omvang en andere vraagstukken van de borgsom' [2023] Tijdschrift voor Strafrecht 207.

Dawson J and Beard J, 'Counter-Terrorism and Sentencing Bill 2019–2021: Lords amendments' (2021) 9169 House of Commons Library Briefing Paper.

D.C.O., 'Commentary: R v G; R v J' [2009] Criminal Law Review 679.

De Coensel S, 'De Wet Diverse Bepalingen in Strafzaken II: Terroristische misdrijven in lijn met de Europese verplichtingen?' (2019) 40 Panopticon 211.

De Coensel S, *Counter-Terrorism & Criminal Law: A Normative Legitimacy Test of Terrorism-Related Offences on Expression, Information and Movement* (Maklu 2020).

De Coensel S, 'Incitement to Terrorism: The Nexus Between Causality and Intent and the Question of Legitimacy – A Case Study of the European Union, Belgium and the United Kingdom' in Christophe Paulussen and Martin Scheinin (eds), *Human Dignity and Human Security in Times of Terrorism* (TMC Asser Press 2020) http://link.springer.com/10.1007/978-94-6265-355-9_12 accessed 14 September 2023.

De Goede M, 'The Politics of Preemption and the War on Terror in Europe' (2008) 14 European Journal of International Relations 161.

de Graaf BA and Eijkman Q, 'Terrorismebestrijding en securitisering: een rechtssociologische verkenning van de neveneffecten' [2011] Justitiële Verkenningen 33.

De Groote J, 'De bovengrens der fout en de ondergrens van het opzet met bijzondere aandacht voor het eventueel opzet: een doctrinale en rechtsvergelijkende analyse' (2017) special number April 2017 Nullum Crimen (NC) 66.

De Herdt J, 'Bijzonder strafrecht en straftoemeting na de Potpourri II-Wet' [2016] Nullum Crimen 189.

De Hert P and Millen J, 'Terrorisme' (2013) VIII.2013 Qualifications et Jurisprudence Penales 1.

De La Serna I, 'Des infractions terroristes', *Les Infractions* (Larcier 2013).

De La Serna I, 'Des infractions terroristes' in Marie-Aude Beernaert and others, *Les infractions. 5: Les infractions contre l'ordre public* (Larcier 2013).

De La Serna I, 'Des infractions terroristes' in Christian De Valkeneer and Ignacio De La Serna, *À la découverte de la justice pénale : Paroles de juriste* (Larcier 2015).

De Nauw A, 'Nieuwe wendingen inzake het lex certa beginsel' in Frank Verbruggen and others (eds), *Strafrecht als roeping: Liber amicorum Lieven Dupont* (Universitaire Pers Leuven 2005).

De Nauw A, 'Titel Iter: Terroristische misdrijven', *Inleiding tot het bijzonder Strafrecht* (sixth edition, Kluwer 2010).

De Nauw A and Deruyck F, *Overzicht van het Belgisch algemeen strafrecht* (die Keure 2015).

De Nauw A and Deruyck F, *Overzicht van het Belgisch algemeen strafrecht* (Die Keure 2017).

De Nauw A and Kuty F, *Manuel de Droit Pénal Spécial* (Wolters Kluwer 2014).

De Nil N, Deruyck F and Meese J, 'Misdrijven', *Strafrecht geannoteerd* (die Keure 2020).

De Roy C, 'De strafbare poging als klassiek leerstuk in het raam van de hedendaagse strijd tegen het terrorisme (noot onder Cass. 3 november 2004)' (2005–2006) 69 Rechtskundig Weekblad 1584.

De Schutter O, 'La Convention Européenne Des Droits de l'Homme à l'épreuve de la lutte contre le terrorisme' in Emmanuelle Bribosia and Anne Weyembergh (eds), *La convention Européenne des droits de l'homme à l'épreuve de la lutte contre le terrorisme* (Bruylant-Nemesis 2002).

De Valkeneer C, 'Les Réponses Face Au Terrorisme : Les Glissements Du Judiciaire Vers l'administratif' [2017] Journal Tribunaux 707.

De Vries U and Francot-Timmermans L, 'As Good as It Gets: On Risk, Legality and the Precautionary Principle' in L Besselink, F Pennings and S Prechal (eds), *The Eclipse of the Legality Principle in the European Union* (Kluwer 2011).

De Wael F, '"Ernstige aanwijzingen van schuld" uit de voorlopige hechteniswet gedefinieerd' (2021) 2021 Rechtspraak Antwerpen Brussel Gent (RABG) 1726.

Decaigny T, 'Nieuwe correctionele hoofdstraffen: de straf onder elektronisch toezicht en de autonome probatiestraf' [2014] Tijdschrift voor Strafrecht 211.

Decaigny T, 'Relatieve zwaarte, toepassingsgebied en duur' in M De Busscher and others (eds), *Strafrecht: duiding* (Larcier 2018).

Decaigny T, 'Vervangende Gevangenisstraf' in M De Busscher and others (eds), *Strafrecht: duiding* (Larcier 2018).

Decaigny T, in M De Busscher and others (eds), *Strafrecht: duiding* (Larcier 2018).

Declercq R, *Beginselen van Strafrechtspleging* (6de herwerkte ed., Kluwer 2014).

Dejemeppe B and Rigaux M-F, 'Lutte contre le terrorisme moderne : le contrôle des droits fondamentaux entre le marteau et l'enclume' in R Leysen and others (eds), *Semper perseverans – Liber amicorum André Alen* (Intersentia 2020).

Dekrem E, 'Naar een veralgemeende strafbaarheid van voorbereidende handelingen?' [2020] Nullum Crimen 133.

Delbrouck I, 'Niet-consensuele seksuele misdrijven – bijzondere strafrechtelijke en strafprocesrechtelijke aspecten' [2023] Postal Memorialis – Lexicon strafrecht, strafvordering en bijzondere wetten N31/1.

Delhaise E, *Infractions terroristes* (Larcier 2019).

Delhaise E and Fievet C, 'Frontières intelligentes et nouvelles incriminations pénales : L'Union Européenne face à la problématique des " foreign terrorist fighters "' [2017] Journal des tribunaux 113.

Delmulle J and Guenter S, 'Gerechtelijke aanpak inzake terrorisme', *Strafrecht en Strafprocesrecht* (Wolters Kluwer 2006).

Delval L, 'Société du risque et gestion des crises: les pouvoirs publics Belges sont-ils organisés pour faire face à un risuqe majeur? type de risque: menace terroriste' in Marc Cools and others (eds), *1915–2015 Het verhaal van de Belgische militaire inlichtingen- en veiligheidsdienst* (Maklu 2015).

Demirsu I, *Counter-Terrorism and the Prospects of Human Rights* (Springer International Publishing 2017).

Dennis I, 'The Rationale of Criminal Conspiracy' (1977) 93 The Law Quarterly review 39.

Deruyck F, 'De impact van het arrest no. 148/2017 van het Grondwettelijk Hof van 21 december 2017 op de voorlopige hechtenis' [2017] Nullum Crimen 54.

Deruyck F, 'Witwassen', *Strafrecht en strafvordering. Artikelsgewijze commentaar met overzicht van rechtspraak en rechtsleer* (Wolters Kluwer).

Deruyck F and De Nauw A, *Inleiding tot het bijzonder strafrecht* (Kluwer 2020).

Devos D, 'Le blanchiment des capitaux d'origine criminelle' [1992] Bank Fin 201.

Devroe W and Rombouts A, 'Wissel als witsel. de beteugeling van het witwassen van gelden via geldwissel in het Belgisch financieel en strafrecht (noot onder corr. Antwerpen 23 februari 1993)' [1994] TRV 199.

Dewandeleer D, "Opzettelijk doden en opzettelijk toebrengen van lichamelijk letsel (Art. 392 t/m 417 Sw.), Algemeen', *Postal Memorialis – Lexicon strafrecht, strafvordering en bijzondere wetten* (2001).

Dhont F, 'Art. 5 EVRM' in J Vande Lanotte and Y Haeck, *Handboek EVRM, Deel 2* (Intersentia 2004).

Dickson B, 'Terrorism Laws and Legal Accountability' in Genevieve Lennon and Clive Walker (eds), *Routledge Handbook of Law and Terrorism* (Routledge 2015).

Dinesson K, '(Un)Reasonable Excuses – On R v Dunleavy, R v Copeland, and Section 58' (2022) 85 Modern Law Review 1550.

Dixon D and others, 'Safeguarding the Rights of Suspects in Police Custody' (1990) 115 Policing and Society 115.

Donkin S, *Preventing Terrorism and Controlling Risk: A Comparative Analysis of Control Orders in the UK and Australia*, vol 1 (Springer New York 2014).

Dragu T, 'Is There a Trade-off between Security and Liberty? Executive Bias, Privacy Protections, and Terrorism Prevention' (2011) 105 American Political Science Review 64.

Du Bois-Pedain A, 'Terrorist Possession Offences: Curiosity Kills the Cat?' (2009) 68 The Cambridge Law Journal 261.

Duff R, 'Pre-Trial Detention and the Presumption of Innocence' in Andrew Ashworth, Lucia Zedner and Patrick Tomlin (eds), *Prevention and the Limits of the Criminal Law* (Oxford University Press 2013).

Duff RA, *Intention, Agency and Criminal Liability: Philosophy of Action and the Criminal Law* (Blackwell 1990).

Duff RA, *Criminal Attempts* (Oxford University Press 1997).

Duff RA, *Answering for Crime: Responsibility and Liability in the Criminal Law* (Hart Publishing 2007).

Dupont L, *Beginselen van behoorlijke strafrechtsbedeling* (Kluwer 1979).

Dupont L, *Beginselen van Strafrecht, Deel I* (Acco 1983).

Dyer P, 'Bail: Criminal Proceedings' [2021] Westlaw UK 11.

Edwards RA, 'Police Powers and Article 5 ECHR: Time for a New Approach to the Interpretation of the Right to Liberty' (2020) 41 Liverpool Law Review 331.

Elliott C and Quinn F, *Criminal Law* (Eleventh edition, Pearson Education Limited 2016).

Espanda DC, 'Sentence: New Cases: Particular Offences Terrorism' CLW/19/46/27.
Ewing KD, 'The Futility of the Human Rights Act' [2004] Public Law 829.
Feldman D, 'Deprivation of Liberty in Anti-Terrorism Law' [2008] The Cambridge Law Journal 4.
Fenwick H, 'The Anti–Terrorism, Crime and Security Act 2001: A Proportionate Response to 11 September?' (2002) 65 The Modern Law Review 724.
Fenwick H, 'Recalibrating ECHR Rights, and the Role of the Human Rights Act Post 9/11: Reasserting International Human Rights Norms in the "War on Terror"?' (2010) 63 Current Legal Problems 153.
Fenwick H, 'Preventive Anti-Terrorist Strategies in the UK and ECHR: Control Orders, TPIMs and the Role of Technology' (2011) 25 International Review of Law, Computers & Technology 129.
Fenwick H, 'Replacing the Human Rights Act with a British Bill of Rights: Creating Greater Parliamentary Autonomy on Human Rights Matters?' in Nicolas Kang-Riou, Jo Milner and Suryia Nayak (eds), *Confronting the Human Rights Act : contemporary themes and perspectives* (Routledge 2012).
Fenwick H, 'The Human Rights Act or a British Bill of Rights: Creating a down-Grading Recalibration of Rights against the Counter-Terror Backdrop?' [2012] Public Law 468.
Fenwick H, 'Designing ETPIMs around ECHR Review or Normalisation of "Preventive" Non-Trial-Based Executive Measures?' (2013) 76 Modern Law Review 876.
Fenwick H, 'Redefining the Role of TPIMs in Combatting "Home-Grown" Terrorism within the Widening Counter-Terror Framework' [2015] European human rights law review 41.
Fenwick H, *Fenwick on Civil Liberties and Human Rights* (Taylor & Francis Group 2016).
Fenwick H, 'Terrorism and the Control Orders/TPIMs Saga: A Vindication of the Human Rights Act or a Manifestation of "Defensive Democracy"?' [2017] Public law. 609.
Fenwick H and Fenwick D, 'The Role of Derogations from the ECHR in the Current "War on Terror"' in Eran Shor and Stephen Hoadley (eds), *International Human Rights and Counter-Terrorism* (Springer 2019).
Fenwick H and Masterman R, 'The Conservative Project to "Break the Link between British Courts and Strasbourg": Rhetoric or Reality?' (2017) 80 The Modern Law Review 1111.
Fenwick H and Phillipson G, 'Covert Derogations and Judicial Deference: Redefining Liberty and Due Process Rights in Counterterrorism Law and Beyond' (2011) 56 McGill Law Journal 863.
Féret J and Peyro Llopis A, 'La lutte contre le terrorisme: instruments et institutions' in Ludovic Hennebel and Damien Vandermeersch (eds), *Juger le terrorisme dans l'État de droit* (Bruylant 2009).
Feyen S, 'Noodzakelijkheid als de schoonmoeder van het proportionaliteitsbeginsel' in R Leysen and others (eds), *Semper perseverans – Liber amicorum André Alen* (Intersentia 2020).
Fiedler S, 'The Right to Rebel: Social Movements and Civil Disobedience' (2009) 1 Cosmopolitan Civil Societies Journal 42.
Fijnaut C, 'De belangrijke rol van het strafrecht bij de bestrijding van (islamitisch) terrorisme' (2005) 2005 Rechtsgeleerd Magazijn THEMIS 210.

Fijnaut C, *De samenhang tussen georganiseerde misdaad en terrorisme en de aanslagen in Parijs en Brussel in 2015–2016* (Intersentia 2020).

Finlay C, *Terrorism and the Right to Resist: A Theory of Just Revolutionary War* (Cambridge University Press 2015)

Flore D, 'La Loi du 19 Décembre 2003 relative aux infractions terroristes: Genèse, principes et conséquences', *Questions d'actualité de droit pénal et de procédure pénale* (Bruylant 2005).

Flore D, *Droit Pénal Européen: Les enjeux d'une justice pénale Européenne* (Larcier 2008).

Forcese C and Roach K, *False Security: The Radicalization of Canadian Anti-Terrorism* (Irwin Law 2015).

Forsyth C, 'Control Orders, Conditions, Precedent and Compliance with Article 6(1)' (2008) 67 The Cambridge Law Journal 1.

Fransen A and Kerkhofs J, 'Het materieel terrorismestrafrecht' in Jan Kerkhofs, Antoon Schotsaert and Philippe Van Linthout (eds), *Contra-terrorisme: De gerechtelijke aanpak van terrorisme in België* (Larcier 2018).

Fransen A and Kerkhofs J, 'Het materieel terrorismestrafrecht in België: De Misdrijven' (2018) 3 Tijdschrift voor Strafrecht 150.

Fransen A, Kerkhofs J and Verrest P, *Terrorisme: Een analyse van het Belgische en Nederlandse Materieel Strafrecht* (Wolf Legal Publishers 2017).

Fransen H, 'Strafwet' [2017] Postal Memorialis – Lexicon strafrecht, strafvordering en bijzondere wetten S180/01.

Franssen V, 'Algemeen' in M De Busscher and others (eds), *Strafrecht: duiding* (Larcier 2018).

Franssen V, 'Begrip Politiek Misdrijf' in M De Busscher and others (eds), *Strafrecht: duiding* (Larcier 2018).

Freeman B, 'Preventive Detention, Extraordinary Rendition and Torture: Counter-Terrorism Initiatives and the Unjustifiable Curtailing of Individual Rights and Liberties' (*Ethics, Terrorism, United States, War & Conlict*, 22 March 2016).

Galli F, 'The War on Terror and Crusading Judges: Re-Establishing the Primacy of the Criminal Justice System' in A Masferrer (ed), *Post 9/11 and the State of Permanent Legal Emergency* (Springer 2012).

Galli F and Weyembergh A, 'Introduction' in Francesca Galli and Anne Weyembergh (eds), *EU counter-terrorism offences: What impact on national legislation and case-law?* (Editions de l'Université de Bruxelles 2012).

Ganor B, 'Defining Terrorism: Is One Man's Terrorist Another Man's Freedom Fighter?' [2002] Police Practice and Research 287.

Garland D, *The Culture of Control: Crime and Social Order in Contemporary Society* (Oxford University Press 2001).

Gearty C, 'Human Rights in an Age of Counter-Terrorism: Injurious, Irrelevant or Indispensable?' (2005) 58 Current Legal Problems 25.

Gearty C, 'The Human Rights Act – an Academic Sceptic Changes His Mind but Not His Heart' [2010] European Human Rights Law Review 582.

Gerards J, 'Freedom of Movement' in P Van Dijk and others, *Theory and Practice of the European Convention on Human Rights* (Intersentia 2018).

Gherbaoui T, 'Criminalising Foreign Fighter Travel in Order to Prevent Terrorism in Europe: An Illegitimate Assault on Human Dignity?' in Christophe Paulussen and

Martin Scheinin (eds), *Human Dignity and Human Security in Times of Terrorism* (TMC Asser Press 2020).

Gibson-Morgan E, 'Police Custody in England and France: A Lawful Deprivation of Liberty?' in Marion Charret-Del Bove and Fabrice Mourlon (eds), *Pre-trial detention in 20th and 21st Century Common Law and Civil Law Systems* (Cambridge Scholars Publishing 2014).

Gioia A, 'The UN Conventions on the Prevention and Suppression of International Terrorism' in Giuseppe Nesi (ed), *International cooperation in counter-terrorism: the United Nations and regional organizations in the fight against terrorism* (Ashgate 2006).

Gless S, 'Fighting Terrorism in a "Rechtsstaat"' in Toine Sapens, Marc Groenhuijsen and Tijs Kooijmans (eds), *Universalis: Liber amicorum Cyrille Fijnaut* (Intersentia 2011).

Gless S, 'The Two Framework Decisions: A Critical Approach' in Francesca Galli and Anne Weyembergh (eds), *EU counter-terrorism offences: What impact on national legislation and case-law?* (Editions de l'Université de Bruxelles 2012).

Greenberg D, 'Terrorism' [2022] Westlaw UK 14.

Greenberg D, 'Terrorist Offences' [2022] Westlaw UK.

Greenberg D, 'Formation of Contract: Consideration' [2023] Westlaw UK.

Günther K, 'Responsibility to Protect and Preventive Justice' in Andrew Ashworth, Lucia Zedner and Patrick Tomlin (eds), *Prevention and the Limits of the Criminal Law* (Oxford University Press 2013).

Gyselaers L, 'La participation des citoyens à la fonction de juger en matière pénale. Etude comparative du droit Anglais, de droit Belge et de droit Français' (PhD thesis, KU Leuven 2011).

Hafner G, 'The Definition of the Crime of Terrorism' in Giuseppe Nesi (ed), *International cooperation in counter-terrorism: the United Nations and regional organizations in the fight against terrorism* (Ashgate 2006).

Hale-Ross S, *Digital Privacy, Terrorism and Law Enforcement: The UK's Response to Terrorist Communication* (1st edn, Routledge 2018).

Hall J, 'Note on Counter-Terrorism and Sentencing Bill: Sentencing Reforms (1)' (2020) Independent Reviewer of Terrorism Legislation.

Hall J, 'Note on Counter-Terrorism and Sentencing Bill: Sentencing Reforms (2)' (2020) Independent Reviewer of Terrorism Legislation.

Hall J, 'The Terrorism Acts in 2020' (2020) Report of the Independent Reviewer of Terrorism Legislation on the Operation of the Terrorism Acts 2000 and 2006, and the Terrorism Prevention and Investigation Measures Act 2011.

Hall J, 'The Terrorism Acts in 2021' (2021) Report of the Independent Reviewer of Terrorism Legislation on the Operation of the Terrorism Acts 2000 and 2006, and the Terrorism Prevention and Investigation Measures Act 2011.

Hallevy G, *A Modern Treatise on the Principle of Legality in Criminal Law* (Springer Berlin Heidelberg 2010).

Halstead P, *Human Rights* (Routledge 2014).

Hameeuw V, 'Strafbaarstelling van terroristische misdrijven: van Europees Kaderbesluit tot het Belgische Strafwetboek' [2005] Tijdschrift voor Strafrecht 2.

Hamilton C, 'The European Union: Sword or Shield? Comparing Counterterrorism Law in the EU and the USA after 9/11' (2018) 22 Theoretical Criminology 206.

Hardy K and Williams G, 'What Is Terrorism – Assessing Domestic Legal Definitions' (2011) 16 UCLA J. Intl. L. Foreign Aff. 77.

Harris L, 'Commentary: R. v LF; R. v DS' [2016] Criminal Law Review 676.

Hayes B and Jones C, 'Taking Stock: The Evolution, Adoption, Implementation and Evaluation of EU Counter-Terrorism Policy' in Fiona de Londras and Josephine Doody (eds), *The Impact, Legitimacy and Effectiveness of EU Counter-Terrorism* (1st edn, Routledge 2015).

Hellemans F, 'Witwassen: een strafbaar maar lonend misdrijf? (Noot onder corr. Antwerpen 14 april 1994)' [1994] TRV 287.

Hennebel L and Tigroudja H, 'Le Juge, Le Terroriste et l'état de Droit' in Ludovic Hennebel and Damien Vandermeersch (eds), *Juger le terrorisme dans l'État de droit* (Bruylant 2009).

Herring J, *Criminal Law: Text, Cases and Materials* (Ninth edition, Oxford University Press 2020).

Hill M, 'The Terrorism Acts in 2017' (2018) Report of the Independent Reviewer of Terrorism Legislation on the Operation of the Terrorism Acts 2000 and 2006, the Terrorism Prevention and Investigation Measures Act 2011, and the Terrorist Asset Freezing Etc Act 2010.

Hirst M, 'Murder under the Queen's Peace' [2008] Criminal Law Review 541.

Hodgson J and Tadros V, 'How to Make a Terrorist Out of Nothing' (2009) 72 Modern Law Review 984.

Hodgson JS and Tadros V, 'The Impossibility of Defining Terrorism' (2013) 16 New Criminal Law Review 494.

Hoet P, 'Werkbare probatie en herroeping' in P Traest and others (eds), *Amicus Curiae* (Intersentia 2013) www.jurisquare.be/en/book/9789400004306/werkbare-probatie-en-herroeping/.

Hoffman B, *Inside Terrorism, Revised and Expanded Edition* (Columbia University Press 2006).

Hoffman D and Rowe J, *Human Rights in the UK: An Introduction to the Human Rights Act 1998* (Third edition, Pearson Education Limited 2010).

Tony Honoré, 'The Right to Rebel' (1988) 8 Oxford J. Legal Stud. 34.

Horseele M and others, 'Recente wijzigingen in het straf(proces)recht: consequent incoherent?', *Recht in beweging – 25ste VRG-Alumnidag* (Gompel&Svacina 2018).

Hudson B, 'Justice in a Time of Terror' (2009) 49 The British Journal of Criminology 702.

Hudson B, 'Who Needs Justice? Who Needs Security?' in Barbara Hudson and Synnove Ugelvik (eds), *Justice in the Risk Society: Challenging and Re-affirming Justice in Late Modernity* (SAGE Publications Ltd 2012).

Hunt A, 'Criminal Prohibitions on Direct and Indirect Encouragement of Terrorism' [2007] Criminal Law Review 441.

Hunt A, 'From Control Orders to TPIMs: Variations on a Number of Themes in British Legal Responses to Terrorism' (2014) 62 Crime, Law and Social Change 289.

Husabø EJ and Bruce I, *Fighting Terrorism through Multilevel Criminal Legislation: Security Council Resolution 1373, the EU Framework Decision on Combating Terrorism and Their Implementation in Nordic, Dutch and German Criminal Law* (Brill | Nijhoff 2009).

Husak D, *Overcriminalization: The Limits of the Criminal Law* (Oxford University Press 2008).

Husak D, 'Negligence, Belief, Blame and Criminal Liability: The Special Case of Forgetting' (2011) 5 Criminal Law and Philosophy 199.

Hustin-Denies N, 'La législation Belge sur le blachiment de capiteaux d'origine criminelle: un instrument d'indemnisation des victimes et de lutte contre la criminalité organisée?' [1995] Ann dr Louv 53.

Huysmans J and others, 'Grondwet (Uitreksel)', *Strafrecht geannoteerd* (die Keure 2020).

Ip J, 'Terrorism Laws and Constitutional Accountability' in Genevieve Lennon and Clive Walker (eds), *Routledge Handbook of Law and Terrorism* (Routledge 2015).

Jackson R, 'In Defence of "Terrorism": Finding a Way through a Forest of Misconceptions' [2011] Behavioral Sciences of Terrorism and Political Aggression 116.

Jayawickrama N (ed), 'The Right to Liberty', *The Judicial Application of Human Rights Law: National, Regional and International Jurisprudence* (Cambridge University Press 2002).

Jespers R, 'La nécessité d'une vision critique sur la lutte contre le terrorisme' (2004) 393 Journal des Procès 12.

Jörg N, Kelk C and Klip A, *Strafrecht met mate* (14th edn, Wolters Kluwer 2019).

Kats R, De Graaf B and Jacobs P, 'Terroristen in detentie: een overzicht van de ontwikkeling en discussie over de terroristenafdelingen in Nederland, 2004–2022' [2022] Justitiele Verkenningen 10.

Kavanagh A, 'Special Advocates, Control Orders and the Right to a Fair Trial'.

Kelly R, 'Sentencing Terrorism Offences: No Harm Intended?' [2019] Criminal Law Review 764.

Kelly R, 'Reforming the Sentencing and Release of Terrorist Offenders' [2023] Criminal Law Review 639.

Kelman D, 'Closed Trials and Secret Allegations: An Analysis of the "Gisting" Requirement' (2016) 80 The Journal of Criminal Law 264.

Kerkhofs J, 'Noot onder corr. Hasselt 27 juli 1999' [1999] Limb. Rechtsl. 264.

Kestemont L and Schoukens P, *Rechtswetenschappelijk Schrijven* (Acco 2012).

Ketels B, 'De strafrechtelijke context van risicovol seksueel gedrag' [2008] Tijdschrift voor Strafrecht 354.

Ketels B, 'Titel Iter Terroristische Misdrijven' in Martine De Busscher and others (eds), *Strafrecht: Duiding* (Larcier 2018).

Khan I, 'Human Rights in an Age of Terror' in Nicolas Kang-Riou, Jo Milner and Suryia Nayak (eds), *Confronting the Human Rights Act : contemporary themes and perspectives* (Routledge 2012).

Kremnitzer M and Saba-Habesch L, 'Executive Measures against the Liberties of Terrorism Suspects' in Genevieve Lennon and Clive Walker (eds), *Routledge Handbook of Law and Terrorism* (Routledge 2015).

Krenc F, 'La Belgique "condamnée" pour la première fois par le Comité Des Droits de l'homme sur fond de lutte contre le terrorisme – Cap sur Genève!' [2009] Journal des tribunaux 621.

Kronenberg MJ and de Wilde B, *Grondtrekken van het Nederlandse strafrecht* (8th edn, Kluwer 2020).

Kuty F, *Principes généraux du droit pénal Belge. Tome 1: La loi pénale* (3rd edn, Larcier 2018).

Laird K, 'Commentary: R v Lane (Sally)' [2019] Criminal Law Review 178.

Lavaux S, 'Terrorisme: la stratégie de l'Union Européenne en matière de radicalisation et de recrutment (suite)' [2011] Vigiles 68.

Lavaux S, 'Terrorisme: La stratégie de l'union Européenne en matière de radicalisation et de recrutement (troisième partie)' [2015] Vigiles 114.

Lavaux S, 'Recente Overheidsmaatregelen i.v.m. de "Foreign Fighters"' [2016] Panopticon 352.

Lazarus L, Goold B and Goss C, 'Control without Punishment: Understanding Coercion' in Jonathan Simon and Richard Sparks, *The SAGE Handbook of Punishment and Society* (SAGE Publications Ltd 2013).

Lee F, 'Sentencing Cases of Preparation of Terrorist Acts (Terrorism Act 2006 s.5): A Call for Proportionality' [2018] Sentencing News 8.

Lee F and Walker C, 'The Counter-Terrorism and Sentencing Act 2021 and the Advance of Intensified Terrorism Punishment' [2022] Criminal Law Review 864.

Lee F and Walker C, 'The Sentencing of Precursor Terrorism Crimes in the United Kingdom' in Clive Walker, Mariona Llobet Anglí and Manuel C Meliá (eds), *Precursor Crimes of Terrorism: The Criminalisation of Terrorism Risk in Comparative Perspective* (Edward Elgar Publishing 2022).

Leestmans D, 'Terrorisme blijft in strafrechtelijke termen deels onvatbaar, interview met Paul Ponsaers' [27 mei 2020] Juristenkrant 8.

Legros R, *Opzet* (Larcier 1959).

Leigh I and others, *Making Rights Real: The Human Rights Act in Its First Decade* (Bloomsbury Publishing Plc 2008).

Liégeois Y and De Smet B, 'Verlenging termijn van arrestatie van 24 uur naar 48 uur' (2018) 20 Rechtskundig Weekblad 762.

Lomell HM, 'Punishing the Uncommitted Crime: Prevention, Pre-Emption, Precaution and the Transformation of Criminal Law' in Barbara Hudson and Synnove Ugelvik (eds), *Justice in the Risk Society: Challenging and Re-affirming Justice in Late Modernity* (SAGE Publications Ltd 2012).

Loveless J, Allen M and Derry C, *Complete Criminal Law* (Seventh edition, Oxford University Press 2020).

Lowe D, *Terrorism: Law and Policy* (Routledge 2018).

Lutz J and Lutz B, *Global Terrorism* (Routledge 2013).

Lynch A, McGarrity N and Williams G, 'The Emergence of a "Culture of Control"' in Nicola McGarrity, Andrew Lynch and George Williams (eds), *Counter-terrorism and beyond: the culture of law and justice after 9/11* (Routledge 2010).

Lynch A, Tulich T and Welsh R, 'Secrecy and Control Orders: The Role and Vulnerability of Constitutional Values in Australia and the United Kingdom' in D Cole, F Fabrini and A Vedaschi (eds), *Secrecy, national security, and the vindication of constitutional law* (Edward Elgar 2013).

Macdonald S and Carlile, Lord, 'Disrupting Terrorist Activity: What Are the Limits to Criminal Methods of Disruption?' in Satvinder S Juss (ed), *Beyond human rights and the war on terror* (Routledge, Taylor & Francis Group 2019).

Machielsen AJ, 'Materiële Verweren' in MF Attinger (ed), *Handboek Strafzaken* (2018).

Macken C, 'Preventive Detention and the Right to Personal Liberty and Security under Article 5 ECHR' (2006) 10 The International Journal of Human Rights 195.

Macken C, *Counter-Terrorism and the Detention of Suspected Terrorists* (Routledge 2011).

Malagnini R, 'La poursuite en Belgique des infractions terroristes commises à l'étranger' [2018] Revue de Jurisprudence de Liège, Mons et Bruxelles (JLMB) 1423.

Mancano L, *The European Union and Deprivation of Liberty: A Legislative and Judicial Analysis from the Perspective of the Individual* (Hart Publishing 2019).

Maras M-H, *Counterterrorism* (Jones and Bartlett 2013).

Marchand C, 'Impact des nouvelles infractions terroristes quant à la qualification de participation à un groupe terroriste et à l'usage d'une preuve secrète devant le tribunal: commentaires d'un avocat' in Francesca Galli and Anne Weyembergh (eds), *EU counter-terrorism offences: What impact on national legislation and case-law?* (Editions de l'Université de Bruxelles 2012).

Marlier G, *Familie in het straf- en strafprocesrecht: afbrokkelende hoeksteen van de samenleving?* (Wolters Kluwer 2018).

Marsavelski A,' The Crime of Terrorism and the Right of Revolution in International Law' (2012–2013) 28 Conn. J. Int'l L. 243.

Martin J, *Criminal Law* (Routledge 2014).

Martin J-C, *Les règles internationales relatives à la lutte contre le terrorisme* (Bruylant 2006).

Martínez-Peñas L and Fernández-Rodríguez M, 'Evolution of British Law on Terrorism: From Ulster to Global Terrorism (1970–2010)' in Aniceto Masferrer (ed), *Post 9/11 and the State of Permanent Legal Emergency: Security and Human Rights in Countering Terrorism*, vol 14 (Springer Netherlands 2012).

Masset A, 'Terrorisme' [2013] Postal Memorialis – Lexicon strafrecht, strafvordering en bijzondere wetten 411.

Masterman R and Murray C, *Constitutional and Administrative Law* (3rd edn, Cambridge University Press 2022).

McBride J, 'Proportionality and the European Convention on Human Rights' in E Ellis (ed), *The Principle of Proportionality in the Laws of Europe* (Hart Publishing 1999).

McConville M, Sanders A and Leng R, *The Case for the Prosecution* (Routledge 1991).

McCormack W, 'Detention of Mega-Terrorists: It's About Crime' (2011) 30 Criminal Justice Ethics 82.

McCulloch J and Pickering S, 'Pre-Crime and Counter-Terrorism: Imagining Future Crime in the "War on Terror"' (2009) 49 The British Journal of Criminology 628.

McCulloch J and Wilson D, *Pre-Crime: Pre-Emption, Precaution and the Future* (Routledge 2016).

McLoughlin JP, Noone GP and Noone DC, 'Security Detention, Terrorism And The Prevention Imperative' (2009) 40 CASE W. RES. J. INT'L L. 463.

Melander S, 'Ultima Ratio in European Criminal Law' (2013) 3 European Criminal Law Review 45.

Meliá MC, 'Terrorism and Criminal Law: The Dream of Prevention, the Nightmare of the Rule of Law' [2011] New Criminal Law Review 108.

Meliá MC and Petzsche A, 'Precursor Crimes of Terrorism' in Genevieve Lennon and Clive Walker (eds), *Routledge Handbook of Law and Terrorism* (Routledge 2015).

Mennes I, 'De Wet van 31 mei 2005: een face-lift van de voorlopige hechtenis?', *Strafrecht en Strafprocesrecht* (Wolters Kluwer 2006).

Middleton B, 'Rebalancing, Reviewing or Rebranding the Treatment of Terrorist Suspects: The Counter-Terrorism Review 2011' (2011) 75 The Journal of Criminal Law 225.

Mitsilegas V, 'The Criminalisation of Travel as a Global Paradigm of Preventive (in) Justice: Lessons from the EU Response to "Foreign Terrorist Fighters"' (2023) 14 New J Eur Crim L 183.

Mols G and De Roos T, 'Naar een algemene strafbaarheid van voorbereidingshandelingen' [1992] N.J.B.

Moreau C, 'Droit pénal de l'ennemi versus droit pénal du citoyen: réflexions sur la fonction sécuritaire du système de droit criminel mise en avant par les infractions terroristes incriminées par les articles 140*sexies* et 140*septies* du Code Pénal' [2021] Revue de Droit Pénal et de Criminologie (Rev. dr. pén.) 101.

Morgan KO, 'The Politics of Pre-Trial Detention in the United Kingdom since 2000' in Marion Charret-Del Bove and Fabrice Mourlon (eds), *Pre-trial detention in 20th and 21st Century Common Law and Civil Law Systems* (Cambridge Scholars Publishing 2014).

Moucheron M, 'Délit politique et terrorisme en Belgique : du noble au vil' [2006] Cultures & conflits 77.

Mucha W, 'Polarization, Stigmatization, Radicalization. Counterterrorism and Homeland Security in France and Germany' [2017] Journal for deradicalization 230.

Mueller TN, 'Preventive Detention as a Counter-Terrorism Instrument in Germany' (2014) 62 Crime, Law and Social Change 323.

Müller J-W, 'Militant Democracy' in Michel Rosenfeld and András Sajó (eds), *The Oxford handbook of comparative constitutional law* (1st ed, Oxford University Press 2012).

Murdoch J, 'Safeguarding the Liberty of the Person: Recent Strasbourg Jurisprudence' [1993] International and Comparative Law Quarterly 494.

Murphy CC, *EU Counter-Terrorism Law: Pre-Emption and the Rule of Law* (1st edn, Hart Publishing 2012).

Mythen G, Walklate S and Khan F, '"Why Should We Have to Prove We're Alright?": Counter-Terrorism, Risk and Partial Securities' [2012] Sociology 383.

Newman E, 'Exploring the "Root Causes" of Terrorism' [2006] Studies in conflict and terrorism 765.

Nouwynck L, 'Institutions de sécurité sociale, travailleus sociaux, secret professionnel et terrorisme: La Cour Constitutionelle remet les pendules à l'heure (noot onder GwH 19 maart 2019)' [2019] Revue de droit communal 21.

Ohana D, 'Responding to Acts Preparatory to the Commission of a Crime: Criminalization of Prevention?' (2006) 25 Crim. Just. Ethics 23.

Onsea I, 'Wet betreffende de criminele organisaties: een eerste effectieve stap in de strijd tegen georganiseerde criminaliteit?' [1999] Panopticon 278.

Onsea I, *De bestrijding van georganiseerde misdaad: de grens tussen waarheidsvinding en grondrechten* (Intersentia 2003).

Ormerod D and Fortson R, 'Serious Crime Act 2007: The Part 2 Offences' [2009] Criminal Law Review 389.

Palmer P, 'Dealing with the Exceptional: Pre-Crime Anti-Terrorism Policy and Practice' (2012) 22 Policing and Society 519.

Parmar A, 'Arrest' in Lucy Welsh, Layta Skinns and Andrew Sanders, *Sanders & Young's Criminal Justice* (Oxford University Press 2021).

Paye J-C, 'De la définition légale de l'organisation criminelle à l'incrimination du terrorisme' (2002) 435 Journal des Procès 9.

Paye J-C, 'Lois Anti-Terroristes. L'exemple Anglais' [2004] Journal des Procès 14.

Perez S and Thibaud T, 'Les instruments de lutte contre le terrorisme au sein de l'Union Européenne', *L'Union Européenne et la lutte contre le terrorisme: état des lieux et perspective* (Larcier 2010).

Peristeridou C, *The Principle of Legality in European Criminal Law* (Intersentia 2015).

Petersen AC, 'Extradition and the Political Offense Exception in the Suppression of Terrorism' (1992) 67 Indiana Law Journal 767.

Petersen J, 'Naar nieuwe verbale uitingsmisdrijven in de strijd tegen terreur?' (2019) 14 Nullum Crimen (NC) 50.

Petzsche A, 'The Penalization of Public Provocation to Commit a Terrorist Offence – Evaluating Different National Implementation Strategies of the International and European Legal Framework in Light of Freedom of Expression' (2017) 7 European Criminal Law Review 241.

Pieterman R, *De voorzorgcultuur: streven naar veiligheid in een wereld vol risico en onzekerheid* (Boom Juridisch 2008).

Ponseille A, 'Les infractions de prévention, argonautes de la lutte contre le terrorisme' [2017] Revue des droits et libertés fondamentaux.

Qureshi T, 'Preparation of Terrorist Acts' [2016] Westlaw UK 5.

Qureshi T, 'Support for Proscribed Organisations' [2022] Westlaw UK 7.

Ramsay P, *The Insecurity State: Vulnerable Autonomy and the Right to Security in the Criminal Law* (Oxford University Press 2012).

Ramsay P, 'Democratic Limits to Preventive Criminal Law' in Andrew Ashworth, Lucia Zedner and Patrick Tomlin (eds), *Prevention and the Limits of the Criminal Law* (Oxford University Press 2013).

Rawls J, *A Theory of Justice* (Harvard University Press 1978).

Redaelli C, 'The Right to Rebel against Violations of Human Rights: A New Role for the Responsibility to Protect?' [2016] Palestine Yearbook of International Law 8.

Reyntjens L, *Ex-citizens and the European convention on human rights: citizenship deprivation examined under the ECHR* (PhD Thesis KU Leuven 2022).

Reyntjens L and Yperman W, 'Terrorisme en internationale mobiliteit: een coherent beleid of nattevingerwerk' [2019] Politie & Recht 99.

Richards A, 'Conceptualizing Terrorism' (2014) 37 Studies in Conflict & Terrorism 213.

Richardson A and Chalk A, 'Possession of Terrorist Materials' [2014] Westlaw UK.

Roach K, 'The Case for Defining Terrorism With Restraint and Without Reference to Political or Religious Motive' in Andrew Lynch, Edwina Macdonald and George Williams (eds), *Law and Liberty in the war on terror* (The Federation Press 2007).

Roach K, 'Must We Trade Rights for Security? The Choice Between Smart, Harsh, or Proportionate Security Strategies in Canada and Britain' in David Dyzenhaus (ed), *Civil rights and security* (Ashgate 2009).

Roach K, *The 9/11 Effect: Comparative Counter-Terrorism* (Cambridge University Press 2011).

Roberts J, 'Sentencing Cases of Failure to Disclose Information about Acts of Terrorism (Terrorism Act 2000 (Section 38B)): A Plea in Mitigation' [2018] Sentencing News 9.

Roelandt J, 'De strijd tegen het terrorisme: een overzicht van de recente wetgevende ingrepen in het straf(proces)recht' [2017] Nullum Crimen 10.

Rosas A, 'The Court of Justice of the European Union: A Human Rights Institution?' (2022) 14 Journal of Human Rights Practice 204.

Rowe JJ, 'The Terrorism Act 2000' [2001] Criminal Law Review 527.

Rowe P, 'The Criminal Liability of a British Soldier Merely for Participating in the Iraq War 2003: A Response to Chilcot Evidence' [2010] Criminal Law Review 752.

Royer S, 'De strijd tegen terroristische propaganda op social media' [2021] Tijdschrift voor Strafrecht 26.

Royer S, Vilain R and Yperman W, 'Grondwetswijziging voor terrorismeprocessen is niet radicaal genoeg' [2020] De Juristenkrant 10.

Rozie J, 'Beklaagde alwetend. Over het criterium van de redelijke voorzienbaarheid als maatstaf van het lex certa-principe in strafzaken' (2012–2013) 21 Rechtskundig Weekblad 802.

Rozie J, 'De werking van verzachtende omstandigheden in strafzaken doorgelicht' (2013) 8 Nullum Crimen 1.

Rozie J, 'Hof van assisen en correctionalisering na Potpourri II: kunst- en vliegwerk of dankbare ingreep van de wetgever?' [2016] Nullum Crimen (NC) 91.

Rozie J, 'De recidivewet van 5 mei 2019: de vergiftigde kers op de repressieve taart' (2019) 14 Nullum Crimen 291.

Rozie M, 'De probatie kan voortaan ook op eigen vleugels vliegen' [2014] Nullum Crimen 349.

Ryan C and Williams K, 'Police Discretion' [1986] Public Law 285.

Samuel Justin S and Daniel A, *The Psychology of Terrorism Fears* (Oxford University Press 2012).

Sánchez Frías A, 'Public Security Derogations to the Free Movement of EU Citizens and Preventive Criminal Law: A Collision between Ever-Expanding Concepts?' [2019] European Journal of Crime, Criminal Law and Criminal Justice 293.

Scheid DE, 'Indefinite Detention of Mega-Terrorists in the War on Terror' (2010) 29 Criminal Justice Ethics 1.

Scheirs V, 'Van binnen naar buiten. de externe rechtspositie van veroordeelde gedetineerden' in Kristel Beyens and Sonja Snacken (eds), *Straffen: Een penologisch perspectief* (Maklu 2017).

Schrijver NJ and Van Den Herik LJ, 'Counter-Terrorism Strategies, Human Rights and International Law: Meeting the Challenges' in ER Muller, U Rosenthal and R De Wijk (eds), *Terrorisme: studies over terrorisme en terrorismebestrijding* (Kluwer 2008).

Shor E and others, 'Terrorism and State Repression of Human Rights: A Cross-National Time-Series Analysis' (2014) 55 International Journal of Comparative Sociology 294.

Silvis J, 'Terrorism and Human Rights' in Koen Lemmens, Stephan Parmentier and Louise Reyntjens (eds), *Human Rights with a human touch: Liber amicorum Paul Lemmens* (Intersentia 2019).

Smeets S and Strebelle C, 'Terrorisme, criminalité organisée et violence urbaine: L'expérience Belge' in Emmanuelle Bribosia and Anne Weyembergh (eds), *Lutte contre le terrorisme et droits fondamentaux* (Bruylant-Nemesis 2002).

Smit DVZ and Ashworth A, 'Disproportionate Sentences as Human Rights Violations' (2004) 67 The Modern Law Review 541.

Smith T, '"Rushing Remand"? Pretrial Detention and Bail Decision Making in England and Wales' (2021) 60 The Howard Journal of Crime and Justice 46.

Smith T, 'The Practice of Pre-Trial Detention in England & Wales – Changing Law and Changing Culture' (2022) 28 European Journal on Criminal Policy and Research 435.

Sottiaux S, *Terrorism and the Limitation of Rights* (Hart Publishing 2008).

Spencer J and Virgo G, 'Encouraging and Assisting Crime: Legislate in Haste, Repent at Leisure' [2008] Arch. News 7.

Spencer JR, '"No Thank You, We've Already Got One!" Why EU Anti-Terrorist Legislation Has Made Little Impact on the Law of the UK' in Francesca Galli and Anne Weyembergh (eds), *EU counter-terrorism offences: What impact on national legislation and case-law?* (Editions de l'Université de Bruxelles 2012).

Sprack J and Engelhardt-Sprack M, *A Practical Approach to Criminal Procedure* (Oxford University Press 2019).

Spreutels J and Velu S, 'La lutte contre le terrorisme dans la jurisprudence de la Cour Consitutionnelle de Belgique' in Koen Lemmens, Stephan Parmentier and Louise Reyntjens (eds), *Human rights with a human touch: Liber amicorum Paul Lemmens* (Intersentia 2019).

Spriet B, 'Het verhandelen van dieren waaraan stoffen met hormonale of antihormonale werking zijn toegediend (noot onder Antwerpen 18 oktober 1990)' [1990] Rechtskundig Weekblad 857.

Spriet B, 'Elk misdrijf- ook dat uit het bijzonder strafrecht – vereist een moreel of schuldbestanddeel (noot onder Cass. 13 december 1994)' (1995) 1995–96 Rechtskundig Weekblad 533.

Spriet B, 'Poging tot misdaad of tot wanbedrijf', *Strafrecht geannoteerd* (die Keure 2020).

Spriet B and De Schepper K, 'De nieuwe witwas(straf)wet – Een schematisch overzicht' [2009–2010] T Fin R 21.

Squires D, 'Terrorism and Pre-Emptive Civil Processes' (2016) 20 The International Journal of Human Rights 684.

Staniforth A, *Preventing Terrorism and Violent Extremism* (Oxford University Press 2014).

Stark F, 'It's Only Words: On Meaning and Mens Rea' (2013) 72 Cambridge Law Journal 155.

Stark F, *Culpable Carelessness: Recklessness and Negligence in the Criminal Law* (Cambridge University Press 2016).

Steiker CS, 'Proportionality as a Limit on Preventive Justice: Promises and Pitfalls' in Andrew Ashworth, Lucia Zedner and Patrick Tomlin (eds), *Prevention and the limits of the criminal law* (Oxford University Press 2013).

Sterkens M, 'Hormonen: De Misdrijven', *Postal Memorialis – Lexicon strafrecht, strafvordering en bijzondere wetten* (2015).

Stessens G, 'Terroristen op reis: over de strafbaarstelling van reizen met terroristisch oogmerk en andere maatregelen ter beperking van de reisvrijheid van (vermeende) terroristen' in Steven Dewulf (ed), *La [CVDW] Liber Amicorum Chris Van den Wyngaert* (Maklu 2017).

Stone R, *Textbook on Civil Liberties & Human Rights* (Tenth edition, Oxford University Press 2016).

Sugman Stubbs K and Galli F, 'Inchoate Offences: The Sanctioning of an Act Prior to and Irrespective of the Commission of Any Harm' in Francesca Galli and Anne Weyembergh (eds), *EU counter-terrorism offences: What impact on national legislation and case-law?* (Editions de l'Université de Bruxelles 2012).

Suzanne O and Yves O, 'Le point sur la legislation antiterroriste' (2005) 501 Journal des Procès 14.

't Hart AC, 'Noot onder Hoge Raad 15 oktober 1996, ECLI:NL:HR:1996:ZD0139'.

Tadros V, 'The System of the Criminal Law' (2002) 22 Legal Studies 448.

Tadros V, 'Justice and Terrorism' [2007] New Criminal Law Review 658.

Tadros V, 'Rethinking the Presumption of Innocence' (2007) 1 Criminal Law and Philosophy 193.

Tadros V, 'Controlling Risk' in Andrew Ashworth, Lucia Zedner and Patrick Tomlin (eds), *Prevention and the Limits of the Criminal Law* (Oxford University Press 2013).

Ten Voorde J, 'Prohibiting Remote Harms: On Endangerment, Citizenship and Control' (2014) 10 Utrecht Law Review 163.

Tersago P, 'Hoofdstuk II. Voorlopige Hechtenis' in T De Meester and others, *Potpourri II – Strafrecht en strafprocesrecht* (Intersentia 2016).

Tersago P, 'Het recidiverisico bij de voorlopige hechtenis: de vreemde eend in de bijt (noot onder Cass. 8 september 2020)' [2021] Tijdschrift voor Strafrecht 85.

Theunis J, 'Le droit à la légalité des incriminations et des peines' in M Verdussen and N Bonbled (eds), *les droits consitutionnels en Belgique* (2nd edn, Bruylant 2011).

Thomas I, 'La mise en oevre en Droit Européen des dispositions internationals de lutte contre le terrorisme' [2004] Revue générale de droit international public 463.

Thomas PA, 'Emergency and Anti-Terrorist Powers' [2002–2003] Fordham Int'l L.J. 1193.

Todts L, *Bestuurlijke en strafrechtelijke vrijheidsbeperkingen ter handhaving van de openbare orde* (die Keure 2021).

Tomkins A, 'National Security and the Role of the Court: A Changed Landscape?' [2010] Law Quarterly Review 543.

Tomkins A, 'National Security and the Due Process of Law' (2011) 64 Current Legal Problems 215.

Traest P, 'Rechts(on)zekerheid in materieel en formeel strafrecht en strafrechtelijk legaliteitsbeginsel' [1993–1994] Rechtskundig Weekblad 1190.

Traest P, 'Ontwikkeling van nieuwe deelnemingsvormen' [2007] Nullum Crimen 24.1

Tsakyrakis S, 'Proportionality: An Assault on Human Rights?' (2009) 7 International Journal of Constitutional Law 468.

Tulkens F and others, *Introduction Au Droit Pénal* (10th edn, Wolters Kluwer 2014).

Van Bavel H, 'De strafrechtelijke aansprakelijkheid van vennootschappen en leidinggevenden: de lege lata, de lege ferenda' [2017] Tijdschrift voor Strafrecht 3.

Van Bavel H and Vandendriessche F, 'Gunningsfraude en de strafrechtelijke bescherming van de vrijheid van opbod' [2013] Tijdschrift voor Strafrecht 283.

Van Cauwenberghe K, 'Kan terrorisme de rechtstaat onderuit halen?' (2015) 318 Juristenkrant 13.

van de Kerchove M, 'Développements récents et paradoxaux du principe de la légalité criminelle et de ses corollaires essentiels' in Yves Poullet and Hendrik Vuye (eds), *Liber Amicorum Jean du Jardin* (Kluwer 2001).

Van Den Berge Y, 'De terbeschikkingstelling van de strafuitvoeringsrechtbank: alweer een nieuwe straf, alweer een nieuwe uitvoering' [2013] Tijdschrift voor Strafrecht 222.

Van Den Berge Y, 'Het Belgische strafrecht: veel aandacht voor de vrijheidsbeneming en de vrijheidsbeperking' [2019] Nullum Crimen 1.

Van Den Steen L, 'De Potpourri II-Wet en de veralgemeende correctionaliseerbaarheid: een prefabbouwwerk met onstabiele fundamenten' [2015–2016] Rechtskundig Weekblad 1604.

Van den Wyngaert C, 'The Political Offence Exception to Extradition: Defining the Issues and Searching a Feasible Alternative' [1983] Revue Belge de Droit International 741.

Van den Wyngaert C, *Strafrecht, strafprocesrecht & internationaal strafrecht in hoofdlijnen* (Maklu 2003).

Van den Wyngaert C, Traest P and Vandromme S, *Strafrecht en strafprocesrecht in hoofdlijnen* (Maklu 2017).

Van den Wyngaert C and Vandromme S, *Strafrecht en strafprocesrecht in hoofdlijnen* (Maklu 2014).

Van den Wyngaert C, Vandromme S and Traest P, *Strafrecht en strafprocesrecht in hoofdlijnen* (11th edn, Gompel&Svacina 2019).

van der Woude MAH, *Wetgeving in een veiligheidscultuur: totstandkoming van antiterrorismewetgeving in Nederland bezien vanuit maatschappelijke en (rechts) politieke context* (Boom Juridische uitgevers 2010).

Van Deuren C, 'Nieuwe straffen bij terroristische misdrijven' (2013) 2013 Rechtspraak Antwerpen Brussel Gent 508.

Van Dijk P and others, 'Chapter 9. Right to Liberty and Security', *Theory and Practice of the European Convention on Human Rights, 5th edition (hardcover)* (Intersentia 2018).

Van Overbeke S, 'Aanwezigheid bij het misdrijf als vorm van strafbare deelneming: je was erbij dus je bent erbij? (noot onder Cass. 17 december 2008)' [2010–2011] Rechtskundig Weekblad 367.

Van Poecke T, *Terrorism and Armed Conflict: A Transnational Criminal Law Framework* (PhD project funded by FWO, 2024).

Van Poecke T, Verbruggen F and Yperman W, 'Terrorist Offences and International Humanitarian Law: The Armed Conflict Exclusion Clause' (2021) 103 International Review of the Red Cross 295.

Van Puyenbroeck L and Claes L, 'Actualia Voorlopige Hechtenis' in P Traest, A Verhage and G Vermeulen (eds), *Strafrecht en strafprocesrecht: doel of middel in een veranderde samenleving?* (Wolters Kluwer 2017).

Van Volsem F, 'Kwalificatieperikelen: Hij die als dief wordt vervolgd, kan worden veroordeeld als heler en omgekeerd (noot onder Cass. 9 december 2008)' [2009] Rechtspraak Antwerpen Brussel Gent 28.

Van Volsem F and others, *Voorlopige hechtenis: commentaar* (Daniel De Wolf ed, INNI publishers 2014).

Vandebroek E, 'Eenvoudig lidmaatschap van criminele vereniging' [2014] Nieuw Juridisch Weekblad 846.

Vander Beken T, *From Brussels with Love: Bespiegelingen over de Invloed van de Europese Unie Op Het Belgische Strafrecht* (VVSR Preadvies 2002).

Vanderheiden K, 'Opschorting, uitstel en probatie' (2016) O155 Postal Memorialis – Lexicon strafrecht, strafvordering en bijzondere wetten 1.

Vandromme S and De Roy C, 'De strafbaarheid van voorbereidingshandelingen en uitvoeringshandelingen: de nieuwste ontwikkelingen in het leerstuk van de strafbare poging en de gevolgen ervan voor het strafprocesrecht', *Strafrecht en Strafprocesrecht* (Wolters Kluwer 2006).

Vanheule J, *Strafbare Deelneming* (Intersentia 2010).

Vanheule J, 'Daden van deelneming die worden omschreven in artikel 67 Sw.' in M De Busscher and others (eds), *Strafrecht: duiding* (Larcier 2018).

Vanheule J, 'Stelsel van de onzelfstandige strafbare deelneming en de voorwaarden voor de strafbare deelneming' in M De Busscher and others (eds), *Strafrecht: duiding* (Larcier 2018).

Vanneste F, 'Het Europese Hof Voor de Rechten van de Mens en de overheden die terrorisme bestrijden: brothers in arms?' (2003–2004) 41 Rechtskundig Weekblad 1665.

Vanneste F and Verbruggen F, 'Symboolstrafwet als vaandel van de strijd tegen terrorisme' [2004] Panopticon 80.

Vansiliette F, 'Mise à la disposition du gouvernement des condamnés' (2014) M 140 Postal Memorialis – Lexicon strafrecht, strafvordering en bijzondere wetten 1.

Velaers J, 'La lutte contre le terrorisme et les Droits de l'homme: Dévelopements récents en Belgique' in P D'Argent, D Renders and M Verdussen (eds), *Les Visages de L'Etat: Liber Amicorum Yves Lejeune* (Bruylant 2017).

Verboon J and Schuurmans KAWM, 'Grenzen aan exonereren voor aansprakelijkheid' [2019] ORP 8.

Verbruggen F, 'Schaduwboksen in het donker: de dogmatische onderbouw van het strafrechtelijk overheidsoptreden tegen georganiseerde criminaliteit' (Faculty of Law of KU Leuven 2001).

Verbruggen F, Prakken E and Roef D, *Voorbereidingshandelingen in het strafrecht* (Wolf legal publishers 2004).

Vereecke V, 'Het eventueel opzet bij de beoordeling van het oogmerk om te doden' (2019) 2019 Rechtspraak Antwerpen Brussel Gent (RABG) 25.

Verhaegen J, 'Le Dol éventuel et sa place en droit pénal Belge', *Liber Amicorum Hermann Bekaert* (Snoeck-Ducaju & Zoon 1977).

Verstraeten R, *Handboek Strafvordering* (5de voll. herz. uitgave, Maklu 2012).

Verstraeten R and Dewandeleer D, 'Witwassen na de wet van 7 april 1995: kan het nog witter?' [1995] Rechtskundig Weekblad 689.

Vervaele J, 'Terorrism and Security' in Steven Dewulf (ed), *la [CVDW] Liber Amicorum Chris Van den Wyngaert* (Maklu 2017).

Verwimp P, 'Foreign Fighters in Syria and Iraq and the Socio-Economic Environment They Faced at Home: A Comparison of European Countries' (2016) 10 Perspectives on Terrorism 68.

Vilain R and Yperman W, 'Grondwettelijk Hof 21 december 2017: it came in like a wrecking ball' [2018] Nullum Crimen 1.

Vilain R and Yperman W, 'Veralgemeende correctionaliseerbaarheid: Rechts(on) zekerheid na het interpretatief arrest van het Grondwettelijk Hof (no. 2018/28)' [2018] Nieuw Juridisch Weekblad 566.

Vladeck S and Walker C, 'Detention and Interrogation in Law and War' in Genevieve Lennon and Clive Walker (eds), *Routledge Handbook of Law and Terrorism* (Routledge 2015).

Vroman F, 'Criminele Organisaties' (2014) C80 Postal Memorialis – Lexicon strafrecht, strafvordering en bijzondere wetten 46.

Waeterinckx P, 'Het collectief misdrijf – De verhouding tussen artikel 65 Sw. en artikel 2, tweede lid Sw.' in M De Busscher and others (eds), *Strafrecht: duiding* (Larcier 2018).

Waeterinckx P, 'Samenloop van verscheidene misdrijven', *Strafrecht geannoteerd* (die Keure 2020).

Waldron J, 'Security and Liberty: The Image of Balance' (2003) 11 Journal of Political Philosophy 191.

Walker C, *Blackstone's Guide to the Anti-Terrorism Legislation* (Oxford University Press 2002).

Walker C, 'Keeping Control of Terrorists without Losing Control of Constitutionalism' (2007) 59 Stanford Law Review 1395.

Walker C, 'Commentary: R v AY' [2010] Criminal Law Review 882.

Walker C, 'Conscripting the Public in Terrorism Policing: Towards Safer Communities or a Police State?' [2010] Criminal Law Review 441.

Walker C, 'Terrorist Offences: R. v Ahmed (Rangzieb); R. v Ahmed (Habib) – Defendant Charged with Terrorist Offences Claiming That Tortured during Detention in Pakistan' [2011] Criminal Law Review 734.

Walker C, 'The Impact of Contemporary Security Agendas Against Terrorism on the Substantive Criminal Law' in Aniceto Masferrer (ed), *Post 9/11 and the State of Permanent Legal Emergency: Security and Human Rights in Countering Terrorism*, vol 14 (Springer Netherlands 2012).

Walker C, 'Foreign Terrorist Fighters and UK Counter Terrorism Laws' in Javaid Rehman and Ayesha Shahid (eds), *The Asian Yearbook of Human Rights and Humanitarian Law: Volume 2* (Brill | Nijhoff 2018).

Walker C, 'Counterterrorism within the Rule of Law? Rhetoric and Reality with Special Reference to the United Kingdom' (2021) 33 Terrorism and Political Violence 338.

Wasmeier M and Thwaites N, 'The "Battle of the Pillars": Does the European Community Have the Power to Approximate National Criminal Laws?' [2004] European Law Review 613.

Wattier I, 'Des infractions terroristes dans le Code Penal' (2004) Janvier Journal du Juriste 6.

Wauters E, 'Het Grondwettelijk Hof over het begrip "terrorisme"' [2007] Vigiles 176.

Webber D, *Preventive Detention of Terror Suspects: A New Legal Framework* (Routledge 2016).

Weber L and Lee M, 'Preventing Indeterminate Threats: Fear, Terror and the Politics of Preemption' in Stephen Farrall and Murray Lee (eds), *Fear of crime: critical voices in an age of anxiety* (Routledge-Cavendish 2009).

Welsh L, Skinns L and Sanders A, 'Detention in the Police Station' in Lucy Welsh, Layla Skinns and Andrew Sanders, *Sanders & Young's Criminal Justice* (Oxford University Press 2021).

Welsh L, Skinns L and Sanders A, 'Prosecutions and Constructing Guilt' in Lucy Welsh, Layla Skinns and Andrew Sanders, *Sanders & Young's Criminal Justice* (Oxford University Press 2021).

Welsh L, Skinns L and Sanders A, 'Summary Justice in the Magistrates' Court' in Lucy Welsh, Layla Skinns and Andrew Sanders, *Sanders & Young's Criminal Justice* (Oxford University Press 2021).

Weyembergh A, 'L'impact du 11 septembre sur l'équilibre sécurité/liberté dans l'espace pénal européen' in Emmanuelle Bribosia and Anne Weyembergh (eds), *La convention Européenne des droits de l'homme à l'épreuve de la lutte contre le terrorisme* (Bruylant-Nemesis 2002).

Weyembergh A and Kennes L, 'Le Titre Iter du Livre II du Code Pénal: Des infractions terroristes', *Droit pénal spécial: tome 1* (Anthémis 2011).

Weyembergh A and Kennes L, 'Domestic Provisions and Case Law: The Belgian Case' in Francesca Galli and Anne Weyembergh (eds), *EU counter-terrorism offences: What impact on national legislation and case-law?* (Editions de l'Université de Bruxelles 2012).

White N, 'Preventive Counter-Terrorism and International Law' [2013] Journal of Conflict & Security Law 181.

Williams G, 'Anti-Terrorism Laws and Human Rights' (2015) 19 Review of Constitutional Studies 127.

Wilson W, *Criminal Law* (Sixth Edition, Pearson Education Limited 2017).

Winants A, 'De invloed van terrorisme op de strafwetgeving: actualia materieel strafrecht' (2019) 14 Nullum Crimen 343.

Wittendorp S and Bakker E, 'Inventarisatie rechtszaken tegen jihadistische buitenlandse strijders: een vergelijking tussen Nederland, België, Denemarken, Duitsland, Frankrijk, het VK en de VS' (2017) ISGA Report.

Wolfendale J, 'Terrorism, Security, and the Threat of Counterterrorism' (2007) 30 Studies in Conflict & Terrorism.

Wood CA, 'Risk Assessment, Counter-Terrorism Law & Policy; A Human Rights-Based Analysis: Assessing the UK's Pre-Emptive and Preventative Measures of Countering Terrorism, Interaction with Article 5 and 6 of the European Convention on Human Rights, and the Potential Role of Risk Assessment,' (Durham University 2017).

Wouters J and Van Poecke T, 'Van strijdkrachten, terroristen en het belgisch strafrecht (noot onder KI Brussel 14 september 2017)' [2017–2018] Rechtskundig Weekblad 1616.

Wouters O, 'Vrijheidsstraf voor het verheerlijken van terrorisme in overeenstemming met artikel 10 EVRM? (noot onder EHRM 23 september 2022)' [2023] Nieuw Juridisch Weekblad 170

Yperman W, 'Heiligt het doel de middelen?' [2018] Nieuw Juridisch Weekblad 304.

Yperman W, 'Terro III dan toch een stap te ver' [2018] Nieuw Juridisch Weekblad 480.

Yperman W, 'Breed concept van deelname met smalle strafschaal' [2019] Nieuw Juridisch Weekblad 673.

Yperman W, 'De bestrijding van terrorisme en strafprocesrecht: vele kleintjes maken een grote' [2019] Tijdschrift voor Strafrecht 8.

Ypperman W, 'Terrorism Offences in Belgian Criminal Law: Is Less More?' [2021] Queen Mary Law Journal 150.

Ypperman W and Royer S, 'Veroordeling Jihadibruid' [2017] Nieuw Juridisch Weekblad 813.

Yukhnenko D, Farouki L and Fazel S, 'Criminal Recidivism Rates Globally: A 6-Year Systematic Review Update – ScienceDirect' (2023) 88 Journal of Criminal Justice https://www.sciencedirect.com/science/article/pii/S0047235223000867#s0020 accessed 23 January 2024.

Zedner L, 'Securing Liberty in the Face of Terror: Reflections from Criminal Justice' (2005) 32 Journal of Law and Society 27.

Zedner L, 'Seeking Security by Eroding Rights: The Side-Stepping of Due Process' in Benjamin Goold and Liora Lazarus (eds), *Security and Human Rights* (Hart Publishing 2007).

Zedner L, 'Preventive Justice or Pre-Punishment? The Case of Control Orders' (2007) 60 Current Legal Problems 174.

Zedner L, 'Fixing the Future? The Pre-Emptive Turn in Criminal Justice' in B McSherry, A Norrie and S Bronitt (eds), *Regulating Deviance: The Redirection of Criminalisation and the Futures of Criminal Law* (Hart Publishing 2009).

Zedner L, *Security* (2009).

Zedner L, 'Terrorizing Criminal Law' (2014) 8 Criminal Law and Philosophy 99.

OTHER

REPORTS, STUDIES AND GUIDES

Amnesty International, 'Veiligheid & Mensenrechten: Maatregelen tegen terrorisme en radicalisering', Letter to the Belgian Chamber of Representatives following a hearing on 12 May 2015 (2015).

Amnesty International report, 'Dangerously disproportionate, the ever-expanding national security state in Europe' (2017).

Article 19, *The Impact of UK Anti-Terror Laws on Freedom of Expression: Submission to ICJ Panel of Eminent Jurists on Terrorism, Counter-Terrorism and Human Rights*, London, April 2006.

Comité T, 'Rapport 2019: Le respect des droits humains dans le cadre de la lutte contre le terrorisme: Un chantier en cours'.

Comité T, 'Rapport 2020: Evaluation des mesures visant à lutter contre le terrorisme à la lumière des droits humains'.

Comité T, 'Rapport 2022: Évaluation des mesures visant à lutter contre le terrorisme à la lumière des droits humains'.

Europol Terrorism Situation and Trend Report in 2017.

FATF IX Special Recommendations, October 2001, 5.

FATF, *Anti-money laundering and counter-terrorist financing measures -Belgium, Fourth Round Mutual Evaluation Report* (2015) 160.

FATF international standards on combating money laundering and the financing of terrorism & proliferation, updated June 2019, 11.

Federaal Parket, Jaarverslag 2021.

Guide on Article 5 of the convention: Right to liberty and security (2014).

Guide on Article 5 of the European Convention on Human Rights: Right to Liberty and Security (2020).

Guide the case-law of the European Court of Human Rights on terrorism (2020).

Human Rights Watch, 'Guantanamo: Facts and Figures' (2017).

M. Scheinn, 'Ten areas of best practices in countering terrorism', report by the Special Rapporteur on the protection of human rights and fundamental freedoms in the fight against terrorism, A/HRC/16/51, 2010.

Report from the Commission to the European Parliament and the Council based on Article 29(1) of Directive (EU) 2017/541 of the European Parliament and of the Council of 15 March 2017 on combating terrorism and replacing Council Framework Decision 2002/475/JHA and amending Council Decision 2005/671/JHA, Brussels 30 September 2020, COM(2020) 619.

Rob Dacre, *'Greater Threats to Society' – The New Draft Guidelines for Terrorism Offences.*

Secretary General of the UN, 'Uniting against terrorism: recommendations for a global counter-terrorism strategy', A/60/825, 2006.
Sentencing Council, *Approach to the assessment of fines, 9. Maximum fines.*
Sentencing Council, *Murder Sentencing Leaflet.*
Sentencing Council, *Terrorism Offences: Definitive Guideline* (2018).
The Court of Appeal Criminal Division, *Review of the Legal Year 2008 / 2009.*
United Nations Human Rights Committee (2008) *Concluding Observations of the Human Rights Committee: United Kingdom of Great Britain and Northern Ireland*, Ninety Third Session, 7–25 July.

NEWSPAPER ARTICLES

Denny Baert, 'Salah Abdeslam en jurylid door ziekte afwezig op terreurproces, proces niet geschorst' (*vrtNWS* 12 December 2022).
Sandra Cardoen, 'Federaal procureur vindt proces aanslagen te complex voor jury: "Je vraagt niet aan iemand op straat om te opereren"' (*vrtNWS* 9 February 2020).
T.D., 'Juryleden proces Nemmouche bezorgd over veiligheid na diefstal dossier' (*Bruzz* 31 January 2019).
Matthias De Backer, 'Waarom we de term "radicalisering" beter weggooien' (*De Morgen* 24 August 2018) 24.
Douglas De Coninck, 'Assisenproces ligt opnieuw onder vuur' (*De Morgen* 11 February 2020).
Douglas De Coninck, 'Rechter terreurproces: "Ik beveel afbraak glazen kooien"' (*De Morgen* 16 September 2022).
H. Decré, 'Rondleiding door slachtoffer', 'half doof' of 'skivakantie': excuses om niet in jury proces-Nemmouche te moeten zitten' (*vrtNWS* 7 January 2019).
Hanne Decré, 'Celstraffen tot 5 jaar (deels met uitstel) voor "doomsday preppers" die zich voorbereidden op einde van de wereld met voedsel, geld en veel wapens' (*vrtNWS* 12 December 2023).
Mark Eeckhaut, '"Mensonterende" kooien op het proces van de aanslagen' (*De Standaard* 12 September 2022).
Mark Eeckhaut, '"Preppers" met arsenaal van honderden wapens staan terecht voor plannen terreuraanslag: "Uit de hand gelopen hobby"' (*De Standaard* 15 November 2023).
Stefan Grommen, 'Proces over aanslagen ligt opnieuw stil: voorzitter vordert politietopman om duidelijkheid te krijgen over nieuwe naaktfouilles' (*vrtNWS* 4 January 2023).
A. Vanrenterghem, 'Burgerlijke partijen en parket over complottheorie Mehdi Nemmouche: "Rookgordijn zonder bewijs, respectloos"' (*vrtNWS* 4 March 2019).
Guy Van Vlierden, 'België gaat terroristen dubbel zo zwaar proberen te straffen: van 5 naar 10 jaar voor "welke beslissing dan ook"' (*Het Laatste Nieuws* 16 November 2021).
F.V.G., 'Geen speciale rechtbank voor terroristen' (*De Standaard* 8 July 2009).
G.V.V., 'België gaat terroristen dubbel zo zwaar proberen te straffen: dit zijn de plannen" (*De Morgen* 16 November 2021).

A.W., K.G. and H.A., 'Jurylid gewraakt op proces tegen Medhi Nemmouche na bizar gesprek met collega' (*Het Laatste Nieuws* 18 February 2019).

Joren Wollants, 'Zaak tegen "preppers", vrienden van doodgeschoten Yannick, wordt in november behandeld' (*Het Laatste Nieuws* 26 September 2023).

G. Wood, 'What ISIS really wants' (*the atlantic* 2015).

X., 'Opnieuw jurylid gewraakt op proces-Nemmouche' (*de standaard* 16 January 2019).

X., 'Zevende jurylid proces Nemmouche gewraakt na gesprek met collega' (*De Morgen* 18 February 2019).

X., 'Meeste Syriëstrijders komen uit België' (*Het Laatste Nieuws* 23 August 2014).

H. Yezza, 'Britain's terror laws have left me and my family shattered' (*The Guardian* 2008).

www.ingramcontent.com/pod-product-compliance
Ingram Content Group UK Ltd.
Pitfield, Milton Keynes, MK11 3LW, UK
UKHW051043120926
8556IPUK00031B/869

9 781839 704383